brief table of contents

detailed table of contents

Whether or not a company wants to participate directly in international business, it cannot escape ever-increasing competition from international firms. We are coming to a situation where hardly any company can claim that it is a domestic one. The globalisation of the marketplace is already a reality, but it led us to some misunderstandings. The concept of the global market, or global marketing, thus needs some clarification. Generally, the concept views the world as one market and is based on identifying and targeting cross-cultural similarities. In our opinion, the global marketing concept is based on the premise of cultural differences and is guided by the belief that each foreign market requires its own culturally adapted marketing strategies. Although consumers dining at McDonald's in New Delhi, Moscow and Beijing is a reality, the idea of marketing a standardised product with a uniform marketing plan remains 'purely theoretical'.

The global marketing strategy is thus different from the globalisation of the market. One has to do with efficiency of operations, competitiveness and orientation, the other with homogeneity of demand across cultures. In this book we consider it important to make this distinction and to see how it affects international marketing strategies.

In Europe, where home markets are smaller, companies like Philips, Unilever, Ericsson, Nokia, Akzo Nobel and Carrefour are deriving up to 80 per cent of their revenues from abroad. The companies that succeed in the twenty-first century will be those capable of adapting to constant change and adjusting to new challenges.

The economic, political and social changes that have occurred over the last decade have dramatically altered the landscape of global business. Consider the present and future impact of:

■ the emergence of China as a full player in the international market
■ the European Union as the biggest single market, with 500 million affluent consumers
■ emerging markets in Eastern Europe, Asia and Latin America where, in spite of economic and political crises, more than 75 per cent of the growth in world trade over the next 20 years is expected to occur
■ the job shift in services from Western to emerging markets
■ the rapid move away from traditional distribution structures in Japan, Europe, the USA and many emerging markets
■ the growth of middle-income households the world over
■ the creation of the World Trade Organization (WTO) and decreasing restrictions on trade
■ the transformation of the Internet from a toy for 'cybernerds' to a major international business tool for research, advertising, communications, exporting and marketing
■ the increased awareness of ethical issues and social responsibility.

As global economic growth occurs, understanding marketing in all cultures is increasingly important. This book addresses global issues and describes concepts relevant to all international marketers, regardless of the extent of their international involvement. Emphasis is on the strategic implications of competition in the markets of different countries. An environmental/cultural approach to international marketing permits a truly global orientation. The reader's horizons are not limited to any specific nation or to the particular ways of doing business in a single country. Instead, we provide an approach and framework for identifying and analysing the important cultural and environmental uniqueness of any country or global region.

The text is designed to stimulate curiosity about the management practices of companies, large and small, seeking market opportunities outside their home country and to raise the reader's consciousness about the importance of viewing international marketing management strategies from a global perspective.

Although this revised edition is infused throughout with a global orientation, export marketing and operations of smaller companies are not overlooked. Issues specific to exporting are discussed where strategies applicable to exporting arise and examples of marketing practices of smaller companies are examined.

new and expanded features in this edition

As a result of extensive review work with the publishers, we evaluated the table of contents and for this new edition have reorganised it so that it better reflects the way topics are taught on most international marketing courses. We have reorganised several chapters, primarily by merging two chapters on the political and legal environment into one chapter, as well as merging the chapters on financial requirements and organising international marketing activities into one chapter.

new content

We have expanded the discussions on cultural issues in Section 2, and brought these chapters forward on the table of contents to really emphasise the importance of culture when marketing internationally. Two new chapters have been added, one on international entry strategies in Section 4 and one on ethics and social responsibility in Section 5. In addition, the chapter on marketing research has been totally revised to include cross-cultural issues in marketing research.

The new and expanded topics in this edition reflect issues in competition, changing marketing structures, the importance of cultural issues, ethics and social responsibility, and negotiations. The global market is swiftly changing from a seller's market to a buyer's market. This is a period of profound social, economic and political change. To remain competitive globally, companies must be aware of all aspects of the emerging global economic order.

Additionally, the evolution of global communications and its known and unknown impact on how international business is conducted cannot be minimised. In the third millennium, people in the 'global village' will grow closer than ever, and will hear and see each other as a matter of course. An executive in Germany will be able to routinely pick up his or her video-phone to hear and see his or her counterpart in an Australian company or anywhere else in the world. In many respects, distance is becoming irrelevant. Telecommunications, video-phones, the Internet, nanotechnology and satellites are helping companies optimise their planning, production and procurement processes. Information – and, in its wake, the flow of goods – is moving around the globe at lightning speed. Increasingly powerful networks spanning the globe enable the delivery of services that reach far beyond national and continental boundaries, fuelling and fostering international trade. The connections of global communications bring people all around the world together in new and better forms of dialogue and understanding.

This dynamic nature of the international marketplace is reflected in the number of new and expanded topics in this edition, including:

- the importance of ethics and social responsibility in marketing
- the European Union of 25 countries and the impact of the euro
- the Internet and its expanding role in international marketing
- big emerging markets (BEMs), particularly China and India
- evolving global middle-income households
- the World Trade Organization and its impact on increasing international trade

- cross-cultural marketing research
- the importance of marketing research for marketing decision making
- trends in channel structures in Europe, Japan, the United States and developing countries
- enhanced emphasis on cultural issues relevant for international marketing
- an expanded chapter on entry strategies
- financial and organisational issues in international marketing, particularly important for small and medium-sized firms.

new features

More than two-thirds of the boxed **Going International** examples are brand new to this edition. These examples are carefully chosen to illustrate the points made in the text. A number of these examples act as provocative mini-cases that can be used as discussion points – featuring questions aimed to initiate exercises and discussion in the classroom. All tables and figures, and the discussions around them, have been updated and a number of new ones added. These are now renamed **exhibits** to reflect their true nature and make navigation around the text easier and quicker.

Also new to this edition are **key terms**, which have been introduced to help readers identify the most important and frequently used terminology. All key terms are emboldened in the text the first time they are used, and definitions provided in the margin for quick reference. A full **glossary** of key terms is provided in the Online Learning Centre (OLC) and at the back of the book.

At the end of each chapter, you'll find a new **Further Reading** feature, where we present a selection of readings that reflect the most classical, most influential and most recent studies in the area covered by the chapter. This new feature will not only encourage students to go deeper into different topics, but will also help teachers in preparing interesting and enriched lectures.

structure of the text

The text is divided into five sections. In **Section 1**, 'An Overview', the two chapters introduce the reader to international marketing and to three international marketing management concepts: the domestic market expansion concept, the multidomestic market concept and the global marketing concept. As companies restructure for the global competitive rigours of the twenty-first century, so too must tomorrow's managers. The successful manager must be globally aware and have a frame of reference that goes beyond a country, or even a region, and encompasses the world. What global awareness means and how it is acquired is discussed early in the text; it is the foundation of global marketing.

Chapter 2 focuses on the dynamic environment of international trade and the competitive challenges and opportunities confronting today's international marketer. The importance of the creation of the World Trade Organization (WTO), as the successor to GATT, is fully explored.

The first three chapters in **Section 2** deal with the impact of culture on international marketing. A global orientation requires the recognition of cultural differences and the critical decision of whether or not it is necessary to accommodate them.

Geography and history (**Chapter 3**) are included as important dimensions in understanding cultural and market differences among countries. Not to be overlooked is concern for the deterioration of the global ecological environment and the multinational company's critical responsibility to protect it.

Chapter 4 presents a broad review of culture and its impact on human behaviour as it relates to international marketing. Specific attention is paid to Geert Hofstede's study of cultural value and behaviour.

Chapter 5 focuses on business customs and practices. Knowledge of the business culture, management attitudes and business methods existing in a country and a willingness to accommodate the differences are important to success in an international market. The chapter provides several examples to deal with these different business practices and customers.

The political climate in a country is a critical concern for the international marketer. In Chapter 6, we take a closer look at the political environment. We discuss the stability of government policies, the political risks confronting a company, and the assessment and reduction of political vulnerability of products. Legal problems common to most international marketing transactions, which must be given special attention when operating abroad, are also discussed in this chapter.

Chapters 7, 8 and 9 in Section 3 are concerned with assessing global market opportunities. As markets expand, segments grow within markets, and as market segments across country markets evolve, marketers are forced to understand market behaviour within and across different cultural contexts. Multicultural research and qualitative and quantitative research are discussed in Chapter 7.

Chapters 8 and 9 explore the impact of the three important trends in global marketing: (1) the growth and expansion of the world's big emerging markets; (2) the rapid growth of middle-income market segments; (3) the steady creation of regional market groups that include the European Union (EU), the North American Free Trade Agreement (NAFTA), the Southern Cone Free Trade Area (Mercosur), the ASEAN Free Trade Area (AFTA) and the Asian–Pacific Economic Cooperation (APEC).

The strategic implications of the shift from socialist-based to market-based economies in Eastern Europe and the returning impact of China on international commerce are examined. Attention is also given to the efforts of the governments of India and many Latin American countries to reduce or eliminate barriers to trade, open their countries to foreign investment and privatise state-owned enterprises.

In Section 4, 'Developing International Marketing Strategies', planning and organising for international marketing are discussed in Chapter 10. Many multinational companies realise that to fully capitalise on the opportunities offered by global markets, they must have strengths that often exceed their capabilities. Here we also deal with positioning and branding as strategic actions. Chapter 11 has been dedicated to entry strategies. Here we provide a model that can be followed to analyse different markets while making decisions on market selection.

In Chapter 12, the special issues involved in moving a product from one country market to another, and the accompanying mechanics of exporting, are addressed. The exporting mechanisms and documentation are explained.

Chapters 13 and 14 focus on product management, reflecting the differences in strategies between consumer and industrial products and the growing importance in world markets for business services. Additionally, the discussion on the development of global products stresses the importance of approaching the adaptation issue from the viewpoint of building a standardised product platform that can be adapted to reflect cultural differences. The competitive importance in today's global market of quality, innovation and technology as the keys to marketing success is explored.

Chapter 15 takes the reader through the distribution process, from home country to the consumer, in the target country market. The structural impediments to market entry imposed by a country's distribution system are examined in the framework of a detailed presentation of the American and European distribution structure. In addition, the rapid changes in channel structure that are occurring in Japan and in other countries, and the emergence of the World Wide Web as a distribution channel, are presented.

Chapter 16 covers advertising and addresses the promotional element of the international marketing mix. Included in the discussion of global market segmentation are recognition of the rapid growth of market segments across country markets and the importance

of market segmentation as a strategic competitive tool in creating an effective promotional message.

Chapter 17 discusses personal selling and sales management, and the critical nature of training, evaluating and controlling sales representatives. Here we also pay attention to negotiating with customers, partners and other actors in our networks. We discuss the factors influencing business negotiations, and varying negotiation styles.

Price escalations and ways in which these can be lessened, countertrade practices and price strategies under varying currency conditions are concepts presented in **Chapter 18**. The factors influencing pricing decisions are thoroughly discussed.

In Section 5, we first deal with ethics and social responsibility in international marketing (Chapter 19). Here we explain what is meant by social responsibility and what implications it has for international marketing activities. The chapter on financing and managing international marketing operations, Chapter 20, deals with the financial aspects of marketing internationally. We look into the capital needs for international marketing, the available sources of funding and the management of financial risk. Organising international marketing activities is also dealt with in Chapter 20. This chapter is particularly relevant for small and medium-sized enterprises.

pedagogical features of the text

The text portion of the book provides a thorough coverage of its subject, with specific emphasis on the planning and strategic problems confronting companies that market across cultural boundaries. The pedagogy we have developed for this textbook is designed to perfectly complement the rest of the book, and has been constructed with the very real needs of students and lecturers in mind.

Current, pithy, sometimes humorous and always relevant examples are used throughout each chapter to stimulate interest and increase understanding of the ideas, concepts and strategies presented, emphasising the importance of understanding the cultural uniqueness and relevant business practices and strategies.

The **Going International** boxes, an innovative feature of the first edition of *International Marketing*, have always been popular with students. This edition includes many new boxes such as these, and all provide up-to-date and insightful examples of cultural differences and international marketing at work, as well as illustrating concepts presented in the text. They reflect contemporary issues in international marketing and real-life marketing scenarios, and can be used as a basis for solo study and as mini-case studies for lectures, as well as to stimulate class discussion. They are unique to this text, lively to read, and will stimulate all who use this book.

As you will have by now noticed, this new edition is four-colour, and features colour pictures that are incorporated into the Going International boxes. In this new edition we've also included an expanded section of maps, which comprises information on regions, plus useful data on trade routes, resources and consumption, languages, transportation and environment in different areas of the world.

'**The Country Notebook: a Guide for Developing a Marketing Plan**', found in **Section 6**, is a detailed outline that provides both a format for a complete cultural and economic analysis of a country and guidelines for a marketing plan.

cases

Building on the success of the case section from the previous edition, we have included a substantial section of excellent case-study material that can be used by students and lecturers to aid learning. You'll find 23 cases in total, 19 of which are brand new to this edition. The cases reflect all regions and by working through them you will encounter all kinds of marketing scenarios in all kinds of companies in all geographical territories. From supermarket chains in Germany to footballers in China; from cereal brands in India to the

wine industry in Australia – each case study is lively, contemporary, thought-provoking and expertly designed to bring out the real issues in international marketing. The shorter cases focus on a single problem, serving as the basis for discussion of a specific concept or issue. The longer, more integrated cases are broader in scope and focus on more than one marketing management problem. Information is provided in a way that enables the cases to be studied as complete works in themselves but, importantly, they also lend themselves to more in-depth analysis that requires students to engage in additional research and data collection.

online supplements

In addition to the resources in this textbook, you'll find more supplements in the **Online Learning Centre (OLC)**, which can be found at: www.mcgraw-hill.co.uk/textbooks/ghauri. A full list of features can be found on page xxiv.

acknowledgements

The success of a text depends on the contributions of many people, especially those who take the time to share their thoughtful criticisms and suggestions to improve the text.

We would especially like to thank the reviewers who gave us valuable insights into this revision:

Kim Rene Bohn, University of Aalborg, Denmark
Peter Dahlin, Malardalen University College, Sweden
Nikos Dimitriadis, University of Sheffield, UK
Peter Forte, ESCEM, France
Jens Graff, UMEA, Sweden
Amjad Hadjikhani, Uppsala University, Sweden
Patricia Harris, Kingston University, UK
Cecilia Lindh, Malardalen University College, Sweden
Dr Ulrike Mayrhofer, IECS Strasbourg, France
Peter Nuttall, UWE, UK
Fred Scharf, University of Ulster, UK
Eric Shui, Birmingham Business School, UK
Dr Rudolf R. Sinkovics, Manchester Business School, UK
John Sisk, Dundalk Institute of Technology, Ireland
Ingemar Tuvesson, Lunds University, Sweden
Fiona Winfield, Nottingham Trent University, UK

We would also like to thank those who contributed to this new edition by writing case studies or examples:

Ulf Elg, Lunds University, Sweden
Richard Gesteland, Global Management, LLC, USA
Sylvie Hertrich, IECS Strasbourg, France
Anna Jonsson, Lunds University, Sweden
Claudia Klausegger, Wirtschaftsuniversität Wien, Austria
Dr Ulrike Mayrhofer, IECS Strasbourg, France
Klaus Meyer, National Chengchi University, Taiwan
Rudolf R. Sinkovics, University of Manchester, UK
Veronika Tarnovskaya, Lunds University, Sweden
Rob van Zanten, University of Adelaide, Australia

In addition, over 200 instructors, unfortunately too many to list here, responded to surveys that helped shape the content and structure of this edition, as well as providing impetus for some very positive changes in the supplement package.

Other than these, we also would like to thank a team of colleagues who helped us in typing, editing and preparing the manuscript. Our special thanks in this regard to Robert-Jan Bulter and Gill Geraghty at Manchester Business School.

We appreciate the help of all the many students and professors who have shared their opinions of past editions, and we welcome their comments and suggestions on this and future editions of *International Marketing*.

A very special thanks to Rachel Crookes at McGraw-Hill, London, who helped us in more than one way to finish this edition on time.

Pervez Ghauri and Philip Cateora

guided tour

Chapter Learning Objectives

What you should learn from Chapter 1

- What is meant by international marketing
- To understand the scope of the international marketing task
- To comprehend the importance of the self-reference criterion (SRC) in international marketing
- To identify and manage the factors influencing the internationalisation of companies
- To evaluate the progression of becoming an international marketer
- To see how international marketing concepts influence international marketers
- To appreciate the increasing importance of global awareness

learning objectives
Each chapter opens with a set of learning objectives, summarising what you will learn from each chapter.

key term

balance of payments
system of accounts that records a nation's international financial transactions

key terms
These are highlighted throughout the chapter and definitions are provided in the margins for quick and easy reference.

Exhibit 3.3 World's oil reserves

Saudi Arabia
Iraq
Kuwait
Russia
Libya
US
Canada
Brazil
Kazakhstan
Azerbaijan
UK

0   50   100   150   200   250   300

Reserves ▓ Years to depletion (at 2004 production rates)

Source: BP, Statistical Review of World Energy, 2004.

exhibits
Each chapter provides a number of figures and tables to illustrate and summarise important information.

GOING INTERNATIONAL 3.1

climate and success

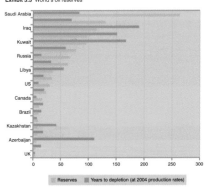

A major food processing company had production problems after it built a pineapple cannery at the delta of a river in Mexico. It built the pineapple plantation upstream and planned to barge the ripe fruit downstream for canning, load them directly on ocean liners, and ship them to the company's various markets. When the pineapples were ripe, however, the company found itself in trouble: crop maturity coincided with the flood stage of the river. The current in the river during this period was far too strong to permit the backhauling of barges upstream; the plan for transporting the fruit on barges could not be implemented. With no alternative means of transport, the company was forced to close the operation. The new equipment was sold for 5 per cent of original cost to a Mexican group, which immediately relocated the cannery. A seemingly simple, harmless oversight of weather and navigation conditions was the primary cause for major losses to the company.

Source: David A. Ricks, Blunders in International Business (Cambridge, MA: Blackwell Publishers, 1993), p. 16.

going international
The book is full of these relevant and contemporary examples of international marketing, which bring the topics to life. Many of them include discussion questions designed to prompt class debates.

summary
These summaries briefly review and reinforce the main topics covered in each chapter to ensure you have acquired a solid understanding of the topics.

summary
One British authority admonishes foreign marketers to study the world until 'the mere mention of a town, country or river enables it to be picked out immediately on the map'. Although it may not be necessary for the student of international marketing to memorise the world map to that extent, a prospective international marketer should be reasonably familiar with the world, its climate and topographic differences. Otherwise, the important marketing characteristics of geography could be completely overlooked when marketing in another country. The need for geographical and historical knowledge goes deeper than being able to locate continents and their countries. For someone who has never been in a tropical rainforest with an annual rainfall of at least 1.5 metres and sometimes more than 5 metres, it is difficult to anticipate the need for protection against high humidity, or to anticipate the difficult problems caused by dehydration in constant 38ºC or more heat in the Sahara region. Without a historical understanding of a culture, the attitudes within the marketplace may not be understood. An understanding of world population and its expected growth in regions and countries can have a profound impact on a company's international marketing strategies. The same goes for the geographic locations of resources and other raw materials.

Aside from the simpler and more obvious ramifications of climate and topography, there are complex geographical and historical influences on the development of the general economy and society of a country. In this case, the need for studying geography

questions
These questions help you test the knowledge you have acquired from each chapter.

questions
1 Why would a country rather domesticate than expropriate?
2 How can government-initiated domestication be the same as confiscation?
3 What are the main factors to consider in assessing the dominant political climate within a country?
4 Why is a working knowledge of political party philosophy so important in a political assessment of a market? Discuss.
5 What are the most frequently encountered political risks in foreign business? Discuss.
6 What are the factors that influence the risk-reduction process in international marketing?
7 Discuss measures a company might take to lessen its political vulnerability.
8 Select a country and analyse it politically from a marketing viewpoint.
9 How does the international marketer determine which legal system will have jurisdiction when legal disputes arise?
10 Discuss some of the reasons why it is probably best to seek an out-of-court settlement in international commercial legal disputes rather than to sue.
11 Illustrate the procedure generally followed in international commercial disputes when settled under the auspices of a formal arbitration tribunal.

further reading
The further reading for each chapter guides you towards the best secondary sources available.

further reading
■ J.J. Boddewyn, 'Political Aspects of MNE Theory', *Journal of International Business Studies*, 1988, 19(3): pp. 341-62.
■ C. Cosset and J. Roy, 'The Determinants of Country Risk Ratings', *Journal of International Business Studies*, 1991, 22(1), pp. 135-42.
■ A. Hadjikhani and P. Ghauri, 'The Behaviour of International Firms in Socio-Political Environments in the European Union', *Journal of Business Research*, 2001, 52(3), pp. 263-75.

country notebook
This feature provides a format for undertaking both a complete cultural and economic analysis of a country, as well as guidelines for a marketing plan.

section 6 supplementary resources

A number of books and articles have described strategic marketing planning at corporate or business unit level. Here we are mainly concerned about a marketing plan for a foreign market or a marketing plan for a particular product in one particular market. The guidelines provided here can be used for different markets; however, depending on the market and the product, the emphasis on different parts of the framework may change.

The first stage in the planning process is a preliminary country analysis. The marketer needs basic information to: (1) evaluate a country market's potential, (2) identify problems that would eliminate a country from further consideration, (3) identify aspects of the country's environment that need further study, (4) evaluate the components of the marketing mix for possible adaptation and (5) develop a strategic marketing plan. One further use of the information collected in the preliminary analysis is as a basis for a country notebook.

Many companies, large and small, have a country notebook for each country in which they do business. The country notebook contains information a marketer should be aware of when making decisions involving a specific country market. As new information is collected, the country notebook is continually updated by the country or product manager. Whenever a marketing decision is made involving a country, the country notebook is the first database consulted. New product introductions, changes in advertising programmes, and other marketing programme decisions begin with the country notebook. It also serves as a quick introduction for new personnel assuming responsibility for a country market.

This section presents four separate guidelines for collection and analysis of market data and preparation of a country notebook: (1) guideline for cultural analysis, (2) guideline for economic analysis, (3) guideline for market audit and competitive analysis, (4) guideline for a preliminary marketing plan. These guidelines suggest the kinds of information a marketer can gather to enhance planning.

The points in each of the guidelines are general. They are designed to provide direction to areas to explore for relevant data. In each guideline, specific points must be adapted to reflect a company's products. The decision as to the appropriateness of specific data and the depth of coverage depends on company objectives, product characteristics, and the country market. Some points in the guidelines are unimportant for some countries and/or some products and should be ignored. Preceding chapters of this book provide specific content suggestions for the topics in each guideline.

Cultural analysis
The data suggested in the cultural analysis include information that helps

the marketer make market planning decisions. However, its application extends beyond product/ market analysis to an important source of information for someone interested in understanding business customs and other important cultural features of the country.

The information in this analysis must be more than a collection of facts. Whoever is responsible for the preparation of this material should attempt to interpret the meaning of cultural information. That is, how does the information help in understanding the effect on the market? For example, the fact that almost all the populations of Italy and Ireland are Catholic is an interesting statistic but not nearly as useful as understanding the effect of Catholicism on values, beliefs and other aspects of market behaviour. Even though both countries are predominantly Catholic, the influence of their individual and unique interpretation and practice of Catholicism can result in important differences in market behaviour.

Guidelines
I Introduction.
Include short profiles of the company, the product to be exported, and the country with which you wish to trade.
II Brief discussion of the country's relevant history.
III Geographical setting.
 A Location.
 B Climate.
 C Topography.
IV Social institutions.
 A Family.
  1 The nuclear family.
  2 The extended family.
  3 Female/male roles (are they changing or static?).
 B Education.
  1 The role of education in society.
  2 Literacy rates.
 C Political system.
  1 Political structure.
  2 Stability of government.
  3 Special taxes.
  4 Role of local government.
 D Legal system.
  1 Organisation of the judiciary system.
  2 Code, common, socialist or Islamic-law country?
  3 Participation in patents, trade marks and other conventions.
 E Social organisations.
  1 Group behaviour.
  2 Social classes.
  3 Race, ethnicity and subcultures.
 F Business customs and practices.
V Religion and aesthetics.

509

section 1
case studies

cases

case 1.1 Starbucks: Going Global Fast

The Starbucks coffee shop on Sixth Avenue and Pine Street in downtown Seattle sits serene and orderly, as unremarkable as any other in the chain bought 15 years ago by entrepreneur Howard Schultz. A little less than three years ago, however, the quiet store-front made front pages around the world. During the World Trade Organization talks in November 1999, protesters flooded Seattle's streets, and among their targets was Starbucks, a symbol, to them, of free-market capitalism run amok, another multinational out to blanket the earth. Amid the crowds of protesters and riot police were black-masked anarchists who trashed the store, leaving its windows smashed and its tasteful green-and-white decor smelling of fear gas instead of espresso. Says an angry Schultz: 'It's hurtful. I think people are ill-informed. It's very difficult to protest against a can of Coke, a bottle of Pepsi, or a can of Folgers. Starbucks is both this ubiquitous brand and a place where you can go and break a window. You can't break a can of Coke.'

The store was quickly repaired, and the protesters have scattered to other cities. Yet cup by cup, Starbucks really is caffeinating the world, its green-and-white emblem beckoning to consumers on three continents. In 1999, Starbucks Corp. had 281 stores abroad. Today, it has about 1200 – and it's still in the early stages of a plan to colonise the globe. If the protesters were wrong in their tactics, they weren't wrong about Starbucks' ambitions. They were just early.

The story of how Schultz & Co. transformed a pedestrian commodity into an upscale consumer accessory has a fairy-tale quality. Starbucks has grown from 17 coffee shops in Seattle 15 years ago to 5689 outlets in 28 countries. Sales have climbed an average of 20 per cent annually since the company went public 10 years ago, to $2.6 billion in 2001, while profits bounded ahead an average of 30 per cent per year, hitting $181.2 million last year. And

This Starbucks store opened in 2000, in the Forbidden City area of Beijing

the momentum continues. In the first three quarters of this fiscal year, sales climbed 24 per cent, year to year, to $2.4 billion, while profits, excluding onetime charges and capital gains, rose 25 per cent, to $159.5 million.

Moreover, the Starbucks name and image connect with millions of consumers around the globe. It was one of the fastest-growing brands in a Business Week survey of the top 100 global brands published 5 August. At a time when one corporate star after another has crashed to earth, brought down by revelations of earnings misstatements, executive greed, or worse, Starbucks hasn't faltered. The company confidently predicts up to 25 per cent annual sales and earnings growth this year. On Wall Street, Starbucks is the last great growth story. Its stock, including four splits, has soared more than 2200 per cent over the past decade, surpassing Wal-Mart, General Electric, PepsiCo, Coca-Cola, Microsoft and IBM in total return. Now

515

---

glossary

accounts-receivable – A comprehensive billing and customer information system that helps you manage your receivables, streamline the collection and control of cash, and separately track individual clients, organisations and funding sources.
act of God – An extraordinary happening of nature not reasonably anticipated by either party to a contract, i.e. earthquakes, floods, etc.
activist groups – See Green activist. Refers to these groups, e.g. Greenpeace.
adaptation – Making changes to fit a particular culture/ environment/conditions; when we produce special/modified products for different markets.
administered pricing – Relates to attempts to establish prices for an entire market.
advertising campaign – Designing and implementing particular advertising for a particular product/purpose over a fixed period.
advertising media – Different alternatives available to a company for its advertising (e.g. TV, magazine).
after-sales service – Services that are available after the product has been sold (e.g. repairs).
air freight – Sending a product by air.
analogy – Reasoning from parallel cases/examples.
Andean Common Market (ANCOM) – A sub-regional economic integration organisation existing out of Bolivia, Colombia, Ecuador, Peru and Venezuela.
anti-trust laws – Laws to prevent businesses from creating unjust monopolies or competing unfairly in the marketplace.
APEC – Asia Pacific cooperation among 21 member states. APEC promotes free trade and economic cooperation between members.
arbitration – Mediation done by a third party in case of a commercial dispute.
ASEAN – The fourth biggest trade area of the world comprising 10 Southeast Asian countries.
Asian crisis – In 1996/1997, stock exchanges and currency values in a number of Asian countries lost a major part of their value.
back translation – When a questionnaire/slogan/ theme is translated into another language, then translated back to the original language by another party. Helps to pinpoint misinterpretation and misunderstandings.

balance of payments – System of accounts that records a nation's international financial transactions.
barriers to exporting – Obstacles/hindrances to export.
barter – Direct exchange of goods between two parties in a transaction.
barter house – International trading company that is able to introduce merchandise to outlets and geographic areas previously untapped.
billboards – Large stands that comprise advertising space, usually found on the sides of roads.
blocked currency – Blockage cuts off all importing or all importing above a certain level. Blockage is accomplished by refusing to allow importers to exchange national currency for the seller's currency.
Boston Consulting Group (BCG) – An international strategy and general management consulting firm, it uses specific models to tackle management problems.
boycott – A coordinated refusal to buy or use products or services of a certain company/country.
brand loyalty – When customers always buy the same brand.
branding – Developing and building a reputation for a brand name.
Bretton Woods Agreement – An agreement made in 1944. It set fixed exchange rates for major currencies and subsequently established the IMF.
bribery – Voluntarily offered payments by someone seeking unlawful advantage.
broker – A catchall term for a variety of middlemen performing low-cost agent services.
business culture – Values and norms followed in business activities.
business services – Services that are sold to other companies (e.g. advertising).
capital account – A record of direct investment portfolio activities, and short-term capital movements to and from countries.
cartel – A cartel exists when various companies producing similar products work together to control markets for the types of goods they produce.
census data – A record of population and its breakdown.
centralisation – When most decisions are made at the top or head office.

635

technology to enhance learning and teaching

Online Learning Centre (OLC)

After completing each chapter, log on to the supporting Online Learning Centre website. Take advantage of the study tools offered to reinforce the material you have read in the text, and to develop your knowledge in a fun and effective way.

Resources for students include:
+ **Self test questions**
+ **Glossary**
+ **Weblinks**
+ **Maps**

Also available for lecturers:
+ **Lecturers' manual**
+ **Solutions to questions**
+ **Case study notes and solutions**
+ **Extra questions**
+ **PowerPoint slides**

If you need to supplement your course with additional cases or content, create a personalised e-book for your students. Visit www.primiscontentcenter.com or e-mail primis_euro@mcgraw-hill.com for more information

Study Skills

Open University Press publishes guides to study, research and exam skills, to help undergraduate and postgraduate students through their university studies.

Visit www.openup.co.uk/ss/ to see the full selection and get a £2 discount by entering the promotional code **study** when buying online

Computing Skills

If you'd like to brush up your computing skills, we have a range of titles covering MS Office applications such as Word, Excel, PowerPoint, Access and more.

Get a £2 discount on these titles by entering the promotional code **app** when ordering online at www.mcgraw-hill.co.uk/app

maps

1 **World**

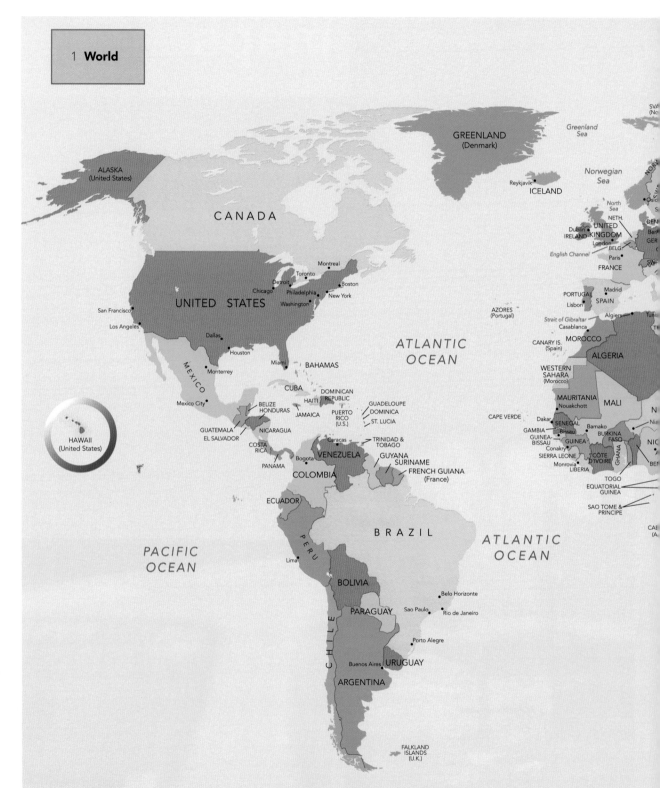

GREENLAND
(Denmark)

Greenland Sea

SVA
(No

Norwegian Sea

Reykjavik•
ICELAND

North Sea

Oslo•

NOR
S

ALASKA
(United States)

Dublin• UNITED
IRELAND KINGDOM
London•
NETH.
BELG.
Paris•

DEN
Berl
GER
SWI

English Channel

CANADA

Montreal•
Toronto•
Detroit•
Chicago•
Philadelphia•
Washington•

Boston•
New York•

PORTUGAL
Lisbon•

Madrid•
SPAIN

Algiers•

Tuni

FRANCE

UNITED STATES

San Francisco•

Los Angeles•

AZORES
(Portugal)

Strait of Gibraltar
Casablanca•

MOROCCO

Dallas•

CANARY IS.
(Spain)

ALGERIA

Houston•

WESTERN
SAHARA
(Morocco)

MEXICO

Monterrey•

Miami•

BAHAMAS

ATLANTIC
OCEAN

MAURITANIA
Nouakchott•

MALI

CUBA

CAPE VERDE

Dakar•

SENEGAL

Nig

Mexico City•

DOMINICAN
REPUBLIC

HAITI

GUADELOUPE
DOMINICA

GAMBIA
GUINEA-
BISSAU

Bissau•
Conakry•
GUINEA

Bamako•

BURKINA
FASO

NIC

BELIZE
HONDURAS

JAMAICA

PUERTO
RICO
(U.S.)

ST. LUCIA

SIERRA LEONE

CÔTE
D'IVOIRE

GHANA

BEI

GUATEMALA
EL SALVADOR

NICARAGUA

Monrovia•
LIBERIA

TOGO

HAWAII
(United States)

COSTA
RICA

Caracas•

TRINIDAD &
TOBAGO

EQUATORIAL
GUINEA

Bogota•

VENEZUELA

GUYANA
SURINAME

SAO TOME &
PRINCIPE

PANAMA

COLOMBIA

FRENCH GUIANA
(France)

ECUADOR

CAE
(A

PACIFIC
OCEAN

PERU

BRAZIL

ATLANTIC
OCEAN

Lima•

BOLIVIA

Belo Horizonte•

Sao Paulo•
PARAGUAY

Rio de Janeiro•

C H I L E

Porto Alegre•

Buenos Aires•
URUGUAY

ARGENTINA

FALKLAND
ISLANDS
(U.K.)

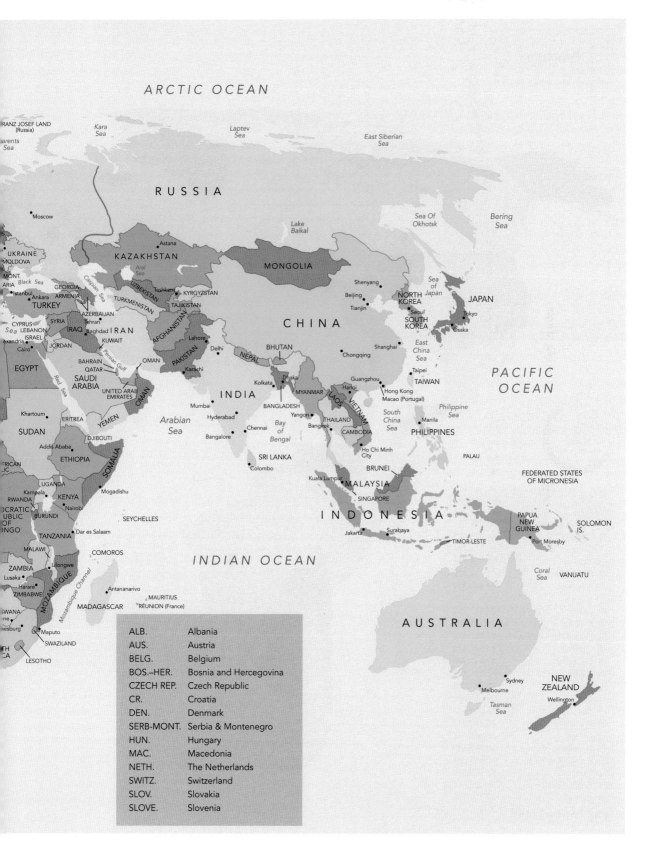

ARCTIC OCEAN

FRANZ JOSEF LAND (Russia)

Kara Sea

Laptev Sea

East Siberian Sea

Barents Sea

RUSSIA

Moscow

Sea Of Okhotsk

Bering Sea

UKRAINE
MOLDOVA

Astana

KAZAKHSTAN

Lake Baikal

MONGOLIA

Aral Sea

MONT.
ARIA

Black Sea

GEORGIA

UZBEKISTAN

Tashkent

KYRGYZSTAN

Shenyang

Sea of Japan

JAPAN

Istanbul
Ankara
TURKEY

ARMENIA

TURKMENISTAN

TAJIKISTAN

Beijing

NORTH KOREA

Tokyo

AZERBAIJAN

Tianjin

SOUTH KOREA

Seoul

Osaka

CYPRUS
Sea LEBANON
ISRAEL
exandria

SYRIA

Tehran

AFGHANISTAN

CHINA

IRAQ
Baghdad

IRAN

Lahore

Shanghai

East China Sea

Cairo

JORDAN

KUWAIT

Delhi

BHUTAN

Chongqing

Taipei

PACIFIC OCEAN

BAHRAIN
QATAR

Persian Gulf

OMAN

PAKISTAN

NEPAL

TAIWAN

EGYPT

Karachi

Kolkata

Dhaka

Guangzhou

SAUDI ARABIA

UNITED ARAB EMIRATES

OMAN

INDIA

MYANMAR

Hanoi

Hong Kong
Macao (Portugal)

Red Sea

Mumbai

BANGLADESH

LAOS

South China Sea

Philippine Sea

Khartoum

ERITREA

YEMEN

Arabian Sea

Hyderabad

Yangon

VIETNAM

Manila

SUDAN

DJIBOUTI

Chennai

Bay of Bengal

Bangkok

THAILAND

PHILIPPINES

Addis Ababa

Bangalore

CAMBODIA

AFRICAN

ETHIOPIA

SOMALIA

SRI LANKA

Ho Chi Minh City

PALAU

UGANDA

Colombo

BRUNEI

FEDERATED STATES OF MICRONESIA

Kampala
RWANDA

KENYA

Mogadishu

Kuala Lumpur

MALAYSIA

OCRATIC
UBLIC
OF
ONGO

Nairobi

SEYCHELLES

SINGAPORE

PAPUA NEW GUINEA

SOLOMON IS.

BURUNDI

TANZANIA

Dar es Salaam

INDONESIA

MALAWI

COMOROS

Jakarta

Surabaya

Port Moresby

ZAMBIA

INDIAN OCEAN

TIMOR-LESTE

Coral Sea

VANUATU

Lusaka
Lilongwe

Antananarivo

Harare
ZIMBABWE

MOZAMBIQUE

Mozambique Channel

MAURITIUS

RÉUNION (France)

GWANA

MADAGASCAR

AUSTRALIA

ne
esburg

Maputo

TH
CA

SWAZILAND

LESOTHO

ALB.	Albania
AUS.	Austria
BELG.	Belgium
BOS.–HER.	Bosnia and Hercegovina
CZECH REP.	Czech Republic
CR.	Croatia
DEN.	Denmark
SERB-MONT.	Serbia & Montenegro
HUN.	Hungary
MAC.	Macedonia
NETH.	The Netherlands
SWITZ.	Switzerland
SLOV.	Slovakia
SLOVE.	Slovenia

Sydney

NEW ZEALAND

Melbourne

Wellington

Tasman Sea

2 Population

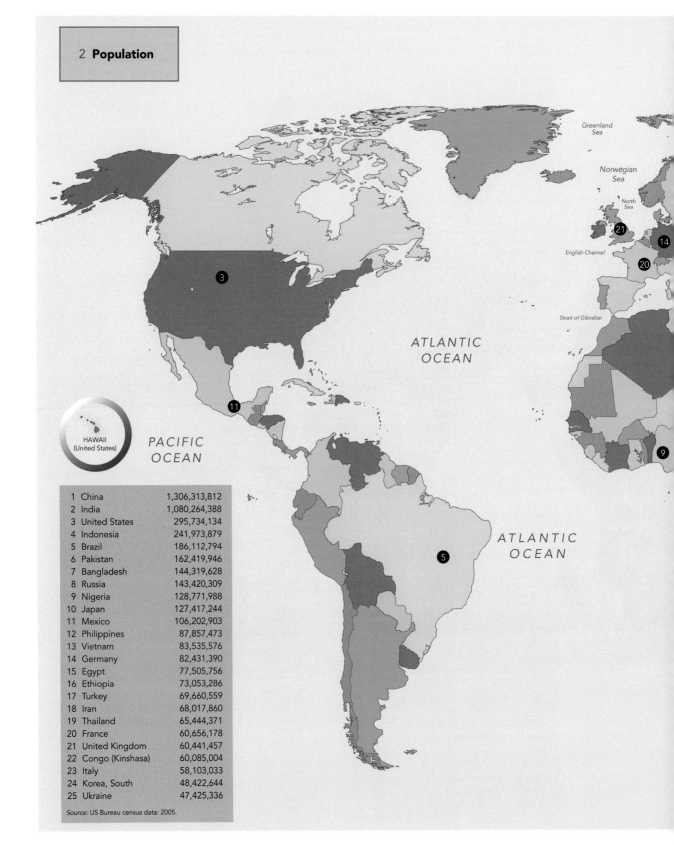

Greenland Sea

Norwegian Sea

North Sea

English Channel

Strait of Gibraltar

ATLANTIC OCEAN

ATLANTIC OCEAN

PACIFIC OCEAN

HAWAII (United States)

1	China	1,306,313,812
2	India	1,080,264,388
3	United States	295,734,134
4	Indonesia	241,973,879
5	Brazil	186,112,794
6	Pakistan	162,419,946
7	Bangladesh	144,319,628
8	Russia	143,420,309
9	Nigeria	128,771,988
10	Japan	127,417,244
11	Mexico	106,202,903
12	Philippines	87,857,473
13	Vietnam	83,535,576
14	Germany	82,431,390
15	Egypt	77,505,756
16	Ethiopia	73,053,286
17	Turkey	69,660,559
18	Iran	68,017,860
19	Thailand	65,444,371
20	France	60,656,178
21	United Kingdom	60,441,457
22	Congo (Kinshasa)	60,085,004
23	Italy	58,103,033
24	Korea, South	48,422,644
25	Ukraine	47,425,336

Source: US Bureau census data: 2005.

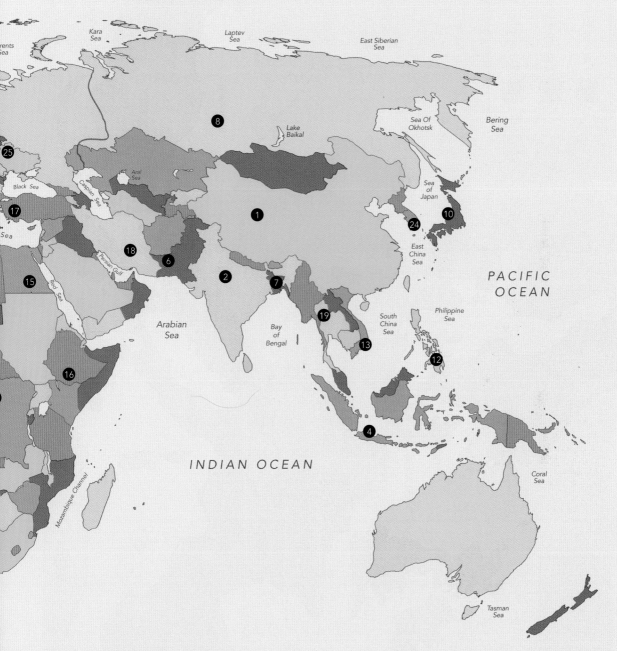

ARCTIC OCEAN

Kara
Sea

Laptev
Sea

East Siberian
Sea

Barents
Sea

Sea Of
Okhotsk

Bering
Sea

Lake
Baikal

8

Aral
Sea

Sea of
Japan

25

Black Sea

Caspian Sea

17

Sea

18

Persian Gulf

6

24

10

East
China
Sea

PACIFIC
OCEAN

15

Red Sea

1

2

7

19

South
China
Sea

Philippine
Sea

Arabian
Sea

Bay
of
Bengal

13

12

16

4

INDIAN OCEAN

Mozambique Channel

Coral
Sea

Tasman
Sea

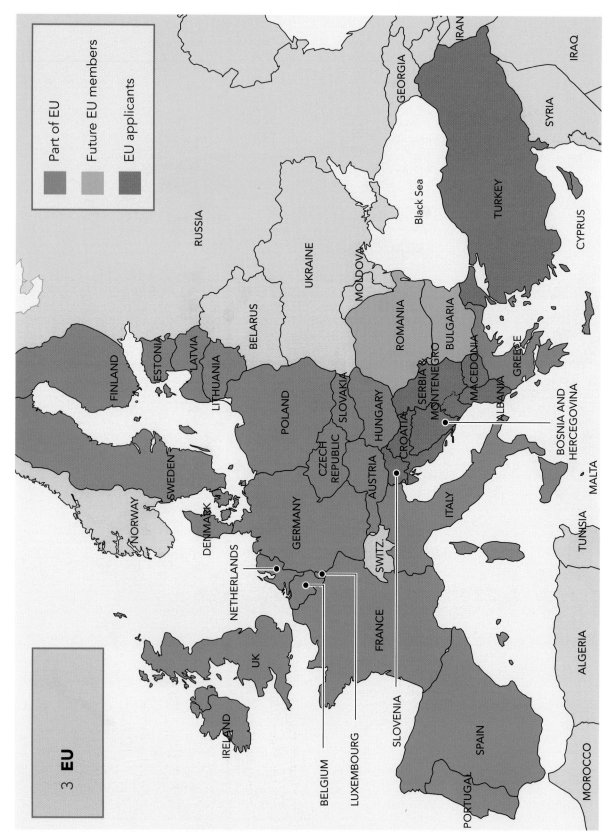

3 **EU**

Part of EU

Future EU members

EU applicants

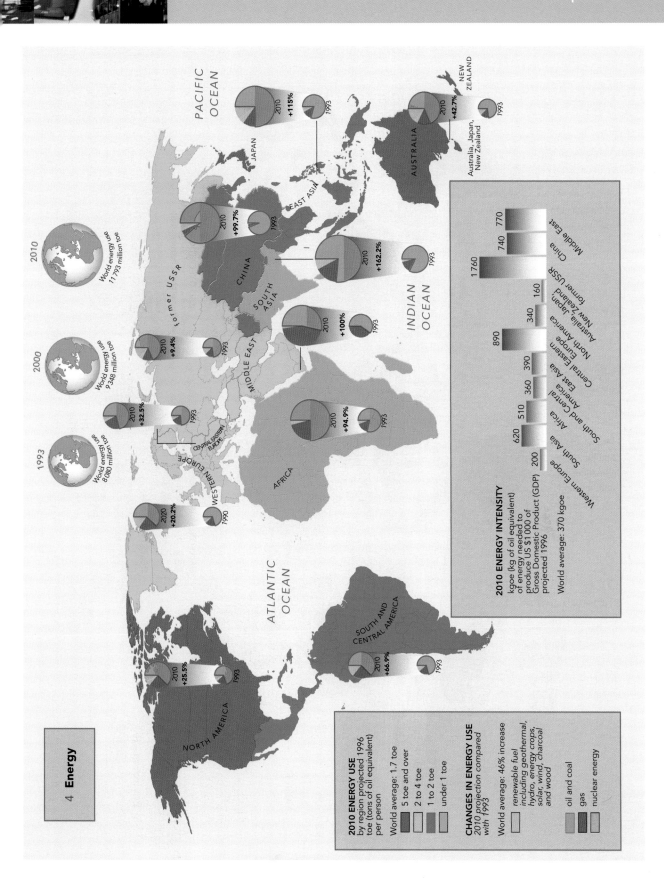

4 Energy

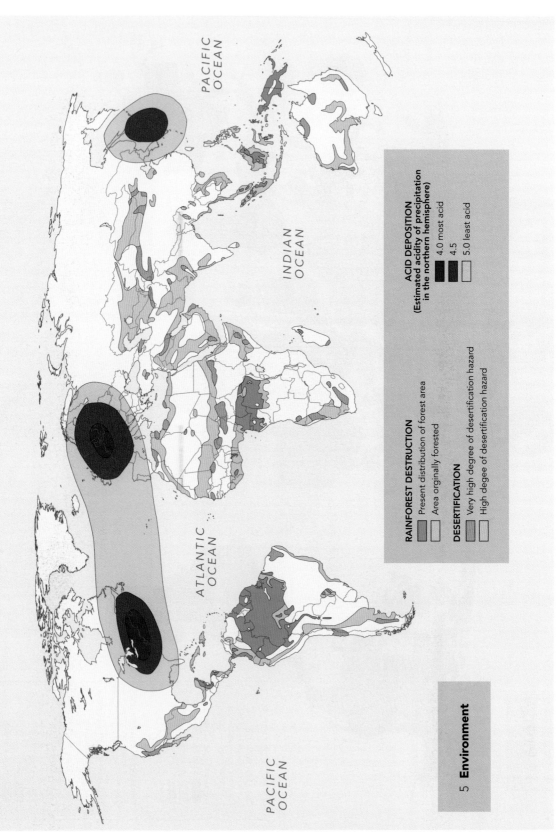

5 **Environment**

RAINFOREST DESTRUCTION

Present distribution of forest area

Area orginally forested

DESERTIFICATION

Very high degree of desertification hazard

High degree of desertification hazard

ACID DEPOSITION
(Estimated acidity of precipitation
in the northern hemisphere)

4.0 most acid

4.5

5.0 least acid

PACIFIC
OCEAN

ATLANTIC
OCEAN

PACIFIC
OCEAN

INDIAN
OCEAN

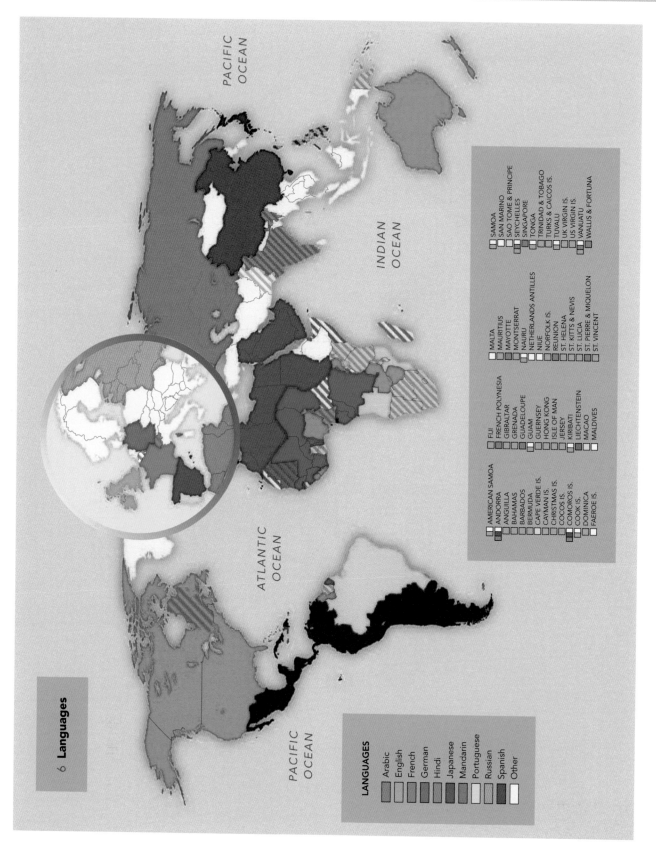

6 **Languages**

LANGUAGES

Arabic
English
French
German
Hindi
Japanese
Mandarin
Portuguese
Russian
Spanish
Other

PACIFIC OCEAN

PACIFIC OCEAN

ATLANTIC OCEAN

INDIAN OCEAN

AMERICAN SAMOA
ANDORRA
ANGUILLA
BAHAMAS
BARBADOS
BERMUDA
CAPE VERDE IS.
CAYMAN IS.
CHRISTMAS IS.
COCOS IS.
COMOROS IS.
COOK IS.
DOMINICA
FAEROE IS.

FIJI
FRENCH POLYNESIA
GIBRALTAR
GRENADA
GUADELOUPE
GUAM
GUERNSEY
HONG KONG
ISLE OF MAN
JERSEY
KIRIBATI
LIECHTENSTEIN
MACAO
MALDIVES

MALTA
MAURITIUS
MAYOTTE
MONTSERRAT
NAURU
NETHERLANDS ANTILLES
NIUE
NORFOLK IS.
REUNION
ST. HELENA
ST. KITTS & NEVIS
ST. LUCIA
ST. PIERRE & MIQUELON
ST. VINCENT

SAMOA
SAN MARINO
SAO TOME & PRINCIPE
SEYCHELLES
SINGAPORE
TONGA
TRINIDAD & TOBAGO
TURKS & CAICOS IS.
TUVALU
UK VIRGIN IS.
US VIRGIN IS.
VANUATU
WALLIS & FORTUNA

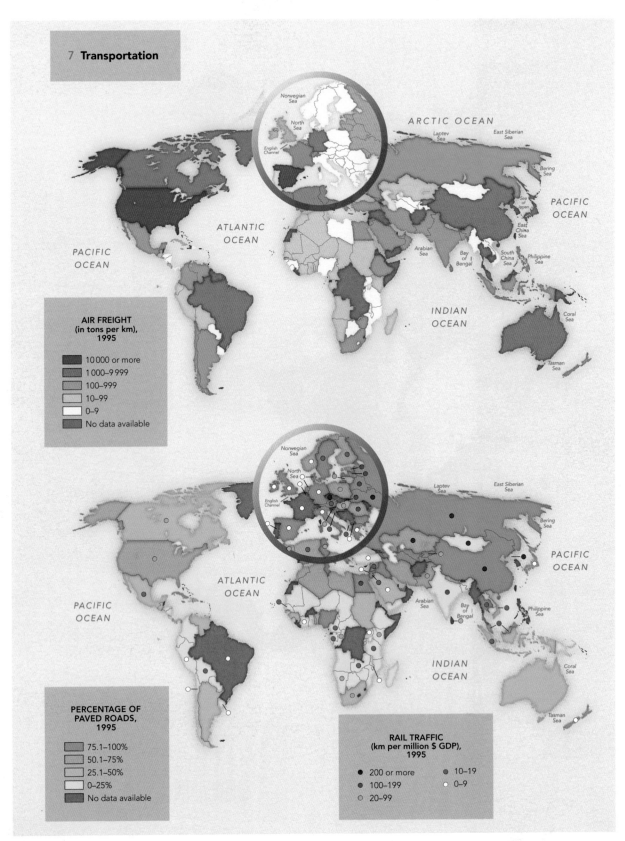

7 Transportation

AIR FREIGHT
(in tons per km),
1995

- 10 000 or more
- 1 000–9 999
- 100–999
- 10–99
- 0–9
- No data available

PERCENTAGE OF
PAVED ROADS,
1995

- 75.1–100%
- 50.1–75%
- 25.1–50%
- 0–25%
- No data available

RAIL TRAFFIC
(km per million $ GDP),
1995

- ● 200 or more
- ● 100–199
- ● 20–99
- ● 10–19
- ○ 0–9

section 1
an overview

chapter 1
The Scope and Challenge of International Marketing

Chapter Outline

Chapter Learning Objectives

What you should learn from Chapter 1

- ■ What is meant by international marketing
- ■ To understand the scope of the international marketing task
- ■ To comprehend the importance of the self-reference criterion (SRC) in international marketing
- ■ To identify and manage the factors influencing the internationalisation of companies
- ■ To evaluate the progression of becoming an international marketer
- ■ To see how international marketing concepts influence international marketers
- ■ To appreciate the increasing importance of global awareness

The modern world is organised on the theory that each nation state is sovereign and independent from other countries. In reality, however, no country can completely isolate its internal affairs from external forces. Even the most inward-looking regimes have realised the limitations of their own resources as well as the benefits of opening up their borders. This major change in the orientation of most regimes has led to an enormous amount of activity in the international marketplace.

A global economic boom in the last decade of the twentieth century has been one of the drivers for efficiency, productivity and open, unregulated markets that has swept the world.[1] Never before in world history have businesses been so deeply involved in and affected by international global developments. Powerful economic, technological, industrial, political and demographic forces are converging to form the foundation of a new global economic order on which the structure of a world economic and market system will be built.[2]

Whether or not a company wants to participate directly in international business, it cannot escape the effect of the ever-increasing number of domestic firms exporting, importing and/or manufacturing abroad; the number of foreign-based firms operating in most markets; the growth of regional trade areas; the rapid growth of world markets; and the increasing number of competitors for global markets. Of all the trends affecting global business today, five stand out as the most dynamic and as the ones that are influencing the shape of international business:

1 the interdependence of the world economies
2 the rapid growth of regional **free-trade areas** such as EU, NAFTA, **ASEAN** and **APEC**
3 the increase in wealth and growth in most parts of the world, causing enhanced purchasing power
4 the evolution of large emerging markets such as Brazil, China, India, Malaysia, Russia, Hungary and Poland
5 availability of advanced methods of communication and transportation due to developments in information technology.

These forces affecting international business have led to a dramatic growth in international trade and have contributed to a perception that the world has become a smaller and more interdependent place.[3] If we look at the Swiss multinational company Nestlé, 'The Food Company of the World', it claims its products are sold in every country in the world. It has factories in more than 80 countries and has many brands that are recognised all over the world.[4] Toyota and its subsidiaries sell their cars in more than 170 countries, giving it a presence in more countries than any other auto manufacturer.[5]

Today most business activities are global in scope. Finance, technology, research, capital and investment flows, production facilities, purchasing and marketing, and distribu-

key terms

free-trade area
where products can move freely, without tariffs and restrictions

ASEAN
the fourth biggest trade area of the world comprising 10 Southeast Asian countries

APEC
Asia Pacific cooperation among 21 member states. APEC promotes free trade and economic cooperation between members

tion networks all have global dimensions. Every business must be prepared to compete in an increasingly interdependent global economic environment, and all business people must be aware of the effects of these trends when managing a multinational conglomerate or a domestic company that exports. As one international expert noted, 'every company is international, at least to the extent that its business performance is conditioned in part by events that occur abroad'.[6] Even companies that do not operate in the international arena are affected to some degree by the success of the European Union, the post 9-11 political economy and the **economic changes** taking place in China and India. The aftermath of 9-11 and the war in Afghanistan and Iraq have changed the political as well as the economic scene. The interdependence among the nations and markets has, however, not been affected. Companies have become even more aggressive to capture new markets in order to compensate for recessions at home or in their traditional markets.

As competition for world markets intensifies, the number of companies operating solely in domestic markets is decreasing. Or, to put it another way, it is increasingly true that the business of any business is international business. The challenge of international marketing is to develop strategic plans that are competitive in the intensifying global markets. These and other issues affecting the world economy, trade, markets and competition will be discussed throughout this text.

key term

economic change change in economic conditions, e.g. recession

the internationalisation of business

Current interest in international marketing can be explained by the changing competitive structures coupled with shifts in demand characteristics in markets throughout the world.

With the increasing globalisation of markets, companies find they are unavoidably enmeshed with foreign customers, competitors and suppliers, even within their own borders. They face competition on all fronts - from domestic firms and from foreign firms. A significant portion of all televisions, DVD players, mobile phones, clothes and tableware sold in Western Europe is foreign made. Sony, Panasonic, Mitsubishi, Nokia, Fujitsu, Toyota

GOING INTERNATIONAL 1.1

evolution of a multinational company

1964 Phil Knight, an accountant at Price Waterhouse, and college track coach Bill Bowerman put in $500 each to start Blue Ribbon Sports.

1970 Bowerman, inspired by the waffle iron, dreams up new shoe treads, which evolve to become the best-selling US training shoe.

1971 Blue Ribbon changes its name to Nike and adopts the swoosh as its logo, designed by a college student for $35. She later gets an undisclosed number of stocks.

1973 Steve Prefontaine, the long-distance runner, becomes the first major athlete to wear Nike in competitions.

1980 Nike goes public with 2.4 million shares at $11. After several splits, stock is worth $78 per share in September 2004.

1985 Air Jordan, the best-selling athletic shoe ever, is introduced.

1987 Nike runs its first advertisement campaign, 'Revolution', based on a Beatles song.

1992 Magic Johnson, sponsored by Nike, wins a gold medal. The first Nike Town opens.

1994 Nike enters the football arena by signing top players such as Ronaldo from Brazil.

1999 Co-founder Bowerman dies and Knight takes total control under allegations of poor working conditions in Asian factories producing Nike goods.

2003 More than half the sales come from outside the US for the first time. It supersedes Adidas as number one football boot in Europe.

With revenues over $12 billion (2004), the company has come a long way from its early years when Phil Knight used to sell sneakers out of his car trunk at tracks. As for advertising, Nike spent $8 million in 1986 and $48 million in 1987. These days it pays $100 million for one endorsement (e.g. Tiger Woods). It has developed sophisticated computer systems to develop and market its products in more places in the world more quickly. It has improved its gross margin from 39.9 per cent in 1998 to 42.9 per cent in 2004. It makes only 3 per cent of shoes without a firm order from a retailer (30 per cent in 1998).

Today, like any other multinational company, Nike is not just one product/brand

company. It started diversifying in 1988 when it bought Cole Haan (dresses and casual shoes) for $88 million; in 1995 it bought Bauer (ice hockey skates) for $409 million; in 2002 it bought Hurley International (skateboard equipment) for $95 million, and Converse (retro-style sneakers) for $305 million in 2003.

As for production, Nike does not own any manufacturing facility. However, factories such as Yue Yuen in an industrial estate in Dongguan, China, are geared towards Nike standards and reflect Nike needs. A particular Nike shoe is made up of 52 different components, coming from five different countries, excluding non-material inputs such as design, transportation and marketing. It will be touched by at least 120 pairs of hands during production. The new production system is a network of logistics; not only do all the materials have to come together, but they also have to come together at the right time. Moreover, constant upgrading of materials, processes and workers is required. The designs and models are changed every week.

What does this mean for the business world? For one thing, it suggests the futility of trying to apply borders to today's business. Nike, for example, is an American firm and though our statesmen and trade negotiators haggle over local content, how would they classify Nike from the Dongguan factory? The leather comes from South Korea; those putting it together are mainland Chinese; the factory is owned by a Taiwanese; some components come from Japan and Indonesia; and the design and marketing come from America. And if this is the case for a simple pair of shoes, imagine what it must be for a computer or a car.

Sources: abstracted from *Far Eastern Economic Review*, 29 August 1996, p. 5; and Stanley Holmes, 'The New Nike', Cover Story, *Business Week*, 20 September 2004, pp. 54-64.

and Nissan are familiar brands in Europe and North America, and, for Western industry, they are formidable opponents in a competitive struggle for European and world markets.

Many familiar domestic companies are now foreign-controlled. When you shop for groceries at Aldi or A&P supermarkets, or buy Alka-Seltzer, you are buying indirectly from a German company. Some well-known brands no longer owned by US companies are Carnation (Swiss), Brooks Brothers clothing (Canada) and the all-American Smith and Wesson handgun, which is now owned by a British firm. There is hardly any country that is not involved in international trade and investment (Exhibit 1.1 shows the top 30 countries). In fact, foreign investment in Western countries by other industrialised countries is quite common. This is illustrated by Exhibit 1.2.

Companies with foreign operations find foreign earnings make an important overall contribution to total corporate profits. Companies that never ventured abroad until recently are now seeking foreign markets. Companies with existing foreign operations realise they

Exhibit 1.1 Top 30 countries for trade and expansion

Rank 2004	Country	GDP per capita US$	Trade blocs/ agreements	Trade bloc totals	Global competition ranking	Population (millions)	Inward direct investment	Export + import/ GDP
1	United States	39 340	NAFTA, WIPO, WTO, APEC, ISRAEL	26	2	293.03	14 1678	24.85
2	United Kingdom	27 920	EU, WIPO, WTO, ISRAEL, MEXICO	25	15	60.50	41 678	62.36
3	Japan	28 160	WIPO, WTO, APEC	14	11	127.33	7 199	33.08
4	Singapore	28 570	WIP, WTO, APEC, ASEAN	16	6	4.26	7 350	311.16
5	Canada	32 180	NAFTA, WIPO, WTO, APEC, CHILE, ISRAEL	28	16	32.01	25 232	60.29
6	Sweden	27 890	EU, WIPO, WTO, SCH, ISRAEL, MEXICO	28	3	9.00	14 916	116.01
7	Taiwan	25 820	WTO, APEC	4	5	22.75	1 878	71.16
8	Denmark	31 060	EU, EMU, WIPO, WTO, ISRAEL, MEXICO	28	4	5.39	9 186	117.07
9	Ireland	34 650	EU, EMU, WIPO, WTO, ISRAEL, MEXICO	32	30	3.95	18 678	169.94
10	Finland	28 630	EU, EMU, WIPO, WTO, ISRAEL, MEXICO	32	1	5.26	10 563	91.08
11	Australia	29 280	APEC, WIPO, WTO	14	10	20.01	9 700	42.05
12	Switzerland	30 770	EFTA, WIPO, WTO	14	7	7.35	8 061	113.20
13	Germany	27 800	EU, EMU, WIPO, WTO, SCH, ISRAEL, MEXICO	33	13	82.24	36 737	78.14
14	Netherlands	29 760	EU, EMU, WIPO, WTO, SCH, ISRAEL, MEXICO	35	12	16.32	32 385	130.12
15	Hong Kong	28 760	WIPO, WTO, APEC	14	24	7.08	17 500	331.19
16	France	28 350	EU, EMU, WIPO, WTO, SCH, ISRAEL, MEXICO	35	26	60.40	47 858	61.09
17	Spain	23 460	EU, EMU, WIPO, WTO, SCH, ISRAEL, MEXICO	35	23	41.05	27 414	52.29
18	Norway	38 360	EFTA, WIPO, WTO	14	9	4.55	3 644	83.58
19	Austria	30 100	EU, EMU, WIPO, WTO, SCH, ISRAEL, MEXICO	14	17	8.22	3 811	117.48
20	Belgium	29 270	EU, EMU, WIPO, WTO, SCH, ISRAEL MEXICO	35	27	10.29	20 733	159.98

Exhibit 1.1 (Top 30 countries for trade and expansion, continued)

Rank 2004	Country	GDP per capita US$	Trade blocs/ agreements	Trade bloc totals	Global competition ranking	Population (millions)	Inward direct investment	Export + import/ GDP
21	Italy	27 700	EU, EMU, WIPO, SCH, ISRAEL, MEXICO	30	41	58.06	14 875	48.84
22	South Korea	18 620	WIPO, WTO, APEC	14	18	48.22	2 789	84.69
23	New Zealand	231 130	WIPO, WTO, APEC	14	14	4.05	1 748	58.44
24	Portugal	18 410	EU, EMU, WIPO, WTO, SCH, ISRAEL, MEXICO	35	25	10.38	5 082	56.20
25	China	5 550	WIPO, WTO, APEC	10	44	1 305.63	57 000	18.34
26	Malaysia	6 840	WIPO, WTO, APEC, ASEAN	16	29	25.46	2 000	135.14
27	Greece	19 390	EU, EMU, WIPO, WTO, ISRAEL, MEXICO	25	35	10.67	554	37.37
28	Chile	11 180	MERCOSUR, WIPO, WTO, APEC, CAN., MEXICO, OTHERS	32	28	15.37	3 729	37.38
29	Thailand	7 880	APEC, WIPO, WTO ASEAN	16	32	64.55	3 000	45.57
30	Czech Republic	16 750	WIPO, WTO, EU, ISRAEL	15	39	10.24	5 000	72.60

Source: Lara L. Sowinski, '30 Top Countries for Trade and Expansion', *World Trade Magazine*, 1 June 2004.

must be more competitive to succeed against foreign multinationals. They have found it necessary to spend more money and time improving their marketing positions abroad because competition for these growing markets is intensifying. For the firm venturing into international marketing for the first time, and for those already experienced, the requirement is generally the same – a thorough and complete commitment to foreign markets and, for many, new ways of operating to handle the uncertainties of foreign markets.

international marketing defined

International marketing is the performance of business activities that direct the flow of a company's goods and services to consumers or users in more than one nation for a profit. The only difference in the definitions of domestic marketing and international marketing is that the marketing activities take place in more than one country. This apparently minor difference accounts for the complexity and diversity found in international marketing operations. Marketing concepts, processes and principles are to a great extent universally applicable, and the marketer's task is the same whether doing business in Amsterdam, London or Kuala Lumpur. The goal of a business is to make a profit by promoting, pricing and distributing products for which there is a market. If this is the case, what is the difference between domestic and international marketing?

The answer lies not with different concepts of marketing, but with the environment within which marketing plans must be implemented. The uniqueness of foreign marketing comes from the range of unfamiliar problems and the variety of strategies necessary to cope with the different levels of uncertainty encountered in foreign markets.

Exhibit 1.2 Direct investment flows around Europe, the United States and Japan, 2002

Countries	Inflow (million $)	Outflow (million $)	Net outflow (million $)
United States	30 030	119 741	89 711
Belgium and Luxembourg	143 912	167 361	23 449
Japan	9 326	31 481	22 155
United Kingdom	24 945	39 703	14 758
France	51 505	62 547	11 042
Norway	872	5 537	4 665
Austria	1 523	5 670	4 147
Italy	14 545	17 123	2 578
Switzerland	9 303	11 787	2 484
Finland	9 148	9 891	743
Sweden	11 081	10 869	–212
Hungary	854	264	–590
Portugal	4 276	3 523	–753
Denmark	5 953	4 839	–1 114
Spain	21 193	18 456	–2 737
The Netherlands	29 182	26 270	–2 912
Czech Republic	9 319	281	–9 038
Germany	38 033	24 534	–13 499

Source: World Investment Report 2003.

Competition, legal restraints, government controls, weather, fickle consumers and any number of other uncontrollable elements can, and frequently do, affect the profitable outcome of good, sound marketing plans. Generally speaking, the marketer cannot control or influence these uncontrollable elements, but instead must adjust or adapt to them in a manner consistent with a successful outcome. What makes marketing interesting is the challenge of moulding the controllable elements of marketing decisions (product, price, promotion and distribution) within the framework of the uncontrollable elements of the marketplace (competition, politics, laws, consumer behaviour, level of technology and so forth) in such a way that marketing objectives are achieved. Even though marketing principles and concepts are universally applicable, the environment within which the marketer must implement marketing plans can change dramatically from country to country. The difficulties created by different environments and culture are the international marketer's primary concern.

the international marketing task

The international marketer's task is more complicated than that of the domestic marketer because the international marketer must deal with at least two levels of uncontrollable uncertainty instead of one. Uncertainty is created by the uncontrollable elements of all business environments, but each foreign country in which a company operates adds its own unique set of uncontrollables. Exhibit 1.3 illustrates the total environment of an international marketer. The inner circle depicts the controllable elements that constitute a marketer's decision area, the second circle encompasses those environmental elements at home that have some effect on foreign-operation decisions, and the outer circles represent the elements of the foreign environment for each foreign market within which the

marketer operates. As the outer circles illustrate, each foreign market in which the company does business can (and usually does) present separate problems involving some or all of the uncontrollable elements. Thus, the greater the number of foreign markets in which a company operates, the greater the possible variety of foreign environmental uncontrollables with which to contend. Frequently, a solution to a problem in country market A is not applicable to a problem in country market B.

marketing controllables

The successful manager constructs a marketing programme designed for optimal adjustment to the uncertainty of the business climate. The inner circle in Exhibit 1.3 represents the area under the control of the marketing manager. Assuming the necessary overall corporate resources, the marketing manager blends price, product, promotion and channels-of-distribution activities to capitalise on anticipated demand. The controllable elements can be altered in the long run and, usually, in the short run, to adjust to changing market conditions or corporate objectives.

The outer circles surrounding the market controllables represent the levels of uncertainty that are created by the domestic and foreign environments. Although the marketer can blend a marketing mix from the controllable elements, the uncontrollables are precisely that and there must be active adaptation. These are the elements that are outside the control of the managers but need to be handled. That effort, the adaptation of the marketing mix to the uncontrollables, determines the ultimate outcome of the marketing enterprise.

domestic uncontrollables

The second circle, representing the domestic environment in Exhibit 1.3, includes home-country elements that are outside the control of the manager and that can have a direct effect on the success of a foreign venture: political forces, legal structure and economic climate.

A political decision involving domestic foreign policy can have a direct effect on a firm's international marketing success. For example, most Western governments imposed restrictions on trade with South Africa to protest about apartheid. In this case the international marketing programmes of such companies as Shell, IBM and British Petroleum (BP) were restricted by domestic uncontrollables. Conversely, positive effects occur when there are changes in foreign policy and countries are given favoured treatment. Such were the cases when South Africa abolished apartheid and the embargo was lifted, and when the Western governments decided to encourage trade with Libya as a reward for not pursuing weapons of mass destruction. In both cases, opportunities were created for international companies.

The domestic economic climate is another important home-based uncontrollable variable with far-reaching effects on a company's competitive position in foreign markets. The capacity to invest in plants and facilities either in domestic or foreign markets is to a large extent a function of domestic economic vitality. It is generally true that capital tends to flow towards optimum use; however, capital must be generated before it can have mobility. Furthermore, if internal economic conditions deteriorate, restrictions against foreign investment and purchasing may be imposed to strengthen the domestic economy.

Inextricably entwined with the effects of the domestic environment are the constraints imposed by the environment of each foreign country.

foreign uncontrollables

In addition to uncontrollable domestic elements, a significant source of uncertainty is the number of uncontrollable foreign business environments (depicted in Exhibit 1.3 by the outer circles). A business operating in its home country undoubtedly feels comfort-

Exhibit 1.3 The international marketing task

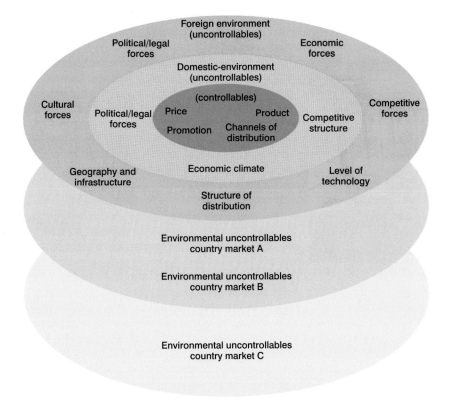

able in forecasting the business climate and adjusting business decisions to these elements. The process of evaluating the uncontrollable elements in an international marketing programme, however, often involves substantial doses of cultural, political and economic shock.

GOING INTERNATIONAL 1.2

McDonald's revolutions

In 2002, McDonald's, the biggest global brand after Coca-Cola, was about to announce its first quarterly loss since going public in 1965. Sales were falling and hundreds of underperforming restaurants were closed; earnings per share had fallen in six out of eight previous quarters. Market share was contested by a new breed of 'quick casual' restaurants such as Panera Bread and Prêt À Manger. The chain ranked at the bottom of the University of Michigan's American Customer Satisfaction Index. To cap it all, it was targeted by a number of lawsuits brought against fast-food companies in the US, and shirts and mugs emblazoned with the words 'Stop super-sizing us' started multiplying across the country. However, as the company responded to the crisis, sales in the US were boosted by new main-course salads and breakfast sandwiches in the first half of 2003, bringing the share prices up by 80 per cent. Nevertheless, it is still for the future to show whether the recovery will be sustainable. Meanwhile, the company is attempting to turn McDonald's into a 'lifestyle' brand, comparable with Apple or Nike, through better products, better marketing and better restaurants.

The company revised its growth targets. Previous targets of 10-15 per cent a year resulted in a focus on opening new restaurants, and service in the existing ones was neglected. Now McDonald's is aiming for annual sales growth of 3-5 per cent from 2005 onwards, with only 2 percentage points coming from new restaurants. The partially lapsed system of sending inspectors round to grade restaurants on quality, service and cleanliness was standardised and toughened up, making it easier to weed out underperforming franchises. Premium salads were added to the menu in March 2003. A 'Salad Plus' menu, offering a variety of low-fat foods, is being tested in Australia. Apple slices are being tested in children's Happy Meals. A new global advertising campaign, featuring the new slogan 'I'm Lovin' It', is the first time McDonald's advertisements in 118 operating countries have used the same slogan.

Other changeover ideas came from one of the most unlikely places - France. Despite the somewhat sour Franco-US relations, France is McDonald's best-performing European subsidiary in terms of operating income per outlet and is in the global vanguard of redesigning restaurants and launching products. French management attributes its success to the adaptation to local tastes and habits. In particular, McDonald's France has an important focus on the 'modernity' of the restaurant image. The company transformed many outlets into so-called 'casual restaurants' by using softer interior materials, and making the seating space more comfortable and attractive. There are lounge chairs in place of hard, fixed plastic seats, and some restaurants have Apple iPod digital music players installed around the walls, so diners can don headphones and listen to music of their choice.

Interior of a 'casual restaurant' McDonald's in France.
Reprinted with permission

Source: adapted from Buckley, N. 'Eyes on the Fries: Will New Products, Restaurant Refits and a Marketing Overhaul Sustain the Golden Arches?'; Minder, R. 'Croques, Leather and Headphones put France in the Vanguard', *Financial Times*, 29 August 2003, p. 15; and 'Battling against Big Food,' *The Economist*, 21 December 2002, p. 116.

A business operating in a number of foreign countries might find polar extremes in political stability, class structure and economic climate - critical elements in business decisions. The dynamic upheavals in some countries further illustrate the problems of dramatic change in cultural, political and economic climates over relatively short periods of time. A case in point is the Soviet Union - a single market that divided into 15 independent republics, 11 of which reformed in a matter of days as the Commonwealth of Independent States (CIS), leaving investors uncertain about the future. They found themselves asking whether contracts and agreements with the Soviet Government were valid in individual independent states. Was the Republic of Russia empowered to represent the CIS, would the rouble survive as the currency of the CIS, and who had the authority to negotiate the sale of property or the purchase of equipment? In a very short period, the foreign investors' enthusiasm for investment in the former USSR and its republics turned to caution in the face of drastic changes as it transformed itself into a market economy.[7] Ever since its liberalisation, Russia, the biggest market among the CIS, has had an inflation rate of 15 per cent per month. This has caused enormous exchange variation, as illustrated by Exhibit 1.4. Such are the uncertainties of the uncontrollable political factors of international business.

The more significant elements in the uncontrollable international environment include (1) political/legal forces, (2) economic forces, (3) competitive forces, (4) level of

technology, (5) structure of distribution, (6) geography and infrastructure, and (7) cultural forces. They constitute the principal elements of uncertainty that an international marketer must cope with in designing a marketing programme. Each is discussed in some detail in subsequent chapters.

Also, a problem for some marketers attuned to one environment is the inability to easily recognise the potential impact of certain uncontrollable elements within another environment, one to which they have not been culturally acclimatised. Road signs of danger and indicators of potential in a foreign market may not always be read or interpreted accurately. The level of technology is an uncontrollable element that can often be misread because of the vast differences that may exist between developed and developing countries. For example, a marketer cannot assume that the understanding of the concept of preventive maintenance for machinery and equipment is the same in other countries as it is in the home country. Thus, in a developing country, where the general population does not have the same level of technical knowledge that exists in a developed country, a marketer will have to take extra steps to ensure that routine maintenance procedures and their importance are understood.

The problem of foreign uncertainty is further complicated by a frequently imposed 'alien status' that increases the difficulty of properly assessing and forecasting the dynamic international business climate. There are two dimensions to the alien status of a foreign business: alien in that the business is controlled by foreigners and alien in that the culture of the host country is alien to the foreign company. The alien status of a business results in greater emphasis being placed on many of the uncontrollable elements than would be found with relation to those same elements in the domestic market.

The political environment offers the best example of the alien status. Domestic marketers must consider the political ramifications of their decisions although the consequences of this environmental element are generally minor. Even a noticeable change in government attitudes towards domestic business with a change of political parties is seldom serious; such is not the case in a foreign country. The political and legal environment can be extremely critical, and shifts in governments often mean sudden changes in attitudes that can result in expropriation, expulsion or major restrictions on operations. The fact is that the foreign company is foreign and thus always subject to the political whims of the government to a greater degree than a domestic firm.

The uncertainty of different foreign business environments creates the need for a close study of the operating environment within each new country relevant for your industry/product. Different solutions to fundamentally identical marketing tasks are

Exhibit 1.4 Rouble exchange rate against the dollar

1989	0.6	1997 (Jan)	5 585.0
1990	1.7	1998 (Jan)	59 980.0
1991 (Jan)	37.6	1999 (Jan)	285 050.0
1992 (Jan)	110.0	2000 (Jan)	274 900.0
1993 (Jan)	417.0	2001 (Jan)	299 300.0
1994 (Jan)	1 400.0	2002 (Jan)	304 701.0
1995 (Jan)	4 500.0	2003 (Jan)	319 578.0
1996 (Jan)	4 999.0	2004 (Jan)	292 400.0
		2005 (Jan)	280 050.0

Sources: Peter Buckley and Pervez Ghauri, *The Economics of Change in Eastern Europe*, 1994, p. 25; xe.com, http://www.xe.com, 2004.

often in order and are generally the result of changes in the environment of the market. Thus, a strategy successful in one country can be rendered ineffective in another by differences in political climate, stages of economic development, level of technology or other cultural variation.

environmental adjustment needed

To adjust and adapt a marketing programme to foreign markets, marketers must be able to interpret effectively the influence and impact of each of the uncontrollable environmental elements on the marketing plan for each foreign market in which they hope to do business. In a broad sense, the uncontrollable elements constitute the culture; the difficulty facing the marketer in adjusting to the culture (i.e. uncontrollable elements of the marketplace) lies in recognising their impact. In a domestic market, the reaction to much of the uncontrollables' (cultural) impact on the marketer's activities is automatic; the various cultural influences that fill our lives are simply a part of our history. We react in a manner acceptable to our society without thinking about it because we are culturally responsive to our environment. The experiences we have gained throughout life have become second nature and serve as the basis for our behaviour.

The task of cultural adjustment is perhaps the most challenging and important one confronting international marketers; they must adjust their marketing efforts to cultures to which they are not attuned. In dealing with unfamiliar markets, marketers must be aware of the frames of reference they are using in making their decisions or evaluating the potential of a market because judgements are derived from experience that is the result of the enculturative process. Once a frame of reference is established, it becomes an important factor in determining or modifying a marketer's reaction to situations – social and even non-social – especially if experience or knowledge of accustomed behaviour is lacking.

When a marketer operates in other cultures, marketing attempts may fail because of unconscious responses based on frames of reference acceptable in one's own culture but unacceptable in different surroundings. Unless special efforts are made to determine local cultural meanings for every market, the marketer is likely to overlook the significance of certain behaviours or activities and proceed with plans that result in a negative or unwanted response.

For example, a Westerner must learn that white is a symbol of mourning in parts of Asia, quite different from Western culture's white for bridal gowns. Also, time-conscious Westerners are not culturally prepared to understand the meaning of time to Latin Americans or Arabs. These differences must be learned in order to avoid misunderstandings that can lead to marketing failures. Such a failure actually occurred in one situation when ignorance led to ineffective advertising on the part of a Western firm; and a second misunderstanding resulted in lost sales when a 'long waiting period' in the outer office of an emerging market customer was misinterpreted by a Western sales executive.

To avoid such errors, the foreign marketer should be aware of the principle of *marketing relativism*, that is, marketing strategies and judgements are based on experience, and experience is interpreted by each marketer in terms of his or her own culture and experience. We take into the marketplace, at home or in a foreign country, frames of reference developed from past experiences that determine or modify our reactions to the situations we face.

Cultural conditioning is like an iceberg – we are not aware of nine-tenths of it. In any study of the market systems of different people, their political and economic structures, religions and other elements of culture, foreign marketers must constantly guard against measuring and assessing the markets against the fixed values and assumptions of their own cultures. They must take specific steps to make themselves aware of the home cultural reference in their analyses and decision making.

self-reference criterion: an obstacle

The key to successful international marketing is adaptation to the environmental differences from one market to another. Adaptation is a conscious effort on the part of the international marketer to anticipate the influences of both the foreign and domestic uncontrollable environments on a marketing mix, and then to adjust the marketing mix to minimise the effects.

The primary obstacle to success in international marketing is a person's **self-reference criterion (SRC)** in making decisions, that is, an unconscious reference to one's own cultural values, experiences and knowledge as a basis for decisions. The SRC impedes the ability to assess a foreign market in its true light.

When confronted with a set of facts, we react spontaneously on the basis of knowledge assimilated over a lifetime – knowledge that is a product of the history of our culture. Quite often we do not know ourselves why we behave in a certain way in a certain situation, as we do that unconsciously. We seldom stop to think about a reaction; we react. Thus, when faced with a problem in another culture, the tendency is to react instinctively, referring only to our SRC for a solution. Our reaction, however, is based on meanings, values, symbols and behaviour relevant to our own culture – and usually different from those of the foreign culture. Such decisions are often not helpful.

To illustrate the impact of the SRC, consider misunderstandings that can occur about personal space between people of different cultures. In the West, unrelated individuals keep a certain physical distance between themselves and others when talking to each other or in groups. We do not consciously think about that distance we just know what feels right without thinking. When someone is too close or too far away, we feel uncomfortable and either move further away or get closer to correct the distance – we are relying on our SRC (see Exhibit 1.5). In some cultures, the acceptable distance between individuals is substantially less than that comfortable to Westerners. When Westerners, unaware of another culture's acceptable distance, are approached too closely by someone from another culture, they unconsciously react by backing away to restore the proper distance (i.e. proper by their own standards) and confusion results for both parties. Westerners assume 'foreigners' are pushy, while foreigners assume Westerners are unfriendly and standoffish. Both react to the values of their own SRCs, making them all victims of a cultural misunderstanding.

Your SRC can prevent you from being aware that there are cultural differences, or from recognising the importance of those differences. Thus, you fail to recognise the need to take action, discount the cultural differences that exist among countries or react to a situation in a way that is offensive to your hosts. A common mistake made by Westerners is to refuse food or drink when offered. In Europe, a polite refusal is certainly acceptable, but in many countries in Asia and the Middle East, a host is offended if you refuse hospitality. While you do not have to eat or drink much, you do have to accept the offering of hospitality. Understanding and dealing with the self-reference criterion are two of the more important facets in international marketing.

If we evaluate every situation through our SRC, then we are ethnocentric. The ethnocentrism and the SRC can influence an evaluation of the appropriateness of a domestically designed marketing mix for a foreign market. If Western marketers are not aware, they may evaluate a marketing mix on Western experiences (i.e. their SRC) without fully appreciating the cultural differences requiring adaptation. ESSO, a brand name for petrol, was a successful name in the United States and would seem harmless enough for foreign countries; however, in Japan, the name phonetically means 'stalled car', an undesirable image for petrol. Another example is 'Pet' in Pet Milk. The name has been used for decades; yet in France, the word *pet* means, among other things, flatulence – again, not the desired image for canned milk. Both of these examples of real mistakes made by major companies stem from relying on SRC in making a decision. In international marketing, relying on one's SRC can produce an inadequately adapted marketing programme that ends in failure.

key term

self-reference criterion (SRC) Considering our own conditions, values and norms

Exhibit 1.5 Four circles of intimacy

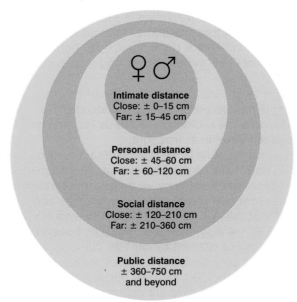

Source: based on Raymond Lesikar and John Pettit, *Business Communication: Theory and Practice* (Homewood, IL: Irwin, 1989).

The most effective way to control the influence of the SRC is to recognise its existence in our behaviour. Although it is almost impossible for someone to learn every culture in depth and to be aware of every important difference, an awareness of the need to be sensitive to differences and to ask questions when doing business in another culture can avoid many of the mistakes possible in international marketing. Asking the appropriate question helped the Vicks Company avoid making a mistake in Germany. It discovered that, in German, 'Vicks' sounds like the crudest slang equivalent of intercourse, so it changed the name to 'Wicks' before introducing the product.[8]

Also be aware that not every activity within a marketing programme is different from one country to another: there are probably more similarities than differences. Such similarities may lull the marketer into a false sense of apparent sameness. This apparent sameness, coupled with our SRC and ethnocentrism, is often the cause of international marketing problems. Undetected similarities do not cause problems; however, the one difference that goes undetected can create a marketing failure. To avoid this, we need to conduct a cross-cultural analysis of each situation and isolate the SRC influence that induces us to be ethnocentric.

becoming international

Once a company has decided to go international, it has to decide the way it will enter a foreign market, and the degree of marketing involvement and commitment it is prepared to make. These decisions should reflect considerable study and analysis of market potential and company capabilities, a process not always followed. Many companies appear to grow into international marketing through a series of phased developments. They gradually change strategy and tactics as they become more involved. Others enter international marketing after much research, with long-range plans fully developed.[9]

phases of international marketing involvement

Regardless of the means employed to gain entry into a foreign market, a company may, from a marketing viewpoint, make no market investment, that is, its marketing involve-

GOING INTERNATIONAL 1.3

you're sick? is it the heart, a virus or liver? it depends where you are from

Pharmaceutical companies have commissioned concurrent studies to help them package and market their products throughout Europe simultaneously, rather than country by country. This is because they know there are deep-rooted national differences in how people think about health, disease and medicine. In the United Kingdom and the Netherlands, people prefer tablets when taking medicine. In France, suppositories are preferred, while in Germany an injection will do.

In different countries, different organs are believed to be the cause of illness. Germans are almost obsessive about the heart and circulation – they are Europe's largest consumers of heart medicine. Southern Europeans assign almost mystical qualities to the liver. In the United Kingdom, doctors tend to look for external agents attacking the body and they prescribe antibiotics. In the central European countries, people turn first to herbal treatments and hot and cold baths, relying on antibiotics only as remedies of last resort. If you say you are tired, the Germans would say that it was cardiac insufficiency. In England they would consider you depressed.

Source: abstracted from Lynn Payer, *Medicine and Culture* (New York: Henry Holt, 1988), p. 265.

ment may be limited to selling a product with little or no thought given to development of market control. Or a company may become totally involved and invest large sums of money and effort to capture and maintain a permanent, specific share of the market. In general, a business can be placed in at least one of five distinct but overlapping phases of international marketing involvement, as outlined below.

No Direct Foreign Marketing In this phase, there is no active cultivation of customers outside national boundaries; however, this company's products may reach foreign markets. Sales may be made to trading companies and other foreign customers who come directly to the firm. Or products reach foreign markets via domestic wholesalers or distributors who sell abroad on their own without explicit encouragement or even knowledge of the producer. An unsolicited order from a foreign buyer is often what piques the interest of a company to seek additional international sales.

Infrequent Foreign Marketing Temporary surpluses caused by variations in production levels or demand may result in infrequent marketing overseas. The surpluses are characterised by their temporary nature; therefore, sales to foreign markets are made as goods are available, with little or no intention of maintaining continuous market representation. As domestic demand increases and absorbs surpluses, foreign sales activity is withdrawn. In this phase, there is little or no change in company organisation or product lines.

Regular Foreign Marketing At this level, the firm has permanent productive capacity devoted to the production of goods to be marketed on a continuing basis in foreign markets. A firm may employ foreign or domestic overseas middlemen or it may have its

own sales force or sales subsidiaries in important foreign markets. The primary focus for products presently being produced is to meet domestic market needs. Investments in marketing and management effort and in overseas manufacturing and/or assembly are generally begun in this phase. Further, some products may become specialised to meet the needs of individual foreign markets, pricing and profit policies tend to become equal with domestic business, and the company begins to become dependent on foreign profits.

International Marketing Companies in this phase are fully committed and involved in international marketing activities. Such companies seek markets throughout the world and sell products that are a result of planned production for markets in various countries. This generally entails not only the marketing but also the production of goods throughout the world. At this point, a company becomes an international or multinational marketing firm dependent on foreign revenues.

Global Marketing At the global marketing level, companies treat the world, including their home market, as their market. This is one step further than the multinational or international company that views the world as a series of country markets (including their home market) with unique sets of market characteristics for which products and marketing strategies must be developed. A global company develops an overall strategy and image to reflect the existing commonalities of market needs among many countries to maximise returns through some global standardisation of its business activities – as much as it is culturally possible to achieve such efficiencies.

changes in international orientation

Experience shows that a significant change in the international orientation of a firm occurs when that company relies on foreign markets to absorb permanent production surpluses and comes to depend on foreign profits. Businesses usually move through the phases of international marketing involvement one at a time, but it is not unusual for a company to skip one or more phases. As a firm moves from one phase to another, the complexity and sophistication of international marketing activity tends to increase and the degree of internationalisation to which management is philosophically committed tends to change. Such commitment affects the specific international strategies and decisions of the firm.

International operations of businesses reflect the changing competitiveness brought about by the globalisation of markets, interdependence of the world's economies, and the growing number of competing firms from developed and developing countries vying for the world's markets. *Global companies* and *global marketing* are terms frequently used to describe the scope of operations and marketing management orientation of these companies. Global markets are evolving for some products but do not exist yet for most products. In many countries, there are still consumers for many products, reflecting the differences in needs and wants, and there are different ways of satisfying these needs and wants based on cultural influences.

international marketing orientations

Although not articulated as such in current literature, it appears that the differences in the international orientation and approach to international markets that guide the international business activities of companies can be described by one of three orientations to international marketing management:

1 domestic market extension orientation
2 multidomestic market orientation
3 global marketing orientation.

It is to be expected that differences in the complexity and sophistication of a company's marketing activity depend on which of these orientations guides its operations. The ideas expressed in each concept reflect the philosophical orientation that also can be associated with successive stages in the evolution of the international operations in a company.

Among the approaches describing the different orientations that evolve in a company as it moves through different phases of international marketing involvement – from casual exporting to global marketing – is the often-quoted **EPRG schema**. The authors of this schema suggest that firms can be classified as having an **E**thnocentric, **P**olycentric, **R**egiocentric or **G**eocentric orientation (EPRG) depending on the international commitment of the firm. Further, the authors state that 'a key assumption underlying the EPRG framework is that the degree of internationalisation to which management is committed or willing to move towards affects the specific international strategies and decision rules of the firm'.[10] The EPRG schema is incorporated into the discussion of the three concepts that follows in that the philosophical orientations described by the EPRG schema help explain management's view when guided by one of the orientations.

domestic market extension orientation

This orientation to international marketing is illustrated by the domestic company seeking sales extension of its domestic products into foreign markets. It views its international operations as secondary to and an extension of its domestic operations; the primary motive is to dispose of excess domestic production. Domestic business is its priority and foreign sales are seen as a profitable extension of domestic operations. Even though foreign markets may be vigorously pursued, the firm's orientation remains basically domestic. Its attitude towards international sales is typified by the belief that if it sells in Manchester it will sell anywhere else in the world. Minimal, if any, efforts are made to adapt the marketing mix to foreign markets; the firm's orientation is to market to foreign customers in the same manner as the company markets to domestic customers. It seeks markets where demand is similar to the home market and its domestic product will be acceptable. This domestic market extension strategy can be very profitable; large and small exporting companies approach international marketing from this perspective. Sporadic export of cheese to Germany and Belgium by some Dutch dairy producers is an example of this concept. Firms with this marketing approach are classified as *ethnocentric* in the EPRG schema.

multidomestic market orientation

Once a company recognises the importance of differences in overseas markets and the importance of offshore business to the organisation, its orientation towards international business may shift to a multidomestic market strategy. A company guided by this concept has a strong sense that country markets are vastly different (and they may be, depending on the product) and that market success requires an almost independent programme for each country. Firms with this orientation market on a country-by-country basis, with separate marketing strategies for each country.

Subsidiaries operate independently of one another in establishing marketing objectives and plans, and the domestic market and each of the country markets have separate marketing mixes with little interaction among them. Products are adapted for each market without coordination with other country markets; advertising campaigns are localised, as are the pricing and distribution decisions.

A company with this concept does not look for similarity among elements of the marketing mix that might respond to standardisation; rather, it aims for adaptation to local country markets. Control is typically decentralised to reflect the belief that the uniqueness of each market requires local marketing input and control. Production and sale of detergents and soaps by Unilever, all over the world, is a typical example of this concept. Firms with this orientation would be classified in the EPRG schema as *polycentric*.

key term

EPRG schema
classifies firms by
their orientation:
ethnocentric,
polycentric,
regiocentric or
geocentric

GOING INTERNATIONAL 1.4

striking a balance between global and local

Multinational companies are often either 'hopelessly local' or 'mindlessly global' in their approach. Unilever tends to be the former, where far away subsidiaries used to work independently with minimal supervision. More recently, however, a new strategy, 'path to growth', has been introduced to correct this. It will ensure that the biggest brands will be managed more centrally.

The best-performing Unilever brands now tend to be those that have undergone this process of globalisation, such as deodorants. But Unilever's €24 billion a year food business is lagging behind the toiletries. The difference lies in the need to accommodate local tastes. The food division has priority brands ranging from Lipton tea to Bertolli olive oil. In spite of best efforts, a local nuance to sales strategies has been missing. The newly installed marketing president for the food division says tomato soup has to taste different in the UK, the Netherlands and Germany.

With thanks to
Unilever Ice Cream
and Frozen Food

One opinion is that Unilever managers are too focused on abstract problems, while they should be aspiring for customer management. As one analyst says, 'They have pretty good brands. It just seems like they have not produced things that the consumer wants.' To overcome this, Unilever has increasingly been poaching staff from rivals to diversify its gene pool. The path to growth strategy, launched in 1999/2000, is designed to conquer a perennial problem of big companies – how to make scale an asset rather than an encumbrance.

One reason that Unilever's performance is questioned is its comparison with Procter & Gamble, its old rival, which has shown vibrant growth after its own restructuring. One analyst believes that breaking up the company into food, and home and personal care would help it to focus on its markets and adapt to local needs, while others say that the group enjoys distribution and purchasing benefits from combining the two businesses worldwide. The management's opinion is, 'The business has been in transformational changes for a number of years. I have no doubt there will be other changes in the future. Nobody can take refuge in saying we haven't quite got the structure right, or we haven't got the brands right, or we haven't got the people right, or we haven't quite got the margins or the cost structure right. All this has been put into place and now we have to build on it.'

■ Do you think Unilever is on the right track for growth? Discuss its path to growth strategy.

Facts on Unilever

■ Employs 234,000 people in around 100 different countries.
■ Worldwide turnover in 2003 was €42.9 billion, 2.5 per cent of which spent on R&D.
■ Food brands include Knorr, Flora/Becel, Hellman's, Lipton, Iglo/Birds Eye/Findus, Rama/Blue Band, SlimFast and Bertolli.
■ Leading personal care brands include Lux, Dove, Sunsilk, Pond's, Axe/Lyns and Rexona.
■ Since the path to growth strategy was launched in 2000, the company has reduced the number of brands from 1 600 to 400 leading brands and 250 smaller brands.

Source: compiled from company information and Adam Jones, 'No Nimble Giant: The Stumbling Blocks Unilever Faces on its Path to Growth', *Financial Times*, 23 August 2004, p. 15.

global marketing orientation

A company guided by this orientation or philosophy is generally referred to as a *global company* – its marketing activity is global and its market coverage is the world. A company employing a global marketing strategy strives for efficiencies of scale by developing a product, to be sold at a reasonable price to a global market, that is, somewhat the same country market set throughout the world. Important to the global marketing concept is the premise that world markets are being 'driven towards a converging commonality',[11] seeking in much the same ways to satisfy their needs and desires. Thus, they constitute significant market segments with similar demands for the same basic product the world over. With this orientation a company attempts to standardise as much of the company effort as is practical on a worldwide basis.

Some decisions are viewed as applicable worldwide, while others require consideration of local influences. The world as a whole is viewed as the market and the firm develops a global marketing strategy, although pricing, advertising or distribution channels may differ in different markets. The development and marketing of the Sony Walkman or PlayStation are good examples of a global marketing orientation. The global marketing company would fit the *regiocentric* or *geocentric* classifications of the EPRG schema.

The global marketing concept views an entire set of country markets (whether the home market and only one other, or the home market and 100 other countries) as a unit, identifying groups of prospective buyers with similar needs as a global market segment, and developing a marketing plan that strives for some level of standardisation wherever it is culturally and cost effective. This might mean a company's global marketing plan has a standardised product but country-specific advertising, or has a standardised theme in all countries with country- or cultural-specific appeals to a unique market characteristic, a standardised brand or image but adapted products to meet specific country needs, and so on. In other words, the marketing planning and marketing mix are approached from a global perspective and, where feasible in the marketing mix, efficiencies of standardisation are sought. Wherever cultural uniqueness dictates the need for adaptation of the product, its image and so on, it is accommodated.

As the competitive environment facing today's businesses becomes more internationalised, the most effective orientation for all firms involved in marketing into another country will be a multidomestic or a global orientation. This means operating as if all the country markets in a company's scope of operations (including the domestic market) are approachable by standardising the overall marketing strategy and adapting the marketing mix as much as possible according to cultural and other uncontrollable factors.

Although the world has not become a homogeneous market, there is strong evidence of identifiable groups of consumers (segments) across country borders with similar purchasing power, needs and behaviour patterns. However, the same product might need a different marketing mix in different countries. Sometimes it is forced by environments, such as government regulations and income levels, and sometimes it is influenced by the fact that the product is in different stages of the product life cycle in different markets. Regardless of the degree to which global markets exist, a company can benefit from a global orientation. The issue of whether marketing programmes should be standardised or localised is not as critical as the recognition that marketing planning processes need to be coordinated across markets.

globalisation of markets

Theodore Levitt's article 'The Globalization of Markets' has spawned a host of new references to marketing activities: global marketing, global business, global advertising and global brands, as well as serious discussions of the processes of international marketing.[12] Professor Levitt's premise is that world markets are being driven 'towards a converging commonality'. Almost everyone everywhere wants all the things they have heard about, seen or experienced via the new technologies. He sees substantial market segments with

common needs, that is, a high-quality, reasonably priced, standardised product. The 'global corporation sells the same thing in the same way everywhere'. Professor Levitt argues that segmenting international markets on political boundaries, and customising products and marketing strategies for country markets or on national or regional preferences are not cost effective. The company of the future, according to Levitt, will be a global company that views the world as one market to which it sells a global product.[13]

As with all new ideas, interpretations abound, and discussions and debates flow. Professor Levitt's article has provoked many companies and marketing scholars to re-examine a fundamental idea that has prevailed for decades; that is, products and strategies must be adapted to the cultural needs of each country when marketing internationally. This approach is contrasted with a global orientation suggesting a commonality in marketing needs and thus a standardised product for all the world. While the need for cultural adaptation exists in most markets and for most products, the influence of mass communications in the world today and its influence on consumer wants and needs cannot be denied.[14]

Certainly, the homogenising effect of mass communications in the European Union has eliminated many of the regional differences that once existed. Based on these experiences, it seems reasonable to believe that to some extent people in other cultures exposed to the same influences will react similarly and that there is a converging commonality of the world's needs and desires. For example, over the last century there has been a significant decrease in number of languages spoken in the world. According to studies in linguistics, in 1900 a population of 1.5 billion people spoke around 6 000 languages. While by the end of the century, a population of 6 billion people spoke fewer than 4 000 languages and many of these are just spoken languages. It is suggested that by 2010, half of these languages will disappear. Also, about half of the world population speaks only the top 10 languages and English is the most commonly taught language.

Does this mean markets are now global? The answer is yes, to some extent; there are market segments in most countries with similar demands for the same product. Levi Strauss, Revlon, Toyota, Ford, Philips, Sony, McDonald's and Coca-Cola are companies that sell a relatively standardised product throughout the world to market segments seeking the same products to satisfy their needs and desires. Does this mean there is no need to be concerned with cultural differences when marketing in different countries? The answer is no, in most of the cases; for some products adaptation is not necessary, but for other products adaptation is still necessary. The issue of modification versus standardisation of marketing effort is, however, more complicated. Even an apparently standardised product such as McDonald's hamburgers needs a different marketing effort and mix. For example, for a McDonald's restaurant in Manhattan, New York, the target customers are working people coming for breakfast or lunch. In Maastricht (the Netherlands) the target customers are families with children; here the restaurant has a big playground with swings and slides attached to it. The restaurant is thus almost empty during the evenings. In Jakarta the target market is more well-to-do youngsters and yuppies. In this case, the restaurant is placed beside the Hard Rock Café and is open 24 hours a day and, in fact, does more business in the night than during the day. The astute marketer always strives to present products that fulfil the perceived needs and wants of the consumer. An apparently standardised product is also modified according to the tastes and wants of the customers in different markets. McDonald's, for example, has restaurants in India, but it serves non-beef 'beefburgers'. In Thailand, it sells pork burgers and in the Philippines chicken and rice is one of the best-selling meals.

Marketing internationally should entail looking for market segments with similar demands that can be satisfied with the same product, standardising the components of the marketing mix that can be standardised and, where there are significant cultural differences that require parts of the marketing mix to be culturally adapted, adapting. Throughout the text, the question of adaptation versus standardisation of products and

GOING INTERNATIONAL 1.5

China: racing ahead or catching up?

The world is anxious about China, its sheer scale and the pace of its growth. A country of 1.3 billion people with per capita income in 2003 that was seven times the level in 1978, China is the only country that simultaneously competes with the US and Africa. In human resources, it is rapidly developing formidable research and development capabilities. Yet, its vast and low-cost labour pool makes it one of the world's most cost-competitive business locations.

There is clearly a need to put things into context. China accounted for one-third of the world's GDP in 1820 and in the thirteenth century was ahead of Europe in terms of per capita income. In the 1960s it was just a few years behind Japan in its technology for machine tools. The main point here is that China's economic achievements have not matched its economic potential. In 2002, China's GDP (in PPP) accounted for 12 per cent of the global GDP. The puzzle for economic historians is not why China has grown so fast, but why it is so poor in the first place.

In the post-Second World War period, China lost a lot of jobs to its Asian rivals by adopting a centrally planned economic system. The market reforms are allowing these jobs to come back. Although some experts may disagree, China's rapid growth has brought benefits worldwide. For example, take trade beyond the question of whether America's huge trade deficit with China actually hurts the US, China ploughs back much of its trade surplus into US treasury bonds. This contributes to a low US interest rate environment.

Moreover, China's rise is complementary rather then competitive with Western interests. It has chosen to rely heavily on foreign direct investment, letting foreign companies share the prosperity. In the first quarter of 2003, US companies' profit from China operations exceeded that from Japan. In 2002, five of the top 15 exporters from China were foreign companies such as Motorola, Logitech and Dell.

China thus runs a huge processing operation for the world on behalf of multinational corporations. In this regard 'Made in China' is fundamentally misleading.

Bicycles and websites are both part of marketing in China
© AFP/CORBIS

■ Do you think China is posing a threat to the Western economies? Discuss.

Source: Y. Huang, 'China is not Racing Ahead, Just Catching Up', *Financial Times*, 8 June 2004, p. 19.

marketing effort will be discussed. International marketing is not a concern of multinational or global firms only. Today all (small and large) firms are involved in or influenced by international marketing activities. Throughout the book, international marketing tasks will be discussed from smaller exporting firms as well as global multinationals.

developing a global awareness

Opportunities in global business abound for those prepared to confront the myriad obstacles with optimism and a willingness to continue learning new ways. The successful business person in the twenty-first century will be globally aware and have a frame of reference that goes beyond a region, or even a country, and encompasses the world. To be globally aware is to have:

- objectivity
- tolerance towards cultural differences[15]
- knowledge of
    cultures
    history
    world market potential
    global economic, social and political trends.

To be globally aware is to be *objective*. Objectivity is important in assessing opportunities, evaluating potential and responding to problems. Millions of dollars were lost by companies that blindly entered the Chinese market in the belief that there were untold opportunities, when, in reality, opportunities were in very select areas and generally for those with the resources to sustain a long-term commitment. Many were caught up in the euphoria of envisioning 1 billion consumers; they made uninformed and not very objective decisions.

To be globally aware is to have *tolerance towards cultural differences*. Tolerance is understanding cultural differences, and accepting and working with others whose behaviour may be different from yours. You do not have to accept, as your own, the cultural ways of another but you must allow others to be different and equal. The fact that punctuality is less important in some cultures does not make them less productive, only different. The tolerant person understands the differences that may exist between cultures and uses that knowledge to relate effectively.

A globally aware person is *knowledgeable* about cultures, history, world market potentials and global economic and social trends. Knowledge of cultures is important in understanding behaviour in the marketplace or in the boardroom. Knowledge of history is important because the way people think and act is influenced by their history.

Over the next few decades there will be enormous changes in market potential in almost every region of the world. A globally aware person will continuously monitor the markets of the world. Finally, a globally aware person will keep abreast of social and economic trends because a country's prospects can change as social and economic trends shift direction or accelerate. Not only the former republics of the USSR, but also Eastern Europe, China and other Asian emerging countries are undergoing social and economic changes that have already altered the course of trade and defined new economic powers. The knowledgeable marketer will identify opportunity long before it becomes evident to others. It is our goal in this text to guide the reader towards acquiring a global awareness.

A number of authors do accept that most people live and behave within their culture and milieu; there are, however, some values that characterise people as converging towards a relatively more globalised culture. The members of a global culture normally possess the following characteristics.[16]

Educated More and more education, particularly higher education, is converging, with universities and schools using the same textbooks and concepts. This is particularly true for business education.

Connected These people are using the most advanced communications, from mobile phones and the internet to frequent travelling.

Pragmatic This new group is more concerned with getting things done as compared to sticking with their principles.

Unintimidated by national boundaries and cultures National cultures or boundaries are not considered obstacles by these people. Instead they are quite keen to explore the world beyond their national boundaries.

GOING INTERNATIONAL 1.6

globalisation: good or bad?

Anti-globalisation protesters and anti-globalisation writers such as Jeff Gates (Democracy at Risk) are often accused of much talk but not actually providing any policy advice on how to change or improve the present global economic and political system. In order to fill this obvious gap in the literature, *The Times* suggested a book by Robert Gilpin, emeritus professor of public and international affairs at Princeton University; *The Challenge of Global Capitalism* provides a cooler outlook on the results of globalisation and what can be done to improve the present system.

Professor Gilpin suggests that to view globalisation as all bad is ridiculous, as such a view ignores the massive increase in income and wealth that globalisation has made possible for the world as a whole. In addition, globalisation is here to stay whether we like it or not, so our task now is to consider ways of maximising the gains from globalisation while minimising the losses. One of the challenges that should be addressed by policy makers now is the weakening of the political elements that supported the open economy in the post-war era, and that were based on strong relations between the Western capitalist powers. After the lifting of the Iron Curtain, the stance of the major superpowers has become more insular, more regionally focused and more unilateralist. These countries need to work together to strengthen the weakening political foundations of the open economy.

On the trading front, the greatest challenge is posed by the increased exposure of national economies to the forces of global competition. The result is increased pressures for protection and more trade disputes, both of which threaten to reverse the gains reaped from trade liberalisation. On the monetary front, removal of restrictions on capital flows left many countries more vulnerable to sudden changes in the mood of investors and conditions on the world financial markets, as the East Asian financial crisis of the 1990s amply demonstrated. Emergence of new trading techniques and greater availability of information means that a crisis occurring in one country is likely to spread quickly to others. The challenge for global policy makers is to devise institutional forums for anticipating such crises, preventing them when possible and providing the countries that are the victims with assistance.

The rise of multinational corporations and the growing concentration of power in the hands of a comparatively small number of giant firms have left consumers and workers feeling overwhelmed by forces outside their control. Exposing firms to more competition and tougher national anti-trust laws combined with international agreements imposing strict codes of conduct on multinationals is likely to be the most effective way of ensuring protection for the interests of consumers and workers.

A danger also exists that the increasingly more pronounced regional groupings such as Europe, North America and Asia will become more closed and inward looking, distorting patterns of global trade and leading to more protectionism, thus damaging the smaller, weaker nations. The solution here would be to build up and strengthen global economic institutions in order to make them more effective in meeting the challenges posed by globalisation – a move completely opposite to the desires of the anti-globalisation protesters.

■ Is globalisation good or bad? Discuss.

Source: N. Grimwade, 'Riders of Capitalism's Storms', *The Times*, 19 January 2001, p. 34.

Flexible and open These people demonstrate a good ability to adapt to changes and unexpected circumstances. They may even seek these situations for gaining novel experiences or new adventures.

Begin from a position of trust These people are able to maintain relationships as they often begin from a position of trust when starting new relationships. This makes them tolerant and more approving of others.

orientation of international marketing

Most problems encountered by the foreign marketer result from the unfamiliar environment within which marketing programmes must be implemented. Success hinges, in part, on the ability to assess and adjust properly to the impact of a strange environment. In light of all the variables involved, with what should a text in international marketing be concerned? In our opinion, a study of foreign marketing environments and cultures, and their influences on the total marketing process is of primary concern and is the most effective approach to a meaningful presentation.

Consequently, the orientation of this text can best be described as an environmental and cultural approach to international strategic marketing. By no means is it intended to present principles of marketing; rather it is intended to demonstrate the unique problems of international marketing. It attempts to relate the foreign environment to the marketing process and to illustrate the many ways in which the environment can influence the marketing task. Although marketing principles are universally applicable, the environment and culture within which the marketer must implement marketing plans can change dramatically from country to country. It is with the difficulties created by different environments and cultural differences that this text is primarily concerned.

Further, the text is concerned with any company marketing in or into any other country or groups of countries, however slight the involvement or the method of involvement. Hence, this discussion of international marketing ranges from the marketing and business practices of small exporters, such as a Groningen-based company that generates more than 50 per cent of its $40 000 (€36 000) annual sales of fish-egg sorters in Canada, Germany and Australia, to the practices of global companies, such as Philips, British Airways, Nokia, ABB and Sony, which generate more than 70 per cent of their annual profits from the sales of multiple products to multiple country-market segments all over the world.[17]

summary

The first section of *International Marketing* offers an overview of international marketing, and a discussion of the global business, political and legal environments confronting the marketer. International marketing is defined as the performance of business activities beyond national borders. The task of the international marketer is explained. Key obstacles to international marketing are not just foreign environments but also our own self-reference criteria (SRC) and ethnocentrism. This section deals exclusively with the uncontrollable elements of the environment and their assessment. The next section offers chapters on assessing international market opportunities. Then, management issues in developing global marketing strategies are discussed. In each chapter the impact of the environment and culture on the marketing process is illustrated. Space prohibits an encyclopaedic approach to all the issues; nevertheless, the authors have tried to present sufficient detail so readers appreciate the real need to make a thorough analysis whenever the challenge arises. The text provides a framework for this task.

questions

1 'The marketer's task is the same whether applied in Amsterdam, London or Kuala Lumpur.' Discuss.
2 How can the increased interest in international marketing on the part of European firms be explained?
3 Discuss the four phases of international marketing involvement.
4 Discuss the conditions that have led to the development of global markets.
5 Differentiate between a global company and a multinational company.
6 Differentiate among the three international marketing orientations.
7 Relate the three international marketing orientations to the EPRG schema.
8 Discuss the three factors necessary to achieve global awareness.
9 What is meant by global markets? How does this influence the adaptation of products and marketing strategies?
10 Define and explain the following:
  – controllable elements in the international marketer's task
  – uncontrollable elements in the international marketer's task
  – self-reference criterion (SRC)
  – international marketing orientation
  – global awareness.

further reading

- Theodore Levitt, 'The Globalization of Markets', *Harvard Business Review*, 1983, May-June, pp. 92-102.
- Peter Buckley and Pervez Ghauri, 'Globalization, Economic Geography and Multinational Enterprises', *Journal of International Business Studies*, 2004, 35(2), pp. 81-98.
- Firat Fuat, 'Educator Insights: Globalization of Fragmentation - A Framework for Understanding Contemporary Global Markets', *Journal of International Marketing*, 5(2), pp. 77-86.

references

1 S. Tamer Cavusgil, Pervez Ghauri and Milind Agarwal, *Doing Business in Emerging Markets: Entry and Negotiation Strategies* (Thousand Oaks: Sage, 2002).
2 Peter Buckley and Pervez Ghauri, 'Globalization, Economic Geography and International Business', *Journal of International Business Studies*, 2004, 35(2), pp. 81-98.
3 Allan Bird and Michael Stevens, 'Towards an Emerging Global Culture and the Effects of Globalisation on Obsolescing National Cultures', *Journal of International Management*, 2003, 6, pp. 395-407, and T. Clark and L.L. Mathur, 'Global Myopia: Globalisation Theory in International Business', *Journal of International Management*, 2003, 9, pp. 361-72.
4 Nestlé: http://www.nestle.com, 2004.
5 Toyota: http://www.toyota.co.jp, 2004.
6 'Borderless Management: Companies Strive to Become Truly Stateless,' *Business Week*, 23 May 1994, pp. 24-6.
7 Gina Gianzero, 'Order from Chaos: Who's Who in the Republics', *Europe*, February 1994, pp. 16-19.
8 David A. Ricks, *Blunders in International Business* (Cambridge, Mass.: Blackwell Publishers, 1993), p. 43.

9 For a report on research that examines the internationalisation of a firm, see Peter Buckley and Pervez Ghauri (eds), *The Internationalization of the Firm: A Reader*, second edition (London: Dryden Press, 1999).

10 Yoram Wind, Susan P. Douglas and Howard V. Perlmutter, 'Guidelines for Developing International Marketing Strategy', *Journal of Marketing*, April 1973, pp. 14-23.

11 Theodore Levitt, 'The Globalization of Markets', *Harvard Business Review*, May–June 1983, pp. 92-102.

12 Levitt, 'Globalization', p. 92.

13 For an opposing view, see Richard A. Kustin, 'Marketing Globalization: A Didactic Examination of Corporate Strategy', *International Executive*, January–February 1994, pp. 79-93.

14 Punkaj Ghemawat, 'Semiglobalisation and International Business Strategy', *Journal of International Business Studies*, 2003, 34(1), pp. 139-52.

15 Webster's unabridged dictionary defines tolerance as a fair and objective attitude towards those whose opinions, practices, race, religion, nationality, etc. differ from one's own: freedom from bigotry. It is with this meaning that the authors are using tolerance.

16 Louis Amato and Ronald Wilder, 'Global Competition and Global Markets: Some Empirical Results', *International Business Review*, 2004, 13(3), pp. 401-16.

17 Here, and in the rest of the book, the euro (€) to dollar ($) exchange rate is that of Friday, 22 September 2004, as given at xe.com (http://www.xe.com/): US$1 = €0.8172; €1 = US$1.2234.

chapter 2
The Dynamics of International Business

Chapter Outline

Chapter Learning Objectives

What you should learn from Chapter 2

- The basis for the re-establishment of world trade following the Second World War
- The emergence of MNCs and their impact on international marketing
- The effects of protectionism on world trade
- The seven types of trade barrier
- The importance of GATT and the emergence of the World Trade Organization
- The role of the International Monetary Fund and the World Bank

Yesterday's competitive market battles were fought in Western Europe, Japan and the United States; tomorrow's competitive battles will extend to Eastern Europe, Russia, China, Asia, Latin America and Africa as these emerging markets become more actively involved in international business. More of the world's people, from the richest to the poorest, will participate in the world's wealth through global trade. The emerging global economy in which we live brings us into worldwide competition with significant advantages for both marketers and consumers, and for both the First World and the Third World.[1] Marketers benefit from new markets opening and smaller markets growing large enough to offer viable business opportunities. Consumers benefit by being able to select the lowest-priced and widest range of goods produced anywhere in the world. Bound together by satellite communications and global companies, consumers in every corner of the world are demanding an ever-expanding variety of goods.

As Exhibit 2.1 illustrates, world trade is an important economic activity, Because of this importance, the inclination is for countries to control international trade to their own advantage. As competition intensifies, the tendency towards protectionism gains momen-

Exhibit 2.1 Top exporters, merchandise exports, 2003, $ billion

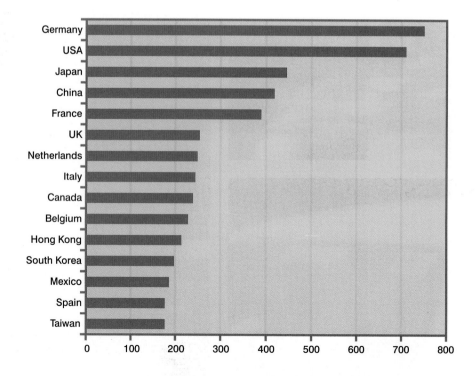

tum. If the benefits of the social, political and economic changes now taking place are to be fully realised, free trade must prevail throughout the global marketplace. The Uruguay round of the General Agreement on Tariffs and Trade (GATT), completed in 1994, was one of the biggest victories for free trade in decades.

the twentieth century

At no time in modern economic history have countries been more economically interdependent, have greater opportunities for international trade existed, or has the potential for increased demand existed than during the last decade of the twentieth century. In the preceding 90 years, world economic development has been erratic.

The first half of the century was marred by a major worldwide economic depression that occurred between the two world wars and that all but destroyed most of the industrialised world. The last half of the century, while free of a world war, was marred by struggles between countries espousing the **Marxist-socialist approach** and those following a democratic, capitalist approach to economic development. As a result of this ideological split, traditional trade patterns were disrupted.

After the Second World War, as a means to dampen the spread of communism, the United States set out to infuse the ideal of capitalism throughout as much of the world as possible. The **Marshall Plan** to assist in rebuilding Europe, financial and industrial development assistance to rebuild Japan and funds channelled through the Agency for International Development and other groups designed to foster economic growth in the underdeveloped world were used to help create a strong world economy. The dissolution of colonial powers created scores of new countries in Asia and Africa. With the striving of these countries to gain economic independence and the financial assistance offered by the Western countries, most of the developing world's economies grew and new markets were created.

The benefits from the foreign economic assistance given by the West flowed both ways. For every dollar the West invested in the economic development and rebuilding of other countries, hundreds of dollars more returned in the form of purchases of Western agricultural products, manufactured goods and services. During this period of economic growth in the rest of the world, the West experienced a major economic boom and an increased standard of living. Certainly a part of Western economic prosperity can be attributed to Western industry supplying the world demand created by economic growth.

In addition to Western economic assistance, a move towards international cooperation among trading nations was manifest in the negotiation of the General Agreement on Tariffs and Trade (GATT). International trade had ground to a halt following the First World War when nations followed the example set by the US enactment of the Smooth-Hawley Law (1930), which raised average US **tariffs** to levels in excess of 60 per cent. In retaliation, other countries erected high tariff walls and international trade stalled, along with most economies. GATT therefore provided a forum for member countries to negotiate a reduction of tariffs and other barriers to trade, and the forum proved successful in reaching those objectives. With the ratification of the Uruguay round agreements, GATT was replaced by the World Trade Organization (WTO) in 1995 and its 117 members moved into a new era of free trade.[2]

world trade and the emergence of multinational corporations

The rapid growth of war-torn economies and previously underdeveloped countries, coupled with large-scale economic cooperation and assistance, led to new global marketing opportunities. Rising standards of living and broad-based consumer and industrial markets in Europe and elsewhere created opportunities for US companies to expand exports and investment worldwide.

The worldwide economic growth and rebuilding after the Second World War was beginning to surface in competition that challenged the supremacy of US industry. Competition arose on all fronts; Japan, Germany, most of the industrialised world and many developing

key terms

Marxist-socialist approach
where a communist or socialist economic system is followed

Marshall Plan
a plan designed to assist in the rebuilding of Europe after the Second World War

tariff
a tax imposed by a government on goods entering at its borders

countries were competing for demand in their own countries and were looking for world markets as well. Countries once classified as less developed were reclassified as newly industrialised countries (NICs). The NICs, such as South Korea, Taiwan, Singapore and Hong Kong, experienced rapid industrialisation in selected industries and became aggressive world competitors in steel, shipbuilding, consumer electronics, automobiles, light aircraft, shoes, textiles, clothing and so forth. In addition to the NICs, a number of developing countries have been reclassified as emerging markets, including China, India, Indonesia, Thailand, Malaysia, Brazil, Mexico and Vietnam. A number of countries from the former Eastern Bloc such as Russia, Poland, Hungary and the Czech Republic are also included in the list. The volume of trade has grown much faster than the world GDP (see Exhibit 2.2).

Exhibit 2.2 The growth of world trade and output since 1950

Source: WTO, www.wto.org.

In short, economic power and potential became more evenly distributed among countries than was the case when Servan-Schreiber warned Europe about US multinational domination.[3] Instead, the US position in world trade is now shared with multinational corporations (MNCs) from other countries. Exhibit 2.3 shows the dramatic change between 1963 and 2004. In 1963, the United States had 67 of the world's largest industrial corporations. By 2004 that number had dropped to 36, while Japan moved from having three of the largest to having 14, South Korea from zero to two and China moved from zero to three. The European Union (EU) has 40 companies among the 100 largest in the world.

Although European markets are quite diverse and constantly changing, Europe, and more so the EU, presents a highly interdependent group of economies in which consumer segments can show a great deal of similarity as well as dissimilarity. Careful thought and analysis is required to plan marketing strategies in Europe. Different industrial sectors, such as capital goods manufacturers, financial services, telecommunications, retail chains and branded goods, show different trends and structures. The restructuring of most industries at European level is posing new challenges for companies within as well as outside Europe.

This heightened competition for European businesses is raising questions such as how to maintain the competitive strength of European business in order to avoid the domination of European markets by foreign multinationals. Among the more important questions raised have been those concerning the ability of European firms to compete in

Exhibit 2.3   The nationality of the world's 100 largest industrial corporations (by country of origin)

	1963	1979	1984	1990	1993	1997	2000	2003	2004
US	67	47	47	33	32	32	36	42	36
Germany	13	13	8	12	14	13	12	11	15
Japan	3	7	12	18	23	26	22	20	14
France	4	11	5	10	6	13	11	7	10
Britain	7	7	5	6	4	2	5	3	6
Switzerland	1	1	2	3	3	3	3	4	4
Italy	2	3	3	4	4	3	3	3	3
China	–	–	–	–	–	–	2	3	3
Netherlands/UK	2	2	2	2	2	2	–	2	2
Netherlands	1	3	1	1	1	3	5	4	2
South Korea	–	–	4	2	4	2	–	2	2
Belgium/Netherlands	–	–	–	–	–	–	–	1	1
Spain	–	–	–	2	2	–	–	1	1
Belgium	–	1	1	1	–	–	1	–	–
Brazil	–	1	–	1	1	–	–	–	–
Canada	–	2	3	–	–	–	–	–	–
India	–	–	1	–	–	–	–	–	–
Kuwait	–	–	1	–	–	–	–	–	–
Mexico	–	1	1	1	1	–	–	–	–
Venezuela	–	1	1	1	1	1	–	–	–
Sweden	–	–	1	2	1	–	–	–	–
South Africa	–	–	1	1	–	–	–	–	–
Turkey	–	–	–	–	1	–	–	3	–

Source: adapted from 'The Fortune 500 Archive', www.fortune.com, 2004.

foreign markets and the fairness of international trade policies of some countries. The EU, a strong advocate of free trade, is now confronted with the dilemma of how to encourage trading partners to reciprocate with open access to their markets without provoking increased protectionism. Equalising trade imbalance without resorting to increased protectionism is a challenge.

the 1990s and beyond

Trends already under way in the last decade of the previous century are destined to change the patterns of trade for decades to come. The economies of the industrialised world have begun to mature and rates of growth will be more modest in the future than they have been for the past 20 years. Conversely, the economies of the developing world will grow at unprecedented rates. As a consequence, there will be a definite shift in economic power and influence away from industrialised countries - Japan, the United States and the European Union - to countries in Asia, Latin America, Eastern Europe and

Africa. According to recent calculations a number of Asian countries will join Western economies as being among the world's largest. This is illustrated in Exhibit 2.4.

Exports and investments are on a steadily accelerating growth curve in emerging markets, where the greatest opportunities for growth will be. China, for example, is projected by the World Bank to have the world's largest economy by 2010. As much as 50 per cent of the expected increase in global exports, from approximately €3.6 trillion ($4.4 trillion) in 1993 to €6.3 trillion ($7.7 trillion) in 2005, will come from developing countries.[4]

Exhibit 2.4 The top 10 economies, GDP at PPP*, 2003, $ trillion

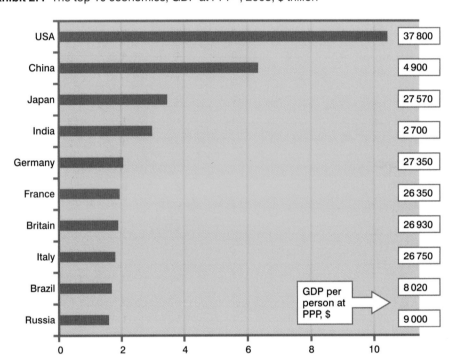

Country	GDP per person at PPP, $
USA	37 800
China	4 900
Japan	27 570
India	2 700
Germany	27 350
France	26 350
Britain	26 930
Italy	26 750
Brazil	8 020
Russia	9 000

*Purchasing-power parity
Source: International Monetary Fund; US Bureau of Economic Analysis; and *The Economist*: 'Scares Ahead for the World Economy: A Survey of World Economy', 2 October 2004, p. 8.

It is estimated that between 1995 and 2000, the number of households with annual incomes approaching $18 000 (€14 710) in Pacific Rim countries has increased from 32.5 million to over 73 million.[5] Demand in Asia for motor vehicles is expected to more than triple, from 16 to 58 million in less than a decade. China is a good example of what is happening in Asia that will make such a prediction reality. The Chinese government has announced a consolidation of its motor vehicle production into a few large manufacturing plants to produce an affordable compact sedan for the masses.[6] Production is expected to double to 3 million units over the next five years.[7] Such increases in consumer demand are not limited to motor vehicles; the shopping lists of the hundreds of millions of households that will enter or approach the middle class over the next decade will include washing machines, televisions and all the other trappings of affluence (see Exhibit 2.5). Similar changes are expected to occur in India, Latin America and Eastern Europe as well.

This does not mean that markets in Europe, Japan and the United States will cease to be important; those economies will continue to produce large, lucrative markets and the companies established in those markets will benefit. It does mean that for a company to be a major player in the next century, now is the time to begin laying the groundwork.

How will these changes that are taking place in the global marketplace impact on international marketing? For one thing, the level and intensity of competition will change as companies focus on gaining entry into or maintaining their position in emerging markets, regional trade areas, and the established markets in Europe, Japan and the United States.

Companies are looking for ways to become more efficient, improve productivity and expand their global reach while maintaining an ability to respond quickly to deliver a product the market demands. For example, large multinational companies, such as Matsushita of Japan, continue to expand their global reach.[8] Nestlé is consolidating its dominance in global consumer markets by acquiring and vigorously marketing local-country major brands;[9] Samsung of South Korea is investing (€450 million/$550 million) in Mexico to secure access to markets in the North American Free Trade Area;[10] and Whirlpool, the US appliance manufacturer, which secured first place in the global appliance business by acquiring the European appliance maker Philips NV, immediately began restructuring itself into its version of a global company.[11] These are a few examples of changes that are sweeping multinational companies as they gear up for the future. Exhibit 2.6 shows the state of the world during the last millennium.

balance of payments

When countries trade, financial transactions among businesses or consumers of different nations occur. Products and services are exported and imported, monetary gifts are exchanged, investments are made, cash payments are made and cash receipts received, and vacation and foreign travel occurs. In short, over a period of time, there is a constant flow of money into and out of a country. The system of accounts that records a nation's international financial transactions is called its **balance of payments**.

A nation's balance-of-payments statement records all financial transactions between its residents and those of the rest of the world during a given period of time – usually one year. Because the balance-of-payments record is maintained on a double-entry book-keeping system, it must always be in balance. As on an individual's financial statement, the assets and liabilities or the credits and debits must offset each other. And, like an individual's statement, the fact that they balance does not mean a nation is in particularly good or poor financial condition. A balance of payments is a record of condition, not a determi-

key term

balance of payments
system of accounts that records a nation's international financial transactions

Exhibit 2.5 Buying boom for Asia, 1995–2000

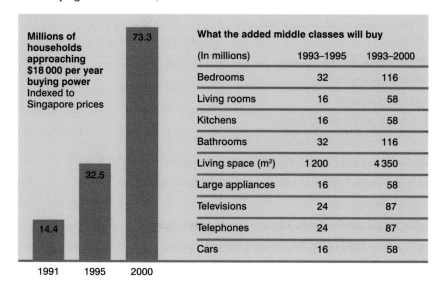

Millions of households approaching $18 000 per year buying power Indexed to Singapore prices	What the added middle classes will buy		
	(In millions)	1993–1995	1993–2000
1991: 14.4	Bedrooms	32	116
1995: 32.5	Living rooms	16	58
2000: 73.3	Kitchens	16	58
	Bathrooms	32	116
	Living space (m²)	1 200	4 350
	Large appliances	16	58
	Televisions	24	87
	Telephones	24	87
	Cars	16	58

Source: Bill Saporito, 'Where the Global Action Is', *Fortune*, Autumn–Winter 1993, p. 64.

nant of condition. Each of the nation's financial transactions with other countries is reflected in its balance of payments.

A nation's balance of payments presents an overall view of its international economic position and is an important economic measure used by treasuries, central banks and other government agencies whose responsibility it is to maintain external and internal economic stability. A balance of payments represents the difference between receipts from foreign countries on one side and payments to them on the other. On the plus side

Exhibit 2.6 A review of the last millennium

1054	Italy and Egypt signed contract for commercial relationship
1081	Venice and Byzantium signed a commercial treaty
1100	China invents marine compass and becomes a trading power
1189	German merchants signed treaty with Novgorod in Russia
1206	Genghis Khan conquers much of Asia including northern China and promotes trade, reviving ancient silk road
1229	German merchants signed trade treaty with Prince of Smolensk in Russia
1358	German Hanseatic League officially formed by Hansa companies for trade and mutual protection. It eventually included 70 cities and lasted for 300 years
1392	England forbids foreigners from trading goods in the country
1404	Chinese forbid private trading in foreign countries, but foreigners could trade in China
1415	Chinese begin trading with Africa through government agencies. Some believe they also sailed to North America in 1421
1479	Venice agreed to pay tribute to the Ottoman Empire in exchange for trading rights; Treaty of Constantinople (now Istanbul)
1500	Rise of mercantilism. States started accumulating wealth to increase power
1500	Slave trade became a major component of world commerce
1520	First chocolate brought from Mexico to Spain
1555	Tobacco trade begins in Europe, introduced by Spanish and Portuguese traders
1561	Dutch traders bring tulips to Europe from the Near East (Turkey)
1597	Holy Roman Empire expels English merchants in retaliation for English treatment of Hanseatic League
1600	Potatoes are brought into Europe from South America, from where they spread all over the world and become one of the main staples
1600	Japan started trading silver for foreign goods
1600	East India Company established in England
1602	Dutch established the East India Company
1612	British East India Company builds its first factory in India
1651	English pass Navigation Act, forcing colonies to trade only with English ships
1719	French consolidate their trade in Asia and establish French East India Company
1750	Industrial Revolution begins with steam engines and increased hardship for workers
1760	China begins strict regulation of foreign trade
1764	Victories in India help Britain to take control of most Eastern trade and trade routes
1764	British started numbering houses to make postal delivery more efficient, opening doors for direct mail merchants

Exhibit 2.6 (A review of the last millennium, continued)

1776	Adam Smith wrote *The Wealth of Nations*, presenting a theory of modern capitalism and free trade
1804	Steam locomotives introduced in England and become dominant force in international trade
1807	US bans trade with Europe
1817	David Ricardo wrote *Principles of Political Economy and Taxation* and proposed a modern trade theory
1821	Britain first to adopt gold standard to back value of its currency
1842	Hong Kong ceded to Britain, the city becomes financial and trading centre for Asia
1848	John Stuart Mill wrote *Principles of Political Economy*, completing the modern theory of trade
1851	First International World Trade Fair held in London
1856	Declaration of Paris recognises principle of free movement of trade even in wartime
1857	Russia and France sign trade treaty
1860	Cobden Treaty to create free trade between Britain and France
1860	First passport issued in the US to regulate foreign travel
1869	Suez Canal completed, cutting travel between Europe and Asia by 4 000 miles
1873	US adopts the gold standard to back the value of dollar
1913	Assembly line introduced by Henry Ford, revolutionising manufacturing
1914	First World War begins
1919	First non-stop flight over Atlantic, paving the way for air cargo around the world
1920	League of Nations established to boost international cooperation and peace
1929	Great Depression starts with crash of US stock market
1939	Second World War begins
1943	First programmable computer (Colossus I) created in England
1944	Bretton Woods Conference creates basis for economic cooperation in 44 countries. IMF founded to help stabilise exchange rates
1947	General Agreement on Tariffs and Trade (GATT) signed by 23 countries
1957	European Economic Community (EEC) established by six European countries (a forerunner of European Union)
1961	Berlin Wall erected to create Eastern and Western Europe
1971	US abandons gold standard, allowing international exchange rate to base on perceived values instead of fixed value
1989	Berlin Wall falls, opening Eastern Europe for trade and commerce
1991	Soviet Union breaks and formally abandons communism
1991	Maastricht Treaty signed among 12 European countries to establish European Union (EU)
1993	North American Free Trade Area (NAFTA) formed between the US, Canada and Mexico
1995	World Trade Organization (WTO) to take over GATT, by 2004 more than 140 members accounting for more than 90 per cent of world trade
1999	Seattle round of WTO puts US vs EU and causes protests against globalisation
2000	Euro as new currency for EU countries introduced in 12 countries
2004	Ten new countries, mainly from Eastern Europe, join EU, making it a union of 25 countries with almost 454 million people, the biggest market in the Western world

are export sales, money spent by foreign tourists, payments to the country for insurance, transportation and similar services, payments of dividends and interest on investments abroad, return on capital invested abroad, new foreign investments in the country and foreign government payments to the country.

A balance-of-payments statement includes three accounts: the **current account** – a record of all merchandise exports, imports and services plus unilateral transfers of funds; the **capital account** – a record of direct investment portfolio transactions, and short-term capital movements to and from countries; and the official reserves account – a record of exports and imports of gold, increases or decreases in foreign exchange, and increases or decreases in liabilities to foreign central banks. Of the three, the current account is of primary interest to international business.

current account

The current account is important because it includes all international trade and service accounts. These are the accounts for the value of all merchandise and services imported and exported, and all receipts and payments from investments (see Exhibit 2.7).

Exhibit 2.7 Trade and current account balance

	Trade balance* (€bn) 2003**	Current account (€bn) 2003**
Australia	−1.5	−11.3
Austria	4.0	1.2
Belgium	3.9	13.8
Britain	−65.1	−36.0
Canada	36.3	14.6
Denmark	7.9	5.3
France	−6.4	11.0
Germany	130.9	64.7
Italy	15.9	−7.0
Japan	101.8	116.3
Netherlands	24.5	11.0
Spain	−39.1	−22.7
Sweden	16.6	10.6
Switzerland	0.8	21.2
USA	−496.7	−508.0

* Imports fob, exports fob. ** Until 3rd quarter of 2003.
Source: based on European Commission, autumn 2003 economic forecasts.

balance of trade

The relationship between merchandise imports and exports is referred to as the *balance of merchandise trade* or **trade balance**. If a country exports more goods than it imports, it has a favourable balance of trade; if it imports more goods than it exports, it has an unfavourable balance of trade. Usually a country that has a negative balance of trade also has a negative balance of payments, unless there is another major cause of inward or outward payments.

protectionism

International business must face the reality that this is a world of tariffs, quotas and non-tariff barriers designed to protect a country's markets from intrusion by foreign compa-

nies. Although the General Agreement on Tariffs and Trade (GATT) and the World Trade Organization (WTO) have been effective in reducing tariffs, countries still resort to protectionist measures. Countries utilise legal barriers, exchange barriers and psychological barriers to restrain entry of unwanted goods. Businesses work together to establish private market barriers, while the market structure itself may provide formidable barriers to imported goods. The complex distribution system in Japan is a good example of a market structure creating a barrier to trade. However, as effective as it is in keeping some products out of the market, in a legal sense it cannot be viewed as a trade barrier.

protection logic and illogic

Countless reasons are espoused by protectionists to maintain government restrictions on trade, but essentially all arguments can be classified as follows:

1 protection of an infant industry
2 protection of the home market
3 need to keep money at home
4 encouragement of capital accumulation
5 maintenance of the standard of living and real wages
6 conservation of natural resources
7 industrialisation of a low-wage nation
8 maintenance of employment and reduction of unemployment
9 national defence
10 increase of business size
11 retaliation and bargaining.

Economists in general recognise as valid only the arguments for infant industry, national defence and the industrialisation of developing countries. The resource conservation argument becomes increasingly valid in an era of environmental consciousness and worldwide shortages of raw materials and agricultural commodities.

Most protectionists argue the need for tariffs on one of the three premises recognised by economists whether or not they are relevant to their products. Proponents are also likely to call on the maintenance of employment argument because it has substantial political appeal. When arguing for protection, the basic economic advantages of international trade are ignored. The fact that the consumer ultimately bears the cost of tariffs and other protective measures is conveniently overlooked. Agriculture and textiles are good examples of protected industries in the United States and a number of European countries that cannot be justified by any of the three arguments. Local prices are artificially held higher than world prices for no sound economic reason (see Exhibit 2.8).

Exhibit 2.8 The price of protectionism

Industry	Total costs to consumers (million $)	Number of jobs saved	Cost per job saved ($)
Textiles and apparel	27 000	640 000	42 000
Carbon steel	6 800	9 000	750 000
Autos	5 800	55 000	105 000
Dairy products	5 500	25 000	220 000
Shipping	3 000	11 000	270 000
Meat	1 800	11 000	160 000

Source: Michael McFadden, 'Protectionism Can't Protect Jobs', *Fortune*, 11 May 1987, p. 125.

GOING INTERNATIONAL 2.1

the price of protectionism

The argument against free trade most often comes down to protecting local jobs. The yearly cost for Russian companies caused by protective measures by foreign countries reaches about $3 billion. Currently, there are 115 restrictions in force on imports into Russia, including 70 anti-dumping restrictions.

Russian politicians are no different in their desire for protection. They point, for example, to a European Union requirement, which requires European car manufacturers to pay the costs of recycling cars that are older than seven years, which will come into force on 1 January 2006. The Russian car manufacturers fear that European producers will sell their old cars to Russian consumers at knock-down prices. Public opinion polls indicate that the majority of Russian consumers prefer an old European car to a new Russian car. Cars that are older than three years currently face import taxes of 50–55 per cent on the declared cost. The Russian government plans to raise the tariffs to 75 per cent for cars three to seven years old, and to 150 per cent for those over seven years, effectively pricing the second-hand European cars out of the market.

Another example of the consequences of protectionism is a candy factory in Holland, Michigan (US). High import tax for foreign sugar has made US sugar enormously expensive. For 70 years sugar has been one of the most protected American commodities, and consequently sugar in America costs three times more than it does in the world market. For this reason, the candy factory is now moving 650 jobs to Quebec, Canada. In general, American consumers are paying a lot more for their sugar-based products every year. Imposing restrictions to protect the sugar-producing industry is destroying jobs in the sugar-related industry. The same logic replays itself with the American administration imposing restrictions against cheap foreign steel to protect local steel-makers in the US. Consequently, there are 50 times more jobs in the steel-using industry than the 200,000 employed in the steel-producing industry. Like the candy factory, Michigan's car industry may be forced to relocate to a less restricted country. Again the consumer is paying the price, a more expensive car or job losses in Michigan.

■ Should countries protect their companies and jobs by keeping foreign products out of the country?

Source: derived from *Pravda*, 'Foreign Countries' Protectionism costs Russian Companies $3bn a Year', 4 December 2002; Michael S. Bernstam and Alvin Rabushka, *The New Protectionism at Work in Russia's Auto Industry*, Hoover Institution, 2001; and *The Detroit News*, 'Protectionism Costs State Jobs', 25 February 2002.

key terms

monetary barriers
putting monetary restrictions on trade, e.g. availability of foreign exchange for imports

market barriers
barriers to trade imposed in an attempt to promote domestic industry

trade barriers

To encourage the development of domestic industry and protect existing industry, governments may establish such barriers to trade as tariffs, quotas, boycotts, **monetary barriers**, non-tariff barriers and **market barriers**. Barriers are imposed against imports and against foreign businesses. While the inspiration for such barriers may be economic or political, they are encouraged by local industry. Whether or not the barriers are economically logical, the fact is that they exist.

Tariffs A tariff, simply defined, is a tax imposed by a government on goods entering at its borders. Tariffs may be used as a revenue-generating tax or to discourage the importation of goods, or for both reasons. In general, tariffs:

- *increase*
  inflationary pressures
  special-interest privileges
  government control and political considerations in economic matters
  the number of tariffs (they beget other tariffs)
- *weaken*
  balance-of-payments positions
  supply-and-demand patterns
  international understanding (they can start trade wars)
- *restrict*
  manufacturers' supply sources
  choices available to consumers
  competition.

GOING INTERNATIONAL 2.2

globalisation: barriers and barricades

The experience of past years shows that globalisation is not an inevitable process and it can be turned back. Earlier in the twentieth century, the two world wars meant that it took 60 years for the world to regain the level of global trade, as a percentage of world output of 1913. Capital flows are catching up but migration has not returned to the early twentieth-century level (and perhaps never will).

The main impact of 9-11 is that it has become difficult for foreigners to enter the United States, a matter of concern to companies and educational institutions. However, the main concern in the public debate in the US is that globalisation is happening too fast, as service-sector jobs are outsourced to developing countries. On the other hand, advocates for future development claim that the 'war on terror' has taken over the resources that were to be spent on the global war on poverty.

The UNCTAD report of 2004 revealed that there was a recovery in world trade in 2002 and 2004; however, 4.9 per cent expansion was still far behind the 6 per cent that prevailed throughout the 1990s. There are a number of barriers that can even worsen the situation. One is the increasing of oil prices to around $50 a barrel, which is a direct effect of the Iraq War and instability in the Middle East. Second, FDI in developing and transition economies has not recovered to the level of 2001. Third, there has been a net outflow of capital from poorer countries to richer countries – $200 billion in 2003. Fourth, there is the danger that global current account imbalances will fuel global tension over trade, e.g. the US trade balance with China.

Positive news is that WTO members reached an agreement on the framework for trade at the WTO Doha meeting. It is important not to prioritise the short-term issue of security at the expense of the long-term goal of poverty reduction and development.

Source: abstracted from Andrew Ball, 'The Mash on Globalisation Comes up Against Barriers and Barricades', *Financial Times*, Special Report: FT World Economy, 1 October 2004, pp. 1-2.

In addition, tariffs are arbitrary, discriminatory and require constant administration and supervision. They are often used as reprisals against protectionist moves of trading partners. In a dispute with the European Community over pasta export subsidies, the United States ordered a 40 per cent increase in tariffs on European spaghetti and fancy pasta. The EC retaliated against US walnuts and lemons. The pasta war raged on as Europe increased tariffs on US fertiliser, paper products and beef tallow, and the United States responded in kind. The war ended when the Europeans finally dropped pasta export subsidies. In March 2002, the American Government imposed 30 per cent tariffs on a range of imported steel products. The tariff was imposed due to findings by the US International Trade Commission that an unexpected surge of imported steel had swamped US markets and damaged US steelmakers. The nine steel-producing countries complained to the World Trade Organization (WTO) with success. The American Government disagrees with the ruling but has not indicated whether it will comply with it. In case the US does not comply with the ruling of the WTO, the countries whose steel imports have been reduced by the US tariffs are entitled to impose retaliatory tariffs equal to the amount of damage the illegal American tariffs caused to their industries.

Non-tariff Barriers Imports are restricted in a variety of ways other than tariffs. These non-tariff barriers include quality standards on imported products, sanitary and health standards, quotas, embargoes and **boycotts**. Exhibit 2.9 provides a list of non-tariff barriers.

key term

boycott
a co-ordinated refusal to buy or use products or services of a certain company/country

---

GOING INTERNATIONAL 2.3

are higher tariffs justified?

According to the development group Oxfam, US tariffs on imports from developing countries are as much as 20 times higher than those charged on imports from other rich nations. The average rate of tariffs on imports from Bangladesh in 2002 was 14 per cent, and duties amounted to $301 million, although the country supplied only 0.1 per cent of total US imports. That value was only slightly smaller than the duties paid on imports from France, which bore an average tariff of 1 per cent and accounted for 2.4 per cent of US imports. Tariffs on imports from India were four times higher than on those from the UK.

The European Union was also said to be discriminating heavily against developing countries. Its duties on imports from India were about four times higher than on those from the US, and more than eight times higher in the case of Sri Lanka and Uruguay.

Oxfam said, 'The overall effect of discriminatory tariff systems is to lower demand for goods produced by the poor, and to exclude them from a stake in global prosperity ... northern tariff structures are designed to undermine developing country exports in precisely those areas where they have a comparative advantage', such as textiles and clothing. Rich countries also charge escalating tariffs on products at each stage of processing: the EU tariff on yarn imports was less than 4 per cent, but 14 per cent on garments. The US and EU charged no tariffs on imports of raw cocoa beans, but as much as 14 per cent on items such as paste and chocolate. As a result, developing countries produced more than 90 per cent of all cocoa beans, but less than 5 per cent of world chocolate output.

■ Do you think developed countries are justified in putting high tariffs on agricultural products?

Source: adapted from Guy de Janquières, 'Oxfam Report: US and EU Tariffs Higher for Third World', *Financial Times*, 2 September 2003, p. 13.

Exhibit 2.9 Types of non-tariff barrier

Specific Limitations on Trade
    Quotas
    Import licensing requirements
    Proportion restrictions of foreign to domestic goods (local content requirements)
    Minimum import price limits
    Embargoes

Customs and Administrative Entry Procedures
    Valuation systems
    Anti-dumping practices
    Tariff classifications
    Documentation requirements
    Fees

Standards
    Standards disparities
    Intergovernmental acceptances of testing methods and standards
    Packaging, labelling, marking standards

Governmental Participation in Trade
    Government procurement policies
    Export subsidies
    Countervailing duties
    Domestic assistance programmes

Charges on Imports
    Prior import deposit requirements
    Administrative fees
    Special supplementary duties
    Import credit discriminations
    Variable levies
    Border taxes

Others
    Voluntary export restraints
    Orderly marketing agreements

Source: A.D. Cao, 'Non Tariff Barriers to US Manufactured Exports', *Columbia Journal of World Business*, Summer 1980, p. 94.

Quotas A quota is a specific unit or dollar limit applied to a particular type of good. There is a limit on imported television sets in the United Kingdom, and there are German quotas on Japanese ball bearings, Italian restrictions on Japanese cars and motorcycles, and US quotas on sugar, textiles and peanuts. **Quotas** put an absolute restriction on the quantity of a specific item that can be imported. Like tariffs, quotas tend to increase prices. In Europe, quotas on textiles are estimated to add 50 to 100 per cent to the wholesale price of clothing.

Voluntary Export Restraints Similar to quotas are voluntary export restraints (**VERs**). Common in textiles, clothing, steel, agriculture and motor vehicles, the VER is an agreement between the importing country and the exporting country for a restriction on the volume of exports. Japan has a VER on vehicles to France, Italy and the United States; that is, Japan has agreed to export a fixed number of these annually. A VER is called voluntary in that the exporting country sets the limits; however, it is generally imposed under the threat of stiffer quotas and tariffs being set by the importing country if a VER is not established.

key terms

quotas
limitations on the quantity of certain goods imported during a specific period

VER
an agreement between the importing country and the exporting country for a restriction on the volume of exports

key terms

Boycott A government boycott is an absolute restriction against the purchase and importation of certain goods from other countries. A public boycott can be either formal or informal and may be government sponsored or sponsored by an industry. It is not unusual for the citizens of a country to boycott goods of other countries at the urging of their government or civic groups. Nestlé products were boycotted by a citizens' group that considered that the way Nestlé promoted baby milk formula to Third World mothers was misleading and harmful to their babies.[12]

Monetary Barriers A government can effectively regulate its international trade position by various forms of **exchange-control** restrictions. A government may enact such restrictions to preserve its balance-of-payments position or specifically for the advantage or encouragement of particular industries. There are three barriers to consider: blocked currency, differential exchange rates and government approval requirements for securing foreign exchange.

Blocked currency is used as a political weapon or as a response to difficult balance-of-payments situations. In effect, blockage cuts off all importing or all importing above a certain level. Blockage is accomplished by refusing to allow importers to exchange national currency for the seller's currency.

The **differential exchange rate** encourages the importation of goods the government deems desirable, and discourages importation of goods the government does not want. The essential mechanism requires the importer to pay varying amounts of domestic currency for foreign exchange with which to purchase products in different categories. For example, the exchange rate for a desirable category of goods might be one unit of domestic money for one unit of a specific foreign currency. For a less desirable product, the rate might be two domestic currency units for one foreign unit. For an undesirable product, the rate might be three domestic units for one foreign unit.

Government approval to secure foreign exchange is often used by countries experiencing severe shortages of foreign exchange. At one time or another, most Latin American and East European, and some Asian countries have required all foreign exchange transactions to be approved by a central ministry or bank. Thus, importers who want to buy a foreign good must apply for an **exchange permit**, that is, permission to exchange an amount of local currency for foreign currency.

GOING INTERNATIONAL 2.4

what's in a name?

© Tom McHugh/ Photo Researchers, Inc.

According to the US Government, you can't call it a 'catfish' unless it's grown in America. The Vietnamese are producing fillets in flooded rice paddies at about $1.80 a pound wholesale. American fish farmers are charging about $2.80. Neither consumers nor ichthyologists can tell the difference between the Asian and American fish, but Uncle Sam has stepped in anyway. The Congressional claim on the 'catfish' name has forced the US to stifle its own protests about Europeans claiming exclusive rights to the name 'herring'.

Standards   Non-tariff barriers of this category include standards to protect health, safety and product quality. The standards are sometimes used in an unduly stringent or discriminating way to restrict trade, but the sheer volume of regulations in this category is a problem in itself. For example, fruit content regulations for jam vary so much from country to country that one agricultural specialist says, 'A jam exporter needs a computer to avoid one or another country's regulations.' Differing standards is one of the major disagreements between the United States and Japan. The size of knotholes in plywood shipped to Japan can determine whether or not the shipment is accepted; if a knothole is too large, the shipment is rejected because quality standards are not met.

The United States, France, Italy and other countries require some products (motor vehicles in particular) to contain a percentage of 'local content' in order to gain admission to their markets. The North American Free Trade Agreement (NAFTA) stipulates that all vehicles coming from member countries must have at least 62.5 per cent North American content to deter foreign manufacturers from using one member nation as the back door to another.[13]

easing trade restrictions

As the global marketplace evolves, trading countries have focused attention on ways of eliminating tariffs, quotas and other barriers to trade. Two ongoing activities to make international trade easier are (1) GATT/WTO and (2) the International Monetary Fund (IMF).

General Agreement on Tariffs and Trade (GATT)

Historically, trade treaties were negotiated on a bilateral (between two nations) basis, with little attention given to relationships with other countries. Further, there was a tendency to raise barriers rather than extend markets and restore world trade. In total, 23 countries signed the General Agreement on Tariffs and Trade (GATT) shortly after the Second World War. Although not all countries participated, this agreement paved the way for the first effective worldwide tariff agreement. The original agreement provided a process to reduce tariffs and created an agency to serve as watchdog over world trade. GATT's agency director and staff offer countries a forum for negotiating trade and related issues. Member countries (117 in 1994) seek to resolve their trade disputes bilaterally; if that fails, special GATT panels are set up to recommend action. The panels are only advisory and have no enforcement powers.

The GATT treaty and subsequent meetings have produced agreements significantly reducing tariffs on a wide range of goods. Since GATT's inception there have been eight 'rounds' of intergovernmental tariff negotiations. The most recently completed was the Uruguay round, which built on the successes of the Tokyo round – the most comprehensive and far-reaching round undertaken by GATT up to that time. The Tokyo round resulted in tariff cuts and set out new international rules for subsidies and countervailing measures, anti-dumping, government procurement, technical barriers to trade (standards), customs valuation and import licensing.

While the Tokyo round addressed **non-tariff barriers**, there were some areas not covered that continued to impede free trade. In addition to market access, there were issues of trade in services, agriculture and textiles, intellectual property rights and investment and capital flows. Based on these concerns, the eighth set of negotiations (the Uruguay round) was begun in 1986 at a GATT trade ministers' meeting in Punta del Este, Uruguay, and finally concluded in 1994. By 1995, 80 GATT members including the United States, the European Union (and its member states), Japan, a number of Asian countries and Canada had accepted the agreement.[14]

The final outcome went well beyond the initial Uruguay-round goal of a one-third reduction in tariffs. Instead, virtually all tariffs in 10 vital industrial sectors[15] with key trading partners were eliminated.[16] This resulted in deep cuts (ranging from 50 to 100 per cent) on

key term

non-tariff barriers hurdles or restrictions on trade that are other than tariff rates, e.g. quotas

electronic items and scientific equipment, and the harmonisation of tariffs in the chemical sector at very low rates (5.5–0 per cent).[17] Once the results of the Uruguay round market-access package are implemented, these high tariffs will be eliminated. One example is Korean tariffs as high as 20 per cent on scientific equipment that will be reduced to an average of 7 per cent, permitting European and US exporters to be more competitive in that market.

An important objective of the Uruguay round was to reduce or eliminate barriers to international trade in services. While there is still much progress to be made before free trade in services will exist throughout the world, the General Agreement on Trade in Services (GATS) is the first multilateral, legally enforceable agreement covering trade and investment in the services sector. It provides a legal basis for future negotiations aimed at eliminating barriers that discriminate against foreign services and deny them market access. Specific market-opening concessions from a wide range of individual countries were achieved, and provision was made for continued negotiations to further liberalise telecommunications and financial services.[18]

Equally significant were the results of negotiations in the investment sector. **Trade-Related Investment Measures (TRIMs)** established the basic principle that investment restrictions can be major trade barriers and are therefore included, for the first time, under GATT procedures. An initial set of prohibited practices included local content requirements specifying that some amount of the value of the investor's production must be purchased from local sources or produced locally; trade balancing requirements specifying that an investor must export an amount equivalent to some proportion of imports or condition the amount of imports permitted on export levels; and foreign exchange balancing requirements limiting the importation of products used in local production by restricting its access to foreign exchange to an amount related to its exchange inflow.

GOING INTERNATIONAL 2.5

round and round: a GATT/WTO chronology

1947	Birth of GATT, signed by 23 countries on 30 October at the Palais des Nations in Geneva.
1948	GATT comes into force. First meeting of its members in Havana, Cuba.
1949	Second round of talks in Annecy, France. Some 5 000 tariff cuts agreed; 10 new countries admitted.
1950–51	Third round in Torquay, England. Members exchange 8 700 trade concessions and welcome four new countries.
1956	Fourth round in Geneva. Tariff cuts worth $1.3 trillion (€1.17 trillion) at today's prices.
1960–62	The Dillon round, named after US Under-Secretary of State Douglas Dillon, who proposed the talks. A further 4 400 tariff cuts.
1964–67	The Kennedy round. Many industrial tariffs halved. Signed by 50 countries. Code on dumping agreed to separately.
1973–79	The Tokyo round, involving 99 countries. First serious discussion of non-tariff trade barriers, such as subsidies and licensing requirements. Average tariff on manufactured goods in the nine biggest markets cut from 7 to 4.7 per cent.
1986–93	The Uruguay round. Further cuts in industrial tariffs, export subsidies, licensing and customs valuation. First agreements on trade in services and **intellectual property**.
1995	Formation of World Trade Organization with power to settle disputes between members.
1997	Agreements concluded on telecommunication services, information technology and financial services.

1998	The WTO has 132 members. More than 30 others are waiting to join.
2001	The Doha agenda. A new round of negotiations, which includes tariffs, agriculture, services and anti-dumping. China becomes the 143rd member of the WTO.
2004	The WTO has 148 members.

Source: WTO, www.wto.org.

Another objective of the EU for the Uruguay round was achieved by an agreement on **Trade-Related Aspects of Intellectual Property Rights (TRIPs)**. The TRIPs agreement establishes substantially higher standards of protection for a full range of intellectual property rights (patents, copyrights, trademarks, trade secrets, industrial designs and semiconductor chip mask works) than are embodied in current international agreements, and it provides for the effective enforcement of those standards both internally and at the border.[19]

The Uruguay round also provides for a better integration of the agricultural and textiles areas into the overall trading system. The reduction of export subsidies, internal supports and actual import barriers for agricultural products are included in the agreement. The Uruguay round also includes another set of improvements in rules covering anti-dumping, standards, safeguards, customs valuation, rules of origin and import licensing. In each case, rules and procedures were made more open, equitable and predictable, thus leading to a more level playing field for trade. Perhaps the most notable achievement of the Uruguay round was the creation of a new institution as a successor to GATT - the World Trade Organization. There have already been several decisions taken by the WTO to resolve international conflicts. For example, when the United States raised tariffs on steel to 30 per cent, the European Union complained to the WTO. The WTO gave the decision that if the US did not take back the tariffs to the normal level, the EU would have the right to increase tariffs on US products. The US then took away the extra tariffs on steel to avoid retaliation.[20]

World Trade Organization (WTO)

The WTO is an institution, not an agreement as was GATT. It sets the rules governing trade between its members, provides a panel of experts to hear and rule on trade disputes between members, and, unlike GATT, issues binding decisions. It requires, for the first time, the full participation of all members in all aspects of the current GATT and the Uruguay round agreements, and, through its enhanced stature and scope, provides a permanent, comprehensive forum to address the trade issues of the twenty-first-century global market.

The membership of GATT rose from 92 in 1986 to 148 in 2004 (see Exhibit 2.10). World trade has also been booming: it grew by 8 per cent in 1995, four times the rate of growth of world GDP. Foreign direct investment (FDI), another measure of international economy integration, also soared: in 1995 cross-border investment flows rose by 40 per cent. Finally, the spread of regional trading agreement, from the EU and NAFTA to APEC, is gaining ground. Almost every member of the WTO is also a member of such a group. According to WTO records, there have been 76 free trade areas or **customs unions** set up since 1948. Of these, more than 50 per cent have come in the 1990s.[21]

All member countries have equal representation in the WTO's ministerial conference, which meets at least every two years to vote for a director-general who appoints other officials. Trade disputes are heard by a panel of experts selected by the WTO from a list of trade experts provided by member countries. The panel hears both sides and issues a decision; the winning side is authorised to retaliate with **trade sanctions** if the losing country does not change its practices. While the WTO has no actual means of enforcement,

key terms

Trade-Related Aspects of Intellectual Property Rights (TRIPS) establishes substantially higher standards of protection for a full range of intellectual property rights than are embodied in current international agreements, and provides for the effective enforcement of those standards

customs union creation of a common external tariff that applies for non-members, the establishment of a common trade policy and the elimination of rules

trade sanctions stringent penalties imposed on a country by means of import tariffs or other trade barriers

Exhibit 2.10 Joining the club: increasing number of GATT/WTO members

Source: WTO, www.wto.org.

international pressure to comply with WTO decisions from other member countries is expected to force compliance. The WTO ensures that member countries agree to the obligations of all the agreements, not just those they like. For the first time, member countries, including developing countries (the fastest-growing markets of the world), will undertake obligations to open their markets and to be bound by the rules of the multilateral trading system. As the number of members is increasing, the trade disputes among countries and regions is also increasing (see Exhibit 2.11).

In the United States, ratification of the WTO was challenged because of concern for the possible loss of sovereignty over its trade laws to the WTO, the lack of veto power (the United States could have a decision imposed on it by a majority of the WTO members) and the role the United States would assume when a conflict arises over an individual state's laws that might be challenged by a WTO member.[22] The GATT agreement was ratified by US Congress and, soon after, the EU, Japan and more than 60 other countries followed. All 117 members of the former GATT supported the Uruguay agreement. Had the Uruguay round not been ratified by the major trading nations, there was concern that countries would lose confidence in global free trade and begin to retreat to regional trade arrangements, risking fragmentation of the world into rival trade blocs. Almost immediately after its inception on 1 January 1995, the WTO's agenda was full of issues ranging from threats of boycotts and sanctions to the membership of new countries, and different trade disputes.[23] The agreements made under the WTO regime have not been very easy. Even the appointment of a director-general is a major source of tension. In spite of all this, the number of WTO members is increasing every year.

International Monetary Fund (IMF)

Inadequate monetary reserves and unstable currencies are particularly vexing problems in world trade. So long as these conditions exist, world markets cannot develop and function as effectively as they should. To overcome these particular market barriers, which plagued international trading before the Second World War, the **International Monetary Fund (IMF)** was formed. Among its objectives were the stabilisation of foreign exchange rates and the establishment of freely convertible currencies. Later, the European Payments Union was formed to facilitate multinational payments. While the IMF has some severe critics, most agree that it has performed a valuable service and at least partially achieved many of its objectives.

key term

International Monetary Fund (IMF) formed to overcome market barriers such as inadequate monetary reserves and unstable currency

GOING INTERNATIONAL 2.6

the US and the EU enter the biggest trade dispute in the history of the WTO

President Bush and his trade representative have brought a complaint about Airbus's subsidies to the WTO. The European trade commissioner is bent on confrontation, his office announced. It is high time to put an end to massive illegal US subsidies to Boeing.

Boeing claims Airbus received launch aid to market its new plane, the A380. Airbus claims that Boeing gets tax breaks from the US Government and support in the shape of government orders. Moreover, Washington State gave it billions of dollars to develop its new plane, the 7E7, in the state. There are allegations and counter-allegations; however, the Boeing-Pentagon relationship is hard to defend. Darleen Druyun, the Pentagon procurement officer, was recently convicted of having favoured Boeing for multi-billion-dollar contracts.

Experts believe that the complaint from the American Government is an election ploy for George Bush, coming just weeks before the 2004 election. These types of case are turning the WTO into another stage for political squabbles, like the United Nations.

The present dispute is also dragging the Japanese aircraft industry into dispute, as the EU commissioner is asking Tokyo to declare its financial aid for the Boeing 7E7. The EU alleges that Tokyo has earmarked $1.6 billion (€1.3 billion, £892 million) in subsidies for the development of the 7E7, 35 per cent of the total cost. Privately, observers believe the total amount is much higher.

Proposed launch funding for the Boeing 7E7

Funding source	$ million	Type of aid	WTO status
State of Washington	3 200	Production subsidy	Actionable
State of Kansas	200	Interest-free bond	Actionable
Japanese Government	1 588	Production subsidy	Prohibited
Italian Government	590	Production subsidy	Actionable
747 special freighters	500	Production subsidy	Actionable
7E7 rail barge	16	Production subsidy	Actionable
Suppliers' support	3 100	Non-recurring cost	Acceptable
Boeing	4 200	Self-financed	Acceptable
Total	13 394		

Source: Mariko Sanchanta, 'Long Relationship with Boeing Drags Japan's Aircraft Industry into Dispute', *Financial Times*, 11 October 2004, p. 2; Amity Shlaes, 'Needless Transatlantic Dogfight', *Financial Times*, 11 October 2004, p. 11; and David Pitchard and Alan MacPherson, 'Industrial Subsidies and Politics of World Trade: The Case of Boeing 7E7', *The Industrial Geographer*, 2004, 1(2), State University of New York.

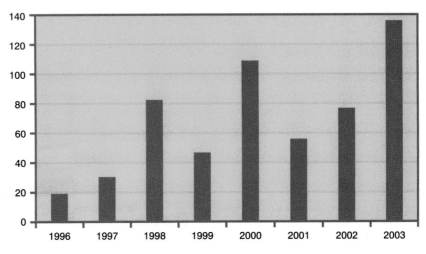

Exhibit 2.11 Number of WTO trade disputes

Source: WTO, www.wto.org.

To cope with universally floating exchange rates, the IMF developed **special drawing rights (SDRs)**, one of its more useful inventions. Because both gold and the US dollar have lost their utility as the basic medium of financial exchange, most monetary statistics relate to SDRs rather than dollars. The SDR is, in effect, 'paper gold' and represents an average base of value derived from the value of a group of major currencies. Rather than being denominated in the currency of any given country, trade contracts are frequently written in SDRs because they are much less susceptible to exchange rate fluctuations. Even floating rates do not necessarily accurately reflect exchange relationships. Some countries permit their currencies to float cleanly without manipulation (clean float) while other nations systematically manipulate the value of their currency (dirty float), thus modifying the accuracy of the monetary marketplace. Although much has changed in the world's monetary system since the IMF was first established, it still plays an important role in providing short-term financing to governments struggling to pay current-account debts, and it will be instrumental in helping to establish free markets in emerging markets.

summary

Regardless of the theoretical approach used in defence of international trade, it is clear that the benefits from absolute or comparative advantage can accrue to any country. Heightened competition around the world has created increased pressure for protectionism from every region of the globe at a time when open markets are needed if world resources are to be developed and utilised in the most beneficial manner for all. It is true that there are circumstances when market protection may be needed and may be beneficial to national defence or the encouragement of infant industries in developing countries, but the consumer seldom benefits from such protection.

Free international markets help participating countries to become full members of world markets and, because open markets provide new customers, most industrialised nations have, since the Second World War, cooperated in working towards freer trade. Such trade will always be partially threatened by various governmental and market barriers that exist or are created for the protection of local businesses. However, the trend has been towards freer trade. The changing economic and political realities are producing unique business structures that continue to protect certain major industries. The emergence of the WTO has played a positive role in easing international trade among different countries and regions. The WTO works on open global markets with controlled and equitable reduction of trade barriers.

questions

1 Discuss the globalisation of the European economy.
2 Differentiate among the current account, balance of trade and balance of payments.
3 'Theoretically, the market is an automatic, competitive, self-regulating mechanism that provides for the maximum consumer welfare and that best regulates the use of the factors of production.' Explain.
4 Why does the balance of payments always balance even though the balance of trade does not?
5 Enumerate the ways in which a country can overcome an unfavourable balance of trade.
6 France exports about 18 per cent of its gross domestic product, while neighbouring Belgium exports 46 per cent. What areas of economic policy are likely to be affected by such variations in exports?
7 Does widespread unemployment change the economic logic of protectionism?
8 The Tokyo round of GATT emphasised the reduction of non-tariff barriers. How does the Uruguay round differ?
9 Discuss the evolution of world trade that has led to the formation of the WTO.
10 What are the major differences between GATT and the WTO?
11 Why do countries use trade barriers? What types of trade barrier are used in what countries?

further reading

■ Gary Hamel and C.K. Prahalad, 'Do you Really Have a Global Strategy?', *Harvard Business Review*, 1985, 63(4), pp. 139-48.
■ Regina Fazio Maruca, 'The Right Way to Go Global: An Interview with Whirlpool CEO David Whitewam', *Harvard Business Review*, 1994, 72(2), pp. 134-45.
■ Alfredo Mauri and Rakesh Sambharya, 'The Impact of Global Integration on MNC Performance: Evidence from Global Industries', *International Business Review*, 2001, 10(4), pp. 421-40.

references

1 Paul Krugman, 'Does Third World Growth Hurt First World Prosperity?', *Harvard Business Review*, July 1994, pp. 113-21.

2 Michael Hunt, 'Free Trade, Free World: The Advent of GATT', *Business History Review*, 2000, 74(2), pp. 350-2.

3 J.J. Servan-Schreiber, *The American Challenge* (New York: Athenaeum, 1968).

4 Bill Saporito, 'Where the Global Action Is', *Fortune*, Autumn-Winter 1993, p. 64.

5 Edward M. Mervosh, 'Winning with the Trade Agreement', *International Business*, January 1994, p. 17.

6 *The Economist*, 'Behind the Mask: A Survey of Business in China', www.economist.com/surveys, September 2004.

7 James Kynge, 'Nissan may Sue Chinese Rivals over Design', *Financial Times*, 28 November 2003, p. 21.

8 Nigel Holden, *Cross-Cultural Management: A Knowledge Management Perspective* (Harlow: FT Prentice Hall, 2002).

9 Allan Bird and Michael Stevens, 'Toward an Emergent Global Culture and the Effects of Globalisation on Obsolescing National Cultures', *Journal of International Management*, 2003, 9, pp. 395-407.

10 'Samsung Putting $500 Million in Mexico', *Associated Press*, 27 September 1994.

11 Regina Fazio Maruca, 'The Right Way to Go Global: An Interview with Whirlpool CEO David Whitwam', *Harvard Business Review*, March-April 1994, pp. 135-45.

12 For a comprehensive review, see Thomas V. Greer, 'International Infant Formula Marketing: The Debate Continues', *Advances in International Marketing*, vol. 4, 1990, pp. 207-25.

13 Anne M. Driscoll, 'Embracing Change, Enhancing Competitiveness: NAFTA's Key Provisions', *Business America*, 18 October 1993, pp. 14-25.

14 Jim Sanford, 'World Trade Organization Opens Global Markets, Protects US Rights', *Business America*, January 1995, p. 4.

15 Construction, agriculture, medical equipment, steel, beer, brown distilled spirits, pharmaceuticals, paper, pulp and printed matter, furniture and toys.

16 European Union, Japan, Austria, Switzerland, Sweden, Finland, Norway, New Zealand, Korea, Hong Kong and Singapore.

17 Sarah E. Shackelton, 'Market Access', *Business America*, January 1994, pp. 7-8.

18 For a complete review of the Uruguay round of GATT, see Louis J. Murphy, 'Successful Uruguay Round Launches Revitalized World Trading System', *Business America*, January 1994, pp. 4-27; and George Pitcher, 'Trade War Looms as West Faces Third World Uprising', *Marketing Week*, 3 April 2003, p. 29.

19 P.M. Rao and P.N. Ghauri, 'Intellectual Property, Multinational Enterprises and the Developing World', paper presented at the Academy of International Business (AIB) Annual Conference, in Stockholm, Sweden, July 2004.

20 Robert G. Matthews, 'US Steel Tariffs Likely to Stay Despite WTO-sanction Threat', *Wall Street Journal*, 31 March 2003, p. A2.

21 *The Economist*, 'All Free Traders Now?', 7 December 1996, pp. 23-5.

22 Ralph Nader, 'WTO Means Rule by Unaccountable Tribunals', *The Wall Street Journal*, 17 August 1994, p. A4; and Elisabeth Becker, 'WTO Rules Against US on Steel Tariff', *New York Times*, 27 March 2003, p. C1.

23 'No End of Woe at the WTO?' *The Economist*, 4 February 1995, p. 59.

section 2
the impact of culture on international marketing

chapter 3
Geography and History: the Foundations of Cultural Understanding

Chapter Outline

Chapter Learning Objectives

What you should learn from Chapter 3

- How geography and history influence the understanding of international markets
- How effects of topography and climate impact on products, population centres, transportation and international trade
- Understand the growing problem and importance of environmental damage to world trade
- Comprehend the social and moral responsibility the international marketer has in terms of protecting the environment
- Evaluate the importance of non-renewable resources for international trade and marketing
- The effects on the world economy of population increases and shifts, and of the level of employment
- Understand the importance and impact of the history of each culture in understanding its response to international marketing

Knowledge of a country's geography and history is essential if a marketer is to interpret a society's behaviour and fundamental attitudes. Culture can be defined as a society's programme for survival, the accepted basis for responding to external and internal events. Without understanding the geographical characteristics to which a culture has had to adapt and to which it must continuously respond, it cannot be completely understood. Nor can one fully appreciate the fundamental attitudes or behaviour of a society without knowledge of the historical events that have shaped its cultural evolution.[1]

Marketers can observe the nuances of a culture but, without an appreciation of the role geography and history play in moulding that culture, they cannot expect to understand fully why it responds as it does. This chapter discusses how geography and history affect behaviour and why they should be taken into account when examining the environmental aspects of marketing in another country.

geography and international markets

Geography, the study of the earth's surface, climate, continents, countries, peoples, industries and resources, is an element of the uncontrollable environment that confronts every marketer but that receives inadequate attention. There is a tendency to study climate, topography and available resources as isolated entities rather than as important causal agents in the marketing environment. The physical character of a nation is perhaps the principal and broadest determinant of both the characteristics of a society and the means by which that society undertakes to supply its needs. Thus, the study of geography is important for the student of marketing when evaluating marketing and its environment.

The purpose of this section is to provide a greater awareness of the world, its complexities and its diversities – an awareness that can mean the difference between success and failure in marketing ventures. Climate and topography are examined as facets of the broader and more important elements of geography. A brief look at the earth's resources and population – the building blocks of world markets – and world trade routes completes the presentation on geography and global markets.

climate and topography

As elements of geography, the physical terrain and climate of a country are important environmental considerations when appraising a market. The effect of these geographical features on marketing ranges from the obvious influences on product adaptation to more profound influences on the development of marketing systems.

Altitude, humidity and temperature extremes are climatic features that affect the uses and functions of products and equipment. Products that perform well in temperate zones may deteriorate rapidly or require special cooling or lubrication to function adequately in tropical zones. Manufacturers have found that construction equipment used in northern Europe requires extensive modification to cope with the intense heat and dust of the Sahara Desert. Within even a single national market, climate can be sufficiently diverse to require major adjustments. In Ghana, a product adaptable to the entire market must operate effectively in extreme desert heat and low humidity and in tropical rainforests with consistently high humidity.

South America represents an extreme but well-defined example of the importance of geography in marketing considerations. The economic and social systems there can be explained, in part, in terms of the geographical characteristics of the area. It is a continent 7242 km (4500 miles) long and 4800 km (3000 miles) wide at its broadest point. Two-thirds of it is comparable to Africa in its climate, 48 per cent of its total area is made up of forest and jungle, and only 5 per cent is arable. Mountain ranges cover South America's west coast for 7242 km (4500 miles), with an average height of 4000m (13000 ft) and a width of 480–650 km (300–400 miles). This is a natural, formidable barrier that has precluded the establishment of commercial routes between the Pacific and Atlantic coasts.

Once the Andes are surmounted, the Amazon basin of 2.5 million square km (2 million square miles) lies ahead. It is the world's greatest rainforest, almost uninhabitable and impenetrable. Through it runs the Amazon, the world's second longest river which, with its tributaries, has almost 65000 km (40000 miles) of navigable water. On the east coast is another mountain range covering almost the entire coast of Brazil, with an average height of 1200m (4000 ft).

There are many other regions of the world that also have extreme topographic and climatic variations. China, the former Soviet Union, India, Pakistan and Canada each have formidable physical and/or climatic conditions within their trading regions.

Rolls-Royce found that fully armour-plated cars from England require extensive body-work and renovations after a short time in Canada. It was not the cold that damaged the cars but the salted sand spread to keep the streets passable throughout the four or five months of virtually continuous snow. The bumpers and side panels corroded and rusted and the oil system leaked. This problem illustrates the harshness of a climate and why it needs to be considered in all facets of product development.

Geographic hurdles must be recognised as having a direct effect on marketing and the related activities of communications and distribution. Furthermore, there may be indirect effects from the geographical ramifications on society and culture that are ultimately reflected in marketing activities. Many of the peculiarities of a country (i.e. peculiar to the foreigner) would be better understood and anticipated if its geography were studied more closely.

The effect of natural barriers on market development is also important. Because of the ease of distribution, coastal cities or cities situated on navigable waterways are more likely to be trading centres than are landlocked cities. Cities not near natural physical trans-portation routes are generally isolated from one another, even within the same country. Consequently, natural barriers rather than actual distance may dictate distribution points.

In discussing distribution in Africa, one marketer pointed out that a shipment from Mombassa on the Kenya east coast to Freetown on the bulge of West Africa could require more time than a shipment from New York or London to Kenya over established freight routes.

Road conditions in Ecuador are such that it is almost impossible to drive a car from the port of Guayaquil to the capital of Quito only 320 km (200 miles) away. Contrast this with more economically advanced countries where formidable mountain barriers have been overcome. A case in point is the 11.6 km (7.2 mile) tunnel that cuts through the base of Mont Blanc in the Alps. This highway tunnel brings Rome and Paris 200 km (125 miles) closer and provides a year-round route between Geneva and Turin of only 270 km (170 miles). Before the tunnel opened, it meant a trip of nearly 800 km (500 miles) when snow closed the highway over the Alps.

Some countries have preserved physical barriers as protection and have viewed them as political as well as economic statements. Increasing globalisation, however, has brought about changes in attitudes. The tunnel beneath the English Channel to connect England and France, and the bridge between Denmark and Sweden are good examples. The bridge to connect Denmark and Sweden over the Baltic strait has connected the Nordic countries with the rest of Europe. The project has made it possible to drive from Lapland in northernmost Scandinavia to Calabria in southern Italy. It has ended millennia of geographic isolation for these Nordic nations. Politically the agreement is seen as a powerful, tangible symbol that they are ending their political isolation from the rest of Europe and are linking themselves economically to the continent's future and membership in the European Union.

After more than 200 years of speculation, a tunnel under the English Channel between Britain and France was officially opened in 1994.[2] Historically, the British have resisted a tunnel; they did not trust the French or any other European country and saw the English Channel as protection. When they became members of the EC, economic reality meant that a tunnel had to be built. The Chunnel, as it is sometimes known, carried more than 17 million tonnes of freight and over 30 million people the first year it was open.[3]

geography, nature and international trade

As countries prosper and expand their economies, natural barriers are overcome. Tunnels are dug, bridges and dams built, and sound environmental practices implemented to control or adapt to climate, topography and the recurring extremes of nature. Man has been reasonably successful in overcoming or minimising the effects of geographical barriers and natural disasters except in the developing countries of the world. Most rich countries have a constant economic growth (see Exhibit 3.1), while growth in poor countries is very uneven.

Always on the slim margin between subsistence and disaster, some developing countries suffer disproportionately from natural and human-assisted catastrophes. Climate and topography coupled with civil wars, poor environmental policies and natural disasters push these countries further into economic ruin. Without irrigation and water management, they are afflicted by droughts, floods, soil erosion and creeping deserts, which reduce the long-term fertility of the land. Population increases, deforestation and overgrazing intensify the impact of drought and lead to malnutrition and ill-health, further undermining the countries' ability to solve their problems. Experts expect mass famine to have killed between 20 million and 30 million Africans in the 1990s. Cyclones cannot be prevented, nor inadequate rainfall, but there are means to control their effects. Unfortunately, each disaster seems to push these countries further away from effective solutions. Countries that suffer the most from major calamities are among the poorest in the world. Many have neither the capital nor the technical ability to minimise the effects of natural phenomena; they are at the mercy of nature.

Industrialised nations have the capital and technical ability to control the harshness of nature, but in striving for more and greater economic wealth, they court other disasters of their own making. Poor hazardous waste management and the increase in industrial pollution are environmental problems for which the industrialised world and those reaching for economic development must assume responsibility. The problems are mostly by-products of processes that have contributed significantly to economic development in many countries and to the lifestyles they seek.[4]

Exhibit 3.1 GDP growth among developed countries, % increase 2004–2005

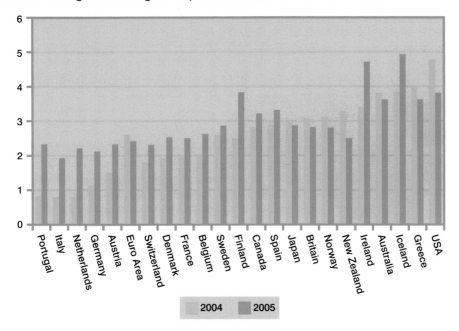

2004   2005

social responsibility and environmental management

The 1990s have been called the **Decade of the Environment**, in that nations, companies and people are reaching a consensus: environmental protection is not an optional extra, 'it is an essential part of the complex process of doing business'.[5] The self-styled **Green activists**, and governments, media and businesses are focusing on ways to stem the tide of pollution and to clean up their decades of neglect. Many view the problem as a global issue rather than a national issue, and one that poses common threats to humankind and thus cannot be addressed by nations in isolation.[6]

Companies looking to build manufacturing plants in countries with more liberal pollution regulations than they have at home are finding that regulations everywhere are becoming stricter. Many Asian governments are drafting new regulations and strictly enforcing existing ones. A strong motivator for Asia and the rest of the world is the realisation that pollution is on the verge of getting completely out of control. An examination of China's rivers, lakes and reservoirs revealed that 21 per cent were polluted by toxic substances and that 16 per cent of the rivers were seriously polluted with excrement. Russia, the EU and a number of other countries have now signed the **Kyoto Agreement** to decrease pollution in the coming years. However, the United States has decided not to sign or comply with the Kyoto Agreement.

Neither Western Europe nor the rest of the industrialised world is free of environmental damage. Rivers are polluted and the atmosphere in many major urban areas is far from clean (e.g. Athens, Los Angeles, Rome and Mexico City, to mention a few). The very process of controlling industrial waste leads to another and perhaps equally critical issue: the disposal of hazardous waste, a by-product of pollution control. Estimates of hazardous waste collected annually exceed 300 million tonnes; the critical question concerns disposal that does not move the problem elsewhere.

The export of hazardous waste by developed countries to developing nations has ethical implications and environmental consequences. Countries finding it more difficult to dispose of such waste at home are seeking countries willing to assume the burden of disposal. Some waste disposal in developing countries is illegal and some is perfectly legal

key terms

Decade of the Environment
the 1990s, when environment was considered the most important issue

Green activists
organisations or individuals who actively want to protect the environment

Kyoto Agreement
agreement signed by the EU, Russia and a number of countries, determining the decrease required in pollution over the coming years

A major food processing company had production problems after it built a pineapple cannery at the delta of a river in Mexico. It built the pineapple plantation upstream and

planned to barge the ripe fruit downstream for canning, load them directly on ocean liners, and ship them to the company's various markets. When the pineapples were ripe, however, the company found itself in trouble: crop maturity coincided with the flood stage of the river. The current in the river during this period was far too strong to permit the backhauling of barges upstream; the plan for transporting the fruit on barges could not be implemented. With no alternative means of transport, the company was forced to close the operation. The new equipment was sold for 5 per cent of original cost to a Mexican group, which immediately relocated the cannery. A seemingly simple, harmless oversight of weather and navigation conditions was the primary cause for major losses to the company.

Source: David A. Ricks, *Blunders in International Business* (Cambridge, MA: Blackwell Publishers, 1993), p. 16.

because of governments that are directly involved in the business of hazardous waste. Illegal dumping is the most reprehensible act since it is done clandestinely and often without proper protection for those who unknowingly come in contact with the poisons.

Governments, organisations and businesses are becoming increasingly concerned with the social responsibility and ethical issues surrounding the problem of generating and disposing of waste. The Organisation for Economic Cooperation and Development (OECD), the United Nations, the European Union and international activist groups are undertaking programmes to strengthen environmental policies. Their influence and leadership are reflected in a broader awareness of pollution problems by businesses and people in general. Responsibility for cleaning up the environment does not rest solely with governments, businesses or **activist groups**; each citizen has a social and moral responsibility to include environmental protection among his or her highest goals. The main issue is whether international trade and economic development can co-exist with protection of the environment. There is thus a lot of discussion on sustainable development – striking a long-lasting balance between trade, environment, technological development and society. More and more companies are realising that sustainable development is of mutual importance to companies and societies.[7]

key term

activist groups
see **green
activists** (p.59);
refers to these
groups, e.g.
Greenpeace

resources

The availability of minerals and the ability to generate energy are the foundations of modern technology. The location of the earth's resources, as well as the available sources of energy, are geographical accidents, and the world's nations are not equally endowed; nor does a nation's demand for a particular mineral or energy source necessarily coincide with domestic supply (see Exhibit 3.2).

Energy is necessary to power the machinery of modern production, and to extract and process the resources necessary to produce the goods of economic prosperity. In much of the underdeveloped world, human labour provides the preponderance of energy. The prin-

Exhibit 3.2 Per capita energy use (commercial and non-commercial), 2000*

Total world energy consumption by region and fuel (quadrillion Btus)

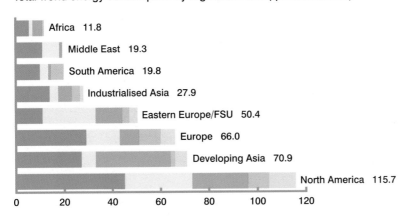

Percentage of world energy consumption by energy sources

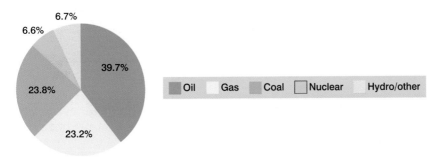

*Total world consumption was 381.8 quadrillion BTUs. The largest portion of the hydro/other category is hydro-electrical energy. Fuels such as wood, peat, animal waste, wind, solar and geothermal account for less than 1.0 quadrillion BTUs in the other portion of the hydro/other category

Source: data compiled from 'Introduction to World Geography', *Oxford Atlas of the World* (NY: Oxford University Press, 2002); Energy Information Administration (EIA), *International Energy Outlook 2002* (Washington DC, December 2001).

cipal supplements to human energy are animals, wood, fossil fuel, nuclear power, and, to a lesser and more experimental extent, the ocean's tides, geothermal power and the sun. Of all the energy sources, petroleum usage is increasing most rapidly because of its versatility and the ease with which it can be stored and transported.

As an environmental consideration in world marketing, the location, quality and availability of resources will affect the pattern of world economic development and trade for at least the remainder of the century. This factor must be weighed carefully by astute international marketers in making worldwide international investment decisions. In addition to the raw materials of industrialisation, there must be an available and economically feasible energy supply to successfully transform resources into usable products.

Because of the great disparity in the location of the earth's resources, there is world trade between those who do not have all they need and those who have more than they need and are willing to sell. Importers of most of the resources are industrial nations with insufficient domestic supplies. Oil is a good example; the Middle East accounts for over 65 per cent of the world's reserves, while Western countries consume most of it. Exhibit 3.3 shows the oil reserves in the world.

Exhibit 3.3 World's oil reserves

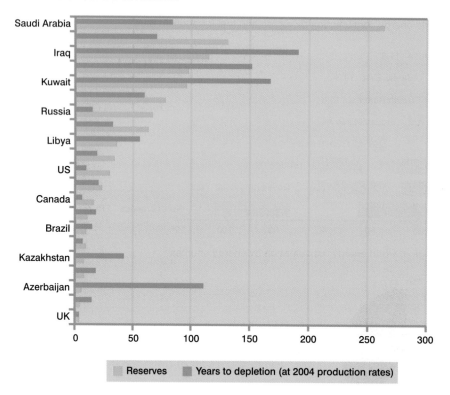

Reserves ■ Years to depletion (at 2004 production rates)

Source: BP, *Statistical Review of World Energy*, 2004.

Aside from the geographical unevenness in which most resources occur, there is no immediate cause for concern about the availability of supply of most resources. Exhibit 3.3 illustrates the approximate time when known oil reserves will be depleted. These estimates of reserves are based on current rates of consumption and will change as new reserves are discovered, as greater proportions are obtained by recycling, as substitutes are introduced, and as rates of consumption increase or abate. Substitutions are already being used to replace many of the minerals. The replacement of steel with fibreglass and plastic in automobile manufacturing is but one example.

One possible source of scarce minerals still untapped can be found in the ocean floors. Undersea mining may provide the world with new reserves of scarce minerals. Nodules of nickel, copper, cobalt and magnesium at the bottom of the Pacific have been estimated to total 10 billion tonnes of rich ore, with 10 million new tonnes formed every year. Similar fields of ore-rich nodules exist in all the world's oceans and seas.

This undersea wealth of minerals will not be easy to exploit because of the cost of undersea mining (higher than traditional mining), disputes over ownership of minerals outside territorial waters and the potential for upsetting the sensitive ocean ecosystem. Yet, like other natural barriers, these too will eventually be overcome as world demand increases and current reserves dwindle.

world population trends

While not the only determinant, the existence of sheer numbers of people is significant in appraising potential consumer demand. Current population, rates of growth, age levels and rural/urban population distribution are closely related to today's demand for various categories of goods. Changes in the composition and distribution of population among the world's countries during the next 40 years will profoundly affect future demand.

Recent estimates claim there are over 6.2 billion people in the world. Exhibit 3.4 presents the population by major areas and the change expected between 2020 and 2150. At present growth rates, world population could leap to 9.3 billion by 2010, from 5.7 billion in 1995.[8] The majority of the people will reside in less developed countries least able to support such population increases. Kenya is a good example of what is happening in many developing countries. The average number of children born to a woman in Kenya is 3.31, a rate that, combined with a declining infant mortality rate, could double the country's population almost overnight, increasing it from 32 million in 2004 to 45 million in 2010. Kenya's present economic growth rate will not support the demands created by such growth. By the year 2025, the World Bank predicts over four-fifths of the world's population will be concentrated in developing countries. Most governments are trying to control the explosive birth rates by encouraging birth control. China has the strictest policy; only one child is allowed per couple except in rural areas where, if the first child is female, a second child is permitted.

Exhibit 3.4 World population projections by major areas, based on a medium fertility scenario,* 1950–2150

	1950 (millions)	1995 (millions)	2010 (millions)	2100 (millions)	2150 (millions)
World	2524	5687	9364	10414	10806
Africa	224	719	2046	2646	2770
Asia (including China and India)	1402	3438	5443	5851	6059
China	555	1220	1517	1535	1596
India	358	929	1533	1617	1669
Europe	547	728	638	579	595
Latin America	166	477	810	889	916
North America	172	297	384	401	414
Oceania	13	28	46	49	51

*The medium-fertility scenario assumes that the total fertility rates will ultimately stabilise by the year 2055 at replacement levels, which are slightly above two children per woman. If fertility rates stay constant at 1990–1995 levels, the world population projection is 14941 million in 2050, 57182 million in 2100 and 296333 million in 2150.
Source: World Population Projections to 2150 (New York: United Nations, Department of Economic and Social Affairs, Population Division, 1998).

Rural/Urban Shifts   A relatively recent phenomenon is a pronounced shift of the world's population from rural to urban areas. In the early 1800s, less than 3.5 per cent of the world's people were living in cities of 20000 or more and less than 2 per cent in cities of 100000 or more. Today, more than 40 per cent of the world's people are urbanites and this trend is accelerating (see Exhibit 3.5).

By 2020, it is estimated that more than 60 per cent of the world's population will live in urban areas, and at least 26 cities will have populations of 10 million or more; most of these will be in the developing world.[9] Tokyo has already overtaken Mexico City as the largest city on earth with a population of 35 million,[10] a jump of almost 9 million since 1975 (see Going International 3.2).[11] Migration from rural to urban areas is largely a result of a desire for greater access to sources of education, healthcare and improved job opportunities. Once in the city, perhaps three out of four migrants make economic gains. The family income of a manual worker in urban Brazil is almost five times that of a farm labourer in a rural area.

Exhibit 3.5 Urban population

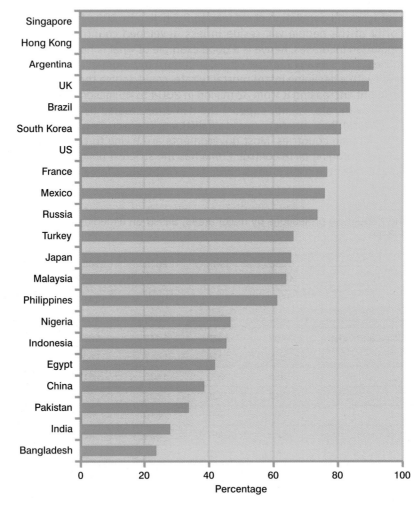

Source: United Nations, *World Urbanization Prospects*, Department of Economics and Social Affairs, 2003.

Although migrants experience some relative improvement in their living standards, intense urban growth without commensurate investment in services eventually leads to profound problems. Slums populated with unskilled workers living hand to mouth puts excessive pressure on sanitation systems, water supplies and other social services. At some point, the disadvantages of unregulated **urban growth** begin to outweigh the advantages for all concerned.

Many fear that, as we approach the year 2020, the bulging cities will become hotbeds of social unrest unless conditions in urban areas are improved. Prospects for improvement are not encouraging because most of the growth will take place in developing countries already economically strained. Further, there is little progress in controlling birth rates in most populous countries.

Increasing Unemployment   Rapid population increases without commensurate economic development create other difficulties. Among the most pressing are the number of new jobs needed to accommodate the flood of people entering the labour pool. During the period 1970 to 2000, one billion people entered the labour market in

GOING INTERNATIONAL 3.2

soon two out of every three people on earth will be living in a city

According to the United Nations the world will soon become predominantly urban. By 2020 at least 23 cities will have passed the 10 million mark. Many parts of Asia-Pacific are facing 'hyper-urbanisation'; while London took 130 years to grow from 1 million to 8 million, Bangkok took 45 years, Dhaka 37 years and Seoul only 25 years. The table below shows the 14 largest cities in 2015.

Population in millions

	City	1975	2004	2015
1	Tokyo	26.6	35.0	36.2
2	Mumbai	7.3	17.4	22.6
3	Delhi	4.4	14.1	20.9
4	Mexico City	10.7	18.7	20.6
5	Sao Paolo	9.6	17.8	20.0
6	New York	15.9	18.3	19.7
7	Dhaka	2.2	11.6	17.9
8	Jakarta	4.8	12.3	17.5
9	Lagos	1.9	10.1	17.0
10	Calcutta	7.9	13.8	16.8
11	Karachi	4.0	11.1	16.2
12	Buenos Aires	9.1	13.0	14.6
13	Cairo	6.4	10.1	13.8
14	Los Angles	8.9	12.0	12.9

Tokyo's famously busy Shibuya crossing
© Mike Wendling

Although some people believe that this urbanisation will bring prosperity and will thus lift many out of poverty, the United Nations believes it will in fact cause growing poverty and deepening inequalities. As the table shows, most of the growth is taking place not in the Western world but in the Third World. It will be increasingly difficult to provide clean water, jobs and infrastructure. Take Lagos, for example, with ever-increasing fumes, smoke, unsanitary water and overcrowded communities. Battered yellow minibuses are the nearest the city has to public transport, with the biblical message of hope decorated all over them: 'No condition is permanent'.

Source: Venessa Houlder, '60 per cent of the World will Live in Cities by 2030', *Financial Times*, 10 September 2004, p. 9; and John Reader, 'No City Limits, Our World in 2020', *Guardian*, 11 September 2004, pp. 2–9.

the Third World; by the year 2020, an additional 1.5 billion will be of working age. The International Labour Organization (ILO) estimates that one billion jobs must be created worldwide by the year 2015.

The mismatch between population growth and economic growth is another major problem to be faced in the next century. Most of the population increases are occurring in the developing world while most of the jobs are being created in the developed world. The vast majority of new workers will be found in developing countries[12] while the majority of jobs will be found in the industrialised world. While it is true that cheap labour costs, brought on in part by vast labour pools in less developed countries, attract labour-intensive manufacturers from higher-cost industrialised countries, the number of new jobs created will not be

sufficient to absorb the projected population growth. The ability to create enough jobs to keep pace with population growth is one problem of uncontrolled growth; another is providing enough to eat.

World Food Production   Having enough food to eat depends on a country's ability to produce sufficient quantities, the ability to buy food from other sources when not self-sufficient, and the physical ability to distribute food when the need arises. The world produces enough food to provide adequate diets for all its estimated 6.2 billion people, yet famine exists, most notably in Africa. Long-term drought, economic weakness, inefficient distribution and civil unrest have created conditions that have led to tens of thousands of people starving.

GOING INTERNATIONAL 3.3

where have all the women gone?

Three converging issues in China have the potential to cause a serious gender imbalance: issue 1 – China, the world's most populous country, has a strict one-child policy to curb population growth; issue 2 – traditional values dictate male superiority and a definite parental preference for boys; and issue 3 – prenatal scanning allows women to discover the sex of their foetuses and thereby abort unwanted female children.

As a consequence, Chinese statisticians have begun to forecast a big marriage gap for the generation born in the late 1980s and early 1990s. In 1990, China recorded 113.8

male births for every 100 female births, far higher than the natural ratio of 106 to 100. In rural areas, where parental preference for boys is especially strong, newborn boys outnumber girls by an average of 144.6 to 100. In one rural township, the ratio was reported to be 163.8 to 100.

Not only is there a gender mismatch on the horizon, but there may also be a social mismatch because most of the men will be peasants with little education, while most of the women will live in cities and more likely have high-school or college degrees. In China, men who do physical labour are least attractive as mates, while women who labour with their minds are least popular.

Thanks to technological advancements (prenatal scanning), India is facing the same problem. Families that are able to pay Rs10 000 ($217, €177, £121) can have the scanning done and abort female foetuses. Traditionally, boys are preferred in Indian culture. According to the latest census report, proportions of Indian girls to boys among children up to six years fell from 945 girls to 1 000 boys (1991) to 927 girls in 2001. The trend is most pronounced in richer states (as people can pay for the test). For example, Punjab has 798 girls and Gujarat 883 to every 1 000 boys. This disparity can have worrying implications especially when, unlike China, India has not been able to impose any family planning.

Source: adapted from 'Sex Determination before Birth', *Reuters News Service*, 3 May 1994; 'Seven Times as Many Men', *AP News Service*, 31 March 1994; Edward Luc, 'Indian Fears Over Falling Female Birth Ratio', *Financial Times*, 15 September 2004, p. 12.

Controlling Population Growth   Faced with the ominous consequences of the population explosion, it would seem logical for countries to take appropriate steps to reduce growth to manageable rates, but procreation is one of the most culturally sensitive uncontrollables. Economics, self-esteem, religion, politics and education all play a critical role in attitudes about family size.

The prerequisites for population control are adequate incomes, higher literacy levels, education for women, better hygiene, universal access to healthcare, improved nutrition and, perhaps most important, a change in basic cultural beliefs about the importance of large families. Unfortunately, progress in providing improved conditions and changing beliefs is hampered by the increasingly heavy demand placed on institutions responsible for change and improvement.

In many cultures, the prestige of a man, whether alive or dead, depends on the number of his progeny, and a family's only wealth is its children. Many religions discourage or ban family planning and thus serve as a deterrent to control. Nigeria has a strong Muslim tradition in the north and a strong Roman Catholic tradition in the east; both faiths discourage family planning. Most traditional religions in Africa encourage large families; in fact, the principal deity for many is the goddess of land and fertility.

Population control is often a political issue. Overpopulation and the resulting problems have been labelled by some as an imperialist myth to support a devious plot by rich countries to keep the developing world population down and maintain the developed world's dominance of the globe. Instead of seeking ways to reduce population growth, some politicians encourage growth as the most vital asset of poor countries. As long as such attitudes prevail, it will be extremely difficult, if not impossible, to control population.

Developed World Population Decline   While the developing world faces a rapidly growing population, it is estimated that the industrialised world's population will decline. Birth rates in Western Europe and Japan have been decreasing since the early or mid-1960s; more women are choosing careers instead of children, and many working couples are electing to remain childless. As a result of these and other contemporary factors, population growth in many countries has dropped below the rate necessary to maintain present levels. The populations of France, Sweden, Italy, Switzerland and Belgium are all expected to drop within a few years. Austria, Denmark, Germany, Japan and several other nations are now at about zero population growth and will probably slip to the minus side in another decade. Exhibit 3.6 reveals the old age dependency in the Europe of the future.

The economic fallout of a declining population has many ramifications. Businesses find their domestic market shrinking for items such as maternity and infant goods, school equipment and selected durables. This leads to reduced production and worker layoffs that affect living standards. Europe, Japan and the United States have special problems because of the increasing percentage of elderly people who must be supported by shrinking numbers of active workers. The elderly require higher government outlays for healthcare and hospitals, special housing and nursing homes, and pension and welfare

Exhibit 3.6 Europe's old age dependency

Country	Population		Dependency ratio[†]	
	2005	**2050**	**2005**	**2050**
	Millions		Millions	
Spain	41.2	37.3	28	72
Italy	57.5	48.1	31	66
Poland	38.5	33.0	20	55
EU	445.2*	431.2*	29**	52**
Germany	83.0	76.0	30	52
France	60.3	62.2	28	50
United States	295.5	419.9	21	39

Notes: [†] Age 65+ as % of those 20–65; * EU 25; ** EU 15.

Source: Eurostat, UN population Division, US Census Bureau and *The Economist*, 2 October, 2004, p. 36.

assistance, but the workforce that supports these costs is dwindling. In addition, a shortage of skilled workers is anticipated in these countries because of the decreasing population. The trends of increasing population in the developing world, with substantial shifts from rural to urban areas and declining birth rates in the industrialised world, will have profound effects on the state of world business and world economic conditions well beyond 2020. And, while world population is increasing, multinational firms could see world markets decreasing on a relative basis because the monied world is losing numbers and poor nations are gaining numbers. Population size is important in marketing, but people must have a means to buy for there to be an effective market.

world trade routes

Major world trade routes have developed among the most industrialised countries of the world: Europe, North America and Japan. It may be said that trade routes bind the world together, minimising distance, natural barriers, lack of resources, and the fundamental differences between peoples and economies. Early trade routes were, of course, overland; later came sea routes and, finally, air routes to connect countries. Trade routes represent the attempts of countries to overcome economic and social imbalances created in part by the influence of geography.

key term

Triad trade
the process of trade undertaken between the EU, North America and Canada, Japan and China

A careful comparison among the world population figures in Exhibit 3.4, the **Triad trade** figures in Exhibit 3.7 and the world trade figures in Exhibit 3.8 illustrate how small a percentage of the world's land mass and population account for the majority of trade. It is no surprise that the major sea lanes and the most developed highway and rail systems link these major trade areas. The more economically developed a country, the better developed the surface transportation infrastructure is to support trade.

Exhibit 3.7 The Triad: merchandise trade between the US and Canada, the EU, Japan and China, 2002 ($ billions)

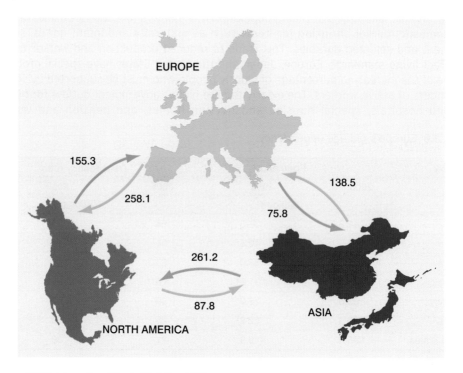

Source: WTO, *International Trade Statistics 2003.*

Exhibit 3.8 Leading exporters and importers in world merchandise trade and commercial service, 2002 ($ millions)

Country*	Exports	Imports	Total
United States	966.5	1 408.0	2 374.5
Germany	712.7	642.8	1 355.5
Japan	481.6	443.8	925.4
France	417.7	460.5	878.2
United Kingdom	402.7	446.7	849.4
China	365.0	341.3	706.3
Italy	310.4	304.5	614.9
Netherlands	298.4	275.5	573.9
Canada	288.7	269.4	558.1
Belgium	248.9	232.3	481.2
Hong Kong	246.4	231.4	477.8
Korea	189.6	187.2	376.8
Spain	181.2	192.3	373.5
Chinese Taipei	156.2	136.9	293.1
Singapore	152.1	137.0	289.1

Note: *Order determined by total dollar value of exports and imports.

Source: World Trade Organization, *International Trade Statistics 2003*.

Although air freight is not extremely important as a percentage of total freight transportation, an interesting comparison between surface routes and air routes is air service to the world's less industrialised countries. Although air routes are the heaviest between points in the major industrial centres, they are also heavy to points in less developed countries. The obvious reason is that for areas not located on navigable waters or where the investment in railways and effective roads is not yet feasible, air service is often the best answer. Air communications have made otherwise isolated parts of the world reasonably accessible.

historical perspective in international trade

To understand, explain and appreciate a people's image of itself and the fundamental attitudes and unconscious fears that are often reflected in its view of foreign cultures, it is necessary to study the culture as it is now as well as to understand the culture as it was, that is, a country's history. An awareness of the history of a country is particularly effective for understanding attitudes about the role of government and business, the relations between managers and the managed, the sources of management authority, and attitudes towards foreign multinational corporations. History helps define a nation's 'mission', how it perceives its neighbours, and how it sees its place in the world.

history and contemporary behaviour

Unless you have a historical sense of the many changes that have buffeted Japan, the isolation before the coming of Admiral Perry in 1853, the threat of domination by colonial powers, the rise of new social classes, Western influences, the humiliation of the Second World War and involvement in the international community, it is difficult to fully understand its contemporary behaviour. Why do the Japanese have such strong loyalty towards

their companies? Why is the loyalty found among participants in the Japanese distribution systems so difficult for an outsider to develop? Why are decisions made by consensus? Answers to such questions can be explained in part by some sense of Japanese history.[13]

history is subjective

History is important in understanding why a country behaves as it does, but history from whose viewpoint? Historical events are always viewed from one's own biases, and thus what is recorded by one historian may not be what another records, especially if the historians are from different cultures. Historians are traditionally objective, but few can help filtering events through their own cultural biases. Not only is history sometimes subjective, but there are other subtle influences on our perspective. Maps of the world sold in the United States generally show the United States as the centre, as maps in Britain show Britain at the centre, while maps in Australia look totally different, with Australia being the centre of the world and the rest lying east, west or north of the centre.

summary

One British authority admonishes foreign marketers to study the world until 'the mere mention of a town, country or river enables it to be picked out immediately on the map'. Although it may not be necessary for the student of international marketing to memorise the world map to that extent, a prospective international marketer should be reasonably familiar with the world, its climate and topographic differences. Otherwise, the important marketing characteristics of geography could be completely overlooked when marketing in another country. The need for geographical and historical knowledge goes deeper than being able to locate continents and their countries. For someone who has never been in a tropical rainforest with an annual rainfall of at least 1.5 metres and sometimes more than 5 metres, it is difficult to anticipate the need for protection against high humidity, or to anticipate the difficult problems caused by dehydration in constant 38°C or more heat in the Sahara region. Without a historical understanding of a culture, the attitudes within the marketplace may not be understood. An understanding of world population and its expected growth in regions and countries can have a profound impact on a company's international marketing strategies. The same goes for the geographic locations of resources and other raw materials.

Aside from the simpler and more obvious ramifications of climate and topography, there are complex geographical and historical influences on the development of the general economy and society of a country. In this case, the need for studying geography and history is to provide the marketer with an understanding of why a country has developed as it has rather than as a guide for adapting marketing plans. Geography and history are two of the environments of foreign marketing that should be understood and that must be included in foreign marketing plans to a degree commensurate with their influence on marketing effort.

questions

1 Study the data in Figure 3.1 and briefly discuss the long-term prospects for industrialisation of an underdeveloped country with a high population growth and minimum resources.
2 Why study geography in international marketing? Discuss.
3 Pick a country and show how employment and topography affect marketing within that country.
4 Discuss the bases of world trade. Give examples illustrating the different bases.

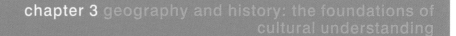

5 The marketer 'should also examine the more complex effect of geography on general market characteristics, distribution systems, and the state of the economy'. Comment.

6 The world population pattern is shifting from rural to urban areas. Discuss the marketing ramifications.

7 Select a country with a stable population and one with a rapidly growing population. Contrast the marketing implications of these two situations.

8 'The basis of world trade can be simply stated as the result of equalising an imbalance in the needs and wants of society on one hand and its supply of goods on the other.' Explain.

9 How do differences in people constitute a basis for trade?

10 'World trade routes bind the world together.' Discuss.

11 Why are the 1990s called the 'Decade of the Environment'? Explain.

12 Some say the global environment is a global issue rather than a national one. What does this mean? Discuss.

further reading

- Nigel Holden, *Cross-Cultural Management: A Knowledge Management Perspective* (Harlow: FT-Prentice Hall, 2002, Chapter 2).
- A.J. Scott, 'Economic Geography: The Great Half Century', in G.L. Clark, M.P. Feldman and M.S. Gertler (eds), *The Oxford Handbook of Economic Geography* (Oxford: Oxford University Press, 2000) pp. 483–504.
- *The Economist, Globalisation – Making Sense of an Integrating World* (London: Profile Books, 2001).

references

1 For an interesting book on the effects of geography, technology and capitalism on an economy, see Dean M. Hanik, *The International Economy: A Geographical Perspective* (New York: Wiley, 1994).

2 'Chunnel Vision', *Europe*, May 1994, p. 43.

3 'Assessing the Channel Tunnel's Benefits', *Business Europe*, 10–16 January 1994, p. 2.

4 World Bank, *World Development Indicators*, CD-ROM, 2003.

5 'A Survey on Development and the Environment', *The Economist*, 21 March 1998.

6 Yoshihide Soeya, 'Balance and Growth', *Look Japan*, January 1994, p. 19.

7 Visit the OECD's website to find out more about sustainable development: www.oecd.org.

8 United Nations, *World Population Projections to 2150*, Department of Economic and Social Affairs, Population Division (New York: United Nations, 1998).

9 'Our World in 2020', Special Survey, *Guardian*, 11 September 2004.

10 This figure represents Tokyo's core suburbs and exurbs.

11 United Nations, *World Urbanization Prospects*, 2003, New York: United Nations.

12 United Nations, *World Population Projections to 2150*, Department of Economic and Social Affairs, Population Division (New York: United Nations, 1998).

13 For insights into some of these questions, see Boye Lafayette DeMente, *Japanese Etiquette and Ethics in Business*, 6th edn (Lincolnwood, IL: NTC Business Books, 1994).

chapter 4
Cultural Dynamics in International Marketing

Chapter Outline

Chapter Learning Objectives

What you should learn from Chapter 4

- How important is the culture to an international marketer and how one can handle cultural differences
- The effects of the self-reference criterion (SRC) on marketing objectives
- What are the elements of culture and how are these related to international marketing
- What is meant by cultural sensitivity and how to handle it
- Can cultural borrowings influence consumer behaviour and attitudes
- How the strategy of planned cultural change works and its consequences

key terms

economic needs
e.g. minimum food, drink, shelter and clothing

economic wants
arise from desire for satisfaction and, due to their non-essential quality, are limitless

culture
a set of values and norms followed by a group of people

collective programming
when groups of people are taught/ indoctrinated with certain values

Humans are born creatures of need; as they mature, want is added to need. **Economic needs** are spontaneous and, in their crudest sense, limited. Humans, like all living things, need a minimum of nourishment and, like a few other living things they need shelter. Unlike any other being, they also need essential clothing. **Economic wants**, however, are for non-essentials and, hence, are limitless. Unlike basic needs, wants are not spontaneous and not characteristic of the lower animals. They arise not from an inner desire for preservation of self or species, but from a desire for satisfaction above absolute necessity. To satisfy their material needs and wants, humans consume.

The manner in which people consume, the priority of needs and the wants they attempt to satisfy, and the manner in which they satisfy them are functions of their culture that temper, mould and dictate their style of living. **Culture** is the human-made part of the human environment – the sum total of knowledge, beliefs, art, morals, laws, customs and any other capabilities and habits acquired by humans as members of society. Culture is 'everything that people have, think and do as members of their society'.[1]

Culture is often defined as 'inherited ethical habit', consisting of values and ideas. Ethical systems create moral communities because their shared languages of good and evil give their members a common moral life.[2]

According to Hofstede,[3] culture is always a collective phenomenon, because it is at least partially shared with people who live or lived within the same environment, which is where it was learned. It is the **collective programming** of the mind that distinguishes the members of one group or category of people from another.

Culture's essence is captured in the above definitions. In sum, the concept is representative when:[4]

- the members of a group share a set of ideas and values
- these are transmitted by symbols from one generation to another
- culture is an outcome of past actions of a group or its members
- culture is learned
- culture shapes behaviour and our perception of the world
- it is reinforced by components such as language, behaviour and 'nation'.

Hofstede's seminal work on culture contains more than 11 600 questionnaires in more than 50 countries. He derived four main conceptual dimensions on which national cultures exhibit significant differences. The dimensions are named *individualism/collectivism*, *power distance*, *masculinity/femininity* and *uncertainty avoidance*. For example, in collective countries there is a close-knit social structure, while in individualistic countries people are basically supposed to care for themselves. Power distance refers to the extent to which a society and its individuals tolerate an unequal distribution of power. A society is masculine when it favours assertiveness, earning money, showing off possessions and

caring little for others, while feminine societies are the opposite. Uncertainty avoidance refers to the degree to which a society feels threatened by uncertain, ambiguous or undefined situations. In high uncertainty avoidance society people look for stable careers and follow rules and procedures. Exhibit 4.1 shows the values of these dimensions for 52 different countries/regions.[5] Exhibit 4.2 shows the grouping of countries according to these differences.

Exhibit 4.1 Values of Hofstede's cultural dimensions for 52 countries or regions

Country/region	Dimensions			
	Power distance	Uncertainty avoidance	Individualism	Masculinity
Arabic countries (ARA)	80	68	38	53
Argentina (ARG)	49	86	46	56
Australia (AUL)	36	51	90	61
Austria (AUS)	11	70	55	79
Belgium (BEL)	65	94	75	54
Brazil (BRA)	69	76	38	49
Canada (CAN)	39	48	80	52
Chile (CHI)	63	86	23	28
Colombia (COL)	67	80	13	64
Costa Rica (COS)	35	86	15	21
Denmark (DEN)	18	23	74	16
East African region (EA)	64	52	27	41
Ecuador (ECUA)	78	67	8	63
Finland (FIN)	33	59	63	26
France (FRA)	68	86	71	43
Great Britain (GB)	35	35	89	66
Greece (GRE)	60	112	35	57
Guatemala (GUA)	96	101	6	37
Hong Kong (HON)	68	29	25	57
India (IND)	77	40	48	56
Indonesia (INDO)	78	48	14	46
Iran (IRA)	58	59	41	43
Ireland (IRE)	28	35	70	68
Israel (ISR)	13	81	54	47
Italy (ITA)	50	75	76	70
Jamaica (JAM)	45	13	39	68
Japan (JAP)	54	92	46	95
Malaysia (MAL)	104	36	26	50
Mexico (MEX)	81	82	30	69
Netherlands (NETH)	38	53	80	14

Exhibit 4.1 (Values of Hofstede's cultural dimensions for 52 countries or regions, continued)

Country/region	Dimensions			
	Power distance	Uncertainty avoidance	Individualism	Masculinity
New Zealand (NZ)	22	49	79	58
Norway (NOR)	31	50	69	8
Pakistan (PAK)	55	70	14	50
Panama (PAN)	95	86	11	44
Peru (PER)	64	87	16	42
Philippines (PHI)	94	44	32	64
Portugal (POR)	63	104	27	31
Salvador (SAL)	66	94	19	40
Singapore (SIN)	74	8	20	48
South Africa (SA)	49	49	65	63
South Korea (KOR)	60	85	18	39
Spain (SPA)	57	86	51	42
Sweden (SWE)	31	29	71	5
Switzerland (SWI)	34	58	68	70
Taiwan (TAI)	58	69	17	45
Thailand (THA)	64	64	20	34
Turkey (TUR)	66	85	37	45
United States (USA)	40	46	91	62
Uruguay (URU)	61	100	36	38
Venezuela (VEN)	81	76	12	73
West African region (WA)	77	54	20	46
West Germany (WG)	35	65	67	66
Overall mean	*57*	*65*	*43*	*49*
Standard deviation	*22*	*24*	*25*	*18*

Source: cited in J.-C. Usunier, *Marketing Across Cultures*, 2nd edn (Hemel Hempstead: Prentice-Hall, 1996) pp. 78–9.

The results of Hofstede's study have been discussed and questioned. It is a valid question that whether the data collected in late 1970s, and the behaviour of people in many countries, have not shifted due to radical changes in the world during the last 30 years. However, Hofstede's study was the first one to systematically study culture relevant to business and management and has thus taken this concept beyond anecdotal references.

Because culture deals with a group's design for living, it is pertinent to the study of marketing, especially international marketing. If you consider for a moment the scope of the marketing concept – the satisfaction of consumer needs and wants at a profit – it becomes apparent that the successful marketer must be a student of culture. What a marketer is constantly dealing with is the culture of the people (the market). When a promotional message is written, symbols recognisable and meaningful to the market (the culture) must be used. When designing a product, the style, uses and other related

marketing activities must be made culturally acceptable (i.e. acceptable to the present society) if they are to be operative and meaningful. In fact, culture is pervasive in all marketing activities – in pricing, promotion, channels of distribution, product, packaging and styling – and the marketer's efforts actually become a part of the fabric of culture. The marketer's efforts are judged in a cultural context for acceptance, resistance or rejection. How such efforts interact with a culture determines the degree of success or failure of the marketing effort.

Exhibit 4.2 The positions of 50 countries and three regions on the power distance and uncertainty avoidance dimensions (for country name abbreviations see Exhibit 4.1)

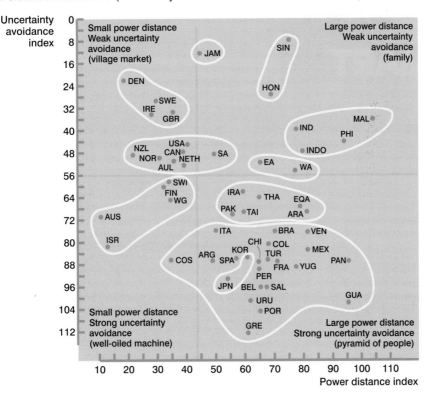

Source: G. Hofstede, *Culture and Organizations: Software of the Mind* (London: McGraw-Hill, 1991), p. 141. Reprinted with permission.

Nie mehr suchen: Niedrigpreise das ganze Jahr!

www.walmartgermany.de

WAL★MART®

'Don't look now: low prices all year round!'

Bolted together from two acquisitions in 1997 and 1998, Wal-Mart Germany is the country's fourth largest hypermarket chain with 10 per cent of the market. Although a drop in the ocean for the world-wide group – it generates less than 2 per cent of Wal-Mart's sales – its poor performance has been a stain on the group's record. Wal-Mart does not publish regional profit figures but the operation is said to be losing $200–300 million (€166–249 million) a year.

'We made mistakes,' says Volker Barth, head of Wal-Mart Germany, 'but one mistake we never made was to underestimate the German market.' Making a mark on Europe's largest and most competitive food retail markets was never going to be easy. But some of Wal-Mart's early mistakes may be impossible to redress. The most glaring one, says an insider, was to disregard the structure of distribution in German food retailing. Drawing on the US model, Wal-Mart decided it wanted to control distribution to stores rather than leave it to suppliers. The result was chaos because suppliers could not adapt to Wal-Mart's centralised demands. With many deliveries failing to arrive in time, out-of-stock rates were sometimes up to 20 per cent, compared to a 7 per cent average for the industry.

Then the group fuelled discontent at Wertkauf, its first acquisition, by filling top positions with US expatriates, a move perceived as arrogant. The ensuing exodus of German managers, which accelerated after the closure of the Wertkauf headquarters in 1999, deprived the group of local expertise.

Dominated by hard discounters and privately owned businesses, and suffering from overcapacity, the German food retail market has long been plagued by microscopic profit margins, oscillating between 1 and 2 per cent, compared with 4 to 6 per cent in the UK. Wal-Mart's low-price message, therefore, had none of the revolutionary ring it carried in the UK when it acquired the Asda chain. Although each of its heavily advertised price cuts in Germany prompted loud complaints from other retailers, they were actually limited in scope and quickly matched by rivals.

Jurgen Elfers, analyst at Commerzbank, blames the failures on the poor quality of the Interspar chain, Wal-Mart's second and largest acquisition. In a Machiavellian twist, Spar-Handels, the seller, extracted a commitment from Wal-Mart to retain 200 hand-picked employees, a large number of whom were later found to be poorly trained, prompting even long-suffering German shoppers to complain of sloppy service. Facing renovation costs up to five times those in the US, and struggling to navigate Germany's Byzantine planning and social regulations, the group has refurbished only a quarter of its 95 stores and many sites remain unattractive, too small, cramped or poorly located. The Kundenmonitor, a yearly survey of customer satisfaction, gave Wal-Mart the poorest mark of all retailers for general customer sentiment in its latest issue – it ranked higher on value for money. 'The problem is that Germany is beginning to raise questions about the group's entire international strategy,' says Andrew Fowler, food retail analyst at Morgan Stanley Dean Witter (see Case Study 4.1 for a more in-depth analysis).

■ What do you think were the main problems Wal-Mart faced in Germany? How can Wal-Mart improve its business in Germany?

Source: Bertrand Benoit, 'Wal-Mart finds German Failures Hard to Swallow', *Financial Times*, 12 October 2000; Erich Culp, 'Juggernaut Wal-Mart Goes Slow in Germany', *The Business*, 26/27 September 2004, p. 4.

The marketer's **frame of reference** must be that markets do not occur or exist naturally – they become, they evolve; they are not static but change, expand and contract in response to marketing effort, economic conditions and other cultural influences. Markets and market behaviour are part of a country's culture. One cannot truly understand how markets evolve or how they react to a marketer's effort without appreciating that markets are a result of culture. Markets are dynamic living phenomena, expanding and contracting not only in response to economic change, but also in response to changes in other aspects of the culture. Markets are the result of the three-way interaction of a marketer's efforts, economic conditions and all other elements of the culture. Marketers are constantly adjusting their efforts to the cultural demands of the market, but they are also acting as agents of change whenever the product or idea being marketed is innovative. Whatever the degree of acceptance in whatever level of culture, the use of something new is the beginning of **cultural change** and the marketer becomes a change agent.

This chapter's purpose is to heighten the reader's sensitivity to the dynamics of culture. It is not a treatise on cultural information about a particular country; rather, it is designed to emphasise the need for study of each country's culture and to point up some relevant aspects on which to focus. This chapter explores briefly the concept of culture related to international marketing. Subsequent chapters explore particular features of each of the cultural elements as they affect the marketing process.

cultural knowledge

There are two kinds of knowledge about cultures. One is **factual knowledge** about a culture; it is usually obvious and must be learned. Different meanings of colour, different tastes and other traits indigenous to a culture are facts that a marketer can anticipate, study and absorb. The other is **interpretive knowledge** – an ability to understand and to appreciate fully the nuances of different cultural traits and patterns. For example, the meaning of time, attitudes towards other people and certain objects, the understanding of one's role in society, and the meanings of life can differ considerably from one culture to another and may require more than factual knowledge to be fully appreciated.

key terms

frame of reference
see **self-reference criterion**
(on page 81)

cultural change
change in cultural conditions, e.g. Americanisation

factual knowledge
something that is usually obvious but that must be learnt, i.e. different meaning of colours

interpretive knowledge
ability to understand and appreciate fully the nuances of different cultural traits and patterns

---

GOING INTERNATIONAL 4.2

can Wal-Mart win in Japan?

Wal-Mart has big plans for Japan. In 2002 the US giant bought a stake in Seiyu, a struggling local retailer, and today owns a controlling 38 per cent interest. At the time it made its move, analysts scoffed that Wal-Mart's model was all wrong for Japan, where shoppers traditionally preferred convenience to knock-down prices, and patronised multi-storey stores with good service in city centres. Moreover, Japan's close-knit network of suppliers and shop owners has given a hostile greeting to outside retailers. However, a decade of economic stagnation has changed Japanese consumer culture. Cut-price outlets such as 100-yen shops have flourished and, like their US counterparts, younger Japanese now spend more time shopping at weekends in malls or discount outlets rather than in small stores close to home. With the economy finally bouncing back, Wal-Mart executives are convinced they can capture a big slice of Japan's $1.3 trillion retail market – the world's second largest. 'Japan's a challenging market, but it's also a very significant growth opportunity,' says Greg Penner, chief financial officer of Wal-Mart Japan.

In the first quarter of 2004, its expenditures fell by 3.6 per cent compared with the same period in the previous year, the result of improved operating efficiency. Furthermore 1600 of Seiyu's full-time employees, 25 per cent of the total, were nudged into voluntary retirement, which will carve $46 million off the annual wage bill. The cuts and new systems have helped Seiyu get back in the black. The company expects to eke out a profit of $4.6 million on sales of $10.2 billion in 2004, compared with losses of $754 million in 2002 and $67 million in 2003.

Staying in the black may be a challenge, given mounting competition from other big-store retailers. France's Carrefour, after some initial missteps, now has eight stores in Japan. Britain's Tesco last year bought C Two-Network a convenience retailer with 78 stores in the Tokyo area, which Tesco could use as a springboard for building a chain of bigger outlets. Local rival Aeon Group expects to have 100 Wal-Mart-style supercentres in suburban areas by the end of 2005, up from four in 2004. Beisia Group hopes to open 75 supercentres by the end of 2005, while supermarket and convenience store operator Ito-Yokado is beefing up its computer systems. 'The biggest threat to Wal-Mart in Japan will be from domestic competition,' says Frank Badillo, chief economist at Retail Forward, a US consulting firm. 'Ito-Yokado and Aeon aren't just going to roll over.'

Wal-Mart may have a bit more trouble with another pillar of its strategy, so-called everyday low prices (EDLP). Japanese retailers typically lure customers into stores with deep discounts on selected items, which they advertise in weekly flyers called *chirashi*. By contrast, Wal-Mart relies less on specials, and instead promises consistently rock-bottom prices. In 2003, Seiyu dropped its *chirashi* for a few weeks because specials didn't fit the Wal-Mart model, but when sales started falling the flyers were quickly reintroduced. The next supercentre isn't slated until 2006, and the company won't discuss plans for more of them.

■ Will Wal-Mart steamroll the opposition? Or will the Japanese get their *sashimi* elsewhere? How can Wal-Mart Japan compete with local and European retailers?

Source: compiled from Ian Rawley, 'Can Wal-Mart Woo Japan?', *Business Week*, 10 May 2004, pp. 24–5.

factual knowledge

Frequently, factual knowledge has meaning as a straightforward fact about a culture, but assumes additional significance when interpreted within the context of the culture. For example, that Mexico is 98 per cent Roman Catholic is an important bit of factual knowledge. But equally important is what it means to be Catholic within Mexican culture versus being Catholic in Spain or Italy. Each culture practises Catholicism in slightly different ways. For example, All Souls' Day is an important celebration among some Catholic countries; in Mexico, however, the celebration receives special emphasis. The Mexican observance is a unique combination of pagan (mostly Indian influence) and Catholic tradition. On the Day of the Dead, as All Souls' Day is called by many in Mexico, it is believed that the dead return to feast. Hence, many Mexicans visit the graves of their departed, taking the dead's favourite foods to place on the graves for them to enjoy. Prior to All Souls' Day, bakeries pile their shelves with bread shaped like bones and coffins, and candy stores sell sugar skulls and other special treats to commemorate the day. As the souls feast on the food, so do the living celebrants. Although the prayers, candles and the idea of the soul are Catholic, the idea of the dead feasting is very pre-Christian Mexican. Thus, a Catholic in

Mexico observes All Souls' Day quite differently from a Catholic in Spain. This interpretive, as well as factual, knowledge about a religion in Mexico is necessary to fully understand Mexican culture.[6]

GOING INTERNATIONAL 4.3

more equal than others

In a peaceful revolution – the last revolution in Swedish history – the nobles of Sweden in 1809 deposed King Gustav IV whom they considered incompetent, and surprisingly invited Jean Baptiste Bernadotte, a French general who served under their enemy Napoleon, to become King of Sweden. Bernadotte accepted and he became King Charles XIV; his descendants occupy the Swedish throne to this day. When the new king was installed he addressed the Swedish parliament in their language. His broken Swedish amused the Swedes and they roared with laughter. The Frenchman who had become king was so upset that he never tried to speak Swedish again. In this incident Bernadotte was a victim of culture shock: never in his French upbringing and military career had he experienced subordinates who laughed at the mistakes of their superior. Historians tell us he had more problems adapting to the egalitarian Swedish and Norwegian mentality (he later became King of Norway as well) and to his subordinates' constitutional rights. He was a good learner, however (except for language!), and he ruled the country as a highly respected constitutional monarch until 1844.

One of the aspects in which Sweden differs from France is the way its society handles *inequality*. There is inequality in any society. Even in the most simple hunter-gatherer band, some people are bigger, stronger or smarter than others. The next thing is that some people have more power than others: they are more able to determine the behaviour of others than vice versa. Some people are given more status and respect than others.

Source: Geert Hofstede, *Cultures and Organizations: Software of the Mind* (London: McGraw-Hill, 1991), p. 23.

---

interpretive knowledge

Interpretive knowledge requires a degree of insight that may best be described as a feeling. It is the kind of knowledge most dependent on past experience for interpretation and most frequently prone to misinterpretation if relying on one's **self-reference criterion (SRC)**.

Ideally, the foreign marketer should possess both kinds of knowledge about a market. Most facts about a particular culture can be learned by researching published material about that culture. This effort can also transmit a small degree of empathy, but to appreciate the culture fully, it is necessary to live with the people for some time. Because this ideal solution is not practical for a marketer, other solutions are sought. Consultation and co-operation with bilingual nationals with marketing backgrounds is the most effective answer to the problem. This has the further advantage of helping the marketer acquire an increasing degree of empathy through association with the people who understand the culture best – the locals.

key term

self-reference criterion (SRC) considering our own conditions, values and norms

key term

cultural sensitivity and tolerance

Successful foreign marketing begins with **cultural sensitivity** – being attuned to the nuances of culture so that a new culture can be viewed objectively, evaluated and appreciated. Cultural empathy must be cultivated carefully. Perhaps the most important step is the recognition that cultures are not right or wrong, better or worse; they are simply different. For every amusing, annoying, peculiar or repulsive cultural trait we find in a country, there is a similarly amusing, annoying or repulsive trait others see in our culture. We find it peculiar that the Chinese eat dogs, while they find it peculiar that we buy packaged, processed dog food in supermarkets and keep dogs as pets. They also find it peculiar that we eat lambs and certain other animals but not dogs and cats.

Just because a culture is different does not make it wrong. Marketers must understand how their own culture influences their assumptions about another culture. The more exotic the situation, the more sensitive, tolerant and flexible one needs to be. Being more culturally sensitive will reduce conflict, improve communications and thereby increase success in collaborative relationships.

It is necessary for a marketer to investigate the assumptions on which judgements are based, especially when the frames of reference are strictly from his or her own culture. As products of our own culture we instinctively evaluate foreign cultural patterns from a personal perspective.

culture and its elements

The student of international marketing should approach an understanding of culture from the viewpoint of the anthropologist. Every group of people or society has a culture because culture is the entire social heritage of the human race: 'the totality of the knowledge and practices, both intellectual and material of society … [it] embraces everything from food to dress, from household techniques to industrial techniques, from forms of politeness to mass media, from work rhythms to the learning of familiar rules'.[7] Culture exists in New York, London and Moscow just as it does among the Gypsies, the South Sea Islanders or the Aborigines of Australia.

elements of culture

The anthropologist studying culture as a science must investigate every aspect of a culture if an accurate, total picture is to emerge. To implement this goal, there has evolved a cultural scheme that defines the parts of culture. For the marketer, the same thoroughness is necessary if the marketing consequences of cultural differences within a foreign market are to be accurately assessed.

Culture includes every part of life. The scope of the term culture to the anthropologist is illustrated by the elements included within the meaning of the term. These are:

1 material culture
  technology
  economics
2 social institutions
  social organisation
  political structures
3 education
  literacy rate
  role and levels
4 belief systems
  religion
  superstitions
  power structure

5 aesthetics
   graphic and plastic arts
   folklore
   music, drama and dance
6 language[8]
   usage of foreign languages
   spoken versus written language.

In the study of humanity's way of life, the anthropologist finds these six dimensions useful because they encompass all the activities of social heritage that constitute culture (Exhibit 4.3). Foreign marketers may find such a cultural scheme a useful framework in evaluating a marketing plan or in studying the potential of foreign markets. All the elements are instrumental to some extent in the success or failure of a marketing effort because they constitute the environment within which the marketer operates. Furthermore, because we automatically react to many of these factors in our native culture, we must purposely learn them in another. Finally, these are the elements with which marketing efforts interact and so are critical to understanding the character of the marketing system of any society. It is necessary to study the various implications of the differences of each of these factors in any analysis of a specific foreign market.

Material Culture   Material culture is divided into two parts: technology and economics. Technology includes the techniques used in the creation of material goods; it is the technical know-how possessed by the people of a society. For example, the vast majority of Western citizens understand the simple concepts involved in reading gauges, but in many countries of the world, this seemingly simple concept is not part of their common culture and is therefore a major technical limitation.

   A culture's level of technology is manifest in many ways. Such concepts as preventive maintenance are foreign in many low-technology cultures. In Germany, the United States, Japan or other countries with high levels of technology, the general population has a broad level of technical understanding that allows them to adapt and learn new technology more easily than populations with lower levels of technology. Simple repairs, preventive maintenance and a general understanding of how things work all constitute a high level of technology. In China, one of the burdens of that country's economic growth is providing the general working population with a modest level of mechanical skill, that is, a level of technology.

Exhibit 4.3 Elements of culture

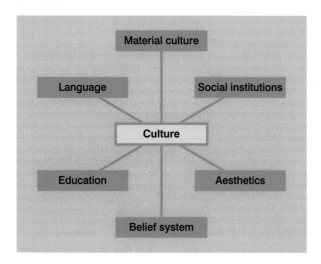

Economics is the manner in which people employ their capabilities and the resulting benefits. Included in the subject of economics are the production of goods and services, their distribution, consumption, means of exchange and the income derived from the creation of utilities.

Material culture affects the level of demand, the quality and types of products demanded and their functional features, as well as the means of production of these goods and their distribution. The marketing implications of the material culture of a country are many: electrical appliances sell in England or France, but have few buyers in countries where less than 1 per cent of the homes have electricity. Even with electrification, economic characteristics represented by the level and distribution of income may limit the desirability of products. Electric can openers and electric juicers are acceptable in the United States, but, in less affluent countries, not only are they unattainable and probably unwanted, they would be a spectacular waste because **disposable income** could be spent more meaningfully on better houses, clothing or food.

key term

disposable income
that proportion of your income that is not already accounted for – for example, by mortgages, loans, bills, and so on

Social Institutions   Social organisation and political structures are concerned with the ways in which people relate to one another, organise their activities to live in harmony with one another and govern themselves. The positions of men and women in society, the family, social classes, group behaviour and age groups are interpreted differently within every culture (see Exhibit 4.4). Each institution has an effect on marketing because each influences behaviour, values and the overall patterns of life. In cultures where social

Exhibit 4.4 Concepts of self and others

Basic problem/cultural orientations	Contrasts across cultures
How should we treat unknown people? (a) Is human nature basically good or bad?	Unknown people are considered favourably and shown confidence or, conversely, they are treated with suspicion when met for the first time

Appraising others
(b)   When appraising others, emphasis placed on:
 	
   (i)   age
 	
   (ii)   sex
   (iii)   social class
	Who are the persons to be considered trustworthy and reliable, with whom it is possible to do business?
	   (i) Older (younger) people are seen more favourably
	   (ii) Trustworthiness is based on sex or not
	   (iii) Social class plays a significant role (or not) in concepts of the self and others

Appraising oneself
(c)   Emphasis placed on the self-concept perceived as culturally appropriate:
   (i)   self-esteem – low/high
 	
   (ii)   perceived potency – low/high
   (iii)   level of activity – low/high
	
	   (i) Shyly and modestly vs extrovert or even arrogant
	   (ii) Power should be shown vs hidden
	   (iii) Busy people are the good ones vs unoccupied/idle people are well thought of

Relating to the group (d) Individualism vs collectivism	The individual is seen as the basic resource and therefore individual-related values are strongly emphasised (personal freedom, human rights, equality between men and women); vs the group is seen as the basic resource and therefore group values favoured (loyalty, sense of belonging, sense of personal sacrifice for the community, etc.)

Source: J.-C. Usunier, *Marketing Across Cultures*, 2nd edn (Hemel Hempstead: Prentice-Hall, 1996), p. 66.

organisation results in close-knit family units, for example, it is more effective to aim a promotional campaign at the family unit than at individual family members. Travel advertising in culturally divided Canada pictures a wife alone for the English audience, but a man and wife together for the French segments of the population because the French are traditionally more closely bound by family ties. The roles and status positions found within a society are influenced by the dictates of social organisation.

Education   In each society, we teach our generation what is acceptable or not acceptable, right or wrong, and other ways of behaviour. The literacy rate in each society is an important aspect and influences the behaviour of people. For a marketer it is important to know the role and level of education in a particular market. It would influence the marketing strategy and techniques used. Which type of advertising and communication is used depends highly on the level of education.

Belief System   Within this category are religion, superstitions and their related power structures. The impact of religion on the value systems of a society and the effect of **value systems** on marketing must not be underestimated. Religion has an impact upon people's habits, their outlook on life, the products they buy, the way they buy them, even the newspapers they read. Acceptance of certain types of food, clothing and behaviour are frequently affected by religion, and such influence can extend to the acceptance or rejection of promotional messages as well. In some countries, too much attention to bodily functions featured in advertisements would be judged immoral or improper and the products would be rejected. What might seem innocent and acceptable in one culture could be considered too personal or vulgar in another.

key term

value systems
values that are
followed
unconsciously

GOING INTERNATIONAL 4.4

religious rituals

Life is filled with little rituals that we do every day or week, and there are some rituals we do only once in our lifetime. Every Muslim is enjoined to make the *hajj*, or pilgrimage, to Mecca once in his or her lifetime if physically and financially able. Here, some 2 million faithful from all over the world gather annually to participate in what is the largest ritual meeting on earth. Catholics have a ritual such as a pilgrimage to Rome, Lourdes, Czestochowa or Santiago de Compostela. Pilgrimages are made to the places where the gods or heroes were born, wrought or died. In some cultures people visit shrines or temples and expect miracles and wonders. In some countries Catholics are supposed to make a pilgrimage on foot to one of these places, and it can take months before they arrive at the holy place.

**The largest ritual
meeting on earth**
© AFP/CORBIS

Religion is one of the most sensitive elements of a culture. When the marketer has little or no understanding of a religion, it is easy to offend, albeit unintentionally. Like all cultural elements, one's own religion is often not a reliable guide of another's beliefs. Many do not understand religions other than their own, and what is 'known' about other religions is often incorrect. The Islamic religion is a good example of the need for a basic understanding. There are more than 1 billion in the world who embrace Islam, yet major multinational companies often offend Muslims. A recent incident involved the French fashion house Chanel, which unwittingly desecrated the Koran by embroidering verses from the sacred book of Islam on several dresses shown in its summer collections. The designer said he took the design, which was aesthetically pleasing to him, from a book on India's Taj Mahal palace and that he was unaware of its meaning. To placate a Muslim group that felt the use of the verses desecrated the Koran, Chanel had to destroy the dresses with the offending designs along with negatives of the photos made of the garments. Chanel certainly had no intention of offending Muslims because some of its most important customers are of that religion. This example shows how easy it is to offend if the marketer, in this case the designer, has not familiarised him- or herself with other religions.[9]

GOING INTERNATIONAL 4.5

struggling McDonald's Japan is trying a new recipe

Passers-by consider the McDonald's half-price sale
AP/Wide World Photos

McDonald's Japan has suffered two consecutive disastrous years, losing a total of $87.5 million, with overall sales falling 4.4 per cent in 2003. When BSE broke out in the US, and Japan imposed a ban on imports of American beef, hamburgers suddenly became unpopular. Given that the Japanese operation generates nearly $2.7 billion in sales and is the biggest franchise of McDonald's Corp. outside the US, the troubles here made headquarters a bit worried, so it ended a 30-year contract with its Japanese partner, taking a one-time charge that contributed to 2003's year's losses. McDonald's US then installed Pat Donahue as chairman, who ran McDonald's Canadian operation, to replace McDonald's Japan's Fujita. (Fujita and his family still own 26 per cent, while McDonald's has a controlling 50 per cent stake.)

Now Makudonarudo, as the Japanese call McDonald's, is on a crash diet. It has cut costs by closing unprofitable franchises and laying off 15 per cent of the staff at the Tokyo headquarters. Three years ago, Fujita boasted that he would have 10 000 McDonald's restaurants by 2010. In 2004 there were 3 752, down from 3 891 in 2002. The company took a $23.4 million loss in 2003 to pull out of a failed high-end sandwich venture with British company Prêt À Manger.

However, the outlook is beginning to improve. Same-store sales in local currency terms increased in 2004. In addition to existing Japanese-style entrees such as the Teriyaki Burger, the company is rolling out spicy Korean-style burgers, a low-calorie tofu sandwich that's being marketed to women, and a bigger Premium Mac aimed at hungry men. The challenge now is getting back the magic that made McDonald's one of the most successful US investments in Japan.

■ Do you think McDonald's can turn things around in Japan? Can you advise it on what to do?

Source: adapted from 'Can Makudonarudo Turn up the Heat?', *Business Week*, 15 March 2004, p. 32.

Superstition plays a much larger role in a society's belief system in some parts of the world than it does in Western culture. What Westerners might consider as mere superstition can be a critical aspect of a belief system in another culture. For example, in parts of Asia, ghosts, fortune-telling, palmistry, head-bump reading, phases of the moon, demons and soothsayers are all integral parts of certain cultures. Astrologers are routinely called on in India and Thailand to determine the best location for a structure. The Thais insist that all wood in a new building must come from the same forest to prevent the boards from quarrelling with each other. Houses should have an odd number of rooms for luck, and they should be one storey because it is unlucky to have another's foot over your head.

One incident reported in Malaysia involved mass hysteria from fear of evil spirits. Most of a factory's labourers were involved and production ground to a halt until a 'bomoh' was called, a goat sacrificed and its blood sprinkled on the factory floor; the goat was then roasted and eaten. The next day the hysteria was over and everyone was back at work.[10]

It can be an expensive mistake to make light of superstitions in other cultures when doing business there. To make a fuss about being born in the right year under the right phase of the moon and to rely heavily on handwriting and palm-reading experts, as in Japan, can be worrisome to a Westerner who seldom sees a 13th floor in a building, refuses to walk under a ladder or worries about the next seven years after breaking a mirror.[11]

Aesthetics   Closely interwoven with the effect of people and the universe on a culture are its aesthetics; that is, the arts, folklore, music, drama and dance. Aesthetics are of particular interest to the marketer because of their role in interpreting the symbolic meanings of various methods of artistic expression, colour and standards of beauty in each culture. The uniqueness of a culture can be spotted quickly in symbols having distinct meanings.

Without a culturally correct interpretation of a country's aesthetic values, a whole host of marketing problems can arise. Product styling must be aesthetically pleasing to be successful, as must advertisements and package designs. Insensitivity to aesthetic values can offend, create a negative impression and, in general, render marketing efforts ineffective. Strong symbolic meanings may be overlooked if one is not familiar with a culture's aesthetic values. The Japanese, for example, revere the crane as being very lucky, for it is said to live a thousand years; however, the use of the number four should be completely avoided since the word for four, *shi*, is also the Japanese word for death.

Language   The importance of understanding the language of a country cannot be overestimated. The successful marketer must achieve expert communication; this requires a thorough understanding of the language as well as the ability to speak it. Advertising copywriters should be concerned less with obvious differences between languages and more with the idiomatic meanings expressed.

A dictionary translation is not the same as an **idiomatic interpretation**, and seldom will the dictionary translation suffice. Quite often there is a difference between spoken and written language. One national food processor's familiar 'Jolly Green Giant' translated into Arabic as 'Intimidating Green Ogre'. One airline's advertising campaign designed to promote its plush leather seats urged customers to 'fly on leather'; when translated for its Hispanic and Latin American customers, it told passengers to 'fly naked'. Pepsi's familiar 'Come Alive with Pepsi', when translated into German, conveyed the idea of coming alive from the grave. Schweppes was not pleased with its tonic water translation into Italian: 'Il Water' idiomatically means the bathroom. Electrolux's advertisement for its vacuum cleaner with the slogan 'Nothing Sucks Better than Electrolux' was not particularly appreciated in Ireland. Carelessly translated advertising statements not only lose their intended meaning, but can suggest something very different, obscene, offensive or just

key term

idiomatic interpretation interpretation according to the characteristics of a particular language

plain ridiculous. One authority suggests, as a cultural translator, a person who translates not only among languages, but also among different ways of thinking and among different cultures.[12]

Many believe that to appreciate the true meaning of a language it is necessary to live with that language for years. Whether or not this is the case, foreign marketers should never take it for granted that they are communicating effectively in another language. Until a marketer can master the vernacular, the aid of a national within the foreign country should be enlisted; even then, the problem of effective communications may still exist. For example, in French-speaking countries, the trademark toothpaste brand name 'Cue' was a crude slang expression for derrière. The intent of a major fountain pen company advertising in Latin America suffered in translation when the new pen was promoted to 'help prevent unwanted pregnancies'. The poster of an engineering company at a Russian trade show did not mean to promise that its oil well completion equipment was dandy for 'improving a person's sex life'.[13]

analysis of elements

Each cultural element must be evaluated in light of how it could affect a proposed marketing programme; some may have only indirect impact, others may be totally involved. Generally, it could be said that the more complete the marketing involvement or the more unique the product, the greater the need for thorough study of each cultural element. If a company is simply marketing an existing product in an already developed market, studying the total culture is certainly less crucial than for the marketer involved in total marketing – from product development, through promotion, to the final selling.

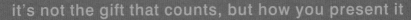

GOING INTERNATIONAL 4.6

it's not the gift that counts, but how you present it

Giving a gift in another country requires careful attention if it is to be done properly. Here are a few suggestions.

Japan
Do not open a gift in front of a Japanese counterpart unless asked and do not expect the Japanese to open your gift.

Avoid ribbons and bows as part of gift wrapping. Bows as we know them are considered unattractive, and ribbon colours can have different meanings.

Do not offer a gift depicting a fox or badger. The fox is the symbol of fertility, the badger, cunning.

Europe
Avoid red roses and white flowers, even numbers and the number 13. Unwrap flowers before presenting.

Do not risk the impression of bribery by spending too much on a gift.

Arab world
Do not give a gift when you first meet someone. It may be interpreted as a bribe.

Do not let it appear that you contrived to present the gift when the recipient is alone. It looks bad unless you know the person well. Give the gift in front of others in less personal relationships.

Latin America

Do not give a gift until after a somewhat personal relationship has developed unless it is given to express appreciation for hospitality.

Gifts should be given during social encounters, not in the course of business.

Avoid the colours black and purple; both are associated with the Catholic Lenten season.

China

Never make an issue of a gift presentation – publicly or privately.

Gifts should be presented privately, with the exception of collective ceremonial gifts at banquets.

Source: adapted from *International Business Gift-Giving Customs*, available from The Parker Pen Company.

While analysis of each cultural element *vis-à-vis* a marketing programme could ensure that each facet of a culture is included, it should not be forgotten that culture is a total picture, not a group of unrelated elements. Culture cannot be separated into parts and be fully understood. Every facet of culture is intricately intertwined and cannot be viewed singly; each must be considered for its synergistic effects. The ultimate personal motives and interests of people are determined by all the interwoven facets of the culture rather than by the individual parts. While some specific cultural elements have a direct influence on individual marketing efforts and must be viewed individually in terms of their potential or real effect on marketing strategy, the whole of cultural elements is manifested in a broader sense on the basic cultural patterns. In a market, basic consumption patterns, that is, who buys, what they buy, frequency of purchases, sizes purchased and so on, are established by cultural values of right and wrong, acceptable and unacceptable. The basic motives for consumption that help define fundamental needs and different forms of decision making have strong cultural underpinnings that are critical knowledge for the marketer.

GOING INTERNATIONAL 4.7

why don't monkeys go bananas?

A number of behavioural scientists concluded an experiment where 10 monkeys were held in a room. A ladder was standing in the middle of the room and on top of the ladder some bananas were placed. It did not take long before one of the monkeys discovered the bananas and tried to reach them. As soon as the monkey climbed the ladder the whole group of monkeys was hosed down with pressured water by the scientists.

The drill was repeated until not one of the monkeys dared to reach for the bananas. Now one monkey was replaced by a new monkey. Of course the new monkey discovered the bananas. On his attempt to reach the bananas, the other monkeys attacked him because they knew what was going to happen to them if this new monkey tried to reach the bananas.

The scientists kept replacing the monkeys that had experienced the hosing until all of them were replaced by new monkeys. Eventually none of the monkeys in the community had experienced the hosing, yet as soon as a new monkey tried to reach for the bananas the other monkeys would pull it down from the ladder and attack it. The monkeys thus declined to get the bananas.

Source: translated from T. Pauka and R. Zunderdorp, *De Banaan Wordt Bespreekbaar. Cultuurverandering in Ambtelijk en Politiek* (Amsterdam: Groningen, 1988).

Culture is dynamic in nature; culture is not static but a living process. That change is constant seems paradoxical in that another important attribute of culture is that it is conservative and resists change. The dynamic character of culture is significant in assessing new markets even though changes occur in the face of resistance. In fact, any change in the currently accepted way of life meets with more initial resistance than acceptance.[14]

cultural change

One view of culture sees it as the accumulation of a series of the best solutions to problems faced in common by members of a given society. In other words, culture is the means used in adjusting to the biological, environmental, psychological and historical components of human existence.

There are a variety of ways a society solves the problems created by its existence. Accident has provided solutions to some of them; invention has solved many others. More commonly, however, societies have found answers by looking to other cultures from which they can borrow ideas. Cultural borrowing is common to all cultures. Although each society has a few truly unique situations facing it, most problems confronting all societies are similar in nature, with alterations for each particular environment and culture.[15]

cultural borrowing

Cultural borrowing is a responsible effort to borrow those cultural ways seen as helpful in the quest for better solutions to a society's particular problems. If what it does adopt is adapted to local needs, once the adaptation becomes commonplace, it is passed on as cultural heritage. Thus, cultures unique in their own right are the result, in part, of borrowing from others. Consider, for example, American culture (United States) and the typical US citizen who:

> ... begins breakfast with an orange from the eastern Mediterranean, a cantaloupe from Egypt, or perhaps a piece of African watermelon ... After his fruit and Colombian coffee he goes on to waffles, cakes made by a Scandinavian technique from wheat domesticated in Asia Minor. Over these he pours maple syrup, invented by the Indians of the Eastern US woodlands. As a side dish he may have the eggs of a species of bird domesticated in Indo-China, or thin strips of the flesh of an animal domesticated in Eastern Asia, which have been salted and smoked by a process developed in northern Europe ...
>
> While smoking, he reads the news of the day, imprinted in characters invented by the ancient Semites upon a material invented in China by a process invented in Germany. As he absorbs the accounts of foreign troubles he will, if he is a good conservative citizen, thank a Hebrew deity in an Indo-European language that he is 100 per cent American.[16]

Actually, this citizen is correct to assume that he or she is 100 per cent American because each of the borrowed cultural facets has been adapted to fit his or her needs, moulded into uniquely American habits, foods and customs. Americans behave as they do because of the dictates of their culture. Regardless of how or where solutions are found, once a particular pattern of action is judged acceptable by society, it becomes the approved way and is passed on and taught as part of the group's cultural heritage. Cultural heritage is one of the fundamental differences between humans and other animals. Culture is learned; societies pass on to succeeding generations solutions to problems, constantly building on and expanding the culture so that a wide range of behaviour is possible. The point is, of course, that although much behaviour is borrowed from other cultures, it is combined in a unique manner, which becomes typical for a particular society. To the foreign marketer, this similar-but-different feature of cultures has important meaning in gaining cultural empathy.

similarities: an illusion

For the inexperienced marketer, the similar-but-different aspect of culture creates illusions of similarity that usually do not exist. Several nationalities can speak the same language or have similar race and heritage, but it does not follow that similarities exist in other respects – that a product acceptable to one culture will be readily acceptable to the other, or that promotional message that succeeds in one country will succeed in the other. Even though people start with a common idea or approach, as is the case among English-speaking Australians, Americans and the British, cultural borrowing and assimilation to meet individual needs translate over time into quite distinct cultures. A common language does not guarantee a similar interpretation of even a word or phrase. Both the British and the Americans speak English, but their cultures are sufficiently different that a single phrase has different meanings to each and can even be completely misunderstood. In England, one asks to be directed to a lift instead of an elevator, and an American, when speaking of a bathroom, generally refers to a toilet, while in England a bathroom is a place to take a tub bath. Also, the English 'hoover' a carpet whereas Americans vacuum clean it.

Differences run much deeper than language differences, however. The approach to life, values and concepts of acceptable and unacceptable behaviour may all have a common heritage and may appear superficially to be the same. In reality, profound differences do exist. Among the Spanish-speaking Latin American countries, the problem becomes even more difficult because the idiom is unique to each country, and national pride tends to cause a mute rejection of any 'foreign-Spanish' language. In some cases, an acceptable phrase or word in one country is not only unacceptable in another, it can very well be indecent or vulgar. In Spanish, *coger* is the verb 'to catch', but in some countries it is used as a euphemism with a baser meaning.

Asians are frequently grouped together as if there were no cultural distinctions among Japanese, Koreans and Chinese, to name but a few of the many ethnic groups in the Pacific region. Asia cannot be viewed as a homogeneous entity and the marketer must understand the subtle and not-so-subtle differences among Asian cultures. Each country (culture) has its own unique national character.

There is also the tendency to speak of the 'European consumer' as a result of growing integration in Europe. Many of the obstacles to doing business in Europe have been or will be eliminated as the EU takes shape, but marketers anxious to enter the market must not jump to the conclusion that a unified Europe means a common set of consumer wants and needs. Cultural differences among the members of the EU are the products of centuries of history that will take further centuries to erase.

Even the United States has many subcultures that today, with mass communications and rapid travel, defy complete homogenisation. It would be folly to suggest that the South is in all respects culturally the same as the northeastern or Midwestern parts of the United States. It also would be folly to assume that the unification of Germany has erased cultural differences that have arisen from over 40 years of political and social separation.[17]

A single geopolitical boundary does not necessarily mean a single culture: Canada is divided culturally between its French and English heritages although it is politically one country. A successful marketing strategy among the French Canadians may be a certain failure among remaining Canadians. Within most cultures there are many subcultures that can have marketing significance.

India is another example: people from the south speak different languages and do not even understand Hindi or other languages of the north, west or east. There are more than 100 languages spoken in India, 25 of which are official languages. In fact, the only language that unites India is English.

resistance to change

A characteristic of human culture is that change occurs. That people's habits, tastes, styles, behaviour and values are not constant but are continually changing can be verified

by reading 20-year-old magazines. This gradual cultural growth does not occur without some resistance. New methods, ideas and products are held to be suspect before they are accepted, if ever, as right.

The degree of resistance to new patterns varies; in some situations new elements are accepted completely and rapidly, and in others, resistance is so strong that acceptance is never forthcoming. Studies show that the most important factor in determining what kind and how much of an innovation will be accepted is the degree of interest in the particular subject, as well as how drastically the new will change the old, that is, how disruptive the innovation will be to presently acceptable values and patterns of behaviour. Observations indicate that those innovations most readily accepted are those holding the greatest interest within the society and those least disruptive. For example, rapid industrialisation in parts of Europe has changed many long-honoured attitudes involving time and working women. Today, there is an interest in ways to save time and make life more productive; the leisurely continental life is rapidly disappearing. With this time-consciousness has come the very rapid acceptance of many innovations that might have been resisted by most just a few years ago. Instant foods, mobile telephones, McDonald's and other fast-food establishments, all supportive of a changing attitude towards work and time, are rapidly gaining acceptance.

Although a variety of innovations are completely and quickly accepted, others meet with firm resistance. India has been engaged in intensive population-control programmes for over 20 years, but the process has not worked well and its population remains among the highest in the world; it has already exceeded 1 billion and is expected to overtake China in the next decade. Why has birth control not been accepted? Most attribute this failure to the nature of Indian culture. Among the influences that help to sustain the high birth rate are early marriage, the Hindu society's emphasis on bearing sons, dependence on children for security in old age and a low level of education among the rural masses. All are important cultural patterns at variance with the concept of birth control. Acceptance of birth control would mean rejection of too many fundamental cultural concepts. For the Indian people, it is easier and more familiar to reject the new idea.

Most cultures tend to be **ethnocentric**, that is, they have intense identification with the known and the familiar of their culture and tend to devalue the foreign and unknown of other cultures. **Ethnocentrism** complicates the process of cultural assimilation by producing feelings of superiority about one's own culture and, in varying degrees, generates attitudes that other cultures are inferior, barbaric or at least peculiar. Ethnocentric feelings generally give way if a new idea is considered necessary or particularly appealing.

Although cultures meet most newness with some resistance or rejection, that resistance can be overcome. Cultures are dynamic and change occurs when resistance yields slowly to acceptance, so the basis for resistance becomes unimportant or forgotten. Gradually there comes an awareness of the need for change, ideas once too complex become less so because of cultural gains in understanding, or an idea is restructured in a less complex way, and so on.

planned cultural change

The first step in bringing about planned change in a society is to determine which cultural factors conflict with an innovation, thus creating resistance to its acceptance. The next step is an effort to change those factors from obstacles to acceptance into stimulants for change. The same deliberate approaches used by the social planner to gain acceptance for hybrid grains, better sanitation methods, improved farming techniques or protein-rich diets among the peoples of underdeveloped societies can be adopted by marketers to achieve marketing goals.[18]

Marketers have two options when introducing an innovation to a culture: they can wait, or they can cause change. The former requires hopeful waiting for eventual cultural

changes that prove their innovations of value to the culture; the latter involves introducing an idea or product and deliberately setting about to overcome resistance and to cause change that accelerates the rate of acceptance.

An innovation that has advantages, but requires a culture to learn new ways to benefit from these advantages, establishes the basis for eventual cultural change. Both a strategy of unplanned change and a strategy of planned change produce cultural change. The fundamental difference is that unplanned change proceeds at its own pace whereas in planned change, the process of change is accelerated by the change agent. While culturally congruent strategy, strategy of unplanned change and strategy of planned change are not clearly articulated in international business literature, the third situation occurs. The marketer's efforts become part of the fabric of culture, planned or unplanned.

Take, for example, the change in diet in Japan since the introduction of milk and bread soon after the Second World War. Most Japanese, who are predominantly fish and rice eaters, have increased their intake of animal fat and protein to the point at which fat and protein now exceed vegetable intake. As many McDonald's hamburgers are apt to be eaten in Japan as the traditional rice ball wrapped in edible seaweed. A Westernised diet has caused many Japanese to become overweight. To counter this, the Japanese are buying low-calorie, low-fat foods to help shed excess weight and are flocking to health studios. All this began when US occupation forces introduced bread, milk and steak to Japanese culture. The effect on the Japanese was unintentional; nevertheless, change occurred. Had the intent been to introduce a new diet – that is, a strategy of planned change – specific steps could have been taken to identify resistances to dietary change and then to overcome these resistances, thus accelerating the process of change. The same process is now under way in China, where people have been introduced to dairy products and bread, since the country opened up its borders.

consequences of an innovation

When product diffusion (acceptance) occurs, a process of social change may also occur. One issue frequently addressed concerns the consequences of the changes that happen within a social system as a result of acceptance of an innovation. The marketer seeking product diffusion and adoption may inadvertently bring about change that affects the very fabric of a social system. Consequences of diffusion of an innovation may be functional or dysfunctional, depending on whether the effects on the social system are desirable or undesirable. In most instances, the marketer's concern is with perceived functional consequences – the positive benefits of product use. Indeed, in most situations, innovative products for which the marketer purposely sets out to gain cultural acceptance have minimal, if any, dysfunctional consequences, but this cannot be taken for granted.

On the surface, it would appear that the introduction of a processed feeding formula into the diet of babies in developing countries where protein deficiency is a health problem would have all the functional consequences of better nutrition and health, stronger and faster growth, and so forth.[19] There is evidence, however, that in at least one situation the dysfunctional consequences far exceeded the benefits. In India, as the result of the introduction of the formula, a significant number of babies annually were changed from breast-feeding to bottle-feeding before the age of six months. In Western countries, with appropriate refrigeration and sanitation standards, a similar pattern exists with no apparent negative consequences. In India, however, where sanitation methods are inadequate, a substantial increase in dysentery and diarrhoea, and a higher infant mortality rate have resulted. A change from breast-feeding to bottle-feeding at an early age without the users' complete understanding of purification has caused dysfunctional consequences. This was the result of two factors: the impurity of the water used with the milk and the loss of the natural immunity to childhood disease that a mother's milk provides.[20]

GOING INTERNATIONAL 4.8

ici on parle Français

Frequently there is a conflict between a desire to borrow from another culture and the natural inclination not to pollute one's own culture by borrowing from others. France offers a good example of this conflict. On the one hand, the French accept such US culture as *The Oprah Winfrey Show* on television, award Sylvester 'Rambo' Stallone the Order of Arts and Letters, listen to Eminem, and dine on all-American gastronomic delights such as the Big Mac and Kentucky Fried Chicken. At the same time, there is an uneasy feeling that accepting so much from America will somehow dilute the true French culture. Thus, in an attempt to somehow control cultural pollution, France is embarking on a campaign to expunge examples of 'franglaise' from all walks of life, including television, billboards and business contracts. If the Culture Ministry has its way, violators will be fined. A list of correct translations include *heures de grande écoute* for 'prime time', *coussin gonflable de protection* for 'airbag', *sablé américain* for 'cookie', and some 3500 other offensive expressions. While the demand for hamburger and US television shows cannot be stemmed, perhaps the French language can be saved.

With a tongue-in-cheek response, an English lawmaker said that he would introduce a bill in Parliament to ban the use of French words in public. Order an 'aperitif' in a British bar or demand an 'encore' at the end of an opera and you might be in trouble – and so goes the 'language war'. The use of foreign words in media and advertising got a last-minute reprieve when France's highest constitutional authority struck down the most controversial parts of the law, saying it applies only to public services and not to private citizens.

Source: adapted from Maarten Huygen, 'The Invasion of the American Way', *World Press Review*, November 1992, pp. 28-9; 'La Guerre Franglaise', *Fortune*, 13 June 1994, p. 14; and 'Briton Escalates French Word-War', Reuters, 21 June 1994.

summary

A complete and thorough appreciation of the dimensions of culture may well be the single most important gain to a foreign marketer in the preparation of marketing plans and strategies. Marketers can control the product offered to a market – its promotion, price and eventual distribution methods – but they have only limited control over the cultural environment within which these plans must be implemented. Because they cannot control all the influences on their marketing plans, they must attempt to anticipate the eventual effect of the uncontrollable elements and plan in such a way that these elements do not preclude the achievement of marketing objectives. They can also set about to effect changes that lead to faster acceptance of their products or marketing programmes. Planning marketing strategy in terms of the uncontrollable elements of a market is necessary in a domestic market as well, but when a company is operating internationally, each new environment influenced by elements unfamiliar and sometimes unrecognisable to the marketer complicates the task. For these reasons, special effort and study are needed to absorb enough understanding of the foreign culture to cope with the uncontrollable features. Perhaps it is safe to generalise that of all the tools the foreign marketer must have, those that help generate empathy for another culture are the most valuable. Each of the cultural elements is explored in depth in subsequent chapters. Specific attention is given to business customs, political culture and legal culture in the following chapters.

questions

1 Which role does the marketer play as a change agent?
2 Discuss the three cultural change strategies a foreign marketer can pursue.
3 'Culture is pervasive in all marketing activities.' Discuss.
4 What is the importance of cultural empathy to foreign marketers? How do they acquire cultural empathy?
5 Why should a foreign marketer be concerned with the study of culture?
6 What is the popular definition of culture? What is the viewpoint of cultural anthropologists? What is the importance of the difference?
7 It is stated that members of a society borrow from other cultures to solve problems, which they face in common. What does this mean? What is the significance to marketing?
8 'For the inexperienced marketer, the "similar-but-different" aspect of culture creates an illusion of similarity that usually does not exist.' Discuss and give examples.
9 Outline the elements of culture as seen by an anthropologist. How can a marketer use this 'cultural scheme'?
10 What is material culture? What are its implications for marketing? Give examples.
11 What are some particularly troublesome problems caused by language in foreign marketing? Discuss.
12 Suppose you were requested to prepare a cultural analysis for a potential market. What would you do? Outline the steps and comment briefly on each.
13 Cultures are dynamic. How do they change? Are there cases where changes are not resisted but actually preferred? Explain. What is the relevance to marketing?
14 How can resistance to cultural change influence product introduction? Are there any similarities in domestic marketing? Explain, giving examples.
15 Defend the proposition that a multinational corporation has no responsibility for the consequences of an innovation beyond the direct effects of the innovation such as the product's safety, performance and so forth.
16 Find a product whose introduction into a foreign culture may cause dysfunctional consequences. Describe how the consequences might be eliminated and the product still profitably introduced.

further reading

- Nigel Holden, *Cross-Cultural Management* (Harlow: Prentice Hall, 2002, Chapter 2).
- Allan Bird and Michael Steven, 'Toward an Emerging Global Culture and the Effects of Globalization on Obsolescing National Cultures', *Journal of International Management*, 2003 (9), pp. 395-407.
- Leonidas Leonidou, 'Product Standardization or Adaptation: The Japanese Approach', *Journal of Marketing Practice: Applied Marketing Science*, 1996, 2(4), pp. 53-71.

references

1 Gary P. Ferraro, *The Culture Dimension of International Business*, 2nd edn (Englewood Cliffs, NJ: Prentice-Hall, 1994), p. 17.

2 Francis Fukuyama, *Trust: The Social Virtues and the Creation of Prosperity* (London: Penguin, 1996).

3 Geert Hofstede, *Cultures and Organizations: Software of the Mind* (London: McGraw-Hill, 1991), p. 5; see also other publications by Hofstede, e.g. *Culture's Consequences: Comparing Values, Behaviours, Institutions and Organisations Across Nations* (Thousand Oaks: Sage, 2001).

4 Nigel Holden, *Cross-Cultural Management* (Harlow: FT Prentice Hall, 2002), pp. 21-2.

5 Cited in Jean-Claude Usunier, *Marketing Across Cultures*, 2nd edn (Hemel Hempstead: Prentice Hall, 1996), pp. 78-9.

6 Lawrence Rout, 'To Understand Life in Mexico, Consider the Day of the Dead', *The Wall Street Journal*, 4 November 1981, p. 1; and John Rice, 'In Mexico, Death Takes a Holiday', Associated Press, 20 October 1994.

7 Colette Guillaumin, 'Culture and Cultures', *Cultures*, vol. 6, no. 1, 1979, p. 1.

8 Melvin Herskovits, *Man and His Works* (New York: Knopf, 1952), p. 634.

9 'Designer Apologizes to Muslim', *The Wall Street Journal*, 21 January 1994, p. A-8.

10 For an interesting article on folklore in Malaysia, see M.S. Hood, 'Man, Forest and Spirits: Images and Survival Among Forest-Dwellers of Malaysia', *Tonan Ajia Kenkyu*, March 1993, p. 444.

11 See, for example, R.W. Scribner, 'Magic, Witchcraft and Superstition', *The Historical Journal*, March 1994, p. 219.

12 For a comprehensive business guide to cultures and customs in Europe, see John Mole, *When in Rome* (New York: Amacom, 1991).

13 For other examples of mistakes, see David A. Ricks, *Blunders in International Business* (Cambridge, MA: Blackwell, 1994).

14 Elizabeth K. Briody, 'On Trade and Cultures', *Trade and Culture*, March-April 1995, pp. 5-6.

15 For an interesting article on cultural change, see Norihiko Shimizu, 'Today's Taboos May Be Gone Tomorrow', *Tokyo Business Today*, January 1995, pp. 29-51.

16 R. Linton, *The Study of Man* (New York: Appleton-Century-Crofts, 1936), p. 327.

17 See, for example, Denise M. Johnson and Scott D. Johnson, 'One Germany ... But is There a Common German Consumer? East-West Differences for Marketers to Consider', *The International Executive*, May-June 1993, pp. 221-8.

18 Chris Halliburton and Reinhard Hünerberg, 'Executive Insights: Pan-European Marketing - Myth or Reality?, *Journal of International Marketing*, 1993, 1(3), pp. 77-92.

19 For an interesting text on change agents, see Gerald Zaltman and Robert Duncan, *Strategies for Planned Change* (New York: Wiley, 1979).

20 For a comprehensive look at this issue, see S. Prakash Sethi, *Multinational Corporations and the Impact of Public Advocacy on Corporate Strategy: Nestlé and the Infant Formula Controversy* (Boston, MA: Kluwer Academic, 1994).

chapter 5
Business Customs and Practices in International Marketing

Chapter Outline

What you should learn from Chapter 5

- How the local customs and traditions of doing business influence international marketing
- The influences of a culture on the modes of doing business abroad
- The effect of high-context, low-context cultures on people's behaviour and on business practices
- How disparate business ethics influence international marketing activities
- How to handle communication in cross-cultural deals and marketing efforts

Business customs are as much a cultural element of a society as is the language. Culture not only establishes the criteria for day-to-day business behaviour but also forms general patterns of attitude and motivation. Executives are to some extent captives of their cultural heritages and cannot totally escape language, heritage, political and family ties or religious backgrounds. One report notes that Japanese culture, permeated by Shinto precepts, is not something apart from business but determines its very essence. Thus, the many business and trade problems between Japan and the West reflect the widespread ignorance of Japanese culture on the part of European and American business people.[1] Although international business managers may take on the trappings and appearances of the business behaviour of another country, their basic frame of reference is most likely to be that of their own people.

In the United States, for example, the historical perspective of **individualism** and 'winning the West' seem to be manifest in individual wealth or corporate profit being dominant measures of success. Japan's lack of frontiers and natural resources, and its dependence on trade have focused individual and corporate success criteria on uniformity, subordination to the group and society's ability to maintain high levels of employment. The feudal background of southern Europe tends to emphasise maintenance of both individual and corporate power and authority while blending those feudal traits with paternalistic concern for minimal welfare for workers and other members of society. Various studies identify North Americans as individualists, Japanese as consensus-oriented and committed to their group, and central and southern Europeans as elitists and rank conscious. While these descriptions are stereotypical, they illustrate cultural differences that are often manifest in business behaviour and practices.[2]

A knowledge of the **business culture**, management attitudes and business methods existing in a country and a willingness to accommodate the differences are important to success in an international market.[3] Unless marketers remain flexible in their own attitudes by accepting differences in basic patterns of thinking, local business tempo, religious practices, political structure and family loyalty, they are hampered, if not prevented, from reaching satisfactory conclusions to business transactions.

This chapter focuses on matters specifically related to the business environment. Besides an analysis of the need for adaptation, it will review the structural elements, attitudes and behaviour of international business processes.

required adaptation

Adaptation is a key concept in international marketing and willingness to adapt is a crucial attitude. **Adaptation**, or at least accommodation, is required on small matters as well as large ones. In fact, the small, seemingly insignificant situations are often the most crucial. More than tolerance of an alien culture is required. There is a need for affirmative acceptance, that is, open tolerance of the concept 'different but equal'. Through such affir-

key terms

individualism
when everybody is concerned only with their own well-being

business culture
values and norms followed in business activities

adaptation
making changes to fit a particular culture/ environment/ conditions

mative acceptance, adaptation becomes easier because empathy for another's point of view naturally leads to ideas for meeting cultural differences.

As a guide to adaptation, there are 10 basic requisites that all who wish to deal with individuals, firms or authorities in foreign countries should be able to meet. These are:

1 open tolerance
2 flexibility
3 humility
4 justice/fairness
5 adjustability to varying tempos
6 curiosity/interest
7 knowledge of the country
8 liking for others
9 ability to command respect
10 ability to integrate oneself into the environment.

In short, add the quality of adaptability to the qualities of a good executive for a composite of the perfect international marketer (see Exhibit 5.1).

Exhibit 5.1 Requisites for cultural adaptation

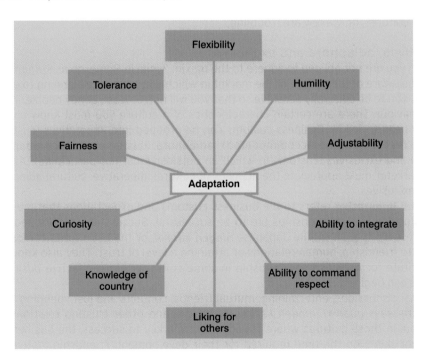

Degree of Adaptation

Adaptation does not require business executives to forsake their ways and change to conform with local customs; rather, executives must be aware of local customs and be willing to accommodate those differences that can cause misunderstanding. Essential to effective adaptation is awareness of one's own culture and the recognition that differences in others can cause anxiety, frustration and misunderstanding of the host's intentions. Also, the differences the host sees in the business executive can create the same potential for misunderstanding. The self-reference criterion (SRC) is especially

operative in business customs. If we do not understand our foreign counterpart's customs, we are more likely to evaluate that person's behaviour in terms of what is acceptable to us.

The key to adaptation is to remain yourself but to develop an understanding and willingness to accommodate differences that exist. A successful marketer knows that in Asia it is important to make points without winning arguments; criticism, even if asked for, can cause a host to 'lose face'. In Germany and the Netherlands it is considered discourteous to use first names unless specifically invited to do so; always address a person as Herr, Frau or Fraulein, and Meneer or Mevrouw with the last name. In Brazil and in Indonesia do not be offended by the Brazilian or Indonesian inclination towards touching during conversation. Such a custom is not a violation of your personal space but the way of greeting, emphasising a point or as a gesture of goodwill and friendship.

A Chinese, Indian or Brazilian does not expect you to act like one of them. After all, you are not Chinese, Indian or Brazilian but a Westerner, and it would be foolish for a Westerner to give up the ways that have contributed so notably to Western success. It would be equally foolish for others to give up their ways. When different cultures meet, open tolerance and a willingness to accommodate each other's differences are necessary. Once a marketer is aware of the possibility of cultural differences and the probable consequences of failure to adapt or accommodate, the seemingly endless variety of customs must be assessed. Where does one begin? Which customs should be adhered to absolutely, which others can be ignored? Fortunately, among the many obvious differences that exist between cultures, only a few are troubling.

imperatives, adiaphora and exclusives

Although you are not obliged to adhere to the maxim 'while in Rome, do as Romans do', you need to be aware of the culture of the market in which you are or are planning to enter. This will allow you to be culturally sensitive so that you will not, at least, annoy people/locals with your behaviour. There are certain characteristics of a culture you must know and certain that you need to follow. Business customs can be grouped into imperatives (customs that must be recognised and accommodated), adiaphora (customs to which adaptation is optional) and exclusives (customs in which an outsider must not participate). An international marketer must appreciate the nuances of cultural imperative, cultural adiaphora and cultural exclusives.

Cultural imperative refers to the business customs and expectations that must be met and conformed to if relationships are to be successful. Successful business people know the Chinese word *guan-xi*, the Japanese *ningen kankei*, or the Latin American *compadre*. All refer to friendship, human relations or attaining a level of trust. They also know there is no substitute for establishing friendship in some cultures before effective business relationships can begin.

Informal discussions, entertaining, mutual friends, contacts and just spending time with others are ways *guan-xi, ningen kankei, compadre* and other trusting relationships are developed. In those cultures where friendships are a key to success, the business person should not skimp on the time required for their development. Friendship motivates local agents to make more sales and friendship helps establish the right relationship with end users, leading to more sales over a longer period.[4] Naturally, after-sales service, price and the product must be competitive, but the marketer who has established *guan-xi, ningen kankei* or *compadre* has the edge. Establishing friendship is an important Asian and Latin American custom. It is imperative that establishing friendship be observed or one risks not earning trust and acceptance, the basic cultural prerequisites for developing and retaining effective business relationships.

Cultural adiaphora relates to areas of behaviour or to customs that cultural aliens may wish to conform to or participate in but that are not required. It is not particularly important, but it is permissible to follow the custom in question; the majority of customs

GOING INTERNATIONAL 5.1

success through cultural customisation

The secret of success in emerging markets is to develop products that are especially designed to meet the needs of the customers in these markets. In 2000, Dell introduced a new consumer PC for the Chinese market called 'Smart PC', different from those it sells anywhere else. It was built by a Taiwanese company, which allowed Dell to sell it at a very low price. It helped Dell to become the number one foreign supplier in China. New markets need new strategies and new products. To develop new products to tap these markets, companies are doing a lot of market research. Intel appointed 10 ethnographers to travel around the world to find out how to redesign its existing or develop new products to fit different cultures and segments in these markets. One of the ethnographers visited

hundreds of families in China and reported that Chinese families were reluctant to buy PCs. Parents were concerned that their children would listen to pop music and surf the web, distracting them from their school work.

Learning from this research, Intel developed a 'Home Learning PC'. It comes with four educational applications and a proper lock and key to allow parents to control computer usage by their children.

The new products developed for new markets need to be simple and capable of operating in harsh environments. For example, India's TVS Electronics has developed an all-inclusive machine for 1.2 million smaller shopkeepers. It is a cash register-cum-computer and it tolerates heat, dust and voltage variations, and costs only $180. Price is often a major factor if a company needs to tap mass markets. HP has set up a pilot programme in rural Africa, where the average person makes less than $1 a day. As many of these people cannot buy computers, HP introduced a solution: 441 (four users for one computer). It is a computer set up in a school or a library but is connected to four keyboards and screens. All four can use the net and send e-mails simultaneously.

When companies modify their products for emerging markets, it can lead to broader improvements. Nokia, for example, developed Smart Radio Technology to cut the number of transmission operators by half in Thailand. This means that operators can build networks with up to 50 per cent less costs. This technology is now exported all over the place by Nokia, from Thailand to Peru.

Source: compiled from Steve Hamm, 'Tech's Future', cover story, *Business Week*, 27 September 2004, pp. 52–9.

fit into this category. One need not adhere to local dress, greet another man with a kiss (a custom in some countries) or eat foods that disagree with the digestive system (so long as the refusal is gracious). On the other hand, a symbolic attempt to participate in adiaphora is not only acceptable, but may also help to establish rapport. It demonstrates that the marketer has studied the culture. A Japanese does not expect a Westerner to bow and to understand the ritual of bowing among Japanese; yet, a symbolic bow indicates interest and some sensitivity to Japanese culture, which is acknowledged as a gesture of goodwill. This may well pave the way to a strong, trusting relationship. At the same time, cultural adiaphora are the most visibly different customs and thus more tempting for the foreigner to try to adapt to when, in fact, adaptation is unnecessary and, if overdone, unwelcome.

GOING INTERNATIONAL 5.2

colours, things, numbers and even smells have symbolic meanings ... often not the ones you think!

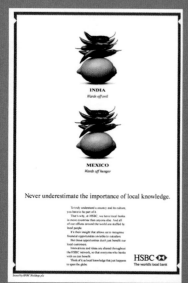

Here, HSBC uses cultural differences to show its local knowledge as a global bank

Green, America's favourite colour for suggesting freshness and good health, is often associated with disease in countries with dense green jungles; it is a favourite colour among Arabs but forbidden in portions of Indonesia. In Japan green is a good high-tech colour, but Americans would shy away from green electronic equipment. Black is not universal for mourning: in many Asian countries white is worn; in Brazil purple, yellow in Mexico and dark red in the Ivory Coast. Americans think of blue as the most masculine colour, but red is manlier in the United Kingdom or France. While pink is the most feminine colour in America, yellow is more feminine in most of the world. Red suggests good fortune in China but death in Turkey. In America a sweet wrapped in blue or green is probably a mint; in Africa the same sweet would be wrapped in red, the US colour for cinnamon ... in every culture, things, numbers and even smells have meanings. Lemon scent in the United States suggests freshness; in the Philippines lemon scent is associated with illness. In Japan the number 4 is like our 13; and 7 is unlucky in Ghana, Kenya and Singapore. The owl in India means bad luck, like our black cat. In Japan a fox is associated with witches. In China a green hat is like a dunce's cap; specifically it marks a man with an unfaithful wife. The stork symbolises maternal death in Singapore, not the kind of message you want to send to a new mother.

Source: from Lennie Copeland and Lewis Griggs, *Going International* (New York: Plume, 1986), p. 63.

Most jokes, even though well intended, don't translate well. Sometimes a translator can help you out. One speaker, in describing his experience, said, 'I began my speech with a joke that took me about two minutes to tell. Then my interpreter translated my story. About 30 seconds later the Japanese audience laughed loudly. I continued with my talk, which seemed well received but at the end, just to make sure, I asked the interpreter, "How did you translate my joke so quickly?" The interpreter replied, "Oh I didn't translate your story at all. I didn't understand it. I simply said our foreign speaker has just told a joke so would you all please laugh".'

Some international managers and marketers argue that interpreters aren't necessary because English is the language of international business. This view is obviously not appreciated in most countries. The Japanese have a joke that goes, 'What do you call a person that can speak two languages? Bilingual, What do you call a person that can speak three languages? Trilingual. What do you call a person that can speak one language? An Englishman.' This may be funny to the Japanese, but is it to English people?[5]

Cultural exclusives are those customs or behaviour patterns reserved exclusively for the local people and from which the foreigner is excluded. For example, a foreigner criticising a country's politics, mores and peculiarities (that is, peculiar to the foreigner) is offensive even though locals may, among themselves, criticise such issues. There is truth in the old adage, 'I'll curse my brother, but if you curse him, you'll have a fight.' There are few cultural traits reserved exclusively for locals, but a foreigner must refrain from participating in those that are reserved. Religion, politics, treatment of women and minorities are some examples of such traits.

key term

cultural exclusives customs or behaviour patterns reserved exclusively for the local people, from which the foreigner is excluded

different business practices

Because of the diverse structures, management attitudes and behaviours encountered in international business, there is considerable latitude in methods of doing business. No matter how thoroughly prepared a marketer may be when approaching a foreign market, there is a certain amount of cultural shock when the uninitiated trader encounters actual business situations. In business transactions, the international marketer becomes aware of the differences in contact level, communications emphasis, tempo and formality of foreign businesses. Ethical standards are likely to differ, as will the negotiation emphasis. In most countries, the foreign trader is also likely to encounter a fairly high degree of government involvement. Quite often people value free time more than a small increase in wage rate. It is, therefore, always an important issue in labour management negotiations. Exhibit 5.2 reveals the number of hours worked in different countries.

Exhibit 5.2 Annual hours worked

Britain	1 719
Canada	1 776
Germany	1 480
Hong Kong	2 287
Japan	1 842
Norway	1 399
Singapore	2 307
United States	1 979

Source: International Labor Organization, 2004.

sources and level of authority

Business size, ownership and public accountability combine to influence the authority structure of business. The international business person is confronted with a variety of authority patterns but most are a variation of three typical patterns: top-level management decisions; decentralised decisions; committee or group decisions.

Top-level management decision making is generally found in those situations where family or close ownership gives absolute control to owners and where businesses are small enough to make such centralised decision making possible. In many European businesses, decision-making authority is guarded jealously by a few at the top who exercise tight control. In many developing countries with a semifeudal, land-equals-power heritage, decision-making participation by middle management tends to be de-emphasised; decisions are made by dominant family members.

In Middle Eastern countries, the top man makes all decisions and prefers to deal only with other executives with decision-making powers. There, one always does business with an individual per se rather than an office or title.

As businesses grow and professional management develops, there is a shift towards decentralised management decision making. **Decentralised decision making** allows executives, at various levels of management, authority over their own functions. This mode is typical of large-scale businesses with highly developed management systems such as those found in the United States. A trader in the United States is likely to be dealing with middle management, and title or position generally takes precedence over the individual holding the job.

Committee decision making is by group or consensus. Committees may operate on a centralised or decentralised basis, but the concept of committee management implies something quite different from the individualised functioning of top management and

key terms

decentralised decision making when every level of the organisation can make its own decisions

committee decision making decision making by group or consensus

103

decentralised decision-making arrangements just discussed. Because Asian cultures and religions tend to emphasise harmony, it is not surprising that **group decision making** predominates there. Despite the emphasis on rank and hierarchy in Japanese social structure, business emphasises group participation, group harmony and group decision making – but at top management level.

The demands these three types of authority system place on a marketer's ingenuity and adaptability are evident. In the case of the authoritative and delegated societies, the chief problem would be to identify the individual with authority. In the committee decision set-up, it is necessary that every committee member be convinced of the merits of the proposition or product in question. The marketing approach to each of these situations differs.

management objectives and aspirations

The training and background (i.e. cultural environment) of managers significantly affect their personal and business outlooks. Society as a whole establishes the social rank or status of management, and cultural background dictates patterns of aspirations and objectives among business people. These cultural influences affect the attitude of managers towards innovation, new products and conducting business with foreigners. To fully understand another's management style, one must appreciate an individual's objectives and aspirations, which are usually reflected in the goals of the business organisation and in the practices that prevail within the company. In dealing with foreign business, a marketer must be particularly aware of the varying objectives and aspirations of management.

Personal Goals   Some cultures emphasise profit or high wages while in other countries security, good personal life, acceptance, status, advancement or power may be emphasised. Individual goals are highly personal in any country, so one cannot generalise to the extent of saying that managers in any one country always have a specific orientation.

Security and Mobility   Personal security and job mobility relate directly to basic human motivation and therefore have widespread economic and social implications. The word security is somewhat ambiguous and this very ambiguity provides some clues to managerial variation. To some, security means good wages and the training and ability required for moving from company to company within the business hierarchy; for others, it means the security of lifetime positions with their companies; to still others, it means adequate retirement plans and other welfare benefits. In European companies, particularly in the countries late in industrialising such as Spain and Italy, there is a strong paternalistic orientation, and it is assumed that individuals will work for one company for the majority of their lives.

key terms

Personal Life   For many individuals, a good personal life takes priority over profit, security or any other goal. In his worldwide study of individual aspirations, David McClelland discovered that the culture of some countries stressed the virtue of a good personal life as being far more important than profit or achievement. The **hedonistic** outlook of Ancient Greece explicitly included work as an undesirable factor that got in the way of the search for pleasure or a good personal life. Perhaps at least part of the standard of living that we enjoy in the Western world today can be attributed to the hard-working ethic from which we derive much of our business heritage.[6]

Social Acceptance   In some countries, acceptance by neighbours and fellow workers appears to be a predominant goal within business. The Asian outlook is reflected in the group decision making so important in Japan, and the Japanese place great importance on fitting in with their group. Group identification is so strong in Japan and some other Asian countries that when a worker is asked what he does for a living, he generally answers by

GOING INTERNATIONAL 5.3

business protocol in a unified Europe

Now that 1992 has come and gone and the European Union is a single market, does it mean that all differences have been wiped away? For some of the legal differences, yes. For cultural differences, no.

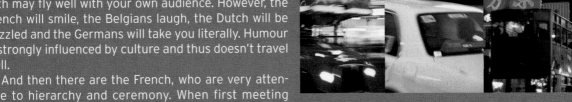

There is always the issue of language and meaning even when both parties speak English. Then there is the matter of humour. The anecdote you open a meeting with may fly well with your own audience. However, the French will smile, the Belgians laugh, the Dutch will be puzzled and the Germans will take you literally. Humour is strongly influenced by culture and thus doesn't travel well.

And then there are the French, who are very attentive to hierarchy and ceremony. When first meeting with a French-speaking business person, stick with *monsieur, madame* or *mademoiselle*: the use of first names is disrespectful to the French. If you don't speak French fluently, apologise. Such apology shows general respect for the language and dismisses any stigma of arrogance.

The formality of dress can vary with each country also. The Brit, the Swede and the Dutchman will take off their jackets and roll up their sleeves; they mean to get down to business. The Spaniard will loosen his tie, while the German disapproves. He thinks they look sloppy and unbusinesslike. He keeps his coat on throughout the meeting. So does the Italian, but that was because he dressed especially for the look of the meeting.

With all that, did the meeting decide anything? It was, after all, a first meeting. The Brits were just exploring the terrain, checking out the broad perimeters and all that. The French were assessing the other players' strengths and weaknesses, and deciding what position to take at the next meeting. The Italians also won't have taken it too seriously. For them it was a meeting to arrange the meeting agenda for the real meeting. Only the Germans will have assumed it was what it seemed and be surprised when the next meeting starts open-ended.

Source: adapted from Barry Day, 'The Art of Conducting International Business', *Advertising Age*, 8 October 1990, p. 46; and Brad Ketchum Jr, 'Faux Pas Go with the Territory', *Inc.*, May 1994, pp. 4–5.

telling you he works for Sumitomo or Mitsubishi or Matsushita, rather than that he is a chauffeur, an engineer or a chemist.

Power   Although there is some power seeking by business managers throughout the world, power seems to be a more important motivating force in the Middle East and South American countries. In these countries, many business leaders are not only profit-oriented, but also use their business positions to become social and political leaders.

communications emphasis

Probably no language readily translates into another because the meanings of words differ widely among languages. Even though it is the basic communication tool of marketers trading in foreign lands, managers, particularly from the United States and the United Kingdom, often fail to develop even a basic understanding of a foreign language, much less master the linguistic nuances that reveal unspoken attitudes and information. One writer comments that 'even a good interpreter doesn't solve the language problem'.

Seemingly similar business terms in English and Japanese often have different meanings. In fact, the Japanese language is so inherently vague that even the well educated have difficulty communicating clearly among themselves. A communications authority on the Japanese language estimates that the Japanese are able to fully understand each other only about 85 per cent of the time. The Japanese prefer English-language contracts, where words have specific meanings.[7]

The translation and interpretation of clearly worded statements and common usage is difficult enough, but when slang is added, the task is almost impossible. In an exchange between an American and a Chinese official, the American answered affirmatively to a Chinese proposal with, 'It's a great idea, Mr Li, but who's going to put wheels on it?' The interpreter, not wanting to lose face but not understanding, turned to the Chinese official and said, 'And now the American has made a proposal regarding the automobile industry'; the entire conversation was disrupted by the misunderstanding of a slang expression.

The best policy when dealing in other languages, even with a skilled interpreter, is to stick to formal language patterns. The use of slang phrases puts the interpreter in the uncomfortable position of guessing at meanings. Foreign language skills are critical in all negotiations, so it is imperative to seek the best possible personnel. Even then, especially in translations involving Asian languages, misunderstandings occur.[8]

Linguistic communication, no matter how imprecise, is explicit, but much business communication depends on implicit messages that are not verbalised. E.T. Hall, professor of anthropology and for decades consultant to business and government on intercultural relations, says, 'In some cultures, messages are explicit; the words carry most of the information. In other cultures ... less information is contained in the verbal part of the message since more is in the context.'[9] Hall divides cultures into high-context and low-context cultures. Communication in a high-context culture depends heavily on the context or non-verbal aspects of communication, whereas the low-context culture depends more on explicit, verbally expressed communications (see Exhibit 5.3). Managers in general probably function best at a low-context level because they are accustomed to reports, contracts and other written communications.

In a **low-context culture**, one gets down to business quickly. In a **high-context culture** it takes considerably longer to conduct business because of the need to know more about a business person before a relationship develops. They simply do not know how to handle a

key terms

low-context culture
cultures that demand explicit communication

high-context culture
cultures that demand implicit communication

Exhibit 5.3 Contextual background of various countries

High context
implicit

Japanese

Arabian

Latin American

Spanish

Italian

English (UK)

French

North American (US)

Scandinavian

German

Swiss

Low context
explicit

Source: patterned after E.T. Hall.

GOING INTERNATIONAL 5.4

Meishi – presenting a business card in Japan

In Japan the business card, or *Meishi*, is the executive's trademark. It is both a mini-résumé and a friendly deity that draws people together. No matter how many times you have talked with a business person by phone before you actually meet, business cannot really begin until you formally exchange cards.

The value of a *Meishi* cannot be overemphasised; up to 12 million are exchanged daily and a staggering 4.4 billion annually. For a business person to make a call or receive a visitor without a card is like a Samurai going off to battle without his sword.

There are a variety of ways to present a card, depending on the giver's personality and style.

Crab style – held out between the index and middle fingers.

Pincer – clamped between the thumb and index finger.

Pointer – offered with the index finger pressed along the edge.

Upside-down – the name is facing away from the recipient.

Platter fashion – served in the palm of the hand.

Not only is there a way to present a card, there is also a way of receiving a card. It makes a good impression to receive a card in both hands, especially when the other party is senior in age or status.

The card should be presented during the earliest stages of introduction, so the Japanese recipient will be able to determine your position and rank, and will know how to respond to you. The normal procedure is for the Japanese to hand you their name card and accept yours at the same time. They read your card and then formally greet you either by bowing or shaking hands or both.

Source: adapted from 'Meishi', *Sumitomo Quarterly*, Autumn 1986, p. 3; and Boye Lafayette DeMente, *Japanese Etiquette and Ethics in Business*, 6th edn (Lincolnwood, IL: NTC Business Books, 1994), p. 24.

low-context relationship with other people. Hall suggests that 'in the Middle East, if you aren't willing to take the time to sit down and have coffee with people, you have a problem. You must learn to wait and not be too eager to talk business. You can ask about the family or ask, "how are you feeling?" but avoid too many personal questions about wives because people are apt to get suspicious. Learn to make what we call chit-chat. If you don't, you can't go to the next step. It's a little bit like a courtship' – the preliminaries establish a firm foundation for a relationship.[10]

Even in low-context cultures, our communication is heavily dependent on our cultural context. Most of us are not aware of how dependent we are on the context and, as Hall suggests, 'since much of our culture operates outside our awareness, frequently we don't even know what we know'.

Probably every business person from the West or other relatively low-context countries who has had dealings with counterparts in high-context countries can tell stories about the confusion on both sides because of the different perceptual frameworks of the communication process. Communication mastery is not only the mastery of a language, but also a mastery of body languages, customs and culture. Such mastery develops only through long association.[11]

Formality and tempo

The breezy informality and haste that seem to characterise the American business relationship appear to be American exclusives that business people from other countries not only fail to share, but also fail to appreciate. This apparent informality, however, does not indicate a lack of commitment to the job. Comparing British and American business managers, an English executive commented about the American manager's compelling involvement in business: 'At a cocktail party or a dinner, the American is still on duty.'

Even though northern Europeans seem to have picked up some American attitudes in recent years, do not count on them being 'Americanised'. As one writer says, 'While using first names in business encounters is regarded as an American vice in many countries, nowhere is it found more offensive than in Germany and France', where formality still reigns. Those who work side by side for years still address one another with formal pronouns.[12]

GOING INTERNATIONAL 5.5

you say you speak English?

The English speak English and the North Americans speak English, but can the two communicate? It is difficult for a North American unless they understand that in England:

- newspapers are sold at bookstalls
- the ground floor is the main floor, while the first floor is what Americans call the second, and so on up the building
- an apartment house is a block of flats
- in England you put your clothes not in a closet, but in a cupboard; A closet usually refers to the WC or water closet, which is the toilet
- when a British friend says she is going to 'spend a penny', she is going to the ladies' room
- a bathing dress or bathing costume is what the British call a bathing suit, and for those who want to go shopping, it is essential to know that a tunic is a blouse; a stud is a collar button, nothing more; and garters are suspenders; suspenders are braces
- if you want to buy a sweater, you should ask for a jumper or a jersey
- a ladder is not always used for climbing, it refers to a run in a stocking
- if someone is called up, it means that you have drafted the person – probably for military service
- to ring someone up is to telephone them
- you put your packages in the boot of your car, not the trunk
- when you table something, you mean you want to discuss it, not postpone it, as in the United States
- any reference to an MD will probably not bring a doctor; the term means managing director in Britain
- when the desk clerk asks what time you want to be knocked up in the morning, he is only referring to your wake-up call.

Source: adapted from Margaret Zellers, 'How to Speak English', *Denver Post*, date unknown; and Lennie Copeland and Lewis Griggs, *Going International* (New York: Plume, 1986), pp. 101-2.

Marketers who expect maximum success have to deal with foreign executives in ways that are acceptable to the foreigner. Latin Americans depend greatly on friendships but establish these friendships only in the South American way: slowly, over a considerable period of time. A typical Latin American is highly formal until a genuine relationship of respect and friendship is established. Even then the Latin American is slow to get down to business and will not be pushed. In keeping with the culture, *mañana* is good enough. How people perceive time helps to explain some of the differences between Western managers and those from other cultures.

P-time versus M-time

The treatment of time is different in different cultures. Westerners are a more time-bound culture than Asian and Latin cultures. Our stereotype of those cultures is 'They are always late', and their view of us is 'You are always prompt'. Neither statement is completely true though both contain some truth. What is true, however, is that we are a very time-oriented society – time is money to us – whereas in other cultures time is to be savoured, not spent. For Westerners the time is running (going), for Asians the time comes. Thus they take it easy and, when asked, respond that they will do a certain thing when the time comes.

Edward Hall defines two time systems in the world – monochronic and polychronic time. **M-time** (monochronic) typifies most North Americans, Dutch, Swiss, Germans and Scandinavians. These Western cultures tend to concentrate on one thing at a time. They divide time into small units and are concerned with promptness. M-time is used in a linear way and is experienced as being almost tangible in that we save time, waste time, bide time, spend time and lose time. Most low-context cultures operate on M-time.

P-time, or polychronic time, is more dominant in high-context cultures where the completion of a human transaction is emphasised more than sticking to schedules. P-time is characterised by the simultaneous occurrence of many things and by 'a great involvement with people'. P-time allows for relationships to build and context to be absorbed as parts of high-context cultures.

key terms

mañana
Spanish for 'tomorrow'

M-time (monochronic)
concentrating on one thing at a time; time is divided up into small units and used in a linear way

P-time (polychronic)
characterised by the simultaneous occurence of many things and by 'a great involvement with people'

GOING INTERNATIONAL 5.6

time: a many cultured thing

Time is cultural, subjective and variable. One of the most serious causes of frustration and friction in cross-cultural business dealings occurs when counterparts are out of sync with each other.

Differences often appear with respect to the pace of time, its perceived nature and its function. Insights into a culture's view of time may be found in their sayings and proverbs. For example:

'Time is money' (United States).
'Those who rush arrive first at the grave' (Spain).
'The clock did not invent man' (Nigeria).
'If you wait long enough, even an egg will walk' (Ethiopia).
'Before the time, it is not yet the time; after the time, it's too late' (France).

Source: adapted from Edward T. Hall and Mildred Reed Hall, *Understanding Cultural Differences* (Yarmouth, ME: Intercultural Press, 1990), p. 196; and Gart M. Wederspahn, 'On Trade and Cultures', *Trade and Culture*, Winter 1993–94, pp. 4–6.

The Westerner's desire to get straight to the point, to get down to business and other indications of directness are all manifestations of M-time cultures. The P-time system gives rise to looser time schedules, deeper involvement with individuals and a wait-and-see-what-develops attitude. For example, two Latins conversing would probably opt to be late for their next appointments rather than abruptly terminate the conversation before it came to a natural conclusion.

Exhibit 5.4 Monochronic (M-time) and polychronic (P-time) behaviour

Monochronic	Polychronic
Do one thing at a time	Do many things at a time
Task oriented	People oriented
Focused and concentrated	Easily distracted and subject to interceptions
Take deadlines seriously	Deadlines are flexible and are followed if possible
Follow schedules and procedures	Schedules and procedures are considered flexible
Make and follow plans	Make plans that can easily be changed and updated
Individualist	Collectivist
Seldom borrow or lend	Borrow and lend often
Exercise promptness	Base promptness on the matter and relationship
Accustomed to short-term relationships	Accustomed to life-long relationships
Treat time as tangible	Treat time as intangible
Value privacy	Like to be surrounded by people (family and friends)

Source: compiled from Edward Hall, 'Monochronic and Polychronic Time', in Larry Samovar and Richard Porter, *International Communication: A Reader* (Belmont, CA: Thompson, 2003), pp. 262–8.

P-time is characterised by a much looser notion of on time or late. Interruptions are routine; delays to be expected. It is not so much putting things off until *mañana* but the concept that human activities are not expected to proceed like clockwork (see Exhibit 5.4).

Most cultures offer a mix of P-time and M-time behaviour, but have a tendency to be either more P-time or M-time in regard to the role time plays. Some are similar to Japan where appointments are adhered to with the greatest M-time precision, but P-time is followed once a meeting begins. The Japanese see Western business people as too time-bound, and driven by schedules and deadlines that thwart the easy development of friendships. The differences between M-time and P-time are reflected in a variety of ways throughout a culture.

When business people from M-time and P-time meet, adjustments need to be made for a harmonious relationship. Often clarity can be gained by specifying tactfully, for example, whether a meeting is to be on Middle Eastern time or Western time. A Westerner who has been working successfully with the Saudis for many years says he has learned to take plenty of things to do when he travels. Others schedule appointments in their offices so they can work until their P-time friend arrives. The important thing for the Western manager to learn is adjustment to P-time in order to avoid the anxiety and frustration that comes from being out of sync with local time. As global markets expand, more business people from P-time cultures are adapting to M-time.

negotiations emphasis

All the above differences in business customs and culture come into play more frequently and are more obvious in the negotiating process than in any other aspect of business. The

basic elements of business negotiations are the same in any country: they relate to the product, its price and terms, services associated with the product and, finally, friendship between vendors and customers. But it is important to remember that the negotiating process is complicated and the risk of misunderstanding increases when negotiating with someone from another culture.[13]

Attitudes brought to the negotiating table by each individual are affected by many cultural factors and customs often unknown to the other individuals and perhaps unrecognised by the individuals themselves. Each negotiator's understanding and interpretation of what transpires in negotiating sessions is conditioned by his or her cultural background.[14] The possibility of offending one another or misinterpreting each other's motives is especially high when one's SRC is the basis for assessing a situation. One standard rule in negotiating is 'know thyself' first and, second, 'know your opponent'. The SRCs of both parties can come into play here if care is not taken.[15]

gender bias in international business

The gender bias against women managers that exists in many countries creates hesitancy among Western multinational companies to offer women international assignments. Questions such as 'Are there opportunities for women in international business?' and 'Should women represent Western firms abroad?' frequently arise as Western companies become more international. As women move up in domestic management ranks and seek career-related international assignments, companies need to examine their positions on women managers in international business.[16]

In many cultures – Asian, Arab, Latin American and even some European ones – women are not typically found in upper levels of management. Traditional roles in male-dominated societies are often translated into minimal business opportunities for women. This cultural bias raises questions about the effectiveness of women in establishing successful relationships with host-country associates. An often-asked question is whether it is appropriate to send a woman to conduct business with foreign customers. To some it appears logical that if women are not accepted in managerial roles within their own cultures, a foreign woman would not be any more acceptable. This is but one of the myths used to support decisions to exclude women from foreign assignments.[17]

It is a fact that men and women are treated very differently in some cultures. In Saudi Arabia, for example, women are segregated, expected to wear veils and forbidden even to drive, while in Kuwait a large number of women are working in managerial positions and they drive and wear Western clothes. Evidence suggests, however, that prejudice towards foreign women executives may be exaggerated and that the treatment local women receive in their own cultures is not necessarily an indicator of how a foreign businesswoman is treated.

When a company gives management responsibility and authority to someone, a large measure of the respect initially shown that person is the result of respect for the firm. When a woman manager receives the strong backing of her firm, she usually receives the respect commensurate with the position she holds and the firm she represents. Thus, resistance to her as a female either does not materialise or is less severe than anticipated. Even in those cultures where a female would not ordinarily be a manager, foreign female executives benefit, at least initially, from the status, respect and importance attributed to the firms they represent. In Japan, where Japanese women rarely achieve even lower-level management positions, representatives of Western firms, for example, are seen first as Germans, second as representatives of firms and then as males or females. Once business negotiations begin, the willingness of a business host to engage in business transactions and the respect shown to a foreign business person grows or diminishes depending on the business skills he or she demonstrates, regardless of gender.[18]

GOING INTERNATIONAL 5.7

lingerie in Saudi Arabia

The Saudi Arabian lingerie market, created by Saudi women's desire for foreign products, oil money, education and exposure to Western lifestyles through the media, has always been good for foreign brands. Since textile manufacturing is virtually non-existent in Saudi Arabia, the lingerie market is wholly dependent on imports. However, building a lingerie store in the mode of Victoria's Secret in a country that

follows the strict Wahhabi principles of Islam means negotiating a thorny path. Featuring a woman's body in ads or using pictures of women wearing lingerie inside the store, or even displaying lingerie on lifelike mannequins, is out of bounds. For three generations, the Al-Mashat family sold lingerie in one corner of the many clothing stores they owned. Entering a store, a woman had to specify her size and colour preference to male sales people, who would then dig under the counter for the merchandise. This changed in November 2001, when Lingerie Perdu, a two-storey, sprawling lingerie emporium, opened in the port city of Jeddah on Tahlia Street, Jeddah's equivalent of London's Bond Street.

To create a brand identity, the store had to have a hip look and feel because Saudi Arabia has an extremely young population: 42.4 per cent are under the age of 15. Additionally, shopping is one of the few recreations available to Saudi women in the complete absence of most other alternatives, even cinemas. For Saudi women, shopping is an experience, a ritual. At the same time, the store design had to be such as not to invite the wrath of the religious police.

First of all, the team concentrated on selecting an appropriate name that would appeal to Saudi women and create an image of luxury in their minds. The name also needed to resonate in multiple languages. It had to be ensured that if someone mispronounced the name, it would not take on a rude meaning. Additionally, a name of a goddess symbolising sensuality could not be chosen because that would amount to idolatry, which is strictly against Islam. In the end, 'Perdu', the French term for 'lost' was chosen. It was felt that it evoked the sense of a man being so swept away by a woman's beauty and sensuality as to feel lost without her. In addition, the name catered to Saudi women's fascination with France.

Not being able to use images of women, Mashat resorted to the use of language: words and poetry. For instance, a large banner was created, visible from outside the store, with the words from a 2000-year-old pre-Islamic Arabic poem that added to the romantic mood, but wouldn't offend Saudi sensibilities.

There were unexpected snags, to be sure. An overzealous airport official stopped the mannequins from being imported into Saudi Arabia despite all efforts to give them a non-lifelike shape. They had to be flown into Bahrain and brought into Jeddah by road in order to circumvent the airport authorities. The religious police also demanded the full-length mirrors in the fitting rooms be taken down.

In addition to making Perdu fashion-forward, Mashat has listened to customers. He hung a thin gauzy material to lightly cover the large glass storefront window to shield the women shopping for intimate wares inside from the intrusive eyes of passers-by. Further, although the male sales people in the store were trained to maintain a distance of 6 feet from female shoppers, to give them some privacy, Mashat realised that customers would be more comfortable with women sales people. Once he'd obtained the special permission needed from the government to allow women to work alongside men, he hired two women, taking the number of women employees in Perdu to three, including the marketing director.

In 2002, after the first full year of the store's existence, Perdu had $3.2 million in revenue, which was expected to grow to $5 million in 2003.

Source: adapted from Arundhati Parmar. 'Out From Under: Saudi Women Sold on Unique Approach to Lingerie', *Marketing News*, 21 July 2003, pp. 1, 9–10.

business ethics

The moral question of what is right and/or appropriate poses many dilemmas for domestic marketers. Even within a country, ethical standards are frequently not defined or always clear. The problem of business ethics is infinitely more complex in the international market-place because value judgements differ widely among culturally diverse groups. What is commonly accepted as right in one country may be completely unacceptable in another. Giving business gifts of high value, for example, is generally condemned in Western countries, but in many countries of the world, gifts are not only accepted but expected.

bribery: variations on a theme

Bribery must be defined because of its limitless variations. The difference between **bribery** and **extortion** must be established: voluntarily offered payments by someone seeking unlawful advantage is bribery; payments extracted under duress by someone in authority from a person seeking only what they are lawfully entitled to is extortion. An example of extortion would be the finance minister of a country demanding heavy payments under the threat that millions of dollars of investment would be confiscated.

Another variation of bribery is the difference between **lubrication** and **subornation**. Lubrication involves a relatively small sum of cash, a gift or a service made to a low-ranking official in a country where such offerings are not prohibited by law; the purpose of such a gift is to facilitate or expedite the normal, lawful performance of a duty by that official (a practice common in many countries of the world). Subornation, on the other hand, generally involves large sums of money, frequently not properly accounted for, designed to entice an official to commit an illegal act on behalf of the one paying the bribe. Lubrication payments accompany requests for a person to do a job more rapidly or more efficiently; subornation is a request for officials to 'turn a blind eye', to not do their jobs or to break the law.

A third type of payment that can appear to be a bribe, but may not be, is an agent's fee. When a business person is uncertain of a country's rules and regulations, an agent may be hired to represent the company in that country. This would be similar to hiring an agent in the home country; for example, an attorney to file an appeal for a variance in a building code on the basis that the attorney will do a more efficient and thorough job than someone unfamiliar with such procedures. Similar services may be requested of an agent in a foreign country when problems occur. However, if a part of that agent's fees is used to pay bribes, the intermediary's fees are being used unlawfully.

The answer to the question of bribery is not an unqualified one. It is easy to generalise about the ethics of political payoffs and other types of payment; it is much more difficult to

make the decision to withhold payment of money when the consequences of not making the payment may affect the company's ability to do business profitably or at all. With the variety of ethical standards and levels of morality that exist in different cultures, the dilemma of ethics and pragmatism that faces international business cannot be resolved until more countries decide to deal effectively with the issue.[19]

Ethical and socially responsible decisions

To behave in an ethically and socially responsible way should be the hallmark of every business person's behaviour, domestic or international. It requires little thought for most of us to know the socially responsible or ethically correct response to questions about knowingly breaking the law, harming the environment, denying someone his or her rights, taking unfair advantage, or behaving in a manner that would bring bodily harm or damage. Unfortunately, the difficult issues are not the obvious and simple 'right' or 'wrong' ones. In many countries, the international marketer faces the dilemma of responding to sundry situations where there is no local law, where local practices appear to condone certain behaviour, or where the company willing to 'do what is necessary' is favoured over the company that refuses to engage in certain practices. In short, being socially responsible and ethically correct is not a simple task for the international marketer operating in countries whose cultural and social values, and/or economic needs are different from those of the marketer.

In normal business operations there are five broad areas where difficulties arise in making decisions, establishing policies and engaging in business operations:

1 employment practices and policies
2 consumer protection
3 environmental protection
4 political payments and involvement in political affairs of the country, and
5 basic human rights and fundamental freedoms.

In many countries, the law may help define the borders of minimum ethical or social responsibility, but the law is only the floor above which one's social and personal morality is tested: 'Ethical business conduct should normally exist at a level well above the minimum required by law.'[20] In fact, laws are the markers of past behaviour that society has deemed unethical or socially irresponsible.[21]

summary

Business customs and practices in different world markets vary so much that it is difficult to make valid generalisations about them; it is even difficult to classify the different kinds of business behaviour that are encountered from country to country. The only safe generalisations are that business people working in another country must be sensitive to the business environment and must be willing to adapt when necessary. Unfortunately, it is not always easy to know when such adaptation is necessary; in some instances adaptation is optional and, in others, it is actually undesirable. Understanding the culture you are entering is the only sound basis for planning.

Business behaviour is derived in large part from the basic cultural environment in which the business operates and, as such, is subject to the extreme diversity encountered among various cultures and subcultures. Environmental considerations significantly affect the attitudes, behaviour and outlook of foreign business people. The motivational patterns of such business people depend in part on their personal backgrounds, their business positions, sources of authority and their own personalities.

Varying motivational patterns inevitably affect methods of doing business in different countries. Marketers in some countries thrive on competition, while in others they do everything possible to eliminate it. The authoritarian, centralised decision-making orientation in some countries contrasts sharply with democratic decentralisation in others. International variation characterises contact level, ethical orientation, negotiation outlook, and nearly every part of doing business. The foreign marketer can take no phase of business behaviour for granted.

The new breed of international business person that has emerged in recent years appears to have a heightened sensitivity to cultural variations. Sensitivity, however, is not enough; the international trader must constantly be alert and prepared to adapt when necessary. One must always realise that, no matter how long the outsider is in a country, that person is not a native; in many countries he or she may always be treated as an outsider. Finally, one must avoid the critical mistake of assuming that knowledge of one culture will provide acceptability in another.

questions

1 'More than tolerance of an alien culture is required; there is a need for affirmative acceptance of the concept "different but equal".' Elaborate.

2 'We should also bear in mind that in today's business-oriented world economy, the cultures themselves are being significantly affected by business activities and business practices.' Comment.

3 'In dealing with foreign businesses, the marketer must be particularly aware of the varying objectives and aspirations of management.' Explain.

4 Suggest ways in which people might prepare themselves to handle unique business customs that may be encountered during a trip abroad.

5 Business customs and national customs are closely interrelated. In which ways would one expect the two areas to coincide and in which ways would they show differences? How could such areas of similarity and difference be identified?

6 Identify both local and foreign examples of cultural imperatives, adiaphora and exclusives. Be prepared to explain why each example fits into the category you have selected.

7 Contrast the authority roles of top management in different societies. How do the different views of authority affect marketing activities?

8 What effects on business customs might be anticipated from the recent rapid integration of Europe?

9 Interview some foreign students to determine the types of cultural shock they encountered when they first came to your country.

10 Compare three decision-making authority patterns in international business.

11 Explore the various ways in which business customs can affect the structure of competition.

12 Why is it important that the business executive be alert to the significance of business customs?

13 Suggest some cautions that an individual from a high-context culture should bear in mind when dealing with someone from a low-context culture. Do the same for facing low- to high-context situations.

14 Political payoffs are a problem. How would you react if you faced the prospect of paying a bribe? What about if you knew that by not paying you would not be able to secure a $10 million contract?

15 Distinguish between P-time and M-time; how can these influence international marketing?

16 Discuss how a P-time person reacts differently from an M-time person in keeping an appointment.

further reading

- T. Clark and L.L. Mathur, 'Global Myopia: Globalisation Theory in International Business', *Journal of International Marketing*, 2003 (6), pp. 361-72.
- G. Darlington, 'Culture – A Theoretical Review', in P. Joynt and M. Warner, *Managing Across Cultures: Issues and Perspective* (London: Thompson, 1996), pp. 33-55.
- Sudhir Kale, 'How National Cultures, Organisational Culture and Personality Impact Buyer–Seller Interaction', in P. Ghauri and J.-C. Usunier, *International Business Negotiations*, 2nd edn (Oxford: Elsevier/Pergamon, 2004), pp. 75-96.

references

1 Yim Yu Wong, 'The Impact of Cultural Differences on the Growing Tensions between Japan and the United States', *SAM Advanced Management Journal*, Winter 1994, pp. 40-8.

2 Edward T. Hall and Mildred Reed Hall, *Understanding Cultural Differences* (Yarmouth, ME: Intercultural Press, 1990), p. 196.

3 Geert Hofstede, 'The Business of International Business is Culture', in Peter J. Buckley and Pervez N. Ghauri (eds), *The Internationalization of the Firm* (London: International Thompson Business Press, 1999), pp. 381-93.

4 Farid Elashmawi, 'China: The Many Faces of Chinese Business Culture', *Trade & Culture*, March–April 1995, pp. 30-2.

5 Haruyasu Ohsumi, 'Cultural Differences and Japan–US Economic Frictions', *Tokyo Business Today*, February 1995, pp. 49-52.

6 *Business Week*, 'Special Report: Mega Europe', 18 November 2002, pp. 24-30.

7 For a discussion of the problems of interpretation of Japanese to English, see Osamu Katayama, 'Speaking in Tongues', *Look Japan*, March 1993, pp. 18-19.

8 Pervez Ghauri and Jean-Claude Usunier, *International Business Negotiations*, 2nd edn (Oxford: Elsevier/Pergamon, 2004).

9 Edward T. Hall, 'Learning the Arabs' Silent Language', *Psychology Today*, August 1979, pp. 45-53. Hall has several books that should be read by everyone involved in international business: *Beyond Culture* (New York: Anchor Press-Doubleday, 1976); *The Hidden Dimension* (New York: Doubleday, 1966); and *The Silent Language* (New York: Doubleday, 1959).

10 For a detailed presentation of the differences in high- and low-context cultures, see Edward T. Hall and Mildred Reed Hall, *Hidden Differences: Doing Business with the Japanese* (New York: Doubleday Anchor Books, 1990), p. 172.

11 Mo Yamin and R. Altunisik, 'A Comparison of Satisfaction Outcomes with Adapted and Non-adapted Products', *International Marketing Review*, 2003, 20(6), pp. 604-21.

12 'Tradition Plays an Important Role in the Business Culture of France', *Business America*, 6 May 1991, pp. 22-3.

13 Stephen Weiss, 'The IBM-Mexico Micro Computer Investment Negotiations', in P. Ghauri and J.-C. Usunier, *International Business Negotiations*, 2nd edn (Oxford: Elsevier/Pergamon, 2004), pp. 327-62.

14 Pervez Ghauri and Tony Fang, 'Negotiations with the Chinese: A Socio-Cultural Analysis', *Journal of World Business*, 2001, 36(3), pp. 303-25.

15 Min Chen, 'Understanding Chinese and Japanese Negotiating Styles', *The International Executive*, March–April 1993, pp. 147–59.

16 Nancy J. Adler, 'Women Managers in a Global Economy', *Training and Development*, April 1994, pp. 31–6.

17 M.T. Claes, 'Women, Men and Management Styles', *International Labor Review*, 1999, 138(4), pp. 431–46.

18 Dafna Izraeli and Yoram Zeira, 'Women Managers in International Business: A Research Review and Appraisal', *Business and the Contemporary World*, Summer 1993, p. 35.

19 For a detailed discussion and guidelines for international business negotiations and ethics, see Pervez Ghauri and Jean-Claude Usunier, *International Business Negotiations* 2nd edn (Oxford: Elsevier/Pergamon, 2004).

20 *A Code of Worldwide Business Conduct and Operating Principles*, published by Caterpillar Inc., p. 4.

21 For a discussion of the guiding principles of ethical and socially responsible behaviour, see Joel Makower and Business for Social Responsibility, *Beyond the Bottom Line: Putting Social Responsibility to Work for Your Business and the World* (New York: Simon & Schuster, 1994).

chapter 6
The International Political and Legal Environment

Chapter Outline

Chapter Learning Objectives

What you should learn from Chapter 6

- How political environment and stability influence international marketing
- Understand what is meant by political risk
- How to evaluate risks and controls associated with investments in foreign markets
- How political vulnerability can be assessed and reduced
- Understand the bases for today's legal systems
- How to protect intellectual property rights

political environments

One of the most undeniable and crucial realities of doing business in a foreign country is that both the host and home governments are partners. Every country has the recognised right to grant or withhold permission to do business within its political boundaries and to control where its citizens conduct business. A government controls and restricts a company's activities by encouraging and offering support or by discouraging and banning its activities – depending on the pleasure of the government. A country's overall goals for its economic, political and social systems form the base for the political environment. Thus, the political climate in a country is a critical concern for the international marketer.[1]

A government reacts to its environment by initiating and pursuing policies deemed necessary to solve the problems created by its particular environment. National environments differ widely. Some countries are economically developed, some underdeveloped; some countries have an abundance of resources, others few or none; some countries are content with the status quo, others seek drastic changes to improve their relative positions in the world community.[2] Reflected in its policies and attitudes towards business are a government's ideas of how best to promote the national interest, considering its own resources and political philosophy. The government is an integral part of every foreign and domestic business activity – a silent partner with nearly total control. Thus, a multinational firm is affected by the political environment of the home country as well as the host country.

The ideal **political climate** for a multinational firm is a stable and friendly government. Unfortunately, governments are not always friendly and stable, nor do friendly, stable governments remain so; changes in attitudes and goals can cause a stable and friendly situation to become risky. Changes are brought about by any number of events: a radical shift in the government when a political party with a philosophy different from the one it replaces ascends to power, government response to pressure from nationalist and self-interest groups, weakened economic conditions that cause a government to recant trade commitments, or an increasing bias against foreign investment. Since foreign businesses are judged by standards as variable as there are countries, the friendliness and stability of the government in each one must be assessed as an ongoing business practice. In so doing, a manager is better able to anticipate and plan for change and to know the boundaries within which the company can operate successfully. This chapter explores some of the more salient political considerations in assessing world markets.

stability of government policies

At the top of the list of political conditions that concern foreign businesses is the stability or instability of prevailing government policies. Governments might change or new political parties might be elected, but the concern of the multinational corporation (MNC) is the continuity of the set of rules or code of behaviour – regardless of which government is in

power. In Italy, for example, there have been more than 50 different governments formed since the end of the Second World War.[3] While the political turmoil in Italy continues, business goes on as usual.

Conversely, radical changes in policies towards foreign business can occur in the most stable governments. If there is potential for profit and if permitted to operate within a country, companies can function under any type of government as long as there is some long-run predictability and stability. PepsiCo operated profitably in the Soviet Union under one of the most extreme political systems. It established a very profitable business with the USSR by exchanging Pepsi syrup for Russian vodka.[4] Socioeconomic and political environments invariably change; these changes are often brought about or reflected in changes in political philosophy and/or a surge in feelings of nationalistic pride.

nationalism

Economic nationalism, which exists to some degree within all countries, is another factor leading to an unfavourable business climate. **Nationalism** can best be described as an intense feeling of national pride and unity, an awakening of a nation's people to pride in their country. Public opinion often tends to become anti-foreign business, and many minor harassments and controls of foreign investment are supported, if not applauded. **Economic nationalism** has as one of its central aims the preservation of national economic autonomy in that residents identify their interests with the preservation of the sovereignty of the state in which they reside. In other words, national interest and security are more important than international consideration.

These feelings of nationalism can be manifest in a variety of ways including 'buy our country's products only', restrictions on imports, restrictive tariffs and other barriers to trade. They may also lead to control over foreign investment which is often regarded with suspicion and may be the object of intense scrutiny and control.[5] Generally speaking, the more a country feels threatened by some outside force, the more nationalistic it becomes in protecting itself against the intrusion. The American Government's behaviour towards foreign trade and the refusal to sign the International Criminal Court (ICC) and Kyoto agreements, after the attack on the Twin Towers, is a good example.[6]

During the period after the Second World War, when many new countries were founded and many others were seeking economic independence, manifestations of militant nationalism were rampant. **Expropriation** of foreign companies, restrictive investment policies and nationalisation of industries were common practices in some parts of the world. This was the period when India imposed such restrictive practices on foreign investments that companies such as Coca-Cola, IBM and many others chose to leave rather than face the uncertainty of a hostile economic climate.[7] By the late 1980s, that level of militant nationalism had subsided and, today, the foreign investor, once feared as a dominant tyrant that threatened economic development, is often sought after as a source of needed capital investment. Nationalism comes and goes as conditions and attitudes change, and foreign companies welcome today may be harassed tomorrow, and vice versa.[8]

While militant economic nationalism has subsided, nationalistic feelings can be found even in the most economically prosperous countries. Nationalism became an issue when Norwegian people said no to membership of the European Union in a referendum. The United Kingdom has been reluctant to adopt the single European currency (the euro) for the same reasons.

It is important to appreciate that attitudes towards foreign companies and investments have totally changed in the last two decades. Today, most countries welcome foreign companies and in fact compete with each other to attract foreign firms by offering different types of benefit such as direct subsidies and tax relief.[9]

key terms

nationalism
an intense feeling of national pride and unity

economic nationalism
the preservation of national economic autonomy

expropriation
taking companies away from their owners and into state ownership (in this case)

key terms

political risks

The kinds of political risk confronting a company range from confiscation through many lesser but still significant government activities such as exchange controls, **import restrictions** and price controls. The most severe political risk is **confiscation** – seizing a company's assets without payment. Another type of risk is **domestication**, when host countries take steps to transfer foreign investments to national control and ownership through a series of government decrees. Governments seek to domesticate foreign-held assets by mandating:

- a transfer of ownership, in part or totally, to nationals
- the promotion of a large number of nationals to higher levels of management
- greater decision-making powers resting with nationals; for example, a number of countries demand that foreign companies can enter their market only through minority **joint ventures**
- a greater number of component products locally produced; for example, a number of countries (also EU and NAFTA) demand that a product must contain 60 per cent of its content to be produced in the country, to be classified as a local product and to avoid taxes or quotas
- specific export regulations designed to dictate participation in world markets; for example, a number of countries, such as China in earlier years, demanded that foreign firms investing in particular regions must export a certain proportion of their production.

A combination of all of these mandates is issued over a period of time and eventually control is shifted to nationals. The ultimate goal of domestication is to force foreign investors to share more of the ownership and management with nationals than was the case before domestication.

GOING INTERNATIONAL 6.1

EU battle over GM imports: new rules, new negotiations

Illustration by Frances Jetter. Used with permission

In 1999, the European Union established a moratorium on imports of new, genetically modified foods. In October 2002, it seemed that the European Union would remain closed to **GM foods** for the foreseeable future, despite the tough regulations on authorising the growing and importation of new GM crops passed on 17 October. The directive set stringent conditions for the use of new GM crops, and was designed to ease fears in some EU states about potential risks of GM foods. However, several EU governments, including those of France and Italy, called for extra rules allowing GM products to be traced and labelled through the food chain before the lifting of the moratorium.

The lack of progress angered the US, where the use of GM crops is widespread. US exporters have been unable to ship to Europe commodities worth millions of dollars. However, after the initial reaction of threatening the EU with litigation through the World Trade Organization, the US decided to try to influence the EU debate on the traceability and labelling legislation, which could potentially permanently block US farmers from selling GM crops in the EU.

> The US will certainly face difficulties in the negotiations with the EU over GM crops. Margot Wallstrom, EU environment commissioner, said: 'In some member states, they are very much against GMOs. They will probably take every chance to move the goalposts and find another obstacle. Others are more constructive.' Negotiations are further complicated by the internal divisions within the EU itself. Washington wants the EU to drop its insistence on labelling processed food derived from GM crops where no traces of GM material remain, a position supported by the UK but few other EU governments. The EU is also divided on the level of accidental GM content that should be allowed in a conventional product or shipment before labelling rules would kick in. In addition, some states are calling for meat and eggs from animals fed on GM feed to be labelled.
>
> ■ Do you think Europe should allow GM foods to be imported and sold in European countries?
>
> *Source:* adapted from M. Mann, and E. Alden, 'EU Ban Stays on New GM Crops', *Financial Times*, 18 October 2002, p. 7.

Risks of confiscation and expropriation have lessened over the last decades because experience has shown that few of the desired benefits materialised after government takeover. Rather than a quick answer to economic development, expropriation and nationalisation often led to nationalised businesses that were inefficient, technologically weak and non-competitive in world markets.

As the world has become more economically interdependent and it has become obvious that much of the economic success of countries such as South Korea, Singapore and Taiwan are tied to foreign investments, countries are viewing foreign investment as a means of economic growth. Countries throughout the world that only a few years ago restricted or forbade foreign investments are now courting them as a much-needed source of capital and technology.

Political risk is still an important issue despite a more positive attitude towards MNCs and foreign investment. The transformation of China, the Commonwealth of Independent States (CIS), and Eastern Europe from Marxist-socialist economies to free market economies is a reality. However, during the transition, companies are facing political and economic uncertainty, currency conversion restrictions, unresponsive bureaucrats and other kinds of political risks. Companies can reduce the political risk through efficient handling of a number of factors (see Exhibit 6.1).

economic risks

Even though expropriation and confiscation are waning in importance as a risk of doing business abroad, international companies are still confronted with a variety of economic risks, often imposed with little warning. Restraints on business activity may be imposed under the banner of national security, to protect an infant industry, to conserve scarce foreign exchange, to raise revenue, to retaliate against unfair trade practices and a score of other real or imagined reasons. These economic risks are an important and recurring part of the political environment that few international companies can avoid.

Exchange Controls   Exchange controls stem from shortages of foreign exchange held by a country. When a nation faces shortages of foreign exchange, controls may be levied over all movements of capital or, selectively, against the most politically vulnerable companies to conserve the supply of foreign exchange for the most essential uses. A recurrent problem for the foreign investor is getting profits and investments into the currency of the home country.

Exhibit 6.1 Factors Influencing the risk-reduction process in international marketing

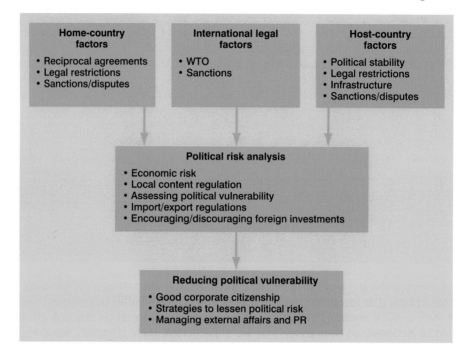

Exchange controls are also extended to products by applying a system of multiple exchange rates to regulate trade in specific commodities classified as necessities or luxuries. Necessary products are placed in the most favourable (low) exchange categories, while luxuries are heavily penalised with high foreign-exchange rates. Venezuela, for example, once had a three-tier exchange rate system to protect scarce foreign reserves. Depending on the transaction, the bolivar had a value in US dollars of 6.5 cents for essential goods, 3.4 cents for non-essential goods, and 0.01 cent for unapproved transactions. South Africa has also until recently had this type of exchange rate for its rand.[10]

key term

local content
to contain locally
made parts

Local Content Laws   In addition to restricting imports of essential supplies to force local purchase, a country often requires a portion of any product sold within that country to have **local content**, that is, to contain locally made parts. This is often imposed on foreign companies that assemble products from foreign-made components. Local-content requirements are not restricted to developing countries. The European Union has had a local-content requirement as high as 65 per cent for 'screwdriver operations', a name often given to foreign-owned assemblers such as Japanese motor vehicle assembly plants in the United Kingdom.

Import Restrictions   Selective restrictions on the import of raw materials, machines and spare parts are fairly common strategies to force foreign industry to purchase more supplies within the host country and thereby create markets for local industry. Although this is done in an attempt to support the development of domestic industry, the result is often to hamstring and sometimes interrupt the operations of established industries. The problem then becomes critical when there are no adequately developed sources of supply within the country.

Tax Controls   Taxes must be classified as a political risk when used as a means of controlling foreign investments. In such cases they are raised without warning and in violation of formal agreements. A squeeze on profits results from taxes being raised signifi-

cantly as a business becomes established. In those developing countries where the
economy is constantly threatened with a shortage of funds, unreasonable taxation of
successful foreign investments appeals to some governments as the handiest and quickest
means of finding operating funds.

Price Controls   Essential products that command considerable public interest, such as
pharmaceuticals, food, petrol and cars, are often subjected to price controls. Such controls
applied during inflationary periods can be used by a government to control the cost of
living. They may also be used to force foreign companies to sell equity to local interests. A
side-effect for the local economy can be to slow or even stop capital investment.

Labour Problems   In many countries, labour unions have strong government support
that they use effectively in obtaining special concessions from business. Layoffs may be
forbidden, profits may have to be shared and an extraordinary number of services may
have to be provided. In fact, in many countries, foreign firms are considered fair game for
the demands of the domestic labour supply. Labour issues are not only a problem in developing countries; they are equally crucial in developed countries (see Exhibit 6.2).

Exhibit 6.2 Labour disputes

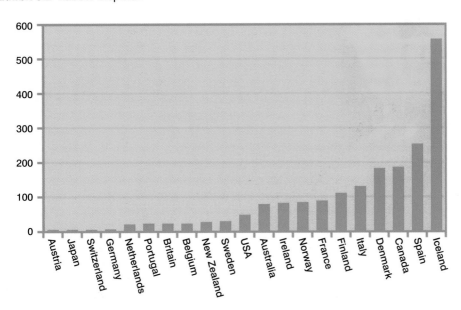

Source: based on *The Economist*, 'Labour Disputes', 24 April 2004, p. 120.

encouraging foreign investment

Governments also encourage foreign investment. In fact, within the same country, some
foreign businesses fall prey to politically induced harassment while others may be placed
under a government umbrella of protection and preferential treatment. The difference lies
in the evaluation of a company's contribution to the national interest.

   The most important reason to encourage foreign investment is to accelerate the development of an economy. An increasing number of countries are encouraging foreign investment with specific guidelines aimed towards economic goals. Multinational corporations
may be expected to create local employment, transfer technology, generate export sales,
stimulate growth and development of local industry, and/or conserve foreign exchange as
a requirement for market concessions.[11] Recent investments in China, India and the former

GOING INTERNATIONAL 6.2

South Korea and China: labour divide

South Korea, generally seen as offering one of the most lucrative investment opportunities for foreign companies in Asia, is in danger of losing the foreign investment to China unless its labour market is made more flexible and unions curbed. Foreign direct investment into South Korea fell from $15.22 billion in 2000 to $9.1 billion in 2001 and $2.66 billion in the first half of 2002. One of the main reasons underlying the fall in investment is worsening relations between foreign companies and local labour following the change of government and the economy's slide into recession.

Nestlé, the Swiss food and drinks group, is considering withdrawing from South Korea because of labour unrest. The company's 450-strong workforce went on strike in July 2003 after the company refused to meet union demands for an inflation-busting 11.7 per cent pay rise and participation in management. Nestlé offered 5.6 per cent. Now

Effigies of General Motors bosses are burnt as dismissed workers clash with police in Seoul

© Reuters newmedia Inc./CORBIS

the company is 'reviewing the necessity' of its factory in South Korea and investigating the legal procedures for closing it, following a 50-day strike that cost the company millions of dollars. The situation in China could not be more different. Increasing competition, falling transport costs and flagging consumer demand are forcing multinational companies to flock to the regions with lowest production costs, such as the Pearl river delta. In 2002, more goods were exported from China's Guangdong province, which encompasses the Pearl river delta, than during the entire 13-year period from 1978 to 1990. Total Chinese exports grew 21 per cent in 2002 to $322 billion and have doubled in just over five years. In contrast, it took Germany 10 years to double exports in the 1960s and seven for Japan in the 1970s. China's inexhaustible supply of land, labour and government encouragement has kept costs down and exported price deflation around the world. Dr Martens, one of many companies driven to China by fierce price competition from firms already manufacturing in China, used small groups of workers assembling complete shoes in its Northampton factory, paid them about $490 a week and has built a stadium for its local football club. Pou Chen, a manufacturer that Dr Martens contracted upon moving its operations to China from the UK, pays about $100 a month, or 36 cents an hour, for up to 69 hours a week and provides dormitories for migrant workers, who must obey strict curfews.

The relentless competition among local suppliers also keeps the profit margins almost invisible. Pou Chen has to worry about more than 800 other shoemakers in the Pearl river delta. However, companies are avoiding labour shortages and rising wages by moving inland where labour is more plentiful. In the words of Mitsuhiko Ikuno, a Japanese managing director, 'There are high levels of engineers and college graduates and plenty of girls with good eyes and strong hands. If we run out of people, we just go deeper into China.'

■ Are labour unions the main reason why jobs are moving to China? Are labour unions to be blamed for falling FDI in South Korea? Are labour unions good?

Source: adapted from Andrew Ward, 'Nestlé Threat to Pull Out of South Korea', *Financial Times*, 4 September 2003, p. 31; and Dan Roberts and James Kynge, 'How Cheap Labour, Foreign Investment and Rapid Industrialisation are Creating a New Workshop of the World', *Financial Times*, 4 February 2003, p. 21.

republics of the USSR include provisions stipulating specific contributions to economic goals of the country that must be made by foreign investors.[12]

The most recent trend in India has been towards dropping preconditions for entry and liberalising requirements in order to encourage further investment. In just the few years between the time Pepsi-Cola was given permission to enter the Indian market and the Coca-Cola company re-entered, requirements were eased considerably.[13]

Pepsi was restricted to a minority position (40 per cent) in a joint venture. In addition, it was required to develop an agricultural research centre to produce high-yielding seed varieties, construct and operate a snack-food processing plant and a vegetable processing plant, and, among other foreign exchange requirements, guarantee that export revenues would be five times greater than money spent on imports. Pepsi agreed to these conditions and by 1994 had captured 26 per cent of the Indian soft drinks market. In contrast, when Coke re-entered the Indian market a few years later, requirements for entry were minimal. Unlike Pepsi, Coca-Cola was able to have 100 per cent ownership of its subsidiary.[14]

Along with direct encouragement from a host country, a Western company may receive assistance from its home government. The intent is to encourage investment by helping to minimise and shift some of the risks encountered in some foreign markets. A number of other facilities are often also available such as **export credit guarantee**.

assessing political vulnerability

Some products appear to be more politically vulnerable than others, in that they receive special government attention. This special attention may result in positive actions towards the company or in negative attention, depending on the desirability of the product. It is not unusual for countries seeking investments in **high-priority industries** to excuse companies from taxes, customs duties, quotas, exchange controls and other impediments to investment.

Conversely, firms marketing products not considered high priority or that fall from favour often face unpredictable government restrictions. Continental Can Company's joint venture to manufacture cans for the Chinese market faced a barrage of restrictions when the Chinese economy weakened. China decreed that canned beverages were wasteful and must be banned from all state functions and banquets. Tariffs on aluminium and other materials imported for producing cans were doubled and a new tax was imposed on canned drink consumption. An investment that had the potential for profit after a few years was rendered profitless by a change in the attitude of the Chinese Government.

politically sensitive products

There are at least as many reasons for a product's political vulnerability as there are political philosophies, economic variations and cultural differences. Unfortunately, there are no absolute guidelines a marketer can follow to determine whether or not a product will be subject to political attention. For products judged non-essential, the risk would be great, but for those thought to be making an important contribution, encouragement and special considerations could be available. Fast-food companies have been subject to protests in India. As McDonald's admitted that it used beef flavours to lace its French fries, a lawsuit was filed against the company for secretly misleading the customers. Beef is forbidden according to Hindu religion. The European Union is quite sensitive about genetically modified (GM) food. Recently Unilever announced that it will stop using GM ingredients in its food products in Britain. Additionally, 11 leading fast-food restaurants, such as McDonald's, Burger King and Pizza Hut, have eliminated GM ingredients in their European branches.

forecasting political risk

In addition to qualitative measures of political vulnerability, a number of firms are employing systematic methods of measuring political risk.[15] **Political risk assessment** is an

key terms

export credit guarantee
when a government/ organisation ensures to give a loan to an exporter

high-priority industries
when some industries are given extra benefits by the authorities because they are considered important

political risk assessment
an attempt to forecast political instability to help management identify and evaluate political events and their potential influence on current and future international business decisions

attempt to forecast political instability to help management identify and evaluate political events and their potential influence on current and future international business decisions. Political risk assessment can:

- help managers decide if risk insurance is necessary
- devise an intelligence network and an early warning system
- help managers develop contingency plans for unfavourable future political events
- build a database of past political events for use by corporate management
- interpret the data gathered by its intelligence network to advise and forewarn corporate decision makers about political and economic situations.

Risk assessment is used not only to determine whether to make an investment in a country, but also to determine the amount of risk a company is prepared to accept. In the Commonwealth of Independent States (CIS) and China the risk may be too high for some companies, but stronger and better-financed companies can make long-term investments that will be profitable in the future. Early risk is accepted in exchange for being in the country when the economy begins to grow and risk subsides.

During the chaos that arose in 1991 after the political and economic changes in the USSR, the newly formed republics were anxious to make deals with foreign investors, yet the problems and uncertainty made many investors take a wait-and-see attitude. Certainly the many companies that are investing in the CIS or China do not expect big returns immediately; they are betting on the future. The unfortunate situation is with the company that does not assess the risk properly. After making a sizeable initial investment they realise they are not financially able to bear all the future risks and costs while waiting for more prosperous times, so they lose their capital. Better political risk analysis might have helped them make the decision not to go into the market, but to make an investment in a country with more predictability and less risk. These days there are a number of political rankings available (see Exhibit 6.3).

There are a variety of methods used to measure political risk. They range from in-house political analysts to external sources that specialise in analysing political risk. Presently, all methods are far from being perfected; however, the very fact that a company attempts to systematically examine the problem is significant.

For a marketer doing business in a foreign country, a necessary part of any market analysis is an assessment of the probable political consequences of a marketing plan – some marketing activities are more susceptible to political considerations than others. Basically, it boils down to evaluating the essential nature of the immediate activity. The following section explores ways businesses can reduce political vulnerability.

reducing political vulnerability

Even though a company cannot directly control or alter the political environment of the country within which it operates, there are measures that can lessen the degree of susceptibility of a specific business venture to politically induced risks. Foreign investors are frequently accused of exploiting a country's wealth at the expense of the national population and for the sole benefit of the foreign investor.

These charges are not wholly unsupported by past experiences, but today's enlightened investor is seeking a return on investment that is commensurate with the risk involved. To achieve such a return, hostile and generally unfounded fears must be overcome.

good corporate citizenship
As long as such fears persist, the political climate for foreign investors will continue to be hostile. Are there ways of allaying these fears? A list of suggestions made years ago is still appropriate for a company that intends to be a good corporate citizen and thereby minimise its political vulnerability.

Exhibit 6.3 Country risk ratings

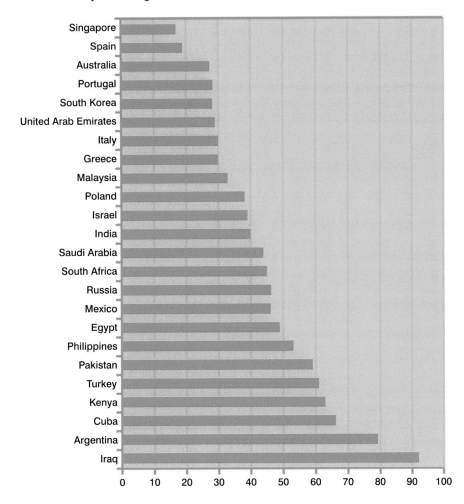

Many companies survive even the most hostile environments; through their operating methods, they have been able to minimise their political vulnerability. There is certainly much to be said for attempting to become more closely identified with the ideals and desires of the host country. To do so might render a marketer's activities and products less politically vulnerable; and, although it would not eliminate all the risks of the political environment, it might reduce the likelihood and frequency of some politically motivated risks. In addition to being good citizens, responsive to various publics, there are other approaches that help minimise the effects of hostile political environments.[16]

strategies to lessen political risk

In addition to corporate activities focused on the social and economic goals of the host country and good corporate citizenship, MNCs can use other strategies to minimise political vulnerability and risk.

Joint Ventures   Typically less susceptible to political harassment, joint ventures can be with either locals or other third-country multinational companies; in both cases, a company's financial exposure is limited. A joint venture with locals helps minimise anti-MNC feeling, and a joint venture with another MNC adds the additional bargaining power of a third country. It is also a preferred entry strategy in countries with relatively higher political risk.

GOING INTERNATIONAL 6.3

Indian court orders tests on Coca-cola and Pepsi's soft drinks

A New Delhi court ordered independent testing of Pepsi soft drinks following allegations that they and those of Coca-Cola's Indian subsidiary were polluted with pesticides. The ruling, which follows a decision of the Indian Parliament to ban the two brands from its premises, was welcomed by PepsiCo.

The Centre for Science and Environment (CSE), the pressure group that made the allegations, said it also welcomed the ruling since it believed it would corroborate its own tests, which it says were conducted under US Government protocols. The CSE alleged that 12 soft drinks owned by the two companies contained traces of deadly pesticide, including DDT, from the groundwater that is used in the drinks.

The pressure group said the threat to public health extended far beyond the quality of soft drinks, since it was the broader contamination of water that was at issue. Indian law does not define clean water. However, the campaign to boycott Pepsi and Coke appears to be gaining momentum in parts of India. The youth wing of the Hindu nationalists has organised demonstrations where bottles of Coke and Pepsi were smashed. The Indian arms of Coca-Cola and PepsiCo hinted strongly that they were planning legal action against the CSE, a non-government body.

Four of the 30 state governments said they would test Pepsi and Coca-Cola for toxins. The two companies placed advertisements in the largest-circulation Indian newspapers seeking to counter the CSE's allegations. But many of the newspapers also carried editorials accusing the two of double standards. 'This is trial by media,' said Rajeev Bakshi, chairman of Pepsi India. 'We are also concerned that there are other players [parliament and government] getting in on the act.' Pepsi said that its regular in-house tests showed that the quality of its products did conform to European Union norms. But India's standards left room for confusion. 'Our aim must surely be to get the Indian Government to establish transparent standards and procedures so that campaigns like this do not happen in this way again,' said the chairman of Pepsi India.

Locals protest against Pepsi © Sharad Saxena/India Today)

■ How should Pepsi and Coca-Cola handle this situation?

Source: Edward Luce, 'Coca-Cola and Pepsi May Take Legal Action Over "Pesticide" Claim', *Financial Times*, 8 August 2003, p. 10; and Edward Luce, 'Indian Court Orders Further Tests on Pepsi's Soft Drinks', *Financial Times*, 12 August 2003, p. 8.

Expanding the Investment Base   Including several investors and banks in financing an investment in the host country is another strategy. This has the advantage of engaging the power of the banks whenever any kind of government takeover or harassment is threatened. This strategy becomes especially powerful if the banks have made loans to the host country; if the government threatens expropriation or other types of takeover, the financing bank has substantial power with the government.

Marketing and Distribution   Controlling distribution in world markets can be used effectively if an investment should be expropriated; the expropriating country would lose access to world markets. This has proved especially useful for MNCs in the extractive industries where world markets for iron ore, copper and so forth are crucial to the success

of the investment. Peru found that when Marcona Mining Company was expropriated, the country lost access to iron ore markets around the world and ultimately had to deal with Marcona on a much more favourable basis than first thought possible.

Licensing   A strategy that some firms find eliminates almost all risks is to license technology for a fee. It can be effective in situations where the technology is unique and the risk is high. Of course, there is some risk assumed because the licensee can refuse to pay the required fees while continuing to use the technology.

Planned Domestication   The strategies just discussed can be effective in forestalling or minimising the effect of a total takeover. However, in those cases where an investment is being domesticated by the host country, the most effective long-range solution is planned phasing out, that is, **planned domestication**. This is not the preferred business practice, but the alternative of government-initiated domestication can be as disastrous as confiscation. As a reasonable response to the potential of domestication, planned domestication can be profitable and operationally expedient for the foreign investor. Planned domestication is, in essence, a gradual process of participating with nationals in all phases of company operations.

Initial investment planning provides for eventual sale of a significant interest (perhaps even controlling interest) to nationals, and incorporation of national economic needs and national managerial talent into the business as quickly as possible. Such a policy is more likely to result in reasonable control remaining with the parent company even though nationals would hold important positions in management and ownership. Company-trained nationals would be more likely to have a strong corporate point of view than a national perspective.

Local suppliers developed over a period of time could ultimately handle a significant portion of total needs, thus meeting government demands for local content. Further, a sound, sensible plan to sell ownership over a number of years would ensure a fair and equitable return on investment in addition to encouraging ownership throughout the populace. Finally, if government concessions and incentives essential in early stages of investment were rendered economically unnecessary, the company's political vulnerability would be lessened considerably.

political payoffs

One approach to dealing with political vulnerability is the **political payoff** – an attempt to lessen political risks by paying those in power to intervene on behalf of the multinational company. Political payoffs or bribery have been used to lessen the negative effects of a variety of problems. Paying heads of state to avoid confiscatory taxes or expulsion, paying fees to agents to ensure the acceptance of sales contracts, and providing monetary encouragement to an assortment of people whose actions can impact the effectiveness of a company's programmes are decisions that frequently confront multinational managers and raise ethical questions.

Bribery poses problems for the marketer at home and abroad. It is illegal to pay a bribe even if it is a common practice in the host country. Further, in most countries, once exposed those involved are punished.[17] There may be short-run benefits to political payoffs but, in the long run, the risks are high and bribery should be avoided.

legal environments

Laws governing business activities within and between countries are an integral part of the legal environment of international business. A Japanese company doing business with France has to contend with two jurisdictions (Japan and France), two tax systems, two legal systems and a third supranational set of European Union laws and regulations that may override French commercial law. Because no single, uniform international commercial

key terms

planned domestication
when a company plans to successively use local staff or components in a foreign market

political payoff
an attempt to lessen political risks by paying those in power to intervene on behalf of the multinational company

GOING INTERNATIONAL 6.4

market-driven political reforms

There have long been two official perceptions of China in the United States: those who welcome economic engagement with the country and those who, by limiting contracts, would restrain its ascending power. Those committed to containment, represented mainly by the Republican Party's right wing, insist that economic engagement does not foster changes to China's repressive political system. The engagement school, on the other hand, holds that as the Chinese become wealthier, so their demands for political representation increase.

Important changes now under way in China support the case for engagement: cities in coastal China, motivated by foreign investors, are embarking on experiments to introduce checks and balances to single-party rule. Yu Youjun, mayor of Shenzhen, says that foreign companies, especially those establishing high-technology factories, are mindful of the need to protect intellectual property: 'Every multinational company and investor is influenced by the investment climate created by governments.' The 'hard environment' of roads, railways, ports and telecommunications was important, but more crucial was the 'soft environment', meaning a government that is 'democratic' and transparent.

**www.
adrianbradshaw.
com**

The crux of the current reform is a strict separation of the roles of the Communist Party, the executive government and the local legislature. The party would be responsible for setting the broad direction of policy, but would be prevented from interfering in its execution. The local legislature would be charged with reviewing and supervising the government's work. In addition, seizing on the trend for greater accountability, many cities last year opened themselves to criticism from local and foreign companies. This practice, known as *wan ren ping zhengfu*, or '10 000 people criticise the government', has become something of a phenomenon. Chaoyang district of Beijing sent questionnaires to companies – 40 per cent of them foreign – asking participants to rate the performance of the local government departments. The top-rated departments will receive a bonus; the bottom ones will have their bonuses reduced. China has decreed that local governments will have to survive purely from tax income, cutting them off from the dividends they used to collect from local state-owned enterprises. This means their income will be decided by how many companies invest in their locality.

■ Do you think the world should force China to adopt a Western-style democracy?

Source: adapted from 'To Woo Investors, Cities Experiment with Political Reform', *Financial Times*, 4 February 2003, p. 21.

law governing foreign business transactions exists, the international marketer must pay particular attention to the legal environment of each country within which it operates.

bases for legal systems

Four common heritages form the bases for the majority of the legal systems of the world:

1 Islamic law, derived from the interpretation of the Koran and found in Iran, Saudi Arabia and some other Islamic states
2 socialist law, derived from the Marxist-socialist system and found in some of the Newly Independent States (NIS) of the former Soviet Union, and in China and other socialist states

3 common law, derived from English law and found in England, Australia, the United States, Canada[18] and other countries once under English influence, and

4 civil or code law, derived from Roman law and found in Germany, Japan, France and the remaining non-Islamic and non-socialist countries.

The differences among these four systems are of more than theoretical importance because due process of law may vary considerably among and within these legal systems. Even though a country's laws may be based on one of the four legal systems, its individual interpretation may vary significantly – from a fundamentalist interpretation of Islamic law as found in Iran or Saudi Arabia to a combination of several legal systems found in the United States, where both common and code law are reflected in their laws.

Islamic and Socialist Law   The basis for the **Shari'ah** (Islamic law) is the interpretation of the Koran. It encompasses religious duties and obligations as well as the secular aspect of law regulating human acts. Broadly speaking, Islamic law defines a complete system that prescribes specific patterns of social and economic behaviour for all individuals. It includes issues such as property rights, economic decision making and types of economic freedom. The overriding objective of the Islamic system is social justice.

Among the unique aspects of Islamic law is the prohibition of the payment of excessive interest. The Islamic law of contracts states that any given transaction should be devoid of **riba**, defined as unlawful advantage by way of excess of deferment, that is, excessive interest or usury. This impacts on banking practices severely; however, a method for payment for the use of money has been developed by Islamic banks through an ingenious compromise.[19] Instead of an interest-bearing loan, banks finance trade by buying some of the borrower's stock, which it then sells back to the company at a higher price. The size of the mark-up is determined by the amount and maturity of the loan and the creditworthiness of the borrower – all traditional yardsticks for determining interest rates. This is practised and is an example of the way Islamic law can be reconciled with the laws of non-Islamic legal systems.[20]

Socialist laws, based on the fundamental tenets of the Marxist-socialist state, cluster around the core concept of economic, political and social policies of the state. Socialist countries are, or were, generally those that formerly had laws derived from the Roman or code-law system. Some of the characteristics of Roman law have been preserved within their legal systems. Although much of the terminology and other similarities of code law have been retained in socialist law, the basic premise on which socialist law is based is that 'law, according to socialist tenets, is strictly subordinate to prevailing economic conditions'.[21] Thus, the words property, contract and arbitration denote different realities because of the collectivisation of the means of production and state planning.

As socialist countries become more directly involved in trade with non-socialist countries, laws governing ownership, contracts and other business realities have been developed to reconcile the differences between socialist law and the common or code law that prevails in most of the industrialised world. China, for example, has had to pass laws covering the protection of intellectual property rights, clarifying ownership rights in joint ventures, and other pieces of commercial legislation necessary for international business.

Common and Code Law   The basis for **common law** is tradition, past practices and legal precedents set by the courts through interpretations of statutes, legal legislation and past rulings. Common law seeks 'interpretation through the past decisions of higher courts, which interpret the same statutes or apply established and customary principles of law to a similar set of facts'.

Code law is based on an all-inclusive system of written rules (codes) of law. Under code law, the legal system is generally divided into three separate codes: commercial, civil and criminal. Common law is recognised as not being all-inclusive, while code law is considered

key terms

Shari'ah
Islamic law

riba
the unlawful advantage by way of excess of deferment; that is, excessive interest or usury

socialist laws
cluster around the core concept of economic, political and social policies of the state; socialist countries are, or were, those whose laws derived from the Roman or code-law system

common law
tradition, past practices and legal precedents set by the courts through interpretations of statutes, legal legislation and past rulings

complete as a result of catchall provisions found in most code-law systems. For example, under the commercial code in a code-law country, the law governing contracts is made inclusive with the statement that 'a person performing a contract shall do so in conformity with good faith as determined by custom and good morals'. Although code law is considered all-inclusive, it is apparent from the foregoing statement that some broad interpretations are possible in order to include everything under the existing code.

As we discuss later in the section on protection of **intellectual property rights**, laws governing intellectual property offer the most striking differences between common-law and code-law systems.[22] Under common law, ownership is established by use; under code law, ownership is determined by registration. Although every country has elements of both common and code law, the differences in interpretation between common- and code-law systems regarding contracts, sales agreements and other legal issues are significant enough that an international marketer familiar with only one system must enlist the aid of legal counsel for the most basic legal questions.

An illustration of where fundamental differences in the two systems can cause difficulty is in the performance of a contract. Under common law in the United States, it is fairly clear that impossibility of performance does not necessarily excuse compliance with the provisions of a contract unless it is impossible to comply for reasons of an **act of God**, such as some extraordinary happening of nature not reasonably anticipated by either party to a contract. Hence, floods, lightning, earthquakes and similar occurrences are generally considered acts of God. Under code law, acts of God are not limited solely to acts of nature but are extended to include 'unavoidable interferences with performance, whether resulting from forces of nature or unforeseeable human acts', including such things as labour strikes and riots.

The international marketer must be concerned with the differences among systems when operating between countries because the rights of the principals of a contract or some other legal document under one law may be significantly different from the rights under the other. It should be kept in mind that there can also be differences between the laws of two countries whose laws are based on the same legal system. Thus, the problem of the marketer is one of anticipating the different laws regulating business, regardless of the legal system of the country.

key terms

intellectual property rights
laws governing intellectual property

act of God
an extraordinary happening of nature not reasonably anticipated by either party to a contract, i.e. earthquakes, floods, etc.

GOING INTERNATIONAL 6.5

České Budéjovice, privatisation, trademarks: what do they have in common with Anheuser-Busch?

Budweiser, that's what!

Anheuser-Busch has launched a massive public relations programme in the small Czech town of České Budéjovice, where a local brewery produces Budweiser Budvar - no relation to Anheuser-Busch. Its goal is to win support for a minority stake in the Czech state-owned brewery, Budéjovic Budvar NP, when the government privatises it. Trees are being planted along main avenues, a new cultural centre was recently opened offering free English courses to citizens and management advice to budding entrepreneurs, and newspaper ads tout the possibilities of future cooperation.

So why the interest in a brewery whose annual production of 500 000 barrels is the equivalent of two days' output for Anheuser-Busch? Part-ownership is critically important to Anheuser-Busch for two reasons. It is in search of new markets and Europe is its target, and it wants to be able to market the Budweiser brand in Europe to achieve a presence there. So what's the connection? It doesn't have the rights to use the Budweiser brand name in Europe since it is owned by Budéjovic Budvar NP, a local brewery in České Budéjovice.

Anheuser-Busch established the name Budweiser in
the United States when German immigrants founded
their St Louis family brewery in the latter part of the
nineteenth century. The Czechs claim they have been
using the name since before Columbus discovered the
New World, even though they did not legally register it
until the 1920s. The Anheuser-Busch Company markets
Budweiser brand beer in North America, but in Europe
it markets Busch brand beer because the Czechs have
the rights to the use of the name Budweiser. The Czech
Government has given Anheuser-Busch the right to negotiate for a minority stake in
Budvar as part of the privatisation of the brewery, which claims to have its roots when
beermaking was licensed by the Bohemian King Otakar II in 1256. The legal battle for the
exclusive right to use the brand names 'Bud' and 'Budweiser' has spread all over the
world and lawsuits are being handled in many countries. In Britain the High Court
allowed both companies to use the brand name while in Switzerland the High Court
banned Anheuser-Busch, the American company, from selling beer under the brand
name 'Bud'. It is not only the brand names but also the marketing slogans that are
causing confusion. The US company uses the slogan 'King of beers' while the Czech
brewery is using the slogan 'Beer of kings', because it comes from a town which once
brewed for the royals and has a large customer base in Germany and the rest of Europe.

■ Who do you think has the right to use the brand name? How do you think this
problem can be solved?

Source: adapted from 'Anheuser-Busch Says Skoal, Salud, Prosit', *Business Week*, 20 September 1993,
pp. 76-7; 'This Bud's for Whom?', *Reuters News Service*, 1 July 1994; Gregory Cancelada, 'Czech Brewery
Retains Right to Use "Budweiser" and "Bud" Trademarks', *St Louis Despatch*, 17 February 2003; also visit
www.budvar.cz and www.anheuser-busch.com.

Determining whose legal system has **jurisdiction** when a commercial dispute arises is
another problem of international marketing. A frequent error is to assume that disputes
between citizens of different nations are adjudicated under some supranational system of
laws. Unfortunately, no judicial body exists to deal with legal commercial problems arising
between citizens of different countries. Confusion probably stems from the existence of
international courts, such as the World Court in The Hague and the International Court of
Justice, the principal judicial organ of the United Nations. These courts are operative in
international disputes between sovereign nations of the world rather than between private
citizens.

Legal disputes can arise in three situations: (1) between governments; (2) between a
company and a government; and (3) between two companies. Disputes between governments can be adjudicated by the World Court and by the WTO, whereas the other two situations must be handled in the courts of the country of one of the parties involved or
through arbitration. Unless a commercial dispute involves a national issue between states,
it is not handled by the International Court of Justice or any similar world court. Because
there is no 'international commercial law', the foreign marketer must look to the legal
system of each country involved – the laws of the home country and/or the laws of the
countries within which business is conducted.

When international **commercial disputes** must be settled under the laws of one of the
countries concerned, the paramount question in a dispute is: Which law governs?
Jurisdiction is generally determined in one of three ways: (1) on the basis of jurisdictional
clauses included in contracts; (2) on the basis of where a contract was entered into; or (3)

key terms

jurisdiction
overall legal
authority

legal disputes
conflicts that are
resolved through
legal means

**commercial
disputes**
conflicts about
commercial
agreements (e.g.
terms of payment,
penalties for
delay)

on the basis of where the provisions of the contract were performed. The most clear-cut decision can be made when the contracts or legal documents supporting a business transaction include a jurisdictional clause. A clause similar to the following establishes jurisdiction in the event of disagreements:

> That the parties hereby agree that the agreement is made in London, UK, and that any question regarding this agreement shall be governed by the law of the United Kingdom.

legal recourse in resolving international disputes

Should the settlement of a dispute on a private basis become impossible, the foreign marketer must resort to more resolute action. Such action can take the form of conciliation, arbitration or, as a last resort, litigation. Most international business people prefer a settlement through arbitration rather than by suing a foreign company.

conciliation

Although arbitration is recommended as the best means of settling international disputes, conciliation can be an important first step for resolving commercial disputes. **Conciliation** is a non-binding agreement between parties to resolve disputes by asking a third party to mediate the differences.

Conciliation is considered to be especially effective when resolving disputes with Chinese business partners because they are less threatened by conciliation than arbitration. The Chinese believe that when a dispute occurs, friendly negotiation should be used first to solve the problem; if that fails, conciliation should be tried. In fact, some Chinese companies may avoid doing business with companies that resort first to arbitration.

Conciliation can be either formal or informal. Informal conciliation can be established by both sides agreeing on a third party to mediate. Formal conciliation is conducted under the auspices of the Beijing Conciliation Centre, which assigns one or two conciliators to mediate. If agreement is reached, a conciliation statement based on the signed agreement is recorded. Although conciliation may be the friendly route to resolving disputes in China, it is not legally binding, so an arbitration clause should be included in all conciliation agreements.

arbitration

International commercial disputes are often resolved by **arbitration** rather than litigation. The usual arbitration procedure is for the parties involved to select a disinterested and informed party or parties as referee(s) to determine the merits of the case and make a judgement that both parties agree to honour.

Tribunals for Arbitration   Although the preceding informal method of arbitration is workable, most arbitration is conducted under the auspices of one of the more formal domestic and international arbitration groups organised specifically to facilitate the mediation of commercial disputes. These groups have experienced arbitrators available and formal rules for the process of arbitration. In most countries, decisions reached in formal mediation are enforceable under the law.

Among the formal arbitration organisations are:

1 the International Chamber of Commerce
2 the London Court of Arbitration; decisions are enforceable under English law and in English courts
3 the American Arbitration Association.

The procedures used by formal arbitration organisations are similar. Arbitration under the rules of the International Chamber of Commerce (ICC) affords an excellent example of how most organisations operate. When an initial request for arbitration is received, the chamber first attempts a conciliation between the disputants. If this fails, the process

key terms

conciliation
a non-binding agreement between parties to resolve disputes by asking a third party to mediate

arbitration
mediation done by a third party in case of a commercial dispute

of arbitration is started. The plaintiff and the defendant select one person each from among acceptable arbitrators to defend their case, and the ICC Court of Arbitration appoints a third member, generally chosen from a list of distinguished lawyers, jurists and/or professors.

The history of ICC effectiveness in arbitration has been spectacular. An example of a case that involved arbitration by the ICC concerned a contract between an English business and a Japanese manufacturer. The English business agreed to buy 100 000 plastic dolls for 80 cents each. On the strength of the contract, the English business sold the entire lot at $1.40 per doll. Before the dolls were delivered, the Japanese manufacturer had a strike; the settlement of the strike increased costs and the English business was informed that the delivery price of the dolls had increased from 80 cents to $1.50 each. The English business maintained that the Japanese firm had committed to make delivery at 80 cents and should deliver at that price. Each side was convinced that it was right. The Japanese, accustomed to code law, felt that the strike was beyond control, was an act of God, and thus compliance with the original provisions of the contract was excused. The English, accustomed to common law, did not accept the Japanese reasons for not complying because they considered a strike the normal course of doing business and not an act of God. The dispute could not be settled except through arbitration or litigation. They chose arbitration; the ICC appointed an arbitrator who heard both sides and ruled that the two parties would share proportionately in the loss. Both parties were satisfied with the arbitration decision and costly litigation was avoided. Most arbitration is successful, but success depends on the willingness of both parties to accept the arbitrator's rulings.

Arbitration Clauses   Contracts and other legal documents should include clauses specifying the use of arbitration to settle disputes. Unless a provision for arbitration of any dispute is incorporated as part of a contract, the likelihood of securing agreement for arbitration after a dispute arises is reduced. An arbitration clause suggested by the International Chamber of Commerce is:

> All disputes arising in connection with the present contract shall be finally settled under the rules of conciliation and arbitration of the International Chamber of Commerce by one or more arbitrators appointed in accordance with the said rules.

litigation

Lawsuits in public courts are avoided for many reasons. Most observers of **litigation** between citizens of different countries believe that almost all victories are spurious because the cost, frustrating delays and extended aggravation that these cases produce are more oppressive by far than any matter of comparable size. The best advice is to seek a settlement, if possible, rather than sue. Other deterrents to litigation are:

key term

litigation
taking the other party to court

1 fear of creating a poor image and damaging public relations
2 fear of unfair treatment in a foreign court (although not intentional, there is justifiable fear that a lawsuit could result in unfair treatment because the decision could be made by either a jury or judge not well versed in trade problems and the intricacies of international business transactions)
3 difficulty in collecting a judgment that may otherwise have been collected in a mutually agreed settlement through arbitration
4 the relatively high cost and time required when bringing legal action
5 loss of confidentiality.

One authority suggests that the settlement of every dispute should follow three steps: first, try to placate the injured party; if this does not work, conciliate, arbitrate; and, finally, litigate. The final step is typically taken only when all other methods fail. Actually, this advice is probably wise whether one is involved in an international dispute or a domestic one.

GOING INTERNATIONAL 6.6

counterfeit, pirated or the original: take your choice

Intellectual properties – trademarks, brand names, designs, manufacturing processes, formulas – are valuable company assets that US officials estimate are knocked off to the tune of $800 million (€720 million) a year due to counterfeiting and/or pirating. Some examples from China are given below.

© Dave Bartruff/
CORBIS

■ Design rip-offs. Beijing Jeep Corporation, a Chrysler Corporation joint venture, found more than 2 000 four-wheel-drive vehicles designed to look nearly identical to its popular Cherokee model.

■ Product rip-offs. Exact copies of products made by Procter & Gamble, Colgate Palmolive, Reebok and Nike are common throughout southern China. Exact copies of any Madonna album are available for as little as $1, as are CDs and movies. One executive says, 'They'll actually hire workers away from the real factories.'

■ Brand name ripoffs. Bausch & Lomb's Ray Ban sunglasses become Ran Bans. Colgate in the familiar bright red becomes Cologate. The familiar Red Rooster on Kellogg's Corn Flakes appears on Kongalu Corn Strips packages that state 'the trustworthy sign of quality which is famous around the world'.

■ Book ripoffs. Even the rich and powerful fall prey to pirating. Soon after *My Father, Deng Xiaoping*, a biography written by Deng Rong, daughter of Deng Xiaoping, was published, thousands of illegal copies flooded the market.

■ Original versions of the products mentioned above are also sold in China by the true owners.

While joining the WTO, China passed a law allowing customers to demand a double refund for fake merchandise sold in department stores. This led to a new business for some. Wang Hai claimed to have made $10 000 buying bogus phones and fax machines and then getting a double refund: 'If I had more money, I would have emptied out every store in Beijing.' The 'Wang Hai Phenomenon' is forcing department stores to stop stocking counterfeit products.

Source: adapted from Marcus W. Brauchli, 'Chinese Flagrantly Copy Trademarks of Foreigners', *The Wall Street Journal*, 26 June 1994, p. B-1; Bob Davis, 'US Plans to Probe Piracy in China, Raising Possibility of Trade Sanctions', *The Wall Street Journal*, 28 June 1994, p. A-2; Chin-Ching Ni, 'Anti-counterfeit Law Allows Chinese Customer to Cash in', *Los Angeles Times*, 14 September 2002, p. A-3.

protection of intellectual property rights: a special problem

Companies spend millions of dollars establishing brand names or trademarks to symbolise quality and a host of other product features designed to entice customers to buy their brands to the exclusion of all others. Such intellectual or industrial properties are among the more valuable assets a company may possess. Names such as Philips, Sony, Swatch, Kodak, Coca-Cola and Gucci, and rights to processes such as xerography and to computer software are invaluable.

Estimates are that more than 10 million fake Swiss watches carrying famous brand names such as Cartier and Rolex are sold every year, netting illegal profits of at least €550

million ($600 million). Although difficult to pinpoint, lost sales from the unauthorised use of Western patents, **trademarks** and copyrights amount to more than €90 billion ($100 billion) annually. That translates into more than a million lost jobs. Software is an especially attractive target for pirates because it is costly to develop but cheap to reproduce. Unauthorised software that sells for €450 ($500) in the United States and United Kingdom can be purchased for less than €9 ($10) in the Far East. To qualify for this list, a brand must have a value greater than $1 billion, derive about one-third of its earnings from outside its home market and have publicly available the brand's marketing and financial data. Some brands might have greater value but have been eliminated due to the above criteria.

GOING INTERNATIONAL 6.7

protection of counterfeited pills

Packets of a Chinese version of the sex-enhancing Viagra pills were put on sale at a park in the Chinese city of Shenyang. The shape and composition of the fake Viagra pills, which has been declared as 'pearl calcium', were similar to the real thing. The Chinese police raided an underground crime ring that was churning out millions of counterfeit Viagra pills to hopeful men across the country's southeast. Since the real Viagra costs more than four times as much as the fake pills, many customers bought the fake pills for use as business gifts.

A Chinese version of the Viagra pill.
©AFP/CORBIS

The failure to protect intellectual or industrial property rights adequately in the world marketplace can lead to the legal loss of these rights in potentially profitable markets. Because **patents**, processes, trademarks and copyrights are valuable in all countries, some companies have found their assets appropriated and profitably exploited in foreign countries without a licence or reimbursement. Further, they often learn that not only are other firms producing and selling their products or using their trademarks, but also that the foreign companies are the rightful owners in the countries where they are operating.

There have been many cases where companies have legally lost the rights to trademarks and have had to buy back these rights or pay royalties for their use. The problems of inadequate protective measures taken by the owners of valuable assets stem from a variety of causes. One of the more frequent errors is assuming that because the company has established rights in the home country, it will be protected around the world, or that rightful ownership can be established should the need arise. Such was the case with McDonald's in Japan. Its 'Golden Arches' trademark was registered by an enterprising Japanese company. Only after a lengthy and costly legal action with a trip to the Japanese Supreme Court was McDonald's able to regain the exclusive right to use the trademark in Japan. After having to 'buy' its trademark for an undisclosed amount, McDonald's maintains a very active programme to protect its trademarks. Many businesses fail to understand that most countries do not follow the principle that ownership is established by prior use or that registration and legal ownership in one country does not necessarily mean ownership in another.

prior use versus registration

In many code-law countries, ownership is established by registration rather than by prior use – the first to register a trademark or other property right is considered the rightful owner. In the United States, a common-law country, ownership of intellectual property

key terms

trademark
registered 'mark' or 'logo' for a company or business

patent
any product or formula/ technology registered with the relevant office that establishes who possesses the right of ownership

rights is established by prior use – whoever can establish first use is typically considered the rightful owner. In Jordan a trademark belongs to whoever registers it first in that country. Thus, you can find a 'McDonald's' restaurant, 'Microsoft' software and 'Safeway' groceries all legally belonging to a Jordanian.[23] A company that believes it can always establish ownership in another country by proving it used the trademark or brand name first is wrong and risks the loss of these assets. It is best to protect intellectual property rights through registration. Several international conventions provide for simultaneous registration in member countries.

international conventions

Many countries participate in international conventions designed for mutual recognition and protection of intellectual property rights. There are three major international conventions.

1 The **Paris Convention** for the Protection of Industrial Property, commonly referred to as the Paris Convention, is a group of 100 nations that have agreed to recognise the rights of all members in the protection of trademarks, patents and other property rights. Registration in one of the member countries ensures the same protection afforded by the home country in all the member countries.

2 The **Madrid Arrangement** established the Bureau for International Registration of Trademarks. There are some 26 member countries in Europe that have agreed to automatic trademark protection for all members. Even though the United States is not a participant of the Madrid Arrangement, if a subsidiary of a US company is located in one of the member countries, the subsidiary could file through the membership of its host country and thereby provide protection in all 26 countries for the US company.

3 The **Inter-American Convention** includes most of the Latin American nations and the United States. It provides protection similar to that afforded by the Paris Convention.

With these three agreements, two multicountry patent arrangements have streamlined patent procedures in Europe. The Patent Cooperation Treaty (PCT) facilitates the application of patents among its member countries. The European Patent Convention (EPC) establishes a regional patent system allowing any nationality to file a single international application for a European patent. Once the patent is approved, it has the same effect as a national patent in each individual country designated on the application.

In addition, the European Union (EU) has approved its Trademark Regulation, which will provide intellectual property protection throughout all member states. Companies have a choice between relying on national systems, when they want to protect a trademark in just a few member countries, or the European system, when protection is sought throughout the EU. Trademark protection is valid for 10 years and is renewable. However, if the mark is not used for five years, protection is forfeited.[24]

commercial law within countries

When doing business in more than one country, a marketer must remain alert to the different legal systems. This problem is especially troublesome for the marketer who formulates a common marketing plan to be implemented in several countries. Although differences in languages and customs may be negated, legal differences between countries may still prevent a standardised marketing programme.

marketing laws

All countries have laws regulating marketing activities in promotion, product development, labelling, pricing and channels of distribution. In some, there may be only a few laws, with lax enforcement; in others, there may be detailed, complicated rules to follow that are stringently enforced. There often are vast differences in enforcement and interpretation

among countries having laws covering the same activities. Laws governing sales promotions in the EU offer good examples of such diversity.

In Austria, **premium offers** to consumers come under the discount law that prohibits any cash reductions that give preferential treatment to different groups of customers. Because most premium offers would result in discriminatory treatment of buyers, they normally are not allowed. Premium offers in Finland are allowed with considerable scope as long as the word 'free' is not used and consumers are not coerced into buying products. France also regulates premium offers, which are, for all practical purposes, illegal because it is illegal to sell for less than cost price or to offer a customer a gift or premium conditional on the purchase of another product. Furthermore, a manufacturer or retailer cannot offer products different from the kind regularly offered (i.e. a detergent manufacturer cannot offer clothing or kitchen utensils). German law covering promotion in general is about as stringent as can be found. Building on an 80-year-old statute against 'unfair competition', the German courts currently prevent businesses from offering all sorts of incentives to lure customers. Most incentives that target particular groups of customers are illegal, as are most offers of gifts.[25]

GOING INTERNATIONAL 6.8

Chinese court hands victory to Nike in trademark case

Nike, the US sports clothing company, has won a controversial court order in China to prevent a Spanish company from manufacturing and exporting clothing from the mainland using the 'Nike' name. The Spanish company, Cidesport, owns the right to use the Nike name in Spain and had been planning to sell the goods made in China solely in its home country, according to evidence before the court.

However, the court ruled that the sample of the goods in China had breached Nike's China registered trademark.

'The protection of the brand [in China] covers not only final consumption, but also the manufacturing of it,' said Tao Xinliang of Shanghai University.

Despite the unusual circumstances, the decision reflects the growing propensity of Chinese courts to uphold the intellectual property rights of foreign brands.

Cidesport had confirmed its right to use the name Nike on apparel in Spain in 1999 after a lengthy court battle with the much larger US company. But the court decision, announced on Chinese websites, will restrict the Spanish company's commercial options by preventing it from manufacturing in China, the global hub of the clothing industry.

The Spanish company argued that, as its products were not sold in China, it did not infringe Nike's China registered trademark. Cidesport had commissioned a factory in eastern China to manufacture a male ski jacket, affixed with the Nike label and Nike packaging. A lawyer advising Nike, Zhou Bin of the Hongqiao law firm in Shanghai, said the US company had found about 300 shipments ready for export in China which it considered were using the trademark illegally. Those shipments will be impounded by Chinese customs, and possibly destroyed, if the Spanish company loses a planned appeal. 'This is a very controversial issue internationally; in Holland, there was an identical case, which Nike lost,' said Mr Zhou.

Source: Richard McGregor, 'Chinese Court Hands Victory to Nike in Trademark Case', *Financial Times,* 21 February 2003, p. 9.

Multinational corporations are facing a growing variety of legislation designed to address environmental issues. Global concern for the environment extends beyond industrial pollution, hazardous waste disposal and rampant deforestation to include issues that focus directly on consumer products. **Green marketing** laws focus on product packaging and its effect on solid waste management and environmentally friendly products.

Germany has passed the most stringent green marketing laws that regulate the management and recycling of packaging waste. The new packaging law was introduced in three phases. The first phase requires all transport packaging such as crates, drums, pallets and Styrofoam containers to be accepted back by the manufacturers and distributors for recycling. The second phase requires manufacturers, distributors and retailers to accept all returned secondary packaging, including corrugated boxes, blister packs, all packaging designed to prevent theft, packaging for vending machine applications and packaging for promotional purposes. The third phase requires all retailers, distributors and manufacturers to accept returned sales packaging including cans, plastic containers for dairy products, foil wrapping, Styrofoam packages and folding cartons such as cereal boxes.[26]

The **green dot programme** mandates that the manufacturer must ensure a regular collection of used packaging materials directly from the consumer's home or from designated local collection points. A green dot on a package will identify those manufacturers participating in this programme. France, Belgium, Denmark and Austria have similar regulations to deal with solid waste disposal.[27]

key terms

Green marketing
marketing decisions that take the environment into consideration

green dot programme
a sign (logo) that shows that the product adheres to Green marketing

anti-trust laws
prevent businesses from creating unjust monopolies or competing unfairly in the marketplace

European Court of Justice
an institution of the European Union

anti-trust: an evolving issue

With the exception of the United States and some European countries, **anti-trust laws** have been either non-existent or unenforced in most of the world's countries for the better part of the twentieth century. However, the European Union has begun to actively enforce its anti-trust laws. Anti-monopoly, price discrimination, supply restrictions and full-line forcing are areas in which the **European Court of Justice** has dealt severe penalties. For example, before Procter & Gamble was allowed to buy VP-Schickedanz AG, a German hygiene products company, it had to agree to sell off one of the German company's divisions that produced Camelia, a brand of sanitary napkin. P&G already marketed a brand in Europe, and the Commission was concerned that allowing it to keep Camelia would give it a controlling 60 per cent of the German sanitary products market and 81 per cent of Spain's.[28] In another instance, Michelin was fined €630 000 ($700 000) for operating a system of discriminatory rebates to Dutch tyre dealers. Similar penalties have been assessed against such companies as United Brands for price discrimination and F. Hoffmann-LaRoche for non-cost-justified fidelity discounts to its dealers.

legal environment of the European Union

The concept of free competition is a fundamental element in the Rome Treaty, which embodies the premise that any restriction on free competition is intrinsically reprehensible. There are in practice some exceptions, but the principle itself is that of positive general condemnation of any limits on competition. Article 85(1) of the Treaty declares:

> The following shall be prohibited as incompatible with the Common Market: all agreements between undertakings, decisions by associations of undertakings and concerted practices which may affect trade between member states and which had as their object or effect the prevention, restriction or distortion of competition within the Common Market.

Article 85 deals with agreements, between two or more parties, that constitute restrictive practices. Article 86 is concerned with the abuse by individual organisations of a dominant trading position enjoyed in the Union, that is to say monopolies. Article 86 of the Rome Treaty declares:

Any abuse by one or more undertakings of a dominant position within the Common Market or
in a substantial part of it shall be prohibited.

the decision-making process

One practice that has developed has been that of giving publicity to any Commission decision in an attempt to influence and educate the market as a whole. Indeed, to the annoy-
ance of a number of firms, commissioners responsible for the competition rules have
often called press conferences to inform the public of decisions actually made, the state of
investigations in progress and, indeed, those about to begin.

When an investigation is launched, the Commission is not required to ask for the cooperation of the company concerned. It can be brusque, enter premises of the company to
examine books and other business records, take copies of extracts from these documents
and ask for oral explanations on the spot. This is known as 'the dawn raid'.

State Aids State aids can result in an artificially low export price, and the consequences to industry in the country where such goods are sold are the same as those
caused by dumped goods. Like products may become uncompetitive and the industry
suffers injury.

In practice, all countries give aid to their export industries, and the Commission must be
aware that it cannot succeed in stamping out such practices. All it can do is to attempt to
reduce the more blatant forms of state aid. The Commission is particularly vigilant in
trying to remove state aid from interstate trade in the Common Market, because such an
aim is a fundamental part of the Rome Treaty.

Mergers The years after 1985 saw a wave of **mergers** in the European Union. However,
such mergers could threaten the existence of competition in important markets by giving
the newly merged company a dominant position. It was clear that national legislation was
inadequate for the control of many of the new mergers, because they were often transfrontier, whereas national legislation was confined to the territory of the individual
member state.

Companies considering merging were obliged to give the Commission prior notification,
after which the Commission was to operate under strict time limits. It had one month after
notification in which to decide whether to initiate proceedings, so that where it saw no
objection, the parties would receive the green light to go ahead promptly. If an investigation into the proposed merger was mounted, the Commission had four months in which
either to approve or block the merger. During the investigation period companies
concerned could propose changes in the merger arrangements that would make the
merger more acceptable to the Commission.

competition policy

Competition policy has three established objectives. As the Commission has stated, it aims
to keep the **Common Market** 'open and unified', i.e. to create a single market for the
benefit of industry and consumers. Second, it must 'ensure that at all stages of the
Common Market's development, there exists the right amount of competition'. By ensuring some degree of commercial rivalry, the Union can help European industry to be
competitive in world markets, as the competition will encourage firms to rationalise and
change. The third objective is to ensure that competition is subject to 'the principles of
fairness in the market place', by which the Commission means 'equality of opportunity for
all operators in the Common Market'. In practice, this means preventing companies from
setting up restrictive agreements and cartels or from abusing a dominant position.

The sheer complexity of the cases imposes a formidable strain on the Commission, as
the Continental Can decision demonstrated. The Continental Can Company, an American
packaging firm, acquired, via its Belgian subsidiary, control of the largest German

key terms

merger
when two
companies decide
to join together

common market
a free-trade area
with a common
external tariff,
international
labour mobility
and common
economic policies
among member
states

143

producer of packaging and metal boxes, Schalbach–Lubeca–Werke AG of Brunswick. It later acquired a majority holding in a Dutch company, Thomassen and Drijver–Verblifa NV of Deventer, which was the leading manufacturer of packaging material in the Benelux countries. The Commission felt that these mergers produced such a dominant position for Continental Can that it constituted an abuse, a violation of Article 86. Continental Can, however, appealed against the Commission decision to the European Court. The Court agreed with the Commission's legal reasoning, but found in favour of the company on the grounds that the Commission had got the facts of the case wrong.

The capacity of the Commission to fine heavily was amply demonstrated in the Tetra-Pak case. In July 1991, this Swedish/Swiss-based packaging company was fined €75 million for abusing its dominant position in breach of Article 86. Following a complaint from Elepak, one of Tetra-Pak's main competitors, the Commission concluded that Tetra-Pak had carried out a deliberate policy of eliminating actual or potential competitors in the aseptic and non-aseptic markets in machinery and cartons. Tetra-Pak's restrictive use of contracts enabled it to segment the European market and therefore charge prices that differed between state members by up to about 300 per cent for machines and up to about 50 per cent for cartons. Evidence gathered during the Commission's inquiry also showed that, at least in Italy and the United Kingdom, Tetra-Pak sold its 'Rex' non-aseptic products at a loss for a long time in order to eliminate competitors.[29]

summary

Vital to every marketer's assessment of a foreign market is an appreciation of the political environment of the country within which he or she plans to operate. Government involvement in business activities, especially foreign-controlled business, is generally much greater than business is accustomed to in the West. The foreign firm must strive to make its activities politically acceptable or it may be subjected to a variety of politically condoned harassment.

In addition to the harassment that can be imposed by a government, the foreign marketer frequently faces the problem of uncertainty of continuity in government policy. As governments change political philosophies, a marketing firm accepted under one administration may find its activities completely undesirable under another. The EU may aid European business in its foreign operations, and if a company is considered vital to achieving national economic goals, the host country often provides an umbrella of protection not extended to others. An unfamiliar or hostile political environment does not necessarily preclude success for a foreign marketer if the marketer's plans are such that the company becomes a local economic asset.

Business faces a multitude of problems in its efforts to develop a successful marketing programme. Not the least of these problems are the varying legal systems of the world and their effect on business transactions. Just as political climate, cultural differences, local geography, different business customs and the stage of economic development must be taken into account, so must such legal questions as jurisdictional and legal recourse in disputes, protection of industrial property rights, extended law enforcement and enforcement of anti-trust legislation by foreign governments. A primary marketing task is to develop a plan that will be enhanced, or at least not adversely affected, by these and other environmental elements. The myriad questions created by different laws and different legal systems indicate that the prudent path to follow at all stages of foreign marketing operations is one leading to competent counsel well versed in the intricacies of the international legal environment.

questions

1 Why would a country rather domesticate than expropriate?
2 How can government-initiated domestication be the same as confiscation?
3 What are the main factors to consider in assessing the dominant political climate within a country?
4 Why is a working knowledge of political party philosophy so important in a political assessment of a market? Discuss.
5 What are the most frequently encountered political risks in foreign business? Discuss.
6 What are the factors that influence the risk-reduction process in international marketing?
7 Discuss measures a company might take to lessen its political vulnerability.
8 Select a country and analyse it politically from a marketing viewpoint.
9 How does the international marketer determine which legal system will have jurisdiction when legal disputes arise?
10 Discuss some of the reasons why it is probably best to seek an out-of-court settlement in international commercial legal disputes rather than to sue.
11 Illustrate the procedure generally followed in international commercial disputes when settled under the auspices of a formal arbitration tribunal.
12 What are intellectual property rights? Why should a company in international marketing take special steps to protect them?

further reading

- J.J. Boddewyn, 'Political Aspects of MNE Theory', *Journal of International Business Studies*, 1988, 19(3): pp. 341-62.
- J.-C. Cosset and J. Roy, 'The Determinants of Country Risk Ratings', *Journal of International Business Studies*, 1991, 22(1), pp. 135-42.
- A. Hadjikhani and P. Ghauri, 'The Behaviour of International Firms in Socio-Political Environments in the European Union', *Journal of Business Research*, 2001, 52(3), pp. 263-75.

references

1 For an account of political change and potential effect on economic growth, see 'China: is Prosperity Creating a Freer Society?', *Business Week*, 6 June 1994, pp. 94-9.
2 Jean J. Boddewyn and Thomas L. Brewer, 'International-Business Political Behavior: New Theoretical Directions', *Academy of Management Review*, vol. 19, no. 1, 1994, pp. 119-43.
3 Niccolo d'Aguino, 'Italy's Political Future', *Europe*, June 1994, pp. 4-8.
4 Visit Pepsi's Russian website for the history of Pepsi in Russia: www.pepsi.ru.
5 Kent Granzin and John Painter, 'Motivational Influences on "Buy Domestic" Purchasing: Marketing Management Implications from a Study of Two Nations', *Journal of International Marketing*, 9(2), 2001, pp. 73-96.
6 Richard Whalen, 'The New Nationalism', *Across the Board*, January/February, 2002; and Harold James, *The End of Globalization: Lessons from the Great Depression* (Boston: Harvard University Press, 2001).
7 Amitaz Ghosh, 'The Mask of Nationalism', *Business India*, 1993 Anniversary Issue, pp. 47-50.
8 Peter J. Buckley and Pervez N. Ghauri (eds), *The Global Challenge for Multinational Enterprises* (Amsterdam: Elsevier, 1999).
9 Lars Oxelheim and Pervez Ghauri (eds), *European Union and the Race for Foreign Direct Investment in Europe* (Oxford: Elsevier, 2004).

10 'South Africa: Mandela's Early Decisions Will Be Key to Luring Outside Investment', *Business Week*, 16 May 1994, pp. 52-4.

11 Lars Oxelheim (ed.), *The Global Race for Foreign Direct Investment: Prospects for Future* (Berlin: Springer-Verlag, 1993).

12 Peter J. Buckley and Pervez N. Ghauri (eds), *The Global Challenge for Multinational Enterprises* (Amsterdam: Elsevier, 1999).

13 Sandeep Tyagi, 'The Giant Awakens: An Interview with Professor Jagdish Bhagwatti on Economic Reform in India', *Columbia Journal of World Business*, Spring 1994, pp. 14-23.

14 Rahul Jacob, 'Coke Adds Fizz to India', *Fortune*, 10 January 1994, pp. 14-15.

15 For a comprehensive review of political risk analysis, see Frederick Stapenhurst, 'Political Risk Analysis in North American Multinationals: An Empirical Review and Assessment', *The International Executive*, March-April 1995, pp. 127-45.

16 For a discussion of problems associated with hostile publics and infrastructure projects, see Amjad Hadjikhani, 'International Businesses and Political Crisis: Swedish MNCs in a Turbulent Market', *Acta Universitatis Uppsaliances*, series Studia Oeconomiae Negotiorum, no. 40, Uppsala, 1996.

17 Masayoshi Kanabayashi, 'Scandal Widens at GE Medical Venture in Japan: Four More Arrested as Firm Apologizes for Bribing Officials at University', *The Wall Street Journal*, 1 March 1991, p. A-10.

18 Goran Therborn, 'The World's Trader, the World's Lawyer: Europe and Global Processes', *European Journal of Social Theory*, November 2002, pp. 403-17.

19 See, for example, Mokhtar M. Metwally, 'Interest Free (Islamic) Banking: A New Concept in Finance', *Journal of Banking and Finance Law and Practice*, June 1994, pp. 119-28.

20 An interesting report on doing business in Islamic countries can be found in 'Fundamental Facts', *Business Traveller*, February 1994, pp. 8-10.

21 Rene David and John E.C. Brierley, *Major Legal Systems in the World Today* (London: The Free Press, 1968), p. 18.

22 Industrial property rights and intellectual property rights are used interchangeably. The more common term used today is intellectual property rights to refer to patents, copyrights, trademarks and so forth.

23 'If It's Fake, This Must Be Jordan', *Reuters News Service*, 27 February 1994.

24 'EU Trademark Regulation', *Business Europe*, 10-16 January 1994, p. 6.

25 'Consumer Protection Swaddled', *The Economist*, 24 July 1993, p. 67.

26 Steve Zwick, 'A Better Package Deal? Germany's Green Dot – a Symbol of Success in Re-cycling Business', *Time International*, 21 May 2001, p. 55.

27 Brandon Mitchener, 'Increasingly, Rules of Global Economy are set in Brussels', *The Wall Street Journal*, 23 April 2002, p. A1.

28 'P&G Will Drop Brand to Gain EU Takeover Clearance', Reuters News Service, 17 June 1994.

29 Keith Perry, *Business and the European Community* (Oxford: Made Simple, Butterworth-Heinemann, 1994), pp. 82-97.

section 3
assessing international market opportunities

chapter 7
Researching International Markets

Chapter Outline

Chapter Learning Objectives

What you should learn from Chapter 7

- Understand the factors involved in international marketing research
- The importance of marketing research in international marketing decisions
- How to handle the problems of availability and use of secondary data
- How to manage the international marketing research process
- Understand the differences in quantitative and qualitative research
- Multicultural sampling and its problems in less-developed countries
- How to estimate market demand
- How to analyse and use research information to draw useful conclusions
- The function of multinational marketing information systems
- How to use sources of available secondary data

Information is the key component in developing successful marketing strategies. Information needs range from the general data required to assess market opportunities to specific market information for decisions about product, promotion, distribution and price. A study of international marketing blunders leads to one conclusion – the majority of mistakes cited could have been avoided if the decision maker had better knowledge of the market.[1] The quality of information available varies from uninformed opinion, i.e. the marketer's self-reference criterion (SRC), to thoroughly researched fact. As an enterprise broadens its scope of operations to include international markets, the need for current, accurate information is magnified. A marketer must find the most accurate and reliable data possible within the limits imposed by time, cost and the present state of the art.[2]

key term

marketing
research
the systematic
gathering,
recording and
analysing of data
to provide
information useful
in marketing
decision making

Marketing research is the systematic gathering, recording and analysing of data to provide information useful in marketing decision making. When operating in foreign markets, the need for thorough information as a substitute for uninformed opinion is at least as important as it is in domestic marketing.

Generally, the tools and techniques for research remain the same for foreign and domestic marketing, but the environments within which they are applied are different. Rather than acquire new and exotic methods of research, the international marketing researcher must develop the ability for imaginative and deft application of tried and tested techniques in sometimes totally strange milieu. The mechanical problems of implementing foreign marketing research might vary from country to country, but the overall objectives for foreign and domestic marketing research are basically the same. Within a foreign environment, the frequently differing emphasis on the kinds of information needed, the often limited variety of appropriate tools and techniques available, and the difficulty of implementing the research process constitute the challenges facing most international marketing researchers.[3]

This chapter deals with the operational problems encountered in gathering information in foreign countries for use by international marketers. Emphasis is on those elements of data generation that usually prove troublesome in conducting research in an environment other than the home market. The section 'Multinational Marketing Information Systems' is followed by a summary of secondary sources available through public and private agencies.

breadth and scope of international marketing research

A basic difference between domestic and international marketing research is the broader scope needed for foreign research. Research can be divided into three types based on information needs:

1 general information about the country, area and/or market
2 information necessary to forecast future marketing requirements by anticipating social, economic and consumer trends within specific markets or countries, and
3 specific market information used to make product, promotion, distribution and price decisions and to develop marketing plans.

In domestic operations, most emphasis is placed on the third type, gathering specific market information, because the other data are often available from secondary sources.

A country's political stability, cultural attributes and geographical characteristics are some of the kinds of information not ordinarily gathered by domestic company marketing research departments but which are required for a sound assessment of a foreign country market. This broader scope of international marketing research entails collecting and assessing information that includes the following:

1 *Economic*: general data on growth of the economy, inflation, business cycle trends and the like, profitability analysis for the division's products, specific industry economic studies, analysis of overseas economies and key economic indicators for the home country and major foreign countries.
2 *Sociological and political climate*: a general non-economic review of conditions affecting the division's business. In addition to the more obvious subjects such as cultural differences, it also covers ecology, safety, leisure time and their potential impact on the division's business.
3 *Overview of market conditions*: a detailed analysis of market conditions the division faces, by market segment, including international.
4 *Summary of the technological environment*: a summary of the state-of-the-art technology as it relates to the division's business, carefully broken down by product segments.
5 *Competitors*: a review of competitors' market shares, methods of market segmentation, products and apparent strategies on an international scale.[4]

For the domestic marketer, most information such as this has been acquired after years of experience with a single market; but in foreign markets this information must be gathered for each new market.

There is a basic difference between information ideally needed and that which is collectible and/or used. Many firms engaged in foreign marketing do not make decisions with the benefit of the information listed. Some have neither the appreciation for information nor adequate time or money for the implementation of research. As a firm becomes more committed to international marketing and the cost of possible failure increases, greater emphasis is placed on research. Consequently, a global firm is or should be engaged in the most sophisticated and exhaustive kinds of research activities. Exhibit 7.1 illustrates the recent growth of foreign marketing research.

the research process

A marketing research study is always a compromise dictated by limits of time, cost and the present state of the art. The researcher must strive for the most accurate and reliable information within existing constraints. A key to successful research is a systematic and orderly approach to the collection and analysis of data. Whether a research programme is conducted in London or Jakarta, the research process should follow these steps:

1 define the research problem and establish research objectives
2 develop a research plan, how you are going to do the research
3 gather the relevant data from secondary and/or primary sources
4 analyse and interpret the collected data
5 draw findings and present the results.

GOING INTERNATIONAL 7.1

marketing research: to err is human (and marketer-like)

Understanding customers and their needs is the central marketing creed. However, it often happens that marketers and managers are very different from their customers – most products are developed by teams of like-minded people who may have little in common with the intended buyer. This can create problems for marketers during the decision-making process – problems that have been highlighted by consumer research, behavioural economics and social psychology. Here we examine two such pitfalls

False consensus

People tend to think that their own attitudes are more common than they really are. When people estimate what others like and do, their own attitudes sway their responses. In a 1993 study, US managers were asked to estimate various attributes of markets, including the percentage of beer sold in US supermarkets that was imported and the percentage of US households that purchased canned chilli. At the time of the study, only about 2 per cent of the beer sold in US supermarkets was imported. The executives, who tended to like and buy imported beer, gave an average estimate of 20 per cent. Canned chilli, on the other hand, was largely disliked and rarely purchased by US executives. While 40 per cent of US households buy it in a given year, the executives' average estimate was only 28 per cent. One explanation for this phenomenon is that it is easy for people to think of what they like and dislike and that they give these preferences extra weight. Another is that when they think of other people, they think of people they know well, who tend to be similar to them. A curious fact is that the false consensus effect occurs even when people are explicitly warned about it. The only way to overcome this effect is to use marketing research and observe the real data.

Overconfidence

The second error lies in failing to identify what we do not know. When executives in the study were asked to indicate how certain they were of their estimates, they were typically overconfident. Along with the estimates, executives provided 90 per cent confidence intervals (or upper and lower bounds for their estimates), representing their belief that the true value would fall, on average, nine out of ten times within these bounds. Overconfidence is not universal, but it is common. The best way to guard against it is to make explicit statements about how confident you are and to check how things turn out. You may start out being just as overconfident as the executives in the survey, but at least you have a chance to learn from your mistakes.

■ How many of your classmates drink coffee and how many drink tea? Write down your answers and then ask the class. Was there a false consensus in your estimate?

Source: adapted from Andrew Gershoff and Eric Johnson, 'Avoid the Trap of Thinking Everyone is Just Like You', *Financial Times Summer School*, 29 August 2003, p. 11.

Although the steps in a research programme are similar for all countries, variations and problems in implementation occur because of differences in cultural and economic conditions. While the problems of research in England or Canada may be similar to those in the United States, research in Germany, South Africa or Mexico may offer a multitude of very different and difficult distinctions. These distinctions become apparent with the first step in the research process – formulation of the problem. Exhibit 7.2 illustrates the marketing research process and its international dimensions.

Exhibit 7.1 Top 10 largest markets in terms of value of marketing research

	Country	2001 (millions)	2002 (millions)
1	United States	€5 082 ($6 129)	€5 229 ($6 307)
2	United Kingdom	€1 378 ($1 662)	€1 455 ($1 755)
3	Germany	€1 141 ($1 376)	€1 235 ($1 490)
4	France	€946 ($1 141)	€1 045 ($1 260)
5	Japan	€914 ($1 102)	€860 ($1 037)
6	Italy	€357 ($430)	€382 ($461)
7	Canada	€347 ($418)	€372 ($449)
8	Spain	€226 ($272)	€251 ($303)
9	China	NA	€250 ($302)
10	Australia	€206 ($249)	€226 ($272)
Emerging countries (excluding China)			
1	Mexico	€197 ($238)	€201 ($243)
2	Brazil	€182 ($220)	€156 ($188)
3	Korea	€90 ($108)	€99 ($120)
4	Taiwan	€67 ($81)	€68 ($82)
5	Hong Kong	€48 ($58)	€50 ($60)
6	India	€40 ($48)	€41 ($50)
7	Colombia	€38 ($46)	€39 ($47)
8	Chile	€33 ($40)	€33 ($40)
9	Singapore	€29 ($35)	€31 ($37)
10	Thailand	€26 ($31)	€26 ($32)

* Expenditure for research by marketing research companies, excluding work conducted in-house or by advertising agencies, universities, government departments or non-profit organisations.

Source: 'Research in Foreign Markets Sees Growth', *Marketing News*, 15 July, 2004, p. 11–13.

defining the problem and establishing research objectives

The research process should begin with a definition of the research problem and the establishment of specific research objectives. The major difficulty here is converting a series of business problems into tightly drawn and achievable research objectives.[5] In this initial stage, researchers often embark on the research process with only a vague grasp of the total problem.

This first step in research is more critical in foreign markets since an **unfamiliar environment** tends to cloud problem definition. Researchers either fail to anticipate the influence of the local culture on the problem or fail to identify the self-reference criterion (SRC) and so treat the **problem definition** as if it were in the researcher's home environment. In assessing some foreign business failures it is apparent that research was conducted, but the questions asked were more appropriate for the home market than for the foreign one. For example, Unilever introduced a super-concentrated detergent to the Japanese market only to find out that a premeasured package on which it was trying to differentiate its product was unacceptable to the market because it didn't dissolve in the wash, the product was not designed to work in a new, popular low-agitation washing machine and the 'fresh smell' positioning of the detergent was not relevant in Japan since most consumers hang their washing outside to dry in the fresh air.[6] Did the company conduct research? Yes. Were appropriate questions asked? No.

key terms

unfamiliar environment
environment with which a company is not familiar, especially when it is a foreign market

problem definition
explaining the research problem

Exhibit 7.2 The marketing research process and the international dimension

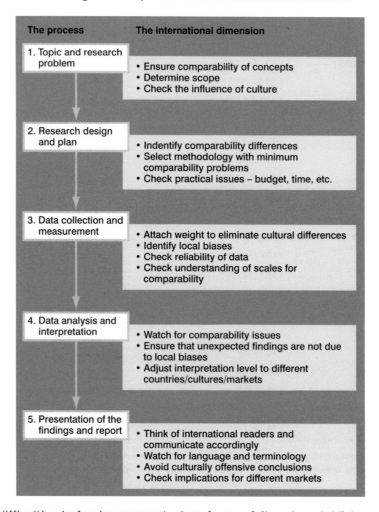

The process	The international dimension
1. Topic and research problem	• Ensure comparability of concepts • Determine scope • Check the influence of culture
2. Research design and plan	• Indentify comparability differences • Select methodology with minimum comparability problems • Check practical issues – budget, time, etc.
3. Data collection and measurement	• Attach weight to eliminate cultural differences • Identify local biases • Check reliability of data • Check understanding of scales for comparability
4. Data analysis and interpretation	• Watch for comparability issues • Ensure that unexpected findings are not due to local biases • Adjust interpretation level to different countries/cultures/markets
5. Presentation of the findings and report	• Think of international readers and communicate accordingly • Watch for language and terminology • Avoid culturally offensive conclusions • Check implications for different markets

key term

consumption patterns
how consumers buy a particular product

Other difficulties in foreign research stem from a failure to establish problem limits broad enough to include all relevant variables. Information on a far greater range of factors is necessary to offset the unfamiliar cultural background of the foreign market. Consider proposed research about **consumption patterns** and attitudes towards hot milk-based drinks. In the United Kingdom, hot milk-based drinks are considered to have sleep-inducing, restful and relaxing properties, and are traditionally consumed prior to bedtime. People in Thailand, however, drink the same hot milk-based drinks in the morning on the way to work and see them as being invigorating, energy-giving and stimulating. If one's only experience is in the United States, the picture is further clouded since hot milk-based drinks are frequently associated with cold weather, either in the morning or the evening, and for different reasons at each time of day. The market researcher must be certain the problem definition is sufficiently defined to cover the relevant range of response possibilities and not be clouded by his or her SRC.

developing a research plan

Once a research problem is clear and its objectives have been defined, it is important to plan the research process. This should be done irrespective of whether the company will undertake the work with its own resources or use outside agencies. The tasks to be undertaken should be specified and alternative methodologies should be evaluated. In this

process an appropriate **methodology** should be selected. For example, which type of research, quantitative or qualitative, should be done. The theories/models we can use to find answers to research questions are also to be identified here. While selecting these methodologies, the comparability of research findings and their usefulness must be kept in mind.

quantitative and qualitative research

Marketing research methods can be grouped into two basic types, quantitative and qualitative research. In both methods, the marketer is interested in gaining knowledge about the market.

In **quantitative research**, the respondent is asked to reply either verbally or in writing to structured questions using a specific response format such as 'yes' or 'no', or to select a response from a set of choices. Questions are designed to get a specific response to aspects of the respondent's behaviour, intentions, attitudes, motives and demographic characteristics. This type of quantitative or survey research provides the marketer with responses that can be presented with precise estimations. The structured responses received in a survey can be summarised in percentages, averages or other statistics. For example, 76 per cent of the respondents prefer product A over product B, and so on. Survey research is generally associated with quantitative research, and the typical instrument used is the questionnaire administered by personal interview, mail or telephone.

Qualitative research, on the other hand, is open-ended, in-depth and seeks unstructured responses that reflect the person's thoughts and feelings on the subject. Qualitative research interprets what the 'people in the sample are like, their outlooks, their feelings, the dynamic interplay of their feelings and ideas, their attitudes and opinions, and their resulting actions'.[7] The most often used forms of qualitative questioning are the focus group, interviews and case studies.

Qualitative research is also used in international marketing research to formulate and define a problem more clearly and to determine relevant questions to be examined in subsequent research. It is used where interest is centred on gaining an understanding of a market, rather than quantifying relevant aspects.

When a British childrenswear subsidiary of Sears was planning to enter the Spanish market, there was concern about the differences in attitudes and buying patterns of the Spanish from those in the United Kingdom, and about market differences that might possibly exist among Spain's five major trading areas of Barcelona, Madrid, Seville, Bilbao and Valencia. Because the types of retail outlet in Spain were substantially different from those in the United Kingdom, 'accompanied shopping interviews'[8] were used to explore shoppers' attitudes about different types of store. In the **interviews**, respondents were accompanied on visits to different outlets selling childrenswear. During the visit to each shop, the respondent talked the interviewer through what she was seeing and feeling. This enabled the interviewer to see the outlet through the eyes of the shopper, and to determine the criteria with which she evaluated the shopping environment and the products available. Information gathered in these studies and other focus group studies helped the company develop a successful entry strategy into Spain.

Qualitative research is also helpful in revealing the impact of sociocultural factors on behaviour patterns and to develop **research hypotheses** that can be tested in subsequent studies designed to quantify the concepts and relevant relationships uncovered in qualitative data collection. Research conducted by Procter & Gamble in Egypt offers an example of how qualitative research leads to specific points that can later be measured by using survey or quantitative research.

For years Procter & Gamble had marketed Ariel Low Suds brand laundry detergent to the 5 per cent of homes in the Egyptian market that had automatic washing machines. It planned to expand its presence in the Egyptian market and commissioned a study to (1) identify the most lucrative opportunities in the Egyptian laundry market and (2) develop

key terms

methodology
way of doing
market research

**quantitative
research**
structured
questioning,
producing answers
that can easily be
converted to
numerical data

**qualitative
research**
open-ended and
in-depth, seeking
unstructured
responses.
Expresses the
respondent's
thoughts and
feelings

interviews
when we talk to
people to get
information on
specific matters

**research
hypothesis**
a theory that can
be proved or
rejected via
research

the right concept, product, price, brand name, package and advertising copy once the decision was made to pursue a segment of the laundry market.

The 'Habits and Practices' study, P&G's name for this phase, consisted of home visits and discussion groups (qualitative research) to understand how the Egyptian housewife did her laundry. They wanted to know her likes, dislikes and habits (the company's knowledge of laundry practices in Egypt had been limited to automatic washing machines). From this study, it was determined that the Egyptian consumer goes through a very laborious washing process to achieve the desired results. Among the 95 per cent of homes that washed in a non-automatic washing machine or by hand, the process consisted of soaking, boiling, bleaching and washing each load several times. Several products were used in the process; bar soaps or flakes were added to the main wash, along with liquid bleach and bluing to enhance the cleaning performance of the poor-quality locally produced powders. These findings highlighted the potential for a high-performing detergent that would accomplish everything that currently required several products. The decision was made to proceed with the development and introduction of a superior-performing high-suds granular detergent.

Once the basic product concept (i.e. one product instead of several to do laundry) was decided on, the company needed to determine the best components for a marketing mix to introduce the new product. The company went back to **focus groups** to assess reactions to different brand names (they were considering Ariel, already in the market as a low-suds detergent for automatic washers, and Tide, which had been marketed in Egypt in the 1960s and 1970s) to get ideas about the appeal and relevant wording for promotions, and to test various price ranges, package design and size. Information derived from focus-group encounters helped the company eliminate ideas with low consumer appeal and focus on those that triggered the most interest. Further, the groups helped refine advertising and promotion wording to ensure clarity of communication through the use of everyday consumer language.

At the end of this stage, the company had well-defined ideas garnered from several focus groups, but did not have a 'feel' for the rest of those in the target market. Would they respond the same way the focus groups had? To answer this question, the company proceeded to the next step, a research programme to validate the relative appeal of the concepts generated from focus groups with a survey (quantitative research) of a large sample from the target market. Additionally, brand name, price, size and the product's intended benefits were tested in large sample surveys. Information gathered in the final **surveys** provided the company with the specific information used to develop a marketing programme that led to a successful product introduction and brand recognition for Ariel throughout Egypt.[9]

Qualitative and quantitative research is not always coupled as in the example of Procter & Gamble's research on Ariel. Qualitative research is also used alone where a small sample of carefully selected consumers is sufficient. For example, it is often difficult for respondents to know whether a product, flavour, concept or some other new idea is appealing if they have no experience with the issue being studied. To simply ask in a direct way may result in no response or, worse, a response that does not reflect how respondents would react if they had more experience.

In another case, Cadbury's, a UK firm, was looking for a way to give its chocolate cream liqueur a unique flavour. One idea was to add a hint of hazelnut flavouring. Yet when the company verbally suggested that the liqueur should be changed in this way consumers reacted negatively because they were unfamiliar with the mix of the two flavours. However, when taste tests were done without revealing what the extra flavours were, consumers loved the result.[10]

gathering secondary data

The breadth of many foreign marketing research studies and the marketer's lack of familiarity with a country's basic socioeconomic and cultural data result in considerable demand

key terms

focus groups
a group of people who are considered relevant for our product and can provide us with useful information

surveys
when we collect information through a list of questions

for information generally available from secondary sources in the Western countries. Unfortunately, such data are not as available in foreign markets. Most Western governments provide comprehensive statistics for their home markets; periodic censuses of population, housing, business and agriculture are conducted and, in some cases, have been taken for over 100 years. Commercial sources, trade associations, management groups, and state and local governments also provide the researcher with additional sources of detailed market information.

While data collection has only recently begun in many countries, it is improving substantially through the efforts of organisations such as the United Nations and the Organisation for Economic Cooperation and Development (OECD). As a country becomes more important as a market, a greater interest in basic data and better collection methods develop. The problems of availability, reliability, comparability of data and validating **secondary data** are described below.

With the emergence of Eastern European countries as potentially viable markets, a number of private and public groups are funding the collection of information to offset a lack of comprehensive market data. Several Japanese consumer goods manufacturers are coordinating market research on a corporate level and have funded 47 research centres throughout Eastern Europe. As market activity continues in Eastern Europe and elsewhere, market information will improve in quantity and quality. To build a **database** on Russian consumers, one Western firm used a novel approach to conduct a survey. It ran a questionnaire in Moscow's *Komsomolskaya Pravda* newspaper asking for replies to be sent to the company. The 350 000 replies received (3 000 by registered mail) attested to the willingness of Russian consumers to respond to market enquiries.

Availability of Data   A critical shortcoming of secondary data on foreign markets is the paucity of detailed data for many market areas. Much of the secondary data a Western marketer is accustomed to having about Western markets is just not available for many countries. Detailed data on the numbers of wholesalers, retailers, manufacturers and facilitating services, for example, are unavailable for many parts of the world; the same applies to data on population and income. Most countries simply do not have governmental agencies that collect, on a regular basis, the kinds of secondary data readily available in, say, the United States, the Netherlands, Germany and the Scandinavian countries. If such information is important, the marketer must initiate the research or rely on private sources of data. One research firm in Israel claims it can provide clients with information on everything from the types of women's undergarments that sell best to the most popular brand of cheese at the local supermarket.[11]

Reliability of Data   Available data may not have the level of reliability necessary for confident decision making for many reasons. Official statistics are sometimes too optimistic, reflecting national pride rather than practical reality, while tax structures and fear of the tax collector often adversely affect data.

China's National Statistics Enforcement Office recently acknowledged that it had uncovered about 60 000 instances of false statistical reports since beginning a crackdown on false data reporting several months earlier.[12] Seeking advantages or hiding failures, local officials, factory managers, rural enterprises and others filed fake numbers on everything from production levels to birth rates. For example, a petrochemical plant reported one year's output to be $20 million (€18 million), 50 per cent higher than its actual output of $13.4 million (€12.1 million).[13] An American survey team verified that 60 million frozen chickens had been imported into Saudi Arabia in one year, even though official figures reported only 10 million. A Japanese company found that 40 000 air conditioners had actually been imported, but official figures were underestimated by 30 000 units. Whether errors of such magnitude are intentional or simply the result of sloppy record keeping is not always clear.

key terms

secondary data
information that somebody else has collected, but that we can use for our purpose

database
a bank/storage of information on a particular issue

The European Union (EU) tax policies can affect the accuracy of reported data also. Production statistics are frequently inaccurate because the countries in the EU collect taxes on domestic sales. Thus, some companies shave their production statistics a bit to match the sales reported to tax authorities. Conversely, foreign trade statistics may be blown up slightly because many countries in the EU grant some form of export subsidy. Knowledge of such 'adjusted reporting' is critical for a marketer who relies on secondary data for forecasting or estimating market demand.

Comparability of Data   Comparability and currency of available data is the third shortcoming faced by international marketers. In most Western countries, current sources of reliable and valid estimates of socioeconomic factors and business indicators are readily available. In other countries, especially those less developed, data can be many years out of date as well as having been collected on an infrequent and unpredictable schedule. Further, even though many countries are now gathering reliable data, there are generally no historical series with which to compare the current information.

A related problem is the manner in which data are collected and reported. Too frequently, data are reported in different categories or in categories much too broad to be of specific value. The term 'supermarket', for example, has a variety of meanings around the world. In Japan a supermarket is quite different from its UK counterpart. Japanese supermarkets usually occupy two- or three-storey structures; they sell foodstuffs, daily necessities and clothing on respective floors. Some even sell furniture, electrical home appliances, stationery and sporting goods, and have a restaurant. General merchandise stores, shopping centres and department stores are different from stores of the same name in the United Kingdom or Germany. Furthermore, data from different countries are often not comparable. One report on the problems of comparing European cross-border retail store audit data states: 'Some define the market one way, others another; some define price categories one way, and others another. Even within the same research agency, auditing periods are defined differently in different countries.'[14] As a result, audit data are largely incomparable.

Validating Secondary Data   The shortcomings discussed here should be considered when using any source of information. Many Western countries have the same high standards of collection and preparation of data, but secondary data from any source, including Western countries, must be checked and interpreted carefully. As a practical matter, the following questions should be asked to judge the **reliability** of data sources effectively.

1 Who collected the data? Would there be any reason for purposely misrepresenting the facts?
2 For what purpose were the data collected?
3 How were the data collected (methodology)?
4 Are the data internally consistent and logical in light of known data sources or market factors?

Checking the consistency of one set of secondary data with other data of known validity is an effective and often used way of judging **validity**. For example, check the validity of the sale of baby products with the number of women of childbearing age and with birth rates, or the number of patient beds in hospitals with the sale of related hospital equipment. Such correlations can also be useful in estimating demand and forecasting sales.

In general, the availability and accuracy of recorded secondary data increase as the level of economic development increases. There are many exceptions: India is at a lower level of economic development than many countries but has accurate and complete development of government-collected data.

key terms

reliability
whether information/results of a study are trustworthy

validity
whether the measures used are reasonable to measure what it is supposed to measure

GOING INTERNATIONAL 7.2

international data: caveat emptor

The statistics used are subject to more than the usual number of caveats and qualifications concerning comparability that are usually attached to economic data. Statistics on income and consumption were drawn from national-accounts data published regularly by the United Nations (UN) and the Organisation for Economic Cooperation and Development (OECD). These data, designed to provide a 'comprehensive statistical statement about the economic activity of a country', are compiled from surveys sent to each of the participating countries (118 nations were surveyed by the UN). However, despite efforts by the UN and the OECD to present the data on a comparable basis, differences among countries concerning definitions, accounting practices and recording methods persist. In Germany, for instance, consumer expenditures are estimated largely on the basis of the turnover tax, while in the United Kingdom, tax-receipt data are frequently supplemented by household surveys and production data.

Even if data-gathering techniques in each country were standardised, definitional differences would remain. These differences are relatively minor except in a few cases; for example, Germany classifies the purchase of a television set as an expenditure for 'recreation and entertainment', while the same expenditure falls into the 'furniture, furnishings and household equipment' classification in the United States.

While income and consumption expenditures consist primarily of cash transactions, there are several important exceptions. Both income and expenditures include the monetary value of food, clothing and shelter received in lieu of wages. Also included are imputed rents on owner-occupied dwellings, in addition to actual rents paid by tenants. Wages and salaries, which make up the largest share of consumer income, include employer contributions to social security systems, private pension plans, life and casualty insurance plans and family allowance programmes. Consumer expenditures include medical services even though the recipient may make only partial payment; if, however, the same services are subsidised wholly by public funds, the transaction is listed as a government rather than a consumer expenditure.

Expenditures, as defined by both the UN (http://www.un.org) and the OECD (http://www.oecd.org), include consumption outlays by households (including individuals living alone) and private non-profit organisations. The latter include churches, schools, hospitals, foundations, fraternal organisations, trades unions and other groups that furnish services to households free of charge or at prices that do not cover costs.

Source: David Bauer, 'The Dimensions of Consumer Markets Abroad', *The Conference Board Record,* reprinted with permission.

gathering primary data

If, after seeking all reasonable secondary data sources, research questions can still not be adequately answered, the market researcher must collect **primary data**. The researcher may question the firm's sales force, distributors, middlemen and/or customers to get appropriate market information. In most primary data collection, the researcher questions respondents to determine what they think about some topic or how they might behave under certain conditions.

key term

primary data
data that has been collected for the systematic research at hand

The problems of collecting primary data in foreign countries are different only in degree from those encountered at home. Assuming the research problems are well defined and objectives are properly formulated, the success of primary research hinges on the ability of the researcher to get correct and truthful information that addresses the research objectives. Most problems in collecting primary data in international marketing research stem from cultural differences among countries, and range from the inability of respondents to communicate their opinions to inadequacies in questionnaire translation (see Exhibit 7.3).

Exhibit 7.3 Problems with gathering primary data

Sampling

Ability to communicate opinions

Willingness to respond

Problems of gathering primary data

Multicultural research – a special problem

Language and comprehension

Ability to Communicate Opinions   The ability to express attitudes and opinions about a product or concept depends on the respondent's ability to recognise the usefulness and value of such a product or concept. It is difficult for a person to formulate needs, attitudes and opinions about goods whose use may not be understood, that are not in common use within the community or that have never been available. For example, it may be impossible for someone who has never had the benefits of some type of air conditioning in the home to express accurate feelings or provide any reasonable information about purchase intentions, or likes and dislikes concerning electric air conditioning. The more complex the concept, the more difficult it is to design research that will help the respondent communicate meaningful opinions and reactions. Under these circumstances, the creative capabilities of the foreign marketing researcher are challenged.

Willingness to Respond   Cultural differences offer the best explanation for the unwillingness or the inability of many to respond to research surveys. The role of the male, the suitability of personal gender-based enquiries, and other gender-related issues can affect willingness to respond. In some countries, the husband not only earns the money, but also dictates exactly how it is to be spent. Because the husband controls the spending, it is he, not the wife, who should be questioned to determine preferences and demand for many consumer goods.

In some cultures, women would never consent to be interviewed by a male or a stranger. A French Canadian woman does not like to be questioned and is likely to be reticent in her responses. In some societies, a man would certainly consider it beneath his dignity to discuss shaving habits or brand preference in personal clothing with anyone and, most emphatically, not with a female interviewer.

Anyone asking questions about any topic from which tax assessment could be inferred is immediately suspected of being a tax agent. Citizens of many Western countries do not feel the same legal and moral obligations to pay their taxes. So, tax evasion is an accepted

practice for many and a source of pride for the more adept. Where such an attitude exists, taxes are arbitrarily assessed by the government, which results in much incomplete or misleading information being reported. One of the problems revealed by the government of India in a recent population census was the under-reporting of tenants by landlords trying to hide the actual number of people living in houses and flats. The landlords had been subletting accommodations illegally and were concealing their activities from the tax department.

In many European countries, such information is seldom if ever released and then most reluctantly. Attempts to enlist the cooperation of retailers in setting up a store sample for shelf inventory and sales information ran into strong resistance because of suspicions and a tradition of competitive secrecy. The resistance was overcome by the researcher's willingness to approach the problem step by step. As the retailer gained confidence in the researcher and realised the value of the data gathered, more and more necessary information was provided.

Although such cultural differences may make survey research more difficult to conduct, it is possible. In some communities, locally prominent people could open otherwise closed doors; in other situations, professional people and local students have been used as interviewers because of their knowledge of the market. As with most of the problems of collecting primary data, the difficulties are not insurmountable to a researcher aware of their existence.

Sampling in Field Surveys   The greatest problem of **sampling** stems from the lack of adequate **demographic data** and available lists from which to draw meaningful samples. If current reliable lists are not available, sampling becomes more complex and generally less reliable. In many countries, telephone directories, cross-index street directories, census tract and block data, and detailed social and economic characteristics of the population being studied are not available on a current basis if at all.

To add to the confusion, in some South American, Mexican and Asian cities, street maps are unavailable, and, in some Asian metropolitan areas, streets are not identified nor are houses numbered. In contrast, one of the positive aspects of research in Japan and Taiwan is the availability and accuracy of **census data** on individuals. In these countries, when a household moves it is required to submit up-to-date information to a centralised government agency before it can use communal services such as water, gas, electricity and education.

The effectiveness of various methods of communication (mail, telephone and personal interview) in surveys is limited. In many countries, telephone ownership is extremely low, making telephone surveys virtually worthless unless the survey is intended to cover only the wealthy. In some countries, fewer than 5 per cent of residents – only the wealthy – have telephones.

The problem of sampling was best summarised by one authority on research in Saudi Arabia who commented that probability sampling there was very difficult, if not impossible. The difficulties are so acute that non-probabilistic sampling becomes a necessary evil.[15] The kinds of problem encountered in drawing a random sample include:

- no officially recognised census of population
- no other listings that can serve as sampling frames
- incomplete and out-of-date telephone directories
- no accurate maps of population centres; thus, no cluster (area) samples can be made.

Furthermore, door-to-door interviewing in Saudi Arabia is illegal. While all the conditions described do not exist in all countries, they illustrate why the collection of primary data requires creative applications of research techniques when expanding into many foreign markets.[16]

key terms

sampling
selection of respondents

demographic data
information on the demographics of a country/city/area

census data
a record of population and its breakdown

Language and Comprehension

The most universal survey sampling problem in foreign countries is the language barrier. Differences in idiom and the difficulty of exact translation create problems in eliciting the specific information desired and in interpreting the respondents' answers. Equivalent concepts may not exist in all languages. Family, for example, has different connotations in different countries. In northern Europe and the United States, it generally means only the parents and children. In Italy and many Latin countries it could mean the parents, children, grandparents, uncles, aunts, cousins and so forth. The names for family members can have different meanings depending on the context within which they are used. In the Italian and many Asian cultures, aunt and uncle are different for the maternal and paternal sides of the family. The concept of affection is a universal idea but the manner in which it is manifest in each culture may differ.

Literacy poses yet another problem; in some developing countries with low literacy rates, written questionnaires are completely useless. Within countries, too, the problem of dialects and different languages can make a national questionnaire survey impractical. In India, there are 25 official languages and more than 50 unofficial ones.

The obvious solution of having questionnaires prepared or reviewed by someone fluent in the language of the country is frequently overlooked. In one such case, a German respondent was asked the number of 'washers' (washing machines) produced in Germany for a particular year; the reply reflected the production of the flat metal disc. Marketers use three different techniques – back translation parallel translation and decentring – to help ferret out translation errors.

- ◼ *Back translation.* In **back translation** the questionnaire is translated from one language to another, then a second party translates it back into the original. This pinpoints misinterpretations and misunderstandings before they reach the public. A soft-drink company wanted to use a very successful Australian advertising theme, 'Baby, it's cold inside', in Hong Kong. It had the theme translated from English into Cantonese by one translator and then retranslated by another from Cantonese into English, where the statement came out, 'Small mosquito, on the inside it is very cold'. Although 'small mosquito' is the colloquial expression for small child in Hong Kong, the intended meaning was lost in translation.
- ◼ *Parallel translation.* Back translations may not always ensure an accurate translation because of commonly used idioms in both languages. **Parallel translation** is used to overcome this problem. In this process, more than two translators are used for the back translation; the results are compared, differences discussed and the most appropriate translation selected.
- ◼ *Decentring.* The **decentring** refers to a successive iteration process of translation and retranslation of a questionnaire, each time by a different translator. The process is as follows: an English version is translated into French and then translated back to English by a different translator. The two English versions are compared and, where there are differences, the original English version is modified and the process is repeated. If there are differences between the two English versions, the original English version of the second iteration is modified and the process of translation and back translation is repeated. The process continues to be repeated until an English version can be translated into French and back translated, by a different translator, into the same English. In this process, the wording of the original instrument undergoes a change and the version that is finally used and its translation have equally comprehensive and equivalent terminologies in both languages.

Because of cultural and national differences, confusion can just as well be the problem of the researcher as of the respondent. The question itself may not be properly worded in the English version. One classic misunderstanding, which occurred in a *Reader's Digest* study of consumer behaviour in Western Europe, resulted in a report that France and Germany

key terms

back translation
text translated into another language, then translated back to the original language by another party. Helps to pinpoint misinterpretation and misunderstandings

parallel translation
when more than two translators are used for a back translation, and a comparison of the results is undertaken

decentring
a successive iteration process of translation and retranslation of a questionnaire, each time by a different translator

GOING INTERNATIONAL 7.3

bringing product development closer to marketing research

Philips, a huge multinational with a net income of €1172 million in the third quarter of 2004, is definitely one of the leaders of European industry and research. The company has 1500 'creative' research staff, mainly scientists, in 13 laboratories, who are funded by a research budget of €300 million a year. It owns 65 000 patents and claims illustrious lists of inventions such as high-speed transistors for mobile phones and plastic semiconductors. However, despite these impressive resources and achievements, the company has a poor record of turning scientific brilliance into profits, and many of the electronics and electrical goods the company helped to invent are being commercialised by US venture capitalists. To combat the problem and to build up a market-oriented research effort, it developed the following strategies.

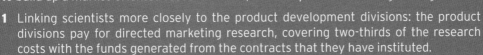

Research at Philips, Eindhoven
Photo: Philips

1 Linking scientists more closely to the product development divisions: the product divisions pay for directed marketing research, covering two-thirds of the research costs with the funds generated from the contracts that they have instituted.

2 Chief technology officers, who work in each product division, scout for new technologies, devised either in Philips or outside, that could help the company's commercial efforts. These people have extensive business experience, which provides them with a different perspective from the scientists. They set targets for the ideas being pursued by the laboratories and timetables for potential commercialisation.

3 Business development officers form a potential conduit between Philips research staff and other businesses with which Philips might want to form a partnership to commercialise particular ideas. Such partnerships are regarded as beneficial for Philips as sometimes other companies are in a better position to take on its scientific ideas than Philips itself.

4 Quantifying output of research employees: this approach is a controversial one because it is difficult to say what constitutes success. However, many think that this effort is worthwhile as part of the interest in getting away from valuing research solely in terms of how much is being spent. Additional factors that are being taken into account are licensing income, patent registrations, publications of scientific papers and revenue coming from scientific ideas.

■ Do you think these changes in Philips' strategy would enable it to capitalise better on its research activities?

Source: adapted from N. Buckley, 'The Need to Harvest Homegrown Creativity', *Financial Times*, 22 March 2001, p. 9.

consumed more spaghetti than did Italy. This rather curious and erroneous finding resulted from questions that asked about purchases of 'packaged and branded spaghetti'. Italians buy their spaghetti in bulk, the French and Germans buy branded and packaged spaghetti. Because the Italians buy little branded or packaged spaghetti, the results under-reported spaghetti purchases by Italians. However, the real question is what the researcher wanted to find out. Had the goal of the research been to determine how much branded and packaged spaghetti was purchased, the results would have been correct. However, because the goal was to know about total spaghetti consumption, the data were incorrect.

Multicultural Research: a Special Problem   As companies become international marketers and seek to standardise various parts of the marketing mix across several countries, multicultural studies become more important. A company needs to determine whether standardisation or adaptation of the marketing mix is appropriate. Thus, market characteristics across diverse cultures must be compared for similarities and differences before a company proceeds with a global marketing strategy. The research difficulties discussed thus far have addressed problems of conducting research within a culture. When engaging in **multicultural studies**, many of these same problems further complicate the difficulty of cross-cultural comparisons.

When designing multicultural studies, it is essential that the differences be taken into account. An important point to keep in mind when designing research to be applied across cultures is to ensure **comparability and equivalence** of results. Different methods may have varying reliabilities in different countries. It is essential that these differences be taken into account in the design of a multicultural survey. Such differences may mean that different research methods should be applied in individual countries. For example, a mail survey may have a high level of reliability in country A but not in country B, whereas a personal interview in country B will have an equivalent level of reliability as the mail survey in country A. Thus, a mail survey should be used in country A and a personal interview in country B. In collecting data from different countries, it is more important to use techniques with equivalent levels of reliability than to use the same techniques.[17]

The adaptations necessary to complete a cross-national study raise a serious question about the reliability of data gathered in cross-national research. There is evidence that insufficient attention is given not only to non-sampling errors and other problems that can exist in improperly conducted multicultural studies, but also to the appropriateness of consumer research measures that have not been tested in multicultural contexts.[18]

analysing and interpreting research information

Once data have been collected, the final steps are the analysis and interpretation of findings in light of the stated marketing problem. Both secondary and primary data collected by the market researcher are subject to the many limitations just discussed. In any final analysis, the researcher must take into consideration these factors and, despite their limitations, produce meaningful guides for management decisions.[19]

Accepting information at face value in foreign markets is imprudent. The meanings of words, the consumer's attitude towards a product, the interviewer's attitude or the interview situation can distort research findings. Just as culture and tradition influence the willingness to give information, they also influence the information given. Newspaper circulation figures, readership and listenership studies, retail outlet figures and sales volume can all be distorted through local business practice. To cope with such disparities, the foreign market researcher must possess three talents to generate meaningful marketing information.

First, the researcher must possess a high degree of cultural understanding of the market in which research is being conducted. In order to analyse research findings, the social customs, semantics, current attitudes and business customs of a society or a subsegment of a society must be clearly understood.

Second, a creative talent for adapting research findings is necessary. A researcher in foreign markets is often travelling for a week or two and is called on to produce results under the most difficult circumstances. Ingenuity and resourcefulness, willingness to use 'catch as catch can' methods to get facts, patience, a sense of humour and a willingness to be guided by original research findings even when they conflict with popular opinion or prior assumptions are all considered prime assets in foreign marketing research.

Third, a sceptical attitude in handling both primary and secondary data is helpful. It might be necessary to check a newspaper press run over a period of time to get accurate circulation figures, or deflate or inflate reported consumer income in some areas by 25 to 50 per cent on the basis of observable socioeconomic characteristics.

key terms

multicultural studies
studies that are performed in different cultures

comparability and equivalence
information that is comparable and is understood in the same way

GOING INTERNATIONAL 7.4

marketing tool: the semantic differential

An important tool in attitudinal research, image studies and positioning decisions is the *semantic differential*. It was originally developed to measure the meaning that a concept – perhaps a political issue, a person, a work of art or, in marketing, a brand, product or company – might have for people in terms of various dimensions. As first presented, the instrument consisted of pairs of polar adjectives with a seven-interval scale separating the opposite members of each pair. For example:

Extremely good   ——————   Extremely bad

This instrument has been refined to obtain greater sensitivity through the use of descriptive phrases. Examples of such bipolar phrases for determining the image of a particular brand of beer are:

Something special   ——————   Just another drink
Local flavour   ——————   Foreign flavour
Really peps you up   ——————   Somehow doesn't pep you up

The number of word pairs varies considerably but may be as many as 50 or more. Flexibility and appropriateness to a particular study are achieved by constructing tailor-made word and phrase lists.

    Semantic differential scales have been used in marketing to compare images of particular products, brands, firms and stores against competing ones. The answers of all respondents can be averaged and then plotted to provide a 'profile', as shown below for three competing beers on four scales (actually, a firm would probably use more scales in such a study).

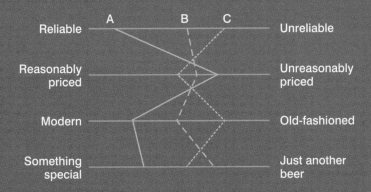

In this profile, brand A shows the dominant image over its competing brands in three of the four categories; however, the negative reaction to its price should alert the company to review pricing practices. Brand C shows a negative image, especially regarding the reliability of its product. The profile indicates that brand C is perceived as being distinctive from the other two brands. Probably the weakest image of all is that of brand B; respondents viewed this brand as having no distinctive image, neither good nor bad.

Simple, easy to administer and analyse, the semantic differential is useful not only in identifying segments and positions where there might be opportunities because these are currently not well covered by competitors, but it is also useful to a well-established firm – such as Coca-Cola – to determine the strength and the various dimensions of attitudes towards its product. Semantic differential scales are also useful in evaluating the effectiveness of a changed marketing strategy, such as a change in advertising theme. Here the semantic differential could be administered before the campaign and again after the campaign, and any changes in perception pinpointed.

■ Develop eight semantic differential scales for soft drinks, and then profile Coke and Pepsi. What differences do you perceive in the two brands? Are they important? Do you see any soft-drink untapped opportunities?

Source: Robert Hartley, *Marketing Mistakes*, 6th edn (New York: Wiley, 1995), pp. 139–40.

presenting the findings and results

Presentation of findings and results in a summarised and easy-to-understand manner is crucial to the success of research. The researcher has to put the research problem, the data collection and findings into a logical, consistent and persuasive report. Before writing the final report of the project, it is necessary to consider the purpose of the report and to whom it is addressed. The researcher has to convince the reader that he or she has done the job in a systematic and logical manner, and that the findings are reliable. This is particularly important in international marketing research, as the results and findings are to be understood and executed by international marketers and managers.

Culturally biased and offensive conclusions need to be avoided, especially in respect of local sensitivities. The report to managers must be concise and convincing. It should include a very short, maximum two pages, executive summary explaining the major issues, some interpretations on data, collected results and managerial implications.

responsibility for conducting marketing research

Depending on size and degree of involvement in foreign marketing, a company in need of foreign market research can rely on an outside foreign-based agency or on a domestic company with a branch within the country in question. It can conduct research using its own facilities or employ a combination of its own research force with the assistance of an outside agency.

Many companies have an executive specifically assigned to the research function in foreign operations; he or she selects the research method and works closely with foreign management, staff specialists and outside research agencies. Other companies maintain separate research departments for foreign operations or assign a full-time research analyst to this activity. For many companies, a separate department is too costly; the diversity of markets would require a large department to provide a skilled analyst for each area or region of international business operations.

A comprehensive review of the different approaches to multicountry research suggests that the ideal approach is to have local researchers in each country, with close coordination between the client company and the local research companies. This cooperation is important at all stages of the research project from **research design**, through data collection, to final analysis. Furthermore, two stages of analysis are necessary. At the individual country level, all issues involved in each country must be identified, and at the multicountry level, the information must be distilled into a format that addresses the client's objectives. Such recommendations are supported on the grounds that two heads are better than one and that multicultural input is essential to any understanding of multicultural

key term

research design
overall plan for relating a research problem to practical empirical research

data. With just one interpreter of multicultural data, there is the danger of one's self-reference criterion (SRC) resulting in data being interpreted in terms of one's own cultural biases.[20] Self-reference bias can affect the research design, **questionnaire design** and interpretation of the data.

If a company wants to use a professional marketing research firm, many are available. Most major advertising agencies and many research firms have established branch offices worldwide. There has also been a healthy growth in foreign-based research and consulting firms. An interesting aside on data collection agencies involves the changing role of the Central Intelligence Agency (CIA) since the demand for military surveillance has diminished in recent years. Members of the US Congress have suggested that the CIA should be active in protecting America's economic commercial interests worldwide and in gathering international trade data to improve the information base for US businesses.

key term

questionnaire design
formulating exact questions to be asked, often in survey research

GOING INTERNATIONAL 7.5

France has stolen a march on the US in economic intelligence

In a report to the US Congress earlier this month, the Central Intelligence Agency named the French services, along with the Israelis, as the most active in launching operations against American interests, both inside and outside the United States. Recently, the DGSE, the French secret service, has stepped up operations in areas such as Bosnia, Algeria and Russia.

The emphasis has continued to shift towards economic intelligence. The ability to intercept secret offers made by US armament firms to Middle Eastern countries has allowed French firms to propose better deals. In 1997, they broke into the lucrative Saudi defence market for the first time by signing a contract for the sale of 12 helicopters built by Eurocopter. The recent CIA report accused the French specifically of launching intelligence operations against US military contractors and high-technology firms. In the report, national security  specialist David E. Cooper describes the intelligence-gathering of a particular country, clearly identifiable as France, which 'recruited agents at the European offices of three US computer and electronic firms'.

According to sources, IBM in Brussels and Texas Instruments were two of those targets. Clearly, France is not the only country to seek such information. In 1994, President Bill Clinton asked the FBI to launch an economic counter-intelligence programme. Former DGSE director Admiral Pierce Lacoste told *The European*:

'It is part of an indirect strategy by the US. They want all the trumps. Initially their target was Japan. But now it is France, for two main reasons. First, France is seen as one of the most vocal and active countries over the strengthening of the European Union and a single currency; and second, because this country is organizing a new economic intelligence system.'

While continuing with traditional intelligence, French President Jacques Chirac set up a special economic and technological intelligence coordination body, inspired by the highly effective Japanese Ministry of International Trade and Industry. The Comité pour la Competitivité et la Securité Économique (CCSE) is led by seven 'wise men', including banker Bernard Esambert, Matra boss Jean-Luc Lagardère and Henri Martre, former chairman of Aérospatiale and author of a detailed study on economic intelligence.

'This is essentially the start of a cultural shift on the part of French industrial and commercial intelligence. But this process will take some time to come to fruition,' said Lacoste. 'Obviously, the French and future European intelligence would play some role in this. They could not allow the CIA to be the only secret service operating in that field'.

■ Do you think companies should have economic intelligence departments, to better forecast the demand?

Source: The European, 29 August–4 September 1996.

estimating market demand

In assessing current product demand and forecasting future demand, reliable **historical data** are required. As previously noted, the quality and availability of secondary data are frequently inadequate. Nevertheless, estimates of market size must be attempted in order to plan effectively. Despite limitations, there are approaches to demand estimation usable with minimum information. The success of these approaches relies on the ability of the researcher to find meaningful substitutes or approximations for the needed economic and demographic relationships. Some of the necessary but frequently unavailable statistics for assessing market opportunity and estimating demand for a product are current trends in market demand.

When the desired statistics are not available, a close approximation can be made using local production figures plus imports, with adjustments for exports and current inventory levels. These data are more readily available because they are commonly reported by the United Nations and other international agencies. Once approximations for sales trends are established, historical series can be used as the basis for projections of growth.[21] In any straight extrapolation, however, the estimator assumes that the trends of the immediate past will continue into the future. For example, if there has been 10 per cent growth per year, on average, in the last five years, we can expect that market will grow by 10 per cent also next year. In a rapidly developing economy, extrapolated figures may not reflect rapid growth and must be adjusted accordingly.

key terms

historical data
information over a period of time

analogy
reasoning from parallel cases/ examples

Analogy   Another technique is to estimate by **analogy**. This assumes that demand for a product develops in much the same way in all countries as comparable economic development occurs in each country. First, a relationship must be established between the item to be estimated and a measurable variable in a country that is to serve as the basis for the analogy. Once a known relationship is established, the estimator then attempts to draw an analogy between the known situation and the country in question. For example, suppose a company wanted to estimate the market growth potential for a beverage in country X, for which it had inadequate sales figures, but the company had excellent beverage data for neighbouring country Y. In country Y it is known that per capita consumption increases at a predictable ratio as per capita gross domestic product (GDP) increases. If per capita GDP is known for country X, per capita consumption for the beverage can be estimated using the relationships established in country Y. Caution must be used with analogy because the method assumes that factors other than the variable used (in this example GDP) are similar in both countries, such as the same culture, tastes, taxes, prices, selling methods, availability of products, consumption patterns and so forth. Despite the apparent drawbacks to analogy, it is useful where data are limited. For example, developments at the Dow Jones Stock Exchange in the US are often used to predict stock development in the UK.

Income Elasticity   Measuring the changes in the relationship between personal or family income and demand for a product can be used in forecasting market demand. In

income-elasticity ratios, the sensitivity of demand for a product to income changes is measured. The elasticity coefficient is determined by dividing the percentage change in the quantity of a product demanded by the percentage change in income. With a result of less than one, it is said that the income–demand relationship is relatively inelastic and, conversely, if the result is greater than one, the relationship is elastic. As income increases, the demand for a product increases at a rate proportionately higher than income increases. For example, if the income elasticity coefficient for recreation is 1.2, it implies that for each 1 per cent change in income, the demand for recreation could be expected to increase by 1.2 per cent; or if the coefficient is 0.8, then for each 1 per cent change in income, demand for recreation could be expected to increase only 0.8 per cent. The relationship also occurs when income decreases, although the rate of decrease might be greater than when income increases. Income elasticity can be very useful, too, in predicting growth in demand for a particular product or product group.

The major problem with this method is that the data necessary to establish elasticities may not be available. However, in many countries, income elasticities for products have been determined and it is possible to use the analogy method described (with all the caveats mentioned) to make estimates for those countries. Income elasticity measurements only give an indication of change in demand as income changes and do not provide the researcher with any estimate of total demand for the product.

As in the case of all methods described in this section, income elasticity measurements are no substitute for original market research when it is economically feasible and time permits. As more adequate data sources become available, as would be the situation in most of the economically developed countries, more technically advanced techniques such as multiple regression analysis or input–output analysis can be used.

multinational marketing information systems

Increased marketing activity by domestic and multinational firms has generated not only more data, but also a greater awareness of its need. In addition to the changes in the quantity and type of information needed, there has been an increase in competent agencies (many of them subsidiaries of Western marketing research firms) whose primary functions are to gather data. As firms become established, and their information needs shift from those necessary to make initial market investment decisions to those necessary for continuous operation, there is a growing demand for continuous sources of information both at the country operational level and at the worldwide corporate level. However, as the abundance of information increases, it reaches a point of 'information overload' and requires some systematic method of storing, interpreting and analysing data.

A company shift from decisions involving market entry to those involved in managing and controlling a number of different growing foreign markets requires greater emphasis on a continuous system designed to generate, store, catalogue and analyse information from sources within the firm and external to the firm for use as the basis of worldwide and country-oriented decision making. In short, companies have a need for a **multinational marketing information system (MMIS)**.

Conceptually, an MMIS embodies the same principle as any information system, that is, an interacting complex of people, machines and procedures designed to generate an orderly flow of relevant information and to bring all the flows of recorded information into a unified whole for decision making. The only differences from a domestic marketing information system are (1) scope – an MMIS covers more than one country – and (2) levels of information – an MMIS operates at each country level, with perhaps substantial differences among country systems, and at a worldwide level encompassing an entire international operation. The system (see Exhibit 7.4) includes a subsystem for each country designed for operational decision making – a country-level marketing information system. Each country

Exhibit 7.4 Multinational marketing information system

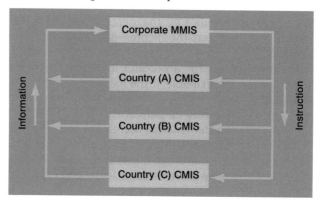

system also provides information to an MMIS designed to provide for corporate control and strategic long-range planning decisions.

In developing an MMIS, it is necessary to design an adequate *country marketing information system (CMIS)* for each country/market. Because of the vast differences among a company's various markets, each CMIS will probably have different data requirements. Once a CMIS is set for each country/market, then an overall MMIS for the worldwide operation is designed. Each level of management has substantially different data needs because country/market systems are designed to provide information for day-to-day operations, while the MMIS is concerned with broader issues of control and long-range strategic planning. However, the CMIS data are used not only for daily operations, but ultimately are transmitted to the MMIS to be included in overall planning decisions. Some of the most challenging tasks facing the developer of the MMIS are determining the kinds of data and the depth of detail necessary, and analysing how it should be processed. This implies that models for decision making have been thought through and are sufficiently specific to be functional.

An MMIS can be designed as a basic system that provides only a source of information or as a highly sophisticated system that includes specific decision models. Experience has shown that success is greater when a company begins with a basic system and continues perfecting it to the desired level of sophistication.

summary

The basic objective of the market research function is providing management with information for more accurate decision making. This objective is the same for domestic and international marketing. In international marketing research, however, achieving that objective presents some problems not encountered on the domestic front.

Consumer attitudes about providing information to a researcher are culturally conditioned. Foreign market information surveys must be carefully designed to elicit the desired data and at the same time not offend the respondent's sense of privacy. The concepts and ideas might have different meanings in different cultures. It is therefore particularly important in cases where research data or results from different markets are compared with each other. Besides the cultural and managerial constraints involved in gathering information for primary data, many foreign markets have inadequate and/or unreliable bases of secondary information.

Three generalisations can be made about the direction and rate of growth of marketing research in foreign marketing. First, both home-based and foreign management are increasingly aware of and accept the importance of marketing research's role in decision making. Second, there is a current trend towards the decentralisation of the research function to put control closer to the area being studied. Third, the most sophisticated tools and techniques are being adapted to foreign information gathering with increasing success. They are so successful, in fact, that it has become necessary to develop structured information systems to appreciate and utilise effectively the mass of information available.

appendix: sources of secondary data

For almost any marketing research project, an analysis of available secondary information is a useful and inexpensive first step. Although there are information gaps, particularly for detailed market information, the situation on data availability and reliability is improving. The principal agencies that collect and publish information useful in international business are presented here, with some notations of selected publications.

international organisations

A number of international organisations provide information and statistics on international markets. The **Statistical Yearbook**, an annual publication of the United Nations, provides comprehensive social and economic data for more than 250 countries around the world. Many regional organisations, such as the Organisation for Economic Cooperation and Development (OECD), the Pan American Union and the European Union, publish information, statistics and market studies relating to their respective regions. The United Nations *Investment Report* and *Development Report* present a lot of information every year. The European Union gathers information on all aspects of European trade issues that are public (see, for example, www.euromonitor.org).

chambers of commerce

In addition to government and organisational publications, many foreign countries maintain chamber of commerce offices in the European Union, functioning as permanent trade missions. These foreign chambers of commerce generally have research libraries available and are knowledgeable regarding further sources of information on specific products or marketing problems.

trade, business and service organisations

Foreign trade associations are particularly good sources of information on specific products or product lines. Many associations perform special studies or continuing services in collecting comprehensive statistical data for a specific product group or industry. Although some information is proprietary in nature and available only to members of an association, non-members frequently have access to it under certain conditions. Up-to-date membership lists providing potential customers or competitors are often available to anyone requesting them, and a listing of foreign trade associations is usually annotated at the end of a specific trade list.

Foreign service industries also supply valuable sources of information useful in international business. Service companies – such as commercial and investment banks, international advertising agencies, foreign-based research firms, economic research institutes, foreign carriers, shipping agencies and freight forwarders – generally regard the furnishing of current, reliable information as part of their service function. The banking industry in foreign countries is particularly useful as a source of information on current local economic situations. The Chase Manhattan Bank in New York periodically publishes a

key term

Statistical Yearbook
an annual publication of the United Nations, provides comprehensive social and economic data for more than 250 countries around the world

newsletter on such subjects as the European Union. There are several good independently published reports on techniques, trends, forecasts and other such current data. Many foreign banks publish periodic or special review newsletters relating to the local economy, providing a first-hand analysis of the economic situation of specific foreign countries. For example, the Krediet Bank in Brussels has published *Belgium, Key to the Common Market*, and the Banco National Commercio Exterior in Mexico has published *Mexico Facts, Figures and Trends*. Even though these publications are sometimes available without charge, they must usually be translated.

US Government

The US Government actively promotes the expansion of US business into international trade. In the process of keeping US businesses informed of foreign opportunities, the US Government generates a considerable amount of general and specific market data for use by international market analysts. The principal source of information from the US Government is the Department of Commerce, which makes its services available to US business in a variety of ways. First, information and assistance are available either through personal consultation in Washington, DC, or through any of the US and FCS (Foreign Commercial Service) district offices of the International Trade Administration (ITA) of the Department of Commerce located in key cities in the United States. Second, the Department of Commerce works closely with trade associations, chambers of commerce and other interested associations in providing information, consultation and assistance in developing international commerce. Third, the department publishes a wide range of information available to interested people at nominal cost.

1 **International Economic Indicators**. Quarterly reports providing basic data on the economy of the United States and seven other principal industrial countries. Statistics included are gross national product, industrial production, trade, prices, finance and labour. This report measures changes in key competitive indicators and highlights economic prospects and recent trends in the eight countries.

2 **Business Information Service for the Newly Independent States (BISNIS)**. This is a one-stop source for firms interested in obtaining assistance on selling in the markets of the Newly Independent States of the former Soviet Union. BISNIS provides information on trade regulations and legislation, defence conversion opportunities, commercial opportunities, market data, sources of financing, government and industry contacts and US Government programmes supporting trade and investment in the region.

3 **National Trade Data Bank (NTDB)**. The Commerce Department provides a number of the data sources mentioned above and others in its computerised information system in the *National Trade Data Bank* (NTDB). The NTDB is a 'one-stop' source for export promotion and international trade data collected by 17 US Government agencies. Updated each month and released on two CD-ROMs, the NTDB enables a user with an IBM-compatible personal computer equipped with a CD-ROM reader to access more than 100 000 trade-related documents. The NTDB contains:

   ■ the latest census data on US imports and exports by commodity and country
   ■ the complete Central Intelligence Agency (CIA) *World Factbook*
   ■ current market research reports compiled by the US and Foreign Commercial Service
   ■ the complete *Foreign Traders Index*, which contains over 55 000 names and addresses of individuals and firms abroad that are interested in importing US products
   ■ State Department country reports on economic policy and trade practices

- the publications *Export Yellow Pages, A Basic Guide to Exporting* and the *National Trade Estimates Report on Foreign Trade Barriers*
- the *Export Promotion Calendar*, and
- many other data series.

This source can be reached through the Internet (http://www.stat-usa.gov/).

A number of research agencies specialising in detailed information on foreign markets provide information services on a subscription basis. A listing of commercial and investment banks in foreign countries, as well as a detailed list of special-purpose research institutes, can be found in *The European World Yearbook* (European Publications, London). Listed below are sources of information that are helpful and available for purchase or subscription.

other sources: abstracts, bibliographies and indexes

The Economist Intelligence Unit, London. Covers Economist Intelligence publications.

F & S Index International and *F & S Europe*. Cleveland: Predicasts. Monthly with quarterly and annual compilations. Indexes foreign companies, and product and industry information with emphasis on sources, giving data or statistics.

Business International. Worldwide Economic Indicators. New York. Annual: economic, demographic, trade and other statistics.

Consumer Europe. London: Euromonitor Publications. Annual: marketing indicators and trends for various markets.

European Marketing Data and Statistics. London: Euromonitor Publications. Annual.

International Marketing Data and Statistics. London: Euromonitor Publications. Annual: covers the Americas, Asia, Africa and Australia. Includes data on retail and wholesale sales, living standards and general consumer marketing data.

The Markets of Asia/Pacific: Thailand, Taiwan, People's Republic of China, Hong Kong, South Korea, the Philippines, Indonesia, Singapore and Malaysia. London: The Asia Pacific Centre Ltd, New York: *Facts on File*, various years. An excellent source for data on prices, retail sales, consumer purchases and other country information.

Internet sources

1 Michigan State University's Center for International Business provides extensive and comprehensive links to a wide range of information sources relevant to international marketing and international business. Links are provided to numerous newspapers and journals (including academic journals) throughout the world; an extremely large number of country/market reports; information on various regional trading blocs; academic papers on international marketing/business; and numerous other linkages. This site can be reached at http://globaledge.msu.edu/ibrd/ibrd.asp.

2 World Class Supersite, provides 'instant free access and step-by-step commentary for 1025 top business sites from 95 countries, chosen based on usefulness to world commerce, timeliness, ease of use, and presentation'. The site comprises seven main sections covering the following areas (and can be reached at http://web.idirect.com/~tiger/supersite.htm).

- Reference (market guides, regional institutions, US government megasites).
- News (world business dailies, world business magazines, business mags by country).
- Learning (Global MBA Elite, notable business institutes).
- Money (world and US stocks, stocks by country, foreign investment).
- Trade (world business directories, cargo, business tools).
- Networking (gathering places, bilateral organisations, leads and tenders).
- World-beaters (MNC manufacturers, MNC services, SMEs, trade services).

3 Since the early 1970s, public opinion surveys have been conducted on behalf of the European Commission at least twice a year in all member states of the European Union. Cross-national comparison of a wide range of social and political issues, including European integration, life satisfaction, social goals, currency issues, working conditions, and travel. This site can be reached at http://www.europa.eu.int.

4 Internet Resources for Exporters is a comprehensive list of export-related resources on the net including links to megasites, country and company information, trade finance, shipping and logistics resources, international legal sites, chambers of commerce, international trade forums, and export reference resources. This site can be reached at http://www.exportusa.com.

5 *The World Factbook* provides macro- and microeconomic data by the CIA, including economic overviews of 260 countries, sectoral briefings, government and defence information. This site can be reached at http://www.odci.gov/cia/publications/factbook.

6 The Web of Culture page is devoted to improving executives' understanding of cross-cultural communications, which is a 'critical success factor' in international marketing, while the other sites reviewed here focus on the economic, business and trade environments of different countries. The site is a useful starting point for those seeking to better their understanding of different national cultures before visiting overseas markets and for students studying the cultural aspects of international marketing. This site can be reached at http://www.webofculture.com.

7 The Organisation for Economic Cooperation and Development provides at its website statistics, economic indicators and other information on member countries. The site can be reached at http://www.oecd.org.

8 The World Bank has more than 14 000 documents containing economic, social, national and regional information on more than 200 countries. The site can be reached at http://www.worldbank.org.

9 The Census Bureau has extensive data at the US level and substantial data for states and counties, somewhat less for cities (e.g. incorporated places). It releases data for the very smallest areas (census tracts, block groups, and blocks). The US Bureau of Census provides several resources available on its Census 2000 Gateway to assist people to narrow their search for Census 2000 data including the release schedules by date, geography and subject. The site can be reached at http://www.census.gov.

10 The British Household Panel Survey began in 1991 and is conducted annually by interview and questionnaire with a national representative sample of some 5 500 households and 10 300 individuals. It covers topics like labour market behaviour, income and wealth, housing, health and socioeconomic values. The site can be reached at http://www.iser.essex.ac.uk/bhps.

11 Euromonitor provides global consumer market intelligence. The website provides consumer industry market reports and online databases about manufacturers, retailers, distributors and suppliers. The databases can be a starting point for researching international markets. The site can be reached at http://www.euromonitor.com.

questions

1 Discuss how the shift from making 'market entry' decisions to 'continuous operations' decisions creates a need for different types of information and data. What assistance does an MMIS provide?

2 Using a hypothetical situation, illustrate how an MMIS might be established and how it would be used at different levels.

3 Discuss the breadth and scope of international marketing research. Why is international marketing research generally broader in scope than domestic marketing research?

4 What is the task of the international market researcher? How is it complicated by the foreign environment?

5 Discuss the stages of the research process in relation to the problems encountered. Give examples.

6 Why is the formulation of the research problem difficult in foreign market research?

7 Discuss the problems of gathering secondary data in foreign markets.

8 What are some of the problems created by language and the ability to comprehend in collecting primary data? How can an international market researcher overcome these difficulties?

9 Discuss how 'decentring' is used to get an accurate translation of a questionnaire.

10 Discuss when qualitative research may be more effective than quantitative research.

11 Sampling offers some major problems in market research. Discuss.

12 Select a country. From secondary sources compile the following information for at least a 10-year period prior to the present:
principal imports
principal exports
gross national product
chief of state
major cities and population
principal agricultural crop.

13 'The foreign market researcher must possess three essential capabilities to generate meaningful marketing information.' Discuss.

further reading

■ Tamer Cavusgil and Ajay Das, 'Methodological Issues in Empirical Cross-cultural Research: a Survey of the Management Literature and Framework', *Management International Review*, 1997, 37(1), pp. 71–96.

■ Samuel Craig and Susan Douglas, 'Conducting International Marketing Research in the Twenty-first Century', *International Marketing Review*, 2001, 18(1), pp. 80–90.

■ Rudolf Sinkovics, Elfriede Penz and Pervez Ghauri, 'Analyzing Textual Data in International Marketing Research', *Qualitative Market Research: An International Journal*, 2005, 8(1), pp. 9–38.

references

1 Tamer Cavusgil, Pervez Ghauri and Milind Agarwal, *Doing Business in Emerging Markets: Entry and Negotiation Strategies* (Thousand Oaks: Sage, 2002).

2 For a complete discussion of marketing research in foreign environments, see Susan P. Douglas and C. Samuel Craig, *International Marketing Research* (Chichester/New York, 2000).

3 John Cantwell, 'The Methodological Problems Raised by the Collection of Foreign Direct Investment Data', *Scandinavian International Business Review*, vol. 1, no. 1, 1992, pp. 86-103.

4 Susan Douglas and Samuel Craig, 'The Changing Dynamic of Consumer Behavior: Implications for Cross-Cultural Research', *International Journal of Research in Marketing*, 1997, 14(4), pp. 373-95.

5 Pervez Ghauri and Kjell Grønhaug, *Research Methods in Business Studies: A Practical Guide*, 3rd edn (Hemel Hempstead: Prentice Hall, 2005).

6 David Kiburn, 'Unilever Struggles with Surf in Japan', *Advertising Age*, 6 May 1991, p. 22.

7 Sidney J. Levy, 'What is Qualitative Research?' in *The Dartnell Marketing Manager's Handbook*, Sidney J. Levy *et al.* (eds) (Chicago: The Dartnell Corporation, 1994), p. 275.

8 N.K. Malhotra, J. Agarwal and F.M. Ulgado, 'Internationalization and Entry Modes: A Multitheoretical Framework and Research Propositions', *Journal of International Marketing*, 2004, 11(4), pp. 1-31.

9 Adapted from Mahmoud Aboul-Fath and Loula Zaklama, 'Ariel High Suds Detergent in Egypt - A Case Study', *Marketing and Research Today*, May 1992, pp. 130-4.

10 Beverly Camp, 'Research Propels Innovation', *Marketing*, 27 January 1994, p. 34.

11 For an example of data available from private sources, see Amy Dockser Marcus, 'As Door Opens to Arab-Israeli Markets, Small Firm Delves into Consumer Quirks', *The Wall Street Journal*, 11 November 1993, p. A-19.

12 'China's Faked Numbers Pile Up', *The Wall Street Journal*, 26 August 1994, p. A-6.

13 'Call for an End to Misreported Statistics', *The New York Times*, 18 August 1994, p. C-17.

14 N.L. Reynold, A.C. Simintiras, and A. Diamantopoulos, 'Theoretical Justification for Sampling Choices in International Marketing Research: Key Issues and Guidelines for Researchers', *Journal of International Business Studies*, 2003, 34(1), pp. 80-9.

15 P. Day, 'Asians Decline Invitations to go out Shopping', *Wall Street Journal*, 30 April 2003, p. A-15.

16 For a complete discussion of questionnaire administration and the resulting problems, see Naresh K. Malhotra, 'Administration of Questionnaires for Collecting Quantitative Data in International Marketing Research', *Journal of Global Marketing*, vol. 4, no. 2, 1991.

17 Susan P. Douglas, and C. Samuel Crag, 'Researching Global Markets', in *The Dartnell Marketing Manager's Handbook*, Sidney J. Levy, *et al.* (eds) (Chicago: The Dartnell Corporation, 1994), pp. 1278-98.

18 An interesting report on problems in cross-cultural replications can be found in Rudolf Sinkovics, Elfriede Penz and Pervez Ghauri, 'Analyzing Textual Data in International Marketing Research', *Qualitative Market Research: An International Journal*, 2005, 8(1), pp. 9-38.

19 B. Lee, S. Saklani and D. Tatterson, 'Top Prospects, State of the Marketing Research Industry in China', *Marketing News*, 10 June 2002, pp. 12-13.

20 P.E. Green, Y. Wind, A.M. Krieger and P. Saatsoglou, 'Applying Qualitative Data', *Marketing Research*, 2000, 12(1), pp. 17-25.

21 N.K. Malhotra and B.C. Bartels, 'Overcoming the Attribute Prespecification Bias in International Marketing Research by Using Non-attribute-based Correspondence Analysis', *International Marketing Review*, 2002, 19(1), pp. 65-79.

chapter 8
Emerging Markets and Market Behaviour

Chapter Outline

The concept of emerging economies is relatively new and most Western managers have realised that emerging economies, besides being large markets, are also becoming competitors and sources of production for Western firms. The World Bank, the IMF and *The Economist* have identified 24 emerging economies based on the size of their gross domestic product (GDP) and the capitalisation of their stock markets, as illustrated in Exhibit 8.1.

Emerging markets will account for 75 per cent of the world's total trade growth in the next decade and beyond, according to estimates by the US Department of Commerce.[1] No more than a decade ago, large parts of the developing world were hostile towards foreign investment and imposed severe regulatory barriers to foreign trade. Today, the view is different. With the collapse of the Marxist-socialist **centrally planned economic model** and the spectacular economic success of Taiwan, South Korea, Singapore and other Asian economies, it became apparent to many that the path to prosperity was open trade and direct investment. As a result, many developing countries are experiencing some degree of industrialisation, urbanisation, rising productivity, higher personal incomes and technological progress, although not all at the same level or rate of development.[2] Few nations are content with the economic status quo; now, more than ever, they seek economic growth, improved standards of living and an opportunity for the good life – most people want to be part of the global consumer world.[3]

Hungary, Poland, China, Brazil, Thailand, Indonesia, Malaysia and India are some of the countries undergoing impressive changes in their economies and emerging as vast markets. In these and other countries, there is an ever-expanding and changing demand for goods and services. Although the **Asian crisis** of 1997 has caused some setbacks in some of the Asian markets, the overall picture for emerging markets is developing positively. Markets are dynamic, developing entities reflecting the changing lifestyles of a culture. As economies grow, markets become different, larger and more demanding.

When economies grow and markets evolve beyond subsistence levels, the range of tastes, preferences and variations of products sought by the consumer increases; they demand more, better and/or different products. As countries prosper and their people are exposed to new ideas and behaviour patterns via global communications networks, old stereotypes, traditions and habits are cast aside or tempered and new patterns of consumer behaviour emerge. Sony televisions with 74 cm (29 in) screens in China, Avon cosmetics in Singapore, Wal-Mart discount stores in Argentina, Brazil, Mexico, China and Thailand, Volvo and BMW being made in Thailand, McDonald's beefless Big Macs in India, Whirlpool washers and refrigerators in Eastern Europe, Sara Lee food products in

key terms

centrally planned economic model
a model that is characterised by state monopoly of all means of production, lack of consumer orientation and lack of competition

Asian crisis
in 1996/1997, stock exchanges and currency values in a number of Asian countries lost a major part of their value

Exhibit 8.1 The emerging economies

	Population 2000 est. (million)**	Literacy rate (%)**	Ave. annual GDP growth rate 1990–99 (%)*	Inflation rate 1999 est. (%)**	Gross domestic savings 1999 (% of GDP)*	GDP 1999 (US$ billion)	Per nominal capita GNP 1999 est. (US$ billion)**	GDP-PPP 1999 est. (US$ billion)**	Per capita GNP-PPP 1999 US = 100*
China	1261.8	81	10.7	−1.3	42	991.2	780	4800.0	10.8
Hong Kong	7.1	92	3.9	−4.0	30	158.6	23520	158.2	68.5
India	1014.0	52	6.1	6.7	20	459.7	450	1805.0	7.0
Indonesia	224.7	83	4.7	2.0	24	140.9	580	610.0	8.0
Malaysia	21.7	83	6.3	2.8	45	74.6	3400	229.1	26.0
Philippines	81.1	94	3.2	6.8	16	75.3	1020	282.0	12.5
Singapore	4.1	91	8.0	0.4	52	84.9	29610	98.0	88.3
South Korea	47.4	98	5.7	0.8	34	406.9	8490	625.7	47.8
Thailand	61.2	93	4.7	2.4	32	123.8	1960	388.7	18.3
Argentina	36.9	96	4.9	−2.0	16	281.9	7600	367.0	37.0
Brazil	172.8	83	2.9	5.0	20	760.3	4420	1057.0	20.6
Chile	15.1	95	7.2	3.4	23	71.0	4740	185.1	27.4
Colombia	39.6	91.3	3.3	9.2	19	46.9	2250	245.1	18.6
Mexico	100.3	89	2.7	15.0	23	474.9	4400	865.5	25.2
Peru	27.0	88.7	5.4	5.5	20	57.3	2390	116.0	14.3
Venezuela	23.5	91	1.7	20.0	17	103.9	3670	182.8	17.2
Israel	5.8	95	5.1	1.3	10	99.0	N/A	105.4	N/A
Portugal	10.0	87	2.5	2.4	17	107.7	10600	151.4	49.5
South Africa	43.4	81	1.9	5.5	18	131.1	3160	296.1	27.2
Turkey	65.6	82	4.1	65.0	21	188.3	2900	409.4	20.0
Czech Republic	10.2	99	0.9	2.5	29	56.3	5060	120.8	40.2
Hungary	10.1	99	1.0	10.0	28	48.3	4650	79.4	34.2
Poland	38.6	99	4.7	8.4	18	154.1	3960	276.5	25.8
Russia	146.0	98	−6.1	86.0	29	375.3	2270	620.3	20.7

Source: *World Bank, *World Development Report,* 2000/2001; **CIA, *World Factbook*, 2000.

Indonesia, VW production in the Czech Republic, and Fiat's 'Pluto' specially developed for emerging markets all represent the opportunities that are arising in these markets.

This chapter explores emerging economies and changing market patterns that are creating opportunities throughout the world. Market behaviour and a rapidly expanding middle-income class in developing and developed countries are examined in the context of a single-country market and as the basis for global market segmentation.

marketing and economic development

The economic level of a country is the single most important environmental element to which the foreign marketer must adjust the marketing task. The stage of economic growth within a

country affects attitudes towards foreign business activity, the demand for goods, distribution systems found within a country and the entire marketing process. In static economies, consumption patterns become rigid, and marketing is typically nothing more than a supply effort. In a dynamic economy, consumption patterns change rapidly. Marketing is constantly faced with the challenge of detecting and providing for new levels of consumption, and marketing efforts must be matched with ever-changing market needs and wants.

Economic development presents a two-sided challenge. First, a study of the general aspects of economic development is necessary to gain empathy for the economic climate within developing countries. Second, the state of economic development must be studied with respect to market potential, including the present economic level and the economy's growth potential. The current level of economic development dictates the kind and degree of market potential that exists, while a knowledge of the dynamism of the economy allows the marketer to prepare for economic shifts in emerging markets.

Economic development is generally understood to mean an increase in national production that results in an increase in the average per capita GDP.[4] Besides an increase in average per capita GDP, most interpretations of the concept also imply a widespread distribution of the increased income. The term 'emerging market', as commonly defined today, tends to mean a country with rapid economic growth – improvements achieved in decades rather than centuries – and considerable increases in consumer demand.

stages of economic development

The best-known model for classifying countries by stage of economic development is that presented by Walt Rostow. He identified five stages of development; each stage is a function of the cost of labour, technical capability of the buyers, scale of operations, interest rates and level of product sophistication. Growth is the movement from one stage to another, and countries in the first three stages are considered to be economically underdeveloped. Briefly, the stages are as follows.

Stage 1: The traditional society. Countries in this stage lack the capability of significantly increasing the level of productivity. There is a marked absence of systematic application of the methods of modern science and technology. Literacy is low, as are other types of social overhead.

Stage 2: The preconditions for take-off. This second stage includes those societies in the process of transition to the take-off stage. During this period, the advances of modern science are beginning to be applied in agriculture and production. The development of transportation, communications, power, education, health and other public undertakings are begun in a small but important way.

Stage 3: The take-off. At this stage, countries achieve a growth pattern that becomes a normal condition. Human resources and social overhead have been developed to sustain steady development. Agricultural and industrial modernisation lead to rapid expansion in these areas.

Stage 4: The drive to maturity. After take-off, sustained progress is maintained and the economy seeks to extend modern technology to all fronts of economic activity. The economy takes on international involvement. In this stage, an economy demonstrates that it has the technological and entrepreneurial skills to produce not everything, but anything it chooses to produce.

Stage 5: The age of high mass consumption. The age of high mass consumption leads to shifts in the leading economic sectors towards durable consumer goods and services. Real income per capita rises to the point where a very large number of people have significant amounts of discretionary income.[5]

While Rostow's classification has met with some criticism because of the difficulty of distinguishing among the five stages, it provides the marketer with some indication of the

relationship between economic development, the types of products a country needs, and the sophistication of its industrial infrastructure.

newly industrialised countries and emerging markets

Some developing countries (LDCs) have grown rapidly in the last few decades and do not fit the traditional pattern of economic development of other LDCs. These countries, referred to as **newly industrialised countries (NICs)**, have shown rapid industrialisation of targeted industries and have per capita incomes that match those of developed countries (for a classification of economies, see Going International 8.1 and Exhibit 8.2). They have moved away from restrictive trade practices and instituted significant free-market reforms; as a result, they attract both trade and foreign direct investment. NICs have become formidable exporters of many products, including steel, automobiles, machine tools, clothing and electronics, as well as being vast markets for imported products.

key term

newly industrialised countries (NICs) developing countries that have grown rapidly in the last few decades and do not fit the traditional pattern of economic development of other LDCs

---

GOING INTERNATIONAL 8.1

what are the First, Second and Third Worlds?

The World Bank defined Third World countries as those with less than $7 300 annual GNP per capita. These included most of the countries of Asia (excluding Japan), Africa, the Middle East, the Caribbean, Central America and South America. These countries were further divided into low-income economies with less than $400, lower-middle-income economies with $400 to $1 700, and upper-middle-income economies with $1 700 to $7 300 (annual GNP per capita).

Industrialised countries, including North America and Western Europe, were often referred to as First World countries, while the Eastern Bloc was referred to as the Second World.

With the breakdown of the communist economies (except China and North Korea), the term Second World has become redundant, and now the terms developed and developing or emerging nations are popularly used.

The more recent classification of country groups by the World Bank (2001) is that low-income economies are those with a GNP per capita of $755 or less in 1999; middle-income economies are those with a GNP per capita of more than $755 but less than $9 266 in 1999 (a further division, at GNP per capita of $2 995 in 1999, is made between lower-middle-income and upper-middle-income economies); and high-income economies are those with a GNP per capita of $9 266 or more in 1999.

Low-income and middle-income economies are sometimes referred to as developing economies. The use of the term is convenient; it is not intended to imply that all economies in the group are experiencing similar development or that other economies have reached a preferred or final stage of development.

Brazil is an example of the growing importance of NICs in world trade, exporting everything from alcohol to carbon steel. Brazilian orange juice, poultry, soybeans and weapons (Brazil is the world's sixth largest weapons exporter) compete with Europe and the United States for foreign markets. Embraer, the Brazilian aircraft manufacturer, provides a substantial portion of the commuter aircraft used in the Western world. Even in automobile production, Brazil is a world player; it ships more than 200 000 cars, trucks and buses to other countries annually. Volkswagen has produced more than 3 million VW Beetles in Brazil and is now investing more than €360 million ($400 million) in a project to produce a two-door compact, code-named the AB9, aimed at the 200 million people in the Mercosur market, the free trade group formed by Argentina, Brazil, Paraguay and Uruguay.[6]

Exhibit 8.2 Classification of economies by income and region, 2004

Income	Sub-group	Sub-Saharan Africa	North Africa	East Asia and Pacific	South Asia	Europe and Central Asia	America and Caribbean	Middle East
Low Income		Angola		Cambodia	Afghanistan	Azerbaijan	Haiti	Yemen, Rep.
		Benin		Indonesia	Bangladesh	Georgia	Nicaragua	
		Burkina Faso		North Korea	Bhutan	Kyrgyz Republic		
		Burundi		Dem. Rep. Lao PDR	Nepal	Moldova		
		Cameroon		Mongolia		Tajikistan		
		Central African Rep.		Myanmar		Uzbekistan		
		Chad		Papua New Guinea				
		Comoros		Solomon Islands				
		Congo, Dem. Rep.		Timor-Leste				
		Congo, Rep.		Vietnam				
		Côte d'Ivoire						
		Equatorial Guinea						
		Eritrea						
		Ethiopia						
		Gambia, The						
		Ghana						
		Guinea						
		Guinea-Bissau						
		Kenya						
		Lesotho						
		Liberia						
		Madagascar						
		Malawi						
		Mali						
		Mauritania						
		Mozambique						
		Niger						
		Nigeria						
		Rwanda						
		São Tomé and Principe						
		Senegal						
		Sierra Leone						

Exhibit 8.2 (Classification of economies by income and region, 2004, continued)

Income	Sub-group	Sub-Saharan Africa	North Africa	East Asia and Pacific	South Asia	Europe and Central Asia	America and Caribbean	Middle East
		Somalia						
		Sudan						
		Tanzania						
		Togo						
		Uganda						
		Zambia						
		Zimbabwe						
Lower middle income		Cape Verde	Algeria	China	Maldives	Albania	Bolivia	Iran, Islamic Rep.
		Namibia	Djibouti	Fiji	Sri Lanka	Armenia	Brazil	Iraq
		South Africa	Egypt	Kiribati	Pakistan	Belarus	Colombia	Jordan
		Swaziland	Morocco	Marshall Islands		Bosnia-Hercegovina	Cuba	Syrian Arab Republic
			Tunisia	Micronesia, Fed. Sts		Bulgaria	Dominican Rep.	West Bank and Gaza
				Philippines		Kazakhstan	Ecuador	
				Samoa		Macedonia FYR	El Salvador	
				Thailand		Romania	Guatemala	
				Tonga		Russian Federation	Guyana	
				Vanuatu		Serbia & Montenegro	Honduras	
						Turkey	Jamaica	
						Turkmenistan	Paraguay	
						Ukraine	Peru	
							St Vincent and the Grenadines	
							Suriname	
Upper middle income		Botswana	Libya	American Samoa		Croatia	Argentina	Lebanon
		Gabon		Malaysia		Czech Rep.	Belize	Libya
		Mauritius		N. Mariana Islands		Estonia	Chile	Oman
		Mayotte		Palau		Hungary	Costa Rica	Saudi Arabia
		Seychelles				Latvia	Dominica	
						Lithuania	Grenada	
						Poland	Mexico	
						Slovak Rep.	Panama	

Exhibit 8.2 (Classification of economies by income and region, 2004, continued)

Income	Sub-group	Sub-Saharan Africa	North Africa	East Asia and Pacific	South Asia	Europe and Central Asia	America and Caribbean	Middle East
							St Kitts and Nevis	
							St Lucia	
							Trinidad and Tobago	
							Uruguay	
							Venezuela	
High Income	OECD			Australia		Austria	Canada	
				Japan		Belgium	United States	
				Korea, Rep.		Denmark		
				New Zealand		Finland		
						France		
						Germany		
						Greece		
						Iceland		
						Ireland		
						Italy		
						Luxembourg		
						Netherlands		
						Norway		
						Portugal		
						Spain		
						Sweden		
						Switzerland		
						United Kingdom		
	Non-OECD			French Polynesia	Brunei	Andorra	Antigua & Barbuda	Bahrain
				Guam	Singapore	Channel Islands	Aruba	Israel
				Hong Kong	Taiwan	Cyprus	Bahamas	Kuwait
						Faeroe Islands	Barbados	Qatar
				Macao		Greenland	Bermuda	United Arab Emirates
				New Caledonia		Isle of Man	Cayman Islands	

Exhibit 8.2 (Classification of economies by income and region, 2004, continued)

Income	Sub-group	Sub-Saharan Africa	North Africa	East Asia and Pacific	South Asia	Europe and Central Asia	America and Caribbean	Middle East
			Puerto Rico			Liechtenstein		
			Virgin Islands			Malta		
						Monaco	Antilles	
						Slovenia		
Total	**217**	**50**	**7**	**38**	**10**	**56**	**39**	**17**

Note: this table classifies all World Bank member economies with populations of more than 30 000. Economies are divided among income groups according to 2002 GNI per capita, calculated using the World Bank Atlas method. Income groups are defined as follows: low income, $375 or less; lower middle income, $736–2 935; upper middle income, $2 936–9 075; and high income, £9 076 or more.

Source: World Bank, *World Development Indicators 2004.*

Among the other NICs, South Korea, Taiwan, Hong Kong and Singapore have had such rapid growth and export performance that they are discussed as the 'Four Tigers' of Southeast Asia. These four countries have become major world competitors as well as major suppliers of many products to Europe, the United States and Japan. Personal incomes in these countries have increased over the last decade to the point at which they are becoming major markets for industrial and consumer goods. They began their industrialisation as assemblers of products for Western and Japanese companies, but are now developing their own product lines and are global competitors. South Korea, for example, exports high-tech goods such as petrochemicals, electronics, machinery and steel that are in direct competition with Japanese, European and US-made products.[7] In consumer products, Hyundai, Samsung and Lucky-Goldstar are among familiar brand names in cars, microwaves and televisions sold in the West. See Exhibit 8.3 for a comparison of NICs and other countries.

Exhibit 8.3 Infrastructure of selected countries

Country	Roads (1 000 km)	Vehicles (per 1 000 people)	Rail lines (km)	Electrical power (kwh per capital)	Mobile phones (per 1 000 people)	Personal computers (per 1 000 people)
United States	6 304	759	160 000	12 331	451	625
Brazil	1 724	79	25 652	1 877	167	63
China	1 403	8	58 656	827	110	19
Colombia	113	51	—	788	76	42
Germany	231	529	36 652	5 963	682	382
India	3 319	7	62 759	354	6	6
Japan	1 162	560	20 165	7 628	588	349
Kenya	64	13	2 634	106	19	6
Mexico	330	151	17 697	1 655	217	69
South Africa	362	143	22 657	3 745	252	69
Spain	664	467	13 866	4 653	655	168

Source: Euromonitor, 2003.

The recent developments in the global markets, and increasing growth and efficiencies in NICs and other developing countries have forced Western countries and firms to realise the existence and importance of emerging markets. Western countries will have to understand the ways of marketing in these markets because these economies, which are growing rapidly, jointly act as markets, sources and competitors. More than two-thirds of the world's population live in emerging markets. Also, the population growth rates are higher in those economies, which will influence the future population balance in coming years.

infrastructure and development

One indicator of economic development is the extent of social overhead capital or infrastructure within the economy. Infrastructure represents those types of capital goods that serve the activities of many industries. Included in a country's infrastructure are paved roads, railways, seaports, communications networks and energy supplies – all necessary to support production and marketing. The quality of infrastructure directly affects a country's economic growth potential and the ability of an enterprise to engage effectively in business.

Infrastructure is a crucial component of the uncontrollable elements facing marketers. Without adequate transportation facilities, for example, distribution costs can increase substantially, and the ability to reach certain segments of the market are impaired. In fact, a market's full potential may never be realised because of inadequate infrastructure.[8] To a marketer, the key issues in evaluating the importance of infrastructure concern the types necessary for profitable trade and the impact on a firm's ability to market effectively if a country's infrastructure is underdeveloped. In addition to the social overhead, capital type of infrastructure described, business efficiency is affected by the presence or absence of financial and commercial service infrastructure found within a country, such as advertising agencies, warehousing storage facilities, credit and banking facilities, marketing research agencies and quality-level specialised middlemen.

As trade develops, a country's infrastructure typically expands to meet the needs of the growing economy. There is some question of whether effective marketing increases the pace of infrastructure development or whether an expanded infrastructure leads to more effective marketing. Infrastructure and effective economic development and marketing activity probably increase concurrently, although seldom progressing at the same pace. While companies continue to market in emerging and developing countries, it is usually necessary to modify offerings and the approach to meet existing levels of infrastructure.[9]

objectives of emerging countries

A thorough assessment of economic development and marketing should begin with a brief review of the basic facts and objectives of economic development. To be capable of adjusting to a foreign economic environment, an international marketer must be able to answer questions such as the following.

1 What are the objectives of the developing countries?
2 What role is marketing assigned, if any, in economic growth plans?
3 What contribution must marketing make, whether overtly planned or not, for a country to grow successfully?
4 Which of the prevailing attitudes might hamper marketing strategies, development and growth?
5 How can the market potential, present and future, be assessed?

The economic growth is not measured solely in economic goals, but also in social achievements. Because foreign businesses are outsiders, they were often feared as having goals in conflict with those of the host country. Today, foreign investors are seen as vital partners in economic development. Experience with state-owned businesses proved to be a disappointment to most governments. Instead of being engines for accelerated economic

growth, **state-owned enterprises (SOEs)** were mismanaged, inefficient drains on state treasuries. Further, the rapid industrialisation of many of the poorest Asian countries pointed towards private-sector investment as the most effective means of economic growth. Most countries deregulated industry, opened their doors to foreign investment, lowered trade barriers and began privatising SOEs. The trend towards privatisation has been a major economic phenomenon in the past two decades, in industrialised as well as in developing countries.[10]

key term

state-owned enterprises (SOEs) companies owned by the government

GOING INTERNATIONAL 8.2

opportunities and threats in the world's biggest market

Wealthy consumers in Shanghai not balking at paying £80 for a bottle of decent chardonnay is a definite sign of China's rise as a major market. Among other signs is Shanghai's opening of a second airport and completing a high-speed electromagnetic train line. Beijing will have its Olympics in 2008, but Shanghai had Bernie Ecclestone's Formula One circus in 2004 and is lobbying hard to secure the Expo trade fair for 2010 ahead of Moscow. Shanghai, Beijing and the coastal cities have been transformed and are as dynamic as perhaps Hong Kong was a few years ago.

Not all multinationals, however, make a profit or even survive in China. While B&Q, helped by the fact that Shanghai residents, who were given a permission to buy their own homes a decade ago, tend to buy empty shells and redecorate them, is close to breaking even, others are not so successful. Foster's has closed three of the four breweries it opened. And Philips found its supposedly revolutionary energy-saving light bulbs were rapidly copied by a local competitor, which offered them at a fraction of the price. Foreign banks, such as Standard Chartered and HSBC are operating under severe regulatory constraints. At the moment, they can offer local and foreign currency loans to foreign investors and foreign-exchange accounts to Chinese. Standard Chartered's new branch in Shanghai, for example, has been visited by local bank managers armed with cameras and tape measures, anxious to copy the latest ideas of Western banking. However, Standard Chartered's managers are unfazed: the worst outcome would be if Chinese consumers are not educated about Western financial services and products. Nobody expects windfall profits in China.

Economic development in China also comes at a price. Currently, there are up to £287 billion of bad loans generated by lending to inefficient state enterprises in the Chinese banking system – or an average of 24.5 per cent of the loan books of the big four state banks. The People's Bank of China, the central bank, is demanding they reduce that figure by three percentage points a year for the next five years. It implies pulling the plug on thousands of state enterprises and risking social unrest. In all, some 25 million state workers were laid off between 1998 and 2002.

China's economic 'miracle' also failed to improve the lot of its vast agricultural population. Though Beijing disputes the numbers, farmers suffered a decline in income in real terms in each year between 1998 and 2002. The disparity in wealth between the rich and poor has never been so great since the communists came to power. Even among industrial enterprises, deflation and price wars have been the order of the day and more than half the state-owned enterprises are reckoned to have seen profits fall in 2001. But, for all that, it is hard to dispute China's attraction for Western companies. China's commitment to economic liberalisation, having joined the WTO and with a population of some 1.3 billion people hungry for economic growth, now looks irresistible.

■ Is China as promising a market as some companies believe?

Source: adapted from Nils Pratley, 'Welcome to the Last Frontier of Untapped Consumerism', *The Sunday Times*, Business, 3 November 2002, pp. 12-13.

marketing's contributions

How important is marketing to the achievement of a country's goals? Unfortunately, marketing (or distribution) is not always considered meaningful to those responsible for planning. Economic planners frequently are more production than marketing oriented, and tend to ignore or regard distribution as an inferior economic activity. Given such attitudes, economic plans are generally more concerned with the problems of production, investment and finance than the problems of efficiency of distribution.

Imagine marketing where there is production but little disposable income, no storage, limited transportation only to the wrong markets, and no middlemen and facilitating agents to activate the flow of goods from the manufacturer to the consumer. When such conditions exist in some emerging markets, marketing and economic progress are retarded. This is, to some degree, the problem of China and many of the republics of the former Soviet Union. In China, for example, most of the 1 billion potential consumers are not accessible because of a poor distribution network. The consumer market in China is probably limited to no more than 20 per cent of those who live in the more affluent cities.

GOING INTERNATIONAL 8.3

Carrefour's expansion into the global retail map

Carrefour, which means 'crossroads' in French, is the world's second biggest retailer after Wal-Mart, with total sales in 1999 of $46.8 billion, net profits of $1 billion, and a

market cap in early June of around $47 billion. The expansion of Carrefour into worldwide markets raises the question of whether it is something more than just a collection of really big stores and whether it can rival Wal-Mart in the retailing market.

For a start, Carrefour is undeniably better than Wal-Mart at certain aspects of retailing, such as fresh food and merchandising. Moreover, the most significant edge of Carrefour on Wal-Mart is its commanding presence in markets where the Americans are the late arrivals on the international retail scene. The global retail map shows that everywhere else, it's Carrefour that sets the pace by having 9 089 locations in Europe, and it has a presence in both Asia and South America, while Wal-Mart has an unremarkable track record outside North America (3 002 stores in the US, 166 in Canada and 461 in Mexico).

However, doubts and worries about Carrefour exist. First of all is the pressure from Wal-Mart's conquering strategy of the rest of Planet Retail. The unmatched computerised sales and distribution systems give Wal-Mart an edge wherever it operates. Second, Carrefour is facing up to the possibility of a takeover threat by its competitor. Moreover, there are doubts about its Internet strategy, and in particular the company's three-year plan to invest more than $900 million in ISPs and portals in 15 European, Latin American and Asian countries, a policy that bears high risk by trying to be all things to all people. Worries about Carrefour also centre on the possibility that its integration with Promodès (Carrefour's rival French group, which was acquired in August 1999) could lead to a slowdown in its 'global store-opening programme', which envisages the launch of at least 55 so-called hypermarkets in 2000, including 40 in Asia and Latin America and 15 in Europe, and also including 120 smaller supermarkets and 365 low-cost discount outlets.

Even though doubts and worries exist, Carrefour is honoured as one of the world's finest retailers and one that has a good chance of growing its way to superstar status. An obsessive attention to detail and a knack for designing stores to meet local tastes contribute to its success. The entry into emerging markets such as Brazil and China represents huge opportunities for growth; while Wal-Mart lags and stumbles on the way. However, a sound legal framework is essential for Carrefour's move into developing markets. Its experience in Russia has taught the company the importance of conducting at least one year's grass-roots research into any challenging market. Another success factor is Carrefour's adaptation to the local culture. It is evident not only in the food and products supplied but also in the selection of local partners. Now the question is whether Carrefour can maintain its present success and fend off the international threat from Wal-Mart.

■ Make a comparative analysis by consulting the websites of Wal-Mart and Carrefour.

Source: abridged from *Fortune*, 'Carrefour on the Global Map', 26 June 2000.

marketing in a developing country

A marketer cannot superimpose a sophisticated marketing programme on an underdeveloped economy. Marketing efforts must be keyed to each situation, custom tailored for each set of circumstances. A promotional programme for a population that is 60 per cent illiterate is vastly different from a programme for a population that is 80 per cent literate. Pricing in a subsistence market poses different problems than pricing in an affluent society. The distribution structure should provide an efficient method of matching productive capacity with available demand. An efficient marketing programme is one that provides for optimum utility at a single point in time, given a specific set of circumstances. In evaluating the potential in a developing country, the marketer must make an assessment of the existing level of marketing development within the country.[11]

level of marketing development

The level of the **marketing function** roughly parallels the stages of economic development. Going International 8.3 illustrates various stages of the marketing process as they develop in a growing economy. Economic cooperation and assistance, technological change, and political, social and cultural factors can and do cause significant deviations in this evolutionary process. However, the focus is on the logic and interdependence of marketing and economic development. The more developed an economy, the greater the variety of marketing functions demanded, and the more sophisticated and specialised the institutions become to perform marketing functions. The evolution of the channel structure illustrates the relationship between marketing development and the stage of economic development of a country.

Advertising agencies, facilities for marketing research, repair services, specialised consumer financing agencies, and storage and warehousing facilities are supportive facilitating agencies created to serve the particular needs of expanded markets and economies. It is important to remember that these institutions do not come about automatically, nor does the necessary marketing institution simply appear. Part of the marketer's task when studying an economy is to determine what in the foreign environment will be useful and how much adjustment will be necessary to carry out stated objectives. In some developing countries it may be up to the marketer to institute the foundations of a modern marketing system.

demand in a developing country

Estimating market potential in less developed countries involves myriad challenges. Most of the difficulty arises from economic dualism – that is, the coexistence of modern and

key term

marketing function marketing activities (often in a company)

traditional sectors within the economy. The modern sector is centred in the cities and has airports, international hotels, new factories and a Westernised middle class. Alongside this modern sector is a traditional sector containing the remainder of the country's population. Although the two sectors may be very close geographically, they are centuries away in terms of production and consumption. This dual economy affects the size of the market and, in many countries, creates two distinct economic and marketing levels. Indonesia, Pakistan and India are good examples. The 11th largest industrial economy in the world, India has a population of over 1 billion, more than 300 million of whom are part of an affluent middle class.[12] The modern sector demands products and services similar to those available in any industrialised country; the traditional sector demands items more indigenous and basic to subsistence. As one authority observed, a rural Indian can live a sound life with few products. Toothpaste, sugar, coffee, washing soap, bath soap and kerosene are bare necessities for those who live in semi-urban and urban areas.[13]

In countries with dual sectors, there are at least two different market segments. Each can prove profitable but each requires its own marketing programme and products appropriate for its market characteristics. Many companies market successfully to both the traditional and the modern market segments in countries with mixed economies. The traditional sector may offer the greatest potential initially, but as the transition from the traditional to the modern takes place (i.e. as the middle-income class grows) an established marketer is better able to capitalise on the growing market.

Tomorrow's markets will include expansion in industrialised countries and the development of the traditional side of emerging and less developed countries, as well as continued expansion of the modern sectors of such countries. The greatest long-range growth potential is to be found in the traditional sector, where the realisation of profit may require a change in orientation and willingness to invest time and effort for longer periods. The development of demand in a traditional market sector means higher initial marketing costs, compromises in marketing methods and sometimes redesigning products, but market investment today is necessary to produce profits tomorrow. The companies that will benefit in the future from emerging markets in Eastern Europe, China, Latin America and elsewhere are the ones that invest when it is difficult and initially unprofitable.[14]

emerging markets

The transition from socialist to **market-driven economies**, the liberalisation of trade and investment policies in developing countries, the transfer of **public-sector enterprises** to the private sector and the rapid development of regional market alliances are changing the way countries will trade and prosper in the next century.

The US Department of Commerce estimates that over 75 per cent of the expected growth in world trade over the next two decades will come from the more than 130 developing and emerging countries. A small core of these countries will account for more than half of that growth.[15] It predicts that the countries identified as big emerging markets (BEMs) alone will be a bigger import market by the end of this decade than the European Union (EU) and, by 2010, will be importing more than the EU and Japan combined.[16] These BEMs, as the US Department of Commerce refers to them, share a number of important traits. They:

■ are all physically large
■ have significant populations
■ represent considerable markets for a wide range of products
■ all have strong rates of growth or the potential for significant growth
■ have all undertaken significant programmes of economic reform
■ are all of major political importance within their regions
■ are 'regional economic drivers'
■ will engender further expansion in neighbouring markets as they grow.

key terms

market-driven economies
economies/ countries that are following the free market economic system

public-sector enterprises
government-owned organisations

GOING INTERNATIONAL 8.4

multinational brands face tough competition from local brands in emerging markets

India has a billion-plus customers and the climate is hot, but Coca-Cola is having a tough time there. After years of mistakes, in 2002 it had 16.5 per cent of the market, behind Pepsi Cola (23.5 per cent) and the number two local rival, Thums Up. Coca-Cola acquired Thums Up in 1993 when it entered India with big plans. In its early years it made all the classic mistakes, overestimating the size of market, misreading consumers and fighting with government rules and regulations. A big dispute with Pepsi, where Coke bottlers hoarded empty Pepsi bottles, gave it a very bad reputation. In the past 10 years, it has had five expatriate CEOs. Pepsi, on the other hand, has had three local CEOs in its 15 years. Coke suffered undeclared losses in the first 10 years and had written off its assets in India by $405 million.

In 2003, however, Coke decided to sell 49 per cent of its Indian bottler, Hindustan Coca-Cola Beverages, for $41 million. The company's overall sales jumped 24 per cent in the same year. India has huge potential. At present soft drink consumption is seven (250 millilitres) servings per head, while in neighbouring Pakistan it is 14 servings per head; in China it is 89 and in Mexico it is 1500 servings. Thus, the potential is huge (see graph).

Local brand Thums Up is now owned by Coca-Cola

Coke in India: room to grow

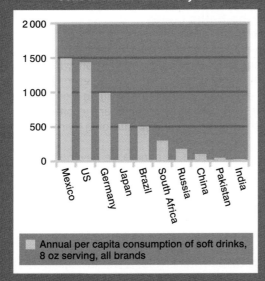

Annual per capita consumption of soft drinks, 8 oz serving, all brands

The key to the new strategy is the new local CEO, who fought with Atlanta to revive the local brand, Thums Up (owned by Coke): $3.5 million was spent on advertising and improving distribution of Thums Up, which within a year jumped to the number two position. Coca-Cola then launched a new 200 ml bottle, selling for 10 cents and aimed at the lower market segments, and the price for normal Coke (300 ml) was dropped to 17 cents from 24 cents. For advertising, a Bollywood movie star, Amir Khan, was hired.

Source: Business Week, 10 February 2003, p. 23.

While these criteria are general in nature and each country does not meet all of them, the US Department of Commerce identified the following as emerging markets: in Asia – China, Indonesia, India, Vietnam, Malaysia, Thailand and South Korea; in Latin America – Mexico, Argentina and Brazil; in Africa – South Africa; in Central Europe – the Czech Republic, Hungary and Poland; and in Southern Europe – Turkey. Although some countries in Asia, such as Malaysia, Thailand and Indonesia, have gone through an economic crisis, these countries are expected to overcome their problems in the same way that Mexico survived the economic crisis of 1994.

These emerging markets differ from other developing countries because they import more than smaller markets and more than economies of similar size. As they embark on economic development, demand for capital goods to build their manufacturing base and develop infrastructure increases. Increased economic activity means more jobs and more income to spend on products not yet produced locally. Thus, as their economies expand, there is an accelerated growth in demand for goods and services, much of which must be imported. Emerging markets' merchandise imports are expected to be nearly 1 trillion dollars; if services are added, the amount jumps beyond that figure.

What is occurring in the emerging markets is analogous to the situation after the Second World War when tremendous demand was created during the reconstruction of Europe. As Europe rebuilt its infrastructure and industrial base, demand for capital goods exploded and, as more money was infused into its economies, consumer demand also increased rapidly. For more than a decade, Europe could not supply its increasing demand for industrial and consumer goods. During that period, the US was the principal supplier because most of the rest of the world was rebuilding or had underdeveloped economies. Meeting this demand produced one of the largest economic booms the United States had ever experienced. Now Japan, Europe and the NICs will become fierce rivals in emerging markets.

Eastern Europe and the Baltic states

Eastern Europe and the Baltic states, satellite nations of the former USSR, are moving rapidly to establish free-market systems (see Exhibit 8.4). New business opportunities are emerging almost daily and the region is described as anywhere from chaotic with big risks to an exciting place with untold opportunities. Both descriptions fit as countries adjust to the political, social and economic realities of changing from the restrictions of a Marxist-socialist system to some version of free markets and capitalism. In the next century, this region will rank among the world's important emerging markets.[17]

Eastern Europe   It is dangerous to generalise beyond a certain point about Eastern Europe because each of the countries has its own economic problems and is at a different point in its evolution from a socialist to a market-driven economy. Most are privatising state-owned enterprises (SOEs), establishing free-market pricing systems, relaxing import controls and wrestling with inflation. The Czech Republic, Poland and Hungary have made more progress towards overhauling their economies than have Bulgaria, Albania and Romania.

The Commonwealth of Russian States (CIS) is still struggling with political instability, and the Asian republics have different levels of ambitions and goals depending upon their location, resources and political leadership. However, in most Eastern European countries, there are democratically elected governments that are committed to establishing market economies on a free-market basis. Most of these countries are trying to attract foreign companies in order to establish technology transfer and trade links. In spite of the reluctance of Western companies to invest, there has been a considerable increase in registered joint ventures and wholly owned subsidiaries.

For the entrepreneur, freedom from communism has provided the opportunity to blossom. Nowhere is this more evident than in Poland. Reforms, coupled with the fact that

Exhibit 8.4 Eastern Europe and the Baltic states

| Part of EU | Members of CIS | Future EU members | EU applicant |

Poland had a relatively large (mostly agricultural) private sector under communism, have led to an explosion of private entrepreneurial activity. For example, 20 per cent of all retail sales in 1989 were private, and by 1991 the private-sale share rose to 80 per cent. A report of a Polish trader who started a business in a warehouse to outfit retail stores typifies the entrepreneurial spirit found in many of the countries. The business, Intercommerce, has scales from Korea, cash registers from Japan, and stack upon stack of German shelves, racks, baskets, hangers, supermarket carts, barcode readers, price-tag tape and checkout counters. When a customer wants furnishings for a new store, the owner of Intercommerce prepares a layout for the store, makes a list of what is needed, and then trucks it all to the new store. 'It takes about an hour,' he says. The company's sales were €9 000 ($10 000) a month in 1990 and €540 000 ($600 000) per month a year later.

Hungary and the Czech Republic, the other two emerging markets, also have promising economic prospects (see Exhibit 8.5) and, along with Poland, were the first to achieve associate status (the transitional stage before full membership) of the EU.[18] The other Eastern European countries are trailing behind these three in their transition from communism to capitalism, and not all are successfully completing the transition to free-market economies. Monetary policy, the transfer of state-owned property to the private sector, restructuring of the legal system to include commercial law and banking reform are issues that are unresolved for many. Even though progress towards reform is patchy, an entrepreneurial class has developed rapidly and the long-term future is bright.[19]

The Baltic States Estonia, Latvia and Lithuania were among the first republics to declare their sovereignty and independence as the Soviet Union began to crumble. Within days of their independence, the European Parliament granted them 'special guest' status in the EU. Trade and cooperation agreements have been signed and eventually they are expected to become associate members. The Baltic states are positioned to be a bridge for trade between the West and the former USSR. With their past experience as exporters to the USSR of manufactured goods made from Russian raw materials, the Baltic states see themselves as a logical location for Western investment seeking markets in the former Soviet Union.[20]

Eastern Europe and the Baltic states are in the sphere of influence of the EU. There is a natural tendency for them to look to the EU for assistance and, eventually, membership. As

Exhibit 8.5 Eastern European markets

	Population (millions)	GDP ($ billions)	GDP ($ per capita)	Exports ($ millions)	Imports ($ millions)
Albania	3.54	16.1	4500	425	1760
Bosnia-Hercegovina	4.00	24.3	6100	1280	4700
Bulgaria	7.50	57.1	7600	7337	9723
Croatia	4.50	47.0	10600	6355	12860
Czech Republic	10.24	161.1	15700	46770	50400
Hungary	10.03	139.8	13900	42030	46190
Macedonia	2.07	13.81	6700	1346	2184
Poland	38.63	427.1	11100	57600	63650
Romania	22.36	155.0	7000	17630	22170
Slovakia	5.42	72.29	13300	21250	21900
Slovenia	2.01	36.82	19000	11980	12630
Serbia & Montenegro	10.83	23.89	2200	2667	7144

Source: World Factbook, www.odci.gov/cia/publications/factbook, 2004.

discussed, the framework for the integration of trade among countries in each of the regions is in place in Europe and the Americas.

Asia

Asia is the fastest-growing market in the world and its share of global output was projected to account for almost one-half of the increase in global output through the year 2000.[21] Both as sources of new products and technology and as vast consumer markets, the Pacific Rim and Asia are just beginning to get into their stride (see Exhibit 8.6).

Exhibit 8.6 Asian markets: selected countries

	Population (millions)	GDP* ($ billions)	GDP* ($ per capita)	Imports of goods and services ($ billions)	Exports of goods and services ($ billions)
Australia	19.4	469.2	24203	105.1	100.5
China	1271.8	1117.2	878	371.4	457.4
Hong Kong	6.7	164.8	24505	260.1	268.5
India	1032.4	492.5	477	80.4	78.0
Indonesia	209.0	216.2	1034	50.4	60.3
Japan	127.0	5647.7	44458	487.6	591.9
South Korea	47.3	639.2	13502	213.8	320.9
Taiwan	22.7	282.2	12261	108.1	125.6

* Constant 1995 dollars.

Source: World Bank, Euromonitor 2003. Copyright 2003 by TRANSACTION PUBS. Reproduced with permission of TRANSACTION PUBS via Copyright Clearance Center.

Asian Pacific Rim   The most rapidly growing economies in this region, other than Japan, are the group of countries referred to as the 'Four Tigers' (or 'Four Dragons'): Hong Kong, South Korea, Singapore and Taiwan. These were the first countries in Asia, besides Japan, to move from a status of developing countries to newly industrialised countries (NICs). They have grown from suppliers of component parts and assemblers of Western products to become major global competitors – in electronics, shipbuilding, heavy machinery, motor vehicles and a multitude of other products. In addition, each has become a major influence in trade and development in the economies of other countries within their spheres of influence.

South Korea is the centre of trade links with north China and the Asian republics of the former Soviet Union. Although North and South Korea do not officially recognise one another, trade between the two, mostly through Hong Kong, is in excess of €112 million ($124 million) annually. There is some likelihood that the two will unite, creating a formidable regional economic power similar to that of Hong Kong and China. The Four Tigers are rapidly extending their trading activity to other parts of Asia.[22]

Japan's role in the Asian Pacific Rim is perhaps the most important in the area. While not part of a common market or any other economic cooperative alliance, Japan's influence is nevertheless increasingly dominant. Sales to Japan account for as much as 12 per cent of GDP in Malaysia and about 7 per cent of GDP in Indonesia, Thailand and South Korea.[23] That these economies influence each other was clearly seen in the 1997–98 Japanese and Asian crisis.

Other Asian countries taking leading positions are China, Indonesia, India, Malaysia and Thailand. Malaysian planners have developed blueprints for new industries ranging from rubber sneakers to colour-television picture tubes. The most elaborate plan calls for Malaysia to become one of the world's foremost producers of word processors, answering machines and facsimile devices. Part of the idea is to limit competition among the region's countries and foster complementary patterns of development. A regional automobile industry might combine transmissions from the Philippines with steering mechanisms from Malaysia and engines from Thailand in a final assembly process in a fourth country.

As these Asian countries continue to develop, in spite of the major 1997–98 crisis, Japanese capital, technology and direction will be paramount. With Japanese leadership, the region is rapidly becoming a major economic power in global trade.[24] Japan's role among the Asian Pacific Rim countries may have the same economic trade impact for developing countries in that region as the EU provides for Eastern Europe and the United States provides for South America – investments, free-trade alliances and markets. In addition, China is gaining ground to become a major player in the world economic scene; see Exhibit 8.7 for a map of the region.

China   The economic and social changes occurring in China since it began actively seeking economic ties with the industrialised world have been dramatic.[25] China's dual economic system, embracing socialism along with many tenets of capitalism, produced an economic boom with expanded opportunity for foreign investment. China remains a socialist economy and anyone doing business there has to contend with the trappings of both capitalist and socialist systems. In the minds of some, China's move towards free enterprise has become a free-for-all with power shifted to provinces, towns and state-owned factories – a country that lacks discipline.[26]

Anyone doing business in China must keep in mind a few fundamentals that have been overshadowed by Western euphoria. First, because of China's size, diversity, political organisation and the return of Hong Kong to China, it is better to think of it as a group of seven regions rather than a single country – a grouping of regional markets rather than a single market.[27] There is no one growth strategy for China. Each region is at a different stage economically and has its own link to other regions as well as links to other parts of the world. Each has its own investment patterns, is taxed differently and has substantial

GOING INTERNATIONAL 8.5

local resistance to global expansion

Since the Asian financial crisis of 1997, a number of Western supermarkets, such as Carrefour and Casino of France, have expanded significantly in Southeast Asia. However, none has moved as fast as Tesco. In Thailand, Tesco's presence has grown from just 13 to 38 stores from 1998 to 2002. Thailand is just one of nine countries that Tesco – the UK's biggest retailer – had entered by 2002. Instead of going for big-bang acquisition in major markets, Tesco has opted for small deals in emerging markets, linking with well-established local operators. Now analysts say that about £37m of the company's £59m overseas profits came from emerging markets in 2002. Although Thailand is one of Tesco's emerging market presences – the others are Hungary, Poland, the Czech Republic, Slovakia, South Korea, Taiwan and Malaysia – it was one of the first, and its experiences there helped form strategy.

A Tesco store in Thailand

Tesco's principle strategy in Thailand was penetration into the heart of small towns using its appealing blend of comfortable surroundings and low prices, which lured confident, cost-conscious Thai consumers from traditional bazaars where vendors sell fresh produce along narrow, crowded aisles. But in spite of increasing popularity with the ordinary consumer, Tesco faces fresh hurdles in Thailand. Weaker local retailers bitterly resent the onslaught of foreign competition and have demanded that the government take action. Many Thais are worried about the disappearance of smaller 'mom and pop' stores; and Tesco, in part because of its success, has become a symbol of what is seen as a broader foreign intrusion into the Thai economy. As the country's economy recovers, small retailers are finding their voice and a receptive audience in a populist government. In response to the vigorous lobbying, the government plans to regulate the retail industry, which could hamper the expansion of foreign hypermarkets as the Thai economy continues to develop. Among many measures, the draft law proposes new limits on the operating hours of foreign hypermarkets, and highly politicised licensing procedures. Separately, Thai authorities are investigating the finances of foreign retailers, after local suppliers complained that they have been forced to sell their goods below cost.

Source: adapted from Amy Kazmin and Susanna Voyle, 'Thailand Adds Some Spice for Tesco', *Financial Times*, 21 September 2002, p. 14.

autonomy in how it is governed. But while each region is separate enough to be considered individually, each is linked at the top to the central government in Beijing.

Second, distribution, manufacturing, banking, transportation and other infrastructure segments of business are out of date and inefficient. Gillette and Coca-Cola, among other companies, are making money in China, but neither can readily send profits home or bring in new equipment because of exchange and import restrictions.[28] Transportation and distribution of goods to inland China vary from good to abysmal. Roads are poor for trucking; breakdowns and delays are common for rail transportation. A World Bank official estimates it will take some 20 years to build an adequate transportation system.[29]

A small segment, however, is becoming very wealthy in China. These wealthy consumers flock to new luxury shops offering Gucci handbags, Benetton sweaters and Adidas sneakers. The Swiss firm Rado sold 10 000 of its top-quality watches in China (excluding Hong

Exhibit 8.7 Asia

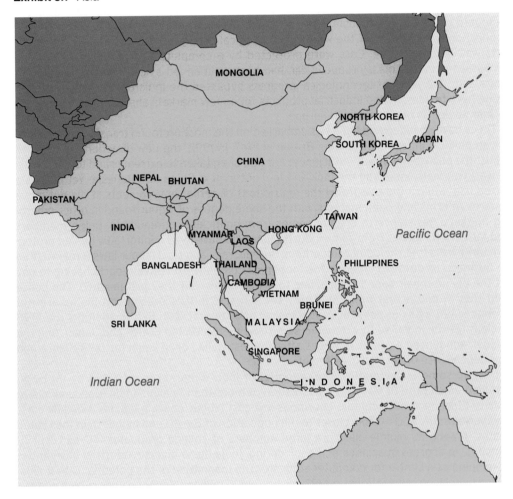

Kong) in a year, and many Chinese are willing to pay up to €45 000 ($50 000) for an Audi
or Mercedes-Benz.[30]

China is not only a huge emerging market, but also an investor. There are thousands of
Chinese companies that have invested heavily in the West, particularly Europe and the
United States. A number of state-owned enterprises such as Sinochem, CITIC and COFCO
have been active in real estate, manufacturing and finance. Also, a number of provincial
and city companies have now set up their own Western trading, manufacturing, investment
and finance companies. Another group active in foreign investments are hybrids working
through wholly owned subsidiaries in Hong Kong.[31]

India   The wave of change that has been washing away restricted trade, controlled
economies, closed markets and hostility to foreign investment in most developing countries finally reached India in the early 1990s. Since its independence, one of the world's
largest markets had set a poor example as a model for economic growth for other developing countries and was among the last of the economically important developing nations to
throw off traditional insular policies. India's growth had been constrained and shaped by
policies of import substitution and an aversion to free markets. Real competition in internal markets was practically eliminated through import bans and prohibitive tariffs on
foreign competition. Industry was so completely regulated that those with the proper

licence could count on a specific share of the market. While other Asian countries were wooing foreign capital, India was doing its best to keep it out. Multinationals, seen as in the vanguard of a new colonialism, were shunned. As a result, India lost its technological connection with the rest of the world. Technological change in many manufactured products was frozen in time. Cars were protected by a complete ban on importation. The Ambassador, India's mass-produced car, had been unchanged since it was introduced 50 years ago – 50 years of technological progress bypassed the Indian automotive industry. Aside from textiles, Indian industrial products found few markets abroad other than in the former Soviet Union and Eastern Europe.

Times have changed and India has embarked on the most profound transformation since it won political independence from Britain in 1947. In 1992, the new direction promised to adjust the philosophy of self-sufficiency that had been taken to extremes and to open India to world markets. India had the look and feel of the next China or Indonesia. Yet India is a mixed bag; while it did overthrow the restrictions of earlier governments, it did not move towards reforms and open markets with the same degree of vigour found in other emerging markets. Resistance to change comes from politicians, bureaucrats, union members and farmers, as well as from some industrialists who have lived comfortably behind protective tariff walls that excluded competition. Bureaucracy and rigid labour laws remain a drag on business, as does corruption. One foreign oil-company executive reports having to pay off the phone repairman: 'I complained to his company, but they just laughed. The police said they would arrest him – but only for a fee.'[32] India's present problems are not economic but a mix of political, psychological and cultural attitudes. In addition, the 1998 nuclear test by India led to **economic sanctions** by the United States and Japan, and the budget, announced a couple of weeks after the test, called once again for self-reliance and less dependence on foreign investments.

Despite some uncertainties, the potential of India's market is reflected by its being included among the BEMs. With a population of more than 1 billion, India is second in size only to China, and both contain enormous low-cost labour pools. India has a middle class numbering some 300 million, closer to the population of the EU and bigger than the United States. Among its middle class are large numbers of college graduates, 40 per cent of whom have degrees in science and engineering. India has a diverse industrial base and is developing as a centre for computer software. The magnitude of the potential is best illustrated by telecommunications: in 1997, fewer than 10 million telephone lines served a population of more than 900 million.

The consumer-goods sector is another important draw for the foreign investor. An estimated 300 million Indians possess sufficient disposable income to form an expanding consumer class. Imported consumer items are still banned, but foreign investment in 22 consumer sectors is now welcome. Several consumer-goods firms have recently been approved for investments, once a virtual impossibility. General Electric's application to form a €36 million ($40 million) joint venture to make refrigerators and washing machines was approved in six weeks. In the past, approval, if it came at all, would have taken three or more years. General Motors, Coca-Cola, Pepsi-Cola, McDonald's and IBM are just a few of the companies that have recently made direct investments in India.

India still presents a difficult business environment. Tariffs are well above those of developing-world norms, although they have been slashed to a maximum of 65 per cent from 400 per cent. Inadequate protection of intellectual property rights remains a serious concern. The anti-business attitudes of India's federal and state bureaucracies continue to hinder potential investors and plague their routine operations.[33]

the Americas

The North American Free Trade Agreement (NAFTA) marks the high point of a silent political and economic revolution that has been taking place in the Americas (see Exhibit 8.8) over the last decade. Most of the countries have moved from military dictatorships to

key term

economic sanctions when it is forbidden to trade with a country

GOING INTERNATIONAL 8.6

the benefits of information technology in village life

Delora Begum's home office is a corrugated metal and straw hut in Bangladesh with a mud floor, no toilet, and no running water. Yet in this humble setting, she reigns as the 'phone lady', a successful entrepreneur and a person of standing in her community. It's all due to a sleek Nokia cell phone. Mrs Begum acquired the handset in 1999. Her telephone 'booth' is mobile: during the day, it's the stall on the village's main dirt road; at night, callers drop by her family hut to use the phone.

After the phone hookup was made, incomes and quality of life improved almost immediately for many villagers. For as long as he can remember, a brick factory manager had to take a two-and-a-half-hour bus ride to Dhaka to order furnace oil and coal for the brick factory. Now, he avoids the biweekly trip: 'I can just call if I need anything, or if I have any problems.' The local carpenter uses the cell phone to check the current market price of wood, so he ensures a higher profit for the furniture he makes.

The only public telecom link to the outside world, this unit allows villagers to learn the fair value of their rice and vegetables, cutting out the middlemen notorious for exploiting them. They can arrange bank transfers or consult doctors in distant cities and, in a nation where only 45 per cent of the population can read and write, the cell phone allows people to dispense with a scribe to compose a letter. It also earns some $600 a year for its owner – twice the annual per capita income in Bangladesh.

When members of the Grand Coast Fishing Operators Cooperative salt and smoke the day's catch to prepare it for market, it may seem light years away from cyberspace, but for these women the Internet is a boon. The cooperative set up a website that enables its 7350 members to promote their produce, monitor export markets and negotiate prices with overseas buyers before they arrive at markets in Senegal. Information technology has thus improved their economic position.

Finally, it seems that new technology can also breed new economic disputes. A disagreement over an unpaid $50 phone bill in a village 110 kilometres northeast of Dhaka, Bangladesh, turned into a gunfight between two groups of villagers that left five dead and 25 injured.

Source: Miriam Jordan, 'It Takes a Cell Phone', *Wall Street Journal*, 25 June 1999, p. B-1; 'A Great Leap: Developing Countries are Finding Ways to Leverage Advances in Information Technology and Help Narrow the North–South Divide', *Time International*, 31 January 2000, p. 42; 'Bangladesh – Five Killed in Shootout over Telephone Bill', *Los Angeles Times*, 31 March 2003, p. A17.

democratically elected governments, while sweeping economic and trade liberalisation is replacing the economic model most Latin American countries followed for decades. Today many of them are at roughly the same stage of liberalisation that launched the dynamic growth in Asia during the last two decades.[34]

The trend towards privatisation of state-owned enterprises (SOEs) follows a period in which governments dominated economic life for most of the twentieth century. State ownership was once considered the ideal engine for economic growth. Instead of economic growth, however, they got inflated public-sector bureaucracies, complicated and unpredictable regulatory environments, the outright exclusion of foreign and domestic private ownership, and inefficient public companies. A study of 35 steel companies in Brazil

Exhibit 8.8 The Americas

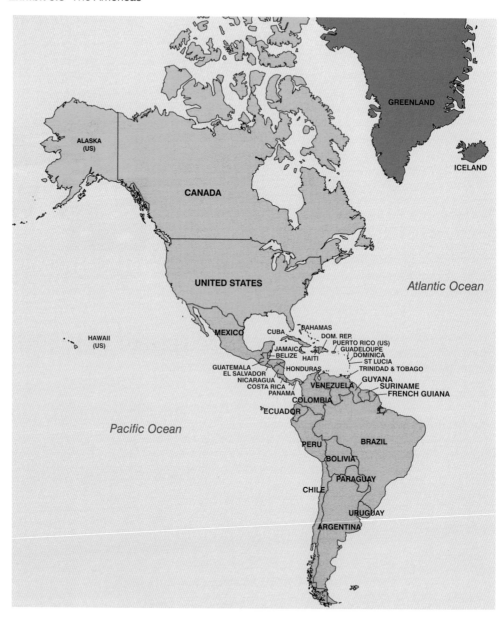

reported that only eight possessed a research lab and just one invested in research and development. As a consequence, productive capacity stood still for a decade.

New leaders have turned away from the traditional closed policies of the past to implement positive market-oriented reforms and seek ways for economic cooperation. **Privatisation** of state-owned enterprises (SOEs) and other economic, monetary and trade policy reforms show a broad shift away from inward-looking policies of import substitution (that is, manufacture products at home rather than import them) and protectionism that were so prevalent earlier. In a positive response to these reforms, investors are spending billions of dollars to buy airlines, banks, public works and telecommunications systems.

Argentina, Brazil, Chile and Mexico are among the countries that have quickly instituted reforms. All have brought inflation under control; Argentina has shown the most spectacular reduction, dropping from a 672 per cent annual rate in 1985 to 7 per cent in 1993.

key term

privatisation
when a
government
company is sold to
private investors

200

GOING INTERNATIONAL 8.7

marketing in the Third World

Much of the marketing challenge in the developing world, which is not accustomed to consumer products, is to get consumers to use the product and to offer it in the right sizes. For example, because many Latin American consumers can't afford a 7 oz bottle of shampoo, Gillette sells it in 0.5 oz plastic bottles. And in Brazil, the company sells Right Guard deodorant in plastic squeeze bottles instead of metal cans.

But the toughest task for Gillette is convincing Third World men to shave. Portable theatres called 'mobile propaganda units' are sent into villages to show movies and commercials that tout daily shaving. In South African and Indonesian versions, a bewildered bearded man enters a locker room where clean-shaven friends show him how to shave. In the Mexican film, a handsome sheriff is tracking bandits who have kidnapped a woman. He pauses on the trail and snaps a double-edged blade into his razor and lathers his face to shave. In the end, of course, the smooth-faced sheriff gets the woman. From packaging blades so that they can be sold one at a time to educating the unshaven about the joys of a smooth face, Gillette is pursuing a growth strategy in the developing world.

What Gillette does for shaving, Colgate-Palmolive does for oral hygiene. Video vans sent into rural India show an infomercial designed to teach the benefits of toothpaste and the proper method of brushing one's teeth. 'If they saw the toothpaste tube, they wouldn't know what to do with it,' says the company's Indian marketing manager. The people need to be educated about the need for toothpaste and then how to use the product. Toothpaste consumption has doubled in rural India in a six-year period.

Educating people to use a product and offering it at an affordable price are important tactics in emerging markets. So is making unaffordable products available through 'community usage'. The idea is that to increase usage of a product or service, a consumer need not own it but need only have access to it. Private telephones, for example, did not produce the income newly privatised companies anticipated. India's 20 million private phones averaged only $229 of revenue per year. The average revenue per payphone (called public call offices), by contrast, exceeds $6870. Community usage provided an unanticipated opportunity, and companies have shifted emphasis to expanding a network of payphones.

There are over 6 million personal computers in Indian households and some 8 million Internet users. Several companies are seeking to tap into this opportunity with community usage. One UK-based company has a contract with the state of Tamil Nadu to set up 13 000 community Internet cafes and is in discussions for similar installations with other state governments.

Source: David Wessel, 'Gillette Keys Sales to Third World Taste', *Wall Street Journal*, 23 January 1986, p. 30; 'Selling to India', *Economist*, 1 May 2000; Raja Ramachandran, 'Understanding the Market Environment of India', *Business Horizons*, January/February 2000, p. 44; World Bank, 2003.

Mexico has been the leader in privatisation and in lowering tariffs even before entering NAFTA. Over 750 businesses, including the telephone company, steel mills, airlines and banks, have been sold. Pemex, the national oil company, is the only major industry Mexico is not privatising, although restrictions on joint projects between Pemex and foreign companies have been liberalised.

In addition to privatisation and lowering tariffs, most Latin American countries are working at creating an environment to attract capital. Chile, Mexico and Bolivia were the first to make deep cuts in tariffs from a high of 100 per cent or more down to a maximum of 10 to 20 per cent. Taxes that act as non-tariff trade barriers are being eliminated, as are restrictions on the repatriation of profits. These and other changes have energised governments, people and foreign investors.[35]

The population of nearly 460 million is one-half greater than that of the United States. Almost 60 per cent of all the merchandise trade in Latin America is transacted with countries in the western hemisphere. The United States alone provides more than 40 per cent of Latin America's imports and buys a similar share of its exports. Economic and trade policy reforms occurring in Latin American countries signify a tremendous potential for trade and investments.[36]

A study by the Institute for International Economics reported that Argentina, Brazil, Bolivia, Chile, Colombia, Paraguay, Uruguay and several Caribbean nations ranked higher on a scale of 'readiness criteria' - price stability, budget discipline, market-oriented policies and a functioning democracy - than did Mexico at the start of the NAFTA talks. Thus, they are viable candidates for a Western Hemisphere Free Trade Agreement (WHFTA) to replace NAFTA. Such an agreement would strengthen trade ties within the region, pre-empt a plethora of smaller trade agreements, increase trade and make economic sense for the region, the United States and Canada. Exhibit 8.9 provides some economic and social data on several countries in the Americas.

Exhibit 8.9 Economic and social data for selected countries in the Americas

Consumer spending					Health and education		
Country	Food ($ millions)	Percentage of total	Clothing ($ million)	Percentage of total	Hospital beds (per 1000)	Physicians (per 1000)	Literacy (%)
United States	535 287	7.1	309 755	4.1	4.0	2.8	97.0
Argentina	20 249	24.3	4 475	5.4	3.3	2.7	97.1
Brazil	49 101	16.6	11 292	3.7	3.1	1.3	86.4
Colombia	14 278	27.2	1 489	2.1	1.5	1.2	92.5
Mexico	109 755	24.4	17 492	3.9	1.2	1.8	92.2
Venezuela	19 359	31.4	1 125	1.8	1.5	2.4	93.4

Source: Euromonitor, World Bank, 2003.

changing market behaviour and market segmentation

As a country develops, profound changes occur that affect its people. Incomes change, population concentrations shift, expectations for a better life adjust to higher standards, new infrastructures evolve, social capital investments are made, and foreign and domestic companies seek new markets or expand their positions in existing markets. Market behaviour changes and eventually groups of consumers with common tastes and needs (i.e. market segments) arise or disappear. Exhibit 8.10 shows consumption patterns in different emerging markets.

Markets evolve from a three-way interaction of the economy, the culture and the marketing efforts of companies. Markets are not static but are constantly changing as they affect and are affected by changes in incomes, awareness of different lifestyles, exposure to new products and exposure to new ideas. Changing incomes raise expectations and the ability to buy more and different goods. The accessibility of global communications, TV, radio and print media means that people in one part of the world are

Exhibit 8.10 Living standards in selected countries

Country	Households (millions)	Persons per household	Colour TV (per 100 households)	Passenger car (per 100 households)	Refrigerator (per 100 households)	Shower (per 100 households)
Brazil	51	3.4	86	45	83	75
Chile	4	3.9	61	45	63	88
Colombia	10	4.2	86	34	67	97
Peru	6	4.7	48	18	46	60
Azerbaijan	2	5.2	55	21	56	64
China	358	3.6	45	3	6	42
Hong Kong	2	3.3	99	74	96	98
India	175	5.9	32	1	13	41
Indonesia	55	4.0	49	4	26	46
Japan	48	2.6	99	81	97	100
Kazakhstan	4	4.1	58	29	80	66
Malaysia	5	4.5	90	64	97	99
Pakistan	22	7.6	36	5	17	64
Phillipines	16	4.9	65	8	41	83
Singapore	1	3.5	99	41	99	100
South Korea	15	3.3	93	44	97	95
Taiwan	7	3.3	99	51	99	98
Thailand	16	3.9	83	36	69	64
Vietnam	16	5.1	37	2	18	36
United States	106	2.6	99	93	100	99

Source: Euromonitor, 2003.

aware of lifestyles in another. Global companies span the globe with new ideas on consumer behaviour and new products to try.

emerging market segments

With the prosperity that results from economic growth, markets grow and distinct segments begin to emerge. A review of the literature suggests that there is a developing middle-income class, a youth market, an elite market, and so on. Evidence supports the notion of an evolving worldwide middle-income class. Do these middle-income classes constitute a worldwide or at least multicountry homogeneous market segment? The evidence is less compelling, but there are some strong suggestions that – for some kinds of products – market segments across countries have more commonalties than differences. It does not, however, mean that we can standardise marketing strategies and efforts.

Another ramification of emerging markets is the creation of a middle-class household that generates new markets for everything from disposable nappies to cars. The middle class in emerging markets differs from the Western middle class. While they do not have two cars and suburban homes, they do have discretionary income, that is, income not needed for food, clothing and shelter.

Furthermore, large households can translate into higher disposable incomes. Young working people in Asia and Latin American usually live at home until they marry. With no

rent to pay, they have more discretionary income and can contribute to household purchasing power. Low per capita incomes are potential markets for a large variety of goods; consumers show remarkable resourcefulness in finding ways to buy what really matters to them. The poorest slums of Calcutta are home to more than 100 000 VCRs and, in Mexico, homes with colour televisions outnumber those with running water.

A London securities firm says a person earning €225 ($250) annually in developing countries can afford Gillette razors, and at €900 ($1000) he can become a Sony television owner. A Nissan or Volkswagen would be possible with a less than €9000 ($10 000) income. Whirlpool estimates that in Eastern Europe a family with an annual income of €900 ($1000) can afford a refrigerator and with $1800 ($2000) they can buy an automatic washer as well.

Exhibit 8.11 Market indicators in selected countries

	Population (millions)	GDP per capita ($)	Highway km (000)	TV stations* total	Telephones in use** (000)	Internet hosts (000)
United States	293.0	37 800	6 406	11 500	181 599	115 312
Argentina	39.1	11 200	215	486	8 009	742
Australia	19.9	29 000	812	104	10.8	2 848
Brazil	184.1	7 600	1 725	138	38.8	3 163
Canada	32.5	29 800	1 409	80	19 951	3 210
China	1 299	5 000	1 403	3 240	263 000	160
France	60.4	27 600	894	10 260	33 905	2 397
Germany	82.4	27 600	231	8 415	54 350	2 686
India	1 065	2 900	3 320	562	48 917	87
Indonesia	238.0	3 200	343	41	7 750	62
Italy	58.0	26 700	480	5 086	26 596	1 438
Japan	127.3	28 200	1 162	7 552	71 149	12 962
Mexico	105.0	9 000	330	236	15 959	1 333
Poland	38.6	11 100	365	435	12 300	804
South Korea	48.6	17 800	87	971	22 877	694
Spain	40.2	22 000	664	2 239	17 567	1 057
UK	60.3	27 700	372	3 751	34 898	3 399

* Including repeater; ** main lines only.

Source: CIA, *World Factbook*, www.odci.gov/cia/publications/factbook, 2004.

key term

segmentation
part of the customer market that is our potential customers/market

international market segmentation
The purpose of market **segmentation** is to identify relatively homogeneous groups of consumers with similar consumption patterns. A market segment has four components: (1) it must be identifiable, (2) it must be economically reachable, (3) it is more homogeneous in its characteristics than the market as a whole and (4) it is large enough to be profitable. International market segmentation is applying those criteria to market segments across country markets. Fundamentally, the international marketer is looking for an identifiable segment of consumers who have the same (or at least mostly similar) needs and wants across several country markets.

When a company does business in more than one country there are two approaches to the market. Target markets can be identified as (1) all consumers within the borders of a country or (2) global market segments – all consumers with the same needs and wants in groups of country markets. Most international marketers have traditionally viewed each country as a single market segment unique to that country.

As economies prosper and living standards improve, consumer attitudes and consumption patterns change. Retail outlets change in response to consumer demands for longer hours, shopping convenience, better service and ease of access. Hypermarkets and department stores are replacing the traditional speciality stores, and quality and service are expected as part of the product offering. Wherever economies are growing, one can expect changes in consumption patterns and the emergence of trends in market behaviour. See Exhibit 8.11 for market indicators in selected countries.

summary

The increasing scope and level of technical and economic growth have enabled many countries to advance their standards of living by as much as two centuries in a matter of decades. As countries develop their productive capacity, all segments of their economies will feel the pressure to improve. The impact of these social and economic trends will continue to be felt throughout the world, causing significant changes in marketing practices. Marketers must focus on devising marketing plans designed to respond fully to each level of economic development. China and the former Soviet Union continue to undergo rapid political and economic changes that have resulted in opening most communist-bloc countries to foreign direct investments and international trade. And although emerging markets present special problems, they are promising markets for a broad range of products.

This ever-expanding involvement of more and more of the world's people with varying needs and wants will test old trading patterns and alliances. The foreign marketer of today and tomorrow must be able to react to market changes rapidly and to anticipate new trends within constantly evolving market segments that may not have existed as recently as last year. Many of today's market facts will probably be tomorrow's historical myths.

questions

1. Is it possible for an economy to experience economic growth as measured by total GNP without a commensurate rise in the standard of living? Discuss fully.
2. Discuss each of the stages of evolution in the marketing process. Illustrate each stage with the example of a particular country.
3. As a country progresses from one economic stage to another, what in general are the marketing effects?
4. Discuss the impact of IT on the emerging markets. How can it influence company strategies?
5. Discuss the significance of economic development to international marketing. Why is the knowledge of economic development of importance in assessing the world marketing environment? Discuss.
6. Considering the developments in the two biggest markets (India and China), discuss the opportunities and threats in these two markets from a foreign company's perspective.
7. The infrastructure is important to the economic growth of an economy. Comment.
8. What is marketing's role in economic development? Discuss marketing's contributions to economic development.

9 Discuss the economic and trade importance of the big emerging markets.
10 What are the traits of those countries considered to be big emerging markets? Discuss.
11 The importance of China as a market and as a competitor to Western companies is widely discussed. You are required to analyse China's emergence as a competitor to the Western markets; would it be able to surpass the US and/or the EU in terms of trade and GDP? Discuss with arguments and examples.
12 What are global market segments? Why are they important to global companies? Discuss.

further reading

- S.T. Cavusgil, P. Ghauri and M. Agarwal, *Doing Business in Emerging Markets* (Thousand Oaks: Sage, 2002), Chapters 1 and 2.
- C.K. Prahalad and K. Lieberthat, 'The End of Corporate Imperialism', *Harvard Business Review*, 1998 (July–August), pp. 69–79.
- P. Krugman, 'Does Third World Growth Hurt First World Prosperity?', *Harvard Business Review*, 1994 (July–August), p. 153.

references

1 'The Big Emerging Markets', *Business America*, March 1994, pp. 4–6.
2 S. Tamer Cavusgil, Pervez Ghauri and Milind Agarwal, *Doing Business in Emerging Markets* (Thousand Oaks: Sage, 2002).
3 For a thorough review of global consumers, see 'The Emerging Middle Class', *Business Week/ 21st Century Capitalism*, 1994, pp. 176–94.
4 Gross domestic product (GDP) and gross national product (GNP) are two measures of a country's economic activity. GDP is a measure of the market value of all goods and services produced within the boundaries of a nation, regardless of asset ownership. Unlike GNP, GDP excludes receipts from that nation's business operations in foreign countries, as well as the share of reinvested earnings in foreign affiliates of domestic corporations.
5 Walt W. Rostow, *The Stages of Economic Growth*, 2nd edn (London: Cambridge University Press, 1971), p. 10. For an interesting discussion, see Peter Buckley and Pervez Ghauri, *The Global Challenge for Multinational Enterprises* (Oxford: Pergamon Press, 1999).
6 'The Battle for Brazil', *Fortune*, 20 July 1998, pp. 48–53.
7 For a description of how competitive South Korea has become, see David P. Hamilton and Steve Glain, 'Silicon Duel: Koreans Move to Grab Memory-chip Market from the Japanese', *Wall Street Journal*, 14 March 1995, p. A-1.
8 For a discussion of the billions of dollars being invested in infrastructure, see Dave Savona, 'Remaking the Globe', *International Business*, March 1995, pp. 30–6.
9 Goitom Tesfom, Clemens Lutz and Pervez Ghauri, 'Comparing Export Marketing Channels: Developed versus Developing Countries', *International Marketing Review*, 2004, 21(4/5), pp. 409–22.
10 For a comprehensive review of one country's move towards a more open economy, see 'Argentina Survey', *The Economist*, 26 November 1994, 18 pages unnumbered beginning on p. 62.
11 For a comprehensive review of channels of distribution in developing countries, see Saeed Samiee, 'Retailing and Channel Considerations in Developing Countries: A Review and Research Propositions', *Journal of Business Research*, vol. 23, 1993, pp. 103–30; and Janeen E. Olsen and Kent L. Granzin, 'Vertical Integration and Economic Development: An Empirical Investigation of Channel Integration', *Journal of Global Marketing*, vol. 7, no. 3, 1994, pp. 7–39.
12 'India: The Poor Get Richer', *The Economist*, 5 November 1994, pp. 39–40.

13 *Business Week*, 'India: How a Thirst for Energy Lead to a Thaw', 15 November 2004, p. 63.

14 When the US Government lifted the trade embargo against Vietnam, many US companies found that their competitors had already made inroads in that market. See Marita Van Oldenborgy; 'Catch-Up Ball', *International Business*, March 1994, pp. 92–4.

15 'Big Emerging Markets', *Business America*, March 1994, pp. 4–6.

16 'Big Emerging Markets' Share of World Exports Continues to Rise', *Business America*, March 1994, p. 28.

17 International Monetary Fund, 'World Economic Outlook on Transitional Economies', http://www.imf.org/external/pubs/ft/weo/2003/02.

18 S. Tamer Cavusgil, Pervez N. Ghauri and Milind R. Agarwal, *Doing Business in Emerging Markets* (Thousand Oaks: Sage, 2002).

19 'Companies Tap EE Luxury Goods Market', *Business Eastern Europe*, 28 April 1994, pp. 4–5.

20 Pervez Ghauri and Karin Holstius, 'The Role of Matching in the Foreign Market Entry Process in the Baltic States', *European Journal of Marketing*, vol. 30, no. 6, 1996, pp. 75–88.

21 John Naisbitt, *Megatrends Asia: Eight Asian Megatrends that are Reshaping Our World* (New York: Simon & Schuster, 1996).

22 Jim Rohwer, *Asia Rising, Why America will Prosper while Asia's Economics Boom* (New York: Simon & Schuster, 1995).

23 'As Japan Goes?' *The Economist*, 20 June 1998, pp. 17–18; and 'Three Futures for Japan', *The Economist*, 21 March 1998, pp. 29–30.

24 Dan Biers, 'Now in First World, Asia's Tigers Act Like It', *Wall Street Journal*, 28 February 1995, p. A-15.

25 'The China Connection', *Business Week*, 5 August 1996, pp. 32–5; and 'China's WTO Accession', *Far Eastern Economic Review*, 2 July 1998, p. 38.

26 'America's Dose of Zinophobia, Japan-Bashing Used to be a Popular Sport in America, Now it is More Fashionable to Worry About China', *The Economist*, 29 March 1997, pp. 67–8.

27 China is divided into 23 provinces (including Taiwan) and five autonomous border regions. The provinces and autonomous regions are usually grouped into six large administrative regions: Northeastern Region, Northern Region (includes Beijing), Eastern Region (includes Shanghai), South Central Region, Southwestern Region, and the Northwestern Region. After Hong Kong's reversion to China, it is considered the seventh autonomous region.

28 'China, Hong Kong, Taiwan', *Trade and Culture*, Winter 1993–94, pp. 52–6.

29 *Business Week*, Cover Story: 'China's Power Brands', 8 November 2004, pp. 44–50.

30 Min Chen, *Asian Management Systems* (New York: Routledge, 1995).

31 'The China Connection', *Business Week*, 5 August 1996, pp. 32–3.

32 'India's Political Struggle', *The Economist*, 5 April 1997, p. 66.

33 *Business Week*, 'China Playing for Keeps-Online', 15 November 2004, pp. 28–9.

34 Matt Moffett, 'Seeds of Reform: Key Finance Ministers in Latin America are Old Harvard-MIT Pals', *Wall Street Journal*, 1 August 1994, p. 1.

35 S. Tamer Cavusgil, Pervez N. Ghauri and Milind R. Agarwal, *Doing Business in Emerging Markets* (Thousand Oaks: Sage, 2002).

36 Paul Magnusson, 'With Latin America Thriving, NAFTA Might Keep Marching South', *Business Week*, 24 July 1994, p. 20.

chapter 9
Multinational Market Regions and Market Groups

During the last three decades an interest in regional integration in Europe, Asia and the Americas has increased. The difficulties faced in the General Agreement on Tariffs and Trade (GATT) in the Uruguay round, the emergence of the WTO and the proliferation of regional arrangements have led to renewed interest in regional integration.[1]

Among the important global trends today is the evolution of the multinational market region – those groups of countries that seek mutual economic benefit from reducing intra-regional trade and tariff barriers. Organisational form varies widely among market regions, but the universal orientation of such multinational cooperation is economic benefit for the participants. Political and social benefits sometimes accrue, but the dominant motive for affiliation is economic. The world is awash with economic cooperative agreements as countries look for economic alliances to expand their access to free markets.

Regional economic cooperative agreements have been around since the end of the Second World War. The most successful has been the European Union (EU); the world's largest multinational market region with 25 member countries is the foremost example of economic cooperation.

Multinational market groups form large markets that provide potentially significant market opportunities for international business. When it became apparent that the EU was to achieve its long-term goal of a single European market, a renewed interest in economic cooperation was sparked. The European Economic Area (EEA), a 27-country alliance between the EU and remaining members of the European Free Trade Area (EFTA), became the world's largest single unified market. Canada, the United States and Mexico entered into a free-trade agreement to form the North American Free Trade Agreement (NAFTA).[2] Many countries in Latin America, Asia, Eastern Europe and elsewhere are either planning some form of economic cooperation or have entered into agreements. With the dissolution of the USSR (Soviet Union) and the independence of Eastern European countries, linkages among the independent states and republics are also forming. The Commonwealth of Independent States (CIS) is an initial attempt at realignment into an economic union of some of the Newly Independent States (NIS) – former republics of the USSR.[3] The growing trend of economic cooperation is increasing concerns about the effect of such cooperation on global competition. Governments and businesses are concerned that the EEA, NAFTA and other cooperative regional groups have become regional trading blocs without trade restrictions internally but with borders protected from outsiders.[4]

Three global regions – Europe, the Americas and the Asian Pacific Rim – are involved in forging a new economic order for trade and development that will dominate world markets for years to come. In Kenichi Ohmae's book, *Triad Power*, he points out that the global

companies that will be Triad powers must have significant market positions in each of the Triad regions.[5] At the economic centre of each Triad region there are one or two economic industrial powers: in the European Triad it is Germany and the United Kingdom; in the American Triad it is the United States; in the Asian Triad it is Japan and China. The Triad regions are the centres of economic activity that provide global companies with a concentration of sophisticated consumer- and capital-goods markets. Within each Triad region there are strong single-country markets and/or multi-country markets (such as the EU) bound together by economic cooperative agreements. Much of the economic growth and development that will occur in these regions and make them such important markets will result from single countries being forged into thriving free trade areas.

The focus of this chapter is on the various patterns of multinational cooperation and the strategic marketing implications of economic cooperation.

la raison d'être

Successful economic union requires favourable economic, political, cultural and geographic factors as a basis for success. Major flaws in any one factor can destroy a union unless the other factors provide sufficient strength to overcome the weaknesses. In general, the advantages of economic union must be clear-cut and significant, and the benefits must greatly outweigh the disadvantages before nations forego any part of their sovereignty. A strong threat to the economic or political security of a nation is often needed to provide the impetus for cooperation. The cooperative agreements among European countries that preceded the European Community (EC) certainly had their roots in the need for economic redevelopment after the Second World War. Many felt that if Europe was to survive there had to be economic unity; the agreements made then formed the groundwork for the European Community.

economic actors

Every type of economic union shares the development and enlargement of market opportunities as a basic orientation; usually markets are enlarged through preferential tariff treatment for participating members and/or common tariff barriers against outsiders. Enlarged, protected markets stimulate internal economic development by providing assured outlets and preferential treatment for goods produced within the customs union, and consumers benefit from lower internal tariff barriers among the participating countries. In many cases, external as well as internal barriers are reduced because of the greater economic security afforded domestic producers by the enlarged market.

Nations with complementary economic bases are least likely to encounter friction in the development and operation of a common market unit. However, for an economic union to survive, it must have in place agreements and mechanisms to settle economic disputes. In addition, the total benefit of economic integration must outweigh the individual differences that are sure to arise as member countries adjust to new trade relationships. The European Union includes countries with diverse economies, distinctive monetary systems, developed agricultural bases and different natural resources. It is significant that most of the problems encountered by the EU have arisen over agriculture and monetary policy. In the early days of the EU, agricultural disputes were common. The British attempted to keep French poultry out of the British market, France banned Italian wine, and the Irish banned eggs and poultry from other member countries. At one point, the EU, not any one country, banned British beef because of the effects of BSE (also called 'mad cow disease') on British animals and its linkages with the human affliction Creutzfeldt-Jakob disease (CJD). In all cases, the reason given was health and safety, but the probable motive, at least in some cases, was the continuation of the age-old policy of market protection. Such skirmishes are not unusual, but they do test the strength of the union.

The demise of the Latin American Free Trade Association (LAFTA) was caused, in part, by its economically stronger members not allowing for the needs of the weaker ones.

Many of the less well-known attempts at common markets have languished because of economic incompatibility that could not be resolved and the uncertainty of future economic advantage.

political factors

Political amenability among countries is another basic requisite for development of a supra-national market arrangement. Participating countries must have comparable aspirations and general compatibility before surrendering any part of their national sovereignty. State sovereignty is one of the most cherished possessions of any nation and is relinquished only for a promise of significant improvement of the national position through cooperation.

Economic considerations provide the basic catalyst for the formation of a customs union group, but political elements are equally important. The uniting of the original European Community countries was partially a response to American dominance and threat of Russia's great political power; the countries of Western Europe were willing to settle their family squabbles to present a unified front. The communist threat no longer exists, but the importance of political unity to fully achieve all the benefits of economic integration has driven the EC countries to form the European Union.[6]

geographic proximity

Although it is not absolutely imperative that cooperating members of a customs union have geographic proximity, such closeness facilitates the functioning of a common market. Transportation networks basic to any marketing system are likely to be interrelated and well developed when countries are close together. One of the first major strengths of the EC was its transportation network: the opening of the Channel tunnel between England and France, and the bridge between Denmark and Sweden further bound this common market. Countries that are widely separated geographically have major barriers to overcome in attempting economic fusion.

cultural factors

Cultural similarity eases the shock of economic cooperation with other countries. The more similar the cultures, the more likely a market is to succeed because members understand the outlook and viewpoints of their colleagues. Although there is great cultural diversity in the EU, key members share a long-established Christian heritage and are commonly aware of being European.

Language, as a part of culture, has not created as much of a barrier for EU countries as was expected. Initially there were seven major languages, but such linguistic diversity did not impede trade because European businesses historically have been multilingual. Nearly every educated European can do business in at least two or three languages; thus, in every relationship, there is likely to be a linguistic common ground. Now even countries such as France, Germany and Italy are switching over to English as a language of trade and science. A number of business schools and universities in these countries are now offering MBAs and other degree programmes in English. This was unthinkable even a decade ago.

patterns of multinational cooperation

Multinational market groups take several forms, varying significantly in the degree of cooperation, dependence and interrelationship among participating nations. There are five fundamental groupings for regional economic integration, ranging from regional cooperation for development, which requires the least amount of integration, to the ultimate of integration, political union. Exhibit 9.1 illustrates different levels of cooperation.

regional cooperation groups

The most basic economic integration and cooperation is the regional cooperation for development (RCD). In the RCD arrangement, governments agree to participate jointly to

Exhibit 9.1 Different levels of multinational cooperation

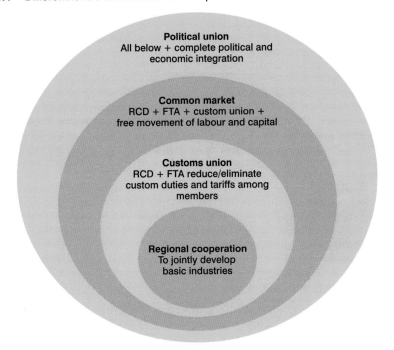

Political union
All below + complete political and
economic integration

Common market
RCD + FTA + custom union +
free movement of labour and capital

Customs union
RCD + FTA reduce/eliminate
custom duties and tariffs among
members

Regional cooperation
To jointly develop
basic industries

develop basic industries beneficial to each economy. Each country makes an advance commitment to participate in the financing of a new joint venture and to purchase a specified share of the output of the venture. An example is the project between Colombia and Venezuela to build a hydro-electric generating plant on the Orinoco river. They shared jointly in construction costs and they share the electricity produced.

free trade area

A free trade area (FTA) requires more cooperation and integration than the RCD. It is an agreement among two or more countries to reduce or eliminate customs duties and non-tariff trade barriers among partner countries while members maintain individual tariff schedules for external countries. Essentially, an FTA provides its members with a mass market without barriers that impede the flow of goods and services. The United States has free trade agreements with Canada and Mexico (NAFTA) and separately with Israel. The seven-nation European Free Trade Association (EFTA), among the better-known free trade areas, still exists although three of its members also belong to the EU and five to the EEA.

customs union

A customs union represents the next stage in economic cooperation. It enjoys the free trade area's reduced or eliminated internal tariffs and adds a common external tariff on products imported from countries outside the union. The customs union is a logical stage of cooperation in the transition from an FTA to a common market. The European Community was a customs union before becoming a common market. Customs unions exist between France and Monaco, Italy and San Marino, and Switzerland and Liechtenstein.

common market

A common market agreement eliminates all tariffs and other restrictions on internal trade, adopts a set of common external tariffs, and removes all restriction on the free flow of capital and labour among member nations. Thus a common market is a common marketplace for goods as well as for services (including labour) and for capital. It is a unified economy and lacks only political unity to become a political union.

GOING INTERNATIONAL 9.1

can McDonald's get cooking in Europe?

Now that McDonald's is sizzling in the US again, can it turn up the heat in Europe? On 13 April 2004, it announced a 14.2 per cent rise in same-store sales for the first quarter in the US. But, after currency-adjusting, growth in Europe was only 3.5 per cent – and sales declined 2.9 per cent in March in the same year. That's no small concern for the fast-

food giant, since European sales were $5.87 billion in 2003, not far behind the $6.04 billion in the US. Time to get the Old World cooking again. McDonald's is already rolling out new offerings, including salads, yoghurt and other fare aimed at health-conscious diners. To develop recipes, the company has opened a test kitchen in the Paris suburbs. It's also planning face-lifts for many of its 6200 European outlets.

Directing this new push is Dennis Hennequin, former head of operations in France, where McDonald's is thriving. Hennequin, who redesigned more than half of McDonald's 1000 French outlets – they now range from faux alpine chalets to sleek music-themed restaurants with head-phones at the tables – was named executive vice-president for Europe in January 2004.

McDonald's plans 160 new restaurants in Europe this year, including 40 in France. But there's still a supersize problem: Britain. Sales at McDonald's 1235 British outlets have been sluggish for years, and the reasons are numerous. New chains such as Yo! Sushi and Nando's Chicken Restaurants, which feature spicy Portuguese chicken, have outpaced McDonald's. Operators such as US-based Subway are pulling in customers with fresh salads and sandwiches on focaccia bread. Starbucks has made McDonald's outlets look sterile and out of date. And the 2001 scare over mad cow disease, along with concerns about rising obesity, make things worse. 'They're being attacked from every angle,' says Jeffrey Young, an industry expert at Allegra Strategies Ltd, a London consultancy.

No surprise, then, that McDonald's chose Britain for the rollout of a Salads Plus menu, which features four varieties of main-course salads topped with warm chicken, a premium chicken sandwich, and a fruit-and-yoghurt dessert. It also wants British franchises to upgrade interiors and exteriors. Outlets in France have reported a 15–20 per cent sales boost after renovations. But Britain is a tougher market than France, where there are few takeout chains to compete with McDonald's.

■ Would new designs revive McDonald's faded image in Europe?

Source: abridged from 'Can McDonald's get it Cooking in Europe?', *Business Week*, 26 April 2004, p. 26.

The Treaty of Rome, the forerunner of the European Union signed in 1957, called for a common market in Europe, eliminating all restrictions on trade, movement of labour and capital. Thus, until the Maastricht Treaty, there was a European Economic Community (EEC). Latin America claims to have three common markets: the Central American Common Market (CACM), the Andean Common Market and the Southern Common Market (Mercosur).

political union

Political union is the most fully integrated form of regional cooperation. It involves complete political and economic integration; it may be voluntary or enforced. The most notable enforced political union was the Council for Mutual Economic Assistance

(COMECON), a centrally controlled group of countries organised by the USSR. With the dissolution of the USSR and the independence of Eastern Europe, COMECON was disbanded.

The Commonwealth of Nations is a voluntary organisation providing for the loosest possible relationship that can be classified as economic integration. The British Commonwealth comprises Britain and countries formerly part of the British Empire. Its members recognise the British monarch as their symbolic head although Britain has no political authority over the Commonwealth. Its member states had received preferential tariffs when trading with Great Britain but, when Britain joined the European Community, all preferential tariffs were abandoned. The Commonwealth can best be described as the weakest of political unions and is mostly based on economic history and a sense of tradition. Heads of state meet every three years to discuss trade and political issues they jointly face, and compliance with any decisions or directives issued is voluntary.

global markets and multinational market groups

The globalisation of markets, the restructuring of Eastern Europe into independent market-driven economies, the dissolution of the Soviet Union into independent states, the worldwide trend towards economic cooperation, and enhanced global competition make it important that market potential be viewed in the context of regions of the world rather than country by country. Formal economic cooperation agreements such as the EC are the most notable examples of multinational market groups, but many new coalitions are forming, old ones are restructuring and the possibility of many new cooperative arrangements is on the horizon.

This section presents basic information and data on markets and market groups in Europe, the Americas, Africa, Asia and the Middle East. Existing economic cooperation agreements within each of these regions will be reviewed. The reader must appreciate that the status of cooperative agreements and alliances among nations has been extremely fluid in some parts of the world. Many are fragile and may cease to exist or may restructure into a totally different form. It will probably take the better part of a decade for many of the new trading alliances that are now forming to stabilise into semi-permanent groups.

Europe

The European Union is the focus of the European region of the first Triad. Within Europe, every type of multinational market grouping exists. The European Union (EU), European Community (EC), European Economic Area (EEA) and the European Free Trade Association (EFTA) are the most-established cooperative groups (see Exhibit 9.2).

Of escalating economic importance are the new members from Eastern Europe, such as Poland, Hungary and the Czech Republic, and the three Baltic states (Estonia, Latvia and Lithuania) that gained independence from the USSR just prior to its break-up. Key issues centre around their economic development and economic integration into the EU.

Also within the European region is the Commonwealth of Independent States. New and untested, this coalition of 12 former USSR republics may or may not survive in its present form to take its place among the other multinational market groups.

European Union

The idea of a united Europe is centuries old; from the Roman Empire to the empire of Charlemagne in the early nineteenth century, or even to the idea of a Catholic Europe with a pope at its head, all aimed at an integrated Europe. At the third Universal Peace Congress in 1849, Victor Hugo officially presented the idea of the United States of Europe. The First World War, with all its senseless bloodshed, brought about a review of the idea of a united Europe. During this period, Count Coudenhove-Kalergi, who was of Greek and Dutch descent but was an Austro-Hungarian diplomat, started a Pan-European Union. He

Exhibit 9.2 The European economic area: EU, EFTA and associates

ICELAND

Norwegian Sea

NORWAY

SWEDEN

FINLAND

White Sea

Gulf of Bothnia

ATLANTIC OCEAN

North Sea

Gulf of Finland

ESTONIA

LATVIA

Baltic Sea

LITHUANIA

DENMARK

IRELAND

NETHERLANDS

UNITED KINGDOM

POLAND

BELGIUM

GERMANY

LUXEMBOURG LIECHTENSTEIN

CZECH REPUBLIC

SLOVAKIA

FRANCE

AUSTRIA HUNGARY

SWITZERLAND

SLOVENIA

ITALY

Black Sea

Adriatic Sea

PORTUGAL

SPAIN

ANDORRA

Tyrrhenian Sea

GREECE

Ionian Sea

Aegean Sea

Mediterranean Sea

MALTA

- ☐ EU
- ☐ EFTA
- ☐ NEW EU MEMBERS

received support from a number of prominent political figures such as Aristide Briand, the French foreign minister, who presented a scheme to the League of Nations in the 1920s for a European Union.

The Second World War finally stimulated the idea of European integration. A group of European politicians worked on the idea with Jean Monet, who is often called the 'Father of Europe', at its head. In addition to being a French diplomat, Monet had been the deputy secretary general of the League of Nations in the interwar years.[7]

Exhibit 9.3 illustrates the evolution of the EU from its beginnings after The Second World War to today. In 1951, six European states (France, West Germany, Italy, the Netherlands, Belgium and Luxembourg) signed the Treaty of Paris to establish the European Coal and Steel Community (ECSC). It was the forerunner of the European Community. In 1955,

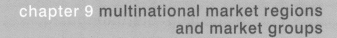

delegates from ECSC states met at Messina in Italy and agreed to form the European Economic Community (EEC), and in March 1957 the Treaty of Rome, formally setting up the EEC, was signed. The purpose was to achieve a customs union of the six countries and by 1969 abolish all tariffs on their mutual trade. The Treaty of Rome had three major political objectives: political unity, peace and democracy. Other objectives included integration, improvement of living standards and encouragement of trade with other countries.[8]

The European Union was created when the 12 nations of the European Community ratified the Maastricht Treaty. The members committed themselves to economic and political

Exhibit 9.3 European Coal and Steel Community to European Union

1951	Treaty of Paris	European Coal and Steel Community (ECSC) (founding members are Belgium, France, Germany, Italy, Luxembourg and the Netherlands)
1957	Treaty of Rome	Blueprint for European Economic Community (EEC)
1958	European Economic Community	Ratified by ECSC founding members. Common Market is established
1960	European Free Trade Area	Established by Austria, Denmark, Norway, Portugal, Sweden, Switzerland and United Kingdom
1973	Expansion	Denmark, Ireland and United Kingdom join EEC
1979	European Monetary System	The European Currency Unit (ECU) is created. All members except the UK agree to maintain their exchange rates within specific margins
1981	Expansion	Greece joins EEC
1985	1992 Single Market Programme	Introduced to European Parliament 'White Paper' for action
1986	Expansion	Spain and Portugal join EEC
1987	Single European Act	Ratified with full implementation by 1992
1992	Treaty on European Union	Also known as Maastricht Treaty. Blueprint for Economic and Monetary Union (EMU)
1993	Europe 1992	Single European Act in force (1 January 1993)
1993	European Union	Treaty on European Union (Maastricht Treaty) in force with monetary union by 1999
1994	European Economic Area	The EEA was formed with EU members and Norway and Iceland
1995	Expansion	Austria, Finland and Sweden join EU
1997	Amsterdam Treaty	Established procedures for expansion to Central and Eastern Europe
1999	Monetary Union	Introduction of the single currency on the foreign exchange markets and for electronic payments
2002	Monetary Union	Euro replaces all national banknotes and coins of EMU members
2004	Expansion	Ten new members join the EU. EC agrees that Turkey can be invited for membership negotiations
2007	Expansion	Bulgaria and Romania are expected to join in 2007

Source: 'Chronology of the EU', http://www.europa.eu.int. Reprinted with permission from the European Communities.

integration. The treaty allows for the free movement of goods, persons, services and capital throughout the member states, a common currency, common foreign and security policies, including defence, a common justice system and cooperation between police and other authorities on crime, terrorism and immigration issues. However, not all the provisions of the treaty have been universally accepted. The dismantling of border controls to permit passport-free movement between countries according to the Schengen Agreement, signed in Schengen (Luxembourg) in 1995, for example, has been implemented by only seven out of 15 EU member states.[9] This group was later joined by most of the members except the United Kingdom and the new members from Eastern Europe.

Of all the multinational market groups, none is more secure in its cooperation or more important economically than the European Union. From its beginning, it has successfully made progress towards achieving the goal of complete economic integration and, ultimately, political union. For a list of EU member countries and related economic data, see Exhibit 9.4.

Historically, standards were used to limit market access effectively. Germany protected its beer market from the rest of Europe with a purity law requiring beer sold in Germany to be brewed only from water, hops, malt and yeast. Italy protected its pasta market by requiring that pasta be made only from durum wheat. Incidentally, both the beer and pasta regulations have been struck down by the European Court of Justice as trade violations. Such restrictive standards effectively kept competing products out of their respective markets whether from other European countries or elsewhere. Sceptics, doubtful that such cultural, legal and social differences could ever be overcome, held little hope for a unified Europe. Their scepticism has proved wrong. Today, many marvel at how far the European Union has come.[10]

The Single European Act   Europe without borders, 'Fortress Europe' and EC 92 refer to the Single European Act – the agreement designed to finally remove all barriers to trade and make the European Community a single internal market. The ultimate goal of the Treaty of Rome, the agreement that founded the EC, was economic and political union, a United States of Europe. The Single European Act moved the EC one step closer to the goal of economic integration.

In addition to dismantling the existing barriers, the Single European Act proposed a wide range of new commercial policies including single European standards, one of the more difficult and time-consuming goals to achieve. Technical standards for electrical products offer a good example of how overwhelming is the task of achieving universal standards. There are 29 types of electrical outlet, 10 types of plug and 12 types of flex used by EU member countries. The estimated cost for all EU countries to change wiring systems and electrical standards to a single European standard is €80 billion, or about US$98 billion. Because of the time it will take to achieve uniform European standards for health, safety, technical and other areas, the Single European Act provides for a policy of harmonisation and mutual recognition.

Mutual recognition extends beyond technical or health standards and includes mutual recognition for marketing practices as well. The European Court of Justice's (ECJ) interpretation of Article 30, which establishes the principle of mutual recognition, is that a product put on sale legally in one member state should be available for sale in the same way in all others. The ECJ's landmark decision involved Germany's ban on the sale of Cassis de Dijon, a French liqueur. Germany claimed that selling the low-alcohol drink would encourage alcohol consumption, considered by authorities to be unhealthy. The Court of Justice rejected the argument, ruling that the restriction represented a non-tariff barrier outlawed by Article 30. In other words, once Cassis de Dijon was legally sold in France, Germany was obligated, under mutual recognition, to allow its sale in Germany.[11]

Food definition problems in particular have impeded progress in guaranteeing free circulation of food products within the EU. For example, several member states maintain

Exhibit 9.4 European market regions

Association	Member	Population (millions)	GDP* ($ billions)	GDP* per capita	Imports of goods and services ($ billions)	Exports of goods and services ($ billions)
European Union (EU)						
	Belgium	1.03	321.1	31 218	233.7	251.5
	Denmark	5.4	207.5	38 710	83.8	92.6
	Germany	82.3	2 701.6	32 813	850.9	941.6
	Greece	10.6	144.8	13 669	46.6	34.8
	Spain	41.1	723.5	17 595	237.0	221.9
	France	59.2	1 804.9	30 492	483.0	815.7
	Ireland	3.8	112.9	29 401	100.3	120.1
	Italy	57.0	1 225.3	21 144	347.3	370.7
	Luxembourg	0.4	24.9	56 382	30.9	35.2
	Netherlands	16.0	502.5	31 333	310.9	339.2
	Austria	8.1	269.8	33 172	310.9	339.2
	Portugal	10.0	131.4	13 109	59.9	46.7
	Finland	5.2	166.7	32 121	57.8	79.0
	Sweden	8.9	281.3	31 627	116.5	143.7
	United Kingdom	58.8	1 334.6	22 697	534.6	455.1
	Czech Republic	10.3	57.1	5 583	51.1	46.1
	Estonia	1.4	6.4	4 707	7.5	6.6
	Cyprus	0.8	57.1	14 592	—	—
	Latvia	2.4	6.6	2 816	4.2	3.7
	Lithuania	3.5	8.0	2 308	7.3	5.6
	Hungary	10.2	56.4	5 540	38.0	36.6
	Malta	0.4	4.0	10 098	—	—
	Poland	38.6	143.6	3 716	56.5	54.1
	Slovenia	2.0	23.9	11 984	15.5	14.6
	Slovak Republic	5.4	23.8	4 405	19.6	18.6
EU candidate countries						
	Bulgaria	7.9	13.1	1 630	10.8	8.5
	Romania	22.4	31.2	1 393	20.1	14.5
	Turkey	68.5	190.3	2 873	56.5	65.2
European Free Trade Area (EFTA)						
	Iceland	0.3	9.0	32 060	3.7	3.5
	Liechtenstein	0.03	—	—	—	—
	Norway	4.5	172.8	38 298	61.5	68.5
	Switzerland	7.2	340.3	47 064	135.6	147.8

* Constant 1995 dollars.

Source: World Bank, 2003. Copyright 2003 by TRANSACTION PUBS. Reproduced with permission of TRANSACTION PUBS via Copyright Clearance Center.

GOING INTERNATIONAL 9.2

how to prevent old Europe becoming a dying continent

The evidence from the UN population division shows that Europe is a continent that has a high degree of population growth. It implies that Europe could become a huge old people's home. There are still high birth rates in northern and western Europe. The fertility rates vary from 1.6 children per woman in the UK to 1.9 for Ireland. The forecast is of a UK population increase of 13 per cent at 136 000 a year. There are low birth rates in southern Europe: 1.27 children per woman in Greece, 1.23 in Italy and 1.15 in Spain. The birth rate is also low in the central European countries: 1.35 in Germany, 1.28 in Austria and 1.41 in Switzerland. The forecast is that the population will drop by 19 per cent in Switzerland and 9 per cent in Austria. Those countries joining the European Union have low birth rates, varying from 1.1 in Latvia to 1.32 in Romania.

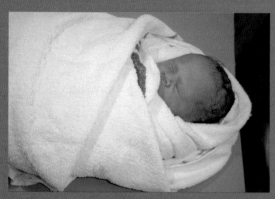

More babies are needed to boost birth rates in Europe

This ageing population has a negative impact on potential economic growth. The overall economic growth rate in the EU declines from 2–2.25 per cent a year to about 1.25 per cent* according to the European Commission. The percentage of people over 60 is 40 per cent, which is significantly more than the percentage of people under 14 (13 per cent). The fertility rate is declining while immigration continues to grow, leading to a threat against cultural continuity.

The solution to these challenges could include promoting more provision for childcare; pension reform to reduce the burden on state welfare provision; governments could reduce large fiscal deficits in order to contribute more towards the accumulation of capital; and immigration could be better managed.

* 'Economic and Financial Market Consequences of Ageing Populations', the EU Economy: 2002 Review, www.europa.eu.int/comm/economy_finance.

Source: adapted from Martin Wolf, 'How to Prevent Old Europe Becoming a Dying Continent', *Financial Times*, 5 March 2003, p. 21.

different definitions of yoghurt. The French insist that anything called *yogurt* must contain live cultures; thus, they prohibited the sale of a Dutch product under the name *yoghurt* because it did not contain live cultures, as does the French product. In March 1996, the European Commission decided that only goat's-milk or ewe's-milk cheese produced in Greece was entitled to be called feta. The ruling brought storms of protest from Danes, who now have five years to rename their cow's-milk feta. Greeks have a solid claim of name, backed by a thousand years of history.[12]

Some of the first and most welcome reforms were the single customs document that replaced the 70 forms originally required for transborder shipments to member countries, the elimination of sabotage rules (which kept a trucker from returning with a loaded truck after delivery), and EU-wide transport licensing. These changes alone were estimated to have reduced distribution costs by 50 per cent for companies doing cross-border business in the EU.

EU Structure   The European Union was created as a result of three treaties that established the European Coal and Steel Community, the European Economic Community and the European Atomic Energy Community. These three treaties are incorporated within the

GOING INTERNATIONAL 9.3

benefits of EU expansion

1 **Stability**   Expansion will promote democracy and rule of law in economies in Eastern Europe and provide the EU region with wider stability.
2 **Bigger market**   The new EU will have almost 500 million citizens, creating the biggest single market of affluent customers. Both old and new members will benefit.
3 **More investment**   The new EU members have already attracted billions of € of foreign capital. The bigger EU will become even more attractive for foreign investors.
4 **Reforms in Central and Eastern Europe**   The accession countries have fully privatised most state industries and have achieved market economies. It will help modernise infrastructure, clean environment and promote efficient industries.
5 **Structural reforms in Western Europe**   The 10 new members will stimulate economies in the smaller (older) EU members. Most countries will reform labour markets, thus restructuring industries and economies toward greater efficiencies.

Source: Business Week, Special Report: 'Mega Europe', 18 November 2002, pp. 24–40.

European Union and serve as the community's constitution. They provide a policy framework and empower the commission and the Council of Ministers to pass laws to carry out EU policy. The union uses three legal instruments: (1) regulations binding the member states directly and having the same strength as national laws; (2) directives also binding the member states but allowing them to choose the means of execution; and (3) decisions addressed to a government, an enterprise or an individual binding the parties named.

EU Authority   Over the years, the European Union has gained an increasing amount of authority over its member states. The Union's institutions (the European Commission, the Council of Ministers, the European Parliament and the European Court of Justice) and their decision-making processes have legal status and extensive powers in fields covered by common policies. Union institutions have the power to make decisions and execute policies in specific areas. They form a federal pattern with executive, parliamentary and judicial branches. A number of private consultant companies specialise in lobbying the different EU institutions (see Exhibit 9.5).

■ The European Commission is a group that initiates policy and supervises its observance by member states. It proposes and supervises the execution of laws and policies. The Commission has a president and four vice presidents; each of its members is appointed for a four-year term by mutual agreement of EU governments. Commission members act only in the interest of the EU. They may not receive instructions from any national government and are subject to the supervision of the European Parliament. Their responsibilities are to ensure that EU rules and the principles of the common market are respected.

■ The Council of Ministers, one from each member country, passes laws based on commission proposals. Because the council is the decision-making body of the EU, it is its responsibility to debate and decide which proposals of the Single European Act to accept as binding on EU members. In concert with the commission's White Paper, the

Exhibit 9.5 Top 10 lobbying consultancies in Europe

Consultancy	Created	Staff	Parent company	Branches
Hill & Knowlton	1967	28	WPP, UK	30 cities in Europe, 35 worldwide
GPC Government Policy Consultants	1988	28	Omnicom, US	London, Edinburgh, associate agencies all over Europe except Luxembourg and Austria
Apco Europe	1995	20	Gray Advertising, US	(With GCI) all EU member states; Washington DC, Seattle, Sacramento, Beijing, Hong Kong, Moscow
Adamson Associates	1981	16	Independent, Belgium	Geneva, Strasbourg
European Public Policy Advisers	1987	16	Private shareholders international	Austria, Belgium, Czech Republic, Finland, France, Hungary, the Netherlands, Norway, Poland, Portugal, Russia, Spain, Sweden, UK, Germany, US (with International Trade Advisers), associated offices in Ireland, Denmark, Italy, Greece
European Strategy	1990	12	Grayling Group, UK	All EU countries (except Portugal, Greece, Austria); NY
Edelman Europe	1995	10	Edelman Public Relations Worldwide, US	Nine offices in Europe, 26 in the Americas and Asia/Pacific region
Robinson, Linton and Associates	1989	9	Burson-Marsteller, US	Uses the Burson-Marsteller network (most European countries, US and Russia)
Entente International Communication	1991	6	Private shareholders	All 15 EU member states, associated offices in other countries
Charles Barker BSMG	1990	3	BSMG, US	UK

Source: based on *The European* and *Marketing News*, several issues, 1998.

Single European Act included the first and only amendment of the original Treaty of Rome (1957), which streamlined decision making. Under provisions in the act, the council can enact into law many of the proposals in the White Paper by majority vote instead of the unanimity formerly required. Requiring only a majority vote by the council for passage of reforms was seen as a necessary change if the Single European Act was to be a reality. However, proposals for changes in tax rates on products and services still require a unanimous vote.

■ The European Parliament has 732 members elected every five years by universal suffrage. It is mainly a consultative body, which passes on most community legislation with limited but gradually increasing budgetary powers. The Single European Act gave Parliament greater powers.[13] After legislation has gone through two readings, Parliament has the right on the second reading to put forward detailed alterations and amendments that, if accepted by the Commission, can be rejected only by the member states and a unanimous vote of the Council of Ministers. Parliament can now influence legislation but it does not have the power to initiate legislation.

■ The European Court of Justice (ECJ) consists of 13 judges and is the Union's Supreme Court. Its first responsibility is challenging any measures incompatible with the Treaty of Rome when they are adopted by the Commission, Council or national governments. Its second responsibility is passing judgment, at the request of a national court, on interpretation or validity of points of EU law. The court's decisions are final and cannot be appealed in national courts. The Court of Justice has increased its presence in the last decade and has become very important in enforcing Union laws and regulations.

GOING INTERNATIONAL 9.4

pros and cons of euro entry

In 2003, *The Financial Times* conducted a survey of 40 UK foreign-owned manufacturers to see how the UK's decision to join or not join the euro might be affecting their plans to invest in the UK. Nineteen of the companies stated that they would be less likely to invest if the UK did not join the euro. Twelve respondents expressed neutral attitudes, and nine declined to comment, either because the question was too difficult or because they preferred to keep their views private. However, the nine included such companies as Ford, Toyota and BMW, whose pro-euro views have been well aired in the past.

Manufacturers who expressed negative attitudes towards the decision not to join the euro tended to be companies with large exports to continental Europe. The poll underlined the fact that many large exporters to continental Europe, hit by the pound's strength against the euro since the late 1990s, believed entry into the single currency would increase their expansion opportunities by reducing currency risks. Companies that operated in highly competitive industries such as automotive manufacturing also said that their investments in the UK might be negatively impacted by the decision not to join the euro. Although these companies may have most of their customers in the UK, and so are not directly affected by the exchange rates, they feel that the health of their businesses will be improved if Britain becomes part of the euro-zone.

A euro-promotion truck in Greece
©AFP/CORBIS

Neutral responses came mostly from companies whose factories sold mainly in the UK (or sold UK-specific products such as boilers and ovens) and were in less competitive industries. Neutral responses were also provided by big exporters from the UK but who sold a considerable amount outside the euro-zone. These businesses said that the euro decision would not make a huge difference to their investment calculations. Possibly the most interesting responses came from companies that might have been expected to say euro entry would help their investment opportunities, but that turned out to be neutral. For example, Geoffrey Lloyd, UK managing director of Heller, a German machine-tool maker, said that 'the most important things for us are issues such as productivity and the skills of our employees'.

■ Do you think the UK's entry into the euro would influence UK companies' competitive position in Europe?

Source: adapted from Peter Marsh, 'Industry Highlights Pros and Cons of Euro Entry', *Financial Times*, 18 February 2003.

Court decisions are binding on EU members; through its judgments and interpretations, the court is helping to create a body of truly EU law that will apply to all EU institutions, member states, national courts and private citizens. Judgments of the court, in the field of EU law, overrule those of national courts. For example, the court overruled Germany's consumer protection rules, which had served as a major trade barrier. Historically, German law has frowned on, if not prohibited, any product advertising that implies medicinal benefits. Estée Lauder Cosmetics was prevented, by German courts, from selling one of its products under the name 'Clinique'. Germany claimed the name would mislead German

consumers, causing them to associate the product with medical treatment. The European Court of Justice (ECJ) pointed out that the product is sold in other member states under the 'Clinique' name without confusing the consumer. Further, if the German court ruling against Estée Lauder was left to stand, it would make it difficult for companies to market their products across borders in an identical manner and thus increase the cost of advertising and packaging for the company and, ultimately, for the consumer.[14] This is but one example of the ECJ's power in the EU and its role in eliminating non-tariff trade barriers.

GOING INTERNATIONAL 9.5

euro five-year report card

Five years after its introduction, most countries that adopted it and companies in the EU are enthusiastic about the euro. 'It knits Europe together economically, and that's good for companies and the economy as a whole,' according to Daniel Gros, director of the Centre for European Policy Studies, a Brussels think-tank.

Europe has abolished exchange-rate risk within the euro-zone to stimulate cross-border trade and investment. The birth of liquid euro-denominated bond and equity markets has cut corporate borrowing costs, thus providing cheaper capital to the industry. It has boosted GDP growth in the poorer countries of the EU, helping them come closer to levels in Germany and France. Most of all, the euro has led to stable prices and the European Central Bank (ECB) has harmonised interest rates to control inflation.

For manufacturers and service providers, one currency makes it easier to compare prices and costs in different countries. This enables companies to easily locate lowest-cost suppliers and hubs for services. Franco-Spanish tobacco company Altadi's, Finnish paper and pulp manufacturer UPM-Kymmene, and France's Axalto (largest maker of Smartcards) are but a few examples of companies that have streamlined production, cut the supply chains short and rationalised distribution networks.

Source: *Business Week*, Finance Europe: 'Happy Birthday Dear Euro', 8 December 2003, pp. 34-5.

The Maastricht Treaty and European Union   The final step in the European Community's march to union was ratification of the Maastricht Treaty. The treaty provided for the Economic and Monetary Union (EMU) and European Union (EU). Under the EMU agreement, in 1998 the EU created a European Central Bank and introduced fixed exchange rates and a single currency.[15] Initially, there was considerable doubt about the viability of a European Union. Surrendering more sovereignty beyond that already relinquished with the provisions of the Single European Act seemed too extreme for many. Denmark and the United Kingdom were the last to ratify the treaty. Despite some last-minute hesitation, Denmark approved the treaty on a second vote and, later, with the UK's approval, the European Union became a reality. Within months of the ratification of the treaty, the EU was expanded when Austria, Finland and Sweden, members of the EEA, became members of the EU in 1995. Norway voted not to join the EU but will remain a member of the European Economic Area.[16] A number of European countries have applied to become members of the EU. Ten of these countries – Poland, Hungary, the Czech Republic, Slovakia, Slovenia, Estonia, Latvia, Lithuania, Malta and Cyprus – were accepted and these countries joined the EU on 1 May 2004 (see Exhibit 9.6).

Exhibit 9.6 The new EU members

Country	Population (millions)	GDP per capita (PPP $)	GDP % annual growth 2003	2004
Cyprus	0.6	13 000	2.0	3.5
Czech Republic	10.3	15 669	2.9	4.0
Estonia	1.4	12 190	4.7	5.5
Hungary	10.0	14 574	2.9	4.0
Latvia	2.3	9 683	7.5	6.0
Lithuania	3.4	11 036	8.9	6.5
Malta	0.3	12 100	4.0	4.5
Poland	38.3	10 854	3.7	4.5
Slovakia	5.4	13 363	4.2	4.4
Slovenia	2.0	19 618	2.3	3.1

Source: compiled from *Business Week*, 'The New Shape of Europe', 18 November 2002, p. 27; and *Financial Times*, Special Report: 'Central and Eastern Europe', 21 September 2004, p. 2.

European Economic Area (EEA)   Because of the success of the EC and concern that they might be left out of the massive European market, five members of the European Free Trade Association (EFTA) elected to join the 12 members of the EC in 1994 to form the European Economic Area (EEA), a single market with free movement of goods, services and capital.[17] The five EFTA countries joining the EEA adopted most of the EC's competition rules and agreed to implement EC rules on company law; however, they maintain their domestic farm policies. The EEA is governed by a special Council of Ministers composed of representatives from EEA member nations.

With nearly 500 million consumers and a gross national product of €6.3 trillion ($7.7 trillion), the EEA is the world's largest consumer market, eclipsing the United States even after the formation of the North American Free Trade Agreement. The EEA is a middle ground for those countries that want to be part of the EU's single internal market but do not want to go directly into the EU as full members or do not meet the requirements for full membership. Of the five founding EFTA members of the EEA, three joined the EU in 1995. Iceland and Norway chose not to become EU members with the other EFTA countries but will remain members of the EEA. Of the other EFTA members, Switzerland voted against joining the EEA but has formally requested membership of the EU, and Liechtenstein has not joined the EEA or requested admission to join the EU. The EEA will probably be the first step for economic unification between the EU and Eastern European countries, and perhaps some of the Newly Independent States.

European Free Trade Association (EFTA)
The European Free Trade Association was conceived by the United Kingdom as a counterpart to the EC before it became a member of the EC. The original members of EFTA were Austria, Denmark, Norway, Portugal, Sweden, Switzerland and the United Kingdom. Iceland became a member in 1970, Finland in 1986 and Liechtenstein in 1991. As discussed earlier, several EFTA countries joined EC countries to form the European Economic Area, and of the original members six went on to join the EU: the United Kingdom and Denmark in 1972, Portugal in 1986, and Austria, Finland and Sweden in 1995. The present members of EFTA are: Iceland, Liechtenstein, Norway and Switzerland. EFTA will most probably dissolve as its members either join the EEA or the EU.

GOING INTERNATIONAL 9.6

the EU constitution: what it does

- Simplifies the EU, bringing together scattered legal texts into one treaty, using supposedly simple language.
- Decision making will be made easier. National vetos removed in some areas, with more qualified majority voting in areas such as asylum and immigration and criminal law.

- New voting system for the Council of Ministers, making it harder to block deals. Votes approved by 55 per cent of countries, representing 65 per cent of the EU's population.
- New role for national parliaments, checking whether proposed EU laws could be better implemented at national level.
- New EU foreign minister heading a new European diplomatic service, merging two EU foreign policy jobs.
- New full-time president of the European Council, the supreme body of the EU, representing member states. Replaces rotating six-month presidency.
- Exit clause, making it clear for first time how a country can leave the EU.
- Enshrines charter of fundamental rights, including right to strike.
- A smaller European Commission from 2014, reducing it from 25 members to two-thirds the number of member countries – 18 in an EU of 27.
- Variable-speed Europe. The treaty will make it easier for small groups of countries to forge ahead with integration in new policy areas, provided others can join in later.

Source: Cathy Newman, 'Delayed Endorsement of Constitution Likely', *Financial Times*, 24 January 2005, p. 3.

The Commonwealth of Independent States (CIS)

The series of events after the aborted coup against Mikhail Gorbachev led to the complete dissolution of the USSR. The first to declare independence were the Baltic states, which quickly gained recognition by several Western nations. The remaining 12 republics of the former USSR,[18] collectively known as the Newly Independent States (NIS), regrouped into the Commonwealth of Independent States (CIS).

The CIS is a loose economic and political alliance with open borders but no central government. The main provisions of the commonwealth agreement are to:

1 repeal all Soviet laws and assume the powers of the old regimes
2 launch radical economic reforms, including freeing most prices
3 keep the rouble, but allow new currencies
4 establish a European Community-style free trade association
5 create joint control of nuclear weapons, and
6 fulfil all Soviet foreign treaties and debt obligations.

The 12 members of the CIS share a common history of central planning, and their close cooperation could make the change to a market economy less painful, but differences over economic policy, currency reform and control of the military may break them apart. How the CIS will be organised and its ultimate importance is anyone's guess.

The three Slavic republics of Russia, Ukraine and Belarus have interests and history in common, as do the five Central Asian Republics. But the ties between these two core groups of the CIS are tenuous and stem mainly from their former Soviet membership. The three Slavic republics are discussing the establishment of an organisation modelled on the European Union to succeed the Commonwealth of Independent States. Kazakhstan and other former Soviet republics may join, which would create a trade bloc that includes most of the former Soviet Union. Moscow would dominate because Russia far outweighs the others in military might and economic resources.[19]

the Americas

The Americas, the second Triad region, has as its centre the United States. Within the Americas, the United States, Canada, Central America and South America have been natural if sometimes contentious trading partners. As in Europe, the Americas are engaged in all sorts of economic cooperative agreements.

United States–Canada Free Trade Agreement (CFTA)

Historically, the United States and Canada have had the world's largest bilateral trade: each is the other's largest trading partner. Despite this unique commercial relationship, tariffs and other trade barriers hindered even greater commercial activity. To further support trade activity, the two countries established the United States–Canada Free Trade Area (CFTA), designed to eliminate all trade barriers between the two countries.

CFTA created a single, continental, commercial market for all goods and most services. The agreement between the United States and Canada is not a customs union such as the European Union; no economic or political union of any kind is involved. It provides only for the elimination of tariffs and other trade barriers.

CFTA was, however, to be short-lived. Not long after both countries had ratified CFTA, Mexico announced that it would seek free trade with the United States. Mexico's overtures were answered positively by the United States, and talks on a US-Mexico free trade area began. Canada, initially ambivalent about joining, agreed to participate and the talks were expanded to a North American Free Trade Agreement – Canada, the United States and Mexico. CFTA became the model after which NAFTA was designed.[20]

North American Free Trade Agreement (NAFTA)

Mexico and the United States have been strong trading partners for decades but Mexico had never officially expressed an interest in a free trade agreement until the President of Mexico, Carlos Salinas de Gortari, announced that Mexico would seek such an agreement with the United States. Because earlier overtures to Mexico from the US had been rebuffed, Salinas's announcement was a surprise to Americans and Mexicans alike. The first signal of change came when Mexico joined the General Agreement on Tariffs and Trade, a move it had opposed earlier. Mexico is now a full member of NAFTA and, according to many studies, the benefits of joining NAFTA are intensively discussed. [21]

Even though Mexico has an abundance of oil and a rapidly growing population, the number of new workers is increasing faster than its economy can create new jobs. The United States needs resources (especially oil) and, of course, markets. The three need each other to compete more effectively in world markets, and they need mutual assurances that their already dominant trading positions in each other's markets are safe from protectionist pressures. When the NAFTA agreement was ratified and became effective in 1994, a single market of 360 million people with a €5.4 trillion ($6 trillion) GNP emerged.

NAFTA requires the three countries to remove all tariffs and barriers to trade, but each will have its own tariff arrangements with non-member countries. All changes already occurring under CFTA will stand and be built on under the NAFTA agreement. Some of the key provisions of the agreement follow.

Market Access   Within 10 years of implementation, all tariffs will be eliminated on North American industrial products traded between Canada, Mexico and the United States. All trade between Canada and the United States is duty free as provided for in CFTA. Mexico immediately eliminated tariffs on nearly 50 per cent of all industrial goods imported from the United States, and remaining tariffs will be phased out entirely within 15 years.

Non-tariff Barriers   In addition to the elimination of tariffs, countries will eliminate non-tariff barriers and other trade-distorting restrictions. NAFTA also eliminates a host of other Mexican barriers such as local content, local production and export performance requirements that have limited US exports.

Rules of Origin   NAFTA reduces tariffs only for goods made in North America. Tough rules of origin will determine whether a good qualifies for preferential tariff treatment under NAFTA. Rules of origin are designed to prevent 'free riders' from benefiting through minor processing or transshipment of non-NAFTA goods. For example, Japan could not assemble cars in Mexico and avoid US or Canadian tariffs and quotas unless the car had a specific percentage of Mexican (i.e. North American) content. For goods to be traded duty free, they must contain substantial (62.5 per cent) North American content.

Customs Administration   Under NAFTA, Canada, Mexico and the United States have agreed to implement uniform customs procedures and regulations. Uniform procedures ensure that exporters who market their products in more than one NAFTA country will not have to adapt to multiple customs procedures. Most procedures governing rules of origin documentation, record keeping and origin verification will be the same for all three NAFTA countries.

Investment   NAFTA will eliminate investment conditions that restrict the trade of goods and service among the three countries. Among conditions eliminated are the requirements that foreign investors export a given level or percentage of goods or services, use domestic goods or services, transfer technology to competitors, or limit imports to a certain percentage of exports.

Services   NAFTA establishes the first comprehensive set of principles governing services trade. Financial institutions are permitted to open wholly owned subsidiaries in each other's markets, and all restrictions on the services they offer had been lifted by 2000.

Intellectual Property   NAFTA will provide the highest standards of protection of intellectual property available in any bilateral or international agreement. The agreement covers patents, trademarks, copyrights, trade secrets, semiconductor integrated circuits, copyrights for North American movies, computer software and records.

Government Procurement   NAFTA guarantees businesses fair and open competition for procurement in North America through transparent and predictable procurement procedures.

The elimination of trade and investment barriers among Canada, Mexico and the United States creates one of the largest and richest markets in the world. Early reports on the effect of NAFTA have been positive although not without a few rough spots. In the first six months after NAFTA's inception, for example, US exports to Mexico rose to $24.5 billion, an increase of 16 per cent over the previous 12 months. Mexican exports to the United States rose 21 per cent in those first six months to €20.2 billion ($23.4 billion). Equally impressive is the increase in trade between Mexico and Canada during the same period: exports from Canada to Mexico increased 33 per cent and Mexican exports to Canada increased by 31

GOING INTERNATIONAL 9.7

Mexico and NAFTA: was it worth it?

On 1 January 2004, NAFTA celebrated its 10th birthday. If we assess the 10 years, NAFTA has been a great success in some areas. The investments flooded in at a rate of $12 billion per year and Mexico's exports grew threefold, from $52 billion to $161 billion. Mexico's per capita income rose by 24 per cent to $4000, which is about 10 times that of China. Mexico's economy was number 15 in the world before NAFTA; now it is the ninth largest economy.

Most Mexicans are, however, soured over NAFTA. Many think that it was oversold and, 10 years on, it has stopped creating any value added. They feel that America, consumed by the so-called 'war on terror', has neglected Mexico. The Mexican envoy to the UN characterised NAFTA as a 'weekend fling'. One recent survey showed that only 45 per cent of Mexicans think that NAFTA has benefited Mexico's economy.

Mexico thought it would become America's biggest workshop, but the job went to China. Local producers of goods from toys to shoes are struggling to survive due to cheaper imports. Mexico has not been able to generate enough jobs to accommodate its fast-growing workforce. Although a lot of investments came in the early years, since 2000 850 factories have been shut down due to decreased demand for their products, partly because many companies are relocating their production to China. Although exports to the US tripled, only a handful of companies enjoyed big gains. Wages have dropped due to the peso crash and government relations have not improved.

The countries around Mexico have gained equally well or more in some cases. Less than 3 per cent of industry parts and components are sourced in Mexico. The infrastructure has not improved; the country needs $50 billion to upgrade its power grid. Moreover, Mexico's gas and energy costs are 40 per cent higher than China's and the availability of skilled (educated) workers is much better in India. India graduates 314 000 science students per annum and China 363 000 as compared to Mexico's 13 300. However, Mexico knows that it has burnt its boats and there is no turning back from NAFTA.

Along with NAFTA came two of Mexico's biggest brand names, Gigante (Mexico's largest supermarket chain) and Grupo Bimbo (a Mexican multinational).

■ Do you think Mexico has benefited from NAFTA? What do you think can be done to enhance the benefits of NAFTA for Mexico?

Source: abridged from Geri Smith and Cristina Lindblad, 'A Tale of What Free Trade Can and Cannot Do', Special Report, *Business Week*, 22 December 2003, pp. 36–43.

per cent. Trade between Canada and the United States has been increasing steadily since 1989 when the Canada Free Trade Agreement (CFTA is now part of NAFTA) became effective.

Latin American economic cooperation

Prior to 1990, most Latin American market groups (see Exhibit 9.7) had varying degrees of success. The first and most ambitious, the Latin American Free Trade Association (LAFTA) gave way to the LAIA (Latin American Integration Association). Plagued with tremendous foreign debt, protectionist economic systems, triple-digit inflation, state ownership of basic industries and overregulation of industry, most countries were in a perpetual state of

economic chaos. Under such conditions there was not much trade or integration among member countries. But, as discussed earlier, there are significant changes occurring in Latin America. There is now a wave of genuine optimism about the economic miracle under way, propagated by political and economic reforms occurring from the tip of Argentina to the Rio Grande river.

In addition to new trade agreements, many of the trade accords that have been in existence for decades, such as the Latin American Integration Association and the Andean Pact, have moved from a moribund to an active state, all of which makes the idea of a common market from Argentina to the Arctic Circle – a Western Hemisphere Free Trade Area (WHFTA) – not as unlikely as it might first appear. An accord reached by Colombia, Mexico and Venezuela, the Group of Three (G-3), typifies the desire for establishing new free trade areas in Latin America. By 2005, G-3 is scheduled to become a tariff-free zone. When approved, the accord will create a free market of 145 million people with a combined

Exhibit 9.7 Latin American market groups

Association	Member	Population (millions)	GDP (US$ billions)	GDP per capita (US$)	Imports (US$ billions)
Andean Common Market (ANCOM)	Bolivia	8.7	21.0	2 400	1.495
	Colombia	42.3	263.2	6 300	13.06
	Ecuador	27.5	45.7	3 300	6.22
	Peru	22.5	146	5 100	8.244
	Venezuela	25.0	117.9	4 800	10.71
	Panama (Associate)	3.0	18.8	6 300	6.622
Central American Common Market (CACM)	Guatemala	14.3	56.5	4 100	5.749
	El Salvador	6.6	31.0	4 800	5.466
	Costa Rica	4.0	35.3	9 100	7.057
	Nicaragua	5.4	11.6	2 300	1.658
	Honduras	6.8	17.6	2 600	3.11
Caribbean Community and Common Market (CARICOM)	Antigua & Barbuda	0.07	0.418	11 000	0.692
	Barbados	0.29	4 355	15 700	1.039
	Belize	0.272	1.280	4 900	0.500
	Dominica	0.07	0.380	5 400	0.098
	Grenada	0.09	0.440	5 000	0.208
	Guyana	0.706	2.797	4 000	0.612
	Jamaica	2.7	10.61	3 900	3.265
	Montserrat	0.009	0.029	3 400	0.017
	St Kitts-Nevis	0.038	0.339	8 800	0.195
	Anguilla	0.013	0.104	8 600	0.081
	St Lucia	0.164	0.866	5 400	0.267
	St Vincent	0.117	0.342	2 900	0.174
	Trinidad & Tobago	1.097	10.62	9 500	3.917
Latin American Integration Association (LAIA)	Argentina*	39.1	435.5	11 200	13.27
	Bolivia	8.7	21.0	2 400	1.495
	Brazil*	184.1	1 375	7 600	48.25
	Chile	15.8	154.7	9 900	17.4
	Colombia	42.3	263.2	6 300	13.06
	Ecuador	27.5	45.7	3 300	6.22
	Mexico	104.9	941.2	9 000	168.9
	Paraguay*	6.2	28.17	4 700	2.77
	Peru	22.5	146	5 100	8.244
	Uruguay*	3.4	4 367	12 800	2.010
	Venezuela	25.0	117.9	4 800	10.71

*Mercosur countries: Southern Cone Common Market (Mercosur) is the newest common market agreement in Latin America.

Source: CIA, *World Factbook*, http://www.odci.gov/cia/publications/factbook, 2004.

GDP of €337 billion ($373 billion).[22] G-3 has already sparked the possibility of expansion to include Ecuador and Chile; both currently have free trade agreements with the G-3 nations.

Latin American Integration Association (LAIA)   The long-term goal of the LAIA is the establishment, in a gradual and progressive manner, of a Latin American Common Market. One of the more important aspects of LAIA is the differential treatment of member countries according to their level of economic development. Over the years, negotiations among member countries have lowered duties on selected products and eased trade tensions over quotas, local-content requirements, import licences and other trade barriers.

The Andean Common Market (ANCOM)   The Andean Pact, as it is generally referred to, has served its member nations with a framework to establish rules for foreign investment, common tariffs for non-member countries, and the reduction or elimination of internal tariffs. The Andean Pact members agreed to go beyond a free trade agreement and implement a customs union in 1996. This revived interest in economic integration by Andean Pact members has resulted in an evaluation of alternatives for member countries to join NAFTA and the possibility of the integration of the Andean Pact and Mercosur (see below) to form a South American Free Trade Area (SAFTA).[23]

Southern Cone Common Market (Mercosur)   Mercosur is the newest common market agreement in Latin America. A successful bilateral trade pact between Argentina and Brazil led to the creation of Mercosur in 1991. Argentina, Brazil, Paraguay and Uruguay are members of Mercosur and seek to achieve free circulation of goods and services, establish a regional common external tariff (targeted at 20 per cent) for third-country imports, and implement harmonised macroeconomic trade and exchange-rate policies among the four partners by 1995. Unfortunately, they were unable to meet the 1995 deadline because the leaders failed to agree on a common external tariff. The most they were able to accomplish was a customs union comprising a free trade zone with a reduction of internal tariffs.

Asia

What is happening in Asia is by far the most important development in the world today. Based on this development a new commonwealth of nations based on economic symbiosis is emerging in the Far East. The Asian continent, from Pakistan to Japan and China down to Indonesia, now accounts for more than half of the world population.[24] Countries in Asia constitute the third Triad region. Japan and China are at the centre of this Triad region, which also includes many of the world's newly industrialised countries (NICs) and emerging economies. After decades of dependence on the United States and Europe for technology and markets, countries in Asia are preparing for the next economic leap, driven by trade, investment and technology aided by others in the region. Though few in number, trade agreements among some of the Asian emerging countries are seen as movement towards a regionwide intra-Asian trade area. This drive was strengthened after the 1996–97 economic crisis in a number of Asian countries.

Presently, there is one multinational trade group, the Association of Southeast Asian Nations (ASEAN),[25] which has evolved into the ASEAN Free Trade Area (AFTA), and one forum, the Asia-Pacific Economic Cooperation (APEC), which meets annually to discuss regional economic development and cooperation.[26]

ASEAN

The Association of Southeast Asian Nations (ASEAN) is the primary multinational trade group in Asia. The goals of the group are economic integration and cooperation through complementary industry programmes, preferential trading including reduced tariff and non-tariff barriers, guaranteed member access to markets throughout the region, and

harmonised investment incentives. Like all multinational market groups, ASEAN has experienced problems and false starts in attempting to unify its combined economies.

Most of the early economic growth came from trade outside the ASEAN group. Similarities in the kinds of products it had to export, in its natural resources and other national assets hampered earlier attempts at intra-ASEAN trade. Steps taken by ASEAN members in the last decade to expand and diversify its industrial base have resulted in the fastest-growing economies in the region.

Four major events account for the vigorous economic growth of the ASEAN countries and their transformation from cheap-labour havens to industrialised nations:

1 the ASEAN governments' commitment to deregulation, liberalisation and privatisation of their economies
2 the decision to shift their economies from commodity based to manufacturing based
3 the decision to specialise in manufacturing components in which they have a comparative advantage (this created more diversity in their industrial output and increased opportunities for trade), and
4 Japan's emergence as a major provider of technology and the capital necessary to upgrade manufacturing capability and develop new industries.

As their economies became more diversified, they signed a framework agreement to create the ASEAN Free Trade Area (AFTA) by 2006. The goal of AFTA is to reduce intra-regional tariffs and remove non-tariff barriers over a 15-year period. Tariffs on all manufactured goods are to be reduced to 5 per cent or less by 2003.[27] The new free trade area consists of 10 countries: Brunei, Cambodia, Indonesia, Malaysia, the Philippines, Singapore, Thailand, Vietnam, Mynamar and Laos. It has a population of 520 million and a GDP of more than €900 billion ($737 billion) (see Exhibit 9.8).

Exhibit 9.8 GDP per capita in ASEAN countries

Members	Population 2004 (million)	GDP per capita 2004 ($)
Indonesia	238	3 200
Vietnam	83	2 500
Philippines	86	4 600
Thailand	65	7 400
Malaysia	24	9 000
Singapore	4	23 700
Brunei	0.37	18 600
Myanmar	0.53	9 605
Laos	6	1 700
Cambodia	13	1 900

Source: Association of Southeast Asian Nations, www.aseansec.org, 2004; and CIA, *World Factbook*, www.odci.gov/cia/publications/factbook, 2004.

APEC

Asia-Pacific Economic Cooperation (APEC) is the other important trade group in the Asian Pacific Rim. It provides a formal structure for the major governments of the region, including the United States and Canada, to discuss their mutual interests in open trade and economic collaboration. APEC is a unique forum that has evolved into the primary regional vehicle for promoting trade liberalisation and economic cooperation. The 18-member

APEC[28] includes the most powerful regional economies in the world (see Exhibit 9.9), whose share of world trade approaches 35 per cent and, as a region, constitutes the United States' most important economic partner. APEC has as its common goal a commitment to open trade, to increase economic collaboration, to sustain regional growth and development, to strengthen the multilateral trading system and to reduce barriers to investment and trade without detriment to other economies.

Exhibit 9.9 Comparison of intra-trade among members of APEC and the EC

	Population, 2004 (millions)	Exports, 1980 (US$ millions)	Exports, 2003 (US$ millions)	GDP, 2003 (US$ billions)
APEC	2582	296809	2950677	19539
North America	417	128608	945484	59835
Asia	1617	150091	1649748	120955
Oceania	23	18110	79223	35059
EU15	382	198917	1103000	8455

Source: APEC, *Outcomes and Outlook*, 2003/2004; EuroStat, 2004.

Africa

Africa's multinational market development activities can be characterised by a great deal of activity, but little progress. Including bilateral agreements, an estimated 200 economic arrangements exist between African countries (see Exhibit 9.10). Despite the large number and assortment of 'paper' organisations, there has been little actual economic integration. This is generally due to the political instability that has characterised Africa in the last decades and the unstable economic base on which it has had to build. Political sovereignty is a new enough phenomenon to most African nations and they are reluctant to relinquish any part of it without specific and tangible benefits in return. Now that South Africa has changed its internal politics, one can speculate about what future role it might play in the economic integration of African countries should it decide to take a leadership position.[29]

Exhibit 9.10 African market groups

Association	Member	Population (millions)	GDP* ($ billions)	GDP* per capita	Imports of goods and services ($ billions)	Exports of goods and services ($ billions)
Afro-Malagasy Economic Union	Benin	6.4	2.7	424	0.8	0.6
	Burkina Faso	11.6	2.9	250	0.7	0.4
	Cameroon	15.2	10.6	696	3.3	3.1
	Central African Republic	3.8	1.3	339	—	—
	Chad	52.4	1.8	230	1.2	0.2
	Congo	16.4	4.5	85	3.3	2.6
	Côte d'Ivoire	1.3	11.7	715	3.7	4.3
	Gabon	11.1	5.5	4379	2.0	2.6
	Mali	2.7	3.2	292	1.3	1.1
	Mauritania	2.7	1.4	502	0.7	0.6
	Niger	11.2	2.3	208	0.4	0.4
	Senegal	9.8	6.1	629	2.4	2.1
	Togo	4.7	1.5	322	0.7	0.4

Exhibit 9.10 (African market groups, continued)

Association	Member	Population (millions)	GDP* ($ billions)	GDP* per capita	Imports of goods and services ($ billions)	Exports of goods and services ($ billions)
East African Customs Union	Ethiopia	54.8	7.9	121	2.1	1.3
	Kenya	30.7	10.0	325	3.8	3.3
	Sudan	31.7	10.4	328	—	—
	Tanzania	34.4	6.8	197	2.2	1.5
	Uganda	22.8	8.1	355	2.3	1.3
	Zambia	10.3	4.2	405	1.5	1.9
Union of Arab Maghreb	Algeria	30.8	49.4	1 616	12.6	14.8
	Libya	5.4	—	—	—	—
	Tunisia	9.7	24.8	2 562	12.5	11.7
	Morocco	29.2	41.9	1 436	16.3	12.1
	Mauritania	as above	—	—	—	—
Economic Community of West African States	Benin	as above	—	—	—	—
	Burkina Faso	as above	—	—	—	—
	Cape Verde	0.4	0.7	1 550	0.4	0.2
	Côte d'Ivoire	as above	—	—	—	—
	Gambia	1.3	0.5	382	0.4	0.3
	Ghana	19.7	8.3	421	3.9	2.9
	Guinea	7.6	4.7	613	1.0	1.0
	Guinea-Bissau	1.2	0.3	206	0.1	0.1
	Liberia	3.2	0.6	196	—	—
	Mali	as above	—	—	—	—
	Mauritania	as above	—	—	—	—
	Niger	as above	—	—	—	—
	Nigeria	1 129.9	33.4	257	21.5	13.5
	Senegal	as above	—	—	—	—
	Sierra Leone	5.1	0.8	158	0.1	0.0
	Togo	4.7	—	—	—	—
Southern African Development Community	Angola	13.5	7.1	525	—	—
	Botswana	1.7	7.0	4 130	3.1	3.5
	Congo	as above	—	—	—	—
	Lesotho	2.1	1.2	563	1.0	0.4
	Namibia	1.8	4.3	2 383	2.5	2.0
	Malawi	10.5	1.7	163	0.7	0.5
	Mauritius	1.2	5.2	4 352	3.3	3.0
	Mozambique	18.1	3.9	213	1.7	1.1
	Seychelles	0.1	0.5	5 939	0.6	0.5
	S. Africa	43.2	175.9	4 068	42.0	46.2
	Swaziland	1.1	1.6	1 529	1.3	1.1
	Tanzania	as above	—	—	—	—
	Zambia	10.3	—	—	—	—
	Zimbabwe	12.8	7.2	559	3.0	3.0

*Constant 1995 dollars.

The Economic Community of West African States (ECOWAS) is the most senior of the African regional cooperative groups and the most successful.[30] A 16-nation group, ECOWAS has an aggregate gross domestic product (GDP) of more than €60 billion ($50 billion) and is striving to achieve full economic integration. Some experts suggest that the economic domination by Nigeria (45 per cent of all the market's exports) may create internal strains that cannot be overcome.

One of the groups becoming strong is the South African Development Community (SADC) with its 14 members. The members are Angola, Congo, Malawi, Tanzania, Zambia, Mozambique, Namibia, Botswana, Zimbabwe, Swaziland, Lesotho, Mauritius, Seychelles and South Africa. The group has a total population of 167.2 million with a GDP of €263.8 billion ($215.6 billion).

Middle East

The Middle East has been less aggressive in the formation of successfully functioning multinational market groups (see Exhibit 9.11). Countries that belong to the Arab Common Market have set goals for free internal trade but have not achieved them. With the possibility of continuing peace in the Middle East, the prospect of a meaningful trade group has improved.

future multinational market groups

With the advent of a single European market and the North American Free Trade Agreement (NAFTA), and with the general concern that these two formidable market groups may be the forerunners of many other regional trading blocs, there is speculation about future alliances.

A conjectural free trade agreement that has emerged is one between the United States and the European Union. Europe fears it will be isolated by free trade agreements that the United States is trying to form with Latin American and Asian countries; the United States is concerned by the fact that Mexico is trying to negotiate its own free trade accord with Europe and that Europe is seeking to establish free trade ties with the countries of Mercosur.

Another more speculative trade group centres around the political and economic unification of China, Taiwan and Hong Kong. Although currently at odds politically, economic integration between Hong Kong, Taiwan and the coastal provinces of southern China, often unofficially referred to as the Chinese Economic Area (CEA), has advanced rapidly in recent years. The current expansion of the triangular economic relationship can be

Exhibit 9.11 Middle East market groups

Association	Member	Populations (millions)	GDP (US$ billions)	GDP per capita (US$)	Imports (US$ millions)
Arab Common Market	Iraq	25.4	37.92	1 500	6.521
	Kuwait	2.3	41.46	19 000	9.606
	Jordan	5.6	23.64	4 300	4.946
	Syria	18.0	58.01	3 300	4.845
	Egypt	76.1	295.2	4 000	14.75
Economic Cooperation Organization (ECO)	Pakistan	159.2	318.0	2 100	12.51
	Iran	69.0	478.2	7 000	25.26
	Turkey	68.9	458.2	6 700	62.43
	Azerbaijan	7.9	26.65	3 400	2.498
	Turkmenistan	4.9	27.88	5 800	2.472
	Uzbekistan	26.4	43.99	1 700	2.31
Gulf Cooperation Council (GCC)	Bahrain	0.678	11.29	16 900	5.126
	Kuwait	2.2	41.46	19 000	9.606
	Oman	2.9	36.7	13 100	5.659
	Qatar	0.840	17.54	21 500	5.711
	Saudi Arabia	25.8	287.8	11 850	30.83
	United Arab Emirates	2.5	57.7	23 200	37.16

Source: CIA, *World Factbook*, www.cia.gov/cia/publications/factbook, 2004.

attributed to a steady transfer of labour-intensive manufacturing operations from Taiwan and Hong Kong to the Chinese mainland. China provides a supply of cheap, abundant labour, and Taiwan and Hong Kong provide capital, technology and management expertise. Hong Kong, now formally part of China, also plays an important role as the financier, investor, supplier and provider of technology, and as a port of entry for China as a whole.[31]

As an economic region, the CEA's economic importance should not be undervalued. Combined exports of the CEA were valued at €254.1 billion ($281.5 billion), accounting for 7.6 per cent of the world's exports and ranking fourth worldwide, behind the United States, Germany and Japan. Their combined imports totalled €240 billion ($266 billion), accounting for 6.9 per cent of the world's imports and ranking third, behind the United States and Germany.[32] The Chinese business empire extends beyond Hong Kong, Taiwan and China itself (see Exhibit 9.12).

Exhibit 9.12 The Chinese empire overseas

	Chinese population as % total of local population	Chinese population (millions)	Business output as % of total local population	GDP contribution ($ billions)
Hong Kong	98	6	80	120
Singapore	76	2	76	62
Taiwan	99	21	95	255
Malaysia	32	6	60	48
Indonesia	4	8	50	98
Philippines	1	1	40	30
Thailand	10	6	50	80
Vietnam	1	1	20	4
Total		51		697

Source: based on 'A Survey of Business in Asia', *The Economist*, 9 March 1996, p. 10.

strategic implications for marketing

The complexion of the entire world marketplace has been changed significantly by the coalition of nations into multinational market groups. To international business firms, multinational groups spell opportunity writ large through access to greatly enlarged markets with reduced or abolished country-by-country tariff barriers and restrictions. Production, financing, labour and marketing decisions are affected by the remapping of the world into market groups.

As goals of the EEA and NAFTA are reached, new marketing opportunities are created; so are new problems. World competition will intensify as businesses become stronger and more experienced in dealing with large market groups. European and non-European multinationals are preparing to deal with the changes in competition in a fully integrated Europe. In an integrated Europe, industries and markets are being restructured. Mergers, acquisitions and joint ventures consolidate operations of European firms in anticipation of the benefits of a single European market. International managers will still be confronted by individual national markets with the same problems of language, customs and instability, even though they are packaged under the umbrella of a common market.

opportunities

Economic integration creates large mass markets for the marketer. Many national markets, too small to bother with individually, take on new dimensions and significance when

combined with markets from cooperating countries. Large markets are particularly important to businesses accustomed to mass production and mass distribution because of the economies of scale and marketing efficiencies that can be achieved. In highly competitive markets, the benefits derived from enhanced efficiencies are often passed along as lower prices, which lead to increased purchasing power.

Another major saving will result from the billions of dollars wasted in developing different versions of products to meet a hotchpotch of national standards. Philips and other European companies invested a total of €18 billion ($20 billion) to develop a common switching system for Europe's 10 different telephone networks. This compares with €2.7 billion ($3 billion) spent in the United States for a common system and €1.35 billion ($1.5 billion) in Japan for a single system.

market barriers

The initial aim of a multinational market is to protect businesses that operate within its borders. An expressed goal is to give an advantage to the companies within the market in their dealings with other countries of the market group. Analysis of the intra-regional and international trade patterns of the market groups indicates that such goals have been achieved. Trade does increase among member nations and decrease with non-member nations.

Local preferences certainly spell trouble for the exporter located outside the market. Companies willing to invest in production facilities in multinational markets may benefit from such protection as they become a part of the market. Exporters, however, are in a considerably weaker position. This prospect confronts many US exporters faced with the possible need to invest in Europe to protect their export markets in the European Union. Recent heavy investments by Japanese (Toyota, Honda and Nissan), American (MCI, GM and Procter & Gamble) and Korean companies (Lucky Goldstar and Samsung) are good examples of such investments.

ensuring EU market entry

Whether or not the European Union will close its doors to outsiders, firms who want to be competitive in the EU will have to establish a presence there. There are four levels of involvement that a firm may have *vis-à-vis* the EU: (1) firms based in Europe with well-established manufacturing and distribution operations in several European countries; (2) firms with operations in a single EU country; (3) firms that export manufactured goods to the EU from an offshore location; and (4) firms that have not actively exported to EU countries. The strategies for effective competitiveness in the EU are different for each type of firm.

The first firm, fully established in several EU countries with local manufacturing, is the best positioned. However, the competitive structure will change under a single Europe. Marketers will have to exploit the opportunities of greater efficiencies of production and distribution that result from lowering the barriers. They will also have to deal with increased competition from European firms as well as other MNCs that will be aggressively establishing market positions. A third area of change will require companies to learn how their customers are changing and, thus, how best to market to them.

European retailers and wholesalers as well as industrial customers are merging, expanding and taking steps to assure their success in this larger market. Nestlé has bought Rowntree, a UK confectionery company, and Britone, the Italian food conglomerate, to strengthen its ties to EU market firms. European banking is also going through a stage of mergers. In one 18-month period, 400 banks and finance firms merged, took stock in one another, or devised joint marketing ventures to sell stocks, mutual funds, insurance or other financial instruments. These mergers are viewed as necessary to compete with Japanese, US and Swiss financial institutions.

A second type of firm – with operations in one European country – is vulnerable when barriers come down and competitors enter the company's market. The firm's biggest problem in this situation is not being large enough to withstand the competition from

outside the country. The answer is to become larger, or withdraw. There are several choices for this firm: expand through acquisition or merger, enter a strategic alliance with a second company, or expand the company beyond being a local single-country firm to being a pan-European competitor.

marketing mix implications

Companies are adjusting their marketing mix strategies to reflect anticipated market differences in a single European market. In the past, companies often charged different prices in different European markets. Non-tariff barriers between member states supported price differentials and kept lower-priced products from entering those markets where higher prices were charged. Colgate-Palmolive has adapted its Colgate toothpaste into a single formula for sale across Europe at one price. Before changing its pricing practices, Colgate sold its toothpaste at different prices in different markets. Badedas Shower Gel, for example, is priced in the middle of the market in Germany and as a high-priced product in the United Kingdom. As long as products from lower-priced markets could not move to higher-priced markets, such differential price schemes worked. Now, however, under the EU rules, companies cannot prevent the free movement of goods, and parallel imports from lower-priced markets to higher-priced markets are more apt to occur. Some price standardisation among country markets will be one of the necessary changes to avoid the problem of parallel imports.

In addition to initiating uniform pricing policies, companies are reducing the number of brands they produce to focus advertising and promotion efforts. For example, Nestlé's current three brands of yoghurt in the EU will be reduced to a single brand.

A major benefit from an integrated Europe is competition at the retail level. Europe lacks an integrated and competitive distribution system that would support small and midsize outlets. The elimination of borders could result in increased competition among retailers and the creation of Europe-wide distribution channels. Retail giants such as France's Carréfour, Germany's Aldi group and Holland's Ahold are planning huge hypermarkets with big advertising budgets.

summary

The experience of the multinational market groups developed since the Second World War points up both the possible successes and the hazards such groups encounter. The various attempts at economic cooperation represent varying degrees of success and failure but, almost without regard to their degree of success, the economic market groups have created great excitement among marketers.

Economic benefits possible through cooperation relate to more efficient marketing and production: marketing efficiency is effected through the development of mass markets, encouragement of competition, the improvement of personal income and various psychological market factors. Production efficiency derives from specialisation, mass production for mass markets and the free movement of the factors of production. Economic integration also tends to foster political harmony among the countries involved; such harmony leads to stability, which is beneficial to the marketer.

The marketing implications of multinational market groups may be studied from the standpoint of firms located inside the market or of firms located outside that wish to sell to the markets. For each viewpoint the problems and opportunities are somewhat different; but regardless of the location of the marketer, multinational market groups provide a great opportunity for the creative marketer who wishes to expand volume. Market groupings make it economically feasible to enter new markets and to employ new marketing strategies that could not be applied to the smaller markets represented by individual countries.

The success of the European Union, the creation of the Canada–Mexico–United States free trade area (NAFTA), the expansion of ASEAN to the ASEAN Free Trade Area (AFTA) and the new Mercosur suggest the growing importance of economic cooperation and integration. Such developments will continue to challenge the international marketer by providing continually growing market opportunities.

questions

1. Elaborate on the problems and benefits for international marketers from multi-national market groups.
2. Explain the political role of multinational market groups. Identify the factors on which one may judge the potential success or failure of a multinational market group.
3. Explain the marketing implications of the factors contributing to the successful development of a multinational market group.
4. Differentiate between a free trade area and a common market. Explain the marketing implication of the differences.
5. Select any three countries that might have some logical basis for establishing a multinational market organisation. Identify the various problems that would be encountered in forming multinational market groups of such countries.
6. US exports to the European Union are expected to decline in future years. What marketing actions may a US company take to counteract such changes?
7. 'Because they are dynamic and because they have great growth possibilities, the multinational markets are likely to be especially rough and tumble for the external business.' Discuss.
8. Why have African nations had such difficulty in forming effective economic unions?
9. Discuss the implications of the European Union for marketing strategy in Europe.
10. Discuss the United States–Canada Free Trade Agreement and compare it with the European Union.
11. What are some of the possibilities for other multinational marketing groups that are forming? Discuss the implications to global marketing if these groups should develop.
12. Using the factors that serve as the basis for success of an economic union (political, economic, social and geographic), evaluate the potential success of the EU, NAFTA, ASEAN, AFTA and Mercosur.

further reading

- Chris Halliburton and Reinhard Hünerber, 'Executive Insights: Pan European Marketing – Myth or Reality?', *Journal of International Marketing*, 1993, 1(3), pp. 77–92.
- Amjad Hadjikhani and Pervez Ghauri, 'The Behaviour of International Firms in Socio-Political Environments in the European Union', *Journal of Business Research*, 2001, 52(3), pp. 263–75.
- Andrew Delios, 'The Race for Japanese FDI in the European Union', in Lars Oxelheim and Pervez Ghauri (eds), *European Union and the Race for Foreign Direct Investment in Europe* (Oxford: Elsevier, 2004), pp. 185–208.

references

1 UNCTAD, *Companies without Borders: Transnational Corporations in the 1990s* (London: Thomson Business Press, 1996).

2 Jay L. Camillo, 'Mexico: NAFTA Opens Door to US Business', *Business America*, March 1994, pp. 14-21.

3 Sabrina Tavernise, 'Buying on Credit is the Latest Rage in Russia', *New York Times*, 20 January 2003, p. 1.

4 The following website provides information on a number of trade blocs: www.mac.doc.org.

5 Kenichi Ohmae, *Triad Power* (New York: The Free Press, 1985), p. 220.

6 The European Community still exists as a legal entity within the broader framework of the European Union.

7 Keith Perry, *Business and the European Community* (Oxford: Butterworth-Heinemann, 1994).

8 James Mehring, 'High Hurdles for New EU Members to Clear', *Business Week*, 5 May 2003, p. 26.

9 *The Economist*, 'Britain and Euro, What a Pity, What a Relief', 14 June 2003, p. 46.

10 Lionel Barber, 'From the Heart of Europe', *Europe*, July-August 1994, pp. 14-17; and 'Pondering Europe's Union', *The Economist*, 20 June 1998, p. 32.

11 T. Buck and R. Waters, 'Commission Talk Tough over Microsoft "Abuses"', *Financial Times*, 7 August 2003, p. 25.

12 *The Economist*, 'All Aboard the EuroTrain', 5 April, 2003, p. 50.

13 F. Guerrera and B. de Jonquieres, 'Something is Rotten Within our System: Europe's Mighty Competition Authorities are Cut Down to Size', *Financial Times*, 28 October 2002, p. 25.

14 'Advertising: Awaiting the Commission's Green Paper', *Business Europe*, 28 March-3 April 1994, pp. 2-3.

15 'The Euro: Will it Create a New European Economy?', *Business Week*, Special Issue, 27 April 1998.

16 *Financial Times*, 'A Year of Planes, Jeans and Price-fixing Deals', 20 March 2002, p. 23.

17 EFTA countries joining the EEA were Austria, Finland, Iceland, Norway and Sweden.

18 The 12 republics of the former USSR, collectively referred to as the Newly Independent States (NIS), are: Russia, Ukraine, Belarus (formerly Byelorussia), Armenia, Moldova (formerly Moldavia), Azerbaijan, Uzbekistan, Turkmenistan, Tajikistan, Kazakhstan, Kyrgystan (formerly Kirghiziya) and Georgia. These same countries, the NIS, are also members of the CIS.

19 Suzanne Crow, 'Russia Promotes the CIS as an International Organization', RFE/RL Research Report, 18 March 1994, pp. 33-7.

20 For more information on NAFTA, see the following website: www.mac.doc.gov.

21 C.J. Chippello, 'NAFTA's Benefits to Firms in Canada May Top Those for Mexico', *Wall Street Journal*, 23 February 2003, p. A2.

22 Paul Magnusson, 'With Latin America Thriving, NAFTA Might Keep Marching South', *Business Week*, 24 July 1994, p. 20.

23 Richard Lapper, 'South American Unity Still a Distant Dream', *Financial Times*, 12 December 2004, p. 8.

24 John Naisbitt, *Mega Trends in Asia* (New York: Simon & Schuster, 1996).

25 ASEAN countries are: Brunei, Indonesia, Malaysia, the Philippines, Singapore and Thailand. Vietnam entered ASEAN in 1996.

26 'A Great Slide Backward in Southeast Asia', *Business Week*, 5 August 1996, p. 23.

27 For details see: www.aseansec.org.

28 APEC members are: Australia, Brunei, Canada, Chile, China, Hong Kong, Indonesia, Japan, the Republic of Korea, Malaysia, Mexico, New Zealand, the Philippines, Papua New Guinea, Singapore, Chinese Taipei (Taiwan), Thailand and the United States.

29 'Opening South Africa: It Should Act Now to Rid Itself and the Region of Apartheid's Economic Remnants', *The Economist*, 8 March 1997, p. 17.

30 'ECOWAS: Last Month ECOWAS Celebrated its 19th Anniversary', *West Africa*, 18 July 1994, pp. 1258-63.

31 For more on China and the Pacific Rim, see www.apec.org.

32 Kenichi Ohmae, 'The New World Order: The Rise of the Region-State', *The Wall Street Journal*, 8 August 1994, p. A-12.

section 4
developing international marketing strategies

chapter 10
International Marketing
Strategies

Chapter Outline

key terms

strategic planning
a systematised way of relating to the future

domestic market extension concept
foreign markets are extensions of the domestic market; the domestic marketing mix is offered, as is, to foreign markets

multidomestic market concept
each country is viewed as being culturally unique; an adapted marketing mix for each country market is developed

global market concept
wherever cost- and culturally effective, an overall standardised marketing strategy is developed for entire sets of country markets; marketing mix elements are adapted where necessary

Chapter Learning Objectives

What you should learn from Chapter 10

- How international marketing management differs from global marketing
- Why adaptation is necessary
- How and when we can use standardised marketing
- What is meant by quality as it relates to products and their use in international markets
- Comprehend the importance of collaborative relationships in international marketing efforts
- The increasing importance of strategic international alliances
- How positioning and branding influences the international marketing strategy
- Understand the factors that influence strategy formulation
- Why there is a need for strategic planning in order to achieve company goals
- Understand the importance of product life cycles for marketing strategy

Confronted with increasing global competition for expanding markets, multinational companies are changing their marketing strategies. Their goals are to enhance their competitiveness and to assure proper positioning in order to capitalise on opportunities in the global marketplace.

A recent study of North American and European corporations indicated that nearly 75 per cent of the companies are revamping their business processes, that most have formalised **strategic planning** programmes and that the need to stay cost competitive was considered to be the most important external issue affecting their marketing strategies.[1] Change is not limited to the giant multinationals but includes small and medium-sized firms as well.[2] In fact, the flexibility of a smaller company may enable it to reflect the demands of international markets and redefine its programmes quicker than larger multinationals. Acquiring a global perspective is easy, but the execution requires planning, organisation and a willingness to try new approaches, from engaging in collaborative relationships to redefining the scope of company operations.[3]

This chapter discusses global marketing management, competition in the global marketplace, strategic planning and strategies.

international marketing management

Determining a firm's overall international strategy to achieve goals and objectives is the central task of international marketing management that defines the level of international integration of the company. Companies must deal with a multitude of strategic issues including the extent of the internationalisation of operations.

As discussed in Chapter 1, a company's international orientation can be characterised as one of three operating concepts:

1 under the **domestic market extension concept**, foreign markets are extensions of the domestic market and the domestic marketing mix is offered, as is, to foreign markets
2 with the **multidomestic market concept**, each country is viewed as being culturally unique and an adapted marketing mix for each country market is developed, and
3 with the **global market concept**, the world is the market and, wherever cost- and culturally effective, an overall standardised marketing strategy is developed for entire sets of country markets, while only marketing mix elements are adapted wherever necessary.

The selection of any one of the approaches to internationalisation produces different effects on subsequent product, promotion, distribution and pricing decisions and strategies.

global versus international marketing management

The primary distinction between global marketing management and international marketing management is orientation[4] (see Exhibit 10.1). **Global marketing** management is guided by the global marketing concept, which views the world as one market and is based on identifying and targeting cross-cultural similarities. International marketing management is based on the premise of cross-cultural differences and is guided by the belief that each foreign market requires its own culturally adapted marketing strategy. Although consumers in New Delhi dining at McDonald's and Western teens plugged into their iPods are a reality, the idea of marketing a standardised product with a uniform marketing plan around the world remains 'purely theoretical'.[5]

key term

global marketing
using global market concepts in marketing decisions

Exhibit 10.1 A Comparison of assumptions about global and multinational companies

	Multinational companies	**Global companies**
Product life cycle	Products are in different stages of the product life cycle in each nation	Global product life cycles; all consumers want the most advanced products
Design	Adjustments to products initially designed for domestic markets	International performance criteria considered during design stage
Adaptation	Product adaptation is necessary in markets characterised by national differences	Products are adapted to global wants and needs; restrained concern for product suitability
Market segmentation	Segments reflect differences Customised products for each segment Many customised markets Acceptance of regional/national differences	Segments reflect group similarities Group similar segments together Fewer standardised markets Expansion of segments into worldwide proportions
Competition	Domestic/national competitive relationships	Ability to compete in national markets is affected by a firm's global position
Production	Standardisation limited by requirements to adapt products to national tastes	Globally standardised production Adaptations are handled through modular designs
The consumer	Preferences reflect national differences	Global convergence of consumer wants and needs
Product	Products differentiated on the basis of design, features, functions, style and image	Emphasis on value-enhancing distinction
Price	Consumers willing to pay more for a customised product	Consumers prefer a globally standardised good if it carries a lower price
Promotion	National product image, sensitive to national needs	Global product image, sensitive to national differences and global needs
Place	National distribution channels	Global standardisation of distribution

Source: adapted with the authors' permission from Gerald M. Hampton and Erwin Buske, 'The Global Marketing Perspective', *Advances in International Marketing*, vol. 2, ed. S. Tamer Cavusgil (Greenwich, Conn.: JAI Press, 1987), pp. 265–6.

As discussed earlier, there is still debate about the extent of global markets today. A reasonable question concerns whether a global marketing strategy is possible and whether a completely standardised marketing mix can be achieved. Keep in mind that global marketing strategy, as used in this text, and the globalisation of markets are two separate, although interrelated, ideas. One has to do with efficiency of operations, competitiveness and orientation, the other with the homogeneity of demand across cultures. There are at least three points that help define a global approach to international marketing:

1 the world is viewed as the market (that is, sets of country markets)
2 homogeneous market segments are sought across country market sets, and
3 standardisation of the marketing mix is sought wherever possible but adapted whenever culturally necessary.

standardisation versus adaptation

Why globalise? Several benefits are derived from globalisation and standardisation of the marketing mix. *Economies of scale in production and marketing* are the most frequently cited benefits. Black & Decker (electrical hand tools, appliances and other consumer products) realised significant production cost savings when it adopted a global strategy. It was able to reduce not only the number of motor sizes for the European market from 260 to eight, but also 15 different models to eight. Ford estimates that by globalising its product development, purchasing and supply activities it can save up to €2.7 billion ($3 billion) a year.[6] The savings in the standardisation of advertising can be substantial. Colgate-Palmolive introduced its Colgate tartar-control toothpaste in over 40 countries, each of which could choose one of two ads. The company estimates that for every country where the standardised commercial runs, it saves €0.9–€1.8 million ($1–2 million) in production costs. However, it soon realised that the standardised ads were not suitable for many countries and were not working. It had to change its strategy and went back to more versions/adaptations of the ads.

Transfer of experience and know-how across countries through improved coordination and integration of marketing activities is also cited as a benefit of globalisation. Unilever, NV, successfully introduced two global brands originally developed by two subsidiaries. Its South African subsidiary developed Impulse body spray and a European branch developed a detergent that cleaned effectively in European hard water. These are examples of how coordination and transfer of know-how from a local market to a world market can be achieved.

The most important benefit derived from globalisation is a *uniform international image*. Global recognition of brand accelerates new product introductions and increases the efficiency and effectiveness of advertising. Uniform global images are increasingly important as satellite communications spread throughout the world. Brands such as Sony, Volvo, Shell, IBM and Ericsson are good examples. Philips International, an electronics manufacturer, had enormous impact with a global product image when it sponsored the soccer World Cup; the same advertisement was seen in 44 countries with voiceover translations in six languages. Adidas acquired the same benefits when it sponsored the soccer World Cup in 2002, which was seen in more then 60 countries.

Global marketing also made a marked difference in accelerating a 3M product launch on a global scale. For example, a high-grade super VHS videotape was introduced in Japan one month and in the United States three months later; it appeared in Europe just six months after its introduction in Japan. In the past, it would have been impossible to get effective media coverage and introduce a new 3M product in all its markets in such a short time.[7] Another example is Microsoft's Windows XP, which was launched simultaneously all over the world, from Chicago to Singapore.

Without doubt, market differences seldom permit complete standardisation. Government and trade restrictions, differences in the availability of media, differences in

customer interests and response patterns, and the whole host of cultural differences presented in earlier chapters preclude complete standardisation of a global marketing mix.

competition in the global marketplace

Global competition is placing new emphasis on some basic tenets of business. It is reducing time frames and focusing on the importance of quality, competitive prices and innovative products. Time is becoming a precious commodity for business, and expanding technology is shortening product life cycles and creating greater opportunities for innovative products. A company can no longer introduce a new product with the expectation of dominating the market for years while the idea spreads slowly through world markets. Consider the effect on Hewlett-Packard's strategies and plans when, in any given year, two-thirds of its revenue comes from products introduced in the prior three years. Shorter product life cycles mean that a company must maximise sales rapidly to recover development costs and generate a profit by offering its products globally. However, companies need to understand the dynamic nature of the global marketplace as well as the culture and environment that cause this dynamism. A failure to understand this results in failure in foreign markets. Wal-Mart's problems in Germany; McDonald's problems in Japan (see Going International 4.5); Nike's problems in late 1980, when its sales fell drastically due to allegations that it exploits labour in its foreign markets; and Marks & Spencer's failure in European markets (France, Netherlands, Sweden, Belgium) are good examples. On the other hand, the German Müller yoghurt in the UK, Toyota's Lexus car in the United States, Tesco's internationalisation into Eastern Europe and McDonald's revival in France are good examples of understanding these forces and adapting marketing strategies to gain success.

Along with technological advances have come enhanced market expectations for innovative products at competitive prices. Today, strategic planning must include emphasis on quality, technology and cost containment.

quality and competitive marketing

As global competition increases for most businesses, many industry and government leaders have warned that a renewed emphasis on quality is a necessity for doing business in growing global markets. In most global markets the cost and quality of a product are among the most important criteria by which purchases are made. Further, the market has gradually shifted from a seller's market to a buyer's market. All over the world, customers have more power because they have more choices as more companies compete for their attention.

Quality is an important criterion for success, but what does quality mean? For many companies, quality is defined internally from the firm's point of view and is measured in terms of compliance with predetermined product specifications or standards and with minimum defects. The concept that quality is measured in terms of conformance to product specifications works if the specifications meet the needs of the market and if the product is delivered to the customer in a manner that fills the customer's needs. The assumption is that a product conforming to exact standards is what the market wants. There is, however, some evidence that quality viewed from within a company may result in 'quality for quality's sake' and yet not fully meet customer expectations of a quality product.[8] Conformance to standards is absolutely necessary for quality, but a customer's perception of quality includes more.

Total quality management (TQM) is a **corporate strategy** that focuses total company effort on manufacturing superior products with continuous technological improvement and zero defects that satisfy customer needs. Defining quality as customer satisfaction means the marketer must continually monitor the customer's changing requirements as well as competitive offerings and adjust product offerings as needed, because the customer evaluates a company's product relative to competing products. Your product

key terms

total quality management (TQM) method that permits continuous improvement of the production of goods and services

corporate strategy strategy of the company as a whole

may be the 'best engineered' in the market with zero defects, but if it does not fulfil all your customer's expectations as well as a competitor's does, the competition wins.[9]

GOING INTERNATIONAL 10.1

war of the laundry titans: how to survive in a no-growth market

In 2000, as the world braced itself for an economic slowdown, $52 billion Unilever and $40 billion Procter & Gamble clashed in the battle for share in the laundry soap market. Eking out growth in tough conditions was not a new experience for the companies. In the late 1990s, as the rest of the world had been growing at hyperspeed, Unilever and P&G had already been living in the slowest of the slow-growth industries – consumer products.

In 2000, the US fabric care market was flat, and at $6 billion a year it was already so big that it could not get much bigger. Americans were just not getting any dirtier. The only way to win market share in such a situation is to take it away from competitors; in this case, even small gains promise large returns – a mere percentage point translates into a $60 million gain in revenues.

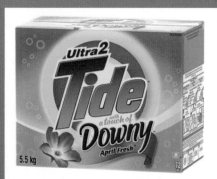

Just one of the 60 variations of Tide products

P&G's Tide has been the undisputed king of the market in the recent years, with 40 per cent share. The key to its success was advertising and an ever-widening product line. Tide spent over $100 million a year on promotion by advertising on TV, billboards, subways, buses, magazines, the Internet, nationwide publicity stunts, such as the Dirtiest Kid in America contest, and sporting events. At the same time, Tide spawned more than 60 variations of itself through developing new, specialised formulations: Tide with Bleach, Tide Free (fragrance free), Tide WearCare (which purports to keep fabrics vibrant for longer), Tide Kick, and so on. Individually, each new mutation does not add up to much (Tide Kick has just 0.005 per cent of the market share), but together they drive the business.

Unilever occupied the laundry throne in overseas markets such as South America and South Asia. However, in the US, the market share of its laundry detergent product, Wisk, dropped from 13 per cent to 9 per cent in 1994 due to cost-cutting efforts and budget freezes. Nevertheless, in 2001, the company's management could not see Unilever in the position of global leadership without a strong position in the US market. Wisk needed to be resurrected for the American public. And the only way to do it, since Tide could out-advertise and out-low-price anyone, was to create something bigger, better and newer. And Wisk thinks it has got it in the new laundry detergent in tablet form that has already been introduced in Europe under the name of Persil and has won a whopping 6 per cent market share. Armed with an 80 per cent promotion budget, Unilever launched Wisk Dual Action Tablets in the US in November 2000. The company predicted that tablets would become a 1 million market over the next five years. Of that, Wisk expects to win 30 per cent share.

However, it is too early to count profits. Shortly after the introduction of Wisk tablets, P&G launched a counter-offensive in the shape of Tide Rapid Action Tablets and aired ads that feature a side-by-side comparison with the Wisk product. The battle rages on.

■ Do you think Unilever can beat P&G in the United States? How?

Source: adapted from K. Brooker, 'A Game of Inches', *Fortune*, 5 February 2001, pp. 98–100.

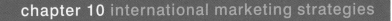
cost containment and international sourcing

As global competition intensifies, profit margins are squeezed. To stay profitable, companies seek ways to keep costs within a range that permits competitive pricing. **Global sourcing**, a major driving force behind companies producing goods around the world, is used to minimise costs and risks. It is rapidly becoming a prerequisite to competing in today's marketplace.

Lower costs are not the only advantage to global sourcing; flexibility and dependability are also important benefits. Worldwide sources strengthen the reliability of quality and supply. Companies can achieve technical supremacy by securing access to innovative technology from offshore sources and perhaps prevent competitors from obtaining the technology as well. The uniqueness of a company's needs and their availability lead a company to source globally. To establish a foothold in markets that might otherwise be closed, companies may source some goods to comply with a country's local-content requirements.

India and China have emerged as prime locations for **outsourcing** all types of jobs. Hundreds of thousands of jobs from the EU and the USA have already moved to these locations. The jobs for which a monthly salary of €3000 is normal in Europe are going for €500 in India or China. For more qualified jobs in computers and software where the average salary in the USA or Europe is around €6000–7000 a month, companies can hire qualified people for €1000 (or less) in India and China.

In addition to these two locations, the new entrants to the EU, such as Poland, Hungary, the Czech Republic and Slovakia, have also joined the race to attract outsourced jobs from the US and the EU. Exhibit 10.2 presents countries that are attracting outsourcing jobs, with an index of attractiveness.

Collaborative Relationships

The accelerating rate of technological progress, market demand created by global industrialisation, and the creation of new middle classes will result in tremendous potential in global markets. But along with this surge in global demand comes an increase in competition as technology and management capabilities spread beyond global companies to new competitors from Asia, Europe and Latin America.[10]

Although global markets offer tremendous potential, companies seeking to function effectively in a fragmented global market of 5 billion people are being forced to stretch production, design and marketing resources and capabilities because of the intensity of competition and the pace of technology. Improving quality and staying on the cutting edge of technology are critical and basic for survival but often are not enough. Restructuring, reorganising and downsizing are all avenues being taken by firms to strengthen their competitive positions.

Additionally, many multinational companies are realising they must develop long-term, mutually beneficial relationships throughout the company and beyond: with competitors, suppliers, governments and customers. In short, multinational companies are developing orientations that focus on building **collaborative relationships** to promote long-term alliances, and they are seeking continuous, mutually beneficial exchanges instead of one-time sales or events.

These collaborative relationships are a mindset characterising an approach to management that can be described as relational exchanges. Relational exchanges occur (1) internally among functional departments, business units, subsidiaries and employees and (2) externally among customers (both intermediary and final), suppliers of goods and services, competitors, government agencies and related businesses where a mutually beneficial goal is sought.[11]

Collaborative relationships[12] can be grouped into two broad categories: relationship marketing – those relationships that focus on the marketing process; and strategic business alliances – those relationships that encompass the other activities of the business enterprise.[13]

key terms

global sourcing
buying components and materials from all over the world

outsourcing
letting other companies take over part of your production process

collaborative relationships
relationships between companies cooperating with each other

249

Exhibit 10.2 Offshore location attractiveness index

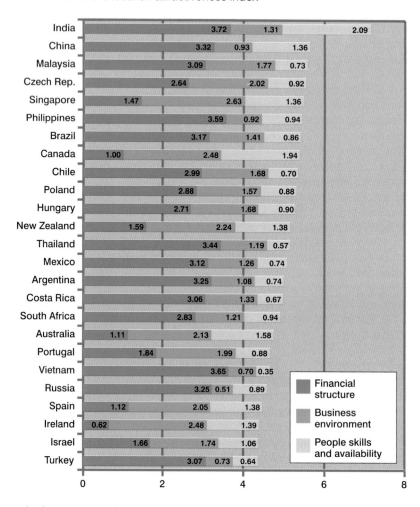

Note: the bars represent index numbers. The weight distribution for the three categories is 40:30:30, meaning that the financial structure is rated on a scale of 1 to 4, and that business environment, and people skills and availability are on a scale of 1 to 3.

Source: Amartya Sen, 'Budapest, the Next Bangalore? New EU Members Join the Outsourcing Race', *Financial Times*, 21 September 2004, p. 19.

GOING INTERNATIONAL 10.2

Toyota's new traction in Europe

Toyota, earlier a marginal player in Europe, is becoming a fearsome market force as it applies itself to winning a big share of the European roadways. Sales in Europe rose 20.6 per cent in the first four months of 2004, following a 10.4 per cent leap in 2003, to 835,000 cars – a dramatic performance given that the European market shrank by 1.3 per cent last year. Those gains, fuelled partly by the redesigned Yaris, pushed Toyota's market share in Western Europe to 5.3 per cent in April 2004, up from 4.5 per cent a year previously, overtaking Mercedes and Audi and edging close to Italy's Fiat.

Toyota is determined to snare even bigger gains in Europe. Its goal is to enhance its market share to 8 per cent by 2010. The world's number two auto-maker spent the 1990s slowly acquiring a hefty 11 per cent chunk of the $457 (€373) billion US auto market. Industry experts say the Japanese giant has a good shot at becoming one of the leading auto brands in Europe and could well exceed its 8 per cent target.

Soaring sales are also helping Toyota's bottom line. European revenues rose 35.3 per cent in 2003, to $19.5 (€16) billion. Operating profit rose nearly ninefold, to $654 (€535) million. Behind the sales surge are investments in local design and production. Half the Toyotas sold in Europe are built at factories in Britain, France and Turkey. In 2005, when a joint-venture plant with PSA Peugeot Citröen starts operations, Toyota's local production will rise to 60 per cent, nearly matching the level of local production in the US. By 2010 the company aims to sell 1.2 million cars in Europe, matching the sales levels of Peugeot and Ford brands.

The New Toyota Corolla Verso
Issued 07/2004

Thanks to its new design studio in southern France, Toyota's recent look is distinctly changing. Its new compact minivan, the Corolla Verso, matches the avant-garde styling pioneered by French and German rivals such as the Renault Scenic or Volkswagen Touran. European auto-makers have more to fear from Toyota than a handful of hot models. While the Japanese powerhouse was figuring out how to build cars attractive to Europeans, it was also bearing down on costs to wield the efficiency needed to prevail in one of the world's lowest-margin auto markets. Toyota's management asked engineers to propose an innovative, cost-saving design for the Valenciennes factory. The result: a compact star-shaped factory that features a production area with limited space to store parts or components. The 2.5 hours' worth of inventory on hand is lower than at any other Toyota factory in the world.

The new factory design was a hit. By putting every production process under one roof – from press machinery to welding, painting, assembly and final quality checks – Toyota cut the overall investment required for the plant by 40 per cent. The design of the French plant is just one example of how Toyota is quietly but relentlessly increasing the standard of efficiency in Europe. European auto-makers such as Fiat, Opel and Ford, which can never seem to get out of the red, will feel the squeeze.

One challenge still facing Toyota is its brand image. Although the Japanese giant regularly ranks first in a variety of quality surveys across Europe, consumers don't perceive Toyota as the quality leader. 'That's our number one headache,' says Toyota. But as Europeans see more Toyotas on the street, opinions are changing. However, the European car makers are giving Toyota a tough battle for every inch of ground.

■ Will Toyota be able to snatch market share from European auto-makers/brands? What can European auto-makers do to constrain Toyota from achieving more market share?

Source: abridged from 'Toyota's New Traction in Europe', *Business Week*, 7 June 2004, p. 21.

A study of CEOs of multinational companies on strategies for 2000 and beyond revealed that most felt that just satisfying the customer will not be enough. The focus will have to be more on the customer, who will be the strongest influence on the corporation.[14] Companies must rid themselves of the one-time-sale orientation, and focus instead on servicing the consumer's needs over time.

relationship marketing

Relationship marketing is the category of collaborative relationships that focuses on the marketing process. Like all relational collaborations, relationship marketing has as its focus the creation, development and support of successful relational exchanges throughout the marketing process. The ultimate goal is to achieve a competitive advantage by establishing long-term, mutually beneficial associations with loyal, satisfied customers.[15]

To build a sustainable relationship with customers, businesses are changing their attitudes towards internal relationships and between themselves and traditional competitors, suppliers, distributors and retailers. It becomes a matter of working with customers and all others involved to produce goods that best serve the customer's needs.

The Whirlpool Corporation, as one example, has formal agreements with Procter & Gamble and Unilever to exchange basic information and ideas. Together they are involved at the engineering and technology levels of product development. The basic rationale for this relationship is that the two industries, washing machines and detergents, are co-dependent – 'they can't be designing detergents 10 years out for washing machines that can't use them', and Whirlpool cannot design satisfactory washing machines without knowledge of the detergents that will be available. Whirlpool also develops relationships with suppliers; instead of working with five steel suppliers, for example, it has partnerships with one or two. It is seeking agreements that will give it access to supplier technologies so they can work together on process improvements.[16]

Why Relationship Marketing?   It helps cement customer loyalty, which means repeat sales and referrals and, thus, market share and revenue growth. A consulting company study estimates that a decrease in customer defection rate of 5 per cent can boost profits by 25 to 95 per cent. The adage that 20 per cent of your customers account for 50 to 80 per cent of your profits has some merit. It has always been good business to focus company resources on the best customers rather than those who are strictly price shoppers.[17] Relationship marketing strengthens that focus.

National Semiconductor Corporation, the multinational chip manufacturer, is forging a partnership with Federal Express Corporation, noted for its worldwide electronic communications and air-truck network. The partnership will allow the chip manufacturer to close its costly global warehouse system, to guarantee just-in-time delivery from its Singapore plant to thousands of customers worldwide within 48 hours, to plan product deliveries precisely and even to divert products to new locations at short notice.

formulating international marketing strategy

Strategic planning means looking at ways to achieve growth of the firm, which often means going to new markets and/or products. It may stem from a saturated home market or development of a competitive product/service that can be tried in new markets. However, the knowledge of the foreign market is necessary to take the firm abroad. It is also restricted by the resources and management perceptions/goals.

Considering the above, a company needs to adopt a **generic strategy** for the company as a whole. It is called generic because it can be applied as an overall strategy across markets and products. Specific marketing strategies for each market/product are used as sub-strategies. Having a generic strategy does not mean having a standardised strategy for all markets and products. In fact, companies often use different marketing strategies for different markets for the same product or business unit. These strategies are influenced by the overall corporate strategy, the particular customer segment, positioning, product life cycle and market environment in the particular market. This is illustrated in Exhibit 10.3.

Companies normally use one of the two generic strategies: **differentiation strategy** or **focus strategy**. Differentiation strategy is one in which the marketer is trying to convince

Exhibit 10.3 Factors influencing international marketing strategy

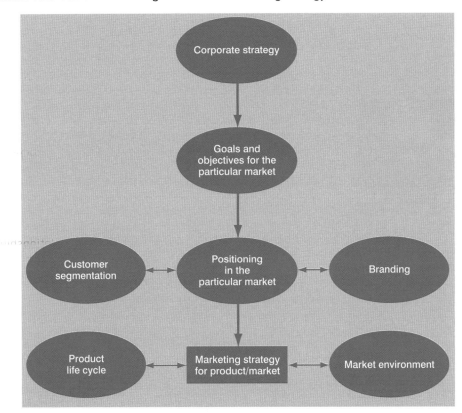

the market/customers that his product is different to that of other competitors. The company tries to give the message that its product offers more value. In some cases it is done as offering premium quality and premier prices while in other cases it is done as low-cost advantage. For example, BMW is using differentiation strategy by conveying to the market that its cars have better quality and other features offering prestige and status. It can thus charge higher prices than its competitors: Volvo, Saab, Honda Accord and Toyota Camry. Wal-Mart and Aldi, on the other hand, are also using differentiation strategies and trying to convince the market/customers that they can provide more value for the money they spend by selling groceries at lowest prices. These companies thus claim to have low-cost strategy. Companies such as easyJet and Ryanair are also good examples. This differentiation offers value to the customer, which has to be visible/verifiable.

Many companies make the mistake of promising to provide value to the customer which is not visible or valued by the customer to justify the premier price or the claims of low cost. Some companies try to offer other features as 'differentiation' such as convenience to order or delivery at home. The key issue is, however, that a company has to develop a differentiation from customer's perspective. In the 'quality and premier pricing' differentiation, the customer has to be convinced that the product is of superior quality as compared to competitors' to justify the premier price. When used properly, it provides **sustainable competitive advantage (SCA)**. In both cases, low-cost or quality differentiation strategies, the company can achieve SCA by being consistent.

Focus strategy is applied when a company decides to focus on a particular market segment or part of the product line. The company using this strategy does not want to compete across the whole market. This may be due to lack of resources, which means that the company cannot support multiple brands. Another reason might be that the company

key term

sustainable competitive advantage (SCA) advantages over other competitors, enjoyed over a long period in the future

GOING INTERNATIONAL 10.3

booming BMW

Looking into the auto world, car fanciers are always drawing attention to any classic or updated models from the big auto-makers – Porsche, Nissan, Toyota, BMW, Mercedes-Benz, Volkswagen and so on. Unlike 10 years ago, when these giants stuck to their classic design, the market is now challenged by frequent new models. The global auto market, from 1990, has been perceived to be fragmented into hot new niches, and demand for luxury models started to shrink as a percentage of total auto sales. The inspiration for a new model is desirable and propels the companies in the market. BMW used to have just a handful of models – essentially the 3, 5, and 7 series – but now it has become an imperative to roll out a new or updated model every three months through 2005 in a ramp-up more ambitious than anything the company has attempted before. BMW aims to expand annual sales by 40 per cent over the next five years, and beat Mercedes-Benz as the number one maker of premium cars in the world.

BMW's expansionist strategy is now well under way. Other than building an exclusive dealer network with Rolls-Royce Phantom, the $37 760 Z4 roadster, the 5 Series sedan and the X3 hit the European showrooms ceaselessly from 2003. It was scheduled that in the fall of 2004 dealers would get their first deliveries of the new 1 Series sub-compact that will go head to head with the Audi 3, the Mercedes A-Class and the high-end versions of Volkswagen's Golf. BMW will also endeavour to introduce a 6 Series convertible and a station wagon version of the new 5 Series. The Bavarian giant has already overtaken Mercedes-Benz in the US market, where it is also ahead of Toyota's Lexus. The profits from these new models are quite impressive. Despite a 53 per cent increase in R&D and a 75 per cent increase in capital expenditures over the past two years, BMW's net profit in 2002 still rose 8.3 per cent, to $2.36 billion, while revenues climbed 9.9 per cent, to $49.5 billion. Operating margins, at 8 per cent in 2002 and 8.7 per cent in 2001 – the heaviest years for investing – were again among the highest in the industry.

BMW has achieved a remarkable performance in the global auto market through the launching of new models, but one must now ask whether the profit margins can be kept against the potential dollar risk in the coming years and whether BMW can maintain the consistently high returns it once achieved with its exclusive portfolio. BMW's manufacturing costs are considered to be higher, its product development process more costly and its purchasing costs higher compared with volume producers. Moreover, BMW is under quality pressure from customers; an engine defect put BMW in an embarrassing situation. Another key doubt lies in the BMW brand. With more updated and new models in the global auto market, is it possible that the brand may suffer through the 'friendly fighting' that exists among the BMW models. In addition, the competitors (Toyota's Lexus, the Mercedes E-Class and Volkswagen's Audi) are also going to be innovative in order to adapt to the fragmented auto market, which adds to the pressure on BMW.

Source: Business Week, 9 June 2003.

wants to provide a better match between its offer and customer needs/wants, thus creating SCA for itself. Companies such as Rolls-Royce, Porsche and Harley-Davidson are good examples of companies using this strategy.

Having decided the overall strategy, a company needs to deal with positioning and branding that is consistent with the strategy chosen. These two aspects become crucial in formulation and then implementation of the strategy.

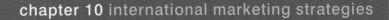
positioning

Positioning is not what you do with the product, but what you do to the customer's mind. The better you understand the mind, the better you understand how positioning works. This means that companies are battling to capture the mind of the customer. This task has become more difficult due to an overload of information and communication by companies and other organisations such as Greenpeace and the WTO. The market is no longer responsive to old strategies due to the fact that there are simply too many companies, too many products and too much communication/information in the market.

The most effective way of positioning a company/product is to know your customer segment and concentrate on understanding this target group, and create an image that matches with their needs/wants. Advertising is only one way to communicate with customers; companies communicate with their markets in many ways. Positioning is thus considered a systematic way to find a window into the customer's mind. It has to be done at the right time and under the right circumstances. Moreover, it has to be done constantly and consistently. Companies such as Sony and Gillette try to position themselves as most innovative and leaders in their industries, and they have consistently tried to do that through communication.

key term

positioning
creating an image of your product and its quality in customers' minds

---

GOING INTERNATIONAL 10.4

Sony's mission: make its own products obsolete

Sony, the creator of the Walkman and the PlayStation, has been synonymous with consumer electronics for most of the past five decades. However, while facing the increasing competition from lower-priced manufacturers in South Korea and China, Sony is frank about the size of the challenge and realises it has to redefine its market strategies. More pressure comes from the digital product industry, where companies with little or no expertise rush into this market due to the rapid commoditisation of hardware products and the ease of access to gain the technologies and know-how.

Kunitake Ando, Sony's president, points out that a networked world influences the consumer electronics industry, and believes that 'Sony's mission is to make our own products obsolete. Otherwise somebody else will do it.' Senior executives aim to transform stand-alone Sony's products (TVs, PCs, camcorders and mobile phones) into the Internet, what they call 'gateways to networks'.

Sony's unique position, based on its broad portfolio of business, enables it to fashion the next generation of high-tech products according to its own vision. Television is believed to be at the heart of Sony's business combination because 'TV is about to be reborn as the centre of broadband entertainment'. Seeking to keep the costs down and to optimise technological gains, the new strategy also centres on software and hardware, an approach that requires better coordination between different divisions. The integration of its audio-visual and IT operations is a good example of the transformation.

Even though Sony is on the way to its new mission, it faces a tough fight on three fronts: against all the other movie studios and music companies; against the might of Microsoft and others in software; and every other electronics company in hardware. And, finally, it will still be a long time before Sony can see whether the new products can survive and compete in the 'networked world'.

■ Do you think it is a good strategy to cannibalise your own product?

Source: 'Sony's Mission is to Make Our Own Products Obsolete. Otherwise Somebody Else Will Do It', an interview with the CEO, *Financial Times*, 10 February 2003.

Every now and then companies need to reposition themselves due to changes in the marketplace or changes in customer tastes. There are several such examples: McDonald's has been trying to reposition itself from a company perceived to be selling 'fast food' or 'junk food' or 'unhealthy food' towards a company selling healthy food. Digital photography is forcing Kodak to reposition itself as more and more customers are moving from film cameras to digital cameras. Toyota had to reposition itself, or create a new positioning, when it wanted to cover the luxury car market, initially in the United States, by introducing the Lexus.

Due to constant changes in technology, consumer tastes and competition, companies are increasingly in danger of losing their positioning. If companies are not proactive in analysing their positioning and repositioning, whenever needed, they lose their markets. The American automobile industry, Sega and Nintendo game consoles, Word Perfect and Lotus spreadsheet software are good examples of companies that lost their positioning. While Macintosh (Apple), IBM and Nokia are good examples of successfully repositioning companies and products.

branding

Companies use brands to be able to convey their marketing strategy and positioning to the markets. Brands are often the most valuable assets companies have. Nike, Coca-Cola, Adidas, Nokia, Philips and Sony are good examples. The best-managed brands increase in value with age and develop personalities of their own. Some even given birth to sub-brands or brand extensions and allow the company to exploit the brand in new areas. Coca-Cola's and Marlboro's clothing lines, different products of Sony and several models of BMW are good examples. Brand extension allows new products to be introduced with lower marketing expenditure. It also allows companies to utilise their existing customer base.

Brands have a profound impact on society, nation/country and customer emotions, thus awarding the brand owner a great responsibility. We have seen that during the Vietnam and Iraq Wars, consumers in many countries boycotted American brands. From a marketer's point of view, the most important impact of brands is that they lead to customer satisfaction and loyalty. A loyal customer base is the biggest asset of a company. The brands are thus the biggest value generators in many companies (see Exhibit 10.4).

Brand loyalty leads to resistance to switching to another company's products. The more satisfied a customer is, the less inclined he or she will be to buy or even try a competing product. Sometimes, switching cost is also an important factor (for example, for software users). However, many companies, by mismanaging their brands, have lost their customers even in this product category. Products such as Word Perfect, Wordstar and Baan software are good examples.

Customer loyalty automatically creates barriers of entry for competitors. To snatch market shares from an established brand would require excessive resources. This is particularly important for companies trying to enter foreign (new) markets. The existence of established brands in the particular market, whether local or foreign, and loyalty of customers, create entry barriers for newcomers. It will also enhance the cost associated with the entrance and consequently the profits.

It is thus important for companies to establish brands. **Branding** means development and building the reputation of a brand name. This is done by understanding the customer segments and creating a brand that can be perceived to satisfy these segments' needs/wants, and then conveying this through communication, advertising and other means. Branding decisions include deciding on the number of brands to be used and how many brands to be used in each market. For example, following the success of the EU, Unilever has decided to cut the number of its brands from 1600 to 400. This will allow the

key terms

brand loyalty
when a customer always buys the same brand

customer loyalty
when a customer always buys one company's products

branding
developing and building the reputation of a brand name

Exhibit 10.4 The world's 25 most valuable brands

Rank 2004		Brand value ($ millions)	Country of ownership
1	Coca-Cola	67394	US
2	Microsoft	61372	US
3	IBM	53791	US
4	GE	44111	US
5	Intel	33499	US
6	Disney	27113	US
7	McDonald's	25001	US
8	Nokia	24041	Finland
9	Toyota	22673	Japan
10	Marlboro	22128	US
11	Mercedes	21331	Germany
12	Hewlett-Packard	20978	US
13	CitiBank	19971	US
14	American Express	16683	US
15	Gillette	16723	US
16	Cisco	15948	US
17	BMW	15886	Germany
18	Honda	14874	Japan
19	Ford	14475	US
20	Sony	12759	Japan
21	Samsung	12553	South Korea
22	Pepsi	12006	US
23	Nescafé	11892	Switzerland
24	Budweiser	11846	US
25	Dell	11500	US

Note: to qualify for this list, a brand must have a value greater than $1 billion, derive about one-third of its earnings from outside its home market, and have publicly available marketing and financial data. Some brands might have greater value but have been eliminated due to the above criteria.

Source: abridged from 'Cult Brands, Business Week Interbrand Annual Ranking', Special Report: *Business Week*, 9 August 2004, pp. 46–53.

company to achieve economies of scale as well as more focused recognition throughout Europe. This will also make distribution and promotion more efficient.

product life cycle and international marketing strategy
Most products go through the different stages of a life cycle; each stage demands different marketing strategies due to different market conditions. There is no fixed length of a **product life cycle (PLC)**, it represents a sale history of a particular product following an

key term

product life cycle (PLC)
different stages in a product's life, from introduction to death

key term

PLC stages
stages in the
product life cycle:
introduction,
growth, maturity
and decline

S-shaped curve, which is divided into four **PLC stages**: introduction, growth, maturity and decline (see Exhibit 10.5). However, all products do not necessarily follow the S-shape through all four stages. Some products die after the first stage, introduction, while others mature very quickly.

Exhibit 10.5 Perspectives of the product life cycle

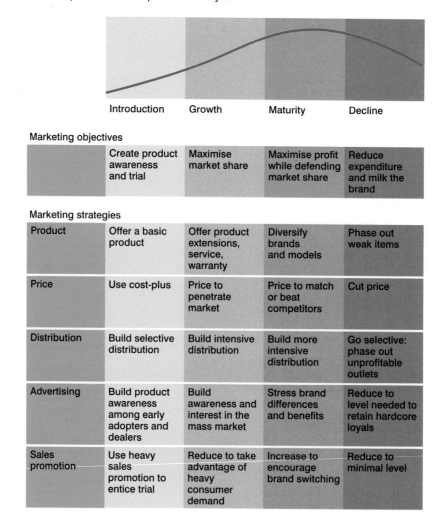

	Introduction	Growth	Maturity	Decline
Marketing objectives				
	Create product awareness and trial	Maximise market share	Maximise profit while defending market share	Reduce expenditure and milk the brand
Marketing strategies				
Product	Offer a basic product	Offer product extensions, service, warranty	Diversify brands and models	Phase out weak items
Price	Use cost-plus	Price to penetrate market	Price to match or beat competitors	Cut price
Distribution	Build selective distribution	Build intensive distribution	Build more intensive distribution	Go selective: phase out unprofitable outlets
Advertising	Build product awareness among early adopters and dealers	Build awareness and interest in the mass market	Stress brand differences and benefits	Reduce to level needed to retain hardcore loyals
Sales promotion	Use heavy sales promotion to entice trial	Reduce to take advantage of heavy consumer demand	Increase to encourage brand switching	Reduce to minimal level

Source: based on Philip Kotler, *Marketing Management: Analysis, Planning, Implementation, and Control*, 9th edn (Upper Saddle River, NJ: Prentice Hall, 1999).

Different stages of the PLC have different characteristics and the marketing objectives in each stage are different. Due to these differences, a marketer has to apply different marketing strategies in different stages. The intensity of competition increases with the stages and finally reaches a point where the market starts declining. At this point, companies can revive the PLC by introducing new features to the product. This is done successfully by automobile companies, by introducing new models every four or five years. Gillette razors are good examples of this strategy, when the company keeps introducing the next generation of shaving razors, from Gillette Sensor to Mach 3 to Mach 3 Turbo and Mach 3 Power.

GOING INTERNATIONAL 10.5

battle of the giants

From 1999 to 2000 Gillette was steadily losing market share to Schick. Traditionally, Gillette owned the razor and blade category in the market, and Jim Kilts, the company CEO, even laid out a strategy to lengthen the amount of time between major new product launches: with little competition in the market, it made sense to slow down spending on R&D. However, the purchase of Schick by Energiser created a serious rival for Gillette. Gillette has already seen its market share in women's blades eroding, and now its share in the male blade market, controlled by its top-selling three-blade razor Mach 3, is being threatened by the introduction of Schick's Quattro four-blade razor.

However, Gillette may have a chance to not only recover market share, but also to lay successful claims to Schick's Quattro-generated revenues: Gillette launched a lawsuit seeking to ban Quattro from the market on the basis of patent infringement. The patent suit against Schick centres on the position of Quattro's blades. In developing Mach 3 in the 1990s, Gillette hit upon a way to achieve a closer shave without irritating the skin: the razor aligned blades progressively closer to the skin so that each one cut closer than the last. Mach 3 is covered by over 50 patents describing the position of the blades in excruciating detail. Gillette claims that the technology applies whether one uses three blades, four or five. If Gillette wins the case, the damages awarded will be more than substantial considering the tremendous sales generated by top-selling razors (in 2002 Mach 3 produced $2 billion in revenues). However, even if Gillette wins, the company must face the fact that it is for the first time dealing with a serious rival. In 2004, Gillette introduced M3 Power, a battery-driven razor. Now, we have to see how Schick is going to counter that move.

■ Do you think Gillette is justified in taking Schick to court for its Quattro?

Source: adapted from Victoria Griffith, 'Schick and Gillette Take Fight to the Edge', *Financial Times*, 16 September 2003, p. 31

strategic planning

Strategic planning is a systematised way of relating to the future. It is an attempt to manage the effects of external, uncontrollable factors on the firm's strengths, weaknesses, objectives and goals to attain a desired end. Further, it is a commitment of resources to a country market to achieve specific goals. In other words, planning is the job of making things happen that may not otherwise occur. There is a lot of discussion on the goals of a company, and scholars often agree that the growth of the firm is the ultimate goal. All the big companies started off as smaller companies and, with clear goals for their growth, they have reached the desired status (see Exhibit 10.6).

Is there a difference between strategic planning for a domestic company and for an international company? The principles of planning are not in themselves different, but the intricacies of the operating environments of the multinational corporation (host country, home and corporate environments), its organisational structure and the task of controlling a multi-country operation create differences in the complexity and process of international planning.

Strategic planning allows for rapid growth of the international function, changing markets, increasing competition and the ever-varying challenges of different national

key term

strategic planning
a systematised way of relating to the future

259

Exhibit 10.6 Mergers and cooperation in the auto industry

The auto industry has been consolidating since the 1960s when there were 42 companies. The number of companies decreased to 11 in 2000 and the consolidation is still going on. In 2004 the following groups were present.		
1	GM	General Motors, Fiat, Alfa Romeo, Ferrari, Subaru, Suzuki, Daewoo, Kia, Lotus, Opel, Cadillac, Chevrolet, Pontiac, Saab, Buick, Saturn, Vauxhall and Isuzu
2	Ford	Ford, Mazda, Volvo, Land Rover, Jaguar, Aston Martin and Lancia
3	VW	VW, SEAT, Audi, Skoda and Bentley
4	Toyota	Toyota, Lexus and Daihatsu
5	Daimler-Chrysler	Mercedes, Chrysler, Mitsubishi, Hyundai and Smart
6	BMW	BMW, Rolls-Royce and Mini
7	Peugeot	Peugeot and Citroën
8	Renault	Renault, Nissan and Samsung
9	Rover	Rover and MG
10	Honda	Honda
11	Porsche	Porsche

Source: compiled from Geutz, M., 'Turning Wheels between Europe, America and Asia: Mergers, Acquisition and Cooperation', paper presented at Carnegie Bosch Institute, Conference, Berlin, October 2001, and Auto Intelligence, 2002.

markets. The plan must blend the changing parameters of external country environments with corporate objectives and capabilities to develop a sound, workable marketing programme. A strategic plan commits corporate resources to products and markets to increase competitiveness and profits.

Planning relates to the formulation of goals and methods of accomplishing them, so it is both a process and a philosophy. Structurally, planning may be viewed as corporate, strategic and/or tactical. International planning at the corporate level is essentially long term, incorporating generalised goals for the enterprise as a whole. Strategic planning is conducted at the highest levels of management, and deals with products, capital and research, and the long- and short-term goals of the company. **Tactical planning** or **market planning** pertains to specific actions and to the allocation of resources used to implement strategic planning goals in specific markets. Tactical plans are made at the local level and address marketing and advertising questions.

A major advantage to a company involved in strategic planning is the discipline imposed by the process. An international marketer who has gone through the planning process has a framework for analysing marketing problems and opportunities, and a basis for coordinating information from different country markets. The process of planning may be as important as the plan itself because it forces decision makers to examine all factors that affect the success of a marketing programme and involves those who will be responsible for its implementation.

company objectives and resources

Evaluation of a company's objectives and resources is crucial in all stages of planning for international operations. Each new market entered can require a complete evaluation, including existing commitments, relative to the parent company's objectives and resources. As markets grow increasingly competitive, as companies find new opportunities, and as the cost of entering foreign markets increases, companies need such planning.

Foreign market opportunities do not always parallel corporate objectives; it may be necessary to change the objectives, alter the scale of international plans or abandon them. One market may offer immediate profit but have a poor long-run outlook, while another may offer the reverse. Only when corporate objectives are clear can such differences be reconciled effectively.

international commitment

The strategic planning approach taken by an international firm affects the degree of internationalisation to which management is philosophically committed. Such commitment affects the specific international strategies and decisions of the firm. After company objectives have been identified, management needs to determine whether it is prepared to make the level of commitment required for successful international operations – commitment in terms of resources to be invested, personnel for managing the international organisation and determination to stay in the market long enough to realise a return on these investments.

the planning process

Whether a company is marketing in several countries or entering a foreign market for the first time, planning is a major factor of success. The first-time foreign marketer must decide what products to develop, in which markets, and with what level of resource commitment. For the company already committed, the key decisions involve allocating effort and resources among countries and products, deciding on new markets to develop or old ones to withdraw from, and which products to develop or drop. Guidelines and systematic procedures are essential for evaluating international opportunities and risks and for developing strategic plans to take advantage of such opportunities. The process illustrated in Exhibit 10.7 offers a systematic guide to planning for the multinational firm operating in several countries.

Phase 1: Preliminary Analysis and Screening – Matching Company/Country

Needs   Whether a company is new to international marketing or already heavily involved, an evaluation of potential markets is the first step in the planning process. A critical first question in the international planning process is deciding in which existing country market to make a market investment. A company's strengths and weaknesses, products, philosophies and objectives must be matched with a country's constraining factors as well as limitations and potential. In the first part of the planning process, countries are analysed and screened to eliminate those that do not offer sufficient potential for further consideration.

The next step is to establish screening criteria against which prospective countries can be evaluated. These criteria are ascertained by an analysis of company objectives, resources and other corporate capabilities and limitations. It is important to determine the reasons for entering a foreign market and the returns expected from such an investment. A company's commitment to international business and objectives for going international are important in establishing evaluation criteria. Minimum market potential, minimum profit, return on investment, acceptable competitive levels, standards of political stability, acceptable legal requirements and other measures appropriate for the company's products are examples of the evaluation criteria to be established.

Once evaluation criteria are set, a complete analysis of the environment within which a company plans to operate is made. The environment consists of the uncontrollable elements discussed earlier and includes both home-country and host-country restraints, marketing objectives and any other company limitations or strengths that exist at the beginning of each planning period. Although an understanding of uncontrollable environments is important in domestic market planning, the task is more complex in foreign marketing because each country under consideration presents the foreign marketer with a different set of unfamiliar environmental constraints. It is this stage in the planning

Exhibit 10.7 The international planning process

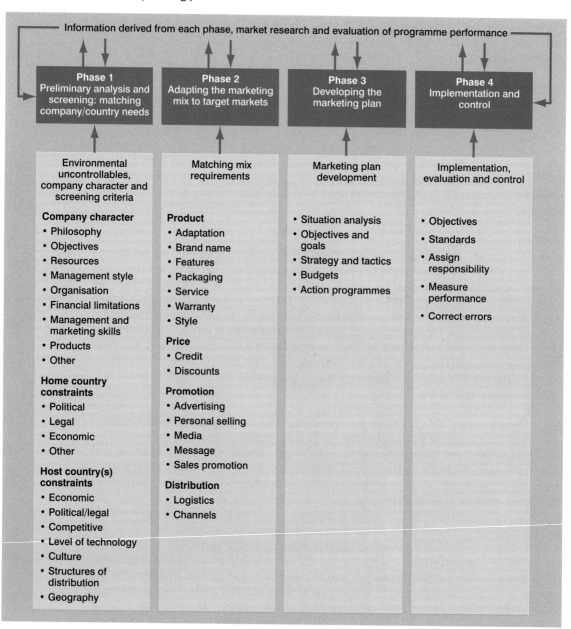

process that more than anything else distinguishes international from domestic marketing planning. The results of phase 1 provide the marketer with the basic information necessary to:

1 evaluate the potential of a proposed country market
2 identify problems that would eliminate the country from further consideration
3 identify environmental elements that need further analysis
4 determine which part of the marketing mix must be adapted to meet local market needs, and
5 develop and implement a marketing action plan.

Information generated in phase 1 helps a company avoid the mistakes that plagued Radio Shack Corporation, a leading merchandiser of consumer electronic equipment in the United States, when it first went international. Radio Shack's early attempts at international marketing in Western Europe resulted in a series of costly mistakes that could have been avoided had it properly analysed the uncontrollable elements of the countries targeted for the first attempt at multinational marketing. The company scheduled its first Christmas promotion for 25 December in the Netherlands, unaware that the Dutch celebrate St Nicholas Day and gift giving on 5 December. Legal problems in various countries interfered with some of its plans; it was unaware that most European countries have laws prohibiting the sale of citizen-band radios, one of the company's most lucrative US products and one it expected to sell in Europe. A free flashlight promotion in German stores was promptly stopped by German courts because giveaways violate German sales laws. In Belgium, the company overlooked a law requiring a government tax stamp on all window signs, and poorly selected store sites resulted in many of the new stores closing shortly after opening.

Phase 2: Adapting the Marketing Mix to Target Markets   A more detailed examination of the components of the **marketing mix** is the purpose of phase 2. When target markets are selected, the market mix must be evaluated in light of the data generated in phase 1. In which ways can the product, promotion, price and distribution be standardised and in which ways must they be adapted to meet target market requirements? Incorrect decisions at this point lead to costly mistakes through efficiency loss from lack of standardisation, products inappropriate for the intended market and/or costly mistakes in improper pricing, advertising and promotional blunders. The primary goal of phase 2 is to decide on a marketing mix adjusted to the cultural constraints imposed by the uncontrollable elements of the environment, which effectively achieves corporate objectives and goals.

An example of the type of analysis done in phase 2 is the process used by Nestlé. Each product manager has a country factbook that includes much of the information suggested in phase 1. The country factbook analyses in detail a variety of culturally related questions. In Germany, the product manager for coffee must furnish answers to a number of questions. How does a German rank coffee in the hierarchy of consumer products? Is Germany a high or a low per capita consumption market? (These facts alone can be of enormous consequence. In Sweden the annual per capita consumption of coffee is 18 pounds, while in Japan it is half a gram!) How is coffee used – in bean form, ground or powdered? If it is ground, how is it brewed? Which coffee is preferred – Brazilian Santos blended with Colombian coffee or robusta from the Ivory Coast? Is it roasted? Do the people prefer dark roasted or blonde coffee? (The colour of Nestlé's soluble coffee must resemble as closely as possible the colour of the coffee consumed in the country.) As a result of the answers to these and other questions, Nestlé produces 200 types of instant coffee (Nescafé), from the dark robust espresso preferred in Latin countries to the lighter blends popular in the United States.

Almost €45 million ($50 million) a year is spent in four research laboratories around the world experimenting with new shadings in colour, aroma and flavour. Do the Germans drink coffee after lunch or with their breakfast? Do they take it black or with cream or milk? Do they drink coffee in the evening? Do they sweeten it? (In France, the answer is clear: in the morning, coffee with milk; at noon, black coffee – i.e. two totally different coffees.) At what age do people begin drinking coffee? Is it a traditional beverage as in France? Is it a form of rebellion among the young as in England where coffee drinking has been taken up in defiance of tea-drinking parents? Or is it a gift, as in Japan? There is a coffee boom in tea-drinking Japan where Nescafé is considered a luxury gift item; instead of chocolates and flowers, Nescafé is toted in fancy containers to dinners and birthday parties. With such depth of information, the product manager can evaluate the marketing mix in terms of the information in the country factbook.

key term

marketing mix
optimal combination of product, price, place (distribution) and promotion

Phase 2 also permits the marketer to determine possibilities for standardisation. By grouping all countries together and looking at similarities, market characteristics that can be standardised become evident.

Frequently, the results of the analysis in phase 2 indicate that the marketing mix would require such drastic adaptation that a decision not to enter a particular market is made. For example, a product may have to be reduced in physical size to fit the needs of the market, but the additional manufacturing cost of a smaller size may be too high to justify market entry. Also, the price required to show a profit might be too high for a majority of the market to afford. If there is no way to reduce the price, sales potential at the higher price may be too low to justify entry.

On the other hand, additional research in this phase may provide information that can suggest ways to standardise marketing programmes among two or more country markets. This was the case for Nestlé when research revealed that young coffee drinkers in England and Japan had identical motivations. As a result, Nestlé now uses principally the same message in both markets.

The answers to three major questions are generated in phase 2: (1) Which elements of the marketing mix can be standardised and where is standardisation not culturally possible? (2) Which cultural/environmental adaptations are necessary for successful acceptance of the marketing mix? (3) Will adaptation costs allow profitable market entry? Based on the results in phase 2, a second screening of countries may take place with some countries dropped from further consideration. The next phase in the planning process is development of a marketing plan.

Phase 3: Developing the Marketing Plan At this stage of the planning process, a marketing plan is developed for the target market – whether a single country or a global market set. It begins with a situation analysis and culminates in a specific action programme for the market. The specific plan establishes what is to be done, by whom, how it is to be done and when. Included are budgets and sales and profit expectations. Just as in phase 2, a decision not to enter a specific market may be made if it is determined that company marketing objectives and goals cannot be met.

Phase 4: Implementation and Control A 'go' decision in phase 3 triggers implementation of specific plans and anticipation of successful marketing. However, the planning process does not end at this point. All marketing plans require coordination and control (phase 4) during the period of implementation. Many businesses do not control marketing plans as thoroughly as they could, even though continuous monitoring and control could increase their success. An evaluation and control system requires performance objective action, that is, to bring the plan back on track should standards of performance fall short. A global orientation facilitates the difficult but extremely important management tasks of coordinating and controlling the complexities of international marketing.

While the model is presented as a series of sequential phases, the planning process is a dynamic, continuous set of interacting variables with information continuously building among phases. The phases outline a crucial path to be followed for effective, systematic planning. Furthermore, it provides the basis for viewing all country markets and their interrelationships as an integrated global unit.[18] By following the guidelines presented in Section 6, 'The Country Notebook – A Guide for Developing a Marketing Plan', the international marketer can put the strategic planning process into operation.[19]

summary

Expanding markets around the world have increased competition for all levels of international marketing. To keep abreast of the competition and maintain a viable position for increasingly competitive markets, a global perspective is necessary. Global competition also requires quality products designed to meet ever-changing customer needs and rapidly advancing technology. Cost containment, customer satisfaction and a greater number of players mean that every opportunity to refine international business practices must be examined in the light of company goals. Collaborative relationships, strategic international alliances and strategic planning are important avenues to global marketing that must be implemented in the planning of global marketing management.

Companies normally follow generic strategies as overall corporate strategies. These strategies are differentiation strategy or focus strategy. The choice of these strategies leads to sub-strategies for each and every product and market. These sub-strategies are influenced by a number of factors, such as branding, positioning and customer segments, the life cycle of the particular product and the market environment. This is achieved through a systematic marketing planning process.

questions

1   Define strategic planning. How does strategic planning for international marketing differ from domestic marketing?
2   Discuss the benefits to an MNC of accepting the global market concept.
3   Define the concept of quality. How do the concept of quality and TQM relate?
4   Cost containment and technological improvement are said to be the basis for competition. Why? Discuss.
5   What is meant by positioning? Explain.
6   Explain the three points that define a global approach to international marketing.
7   Branding is considered a part of strategy – discuss how valuable branding is for a consumer products company. Give examples.
8   What is the importance of collaborative relationships to competition?
9   Discuss what is meant by relationship marketing and how it differs from traditional marketing.
10 In phases 1 and 2 of the international planning process, countries may be dropped from further consideration as potential markets. Discuss some of the conditions in each phase that may exist in a country that would lead a marketer to exclude it.
11 Assume that you are the director of international marketing for a company producing refrigerators. Select one country in Asia and one in Europe and develop screening criteria to use in evaluating the two countries. Make any additional assumptions that are necessary about your company.

further reading

- G. Hamel and C.K. Prahalad, 'Do You Really Have a Global Strategy?', *Harvard Business Review*, 1985, 63(4), pp. 139-48.
- J.K. Johanson and H.B. Thorelli, 'International Product Positioning', *Journal of International Business Studies*, 1985, Fall, pp. 57-75.
- C.K. Prahalad and K. Lieberthal, 'The End of Corporate Imperialism', *Harvard Business Review*, 2003, 81(8), pp. 109-17.

references

1 John Dunning, *Making Globalization Good: The Moral Challenges of Global Capitalism* (Oxford: Oxford University Press, 2003).

2 S. Ghoshal and C.A. Bartlett, 'Integrating the Enterprise', *Sloan Management Review*, 2002, 44(1), pp. 31-8.

3 John Dunning and J.-L. Muschielli (eds), *Multinational Firms: The Global-Local Dilemma* (London: Routledge, 2002).

4 Cyndee Miller, 'Chasing the Global Dream', *Marketing News*, 2 December 1996, pp. 1-2.

5 Peter Buckley, *Multinational Firms, Cooperation and Competition in the World Economy* (Houndsmill, Basingstoke: Macmillan).

6 'Ford: Alex Trotman's Daring Global Strategy', *Business Week*, 3 April 1995, pp. 94-104.

7 S. Tariq Anwar, 'Cases: Vodafone and Wireless Industry: A Case in Market Expansion and Global Strategy', *Journal of Business and Industrial Marketing*, 2003, 18(3), pp. 270-88.

8 S.T. Cavusgil, S. Yeniyurt and J.D. Townsend, 'The Framework of a Global Company: A Conceptualization and Preliminary Validation', *Industrial Marketing Management*, 33(8), pp. 711-16.

9 'Tearing Up Today's Organization Chart', *Business Week*, 21st Century Capitalism Issue, 1994, pp. 80-2.

10 This section draws from Robert M. Morgan and Shelby D. Hunt, 'The Commitment-Trust Theory of Relationship Marketing', *Journal of Marketing*, July 1994, pp. 20-38.

11 David Whitwam, Regina Fazio Maruca, 'The Right Way to Go Global: An Interview with Whirlpool CEO David Whitwam', *Harvard Business Review*, March-April 1994, 72(2), pp. 135-43.

12 The authors prefer to use the term *collaborative relationship* to refer to all forms of collaborative effort between a company and its customers, markets, suppliers, manufacturing partners, research and development partners, government agencies and all other types of alliance. Consumer orientation, *Keiretsu* and strategic alliances can all be grouped under the broad rubric of collaborative relationships. All seek similar universal 'truths': participant satisfaction, long-term ties, loyalty and mutually beneficial exchanges, yet there are some fundamental differences among them.

13 Jagdish Seth and Atul Parvatiyar, 'The Evolution of Relationship Marketing', *International Business Review*, 1995, 5(4), pp. 625-45.

14 Saeed Smiee and Peter Walters, 'Relationship Marketing in an International Context', *International Business Review*, 2003, 12(2), pp. 193-214.

15 For a complete discussion of the logic of SIAs, see Kenichi Ohmae, *The Borderless World* (New York: Harper Business, 1990), Chap. 8, 'The Global Logic of Strategic Alliances', pp. 114-36; and Kenichi Ohmae, 'Putting Global Logic First', *Harvard Business Review*, January 1995, 73(1), pp. 119-25.

16 This section draws on Subhath Jain, *Marketing: Planning and Strategy*, 6th edn (Cincinnati, Ohio: Thomson Learning, 2002), Chapter 9.

17 This section draws on Michael Porter, *Competitive Advantage; Creating and Sustaining Superior Performance* (The Free Press, 1985); and Harold Chee and Rod Haris, *Global Marketing Strategy* (FT Management, 1998).

18 Roger Kashlak, Rajan Chandran and Anthony Di Benedetto, 'Reciprocity in International Business: A Study of Telecommunications Alliances and Contracts', *Journal of International Business Studies*, vol. 29, no. 2, 1998, pp. 281-304.

19 C.K. Prahalad and K. Lieberthal, 'The End of Corporate Imperialism', *Harvard Business Review*, 1998, 81(8), pp. 109-17.

chapter 11
International Market Entry Strategies

Chapter Outline

why firms go abroad

Internationalisation of the firm – why and how firms go to foreign markets – has been the most important issue in international business and international marketing. As we argued earlier, growth of the firm is the main driver of internationalisation. Do firms go international through a gradual, incremental process? Is this 'stage of internationalisation model' valid for smaller as well as bigger firms? Can multinational companies, having earlier experience, leapfrog these stages or should they go step by step, first to closer markets and then to far-away markets? And how can companies analyse the suitability of a market for their product? These are some of the questions that interest all companies that are active or are planning to be active in cross-border markets.[1]

A number of studies have already addressed these questions. The **establishment chain model**, one of the earlier studies, presented gradual internationalisation, from no regular export to manufacturing subsidiaries. It states that companies gradually develop their operations abroad.[2] The firm first grows in the domestic market and then expands into close-by foreign markets. The obstacles to internationalisation include a lack of knowledge of foreign markets and resources. The **psychic distance**, that some markets are perceived far away and difficult due to different culture and environments, is considered another obstacle. Psychic distance is sometimes correlated with geographic distance but not always. For example, Britain and Australia are geographically far away but have very little psychic distance. France and Britain are, however, in an opposite situation. This psychic distance is not constant and changes due to communication and experience. The establishment chain model suggests four different stages of going abroad:

1 no regular export
2 export via representatives (e.g. agent)
3 sales subsidiary
4 production/manufacturing subsidiary.

This means the more experience a firm gets in a market, the more knowledge (of the market) it acquires and the more resources it is willing to commit. In stage one the firm has not committed any resources, while resource commitment increases with every stage. Whether a firm will proceed from stage 1 to 4 depends on the psychic distance and the size of the market as well as the need for control. With some industries/products it is crucial for the company to have control of its activities; for example, to ensure consistent positioning or brand image. This is illustrated by Exhibit 11.1.

The other main obstacle to going abroad is the psychic distance that a company can perceive in a particular market when it is thought to be psychologically far away. If this is the case, then the company would not like to commit a large amount of resources in that market. It would prefer to choose a successive involvement and follow an establishment chain model (see Exhibit 11.1). In such a market it might even like to use a licensee as an entry strategy.

Exhibit 11.1 The establishment chain model

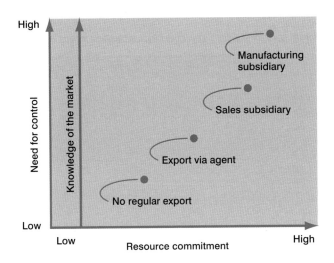

market servicing strategies

Company resources and psychic distance are not the only reasons why a company enters a particular market. A particular market can attract foreign companies and a particular mode of entry. In other words, how a particular market will be served, by domestic or foreign firms or a certain combination of the two, depends on company objectives and market characteristics.

Normally companies have three main objectives when entering a foreign market:[3]

1 market seeking
2 efficiency seeing
3 resource seeking.

A **market seeking** strategy means that the company is looking for a considerable market for its products/offers. This can be due to a saturated market at home, or because the company believes that it has a strong product/brand that can penetrate into new markets. The firm thus wants to enter large or rapidly growing markets – for example, China and India.

Efficiency seeking means that firms want to enter countries/markets where they can achieve efficiency in different ways, e.g. R&D and other infrastructural effects. Efficiencies can also be achieved due to the fact that a certain industry has gathered at a place, creating a beneficial infrastructure, such as Silicon Valley. Philips and other consumer electronic product companies invested in Singapore and Malaysia, for example.

Resource seeking firms try to enter into countries to get access to raw materials or other crucial inputs that can provide cost reduction and lower operation costs; for example, investment by most oil companies in the Middle East or textiles and garment companies in India and Pakistan.

In some markets companies may achieve more than one of these strategies. They will, however, influence the location decisions of companies. Moreover, depending on the knowledge and the need for control, the companies will like to increase resource commitment and would or would not want to own their operations in a particular foreign market. Here, benefits/incentives provided by host governments also play a major role. Several governments provide tax benefits; for example, foreign companies are exempt from any tax for the first few years, free land or other benefits.

A number of studies have looked into the location decision-making process of firms. Most conclude that the selection for a market entry, particularly foreign direct investment,

key terms

market seeking
companies that venture into new countries/become international because they are looking for new markets, actively seeking customers worldwide

efficiency seeking
firms want to enter countries/ markets where they can achieve efficiency in different ways

resource seeking
firms try to enter countries to get access to raw materials or other crucial inputs for cost reduction/lower operation costs

depends on factors such as the availability of infrastructure, language and supportive attitude of the home market (see the example in Exhibit 11.2).[4]

Exhibit 11.2 Important factors in country selection for Japanese entry into Europe

Aspect	UK	Germany	France	Netherlands
Labour availability	8	7	7	7
Wage level	9	6	8	6
Labour unions	8	8	8	8
Supporting industries	9	8	6	7
Support of Development Agency	10	7	4	7
Investment incentives	6	9	8	8
Language	10	7	4	8
Feelings against Japanese	8	7	3	7
Presence of other Japanese manufacturers	8	7	4	4
Total score	**76**	**66**	**52**	**62**

Source: N. Hood and T. Truijens, 'European Location Decisions of Japanese Manufacturers', *International Business Review*, 1993, 2(1), pp. 39–63; P.N. Ghauri, U. Elg and R.R. Sinkovics, 'Foreign Direct Investment – Location Attractiveness for Retailing Firms in the European Union', in L. Oxelheim and P. Ghauri (eds), *European Union and the Race for Foreign Direct Investment in Europe* (Oxford: Elsevier, 2004), pp. 407–28.

Depending upon the main objective of the company to enter a particular market, different factors become more or less important. For market entry, the marketer needs to carry out a competition analysis to establish whether it will be possible to achieve desired market share or not. For resource-seeking firms we have to look at suppliers of those resources and their existing relationships and network, and whether it will be possible for the company to penetrate into these networks or not. For efficiency-seeking firms the marketer has to look at efficiencies that can be achieved and sustained for a long period.

While making entry decisions a company also has to see whether it is the first foreign company in the particular product group or not. To be the first in the market entails first-mover advantages: if the product is accepted by the market, it can gain a major share of the market. This was the case for Pepsi Cola, which entered Russia and India as the first mover. Coca-Cola entered these markets after few years and had to struggle harder to gain respectable market share. Moreover, the first mover gains valuable experience/knowledge of the market, enabling it to lessen uncertainties and gain cost advantage. However, the first mover can also face certain disadvantages, such as convincing and educating the market that the new product is useful. The first mover thus takes the initial costs and if the market reacts positively, other companies can come in and reap the benefits. For example, Royal Crown was the pioneer company to market diet colas, which were mainly sold to diabetics. When Coca-Cola and Pepsi Cola realised the market opportunity, they came with big advertising budgets and pushed Royal Crown out of the market. It took only one year for Coca-Cola to become the market leader.

First mover advantage is also important when a market first opens for foreign companies. When the Soviet Union broke up and China opened its market, a number of companies wanted to be first to enter these countries in order to gain market recognition and share. Many companies, such as Philips and IKEA, entered these markets knowing that they would not make any profits in the first few years.

GOING INTERNATIONAL 11.1

Volvo maps route to enter Asia

Volvo, the Swedish truck maker, has been on the offensive since it sold its car operations to Ford. As the world's second largest heavy trucks producer, it made a number of acquisitions in Europe and America (Mack in the US and Renault Trucks in France) with the money it raised from the sale. Its truck sales reached record levels in 2004, but less than 10 per cent of these came from Asia.

According to the CEO, Volvo wants to enter the Asian market with medium-duty trucks. At present it does not have a medium-duty truck operation in Asia, which is the biggest market. Smaller trucks are also popular in Japan, where Volvo wants to achieve 5 per cent market share from 1 per cent at present.

Volvo is looking for a joint venture partner in Japan, although some believe that the best way to increase sales in Asia is to find a partner in China and produce local-style trucks, rather than producing European-style sophisticated trucks. Cash is not a problem; with no debts and a reserve of more than B1.3 billion, Volvo is under pressure to invest that money wisely.

■ What do you think is the right way for Volvo to enter Asia?

Source: N. George, 'Volvo Maps Route to Asia Expansion', *Financial Times*, 26 November 2004, p. 28 (photo from same source).

market opportunity assessment

The main purpose of market opportunity assessment is to answer questions such as: Should we enter a particular country or not? Is there a potential in that market for the particular industry and for a new competitor? Is there market/sale potential for the particular product?

The first question helps the company to screen the market in relation to the company's overall strategy, and the economic, cultural and legal environment of the country. The second question helps the company to assess whether the market is economically attractive or not. If it is a market where there is already fierce competition and overcapacity, it will be difficult to gain any market share from the existing competitors. The third question helps the company to make an advanced in-depth analysis of market opportunity for its particular product.[5]

Moreover, if the objective of the company is to seek efficiency when going into a particular market, it needs to do a different type of analysis. What type of efficiencies is it looking for, R&D or agglomeration? Most top companies in a particular sector gravitate to a certain market/area and create an efficient infrastructure for that particular industry, such as Silicon Valley in the US and Bangalore in India for software, and Singapore/Malaysia for consumer electronics. If a company is moving to a market to achieve cost advantages, the analysis has to deal with the cost factors that are important for the particular product, such as cheap labour, cheap raw material, taxation rules, and so on.[6]

Market opportunity assessment and country selection for an entry also depend upon the proactive versus reactive approaches of the company. In a **proactive market selection**, a company is involved in a systematic approach. The marketer in this case proactively makes visits and does marketing research to assess the potential of a market. A number of

key term

proactive market selection
actively and systematically selecting a market

companies with marketing research departments continuously collect information on different markets to detect a potential market at an early stage.

In a **reactive market selection**, the company is not actively collecting information or analysing any market to assess its potential. Companies following this approach, often wait for an unsolicited order, or an initiative taken by importers from a potential market. Often these companies wait for other companies (their competitors) to enter the market first. Such companies believe that the first movers will have to pave the way and handle initial problems, and then they can enter the market. This approach, however, is not always a wise choice as it is very difficult to snatch market share from existing foreign and domestic companies. Moreover, a company has to do its own assessment according to its objective, product and positioning.

market/country selection

There are several methods to analyse a country for investment decisions. The **Boston Consulting Group (BCG)** provides one such method. Basically, it is used to decide on the best mix of businesses or products in order to maximise the long-term profit and growth of the firm. It helps managers to analyse each and every business or product of the company and thus supports the designing of each business/product strategy. The main benefit is that it relates company products to the competition instead of analysing each product in isolation.

In international marketing, this model is used successfully to analyse each market/country (instead of business or product), which is then put into the context of competition and the company's own capabilities. It analyses two determining factors:

1 country attractiveness
2 competitive strength of the company.

Here the BCG portfolio analysis has been modified to include the above two factors: instead of products and relative market shares, we use country attractiveness and company strength to achieve market share in the new market. In spite of the limitations of using standardised models for different problems, this analysis can provide useful information when selecting a country/market in a marketing entry context.[5]

The factors that would influence the attractiveness of the country might include the market size, the market growth, competitive conditions and uncontrollable elements (e.g. the cultural, legal and political environments) (see Exhibit 11.3).

Assessing **competitive strength** means looking at whether the company has the resources and potential to achieve its goals in the particular market or not. For instance, is it possible to gain some market share? Do we have the marketing ability and resources? Is there a fit between the product and its positioning, and the market? There has to be some weighting of these factors to find the match between the market and the company. Exhibit 11.4 presents a nine-cell matrix depicting relative market investment opportunities for different types of match.[6]

Exhibit 11.3 Dimensions of country attractiveness and competitive strength

Country attractiveness	Competitive strength of the company
■ Market size (total and segments)	■ Market share
■ Market growth (total and segments)	■ Marketing ability and capacity
■ Competitive conditions	■ Product and positioning fit
■ Market uncontrollables (cultural, legal and political environments)	■ Quality of distribution services

Exhibit 11.4 Market portfolio analysis: country attractiveness/competitive strength

The matrix reveals that, depending on the careful use of this analysis, a company may have several choices when making an entry decision.

Invest: This represents a country that is very attractive due to the size of the market and the growth. Moreover, this is a market where the company can attain the competitive strength to achieve its objectives. The analysis thus suggests that this country is suitable for entry and major investment.

Divest/license: This represents a market where the company should not invest. Moreover, if the company is already there, it should divest and get out. This is a market where the company will have problems or need to make heavy investments to gain some market share. It is therefore suggested that if the company wants to enter this market, it is better to do it through 'licensing', the mode of entry that is least demanding of resources.

Joint venture: This refers to a market that is quite attractive but difficult. It demands huge investments/resources to gain considerable/acceptable market share. It is therefore suggested that if you cannot dominate the market (have major market share), then it is better not to enter or to enter through a joint venture, i.e. share the costs and local difficulties with a local partner.

Selective strategy: This is a category of markets where there is fierce competition and it is therefore difficult to maintain a stable market share. However, if the company has other strengths, such as product/positioning fit with the market or a powerful brand, it can decide to invest. As is clear from Exhibit 11.4, the market is moderately attractive.

It is clear that the use of BCG portfolio analysis, as applied above for entry strategies, is useful as it provides some useful insights into company/country match and compatibility. Together with other models/methods given in this chapter, this can be a useful tool in international entry strategy decision making. Although each company might give different ratings or weights to each of the factors in country attractiveness and competitive strength, it can provide useful analysis for each entry decision. Its major strength is that a company can compare different markets, thus revealing which one is most suitable, and it helps the company to look at its capabilities in the context of international competition in each market.

strategic international alliances

Strategic international alliances (SIAs) are sought as a way to shore up weaknesses and increase competitive strengths. Opportunities for rapid expansion into new markets, access to new technology, more efficient production and marketing costs, and additional sources of capital are all motives for engaging in strategic international alliances.

An SIA is a business relationship established by two or more companies to cooperate out of mutual need and to share risk in achieving a common objective. A strategic international alliance implies (1) that there is a common objective, (2) that one partner's weakness is offset by the other's strength, (3) that reaching the objective alone would be too costly, take too much time or be too risky and (4) that together their respective strengths make possible what otherwise would be unattainable. In short, an SIA is a synergistic relationship established to achieve a common goal where both parties benefit.

Opportunities abound the world over but, to benefit, firms must be current in new technology, have the ability to keep abreast of technological change, have distribution systems to capitalise on global demand, have cost-effective manufacturing and have capital to build new systems as necessary. Other reasons to enter into strategic alliances are to:[7]

1 acquire needed current market bases
2 acquire needed technological bases
3 utilise excess manufacturing capacity
4 reduce new market risk and entry costs
5 accelerate product introductions demanded by rapid technological changes and shorter product life cycles
6 achieve economies of scale in production, research and development or marketing
7 overcome cultural and trade barriers
8 extend the existing scope of operations.

The scope of what a company needs to do and what it can do is at a point where even the largest firms engage in alliances to maintain their competitiveness. Exhibits 11.5 and 11.6 show the different alliances in the airline industry and in the European television broadcast market.

A company enters a **strategic alliance** to acquire the skills necessary to achieve its objectives more effectively, and at a lower cost or with less risk than if it acted alone.[8] For example, a company strong in research and development skills and weak in the ability or capital to successfully market a product will seek an alliance to offset its weakness – one partner to provide marketing skills and capital and the other to provide technology and a product. The majority of alliances today are designed to exploit markets and/or technology.[9]

Many companies are entering SIAs to be in a strategic position to be competitive and to benefit from the expected growth in the single European market. One example is General Mills, which wants a share of the rapidly growing breakfast-cereal market in Europe. It could be worth hundreds of millions of dollars as health-conscious Europeans change their breakfast diet from eggs and bacon to dry cereal. Kellogg's has been in Europe since 1920 and controls about half the market. General Mills, Kellogg's major US competitor, has set its sights on a 20 per cent share of the EU market and it plans to achieve that goal with Cereal Partners Worldwide (CPW), a joint venture between General Mills and Nestlé.

It would be extremely costly to enter the market from scratch. Although the cereal business uses cheap commodities as its raw materials, it is both capital and marketing intensive; sales volume must be high before profits begin to develop. Only recently has Kellogg's earned significant profits in Europe.

General Mills wanted a part of this large and rapidly growing market. To reach its goal would have required a manufacturing base and a massive sales force. Further, Kellogg's stranglehold on supermarkets would have been difficult for an unknown to breach easily. The solution was a joint venture with Nestlé. Nestlé had everything General Mills lacked – a well-known brand name, a network of plants, a powerful distribution system – except the one thing General Mills could provide – strong cereal brands.[10]

Of course, not all SIAs are successful; some fail and others are dissolved after reaching their goals. Failures can be attributed to a variety of reasons, but all revolve around lack of

Exhibit 11.5 The biggest airline alliances

Alliance	Aircraft fleet	Turnover (€ billion) ($)	GDP passenger (million)	Kilometre* (million)	Close relationships with:
Oneworld American Airlines British Airways Cathay Pacific (Hong Kong) Qantas (Australia) Canadian Airlines	1 157	64 (71)	159.4	390	Aerolineas (Arg.); Avianca (Col.); Taca, Tam (Brazil); LanChile; Iberia (Spain); Finair; Lot (Poland); Japan Airlines; US Airways
Star Alliance United Airlines (US) Lufthansa (Germany) SAS (Sweden) Air Canada Thai Airways Varig (Brazil)	578	58.7 (65)	188.5	335	Singapore Airlines; Air New Zealand; Ansett (Australia)
Sky Team Northwest KLM Air France Alitalia Continental Korean Air Delta Cza – Czech Airlines Aero Mexico	989	31 (34.4)	134.0	253	Kenya Airways (35 per cent); Japan Air System, Nippon Cargo (Japan); Malaysian Airline System (*16 mn passengers*); America West; Aces (Col.); Braathens (Nor.); Eurowings (Ger.); (Southern China Airlines)
Global Alliance Delta Airlines (US) Swissair THY Turkish Airlines TAP Air Portugal Austrian Airlines AOM (France)	830	25.3 (28)	149.5	194	Aeromexico; AeroPeru

*A 'passenger/kilometre' is 1 kilometre flown with one passenger. The figures give the total amount of passenger/kilometres flown by the alliance.

Source: based on 'Vier Allianties Beheersen Helft van Luchtvaart', *De Volkskrant*, 22 September, p. 16; and 'Clubable Class Books Slots for Take-off', *The European*, 28 September–4 October 1998, pp. 18–19.

perceived benefits to one or more of the partners. Benefits may never have been realised in some cases, and different goals and management styles have caused dissatisfaction in other alliances. Such was the case with an alliance between Rubbermaid and the Dutch chemical company DSM; the two differed on management and strategic issues. Rubbermaid wanted to invest in new products and expansion to combat sluggish demand as the result of a European recession, while DSM baulked at any new investments.[11] In other cases, an alliance may have outlived its usefulness even though it had been successful.[12]

market entry strategies

When a company makes the commitment to go international, it must choose an entry strategy. This decision should reflect an analysis of market potential, company capabilities, and the degree of marketing involvement and commitment management is prepared to make. A company's approach to foreign marketing can require minimal investment and be limited to infrequent exporting with little thought given to market development. Or a company can

Exhibit 11.6 Europe's major pay-TV players

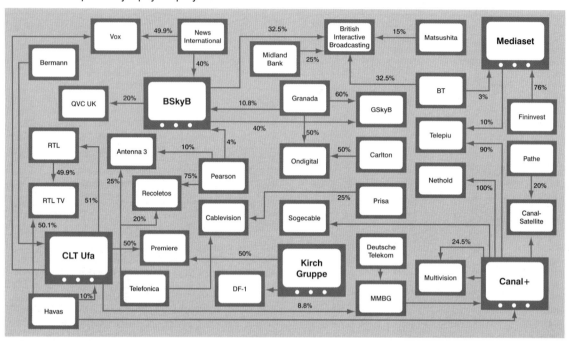

The tangled web. A look at major movers and shakers reveals some of the alliances they have formed. It also shows the variety of players entering the market, ranging from broadcasters such as CLT-Ufa to telcos such as BT to banks such as Midland. Companies are competing and cooperating at the same time. In Britain, News International and Granada are partners in GSkyB, but Granada's stake in the planned Ondigital service will be in direct competition with BSkyB, part-owned by News International. The arrows point towards subsidiaries and the percentages show the stake held in the subsidiaries – a complicated picture.

Source: ARC Chart, *The European*, 10–16 August 1998, p. 10.

GOING INTERNATIONAL 11.2

entering the luxury car market: from Toyota Crown to Lexus

1958   Toyota launches its first luxury sedan, named Crown in the US. But it was a flop and was soon withdrawn.

1983   In a secret board meeting Toyota decided to create a top luxury car, code name 'F1'.

1985   Toyota sends a number of its designers to California to understand American luxury car customers and to develop the car.

1988   Lexus brand and logo made public, which was challenged for trademark infringement by computer company Lexis.

1989   First Lexus sedan introduced, priced at $10 000 – below Mercedes' similar model.

1990   Lexus select 121 special dealers for the car. J.D. Power ranks Lexus number one in quality survey.

1991   Lexus sells 71 206 cars, becoming America's top-selling luxury imported car.

1995   US Government threatens to impose 100 per cent duty on Japanese import brand. Customers complain of uninspiring models. Mercedes takes over as number one luxury import.

1996   Lexus launches LX450 SUV and passes Range Rover in sales within two months of introduction.

1998   RX300 launched and became a big success, boosting total sales by 60 per cent.

2001 Lexus ranked number one by J.D. Power on customer satisfaction for the 10th time in 11 years.

2002 Lexus slides to number three in J.D. Power ranking, overtaken by Nissan's Infinity and Honda's Saturn. BMW close to becoming number one luxury import.

2003 Toyota starts selling Lexus brand in Japan.

The above chronology presents the planned market entry by Toyota into the US luxury car market segment. Now Toyota is about to announce yet another super-luxury car. At present it is nicknamed 'Mount Everest' and would have a V10 engine (derived from its V12 Formula One race car) and, with a price tag of €150 000 ($183 510), it will compete with the Aston Martin DB7 (€141 800/$173 478) and the Mercedes-Benz SL55 (€113 250/$138 550).

Toyota is, however, facing a big problem; with the price as high as Mount Everest, it is planning to introduce the car as a Lexus model. The average buyer of Lexus is, however, 52 years old (which is four years older than an average Mercedes-Benz buyer and nine years older than a BMW buyer).

Existing Lexus models go for between €30 000/$36 702 (IS300) and €60 000/$73 404 (SC430). It is wondered whether the sporty 'Mount Everest' Lexus would attract the wealthy younger buyer. Normal impressions in the US are that 'Grandpa drives a Lexus' and 'It look likes a grown-up's car'.

One idea at Toyota is to introduce it as 1960s popular sport model Toyota 2000GT. Others say, 'We are creating something beyond the ordinary, not another Toyota!'

■ Can you help Toyota in deciding which is the most suitable market (segment) to enter with this new model? How should it be named and positioned? Consult the Toyota/Lexus website and analyse its strategies.

Source: Business Week, Special Report, 'Lexus's Big Test: Can it Keep its Cachet?', 24 March 2004, pp. 48–51.

make large investments of capital and management effort to capture and maintain a permanent, specific share of world markets. Both approaches can be profitable.

There is a variety of foreign market entry strategies from which to choose. Each has particular advantages and shortcomings, depending on company strengths and weaknesses, the degree of commitment the company is willing or able to make and market characteristics, as depicted by Exhibit 11.7.

exporting

A company might decide to enter the international arena by exporting from the home country. This means of foreign market development is the easiest and most common approach employed by companies taking their first international step because the risks of financial loss can be minimised. Exporting is a common approach for the mature international company as well. Several companies engage in exporting as their major market entry method. Generally, early motives are to skim the cream from the market or gain business to absorb overheads. Even though such motives might appear opportunistic, exporting is a sound and permanent form of operating in international marketing. The mechanics of exporting and the different middlemen available to facilitate the exporting process are discussed in detail in the next chapters.

Piggybacking   Piggybacking occurs when a company (supplier) sells its product abroad using another company's (carrier) distribution facilities. This is quite common in industrial

Exhibit 11.7 Factors influencing market entry strategies

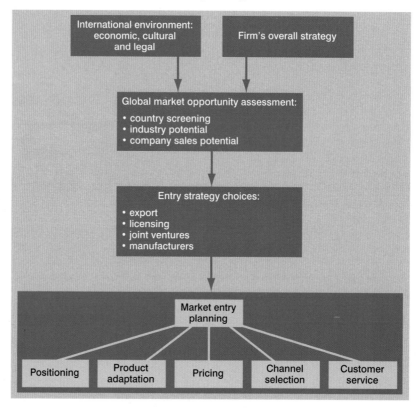

products, but all types of product are sold using this method. Normally, piggybacking is used when the companies involved have complementary but non-competitive products.

There has to be some benefit for the exporting (carrier) company. Some companies, such as General Electric or big retailers such as Wal-Mart or Tesco, use this as a way of broadening the product lines that they can offer to their foreign customers. These companies believe that offering a broader range of products will help them in boosting the sales of their own products. Some companies use this to share transportation costs and some companies do it purely for the profits, as they can make profit on other companies' (suppliers) products. This is done either through adding on their margins or by getting commission from the suppliers. Some governments or regional development agencies also encourage their companies to use this method to support weaker or smaller companies. This can also be used as a first step towards a company's own international activities to test the market. This is particularly advantageous for smaller firms, as they often lack the necessary resources. Once they realise the market potential, they can start their own exporting.

licensing

A means of establishing a foothold in foreign markets without large capital outlays is **licensing. Patent rights**, trademark rights and the rights to use technological processes are granted in foreign licensing. It is a favourite strategy for small and medium-sized companies although by no means limited to such companies. Not many confine their foreign operations to licensing alone; it is generally viewed as a supplement to exporting or manufacturing, rather than the only means of entry into foreign markets. The advantages of licensing are most apparent when capital is scarce, when import restrictions forbid other means of entry, when a country is sensitive to foreign ownership, or when it is neces-

sary to protect patents and trademarks against cancellation for non-use. Although this may be the least profitable way of entering a market, the risks and headaches are less than for direct investments; it is a legitimate means of capitalising on intellectual property in a foreign market.

Licensing takes several forms. Licences may be granted for production processes, for the use of a trade name or for the distribution of imported products. Licences may be closely controlled or be autonomous, and they permit expansion without great capital or personnel commitment if licensees have the requisite capabilities. Not all licensing experiences are successful because of the burden of finding, supervising and inspiring licensees.[13]

GOING INTERNATIONAL 11.3

Vuitton is bagging new markets

Flip through *Vogue*, *Vanity Fair* or *Elle* and you'll find pages and pages of half-naked models, legs splayed, dangling handbags from Vuitton and rivals Gucci, Prada and Hermès. In the glam department, Vuitton is great but not alone. You have to peek behind the glittery façade to see what makes Vuitton unique – what makes it, in fact, the most profitable luxury brand on the planet. There's the relentless focus on quality. (That robot makes sure Vuitton rarely has to make good on its lifetime repair guarantee.) There's the rigidly controlled distribution network. (No Vuitton bag is ever marked down, ever.) Above all, there's the efficiency of a finely tuned machine, fuelled by ever-increasing productivity in design and manufacturing – and, as Vuitton grows ever bigger, the ability to step up advertising and global expansion without denting the bottom line.

The Vuitton machine is running mighty smoothly right now. With $3.8 billion in annual sales, it's about twice the size of runners-up Prada and Gucci Group's Gucci division. Vuitton has maintained double-digit sales growth and the industry's fattest operating margins as rivals have staggered through a global downturn the past two years. That power was underscored anew, when parent LVMH Moët Hennessy Louis Vuitton reported a 30 per cent earnings increase for 2003, fuelled by a record high 45 per cent operating margin at Vuitton. The average margin in the luxury accessories business is 25 per cent.

LVMH chairman Bernard Arnault says the brand will keep roaring ahead, even though it has already quintupled sales and increased margins sixfold since he bought the company in 1989. Although LVMH doesn't disclose sales for Vuitton alone, analysts reckon they grew at least 16 per cent worldwide in 2003 and are likely to repeat that feat in 2004.

Does Vuitton – which started as a maker of steamer trunks during the reign of Napoleon III – have its best days ahead of it? It still needs to wean itself from Japanese customers, who account for an estimated 55 per cent of sales. Vuitton must build sales in the US while tapping into rising affluence in China and India. It also needs to fight increasingly sophisticated global counterfeiting rings. Most of all, because Vuitton markets itself as an arbiter of style, it needs to keep convincing customers that they're members of an exclusive club. Vuitton has some serious strengths. One is the loyalty of its clients, shoppers who think one Vuitton bag in the closet just looks too lonely.

Another threat would be the departure of key personnel. For Vuitton, the biggest challenge may be to keep this powerful machine under control. The company opened 18 stores last year, about twice the rate of store openings a decade ago. Arnault promises that Vuitton will never lose its discipline or its focus on quality. 'That's what differentiates Louis Vuitton,' he says. The message seems to be getting across. Just ask Ariella Cohen, a 24-year-old Manhattan legal assistant who already owns a Vuitton messenger bag and several Vuitton accessories, and now covets high-heeled Vuitton sandals – even though she'll have to put her name on a waiting list. 'Louis Vuitton never goes out of style,' she says as she leaves its Fifth Avenue store.

■ Would the Louis Vuitton machine ever run out of steam?

Source: Business Week, 'Money Machine', 22 March 2004.

franchising

Franchising is a rapidly growing form of licensing in which the franchiser provides a standard package of products, systems and management services, and the franchisee provides market knowledge, capital and personal involvement in management. The combination of skills permits flexibility in dealing with local market conditions and yet provides the parent firm with a reasonable degree of control. The franchiser can follow through on marketing of the products to the point of final sale. It is an important form of vertical market integration. Potentially, the franchise system provides an effective blending of skill centralisation and operational decentralisation, and has become an increasingly important form of international marketing. In some cases, franchising is having a profound effect on traditional businesses. In England, for example, it is estimated that annual franchised sales of fast foods is nearly €1.8 billion ($2 billion), which accounts for 30 per cent of all foods eaten outside the home.

Prior to 1970, international franchising was not a major activity. A survey by the International Franchising Association revealed that only 14 per cent of its member firms had franchises outside the United States, and the majority of those were in Canada. By the 1990s, more than 30 000 franchises of US firms were located in countries throughout the world. Franchises include soft drinks, motels, retailing, fast foods, car rentals, automotive services, recreational services and a variety of business services from print shops to sign shops. Franchising is the fastest-growing market entry strategy. It is often among the first types of foreign retail business to open in the emerging market economies of Eastern Europe, the former republics of Russia and China. McDonald's is in Moscow (its first store seats 700 inside and has 27 cash registers), and Kentucky Fried Chicken is in China (the Beijing KFC store has the highest sales volume of any KFC store in the world).

There are three types of franchise agreement used by franchising firms – master franchise, joint venture and licensing – any one of which can have a country's government as one partner. The master franchise is the most inclusive agreement and the method used in more than half of the international franchises. The master franchise gives the franchisee the rights to a specific area (many are for an entire country) with the authority to sell or establish subfranchises. The McDonald's franchise in Moscow is a master agreement owned by a Canadian firm and its partner, the Moscow City Council Department of Food Services.

joint ventures

Joint ventures (JVs), one of the more important types of collaborative relationship, have accelerated sharply during the past 20 years. Besides serving as a means of lessening political and economic risks by the amount of the partner's contribution to the venture, joint ventures provide a less risky way to enter markets that pose legal and cultural barriers than would be the case in the acquisition of an existing company.

In the Asian Pacific Rim, US companies face less familiar legal and cultural barriers than they find in Western Europe, and thus prefer joint ventures to buying existing businesses. In 1993, for example, US companies acquired 225 European firms and entered into 67 joint ventures, whereas in Asia, US firms acquired only 27 existing companies but formed 97 joint ventures.[14]

Local partners can often lead the way through legal mazes and provide the outsider with help in understanding cultural nuances. A joint venture can be attractive to an international marketer:

1 when it enables a company to utilise the specialised skills of a local partner
2 when it allows the marketer to gain access to a partner's local distribution system
3 when a company seeks to enter a market where wholly owned activities are prohibited
4 when it provides access to markets protected by tariffs or quotas, and
5 when the firm lacks the capital or personnel capabilities to expand its international activities.

In China, a country considered to be among the riskiest in Asia, there have been 49400 joint ventures established in the first 15 years since they began allowing JVs. Among the many reasons JVs are so popular is that they offer a way of getting around high Chinese tariffs, allowing a company to gain a competitive price advantage over imports. By manufacturing locally with a Chinese partner rather than importing, China's high tariffs (the tariff on motor vehicles is 200 per cent, 150 per cent on cosmetics and the average on miscellaneous products is 75 per cent) are bypassed and additional savings are achieved by using low-cost Chinese labour.[15] Many Western brands are manufactured and marketed in China at prices that would not be possible if the products were imported.

A joint venture is differentiated from other types of strategic alliance or collaborative relationship in that a joint venture is a partnership of two or more participating companies that have joined forces to create a separate legal entity. Joint ventures should also be differentiated from minority holdings by an MNC in a local firm. Four factors are associated with joint ventures:

1 JVs are established, separate, legal entities
2 they acknowledge intent by the partners to share in the management of the JV
3 they are partnerships between legally incorporated entities, such as companies, chartered organisations or governments, and not between individuals
4 equity positions are held by each of the partners.

Nearly all companies active in world trade participate in at least one joint venture somewhere; many number their joint ventures in the dozens. A recent Conference Board study indicated that more than 50 per cent of *Fortune* 500 companies were engaged in one or more international joint ventures. In Japan alone, Royal Dutch Shell has more than 30 joint ventures; IBM has more than 35.

consortia

The consortium and syndicate are similar to the joint venture and could be classified as such except for two unique characteristics: (1) they typically involve a large number of participants; (2) they frequently operate in a country or market in which none of the participants is currently active. Consortia are developed for pooling financial and managerial resources and to lessen risks. Often, huge construction projects are built under a consortium arrangement in which major contractors with different specialities form a separate company specifically to negotiate for and produce one job. One firm usually acts as the lead firm or the newly formed corporation may exist quite independently of its originators.

GOING INTERNATIONAL 11.4

Renault enters India with a joint venture

Renault, the French auto-maker, is partnering with Mahindra and Mahindra, the Indian tractor and SUV maker, to launch its 'Logan'. It has developed the Logan especially for emerging markets. The four-door saloon car is already sold in Romania and is a low-cost car suitable for emerging market purchasing power.

Logan will enter India's mid-market and will compete head to head with Tata, Ford and Hyundai. The mid-market segment represents 20 per cent of the total auto market, which reached 1 million cars in 2004.

Renault's partnership with Mahindra and Mahindra will force the latter to dispose of its small stake in the Indian Ford subsidiary. Renault, together with Nissan (now 44 per cent owned by Renault), is focusing on growing auto markets in emerging countries.

Source: K. Merchant, 'Renault/Mahindra to Launch Logan in India', *Financial Times*, 23 November 2004, p. 28.

manufacturing

Another means of foreign market development and entry is manufacturing within a foreign country. A company may manufacture locally to capitalise on low-cost labour, to avoid high import taxes, to reduce the high costs of transportation to market, to gain access to raw materials, and/or as a means of gaining market entry. Seeking lower labour costs offshore is no longer an unusual strategy. A hallmark of global companies today is the establishment of manufacturing operations throughout the world. This is a trend that will increase as barriers to free trade are eliminated and companies can locate manufacturing wherever it is most cost effective.

There are three types of manufacturing investment by firms in foreign countries: (1) market seeking; (2) resource seeking; (3) efficiency seeking. Investments in China, for example, are of the first kind, where companies are attracted by the size of the market. Investment in India, especially by a number of fashion garment producers such as Mexx and Marc O'Polo, are of the second type, while investments in Malaysia and Singapore by electronics manufacturers such as Philips and Motorola are of the third type.

countertrade

Countertrade deals are now on the increase and represent a significant proportion of world trade. Countertrade ties the export and other foreign sales to an undertaking from the seller to purchase products from the buyer or a third party in the buyer's country. There are several reasons behind the demand for countertrade, such as promotion of local exports, saving scarce foreign exchange, balancing trade flows and/or ensuring guaranteed supplies. The terms and conditions for countertrade are not standardised and may be different from market to market. Other terms used for countertrade include counterpurchase, buyback, compensation and offset, and barter. In the 1960s, Eastern European countries started demanding countertrade to achieve a balance in foreign trade. Nowadays, however, it is common practice in developing as well as in developed markets, and there are a number of companies that specialise in advising on countertrade and a number of trading houses that act as clearing houses for countertrade products.[16]

GOING INTERNATIONAL 11.5

change is on the cards for global brands

As the cultural landscape of the world is changing and people increasingly reject being seen as 'normal' and desire to be seen as individuals, the multinational brands and mass marketing that made them so successful are experiencing a decline. The days have passed when consumer goods companies could invent blockbuster products, advertise them to a waiting public on peak-time television and watch the goods fly off the shelves.

Of the 74 brands that appeared in the 2001 and 2000 rankings in *Business Week*, 41 were calculated to have lost value. And the total value of those 74 brands was estimated to have fallen by a staggering $49 billion to $851.6 billion, a decline of more than 5 per cent. Coca-Cola was down 5 per cent, McDonald's 9 per cent, Gillette 12 per cent and Nike 5 per cent.

The fall of the Berlin Wall in 1989 seemed to present limitless growth opportunities as the closed economies of Russia, China and other countries opened up to the

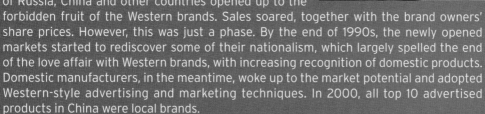

forbidden fruit of the Western brands. Sales soared, together with the brand owners' share prices. However, this was just a phase. By the end of 1990s, the newly opened markets started to rediscover some of their nationalism, which largely spelled the end of the love affair with Western brands, with increasing recognition of domestic products. Domestic manufacturers, in the meantime, woke up to the market potential and adopted Western-style advertising and marketing techniques. In 2000, all top 10 advertised products in China were local brands.

In the developed world, populations have stopped growing or even gone into decline and consumers have most of the basic products they need. Established consumer brands are also under attack from the retailers who introduce cheaper, private-label versions of branded products. Competition is on the increase: almost all of the 31 432 new products introduced in North American in 2000 competed with products in existing categories. Consolidation in the industry allows retailers to dictate harsher terms to the manufacturers.

Some brand owners responded to the situation by introducing local brands in the developing world or by buying smaller brands, such as the purchase of Ben & Jerry's Homemade Ice-cream by Unilever. Some academics also suggest that in order to restore growth, companies must abandon the one-size-fits-all approach and find out how they can make their brands meaningful to different kinds of people. However, this approach is likely to involve a lot of costly market research and development. Nevertheless, the global brands seem to be in for a change.

Source: R. Tomkins, 'No Logo', *Financial Times*, 7 August 2001, p. 2.

summary

Expanding markets around the world have increased competition for all levels of international marketing. To keep abreast of the competition and maintain a viable position for increasingly competitive markets, a global perspective is necessary. Global competition also requires quality products designed to meet ever-changing customer needs and rapidly advancing technology. Cost containment, customer satisfaction and a greater number of players mean that every opportunity to refine international business practices must be examined in the light of company goals. Collaborative relationships, strategic international alliances, strategic planning and alternative market entry strategies are important avenues to global marketing that must be implemented in the planning of global marketing management.

questions

1 How will entry into a developed foreign market differ from entry into a relatively untapped market?
2 Explain the popularity of joint ventures.
3 Assume you are marketing director of a company producing refrigerators. Select one country in Asia and one in Latin America and develop screening criteria to evaluate the two markets. Based on these criteria make an analysis and select the country you should enter.
4 What are the factors that influence the attractiveness of a country as a market? How can you do the analysis to select a market to enter?
5 Explain the popularity of strategic alliances – why do companies enter these agreements?

further reading

■ F.R. Root, *Entry Strategies for International Markets* (Lexington, MA: Lexington Books, 1994).
■ K.R. Robertson and V.R. Wood, 'The Relative Importance of Types of Information in the Foreign Market Selection Process', *International Business Review*, 2001, 10(3), pp. 363-79.
■ R. Mudambi and S.M. Mudambi, 'Diversification and Market Entry Choices in the Context of Foreign Direct Investment', *International Business Review*, 2002, 11(1), pp. 35-55.

references

1 This section draws on Peter Buckley and Pervez Ghauri (eds), *The Internationalization of the Firm: A Reader* (London: Thomson Learning, 2004).
2 Jan Johanson and Finn Wiethersheim-Paul, 'The Internationalization of the Firm: Four Swedish Cases', *Journal of Management Studies*, 1975 (October), pp. 305-22.
3 This section draws on Pervez Ghauri and Peter Buckley, 'Globalization and the End of Competition', in V. Havila, M. Forsgren and H. Håkansson (eds), *Critical Perspectives on Internationalisation* (Oxford: Elsevier, 2002), pp. 7-28.

4 Lars Oxelheim and Pervez Ghauri (eds), *European Union and the Race for Foreign Direct Investment in Europe* (Oxford: Elsevier, 2004).

5 G.D. Harrel and R.O. Kiefer, 'Multinational Strategic Portfolios', *MSU Business Topics*, 1981 (winter), pp. 51-5.

6 This section draws on G. Albaum, J. Strandskov and E. Duerr, *International Marketing and Export Management* (London: FT-Prentice Hall, 2002).

7 Subhath Jain, *Marketing: Planning and Strategy* (Cincinnati, Ohio: Thomson Learning, 2000).

8 Brian Toyne and Peter Walters, *Global Marketing Management: A Strategic Perspective* (Boston: Alan & Bacon, 1989).

9 For a useful guide on SIAs, see e.g. David Faulkner, *International Strategic Alliances; Co-operating to Compete* (London: McGraw Hill, 1995).

10 John Tagliabue, 'Spoon-to-Spoon Combat Overseas', *The New York Times*, 1 January 1995, p. 17.

11 Raju Narisetti, 'Rubbermaid Brings to End Europe Venture', *Wall Street Journal*, 1 June 1994, p. A-4.

12 Roger Kashlak, Rajan Chandran and Anthony Di Benedetto, 'Reciprocity in International Business: A Study of Telecommunications Alliances and Contracts', *Journal of International Business Studies*, vol. 29, no. 2, 1998, pp. 281-304.

13 Preet Aulakh, Tamer Cavusgil and M.B. Sarkar, 'Compensation in International Licensing Agreements', *Journal of International Business Studies*, vol. 29, no. 2, 1998, pp. 409-20.

14 Joel Bleeke and David Ernst (eds), *Collaborating to Compete* (New York: Wiley, 1993).

15 Steve Lanier, 'China: Joint Ventures are Not Just for Giants', *Trade & Culture*, September–October 1994, pp. 17-18.

16 For further details on this topic see Michael Row, *Countertrade* (London: Euromoney Books, 1989).

chapter 12
Exporting, Managing and Logistics

Chapter Outline

Most countries control the movement of goods crossing their borders, whether leaving (exports) or entering (imports). Export and import documents, tariffs, quotas and other barriers to the free flow of goods between independent sovereignties are requirements that must be met by either the exporter or importer, or both.

The mechanics of exporting adds extra steps and costs to an international marketing sale that are not incurred when marketing domestically. In addition to selecting a target market, designing an appropriate product, establishing a price, planning a promotional programme and selecting a distribution channel, the international marketer must meet the legal requirements of moving goods from one country to another. The exporting process (see Exhibit 12.1) includes the licences and documentation necessary to leave the country, an international carrier to transport the goods, and fulfilment of the requirements necessary to get the shipment into another country legally. These mechanics of exporting are sometimes considered the essence of foreign marketing. Although their importance cannot be minimised, they should not be seen as the primary task of international marketing.

Exhibit 12.1 The exporting process

Leaving the exporting country	Physical distribution	Entering the importing country
Licences	*International shipping*	*Tariffs, taxes*
General	*and logistics*	*Non-tariff barriers*
Validated	*Packing*	Standards
Documentation	*Insurance*	Inspection
Export declaration		Documentation
Commercial invoice		Quotas
Bill of lading		Fees
Consular invoice		Licences
Special certificates		Special certificates
Other documents		Exchange permits
Other barriers		

key term

export regulations
rules and regulations for export

The rules and regulations that cover the exportation and importation of goods, and the physical movement of those goods between countries are the special concerns of this chapter.

regulations and restrictions of exporting and importing

There are many reasons why countries impose some form of regulation and restriction on the exporting and importing of goods. **Export regulations** can be designed to conserve

scarce goods for home consumption or to control the flow of strategic goods to actual or potential enemies. **Import regulations** may be imposed to protect health, conserve foreign exchange, serve as economic reprisals, protect home industry or provide revenue in the form of tariffs. To comply with various regulations, the exporter may have to acquire licences or permits from the home country and ascertain that the potential customer has the necessary permits for importing goods.

export controls
Delivering a product or service is a vital aspect of marketing, and product availability is an important part of customer satisfaction. In the case of EC cross-border restrictions, the Single Europe Act 1986 was quite clear: from 31 December 1992 the EC will be 'an area without internal frontiers, in which free movement of goods, persons, services and capital is ensured'. In this respect real progress has been made. The Single Administrative Document was introduced in 1993 to replace a number of customs documents. There are no foreign exchange restrictions on transactions across Europe. There are standardised rules and regulations for transport methods and working conditions. However, civil law codes vary across Europe and implication of contract law is not the same in EU countries. It is thus advised that each contract should specify which country's law is to apply.

The major trends over the last few years include: an increased volume of trade using road transport, more use of special cargoes instead of bulk trade and a shift from rail or road transport to a combination of road, rail, air and sea transport to cover the distances more efficiently and to provide door-to-door service.[1]

import restrictions
When an exporter plans a sale to a foreign buyer, it is necessary to examine the export restrictions of the home country as well as the import restrictions and regulations of the importing country. Although the responsibility for import restrictions may rest with the importer, the exporter does not want to ship goods until it is certain that all import regulations have been met. Goods arriving without proper documentation can be denied entry.

There are many types of trade restriction besides import tariffs imposed by the foreign country. A few examples of the 30 basic **barriers to exporting** considered important by *Business International* include:

1 import licences, quotas and other quantitative restrictions
2 currency restrictions and allocation of exchange at unfavourable rates on payments for imports
3 devaluation
4 prohibitive prior import deposits, prohibition of collection-basis sales and insistence on cash letters of credit
5 arbitrarily short periods in which to apply for import licences, and
6 delays resulting from pressure on overworked officials or from competitors' influence on susceptible officials.

The most frequently encountered trade restrictions, besides tariffs, are such non-tariff barriers as exchange permits, quotas, import licences, boycotts, standards and voluntary agreements.

The various market barriers that existed among members of the European Union created a major impediment to trade. One study of 20 000 EU exporting firms indicated that the most troublesome barriers were administrative roadblocks, border-crossing delays and capital controls. One such barrier was imposed by the French Government against Japanese VCRs. All Japanese VCRs were directed to land at only one port where only one inspector was employed; hence, only 10 or 12 VCRs could enter France each day.[2]

key terms

import regulations rules and regulations for import

barriers to exporting obstacles/hindrances to export

289

GOING INTERNATIONAL 12.1

free trade or hypocrisy?

Much has been written about trade problems between the United States, Europe and other countries. The impression is that high tariffs, quotas and export trade subsidies  are restrictions used by other countries – that the United States is a free, open market while the rest of the world's markets are riddled with trade restrictions. Neither impression is completely true. The United States does engage in trade restrictions. One estimate is that over 25 per cent of manufactured goods sold in the United States are affected by trade barriers. The cost to US consumers is $50 billion (€45 billion) more annually than if there were no restrictions. Consider a sample of US trade hypocrisy.

Quotas: Sugar quotas imposed by the United States result in a pound of sugar costing 10 cents in Canada versus 35 cents in the United States. US beef quotas cost consumers $873 million (€788 million) a year in higher prices. There are quotas with all major clothing-producing nations and on steel with the EU.

Tariffs: Tariffs average 26 per cent of the value of imported clothing, 40 per cent on orange juice, 40 per cent on peanuts, 115 per cent on low-priced watch parts imported from Taiwan and 40 per cent on leather imports from Japan.

Shipping: Foreign ships are barred from carrying passengers or freight between any two US ports. Food donations to foreign countries cost an extra $100 million (€90 million) because they must be shipped on US carriers.

Subsidies: The United States provided export subsidies to US farmers of 111 per cent for poultry exports, 78 per cent for wheat and flour, and more than 100 per cent for rice. According to the EU, the US Government is paying billions of dollars to Boeing as launching funds for its new 7E7 plane. The American Government is in turn blaming the EU for subsidising Airbus's new jumbo A380. The battle is on in the WTO.

Many of these restrictions will begin to disappear as the provisions of the Uruguay round of GATT and the WTO apply, but even then countries will have tariffs, quotas and other barriers to trade.

Sources: abstracted from 'Import Tariffs Imposed by a Protectionist US', *Fortune*, 12 December 1991, p. 14; James Bovard, 'A US History of Trade Hypocrisy', *Wall Street Journal*, 8 March 1994, p. 36; M. Sanchanta, 'Long Relationship with Boeing Drags Japan's Aircraft Industry into Dispute', *Financial Times*, 11 October 2004, p. 2.

As the EU becomes a single market, many of the barriers that existed among member countries have been erased. The single European market has no doubt made trade easier among its member countries but due to reluctance by some member countries, such as the UK, Sweden and Denmark, a number of hidden barriers still exist. The success of the euro is in fact contributing positively towards a complete integration and elimination of barriers. There is, however, a rising concern that a fully integrated EU will become a market with strong protectionist barriers towards non-member countries.

Tariffs   Tariffs are the taxes or customs duties levied against goods imported from another country. All countries have tariffs for the purpose of raising revenue and protecting home industries from the competition of foreign-produced goods. Tariff rates are based on value or quantity, or a combination of both.

The EU is the largest member of the WTO in terms of trade; including intra-EU trade, it accounts for almost 40 per cent of world merchandise trade. However, with increasing integration the EU's trade with third countries is decreasing. The Treaty of Rome required the EC to develop a **Common Commercial Policy (CCP)**, the aim of which is to liberalise world trade. The key element of CCP is the Common External Tariff (CET), which all member states must apply. The community has a number of preferential trade agreements, for example with EFTA and Turkey. But at the same time, it has variable levies on imported food and quotas on imported textiles through the Multi-Fibre Agreement (MFA), as well as a number of other restrictions on imports that harm sensitive domestic industries such as agriculture and cars. On the other hand, the American administration created a climate of uncertainty for a number of EU firms. The government proposed that no federal agencies should award contracts to companies from a number of EU states. The American government also proposed that all four-wheel-drive cars should be considered as trucks and thus attract a 25 per cent tariff instead of the 2.5 per cent for cars. Although the main purpose was to stop Japanese four-wheel-drive cars, EU manufacturers such as Land Rover, Mercedes-Benz and Volkswagen would also be affected. It was also feared that the American administration would increase tariffs on 'gas-guzzling' cars. This would directly influence Rolls-Royce, BMW, Jaguar and Mercedes-Benz.

Exchange Permits   Especially troublesome to exporters are **exchange restrictions** placed on the flow of currency by some foreign countries. To conserve scarce foreign exchange and alleviate balance-of-payment difficulties, many countries impose restrictions on the amount of their currency they will exchange for the currency of another country. In effect, they ration the amount of currency available to pay for imports. Exchange controls may be applied in general to all commodities, or a country may employ a system of multiple exchange rates based on the type of import. Essential products might have a very favourable exchange rate, while non-essentials or luxuries would have a less favourable rate of exchange. South Africa, for example, until recently had a two-tier system for foreign exchange, commercial rand and financial rand. At times, countries may not issue any exchange permits for certain classes of commodity.

In countries that use exchange controls, the usual procedure is for the importer to apply to the control agency of the importing country for an import permit; if the control agency approves the request, an import licence is issued. On presentation to the proper government agency, the import licence can be used to have local currency exchanged for the currency of the seller.

Receiving an **import licence**, or even an exchange permit, however, is not a guarantee that a seller can exchange local currency for the currency of the seller. If local currency is in short supply – a chronic problem in some countries – other means of acquiring home-country currency are necessary. For example, in a transaction between the government of Colombia and a US truck manufacturer, there was a scarcity of US currency to exchange for the 1000 vehicles Colombia wanted to purchase. The problem was solved through a series of exchanges. Colombia had a surplus of coffee that the truck manufacturer accepted and traded in Europe for sugar; the sugar was traded for pig iron, and finally the pig iron for US dollars.

This somewhat complicated but effective countertrade transaction has become more common. As discussed in other chapters, countertrade deals are often a result of the inability to convert local currency into home-country currency and/or the refusal of a government to issue foreign exchange.

Quotas   Countries may also impose limitations on the quantity of certain goods imported during a specific period. These quotas may be applied to imports from specific countries or from all foreign sources in general. Most European Union countries, for example, have specific quotas for importing cotton, tobacco, textiles and cars; in the case

GOING INTERNATIONAL 12.2

export methods need to be reassessed and adjusted constantly

All companies need to rethink their export strategy periodically. A surprising number of firms and small potential exporters need to develop one for the first time. This means

tailoring marketing and product strategies to the markets they work in or want to penetrate. In Europe, in order to succeed it is vital, at least in some industries, to be less dependent on the home market. According to Chris Walkey, Rover's director for external affairs, 'As recently as 1991 Rover allocated no resources to exploring markets overseas. Now we are exporters investing resources to find opportunities in international markets and we are now making substantial adaptations for foreign markets.' Paul Brauklin, from Oxford

Instruments and an export promoter for UK firms seeking opportunities in Japan, considers top management's commitment as an essential for exporting. He argues, 'They must have a clear strategy, an effective management team and they must be continually monitoring progress ... If you come across a company not doing well in, say, Japan, it is because one of these elements is missing.'

The London-based Institute of Export recommends that its members follow six points of strategy.

1 Know the market by conducting extensive market research.
2 Know the documentation; sales executives often neglect to build in the cost of documentation and squeeze margins to the point where the deal becomes problematic and future orders are endangered.
3 Examine the potential for currency fluctuations. UK exporters should not necessarily invoice in sterling.
4 Consider credit insurance. It may prove expensive for a small company working on 10–15 per cent margins.
5 Ensure staff are fully trained. This can range from one-day courses to long-term professional qualifications.
6 Use official bodies such as the Department of Trade and Industry (DTI) in the UK or Export Promotion Bureaux in other countries. In some cases financial support for business development will be available.

Source: Financial Times: FT Exporter, Autumn 1995, p. 11.

of some of these items, there are also limitations on the amount imported from specific countries. Most Western countries (e.g. the EU and the US) have imposed quotas on the biggest textile/garments producers, as to how much they can export to these markets (see Exhibit 12.2).

The most important reasons to set quotas are to protect domestic industry and to conserve foreign exchange. Some importing countries also set quotas to ensure an equitable distribution of a major market among friendly countries.

Import Licences   As a means of regulating the flow of exchange and the quantity of a particular imported commodity, countries often require import licences. The fundamental difference between quotas and import licences as a means of controlling imports is the

Exhibit 12.2 Top 10 clothing exporters

	Exports growth ($ billions)	As % total per year 2000–08	Exports
China	124	18	21
India	14	9	29
Hong Kong	8	–4	NA
Bangladesh	6	1	82
Pakistan	4	6	70
Indonesia	4	–4	NA
South Korea	4	–4	NA
Sri Lanka	3	–3	55
Vietnam	3	2	NA
Thailand	2.7	–4	NA

* Forecast.

Source: compiled from *The Economist*, 'The Looming', Special Report on the Textile Industry, 13 November 2004, pp. 91–3.

greater flexibility of import licences over quotas. Quotas permit importing until the quota is filled; licensing limits quantities on a case-by-case basis.

Boycott   A boycott is an absolute restriction against trade with a country, or trade of specific goods. Countries can refuse to trade (buy or sell) with other countries; for example, the United States imposed, with the help of the United Nations, a boycott on trade with Libya, which was respected by most countries. This was, however, taken away after Libya gave up its plan to develop nuclear weapons. The United Nations also imposed a boycott on trade with Iraq after the first Gulf War. The United States has also had a boycott on trade with Cuba, due to the latter's communist regime. This boycott was also respected by Western European countries. However, lately the WTO and the European Union want to open trade with Cuba, but America is pushing against it.

Standards   Health standards, safety standards and product quality standards are necessary to protect the consuming public, and imported goods are required to comply with local laws. Unfortunately, standards can also be used to slow down or restrict the procedures for importing to the point that the additional time and cost required to comply become, in effect, trade restrictions. Safety standards are a good example. Most countries have safety standards for electrical appliances and require that imported electrical products meet local standards. However, the restrictiveness of safety standards can be escalated to the level of an absolute trade barrier by manipulating the procedures used to determine if products meet the standards. The simplest process for the importing nation is to accept the safety standard verification used by the exporting country. In some industries, such as clothing, most parties are familiar with these standards and there are hardly any problems arising due to this fact. The European Union has certain standards for electronic products and each company selling into the EU has to comply with these.

GOING INTERNATIONAL 12.3

export restrictions on technology

© Roger
Ressimeyer/
CORBIS

Most Western countries impose restrictions on the export of sensitive advanced technology to a number of countries. For example, while India and Pakistan were working to develop uranium enrichment capabilities, all export of technology related to uranium enrichment could not be exported to these countries. Libya has had total export restrictions for similar reasons. However, now that Libya has promised to give up its nuclear ambitions, these restrictions have been relaxed.

China successfully fired a new type of long-range ground-to-ground missile and is running an extensive training programme for air force officers. At the same time, tensions between China and Taiwan have intensified after Taiwan's president declared that relationships between Taipei and Beijing should be based on 'state-to-state' relationship principles.

The United States, being an ally of Taiwan, has restrictions on technology export to China, particularly technology that can be used in military applications. While most of the technology can be used for both civilian and military applications, it's the responsibility of the exporters to ensure that the technology exported is not used for military purposes.

Source: compiled from various sources.

Voluntary Agreements   Foreign restrictions of all kinds abound and the United States can be counted among those governments using restrictions. For decades, US Government officials have been arranging 'voluntary' agreements with the Japanese steel and automotive industries to limit sales to the United States. Japan entered these voluntary agreements under the implied threat that if it did not voluntarily restrict the export of automobiles or steel to an agreed limit, the United States might impose even harsher restrictions including additional import duties. Similar negotiations with the governments of major textile producers have limited textile imports as well. It is estimated that the cost of tariffs, quotas and voluntary agreements on all fibres is as much as €36 billion ($44 billion) at the retail level. This works out to be a hidden tax of almost €450 ($550) a year for every American family.

Other Restrictions   Restrictions may be imposed on imports of harmful products, drugs, medicines, and immoral products and literature. Products must also comply with government standards set for health, sanitation, packaging and labelling. For example, in the Netherlands all imported hen and duck eggs must be marked in indelible ink with the country of origin; in Spain, imported condensed milk must be labelled to show fat content if it is less than 8 per cent fat; and in EU countries, all animals imported from outside the European Union must be accompanied by a sanitary certificate issued by an approved veterinary inspector; even then the animals have to spend a specified period in quarantine. Failure to comply with regulations can result in severe fines and penalties.

While sanitation certificates, **content labelling** and other such regulations serve a legitimate purpose, countries can effectively limit imports by using such restrictions as additional trade barriers. Most of the economically developed world encourages foreign trade and works through the WTO to reduce tariffs and non-tariff barriers to a reasonable rate.

key term

content labelling
mention of the contents/
ingredients of a product on the package

GOING INTERNATIONAL 12.4

Astra-Zeneca fails to get FDA approval

The Food and Drug Advisory (FDA) committee in the United States approves all import of food and drugs (pharmaceuticals) into the US.

Astra-Zeneca, the UK-Swedish pharmaceutical company, is very upbeat about its new drug Exanta, which can prevent strokes and blood clots. Exanta is the first new type of oral anti-coagulant treatment in 50 years and is considered a good alternative to existing drugs that require extensive monitoring of patients. It has already been approved by 14 European countries.

The FDA has, however, refused to grant approval to Exanta. It says that Astra-Zeneca needs to monitor Exanta's side effects on lives. According to FDA claims, evidence of its potential risks outweigh the benefits. The objection is related to potential liver toxicity, which the company has already disclosed. The FDA criticised the design of clinical trials to show the drug prevented strokes. It said, that although the statistical evidence supported the efficiency of Exanta, the criteria used to compare it with the existing treatment (warfarin) were too liberal.

This decision is considered a big blow to Astra-Zeneca. At the announcement of the decision, its shares fell by 4 per cent. Astra-Zeneca was hoping that Exanta would become one of its blockbuster drugs and fill the gap left by Prilosec, the ulcer medicine whose patent expired. Prilosec's sales peaked at about €8 billion and Exanta was expected to bring in a similar figure.

Source: abridged from, C. Bowe, 'Astra-Zeneca Fails to Get the US Nod for Antistroke Drug', *Financial Times*, 9 September 2004, p. M1.

Yet, in times of economic recession, countries revert to a protectionist philosophy and seek ways to restrict the importing of goods. Non-tariff barriers have become one of the most potent ways for a country to restrict trade. The elimination of non-tariff barriers has been a major concern of GATT negotiations in the Uruguay round, and the WTO will place more emphasis on these issues as well as on tariffs and trade in services.[3]

customs-privileged facilities

To facilitate export trade, countries designate areas within their borders as customs-privileged areas, that is, areas where goods can be imported for storage and/or processing with tariffs and quota limits postponed until the products leave the designated areas. Foreign-trade zones (also known as free-trade zones), free ports and in-bond arrangements are all types of customs-privileged facilities that countries use to promote foreign trade.

foreign-trade zones

The number of countries with **foreign-trade zones (FTZs)** has increased as trade liberalisation has spread through Latin America, Eastern Europe and other parts of Europe and Asia. Most FTZs function in a similar manner regardless of the host country. The FTZs

key term

foreign-trade zones (FTZs) where products are produced mostly for exporting purposes

GOING INTERNATIONAL 12.5

privileged companies

Cartel arrangements, where competitors or would-be competitors join together, are often illegal in most countries but especially in the United States and Europe. This is done according to anti-trust regulations to restrict the competitors from price fixing and other activities that may not be beneficial for the consumers and for free competi-

tion. However, many countries pass legislation to allow such collaborative ventures to strengthen domestic companies. For example, in the United States, so called 'Webb-Promerene Associations' and 'Export Trading Companies' formed under the Export Trading Company Act are exempt from anti-trust regulations if they meet certain conditions.

These arrangements are agreed by governments that want to promote exports from their country. Some governments also use 'tax incentives' by allowing certain types of organisational arrangement. The United States Government is doing this through fostering of Foreign Sales Corporations (FSCs). Here tax incentives/exemptions are given to companies that export to other countries.

Although a number of other countries are also using these methods to promote exports, many of these arrangements have been less successful than expected.

Source: based on G. Albaum, J. Strandkov and E. Derr, *International Marketing and Export Management* (Harlow: FT Prentice Hall, 2002) p. 291.

extend their services to thousands of firms engaged in a spectrum of international trade-related activities ranging from distribution to assembly and manufacturing.

In situations where goods are imported into a country to be combined with local-made goods and re-exported, the importer or exporter can avoid payment of local import duties on the foreign portion and eliminate the complications of applying for a 'drawback', that is, a request for a refund from the government of the duties paid on imports later re-exported. Other benefits for companies utilising foreign-trade zones include:

1 lower insurance costs due to the greater security required in FTZs
2 more working capital since duties are deferred until goods leave the zone
3 the opportunity to stockpile products when quotas are filled or while waiting for ideal market conditions
4 significant savings on goods or materials rejected, damaged or scrapped for which no duties are assessed, and
5 exemption from paying duties on labour and overhead costs incurred in an FTZ, which are excluded in determining the value of the goods.

The Special Economic Zone (SEZ) in Shenzhen, China, is an example of China's economic development programme that established SEZs as a means of attracting foreign capital and technology. In 10 years, Shenzhen's population grew from 30 000 to over 1 million. Hundreds of thousands of Chinese work in the Special Economic Zone. Hourly manufacturing labour costs in China are very low compared with the Western minimum wage; average per capita labour costs, including benefits, run between €54 ($60) and €81 ($95) per month.

export documents

Each export shipment requires various documents to satisfy government regulations controlling exporting as well as to meet requirements for international commercial payment transactions. The most frequently required documents are export declarations, consular invoices or certificates of origin, bills of lading, commercial invoices and insurance certificates. In addition, documents such as import licences, export licences, packing lists and inspection certificates for agricultural products are often necessary.

The paperwork involved in successfully completing a transaction is considered by many to be the greatest of all non-tariff trade barriers. Generally, preparation of documents can be handled routinely, but their importance should not be minimised; incomplete or improperly prepared documents lead to delays in shipment. In some countries, there are penalties, fines and even confiscation of goods as a result of errors in some of these documents. Export documents are the result of requirements imposed by the exporting government, of requirements set by commercial procedures established in foreign trade and, in some cases, of the supporting import documents required by the foreign government. Descriptions of the principal export documents follow.

Export Declaration   To maintain a statistical measure of the quantity of goods shipped abroad and to provide a means of determining whether regulations are being met, most countries require shipments abroad to be accompanied by an export declaration. Usually such a declaration, presented at the port of exit, includes the names and addresses of the principals involved, the destination of the goods, a full description of the goods and their declared value.

Bill of Lading   The bill of lading is the most important document required to establish legal ownership and facilitate financial transactions. It serves the following purposes: (1) as a contract for shipment between the carrier and shipper; (2) as a receipt from the carrier for shipment; and (3) as a certificate of ownership or title to the goods. Bills of lading are issued in the form of straight bills, which are non-negotiable and are delivered directly to a consignee, or order bills, which are negotiable instruments. Bills of lading are frequently referred to as being either clean or foul. A clean bill of lading means the items presented to the carrier for shipment were properly packaged and clear of apparent damage when received; a foul bill of lading means the shipment was received in damaged condition and the damage is noted on the bill of lading.

Commercial Invoice   Every international transaction requires a commercial invoice, that is, a bill or statement for the goods sold. This document often serves several purposes; some countries require a copy for customs clearance, and it is one of the financial documents required in international commercial payments.

Insurance Policy or Certificate   The risks of shipment due to political or economic unrest in some countries, and the possibility of damage from sea and weather, make it absolutely necessary to have adequate insurance covering loss due to damage, war or riots. Typically the method of payment or terms of sale require insurance on the goods, so few export shipments are uninsured. The insurance policy or certificate of insurance is considered a key document in export trade.

Licences   Export or import licences are additional documents frequently required in export trade. In those cases where import licences are required by the country of entry, a copy of the licence or licence number is usually required to obtain a consular invoice. Whenever a commodity requires an export licence, it must be obtained before an export declaration can be properly certified.

Others Sanitary and health inspection certificates attesting to the absence of disease and pests may be required for certain agricultural products before a country allows goods to enter its borders. Packing lists with correct weights are also required in some cases.

GOING INTERNATIONAL 12.6

you don't look like a Mexican peanut to me!

The US Government is serious about its import restrictions, especially on agricultural products. It doesn't look kindly, for example, on peanuts from China being shipped as Mexican peanuts. But how do you tell where peanuts, orange juice and other agricultural products come from? With an 'inductively coupled plasma mass spectrometer', that's how.

The US Customs Service uses such a machine to determine whether a peanut headed for Safeway matches a peanut grown in Mexico or Georgia. It's a little like DNA testing for plants. While the machine can't tell exactly whether the peanuts come from a specific country, it can tell if the peanuts in a sample match a sample of peanuts known to come from a specific country. This process began about 10 years ago with the analysing of frozen orange juice. Since frozen orange juice from different countries has different tariff schedules, transshipment through a lower-tariff country can make a big difference in tariffs paid.

In a little over a year, with the help of the machine, US Customs was able to build a case of 'dumping' against Chinese garlic, an illegal transshipment case against Argentine peanuts, and a case against a California coffee distributor who was adulterating Hawaiian Kona coffee with cheaper Central American beans and selling the result as pure Kona.

Source: Guy Gugliotta, 'High-tech Trade Enforcement Tracks Peanuts Across Borders', *Washington Post*, 4 December 1997, p. A21; and Bob Dart, 'US Takes Aim at Peanut Traffickers: High-tech Equipment is Helping to Detect Illegal Over-the-border Shipments: Undercutting NAFTA', *Atlanta Journal and Constitution*, 9 December 1997, p. A12.

terms of sale

Terms of sale, or trade terms, differ somewhat in international marketing from country to country. In some countries it is customary to ship FOB (free on board, meaning that the price is established at the door of the factory), while in others CIF (cost, insurance and freight) is more common. International trade terms often sound similar to those used in domestic business but generally have different meanings. International terms indicate how buyer and seller divide risks and obligations and, therefore, the costs of specific kinds of international trade transaction. When quoting prices, it is important to make them meaningful. The most commonly used international trade terms include the following.

CIF (cost, insurance, freight) to a named overseas port of import. A CIF quote is more meaningful to the overseas buyer because it includes the costs of goods, insurance, and all transportation and miscellaneous charges to the named place of debarkation.
C&F (cost and freight) to named overseas port. The price includes the cost of the goods and transportation costs to the named place of debarkation. The cost of insurance is borne by the buyer.

FAS (free alongside) at a named port of export. The price includes cost of goods and charges for delivery of the goods alongside the shipping vessel. The buyer is responsible for the cost of loading on to the vessel, transportation and insurance.

FOB (free on board) at a named inland point of origin; at a named port of exportation; or a named vessel and port of export. The price includes the cost of the goods and delivery to the place named.

EX (named port of origin). The price quoted covers costs only at the point of origin (for example, EX Factory). All other charges are the buyer's concern.

A complete list of terms and their definitions can be found in *Incoterms*, a booklet published by the International Chamber of Commerce. It is important for the exporter to understand exactly the meanings of terms used in quotations. A simple misunderstanding regarding delivery terms may prevent the exporter from meeting contractual obligations or make that person responsible for shipping costs he or she did not intend to incur. Exhibit 12.3 indicates who is responsible for a variety of costs under various terms.

Exhibit 12.3 Who is responsible for costs under various terms

Cost items/terms	FOB (free on board) inland carrier at factory	FOB (free on board) inland carrier at point of shipment	FAS (free alongside) vessel or plane at port of shipment	CIF (cost, insurance, freight) at port of destination
Export packing*	Buyer	Seller	Seller	Seller
Inland freight	Buyer	Seller	Seller	Seller
Port charges	Buyer	Buyer	Seller	Seller
Forwarder's fee	Buyer	Buyer	Buyer	Seller
Consular fee	Buyer	Buyer	Buyer	Buyer†
Loading on vessel or plane	Buyer	Buyer	Buyer	Seller
Ocean freight	Buyer	Buyer	Buyer	Seller
Cargo insurance	Buyer	Buyer	Buyer	Seller
Customs duties	Buyer	Buyer	Buyer	Buyer
Ownership of goods passes	When goods on board an inland carrier (truck, rail, etc.) or in hands of inland carrier	When goods unloaded by inland carrier	When goods alongside carrier, in hands of air or ocean carrier	When goods on board air or ocean carrier *at port of shipment*

* Who absorbs export packing? This charge should be clearly agreed on. Charges are sometimes controversial.
† The seller has responsibility to arrange for consular invoices (and other documents requested by the buyer's government). According to official definitions, buyer pays fees, but sometimes, as a matter of practice, seller includes in quotations.

Letter of Credits   These days most import and export is done through **letter of credits (LC)**. The letter of credit shifts the buyer's credit risk to the bank issuing the LC. When an LC is issued, the seller draws a draft against the bank issuing the credit and receives money by presenting shipping documents to show that he has already shipped the goods. The LC provides the greatest degree of protection to the seller – that he will receive his money once he has shipped the goods.

The procedure for LC starts at the signing of the contract, as it stipulates how the cash will be paid for goods (see Exhibit 12.4). The buyer/importer goes to the local bank and arranges for the letter of credit, the buyer bank notifies its corresponding bank in the seller's country (seller's bank) with the conditions set forth in the LC. The seller can draw a draft against the LC for the payment of goods.

Exhibit 12.4 A letter-of-credit transaction

Here is what typically happens when payment is made by an irrevocable letter of credit confirmed by a US bank. Follow the steps in the illustration below.

1 Exporter and customer agree on terms of sale.
2 Buyer requests its foreign bank to open a letter of credit.
3 The buyer's bank prepares an irrevocable letter of credit (LC), including all instructions, and sends the irrevocable letter of credit to a US bank.
4 The US bank prepares a letter of confirmation and letter of credit and sends to seller.
5 Seller reviews LC. If acceptable, arranges with freight forwarder to deliver goods to designated port of entry.
6 The goods are loaded and shipped.
7 At the same time, the forwarder completes the necessary documents and sends documents to the seller.
8 Seller presents documents, indicating full compliance, to the US bank.
9 The US bank reviews the documents. If they are in order, issues seller a cheque for amount of sale.
10 The documents are airmailed to the buyer's bank for review.
11 If documents are in compliance, the bank sends documents to buyer.
12 To claim goods, buyer presents documents to customs broker.
13 Goods are released to buyer.

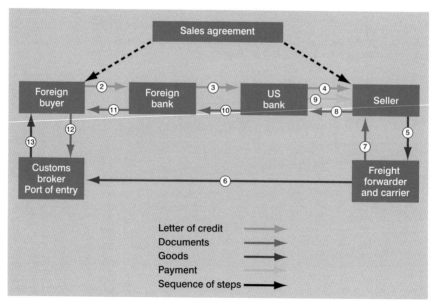

Source: based on 'A Basic Guide to Exporting', US Department of Commerce, International Trade Administration, Washington, DC, 2004.

packing and marking

Special packing and marking requirements must be considered for shipments destined to be transported over water, subject to excessive handling or destined for parts of the world with

extreme climates or unprotected outdoor storage. Packing adequate for domestic shipments often falls short for goods subject to the conditions mentioned. Protection against rough handling, moisture, temperature extremes and pilferage may require heavy crating, which increases total packing costs as well as freight rates because of increased weight and size. Since some countries determine import duties on gross weight, packing can add a significant amount to import fees. To avoid the extremes of too much or too little packing, the marketer should consult export brokers, export freight forwarders or other specialists.

export shipping

Whenever and however title to goods is transferred, those goods must be transported. Shipping goods to another country presents some important differences from shipping to a domestic site. The goods can be out of the shipper's control for longer periods of time than in domestic distribution, more shipping and collection documents are required, packing must be suitable and shipping insurance coverage is necessarily more extensive. The task is to match each order of goods to the shipping modes best suited for swift, safe and economical delivery. Ocean shipping, air freight, air express and parcel post are all possibilities. Ocean shipping is usually the least expensive and most frequently used method for heavy bulk shipment. For certain categories of goods, air freight can be the most economical and certainly the speediest.

Shipping costs are an important factor in a product's price in export marketing; the transportation mode must be selected in terms of the total impact on cost. One estimate is that logistics account for between 19 and 23 per cent of the total cost of a finished product sold internationally. In ocean shipping, one of the important innovations in reducing or controlling the high cost of transportation is the use of containerisation. **Containerised shipments**, in place of the traditional bulk handling of full loads or breakbulk operations, have resulted in intermodal transport between inland points, reduced costs and simplified handling of international shipments.

With increased use of containerisation, rail container service has developed in many countries to provide the international shipper with door-to-door movement of goods under seal, originating and terminating inland. This eliminates several loadings, unloadings and changes of carriers and reduces costs substantially. Containerised cargo handling also reduces damage and pilferage in transit.

For many commodities of high unit value and low weight and volume, international air freight has become important. Air freight has shown the fastest growth rate for freight transportation even though it accounts for only a fraction of total international shipments.[4] While air freight can cost two to five times surface charges for general cargo, some cost reduction is realised through reduced packing requirements, paperwork, insurance and the cost of money tied up in inventory. Although usually not enough to offset the higher rates charged for air freight, if the commodity has high unit value or high inventory costs, or if there is concern with delivery time, air freight can be a justifiable alternative. Many products moving to foreign markets meet these criteria.

The selection of transportation mode has an important bearing on the cost of export shipping, but it is not the only cost involved in the physical movement of goods from point of origin to ultimate market. Indeed, the selection of mode, the location of inventory, warehouses and so forth, all figure in the cost of the physical movement of goods. A narrow solution to the physical movement of goods is the selection of transportation; a broader application is the concept of logistics management or physical distribution.

logistics

When a company is primarily an exporter from a single country to a single market, the typical approach to the physical movement of goods is the selection of a dependable mode of transportation, which ensures safe arrival of the goods within a reasonable time for a reasonable carrier cost. As a company becomes global, such a solution to the movement of

products could prove costly and highly inefficient for seller and buyer. At some point in the growth and expansion of an international firm, costs other than transportation are such that an optimal cost solution to the physical movement of goods cannot be achieved without thinking of the physical distribution process as an integrated system. When a foreign marketer begins producing and selling in more than one country and becomes a global marketer, it is time to consider the concept of logistics management, that is, a total systems approach to management of the distribution process that includes all activities involved in physically moving raw material, in-process inventory and finished goods inventory from the point of origin to the point of use or consumption.[5]

interdependence of physical distribution activities

Distribution viewed as a system involves more than the physical movement of goods. It includes location of plants and warehousing (storage), transportation mode, inventory quantities and packing. The concept of physical distribution takes into account that the costs of each activity are interdependent, and a decision involving one affects the cost and efficiency of one or all others.[6]

The idea of interdependence can be illustrated by the classic example of **air freight**. Exhibit 12.5 is an illustration of an actual company's costs of shipping 44 000 peripheral boards worth €6.9 million ($7.7 million) from a Singapore plant to the US west coast using two modes of transportation: **ocean freight** and the more expensive air freight. When total costs are calculated, air freight is actually less costly than ocean freight. When considering only rates for transportation and carrying costs for inventory in transit, air transportation costs are approximately €51 000 ($57 000) higher than ocean freight. However, there are other costs involved. To offset the slower ocean freight and the possibility of unforeseen delays and still ensure prompt customer delivery schedules, the company has to continuously maintain 30 days of inventory in Singapore and another 30 days' inventory at the company's distribution centres. Costs of financing 60 days of inventory and additional warehousing costs at both points – that is, real physical distribution costs – would result in the cost of ocean freight exceeding air by more than €67 000 ($75 000). There may even be additional costs associated with ocean freight – for example, higher damage rate, higher insurance and higher packing rates for ocean freight. Substantial savings can result from the systematic examination of logistics costs and the calculation of total physical distribution costs.[7]

key terms

air freight
in this case, the cost of sending a product by air

ocean freight
in this case, the cost of sending a product by ship

Exhibit 12.5 Real physical distribution costs between air and ocean freight: Singapore to the United States

In this example 44 000 peripheral boards worth $7.7 million (€6.9 million) are shipped from a Singapore plant to the US west coast. Cost of capital to finance inventories is 10 per cent annually: $2109 per day to finance $7.7 million.		
	Ocean	**Air**
Transport costs	$31 790 (in transit 21 days)	$127 160 (in transit 3 days)
In-transit inventory financing costs	$44 289	$6 328
Total transportation costs	$76 079	$133 487
Warehousing inventory costs	(60 days @ $2 109 per day)	
Singapore and US	$126 540	
Warehouse rent	$6 500	
Real physical distribution costs	$209 119	$133 487

Source: adapted from 'Air and Adaptec's Competitive Strategy', *International Business*, September 1993, p. 44.

Although a cost difference will not always be the case, the example serves to illustrate the interdependence of the various activities in the physical distribution mix and the total cost. A change of transportation mode affected a change in packaging and handling, inventory costs, warehousing time and cost, and delivery charges.

Distribution problems confronting the international marketer are compounded by additional variables and costs that are also interdependent and must be included in the total physical distribution decision. As the international firm broadens the scope of its operations, the additional variables and costs become more crucial in their effect on the efficiency of the distribution system.

One of the major benefits of European unification is the elimination of transportation barriers among member countries. Instead of approaching Europe on a country-by-country basis, a centralised logistics network can be developed. Studies indicate that companies operating in Europe may be able to cut 20 warehousing locations to three and maintain the same level of customer service.[8] A German **white goods** manufacturer was able to reduce its European warehouses from 39 to 10 as well as improve its distribution and enhance customer service. By cutting the number of warehouses, it reduced total distribution and warehousing costs, brought down staff numbers, held fewer items of stock, provided greater access to regional markets, made better use of transport networks and improved service to customers, all with a 21 per cent reduction in total logistics costs.[9]

benefits of physical distribution systems

A physical distribution system may also result in better (more dependable) delivery service to the market; when production occurs at different locations, companies are able quickly to determine the most economical source for a particular customer. As companies expand into multinational markets and source these markets from multinational production facilities, they are increasingly confronted with cost variables that make it imperative to employ a total systems approach to the management of the distribution process to achieve efficient operation. Finally, a physical distribution system can render the natural obstructions created by geography less economically critical for the multinational marketer.

the foreign-freight forwarder

The foreign-freight forwarder, licensed by the government, arranges for the shipment of goods as the agent for an exporter. The forwarder is an indispensable agent for an exporting firm that cannot afford an in-house specialist to handle paperwork and other export trade mechanics. Even in large companies with active export departments capable of handling documentation, a forwarder is useful as a shipment coordinator at the port of export or at the destination port. Besides arranging for complete shipping documentation, the full-service **foreign-freight forwarder** provides information and advice on routing and scheduling, rates and related charges, consular and licensing requirements, labelling requirements and export restrictions. Further, the agent offers shipping insurance, warehouse storage, packing and containerisation, and ocean cargo or air freight space. Both large and small shippers find freight forwarders' wide range of services useful and well worth the fees normally charged. In fact, for many shipments, forwarders can save on freight charges because they can consolidate shipments into larger, more economical quantities. Experienced exporters regard the foreign-freight forwarder as an important addition to in-house specialists (see Exhibit 12.6).

key terms

white goods
often refers to
kitchen machines
(e.g. refrigerators,
freezers)

**foreign-freight
forwarder**
a company that
helps other
companies in
transportation and
export/import
matters

Exhibit 12.6 Major services rendered by international freight forwarders

- Develops most economic methods of shipment. Figures costs, FOB, CIF, etc.
- Arranges export licences or import permits.
- Arranges transport from plant to port/airport and beyond.
- Prepares export declaration, bill of lading and other necessary documents.
- Arranges and executes formalities with authorities such as port and customs.
- Prepares or arranges documents in foreign language, if necessary.
- Assembles all documents necessary for export/import and presents them to relevant authorities when required.
- Prepares and presents documents to the bank for letter of credit or payment.

Source: based on Subhash Jain, *Export Strategy, Westpol* (Connecticut: Quorum, 1989).

summary

An awareness of the mechanics of export trade is indispensable to the foreign marketer who engages in exporting goods from one country to another. Although most marketing techniques are open to interpretation and creative application, the mechanics of exporting are very exact; there is little room for interpretation or improvisation with the requirements of export licences, quotas, tariffs, export documents, packing, marketing and the various uses of commercial payments. The very nature of the regulations and restrictions surrounding importing and exporting can lead to frequent and rapid change. In handling the mechanics of export trade successfully, the manufacturer must keep abreast of all foreign and domestic changes in requirements and regulations pertaining to the product involved. For firms unable to maintain their own export staffs, foreign-freight forwarders can handle many details for a nominal fee.

With paperwork completed, the physical movement of goods must be considered. Transportation mode affects total product cost because of the varying requirements of packing, inventory levels, time requirements, perishability, unit cost, damage and pilfering losses, and customer service. Transportation for each product must be assessed in view of the interdependent nature of all these factors. To assure optimum distribution at minimal cost, a physical distribution system determines everything from plant location to final customer delivery in terms of the most efficient use of capital investment, resources, production, inventory, packing and transportation.

questions

1 Explain the reasoning behind the various regulations and restrictions imposed on the exportation and importation of goods.
2 What is the purpose of an import licence? Discuss.
3 Explain foreign-trade zones and illustrate how they may be used by an exporter/by an importer. How do foreign-trade zones differ from bonded warehouses?
4 Explain each of the following export documents:
   a bill of lading
   b consular invoice or certificate of origin
   c commercial invoice
   d insurance certificate.
5 Why would an exporter use the services of a foreign-freight forwarder? Discuss.
6 Besides cost advantages, what are the other benefits of an effective physical distribution system?

further reading

- S.T. Cavusgil, 'Differences Among Exporting Firms Based on Degree of Internationalization', *Journal of Business Research*, 1984, 12(2) pp. 195-208.
- C.A. Solberg and E. Nes, 'Export Trust, Commitment and Marketing Control in Integrated and Independent Export Channels', *International Business Review*, 2002, 11(4) pp. 385-405.
- V.V. Miller and K. Loess, 'An Institutional Analysis of the US Foreign Sales Corporations', *International Business Review*, 2002, 11(6), pp. 753-63.

references

1 S.T. Cavusgil, 'Guidelines for Export Market Research', *Business Horizon*, 1985, November/December, pp. 283-95.
2 Fahri Karakaya, 'Barriers to Entry in International Markets', *Journal of Global Marketing*, vol. 7, no. 1, 1993, p. 10.
3 Alan Rugman and Alain Verbeke, 'Multinational Enterprises and Public Policy', *Journal of International Business Studies*, vol. 29, no. 1, 1998, pp. 115-36.
4 John Gorsuch, 'Air Cargo', *Trade and Culture*, March-April 1995, pp. 21-6.
5 G. Albaum, J. Strandkov and E. Derr, *International Marketing and Export Management* (Harlow: FT Prentice Hall, 2002).
6 Constantine Katsikeas, Ali Al-Khalifa and Dave Crick, 'Manufacturers' Understanding of their Overseas Distributors: The Relevance of Export Involvement', *International Business Review*, vol. 6, no. 2, 1997, pp. 147-64.
7 M. Posner, 'Exports, Opportunities and Risks', *Credit Management*, April 2003, p. 18.
8 J.D. Coates, 'International Logistics', *World Trade*, 1 March 2003, p. 28.
9 'Cross-border Logistics: How Bosch-Siemens Saved Time and Costs', *Business Europe*, 23-29 May 1994, p. 7.

chapter 13
Developing Consumer Products for International Markets

Chapter Outline

Chapter Learning Objectives

What you should learn from Chapter 13

- How important it is to offer a product suitable to the intended market
- The current dichotomy of standardised versus adapted products in international marketing
- How to manage the relationship between product acceptance and the market into which it is introduced
- How country of origin effect impacts on product image
- How to identify physical, mandatory and cultural requirements for product evaluation
- How to identify and comply with physical, mandatory and cultural requirements for product adaptation
- To comprehend the need to view all attributes of a product in order to overcome or modify resistance to its acceptance
- To understand the impact of environmental awareness on product decisions

The opportunities and challenges for international marketers of **consumer goods** today have never been greater or more diverse. New consumers are springing forth in emerging markets from Eastern Europe, the Commonwealth of Independent States, China, India, other Asian countries and Latin America – in short, globally.[1] Emerging markets promise to be huge markets in the future.[2] In the more mature markets of the industrialised world, opportunity and challenge also abound as consumers' tastes become more sophisticated and complex, and as increases in purchasing power provide them with the means of satisfying new demands.

Never has the question 'Which products should we sell?' been more critical than it is today. For the company with a domestic-market-extension orientation, the answer generally is, 'Whatever we are selling at home'. The company with a multidomestic-market orientation develops different products to fit the uniqueness of each country market; the global orientation seeks commonalties in needs among sets of country markets and responds with a somewhat global product.

All three strategies are appropriate somewhere but, because of the enormous diversity in international markets, the appropriate strategy for a specific market is determined by the company's resources, the product and the target market. Consequently, each country market must be examined thoroughly or a firm risks marketing poorly conceived products in incorrectly defined markets with an inappropriate marketing effort.[3]

The trend for larger firms is towards becoming global in orientation and strategy. However, product adaptation is as important a task in a smaller firm's marketing effort as it is for global companies. As competition for world markets intensifies and as market preferences become more global, selling what is produced for the domestic market in the same manner as it is sold at home proves to be increasingly less effective. Most products cannot be sold at all in foreign markets without modification; others may be sold as is but their acceptance is greatly enhanced when tailored specifically to market needs. In a competitive struggle, quality products that meet the needs and wants of a market at an affordable price should be the goal of any marketing firm. For some product category groups and some country markets, this means **differentiated products** for each market. Other product groups and country market segments do well competitively with a global or standardised product but, for both, an effective marketing strategy is essential. Even standardised products may have to be sold by different and adapted marketing strategies.

key terms

consumer goods
goods that consumers buy to consume

differentiated products
products that are considered different from other similar products

This chapter explores some of the relevant issues facing an international marketer when planning and developing consumer products for international markets. The questions about product planning and development range from the obvious – which product to sell – to the more complex – when, how and if products should be adapted for different markets.

international markets and product development

There is a recurring debate about product planning and development that focuses on the question of standardised or **global products** marketed worldwide versus differentiated products adapted, or even redesigned, for each culturally unique market. One extreme position is held by those with strong production and unit-cost orientation who advocate global standardisation, while at the other extreme are those, perhaps more culturally sensitive, who propose a different or adapted product for each market.[4]

Underlying the arguments offered by the proponents of standardised products is the premise that global communications and other worldwide socialising forces have fostered a homogenisation of tastes, needs and values in a significant sector of the population across all cultures. This has resulted in a large global market with similar needs and wants that demands the same reasonably priced products of good quality and reliability.[5]

GOING INTERNATIONAL 13.1

IKEA's new game plan

Ingvar Kamprad, the 71-year-old founder, set up IKEA, an acronym for Ingvar Kamprad Elmtaryd Agunnaryd, in 1943. Elmtaryd is the name of his family's farm and Agunnaryd his village in Sweden. He started selling furniture in the 1950s, with 'well-designed furniture at low prices' as his slogan.

When it opened its first store in the US market (Philadelphia) in 1985, it sold European-size curtains that did not fit American windows. In 1990, it snapped up five stores owned by Store Furnishings International in California. The new stores were a big fiasco and analysts said that IKEA came in with a certain arrogance, without adapting its products or marketing for the American market. So in 1995 and 1996, it shook up its North American operations, shutting two of its 21 stores and slashing office staff. Now it designs about one-third of its products especially for the US market; sofas are firmer and kitchen cabinets are deeper to match American appliances. In 1996, the North American unit turned a profit on $859 million (€775 million) sales.

For the year ending August 1997, IKEA's sales jumped 21 per cent. Although its furniture, toys and housewares are priced from 20 per cent to 30 per cent below rivals, its sales per square metre are three times the industry average and its 8 per cent to 10 per cent pre-tax margin is twice as high.

Now IKEA has launched a big expansion into new products and markets. It is rolling out a major new product line of children's furniture and toys. It is opening up eight new stores from Shanghai to Warsaw, thus going beyond its traditional Western European base. It envisions an IKEA that grabs customers in childhood and holds on to them for life. In the past two decades, IKEA has grown more than tenfold, to 139 stores in 28 countries. Kamprad is still the chief strategy officer and he embodies the company's value and vision. As he hustles to expand his empire, Kamprad is also acting to protect it from his own family. He decided long ago that none of his three sons, although working as IKEA managers, would ever control the company. So he transferred 100 per cent of his IKEA equity to a Dutch-based charitable foundation as an irrevocable gift in 1984. IKEA is valued by the analysts at more than $6 billion (€5.4 billion) or 18 times its earnings of $340 million (€307 million) in 1997.

■ Can IKEA capture the children's toy market? Discuss.

Source: Julia Flynn and Lori Bongiorno, 'IKEA's New Game Plan', *Business Week*, 6 October 1997, pp. 99–100.

In support of this argument, a study found that products targeted for urban markets in less developed countries needed few changes from products sold to urban markets in developed countries: 'Modern products usually fit into lifestyles of urban consumers wherever they are.'[6] Other studies identify a commonality of preferences among population segments across countries. Families in New York need the same dishwashers as families in Paris, and families in Rome make similar demands on a washing machine as do families in London. However, the sizes, colours, voltage requirements, switches and advertising may need to be adapted to each market.

Although recognising some cultural variations, advocates of **standardisation** believe that product standardisation leads to production economies and other savings that permit profits at prices that make a product attractive to the global market. Economies of production, better planning, more effective control and better use of creative managerial personnel are the advantages of standardisation. Such standardisation can result in significant cost savings but it makes sense only when there is adequate demand for the standardised product.

Those who hold the opposing view stress that substantial cultural variation among countries dictates a need for differentiated products to accommodate the uniqueness of cultural norms and product use patterns. For example, Electrolux, the appliance manufacturer, finds the refrigerator market among European countries far from homogeneous. Northern Europeans want large refrigerators because they shop only once a week in supermarkets; Southern Europeans prefer small ones because they pick through open-air markets almost daily. Northerners like their freezers on the bottom, Southerners on top. And Britons, who devour huge quantities of frozen foods, insist on units with 60 per cent freezer space. Further, 100 appliance makers compete for that market. To be competitive, Electrolux alone produces 120 basic designs with 1500 variations. Compare such differences to the relatively homogeneous United States market where most refrigerators are standardised, have freezers on top, and come in only a few sizes, and where 80 per cent are sold by four firms. Can Electrolux standardise its refrigerator line for the European market? Management thinks not, so long as the market remains as it is.[7]

The issue between these two extremes cannot be resolved with a simple either/or decision since the prudent position probably lies somewhere in the middle. Most astute marketers concede that there are definable segments across country markets with some commonality of product preferences, and that substantial efficiencies can be attained by standardising, but they also recognise that there may be cultural differences that remain

key term

standardisation when the same products are produced for many markets

important. The key issue is not whether to adapt or standardise, but how much adaptation is necessary and to what point a product can be standardised.

Most products are adapted, at least to some degree, even those traditionally held up as examples of standardisation. Although the substantial portion of its product is standardised worldwide, McDonald's does not sell beefburgers but includes vegetarian and lamb-burgers in its Indian stores, to accommodate dietary and religious restrictions, and wine and beer in European stores. In Norway, it sells a salmonburger that is not sold in other markets. In Indonesia and the Philippines it sells chicken and rice meals. Pepsi Cola reformulated its diet cola to be sweeter and more syrupy, and changed its name from Diet Pepsi to Pepsi Light and Pepsi Max to appeal to international markets where the idea of 'diet' is often shunned and a sweeter taste is preferred.[8]

Even if different products are necessary to satisfy local needs, as in the case of Electrolux, this does not exclude a standardisation approach. A fully standardised product may not be appropriate, but some efficiencies through standardising some aspects of the product may be achieved. Whirlpool faced this problem when it acquired NV Philips, a division of Philips, the European appliance manufacturer, whose approach to the European market was to make a different product for each country market. Whirlpool found that the Philips German plant produced feature-rich washing machines that sold at higher prices, while washers from the Italian plants ran at lower RPMs and were less costly. Each plant operated independently of the other and they produced **customised products** for their respective markets. The washing machines made in the Italian and German facilities differed so much that 'they did not have one screw in common', yet the reality was that the insides of the machines were very similar. Immediate steps were taken to standardise and simplify both the German and Italian machines by reducing the number of parts and using as many common parts as possible. New products were developed in a way to ensure that a wide variety of models could be built on a standardised platform. The same approach was taken for dryers and other product categories. Although complete standardisation could not be achieved, efficiencies were attained by standardising the platform (the core product) and customising other features to meet local preferences.[9]

As companies gain more experience of the idea of global markets, the approach is likely to be to standardise where possible and adapt where necessary. To benefit from standardisation as much as possible and still provide for local cultural differences, companies are using an approach to product development that allows for such flexibility. The idea is to develop a core platform containing the essential technology, and then base variations on this platform. Sony of Japan has used this approach for its Walkman. The basic Walkman platform gives it the flexibility to rapidly adjust production to shifts in market preference. The Apple iPod is a good example of standardised product, but it uses different marketing channels and strategies in different countries. In the US it is opening its own retail outlets, while in Europe it is sold via distributors.

To differentiate for the sake of differentiation is not a solution, nor is adaptation for the sake of adaptation or standardisation for the sake of standardisation. Realistic business practice requires that a company strives for uniformity in its marketing mix whenever and wherever possible, while recognising that cultural differences may demand some accommodation if the product is to be competitive.[10]

global brands

Hand in hand with global products are global brands. A **global brand** is defined as the worldwide use of a name, term, sign, symbol, design or combination thereof intended to identify goods or services of one seller and to differentiate them from those of competitors. Much like the experience with global products, there is no single answer to the question of whether or not to establish global brands. There is, however, little question of the importance of a brand name.

key terms

customised products
products that are modified for each customer

global brand
the worldwide use of a name, term, sign, symbol, design or combination thereof, to identify goods or services of one seller and differentiate them from those of competitors

GOING INTERNATIONAL 13.2

in Germany, video games showing frontal nudity are OK, but blood is *verboten*

Video game heroine Lara Croft is an adrenaline junkie unafraid of getting bloody. But in Germany, the buxom starlet of the 'Tomb Raider' series doesn't bleed – even if she's being mauled by a tiger.

Although the $25-billion video game industry is global, the games themselves aren't.

They reflect the distinct cultures and traditions of different markets, and game publishers carefully tweak their titles and other details to tone down offensive materials. And 'offensive' varies from country to country.

Red blood in a game sold in the United States turns green in Australia. A topless character in a European title acquires a bikini in the United States. Human enemies in an American game are changed into robots in Germany. Violent sex scenes in a Japanese game disappear in the American version.

Of all countries, Germany is one of the trickiest to tackle, publishers say. The country spent five decades developing one of the world's strictest decency standards for virtually all media, from books and comics to music and games.

If a game features blood splatterings, decapitations or death cries, it runs the risk of being placed on a government list known as 'the index'. Being indexed means it can't be sold to anyone under 18, displayed in stores or advertised on television, in newspapers, or in magazines. Games containing pornography or glorifications of war, Nazism and racial hatred face the same fate. The scariest part of this story is not the games themselves, but the newest use of them as political tools. One game indexed in Germany involves a prisoner of war camp for Turkish detainees. On the other side, Hizbollah, the terrorist organisation best known for killing 240 American marines in Lebanon in 1983, also published a new 'click-and-kill' game. When are such games more than just entertainment?

Sources: A. Phan, S. Sandell, 'Germany, Video Games Showing Frontal Nudity are OK, but Blood is *Verboten*', *Los Angeles Times*, 9 June 2003, p. C1; and 'Jihad in Cyperspace in Hizbollah's New Video Game', *The Economist*, 15 March 2003, p. 42.

A successful brand is the most valuable resource a company has. The brand name encompasses the years of advertising, good will, quality evaluation, product experience and the other beneficial attributes the market associates with the product. The value of Philips, Kodak, Sony, Coca-Cola, McDonald's, Nike, Adidas, Toyota and Shell is indisputable. One estimate of the value of 112-year-old Coca-Cola, the world's most valuable brand, places it at over $67 billion, Microsoft at over $60 billion and Nokia at over $24 billion.[11]

Naturally, companies with such strong brands strive to use those brands globally. Even for products that must be adapted to local market conditions, a global brand can be used successfully. Philips produces several models of TVs and vacuum cleaners for different markets using the same brand name. Toyota markets several models in different countries using the same brand names. And Sony is, of course, a global brand.

A global brand generally means substantial cost savings and gives a company a uniform worldwide image that enhances efficiency and cost savings when introducing other products associated with the brand name, but not all companies believe a global approach is

GOING INTERNATIONAL 13.3

local brands giving tough time to global brands

Domestic companies in emerging markets are developing their
own brands to dominate both at home and abroad.

In China billion-dollar companies are emerging with brands in
a number of industries (see the table below). The experts say it is
just the beginning. However, brand awareness of Chinese brands
in the US and Europe is rather low. But China's huge domestic
market provides these companies with a fierce battleground and
the opportunity to emerge as formidably competitive. According
to McKinsey and Co, 'There is no doubt that world-class Chinese
brands will emerge.' The following brands are already winners:

The new QQ car
model from
Chinese car
company Chery.
© Kevin
Lee/Bloomberg
news/Landov

Brand	Revenues ($ million)	Profit ($ million)	Slogan
Haier (Appliances, TVs)	9750	193	Honest and trustworthy for ever
Lenova (Computers)	3000	128	Innovation and excellence
TCL (TVs, mobile phones)	3400	163	Technology that caters for you
WAHAHA (Beverages)	1230	196	Youth knows no failure
Gome (Electronics)	2150	151	Wherever we are needed, we are there
Geely (Cars)	484	58	A happy life comes with Geely
Bird (Mobile phones)	1300	42.3	The fighter plane of mobile phones
Tsingtao (Beer)	907	31	Enthusiasm everywhere
Li-ning (Clothing, shoes)	121	11	Anything is possible
Yongheking (Fast food)	36	0.386	Delicious food, new concept

■ Do you think these brands will be as successful abroad as they are at home? What do
you think is the success factor for these brands?

Source: compiled from *Business Week*, Cover Story: 'China's Powerful Brands', 8 November 2004, pp.
44–50.

the best. Except for companies such as Philips, Kodak, Coca-Cola, Caterpillar, Sony and
Levi's, which use the same brands worldwide, other multinationals such as Nestlé, Mars,
Procter & Gamble, Unilever and Gillette have some brands that are promoted worldwide
and others that are country specific. Unilever never uses the name 'Unilever' for any of its
products. Among companies that have faced the question of whether or not to make all
their brands global, not all have followed the same path.

Companies that already have successful **country-specific brand** names must balance
the benefits of a global brand against the risk of losing the benefits of an established
brand. The cost of re-establishing the same level of brand preference and market share for
the global brand that the local brand had must be offset against the long-term cost savings
and benefits of having only one brand name worldwide.

key term

**country-specific
brand**
a brand that is
sold in only one
country

A different strategy is followed by Nestlé, which has a stable of global and country-specific brands in its product line. The Nestlé name itself is promoted globally but its global brand expansion strategy is two-pronged. It acquires well-established local brands when it can and builds on their strengths; in other markets where there are no strong brands it can acquire, it uses global brand names. The company is described as preferring brands to be local, people regional and technology global. It does, however, own some of the world's largest global brands; Nescafé is but one (see Exhibit 13.1).

Exhibit 13.1 Nestlé's branding strategy

Level 1	10 worldwide corporate brands	*For example*: Nestlé; Carnation; Buitoni; Maggi; Perrier
Level 2	45 worldwide strategic brands	*For example:* Kit-Kat; Polo; Cerelac; Baci; Mighty Dog; Smarties; After Eight; Coffee-Mate
Level 3	140 regional strategic brands	*For example:* Mackintosh; Vittel; Contadina; Stouffer's; Herta; Alpo; Findus
Level 4	7500 local brands	*For example:* Texicana; Brigadeiro; Rocky; Solis

Source: based on Andrew Parsons, 'Nestlé: The Visions of Local Managers', An Interview with Peter Brabeck-Letmathe, CEO Nestlé', *The McKinsey Quarterly*, 2 November 1996, pp. 5–29.

Unilever is another company that follows a similar strategy of a mix of local and global brands. In Poland, Unilever introduced its Omo brand detergent (sold in many other countries), but it also purchased a local brand, Pollena 2000. Despite a strong introduction of two competing brands, Omo by Unilever and Ariel by Procter & Gamble, a refurbished Pollena 2000 had the largest market share a year later. Unilever's explanation was that Eastern European consumers are wary of new brands; they want brands that are affordable and in keeping with their own tastes and values. Pollena 2000 is successful not just because it is cheaper but because it chimes with local values.[12] More recently, Unilever has decided to focus on fewer brands, and has cut the number of brands from 1600 to 400 in its hygiene product group.

country-of-origin effect and global brands

As discussed earlier, brands are used as external cues to taste, design, performance, quality, value, prestige and so forth. In other words, the consumer associates the value of the product with the brand. The brand can convey either a positive or a negative message about the product to the consumer and is affected by past advertising and promotion, product reputation and product evaluation and experience. In short, many factors affect brand image, and one factor that is of great concern to multinational companies that manufacture worldwide is the **country-of-origin effect (COE)** on the market's perception of the product.[13]

Country-of-origin effect can be defined as any influence that the country of manufacture has on a consumer's positive or negative perception of a product. Today a company competing in global markets will manufacture products worldwide and, when the customer is aware of the country of origin, there is the possibility that the place of manufacture will affect product/brand image.

The country, the type of product and the image of the company and its brands all influence whether or not the country of origin will engender a positive or negative reaction. There are a variety of generalisations that can be made about country-of-origin effects on products and brands. Consumers tend to have stereotypes about products and countries that have been formed by experience, hearsay and myth. We will now look at some of the more frequently cited generalisations.

Consumers have broad but somewhat vague stereotypes about specific countries and specific product categories that they judge 'best': English tea, French fashion garments

key term

country-of-origin effect (COE)
influence of country of manufacture on a consumer's positive or negative perception of a product

and perfumes, Chinese silk, Italian leather, Japanese electronics, Jamaican rum, and so on. Stereotyping of this nature is typically product specific and may not extend to other categories of products from these countries.

GOING INTERNATIONAL 13.4

new products challenging the imperialists

Boycotts are often used to demonstrate disapproval of policies at all levels. When France did not support the Iraq War, the US administration and consumers openly boycotted French products. No official party was to serve French wine and French cheese. French fries were renamed freedom fries. After the war on Iraq, Muslim consumers in many countries also started boycotting American products. Some companies/entrepreneurs detected the opportunity and started providing alternatives. Mecca-Cola is perhaps the most famous example. Introduced by a French-Tunisian businessman in France, it targets consumers who do not want 'coca-colonisation' and those who want to boycott American products due to its foreign policy or any other reason.

Mecca-Cola has been a big success; the launch in the British market was delayed twice as the manufacturing capacity could not cope with the excessive demand all over Europe.

The market for political food goes beyond fizzy drinks. Those moved by the plight of Palestinian farmers can now buy 'Zayton olive oil', harvested from the West Bank. The demand, according to importers, has been enormous; the first two shipments were pre-sold to distributors and shops.

Source: compiled from: *The Economist*, 'Political Food: Mullah Moolah', 30 October 2004, p. 37.

Ethnocentrism can also have country-of-origin effects; feelings of national pride – the 'buy American' effect, for example – can influence attitudes towards foreign products. Honda, which manufactures one of its models almost entirely in the United States, recognises this phenomenon and points out how many component parts are made in America in some of its advertisements. On the other hand, others have a stereotype of Japan as producing the 'best' cars. A recent study found that US car producers may suffer comparatively tarnished in-country images regardless of whether they actually produce superior products.[14]

Countries are also stereotyped on the basis of whether they are industrialised, or in emerging or less developed economies. These stereotypes are less country-product specific; they are more a perception of the quality of goods in general produced within the country. Industrialised countries have the highest quality image, and there is generally a bias against products from developing countries. However, within countries grouped by economic development there are variations of image. For example, one study of COE between Mexico and Taiwan found that a microwave oven manufactured in Mexico was perceived as significantly more risky than an oven made in Taiwan. However, for jeans there was no difference in perception between the two countries.[15]

One might generalise that the more technical the product, the less positive is the perception of one manufactured in a less developed country. There is also the tendency to favour **foreign-made products** over **domestic-made products** in less developed countries. Not all foreign products fare equally well because consumers in developing countries have

key terms

foreign-made products
those products made in a different country from the one they are being sold in

domestic-made products
those products sold in the country in which they were made

stereotypes about the quality of foreign-made products even from industrialised countries. A survey of consumers in the Czech Republic found that 72 per cent of Japanese products were considered to be of the highest quality, German goods followed with 51 per cent, Swiss goods with 48 per cent, Czech goods with 32 per cent and, last, the United States with 29 per cent.[16]

One final generalisation about COE involves fads that often surround products from particular countries or regions in the world. These fads are most often product specific and generally involve goods that are themselves faddish in nature. European consumers are apparently enamoured with a host of American-made products ranging from Jeep Cherokees to Bose sound systems.[17] In the 1970s and 1980s, there was a backlash against anything American, but in the 1990s American was in. In China, anything Western seems to be the fad. If it is Western, it is in demand, even at prices three or four times higher than domestic products.[18] In most cases, such fads wane after a few years as some new fad takes over.

Country stereotyping can be overcome with good marketing. The image of Korean electronics improved substantially in Western countries once the market gained positive experience with Korean brands. All of which stresses the importance of building strong global brands like Sony, General Electric, Samsung and Levi's. Brands effectively advertised and products properly positioned can help ameliorate a less than positive country stereotype. Consumers perceive **pioneering brands** more positively than **follower brands**, irrespective of COE. Apple's iPod is a good example.[19]

own brands

Growing as challenges to manufacturers' brands, whether global or country-specific, are brands owned by retailers. In the food-retailing sector in Britain, the Netherlands and many European countries, manufacturers' brands are increasingly confronted by brands owned by national retailers. From blackberry jam, coffee, tea and vacuum-cleaner bags to smoked salmon and sun-dried tomatoes, **own brand** products dominate grocery stores in Britain and in many of the hypermarkets of Europe. It is estimated that own-brand products have captured nearly 30 per cent of the British and Swiss markets, and more than 20 per cent of the French and German markets. In some European markets, own-brand market share has doubled in just the past five years.

Sainsbury's, for example, one of Britain's largest grocery retailers with 420 stores, reserves the best shelf space for its own brands. A typical Sainsbury's store has about 16 000 products, of which 8000 are Sainsbury's own brands. The company avidly develops new products, launching 1400 to 1500 new own-brand items each year, and weeds out hundreds of others that are no longer popular. It launched its own Novon-brand laundry detergent and, in the first year, its sales climbed past Procter & Gamble's and Unilever's top brands to make it the top-selling detergent in Sainsbury's stores and the second-best seller nationally with a 30 per cent market share.[20] The 15 per cent margin on own-brand labels that chains such as Sainsbury boast about helps explain why their operating profit margins are as high as 8 per cent, or eight times the profit margins of their US counterparts.

Own-brand penetration has traditionally been high in Britain and, more recently, high in Europe as well. Own brands, with their high margins, will become even more important as the trend in consolidation of retailers continues and as discounters such as Ahold of the Netherlands, Aldi of Germany, Wal-Mart of the United States and Carréfour of France expand throughout Europe, putting greater pressure on prices.

As it stands now, own brands are formidable competitors. They provide the retailer with high margins, they receive preferential shelf space and strong in-store promotion and, perhaps most important for consumer appeal, they are quality products at low prices. Contrast this with manufacturers' brands, which are traditionally premium priced and offer the retailer lower margins than they get from their own brands. Exhibit 13.2 shows the market share and growth rate for own brands.

Exhibit 13.2 Market share and growth rate for own brands

	Market share (%)	Growth rate (annual % 2003)
Global	15	4
Europe	22	6
North America	16	0
Asia Pacific	4	14
Emerging markets	4	48
Latin America	1	16

Source: compiled from Gary Silverman, 'Retailers Pack New Punch in Battle with Brands', *Financial Times*, 15 November 2004, p. 20.

To maintain market share, global brands will have to be priced competitively and provide real consumer value. Global marketers must examine the adequacy of their brand strategies in the light of such competition. This may make the cost and efficiency benefits of global brands even more appealing.

products and culture

To appreciate the complexity of standardised versus adapted products, one needs to understand how cultural influences are interwoven with the perceived value and importance a market places on a product. A product is more than a physical item; it is a bundle of satisfactions (or utilities) the buyer receives. This includes its form, taste, colour, odour and texture, how it functions in use, the package, the label, the warranty, manufacturer's and retailer's servicing, the confidence or prestige enjoyed by the brand, the manufacturer's reputation, the country of origin and any other symbolic utility received from the possession or use of the goods. In short, the market relates to more than a product's physical form and primary function (see Exhibit 13.3).

Its **physical attributes** generally are required to create the primary function of the product. The primary function of a car, for example, is to move passengers from point A to point B. This ability requires an engine, transmission and other physical features to achieve its primary purpose. The physical features and primary function of a car are generally in demand in all cultures where there is a desire to move from one point to another, other than on foot or by animal power. Few changes to the physical attributes of a product are

key term

physical attributes physical characteristics of a product

Exhibit 13.3 Factors influencing international product decisions

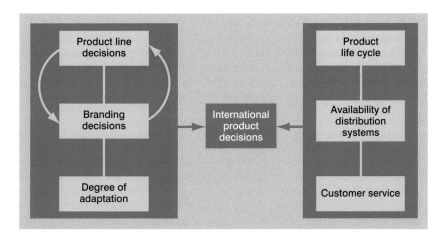

required when moving from one culture to another. However, a car has a bundle of psychological features as important in providing consumer satisfaction as its physical features. Within a specific culture, other features (colour, size, design, brand name) have little to do with the car's primary function, the movement from point A to B, but do add value to the satisfaction received.

The meaning and value imputed to the psychological attributes of a product can vary among cultures and are perceived as negative or positive. To maximise the bundle of satisfactions received and to create positive product attributes rather than negative ones, adaptation of the **non-physical features** of a product may be necessary.

Coca-Cola, frequently touted as a global product, found it had to change Diet Coke to Coke Light when it was introduced in Japan and a number of European countries. Japanese women do not like to admit to dieting and, further, the idea of diet implies sickness or medicine. This also applies in some European countries. So, instead of emphasising weight loss, 'figure maintenance' is stressed.

The adoption of some products by consumers can be affected as much by how the product concept conflicts with norms, values and behaviour patterns as by its physical or mechanical attributes. As one authority states:

> In short, it is not just lack of money, nor even differences in the natural environment, that constitutes major barriers to the acceptance of new products and new ways of behaving. A novelty always comes up against a closely integrated cultural pattern, and it is primarily this that determines whether, when, how and in what form it gets adopted. The Japanese have always found all body jewellery repugnant. The Scots have a decided resistance to pork and all its associated products, apparently from days long ago when such taboos were decided by fundamentalist interpretations of the Bible.[21]

When analysing a product for a second market, the extent of adaptation required depends on cultural differences in product use and perception between the market the product was originally developed for and the new market. The greater these cultural differences between the two markets, the greater the extent of adaptation necessary.

An example of this involves an undisputed American leader in cake mixes, which tacitly admitted failure in the English market by closing down operations after five unsuccessful years. Taking its most successful mixes in the US market, the company introduced them into the British market. A considerable amount of time, money and effort was expended to introduce its variety of cake mixes to this new market. Hindsight provides several probable causes for the company's failure. The British eat most of their cake with tea instead of dinner and have always preferred dry sponge cake, which is easy to handle; the fancy, iced cakes favoured in the United States were the type introduced. Fancy, iced cakes are accepted in Britain, but they are considered extra special and purchased from a bakery or made with much effort and care at home. Homemakers felt guilty about not even cracking an egg, and there was suspicion that dried eggs and milk were not as good as fresh ones. Therefore, when the occasion called for a fancy cake, an easy cake mix was simply not good enough.

When instant cake mixes were introduced in Japan, consumers' response was less than enthusiastic. Not only do Japanese reserve cakes for special occasions, they prefer them to be beautifully wrapped and purchased in pastry shops. The acceptance of instant cakes was further complicated by another cultural difference – most Japanese homes do not have ovens.

innovative products and adaptation

An important first step in adapting a product to a foreign market is to determine the degree of newness perceived by the intended market. How people react to newness and how new a product is to a market must be understood. In evaluating the newness of a product, the international marketer must be aware that many products successful in Western countries, having reached the maturity or even decline stage in their life cycles,

---

key term

non-physical features characteristics of a product that are not physical but perceptional

GOING INTERNATIONAL 13.5

why Coca-Cola became so popular

When Atlanta pharmacist John Pemberton invented Coca-Cola in 1886, he named it that
for a reason. His 'brain tonic' included extracts of the kola nut, a high-caffeine stimulant
thought to be an aphrodisiac, and coca leaf extract, containing a small
amount of cocaine. It's been a hundred years since Coke included that particular ingredient.

Before Coca-Cola, Pemberton had created a version of coca wine, a
popular cocaine-laced beverage endorsed by Queen Victoria and Pope Leo
XIII. In his new cola beverage, he eliminated alcohol in a nod to the temper-
ance movement but kept the coca extract. When pharmacies began mixing
his syrup with carbonated water, sales bubbled up.

In the late nineteenth century cocaine was hailed as a painkilling breakthrough and found in dozens of products, from throat lozenges to suppositories. But public concern began to grow about its safety, and by 1904
Coca-Cola was completely 'decocainised' (though coca extract, with all traces
of the drug removed, remains an ingredient to this day).

Despite the omission, Coke's popularity continued to rise, owing in part to
a successful promotion campaign. Growing suspicious of the drink's success,
officials at the US Bureau of Chemistry (precursor to the Food and Drug
Administration) had a shipment of Coke syrup seized in Chattanooga, Tennessee, in
1909. The product, they charged, violated the Pure Food and Drug Act of 1906, prohibiting sale of 'adulterated or misbranded' foods. The 'adulterating' chemical: caffeine. The
government lost its case.

Source: M.G. Zackowitz, 'More Than Just a Sugar Buzz', *National Geographic*, October 2004, p. 4.

---

may be perceived as new in another country or culture and, thus, must be treated as innovations. A new product would therefore demand a different type of marketing strategy
than the one used at home for a rather mature product.

Whether or not a group accepts an **innovation**, and the time it takes, depends on its
characteristics. Products new to a social system are innovations, and knowledge about the
diffusion (i.e. the process by which innovation spreads) of innovation is helpful in developing a successful product strategy.

Another US cake mix company entered the British market but carefully eliminated most
of the newness of the product. Instead of introducing the most popular American cake
mixes, the company asked 500 British housewives to bake their favourite cake. Since the
majority baked a simple, very popular dry sponge cake, the company brought to the
market a similar easy mix. The sponge cake mix represented familiar tastes and habits that
could be translated into a convenience item, and did not infringe on the emotional aspects
of preparing a fancy product for special occasions. Consequently, after a short period of
time, the second company's product gained 30 to 35 per cent of the British cake-mix
market. Once the idea of a mix for sponge cake was acceptable, the introduction of other
flavours became easier.

The goal of a foreign marketer is to gain product acceptance by the largest number of
consumers in the market in the shortest span of time. However, as many of the examples
cited have illustrated, new products are not always readily accepted by a culture; indeed,
they often meet resistance. Although they may ultimately be accepted, the time it takes for
a culture to learn new ways, to learn to accept a new product, are of critical importance to
the marketer since planning reflects a time frame for investment and profitability.

key term

innovation
new product/
technology/
method

319

GOING INTERNATIONAL 13.6

Europe's luxury brands are digging for gold in Asia

Japanese consumers are the most affluent in Asia and the most finicky about quality and service. But, if won, the Japanese clientele can be most rewarding. Few luxury brands disclose their country-specific sales figures, but retail analysts in Japan estimate 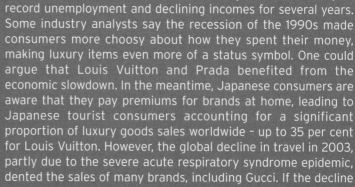 that the leading luxury brands make 15–25 per cent of their global sales there. For Louis Vuitton, part of the LVMH empire, the figure is as high as 30 per cent. Merrill Lynch estimates that 21 per cent of Bulgari's sales are to Japan, making it the Italian accessory-maker's largest single market.

Japanese women have chased designer brands despite record unemployment and declining incomes for several years. Some industry analysts say the recession of the 1990s made consumers more choosy about how they spent their money, making luxury items even more of a status symbol. One could argue that Louis Vuitton and Prada benefited from the economic slowdown. In the meantime, Japanese consumers are aware that they pay premiums for brands at home, leading to Japanese tourist consumers accounting for a significant proportion of luxury goods sales worldwide – up to 35 per cent for Louis Vuitton. However, the global decline in travel in 2003, partly due to the severe acute respiratory syndrome epidemic, dented the sales of many brands, including Gucci. If the decline

The Louis Vuitton store in the Ginza district of Tokyo
With thanks to Louis Vuitton

in overseas travel continues it may bolster sales in Japan, but undermine sales elsewhere, particularly in Hawaii and France, two hotspots for Japanese in need of high-end retail therapy.

At the same time as Japan is seeming to approach saturation point, European brands such as Gucci and Louis Vuitton are increasingly looking to China, predicting that in 15 years the Chinese traveller will be more important for the luxury goods market than the Japanese traveller. Chinese consumers are already Louis Vuitton's fifth largest clientele group worldwide. Gucci Group is looking at China as its main engine of growth in the next decades for two of its brands, Gucci and Yves Saint Laurent. In 2004, the company is planning to open two Gucci stores outside Beijing and Shanghai in Chengdu and Hangzhou.

■ Do you think Asians will keep on buying global brands or will they turn over to local brands (see also Going International 13.3)?

Source: compiled from 'A Japanese Obsession Spreads Across Asia', *Financial Times*, 12 December 2003, p. 14; and Mackay, A. 'Asia Becomes Gucci's Main Engine of Growth', *Financial Times*, 23 September 2003, p. 19.

diffusion of innovations

There is ample evidence of the fact that product innovations have a varying rate of acceptance. Some diffuse from introduction to widespread use in a few years, others take decades. Microwave ovens, introduced in the 1950s, reached widespread acceptance in the 1980s. The contraceptive pill was introduced during that same period and gained acceptance several years later. There is also a growing body of evidence that the understanding of diffusion theory may provide ways in which the process of diffusion can be accelerated. Knowledge of this process may provide the foreign marketer with

GOING INTERNATIONAL 13.7

new products for better hygiene

Japanese companies are very active in developing new products – the Sony Walkman, PlayStation and Toyota Prius are not the only ones. In developing new types of toilet, they are competing with Dutch manufacturers.

Japan's abundance of water has allowed it to focus on cleanliness, frequent bathing and high-tech bathrooms. Matsushita's toilets read your body temperature and blood pressure. It will soon be able to tell you about glucose and protein levels in your urine. The toilet also washes and dries your bottom.

The Dutch, on the other hand, are worried about using too much water, as most of their country is below sea level. They do not want to throw too much water into the ground. Sphinx in Maastricht has developed a urinal for women that reduces the usage of water, and a fly embedded in the porcelain for its men's urinal. The latter reduces maintenance costs as the company's research has shown that most men will aim for the fly, which is strategically placed to minimise splash. These Dutch innovations can be seen at Schiphol Airport in Amsterdam.

Source: compiled from several sources.

key terms

rate of diffusion
speed at which a product spreads out in a specific area

congruent innovation
when the product concept is accepted by the culture; the innovativeness is typically one of introducing variety and quality, or functional features or style

continuous innovation
usually alteration of a product rather than creation of a new one

the ability to assess the time it takes for a product to diffuse – before it is necessary to make a financial commitment.

At least three extraneous variables affect the **rate of diffusion** of an object: the degree of perceived newness, the perceived attributes of the innovation, and the method used to communicate the idea. Each variable has a bearing on consumer reaction to a new product and the time needed for acceptance. An understanding of these variables can produce better product strategies for the international marketer.

degree of newness
As perceived by the market, varying degrees of newness categorise all new products. Within each category, myriad reactions affect the rate of diffusion. In giving a name to these categories, one might think of (1) congruent innovations, (2) continuous innovations, (3) dynamically continuous innovations and (4) discontinuous innovations.

1 A **congruent innovation** is actually not an innovation at all because it causes absolutely no disruption of established consumption patterns. The product concept is accepted by the culture and the innovativeness is typically one of introducing variety and quality or functional features, style or perhaps an exact duplicate of an already existing product – exact in the sense that the market perceives no newness, such as cane sugar versus beet sugar.

2 A **continuous innovation** has the least disruptive influence on established consumption patterns. Alteration of a product is almost always involved rather than the creation of a new product. Generally, the alterations result in better use patterns – perceived improvement in the satisfaction derived from its use. Examples include fluoride toothpaste, disposable razors and flavours in coffee. A continuous improvement in Gillette and Wilkinson Sword razors is another example.

3 A **dynamically continuous innovation** has more disruptive effects than a continuous innovation, although it generally does not involve new consumption patterns. It may

mean the creation of a new product or considerable alteration of an existing one designed to fulfil new needs arising from changes in lifestyles or new expectations brought about by change. It is generally disruptive and therefore resisted because old patterns of behaviour must change if consumers are to accept and perceive the value of the dynamically continuous innovation. Examples include electric toothbrushes, electric hair-curlers, central air-conditioning and frozen dinners.

4 A **discontinuous innovation** involves the establishment of new consumption patterns and the creation of previously unknown products. It introduces an idea or behaviour pattern where there was none before. Examples include television, the computer, the fax machine, the electric car and microwave ovens.

GOING INTERNATIONAL 13.8

new products in the auto industry

Toyota Prius - 2005 European Car of the Year
Issued 11/2004

Toyota launched its hybrid car, the Toyota Prius, in 2001 and sold 15 556 models in the first year. In 2005 it is expected to sell more than 100 000. The Prius cuts fuel consumption by combining an electric motor with a gas engine. It is not only cheaper to run but also environmentally friendly as compared to other autos.

Now Toyota is moving its hybrid technology to its main product lines. First it is being incorporated in Lexus models (RX SUVs); the Camry is next in line, which is America's best-selling car. Honda has also started using the technology in its Civics and Accord models. The American auto industry is, however, far behind. In the age of high gas/oil prices, it is expected that hybrid autos will capture 20 per cent of the US car market. This will allow Toyota and Honda to achieve economies of scale, and means that customers will not have to pay any extra for the new technology. Both companies are focusing on power and luxury to attract more customers: the Toyota Highlander SUV features 270 horsepower and a better economy than a normal compact sedan.

Ford is the only American auto-maker to launch a hybrid SUV, the Ford Escape; but, in applying the technology as a strategy, it is far behind. Land Rover, now a Ford brand, is next in line for the hybrid technology.

Source: Business Week, 'How Hybrids are Going Mainstream', 1 November 2004, p. 37.

key terms

discontinuous innovation
Introduces an idea or behaviour that wasn't present before

dynamically continuous innovation
this may mean the creation of a new product or considerable alteration of an existing one

The extent of a product's diffusion and its rate of diffusion are partly functions of the particular product's attributes. Each innovation has characteristics by which it can be described, and each person's perception of these characteristics can be utilised in explaining the differences in perceived newness of an innovation. These attributes can also be utilised in predicting the rate of adoption, and the adjustment of these attributes, or product adaptation can lead to changes in consumer perception and thus to altered rates of diffusion. Emphasis given to product adaptation for local cultural norms and the overall brand image created are critical marketing decision areas. Due to these adaptation issues, more and more products/brands are being developed in emerging markets. These brands and innovations are more adapted to local needs and demands (see Exhibit 13.4).

Exhibit 13.4 The world's rising innovation hotspots

Country	US patents 1993	1994	R&D spending ($ billion)	Science and engineering graduates	Strengths
India	30	354	10	316 000	Software, drugs and chips
China	60	366	1.2	337 000	Engineering, computers, graphics software
Russia	62	268	1.2	216 000	Aerospace, software, laser optics, energy and chemistry
Singapore	39	438	2.2	5 600	Broadband, computing, biotech, computer peripherals
Taiwan	62	5 300	2.3	4 900	Chips, PCs, multimedia devices and network equipment
South Korea	764	3 952	2.9	9 700	Digital displays, chips, computer games, wireless telecom and broadband

Source: compiled from Steve Hamm, 'Tech's Future', Cover Story, *Business Week*, 27 September 2004, pp. 52–9.

GOING INTERNATIONAL 13.9

can iPod keep leading the brand?

Apple's continued innovation strategy has paid off: it is expanding its chain of retail stores and capturing huge markets for its add-ons and accessories. In October 2004, it launched the iPod Photo, at the same time launching a special black and red version of the iPod, marketed using rock band U2. It seems the Apple can go on to out-innovate its rivals for a long time to come.

History is, however, against this notion, and 'everything that goes up – comes down'. Just look at brands such as Psion handhelds, Palm PDAs, Nintendo game consoles and Apple's own PCs. Rivals are working hard to challenge iPods: Sony, with its Sony network Walkman; Dell, with its Pocket DJ; Zen micro, with its creative Zen micro; as well as companies such as Samsung and Microsoft getting set to take the iPod lead away from Apple.

At the moment, however, iPod is doing fine, and even more so with its accessories costing $10 to $300. BMW (US) has sold 12 000 adapters to integrate the iPod into its sound systems. The new iPod Photo at a price of $600 and sound-dock iPod speakers by Bose are attracting a lot of high-end customers. iPod Photo can also be hooked up to computers or televisions. The company is now facing a tough choice: should it keep iPod's proprietary system closed, only for Apple, or would it be better to keep the lead by licensing its technology to newcomers?

■ Could you help Apple to make this decision? Explain.

Source: compiled from *Business Week*, 'Assault on the iPod' (p. 74) and 'Can the iPod Keep Leading the Brand?' 8 November 2004, p. 81.

key term

mandatory requirements
requirements that a company must meet

physical or mandatory requirements and adaptation

A product may have to change in a number of ways to meet the physical or **mandatory requirements** of a new market; these can range from simple package changes to total redesign of the physical core product. Some changes are obvious with relatively little analysis; a cursory examination of a country will uncover the need to rewire electrical goods for a different voltage system, simplify a product when the local level of technology is not high, or print multilingual labels where required by law. Electrolux, for example, offers a cold-wash-only washing machine in Asian countries in which electric power is expensive or scarce.[22]

Legal, economic, technological and climatic requirements of the local marketplace often dictate product adaptation. Specific package sizes and safety and quality standards are usually set by laws that vary among countries. To make a purchase more affordable in low-income countries, the number of units per package may have to be reduced from the typical quantities offered in high-income countries. Razor blades, cigarettes, chewing gum and other multiple-pack items are often sold singly or two to a pack instead of the more customary 10 or 20.

Changes may also have to be made to accommodate climatic differences. General Motors of Canada, for example, experienced major problems with several thousand Chevrolet cars shipped to a Middle East country; it was quickly discovered they were unfit for the hot, dusty climate. Supplementary air filters and different clutches had to be added to adjust for the problem. Even peanuts and crackers have to be packaged in tins for humid areas.

The less economically developed a market is, the greater degree of change a product may need for acceptance. One study found only 1 in 10 products could be marketed in developing countries without modification of some sort. Of the modifications made, nearly 25 per cent were mandatory; the other modifications were made to accommodate variations in cultures.[23]

product life cycle and adaptation

Even between markets with few cultural differences, substantial adaptation could be necessary if the product is in a different stage of its life cycle in each market. Product life cycle and the marketing mix are interrelated; a product in a mature stage of its life cycle in one market can have unwanted and/or unknown attributes in a market where the product is perceived as new and thus in its introductory stage. Marketing history is replete with examples of mature products in one market being introduced in another and failing (see Exhibit 13.5).

Certainly an important approach in analysing products for foreign markets is determining the stage of the product's life cycle. All subsequent marketing plans must then include adaptations necessary to correspond to the stage of the product life cycle in the new market.

The success of these alternatives depends on the product and the fundamental need it fulfils, its characteristics, its perception within the culture and the associated costs of each programme. To know that foreign markets are different and that different product strategies may be needed is one thing; to know when adaptation of your product line and marketing programme is necessary is another and more complicated problem.

screening products for adaptation

Evaluating a product for marketing in another country requires a systematic method of screening products to determine if there are cultural resistances to overcome and/or physical or mandatory changes necessary for product acceptance. Only when the psychological (or cultural) and physical dimensions of the product, as determined by the country market, are known can the decision for adaptation be made. Products can be screened on two

Exhibit 13.5 Life cycle for products in international markets

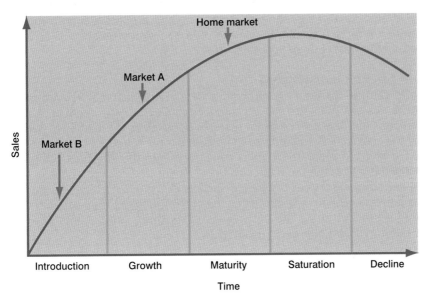

different bases by using 'analysis of characteristics of innovations' to determine if there
are cultural-perceptual reasons why a product will be better accepted if adapted, and/or
'analysis of product components' to determine if there are mandatory or physical reasons
why a product must be adapted.

analysis of characteristics of innovations

Attributes of a product that cause **market resistance** to its acceptance and affect the rate
of acceptance can be determined if a product is analysed by the five characteristics of an
innovation:

1 relative advantage – the perceived marginal value of the new product relative to the
   old
2 compatibility – its compatibility with acceptable behaviour, norms, values, and so
   forth
3 complexity – the degree of complexity associated with product use
4 trialability – the degree of economic and/or social risk associated with product use,
   and
5 observability – the ease with which the product benefits can be communicated.[24]

In general, it can be postulated that the rate of diffusion is positively related to relative
advantage, compatibility, trialability and observability, but negatively related to complexity.

The evaluator must remember it is the perception of product characteristics by the
potential adopter, not the marketer, that is crucial to the evaluation. A market analyst's
self-reference criterion may cause a perceptual bias when interpreting the characteristics
of a product. Thus, instead of evaluating product characteristics from the foreign user's
frame of reference, it is analysed from the marketer's frame of reference, leading to a
misinterpretation of the cultural importance.

Once the analysis has been made, some of the perceived newness or cause for resistance can be minimised through adroit marketing. The more congruent with current
cultural values the perceptions of the product can be, the less the probable resistance and
the more rapid the diffusion or acceptance of the product. A product can frequently be
modified physically to improve its relative advantage over competing products, enhance its

key term

**market
resistance**
when customers
are reluctant to
accept a new
product/service

compatibility with cultural values and even minimise its complexity. Its relative advantage and compatibility can also be enhanced and some degree of complexity lessened through advertising efforts. Small sizes, samples, packaging and product demonstrations are all sales promotion efforts that can be used to alter the characteristics of an innovative product and accelerate its rate of adoption.

analysis of product components

In addition to cultural resistance to product acceptance, which may require adaptation, physical attributes can influence the acceptance or rejection of a product. A product is multidimensional, and the sum of all its features determines the bundle of satisfactions received by the consumer. To identify all the possible ways a product may be adapted to a new market, it helps to separate its many dimensions into three distinct components, as illustrated in Exhibit 13.6, the product component model. The core component, packaging component and support services component include all a product's tangible and intangible elements and provide the bundle of utilities the market receives from use of the product. By analysing a product along the dimensions of its three components, the marketer focuses on different levels of product adaptation.

The Core Component   This component consists of the physical product – the platform that contains the essential technology – and all its design and functional features. It is on the product platform that product variations can be added or deleted to satisfy local differences. Major adjustments in the platform aspect of the core component may be costly because a change in the platform can affect product processes and thus require additional capital investment. However, alterations in design, functional features, flavours,

Exhibit 13.6 Product component model

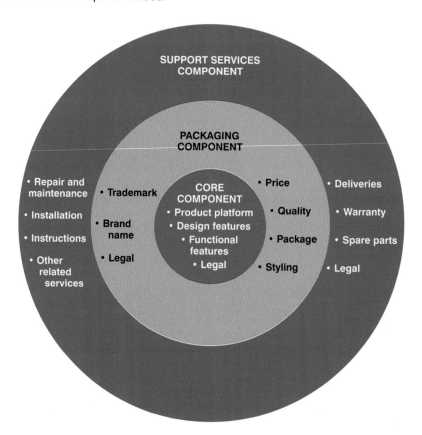

colour and other aspects can be made to adapt the product to cultural variations. In Japan, both Nestlé and Kellogg's sold the same kind of Corn Flakes and Sugar Pops that they sold in Western countries, but Japanese children ate them mostly as snacks instead of for breakfast. In order to move its product into the large breakfast market, Nestlé reformulated its cereals to fit Japanese tastes more closely. The Japanese traditionally eat fish and rice for breakfast, so Nestlé developed cereals with familiar tastes – seaweed, carrots and zucchini, and coconuts and papaya. The result was a 12 per cent share of a growing market.[25]

Functional features can be added or eliminated depending on the market. In markets where hot water is not commonly available, washing machines have heaters as a functional feature. In other markets, automatic soap and bleach dispensers may be eliminated to cut costs and/or to minimise repair problems. Additional changes may be necessary to meet safety and electrical standards or other mandatory requirements. The physical product and all its functional features should be examined as potential candidates for adaptation.

The Packaging Component   The packaging component includes style features, packaging, labelling, trademarks, brand name, quality, price and all other aspects of a product's package. As with the core component, the importance of each of these elements in the eyes of the consumer depends on the need that the product is designed to serve. Packaging components frequently require both discretionary and mandatory changes. For example, some countries require labels to be printed in more than one language while others forbid the use of any foreign language. Elements in the packaging component may incorporate symbols that convey an unintended meaning and thus must be changed. One company's red-circle trademark was popular in some countries but was rejected in parts of Asia where it conjured up images of the Japanese flag. Yellow flowers used in another company trademark were rejected in Mexico where a yellow flower symbolises death or disrespect.

Care must be taken to ensure that corporate trademarks and other parts of the packaging component do not have unacceptable symbolic meanings. Particular attention should be given to translations of brand names and colours used in packaging. White, the colour for purity in Western countries, is the colour for mourning in others. When Coca-Cola went to China, translators chose characters that sounded like Coca-Cola, but to the Chinese they read 'bite the wax tadpole'.

There are countless reasons why a company might have to adapt a product's packaging. In some countries, specific bottle, can and package sizes are stipulated by law, as are measurement units. Such descriptive words as 'giant' or 'jumbo' on a package or label may be illegal. High humidity and/or the need for long shelf life because of extended distribution systems may dictate extra-heavy packaging for some products. A poorly packaged product conveys an impression of poor quality. It is also important to determine if the packaging has other uses in the market. Again in Japan, Lever Brothers sells Lux soap in stylish boxes because in Japan more than half of all soap cakes are purchased during the two gift-giving seasons. Size of package is also a factor that may make a difference to success in Japan. Soft drinks are sold in smaller-size cans than in the United States and Western Europe to accommodate local consumption patterns and the smaller Japanese hand.

Labelling laws vary from country to country and do not seem to follow any predictable pattern. In Saudi Arabia, for example, product names must be specific. 'Hot Chilli' will not do, it must be 'Spiced Hot Chilli'. Prices are required to be printed on the labels in many countries, but in Chile it is illegal to put prices on labels or in any way suggest retail prices. Coca-Cola ran into a legal problem in Brazil with its Diet Coke. Brazilian law interprets diet to have medicinal qualities. Under the law, producers must give daily recommended consumption on the labels of all medicines. Coke had to get special approval to get around this restriction.

The Support Services Component   This component includes repair and maintenance, instructions, installation, warranties, deliveries and the availability of spare parts.

key term

labelling laws indicate what should be mentioned on the package

Many otherwise successful marketing programmes have ultimately failed because little attention was given to this product component. Repair and maintenance are especially difficult problems in developing countries. In Europe and the United States, a consumer has the option of company service as well as a score of competitive service retailers ready to repair and maintain anything from cars to lawn mowers. Equally available are repair parts from company-owned or licensed outlets or the local hardware store. Consumers in a developing country and many developed countries may not have even one of the possibilities for repair and maintenance available in the West.

Literacy rates and educational levels of a country may require a firm to change a product's instructions. A simple term in one country may be incomprehensible in another. In rural Africa, for example, the consumer had trouble understanding that Vaseline Intensive Care lotion is absorbed into the skin. Absorbed was changed to soaks into, and the confusion was eliminated. The Brazilians have successfully overcome low literacy and technical skills of users of the sophisticated military tanks it sells to Third World countries. They include video-cassette players and videotapes with detailed repair instructions as part of the standard instruction package. They also minimise spare parts problems by using standardised, off-the-shelf parts available throughout the world.

quality products

The debate about product standardisation versus product adaptation is not just a textbook exercise. It can mean the difference between success and failure in today's markets. As discussed in an earlier chapter, a quality product is one that satisfies consumer needs, has minimum defects and is priced competitively. Gone are the days when the customer's knowledge was limited to one or at best just a few different products. Today the customer knows what is best, cheapest and best quality. The power in the marketplace is shifting from a seller's market to the customers, who have more choices because there are more companies competing for their attention. It is the customer who defines quality in terms of his or her needs and resources. Quality is not just desirable, it is essential for success in today's competitive international market, and the decision to standardise or adapt a product is crucial in delivering quality.

summary

The growing globalisation of markets that gives rise to standardisation must be balanced with the continuing need to assess all markets for those differences that might require adaptation for successful acceptance. Each product must be viewed in light of how it is perceived by each culture with which it comes into contact. What is acceptable and comfortable within one group may be radically new and resisted within others depending on the experiences and perceptions of each group. Understanding that an established product in one culture may be considered an innovation in another is critical in planning and developing consumer products for foreign markets. Analysing a product as an innovation and using the product component model may provide the marketer with important leads for adaptation.

In some cases, the marketer needs only to adapt the packaging, while in others product characteristics and features need to change to make it compatible for the foreign market. More and more consumers and societies/governments are becoming aware of environmental issues. Many countries/markets have put these responsibilities on the shoulders of companies that sell the products to ensure that their products and packaging are not causing environmental problems. The marketer thus has to check these rules and regulations when entering these markets.

questions

1 Debate the issue of global versus adapted products for the international marketer.
2 Define the country-of-origin effect and give examples.
3 The text discusses stereotypes, ethnocentrism, degree of economic development and fads as the basis for generalisations about country-of-origin effect on product perception. Explain each and give an example.
4 Discuss how different stages in the life cycle of a product can influence the standardisation/adaptation decision. Give three examples.
5 Discuss the different promotional/product strategies available to an international marketer.
6 Assume you are deciding to 'go international'; outline the steps you would take to help you decide on a product line.
7 Products can be adapted physically and culturally for foreign markets. Discuss.
8 What are the three major components of a product? Discuss their importance to product adaptation.
9 How can knowledge of the diffusion of innovations help a product manager plan international investments?
10 Discuss the characteristics of an innovation that can account for differential diffusion rates.
11 Give an example of how a foreign marketer can use knowledge of the characteristics of innovations in product adaptation decisions.
12 Discuss 'environmentally friendly' products and product development.

further reading

- L. De Chernatony, C. Halliburton and R. Bernath, 'International Branding: Demand or Supply-driven Opportunity', *Harvard Business Review*, 1989, 12(2), pp. 9-21.
- M. Kotabe, 'Corporate Product Policy and Innovation Behaviour of European and Japanese Multinationals: An Empirical Investigation', *Journal of Marketing*, 1990, 54, pp. 19-33.
- S. Zhang and B.H. Schmitt, 'Brand Name Translation: Language Constraints, Product Attributes and Consumer Perceptions in East and South East Asia', *Journal of International Marketing*, November 2002, 10(2), pp. 29-45.

references

1 Rahul Jacob, 'The Big Rise: Middle Classes Explode Around the Globe Bringing New Markets and New Prosperity', *Fortune*, 30 May 1994, pp. 74-90; and 'Consumers Have Money to Burn', *Business Week*, 20 April 1998, pp. 30-1.
2 'Brazil's New Look: A Sounder Economy is Emerging', *Business Week*, 4 May 1998, pp. 22-6; and 'What to do about Asia', *Business Week*, 26 January 1998, pp. 48-50.
3 For an empirical study of the debate, see David M. Szymanski, Sundar G. Bharadwaj and Rajan P. Varadarajan, 'Standardization versus Adaptation of International Marketing Strategy: An Empirical Investigation', *Journal of Marketing*, October 1993, pp. 1-17.
4 For a balanced view, see S. Tamer Cavusgil, Shaoming Zou and G.M. Naidu, 'Product and Promotion Adaptation in Export Ventures: An Empirical Investigation', *Journal of International Business Studies*, Third Quarter 1993, pp. 479-506.
5 J. Quelch and D. Harding, 'Brand vs Product Labels - Fighting to Win', *Harvard Business Review*, 1996, January-February.

6 An interesting comment on the increasing importance of consistency in product design for the European market is covered in 'Cross-Border Design', *Business Europe*, 9–15 January 1995, pp. 6–7; and Pervez Ghauri, 'Recent Trends in Global Business and the Asian Crisis: Cooperation vs Competition', *KELOLA*, Journal of Gajah Mada University, Indonesia, 1998, 18/VII, pp. 1–15.

7 William Echikson, 'Electrolux: The Trick to Selling in Europe', *Fortune*, 20 September 1993, p. 82.

8 Laurie M. Grossman, 'PepsiCo Plans Big Overseas Expansion in Diet Cola Wars with its Pepsi Max', *Wall Street Journal*, 4 April 1994, p. B4.

9 Regina Fazio Maruca, 'The Right Way to Go Global', *Harvard Business Review*, March–April 1994, p. 136.

10 Adrian Palmer, 'Relationship Marketing: Local Implementation of Universal Concept', *International Business Review*, vol. 4, no. 4, 1995, pp. 471–82.

11 *Business Week*, Special Report: 'Branding in the Age of Anti-Americanism', 4 August 2003, pp. 45–50.

12 'Unilever Chief: Refresh Brands', *Advertising Age*, 19 July 1994, pp. 1–20.

13 For a comprehensive review of the literature on country-of-origin effects, see e.g. Warren Bilky and Erik Nes, 'Country-of-origin Effects in Product Evaluations', *Journal of International Business Studies*, 1982, vol. 13, no. 1, pp. 89–99; Aysegul Ozsomer and Tamer Cavusgil, 'Country-of-origin Effects on Product Evaluation: A Sequel to Bilky and Nes Review', in M.C. Gilly *et al.* (eds), *Proceedings of the American Marketing Association, Annual Conference, 1991*, pp. 69–77; and Robert Peterson and Alain Jolibert, 'A Meta Analysis of Country-of-origin Effects', *Journal of International Business Studies*, vol. 26, no. 4, 1996, pp. 883–900.

14 David Strutton, Lou E. Pelton and James R. Lumpkin, 'Internal and External Country of Origin Stereotypes in the Global Marketplace for the Domestic Promotion of US Automobiles', *Journal of Global Marketing*, vol. 7, no. 3, 1994, pp. 61–77.

15 Jerome Witt and C.P. Rao, 'The Impact of Global Sourcing on Consumers: Country-of-origin Effects on Perceived Risk', *Journal of Global Marketing*, vol. 6, no. 3, 1992, pp. 105–28.

16 'Czech Republic: Consumers Think Foreign Goods are Overpriced', *Crossborder Monitor*, 3 August 1994, p. 4.

17 Dana Milbank, 'Made in America Becomes a Boast in Europe', *Wall Street Journal*, 19 January 1994, p. B1.

18 Sheila Tefft, 'China's Savvy Shoppers Load Carts with Expensive Imported Goods', *Advertising Age*, 20 June 1994, pp. 1–21.

19 See Frank Alpert and Michael Kamins, 'An Empirical Investigation of Consumer Memory, Attitude, and Perceptions Towards Pioneer and Follower Brands', *Journal of Marketing*, vol. 59, no. 4, 1995, pp. 34–45.

20 Eleena de Lisser and Kevin Helliker, 'Private Labels Reign in British Groceries', *Wall Street Journal*, 3 March 1994, p. B1.

21 L. Alvarez, 'Consumers in Europe Resist Gene-altered Food', *New York Times*, 11 February 2003. p. 43.

22 'Electrolux Targets Southeast Asia', *Dow Jones News Service*, 4 January 1995.

23 Jagdish Sheth and Babwari Mittal, 'A Framework for Managing Customer Expectations', *Journal of Market Focused Management*, vol. 1, no. 2, 1996, pp. 137–58.

24 For a good reference book on new product development, see E.M. Rogers, *Diffusion of Innovations*, 5th edn (New York: Free Press, 2003).

25 G.M. Eckhardt and M.J. Houston, 'Cultural Paradoxes Reflected in Brand Meaning: McDonald's in Shanghai, China', *Journal of International Marketing*, 2001, 9(2), pp. 97–114.

chapter 14
Marketing Industrial Products and Business Services

Chapter Outline

The interest in industrial marketing, also referred to as business-to-business (B2B) marketing or interorganisational buying and selling, gained real momentum in the 1970s. It is argued that marketing of **industrial products** is different from marketing of consumer products. In industrial markets buyers are well informed, highly organised and sophisticated in their purchasing behaviour. Moreover, multiple influences participate actively in purchasing decisions. While in consumer marketing buyers are often passive and the relationship between the buyers and sellers is indirect. In industrial marketing, the buyer most often is not the end user of the product and sells it to the next stage in the supply chain, as it is or as a part of a package/product assembled or produced by him. In this type of market, interaction between the organisations and a network of relationships is considered more important than finding a marketing mix.[1]

Industrial products and services, from computers and photocopiers to machine tools and air freight or telecommunications, are different in nature. First, industrial goods are goods and services often used in the process of creating other goods and services. Consumer goods are in their final form and are consumed by individuals. Second, the motives are different: industrial buyers are seeking profits while final consumers are seeking satisfaction. Moreover, while in consumer markets the number of customers is huge, in industrial markets the number of buyers and sellers is small. These factors are manifest in specific buying patterns and demand characteristics, and in special emphasis on relationship marketing as a tool.[2]

Industrial goods can be categorised in a variety of ways. A typical scheme involves construction material, heavy equipment, light equipment, components and subassemblies, raw materials, processed materials, maintenance materials and operating supplies.[3]

Along with industrial goods, **business services** are a highly competitive growth market seeking quality and value. Manufactured products generally come to mind when we think of international trade. Yet the most rapidly growing sector of international trade today consists of business and consumer services – accounting, advertising, banking, consulting, construction, hotels, insurance, law, transportation, travel, television programmes and films sold internationally. The intangibility of business services creates a set of unique problems to which the service provider must respond. A further complication is a lack of uniform laws that regulate market entry. Protectionism, while prevalent for industrial goods, can be much more pronounced for the business service provider, such as airlines and telecommunications.[4]

This chapter discusses the special problems in marketing industrial goods and business services internationally, the increased competition and demand for quality in those goods and services, and the implications for the international marketer.

key terms

industrial products
products developed for the industrial market, not the consumer market

business services
services that are sold to other companies (e.g. advertising)

the industrial product market

technology and market demand

Not only is technology the key to economic growth, for many products it is also the competitive edge in today's global markets. As precision robots, sophisticated computer programs and digital control systems take over the factory floor, manufacturing is becoming more science-oriented and access to inexpensive labour and raw materials is becoming less important. The ability to develop the latest technology and to benefit from its application is a critical factor in the international competitiveness of countries and companies.[5]

Demand and Technology Three interrelated trends will spur demand for technologically advanced products: (1) expanding economic and industrial growth in emerging markets; (2) the liberalisation of *most* markets; and (3) the privatisation of government-owned industries.

Japan and many Asian countries have been in a state of rapid economic growth over the last 25 years. Japan has become the most advanced industrialised country in the region, while South Korea, Hong Kong, Singapore and Taiwan (the 'four tigers') have successfully moved from being cheap-labour sources to industrialised nations. The emerging markets of Brazil, Mexico, Malaysia, Thailand and Indonesia are exporters of semi-manufactured and manufactured products to Japan, Europe and the United States, but they are methodically gearing up for greater industrialisation.[6]

Besides demand for goods to build new manufacturing plants, many of the emerging countries are making much-needed investments in infrastructure.[7]

As a market economy develops in the Newly Independent States (former republics of the USSR) and other Eastern European countries, new privately owned businesses are creating a demand for the latest technology to revitalise and expand manufacturing facilities. The big emerging markets (BEMs) are estimated to account for more than €1.3 trillion ($1.5 trillion) of trade by 2010.[8] These countries are demanding the latest technology to expand their industrial bases and build modern infrastructures. Telmex, a €3.6 billion ($4 billion) joint venture between Southwestern Bell, France Telecom and Telefonos de Mexico, has invested hundreds of millions of dollars to bring the Mexican telephone system up to the most advanced standards. Telmex is only one of scores of new privatised companies from Poland to Patagonia that are creating a mass market for the most advanced technology.

the volatility of demand in industrial markets

In consumer products, firms are exposed to customers more directly and have better control over their strategies towards consumer demand, product life cycle extension and demand fluctuations. For industrial product companies, however, the firms do not sell their products directly to consumers and therefore are not fully aware of the **volatility in demand**. Their customers – other industrial buyers – act according to the demand situation for their own products. The producer of industrial products thus faces a derived demand situation. For example, Philips' semiconductor division, whose main customers are computer and consumer electronics producers, is dependent on the general demand conditions in these two markets. The monitor demand for PCs or television sets would indirectly influence the demand for Philips semiconductors. Simply speaking, derived demand can be defined as demand dependent on another source.

Demand for airplanes, for instance the Airbus A380 or Boeing 7E7, depends on the demand for air travel and the potential/expected growth in that demand. Sometimes minor changes in consumer demands mean major changes in the related industrial demand. In Exhibit 14.1, a 10 per cent increase in consumer demand for shower stalls in two years translates into a 100 per cent increase in demand for machines making shower stalls. A 15 per cent decrease in shower stalls in year five, results in a complete shutdown of demand for shower stall-making machines.

key term

volatility in demand
changes in demand

Exhibit 14.1 Derived demand example

Time period	Consumer demand for premoulded fibreglass shower stalls			Number of machines in use to produce the shower stalls			Demand for the machines		
Year	Previous year	Current year	Net change	Previous year	Current year	Net change	Replacement	New	Total
1	100 000	100 000	—	500	500	—	50	—	50
2	100 000	110 000	+10 000	500	550	+50	50	50	100
3	110 000	115 000	+5 000	550	575	+25	50	25	75
4	115 000	118 000	+3 000	575	590	+15	50	15	65
5	118 000	100 000	−18 000	590	500	−90	—	−40	−40
6	100 000	100 000	—	500	500	—	10	—	10

Source: adapted from R.L. Vaile, E.T. Grether and R. Cox, *Marketing in the American Economy* (New York: Ronald Press, 1952), p. 16. Appears in Robert W. Haas, *Business Marketing,* 6th edn (Cincinnati, OH: Southwestern, 1995), p. 115.

attributes of product quality

As discussed earlier, the concept of quality encompasses many factors, and the perception of quality rests solely with the customer. The level of technology reflected in the product, compliance with standards that reflect customer needs, support services and follow-through, and the price relative to competitive products are all part of a customer's evaluation and perception of quality. As noted, these requirements are different for ultimate consumers and for industrial customers because of differing end uses. The factors themselves also differ among industrial goods customers because their needs are varied.

Industrial marketers frequently misinterpret the concept of quality. Good quality is not the same as *technically* good quality. For example, an African government had been buying hand-operated dusters to distribute pesticides in cotton fields; the dusters were loaned to individual farmers. The duster supplied was a finely machined device requiring regular oiling and good care. But the fact that this duster turned more easily than any other on the market was relatively unimportant to the farmers. Furthermore, the requirement for careful oiling and care simply meant that in a relatively short time of inadequate care the machines froze up and broke. The result? The local government went back to an older type of French duster that was heavy, turned with difficulty and gave a poorer distribution of dust, but lasted longer because it required less care and lubrication. In this situation, the French machine possessed more relevant quality features and therefore, in marketing terms, possessed the higher quality for the particular customer.

It must be kept in mind that the concept of quality is not an absolute measure but one relative to use patterns and/or predetermined standards. Best quality is best because the product adheres exactly to specified standards that have been determined by expected use of the product. Since use patterns are frequently different from one buyer to another, standards vary so that superior quality for one customer falls short of superior quality as determined by the needs of another customer. Total quality management (TQM) includes customer satisfaction as well as conformance to standards. Customer needs are as much a part of the concept of quality as are standards. One research report examining the purchase decision variables of import managers found that product quality, including dependability of suppliers and timely delivery, were the most important variables influencing purchase decisions.

GOING INTERNATIONAL 14.1

your hoses are a threat to public security!

Universal standards made life miserable for Evan Segal. He is president of Dormont Manufacturing Company, which makes hoses that hook up deep-fat fryers and the like to gas outlets and once sold these hoses throughout Europe. Then one day one of his top customers, Frymaster Corporation of Shreveport, Louisiana, called to alert him that McDonald's was being told it could no longer use his hoses in its British restaurants. Similar problems popped up elsewhere, including EuroDisney outside Paris; shortly before the theme park opened, French inspectors demanded that Dormont's hoses be replaced with French-approved equipment.

The disparate national standards stemmed from the fact that the hoses are crucial to the safe operation of gas appliances and thus fell under the product-safety provisions, allowing each country to set its own standards. In Dormont's case, the specifications were written by committees often dominated by domestic European producers. They spell out the minutiae of each country's acceptable gas hose design – such as the colour of plastic coating or how the end pieces should be attached to the rest of the hose.

Mr Segal thought he had made a major breakthrough when the British Standards Institute, one of the European agencies that test equipment and hand out approvals, issued Dormont a certificate authorising the company to paste a seal of approval on its products signifying that the hoses conformed with European Union rules for gas appliances, enabling the company to sell them throughout the region. But the victory was short-lived. A miffed German competitor fired off a formal complaint to the European Commission, the EU's Brussels-based executive body. Commission officials familiar with the case say the rival argued that the British office erred because hoses are not really part of a gas appliance. The approval was withdrawn.

Source: Timothy Aeppel, 'Europe Unity Undoes a US Exporter', *Wall Street Journal*, 1 April 1996, p. B1; and Brandon Mitchener, 'Standard Bearers Increasingly Rules of Global Economy are Set in Brussels', *Wall Street Journal*, 23 April 2002, p. A1. Copyright 1996 by Dow Jones & Co. Inc. Reproduced with permission of Dow Jones & Co. Inc. Copyright Clearance Center.

price–quality relationship

There is a price–quality relationship that exists in an industrial buyer's decision. One important dimension of quality is how well a product meets the specific needs of the buyer. When a product falls short of performance expectations, its poor quality is readily apparent. However, it is less apparent but nonetheless true that a product that exceeds performance expectations is also of poor quality. A product whose design exceeds the wants of the buyer's intended use generally means a higher price that reflects the extra capacity. Quality for many goods is assessed in terms of fulfilling specific expectations, no more and no less. A product that produces 20 000 units per hour when the buyer needs one that produces only 5000 units per hour is not a quality product in that the extra capacity of 15 000 units is unnecessary to meet the buyer's use expectations.

This does not mean quality is unimportant or that the latest technology is not sought by some buyers. Rather, it means that those buyers require products designed to meet their specific needs, not products designed for different uses and expectations, especially if the additional features result in higher prices. This attitude was reflected in a study of the

purchasing behaviour of Chinese import managers, who ranked product quality first, followed in importance by price. Timely delivery was third and product style/features ranked 11th out of 17 variables studied.[9] Hence, a product whose design reflects the needs and expectations of the buyer – no more, no less – is a quality product.

product design–quality relationship

Industrial marketers must keep in mind that buyers of industrial goods judge products by their contribution to profit or to the improvement of the buyer's own products and production processes. Consequently, products designed to meet the needs of individual industrial users are critical to competitive advantage. Competitors from Japan, the US and even the emerging countries stand ready to provide the customer with a product that fits its exact needs and is offered at a competitive price.

The design of a product must be viewed from all aspects of use. Extreme variations in climate create problems in designing equipment that is universally operable. Products that function effectively in Western Europe may require major design changes to operate as well in the hot, dry Sahara region or the humid tropical rainforests of Latin America. Trucks designed to travel the autobahns of Germany will almost certainly experience operational difficulties in the mountainous regions of Asia on roads that barely resemble jeep trails. Manufacturers must consider many variations in making products that will be functional in far-flung markets.

In the light of today's competition, a company must consider the nature of its market and the adequacy of the design of its products. Effective competition in global markets means that overengineered and overpriced products must give way to products that meet the specifications of the customer at competitive prices. Success is in offering products that fit a customer's needs, technologically advanced for some and less sophisticated for others, but all of high quality. In most industrial markets, especially for components and parts, the buyer normally decides and gives specifications for design and other characteristics of the product.

service and replacement parts

Effective competition abroad not only requires proper product design but effective service, prompt deliveries and the ability to furnish spare and replacement parts without delay.[10] In highly competitive markets such as Japan, for example, it is imperative to give the same kind of service a domestic company or a Western company can give.

For many technical products, the willingness of the seller to provide installation and training may be the deciding factor for the buyers in accepting one company's product over another's. South Korean and other Asian business persons are frank in admitting they prefer to buy from Western firms, but the Japanese get the business because of service. Frequently heard tales of conflicts between Western and foreign firms over assistance expected from the seller are indicative of the problems of after-sales service and support. A South Korean businessman's experiences with a German engineer and some Japanese engineers typify the situation. The Korean electronics firm purchased semiconductor chip-making equipment for a plant expansion. The German engineer was slow in completing the installation; he stopped work at five o'clock and would not work at the weekends. The Japanese, installing other equipment, understood the urgency of getting the factory up and running; without being asked they worked day and night until the job was finished.

Unfortunately this is not an isolated case; Hyundai Motor Company bought two multi-million-euro presses to stamp body parts for cars. The 'presses arrived late, the engineers took much longer than promised to set up the machines, and Hyundai had to pay the Western workers extra to get the machines to work right'. The impact of such problems translates into lost business for Western firms. Samsung Electronics Company, Korea's largest chip maker, used Western equipment for 75 per cent of its first memory-chip plant. When it outfitted its most recent chip plant, it bought 75 per cent of the equipment from Japan.

GOING INTERNATIONAL 14.2

Nike's future: design and customisation

After the record revenues of $9.5 billion in 1998, Nike's sales dropped to $8.8 billion the next year. Finding growth since has not been easy, particularly in the domestic market. In 2002, this became the job of Mark Parker, one of the two co-presidents, who was put in charge of the entire global product and brand management and is also a footwear designer. Parker's appointment as president signified the growing importance played by

design in Nike's fortunes. The challenge that is facing Nike now is to keep applying its skills of reinvention to the way the brand is perceived by its public, creating new connections and extending its reach. The future is not simply about selling more and better products – it's more dimensionalised.

One of the new dimensions is selling services. The company began to explore the viability of selling on-brand services in areas such as sports coaching or information. Such a move would give Nike access to top minds and methodologies in sport, which makes solid

strategic sense for business. Second, Nike is planning to extend its sponsorship of athletes into events sponsorship. And, third, the company is exploring the possibilities in personalisation and customisation of its products.

Nike's aim now is to devote time and resources to tomorrow's game plan. For this Mark Parker has set up a crack team called the 'explore group'. 'The explore group is way out there in what we call "deep space". It's a small group of Green Beret-Navy Seal-type operatives who are really big thinkers and are supported by a network of some of the most leading-edge technology specialists. We don't talk a lot about this, but it's really big,' Parker says. 'Together with the Massachusetts Institute of Technology, Nasa and digital companies like Philips, they are exploring things like smart products that can feed into networks,' he continues. 'One of the biggest items on the agenda is customisation and personalisation.'

■ What advice would you give on Nike's plan for the future?

Source: adapted from 'Design's Great Leap Forward', *Financial Times, Creative Business*, 3 December 2002, pp. 2–3.

Technical training is rapidly becoming a major **after-sales service** when selling technical products in countries that demand the latest technology but do not always have trained personnel. China demands the most advanced technical equipment but frequently has untrained people responsible for products they do not understand. Heavy emphasis on training programmes and self-teaching materials to help overcome the common lack of skills to operate technical equipment is a necessary part of the after-sales service package in much of the developing world.

A recent study of international users of heavy construction equipment revealed that, next to the manufacturer's reputation, quick delivery of replacement parts was of major importance in purchasing construction equipment. Furthermore, 70 per cent of those questioned indicated they bought parts not made by the original manufacturer of the equipment because of the difficulty of getting original parts. Smaller importers complain of Western exporting firms not responding to orders or responding only after extensive delay. It appears that the importance of timely availability of spare parts to sustain a

key term

after-sales service
service available after the product has been sold (e.g. repairs)

market is forgotten by some Western exporters. When companies are responsive, the rewards are significant.

Some international marketers also may be forgoing the opportunity of participating in a lucrative aftermarket. Certain kinds of machine tools use up five times their original value in replacement parts during an average lifespan and thus represent an even greater market. One international machine tool company has capitalised on the need for direct service and available parts by changing its distribution system from the 'normal' to one of stressing rapid service and readily available parts. Instead of selling through independent distributors, as do most machine tool manufacturers in foreign markets, this company has established a series of company stores and service centres similar to those found in the home market. This company can render service through its system of local stores, while most competitors despatch service people from their home-based factories. The service people are kept on tap for rapid service calls in each of its network of local stores, and each store keeps a large stock of standard parts available for immediate delivery. The net result of meeting industrial needs quickly is keeping the company among the top suppliers in foreign sales of machine tools.

universal standards

A lack of universal standards is another problem in international sales of industrial products. The United Kingdom and the United States have two major areas of concern for the industrial goods exporter: one is a lack of common standards for manufacturing highly specialised equipment such as machine tools and computers, and the other is the use of the inch-pound or English system of measurement.[11] Domestically, the use of the inch-pound and the lack of a universal manufacturing standard are minor problems, but they have serious consequences when affected products are scheduled for export. Conflicting standards are encountered in test methods for materials and equipment, quality control systems and machine specifications. In the telecommunications industry, the vast differences in standards among countries create enormous problems for expansion of that industry. Efforts are being made through international organisations to create international standards; for example, the International Electrotechnical Commission (IEC) is concerned with standard specifications for electrical equipment for machine tools. The UK has now adopted the metric system in a number of industries. For example, litres are replacing pints and kilograms are replacing pounds.

In addition to industry and international organisations setting standards, countries often have standards for products entering their markets. Saudi Arabia has been working on setting standards for everything from light bulbs to lemon juice, and it has asked its trading partners for help. The standards will most likely be adopted by the entire Arab world. Most countries sent representatives; even New Zealand sent a representative to help write the standards for the shelf life of lamb.

ISO 9000 certification: an international standard of quality

With quality becoming the cornerstone of global competition, companies are requiring assurance of standard conformance from suppliers just as their customers are requiring the same from them. **ISO 9000**, a series of five international industrial standards (ISO 9000–9004) originally designed to meet the need for product quality assurances in purchasing agreements, is becoming a quality assurance certification programme that has competitive and legal ramifications when doing business in the European Union and elsewhere.[12]

ISO 9000 refers to the registration and certification of a manufacturer's quality system. It is a certification of the existence of a quality control system a company has in place to ensure it can meet published quality standards. ISO 9000 standards do not apply to specific products. They relate to generic system standards that enable a company, through a mix of internal and external audits, to provide assurance that it has a quality control system. It is a certification of the production process only, and does not guarantee a

key term

ISO 9000
quality assurance certification of the production process

manufacturer produces a 'quality' product. The series describes three quality system models, defines quality concepts and gives guidelines for using international standards in quality systems.[13]

A company requests a certifying body (a third party authorised to provide an ISO 9000 audit) to conduct a registration assessment, that is, an audit of the key business processes of a company. The assessor asks questions about everything from blueprints to sales calls to filing. 'Does the supplier meet promised delivery dates?' and 'Is there evidence of customer satisfaction?' are some of the questions asked and the issues explored. The object is to develop a comprehensive plan to ensure minute details are not overlooked. The assessor helps management create a quality manual, which will be made available to customers wishing to verify the organisation's reliability. When accreditation is granted, the company receives certification. A complete assessment for recertification is done every four years with intermediate evaluations during the four-year period.

ISO 9000 is not a legal requirement for access to the European market, but ISO 9000 certification is required under EU law for product certification on a few highly regulated, high-risk products such as medical devices, telecommunication terminal equipment, gas appliances and personal protective equipment.

Although ISO 9000 is voluntary, except for regulated products, the EU Product Liability Directive puts pressure on all companies to become certified. The directive holds that a manufacturer, including an exporter, will be liable, regardless of fault or negligence, if a person is harmed by a product that fails because of a faulty component. Thus, customers in the EU need to be assured that the components of their products are free of defects or deficiencies. A manufacturer with a well-documented quality system will be better able to prove that its products are defect-free and thus minimise liability claims.

A strong level of interest in ISO 9000 is being driven more by 'marketplace' requirements than by government regulations, and ISO 9000 is becoming an important competitive marketing tool in Europe. As the market demands quality and more and more companies adopt some form of TQM (total quality management), manufacturers are increasingly requiring ISO 9000 registration of their suppliers. Companies manufacturing parts and components in China are quickly discovering that ISO 9000 certification is a virtual necessity. More and more buyers, particularly those in Europe, are refusing to buy from manufacturers that do not have internationally recognised third-party proof of their quality capabilities.[14]

Outside regulated product areas, the importance of ISO 9000 registration as a competitive market tool in the EU varies from sector to sector. In some sectors, European companies may require suppliers to attest that they have an approved quality system in place as a condition for purchase. ISO 9000 may be used to serve as a means of differentiating different 'classes' of suppliers (particularly in high-tech areas) where high product reliability is crucial. In other words, if two suppliers are competing for the same contract, the one with ISO 9000 registration may have a competitive edge.

Manufacturers in developing countries are seeking ISO certification to offset concern among buyers about their quality capabilities. In Brazil, over 400 companies have been certified, compared with only 18 three years earlier. ISO certification has been credited as a major contributor to Brazil's positive trade surplus.[15] If a company practises total quality management, the system probably meets ISO 9000 standards but it would have to be audited and certified as such.[16]

relationship marketing

Relationship marketing has gained considerable attention in recent years. A number of studies on relational selling (key account management, database marketing, etc.), customer and supplier retention (in industrial as well as consumer products), cooperative marketing arrangements (cobranding, just-in-time supplies, EDI, shared logistics, etc.) and strategic partnerships (comarketing, codesign, coproduction, joint R&D, etc.) have

appeared in this area. Scholars from all parts of the world – Europe, America, Asia and Australia – are stressing relationship marketing.[17]

While traditional transactional marketing is believed to be based on competition and self-interest, relationship marketing is based more on mutual cooperation, trust and joint benefits.[18] The purpose of relationship marketing is considered to enhance marketing productivity by achieving efficiency and effectiveness.[19] Through interdependence and partnering, a lower cost and competitive advantages are achieved.

Relationship marketing is believed to be useful for both consumer products and industrial or business-to-business products. The relationship of consumers to business organisations is best described as that of membership.[20] The differences in the type of relationship and interdependence between the parties in business–consumer versus business-to-business relationships is explained in Exhibit 14.2. The table reveals that while business-to-consumer and business-to-business relationships have similarities, there are also major differences. It seems that the latter type of relationship is more long term and thus demands a higher level of relationship and commitment.

The marketing strategy of a firm will depend on the nature of its products (the more complex the product, the more need there is for the relationship), the nature of its customers (according to the importance individuals attach to the economic versus social aspects of exchange, e.g. in different cultures) and on the nature of the organisations involved (orientation of the organisations towards networks and collaborations).

Relationship marketing is not new, but it has become increasingly important in international marketing activities. The importance of relationships in China, *guanxi* (connections), has been reported by a number of scholars, where a business relationship often started with a social relationship. The development of a good relationship 'with a friend' was usually considered as a prerequisite for a business relationship. Due to recent decentralisation of economic decision making in China, relationships have become even more important.[21]

The characteristics that define the uniqueness of industrial products discussed above lead naturally to relationship marketing.[22] The long-term relationship with customers, which is at the core of relationship marketing, fits the characteristics inherent in industrial products and is a viable strategy for industrial goods marketing. The first and foremost characteristic of industrial goods markets is the motive of the buyer – to make a profit. Industrial products fit into a business or manufacturing process, and their contributions will be judged on how well they contribute to that process. In order for an industrial marketer to fulfil the needs of its customer, the marketer must understand those needs as they exist today and how they will change as the buyer strives to compete in global markets that call for long-term relationships.[23]

Relationship marketing ranges all the way from gathering information on customer needs to designing products and services, channelling products to the customer in a timely and convenient manner, and following up to make sure the customer is satisfied. For example, SKF, the bearing manufacturer, seeks strong customer relations with after-sales follow-through. The end of the transaction is not delivery; it continues as SKF makes sure the bearings are properly mounted and maintained. This helps customers reduce downtime, thus creating value in the relationship with SKF. SKF's marketing efforts encompass an array of activities to support long-term relationships that go beyond 'merely satisfying the next link in the distribution chain to meeting the more complex needs of the end user, whether those needs are technical, operational, or financial'.[24]

The industrial customer's needs in global markets are continuously changing, and suppliers' offerings must also continue to change. The need for the latest technology means that it is not a matter of selling the right product the first time but one of continuously changing the product to keep it right over time. The objective of relationship marketing is to make the relationship an important attribute of the transaction, thus differentiating oneself from competitors. It shifts the focus away from price to service and long-term benefits. The reward is loyal customers that translate into substantial profits.

Exhibit 14.2 Comparison of business-to-consumer and business-to-business relationships

	Characteristics	Business-to-consumer	Business-to-business
1	Relationship form	Membership	Working partnership, just-in-time exchange, comarketing, alliance, strategic alliance, distribution channel relationship
2	Average sale size; potential lifetime value of the customer to the selling firm	Normally small sale size; relatively small and predictable lifetime value of the customer; limit on the amount of investment in relationship for any single customer	Normally large and consequential; allows for large and idiosyncratic investments in single relationship
3	Number of customers	Large number; requires large overall investments in relationship management, but low investment per customer	Relatively fewer customers to spread investments in relationships over; investments often idiosyncratic
4	Seller's ability and cost to replace lost customer	Can normally be replaced quickly and at relatively low cost	Large customers can be difficult and time consuming to replace
5	Seller's dependence on buyer	Low for any single customer	Varies based on customer size; can be devastating
6	Buyer dependence on seller	Normally has viable alternatives, low switching costs and switch can be made quickly	Viable alternatives can take time to find, switching costs can be high and changes impact multiple people in the organisation
7	Purchasing time frame, process and buying centre complexity	Normally a short time frame, simple process, and simple buying centre, where one or two individuals fill most buying roles	Often a long time frame, complex process; may have multiple individuals for a single buying role; may be subject to organisation budget cycles
8	Personal knowledge of other party	Relatively few contact points with seller, even when loyal user; seller's knowledge of buyer often limited to database information	Multiple personal relationships; multiple inter-organisational linkages
9	Communication means to build and sustain relationships	Dependence on non-personal means of contact; seller's knowledge generally limited to database information of customer	Emphasis on personal selling and personal contact; customer knowledge held in different forms and places
10	Relative size	Seller normally larger than buyer	Relative size may vary
11	Legal	Consumer protection laws unbalanced to favour consumer	Relationships governed by prevailing contract law as well as industry standard regulations and ethics

Source: Thomas Gruen, 'The Outcome of Relationship Marketing in Consumer Markets', *International Business Review*, 1995, vol. 4, no. 4, pp. 447–69.

Relationship marketing can often give a company the competitive edge when a customer's ultimate success depends on more than technical expertise. For example, Pacific Telesis Group (Pactel), the San Francisco Baby Bell, won the right to build and partly own a €1.4 billion ($2 billion) cellular-phone network in Germany. Other bidders had the technical expertise to build the system, but the Pactel unit offered after-sale support systems, such as accounting software, management information systems and customer service procedures, critical to building the business and making it user-friendly.[25]

IBM of Brazil stresses stronger ties with its customers by offering planning seminars that address corporate strategies, competition, quality and how to identify marketing

how Intel got inside

In microprocessors Intel has the kind of monopoly that any company would be proud to control. More than 85 per cent of all personal computers (PCs) rely on Intel technology. Intel's current and very challenging goal is to maintain its PC monopoly while dominating the market for the new high-performance chips that promise to put PCs on a par with high-end workstations. Many computer analysts think that Intel could eventually control more than 90 per cent of the desktop market, including workstations.

By aggressively promoting the Pentium processor in the media, Intel bypassed its traditional customers – the computer manufacturers – and directly targeted PC users. This 'awareness campaign' for its processors has led the majority of PC buyers – especially business users – to specifically demand an Intel processor in their computers. In turn this has created an additional barrier for Intel's competitors: they not only have to deliver processors that are faster and cheaper than Intel's but, more importantly, they also have to convince consumers that their products are fully compatible with Intel's. Andy Grove, Intel's chairman and until recently CEO, says, 'It was an attitude change, a change we actually stimulated, but one whose impact we did not fully comprehend.'

However, as Intel's business model is essentially based around selling a continuous stream of faster microprocessors, its investment in production, R&D and marketing has reflected this at every stage. But growth in high-powered (read high-margin) Pentium II chips has slowed down, mainly as consumers have flocked to sub-thousand-dollar PCs. In this price-sensitive segment, Pentium's premium image doesn't stand for much. Customers look at the best price-performance. This is where AMD seems to have a slight edge; only time will tell if Intel can manage to repeat its success in this highly cut-throat market with its recently introduced Celeron processors.

Source: European Business Report, Spring 1Q, 1998, p. 31.

opportunities. One of these seminars showed a food import/export firm how it could increase efficiency by decentralising its computer facilities to better serve its customers. The company's computers were centralised at headquarters while branches took orders manually and mailed them to the home office for processing and invoicing. It took several days before the customer's order was entered and added several days to delivery time. The seminar helped the company realise it could streamline its order processing by installing branch office terminals that were connected to computers at the food company's headquarters. A customer could then place an order and receive an invoice on the spot, shortening the delivery time by several days or weeks. Not all participants who attend the 30 different seminars offered annually become IBM customers, but it creates a continuing relationship among potential customers. 'So much so,' as one executive commented, 'that when a customer does need increased computer power, he will likely turn to us.'[26]

promoting industrial products

The promotional problems encountered by foreign industrial marketers are little different from the problems faced by domestic marketers. Until recently there has been a paucity of

GOING INTERNATIONAL 14.4

adaptation in industrial products

Many manufacturers participating in today's global business face the same issue: how to customise products to meet local preferences. Some companies' bottom lines and market shares suffer because of failure to customise. For example, Adidas-Salomon, the German sportswear maker, lost sales in the US due to its inability to meet local consumers' tastes. Other companies, on the other hand, are succeeding.

Behr, a German company and a world leader in radiators and air-conditioning systems for cars, chooses to adapt its products to climatic conditions and consumer preferences in different countries. Its €3.8m laboratory in Stuttgart is capable of simulating wind speeds of up to 130 kph and temperatures from –30°C to +50°C, which covers driving conditions in just about every part of the world. Allowing for the driver's ability to 'tune' the conditions inside the vehicle to suit their individual tastes, the overall design of the company's units is influenced by national traits. 'German drivers like warm legs, the Japanese favour air being blown at their face to keep them cool, while Americans prefer an all-round effect in which air is directed over their entire bodies,' says Rudolf Riedel, manager of Behr's vehicle test operations. With the help of data from the laboratory, company engineers can work out how to alter key components inside standard air-conditioning systems so as to fit national preferences.

Bialetti is a much smaller company, but one of Europe's biggest makers of cooking utensils. About half of its production is exported. While Behr's focus is on its design laboratory, Bialetti has based its approach to variation on highly flexible production equipment. Across its range of aluminium pans, which account for about 70 per cent of sales, the company makes 2500 variants, most of them based on standard designs, with changes to such details as the pan's dimensions and the type of handle. 'For Russia, we have to make very deep pans because of the interest in cooking casseroles on a stove; in Japan or China we have the wok variants, while among the types we sell in Italy is a special Grande Famiglia range for large households,' says Francesco Ranzoni, the company's chairman. To make such customisations possible, Bialetti invested heavily in automatic press machines. These make individual items in relatively short production runs, of perhaps 5000 items per batch. The production equipment is sufficiently flexible to be switched to making a different kind of product, often within minutes.

■ Do companies need to adapt their products in a B2B market?

Source: adapted from Peter Marsh, 'One Size Fits All: Except for Local Preferences', *Financial Times*, 27 December 2002, p. 9; and Uta Harnischfeger, 'Failure to Meet US Tastes Cuts Sales at Adidas', *Financial Times*, 7 August 2003, p. 23.

specialised advertising media in many countries. In the last decade, however, specialised industrial media have been developed to provide the industrial marketer with a means of communicating with potential customers, especially in Western Europe and to some extent in Eastern Europe, the Commonwealth of Independent States (CIS) of the former USSR, and China. In addition to advertising in print media and reaching industrial customers through catalogues and direct mail, the trade show has become the primary vehicle for doing business in many foreign countries.

industrial trade shows

One of the most powerful international promotional media is the trade show or **trade fair**. As part of their international promotion activities, the European Union, Germany and the US Department of Commerce and many other countries sponsor trade fairs in many cities around the world. Additionally, there are annual trade shows sponsored by local governments in most countries. African countries, for example, host more than 70 industry-specific trade shows.

Trade shows serve as the most important vehicles for selling products, reaching prospective customers, contacting and evaluating potential agents and distributors, and marketing in most countries. They have been at the centre of commerce in Europe for centuries and are where most prospects are found. European trade shows attract high-level decision makers who are not attending just to see the latest products but are there to buy.[27] The importance of trade shows to Europeans is reflected in the percentage of their media budget spent on participating in trade events. On average, Europeans spend 22 per cent of their total annual media budget on trade events, while American firms typically spend less than 5 per cent. The Hannover Industry Fair (Germany), the largest trade fair in the world, has nearly 6000 exhibitors who show a wide range of industrial products to 600 000 visitors.

Trade shows provide the facilities for a manufacturer to exhibit and demonstrate products to potential users. They are an opportunity to create sales and establish relationships with agents and distributors that can lead to more permanent distribution channels in foreign markets. In fact, a trade show may be the only way to reach some prospects. Trade show experts estimate that 80 to 85 per cent of the people seen on a trade show floor never have a sales person call on them.

The number and variety of trade shows is such that almost any target market in any given country can be found through this medium. In the CIS, fairs and **exhibitions** offer companies the opportunity to meet new customers, including private traders, young entrepreneurs and representatives of non-state organisations. The exhibitions in the CIS offer a cost-effective way of reaching a large number of customers who might otherwise be difficult to target through individual sales calls. Specialised fairs in individual sectors such as computers, the automotive industry, fashion and home furnishings regularly take place. These days some trade shows are held online, providing excellent access with the minimum of expense.[28]

Thirty-nine American firms participated in a seven-day electronics production equipment exhibition in Osaka, Japan, and came home with €1.4 million ($1.6 million) in confirmed orders along with estimates for the following year of €9 million ($10 million). Five of the companies were seeking Asian agents/distributors through the show, and each was able to sign up a representative before the show closed. Trade shows and trade fairs are scheduled periodically and any interested business can reserve space to exhibit.[29]

countertrade: a pricing tool

Willingness to accept countertrades, the inclusive term used to describe transactions where all or partial payment is made in kind rather than cash, is an important price advantage in international trade.[30] While not unique to industrial goods markets, countertrading will continue to be important when marketing to the emerging markets – in Eastern Europe, the former republics of Russia, China and some countries in Asia and South America.[31] In most rapidly industrialising countries, there is a shortage of hard currencies, and those that exist are reserved for top-priority projects; goods of less importance, and even some priority goods, are instead acquired with some form of countertrade. A marketer unwilling to accept countertrades will probably lose the sale to a competitor who already includes countertrading as an important pricing tool.

key terms

trade fair
exhibition where participants are able to show/sell their products and services. Also used to establish and maintain contacts

exhibitions
used to promote product range extensions and to launch activities in new markets

marketing services globally

The service sectors in many industrial nations collectively account for up to 70 per cent of the gross national product. This includes a broad range of industries as well as many government and non-profit activities. The changing patterns of government regulations, privatisation of public corporations and **non-profit organisations**, computerisation and technological innovations and the internationalisation of service businesses are some of the factors that are transforming service sectors in the European Union, the United States, Japan and many emerging economies. In many cases services are competing with products as they provide similar benefits. For example, buying a service may be an alternative to doing it yourself – jobs such as lawn care, equipment maintenance, etc. Using a rental service is an alternative to buying a product. Moreover, the service content of a number of products ranging from fast-food restaurants to automobile manufacture is increasing.[32]

Unlike merchandise trade, which requires a declaration of value when exported, most services do not have to have an export declaration; nor do they always pass through a tariff or customs barrier when entering a country. Consequently, an accurate tally of service trade exports is difficult to determine. Services not counted include advertising, accounting, management consulting, legal services and most insurance; ironically, these are among the fastest growing.[33]

key term

non-profit organisations organisations whose purpose is not profit-oriented (e.g. Worldwide Fund for Nature, universities)

GOING INTERNATIONAL 14.5

keys to success in the European entertainment market

Despite increased competition throughout the industry, Europe is still an attractive market for entertainment companies. This is partly due to more vacation days (the European Union standard is at least 20 days), higher disposable incomes and leisure developments encouraged by city and county planning authorities.

Europe has a long and extensive history of theme parks and attractions, which historically were family-owned, small-scale operations. Although many of these mum-and-dad parks and attractions have disappeared, Europe still boasts the oldest operating amusement park – in Bakken, Denmark.

Many family entertainment projects – such as Disneyland Paris, Port Aventura in Spain and LegoLand in Windsor, England – emerged within the last decade through various public and privately funded bodies.

© AP/Wide World Photos

Their success in Europe is often driven by weather considerations, the addition of rides and attractions, retail propositions linked to a park, and movie or intellectual property that enhance the overall brand.

Based on our work with many US entertainment companies, we have developed the 'Top 10 Predictors of Success' for an entertainment venture in Europe.

10 Do your homework. Make sure you are aware of past case studies, regional and national consumer tastes, preferences and traditions.

9 Get your relationship right with HQ. Strike a balance between the amount of autonomy or control your headquarters and European teams are given, and develop a reporting structure that enables all involved to share best marketing practices with colleagues across geographic boundaries.

8 Manage expectations within your company about when your European activities will start showing a profit (or, at least, break even).

7 'Glocalise' your concepts, striking a balance between how much of your US ideas should be brought to Europe, while still making them appeal to 'local' European tastes.

6 Set realistic payback periods.

5 Understand that the different business customs across these 25 distinct markets mean that you have at least 25 different customer tastes, and therefore need to consider how 'entertainment' is defined by and made relevant to such a disparate population.

4 There is no such thing as the 'United States of Europe'. Because of differing consumer tastes, the implementation of your marketing plans within each of the EU countries will vary significantly.

3 Use local experts wherever possible, to ensure you've been given an accurate, current picture of your target market trends and concerns.

2 Test your concepts and ideas with your target guests to learn what they like, their propensity to pay various entry fees, promotional tie-ins and other marketing activities.

1 Plan, plan, plan!

Source: Allyson L. Stewart-Allen, 'Marketing Perspective', *Marketing News*, 17 August 1998, p. 9.

characteristics of services

In contrast to industrial and consumer goods, services are distinguished by unique characteristics and thus require special consideration. Products are classified as tangible or intangible. Cars, computers, furniture, and so on, are examples of *tangible products* that have a physical presence; they are a thing or object that can be stored and possessed, and whose intrinsic value is embedded within its physical presence. Insurance, dry cleaning, hotel accommodation and airline passage or freight service are *intangible products* whose intrinsic value is the result of a process, a performance or an occurrence that exists only while it is being created. The intangibility of services results in characteristics unique to a service: it is *inseparable* in that its creation cannot be separated from its consumption; it is *heterogeneous* in that it is individually produced and is thus virtually unique; it is *perishable* in that once created it cannot be stored but must be consumed simultaneously with its creation. Contrast these characteristics with a tangible product that can be produced in one location and consumed elsewhere, that can be standardised, whose quality assurance can be determined and maintained over time, and that can be produced and stored in anticipation of fluctuations in demand.[34]

Services can be classified as being either consumer or industrial in nature. Additionally, the same service can be marketed both as industrial and consumer, depending on the motive of, and use by, the purchaser. For example, travel agents and airlines sell industrial services to a business person and a consumer service to a tourist. Financial services, hotels, insurance, legal services and others all may be industrial or consumer services.

These fundamental characteristics explain why it is important that services be discussed separately from industrial and consumer goods and why their very nature affects the manner in which they are marketed internationally.

entering international markets

Client Followers and Market Seekers   Most Western service companies entered international markets to service their Western clients, business travellers and tourists. Banks, accounting and advertising firms were among the earlier companies to establish branches or acquire local affiliations abroad to serve their Western multinational clients. Hotels and car-rental agencies followed the business traveller and tourist to fill their needs.[35] Their primary purpose for marketing their services internationally was to service

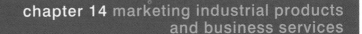
home-country clients. Once established, many of these **client followers**, as one researcher refers to them, expanded their client base to include local companies. As global markets grew, creating greater demand for business services, service companies became market seekers in that they actively sought customers for their services worldwide. One study of select types of service industries shows that the relative importance of client following or market seeking as a motive for entry into foreign markets varies by type of service.[36]

Exhibit 14.3 shows that, today, the most important motive for engaging in international business for most business service firms is to seek new markets. The notable exceptions are accounting and advertising firms whose motives are about equally divided between being client followers and market seekers.

Exhibit 14.3 Entry motive by type of service offered (per cent selected as follower or seeker)

Entry motive	Advertising, accounting	Computer needs	Engineering, architecture	Management consulting	Consumer	Bank	Misc.
Client followers	46.15%	22.01%	24.35%	21.48%	00.0%	30.77%	27.45%
Market seekers	53.65	77.99	75.65	78.52	100.0	69.23	72.55
Total: 100%							

Source: M. Krishna Erramilli, 'Entry Mode Choice in Service Industries', *International Marketing Review*, vol. 7, no. 5, 1991, p. 58.

Entry Modes Because of the varied characteristics of business services, not all of the traditional methods of market entry discussed earlier are applicable to all types of services. Although most services have the inseparability of creation and consumption just discussed, there are those where these occurrences can be separated. Such services are those whose intrinsic value can be 'embodied in some tangible form (such as a blueprint or document) and thus can be produced in one country and exported to another'. Data processing and data analysis services are other examples. The analysis or processing is completed on a computer located in a Western country and the output (the service) is transmitted via satellite to a distant customer. Some banking services could be exported from one country to another on a limited basis through the use of ATMs (automatic teller machines). Architecture and engineering consulting services are exportable when the consultant travels to the client's site and later returns home to write and submit a report or a blueprint. In addition to exporting as an entry mode, these services also use franchising, direct investment (joint ventures and wholly owned subsidiaries) and licensing.

Most other services – car rentals, airline services, entertainment, hotels and tourism, to name a few – are inseparable and require production and consumption to occur almost simultaneously and, thus, exporting is not a viable entry method for them. The vast majority of services enter foreign markets by licensing, franchising and/or direct investment.

market environment for business services

Service firms face most of the same environmental constraints and problems confronting merchandise traders. Protectionism, control of transborder data flows, competition and the protection of trademarks, processes and patents are possibly the most important problems confronting the MNC in today's international services market.

Protectionism The most serious threat to the continued expansion of international services trade is **protectionism**. The growth of international services has been so rapid during the last decade that it has drawn the attention of domestic companies and governments. As a result, direct and indirect trade barriers have been imposed to restrict foreign companies from domestic markets. Every reason, from the protection of infant industries

key terms

client followers
companies that have followed their clients to other countries (become international) to service primary clients while they are abroad

protectionism
when governments do not allow freedom of activity for foreign companies, to protect their own companies

to national security, has been used to justify some of the restrictive practices. The General Agreement on Trade in Services (GATS), part of the Uruguay round package, provides for most-favoured-nation treatment, national treatment, market access, transparency and the free flow of payments and transfers.

Until the GATT and WTO agreements there were few international rules of fair play governing trade in services. Service companies faced a complex group of national regulations that impeded the movement of people and technology from country to country. The industrialised nations want their banks, insurance companies, construction firms and other service providers to be allowed to move people, capital and technology around the globe unimpeded.

Restrictions designed to protect local markets range from not being allowed to do business in a country to requirements that all foreign professionals pass certification exams in the local language before being permitted to practise.

The European Union has made considerable progress towards establishing a single market for services. Legal services and the film industry seem to be two that are very difficult to negotiate. A directive regarding Transfrontier Television Broadcasting created a quota for European programmes requiring EU member states to ensure that at least 50 per cent of entertainment air time is devoted to 'European works'. The EU argues that this set-aside for domestic programming is necessary to preserve Europe's cultural identity. The consequences for the US film industry are significant because over 40 per cent of US film industry profits come from foreign revenues.

Transborder Data Flow Restrictions on transborder data flows are potentially the most damaging to both the communications industry and other multinationals that rely on data transfers across borders to conduct business. Some countries impose tariffs on the transmission of data and many others are passing laws forcing companies to open their computer files to inspection by government agencies.

Most countries have a variety of laws to deal with the processing and electronic transmission of data across borders. There is intense concern about how to deal with this relatively new technology. In some cases, concern stems from not understanding how best to tax transborder data flows and, in other cases, there is concern over the protection of individual rights when personal data are involved. The European Commission is concerned that data on individuals (such as income, spending preferences, debt repayment histories, medical records and employment data) are being collected, manipulated and transferred between companies with little regard for the privacy of the individuals about whom the data are collected. A proposed directive by the Commission would require the consent of the individual before data are collected or processed. A wide range of foreign service companies would be affected by such a directive; insurance underwriters, banks, credit reporting firms, **direct marketing** companies and tour operators are a few examples. The directive would have a wide-ranging effect on data-processing and data-analysis firms because it will prevent a firm from transferring information electronically to other countries for computer processing if it concerns individual European consumers.

Competition As mentioned earlier, competition in all phases of the service industry is increasing as host-country markets are invaded by many foreign firms. The practice of following a client into foreign markets and then expanding into international markets is followed by German, British, Japanese, Swedish and American service firms, along with many others. Telecommunications, banking, advertising, construction and hotels are services that face major global competition, not only among European and Japanese companies but also from representatives of Brazil, China and other parts of the world. In recent years, a number of Western companies have been outsourcing service jobs to emerging markets. This is perceived as a new kind of competition. A number of labour organisations are protesting against this.

GOING INTERNATIONAL 14.6

impact of globalisation on job shift

As the wave of globalisation has swept the whole world and reshaped the global economy, it has also had great impact on what jobs are done where. Two decades ago the first wave started with an exodus of jobs making shoes, cheap electronics and toys, from the West to developing countries. Simple service work, such as processing credit-card receipts, and mind-numbing digital toil, such as writing software code, began fleeing high-cost countries too.

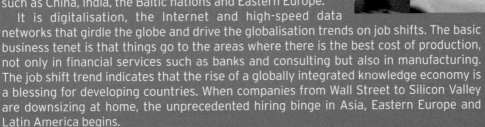

Now, the trend is characterised by all kinds of knowledge work that is now done almost anywhere. Forrester Research Inc. analyst John C. McCarthy predicts at least 3.3 million white-collar jobs and $136 billion in wages will shift from the US to low-cost countries by 2015. It is the same story within Europe. Huge back offices for these developed countries have been established and continue to grow in emerging markets such as China, India, the Baltic nations and Eastern Europe.

It is digitalisation, the Internet and high-speed data networks that girdle the globe and drive the globalisation trends on job shifts. The basic business tenet is that things go to the areas where there is the best cost of production, not only in financial services such as banks and consulting but also in manufacturing. The job shift trend indicates that the rise of a globally integrated knowledge economy is a blessing for developing countries. When companies from Wall Street to Silicon Valley are downsizing at home, the unprecedented hiring binge in Asia, Eastern Europe and Latin America begins.

However, for security and practical reasons, corporations are likely to keep crucial R&D and the bulk of back-office operations close to home, so as to adjust the job distribution. In addition, companies may have comparative advantages shift to other fields by possessing big foreign markets for their services and goods. Meanwhile, the benefits can be huge for the companies most adept at managing a global workforce, handling everything from product design and tech support to employee benefits.

On the other side of the coin there are issues of losing control of core business and the difficulty of coordinating manufacturing and design work overseas. Opposition to free trade could broaden if globalisation, having already made blue collars in developed countries adverse to some extent, continues to unfavourably influence more politically powerful middle-class white collars. In developing countries it might be different, especially for those loaded with college grads who speak Western languages. Outsourced white-collar work will likely contribute to the economic development even more than new factories making sneakers or mobile phones. A tremendous pool of well-trained graduates such as those in India and China entice corporations to dip in, not only in IT but finances and architecture as well.

It is difficult to conclude whether this globalisation trend benefits more the employees in developing countries or harms those in the West. What can be noted is that with the rise of the global knowledge industry the big beneficiaries will be those companies offering the speediest and cheapest telecom links, the investor-friendly policies and ample college graduates.

■ Do you think this trend of job shift is good for developed countries? Do you think it is good for developing countries?

Source: 'The New Global Job Shift', *Business Week*, 3 February 2003.

Protection of Intellectual Property An important form of competition difficult to combat is pirated trademarks, processes and patents. Computer design and software, trademarks, brand names and other intellectual properties are easy to duplicate and difficult to protect. The protection of intellectual property rights is a major problem in the services industries. Countries seldom have adequate - or any - legislation; any laws they do have are extremely difficult to enforce. The Trade Related Intellectual Property Rights part of the GATT agreement obligates all members to provide strong protection for copyright and related rights, patents, trademarks, trade secrets, industrial designs, geographic indications and layout designs for integrated circuits.

The TRIPS agreement is helpful in the protection of services but the key issue is that enforcement is very difficult without the full cooperation of host countries. The situation in China has been especially slow because that country has only recently been trying to enforce rights of intellectual property. The total annual cost for US businesses of pirated software, CDs, books and films in China alone totals more than €2235 million ($2476 million). Industry estimates are that Western companies lose over €54 billion ($60 billion) annually on piracy of all types of intellectual property. As it is so easy to duplicate electronically recorded music and films, pirated copies are often available within a few days of their release. In Thailand, for example, illegal copies of films are available within 10 days of their release in the Western markets.

Things are, however, improving. Beijing authorities have destroyed 800 000 pirated videos and audio cassettes, and more than 40 000 software programs. In one particular year, they also imposed fines totalling some €2.7 million ($3 million) in connection with some 9000 cases of trademark violation.

summary

Industrial goods marketing requires close attention to the exact needs of customers. Basic differences across various markets are less than for consumer goods but the motives behind purchases differ enough to require a special approach. Global competition has risen to the point that industrial goods marketers must pay close attention to the level of economic and technological development for each market to determine the buyer's assessment of quality. Companies that adapt their products to these needs are the ones that should be the most effective in the marketplace. Industrial markets are lucrative and continue to grow as more countries strive for at least a semblance of industrial self-sufficiency. The derived nature of demand for industrial products encourages these companies to have close relationships with their customers. Relationship marketing is therefore becoming important in this sector.

One of the fastest-growing areas of international trade is business services. This segment of marketing involves all countries at every level of development; even the least-developed countries are seeking computer technology and sophisticated data banks to aid them in advancing their economies. Their rapid growth and profit profile make them targets for protectionism and piracy. The increasing competition in the form of outsourcing of service jobs is resulting in some job losses in the service sector in developed countries. More qualified and sensitive jobs, such as R&D and design, are kept at home.

questions

1   What are the differences between consumer and industrial goods, and what are the implications for international marketing? Discuss.
2   'The adequacy of a product must be considered in relation to the general environment within which it will be operated rather than solely on the basis of technical efficiency.' Discuss the implications of this statement.
3   What role do service, replacement parts and standards play in competition in foreign marketing? Illustrate.
4   Discuss the part industrial trade fairs play in international marketing of industrial goods.
5   Describe the reasons an MNC might seek ISO 9000 certification.
6   What ISO 9000 legal requirements are imposed on products sold in the EC? Discuss.
7   Discuss how the characteristics that define the uniqueness of industrial products lead naturally to relationship marketing. Give some examples.
8   Select several countries, each at a different stage of economic development, and illustrate how the stage affects the usage of relationship marketing.

further reading

- J. Sheth and A. Parvatiyar, 'The Evolution of Relationship Marketing', *International Business Review*, 1995, 4(4), pp. 471–81.
- W. Ulaga and S. Chacour, 'Measuring Customer-perceived Value in Business Markets: A Prerequisite for Marketing Strategy Development and Implementation', *Industrial Marketing Management*, 2001, 30(6), pp. 525–40.
- F. Contractor, S.K. Kundu and C.C. Hu, 'A Three Stage Theory of International Expansion: The Link between Multinationality and Performance in the Service Sector', *Journal of International Business Studies*, 2003, 34, pp. 5–19.

references

1   For a discussion on networks in industrial marketing see e.g. Pervez Ghauri (ed.), *Advances in International Marketing: From Mass Marketing to Relationships and Networks* (Greenwich, NY: JAI Press, 1999).
2   Hans Gemünden, Thomas Ritter and Achim Walter (eds), *Relationships and Networks in International Markets* (Oxford: Pergamon), 1997.
3   Frederick Webster, *Industrial Marketing Strategy*, 3rd edn (New York: Wiley, 1991).
4   Karin Venetis, 'Service Quality and Customer Loyalty in Professional Business Service', PhD dissertation, Maastricht University, 1997.
5   John Naisbitt, *Mega Trends Asia* (New York: Simon & Schuster, 1996).
6   Philippe Lasserre and Helmut Schütte, *Strategies for Asia Pacific* (London: Macmillan, 1995).
7   Gregory Ingram and Christine Kessides, 'Infrastructure for Development', *Finance and Development*, September 1994, pp. 18–21.
8   'The Big Emerging Markets', *Business America*, March 1994, pp. 4–6.
9   Kyung-Il Ghymn, Paul Johnson and Weijiong Zhang, 'Chinese Import Managers' Purchasing Behaviour', *Journal of Asian Business*, vol. 9, no. 3, Summer 1993, pp. 35–45.
10   J. Carbone, 'Who Will Survive?' *Purchasing*, 15 May 2003, pp. 33–42.
11   Tom Reilly, 'The Harmonization of Standards in the European Union and the Impact on US Business', *Business Horizons*, March–April 1995, pp. 28–34.

12 Neil Morgan and Nigel Piercy, 'Interactions Between Marketing and Quality at the SBU Level: Influences and Outcomes', *Journal of the Academy of Marketing Science*, vol. 26, no. 3, 1998, pp. 190-208.

13 Robert W. Peach (ed.), *The ISO 9000 Handbook*, 2nd edn (Fairfax, VA: CEEM Information Services, 1994).

14 'Quality: ISO 9000 Certification Standardization', *Business China*, 30 May 1994, p. 4.

15 T. Witkowski and M. Wolfinbearger, 'Comparative Service Quality: German and American Ratings of Five Different Service Settings', *Journal of Business Research*, 2002, November, pp. 875-81.

16 M. Terziovski, D. Power and A.S. Sohal, 'The Longitudinal Effects of the ISO 9000 Certification Process on Business Performance', *European Journal of Operations Research*, May 2003, pp. 580-95.

17 Jagdish Sheth and Atul Parvatiyar, 'The Evolution of Relationship Marketing', *International Business Review*, vol. 4, no. 4, 1995, pp. 397-418.

18 R.M. Morgan and S.D. Hunt, 'The Commitment-Trust Theory of Relationship Marketing', *Journal of Marketing*, vol. 58, July 1994, pp. 20-38.

19 J.N. Sheth and R. Sisodia, 'Improving the Marketing Productivity', in *Encyclopaedia of Marketing for the Year 2000* (Chicago, IL: American Marketing Association - NTC, 1995).

20 R. Salle, B. Cova, and C. Pardo, 'Portfolio of Supplier-Customer Relationships', in A.G. Woodside (ed.), *Advances in Business Marketing and Purchasing*, vol. 9, 2000, pp. 419-42.

21 See, e.g. Ingemar Björkman and Sören Kock, 'Social Relationships and Business Networks: The Case of Western Companies in China', *International Business Review*, vol. 4, no. 4, 1995, pp. 519-35.

22 Adrian Palmer, 'Relationship Marketing: Local Implementation of a Universal Concept', *International Business Review*, vol. 4, no. 4, 1995, pp. 471-81.

23 For a comprehensive review of relationship literature, see Robert M. Morgan, and Shelby D. Hunt, 'The Commitment-Trust Theory of Relationship Marketing', *Journal of Marketing*, July 1994, pp. 20-38; and special issue of *International Business Review* on Relationship Marketing, vol. 4, no. 4, 1995.

24 Rahul Jacob, 'Why Some Customers Are More Equal than Others', *Fortune*, 19 September 1994, p. 215.

25 Ralph T. King Jr, 'US Service Exports Are Growing Rapidly, But Almost Unnoticed', *Wall Street Journal*, 21 April 1993, p. A1.

26 S. Leek, P.W. Turnbull and P. Naude, 'How is Information Technology Affecting Business Relationships?', *Industrial Marketing Management*, 2003, 32(2), pp. 119-26.

27 Marnik G. Dekimpe, Pierre François, Srinath Gopalakrishna, Gary L. Lilien and Christophe van den Bulte, 'Generalizing About Trade Show Effectiveness: A Cross-National Comparison', *Journal of Marketing*, vol. 61, no. 4, 1997, pp. 55-64.

28 J. Saranow, 'The Show Goes On: Online Trade Shows Offer Low Cost, Flexible Alternatives for Organizers', *Wall Street Journal*, 13 June 2003, p. B4.

29 'Africa: Marketing Through Trade Shows', *Trade and Culture*, Spring 1994, pp. 55-6.

30 Countertrades are discussed in depth in Chapter 18.

31 'Financing CIS Sales: Reinventing Countertrade', *Business Eastern Europe*, 17 January 1994, pp. 1-2.

32 Christopher Lovelock, *Service Marketing: Text, Cases and Readings*, 2nd edn (Englewood Cliffs, NJ: Prentice Hall, 1991).

33 'Service Exports', *Business America*, Annual Report to the US Congress, October 1994, p. 87.

34 J. Conley, 'What Happened to Customer Service?', *Risk Management*, April 2003, pp. 22-6.

35 Christine Domegan, 'The Adoption of Information Technology in Customer Service', *European Journal of Marketing*, vol. 30, no. 6, 1996, pp. 52-69.

36 For an insightful study of entry-mode choice by service firms, see M. Krishna Erramilli and C.P. Rao, 'Service Firms' International Entry-mode Choice: A Modified Transaction-Cost Analysis', *Journal of Marketing*, July 1993, pp. 19-38.

chapter 15
The International Distribution System

Chapter Outline

If expected marketing goals are to be achieved, a product must be made accessible to the target market in an efficient manner. In many markets, the biggest constraint to successful marketing is distribution.[1] Getting the product to the target market can be a costly process if inadequacies within the distribution structure cannot be overcome. Forging an efficient and reliable channel of distribution may be the most critical and challenging task facing the international marketer.

Each market contains a **distribution network** with many channel choices whose structures are unique and, in the short run, fixed. In some markets, the distribution structure is multilayered, complex and difficult for new marketers to penetrate; in others, there are few specialised middlemen except in major urban areas; and in yet others, there is a dynamic mixture of traditional and new, evolving distribution institutions available. Regardless of the predominating distribution structure, competitive advantage will reside with the marketer best able to build the most efficient channel from among the alternatives available.

This chapter discusses the basic points involved in making channel decisions: (1) channel structures; (2) available alternative middlemen; (3) locating, selecting, motivating and terminating middlemen; and (4) controlling the channel process.

key term

distribution network
how the product moves from the producer to the customer

channel of distribution structures

In every country and in every market, urban or rural, rich or poor, all consumer and industrial products eventually go through a distribution process. The process includes the physical handling and distribution of goods, the passage of ownership (title), and – most important from the standpoint of marketing strategy – the buying and selling negotiations between producers and middlemen and between middlemen and customers.[2]

A host of policy and strategy channel-selection issues confronts the international marketing manager. These issues are not in themselves very different from those encountered in domestic distribution, but the resolution of the issues differs because of different channel alternatives and market patterns.

Each country market has a channel structure through which goods pass from producer to user. Within this structure are a variety of middlemen whose customary functions, activities and services reflect existing competition, market characteristics, tradition and economic development. In short, the behaviour of channel members is the result of the interactions between the cultural environment and the marketing process. Channel structures range from those with little developed marketing infrastructure found in many emerging markets to the highly complex, multilayered system found in Japan.[3]

import-oriented distribution structure

Traditional channels in developing countries evolved from economies with a strong dependence on imported manufactured goods. Typically, an importer controls a fixed supply of goods and the marketing system develops around the philosophy of selling a limited supply of goods at high prices to a small number of affluent customers. In the resulting seller's market, market penetration and mass distribution are not necessary because demand exceeds supply and, in most cases, the customer seeks the supply. This produces a channel structure with a limited number of middlemen.

Contrast this with the mass consumption distribution philosophy that prevails in Europe and other industrialised nations. In these markets, supply is not dominated by one supplier, supply can be increased or decreased within a given range, and profit maximisation occurs at or near production capacity. Generally a buyer's market exists and the producer strives to penetrate the market and push goods out to the consumer, resulting in a highly developed channel structure that includes a variety of intermediaries.

This import-oriented philosophy permeates all aspects of market activities and behaviour. For example, a Brazilian bank had ordered piggy banks for a local promotion; because it went better than expected, the banker placed a reorder of three times the original. The local manufacturer immediately increased the price and, despite arguments pointing out reduced production costs and other supply-cost factors, could not be dissuaded from this action. True to an import-oriented attitude, the notion of economies of scale and the use of price as a demand stimulus escaped the manufacturer who was going on the theory that with demand up, the price also had to go up. A one-deal mentality of pricing at retail and wholesale levels exists because in an import-oriented market, goods come in at a landed price and pricing is then simply an assessment of demand and diminishing supply. If the producer or importer has control of supply, then the price is whatever the market will bear.

This attitude affects the development of intermediaries and their functions. Distribution systems are local rather than national in scope and the relationship between the supplier and any **middleman** in the marketplace is considerably different from that found in a mass-marketing system. The idea of a channel as a chain of intermediaries performing specific activities and each selling to a smaller unit beneath it until the chain reaches the ultimate consumer is not common in an import-oriented system.[4]

European distribution structure

The unified Europe has a larger population than the United States or Japan. However, this population is located in an area that is only 12 per cent of the land area of the United States. In spite of this concentration, transportation in the EU was overburdened with regulations and administrative routines. A truck from Glasgow to Athens was spending 30 per cent of its time on border crossings, waiting and filling out some 200 forms. These inefficiencies are now gone and now only one piece of paper is required to move goods between EU member states. Transit documents have been simplified and custom formalities have been eliminated. As a result companies are now working with centralised warehouses and distribution centres. More and more companies are implementing **just-in-time (JIT)** production and purchasing methods. Pan-European franchising has increased following the removal of trade barriers. Retailers and supermarkets have undergone some restructuring, and companies like Hennes & Mauritz, Zara, Ahold, Aldi and Carréfour are now present in most major cities around Europe. As distribution becomes easier, concentration of production is becoming common. Nestlé, for example, is now producing candy bars in Berlin for distribution throughout Europe. The distributor's power is thus increasing.

United States and Japanese distribution structure

In the United States, the distribution system is most advanced and it is not difficult to reach all corners of the market. The huge size of the market has led to large-sized retailers who often buy direct from manufacturers. At the same time, many manufacturers have their own distribution channels or retail stores.

key terms

middleman
businessman, other than the producer and consumer, involved in exchange of goods

just-in-time (JIT)
deliveries made at a time when the component is to be used and not before (often in manufacturing)

Distribution in Japan has long been considered the most effective non-tariff barrier to the Japanese market.[5] The distribution system is different enough from its United States or European counterparts that it should be carefully studied by anyone contemplating entry. The Japanese system has four distinguishing features: (1) a structure dominated by many small wholesalers dealing with many small retailers; (2) channel control by manufacturers; (3) a business philosophy shaped by a unique culture; and (4) laws that protect the foundation of the system – the small retailer.[6] A comparison of the US, Japan and Germany, the biggest market in Europe, is presented in Exhibit 15.1.

Exhibit 15.1 Retail structure in three countries

	Retail outlets (000s)		
	Germany	Japan	United States
Food stores			
Supermarkets	9.0	15.0	43.7
Hypermarkets	2.3	1.5	3.1
Discounters	15.4	1.0	29.1
Independent grocers	34.2	62.0	9.7
Bakers	47.2	74.7	2.8
Butchers	44.3	16.4	8.0
Fishmongers	27.1	27.0	1.6
Greengrocers	16.1	27.7	3.3
Non-food stores			
Booksellers	25.6	37.0	12.7
Chemists	39.4	83.3	47.4
Department stores	1.2	0.3	13.5
Electronics, computers	30.6	61.9	30.3
Home furnishings	11.7	38.7	28.2
Sporting goods	8.3	19.3	23.2
Toy shops	3.6	12.1	18.0

Source: Euromonitor, 2003.

High Density of Middlemen There is a density of middlemen, retailers and wholesalers in the Japanese market unparalleled in any Western industrialised country. The traditional structure serves consumers who make small, frequent purchases at small, conveniently located stores. Exhibit 15.2 illustrates the contrast between shorter US channels and the long Japanese channels.

In Japan, small stores (95.1 per cent of all retail food stores) account for 57.7 per cent of retail foods sales, whereas in the United States small stores (69.8 per cent of all retail food stores) generate 19.2 per cent of food sales. A disproportionate percentage of non-food sales are made in small stores in Japan as well. In the United States, small stores (81.6 per cent of all stores) sell 32.9 per cent of non-food items; in Japan, small stores (94.1 per cent of all stores) sell 50.4 per cent.[7]

Channel Control In Japan, manufacturers depend on wholesalers for a multitude of services to other members of the distribution network. Financing, physical distribution, warehousing, inventory, promotion and payment collection are provided to other channel members by wholesalers. The system works because wholesalers and all other middlemen

Exhibit 15.2 Comparison of distribution channels between the United States and Japan

Car parts: Japan

| Car makers' affiliated parts makers | Independent parts makers | Repair parts makers |

Car makers — Wholesalers — Special agents

Dealers — Cooperative sales companies — 2nd-level wholesalers

Sub-dealers — Retailers

Large users — Petrol stations

Car repair shops

End users

Car parts: United States

Manufacturer — 51% — Warehouse distributor — Jobber buying groups — Jobber — Installer — Customer

10%

18% — Mass merchandiser

21% — Repair specialist

——— Primary channel   - - - - Secondary channel

Source: McKinsey Industry Studies.

downstream are tied to manufacturers by a set of practices and incentives designed to ensure strong marketing support for their products and to exclude rival competitors from the channel.[8]

Business Philosophy   Coupled with the close economic ties and dependency created by trade customs and the long structure of Japanese distribution channels is a unique business philosophy that emphasises loyalty, harmony and friendship. The value system supports long-term dealer/supplier relationships that are difficult to change as long as each party perceives economic advantage. The traditional partner, the insider, generally has the advantage.

A general lack of price competition, the provision of costly services and other inefficiencies render the cost of Japanese consumer goods among the highest in the world.

GOING INTERNATIONAL 15.1

Mitsukoshi department store, established 1611 – but will it be there in 2011?

Japanese department stores have a long history in Japanese retailing. Mitsukoshi department store, the epitome of Japanese retailing, began as a dry goods store in 1611. To visit a Japanese department store is to get a glimpse of Japanese life. In the basements and sub-basements, food abounds with everything from crunchy Japanese pickles to delicate French pastry and soft-coloured, seasonally changing forms of Japanese candies. Besides the traditional floors for women's and men's clothing and furniture, most stores have a floor devoted to kimonos and related accessories, and another floor dedicated to children's needs and wants. On the roof there may be miniature open-air amusement parks for children.

But wait, there's more. Department stores are not merely content to dazzle with variety, delight with imaginative displays and accept large amounts of yen for clothes and vegetables. They also seek to serve up a bit of culture. Somewhere between the floors of clothing and the roof, it is likely that you will find a banqueting hall, an art gallery, an exhibition hall and one or two floors of restaurants serving everything from *doria* (creamy rice with cheese) to *tempura*. Department stores aim to be 'total lifestyle enterprises,' says one manager. 'We try to be all-inclusive, with art, culture, shopping and fashion. We stress the philosophy of *i-shoku-ju*, the three big factors in life: what you wear, what you eat and how you live.'

Japanese retailing is dominated by two kinds of store, giant department stores like Mitsukoshi and small neighbourhood shops, both kept alive by a complex distribution system that translates into high prices for the Japanese consumer. In exchange for high prices, the Japanese consumer gets variety, services and, what may be unique to Japanese department stores, cultural enlightenment.

But there are winds of change. Sales for department stores have been down. The Japanese like the amenities of department stores but they are beginning to take notice of the wave of 'new' discount stores that are challenging the traditional retail system by offering quality products at sharply reduced prices. Aoyama Trading Company, which opened a discount men's suit store in the heart of Ginza, where Tokyo's most prestigious department stores are located, may be the future. The owner says he can sell suits for two-thirds the department store price by purchasing directly from manufacturers. Another omen may be Toys 'R' Us, which has opened 16 discount toy stores in Japan. Department store response has been to discount toy prices, for the first time, by as much as 30 per cent.

■ As one discounter after another 'cherry picks' item after item to discount, can department stores continue to be 'total lifestyle enterprises'? Will there be a Mitsukoshi, as we know it today, in 2011?

Source: 'A World in Themselves', *Look Japan*, January 1994, pp. 40-2; 'From Men's Suits to Sake, Discounting Booms in Japan', *Advertising Age International*, 21 March 1994, pp. 1-4; F. Crawford, 'Business Without Borders', *Chain Store Age*, December 2001, pp. 86-96.

Large-scale Retail Store Law   Competition from large retail stores has been almost totally controlled by *Daitenho* – the large-scale retail store law. Designed to protect small retailers from large intruders into their markets, the law requires that any store larger than 500 square metres (5382 square feet) must have approval from the prefectural government to be 'built, expanded, stay open later in the evening, or change the days of the month they must remain closed'.[9]

Agreements between the European Union, the United States and Japan have had a profound impact on the Japanese distribution system, leading to deregulation of retailing and by strengthening rules on monopoly business practices.[10] The retailing law has been relaxed to permit new outlets as large as 1000 square metres without prior permission. Limits on store hours and business days per year have also been lifted.[11] Officially relaxing laws and regulations on retailing is but one of the important changes signalling the beginning of profound changes in how the Japanese shop.[12]

trends: from traditional to modern channel structures

Today, few countries are so sufficiently isolated that they are unaffected by global economic and political changes. These currents of change are altering all levels of economic fabric, including the distribution structure. Traditional channel structures are giving way to new forms, new alliances and new processes – some more slowly than others, but all changing. Pressures for change in a country come from within and without. Multinational marketers are seeking ways to profitably tap market segments that are served by costly, traditional distribution systems. Direct marketing, door-to-door selling, hypermarkets, discount houses, shopping malls, catalogue selling and selling through the Internet are being introduced in an attempt to provide efficient distribution channels.[13]

In anticipation of a single European market, national and international retailing networks are developing throughout Europe. An example is Sainsbury's, the UK supermarket giant, which has entered an alliance with Esselunga of Italy (supermarkets), Docks de France (hypermarkets, supermarkets and discount stores) and Belgium's Delhaize (supermarkets). The alliance provides the opportunity for the four to pool their experience and buying power and prepare to expand into other European markets.[14] Ahold (Albert Heijn) of the Netherlands is expanding globally from the United States to Asia. More than 60 per cent of its revenue is coming from abroad. While European retailers see a unified Europe as an opportunity for pan-European expansion, foreign retailers are attracted by the high margins and prices characterised as 'among the most expensive anywhere in the world'. Costco, the US-based warehouse retailer, saw the high gross margins British supermarkets command, 7 to 8 per cent compared with 2.5 to 3 per cent in the United States, as an opportunity. Costco prices will be 10 to 20 per cent cheaper than rival local retailers. The impact of these and other trends is to change traditional distribution and marketing systems, leading to greater efficiency in distribution. Competition will translate those efficiencies into lower consumer prices. Exhibit 15.3 gives you an idea of the retail structures found in selected countries.

Exhibit 15.3 Retail structure in selected countries

Country	All retailers (000)	People served per retailer	Internet users (per 1 000)
United States	702	395	501
Canada	112	276	434
Argentina	296	127	88
Germany	410	200	374
Poland	390	99	98
Israel	53	119	281
South Africa	93	482	71
China	21 188	61	11
Japan	1 202	106	440
Australia	93	208	371

Source: Euromonitor, World Bank 2003.

the Internet

The Internet is an important distribution method for multinational companies and a source of products for businesses and consumers. Computer hardware and software companies and book and music retailers were the early e-marketers to use this method of distribution and marketing. More recently there was an expansion of other types of retailing and business-to-business (B2B) services into **e-commerce**. Technically,

key term

e-commerce is a form of direct selling; however, because of its newness and the unique issues associated with this form of distribution, it is important to differentiate it from other types of direct marketing.

E-commerce is used to market business-to-business services, consumer services and consumer and industrial products via the World Wide Web. It involves the direct marketing from a manufacturer, retailer, service provider or some other intermediary to a final user. Some examples of e-marketers with an international presence are Dell Computer Corporation (www.dell.com), which generates nearly 50 per cent of its total sales, an average of about €84 million a day, online, and Cisco Systems (www.cisco.com), which generates more than €1.2 billion in sales annually. Cisco's website appears in 14 languages and has country-specific content for 49 nations. Gateway has global sites in Japan, France, the Netherlands, Germany, Sweden, Australia, the United Kingdom and the United States, to name a few (www.gateway.com).

Besides consumer goods companies such as Levi's, Nike and others, many smaller and less well-known companies have established a presence on the Internet beyond their traditional markets. An Internet customer from the Netherlands can purchase a pair of brake levers for his mountain bike in California-based Price Point. He pays $159 (€130) in America instead of the $232 (€190) that the same items would cost in a local bike store.

For a Spanish shopper in Pamplona, buying sheet music used to mean a 400-kilometre trip to Madrid. Now he crosses the Atlantic to shop – and the journey takes less time than a trip to the corner store. Via the Internet he can buy directly from specialised stores and high-volume discounters in London, and almost anywhere else.

E-commerce is more developed in the United States than the rest of the world, partly because of the vast number of people who own personal computers and because of the much lower cost of access to the Internet than found elsewhere. However, according to some estimates, Europeans actually spent as much on e-commerce in 2002 as Americans, both at about $19.3 billion (€15.8 billion).[15]

Small and middle-sized firms are expected to generate substantial growth in international transactions, as well as to pool their purchases through various Internet exchanges for everything from telephone services and office furniture to electricity. Although each order is individually small, such purchases combined account for 30 to 60 per cent of firms' total non-labour costs and are usually bought inefficiently and expensively. Overall costs are reduced by bulk buying through an online intermediary and the savings resulting from placing and processing orders online, which is much cheaper and faster than the traditional way. One study estimates that if all small and medium-sized firms in Britain used the Internet to buy indirect inputs, they could save more than $36.7 billion (€30 billion) a year.

Services, the third engine for growth, are ideally suited for international sales via the Internet. All types of services – banking, education, consulting, retailing, gambling – can be marketed through a website that is globally accessible. As outsourcing of traditional in-house tasks such as inventory management, quality control, accounting, secretarial, translation and legal services has become more popular among companies, the Internet providers of these services have grown internationally. The introduction of broadband has facilitated the usage of the Internet. Exhibit 15.4 shows broadband penetration in the top 10 countries.

E-commerce enables companies to cut costs in three ways. First, it reduces procurement costs, making it easier to find the cheapest supplier, and it cuts the cost of processing the transactions. Estimates are that a firm's possible savings from purchasing over the Internet vary from 2 per cent in the coal industry to up to 40 per cent in electronic components. British telecom claims that procuring goods and services online will reduce the average cost of processing a transaction by 90 per cent and reduce the direct costs of goods and services it purchases by 11 per cent. The Ford, GM, and DaimlerChrysler exchange network for buying components from suppliers could reduce the cost of making

361

Exhibit 15.4 Top 10 markets with most broadband penetration (2003) (percentage of total households)

South Korea	70.5
Hong Kong	50.3
Taiwan	43.2
Canada	36.2
Singapore	28.6
Japan	28.0
Denmark	25.7
Belgium	24.7
Switzerland	23.1
United States	22.5

Source: e-Marketer Inc., New York; and *Marketing News*, 'Wired and Wireless Activity, Forces Ahead in the Global Arena', 15 July 2004, p.16.

a car by as much as 14 per cent. Second, it allows better supply-chain management. And, third, it makes possible tighter inventory control. With Wal-Mart's direct Internet links between its inventory control system and its suppliers, each sale automatically triggers a replenishment request. The results are fewer out-of-stock situations, the ability to make rapid inventory adjustments, and reduced ordering and processing costs.

The World Wide Web, as a market, is rapidly moving through the stage where the novelty of buying on the Web is giving way to a more sophisticated customer who has more and constantly improving websites to choose from. In short, Web merchants are facing more competition, and Web customers have more choice. This means that if a company is going to be successful in this new era of marketing, the basics of good marketing cannot be overlooked.

By its very nature, e-commerce has some unique issues that must be addressed if a domestic e-vendor expects to be a viable player in the international cyber-marketplace. Many other issues arise because the host-country intermediary who would ordinarily be involved in international marketing is eliminated. An important advantage of selling direct is that total costs can be lowered so that the final price overseas is considerably less than it would have been through a local-country middleman.

factors influencing marketing through the Internet

1 **Culture.** The website and the product must be culturally neutral or adapted to fit the uniqueness of a market, because culture does matter. In Japan, the pickiness of Japanese consumers about what they buy and their reluctance to deal with merchants at a distance must be addressed when marketing on the web. Even a Japanese-language site can offend Japanese sensibilities. As one e-commerce consultant warns, in a product description, you wouldn't say 'Don't turn the knob left', because that's too direct. Instead you would say something like: 'It would be much better to turn the knob to the right.' Too many European sites are more consumer oriented. The different cultural reactions to colour can be a potential problem for websites designed for global markets. While red may be highly regarded in China or associated with love in the United States, in Spain it is associated with socialism. The point is that when designing a website, culture cannot be forgotten.

2 **Adaptation.** Ideally, a website should be translated into the languages of the target markets. This may not be finally feasible for some companies, but at least the most important pages of the site should be translated. Simple translation of important pages is only a stopgap, however. If companies are making a long-term commitment to sales in another country, web pages should be designed (in all senses of the term – colour, use of features, etc.) for that market. One researcher suggests that if a website does not have at least multiple languages, a company is losing sales. It is the company's responsibility to bridge the language and cultural gap; the customer will not bother – he or she will simply go to a site that speaks his or her language. As discussed earlier, culture does count, and as competition increases, a country-specific website may make the difference between success and failure.[16]

3 **Local contact.** Companies fully committed to foreign markets are creating virtual offices abroad; they buy server space and create mirror sites, whereby a company has a voicemail or fax contact point in key markets. Foreign customers are more likely to visit sites in their own country and in the local language. In Japan, where consumers seem particularly concerned about the ability to return goods easily, companies may have outlets where merchandise can be returned and picked up. These so-called clicks-and-mortar models have gained a large following.

4 **Payment.** The consumer should be able to use a credit card number – by e-mail (from a secure page on the website), by fax or over the phone.

5 **Delivery.** For companies operating in Europe, surface postal delivery of small parcels is most cost effective but takes the longest time. For more rapid but more expensive deliveries, Federal Express, United Parcel Service and other private delivery services provide delivery worldwide. For example, Tom Clancy's bestseller *Executive Orders*, shipped express to Paris from Seattle-based Amazon.com, would cost a reader €67.92. The same book delivered in four to 10 weeks via surface mail costs €31.22, which is a substantial saving over the cost of the book in a Paris bookstore, where it sells for €43.28.

Once sufficient volume in a country or region is attained, container shipments to free trade zones or bonded warehouses can be used for distribution of individual orders via local delivery services within the region. These same locations can also be used for such after-sales services as spare parts, defective product returns and supplies. Companies such as FedEx, UPS and similar small-package delivery services also have overseas storage and fulfilment centres for individual orders that e-commerce companies can use to provide faster and less costly in-country delivery.

6 **Promotion.** Although the web is a means of promotion, if you are engaging in e-commerce you also need to advertise your presence and the products or services offered. How do you attract visitors from other countries to your website? The same way you would at home – except in the local language. Search engine registration, press releases, local newsgroups and forums, mutual links and banner advertising are the traditional methods. A website should be seen as a retail store, with the only difference between it and a physical store being that the customer arrives over the Internet instead of on foot.

When discussing the Internet and international channels of distribution, the question of how traditional channels will be changed by the Internet must be considered. Already, comparison shopping across the continent via the Internet is wrenching apart commercial patterns cobbled together over centuries.

electronic commerce

The Internet has connected hundreds of millions of the world's people through a seamless digital network. A store placed on the Internet anywhere is in fact everywhere. If the store sells digital products, such as Netscape, it can deliver the products as easily as handing them over the counter. Cisco Computers, a network equipment maker, is already selling

products from its website at the rate of $1 billion (€900 million) a year. General Electric is saving a fortune by buying $1 billion (€900 million) worth of components from its suppliers online. Dell is selling more than $1 million worth of PCs a day on the web.

According to surveys by Nielsen and from international data, 73 per cent of Internet users had used the web for shopping in 1997. It is estimated that by 2007, some 114 million consumers will be buying online, in Europe alone, spending an average of €120 a year.

Electronic commerce does not only mean buying online – many consumers search for their purchase online and then buy in another way. The Internet is just one source of **electronic commerce**. Credit cards, automatic teller machines, telephone banking, electronic data interchange (EDI) and other commercial online services from France's Minitel to Compuserve are all examples of electronic commerce. All these have changed their own markets and competition in a radical way.

Credit cards initiated home shopping by creating a virtual payment system that transcended national borders. The Internet extends this beyond the transaction itself to everything that comes before and after, from marketing to product display to order tracking and even delivery. And, unlike the commercial services, which are open only to their subscribers, the Internet is open to everyone. If we consider e-mail, it is much the same as regular mail but it is faster. It is so much faster that it has reshaped companies, curtailed distances and has revitalised letter writing.

Electronic commerce has already had a profound impact on retailing. There are now thousands of online shopping malls, supermalls and malls-of-malls, which are competing directly with traditional retailers.

Other than financial services, travel and adult entertainment, retailing has been affected most by electronic commerce. The most obvious advantage of electronic shops is that their costs are lower and they are less constrained for space as compared to traditional retailers. A number of traditional retailers have also opened their electronic shops on the Internet but their offerings are often limited, hard to find and slow to download or see on the screen. Building an online shopping site that is attractive and convenient to buyers is not an easy task.

Advertising and marketing, although not strictly in the category of electronic commerce, have also been profoundly affected by this development. Unlike traditional advertising, **Internet advertising** is interactive and can be customised for each viewer. Internet advertising cannot replace mass advertising in other media but is a good alternative to direct mail, which is normally quite expensive. The Internet makes it easier both to communicate with and target potential customers.[17]

Financial services and travel are two of the many sectors that are already using the Internet for marketing and customer services. An Internet advertising banner provides a direct link to the advertiser's website for more information and alternatives. Compare it with television advertising where a customer sees the advertisement for a minute or less and may have to remember it for days until he or she next goes shopping. The Internet advertisement allows not only for more information, but also for an immediate response or purchase. The total Internet advertising revenues were $267 million (€241 million) as compared to $33 billion (€30 billion) for television advertising in America alone.

It is not only retailers who believe that the traditional shop may soon become a rarity; manufacturers are equally worried. Procter & Gamble, one of the largest advertisers in the world, has revealed that it is considering moving 80 per cent of its $3 billion (€2.7 billion) advertising budget to the Internet. The Internet is considered the most important marketing media in history.

The amount of goods and services sold through electronic commerce is growing at an amazing rate. In 1998, goods and services sold online in Europe and the United States exceeded $5 billion (€4.5 billion), double the figure for 1997.[18] It is estimated that online commerce was worth around $65 billion (€59 billion) in 2001.

key terms

electronic commerce
buying/selling a product via the Internet

internet advertising
advertising on and through websites

GOING INTERNATIONAL 15.3

big-box cookie-cutter stores don't always work

Wal-Mart, JCPenney and Office Depot are all going global with their successful US operating strategy. Friendly service, low prices, extensive variety and apples-to-appliance
offerings – all hallmarks of such stores – make tradition-bound retail foreign markets
look ripe to pick with their poor service, high prices and limited products. Counting on
their tremendous buying power and operating efficiency to enable them to lower prices,
such large retailers went global. But not all is the same the world over. Adaptation is still
important, and many had to adapt their operating strategy to accommodate cultural
and business differences. Growth strategies must be
supported by three foundations: (1) the retailer must
offer a competitively superior product as defined by
local customers, (2) the retailer must be able to develop
superior economies across the value chain that delivers
the product to the local consumer, and (3) global retailers must be able to execute in the local environment.

Consider, for example, some of the problems US
retailers had when building their global strategies on
these three pillars.

- In fashion and clothing markets, personal taste is critically important in the buying
  decision. Distinctions in culture, climate and even physiology demand that products
  be tailored to each market. Tight skirts, blouses and any other article that tightly
  hugs the female silhouette are sure sellers in southern Europe and sure losers in the
  north. Dutch women bicycle to work, so tight skirts are out, French men insist that
  trousers be suitable for cuffs; German men cannot be bothered with cuffs. Rayon and
  other artificial fabrics are impossible to sell in Germany, but next door in Holland artificial fabrics are popular because they are much cheaper.
- The best-selling children's lines in northern Europe don't have a significant following
  in France; the French dress their children as little adults, not as kids. One of the best
  sellers is a downsized version of a women's clothing line for girls.
- The lack of sunshine in northern Europe means that lime-green fashions don't sell
  well there; consumers sense that the colour leaves a rather sickly impression. But in
  the south, lime green looks great with a St Tropez tan.
- Operational costs vary too. Costs in the United States, where the minimum wage is
  $5.15 per hour, are dramatically different than in France, where the minimum wage is
  over $10.00, including employer social charges. As a consequence, Toys 'R' Us was
  forced to adapt its operating structure in France, where it uses one-third fewer
  employees per store than it does in the United States.
- The image of Sam Walton's English setter on packages of its private-label dog food,
  Ol' Roy, was replaced with a terrier after Wal-Mart's German executives explained
  that terriers are popular in Germany, while setters aren't familiar.
- JCPenney is closing its five home-furnishing stores in Japan, in part because so
  many products, from curtains to bed sheets, had to be made differently there.
- Office Depot closed its US-style cookie-cutter stores in Japan and reopened stores
  one-third the size of the larger ones. Customers were put off by the warehouse-like
  atmosphere and confused by the English-language signs. The new stores have signs
  in Japanese and are stocked with office products more familiar to the Japanese and
  purchased locally, such as two-ring loose-leaf binders rather than the typical three-
  ring binders sold in the United States.

■ After initially doing well, Starbucks is no longer making a profit in Japan. It appears to be a matter of taste. One consumer reports, 'The coffee tastes artificial.'

Source: Ernest Beck and Emily Nelson, 'As Wal-Mart Invades Europe, Rivals Rush to Match its Formula', *Wall Street Journal*, 6 October 1999; John C. Koopman, 'Successful Global Retailers: A Rare Breed', *Canadian Manager*, April 2000, p. 22; Yumiko Ono, 'US Superstores Find Japanese Are a Hard Sell', *Wall Street Journal*, 14 February 2000, p. C1; and Stanley Holmes, Irene M. Kunii, Jack Ewing and Kerry Capell, 'For Starbucks, There's No Place Like Home', *Business Week*, 9 June 2003, p. 48.

Across Europe, electronic commerce has become a reliable alternative to traditional shopping. It has revived catalogue shopping, which was earlier considered a downmarket and lower-quality provider that would take weeks or months to arrive. With the help of the Internet, this method has become trendy for buying anything from a dress to computers. The Internet offering promises delivery within 24–48 hours.

Two years of research by the Consumer Direct Cooperative (CDC), a consortium of 31 organisations including Coca-Cola, Nabisco and Procter & Gamble, identified six major groups of potential online shoppers.

1 *Shopping avoiders*: customers who dislike the routine of regular grocery shopping.
2 *Necessity users*: people who are limited in their ability to go shopping, due to their working hours or having young children.
3 *New technologists*: younger customers who are eager to embrace and feel comfortable with new technologies.
4 *Time-starved*: people who do not worry much about the price and are willing to pay extra to save time.
5 *Responsibles*: customers who have a lot of free time and enjoy shopping.
6 *Traditional customers*: often older people who normally avoid new technologies and enjoy shopping in high-street shops.

According to this research, the first four groups are real potential online shoppers as they see a clear advantage in electronic commerce. The last two groups are initially reluctant, but CDC believes even they will change over time.

distribution patterns

International marketers need a general awareness of the patterns of distribution that confront them in world marketplaces. Nearly every international trading firm is forced by the structure of the market to use at least some middlemen in the distribution arrangement. It is all too easy to conclude that, because the structural arrangements of foreign and domestic distribution seem alike, foreign channels are the same as or similar to domestic channels of the same name. This is misleading. Only when the varied intricacies of actual distribution patterns are understood can the complexity of the distribution task be appreciated.

general patterns

Generalising about the internal distribution channel patterns of various countries is almost as difficult as generalising about the behaviour patterns of people. Despite similarities, marketing channels are not the same throughout the world. Marketing methods taken for granted in most European Union markets are rare in many countries. Even within Europe there are differences, as illustrated by Exhibit 15.5. However, these rules are changing in many countries. A number of countries, such as France and the Netherlands, are changing these rules to protect small independent retailers from bigger chain stores.

Exhibit 15.5 Shopping around: permitted shopping hours in Europe

Country	Monday–Friday	Saturday	Sunday
Austria	07.00–19.30	07.00–13.00	Closed (exceptions in tourist areas)
Belgium	05.00–20.00	05.00–20.00	05.00–13.00
Britain	No restriction	No restriction	No restriction (large shops can open for only six hours)
Denmark	05.00–17.00	06.00–17.00	Closed (except small shops)
Germany	06.00–20.00	06.00–16.00	Closed (except small shops)
Finland	07.00–21.00	07.00–18.00	Closed (except 12.00–21.00 in June to August and December)
France	No restriction	No restriction	No restriction (but no obligation for employees to work)
Ireland	No restriction	No restriction	No restriction
Italy	09.00–20.00*	09.00–20.00	Closed
Luxembourg	06.00–20.00	06.00–18.00	06.00–13.00
Netherlands	06.00–22.00	06.00–22.00	Closed (shops may open 12 Sundays a year)
Norway	06.00–20.00	06.00–18.00	Closed
Sweden	No restriction	No restriction	No restriction

*Must close for half a day once a week.

Source: based on 'Il Sole 24 Ore', *The Economist*, 14 March 1998, p. 41.

Middlemen Services   Service attitudes of trades people vary sharply at both the retail and wholesale levels from country to country. In Egypt, for example, the primary purpose of the simple trading system is to handle the physical distribution of available goods. On the other hand, when margins are low and there is a continuing battle for customer preference, both wholesalers and retailers try to offer extra services to make their goods attractive to consumers. When middlemen aren't interested in promoting or selling individual items of merchandise, the manufacturer must provide adequate inducement to the middlemen, or undertake much of the promotion and selling effort.

Line Breadth   Every nation has a distinct pattern relative to the breadth of line carried by wholesalers and retailers. The distribution system of some countries seems to be characterised by middlemen who carry or can get everything. In others, every middleman seems to be a specialist dealing only in extremely narrow lines. Government regulations in some countries limit the breadth of line that can be carried by middlemen, and licensing requirements to handle certain merchandise are not uncommon.

Costs and Margins   Cost levels and middleman margins vary widely from country to country, depending on the level of competition, services offered, efficiencies or inefficiencies of scale, and geographic and turnover factors related to market size, purchasing power, tradition and other basic determinants. In India, competition in large cities is so intense that costs are low and margins thin; but in rural areas, the lack of capital has permitted the few traders with capital to gain monopolies, with consequent high prices and wide margins.

Channel Length   Some correlation may be found between the stage of economic development and the length of marketing channels. In every country, channels are likely to be shorter for industrial goods and for high-priced consumer goods than for low-priced products. In general, there is an inverse relationship between channel length and the size

of the purchase. Combination wholesaler–retailers or semi-wholesalers exist in many countries, adding one or two links to the length of the distribution chain. In China, for example, the traditional distribution system for over-the-counter drugs consists of large local wholesalers divided into three levels. First-level wholesalers supply drugs to major cities such as Beijing and Shanghai. Second-level ones service medium-sized cities, while the third level distributes to counties and cities with 100 000 people or fewer. It can be profitable for a company to sell directly to the top two levels of wholesalers and leave them to sell to the third level, which is so small that it would be unprofitable for the company to seek out.[19]

GOING INTERNATIONAL 15.4

changing the nature of retailing

A partnership between academic researchers and business called the Auto-ID Center, based in Cambridge, Massachusetts, and founded in 1999, has been developing a new 'smart tag' technology that is likely to replace the barcodes on consumer goods. The

smart tags are a new, supercheap version of an old tracking technology called Radio Frequency Identification (RFID). RFID systems are made up of readers and smart tags – or microchips attached to antennas. When the tag nears a reader, it broadcasts the information contained in its chip. From 1999 to 2003, the price of the cheapest tags plummeted from $2 to 20 cents. The technology is already widely used to track pets, livestock, parts in car factories and luggage at airports. Gillette announced that it had put in an order for half a billion smart tags, signalling the start of their adoption by the consumer-goods industry.

The smart tags can be combined with smart shelves, which are fitted with tag readers. Gillette says that retailers and consumer-goods firms in America lose around $30 billion a year in sales because shop shelves run out of products and stand empty. With smart tags and readers, shop shelves will be able to keep count of the products and let the store staff know when the stock runs low. Gillette is also piloting the use of smart tags to track products as they move from factory to supermarket, as using barcodes is an error-prone and labour-intensive task. That is expected to reduce shipment errors and cut theft. Because manufacturers will be sure that they are shipping the right quantities of goods to the right place, they can also afford to shrink the inventories they maintain in case of error, thus increasing efficiencies in managing stocks.

The biggest worry is that consumers will reject the smart tags because of privacy concerns. If firms link products to consumers at the checkout, ordinary objects could become traceable after their purchase. To address this problem, the Auto-ID Center included a 'kill command' in its chip specifications that can permanently disable the tag at the checkout.

Source: adapted from 'The IT Revolution: The Best Thing Since the Bar-code', *The Economist*, 8 February 2003, pp. 71–2.

Non-existent Channels   One of the things companies discover about international channel-of-distribution patterns is that, in many countries, adequate market coverage through a simple channel of distribution is nearly impossible. In many instances, appropriate channels do not exist; in others, parts of a channel system are available but other parts are not. Several distinct distribution channels are necessary to reach different segments of

a market; channels suitable for distribution in urban areas seldom provide adequate rural coverage.

Eastern Europe presents a special problem. When communism collapsed, so did the government-run distribution system. Local entrepreneurs are emerging to fill the gap but they lack facilities, training and product knowledge, and they are generally undercapitalised. Companies that have any hope of getting goods to customers profitably must be prepared to invest heavily in distribution.[20]

Blocked Channels   International marketers may be blocked from using the channel of their choice. Channel blockage can result from competitors' already-established lines in the various channels and trade associations or cartels having closed certain channels. Associations of middlemen sometimes restrict the number of distribution alternatives available to a producer. Drug manufacturers in many countries have inhibited distribution of a wide range of goods through any retail outlets except pharmacies. The pharmacies, in turn, have been supplied by a relatively small number of wholesalers who have long-established relationships with their suppliers. Thus, through a combination of competition and association, a producer may be kept out of the market completely.

Stocking   The high cost of credit, danger of loss through inflation, lack of capital and other concerns cause foreign middlemen in many countries to limit inventories. This often results in out-of-stock conditions and sales lost to competitors. Physical distribution lags intensify their problem so that, in many cases, the manufacturer must provide local warehousing or extend long credit to encourage middlemen to carry large inventories. Considerable ingenuity, assistance and, perhaps, pressure are required to induce middlemen in most countries to carry adequate or even minimal inventories.

Power and Competition   Distribution power tends to concentrate in countries where a few large wholesalers distribute to a mass of small middlemen. Large wholesalers generally finance middlemen downstream. The strong allegiance they command from their customers enables them to effectively block existing channels and force an outsider to rely on less effective and more costly distribution.

retail patterns

Retailing shows even greater diversity in its structure than does wholesaling. In Italy and Morocco, retailing is largely composed of speciality houses that carry narrow lines, while in Finland most retailers carry a more general line of merchandise. Retail size is represented at one end by Japan's giant Mitsukoshi, which reportedly enjoys the patronage of more than 100 000 customers every day. The other extreme is represented in the market of Ibadan, Nigeria, where some 3000 one- or two-person stalls serve not many more customers.

Size Patterns   The extremes in size in retailing are similar to those that predominate in wholesaling. The retail structure and the problems it engenders cause real difficulties for the international marketing firm selling consumer goods. In Italy, official figures show there are 865 000 retail stores, or one store for every 66 Italians. Of the 340 000 food stores, fewer than 1500 can be classified as large. Thus, middlemen are a critical factor in adequate distribution in Italy.

Emerging countries present similar problems. Among the large supermarket chains in South Africa there is considerable concentration. One thousand of the country's 31 000 stores control 60 per cent of all grocery sales, leaving the remaining 40 per cent of sales to be spread among 30 000 stores. It may be difficult to reach the 40 per cent of the market served by those 30 000 stores. Predominantly in black communities, retailing is on a small scale - cigarettes are often sold singly, and the entire fruit inventory may consist of four apples in a bowl.[21]

GOING INTERNATIONAL 15.5

worldwide wholesalers

**The late Pope
John Paul II in St.
Peter's square**
©Giansanti
Gianni/CORBIS
SYGMA)

In some industries there are worldwide wholesalers who buy and distribute the products throughout the world. For example, in the flower industry, the Netherlands has historically been the place for trading. Dutch traders bought tulips from the Ottoman Empire in 1593. They used to sell promissory notes to guarantee future delivery of tulips and bulbs. At today's present value, these promissory notes were priced around €1 million for a single black tulip bulb – enough money to buy a five-storey house in central Amsterdam today.

Today at Amsterdam flower market you can buy a black tulip for about €1. From the wholesale warehouse at Aalsmeer, 150 football fields of cut flowers worth €20 million are auctioned every day. The bidders in four huge auction rooms pay attention to the 'clock' as high starting prices tick down. The wholesaler-buyer that stops the clock pays the indicated price. Thus, at Aalsmeer the prices are set for flowers all over the world. The Dutch are the biggest exporter of flowers (60 per cent of the world total).

Outside Aalsmeer auction house, trucks are constantly loaded for shipments by land across Europe and by air freight worldwide. The US, Japan and Germany are the big buyers. Every Easter Sunday, the Pope addresses the world from St Peter's Square in Rome, reciting 'Bedank voor bloemen.' Thus every Easter he thanks the Dutch nation for providing the flowers for this key Catholic ritual.

Direct Marketing　　Retailing around the world has been in a state of active ferment for several years. The rate of change appears to be directly related to the stage and speed of economic development, and even the least-developed countries are experiencing dramatic changes. Supermarkets of one variety or another are blossoming in developed and developing countries alike. Discount houses that sell everything from powdered milk and canned chilli to Korean TVs and VCRs are thriving and expanding worldwide. Selling directly to the consumer through the mail, by telephone or door-to-door is becoming the distribution-marketing approach of choice in markets with insufficient and/or underdeveloped distribution systems. Avon has successfully expanded into Eastern Europe, Latin America and Asia with its method of direct marketing. Companies that enlist individuals to sell their products, such as Avon, are proving to be especially popular in Eastern Europe and other countries where many are looking for ways to become entrepreneurs.[22]

Direct sales through catalogues have proved to be a successful way to enter foreign markets. In Japan, it has been an important way to break the trade barrier imposed by the Japanese distribution system. For example, a US mail-order company, Shop America, has teamed up with 7-Eleven in Japan to distribute catalogues in its 4000 stores. Shop America sells items such as compact discs, Canon cameras and Rolex watches for 30 to 50 per cent less than Tokyo stores.

Resistance to Change　　Efforts to improve the efficiency of the distribution system, new types of middlemen, and other attempts to change traditional ways are typically viewed as threatening and thus resisted. Laws abound that protect the entrenched in their positions. In Italy, a new retail outlet must obtain a licence from a municipal board composed of local trades people. In a two-year period, some 200 applications were made and only 10 new licences granted. Opposition to retail innovation prevails everywhere, yet in the face of all the

Exhibit 15.6 International channel-of-distribution alternatives

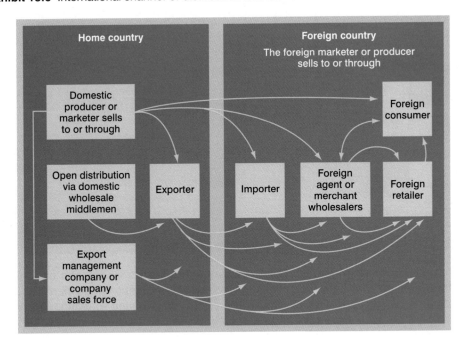

restrictions and hindrances, self-service, discount merchandising, liberal store hours and large-scale merchandising continue to grow because they offer the consumer convenience and a broad range of quality product brands at advantageous prices.

alternative middleman choices

A marketer's options range from assuming the entire distribution activity (by establishing its own subsidiaries and marketing directly to the end user) to depending on intermediaries for distribution of the product. Channel selection must be given considerable thought since, once initiated, it is difficult to change, and if it proves inappropriate, future growth of market share may be affected.[23]

Exhibit 15.6 shows some of the possible channel-of-distribution alternatives. The arrows show those to whom the producer and each of the middlemen may sell. In the home country, the seller must have an organisation (generally the international marketing division of a company) to deal with channel members needed to move goods between countries. In the foreign market, the seller must supervise the channels that supply the product to the end user.

Once the marketer has clarified company objectives and policies, the next step is the selection of specific intermediaries needed to develop a channel.[23] External middlemen are differentiated on whether or not they take title to the goods. Agent middlemen represent the principal rather than themselves, and merchant middlemen take title to the goods and buy and sell on their own account. The distinction between agent and merchant middlemen is important because a manufacturer's control of the distribution process is affected by who has title to the goods in the channel.

■ **Agent middlemen** work on commission and arrange for sales in the foreign country but do not take title to the merchandise. By using agents, the manufacturer assumes trading risk but maintains the right to establish policy guidelines and prices, and to require its agents to provide sales records and customer information.

Remember for a moment the scene in the Pixar movie *Monsters, Inc.* – millions of doors on conveyor belts. That scene is reminiscent of the inside of Nike's European distribution centre in Laakdal, Belgium. The shoes come from a variety of Asian low-cost manufacturers and arrive at the centre via Rotterdam and Antwerp and the adjacent canal. Some 12 000 people work at the heavily automated facility where 8 million pairs of shoes are sorted and then shipped to customers all over the continent by truck. Even as sales grow the company will not need to expand the centre because the trend is for the factories to ship directly to the major European retailers, including Nike Sport in St Petersburg.

■ **Merchant middlemen** actually take title to manufacturers' goods and assume the trading risks, so they tend to be less controllable than agent middlemen. Merchant middlemen provide a variety of import and export wholesaling functions involved in purchasing for their own account and selling in other countries. Because merchant middlemen are primarily concerned with sales and profit margins on their merchandise, they are frequently criticised for not representing the best interests of a manufacturer. Unless they have a franchise or a strong and profitable brand, merchant middlemen seek goods from any source and are likely to have low brand loyalty. Ease of contact, minimised credit risk and elimination of all merchandise handling outside the home market are some of the advantages of using merchant middlemen.

Middlemen are not clear-cut, precise, easily defined entities. It is exceptional to find a firm that represents one of the pure types identified here. What functions are performed by the British middleman called a *stockist*, or one called an *exporter* or *importer*? One company engages in both importing and exporting, acts as an agent and a merchant middleman, operates from offices in the United States, Germany and the United Kingdom, provides financial services and acts as a freight forwarder. It would be difficult to put this company into an appropriate pigeonhole. Many firms work in a single capacity, but the conglomerate type of middleman described here is a major force in some international business.

Only by analysing middlemen functions in skeletal simplicity can the nature of the channels be determined. Three alternatives are presented: first, middlemen physically located in the manufacturer's home country; next, middlemen located in foreign countries; and, finally, a company-owned system.

home country middlemen

Home country, or domestic, middlemen, located in the producing firm's country, provide marketing services from a domestic base. By selecting **domestic middlemen** as intermediaries in the distribution processes, companies relegate foreign-market distribution to others. Domestic middlemen offer many advantages for companies with a small international sales volume, those inexperienced with foreign markets, those not wanting to become immediately involved with the complexities of international marketing and those wanting to sell abroad with minimum financial and management commitment. A major trade-off for using domestic middlemen is limited control over the entire process. Domestic middlemen are most likely to be used when the marketer is uncertain and/or desires to

minimise financial and management investment. A brief discussion of the more frequently used domestic middlemen follows.

Export Management Companies The **export management company (EMC)** is an important middleman for firms with relatively small international volume or those unwilling to involve their own personnel in the international function. EMCs range in size from one person up to 100 and handle about 10 per cent of the manufactured goods exported.

Whether handling five clients or 100, the EMC's stock-in-trade is personalised service. Typically, the EMC becomes an integral part of the marketing operations of the client companies. Working under the names of the manufacturers, the EMC functions as a low-cost, independent marketing department with direct responsibility to the parent firm. The working relationship is so close that customers are often unaware they are not dealing directly with the export department of the company (see Exhibit 15.7).

Exhibit 15.7 How does an EMC operate?

> **Most export management companies offer a wide range of services and assistance, including:**
>
> - researching foreign markets for a client's products
>
> - travelling overseas to determine the best method of distributing the product
>
> - appointing distributors or commission representatives as needed in individual foreign countries, frequently within an already existing overseas network created for similar goods
>
> - exhibiting the client's products at international trade shows, such as US Department of Commerce-sponsored commercial exhibitions at trade fairs and US Export Development Offices around the world
>
> - handling the routine details in getting the product to the foreign customer – export declarations, shipping and customs documentation, insurance, banking and instructions for special export packing and marking
>
> - granting the customary finance terms to the trade abroad and assuring payment to the manufacturer of the product
>
> - preparing advertising and sales literature in cooperation with the manufacturer and adapting it to overseas requirements for use in personal contacts with foreign buyers
>
> - corresponding in the necessary foreign languages
>
> - making sure that goods being shipped are suitable for local conditions, and meet overseas legal and trade norms, including labelling, packaging, purity and electrical characteristics
>
> - advising on overseas patent and trademark protection requirements.

Source: 'The Export Management Company', US Department of Commerce, Washington, DC.

Two of the chief advantages of EMCs are (1) minimum investment on the part of the company to get into international markets, and (2) no company personnel or major expenditure of managerial effort. The result, in effect, is an extension of the market for the firm with negligible financial or personnel commitments.

Trading Companies Trading companies have a long and honourable history as important intermediaries in the development of trade between nations. **Trading companies** accumulate, transport and distribute goods from many countries. In concept, the trading company has changed little in hundreds of years.

The British firm Gray MacKenzie & Company is typical of companies operating in the Middle East. It has some 70 sales people and handles consumer products ranging from toiletries to outboard motors and Scotch whisky. The key advantage to this type of trading company is that it covers the entire Middle East.

key terms

export management company (EMC) important middleman for firms with relatively small international volume or those unwilling to involve their own personnel in the international function

trading companies accumulate, transport and distribute goods from many countries

373

Large, established trading companies are generally located in developed countries; they sell manufactured goods to developing countries, and buy raw materials and unprocessed goods. Japanese trading companies (*sogo shosha*), dating back to the early 1700s, operate both as importers and exporters. Some 300 are engaged in foreign and domestic trade through 2000 branch offices outside Japan and handle over $1 trillion (€0.9 trillion) in trading volume annually.[24]

Complementary Marketers   Companies with marketing facilities or contacts in different countries with excess marketing capacity or a desire for a broader product line sometimes take on additional lines for international distribution; although the generic name for such activities is complementary marketing, it is commonly called **piggybacking**.[25] General Electric Company has been distributing merchandise from other suppliers for many years. It accepts products that are non-competitive but complementary and that add to the basic distribution strength of the company itself.

Most piggyback arrangements are undertaken when a firm wants to fill out its product line or keep its seasonal distribution channels functioning throughout the year. Companies may work either on an agency or merchant basis, but the greatest volume of piggyback business is handled on an ownership (merchant) purchase-resale arrangement.

The selection process for new products for piggyback distribution determines whether (1) the product relates to the product line and contributes to it, (2) the product fits the sales and distribution channel presently employed, (3) there is an adequate margin to make the undertaking worthwhile and (4) the product will find market acceptance and profitable volume. If these requirements are met, piggybacking can be a logical way of increasing volume and profit for both the carrier and the piggybacker.

Manufacturer's Export Agent   The **manufacturer's export agent (MEA)** is an individual agent middleman or an agent middleman firm providing a selling service for manufacturers. Unlike the EMC, the MEA does not serve as the producer's export department but has a short-term relationship, covers only one or two markets, and operates on a straight commission basis. Another principal difference is that MEAs do business in their own names rather than in the name of the client.

Home Country Brokers   The term **broker** is a catchall for a variety of middlemen performing low-cost agent services. The term is typically applied to import-export brokers who provide the intermediary function of bringing buyers and sellers together and who do not have a continuing relationship with their clients. Most brokers specialise in one or more commodities for which they maintain contact with major producers and purchasers throughout the world.

Buying Offices   A variety of agent middlemen may be classified simply as buyers or buyers for export. Their common denominator is a primary function of seeking and purchasing merchandise on request from principals; as such, they do not provide a selling service. In fact, their chief emphasis is on flexibility and the ability to find merchandise from any source. They do not often become involved in continuing relationships with domestic suppliers and do not provide a continuing source of representation.

Export Merchants   Export merchants are essentially domestic merchants operating in foreign markets. As such, they operate much like the domestic wholesaler. Specifically, they purchase goods from a large number of manufacturers, ship them to foreign countries and take full responsibility for their marketing. Sometimes they utilise their own organisations, but, more commonly, they sell through middlemen. They may carry competing lines, have full control over prices, and maintain little loyalty to suppliers, although they continue to handle products as long as they are profitable.

key terms

sogo shosha
Japanese trading and investment organisations that also perform a unique and important role as risk takers

piggybacking
using another company's channels to export products

manufacturer's export agent (MEA)
individual agent middleman or agent middleman firm providing a selling service for manufacturers

broker
catchall for a variety of middlemen performing low-cost agent services

Export Jobbers   Export jobbers deal mostly in commodities; they do not take physical possession of goods but assume responsibility for arranging transportation. Because they work on a job-lot basis, they do not provide a particularly attractive distribution alterna-tive for most producers.

Exhibit 15.8 summarises information pertaining to the major kinds of domestic middlemen operating in foreign markets. No attempt is made to generalise about rates of commission, mark-up or pay because so many factors influence compensation.[26]

foreign country middlemen

The variety of agent and merchant middlemen in most countries is similar to those in Europe and the United States. An international marketer seeking greater control over the distribution process may elect to deal directly with middlemen in the foreign market. They gain the advantage of shorter channels and deal with middlemen in constant contact with

Exhibit 15.8 Characteristics of domestic middlemen serving overseas markets

Types of duty	Agent — EMC	MEA	Broker	Buying offices	Selling groups	Export merchant	Merchant export jobber	Import and trading companies	Complementary marketers
Take title	No*	No	No	No	No	Yes	Yes	Yes	Yes
Take possession	Yes	Yes	No	Yes	Yes	Yes	No	Yes	Yes
Continuing relationship	Yes	Yes	No	Yes	Yes	No	Yes	Yes	Yes
Share of foreign output	All	All	Any	Small	All	Any	Small	Any	Most
Degree of control by principal	Fair	Fair	Nil	Nil	Good	None	None	Nil	Fair
Price authority	Advisory	Advisory	Yes (at market level)	Yes (to buy)	Advisory	Yes	Yes	No	Some
Represent buyer or seller	Seller	Seller	Either	Buyer	Seller	Self	Self	Self	Self
Number of principals	Few – many	Few – many	Many	Small	Few	Many sources	Many sources	Many sources	One per product
Arrange shipping	Yes	Yes	Not usually	Yes	Yes	Yes	Yes	Yes	Yes
Type of goods	Manufactured goods and commodities	Staples and commodities	Staples and commodities	Staples and commodities	Complementary to their own lines	Manufactured goods	Bulky and raw materials	Manufactured goods	Complementary to line
Breadth of line	Speciality – wide	All types of staples	All types of staples	Retail goods	Narrow	Broad	Broad	Broad	Narrow
Handle competitive lines	No	No	Yes	Yes – utilises many sources	No	Yes	Yes	Yes	No
Extent of promotion and selling effort	Good	Good	One shot	n.a.	Good	Nil	Nil	Good	Good
Extend credit to principal	Occasionally	Occasionally	Seldom	Seldom	Seldom	Occasionally	Seldom	Seldom	Seldom
Market information	Fair	Fair	Price and market conditions	For principal not for manufacturer	Good	Nil	Nil	Fair	Good

Note: n.a. = not available.

* The EMC may take title and thus becomes a merchant middleman.

the market. As with all middlemen, particularly those working at a distance, effectiveness is directly dependent on the selection of middlemen and on the degree of control the manufacturer can and/or will exert.

Using **foreign-country middlemen** moves the manufacturer closer to the market and involves the company more closely with problems of language, physical distribution, communications and financing. Foreign middlemen may be agents or merchants; they may be associated with the parent company to varying degrees; or they may be temporarily hired for special purposes. Some of the more important foreign-country middlemen are manufacturers' representatives and foreign distributors.

Manufacturers' Representatives   Manufacturers' representatives are agent middlemen who take responsibility for a producer's goods in a city, regional market area, entire country or several adjacent countries. When responsible for an entire country, the middleman is often called a sole agent. The well-chosen, well-motivated, well-controlled

manufacturers' representative can provide excellent market coverage for manufacturers in certain circumstances. The manufacturers' representative is widely used in distribution of industrial goods overseas and is an excellent representative for any type of manufactured consumer goods.

Foreign **manufacturers' representatives** have a variety of titles including sales agent, resident sales agent, exclusive agent, commission agent and indent agent. They take no credit, exchange or market risk but deal strictly as field sales representatives. They do not arrange for shipping or for handling and usually do not take physical possession. Manufacturers who desire the type of control and intensive market coverage their own sales force would afford, but who cannot field one, may find the manufacturers' representative a satisfactory choice.

Distributors   A foreign distributor is a merchant middleman. This intermediary often has exclusive sales rights in a specific country and works in close cooperation with the manufacturer. The distributor has a relatively high degree of dependence on the supplier companies, and arrangements are likely to be on a long-term, continuous basis. Working through distributors permits the manufacturer a reasonable degree of control over prices, promotional effort, inventory, servicing and other distribution functions. If a line is profitable for distributors, they can be depended on to handle it in a manner closely approximating the desires of the manufacturer.

Foreign-country Brokers   Like the export broker discussed earlier, brokers are agents who deal largely in commodities and food products. The **foreign brokers** are typically part of small brokerage firms operating in one country or in a few contiguous countries. Their strength is in having good continuing relationships with customers and providing speedy market coverage at a low cost.

Managing Agents   A managing agent conducts business within a foreign nation under an exclusive contract arrangement with the parent company. The **managing agent** in some cases invests in the operation and in most instances operates under a contract with the parent company. Compensation is usually on the basis of cost plus a specified percentage of the profits of the managed company.

Dealers   Generally speaking, anyone who has a continuing relationship with a supplier in buying and selling goods is considered a dealer. More specifically, dealers are middlemen selling industrial goods or durable consumer goods direct to customers; dealers are the last step in the channel of distribution. **Dealers** have continuing, close working relationships with their suppliers and exclusive selling rights for their producer's products within a given geographic area. Finally, they derive a large portion of their sales volume from the products of a single supplier firm. Usually a dealer is an independent merchant middleman, but sometimes the supplier company has an equity in its dealers.

Some of the best examples of dealer operations are found in the farm equipment, earthmoving and automotive industries. These categories include Massey Ferguson, with a vast, worldwide network of dealers; Caterpillar Tractor Company, with dealers in every major city of the world; and the various car companies.

Import Jobbers, Wholesalers and Retailers   Import jobbers purchase goods directly from the manufacturer and sell to wholesalers and retailers and to industrial customers. Large and small **wholesalers and retailers** engage in direct importing for their own outlets and for redistribution to smaller middlemen. The combination retailer-wholesaler is more important in foreign countries than in Western countries. It is not uncommon to find large retailers wholesaling goods to local shops and dealers. Exhibit 15.9 summarises the characteristics of foreign-country middlemen.

key terms

manufacturers' representatives represent the producing company in another country

foreign brokers agents who deal largely in commodities and food products, typically part of small firms operating in one or a few countries

managing agent conducts business within a foreign nation under exclusive contract to the parent company

dealer anyone who has a continuing relationship with a supplier in buying and selling goods

wholesalers and retailers facilitate the exchange of goods between manufacturer and consumer

Exhibit 15.9 Characteristics of foreign-country middlemen

Type of duty	Agent Broker	Manufacturers' representative	Managing agent	Merchant distributor	Dealer	Import jobber	Wholesaler and retailer
Take title	No	No	No	Yes	Yes	Yes	Yes
Take possession	No	Seldom	Seldom	Yes	Yes	Yes	Yes
Continuing relationship	No	Often	With buyer, not seller	Yes	Yes	No	Usually not
Share of foreign output	Small	All or part for one area	n.a.	All, for certain countries	Assignment area	Small	Very small
Degree of control by principal	Low	Fair	None	High	High	Low	Nil
Price authority	Nil	Nil	Nil	Partial	Partial	Full	Full
Represent buyer or seller	Either	Seller	Buyer	Seller	Seller	Self	Self
Number of principals	Many	Few	Many	Small	Few major	Many	Many
Arrange shipping	No	No	No	No	No	No	No
Type of goods	Commodity and food	Manufactured goods	All types manufactured goods	Manufactured goods	Manufactured goods	Manufactured goods	Manufactured consumer goods
Breadth of line	Broad	Allied lines	Broad	Narrow to broad	Narrow	Narrow to broad	Narrow to broad
Handle competitive lines	Yes	No	Yes	No	No	Yes	Yes
Extent of promotion and selling effort	Nil	Fair	Nil	Fair	Good	Nil	Nil usually
Extend credit to principal	No	No	No	Sometimes	No	No	No
Market information	Nil	Good	Nil	Fair	Good	Nil	Nil

Note: n.a. = not available.

government-affiliated middlemen

Marketers must deal with governments in every country of the world. Products, services and commodities for the government's own use are always procured through government purchasing offices at federal, regional and local levels. As more and more social services are undertaken by governments, the level of government purchasing activity escalates. In the Netherlands, the state's purchasing office deals with more than 10 000 suppliers in 20 countries. About one-third of the products purchased by that agency are produced outside the Netherlands; 90 per cent of foreign purchases are handled through Dutch representatives. The other 10 per cent are purchased directly from producing companies. In Sweden and Norway, the state has a monopoly on all alcoholic drinks and they can be bought only in state-monopoly stores.

factors affecting choice of channel

The international marketer needs a clear understanding of market characteristics and must have established operating policies before beginning the selection of channel middlemen. The following points should be addressed prior to the selection process.

1 Identify specific target markets within and across countries.
2 Specify marketing goals in terms of volume, market share and profit margin requirements.

3 Specify financial and personnel commitments to the development of international distribution.
4 Identify control, length of channels, terms of sale and channel ownership.

Once these points are established, selecting among alternative middlemen choices to forge the best channel can begin. Marketers must get their goods into the hands of consumers and must choose between handling all distribution or turning part or all of it over to various middlemen. Distribution channels vary depending on target market size, competition and available distribution intermediaries.

Although the overall marketing strategy of the firm must embody the company's profit goals in the short and long run, channel strategy itself is considered to have six specific strategic goals. These goals can be characterised as the 'six Cs' of channel strategy – cost, capital, control, coverage, character and continuity, as illustrated in Exhibit 15.10. In forging the overall channel-of-distribution strategy, each of the six Cs must be considered in building an economical, effective distribution organisation within the long-range channel policies of the company.

Exhibit 15.10 Factors influencing choice of channel

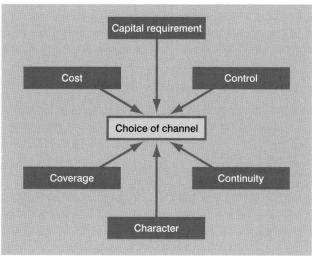

cost

There are two kinds of channel cost: the capital or investment cost of developing the channel and the continuing cost of maintaining it. The latter can be in the form of direct expenditure for the maintenance of the company's selling force or in the form of margins, mark-up or commissions of various middlemen handling the goods. Marketing costs (a substantial part of which is channel cost) must be considered as the entire difference between the factory price of the goods and the price the customer ultimately pays for the merchandise. The costs of middlemen include transporting and storing the goods, breaking bulk, providing credit, and the cost of local advertising, sales representation and negotiations.

capital requirement

The financial ramifications of a distribution policy are often overlooked. Critical elements are capital requirement and cash-flow patterns associated with using a particular type of middleman. Maximum investment is usually required when a company establishes its own internal channels, its own sales force. Use of distributors or dealers may lessen the cash investment, but manufacturers often provide initial inventories on consignment, loans, floor plans or other arrangements.

control

The more involved a company is with the distribution, the more control it exerts. A company's own sales force affords the most control but often at a cost that is not practical. Each type of channel arrangement provides a different level of control and, as channels grow longer, the ability to control price, volume, promotion and types of outlet diminishes. If a company cannot sell directly to the end user or final retailer, an important selection criterion of middlemen should be the amount of control the marketer can and wants to maintain.[27]

coverage

Another major goal is full-market coverage to (1) gain the optimum volume of sales obtainable in each market, (2) secure a reasonable market share, and (3) attain satisfactory market penetration. Coverage may be assessed on geographic and/or market segments. Adequate market coverage may require changes in distribution systems from country to country or time to time. Coverage is difficult to develop both in highly developed areas and in sparse markets – the former because of heavy competition and the latter because of inadequate channels.

Many companies do not attempt full-market coverage but seek significant penetration in major population centres. In some countries, two or three cities constitute the majority of the national buying power. For instance, 60 per cent of the Japanese population lives in the Tokyo-Nagoya-Osaka market area, which essentially functions as one massive city.

In China, for example, the often-quoted 1 billion-person market is, in reality, fewer than 25 to 30 per cent of the population of the most affluent cities. Even as personal incomes increase in China, distribution inadequacies limit marketers in reaching all those who have adequate incomes.

character

The channel-of-distribution system selected must fit the character of the company and the markets in which it is doing business. Some obvious product requirements, often the first considered, relate to perishability or bulk of the product, complexity of sale, sales service required and value of the product.

Channel commanders must be aware that channel patterns change; they cannot assume that once a channel has been developed to fit the character of both company and market no more need be done. The United Kingdom, for example, has epitomised distribution through speciality-type middlemen, distributors, wholesalers and retailers; in fact, all middlemen have traditionally worked within narrow product speciality areas. In recent years, however, there has been a trend towards broader lines, conglomerate merchandising and mass marketing.

continuity

Channels of distribution often pose longevity problems. Most agent middlemen firms tend to be small institutions. When one individual retires or moves out of a line of business, the company may find it has lost its distribution in that area. Wholesalers, and especially retailers, are not noted for their continuity in business either. Most middlemen have little loyalty to their vendors. They handle brands in good times when the line is making money, but quickly reject such products within a season or a year if they fail to produce during that period. Distributors and dealers are probably the most loyal middlemen, but even with them manufacturers must attempt to build brand loyalty downstream in a channel lest middlemen shift allegiance to other companies or other inducements.

locating, selecting and motivating channel members

The actual process of building channels for international distribution is seldom easy and many companies have been stopped in their efforts to develop international markets by their inability to construct a satisfactory system of channels.

Despite the chaotic condition of international distribution channels, international marketers can follow a logical procedure in developing channels. After general policy guides are established, marketers need to develop criteria for the selection of specific middlemen. Construction of the middleman network includes seeking out potential middlemen, selecting those who fit the company's requirements and establishing working relationships with them.

In international marketing, the channel-building process is hardly routine. The closer the company wants to get to the consumer in its channel contact, the larger the sales force required. If a company is content with finding an exclusive importer or selling agent for a given country, channel building may not be too difficult; but if it goes down to the level of subwholesaler or retailer it is taking on a tremendous task and must have an internal staff capable of supporting such an effort.

locating middlemen

The search for prospective middlemen should begin with study of the market and determination of criteria for evaluating middlemen servicing that market. The company's broad policy guidelines should be followed, but expect expediency to override policy at times. The checklist of criteria differs according to the type of middlemen being used and the nature of their relationship with the company. Basically, such lists are built around four subject areas: (1) productivity or volume; (2) financial strength; (3) managerial stability and capability; and (4) the nature and reputation of the business. Emphasis is usually placed on either the actual or potential productivity of the middleman.

selecting middlemen

Finding prospective middlemen is less a problem than determining which of them can perform satisfactorily. Most prospects are hampered by low volume or low potential volume, many are underfinanced, and some simply cannot be trusted. In many cases, when a manufacturer is not well known abroad, the reputation of the middleman becomes the reputation of the manufacturer, so a poor choice at this point can be devastating.

Screening   The screening and selection process itself should follow this sequence: (1) a letter including product information and distributor requirements in the native language to each prospective middleman; (2) a follow-up to the best respondents for more specific information concerning lines handled, territory covered, size of firm, number of sales people and other background information; (3) check of credit and references from other clients and customers of the prospective middleman; and (4) if possible, a personal check of the most promising firms.

One source suggests that the only way to select a middleman is to go personally to the country and talk to ultimate users of your product to find whom they consider to be the best distributors. Visit each one before selecting the one to represent you; look for one with a key person who will take the new line of equipment to their heart and make it their personal objective to make the sale of that line a success.

The Agreement   Once a potential middleman has been found and evaluated, there remains the task of detailing the arrangements with that middleman. So far the company has been in a buying position, now it must shift into a selling and negotiating position to convince the middleman to handle the goods and accept a distribution agreement that is workable for the company. Agreements must spell out the specific responsibilities of the manufacturer and the middleman, including an annual sales minimum. The sales minimum serves as a basis for evaluation of the distributor and failure to meet sales minimums may give the exporter the right of termination.

Some experienced exporters recommend that initial contracts be signed for one year only. If the first year's performance is satisfactory, they should be reviewed for renewal for

a longer period. This permits easier termination and, more important, after a year of working together in the market, a more workable arrangement can generally be reached.

motivating middlemen

Once middlemen are selected, a promotional programme must be started to maintain high-level interest in the manufacturer's products. A larger proportion of the advertising budget must be devoted to channel communications than in the head office because there are so many small middlemen to be contacted. Consumer advertising is of no avail unless the goods are actually available. On all levels, there is a clear correlation between the middle-man's motivation and sales volume. The hundreds of motivational techniques that can be employed to maintain middleman interest and support for the product may be grouped into five categories: financial rewards, psychological rewards, communications, company support and corporate rapport.

Obviously, margins or commissions must be competitive and set to meet the needs of the middleman, and may vary according to the volume of sales and the level of services offered. Without a combination of adequate margin and adequate volume, a middleman cannot afford to give much attention to a product.

Being human, middlemen and their sales people respond to psychological rewards and recognition for the jobs they are doing. A trip to the parent company's home or regional office is a great honour. Publicity in company media and local newspapers also builds esteem and involvement among foreign middlemen.

terminating middlemen

When middlemen do not perform up to standards or when market situations change, requiring a company to restructure its distribution, it may be necessary to terminate rela-tionships with certain middlemen or certain types of middlemen. In Western markets, it is usually a simple action regardless of the type of middleman – agent or merchant, they are simply dismissed. However, in other parts of the world, the middleman typically has some legal protection that makes it difficult to terminate relationships. Some companies give all middlemen contracts for one year, or for another specified period, to avoid such problems. But as many experienced international marketers know, the best rule is to avoid the need to terminate distributors by screening all prospective middlemen carefully. A poorly chosen distributor may not only fail to live up to expectations but may also adversely affect future business and prospects in the country.

controlling middlemen

The extreme length of channels typically used in international distribution makes control of middlemen particularly difficult. Some companies solve this problem by establishing their own distribution systems; others issue franchises or exclusive distributorships in an effort to maintain control through the first stages of the channels.

Until the various world markets are more highly developed, most international marketers cannot expect to exert a high degree of control over their international distribu-tion operations. Although control is difficult, a company that succeeds in controlling distri-bution channels is likely to be a successful international marketer.

Some manufacturers have lost control through 'secondary wholesaling' – when rebuffed discounters have secured a product through an unauthorised outlet. A manu-facturer may then find some of the toughest competition from its own products that have been diverted through other countries or manufactured by subsidiaries and exported or bootlegged into markets the parent would prefer to reserve. Such action can directly conflict with exclusive arrangements made with distributors in other coun-tries and may undermine the entire distribution system by harming relationships between manufacturers and their channels.[28]

summary

From the foregoing discussion, it is evident that the international marketer has a broad range of alternatives for developing an economical, efficient, high-volume international distribution system. To the uninitiated, however, the variety may be overwhelming.

Careful analysis of the functions performed suggests more similarity than difference between international and domestic distribution systems; in both cases there are three primary alternatives of using agent middlemen, merchant middlemen or a company's own sales and distribution system. In many instances, all three types of middleman are employed on the international scene, and channel structure may vary from nation to nation or from continent to continent. The neophyte company in international marketing can gain strength from the knowledge that information and advice are available relative to the structuring of international distribution systems and that many well-developed and capable middleman firms exist for the international distribution of goods. Within the past decade, international middlemen have become more numerous, more reliable, more sophisticated and more readily available to marketers in all countries. Such growth and development offer an ever-wider range of possibilities for entering foreign markets, but the international business person should remember that it is just as easy for competitors.

questions

1 Discuss the distinguishing features of the European distribution system.
2 Discuss the ways Japanese manufacturers control the distribution process from manufacturer to retailer.
3 Discuss how the globalisation of markets, especially in the European Union, affects retail distribution.
4 In what ways and to what extent do the functions of domestic middlemen differ from those of their foreign counterparts?
5 Why is the EMC sometimes called an independent export department?
6 Discuss how physical distribution relates to channel policy and how they affect one another.
7 Explain how and why distribution channels are affected as they are when the stage of development of an economy improves.
8 In what circumstances is the use of an EMC logical?
9 In what circumstances are trading companies likely to be used?
10 How is distribution-channel structure affected by increasing emphasis on the government as a customer and by the existence of state trading agencies?
11 Review the key variable that affects the marketer's choice of distribution channels.
12 Account, as best you can, for the differences in channel patterns that might be encountered in a highly developed country and an emerging country.
13 One of the first things companies discover about international channel-of-distribution patterns is that in most countries it is nearly impossible to gain adequate market coverage through a simple channel-of-distribution plan. Discuss.
14 Discuss the factors influencing marketing via the Internet.

further reading

- A. Nicholas, 'Retailers and International Markets', *International Marketing Review*, 1990, 7(4), pp. 75–85.
- B. Petersen and L.S. Welch, 'International Retailing Operations: Downstream Entry and Expansion via Franchising', *International Business Review*, 2000, 9(1), pp. 479–96.
- P.Y.K. Chau, M. Cole, A.P. Messey, M. Montoya-Weiss and R. O'Keefe, 'Cultural Differences in Online Behaviour of Consumers', *Communication of the ACM*, 2002, 45(1), pp. 138–43.

references

1 J. Evans, A. Treadgold and F.T. Movondo, 'Psychic Distance and the Performance of International Retailers: A Suggested Theoretical Framework', *International Marketing Review*, 2000, 17(4/5), pp. 297–309.

2 D. Ford, 'Distribution, Internationalisation and Networks', *International Marketing Review*, 2002, 19(2/3), pp. 225–35.

3 P. Ellis, 'Are International Trade Intermediaries Catalysts in Economic Development?', *Journal of International Marketing*, 2003, 112(12), pp. 73–96.

4 For a report on research on a nation's level of economic development and marketing channels, see Janen E. Olsen and Kent L. Granzin, *Journal of Global Marketing*, vol. 7, no. 3, 1994, pp. 7–39.

5 Constantine Katsikeas, Ali Al-Khalifa and Dave Crick, 'Manufacturers' Understanding of their Overseas Distributors: The Relevance of Export Involvement', *International Business Review*, vol. 6, no. 2, 1997, pp. 147–64.

6 A comprehensive review of the changing character of the Japanese distribution system is presented in John Fahy and Fuyuki Taguchi, 'Reassessing the Japanese Distribution System', *Sloan Management Review*, Winter 1995, pp. 49–61.

7 Arieh Goldman, 'Japan's Distribution System: Institutional Structure, Internal Political Economy, and Modernization', *Journal of Retailing*, Summer 1991, pp. 156–61.

8 Gregory L. Miles, 'Unmasking Japan's Distributors', *International Business*, April 1994, pp. 30–42.

9 Robert E. Weigand, 'So you Think our Retailing Laws are Tough?', *Wall Street Journal*, 13 November 1989, p. A12; and 'The Euro Effect: The Race to Rule Retailing Heats Up as New Currency Looms', *Business Week*, 19 January 1998, pp. 16–17.

10 Masami Kogayu, 'Fair is Free and Free is Fair', *Look Japan*, July 1994, pp. 12–13; and Marnik G. Dekimpe, Pierre François, Srinath Gopalakrishna, Gary L. Lilien and Christophe van den Bulte, 'Generalizing About Trade Show Effectiveness: A Cross-national Comparison', *Journal of Marketing*, vol. 61, no. 4, 1997, pp. 55–64.

11 Fumio Matsuo, 'Trade with a Moral Compass', *Wall Street Journal*, 6 December 1994, p. A20.

12 L. Bannon and C. Vizthum, 'Small World: One-Toy-Fits-All: How Industry Learned to Love the Global Kid', *Wall Street Journal*, 29 April 2003, p. A1.

13 T. Li, A.F.J. Nicholls and S. Roslow, 'Organisational Motivation and the Global Concurrent Launch in Markets with Accelerated Technology', *International Business Review*, 2003, 12(5), pp. 523–42.

14 'Stores Form New Euro-Retail Alliance', *Business Europe*, 18–24 April 1994, pp. 7–8.

15 'Distribution', *Business Asia*, 17 January 1994, p. 7.

16 M. Newman, 'E-commerce: The Rules – So Many Countries, So Many Laws', *Wall Street Journal*, 28 April 2003, p. R28.

17 S. Dutta and B. Biren, 'Business Transformation on the Internet: Results from the 2000 Study', *European Management Journal*, 2001, 19(5), pp. 449–62.

18 G. Bergendahl, 'Models for Investment in Electronic Commerce – Financial Perspectives with Empirical Evidence', *Omega*, 2005, p. 33.

19 'Moving Goods in Beijing and Tianjin: Market Making', *Business China*, 5 September 1994, pp. 8–9.

20 'Poland, Stocking the Corner Shop', *Business Eastern Europe*, 9 January 1995, p. 1.

21 See, for example, 'Consumer Marketing in Indonesia: A Market Too Far', *Business Asia*, 14 February 1994, pp. 6-7.

22 Avon Products, Inc., 'Earning Forecast is Raised on International Performance', *Wall Street Journal*, 31 March 2003, p. B4.

23 M. Harvey and M. Novicevic, 'Seeking Marketing Managers to Effectively Control Global Channel of Distribution', *International Marketing Review*, 2002, 129(4), pp. 525-44.

24 Yukio Onuma, 'Myths and Realities of the *Sogo-Shosha*', *Trade and Culture*, September-October 1994, pp. 33-4.

25 G.I. Balabaris, 'Factors Affecting Export Intermediaries Service Offerings: The British Example', *Journal of International Business Studies,* 2000, 31(1), pp. 83-94.

26 N.C. Williamson, D.C. Bello, T. Wingler, D. Ludwig and I. Basu, 'Vertical Integration in the Indirect Export Channel: An Empirical Test of Some Operating Variables', *International Business Review*, 1994, 3(2), pp. 1449-63.

27 C. Pahud de Mortanges and J. Vossen, 'Mechanisms to Control the Marketing Activities of Foreign Distributors', *International Business Review*, 1999, 8(1), pp. 75-97.

28 G.A. Fuentes, 'Middlemen and Agents in the Procurement of Paddy: Institutional Arrangements from the Rural Philippines', *Journal of Asian Economics*, 2002, 9(2), pp. 307-31.

chapter 16
International Advertising and Promotion

Chapter Outline

Chapter Learning Objectives

What you should learn from Chapter 16

■ How to evaluate local market characteristics that affect the advertising and promotion of products

■ Whether pan-European advertising is possible

■ When global advertising is most effective and when modified advertising is necessary

■ To understand the effects of a single European market on advertising

■ What the impact is of limited media, excessive media, and government regulations on advertising and promotion budgets

■ How to understand and handle the creative challenges in international advertising

■ How sales promotions can be used efficiently in foreign markets

■ How to handle the communication process and avoid advertising misfires

Advertising, sales promotion, personal selling and public relations, the mutually reinforcing elements of the promotional mix, have as their common objective successful sale of a product or service. Once a product is developed to meet target market needs and is properly distributed, intended customers must be informed of the product's value and availability. Advertising and promotion are basic ingredients in the marketing mix of an international company (see Exhibit 16.1). Exhibit 16.2 presents worldwide spending on sponsorship, which is becoming an increasingly important promotional activity.

Of all the elements of the marketing mix, decisions involving advertising are those most often affected by cultural differences among country markets. Consumers respond in terms of their culture, its style, feelings, value systems, attitudes, beliefs and perceptions.[1] Because advertising's function is to interpret or translate the need/want-satisfying qualities of products and services in terms of consumer needs, wants, desires and aspirations, the emotional appeals, symbols, persuasive approaches and other characteristics of an advertisement must coincide with cultural norms if it is to be effective. Because advertising is mainly based on language and images, it is influenced by culture.[2]

Exhibit 16.1 World advertising spending

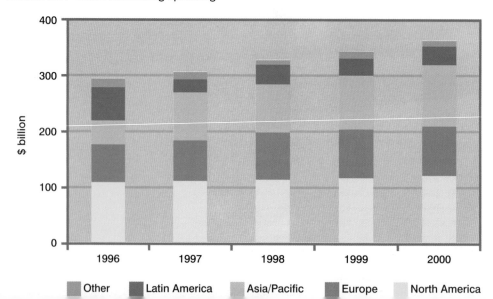

Exhibit 16.2 Sponsorship spending worldwide 2002–2004 ($ billion)

	2002	2003	2004
Worldwide	24.4	25.9	28.0
North America	9.7	10.2	11.1
Europe	7.1	7.4	7.9
Pacific Rim	4.3	4.7	5.2
Central, South America	2.1	2.2	2.3
Others	1.3	1.4	1.5

Source: compiled from *Marketing News*, 'International Events and Sponsorship', 15 July 2004, p. 18.

Reconciling an international advertising and sales promotion effort with the cultural uniqueness of markets is the challenge confronting the international marketer. The basic framework and concepts of international promotion are essentially the same wherever employed. Six steps are involved:

1 study the target market(s)
2 determine the extent of worldwide standardisation
3 determine the promotional mix (the blend of advertising, personal selling, sales promotions and public relations) in national or global markets
4 develop the most effective message(s)
5 select effective media
6 establish the necessary controls to assist in monitoring and achieving worldwide marketing objectives (see Exhibit 16.3).

Exhibit 16.3 A framework for international promotion

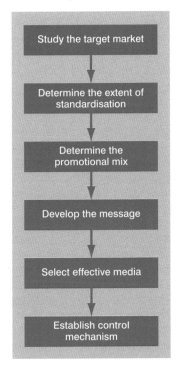

Source: 'Zenith Media', *The Economist*, 17 January 1998, p. 102.

A review of some of the global trends that can impact international advertising is followed by a discussion of global versus modified advertising. A survey of problems and challenges confronting international advertisers – including basic creative strategy, media planning and selection, sales promotions and the communications process – concludes the chapter.

international advertising

Intense competition for world markets and the increasing sophistication of foreign consumers have led to a need for more sophisticated advertising strategies. Increased costs, problems of coordinating advertising programmes in multiple countries, and a desire for a common worldwide company or product image have caused companies to seek greater control and efficiency without sacrificing **local responsiveness**. In the quest for more effective and responsive promotion programmes, the policies covering centralised or decentralised authority, use of single or multiple foreign or domestic agencies, appropriation and allocation procedures, copy, media and research are being examined.

One of the most widely debated policy areas pertains to the degree of specialised advertising necessary from country to country.[3] One view sees advertising customised for each country or region because every country is seen as posing a special problem. Executives with this viewpoint argue that the only way to achieve adequate and relevant advertising is to develop separate campaigns for each country. At the other extreme are those who suggest that advertising should be standardised for all markets of the world and who overlook regional differences altogether.[4]

Debate on the merits of standardisation compared to modification of international advertising has been going on for decades. Theodore Levitt's article 'The Globalisation of Markets' caused many companies to examine their international strategies and to adopt a global marketing strategy.[5] Levitt postulated the existence and growth of the global consumer with similar needs and wants, and advocated that international marketers should operate as if the world were one large market, ignoring superficial regional and national differences. In our opinion, although we do have some global products and brands, we need to adapt our marketing approach and tactics according to cultural differences and segments. Even in the EU, a truly integrated market, the buying behaviour for global products, such as Sony TVs or Philips vacuum cleaners, is different.

Another example is Gillette, which sells 800 products in more than 200 countries. It has a consistent worldwide image as a masculine, sports-oriented company, but its products have no such consistent image. Its razors, blades, toiletries and cosmetics are known by many names. Trac II blades in the United States are more widely known worldwide as G-II, and Atra blades are called Contour in Europe and Asia. Silkience hair conditioner is known as Soyance in France, Sientel in Italy and Silkience in Germany. Whether or not a global brand name could have been chosen for Gillette's many existing products is speculative. However, Gillette's current corporate philosophy of globalisation provides for an umbrella statement, 'Gillette, the Best a Man Can Get', in all advertisements for men's toiletries products in the hope of providing some common image.

It would be difficult for Gillette or Unilever to standardise their brand names across different markets, since each brand is established in its market. Yet, with such a diversity of brand names it is easy to imagine the problem of coordination and control, and the potential competitive disadvantage against a company with global brand recognition.

As discussed earlier, there is a fundamental difference between a multidomestic marketing strategy and a global marketing strategy. One is based on the premise that all markets are culturally different and a company must adapt marketing programmes to accommodate the differences, whereas the other assumes similarities as well as differences, and standardises where there are similarities but adapts where culturally required. Further, it may be possible to standardise some parts of the marketing mix and not others. Also, the

GOING INTERNATIONAL 16.1

economists assume that people know what they want. advertisers assume that they do not. who is right?

Companies such as Coca-Cola, Kodak and McDonald's believe that the huge sums they spend on advertising are an investment in their valuable brands. They are not the only ones, however, who pay close attention to advertising. To economists - the official sponsors of rational decision making - the motives and methods of advertisers raise doubts about a fundamental claim: that people are good at making decisions for themselves.

In the economist's view of the world there is little need for firms to spend so much money cajoling consumers into buying their wares. Of course, people need good information to make good choices and it is often too costly or time-consuming to collect it themselves. So advertising a product's features, its price or even its existence can provide genuine value. But many ads seem to convey no such 'hard' information. Moreover, most advertising firms place a huge emphasis on creativity and human psychology when designing campaigns.

Economists need to explain, therefore, why a rational consumer would be persuaded by an ad that offers nothing but an enticing image or a good laugh. If consumers are rational, they should ignore such obvious gimmicks. If producers are rational, they should not waste money on ads that consumers will ignore.

Companies such as Kodak and McDonald's are willing to spend huge sums convincing people their products are the best around. This explanation was first developed by Phillip Nelson in a classic paper written in 1974. He argued that a great deal of seemingly wasteful advertisement is in fact intended to send a 'signal' to consumers - that even though a product's quality is hard to verify in advance, it really is one of the best on the market. From this perspective, it does not matter what an advertisement says - so long as consumers can see the firm spending big sums on advertising.

On the whole, economists find Nelson's account convincing. But they believe that he had only half the story: companies need pricing as well as advertising to convey quality to consumers. However, they have not been able to agree how prices and advertising should be related.

Part of the problem is that it is extremely difficult to measure the amount firms spend on advertising 'hard' information about a product's price, say, or how it works, as opposed to their spending on 'signal' advertising of the touchy-feely sort. Moreover, some kinds of product - those whose quality can be verified only through experience - should have more 'signal' advertising. But what is quality? And can an economist tell how easily it can be verified? In fact, two economists recently conducted a different kind of study, which suggests that the 'signalling' theory may be wrong. Sridhar Moorthy and Scott Hawkins ran an experiment in which people read foreign-language magazines with ads for unfamiliar brands in several product categories: cookware, overcoats, nasal spray and yoghurt. The ads were real, but the magazines were altered to change the frequency with which they appeared.

Pizza Hut gets a slice of the action on a Russian rocket
AP/WideWorld Photos

Although they did not understand the ads' content, the subjects associated a high frequency of advertising with high quality. However, a control group saw each ad only once, with a message attached telling them how often it appeared in other magazines. Even though the control group could remember the frequency of the ads, they did not assume – as their peers had done – that more ads meant higher quality. This suggests that people do indeed associate more ads with higher quality, but not because they have a sophisticated understanding of the signal companies are trying to send. They simply see lots of ads for a product and want to buy it. The distinction is crucial. If seeing is truly believing, then even low-quality firms may be able to create the impression of high quality by advertising, confounding the signal. Or perhaps not.

■ Can everything be sold through advertising? Can a low-quality producer convince the market, through advertising, that it is in fact selling high-quality products?

Source: Phillip Nelson, 'Advertising as Information', *Journal of Political Economy*, July 1974; Sridhar Moorthy and Scott Hawkins, 'Advertising Repetition and Quality Perceptions', Working Paper, February 1998; *The Economist*, 14 February 1998, p. 92.

same standardised products may be marketed globally but, because of differences in cultures, target segments or stages in the product life cycle, have a different advertising appeal in different markets.

The Parker Pen Company sells the same pen in all markets, but advertising differs dramatically from country to country. Print ads in Germany simply show the Parker pen held in a hand that is writing a headline – 'This is how you write with precision'. In the United Kingdom, where it is the brand leader, the exotic processes used to make pens, such as gently polishing the gold nibs with walnut chips, is emphasised. In the United States, the ad campaign's theme is status and image. The headlines in the ads are, 'You walk into a boardroom and everyone's naked. Here's how to tell who's boss', and 'There are times when it has to be a Parker'. The company considers the different themes necessary because of the different product images and different customer motives in each market. On the other hand, its most expensive Duofold Centennial pen (about €180, or $200), created to coincide with the company's 100th anniversary and targeted for an upscale market in each country, is advertised the same way throughout the world. The advertising theme is designed to convey a statement about the company as well as the pricey new product. The importance of advertising is, however, different for different industries/product groups. Exhibit 16.4 shows advertising spending in different industries.

The seasoned international marketer or advertiser realises the decision for standardisation or modification depends more on motives for buying than on geography. Advertising must relate to motives. If people in different markets buy similar products for significantly different reasons, advertising must focus on such differences. An advertising programme developed by Chanel, the perfume manufacturer, failed in the United States although it was very popular in Europe. Admitting failure in its attempt to globalise the advertising, one fragrance analyst commented, 'There is a French-American problem. The French concept of prestige is not the same as America's.'

pattern advertising: plan globally, act locally

As discussed in Chapter 13, a product is more than a physical item; it is a bundle of satisfactions the buyer receives. This package of satisfactions or utilities includes the primary function of the product along with many other benefits imputed by the values and customs of the culture. Different cultures often seek the same value or benefits from the primary

Exhibit 16.4 Top 100 advertisers' global spending by category ($ million)

Category	2001	Percent change from 2000	Per cent total
Automotive	19 334.4	–3.3	27.3
Food	11 220.7	–6.9	15.8
Personal care	10 300.2	5.2	14.5
Electronics, computers	6 557.5	–8.0	9.2
Media and entertainment	6 285.4	3.2	8.9
Pharmaceuticals	5 655.8	3.6	8.0
Fast food	2 989.4	–2.3	4.2
Household cleaners	2 203.5	6.6	3.1
Telecommunications	1 733.0	–19.7	2.4
Financial services, credit	1 156.3	–14.8	1.6
Retail	987.3	–6.4	1.4
Beer, wine and liquor	951.3	1.5	1.3
Toys	529.2	–12.2	0.7
Photo film	490.4	4.9	0.7
Miscellaneous	556.3	–10.7	0.8

Source: 'Special Report: Global Marketers', *Advertising Age*, supplement to the *Ad Age* Special Report, 11 November 2002. Copyright, Crain Communications, Inc. 2002.

function of a product; for example, the ability of a car to get from point A to point B, a camera to take a picture or a wristwatch to tell the time. But while agreeing on the benefit of the primary function of a product, other features and psychological attributes of the item can have significant differences.

Consider the different market – perceived needs for a camera. In the United Kingdom, excellent pictures with easy, foolproof operation are expected by most of the market; in most countries of Europe, the United States and Japan, a camera must take excellent pictures but the camera must also be state-of-the-art in design. In Africa, where penetration of cameras is less than 20 per cent of the households, the concept of picture-taking must be sold. In all three markets, excellent pictures are expected (i.e. the primary function of a camera is demanded) but the additional utility or satisfaction derived from a camera differs among cultures. There are many products that produce these different expectations beyond the common benefit sought by all. Thus, many companies follow a strategy of **pattern advertising**, a global advertising strategy with a standardised basic message allowing some degree of modification to meet local situations. As the popular saying goes, 'Think globally, act locally.' In this way, some economies of standardisation can be realised while specific cultural differences are accommodated.

Evidence indicates that no generalised recommendation can be made about whether to adapt or standardise international advertising. The only answer is 'it depends'. It depends on the product, the culture, use patterns, and so on. A review of business practices indicates that few companies adopt either extreme of adapting or standardising all their advertising efforts and those that have are moving towards a more centralist position: standardise where possible and adapt where necessary, which generally translates into pattern advertising.

key term

pattern advertising
global advertising strategy with a standardised basic message allowing some degree of modification to meet local situations

international advertising and world brands

Global brands generally are the result of a company that elects to be guided by a global marketing strategy. Global brands carry the same name, same design and same creative strategy everywhere in the world; Sony, Philips, Marks & Spencer, Jaguar, BMW, Volvo, Coca-Cola, Pepsi Cola and McDonald's are a few of the global brands. Even when cultural differences make it ineffective to have a standardised advertising programme or a standardised product, a company may have a world brand. Nescafé, the world brand for Nestlé Company's instant coffee, is used throughout the world even though advertising messages and formulation (dark roast and light roast) vary to suit cultural differences. In Japan and the United Kingdom, advertising reflects each country's preference for tea; in France, Germany and Brazil, cultural preferences for ground coffee call for a different advertising message and formulation.

Colgate-Palmolive announced it was decentralising its advertising; marketing in future would be tailored specifically to local markets and countries. An industry analyst reported that 'There will be little, if any, global advertising.' This appeared to be a reversal for Colgate, one of the first companies to embrace worldwide standardised advertising.[6] The apparent reversal in policy represents what is happening in many companies that initially took extreme positions on standardising their marketing efforts. Companies have discovered that the idea of complete global standardisation is more myth than reality.

As discussed earlier, markets are constantly changing and are in the process of becoming more alike, but the world is still far from being a homogeneous market with common needs and wants for all products. Myriad obstacles to strict standardisation remain. Nevertheless, the lack of commonality among markets should not deter a marketer from being guided by a global strategy, that is, a marketing philosophy that directs products and advertising towards a worldwide rather than a local or regional market, seeking standardisation where possible and modifying where necessary. To achieve global advertising huge sums are being spent on a worldwide basis. Top companies spend billions on advertising (see Exhibit 16.5).

pan-European advertising

The attraction of a single European market will entice many companies to standardise as much of their promotional effort as possible. As media coverage across Europe expands, it will become more common for markets to be exposed to multiple advertising messages and brand names of the same product. To avoid the confusion that results when a market is exposed to these, as well as for reasons of efficiency, companies will strive for harmony in brand names, advertising and promotions across Europe.

Mars, the confectionery company, traditionally used several brand names for the same product but recently has achieved uniformity by replacing them with a single name. A chocolate bar sold in some parts of Europe under the brand name Raider was changed to Twix, the name used in the United States and the United Kingdom.

Along with changes in behaviour patterns, legal restrictions are gradually being eliminated, and viable market segments across country markets are emerging. While Europe will never be a single homogeneous market for every product, it does not mean that companies should shun the idea of developing European-wide promotional programmes especially for global, European brands and for corporate image. A pan-European promotional strategy would mean identifying a market segment across all European countries and designing a promotional concept appealing to market segment similarities.

key term

promotional strategy systematic planning to promote a product

international market segmentation and promotional strategy

Rather than approach a **promotional strategy** decision as having to be either standardised or adapted, a company should first identify market segments. Market segments can be defined within country boundaries or across countries. Global market segmentation involves identifying homogeneous market segments across groups of countries.

Exhibit 16.5 Top 20 global advertisers ($ millions)*

2001	2000	Advertiser	Headquarters	2001	Per cent Change
1	2	Procter & Gamble Co.	Cincinnati	3820.2	6.6
2	1	General Motors Corp.	Detroit	3028.9	−20.1
3	3	Unilever	London/Rotterdam	3005.5	2.6
4	6	Ford Motor Co.	Dearborn, MI	2309.0	3.0
5	5	Toyota Motor Corp.	Toyota City, Japan	2213.3	−3.1
6	8	AOL Time Warner	New York	2099.8	9.5
7	4	Philip Morris Cos.	New York	1934.6	−19.0
8	7	DaimlerChrysler	Stuttgart	1835.3	−12.4
9	9	Nestlé	Vevey, Switzerland	1798.5	3.2
10	10	Volkswagen	Wolfsburg, Germany	1574.1	−2.0
11	13	Honda Motor Co.	Tokyo	1426.0	5.6
12	11	McDonald's Corp.	Oak Brook, IL	1405.3	−3.6
13	14	Coca-Cola Co.	Atlanta	1402.4	6.5
13	12	L'Oréal	Paris	1348.8	−2.1
15	16	Walt Disney Co.	Burbank, CA	1,260.4	−1.6
16	18	Johnson & Johnson	New Brunswick, NJ	1227.3	−0.4
17	17	Nissan Motor Co.	Tokyo	1224.0	−3.8
18	15	Sony Corp.	Tokyo	1218.9	−4.9
19	20	GlaxoSmithKline	Greenford, Middlesex, UK	1130.1	6.0
20	21	PepsiCo	Purchase, NY	1025.8	8.3

*Figures are US dollars in millions and are *Advertising Age* estimates.

Source: 'Special Report: Global Marketers', *Advertising Age*, supplement to the *Ad Age* Special Report, 11 November 2002. Copyright, Crain Communications, Inc., 2002.

Procter & Gamble is an example of a company that identified mass-market segments across the world and designed brand and advertising concepts that apply to all. The company's shampoo positioning strategy, 'Pro-V vitamin formula strengthens the hair and makes it shine', was developed for the Taiwan market, and then launched successfully in several other countries with only minor adaptation for hair types and languages. L'Oréal's 'It's expensive and I'm worth it' brand position also works well worldwide. Unilever's fabric softener's teddy bear brand concept has worked well across borders, even though the 'Snuggle' brand name changes in some countries; it is Kuschelweich in Germany, Coccolino in Italy and Mimosin in France.[7]

Other companies have identified niche segments too small for country-specific development but, when taken in aggregate, they have become profitable markets. The luxury-brand luggage Vuitton is an example of a product designed for a niche segment. It is marketed as an exclusive, high-priced, glamorous product worldwide to relatively small segments in most countries.

While there are those who continue to argue the merits of standardisation versus adaptation, most will agree that identifiable market segments for specific products exist across country markets, especially in some types of product, and that companies should approach promotional planning from a global perspective, standardise where feasible and adapt where necessary.

GOING INTERNATIONAL 16.2

selling Levi's around the world

Levi's clothing is sold in more than 70 countries, with different cultural and political aspects affecting advertising appeals. Here are some of the appeals used.

In Indonesia, ads show Levi's-clad teenagers cruising around Dubuque, Iowa, in 1960s convertibles.

In the United Kingdom, ads emphasise that Levi's is an American brand and star an all-American hero, the cowboy, in fantasy wild west settings.

In Japan, local jeans companies had already positioned themselves as American. To differentiate Levi's, the company positioned itself as legendary American jeans with commercials themed 'Heroes Wear Levi's', featuring clips of cult figures such as James Dean. The Japanese responded – awareness of Levi's in Japan went from 35 per cent to 95 per cent as a result of this campaign.

In Brazil, the market is strongly influenced by fashion trends emanating from the continent rather than from America. Thus, the ads for Brazil are filmed in Paris, featuring young people, cool amid a wild Parisian traffic scene.

In Australia, commercials were designed to build brand awareness with product benefits. The lines 'fit looks tight, doesn't feel tight, can feel comfortable all night' and 'a legend doesn't come apart at the seams' highlighted Levi's quality image, and 'since 1850 Levi's jeans have handled everything from bucking broncos ...' emphasised Levi's' unique positioning.

With thanks to Levi.

Source: adapted from 'Exporting a Legend', *International Advertiser*, November–December 1981; and 'For Levi's, a Flattering Fit Overseas', *Business Week*, 5 November 1990, p. 76.

challenges of international advertising

The growing intensity of international competition, coupled with the complexity of marketing multinationally, demands that the international advertiser function at the highest creative level. Advertisers from around the world have developed their skills and abilities to the point that advertisements from different countries reveal basic similarities and a growing level of sophistication. To complicate matters further, boundaries are placed on creativity by legal, tax, language, cultural, media, production and cost limitations.

key term

comparative advertising
directly compares you with your competitors

legal and tax considerations

Laws that control **comparative advertising** vary from country to country in Europe. In Germany, it is illegal to use any comparative terminology; you can be sued by a competitor if you do. Belgium and Luxembourg explicitly ban comparative advertising, whereas it is clearly authorised in the United Kingdom, Sweden, Ireland, Spain and Portugal. The European Commission is issuing several directives to harmonise the laws governing advertising. Many fear that if the laws are not harmonised, member states may close their borders to advertising that does not respect their national rules. The directive covering comparative advertising will allow implicit comparisons that do not name competitors, but will ban explicit comparisons between named products. In Asia, an advertisement showing chimps choosing Pepsi over Coke was banned from most satellite television. The term 'the leading cola' was accepted only in the Philippines.[8]

Advertising on television is strictly controlled in many countries. In Kuwait, the government-controlled TV network allows only 32 minutes of advertising per day, in the evening. Commercials are controlled to exclude superlative descriptions, indecent words, fearful or shocking shots, indecent clothing or dancing, contests, hatred or revenge shots, and attacks on competition. It is also illegal to advertise cigarettes, lighters, pharmaceuticals, alcohol, airlines, and chocolates or other sweets. In the United States, advertising pharmaceuticals is allowed (see Exhibit 16.6).

Exhibit 16.6 Direct to consumer prescription drug advertising in the United States

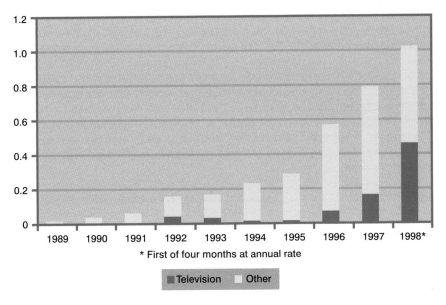

* First of four months at annual rate

■ Television   □ Other

Source: 'Competitive Media Reporting', *The Economist*, 8 August 1998, p. 58.

Some countries have special taxes that apply to advertising, which might restrict creative freedom in media selection. The tax structure in Austria best illustrates how advertising taxation can distort media choice by changing the cost ratios of various media. In federal states, with the exception of Bergenland and Tyrol, there is a 10 per cent tax on ad insertions; for posters, there is a 10–30 per cent tax according to state and municipality. Radio advertising carries a 10 per cent tax, except in Tyrol where it is 20 per cent. In Salzburg, Steiermark, Karnten and Voralbert there is no tax. There is a uniform tax of 10 per cent throughout the country on television ads. Cinema advertising has a 10 per cent tax in Vienna, 20 per cent in Bergenland and 30 per cent in Steiermark. There is no cinema tax in the other federal states.

language limitations

Language is one of the major barriers to effective communication through advertising. The problem involves different languages of different countries, different languages or dialects within one country, and the subtler problems of linguistic nuance and vernacular.

Incautious handling of language has created problems in nearly every country. Some examples suffice. Chrysler Corporation was nearly laughed out of Spain when it translated the US theme advertising 'Dart Is Power'. To the Spanish, the phrase implied that buyers sought but lacked sexual vigour. The Bacardi Company concocted a fruity bitters with a

made-up name, 'Pavane', suggestive of French chic. Bacardi wanted to sell the drink in Germany, but 'Pavane' is perilously close to 'pavian', which means 'baboon'. A company marketing tomato paste in the Middle East found that in Arabic the phrase 'tomato paste' translates as 'tomato glue'. In Spanish-speaking countries you have to be careful of words that have different meanings in the different countries. The word 'ball' translates in Spanish as 'bola'. Bola means ball in one country, revolution in another, a lie or fabrication in another and in yet another it is an obscenity. Tropicana-brand orange juice was advertised as 'jugo de China' in Puerto Rico, but when transported to Miami's Cuban community it failed. To the Puerto Rican, 'China' translated into orange, but to the Cuban it was 'China' and the Cubans were not in the market for Chinese juice. One Middle East advertisement features a car's new suspension system that, in translation, said the car was 'suspended from the ceiling'. Since there are at least 30 dialects among Arab countries, there is ample room for error. What may appear as the most obvious translation can come out wrong. 'A whole new range of products' in a German advertisement came out as 'a whole new stove of products'.

Low literacy in many countries seriously impedes communications and calls for greater creativity and use of verbal media. Multiple languages within a country or advertising area provide another problem for the advertiser. Even a tiny country such as Switzerland has four separate languages. The melting-pot character of the Israeli population accounts for some 50 languages. A Tel Aviv commentator says that even though Hebrew 'has become a negotiable instrument of daily speech, this has yet to be converted into advertising idiom'. As revealed by one study:

> In industrialised countries such as Canada and Sweden, advertising copy in general contains more writing and technical information, because most consumers have a high level of literacy and education and like to compare technical details and specifications. Comparative shopping practices are limited in Turkey, and the general level of education is not that high. Unlike Canada and Sweden most of the advertising copy used by the Turkish agencies is persuasive in nature rather than informative or comparative.[9]

cultural diversity

The problems of communicating to people in diverse cultures is one of the great creative challenges in advertising. Communication is more difficult because cultural factors largely determine the way various phenomena are perceived. If the perceptual framework is different, perception of the message itself differs.

International marketers are becoming accustomed to the problems of adapting from culture to culture. Knowledge of differing symbolisms of colours is a basic part of the international marketer's encyclopaedia. An astute marketer knows that, as we have already seen, white in Europe is associated with purity but in Asia it is commonly associated with death. The marketer must also be sophisticated enough to know that the presence of black in the West or white in Eastern countries does not automatically connote death. Colour is a small part of the communications package, but if the symbolism in each culture is understood, the marketer has an educated choice of using or not using various colours.

Knowledge of cultural diversity must encompass the total advertising project. Existing perceptions based on tradition and heritage are often hard to overcome. Marketing researchers in Hong Kong found that cheese is associated with *Yeung-Yen* (foreigners) and rejected by some Chinese. The concept of cooling and heating the body is important in Chinese thinking; malted milk is considered heating, while fresh milk is cooling; brandy is sustaining, whisky harmful. A soap commercial featuring a man touching a woman's skin while she bathes, a theme used in some European countries and in the United States, would be rejected in countries where the idea of a man being in the same bathroom with a female would be taboo.

As though it were not enough for advertisers to be concerned with differences among nations, they find subcultures within a country require attention as well. In India, there are

GOING INTERNATIONAL 16.3

sex doesn't sell any more!

The advertisers all over Europe are realising that sex does not sell the way it used to. Experts believe that people are looking for things that are more real, more wholesome and more pure. According to the Chartered Institute of Marketing (CIM), 'using sex to sell has been overdone and has reached saturation point'.

The agencies that specialised in this type of advertising, e.g. TBWA, which invented 'FCUK' for French Connection, a UK clothing brand, also agree. There has

With thanks to FCUK

been a shift: sex does not shock people any more. A recent research by CIM revealed that only 6 per cent of consumers were positively influenced by sexual images in advertising. Most consumers find explicit sexual images boring and repelling; subtle cues and suggestions are much more powerful. Women consumers are particularly offended by explicit sexual images.

easyJet, the low-priced airline, learnt its lesson when it was ridiculed for a poster it produced featuring a bulging bikini top with the slogan 'Discover weapons of mass-distraction'.

■ Do you think sex sells?

Source: compiled from *The Economist*, 'Sex Doesn't Sell', 30 October 2004, pp. 36–7.

several patterns of breakfast eating. The youth of a country almost always constitute a different consuming culture from the older people, and urban dwellers differ significantly from rural dwellers. Besides these differences, there is the problem of changing traditions. In all countries, people of all ages, urban or rural, cling to their heritage to a certain degree but are willing to change some areas of behaviour.

production and cost limitations

Creativity is especially important when a budget is small or where there are severe production limitations, poor-quality printing and a lack of high-grade paper. For example, the poor quality of high-circulation glossy magazines and other quality publications has caused Colgate-Palmolive to depart from its customary heavy use of print media in the West for other media in Eastern Europe. The necessity for low-cost reproduction in small markets poses another problem in many countries. For example, hand-painted **billboards** must be used instead of printed sheets because the limited number of billboards does not warrant the production of printed sheets. In Western societies, the increasing cost of advertising in television and radio is forcing companies to look for alternative advertising methods. The increasing cost of advertising through sports events is illustrated by Olympic broadcast rights fees over the years (Exhibit 16.7).

key term

billboards
large stands that comprise advertising space, usually found at the sides of roads

media planning and analysis

tactical considerations

Although nearly every sizeable nation essentially has the same kind of media, there are a number of specific considerations, problems and differences encountered from one nation to another. In international advertising, an advertiser must consider the availability, cost

GOING INTERNATIONAL 16.4

Sharapova sparks outrage in Los Angeles

Los Angeles, the city of *Playboy* magazine and lap-dance clubs, was mortified by an advertising campaign that featured a scantily clad Maria Sharapova simply sitting on a tennis court. Sharapova, the 2004 Wimbledon women's champion, was considered to be the perfect model to market the World Women's Tennis Association (WTA) tournament in Los Angeles, which she later won. She is attractive and talented and what tournament director would not use her image to promote the event?

The tournament took place at the Staple Center, the LA Lakers' (basketball team) home. The nearby Convention Center was to stage the United States' annual trade fair for adult entertainment soon after.

Previously it had been difficult to attract people to this tournament; it has been difficult to spot a full row at the 19 000-seat arena. Yet the reactions to the advertising campaign have been appalling. A *Los Angeles Times*' sport columnist wrote, 'Take a look at this picture of Maria Sharapova. What do you think? Can you say it out loud?' Even the number one female player, Lindsay Davenport, said, 'I would not do it, and I would not allow my daughter to do it either.' However, Serena Williams spoke out, 'It's a wonderful picture. But it's unfortunate that if you're a female actress or singer, it's the sexiest ones that sell more tickets. I hate it, but sex sells.'

The WTA chief executive replied, 'I don't think those advertisements are racy or inappropriate. I also find it a bit ironic that in LA, the home of entertainment industry, somebody finds it out of line.' John Lloyd, former British tennis number one and a resident of LA, agreed: 'Anybody who finds the picture offensive must have a strange mind.'

Sharapova doesn't seem to be bothered. After the first week of the tournament she got another $6 (€5.2) million endorsement from Canon. Maria's trainer, however, revealed that she was furious that the writer in the newspaper thought they couldn't sell her as a winner but only as sexy.

■ Do you think the picture sounds inappropriate? Do you think the WTA is trying to sell itself using sex?

Source: Barry Flatman, 'More Than Just a Pretty Face', *The Times*, 14 November 2004, p. 218.

and coverage of the media. Local variations and lack of market data provide areas for additional attention.

Imagine the ingenuity required of advertisers confronted with the following situations.

1 TV commercials are sandwiched together in a string of 10-50 commercials within one station break in Brazil.
2 In many countries, national coverage means using as many as 40-50 different media.
3 Specialised media reach small segments of the market only. In some countries of Europe, there are socialist, neutral and other specialised broadcasting systems.
4 In Germany, TV scheduling for an entire year must be arranged by 30 August of the preceding year, and there is no guarantee that commercials intended for summer viewing will always be run in the specified period.
5 In Vietnam, advertising in newspapers and magazines will be limited to 10 per cent of space and to 5 per cent of time, or three minutes an hour, on radio and TV.

Exhibit 16.7 Olympic broadcast rights fees* ($million)

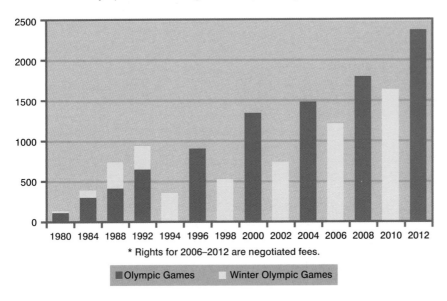

* Rights for 2006–2012 are negotiated fees.

■ Olympic Games   ☐ Winter Olympic Games

Source: International Olympic Committee (IOC), 2004.

Availability   One of the contrasts of international advertising is that some countries have too few advertising media and others have too many. In some countries, certain **advertising media** are forbidden by government edict to accept some advertising materials. Such restrictions are most prevalent in radio and television broadcasting. In many countries, there are too few magazines and newspapers to run all the advertising offered to them. Conversely, some nations segment the market with so many newspapers that the advertiser cannot gain effective coverage at a reasonable cost. Gilberto Sozzani, head of an Italian advertising agency, comments about his country: 'One fundamental rule. You cannot buy what you want.'

Cost   Media prices are susceptible to negotiation in most countries. Agency space discounts are often split with the client to bring down the cost of media. The advertiser may find the cost of reaching a prospect through advertising depends on the agent's bargaining ability. The per-contract cost varies widely from country to country. One study showed the cost of reaching a thousand readers in 11 different European countries ranged from €1.43 ($1.75) in Belgium to €5.33 ($6.52) in Italy; in women's service magazines, the page cost per thousand circulation ranged from €2.27 ($2.78) in Denmark to €9.81 ($12.00) in Germany. In some markets, shortages of advertising time on commercial television have caused substantial price increases.

Coverage   Closely akin to the cost dilemma is the problem of coverage. Two points are particularly important: one relates to the difficulty of reaching certain sectors of the population with advertising and the other to the lack of information on coverage. In many world marketplaces, a wide variety of media must be used to reach the majority of the markets. In some countries, large numbers of separate media have divided markets into uneconomical advertising segments. With some exceptions, a majority of the native population of developing countries cannot be reached readily through the medium of advertising. In Brazil, an exception, television is an important medium with a huge audience. One network, in fact, can reach 90 per cent of Brazil's more than 17 million TV households.

Because of the lack of adequate coverage by any single media in Eastern European countries, it is necessary for companies to resort to a multimedia approach. In the Czech

key term

advertising media different alternatives available to a company for its advertising (e.g. TV, magazine)

GOING INTERNATIONAL 16.5

how do we measure the effectiveness of advertising?

A firm can spend millions of dollars on advertising, and it is only natural to want some feedback on the results of such an expenditure: to what extent did the advertising really pay? Yet, many problems confront the firm trying to measure this.

Most of the methods for measuring effectiveness focus not on sales changes but on how well the communication is remembered, recognised or recalled. Most evaluative methods simply tell which ad is the best among those being appraised. But even though one ad may be found to be more memorable or to create more attention than another, that fact alone gives no assurance of relationship to sales success. A classic example of the dire consequences that can befall advertising people as a result of the inability to directly measure the impact of ads on sales is reflected in the following example.

The Doyle Dane Bernbach advertising agency created memorable TV commercials for Alka-Seltzer, such as the 'spicy meatball man' and the 'poached oyster bride'. These won professional awards as the best commercials of their year and received high marks for humour and audience recall. But the $22 million (€20 million) account was abruptly switched to another agency. The reason? Alka-Seltzer's sales had dropped somewhat. Of course, no one will ever know whether the drop might have been much worse without these notable commercials.

So, how do we measure the value of millions of dollars spent on advertising? Not well. Nor can we determine what is the right amount to spend for advertising (versus what is too much or too little).

■ Can a business succeed without advertising? Why or why not?

Source: Robert Hattley, *Marketing Mistakes*, 6th edn (New York: Wiley, 1995), p. 134.

Japanese beverage company Suntory use LCD displays in unusual ways to promote their drinks at a sports event.
Tatsuyuki Tayama/Fujifotos/The Image Works

Republic, for example, TV advertising rates are high and unavailable prime-time spots have forced companies to use billboard advertising. Outdoor advertising has become popular and in Prague alone billboards have increased from 50 in 1990 to over 5000 in 1996.[10]

Lack of Market Data Verification of circulation or coverage figures is a difficult task. Even though many countries have organisations similar to the Audit Bureau of Circulation (ABC), accurate circulation and audience data are not assured. For example, the president of the Mexican National Advertisers Association charged that newspaper circulation figures are 'grossly exaggerated'. He suggested that 'as a rule agencies divide these figures in two and take the result with a grain of salt'. The situation in China is no better: surveys of habits and penetration are available only for the cities of Beijing, Shanghai and Guangzhou. Radio and television audiences are always difficult to measure, but at least in most countries geographic coverage is known.

specific media information

An attempt to evaluate the specific characteristics of each medium is beyond the scope of this discussion. Furthermore, such information would quickly become outdated because of the rapid changes in the international advertising media field. It may be interesting, however, to examine some of the unique international characteristics of various advertising media. In most instances, the major implications of each variation may be discerned from the data presented.

Newspapers   The newspaper industry is suffering in some countries from lack of competition, and choking because of it in others. Most European cities have just one or two major daily newspapers but, in many countries, there are so many newspapers that an advertiser has trouble reaching even partial market coverage. Uruguay, population 3 million, has 21 daily newspapers with a combined circulation of 553 000. Norway, on the other hand, with a population of more than 4 million, has only one national daily morning newspaper. Turkey has 380 newspapers, and an advertiser must consider the political position of each newspaper so the product's reputation is not harmed through affiliations with unpopular positions. Japan has only five national daily newspapers, but the complications of producing a Japanese-language newspaper are such that they each contain just 16-20 pages. Connections are necessary to buy advertising space; *Asahi*, Japan's largest newspaper, has been known to turn down over a million dollars a month in advertising revenue.

Separation between editorial and advertising content in newspapers provides another basis for contrast on the international scene. In some countries, it is possible to buy editorial space for advertising and promotional purposes. The news columns are for sale not only to the government but to anyone who has the money. Since there is no indication that the space is paid for, it is impossible to tell exactly how much advertising appears in a given newspaper.

Magazines   The use of foreign national consumer magazines by international advertisers has been notably low for many reasons. Few magazines have large circulations or provide dependable circulation figures. Technical magazines are used extensively to promote export goods; but, as in the case of newspapers, paper shortages cause placement problems.

Increasingly, Western publications are publishing overseas editions. *Reader's Digest International* has added a new Russian-language edition to its more than 20 languages. Other print media available in international editions range from *Playboy* to *The Economist*. Advertisers have three new magazines to reach females in China: Hachette Filipacfchi Presse, the French publisher, is expanding Chinese-language editions of *Elle*, a fashion magazine; *Woman's Day* is aimed at China's 'busy modern' woman; and *L'Événement Sportif* is a sports magazine.[11] These media offer alternatives for multinationals as well as for local advertisers.

Radio and Television   Possibly because of their inherent entertainment value, radio and television have become major communications media in most nations. Most populous areas have television broadcasting facilities. In some markets, such as Japan, television has become almost a national obsession and thus finds tremendous audiences for its advertisers. In China, for example, virtually all homes in major cities have a television, and most adults view television and listen to radio daily.[12] Radio has been relegated to a subordinate position in the media race in countries where television facilities are well developed. In many countries, however, radio is a particularly important and vital advertising medium when it is the only one reaching large segments of the population.

Entrepreneurs in the radio/television field have discovered that audiences in commercially restricted countries are hungry for commercial television and radio, and that marketers are eager to bring their messages into these countries. A major study in 22 countries revealed that the majority were favourable towards advertising. Individuals in former communist countries were among the more enthusiastic supporters. In a 22-country survey, Egypt was the only one where the majority of responses were anti-advertising. Only 9 per cent of Egyptians surveyed agreed that many TV commercials are enjoyable, compared to 80 per cent or more in Italy, Uruguay and Bulgaria.[13] Italy, which had no private/local radio or TV until 1976, currently has some 300 privately owned stations.

Satellite and Cable TV   Of increasing importance in TV advertising is the growth and development of satellite TV broadcasting. Sky, a UK-based commercial satellite TV station,

beams its programmes and advertising into most of Europe via cable TV subscribers. New technology now permits households to receive broadcasts directly from the satellite via a dish the 'size of a dinner plate' costing about €315 ($350). This innovation adds possibilities of greater coverage and the ability to reach all of Europe with a single message.[14]

Parts of Asia and Latin America receive TV broadcasts from satellite television networks. Univision and Televisa are two Latin-American satellite television networks broadcasting via a series of affiliate stations in each country to most of the Spanish-speaking world, including the United States. *Sabado Gigante*, a popular Spanish-language programme broadcast by Univision, is seen by tens of millions of viewers in 16 countries. Star TV, a new pan-Asian satellite television network, has a potential audience of 2.7 billion people living in 38 countries from Egypt through India to Japan, and from the Soviet Far East to Indonesia. Star TV was the first to broadcast across Asia but was quickly joined by ESPN and CNN. The first Asian 24-hour all-sports channel was followed by MTV Asia and a Mandarin Chinese-language channel that delivers dramas, comedies, films and financial news aimed at the millions of overseas Chinese living throughout Asia. Programmes are delivered through cable networks but can be received through private satellite dishes.[15]

Direct Mail   Direct mail is a viable medium in many countries. It is especially important when other media are not available. As is often the case in international marketing, even such a fundamental medium is subject to some odd and novel quirks. Despite some limitations with direct mail, many companies have found it a meaningful way to reach their markets. The Reader's Digest Association has used **direct-mail advertising** in many countries to successfully market its magazines.

In Southeast Asian markets where print media are scarce, direct mail is considered one of the most effective ways to reach those responsible for making industrial goods purchases, even though accurate mailing lists are a problem in Asia as well as in other parts of the world. **Industrial advertisers** are heavy mail users and rely on catalogues and sales sheets to generate large volumes of international business. Even in Japan, where media availability is not a problem, direct mail is used successfully by marketers such as Nestlé Japan and Dell Computer. To promote its Buittoni fresh chilled pasta, Nestlé is using a 12-page colour direct-mail booklet of recipes, including Japanese-style versions of Italian favourites.

Other Media   Restrictions on traditional media or their availability cause advertisers to call on lesser media to solve particular local-country problems. The cinema is an important medium in many countries, as are billboards and other forms of outside advertising. Billboards are especially useful in countries with high illiteracy rates.

In Haiti, sound trucks equipped with powerful loudspeakers provide an effective and widespread advertising medium. Private contractors own the equipment and sell advertising space much as a radio station would. This medium overcomes the problems of illiteracy, lack of radio and television set ownership and limited print media circulation. In Ukraine, where the postal service is unreliable, businesses have found that the most effective form of direct business-to-business advertising is direct faxing.[16]

sales promotion

Other than advertising, personal selling and publicity, all marketing activities that stimulate consumer purchases and improve retailer or middlemen effectiveness and cooperation are sales promotions. In-store demonstrations, samples, coupons, gifts, product tie-ins, contests, sweepstakes, sponsorship of special events, such as concerts and fairs, and point-of-purchase displays are types of sales promotion devices designed to supplement advertising and personal selling in the promotional mix. Multinational companies spend millions of dollars to get exposure through big events such as the soccer World Cup.

key terms

direct-mail advertising
advertising that comes through the post, directly addressed to the recipient

industrial advertisers
companies that advertise industrial products

Sales promotions are short-term efforts directed to the consumer and/or retailer to achieve such specific objectives as:

1 consumer product trial and/or immediate purchase
2 consumer introduction to the store
3 gaining retail point-of-purchase displays
4 encouraging stores to stock the product, and
5 supporting and augmenting advertising and personal sales efforts.

key term

sales promotions
activities to
attract consumers
and promote
products

An example of sales promotion is the African cigarette manufacturer that, in addition to regular advertising, sponsors musical groups and river explorations, and participates in local fairs in attempts to make the public aware of the product. Procter & Gamble's introduction of Ariel detergent in Egypt included the 'Ariel Road Show'. This puppet show was taken to local markets in villages where more than half of the Egyptian population still live. The show drew huge crowds, entertained people, told about Ariel's better performance without the use of additives, and sold the brand through a distribution van at a nominal discount. Besides creating brand awareness for Ariel, the road show helped overcome the reluctance of the rural retailers to handle the premium-priced Ariel.

An especially effective promotional tool when the product concept is new or has a very small market share is product sampling. Nestlé Baby Foods faced such a problem in France

GOING INTERNATIONAL 16.6

mobile brand ambassadors (at a discount)

Advice on skin care or your next holiday destination is the last thing you would expect when you hop into a black cab. But at Taxi Media, which controls over 85 per cent of taxi ads in the UK, the cabbie is not just a taxi driver but a 'brand ambassador'. In the age of digital TV, where consumers can fast-forward during ads, and SMS, advertisers are looking for new ways to catch consumers' attention.

Bus and taxi ads fall within the outdoor advertising category. Brand owners can pay to have ads on the sides of vehicles or opt for a full deal, which includes ads right across the cab's exterior and on receipts and tip-up seats. And the idea is that drivers provide the added value, promoting the brand with the passenger. Knowledge of the brand comes courtesy of the advertisers. For example, drivers who carry ads for Clinique were given facials and seminars on the company's 'three-step skin care system'. Qantas, the airline, offered free air tickets to Australia for the 40 cabbies carrying its ads, and the South African Tourist Board organised a trip to South Africa. The apparently good-natured and chatty character of the drivers makes them perfect brand ambassadors if they are enthusiastic about the product or service advertised on their cab.

With thanks to Taxi Media & Clear Channel UK

Taxi Media, which has about 10 000 drivers on its books, says the market, which is worth about £17 million in the UK, was flat in 2002, and would grow slightly in 2003. Of the 16 000 licensed cabs in London, 10 per cent carry advertisements. Compared to other outdoor media, taxi ads can be relatively cheap – £3000 to £5000 for a full livery per taxi for 12 months, of which £1000 will go to the driver. An outdoor poster in London can cost more than double that, depending on the location, for only a few weeks. Buses and taxis also cover areas often denied to other outdoor media. They are seen in every tourist spot as well as the royal parks, residential areas and the City of London.

Source: adapted from Emiko Terazono. 'Do Ask Me, Guv', *Financial Times Creative Business*, 12 August 2003, p. 6.

in its attempt to gain share from Gerber, the leader. The company combined sampling with a novel sales promotion programme to gain brand recognition and to build goodwill.

Most Frenchmen take off for a long vacation in the summertime. They pile the whole family into the car and roam around France, or head for Spain or Italy, staying at well-maintained campgrounds found throughout the country. It is an inexpensive way to enjoy the month-long vacation. However, travelling with a baby still in nappies can be a chore. Nestlé came up with a way to dramatically improve the quality of life for any parent and baby on the road.

It provides rest-stop structures along the road where parents can feed and change their babies. Sparkling clean Le Relais Bébés are located along main travel routes. Sixty-four hostesses at these rest stops welcome 120 000 baby visits and dispense 600 000 samples of baby food each year. There are free disposable nappies, a changing table and high-chairs for the babies to sit in during meals. A strong tie between Nestlé and French mothers developed as a result of Le Relais Bébé. The most recent market research survey showed an approval rating of 94 per cent and Nestlé's share of the market has climbed to more than 43 per cent – close to a 24 share-point rise in under seven years.

As is true in advertising, the success of a promotion may depend on local adaptation. Major constraints are imposed by local laws, which may not permit premiums or free gifts to be given. Some countries' laws control the amount of discount given at retail, others require permits for all sales promotions and in at least one country no competitor is permitted to spend more on a sales promotion than any other company selling the product. Effective sales promotions can enhance the advertising and personal selling efforts and, in some instances, may be effective substitutes when environmental constraints prevent full utilisation of advertising.

international advertising and the communications process

Promotional activities (advertising, personal selling, sales promotions and public relations) are basically a communications process. All the attendant problems of developing an effective promotional strategy in domestic marketing plus all the cultural problems discussed earlier must be overcome to have a successful international promotional programme. A major consideration for foreign marketers is to ascertain that all constraints (cultural diversity, media limitations, legal problems, and so forth) are controlled so the right message is communicated to and received by prospective consumers. International communications may fail for a variety of reasons: a message may not get through because of media inadequacy, the message may be received by the intended audience but not be understood because of different cultural interpretations or the message may reach the intended audience and be understood but have no effect because the marketer did not correctly assess the needs and wants of the target market.[17]

The effectiveness of promotional strategy can be jeopardised by so many factors that a marketer must be certain no influences are overlooked. Those international executives who understand the communications process are better equipped to manage the diversity they face in developing an international promotional programme.[18]

In the communications process, each of the seven identifiable segments can ultimately affect the accuracy of the process. As illustrated in Exhibit 16.8 the process consists of:

1 an information source – an international marketing executive with a product message to communicate
2 encoding – the message from the source converted into effective symbolism for transmission to a receiver
3 a message channel – the sales force and/or advertising media that conveys the encoded message to the intended receiver

4 decoding - the interpretation by the receiver of the symbolism transmitted from the information source

5 receiver - consumer action by those who receive the message and are the target for the thought transmitted

6 feedback - information about the effectiveness of the message, which flows from the receiver (the intended target) back to the information source for evaluation of the effectiveness of the process, and to complete the process, and

7 noise - uncontrollable and unpredictable influences such as competitive activities and confusion detracting from the process and affecting any or all of the other six steps.

Exhibit 16.8 The international communication process

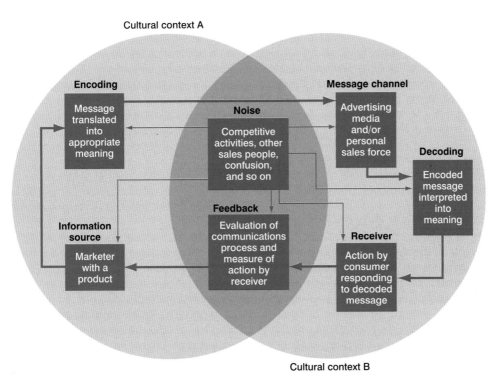

Unfortunately, the process is not as simple as just sending a message via a medium to a receiver and being certain that the intended message sent is the same one perceived by the receiver. In Exhibit 16.8, the communications-process steps are encased in cultural context A and cultural context B to illustrate the influences complicating the process when the message is encoded in one culture and decoded in another. If not properly considered, the different cultural contexts can increase the probability of misunderstandings. According to one researcher, effective communication demands that there exist a psychological overlap between the sender and the receiver; otherwise a message falling outside the receiver's perceptual field may transmit an unintended meaning. It is in this area that even the most experienced companies make blunders.[19]

Most **promotional misfires**, or mistakes, in international marketing are attributable to one or several of these steps not properly reflecting cultural influences and/or a general lack of knowledge about the target market. A review of some of the points discussed in this chapter serves to illustrate this. The information source is a marketer with a product to sell to a specific target market. The product message to be conveyed should reflect the needs and

key term

promotional misfires
mistakes made in the advertising activities of a company

wants of the target market; however, as many previous examples have illustrated, the marketer's perception of market needs and actual market needs do not always coincide. This is especially true when the marketer relies more on the self-reference criterion (SRC) than on effective research. It can never be assumed that 'If it sells well in one country, it will sell in another.' Bicycles designed and sold in the United States to consumers fulfilling recreational-exercise needs are not sold as effectively for the same reasons in a market where the primary use of the bicycle is transportation. From the onset of the communications process, if basic needs are incorrectly defined, communications fail because an incorrect or meaningless message is received even though the remaining steps in the process are executed properly.

The encoding step causes problems even with a proper message. At this step such factors as colour, values, beliefs and tastes can cause the international marketer to symbolise the message incorrectly. For example, the marketer wants the product to convey coolness, so the colour green is used; however, people in the tropics might decode green as dangerous or associate it with disease. Another example of the encoding process misfiring is a perfume presented against a backdrop of rain which, for Europeans, symbolised a clean, cool, refreshing image, but to Africans was a symbol of fertility. The ad prompted many viewers to ask if the perfume was effective against infertility.

Message channels must be selected carefully if an encoded message is to reach the consumer. Media problems are generally thought of in terms of the difficulty in getting a message to the intended market. Problems of literacy, media availability and types of media create problems in the communications process at this step. Errors such as using television as a medium when only a small percentage of an intended market is exposed to TV, or using print media for a channel of communications when the majority of the intended users cannot read, are examples of ineffective media channel selection in the communications process. Decoding problems are generally created by improper encoding, causing such errors as a translation that was supposed to be decoded as 'hydraulic ram' but was instead decoded as 'wet sheep'.

Decoding errors may also occur accidentally. In some cases, the intended symbolism has no meaning to the decoder. One soft drink manufacturer's advertisement promised a thirst-quenching reward based on the concepts 'Glacier Fresh' or 'Avalanche of Taste' in a part of the world where wintry mountain temperatures are an unknown experience. Errors at the receiver end of the process generally result from a combination of factors: an improper message resulting from incorrect knowledge of use patterns, poor encoding producing a meaningless message, poor media selection that does not get the message to the receiver or inaccurate decoding by the receiver so that the message is garbled or incorrect.

Finally, the feedback step of the communications process is important as a check on the effectiveness of the other steps. Companies that do not measure their communications efforts are apt to allow errors of source, encoding, media selection, decoding or receiver to continue longer than necessary. In fact, a proper feedback system allows a company to correct errors before substantial damage occurs.

In addition to the problems inherent in the steps outlined, the effectiveness of the communications process can be impaired by noise. Noise comprises all other external influences such as competitive advertising, other sales personnel and confusion at the receiving end that can detract from the ultimate effectiveness of the communications. Noise is a disruptive force interfering with the process at any step and is frequently beyond the control of the sender or the receiver. The significance is that one or all steps in the process, cultural factors, or the marketer's SRC, can affect the ultimate success of the communication. In designing an international promotional strategy, the international marketer can effectively use this model as a guide to help ensure all potential constraints and problems are considered so that the final communication received and the action taken correspond with the intent of the source.

GOING INTERNATIONAL 16.7

guerrilla marketing

For the past 10 years, the effectiveness of television advertising and other traditional techniques in reaching younger consumers in the developed world has been in decline. As a result, companies are turning to new approaches such as guerrilla marketing, also called buzz marketing.

The traditional media have become less effective for several reasons. First is increasing fragmentation: as the number of television channels, radio stations and consumer publications proliferates, audiences split into smaller groups, making it more difficult and expensive to reach an audience of a given size. Second is competition from other media: computer games and the Internet draw people away from TV. Third, people have grown cynical towards brands and multinational companies. Protesters against such global organisations as the World Trade Organization and the International Monetary Fund attract growing support for their attacks on perceived collaboration between governments and big business.

With thanks to
Red Bull

Yet, while the younger generation is turned off by slick advertising and suspicious of corporate manipulation, it remains conscious of brands and image. Buzz marketing – also known as word-of-mouth or stealth marketing – has emerged as a way for companies to get on the right side of consumers in the battle for sales. Buzz marketing involves getting trendsetters in any community to carry the brand's message, creating interest with no overt promotion. The message can be transmitted physically (people seen with the brand), verbally (through conversation) or virtually (via the Internet).

Red Bull is a company at the forefront of guerrilla marketing. When the drink was originally formulated, bars refused to stock it, seeing it as a medicinal or health-related product rather than a mixer. But snowboarders and clubbers soon recognised the boost it gave them and began taking it to alcohol-free discos, and before long bars began stocking the drink. Red Bull also hired student brand managers at university campuses, giving each a case of Red Bull and encouraging them to throw a party. It hired hip locals to drive around in cars emblazoned with the logo and equipped with a four-foot model of the Red Bull can. The cars carried fridges stocked with more than 250 cans of Red Bull, to be distributed to 'those in need of energy': shift workers, truck drivers, university students, executives, clubbers and athletes. Red Bull also sponsors a number of 'extreme' sports, backed by TV and press advertisements, and allied itself with those who push boundaries. Today, it has a 65 per cent share of the US energy drink market. The company keeps tight control on how it markets itself to clubs and bars. In the US, its representatives scout out hot spots – the bars and clubs frequented by trendsetters. They then offer them branded refrigerators and offer free goods along with their first order.

Red Bull is not alone in using buzz marketing. Among others are the following.

■ **Piaggio:** During its Vespa campaign, Piaggio had models drive around Los Angeles on Vespa scooters and chat up customers in cafés and bars. If asked about the Vespa, they would casually mention its various qualities and drop the names of celebrities who had recently purchased one. If anyone showed interest, the model would give them details of the nearest Vespa dealer.

- **Ford:** Ford identified 120 people in six core markets as trendsetters (for example, local DJs). Each was given a Focus to drive for six months as well as promotional material to distribute to anyone who expressed interest.
- **Hasbro:** Hasbro enlisted 'cool' pre-teenage boys to play its POX game, then sent them back to school to tell their jealous friends. They were given $30 and copies of the games to give out.

Buzz is useful in many contexts but is particularly effective for products that generate conversation – in other words, products with which consumers are emotionally involved. It can be a perfect tool to create an underground campaign, yet it can backfire badly if it appears contrived, turning off precisely those consumers it wishes to attract.

- Do you think guerrilla marketing is a successful way to market products like Red Bull?

Source: adapted from Nirmalya Kumar and Sophie Linguri, 'Buzz, Chat and Branding Give Red Bull Wings', *Financial Times Summer School*, 8 August 2003, p. 13.

the advertising agency

Just as manufacturing firms have become international, US, Japanese and European advertising agencies are expanding internationally to provide sophisticated agency assistance worldwide. Local agencies have also expanded as the demand for advertising services by MNCs has developed. Thus, the international marketer has a variety of alternatives available. In most commercially significant countries, an advertiser has the opportunity to employ (1) a local domestic agency, (2) its company-owned agency or (3) one of the multinational advertising agencies with local branches.

A local domestic agency may provide a company with the best cultural interpretation in situations where local modification is sought, but the level of sophistication can be weak. Another drawback of local agencies is the difficulty of coordinating a worldwide campaign. One drawback of the company-owned agency is the possible loss of local input when it is located outside the area and has little contact within the host country. The best compromise is the multinational agency with local branches because it has the sophistication of a major agency with local representation. Further, the multinational agency with local branches is better able to provide a coordinated worldwide **advertising campaign**. This has become especially important for firms doing business in Europe. With the interest in global or standardised advertising, many agencies have expanded to provide worldwide representation. Many companies with a global orientation employ one or perhaps two agencies to represent them worldwide.

Compensation arrangements for advertising agencies throughout the world are based on 15 per cent commissions. However, agency commission patterns throughout the world are not as consistent as they are in Europe or the United States; in some countries, agency commissions vary from medium to medium. Services provided by advertising agencies also vary greatly but few foreign agencies offer the full services found in Western agencies.

international control of advertising

European Union officials are establishing directives to provide controls on advertising as cable and satellite broadcasting expands. Deception in advertising is a major issue because most member countries have different interpretations of what constitutes a **misleading advertisement**. Demands for regulation of advertising aimed at young consumers is a trend appearing in both industrialised and developing countries.

Decency and the blatant use of sex in advertisements are also receiving public attention. One of the problems in controlling decency and sex in ads is the cultural variations around the world. An ad perfectly acceptable to a Westerner may be very offensive to someone

key terms

advertising campaign
designed and implemented for a particular product/purpose over a fixed period

misleading advertisement
gives incorrect message/ impression of a product/company

from the United States or, for that matter, a Spaniard. Standards for appropriate behaviour as depicted in advertisements vary from culture to culture. Regardless of these variations, there is growing concern about decency, sex and ads that demean women and men.

The difficulty that business has with self-regulation and restrictive laws is that sex can be powerful in some types of advertisement. European advertisements for Häagen-Dazs, a premium ice cream, and LapPower, a Swedish laptop computer company, received criticism for their ads as being too sexy. The Häagen-Dazs ad shows a couple, in various states of undress, in an embrace feeding ice cream to one another. Some British editorial writers and radio commentators were outraged. One commented that 'the ad was the most blatant and inappropriate use of sex as a sales aid'. The ad for LapPower personal computers that the Stockholm Business Council on Ethics condemned featured the co-owner of the company with an 'inviting smile and provocative demeanour displayed'. (She was bending over a LapPower computer in a low-cut dress.)

The bottom line for both these companies was increased sales. In the United Kingdom, sales soared after the 'Dedicated to Pleasure' ads appeared, and in Sweden the co-owner stated that 'Sales are increasing daily.' Whether laws are passed or the industry polices itself, there is an international concern about advertising and its effect on people's behaviour.

The advertising industry is sufficiently concerned with the negative attitudes of consumers and governments and with the poor practices of some advertisers that the International Advertising Association and other national and international industry groups have developed a variety of self-regulating codes. Sponsors of these codes feel that unless

GOING INTERNATIONAL 16.8

luxury brands in the film business

The focus on traditional advertising is changing. Luxury brands are moving from celebrity endorsements and using their pictures to making real films. Advertisers believe that target customers for brands are becoming resistant to the traditional advertising methods and have therefore moved to other methods such as product placement in movies (e.g. Omega and BMW in James Bond), direct marketing and sponsorship.

Louis Vuitton has donated an Olivier Debré stage curtain to the Hong Kong Opera. Max Mara has announced its sponsorship of the 'Max Mara Art Prize for Women'.

Chanel started its 2004 Christmas campaign with a short movie directed by Baz Luhrmann. It is a shorter version of *Love Story*, which tells a tale of one of the most famous women (Nicole Kidman) in the world, who flees the paparazzi and jumps into a taxi where she meets a young writer (Brazilian actor Rodrigo Santoro), who does not know who she is. They spend a weekend together in his garret, before she reveals who she is and returns to the real world.

Although she is wearing a 'No. 5' diamond necklace and there is a double 'C' illuminated outside the room, Chanel No. 5 is not actually featured in the movie.

Advertisers believe this approach creates a very solid connection to consumers. The ad will place Chanel No. 5 as the ultimate luxury brand in the market. Some say it will also position Nicole Kidman as the most desirable woman. It will also place her in the elite group of fashion icons, such as Catherine Deneuve (also a Chanel 'face').

Source: Vennessa Friedman, 'Coming Soon, Nicole Kidman in Chanel No. 5', *Financial Times*, 11 November 2004, p. 132.

411

the advertisers themselves come up with an effective framework for control, governments will intervene. This threat of government intervention has spurred interest groups in Europe to develop codes to ensure that the majority of ads conform to standards set for 'honesty, truth and decency'. In those countries where the credibility of advertising is questioned and in those where the consumerism movement exists, the creativity of the advertiser is challenged.

In many countries, there is a feeling that advertising, and especially TV advertising, is too powerful and persuades consumers to buy what they do not need. South Korea, for example, has threatened to ban advertising of bottled water because the commercials may arouse public mistrust of tap water.[20]

summary

Global advertisers face unique legal, language, media and production limitations in every market that must be considered when designing a promotional mix. As the world and its markets become more sophisticated, there is greater emphasis on international marketing strategy. The current debate among marketers is the effectiveness of standardised versus modified advertising for culturally varied markets. And, as competition increases and markets expand, greater emphasis is being placed on global brands and/or image recognition.

The most logical conclusion seems to be that, when buying motives and company objectives are the same for various countries, the advertising orientation can be the same. When they vary from nation to nation, the advertising effort will have to reflect these variations. In any case, variety in media availability, coverage and effectiveness will have to be taken into consideration in the advertiser's plans. If common appeals are used, they may have to be presented by a radio broadcast in one country, by cinema in another, and by television in a third.

A skilled advertising practitioner must be sensitive to the environment and alert to new facts about the market. It is also essential for success in international advertising endeavours to pay close attention to the communications process and the steps involved.

questions

1 'Perhaps advertising is the side of international marketing with the greatest similarities from country to country throughout the world. Paradoxically, despite its many similarities, it may also be credited with the greatest number of unique problems in international marketing.' Discuss.
2 Discuss the difference between advertising strategy when a company follows a multidomestic strategy rather than a global market strategy.
3 With satellite TV able to reach many countries, discuss how a company can use it and deal effectively with different languages, different cultures and different legal systems.
4 Outline some of the major problems confronting an international advertiser.
5 Defend either side of the proposition that advertising can be standardised for all countries.
6 Review the basic areas of advertising regulation.
7 How can advertisers overcome the problem of low literacy in their markets?
8 What special media problems confront the international advertiser?
9 Discuss the reason for pattern advertising.

10 Will the ability to broadcast advertisements over TV satellites increase or decrease the need for standardisation of advertisements? What are the problems associated with satellite broadcasting? Comment.

11 'Foreign newspapers cannot be considered homogeneous advertising entities.' Elaborate.

12 What is sales promotion and how is it used in international marketing?

13 Show how the communications process can help an international marketer avoid problems in international advertising.

14 Take each of the steps of the communications process and give an example of how cultural differences can affect the final message received.

15 Discuss the problems created when the communications process is initiated in one cultural context and ends in another.

further reading

- M. Agarwal, 'A Review of the 40-year Debate in International Advertising: Practitioner and Academician Perspectives to the Standardization vs Adaptation Issue', *International Marketing Review*, 1995, 12(1), pp. 26-48.

- M. De Mooij, 'New Directions in International Advertising Research', *International Marketing Review*, 2003, 20(6), pp. 678-80.

- S. Brown, 'O Customer, Where Art Thou?', *Business Horizon*, 2004, 47(4), pp. 61-70.

references

1 Laurent Gallissor, 'The Cultural Significance of Advertising: A General Framework of the Cultural Analysis of the Advertising Industry in Europe', *International Sociology*, March 1994, pp. 13-28.

2 Jean-Claude Usunier, *Marketing Across Cultures* (Hemel Hempstead: Prentice Hall, 1996).

3 Michael G. Harvey, 'Point of View: A Model to Determine Standardization of the Advertising Process in International Markets', *Journal of Advertising Research*, July-August 1993, pp. 57-63.

4 Michel Laroche, V.H. Kirpalani, Frank Pons and Lianxi Zhou, 'A Model of Advertising Standardization in Multinational Corporations', *Journal of International Business Studies*, 2001, 32(2), pp. 249-66.

5 Theodore Levitt, 'The Globalization of Markets', *Harvard Business Review*, May-June 1983, pp. 92-102.

6 'How Colgate-Palmolive Crafts Ad Strategies in Eastern Europe', *Crossborder Monitor*, 2 March 1994, p. 8.

7 Carl Arthur Solberg, 'The Perennial Issue of Adaptation or Standardization of International Marketing Communication: Organisational Contingencies and Performance', *Journal of International Marketing*, 2002, 10(3), pp. 1-21.

8 'Pepsi Spots Banned in Asia', *Advertising Age International*, 21 March 1994, pp. 1-2.

9 Erdener Kaynak and Pervez Ghauri, 'A Comparative Analysis of Advertising Practices in Unlike Environments: A Study of Agency–Client Relationships', *International Journal of Advertising*, vol. 5, 1986, pp. 121-46.

10 George Zinkhan and Madeline Johnson, 'The Use of Parody in Advertising', *Journal of Advertising*, 1994, 23(3), III.

11 N.S. Hong and C.Y. Poon, *Business Restructuring in Hong Kong* (Oxford: Oxford University Press, 2004).

12 E.C. Hirschman, 'Men, Dogs, Guns and Cars: The Semiotics of Rugged Individualism', *Journal of Advertising*, 32(1), pp. 9-22.

13 Swee Hoon Ang, 'Advertising Strategy and Advertising: Comparing USA and Australia', *The Journal of Marketing Communications*, 2002, 8(3), pp. 179-88.

14 H.J. Rotfeld, *Adventures in Misplaced Marketing* (Westport: Quoram Books, 2001).

15 S. Samee, I. Jeong, J.H. Pae and S. Tai, 'Advertising Standardization in Multinational Corporations: The Subsidiary Perspective', *Journal of Business Research*, 2003, 56(8), pp. 613–26.

16 C.A. Solberg, 'The Perennial Issue of Adaptation or Standardization of International Marketing Communication: Organisational Contingencies and Performance', *Journal of International Marketing*, 2002, 10(3), pp. 1–21.

17 A.S. Hoon, 'Advertising Strategy and Effective Advertising: Comparing the USA and Australia', *The Journal of Marketing Communications*, 2002, 8(3), pp. 179–88.

18 R.A. Kustin, 'Marketing Mix Standardization: A Cross-Cultural Study of Four Countries', *International Business Review*, 2004, 13(5), pp. 637–49.

19 Sudhir H. Kale, 'How National Culture, Organizational Culture and Personality Impact Buyer–Seller Interactions', in Pervez Ghauri and Jean-Claude Usunier (eds), *International Business Negotiations* (Oxford: Pergamon, 1996).

20 Marieke de Mooij, *Consumer Behaviour and Culture: Consequences for Global Marketing and Advertising* (Thousand Oaks: Sage, 2004).

chapter 17
Personal Selling and Negotiations

Chapter Outline

There are four ways of achieving marketing communication: advertising, sales promotions, personal selling and public relations. Cultural differences as well as the type of product have a major impact on how an optimal mix is found among the above-mentioned four ways to achieve the objectives of a company. People who want to take into account cultural differences have to be **relationship-centred** rather than purely **deal-centred**.[1]

The sales person provides a company's most direct contact with the customer and, in the eyes of most customers, the sales person *is* the company. As the presenter of the company's offerings and gatherer of customer information, the sales person is the final link in the culmination of a company's marketing and sales effort.

The tasks of building, training, compensating and motivating an international marketing group generate unique problems at every stage of management and development. This chapter discusses the importance of communications and negotiations in building marketing relationships with international customers.

selling in international markets

Increased global competition coupled with the dynamic and complex nature of international business increases the need for closer ties with both customers and suppliers. Selling in international marketing, built on effective communications between the seller and buyer, focuses on building long-term alliances rather than treating each sale as a one-time event.[2] This approach is becoming increasingly important for successful international marketers, especially in industrial buyer–seller interactions.[3] In **personal selling**, persuasive arguments are presented directly in a face-to-face relationship between sellers and potential buyers. To be effective, sales people must be certain that their communication and negotiation skills are properly adapted to a cross-cultural setting.

In many countries a low status is associated with selling. It is associated with the negative connotation of taking money from people rather than usefully bringing products and services to them. Seller status can also be associated with a particular group of people, e.g. Chinese, Dutch or Lebanese. In this perception, the seller's role is to convince and show the buyer the worth of the product on offer. In marketing, however, one of the seller's roles is to recognise the customer's needs and make them known to his or her company. The style of selling is often related to national culture, but it also depends on the personality of the sales person and the type of industry. Selling styles can also depend on which types of result or achievement are sought – for example, whether it is to win a new customer or maintaining an old relationship. According to Usunier, when preparing arguments, a

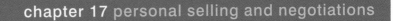

sales person has two main concerns: one is for the customers and their needs, the other is for achieving the sales.[4] This is illustrated in Exhibit 17.1.

Exhibit 17.1 Selling orientations

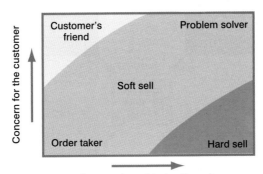

Source: Jean-Claud Usunier, *Marketing Across Cultures* (Hemel Hempstead: Prentice Hall, 1996), p.464.

If we separate the seller's role from that of the negotiator, the role of the sales person is mainly persuasion. There are, however, differences between persuasion and rather insistent and annoying behaviour. The main issue here is to understand what arguments will be best and quickest to persuade a particular customer.

In addition to the above factors, the two main components of personal selling are content and style. Content refers to the substantive aspects of the interaction for which the buyer and the seller come together. It includes suggesting, offering and negotiating. Style refers to the rituals, format, mannerisms and ground rules that the buyer and the seller follow in their encounter. A satisfactory interaction between the buyer and the seller is contingent upon buyer-seller compatibility with respect to both the content and the style of communication. The level of this compatibility is determined by cultural and personality factors.[5] The effectiveness of personal selling in international marketing is influenced by a number of factors, such as the nature of the sales person-customer relationship, the behaviour of the sales person, the resources of the sales person and the nature of the customer's buying task, as illustrated by Exhibit 17.2.

The Nature of the Sales Person–Customer Relationship The sales person-customer relationship is very important in international marketing as keeping a sales force in a foreign market means that the company is concerned about the continuity in the relationship with its customers and that it wants to meet people face-to-face rather than through printed material and advertising. The relationship development thus becomes very important. The sales person has to develop a relationship of trust and friendship with its customers. In most relationships one party is more dominant than the other; this is also true in the sales person-customer relationship.

Here the salesperson should seek to create a balance in this power/dependence situation. Depending on the above and the nature of the relationship, the parties perceive it as cooperative or conflicting. This issue is directly related to the bargaining power of the parties. The sales person's job is to drive the relationship towards a cooperative one. The nature of this relationship and willingness to cooperate also depends on what the parties expect from each other in the future. The more they anticipate a future beneficial interaction, the more the relationship is improved.

Behaviour of the Sales Person The behaviour of the sales person in international marketing interaction is highly dependent on his or her awareness of the local culture, values and norms. Due to this, companies normally use a local sales force. Whether the sales person is an **expatriate** or a local, the sales message, approach and behaviour to the

key term

expatriate
employee of the company/ organisation sent to another country to work

417

Exhibit 17.2 Factors influencing the effectiveness of personal selling

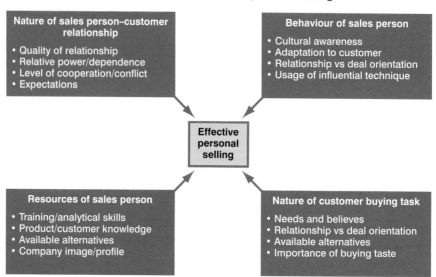

customer should be adapted in terms of language, level of argument and local norms. A relationship orientation instead of a one-shot deal orientation is essential in interaction with customers. In fact, this is often the main reason behind having a sales force. Sales people should also use the influential techniques mentioned earlier and in the negotiation section of this chapter. One should be aware that these techniques can be different in different markets, depending on culture, type of product and company.

Resources of the Sales Person   The sales person to be used in international marketing needs to be trained not only for a particular market/culture but also for general skills such as analytical techniques and negotiation. These skills are essential for international marketing activities and for developing relationships with customers. The sales force should be fully aware of the company's products and customers' needs, and how these two could be matched. A holistic view of the company's capabilities and resources is essential for representing the company fully and efficiently. The sales person should have full knowledge of the market and customer segmentation, not only of existing customers. Having a full picture of all available alternatives is a good resource that helps customer relationships. The image and positioning of a company in a particular market is of the utmost importance and is good baggage for the sales person. There should be some consistency in the company image and the message a sales person is taking to customers.

Nature of Customer's Buying Task   Another important factor, external to the sales person, is the nature and characteristic of the customer's buying task. Although it is beyond the sales person's control, he or she can in fact influence it. One way is to make the customer believe that there is a perfect match between his or her needs and what the sales person is offering. Another way is to work with the customer in defining those needs. The relationship orientation from both sides is thus crucial, as it can allow the sales person to get involved at an early stage of the customer's buying process. The number of alternatives available to customers would influence this aspect. The more options a customer has, the harder the sales person has to work to convince the customer. The importance of the buying task in the customer's organisation is also valuable information a sales person should have. The more important the buying task, the earlier the customer should be directed towards relationship orientation, which will lead to an earlier involvement of the sales organisation in the customer's internal decision making.

GOING INTERNATIONAL 17.1

are international assignments glamorous?

'Glamorous' is probably not the adjective the following executives would use.

'The problem as I see it with the company's talk about international managers is that they were just paying lip-service to it. When I applied for the posting to Malaysia they gave me all this stuff about the assignment being a really good career move and how I'd gain this valuable international experience and so on. And don't get me wrong, we really enjoyed the posting. We loved the people and the culture and the lifestyle and when it came to returning home, we weren't really all that keen ... The problem was that while I had been away, the company had undergone a wholesale restructuring ... This meant that when I got back, my job had effectively been eliminated.'

'We have been in the United States for 11 months and I reckon it will be another six to 12 months before my wife and the kids are really settled here. I'm still learning new stuff every day at work and it has taken a long time to get used to American ways of doing things ... I mean if the company said, "Oh, we want you to move to South Africa in a year's time," I would really dig my heels in because it was initially very disruptive for my wife when she first came here.'

And 'glamorous' would not be on the tip of these expatriate spouses' tongues either.

'I found I haven't adapted to Spanish hours. I find it a continual problem because the 2–5 pm siesta closure is really awkward. I always find myself where I have to remind myself that from 2–5 I have a blank period that I can't do anything ... We started adjusting to the eating schedule. Whether we like it or not, we eat a lot later.'

'Well, we went down to Club Med for a vacation and the French were all topless and my eight-year-old son didn't say anything by my four-year-old daughter now refuses to wear a top. I will not let her get away with it back in the US.'

'We've been really fortunate we haven't had to use health care services here ... The thought of going to, needing to go a doctor is scary because for me it would have to be someone English speaking or I wouldn't, you know, feel comfortable.'

■ Given these kinds of problems, is that international sales position being offered to you as attractive as it looks? Will it really help your career?

Sources: Nick Forster, 'The Myth of the "International Manager"', *International Journal of Resource Management*, February 2000, 11(1), pp. 126–42; and Mary C. Gilly, Lisa Penaloza and Kenneth M. Kambara, 'The Role of Consumption in Expatriate Adjustment and Satisfaction', Working Paper, Graduate School of Management, University of California, Irvine, 2004.

the international selling sequence

Knowing the customer in international sales means more than understanding the customer's product needs. It includes knowing the customer's culture. A cosmopolitan sales person will become more adept at cross-cultural selling if given a thorough grounding in the sequence that should be followed. Exhibit 17.3 presents a flowchart of international selling transactions. This step-by-step approach can be utilised for salesforce planning and training.[6]

The selling sequence starts with a self-appraisal, which is quite similar to the self-reference criteria (SRC) discussed in earlier chapters. The aim of self-appraisal is to develop a frame of reference whereby one's own communication preferences with regard to content

Exhibit 17.3 The international selling sequence

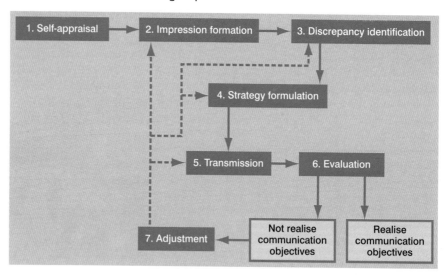

Source: Sudhir Kalé, 'How National Culture, Organizational Culture and Personality Impact Buyer–Seller Interactions', Pervez Ghauri and Jean-Claud Usunier, *International Business Negotiations* (Oxford: Pergamon, 1996), p. 35.

and style could be understood. Dimensions of SRC (that is, an unconscious reference to one's own cultural values, experience and knowledge) serve as a basis for self-awareness (see Chapter 1).

Impression formation involves understanding the buyer's cultural position. Typically, national culture and **organisational culture** can be assessed even before the seller meets with the buyer. Hofstede provides scores and ranks for 50 countries on the basis of positions on the four dimensions of national culture.[7] The organisational culture of most large and medium-sized companies can be gleaned from their press releases, annual reports and from popular literature. A trained sales person can assess a buyer's temperament with a fair degree of accuracy in a relatively short period of interaction. An accurate impression of the buyer in terms of national culture, organisational culture and temperament lays the foundation for relationship building, which is so critical to successful selling.

In the third step, the seller goes through the mental exercise of 'discrepancy identification'. This involves comparing the buyer's estimated position on the various dimensions of culture with one's own. This alerts the seller to potential problem areas in communication arising out of differences in temperament and cultural conditioning.

Strategy formulation involves minimising the impact of problem areas identified in the earlier step. For instance, if the buyer is a feeler, and the seller is a thinker, the seller needs to modify his persuasion style. While his preferred persuasion style is logical and impersonal, this may not fit well with the buyer. The appropriate style in this instance would be to appeal to the buyer's feelings and emotions, and to point out the people-benefits behind the seller's offering. Similar adjustments need to be made on other dimensions as well where discrepancies exist between the seller and the buyer.

Transmission involves implementation of the communication/persuasion strategy. During the course of transmission, the seller should be sensitive to the verbal and non-verbal feedback received from the buyer. If the seller has correctly identified the seller's mindset based on temperament and culture, the strategy should be on target and the feedback received from the buyer will be encouraging.

Assessing the effect of the communication strategy constitutes the 'evaluation' phase. If the seller's communication objectives are realised then the encounter has been successful. If not, the seller goes through the 'adjustment' process where buyer impres-

key term

organisational culture
values and norms of working in an organisation

sions, discrepancies and strategy are re-evaluated and the transmission is modified. At the evaluation and adjustment phase, the seller always has the choice of cutting short the encounter, and trying again at some time in the future. Regardless of the outcome, every encounter adds to the seller's repertoire of experiences, skills, strategies and alternative transmission approaches.

understanding the nuances of cross-cultural communications

Communications and the art of persuasion, knowledge of the customer and product, the ability to close a sale and after-sale service are all necessary for successful selling. These are the attributes sought when hiring an experienced person and those taught to new employees. Since culture impacts on the international sales effort just as it does on international advertising and promotion, the marketer must be certain that all international sales personnel have an understanding of the influence of culture on communications. After all, selling is communication and, unless the sales person understands the overtones of cross-cultural communications, the sales process could be thwarted.

Effective communication requires an understanding of the nuances of the spoken language as well as the silent language.[8] Perhaps more important than language nuances are the meanings of different **silent languages** spoken by people from different cultures. They may think they are understanding one another when, in fact, they are misinterpreting one another. For example:

> A Briton visits a Saudi official to convince him to expedite permits for equipment being brought into the country. The Saudi offers the Briton coffee, which is politely refused (he had been drinking coffee all morning at the hotel while planning the visit). The latter sits down and crosses his legs, exposing the sole of his shoe. He passes the documents to the Saudi with his left hand, enquires after the Saudi's wife and emphasises the urgency of getting the needed permits.

In less than three minutes, the Briton unwittingly offended the Saudi five times. He refused his host's hospitality, showed disrespect, used an 'unclean' hand, implied a familial familiarity and displayed impatience with his host. He had no intention of offending his host and probably was not aware of the rudeness of his behaviour. The Saudi might forgive his British guest for being ignorant of local custom, but the forgiven sales person is in a weakened position.

Knowing your customer in international sales means more than knowing your customer's product needs; it includes knowing your customer's culture. One international consultant suggests five rules of thumb for successful selling abroad.

1 **Be prepared** and do your homework. Learn about the host's culture, values, geography, religion and political structure. In short, do as complete a cultural analysis as possible to avoid cultural mistakes.
2 **Slow down**. Westerners are slaves to the clock. Time is money to a Westerner but, in many countries, emphasis on time implies unfriendliness, arrogance and untrustworthiness.
3 **Develop relationships** and trust before getting down to business. In many countries, business is not done until a feeling of trust has developed.
4 **Learn the language,** its nuances and the idiom, and/or get a good interpreter. There are just too many ways for miscommunication to occur.
5 **Respect the culture.** Manners are important. You are the guest, so respect what your host considers important.[9]

Anyone being sent into another culture as a sales person or company representative should receive training to develop the cultural skills discussed. In addition, they should receive *specific* schooling on the customs, values, and social and political institutions of the host country.

In international sales and purchase transactions, the responsibilities need to be clearly defined. For example, who is responsible for freight and insurance and from which point (ex-factory, on board, etc.) to which point are crucial issues and, if ignored, can lead to serious problems. What are the penalties for delays, and how is responsibility for delays to be determined, for example, in the case of strike, accident or fire? What if the goods do not correspond to the agreed sample or specifications? What if the payment is not made on time? Although a number of middlemen, such as clearing agents, are available to handle these issues, the sales person is solely responsible for negotiating these terms. The price or terms might be different with different responsibilities.

recruitment of an international sales force

The number of marketing management personnel from the home country assigned to foreign countries varies according to the size of the operation and the availability of qualified locals. Increasingly, the number of home-country nationals (expatriates) assigned to foreign posts is smaller as the pool of trained, experienced locals grows.

The largest personnel requirement abroad for most companies is the sales force, drawn from three sources: expatriates, **local nationals** and **third-country nationals**. A company's staffing pattern may include all three types in any single foreign operation, depending on qualifications, availability and a company's needs.

Expatriates   The number of companies relying on expatriate personnel is declining as the volume of world trade increases and as more companies use locals to fill marketing positions. However, when products are highly technical, or when selling requires an extensive background of information and applications, an expatriate sales force remains the best choice. The expatriate sales person may have the advantages of greater technical training, better knowledge of the company and its product line and proven dependability and effectiveness. And, because they are not locals, expatriates sometimes add to the prestige of the product line in the eyes of local customers.

Local Nationals   The historical preference for expatriate managers and sales people from the home country is giving way to a preference for locals. At the sales level, the picture is clearly biased in favour of the locals because they transcend both cultural and legal barriers. More knowledgeable about a country's business structure than an expatriate would be, local sales people are better able to lead a company through the maze of unfamiliar distribution systems. Furthermore, there is now a pool of qualified local personnel available that costs less to maintain than a staff of expatriates. In Asia, many locals will have earned Master's or MBA degrees in Europe or the United States; thus you get the cultural knowledge of the local meshed with an understanding of Western business management. Although expatriates' salaries may be no more than those of their national counterparts, the total cost of keeping comparable groups of expatriates in a country can be considerably higher because of special cost-of-living benefits, moving expenses, taxes and other costs associated with keeping an expatriate abroad.

Third-country Nationals   The internationalisation of business has created a pool of third-country nationals (TCNs), expatriates from their own countries working for a foreign company in a third country. The TCNs are a group whose nationality has little to do with where they work or for whom. An example would be a German working in Malaysia for a US company. Historically, there have been a few expatriates or TCNs who have spent the majority of their careers abroad, but now a truly 'global executive' has begun to emerge. The recently appointed chairman of a division of a major Dutch company is a Norwegian who gained that post after stints in the United States, where he was the US subsidiary's chairman, and in Brazil, where he held the position of general manager. At one time,

key terms

local nationals
employees of a company that are local to the market

third-country nationals
expatriates from the business's own country working for a foreign company in a third country

Burroughs Corporation's Italian subsidiary was run by a Frenchman, the Swiss subsidiary by a Dane, the German subsidiary by an Englishman, the French subsidiary by a Swiss, the Venezuelan subsidiary by an Argentinean, and the Danish subsidiary by a Dutchman. The CEO of Up John-Pharmacia, an American-Swedish pharmaceutical multinational with its head office in Michigan, is a Pakistani.

Development of TCN executives reflects not only a growing internationalisation of business but also acknowledges that personal skills and motivations are not the exclusive property of one nation.[10] TCNs are often sought because they speak several languages and know an industry or foreign country well. More and more companies are realising that talent flows to opportunity regardless of nationality.

Host Country Restrictions   The host governments' attitudes towards foreign workers complicate flexibility in selecting expatriate nationals or local nationals. Concern about foreign corporate domination, local unemployment and other issues cause some countries to restrict the number of non-nationals allowed to work within the country. Most countries have specific rules limiting work permits for foreigners to positions that cannot be filled by a national. Further, the law often limits such permits to periods just long enough to train a local for a specific position. Such restrictions mean that MNCs have fewer opportunities for sending home-country personnel to sales positions abroad.

selecting an international sales force

To select personnel for international positions effectively, management must define precisely what is expected of its people. A formal job description can aid management in expressing those desires for long-range needs as well as for current needs. In addition to descriptions for each marketing position, the criteria should include special requirements indigenous to various countries.[11]

People operating in the home country need only the attributes of effective sales persons, whereas a transnational manager can require skills and attitudes that would challenge a diplomat. Personnel requirements for various positions vary considerably, but despite the range of differences, some basic requisites leading to effective performance should be considered because effective executives and sales people, regardless of the foreign country in which they are operating, share certain characteristics. Special personal characteristics, skills and orientations are demanded for international operations.

Maturity is a prime requisite for expatriate and third-country personnel. Sales personnel working abroad must typically work more independently than their domestic counterparts. The company must have confidence in their ability to make decisions and commitments without constant recourse to the home office, or they cannot be individually effective.

Also, sales people operating in foreign countries need *considerable breadth of knowledge of many subjects both on and off the job*. The ability to speak several languages is becoming a necessity. In addition to the intangible skills necessary in handling interpersonal relationships, international marketers must also be effective sales people. Every marketing person in a foreign position is directly involved in the selling effort and must possess a sales sense that cuts through personal, cultural and language differences, and deals effectively with the selling situation.

The marketer who expects to be effective in the international marketplace needs to have a positive outlook on an international assignment. People who do not like what they are doing and where they are doing it stand little chance of success. Failures are usually the result of overselling the assignment, showing the bright side of the picture, and not warning about the bleak side.

Successful adaptation in international affairs is based on a combination of attitude and effort. A careful study of the customs of the market country should be initiated before the marketer arrives, and should continue as long as there are facets of the culture that are not clear. One useful approach is to listen to the advice of national and foreign business

GOING INTERNATIONAL 17.2

how important are those meetings?

Selling in East Asia: guanxi in action

You are the newly-hired marketing manager of Glorious Paints, a Singapore manufacturer of marine paints. It is a fast-growing company headed by three young, Western-educated directors.

Last year the marketing director led Glorious Paints to its first overseas sale, selling a large quantity of paint to Australia and New Zealand. Director Tan achieved this success by first sending information to potential distributors along with covering letters requesting appointments.

After receiving replies, Tan met with the interested candidate firms at their offices to negotiate a distribution agreement with the company best qualified to handle that market area. This process took about four months and today sales volume already exceeds expectations. Following that success you were hired to expand exports to other Pacific Rim markets. The director called you into his office to discuss market research showing that

© Charles Gupton/
CORBIS

Taiwan is a very promising market with high demand and little local competition. So you were instructed to set up distribution there using the approach that had worked in Australia/New Zealand.

By searching a number of databases you came up with the names and contact information of a number of Taiwanese importers, agents, representatives and wholesalers involved in the paint business. Next you sent off brochures and product information to these prospects, enclosing a covering letter requesting an appointment to discuss possible representation.

To your surprise, six weeks went by without a single response. At a strategy session Mr Tan pointed out that many Taiwanese are not comfortable corresponding in English, so you fired off a second mailing, this time in Chinese. But after another two months not a single prospective distributor has answered your request for an appointment. Mr Tan is upset with your lack of progress in this attractive market. He has called an urgent meeting for this afternoon and expects you to come up with a solution. As you sit stirring your tea the questions revolve in your head like the spoon in the teacup. 'What have I done wrong? This strategy worked fine with the Aussies. Why not with the Taiwanese? What do we do now?'

Source: © Copenhagen Business School Press, 2002. With thanks to the author, Richard R. Gesteland, Global Management LLC: 2002, and CBS Press (www.cbspress.dk/).

people operating in that country. Cultural empathy is clearly a part of basic orientation because it is unlikely that anyone can be effective if antagonistic or confused about the environment.

The personal characteristics, skills and orientation that identify the potentially effective sales person have been labelled in many different ways. Each person studying the field has a preferred list of characteristics, yet rising above all the characteristics there is an intangible something that some have referred to as a 'sixth sense'. This implies that, regardless of individual attributes, there is a certain blend of personal characteristics, skills and orientation that is hard to pinpoint and that may differ from individual to individual, but that produces the most effective overseas personnel.

Getting the right person to handle the job is a primary function of personnel management. It becomes especially important in the selection of locals to work for foreign companies within their home country. Most developing countries and many European countries have stringent laws protecting workers' rights. These laws are specific as to penalties for the dismissal of employees.

GOING INTERNATIONAL 17.3

personal selling tips, from Brussels to Bangkok

The best training programmes are much more than just a list of tips. But a quick read-through of such tips provides a glimpse of the cultural variation facing sales representatives around the globe.

Belgium: Be able to identify the decision makers. In Flanders (Dutch-speaking region) group decisions are common, but in Wallonia (French-speaking region) the highest-level execs have the final say.

China: Expect to continue negotiations after a deal is inked. To Chinese, signing a contract is just the beginning of the business relationship; therefore, they expect both sides to continue working together to fix problems that arise.

Colombia: Business counterparts want to get to know you personally and form a strong friendship with you. Be sure not to change reps in midstream, because a switch often puts an end to negotiations.

Germany: Be prepared with data and empirical evidence that supports your sales proposition. German business people are unimpressed by flashy advertising and brochures, so keep them serious and detailed, with unexaggerated information.

Japanese salesmen save on expenses by using "capsule hotels" as lodgings.
©Roger Ressmeyer/CORBIS

India: Make sure your schedule remains flexible. Indians are more casual about time and punctuality. Because of India's rigid hierarchy, decisions are made only by the highest-level boss.

Mexico: When planning a meeting, breakfast and lunch are preferable. Take your time and cultivate relationships with business contacts. Those relationships are generally considered more important than professional experience.

Peru: Peruvians relate to individuals and not corporate entities. Establish personal rapport and don't switch your representative in the middle of negotiations.

Russia: Your first meeting will be just a formality. Your Russian counterparts will take this time to judge your credibility, so it's best to be warm and approachable.

Scotland: Scottish people tend to be soft-spoken and private. It takes time to build relationships, but business counterparts seem friendlier after bonds are established. (By the way, Scotch is a drink, not a nationality – it's Scottish.)

South Korea: Status is important. Make sure your business card clearly indicates your title. Don't send a rep to meet with a Korean executive of higher status – it could be viewed as disrespectful.

Thailand: The Thai culture emphasises non-conflict, so don't make assertive demands when making sales pitches.

Source: Sales and Marketing Management publishes these tips regularly in its magazine and on its website (www.salesandmarketing.com).

training and motivation

The nature of a training programme depends largely on whether expatriate or local personnel are being trained as sales people. Training for the expatriates focuses on the customs and the special foreign sales problems that will be encountered, whereas local personnel require greater emphasis on the company, its products, technical information and selling methods. In training either type of personnel, the sales training activity is burdened with problems stemming from long-established behaviour and attitudes. Local personnel cling to habits continually reinforced by local culture. Nowhere is the problem greater than in China, where the legacy of the communist tradition lingers. The attitude that whether you work hard or not, you get the same rewards, has to be changed if training is going to hold. Expatriates as well are captives of their own habits and patterns. Before any training can be effective, open-minded attitudes must be established. Exhibit 17.4 shows the similarities and dissimilarities in the reward systems of different countries.

Continual training may be more important in foreign markets than in domestic ones because of the lack of routine contact with the parent company and its marketing personnel. One aspect of training is frequently overlooked: home-office personnel dealing with international marketing operations need training designed to make them responsive to the needs of the foreign operations. In most companies, the requisite sensitivities are expected to be developed by osmosis in the process of dealing with foreign affairs; a few companies

Exhibit 17.4 Global similarity to US compensation plans

Countries/regions		Eligibility	Degree of plan similarity with the United States				
			Performance measures	Weighting	Plan mechanics	Mix/ leverage	Payout frequency
Europe	United Kingdom						
	Scandinavia						
	France						
	Germany						
	Spain/Italy						
Southeast Asia	Hong Kong						
	Korea						
	Taiwan						
	Malaysia Indonesia (Singapore)						
	Australia						
Japan							
Canada							
South America							

☐ Similar ☐ Varies ☐ Dissimilar

Data represent multiple client projects conducted by the Alexander Group, Inc. for primarily high-technology industry sales organisations.

Source: David G. Schick and David J. Cichelli, 'Developing Incentive Compensation Strategies in a Global Sales Environment', *ACA Journal*, Autumn 1996; updated based on interview with David J. Cichelli, vice president of the Alexander Group, in May 2003.

send home-office personnel abroad periodically to increase their awareness of the problems of the foreign operations.[12]

Marketing is a business function requiring high motivation regardless of the location of the practitioner. Marketing managers and sales managers typically work hard, travel extensively and have day-to-day challenges. Selling is hard, competitive work wherever undertaken, and a constant flow of inspiration is needed to keep personnel functioning at an optimal level. National differences must always be considered in motivating the marketing force. One company found its sales people were losing respect and had low motivation because they did not have girls to pour tea for customers in the Japanese branch offices. The company learned that when male personnel served tea, they felt they lost face; tea girls were authorised for all branches.

The behaviour of a sales force is dependent on a number of factors such as: *background* – their education, general knowledge and ability to speak more than one language. It is also important how they dress and talk and that they deal tactfully with people. *Well informed* – first of all about the product and company they are selling. Buyers are never satisfied with information they get from brochures and ask the sales people all kinds of questions. If the latter are not well informed they will not be able to provide satisfactory information to the customer. Sales people should also have full knowledge of the local market, competing products and new developments in the field. *Morale* – to keep people going, their morale should be kept high. A common complaint among international sales people is that their head office does not understand them. They often feel left alone or deserted. Their morale can be boosted through realistic sales targets, giving them full support and making them feel that head office is fully behind them. Their achievements should be properly rewarded in accordance with their career goals. *Job stability* – sales people often have an uneasy feeling that while they are on the road other people at the office are getting all the benefits with regard to promotions and job stability. They may also be afraid about what will happen if they do not meet their target. Sales people worried about these issues cannot be very effective; it is therefore very important to select sales people with care, train them, and then support them with confidence and backing.

As the cultural differences reviewed in earlier chapters affect the motivational patterns of a sales force, a manager must be extremely sensitive to the personal behaviour patterns of employees. Individual incentives that work effectively in the West can fail completely in other cultures. For example, with Japan's emphasis on paternalism and collectivism, and its system of lifetime employment and seniority, motivation through individual incentive does not work because Japanese employees seem to derive the greatest satisfaction from being comfortable members of a group. Thus, an offer of financial reward for outstanding work could be turned down because an employee would prefer not to appear different from peers and possibly attract their resentment.

cross-cultural negotiations

The keystone of effective marketing and buyer–seller interactions is effective negotiation. Poorly conducted negotiations can leave the seller and the buyer frustrated, and do more to destroy effective relationships than anything else. Negotiation should be handled in such a way that a long-term relationship between buyer and seller is ensured.[13]

The basic elements of business negotiations are the same in every country; they relate to the product, its price and terms, services associated with the product and, finally, friendship between vendors and customers. Selling is often thought of as a routine exchange with established prices and distribution networks from which there is little deviation. But, particularly in international sales, the selling transaction is almost always a negotiated exchange. Price, delivery dates, quality of goods or services, volume of goods sold, financing, exchange rate risk, shipping mode, insurance, and so on, are all set by bargaining or negotiations. Such negotiations should not be conducted in a typical 'win-lose' situation but as a shared benefit that will ensure a long-term relationship.[14]

GOING INTERNATIONAL 17.4

cross-cultural selling

Some stereotypes of selling styles are often associated with different markets. Here are some examples.

In Asian countries, where arrogance and showing of extreme confidence are not appreciated, sales people should make modest, rational, down-to-earth points. They should avoid trying to win arguments with the customers, who could suffer from a 'loss of face' and react negatively. In Japan, one is expected to play golf with one's customers.

In Italy, on the contrary, the lack of self-confidence would be perceived as a clear sign of lack of personal credibility and reliability; thus one needs to argue strongly in order to be taken seriously.

In Switzerland, you have to speak precisely and your words will be taken quite literally.

In the United Kingdom, it is advisable to use the *soft sell* approach. Do not be pushy, instead try to 'chat' and convince.

In Germany, you should use the *hard sell* approach by being persistent. Make visits, offer trials and be very visible.

Golf course negotiations are common in many different business cultures
© Macduff Everton/CORBIS

Blending company sales objectives and the personal objectives of sales people is a task worthy of the most skilled manager. The Western manager must be constantly aware that many of the techniques used to motivate Western personnel and their responses to these techniques are based on Western cultural premises and may not work in other countries.

Simply stated, to negotiate is to confer, bargain or discuss with a view to reaching an agreement. It is a sequential rather than simultaneous give-and-take discussion resulting in a mutually beneficial understanding. Most authorities on negotiating include three stages in the negotiating process: (1) pre-negotiation stage; (2) negotiation stage; and (3) post-negotiation stage. In the pre-negotiation stage, parties attempt to understand each other's needs and offers, which is done through informal meetings and arrangements. The negotiation stage refers to face-to-face negotiations, and the post-negotiation stage refers to the stage when parties have agreed to most of the issues and are to agree on contract language and format, and signing of the contract, how it leads to more business and relationship development.

In addition to these stages, the process of international business negotiation has two more dimensions: (1) strategic factors and (2) cultural factors (see Exhibit 17.5).

As explained earlier, cultural factors play an important role in each and every stage of the international negotiation process. Cultural factors include time, pattern of communication and emphasis on personal relationships. While 'time is money' in Western cultures, it has no such value attached to it in Asia, Latin America and Africa. Knowing whether the other party is looking for a collective solution or an individual benefit is very important. According to Hofstede's studies, we can place different countries on different scales of individual and collective behaviour.[15] Different cultures have different patterns of communication as regards direct versus indirect and explicit versus implicit communication. Some languages are traditionally vague, others exaggerate, which makes communication difficult for those from outside who are not familiar with the language. Finally, different cultures give different importance to personal relations in negotiations. In the West, the

Exhibit 17.5 The process of international sales negotiations

negotiators are more concerned with the issue at hand, irrespective of who is representing the other side.

pre-negotiation stage

Before entering an international negotiation process, the two parties should know which type of decision-making procedure is going to be followed by the other party and which type of strategy should be used to match it. How should a party present its offer and capabilities? The formal versus informal and argumentative versus informative presentation style is very distinct in many countries. If not prepared, negotiators can make serious blunders. In negotiations people refer to different types of strategy, such as tough, soft or intermediate. In this respect too it is important to have information on the other party's strategy, so that you can match it. Furthermore, it is important to know who makes the decisions, and whether the negotiators taking part in the negotiation have decision-making powers.

Under strategic factors, it is also important to evaluate your position and realise whether there is a need for an agent or consultant for a particular negotiation process. It is a generally held opinion that the more unfamiliar or complex the other party or market is, the greater is the need for an agent or consultant.

Business people have to understand the cultural context of negotiations. An authoritative source on cross-cultural negotiating suggests that one of the major difficulties in any cross-cultural negotiation is that expectations about the normal process of negotiations differ among cultures. Two important areas where differences can arise in cross-cultural negotiating are rapport and the degree of emphasis placed on each of the stages in the negotiating process by those involved in a negotiation.[16]

In the pre-negotiation stage the parties gather as much relevant information as possible on each other. Some informal meetings are held to check each other's positions and capabilities. This stage is often more important than the formal negotiation stage, as buyers and sellers can develop social, informal relationships. Trust and confidence gained from these relationships increase the chances of an agreement.

The most important issue at this stage, however, is to do the preparation thoroughly. An insight into the buying behaviour of the customer and his or her priorities is crucial, as it is necessary to present the product/service in a manner consistent with those priorities and behaviour. For a new customer, the amount of homework to be done is quite heavy, but it will help in subsequent interactions. The idea is to read the map before getting lost. The necessary first step in getting started in an overseas venture is to 'study the map' and learn as much as possible about the target country, culture and individuals before leaving home. Preparation on some practical details such as availability of office equipment and computers in the new country or the necessity of having an agent, and so on, are also some of the essentials of this stage.

GOING INTERNATIONAL 17.5

how to insult a Mexican customer

Señor Jose Garcia Lopez, a Mexican importer-distributor, had been negotiating with a Danish manufacturing company for several months when he decided to visit Copenhagen to finalise a distribution agreement and purchase contract. He insisted on coming over as soon as possible.

To accommodate his potential customer, Flemming, the 40-year-old export manager, welcomed Sr Garcia to Denmark for meetings on Thursday and Friday. Flemming warned Sr Garcia that he had a long-scheduled flight to Tokyo early Saturday, but the Mexican customer saw no problem at all since he was also booked to leave Denmark that Saturday morning.

The business meetings went very smoothly, so on Friday afternoon Sr Garcia confided that he looked forward to signing the contract after his return to Mexico City. That evening the Danes invited Sr Garcia out for an evening on the town. Flemming and his 21-year-old assistant Margrethe hosted an excellent dinner and then took their Mexican prospect on a tour of Copenhagen nightspots. Around midnight Flemming glanced at his watch. 'Sr Garcia, as you know, I have a very early flight tomorrow to Tokyo. I hope you'll forgive me if I leave you now. When you are ready, Margrethe will make sure you get back to your hotel all right. And then she will drive you to the airport tomorrow morning. Have a good flight!'

Next morning in the car on the way to the airport Jose Garcia was uncharacteristically silent. Then he turned to the young assistant: 'Margrethe, would you please tell your boss that I have decided not to sign that contract after all. It is not your fault of course. If you think about what happened last evening I believe you will understand why I no longer want to do business with your company.'

Source: © Copenhagen Business School Press, 2002. With thanks to the author, Richard R. Gesteland, Global Management LLC: 2002, and CBS Press (http://www.cbspress.dk/).

face-to-face negotiation stage

In the formal face-to-face negotiation stage, parties evaluate alternatives. The differences in preferences and expectations are explored and possibilities of coming closer to each other are sought. Negotiators give and take and come to their final positions. In this stage, a balance between firmness and credibility is important, and parties give and receive signals for further movement in the process.

Time plays an important role in cross-cultural negotiation. In a culture where time is money, little importance is given to relationship building and small talk. In the West, people are constantly on the move, while Asians believe that considerable time should be spent in building general understanding, trust and relationships. Selling in international markets takes much longer than in domestic transactions, not only due to culture, but also because the tempo is generally slower. In some countries there are long religious or national holidays. In Muslim countries, Ramadan is not really appropriate for negotiations. In Europe, the months of July and August are not suitable as most people are on holiday. In the United States, the period between Thanksgiving and New Year is considered difficult. And so on. All these aspects need to be considered when planning for negotiations.

While negotiating in other countries a combination of solid know-how, experience and common sense is required to master the process. Now that an extensive literature on such

negotiations exists, it is possible to acquire this know-how and learn from others' experience. Some of the literature that is available is general in nature, but there are also specialist books on regional negotiation styles.[17] When negotiating, it is important to remember the following points.

1 **Understand the value of the particular deal.** The first step in each negotiation process is to realise the implication of that deal in the short run as well as in the long run. Unless you have a clear picture of the deal you cannot formulate a true strategy towards transactions versus relational approach.

2 **Evaluate the competition.** If you know what range of alternatives the other party has, you can see more clearly how important the deal is for them. In this way, you can create arguments and alternatives that match or compete with the alternatives the other party has.

3 **Check your language and communication capabilities.** Depending on the other party and the market/country involved, you have to decide how best you can manage the communication process. The messages should be adapted to the level and culture of the other party. Also consider non-verbal communication, especially those things you cannot/should not do.[18]

4 **Understand the decision-making process,** your own and that of the other party. It is clear that you can make all decisions while you are out there. Do you know that the negotiators coming from the other side can make all decisions? Who in their team or head office is in fact the decision maker?

5 **Patience is an asset in international business negotiations.** In many cultures, Asian, Middle Eastern and even in Eastern Europe, things take their time. Negotiators from these cultures are not to be hurried; they really need to feel the negotiation process before they are ready to make a decision. In such cases it is not useful to push them to make a decision.

GOING INTERNATIONAL 17.6

Russia: opportunities and rules of engagement

Russia is the world's biggest country – it crosses 11 time zones and has 150 million inhabitants. Although it remains difficult to crack, the Russian market holds attraction for foreign investors, not least because of its high potential and abundance of raw materials. At present, more than 900 North American and more than 700 German companies are registered in Moscow. As purchasing power is recovering from the 1998 crisis that wiped out people's savings, sales are rising for everything from beer to hair colouring. In 2001, sales of Carlsberg's popular Baltika beer soared 60 per cent and L'Oréal's sales jumped 52 per cent.

Hypermarkets are gaining a hold in the retailing arena as Russian consumers, who do not have mortgages and loans to pay off due to underdeveloped banking systems, spend most of their income on food and other household products. Economic growth fostered by FDI has created a new social class in Moscow and St Petersburg: *Novye Bysinessmeny*, the new business people.

On the downside, the cost of living has risen considerably in recent years, making Moscow the most expensive city in the world after Tokyo and London. Rising inflation has meant that ordinary people can afford less now than before. The chaos and corruption of Russia's labyrinthine bureaucracy has had a serious effect on business life, while crime has reached alarming proportions in some parts of the country. However, those who are prepared to brave the difficulties and take advantage of the opportunities that Russia offers may find the following advice from the *Financial Times* useful.

■ During business negotiations in Russia, the relaxed and humorous Western way of communicating is not really appropriate. Negotiations are a serious matter and should be treated accordingly. The first encounter is usually calm and formal. However, subsequent meetings can be lively and spirited – occasional emotional outbursts are not uncommon.

■ Personal relationships are very important, and in many cases the success of the venture depends on them rather than on official petitions or applications. Russian negotiators generally do not expect help from bureaucracy.

■ Most Russians are suspicious of public authorities and red tape, and will be mistrustful of any changes to contracts. If you have to make changes to meet laws or regulations, you will have to offer a good explanation.

■ The dress code in Russia is rather formal and conservative. When you are introduced to a business partner, use your family name and your title, not your first name. Later on, during the conversation, you can switch to the Russian style of combining your own and your father's first name, although the *Novye Bysinessmeny* usually address each other by their first names.

■ It is a good idea to bring a supply of business cards showing your title and academic qualifications.

■ Business meetings usually take place in restaurants. Invitations to private houses are rare, but if invited you should not refuse such an opportunity.

■ Russians drink a lot of vodka. Be careful to take part in a toast, which is an important ritual. The host has the honour of performing the first toast. Think about an honest toast in reply and use it to create a positive feeling and move the business along.

■ Russian business partners are rather slow, but once you have won their sympathy, you will have formed a long-lasting relationship.

■ Negotiation can be difficult outside big cities because the use of foreign languages is not as widespread there. Do not expect your business partner to speak English. Interpreters play an important role when doing business in Russia; it is worth spending some time to find a good one.

■ Negotiations can be protracted, starting up to an hour late. They are often interrupted and sometimes two or more talks are held at the same time, which can distract your business partner. However, your partner will take all the time they need to consider the information - Russians believe you can never gather enough information about a prospective deal.

■ Enterprises operating in Russia commonly encounter fiscal obscurities, problematic legal issues and difficulties in dealing with public authorities. New laws and regulations have only added to the complications. Some licences - especially for export - are hard to obtain. Make sure you have trustworthy professionals such as lawyers and accountants on your side.

Source: adapted from Sergey Frank, 'A Market Emerging From a Country in Turmoil', *Financial Times*, 19 February 2001, p. 7; and 'To Russia, With Love: It's the Multinationals' New Darling', *Business Week*, 16 September 2002, pp. 20-1.

post-negotiation stage

In the post-negotiation stage the contract is drawn up. Experience shows that writing the contract and its language and formulations can be a negotiation process in itself as meanings and values differ between the two parties. If not properly handled, this stage can lead to renewed face-to-face negotiations. The best way to avoid this is to make sure that both parties thoroughly understand what they have agreed on before leaving each negotiation session.

summary

An effective international sales force constitutes one of the international marketer's greatest concerns. The company sales force represents the major alternative method of organising a company for foreign distribution and, as such, is on the front line of a marketing organisation.

The role of marketers in both domestic and foreign markets is changing rapidly, along with the composition of international managerial teams and sales forces. These last two have many unique requirements that are being filled by expatriates, locals, third-country nationals, or a combination of the three. In recent years, the pattern of development has been to place more emphasis on local personnel operating in their own countries.

The importance of negotiations is more evident in international as compared to domestic marketing. The sales force needs to be trained in cross-cultural communication and negotiation for successful marketing performance. For successful negotiations in an international context, you have to understand the other party and its priorities. The impact of culture on the decision-making process of the parties involved is of utmost importance and should be fully understood in order to handle the negotiations efficiently. Moreover, you need to adapt your communication pattern to one that is easily understandable by the other party.

questions

1. What are the factors that influence the effectiveness of personal selling in international marketing? Explain.
2. Define the following: expatriate, third-country national, non-verbal feedback, cultural empathy.
3. Why might it be difficult to adhere to set job criteria in selecting foreign personnel? What compensating actions might be necessary?
4. Under what circumstances should expatriate sales people be utilised?
5. Discuss the problems that might be encountered in having an expatriate sales person supervising foreign sales people.
6. 'It is costly to maintain an international sales force.' Comment.
7. Adaptability and maturity are traits needed by all sales people. Why should they be singled out as especially important for international sales people?
8. Discuss the stages in cross-cultural negotiations. How can you effectively manage an international negotiation process? Discuss.
9. Why is sound negotiation the key to effective relationship marketing? Discuss.

further reading

- P.N. Ghauri, 'Guidelines for International Business Negotiations', *International Marketing Review*, 1986, 3(3), pp. 72-82.
- S. Kale, 'How National Culture, Organisational Culture and Personality Impact Buyer-Seller Interaction', in P. Ghauri and J.-C. Usunier, *International Business Negotiations*, 2nd edn (Oxford: Elsevier, 2004).
- G.S. Insch and J.D. Daniel, 'Causes and Consequences of Declining Early Departure from Foreign Assignments', *Business Horizon*, 2003, 45(6), pp. 39-48.

references

1   Jean-Claude Usunier, *Marketing Across Cultures* (Hemel Hempstead: Prentice Hall, 1996).
2   R.B. Money, M.C. Gilly and J.L. Graham, 'National Culture and Referral Behaviour in the Purchase of Industrial Services in the United States and Japan', *Journal of Marketing*, 1998, 62(4), pp. 76-87.
3   Harald Biong and Fred Selnes, 'Relational Selling Behavior and Skills in Long-Term Industrial Buyer–Seller Relationships', *International Business Review*, vol. 4, no. 4, 1995, pp. 483-98.
4   Jean-Claude Usunier, *Marketing Across Cultures* (Hemel Hempstead: Prentice-Hall, 1996).
5   Jagdish Sheth, 'Cross-cultural Influences on the Buyer–Seller Interaction/Negotiation Process', *Asia Pacific Journal of Management*, vol. 1, no. 1, 1983, pp. 46-55.
6   This section is based on Sudhir Kalé, 'How National Culture, Organizational Culture and Personality Impact Buyer–Seller Interactions', in Pervez Ghauri and Jean-Claude Usunier, *International Business Negotiations* (Oxford: Pergamon, 1996), pp. 21-37.
7   Geert Hofstede, 'National Cultures in Four Dimensions: A Research-based Theory of Cultural Differences Among Nations', *International Studies of Management and Organization*, vol. xii, nos 1-2, 1983, pp. 46-74.
8   See, for example, 'Nonverbal Negotiation in China: Cycling in Beijing', *Negotiation Journal*, January 1995, pp. 11-18.
9   This section draws on Lennie Copeland, 'The Art of International Selling', *Business America*, 25 June 1984, pp. 2-7; and Roger E. Axtell, *The Do's and Taboos of International Trade* (New York: Wiley, 1994).
10 D. Rouzies, M. Segalla and B.A. Weitz, 'Cultural Impact on European Staffing Decisions in Sales Management', *International Journal of Research in Marketing*, 2003, 20(1), pp. 67-85.
11 C. Bartlett and S. Ghaoshal, 'Lessons from Late Movers', *Harvard Business Review*, 2000, 78(2), pp. 132-42.
12 For a comprehensive review of the difference between human resource management in Europe and the United States, see Chris Brewster, 'Towards a "European Model of Human Resource Management"', *Journal of International Business Studies*, First Quarter 1995, pp. 1-21.
13 This section draws on Pervez Ghauri and Jean-Claude Usunier (eds), *International Business Negotiations,* 2nd edn (Oxford: Elsevier, 2004).
14 S.C. Schneider and J.-L. Barsoux, *Managing Across Cultures*, 2nd edn (Harlow, UK: Pearson, 2003).
15 Geert Hofstede, 'National Cultures in Four Dimensions: A Research-based Theory of Cultural Differences Among Nations', *International Studies of Management and Organization*, vol. xii, nos 1-2, 1983, pp. 46-74.
16 A. Rugman and R. Rodgetts, 'The End of Global Strategy', *European Management Journal*, 19(4), pp. 333-43.
17 See, for example, Lennie Copeland and Lewis Griggs, *Going International* (New York: Plume, 1985); John L. Graham and Yoshihiro Sano, *Smart Bargaining: Doing Business with the Japanese*, rev. edn (New York: Harper, 1990); and Pervez Ghauri and Jean-Claude Usunier, *International Business Negotiations* (Oxford: Elsevier, 2004).
18 T. Fang, C. Fridh and S. Schutzberg, 'Why did the Telia–Telenor merger fail?', *International Business Review*, 2004, 13(5), pp. 573-94.

chapter 18
Pricing for International Markets

Chapter Outline

Even when the international marketer produces the right product, promotes it correctly and initiates the proper channel of distribution, the effort fails if the product is not properly priced. Setting the right price for a product can be the key to success or failure. While the quality of Western products is widely recognised in global markets, foreign buyers, like domestic buyers, balance quality and price in their purchase decisions. A product's price must reflect the quality/value the consumer perceives in the product. Of all the tasks facing the international marketer, determining what price to charge is one of the most difficult decisions. It is further complicated when the company sells its product to customers in different country markets.[1]

A unified Europe, economic reforms in Eastern Europe and the economic growth in Asian and Latin American countries are creating new marketing opportunities with enhanced competition. As global companies vie for these markets, price becomes increasingly important as a competitive tool. Whether exporting or managing overseas operations, the international marketing manager is responsible for setting and controlling the actual price of goods as they are traded in different markets. The marketer is confronted with new sets of variables to consider with each new market: different tariffs, costs, attitudes, competition, currency fluctuations, methods of price quotation and the marketing strategy of the firm.

This chapter focuses on pricing considerations of particular concern in the international marketplace. Basic pricing policy questions that arise from the special cost, market and competitive factors in foreign markets are reviewed. A discussion of **price escalation** and its control and factors associated with price setting is followed by a review of the mechanics of international price quotation.

key term

price escalation
an increase in
price

pricing policy

Active marketing in several countries compounds the number of pricing problems and variables relating to price policy. Unless a firm has a clearly thought-out, explicitly defined price policy, prices are established by expediency rather than design. Pricing activity is affected by the country in which business is being conducted, the type of product, variations in competitive conditions and other strategic factors. Price and terms of sale cannot be based on domestic criteria alone.[2]

parallel imports

The broader the product line and the larger the number of countries involved, the more complex the process of controlling prices to the end user. Besides having to meet price competition country by country and product by product, companies have to guard against competition from within the company and by their own customers. If a large company does not have effective controls, it can find its products in competition with its own subsidiaries

or branches. Because of different prices that can exist in different country markets, a product sold in one country may be exported to another and undercut the prices charged in that country. For example, to meet economic conditions and local competition, a British pharmaceutical company sells its drugs in a developing country at a low price only to discover that these discounted drugs are exported to a third country where they are in direct competition with the same product sold for higher prices by the same firm.[3] These **parallel imports** (sometimes called the grey market) upset price levels and result from ineffective management of prices and lack of control.

Parallel imports develop when importers buy products from distributors in one country and sell them in another to distributors who are not part of the manufacturer's regular distribution system. This practice is lucrative when wide margins exist between prices for the same products in different countries (see Exhibit 18.1). A variety of conditions can create the profitable opportunity for a parallel market.

Exhibit 18.1 Showroom tactics: new car prices (cheapest European country equals 100)

	Germany	Spain	France	Italy	UK
VW Golf	107.4	102.6	103.9	106.7	130.9
VW Passat	125.3	104.3	108.6	111.1	126.9
Opel Corsa	109.3	102.8	102.7	101.9	124.1
Opel Astra	116.3	100.0	105.2	108.3	121.5
Opel Vectra	119.5	100.0	108.0	112.2	114.1
Ford Escort	125.3	115.0	113.1	120.5	133.3
Ford Mondeo	119.0	100.0	117.4	127.7	123.9
Renault Clio	107.3	107.3	114.8	103.0	124.0
Renault Mégane	101.2	109.3	115.8	106.0	129.8
Peugeot 306	110.3	104.4	123.6	114.9	137.6
Fiat Punto	126.2	107.5	100.0	113.3	127.3
Fiat Bravo	115.2	108.3	107.1	123.2	135.9

Source: based on the European Commission, in *The European*, 2–8 February 1998, p. 22.

Variations in the value of currencies between countries frequently lead to conditions that make parallel imports profitable. When the dollar was high relative to the German mark, Cabbage Patch Kid dolls were purchased from German distributors at what amounted to a discount and resold in the United States.

Purposefully restricting the supply of a product in a market is another practice that causes abnormally high prices and thus makes a parallel market lucrative. Such was the case with the Mercedes-Benz cars whose supply was limited in the United States. The grey market that evolved in Mercedes cars was partially supplied by Americans returning to the United States with cars they could sell for double the price they had paid in Germany. This situation persisted until the price differential that had been created by limited distribution evaporated.

Restrictions brought about by import quotas and high tariffs can lead to parallel imports and make illegal imports attractive. India has a three-tier duty structure on computer parts ranging from 50 to 80 per cent on imports. As a result, estimates are that as much as 35 per cent of India's domestic computer hardware sales are accounted for by the grey market.[4]

Large **price differentials** between country markets is another condition conducive to the creation of parallel markets. Japanese merchants have long maintained very high prices for consumer products sold within the Japanese market. As a result, prices for

key terms

parallel imports
when products are
imported into a
country without
the consent of the
brand owner

price differentials
difference in price
of a product

Japanese products sold in other countries are often lower than they are in Japan. For example, the Japanese can buy Canon cameras from New York catalogue retailers and have them shipped to Japan for a price below that of the camera purchased in Japan. In addition to the higher prices for products at home, the rising value of the yen makes these price differentials even wider. When the New York price for Panasonic cordless telephones was €54.10 ($59.95), they cost €137.20 ($152) in Tokyo, and when the Sony Walkman was €80.30 ($89), it was €149.14 ($165.23) in Tokyo.

GOING INTERNATIONAL 18.1

driving a Golf through the grey market

Estimates of the grey market's current share of car sales range from 3 per cent to 10 per cent, depending on the country. Assuming a conservative 5 per cent, the total only in Europe could hit 600 000 vehicles' worth in just one year, which would total €10.8

billion. The biggest source of grey market cars is Italy, where more than 10 per cent of the cars sold, roughly 185 000, end up in other countries. Re-importers also handle cars from the Netherlands and even from countries outside the European Union, such as Canada. The major destination is Germany, where about 330 000 grey market cars are sold annually. The grey market has benefited consumers while giving fits to traditional dealers and car makers. Competition from the grey market is forcing dealers to negotiate lower prices, while producers have cancelled or delayed planned price increases. Because most of the re-importers are legitimate, the car manufacturers' only hope of stopping them is to block renegade dealers from selling to the grey market. In 1994, for example, Peugeot asked the European Commission to ban sales to re-importers, but was not successful.

Car makers can withdraw a dealer's franchise, as Peugeot did when it pulled its dealer in Italy. But it is almost impossible to spot and stop these side deals. Golf is a typical example: VW ships Golfs from its plant in Wolfsburg, Germany, to a VW distributor in Italy, pricing it low to compete locally. The distributor sells the car to a franchised VW dealer in, let's say, Florence. An independent re-importer buys the car from the Italian dealer and ships it back to Germany. A German consumer then buys the car from the re-importer for some €3000–3500 less than it would cost at a German VW dealer.

Source: 'Carmakers Think Monetary Union is the Answer', *Business Week*, 20 November 1995, p. 21.

Foreign companies doing business in Japan generally follow the same pattern of high prices for the products they sell in Japan, thus creating an opportunity for parallel markets in their products. Eastman Kodak prices its film higher in Japan than in other parts of Asia. Enterprising merchants buy Kodak film in South Korea for a discount and resell it in Japan at 25 per cent less than the authorised Japanese Kodak dealers. For the same reason, Coca-Cola imported from the United States sells for 27 per cent less through discounters than Coke's own made-in-Japan product.[5]

The possibility of a parallel market occurs whenever price differences are greater than the cost of transportation between two markets. In Europe, because of different taxes and competitive price structures, prices for the same product vary between countries. When this occurs, it is not unusual for companies to find themselves competing in one country with their own product imported from another country at lower prices. Presumably such price differentials will cease to exist once all restrictions to trade are

eliminated in the European Union and a full monetary union is achieved, stabilising prices in the EU countries.[6]

Perfume and designer brands such as Gucci and Cartier are especially prone to grey markets. To maintain the image of quality and exclusivity, prices for such products traditionally include high profit margins at each level of distribution, differential prices among markets and limited quantities, as well as distribution restricted to upmarket retailers. In the United States, wholesale prices for exclusive brands of fragrance are often 25 per cent more than wholesale prices in other countries. These are the ideal conditions for a lucrative grey market for unauthorised dealers in other countries who buy more than they need at wholesale prices lower than US wholesalers pay. They then sell the excess at a profit to unauthorised US retailers, but at a price lower than the retailer would have to pay to an authorised US distributor.

GOING INTERNATIONAL 18.2

how do Levi's 501s get to international markets?

Levi Strauss sells in international markets – how else would 501 jeans get to market? The answer is via the grey market, or 'diverters'. Diverters are enterprising people who legally buy 501s at retail prices, usually during sales, and then resell them to foreign buyers. It is estimated that Levi Strauss sells millions of dollars of Levi's abroad at discount prices – all authorised sales. US retail prices for Levi's 501s are $30 to $40 a pair; in Germany, they are sold to authorised wholesalers for about $40, and authorised retailers sell them at about $80. The difference of $40 or so makes it economically possible for a diverter to buy 501s in the United States and sell them to unauthorised dealers who then sell them for $60 to $70, undercutting authorised German retailers. Similar practices happen around the world, but how do diverters work?

Here is an example of what is repeated in city after city all over the United States. 'They come into a store in groups and buy every pair of Levi's 501 jeans they can,' says one store manager. He has seen two or three vans full of people come to the store when there is a sale and buy the six-pair-a-day limit, returning day after day until the sale is over. In another retail chain store, where a similar thing was happening, a month-long storewide sale was stopped, at the behest of Levi's, after only two weeks. The Levi's are then channelled to a diverter, who exports them to unauthorised buyers throughout the world. Many eventually end up in discount stores and are sold at discounted prices relative to those distributed through approved channels. This is but one way diverters acquire merchandise. Another is for wholesalers to buy quantities in excess of their needs and then divert the excess to foreign buyers.

These practices are feasible because of the lower mark-ups and prices of US and other retailers compared with the higher costs and the resulting higher mark-ups and prices that retailers charge in many other countries (Levi's has a higher wholesale price for foreign sales than for domestic sales).

Retail prices in the United States are often more competitive than in other countries where, historically, price competition is not as fierce. For example, Levi's 501s sell for $73 in Britain versus $45 in the United States. Some, but not all, of the price differences can be attributed to price escalation – that is, tariffs, shipping and other costs associated with exporting – but that portion of the difference attributable to higher margins creates an opportunity for profitable diverting.

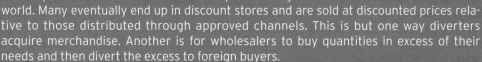

In an attempt to stop discount stores not in the manufacturer's official distribution channel from selling 'unauthorised Levi's', Tesco, a UK supermarket chain, was sued by Levi-Strauss & Company. After a four-year court battle, Levi's won when it was ruled that the supermarket has been selling Levi's illegally. However, Tesco, Costco, Wal-Mart and other mass retailers cater to a vast market interested in value-priced, quality products – a market LS&Co misses if its products are not sold there. Consequently, Levi developed a Signature brand for Tesco that sells for about £25 a pair – £20 less than ordinary Levi's. The Levi Strauss Signature® brand is distinct from the Levi's® brand in both retail availability and product design, and in the UK sells in value-channel retailers such as Asda, Tesco and Makro. It seems the old adage 'If you can't beat them, join them' applies.

According to the president of Levi Strauss Europe, the Levi's brand is the most valuable asset the company has, which has been built over a period of 130 years. The London ruling was based on the European Court of Justice's clarification of the trademark law. That decision confirmed that unauthorised retailers cannot sell trademarked goods from outside the EEA unless they have the explicit consent of the trademark owner, who has the right to control the distribution of its products within the European Economic Area.

Sources: Jim Hill, 'Flight of the 501s', *Oregonian*, 27 June 1993, p. G1; 'Diversion!', *Journal of Commerce*, 26 June 2000, p. WP; Jean Eaglesham and Deborah Hargreaves, 'Court Left to Iron Out Brand Import Wrinkle: Levi's v. Tesco', *National Post*, 24 January 2001, p. C3; 'Levi's Win in Court', *Daily Record*, 1 August 2002; 'Levi Plans Tesco Line', *The Mirror*, 25 April 2003, p. 4; www.levistrauss.com/news, 2005.

To prevent parallel markets from developing when such marketing and pricing strategies are used, companies must maintain strong control systems. These control systems are difficult to maintain and there remains the suspicion that some companies are less concerned with controlling grey markets than they claim. For example, in one year a French company exported €36 million ($40 million) of perfume to Panamanian distributors. At that rate, Panama's per capita consumption of that one brand of perfume alone was 35 times that of the European Union.

key terms

skimming
charging a high price to maximise profit in the early stages of a product's introduction

penetration pricing
charging lower prices to gain market share in a new market

skimming versus penetration pricing

Firms must also decide when to follow a **skimming** or a **penetration-pricing** policy. Traditionally, the decision on which policy to follow depends on the level of competition, the innovativeness of the product, and market characteristics (see Exhibit 18.2).[7]

A company skims when the objective is to reach a segment of the market that is relatively price-insensitive and thus willing to pay a premium price for the value received. If limited supply exists, a company may follow a skimming approach in order to maximise revenue and to match demand to supply. When a company is the only seller of a new or innovative product, a skimming price may be used to maximise profits until competition forces a lower price. Skimming is often used in those markets where there are only two income levels, the wealthy and the poor. Costs prohibit setting a price that will be attractive to the lower income market so the marketer charges a premium price and directs the product to the high-income, relatively price-inelastic segment. Today, such opportunities are fading away as the disparity in income levels is giving way to growing middle-income market segments.

A penetration-pricing policy is used to stimulate market growth and capture market share by deliberately offering products at low prices. Penetration pricing is most often used to acquire and hold share of a market as a competitive manoeuvre. However, in country markets experiencing rapid and sustained economic growth and where large parts of the population move into middle-income classes, penetration pricing may be used to stimulate market growth even with minimum competition. Penetration pricing may be a

Exhibit 18.2 Skimming versus penetration strategies in marketing

		Promotion	
		high	*low*
Price	**high**	Rapid-skimming strategy	Slow-skimming strategy
	low	Rapid-penetration strategy	Slow-penetration strategy

more profitable strategy than skimming if it maximises revenues and builds market share as a base for the competition that is sure to come.

As many of the potential market growth trends that were set in place in the early 1990s begin to pay dividends with economic growth and a more equitable distribution of wealth within local economies, and as distinct market segments emerge within and across country markets, global companies will have to make more sophisticated pricing decisions than were made when companies directed their marketing efforts only towards single market segments.

leasing in international markets

An important selling technique to alleviate high prices and capital shortages for capital equipment is the leasing system. The concept of equipment **leasing** has become increasingly important as a means of selling capital equipment in overseas markets. In fact, it is estimated that €45 billion ($50 billion) worth (original cost) of foreign-made equipment is on lease in Western Europe.

The system of leasing used by industrial exporters is quite simple. Terms of the leases usually run from one to five years, with payments made monthly or annually; included in the rental fee are servicing, repairs and spare parts. Just as contracts for domestic and overseas leasing arrangements are similar, so are the basic motivations and the short-comings. Here are some examples.

1 Leasing opens the door to a large segment of nominally financed foreign firms that can be sold on a lease option but might be unable to buy for cash.
2 Leasing can ease the problems of selling new, experimental equipment, because less risk is involved for the users.
3 Leasing helps guarantee better maintenance and service on overseas equipment.
4 Equipment leased and in use helps to sell to other companies in that country.
5 Lease revenue tends to be more stable over a period of time than direct sales would be.

The disadvantages or shortcomings take on an international flavour. Besides the inherent disadvantages of leasing, some problems are compounded by international relationships. In a country beset with inflation, lease contracts that include maintenance and supply parts, as most do, can lead to heavy losses towards the end of the contract period. Further, countries where leasing is most attractive are those where spiralling inflation is most likely to occur. The added problems of currency devaluation, expropriation or other political risks are operative longer than if the sale of the same equipment is made outright. In the light of these perils, there is greater risk in leasing than in outright sale; however, there is a definite trend towards increased use of this method of selling internationally.[8]

key term

leasing
borrowing/renting

GOING INTERNATIONAL 18.3

when is a car a truck and a daily planner a diary? when the US Customs Service says so

How an import is classified can mean a big difference in the tariffs paid. But it is not always apparent how a product should be classified, at least to the US Customs Service. Here are two cases.

The US Customs Service classified multipurpose vehicles as trucks, that is, vehicles designed to transport cargo or other goods. Trucks pay a 25 per cent tariff, whereas passenger vehicles pay only a 2.5 per cent tariff. The two-door Nissan Pathfinder was initially classified as a truck rather than as a passenger vehicle, but Nissan challenged the classification. The Justice Department argued that the Pathfinder was built with the same structural design as the Nissan pickup truck despite all the options added later in production, and should therefore be considered a truck for tariff purposes. The court said that doesn't matter; it's how the vehicle is used that counts. The judge declared that the Pathfinder 'virtually shouts to the consumer, "I am a car, not a truck!"' The ruling means a $225 saving for every $1000 the consumer spends on a Pathfinder.

The Mead Corporation imports what it considers to be a loose-leaf daily planner that contains a section for daily notes, phone numbers and addresses. Customs classified the planners as 'Bound Diaries' on which a 4 per cent duty applies. Mead challenged the decision and contended that the product should be classified as a daily planner on which there is no duty. The US Supreme Court ruled in favour of Mead.

Sources: 'Nissan Wins US Customs Suit', *Associated Press*, 9 September 1994; 'US High Court: No Deference to Customs on Tariffs', *Reuters News Service*, 18 June 2001; R.G. Edmonson, 'Importers Laud Mead Ruling', *The Journal of Commerce*, 19 June 2001; and 'Mead Hails Tariff Ruling by High Court', *Associated Press*, 19 June 2001.

factors influencing international pricing

People travelling abroad are often surprised to find goods that are relatively inexpensive in their home country priced outrageously higher in other countries. It is also possible that goods priced reasonably abroad may be priced enormously high in the home market. Beginning with the import tariff, each time a product changes hands an additional cost is incurred. First, the product passes through the hands of an importer, then to the company with primary responsibility for sales and service, then to a secondary or even a tertiary local distributor, and finally to the retailer and the consumer. The factors influencing pricing in international markets include the objective of the firm in a particular market, price escalation, competition, target customer segment and pricing control (see Exhibit 18.3).

pricing objectives

In general, price decisions are viewed two ways: pricing as an active instrument of accomplishing marketing objectives or pricing as a static element in a business decision. If the former view is followed, the company uses price to achieve a specific objective, whether a targeted return on profits, a targeted market share or some other specific goal. The company that follows the second approach probably exports only excess inventory, places a low priority on foreign business and views its export sales as passive contributions to

Exhibit 18.3 Factors influencing international pricing

sales volume. Profit is by far the most important pricing objective. Pricing objectives should be consistent with the marketing objectives of the firm in a particular market as well as the overall strategy of the firm. Essentially, objectives are defined in terms of profit, market share or positioning.

The more control a company has over the final selling price of a product, the better it is able to achieve its marketing goals. However, it is not always possible to control end prices, and in this case, companies may resort to 'mill net pricing', that is, the price received at the plant.

price escalation

Excess profits do exist in some international markets, but generally the cause of the disproportionate difference in price between the exporting country and the importing country, here termed *price escalation*, is the added costs incurred as a result of exporting products from one country to another. Specifically, the term relates to situations where ultimate prices are raised by shipping costs, insurance, packing, tariffs, longer channels of distribution, larger middlemen margins, special taxes, administrative costs and exchange-rate fluctuations (see Exhibit 18.4). The majority of these costs arise as a direct result of moving goods across borders from one country to another and combine to escalate the final price to a level considerably higher than in the domestic market.

Taxes, Tariffs and Administrative Costs   'Nothing is surer than death and taxes' has a particularly familiar ring to the ears of the international trader because taxes include tariffs, and tariffs are one of the most pervasive features of international trading. Taxes and tariffs affect the ultimate consumer price for a product and, in most instances, the consumer bears the burden of both. Sometimes, however, the consumer benefits when manufacturers selling goods in foreign countries reduce their net return to gain access to a foreign market. Absorbed or passed on, taxes and tariffs must be considered by the international business person.

A tariff, or duty, is a special form of taxation and, like other forms of taxes, may be levied for the purpose of protecting a market or for increasing government revenue. A tariff is a fee charged when goods are brought into a country from another country. The level of tariff is typically expressed as the rate of duty and may be levied as specific, *ad valorem*, or a combination. A *specific* duty is a flat charge per physical unit imported, such as 15 cents per bushel of rye. *Ad valorem* duties are levied as a percentage of the value of the goods imported, such as 20 per cent of the value of imported watches. *Combination* tariffs include both a specific and an *ad valorem* charge, such as €1 per camera plus 10 per cent of its value.

Exhibit 18.4 Factors influencing price escalation

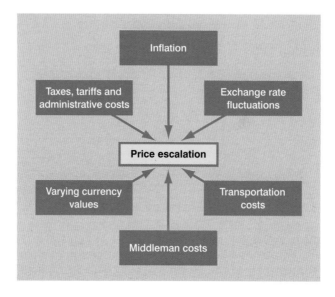

In addition to taxes and tariffs, there are a variety of administrative costs directly associated with exporting and importing a product. Acquiring export and import licences and other documents and the physical arrangements for getting the product from port of entry to the buyer's location mean additional costs. While such costs are relatively small, they add to the overall cost of exporting.

Inflation   The effect of inflation on cost must be taken into account. In countries with rapid inflation or **exchange variation**, the selling price must be related to the cost of goods sold and the cost of replacing the items. Goods are often sold below their cost of replacement plus overhead, and sometimes are sold below replacement cost. In these instances, the company would be better off not to sell the products at all. When payment is likely to be delayed for several months or is worked out on a long-term contract, inflationary factors must be figured into the price.

Because inflation is beyond the control of companies, they use a variety of techniques to inflate the selling price to compensate for inflation pressure and price controls. They may charge for extra services, inflate costs in transfer pricing, break up products into components and price each component separately, or require the purchase of two or more products simultaneously and refuse to deliver one product unless the purchaser agrees to take another, more expensive, item as well. Exhibit 18. 5 focuses on the different price strategies a company might employ under a weak or strong domestic currency.

Exchange-rate Fluctuations   At one time, world trade contracts could be easily written and payment was specified in a relatively stable currency. The American dollar was the standard and all transactions could be related to it. Now that all major currencies are floating freely relative to one another, no one is quite sure of the value of any currency in the future. Increasingly, companies are insisting that transactions be written in terms of the vendor company's national currency, and forward **hedging** is becoming more common. If exchange rates are not carefully considered in long-term contracts, companies find themselves unwittingly giving 15–20 per cent discounts. The added cost incurred as exchange rates fluctuate on a day-to-day basis must be taken into account, especially where there is a significant time lapse between signing the order and delivery of the goods. Exchange-rate differentials mount up. Due to exchange rate fluctuations in one year,

key terms

exchange variation
variation in the exchange rate of two currencies

hedging
insuring against a negative event

Exhibit 18.5 Pricing strategies under varying currency conditions

When domestic currency is WEAK …	When domestic currency is STRONG …
Stress price benefits	Engage in non-price competition by improving quality, delivery and after-sale service
Expand product line and add more costly features	Improve productivity and engage in vigorous cost reduction
Shift sourcing and manufacturing to domestic market	Shift sourcing and manufacturing overseas
Exploit export opportunities in all markets	Give priority to exports to relatively strong-currency countries
Conduct conventional cash-for-goods trade	Deal in countertrade with weak-currency countries
Use full-costing approach, but use marginal-cost pricing to penetrate new/competitive markets	Trim profit margins and use marginal-cost pricing
Speed repatriation of foreign-earned income and collections	Keep the foreign-earned income in host country, slow collections
Minimise expenditures in local, host-country currency	Maximise expenditures in local, host-country currency
Buy needed services (advertising, insurance, transportation, etc.) in domestic market	Buy needed services abroad and pay for them in local currencies
Minimise local borrowing	Borrow money needed for expansion in local market
Bill foreign customers in domestic currency	Bill foreign customers in their own currency

Source: S. Tamer Cavusgil, 'Unravelling the Mystiques of Export Pricing', Chapter 71 in Sidney J. Levy *et al.* (eds), *Marketing Manager's Handbook* (New York: Dartnell, 1994), Figure 2, p. 1362.

Nestlé lost a million dollars in six months, while other companies have lost and gained even larger amounts. In June 1996, the pound sterling was worth 2.55 Dutch guilders, while in June 1997 it was worth 3.50, which created huge problems for British and Dutch firms selling in each other's markets (see Exhibit 18.6).

Exhibit 18.6 The gaps that the euro could close: prices on selected goods and services ($)

	Belgium	France	Germany	Italy	Spain
1.5 litre bottle of Coca-Cola	2.05	1.05	1.89	1.65	1.14
Big Mac	2.86	3.08	2.67	2.48	2.38
Volkswagen Golf GL[a]	13 553	16 317	13 999	17 056	17 356
Litre of unleaded petrol	0.93	1.03	0.87	0.94	0.73
Dry-cleaned men's shirt	3.68	4.67	2.43	2.75	2.92
Subway or bus ticket	1.32	1.20	2.10	0.83	0.82
Pair of Levi's 501 jeans	71	83	81	69	70
Compaq Pressario 2240 computer	1 316	1 348	917	1 208	1 267[c]
One-day rental car, Mercedes C-class[b]	154	110	103	243	113
One hour of translation	89	104	78	55	39

[a]Two-door model; [b]Without insurance; [c]Model 4504.

Source: Business Week, 27 April 1998, p. 44.

Varying Currency Values   In addition to risks from exchange-rate variations, other risks result from the changing values of a country's currency relative to other currencies. Consider the situation in Germany for a purchaser of US-manufactured goods for the period 2001–2004. During this period, the value of the US dollar relative to the euro went from a very strong position ($0.80 to €1) in 2001 to a weaker position in late 2004 ($1.30 to €1). A strong dollar produces price resistance because it takes a larger quantity of local currency to buy a US dollar. Conversely, when the US dollar is weak, demand for US goods increases because fewer units of local currency are needed to buy a US dollar. The weaker US dollar, compared to most of the world's stronger currencies that existed during 2003 and 2004 helped the US economy to recover from the shocks of 9/11.[9]

When the value of the dollar is weak relative to the buyer's currency (i.e. it takes fewer units of the foreign currency to buy a dollar), companies generally employ cost-plus pricing. To remain price competitive when the dollar is strong (i.e. when it takes more units of the foreign currency to buy a dollar), companies must find ways to offset the higher price caused by currency values. By comparing the price of a relatively standardised product, it is possible to gain an insight into the under- or over-valuation of currencies (see Exhibit 18.7).

Middleman   Channel length and marketing patterns vary widely. In some countries, channels are longer and middleman margins higher than is customary. The diversity of channels used to reach markets and the lack of standardised middleman mark-ups leave many producers unaware of the ultimate price of a product.

Besides channel diversity, the fully integrated marketer operating abroad faces various unanticipated costs because marketing and distribution channel infrastructures are under-developed in many countries. The marketer can also incur added expenses for warehousing and handling of small shipments, and may have to bear increased financing costs when dealing with underfinanced middlemen. Because no convenient source of data on middleman costs is available, the international marketer must rely on experience and marketing research to ascertain middleman costs.

Transportation   Exporting also incurs increased transportation costs when moving goods from one country to another. If the goods go over water, there are additional costs for insurance, packing and handling not generally added to locally produced goods. Such costs add yet another burden because import tariffs in many countries are based on the landed cost that includes transportation, insurance and shipping charges. These costs add to the inflation of the final price. The next section details how a reasonable price in the home market may more than double in the foreign market.

Exhibit 18.8 illustrates some of the effects these factors may have on the end price of a consumer item. Because costs and tariffs vary so widely from country to country, a hypothetical but realistic example is used. It assumes (1) that a constant net price is received by the manufacturer, (2) that all domestic transportation costs are absorbed by the various middlemen and reflected in their margins and (3) that the foreign middlemen have the same margins as the domestic middlemen. In some instances, foreign middlemen margins are lower, but it is equally probable that these margins could be greater. In fact, in many instances, middlemen use higher wholesale and retail margins for foreign goods than for similar domestic goods.

key term

price control
when prices are
regulated/fixed by
an authority

Notice that the retail prices in Exhibit 18.8 range widely, illustrating the difficulty of **price control** by manufacturers in overseas retail markets. No matter how much the manufacturer may wish to market a product in a foreign country for a price equivalent to €9, there is little opportunity for such control. Even assuming the most optimistic conditions for Foreign example 1, the producer would need to cut net by more than one-third to absorb freight and tariff costs if the goods are to be priced the same in both foreign and domestic markets.

Exhibit 18.7 The hamburger standard

	Big Mac price in $	Implied PPP* of the $	Umder (–)/over (+) valuation against the $ (%)
United States	2.90	–	–
Argentina	1.48	1.50	–49
Australia	2.27	1.12	–22
Brazil	1.70	1.86	–41
Britain	3.37	1.54	+16
Canada	2.33	1.1	–20
Chile	2.18	483	–25
China	1.26	3.59	–57
Czech Republic	2.13	19.5	–27
Denmark	4.46	9.57	+54
Egypt	1.62	3.45	–44
Euro area	3.28	1.06	+13
Hong Kong	1.54	4.14	–47
Hungary	2.54	183	–13
Indonesia	1.77	5 552	–39
Japan	2.33	90.3	–20
Malaysia	1.33	1.74	–54
Mexico	2.08	8.28	–28
New Zealand	2.65	1.50	–8
Peru	2.57	3.10	–11
Philippines	1.23	23.8	–57
Poland	1.63	2.17	–44
Russia	1.45	14.5	–50
Singapore	1.92	1.14	–34
South Africa	1.86	4.28	–36
South Korea	2.72	1,103	–6
Sweden	3.94	10.2	+36
Switzerland	4.90	2.17	+69
Taiwan	2.24	25.9	–23
Thailand	1.45	20.3	–50
Turkey	2.58	1 362 069	–11
Venezuela	1.48	1,517	–49

* Purchasing-power parity

Source: McDonald's; *The Economist*, 'Food for Thought', 27 May 2004.

Unless price escalation can be reduced, marketers find that the only buyers left are the wealthier ones. If marketers are to compete successfully in the growth of markets around the world, cost containment must be among their highest priorities. If costs can be reduced anywhere along the chain from manufacturer's cost to **retailer mark-ups**, price escalation will be reduced. A discussion of some of the approaches to lessening price escalation follows.

key term

retailer mark-ups
the profit margin
of the retailer

Exhibit 18.8 Sample causes and effects of price escalation ($)

	Domestic example	Foreign example 1: assuming the same channels with wholesaler importing directly	Foreign example 2: importer and same margins and channels	Foreign example 3: same as 2 but with 10 per cent cumulative turnover tax
Manufacturing net	5.00	5.00	5.00	5.00
Transport cif	n.a.	6.10	6.10	6.10
Tariff (20 per cent cif value)	n.a.	1.22	1.22	1.22
Importer pays	n.a.	n.a.	7.32	7.32
Importer margin when sold to wholesaler (25 per cent) on cost	n.a.	n.a.	1.83	1.83
Wholesaler pays landed cost	5.00	7.32	9.15	+ 0.73 turnover tax 9.88
Wholesaler margin ($33^1/_3$ per cent on cost)	1.67	2.44	3.05	3.29
Retailer pays	6.67	9.76	12.20	+ 0.99 turnover tax 14.16
Retail margin (50 per cent on cost)	3.34	4.88	6.10	7.08
Retail price	$10.01	$14.64	$18.30	+ 1.42 turnover tax $22.66

Notes: *a* All figures in US dollars; cif = cost, insurance and freight; n.a. = not applicable.
b The table assumes that all domestic transportation costs are absorbed by the middleman.
c Transportation, tariffs and middleman margins vary from country to country, but for purposes of comparison, only a few of the possible variations are shown.

Approaches to Lessening Price Escalation There are four efforts whereby costs may be reduced in attempting to lower price escalation: (1) lower the cost of goods; (2) lower the tariffs; (3) lower the distribution costs; and (4) using foreign-trade zones.

Lower the cost of goods
If the manufacturer's price can be lowered, the effect is felt throughout the chain. One of the important reasons for manufacturing in a third country is an attempt to reduce manufacturing costs and, thus, price escalation. The impact can be profound if you consider that the hourly cost of skilled labour in India is less than €1.8 ($2) an hour including benefits, compared with more than €13 ($15) in Germany.

For the US General Electric Company (GE), the costs of manufacturing a typical microwave oven are GE €197 ($218), compared to €140 ($155) for Samsung, a Korean manufacturer. A breakdown of costs reveals that assembly labour cost GE €7.2 ($8) per oven and the Korean firm only €0.57 ($0.63). Overhead labour for supervision, maintenance and set-up was €27 ($30) per GE oven and €0.66 ($0.73) for the Korean company. The largest area of difference was for line and central management; that came to €18 ($20) per oven for GE versus €0.02 ($0.02) for Samsung. Perhaps the most disturbing finding was that Korean labourers delivered more for less cost. GE produced four units per person whereas the Korean company produced nine.

Lowering manufacturing costs can often have a double benefit – the lower price to the buyer may also mean lower tariffs, since most tariffs are levied on an *ad valorem* basis.

Lower the tariffs
When tariffs account for a large part of price escalation, as they often do, companies seek ways to lower the rate. Some products can be reclassified into a different, and lower, customs classification. An American company selling data communications equipment in

Australia faced a 25 per cent tariff, which affected the price competitiveness of its products. It persuaded the Australian Government to change the classification for the types of product the company sells from 'computer equipment' (25 per cent tariff) to 'telecommunication equipment' (3 per cent tariff). Like many products, this company's products could be legally classified under either category.

There are often differential rates between fully assembled, ready-to-use products and those requiring some assembly, further processing, the addition of locally manufactured component parts or other processing that adds value to the product and can be performed within the foreign country. A ready-to-operate piece of machinery with a 20 per cent tariff may be subject to only a 12 per cent tariff when imported unassembled. An even lower tariff may apply when the product is assembled in the country and some local content is added.

Lower the distribution costs

Shorter channels can help keep prices under control. Designing a channel that has fewer middlemen may lower distribution costs by reducing or eliminating middleman mark-up. Besides eliminating mark-ups, fewer middlemen may mean lower overall taxes. Some countries levy a value-added tax on goods as they pass through channels. Each time goods change hands, they are taxed. The tax may be cumulative or non-cumulative. The cumulative value-added tax is based on total selling price and is assessed every time the goods change hands. Obviously, in countries where value-added tax is cumulative, tax alone provides a special incentive for developing short distribution channels. Where that is achieved, tax is paid only on the difference between the middleman's cost and the selling price.

Using foreign-trade zones

Some countries have established foreign or free-trade zones (FTZs) or free ports to facilitate international trade. There are more than 300 of these facilities in operation throughout the world where imported goods can be stored or processed. As free-trade policies in Asia, Eastern Europe and other developing regions expand, there has been an equally rapid expansion in the creation and use of FTZs. In a free port or FTZ, payment of import duties is postponed until the product leaves the FTZ area and enters the country. An FTZ is, in essence, a tax-free enclave and not considered part of the country as far as import regulations are concerned. When an item leaves an FTZ and is officially imported into the host country of the FTZ, all duties and regulations are imposed.[10]

By shipping unassembled goods to an FTZ in an importing country, a marketer can lower costs in a variety of ways.

1 Tariffs may be lower because duties are typically assessed at a lower rate for unassembled versus assembled goods.
2 If labour costs are lower in the importing country, substantial savings may be realised in the final product cost.
3 Ocean transportation rates are affected by weight and volume; thus, unassembled goods may qualify for lower freight rates.
4 If local content, such as packaging or component parts, can be used in the final assembly, there may be a further reduction of tariffs.

All in all, an FTZ is an important method for controlling price escalation. Incidentally, all the advantages offered by an FTZ for an exporter are also advantages for an importer. These zones are used in many countries in the West as well as in the emerging markets. Over 100 FTZs in the United States are used by US importers to help lower their costs of imported goods.[11]

competition

The nature of market structure in particular is an important determinant of price. It refers to the number of competing firms, their size and relative position. In the case of an

oligopoly structure, the entering firm would have little freedom to choose a price. Depending on the income levels, a certain market can take only a certain level of pricing. The prices have thus to be set at the level of the competing products. A company can also use competitors' prices as a landmark for positioning its products as compared to competitors. For example, if it wants to position its product as being of higher quality than its competitors, it has to price it accordingly. On the other hand, if a company decides to compete with its competitors on price, it has to set a competitive price. When entering a market and using competitive pricing, a company needs also to check on the cost structure of its competitors. The price is just one of the elements of the marketing mix and has thus to be matched with other elements of it. When a higher price is charged, the company should be able to convince the market that it has a better product, thereby justifying its higher price.

target customer

Marketers have to evaluate and understand a particular segment or target customer group in the market that they are entering. Knowledge of **demand elasticity** and price is essential, as is knowledge of how customers would react in the case of price change. Demand for a product is *elastic* if demand can be considerably increased by lowering the price. If a

key term

demand elasticity
when demand for a product changes due to minor changes in the price

decrease in price would have little effect on demand, it will be considered *inelastic*. Other than the buying behaviour, the ability of customers to buy, prices of substitute and competing products, and the nature of non-price competition are of the utmost importance. In the case of undifferentiated products, the competition is more on pricing, but with differentiated products, market share of a company can even be enhanced through higher prices. Brand names and an image of high quality are two of the factors that characterise differentiated products that can be sold at premium prices.

pricing controls

Companies doing business in foreign countries encounter a number of different types of government price setting. To control prices, governments may establish margins, set prices and floors or ceilings, restrict price changes, compete in the market, grant subsidies or act as a purchasing **monopsony** or selling monopoly. The government may also influence prices by permitting, or even encouraging, businesses to collude in setting manipulative prices.

In most countries, governments regulate pricing. All these rules and regulations need to be considered while setting prices. A number of governments, although liberal on price setting, restrict price changes. A company entering a foreign market with a penetration strategy with a lower price, hoping to increase the price after achieving a certain market share might not be able to change its price. In Europe, a number of rules and regulations are being changed and standardised. Price controls are normally exercised for political and social reasons such as to control inflation, protect consumers from unjustified price increases and stimulate equal distribution of wealth. Price controls are not only limited to developing countries. In the 1980s, countries such as France, Sweden and the United States enforced **price freezes** to control inflation and balance of payments. To cover against the impact of price freezes and controls, firms should regularly review prices in inflationary markets. Firms should watch out for such measures and pre-empt such controls. One way out of them is to keep introducing new products. Another way is to review payment terms and other conditions of sale such as discounts and credits.

administered pricing

Administered pricing relates to attempts to establish prices for an entire market. Such prices may be arranged through the cooperation of competitors, through national, state or local governments or by international agreement. The legality of administered pricing arrangements of various kinds differs from country to country and from time to time. A country may condone price fixing for foreign markets but condemn it for the domestic market.

In general, the end goal of all administered pricing activities is to reduce the impact of price competition or eliminate it. Price fixing by business is not viewed as an acceptable practice but when governments enter the field of price administration, they presume to do it for the general good - to lessen the effects of 'destructive' competition.

price setting by industry groups

The pervasiveness of **price fixing** attempts in business is reflected by the diversity of the language of administered prices; pricing arrangements are known as agreements, arrangements, combines, conspiracies, cartels, communities of profit, profit pools, licensing, trade associations, price leadership, customary pricing or informal interfirm agreements. The arrangements themselves vary from the completely informal, with no spoken or acknowledged agreement, to highly formalised and structured arrangements. Any type of price-fixing arrangement can be adapted to international business; but of all the forms mentioned, the three most directly associated with international marketing are licensing, cartels and trade associations.

key terms

monopsony
the buying-side of
a selling-side
monopoly

price freezes
when the price of
a product cannot
be increased

**administered
pricing**
relates to
attempts to
establish prices
for an entire
market

price fixing
when competing
companies agree
to set a price for
their products

Licensing Agreements In industries where technological innovation is especially important, patent or process agreements are the most common type of international combination. In most countries, licensing agreements are legally acceptable because the owners of patents and other processes are granting an exclusive licence to someone in another country to produce a product. By contractual definition, a patent holder can control territorial boundaries and, because of the monopoly, can control pricing. Often such arrangements go beyond a specific licensing agreement to include a gentlemen's agreement to give their foreign counterparts first rights on patents and new developments. Such arrangements can lead to national monopolies that significantly restrict competition and thereby raise product prices. Like so many other agreements related to restricting competition, the legality of licensing agreements is difficult to discuss outside the context of a specific situation. Licensing arrangements have been an important factor in international marketing in the past and continue to be important despite numerous restrictions.

Cartels A cartel exists when various companies producing similar products work together to control markets for the types of goods they produce. Generally, a cartel involves more than a patent licensing agreement and endows the participants with greater power. The cartel association may use formal agreements to set prices, establish levels of production and sales for the participating companies, allocate market territories and even redistribute profits. In some instances, the cartel organisation itself takes over the entire selling function, sells the goods of all the producers and distributes the profits.

The economic role of **cartels** is highly debatable, but their proponents argue that they eliminate cut-throat competition and 'rationalise' business, permitting greater technical progress and lower prices to consumers. However, in the view of most experts, it is doubtful that the consumer benefits very often from cartels.

The Organization of Petroleum Exporting Countries (OPEC) is probably the best-known international cartel. Its power in controlling the price of oil resulted from the percentage of oil production it controlled. In 2004, a sudden rise in price, due to the Iraq War, from $18 (€15) a barrel to $50 (€45) or more a barrel, was one of the factors in throwing the world into a major recession. Non-OPEC oil exporting countries benefited from the price increase while net importers of foreign oil suffered economic downturns. Among less developed countries, those producing oil prospered while oil importers suffered economically from the high prices.[12]

The legality of cartels is not clearly defined at present. Domestic cartelisation is illegal in most Western countries, and the European Union has specific provisions for controlling cartels. The United States, however, does permit firms to take cartel-like actions in foreign markets. Increasingly, it has become apparent that many governments have concluded that they cannot ignore or destroy cartels completely, so they have chosen to establish ground rules and regulatory agencies to oversee the cartel-like activities of businesses within their jurisdiction.

Trade Associations The term **trade association** is so broad that it is almost meaningless. Trade associations may exist as hard, tight cartels or merely informal trade organisations having nothing to do with pricing, market share or levels of production. In many countries, trade associations gather information about prices and transactions within a given industry. Such associations have the general goal of protecting and maintaining the pricing structure most generally acceptable to industry members.

In most industrial nations manufacturers' associations frequently represent 90 to 100 per cent of an industry. The association is a club one must join for access to customers and suppliers. It often handles industrywide labour negotiations and is capable of influencing government decisions relating to the industry.

key terms

cartels
exist when various companies producing similar products work together to control markets for the types of goods they produce

trade association
association of companies belonging to the same industry

international agreements

Governments of producing and consuming countries seem to play an ever-increasing role in the establishment of international prices for certain basic commodities. There is, for example, an international coffee agreement, an international cocoa agreement and an international sugar agreement. The world price of wheat has long been at least partially determined by negotiations between national governments.

Despite the pressures of business, government and international price agreements, most marketers still have wide latitude in their pricing decisions for most products and markets.

transfer pricing

As companies increase the number of worldwide subsidiaries, joint ventures, company-owned distributing systems and other marketing arrangements, the price charged to different affiliates becomes a pre-eminent question. Prices of goods transferred from operations or sales units in one country to a company's units elsewhere may be adjusted to enhance the ultimate profit of the company as a whole. The benefits of **transfer pricing** are as follows.

1 Lowering duty costs by shipping goods into high-tariff countries at minimal transfer prices so duty base and duty are low.
2 Reduction of income taxes in high-tax countries by overpricing goods transferred to units in such countries; profits are eliminated and shifted to low-tax countries. Such profit shifting may also be used for 'dressing up' financial statements by increasing reported profits in countries where borrowing and other financing are undertaken.
3 Facilitation of dividend repatriation. When dividend repatriation is curtailed by government policy, invisible income may be taken out in the form of high prices for products or components shipped to units in that country.
4 To show more or less profit in crucial times; for example, in the case of new emission, government rules, to please shareholders or to show the good performance of new/old management.

key term

transfer pricing
when a company uses selective prices for internal transactions (e.g. between two subsidiaries)

The tax and financial manipulation possibilities of transfer pricing have not been overlooked by government authorities. Transfer pricing can be used to hide subsidiary profits and to escape foreign market taxes. Transfer pricing is managed in such a way that profit is taken in the country with the lowest tax rate. For example, a foreign manufacturer makes a VCR for €45 ($50) and sells it to its European subsidiary for €135 ($150). The European subsidiary sells it to a retailer for €180 ($200), but it spends €45 ($50) on advertising and shipping so it shows no profit and pays no taxes. Meanwhile, the parent company makes a €90 ($100) gross margin on each unit and pays a lower tax rate in the home country. If the tax rate was lower in the country where the subsidiary resides, the profit would be taken there and no profit taken in the home country.[13]

The overall objectives of the transfer pricing system include: (1) maximising profits for the corporation as a whole, (2) facilitating parent-company control, and (3) offering management at all levels, both in the product divisions and in the international divisions, an adequate basis for maintaining, developing and receiving credit for their own profitability.

An intracorporate pricing system should employ sound accounting techniques and be defensible to the tax authorities of the countries involved. All of these factors argue against a single uniform price or even a uniform pricing system for all international operations.

Four arrangements for pricing goods for intracompany transfer are:

1 sales at the local manufacturing cost plus a standard mark-up
2 sales at the cost of the most efficient producer in the company plus a standard mark-up
3 sales at negotiated prices
4 arm's-length sales using the same prices as quoted to independent customers.

Of the four, the arm's-length transfer is most acceptable to tax authorities and most likely to be acceptable to foreign divisions, but the appropriate basis for intracompany transfers depends on the nature of the subsidiaries and market conditions.

dumping

A logical outgrowth of a market policy in international business is goods priced competitively at widely differing prices in various markets. Marginal (variable) cost pricing, as discussed above, is one way prices can be reduced to stay within a competitive price range. The market and economic logic of such pricing policies can hardly be disputed, but the practices are often classified as dumping and are subject to severe penalties and fines (see Exhibit 18.9). **Dumping** is defined differently by various economists. One approach classifies international shipments as dumped if the products are sold below their cost of production. The other approach characterises dumping as selling goods in a foreign market below the price of the same goods in the home market. Even rate cutting on cargo shipping has been called dumping.

In the 1960s and 1970s, dumping was hardly an issue because world markets were strong. But since the 1980s, dumping became a major issue for a large number of industries. Excess production capacity relative to home-country demand caused many companies to price their goods on a marginal-cost basis, figuring that any contribution above variable cost was beneficial to company profits. In a classic case of dumping, prices are maintained in the home-country market and reduced in foreign markets. For example, the European Union charged that differences in prices between Japan and EU countries ranged from 4.8 to 86 per cent. To correct for this dumping activity, a special import duty of 33.4 per cent was imposed on Japanese computer printers.

Assembly in the importing country is one way companies attempt to lower prices and avoid dumping charges. However, these screwdriver plants, as they are often called, are subject to dumping charges if the price differentials reflect more than the cost savings that

Exhibit 18.9 Anti-trade: summary of anti-dumping actions, 1996

	New actions	Measures in force*
South Africa	30	31
Argentina	23	30
EU	23	153
United States	21	311
India	20	15
Australia	17	47
Brazil	17	24
Korea	13	14
Indonesia	8	n.a.
Israel	6	n.a.
Canada	5	96
Peru	5	4
New Zealand	4	27
Chile	3	0
Mexico	3	95
Venezuela	3	3
Malaysia	2	n.a.
Colombia	1	7
Guatemala	1	n.a.
Thailand	1	1
Japan	–	3
Singapore	–	2
Turkey	–	37
Total	206	900

*31 December 1996.

Source: based on WTO, *The Economist*, 8 November 1997.

result from assembly in the importing country. The increased concern and enforcement in the European Union reflects the changing attitudes among all countries towards dumping. The EU has had anti-dumping legislation from its inception and the Department of Trade of the EU has imposed duties on a variety of products.

price quotations

In quoting the price of goods for international sale, a contract may include specific elements affecting the price, such as credit, sales terms and transportation. Parties to the transaction must be certain that the quotation settled on appropriately locates responsibility for the goods during transportation, and spells out who pays transportation charges and from what point. Price quotations must also specify the currency to be used, credit terms and the type of documentation required. Finally, the price quotation and contract should define quantity and quality. A quantity definition might be necessary because different countries use different units of measurement.[14]

countertrade as a pricing tool

The challenges of **countertrade** must be viewed from the same perspective as all other variations in international trade. Marketers must be aware of which markets will be likely to require countertrades just as they must be aware of social customs and legal requirements. Assessing this factor along with all other market factors will enhance a marketer's competitive position.

Ben and Jerry's Homemade Ice Cream, Inc., a well-known US ice cream vendor, is manufacturing and selling ice cream in Russia. With the roubles it earns, it is buying Russian walnuts, honey and *matryoshky* (Russian nesting dolls) to sell in the United States. This was the only means of getting its profit out of Russia because there was a shortage of hard currency in Russia, making it difficult to convert roubles to dollars. PepsiCo sold Pepsi to Russians in exchange for the exclusive rights to sell Stolichnaya vodka in the United States. In neither transaction did cash change hands; these were barter deals, a type of countertrade. Although cash may be the preferred method of payment, countertrades are becoming an important part of trade with Eastern Europe, China and, to a varying degree, some Latin American and African nations.[15] Today, an international company must include in its market-pricing toolkit some understanding of countertrading.

types of countertrade

Countertrade includes four distinct transactions: barter, compensation deals, counter-purchase and buy-back.[16]

- ■ **Barter** is the direct exchange of goods between two parties in a transaction. One of the largest barter deals to date involved Occidental Petroleum Corporation's agreement to ship superphosphoric acid to the former Soviet Union for ammonia urea and potash under a two-year, €18 billion ($20 billion) deal. No money changed hands, nor were any third parties involved. Obviously, in a barter transaction, the seller (Occidental Petroleum) must be able to dispose of the goods at a net price equal to the expected selling price in a regular, for-cash transaction. Further, during the negotiation stage of a barter deal, the seller must know the market and the price for the items offered in trade. In the Russian barter trade example, the price and a market for the ammonia urea and potash were established because Occidental could use the products in its operations. But bartered goods can range from hams to iron pellets, mineral water, furniture or olive oil – all somewhat more difficult to price and market when potential customers must be sought.

- ■ **Compensation deals** involve payment in goods and in cash. A Western seller delivers lathes to a buyer in Pakistan and receives 70 per cent of the payment in convertible currency and 30 per cent in tanned hides and raw cotton. In an actual deal, General Motors Corporation sold €11.8 million ($12 million) worth of locomotives and diesel engines to the former Yugoslavia and took cash and €3.6 million ($4 million) in Yugoslavian cutting tools as payment.

  An advantage of a compensation deal over barter is the immediate cash settlement of a portion of the bill; the remainder of the cash is generated after successful sale of the goods received. If the company has a use for the goods received, the process is relatively simple and uncomplicated. On the other hand, if the seller has to rely on a third party to find a buyer, the cost involved must be anticipated in the original compensation negotiation if the net proceeds to the seller are to be equal to the market price.

- ■ Counter-purchase or offset trade is probably the most frequently used type of countertrade. For this trade, two contracts are negotiated. The seller agrees to sell a product at a set price to a buyer and receives payment in cash. However, the first contract is contingent on a second contract that is an agreement by the original seller to buy goods from the buyer for the total monetary amount involved in the first contract or for a set percentage of that amount. This arrangement provides the seller with more flexibility

key terms

countertrade
when products are exchanged for other products instead of cash

barter
direct exchange of goods between two parties

compensation deals
involve payment in goods and in cash

than the compensation deal because there is generally a time period – 6 to 12 months or longer – for completion of the second contract. During the time that markets are sought for the goods in the second contract, the seller has received full payment for the original sale. Further, the goods to be purchased in the second contract are generally of greater variety than those offered in a compensation deal.

The offset trades, as they are sometimes called, are becoming more prevalent among economically weak countries. Several variations of a counter-purchase or offset have developed to make it more economical for the selling company. For example, the Lockheed Corporation goes so far as to build up offset trade credits before a counter-purchase deal is made. Knowing that some type of countertrade would have to be accepted to make aircraft sales to Korea, it actively sought the opportunity to assist in the sale of Hyundai personal computers even though there was no guarantee that Korea would actually buy aircraft from it. Lockheed has been involved in countertrades for over 20 years. During that time, countertrade agreements have totalled over €1.2 billion ($1.3 billion) and have included everything from tomato paste to rugs, textiles and automotive parts.

■ **Product buy-back** agreement is the last of the four countertrade transactions. This type of agreement is made when the sale involves goods or services that produce other goods and services, that is, production plant, production equipment or technology. The buy-back agreement usually involves one of two situations: the seller agrees to accept as partial payment a certain portion of the output, or the seller receives full price initially but agrees to buy back a certain portion of the output. When Massey Ferguson, a British farm equipment manufacturer, sold a tractor plant to Poland it was paid part in hard currency and the balance in Polish-built tractors. In another situation, General Motors built a motor vehicle manufacturing plant in Brazil and was paid under normal terms but agreed to the purchase of resulting output when the new facilities came on stream. Levi Strauss took Hungarian-made blue jeans, which it sells abroad, in exchange for setting up a jeans factory near Budapest.[17]

A major drawback to product buy-back agreements comes when the seller finds that the products bought back are in competition with its own similarly produced goods. On the other hand, some have found that a product buy-back agreement provides them with a supplemental source in areas of the world where there is demand but where they have no available supply.[18]

Western firms and countertrade

Countertrade transactions are on the increase in world trade; some estimates of countertrade in international trade go as high as 30 per cent. More conservative estimates place the amount closer to 20 per cent. Regardless, a significant amount of all international trade now involves some type of countertrade transaction, and this percentage is predicted to increase substantially in the near future. Much of that increase will come in trading with emerging countries; in fact, some require countertrades of some sort with all foreign trade. Countertrade arrangements are involved in an estimated 50 per cent or more of all international trade with Eastern European and developing countries.[19]

Western European and Japanese firms have the longest history of countertrade. Western Europe has traded with Eastern Europe and Japan through its *soga shosha* (trading companies) worldwide.[20]

The crucial problem confronting a seller in a countertrade negotiation is determining the value of and potential demand for the goods offered. Frequently there is inadequate time to conduct a market analysis; in fact, it is not unusual to have sales negotiations almost completed before countertrade is introduced as a requirement in the transaction.

Although such problems are difficult to deal with, they can be minimised with proper preparation. In most cases where losses have occurred in countertrades, the seller has been unprepared to negotiate in anything other than cash. Some preliminary research

GOING INTERNATIONAL 18.6

why purchasers impose countertrade

To preserve hard currency. Countries with non-convertible currencies look to counter-trade as a way of guaranteeing that hard currency expenditures (for foreign imports) are offset by hard currency (generated by the foreign party's obligation to purchase domestic goods).

To improve balance of trade. Nations whose exports have not kept pace with imports increasingly rely on countertrade as a means to balance bilateral trade ledgers.

To gain access to new markets. As a non-market or developing country increases its production of exportable goods, it often lacks a sophisticated market-ing channel to sell the goods to the West for hard currency. By imposing countertrade demands, foreign trade organisations utilise the marketing organisations and expertise of Western companies to market their goods for them.

To upgrade manufacturing capabilities. By entering compensation arrangements under which foreign (usually Western) firms provide plant and equipment and buy back resultant products, the trade organisations of less developed countries can enlist Western technical cooperation in upgrading industrial facilities.

To maintain prices of export goods. Countertrade can be used as a means to dispose of goods at prices that the market would not bear under cash-for-goods terms. Although the Western seller absorbs the added cost by inflating the price of the original sale, the nominal price of the counterpurchased goods is maintained, and the seller need not concede what the value of the goods would be in the world supply-and-demand market. Conversely, if the world price for a commodity is artificially high, such as the price for crude oil, a country can barter its oil for Western goods (e.g. weapons) so that the real 'price' the Western partner pays is below the world price.

To force reinvestment of proceeds from weapon deals. Many Arab countries require that a portion of proceeds from weapons purchases be reinvested in facilities desig-nated by the buyer - everything from pipelines to hotels and sugar mills.

Source: Leo G.B. Welt, 'Countertrade? Better Than No Trade', *Export Today*, Spring 1985, p. 54; and Anne Marie Squeo and Daniel Pearl, 'The Big Sell: How a Gulf Sheikdom Landed its Sweet Deal with Lockheed Martin', *Wall Street Journal*, 20 April 2000.

key term

barter houses
international
trading companies
able to introduce
merchandise to
outlets and
geographic areas
previously
untapped

should be done in anticipation of being confronted with a countertrade proposal. Countries with a history of countertrading are easily identified and the products most likely to be offered in a countertrade can often be ascertained.[21]

Barter houses specialise in trading goods acquired through barter arrangements and are the primary outside source of aid for companies beset by the uncertainty of a counter-trade. While barter houses, most of which are found in Europe and Asia, can find a market for bartered goods, it requires time, which puts a financial strain on a company because capital is tied up longer than in normal transactions. Seeking loans to tide it over until sales are completed usually solves this problem.

There are many examples of companies losing sales to competitors who were willing to enter into countertrade agreements. A Western oilfield equipment manufacturer claims it submitted the lowest dollar bid in an Egyptian offer but lost the sale to a bidder who offered a counter-purchase arrangement. Incidentally, the successful company was

Japanese, with a sizeable established trading company to dispose of the Egyptian goods received in the counter-purchase arrangement.

proactive countertrade strategy

Some authorities suggest that companies should have a defined countertrade strategy as part of their marketing strategy rather than be caught unprepared when confronted with a countertrade proposition. Currently most companies have a reactive strategy, that is, they use countertrade when they believe it is the only way to make a sale. Even when these companies include countertrade as a permanent feature of their operations, they use it to react to a sales demand rather than using countertrade as an aggressive marketing tool for expansion.[22]

Successful countertrade transactions require that the marketer (1) accurately establishes the market value of the goods being offered and (2) disposes of the bartered goods once they are received. Most countertrades judged unsuccessful result from not properly resolving one or both of these factors.

In short, unsuccessful countertrades are generally the result of inadequate planning and preparation. One experienced countertrader suggests answering the following questions before entering into a countertrade agreement: (1) Is there a ready market for the goods bartered? (2) Is the quality of the goods offered consistent and acceptable? (3) Is an expert needed to handle the negotiations? (4) Is the contract price sufficient to cover the cost of barter and net the desired revenue?

summary

Pricing is one of the most complicated decision areas encountered by international marketers. Rather than deal with one set of market conditions, one group of competitors, one set of cost factors and one set of government regulations, international marketers must take all these factors into account, not only for each country in which they are operating, but often for each market within a country. The continuing growth of the less developed country markets, coupled with their lack of investment capital, has increased the importance of countertrades for most marketers, making it an important tool to include in pricing policy.

Market prices at the consumer level are much more difficult to control in international than in domestic marketing, but the international marketer must still approach the pricing task on a basis of objectives and policy, leaving enough flexibility for tactical price movements. Pricing in the international marketplace requires a combination of intimate knowledge of market costs and regulations, an awareness of possible countertrade deals, infinite patience for detail and a shrewd sense of market strategy.

questions

1 Discuss the causes of and solutions for parallel imports and their effect on price.
2 Why is it so difficult to control consumer prices when selling overseas?
3 What are the causes of price escalation? Do they differ for exports and goods produced and sold in a foreign country?
4 Define the following: parallel imports, skimming, price escalation, dumping, transfer pricing and cartel.
5 Price escalation is a major pricing problem for the international marketer. How can this problem be counteracted? Discuss.
6 Changing currency values have an impact on pricing strategies. Discuss.

7 'Regardless of the strategic factors involved and the company's orientation to market pricing, every price must be set with cost considerations in mind.' Discuss.

8 'Price fixing by business is not generally viewed as an acceptable practice (at least in the domestic market); but when governments enter the field of price administration, they presume to do it for the general welfare, to lessen the effects of destructive competition.' Discuss.

9 Do value added taxes discriminate against imported goods?

10 Explain specific tariffs, *ad valorem* tariffs and combination tariffs.

11 Suggest an approach a marketer may follow in adjusting prices to accommodate exchange-rate fluctuations.

12 Why has dumping become such an issue in recent years?

13 Discuss the various ways in which governments set prices. Why do they engage in such activities?

14 Discuss the alternative objectives possible in setting transfer prices.

15 Why do governments scrutinise transfer pricing arrangements so carefully?

16 Why are costs so difficult to assess in marketing internationally?

17 Discuss why countertrading is on the increase.

18 Discuss the major problems facing a company that is countertrading.

19 If a country you are trading with has a shortage of hard currency, how should you prepare to negotiate price?

20 Of the four types of countertrade discussed in the text, which is the most beneficial to the seller? Explain.

21 Why should a knowledge of countertrades be part of an international marketer's pricing toolkit? Discuss.

further reading

■ S.T. Cavusgil, 'Unravelling the Mystique of Export Pricing', *Business Horizon*, 1988, 31(3), pp. 54-63.

■ M. Theodosiou and C.S. Katsikeas, 'Factors Influencing the Degree of International Pricing Strategy Standardization of Multinational Corporations', *Journal of International Marketing*, 2001, 9(3), pp. 1-11.

■ M.B. Myers, 'Implication of Pricing Strategy - Venture Strategy Congruence: An Application Using Optimal Models in an International Context', *Journal of Business Research*, 2004, 57(6), pp. 591-600.

references

1 For a comprehensive review of pricing and the integration of Europe, see Wolfgang Gaul and Ulrich Luz, 'Pricing in International Marketing and Western European Economic Integration', *Management International Review*, vol. 34, no. 2, 1994, pp. 101-24.

2 S. Tamer Cavusgil, 'Unravelling the Mystiques of Export Pricing', in Sidney J. Levy *et al.* (eds), *Marketing Manager's Handbook* (New York: Dartnell, 1994), pp. 1357-74; and 'The Debate on Export Subsidies', *European Business Report*, Spring IQ, 1998, p. 58.

3 For a complete and thorough discussion of parallel markets, see Robert E. Weigand, 'Parallel Import Channels - Options for Preserving Territorial Integrity', *Columbia Journal of World Business*, Spring 1991, pp. 53-60.

4 S.T. Cavusgil, K. Chan and C. Zhang, 'Strategic Orientations in Export Pricing: A Clustering Approach to Create Firm Taxonomies', *Journal of International Marketing*, 2003, 11(1), pp. 47-72.

5 R.A. Kustin, 'Marketing Mix Standardization: A Cross-cultural Study of Four Countries', *International Business Review*, 13(5), pp. 637–49.

6 'Cross-border Pricing: Is the Price Right?', *Business Europe*, 6–12 February 1995, pp. 6–7; and 'Showroom Tactics: New Car Prices', *The European*, 2–8 February 1998, p. 22.

7 For a comprehensive review of pricing in foreign markets, see James K. Weekly, 'Pricing in Foreign Markets: Pitfalls and Opportunities', *Industrial Marketing Management*, May 1992, pp. 173–9.

8 See, for example, Joseph Neu, 'Profiting from Leasing Abroad', *International Business*, April 1995, pp. 56–8.

9 'US-based MNCs Say Weak Dollar is Nothing to Cry About', *Crossborder Monitor*, 20 July 1994, pp. 1–2.

10 'Special Section: FTZs', *Global Trade and Transportation*, September 1994, pp. 24–7.

11 D. Scott Freeman, 'Foreign Trade Zones: An Underutilized US Asset', *Trade and Culture*, September–October 1994, pp. 94–5.

12 P. Verburg, 'Diamond Cartels Are Forever', *Canadian Business*, 10 July 2000, p. 135.

13 L.W. Siegel, 'Critics Believe DeBeers Manipulates the Market to Keep Diamonds High', *All Things Considered* (NPR), 11 November 2001.

14 H. Ramakrishnan and S. Vikraman, 'Transfer Pricing Norms May Not Be Eased Yet', *Economic Times*, 18 February 2003.

15 Most countertrade is found in countries with shortages of foreign exchange, which is often given as the reason why countertrades are mandated by these countries. An interesting study, however, casts some doubt on this thesis and suggests instead that countertrades may be a reasonable way for countries to minimise transaction costs. For an insightful report on this research, see Jean-Francois Hennart and Erin Anderson, 'Countertrade and the Minimization of Transaction Costs: An Empirical Examination', *The Journal of Law, Economics, and Organization*, vol. 9, no. 2, 1993, pp. 290–313.

16 A variety of terms are used to describe the transactions the authors classify as countertrades. Switch trading, parallel trades, offset trades and clearing agreements are other terms used to describe countertrade, but they are only variations of the four types mentioned here. In order not to further confuse the issue but to help standardise terminology, the authors have used the terms developed by *Business International*.

17 D. West, 'Countertrade', *Business Credit*, April 2002, p. 48.

18 M.R. Snyder, 'Doing Business in Russia Again?', *Moscow Times*, 9 January 2002.

19 A report on risk sharing in countertrade is found in Erwin Amann and Dalia Marin, 'Risk-sharing in International Trade: An Analysis of Countertrade', *The Journal of Industrial Economics*, March 1994, pp. 63–77.

20 D. Hew, 'Time for Asia to Cash in on Countertrade', *Business Times*, Singapore, 4 September 2002.

21 See, for example, the study by Aspy P. Palia and Heon Deok Yoon, 'Countertrade Practices in Korea', *Industrial Marketing Management*, July 1994, pp. 205–14, which examines the kinds of countertrade practices most appropriate in Korea.

22 B. Meyer, 'The Original Meaning of Trade Meets the Future in Barter', *World Trade*, January 2000, p. 46.

section 5
ethical, financial and organisational issues in international marketing

chapter 19
Ethics and Social Responsibility in International Marketing

Chapter Outline

Ethical issues and social responsibility together comprise a difficult but important task for international marketers. Consumer awareness about ethics, particularly in the case of multinational companies (MNCs) and foreign firms has increased. In addition a number of organisations (such as Greenpeace), consumer associations and national health organisations have entered the debate and are questioning MNC strategies and operations in different countries. Although most of the criticism is directed towards the strategic level of the companies, it is normally the marketing department that has to convince the market that the company is socially responsible and follows ethical principles.

ethical environment

Multinational companies (MNCs) operate in a number of countries, where legal and ethical standards may differ. There are huge differences as to right and wrong between the United States and Europe. Different countries in Europe also have different rules and regulations regarding Green marketing, marketing of cigarettes and alcoholic drinks, and packaged food. Huge investments made by MNCs in developing countries contribute towards their economic development but may have a huge impact on the environment (pollution) and other social issues. Some MNCs believe that while in developing countries, they do not have to follow the same standards of social responsibility as in their home markets, which is in itself morally wrong. Depending on history, geography, religion and economic systems, countries such as the US and Japan do have different attitudes towards work, leisure and pollution. The existence of diverse nationalities within Europe means that attitudes are not quite homogeneous. In spite of the Protestant values of hard work, self-control and saving for the future, four-week vacations, two-hour lunch breaks, 35-hour working weeks and excessive spending based on borrowing are quite common. This from an American or Japanese perspective can be considered lazy or perhaps even immoral. In Japan, a senior executive leaving a company and joining a competing firm is considered unethical.

Managers have also realised that instead of being defensive and reactive, they can proactively use ethical issues as marketing tools in many countries. Royal Shell, for example, has used this strategy for a number of years, where most of its advertising campaigns emphasise the role it is playing in the development of societies, particularly in developing countries. McDonald's has also changed its marketing strategies after being accused of selling 'junk food' to children. Not only did it change its product mix (e.g. adding fruit to its happy meals and salads to normal offerings), but it also ran an advertising campaign throughout 2004, aiming to convince the market that it is a socially responsible company. One study asserts that two-thirds of consumers claim that their purchasing decision is influenced by ethical considerations.

GOING INTERNATIONAL 19.1

who is responsible for social responsibility?

Managers often complain of being held responsible for the well-being of society. They claim that according to the free market economic system (capitalism), by running a profitable company, they are advancing the public good. They also claim that by having 'good management', i.e. dealing honestly with employees, customers and suppliers, they are doing their job. They have responsibility towards their investors (owners) and if they reduce profits to raise social welfare then perhaps they are not honest with their investors.

Rich multinationals operating in developing countries also claim that they in fact typically want to employ local people, and pay substantially higher wages and provide better benefits than the local norms. But how much more of this is required in order to be labelled a good corporate citizen? According to Joel Bakan, a professor at the University of Columbia:

> Today, corporations govern our lives. They determine what we eat, what we watch, what we wear, where we work and what we do. We are inescapably surrounded by their culture, iconography and ideology. And, like the church and the monarchy in other times, they posture as infallible and omnipotent, glorifying themselves in imposing buildings and elaborate displays. Increasingly, corporations dictate the decisions of their supposed overseers in government and control domains of society once firmly embedded in the public sphere. Corporations now govern society, perhaps more than governments themselves do; yet ironically it is their very power, much of which they have gained through economic globalisation, that makes them vulnerable. As is true of any ruling institution, the corporation now attracts mistrust, fear and demands for accountability from an increasingly anxious public. Today's corporate leaders understand, as did their predecessors, that work is needed to regain and maintain the public's trust. And they, like their predecessors, are seeking to soften the corporation's image by presenting it as human, benevolent and socially responsible.

Economist and philosopher Adam Smith.
© Bettmann/ CORBIS

According to Adam Smith, the father of the free market economic system:

> Every individual necessarily labours to render the annual revenue of the society as great as he can. He generally, indeed, neither intends to promote the public interest, nor knows how much he is promoting it; he intends only his own gain, and he is in this, as in many other cases, led by an invisible hand to promote an end which was no part of his intention. Nor is it always the worse for the society that it was no part of it. By pursuing his own interest he frequently promotes that of the society more effectually than when he really intends to promote it. I have never known much good done by those who affected to trade for the public good.
>
> It is not from the benevolence of the butcher, the brewer, or the baker, that we expect our dinner, but from their regard to their own interest. We address ourselves, not to their humanity but to their self-love, and never talk to them of our own necessities but of their advantages.

Although he promotes selfishness, he admires benevolence. But his main thesis is that benevolence is not necessary to advance public interest, as long as people are free to engage with each other in voluntary economic interactions.

■ Does Adam Smith's invisible hand, the private search for profit, advance public interest? Who, in your opinion, should be responsible for the well-being of society?

Source: The Economist, 'A Survey of Corporate Responsibility: The Good Company', 22 January 2005, pp. 1-18.

what is social responsibility?

Ethics and social responsibility go hand in hand. If a company is misleading its consumers, not telling the truth about the serious negative impact of its products (e.g. in case of pharmaceutical and food companies) or, once realising that its product has caused damage to consumer health or well-being, refuses to accept and take responsibility, then that company has not been socially responsible. The different views on these two concepts have been summarised by Fisher (2004) as follows.

- Social responsibility is ethics in an organisational context.
- Social responsibility focuses on the impact that business activity has on society while ethics is concerned with the conduct of people within organisations.
- Social responsibility and ethics are unrelated concepts.
- Social responsibility has various dimensions, one of which is ethics.

One problem is understanding what social responsibility is, and that ideas about right and wrong and what is ethical and what is not may differ from country to country. For instance, even within Europe there are different opinions on under-age sex, bribes and lying to serve self-interest. These standards differ from Scandinavia in the north to Italy and Greece in the south. Some countries stress individual responsibility while others think it is society's responsibility to ensure that companies operate in a socially responsible manner.

GOING INTERNATIONAL 19.2

the US takes on global standards to fight obesity: 'personal responsibility'

How do you change the eating habits of several hundred million people? That's the daunting problem the World Health Organization (WHO) is trying to solve with a proposal for fighting obesity worldwide. It's a bold and necessary effort but, unfortunately, it may be undermined by the world's fattest nation: the US.

The UN estimates that 300 million people worldwide are obese and a further 750 million are overweight, including 22 million children under five. Health experts around the world are unanimous in saying that something must be done. But that's where the unanimity ends. The WHO has spent the past year hammering out a series of non-binding actions that governments could undertake. The initiative is scheduled for adoption in May, but the US, with backing from the powerful food lobby, is working furiously to water down the proposals. These include restrictions on advertising, changes in labelling, increased taxes on junk food and the elimination of sugar subsidies.

The playbook for the Administration's attack is much the same as the one it used to block international action on global warming. It is charging that the WHO's conclusions are not supported by 'sufficient scientific evidence' that fats and sugars cause obesity. Technically, the US has a point. William R. Steiger, the lead delegate to the WHO from the Health and Human Services Dept (HHS), complained in a letter to the organisation that the evidence linking sugar and fats to obesity comes from epidemiological studies rather than stringently controlled clinical trials. 'In this country, you can't make a scientific claim unless you have the evidence to back it up,' argues an HHS spokesman.

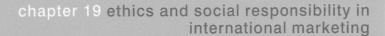

Even the US does not advocate doing nothing. The Center for Disease Control estimates that one in every three adults in the US is obese, and 15 per cent of children are
overweight – double the rate of 10 years ago. Poor self-control is only one aspect of the
obesity problem, however. There are huge obstacles to making healthier choices.
Among them: larger portions, inadequate nutritional information on food labels, fast
foods sold in schools, and cutbacks in physical education programmes. 'Food is something we need to live,' says Dr C. Ronald Kahn, president of the Joslin Diabetes Center in
Boston. 'What we really need to do is eat less of it.'

The WHO, however, does recommend restrictions on advertisements that exhort us
to eat more, particularly those aimed at children. 'Advertising junk food to children is
unethical and immoral,' says Dr Walter C. Willett, head of the Department of Nutrition at
Harvard University's School of Public Health.

Ultimately, the WHO proposals form a multifaceted approach, combining education
and regulations. With the same combination, the US was able to cut the smoking rate in
half, even though it took 40 years. 'It will take at least that long to cut obesity rates by
half,' Willet predicts, and then only if the US Government gets serious about tackling the
problem. So far, there is little scientific evidence proving that it is.

■ Do you think it is government's responsibility to control the food industry?

Source: Business Week, 'Let Them Eat Cake – if They Want to', 23 February 2004.

Social responsibility thus means that a company plays a role in society that is beyond its
economic goals and that makes a constructive contribution towards society's well-being in
the long term. A few decades ago, a number of authors stated that the main responsibility
of a company is to maximise its profits within the rules of law.[1] Some even stated that if a
company engages in activities other than profit maximisation, it is working against share-
holder interests. They believe that society's well-being is the responsibility of the state.[2]

Later studies, however, stress that the role played by a company has to go beyond profit
maximisation and self-interest. This view believes that the more a company behaves
responsibly, the more it will create goodwill and its positive corporate image will help its
positioning in customers' minds and thus its competitive advantage.[3]

As Friedman (1970: 2, see reference 3) comments, 'there is only one social responsibility
of business, to use its resources and engage in activities designed to increase profits so
long as it stays within the rules of the game, and engages in open and free competition
without deception or fraud'.

From the marketer's point of view we believe in the latter. It is important to realise that
each company has its **stakeholders** who benefit or are harmed or whose rights are
violated or respected by its actions.[4] Just as owners have a right to demand that a
company does not jeopardise their interests, so do other stakeholders have the right to
demand the same. Even in the 'narrow definition', the stakeholders include owners,
employees, management, suppliers, customers and the local community (see Exhibit 19.1).

Owners are the investors and they want some return on their investment. Sometimes
pension funds or other organisational advisers also invest in corporations. This means that
the future well-being of lots of people is dependent on how the company performs.
Employees have their, and often their families', livelihoods to support and expect wages,
security and other benefits. Employers have to follow management instructions and they
represent the company with their behaviour inside and outside the firm. *Suppliers* are
important for firms and this relationship is in fact mutual and reciprocal. While suppliers'
components and materials influence the quality and reputation of the firm, the firm's
performance influences supplier success.

key terms

**social
responsibility**
when a company is
concerned about
the implications of
its decisions on
society in general

stakeholders
parties that have
an interest in the
company's
activities

Exhibit 19.1 Stakeholders of a firm

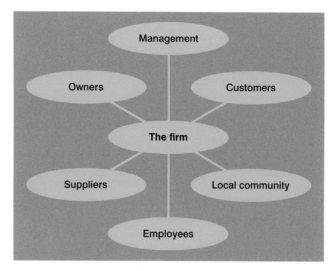

Source: Freeman, 2002, p. 175 (see reference 8).

Customers are involved in the actual exchange with the firm as they pay to acquire its products. This payment is the lifeblood of the firm as it provides it with revenue. Understanding and satisfying customers' needs and wants are the main tasks of marketers. The better a firm can satisfy customers, the more successful it will be and the better it can serve the interests of other stakeholders. The *local community* benefits from the activities of the firm as it pays tax and provides job opportunities; it thus contributes towards the economic and social well-being of the local community. From a resident's perspective, the firm is expected to be a good citizen, just like all other citizens, individuals as well as organisations. It cannot endanger the community by its anti-social behaviour, such as causing pollution, dumping toxic waste or not paying taxes.

In case companies are not taking due care of their stakeholders or are violating the rules of good citizenship, the government intervenes and/or regulates company behaviour through industrial policy and taxation.

analysing ethical issues and social responsibility

In international marketing, there is a tendency to find reasons to support company decision making. In the case of a company deciding to enter a particular market, its marketing research will show how lucrative the market is. It can make even small numbers look good. The dilemmas and temptations in market research to give in to unethical behaviour are well documented.[5]

Respecting the rights of respondents in marketing research is a matter of ethics. Collecting information on consumers without their consent (e.g. through observations) is considered unethical.

After a poisoning scandal in 1982, where several deaths were reported from taking cyanide-laced Tylenol-extra-strength pain reliever capsules, Johnson & Johnson learnt its lesson. The company convinced the market that the cyanide had been placed in the capsules by criminals. Johnson & Johnson was able to do this due to the trust it had developed with the market and local communities. As a result, it now openly states its code of conduct (see Exhibit 19.2).

The company continued to market Tylenol-extra-strength, as it was a very successful brand with an annual market of $350 million. However, after another tampering incident in 1986, where one person died, the company decided to terminate the marketing of this product and launched a new brand, Tylenol-caplets, in tablet form.[6]

Exhibit 19.2 Johnson & Johnson: 'Our Credo'

We believe our first responsibility is to the doctors, nurses and patients, to mothers and fathers and all others who use our products and services. In meeting their needs everything we do must be of high quality. We must constantly strive to reduce our costs in order to maintain reasonable prices. Customers' orders must be serviced promptly and accurately. Our suppliers and distributors must have an opportunity to make a fair profit.

We are responsible to our employees, the men and women who work with us throughout the world. Everyone must be considered as an individual. We must respect their dignity and recognise their merit. They must have a sense of security in their jobs. Compensation must be fair and adequate, and working conditions clean, orderly and safe. We must be mindful of ways to help our employees fulfil their family responsibilities. Employees must feel free to make suggestions and complaints. There must be equal opportunity for employment, development, and advancement for those qualified. We must provide competent management, and their actions must be just and ethical.

We are responsible to the communities in which we live and work and to the world community as well. We must be good citizens – support good works and charities and bear our fair share of taxes. We must encourage civic improvements and better health and education. We must maintain in good order the property we are privileged to use, protecting the environment and natural resources.

Our final responsibility is to our stockholders. Business must make a sound profit. We must experiment with new ideas. Research must be carried on, innovative programs developed and mistakes paid for. New equipment must be purchased, new facilities provided and new products launched. Reserves must be created to provide for adverse times. When we operate according to these principles, the stockholders should realise a fair return.

Johnson & Johnson, the statement, 'Our Credo', reprinted by permission.

Source: J.R. Boatright, 2003, p. 11 (see reference 6).

GOING INTERNATIONAL 19.3

Toys 'R' Us: fair or foul?

Hardball tactics are often applauded in business, but when Child World was the victim, the toy retailer cried foul. Its complaint was directed against a major competitor, Toys 'R' Us, whose employees allegedly bought Child World inventory off the shelves during a promotion in which customers received $25 gift certificates for buying merchandise worth $100. The employees of Toys 'R' Us were accused of selecting products that Child World sells close to cost, such as diapers, baby food and infant formula. These items could be resold by Toys 'R' Us at a profit, because the purchase price at Child World was barely above what a wholesaler would charge, and then Toys 'R' Us could redeem the certificates for additional free merchandise, which could be resold at an even higher profit. Child World claims that its competitor bought up to $1.5 million worth of merchandise in this undercover manner and received as much as $375 000 worth of gift certificates. The practice is apparently legal, although Child World stated that the promotion excluded dealers, wholesalers and retailers. Executives at Toys 'R' Us do not deny the accusation and contend that the practice is common in the industry. Child World may have left itself open to such a hardball tactic by slashing prices and offering the certificates in an effort to increase market share against its larger rival.

■ Who do you think is behaving unethically, Toys 'R' Us or Child World? Discuss.

Source: J.R. Boatright, 2003, p. 12 (see reference 6).

Social responsibility refers to voluntary responsibilities that go beyond the purely economic and legal responsibilities of a firm. This means that the firm is willing to sacrifice part of its profit for the benefit of its stakeholders. It can thus be defined as corporate behaviour up to a level where it is congruent with the prevailing social norms, values and expectations of performance.[7]

These responsibilities can be presented as different levels (Exhibit 19.3). The inner circle in Exhibit 19.3 refers to the absolute minimum responsibility of a firm, where it has to efficiently perform the economic functions such as products, job creation and growth. The second circle refers to the awareness of changing social values and priorities with regard to the environment, safety of employees and customers, and relationships with employees. The third circle refers to emerging priorities that a firm should adhere to. This includes improving the life of local communities and helping them solve problems such as poverty and injustice. Companies can make a considerable contribution in this respect.

Exhibit 19.3 Levels of social responsibility

Social values and priorities

Environment

Economic functions and growth

Social priorities of the local community

Solving problems related to poverty and injustice

Contribute towards community's well-being

Source: based on J.R. Boatright, 2003, pp. 374–5 (see reference 6).

business ethics

In the real world of business, companies do generally behave.[8] With an increasing awareness of ethics among all the stakeholders, those companies that are more ethical are believed to perform better. Ethics refers to a standard of behaviour or code of conduct that is based on moral duties and obligations. These standards are based on values, beliefs, industry, society and government regulations.

There are two views on ethics: one is that you follow some absolute principles (e.g. based on religion); the other is that you follow a more consequential approach – you evaluate the consequences of your decisions and if they do not violate the ethical standards then they are fine. Many managers follow this approach as it fits into their normal decision-making models.[9] In reality, however, managers use a mixed approach.

GOING INTERNATIONAL 19.4

ethics and social responsibility after an industrial accident

Victims of the Bhopal disaster are still awaiting justice more than 20 years after a gas leak from US company Union Carbide's pesticide plant, which killed more than 7000 people in the world's worst industrial accident. Almost all parties, including the Indian Government, continue to evade their responsibilities.

The gas leaked into the slums adjoining the plant and has killed another 15 000 in the last two decades. Amnesty International estimates that fatalities have been caused by respiratory problems, breakdown of immune systems, breast and cervical cancer, and neurological disorders.

Yet the site, Union Carbide's largest plant in the developing world, has still not been decontaminated. Independent studies show that the groundwater system, which continues to be used by slum-dwellers, remains polluted and that numerous health disorders continue to arise.

In 1989, the government of India negotiated a €353 million (£248 million) out-of-court settlement with Union Carbide, which has since been bought by Dow Chemical. Due to bureaucratic slowness, most of the money is still held in India's central bank in Mumbai.

The Indian Government has failed to ensure that survivors receive adequate compensation and medical assistance or to prevent widespread corruption affecting the compensation process. Amnesty International says the compensation was a fraction of Union Carbide's true liability by international norms; Dow Chemical declines any liability. India continues to press for extradition of Warren Anderson, Union Carbide's CEO. His whereabouts are disputed. Amnesty says the tragedy underlines the need to develop an international human rights framework that could govern the duties and liabilities of private companies.

Activists of the Bharatiya Janata Party wearing maks protest in Bhopal on the eve of World Environment Day, 2003
© Reuters NewMedia, Inc./ CORBIS

■ Do you think Union Carbide has behaved ethically in this case? Has it been socially responsible?

■ Who, do you think is to be blamed for the misery of the victims and the fact that majority of them still haven't received compensation or medical assistance?

Source: Edward Luc, 'Victims of Bhopal Disaster Still Awaiting Justice', *Financial Times*, 29 November 2004, p. 8.

Ethics have also become a matter of not violating basic human rights. The norms of morality are time and place bound. This means that they can change with time and increased awareness. For example, some decades ago it was considered all right for factories to throw their liquid waste into lakes and rivers, while at present it is considered totally wrong and unethical. In Europe, a couple of decades ago, all such factories were required to install anti-pollution systems to clean any such waste before dumping it into natural surroundings. No longer can ethics be confused with legality. Law and written codes of conduct are the minimum requirements; they provide only basic guidelines. All that is legal is not necessarily ethical. If a company is acquitted of any wrongdoing, this does not necessarily mean that it has been ethical.[10] An ethical company is not looking to meet minimum standards but instead is looking to do the maximum it can for the well-being of its stakeholders.

ethics and international marketing

Consumers and societies have become increasingly wary (read sceptical) of the marketing activities of firms. The main purpose of marketing and advertising is to communicate with consumers and make them aware of the existence and characteristics of products. However, the type of information conveyed in these advertisements, and whether the claims made (e.g. Coke is the real thing or that a certain cosmetic will make you look 10 years younger) are correct, realistic and justified, is often questioned. It was once a common view that companies not only satisfy consumer demands but they also create consumer demand: the 'dependence effect'. A number of scholars regard excessive advertising campaigns for cigarettes as an example of this unnecessary or 'unethical' demand creation.[11]

In recent years, however, it has been widely accepted that marketing and advertising are essential parts of company activities and play important roles in modern society. Marketing should not, however, be deceiving, manipulating or exaggerative. Failure to tell the whole truth about a product, and misleading or unjustified pricing or packaging are considered unethical marketing practices. Product safety is a responsibility of the manufacturing company and if there are any dangers, it is the company's responsibility to properly inform the customer. Moreover, despite being careful, if the company has not properly conveyed the dangers or possible risks of a product usage, it will be held responsible for any hardship caused to anyone.[12] That is why car companies often call back a particular model to replace parts, if they suspect they might malfunction and hurt someone.

GOING INTERNATIONAL 19.5

Cadbury's clean conscience

On top of a truck festooned with Cadbury's cocoa logos, two contestants are competing to organise six boxes into a pyramid. In the right order, these explain how to transform cow dung, grass and banana leaves into cheap but effective compost. It is a simple game but it has the audience spellbound; 700 farmers and traders hoot with laughter as the contestants struggle to complete the task. When one arranges a picture of a cow back to front, they are beside themselves.

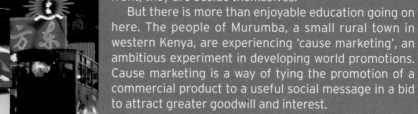

But there is more than enjoyable education going on here. The people of Murumba, a small rural town in western Kenya, are experiencing 'cause marketing', an ambitious experiment in developing world promotions. Cause marketing is a way of tying the promotion of a commercial product to a useful social message in a bid to attract greater goodwill and interest.

Cadbury has formed a partnership with Mediae Trust, an organisation that works on new techniques to foster development through the media, alongside Britain's Department of International Development. Under the deal, Cadbury pays for the radio and TV channel TnM's air time in return for advertising. It has also introduced mobile vans to carry actors around rural Kenya to perform live shows exploring the themes raised in the soap opera relayed on the TV channel.

In theory everyone benefits: Cadbury from its association with social responsibility and a large, engaged rural audience; the development agencies from co-funding and exposure to commercial communication techniques.

Unfortunately, as the compost message was delivered, the need for strict monitoring became clear. The presentation's designated time had been severely squeezed by a new marketing promotion in which people were given raffle tickets if they bought a Cadbury product. Some of the audience appeared to become confused between the educational and promotional content. 'I like the show because it educates us, like what to do if your child is mistreated,' said Linnet Nafula. 'It also teaches us how useful Cadbury's is; that it builds healthy bodies.'

■ Do you think Cadbury's marketing campaign is ethical? How could this approach be made more beneficial for local populations?

Source: M. Turner, 'Cadbury's Clean Conscience', *Financial Times*, 18 February 2004, p. 18.

Green marketing

The twenty-first century has been dubbed 'the century of environmental awareness'. Consumers, business people and public administrators must now demonstrate a sense of 'Green' responsibility by integrating environmental habits into individual behaviour.

Europe has been at the forefront of the '**Green movement**' (www.greendot.ie), with strong public opinion and specific legislation favouring environmentally friendly marketing. Green marketing is a term used to identify concern with the environmental consequences of a variety of marketing activities. The European Union, concerned that national restrictions on waste would create 15 different codes that could become clear barriers to trade, has passed legislation to control all kinds of packaging waste throughout the EU. Two critical issues that affect product development are the control of the packaging component of solid waste and consumer demand for environmentally friendly products.[13]

Germany has a strict **eco-labelling** programme to identify, for the concerned consumer, products that have a lesser impact on the environment than similar products. Under German regulation, a manufacturer is permitted to display a logo, called the 'Blue Angel', on all products that comply with certain criteria that make them environmentally friendly. More than 3400 products in 85 product categories have been examined and awarded the Blue Angel logo (www.blauer-engel.de). While for the European eco-label there are 23 product groups with 236 companies being awarded the label. While it is difficult to judge the commercial value of a Blue Angel designation, manufacturers are seeking the eco-label for their products in response to growing consumer demand for environmentally friendly products. Similar national labels exist in France, Denmark, the Netherlands, Finland, Norway, Austria, the Czech Republic and Hungary.

Partly to offset an onrush of eco-labels from every European country, the European Commission issued guidelines for eco-labelling that became operational in October 1992. Under the EC directive, a product is evaluated on all significant environmental effects throughout its life cycle, from manufacturing to disposal – a cradle-to-grave approach.[14]

Companies will be encouraged to continuously update their environmental technology because eco-labels will be granted for a limited period only. As more environmentally friendly products come onto the market, the standards will become tougher, and products that have not been improved will lose their eco-labels (see Exhibit 19.4).[15]

The Blue Angel and similar eco-labels are awarded on the basis of a product's environmental friendliness, that is, how 'friendly' it is when used and when its residue is released into the environment (see Exhibit 19.5). A detergent formulated to be biodegradable and not to pollute would be judged friendlier than a detergent whose formulation would be harmful when discharged. Aerosol propellants that do not deplete the ozone layer are another example of environmentally friendly products. No country's laws yet require products to carry an eco-label for them to be sold. The designation that a product is 'environmentally friendly' is voluntary and its environmental success depends on the consumer selecting the eco-friendly product. However, laws that mandate systems to control solid waste, while voluntary in one sense, do carry penalties, albeit indirect ones.

key terms

Green movement
political/consumer movement favouring environment-friendly approaches

eco-labelling
a label or logo to show that a company is socially responsible

475

Exhibit 19.4 Examples of EC environmental symbols (eco-labels)

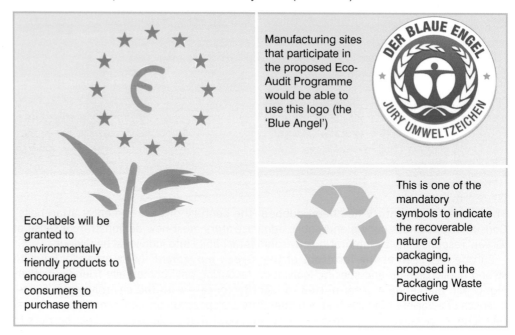

Manufacturing sites that participate in the proposed Eco-Audit Programme would be able to use this logo (the 'Blue Angel')

Eco-labels will be granted to environmentally friendly products to encourage consumers to purchase them

This is one of the mandatory symbols to indicate the recoverable nature of packaging, proposed in the Packaging Waste Directive

Source: Catherine Vial, 'Why Policy Will Affect American Business', *Business America*, 8 March 1993, p. 27.

Exhibit 19.5 How long will litter last?

	Number of years
Cigarette butts	1–5
Aluminium cans and tabs	500
Glass bottles	1000
Plastic bags	10–20
Plastic-coated paper	5
Plastic film containers	20–30
Nylon fabric	30–40
Leather	up to 50
Orange and banana peels	up to 2
Tin cans	50
Plastic holders	100
Plastic bottles and Styrofoam	indefinitely

Source: based on Grame Pole, *Au Altitude Super Guide: Canadian Rockies* (Vancouver: Altitude Publishing, 1993), p. 29.

Germany's law requires that packaging materials through all levels of distribution, from the manufacturer to the consumer, must be recycled or reused. Each level of the distribution chain is responsible for returning, back upstream, all packaging, packing and other waste materials. The biggest problem is with the packaging the customer takes home; by law the retailer must take back all packaging from the customer if no central recycling locations are available. To save retailers from having to shoulder the burden of

the recovery of sales packaging alone, a parallel or dual waste collection system is part of German law. For the manufacturer's product to participate in direct collection and not have to be returned to the retailer for recycling, the manufacturer must guarantee financial support for kerbside or central collection of all materials. For participating manufacturers, a green dot can be displayed on the package, which signals to the consumer that a product is eligible for kerbside or central-location pick-up.

Packaging without the green dot must be returned to the retailer for recycling. Goods sold without the green dot are not illegal; however, retailers will be reluctant to stock such products because they are responsible for their recycling. It is likely that the market – retailers, wholesalers and importers – will refuse packaged goods without the green dot, even those with recyclable packaging. The growing public and political pressure to control solid waste is a strong incentive for manufacturers to comply.

Packaging used by fast-food outlets is not covered by the German green dot programme, and one German city, concerned about its waste disposal, imposed a tax on all fast-food containers. The local law requires fast-food restaurants to pay a tax equivalent to €0.27 for each paper plate, €0.22 for each can or non-returnable bottle, and €0.05 for each plastic spoon, fork or knife. The law was challenged by two McDonald's restaurants and two vending machine companies, but the German court upheld the tax. The impact has led some snack bars and fast-food outlets to adopt new packaging techniques. Cream is now served in reusable metal pitchers, and jam and yoghurt in glass jars. French fries are sold on plates made of edible wafers, and soft drinks are offered in returnable bottles rather than in cans. The city is happy with the results.[16]

To stave off a multitude of individual country laws controlling solid waste disposal, the European Commission has issued a global packaging directive. This law is considered weaker than the German law, but the limits of the law on total recovery of solid waste are seen as more workable than the German law, and collection of sales packaging materials by retailers is not mandated. The law leaves rules on collection up to individual member states, so the German green dot programme is permissible.

ethical behaviour in international marketing

Marketers need to adhere to their individual as well as collective responsibilities. They cannot just look at their own marketing campaign but have the put it in the context of all marketing campaigns targeting the same customer segment.[17] The marketers have responsibility towards the entire market segment and not just those who are affected by their product. This is true for cigarette and liquor advertising and its impact on younger members of the market.

In salesman/buyer relationships, bribery and other illegal/immoral payments are common issues. It is quite prevalent in many societies. In Hong Kong, it is said to be around 5 per cent, in Russia around 20 per cent and in Indonesia it can sometimes be as high as 30 per cent.[18] In many countries there is a formal way of doing business and there is also an informal way of doing business. The informal way often works faster, but might include bribes or 'commission' to be paid to 'experts'.[19]

A number of countries have signed a convention against bribery (see Exhibit 19.6) but, as it is an illegal activity, there is no guarantee that in these countries bribery does not take place.

Product safety is a major issue in marketing ethics. Consumers have the right to be protected from harmful products. It is the responsibility of the marketer to ensure that the products meet these criteria. Consumers need to be informed sufficiently (e.g. on the package) to make a rational decision. The package must include crucial information about the product, e.g. the net quantity/weight and value comparison. Food articles should also include nutrition values and contents. Exhibit 19.7 explains non-ethical behaviour in international marketing activities.

Exhibit 19.6 OECD anti-bribery convention: signatory countries

Argentina	Japan
Australia	Korea
Austria	Luxembourg
Belgium	Mexico
Brazil	The Netherlands
Bulgaria	New Zealand
Canada	Norway
Chile	Poland
Czech Republic	Portugal
Denmark	Slovak Republic
Finland	Slovenia
France	Spain
Germany	Sweden
Greece	Switzerland
Hungary	Turkey
Iceland	United Kingdom
Ireland	United States
Italy	

Source: Report on Anti-Bribery Convention 2003. Cited in Blythe and Zimmerman, 2005, p. 361 (see reference 10).

Exhibit 19.7 Ethical issues in international marketing activities

Marketing activity	(Un)Ethical issues
Positioning	Positioning a low-quality product as a high-quality product Product positioned to perform a function that is not true, e.g. cholesterol-reducing food, anti-ageing cosmetics Blackmailing customers that if they do not use the product they will be harmed/disadvantaged in some way
Product	Product that can cause harm to customers/users, e.g. children's toys Products that pose a safety risk for the users, e.g. electric goods, automobiles Products that can cause health problems, e.g. side-effects of medicines When customers are not fully informed about product content, e.g. in food articles, nuts, GM ingredients or sugar/salt level Use of environment-friendly packaging
Price	Price cartels, where two or more competitors fix a price that is higher than competitive pricing Charging discriminatory prices without any extra value provided Transfer pricing; over/underpricing internal invoices for taxation purposes Charging high monopolistic prices, e.g. medicines for epidemic diseases, such as AIDS in Africa Pay bribery/illegal payments or gifts to acquire sales
Promotion	Claiming inaccurate product benefits through advertising Not informing the customer fully through different communication Using inappropriate language in advertising Using discriminatory or degrading slogans Advertising directed towards younger children Paying illegal kickbacks to promote the product
Place/ distribution	Discriminatory distribution, e.g. forcing wholesalers and retailers to discriminate among customers (to whom the product can be sold) Demanding unfair benefits/kickbacks/advances from retailers or suppliers Taking responsibility for after-sales service, e.g. in electronic goods

These days the usage of universal price codes (UPCs) or barcodes does not always allow the customer to see and compare the price. It is the duty of the seller/retailer to provide information on price on each product. In case there is an operational cost (e.g. electric appliances, tyres, etc.) the customer has to be informed about these 'hidden costs'.

Advertising is considered the most crucial aspect of marketing with regard to ethical issues. Quite often advertising is misleading or deceptive and customers are led to believe a false claim. Advertising is deceptive when it shows packaging that does not correspond with the price mentioned, e.g. the size and quantity versus price. A number of countries find slogans such as 'buy one, get one free' or '30 per cent free' manipulative and misleading.[20]

Moreover, it is unethical to market food knowing that it is unhealthy or harmful. It is not the customer's responsibility to check before buying.

In terms of guidelines for future managers, the ethical test, shown below, drawn up by the Institute of Business Ethics is useful because of its simplicity and clarity.

Simple ethical test for a business decision:

- *Transparency*
  Do I mind others knowing what I have done?
- *Effect*
  Who does my decision affect or hurt?
- *Fairness*
  Would my decision be considered fair by others?

GOING INTERNATIONAL 19.6

ethics and pragmatics in the junk-food industry

The UK Government definitely thinks that pop stars should be used to promote healthy food instead of junk food, which has contributed to a doubling in the number of children with weight problems in the past 10 years. In conjunction with this philosophy, the Food Standards Agency is proposing to ban junk-food companies from sponsoring pop concerts and sporting events. The Agency's targets would include Pepsi Cola (which sponsored concerts by Britney Spears, Ms Dynamite and Beyoncé), Coca-Cola (which has sponsored the boy band Busted and the girl band Mis-Teeq), McDonald's (the sponsor of Justin Timberlake and ITV's *Pop Stars: the Rivals*) and Nestlé (which supports ITV's *Pop Idol*). The football club Sheffield Wednesday would lose its sponsorship from Chupa Chups lollipops.

The proposed ban would cover television and radio advertising, and would prevent 'unhealthy' food manufacturers from making links with cartoon characters and sporting personalities. Billboard and magazine advertising aimed at children, and 'pop-up' advertisements on the Internet would be banned, and junk-food companies would be barred from linking up with computer games and competitions. They would also not be allowed to target mobile telephones by text message when their owners are near a food outlet. The agency also proposes curbs on links between 'unhealthy' food manufacturers and schools, citing Cadbury's 'Get Active' campaign and the Walkers 'books for schools' scheme.

The Agency's proposals have shocked the fast-food companies. Officially, most executives said that they would 'study the proposals with interest' and would conform with any changes in the law. Privately, however, many said that if implemented the rules

would be 'disastrous' and could cost thousands of jobs. The companies are expected to resist any attempt to interfere with sponsorship. Some defend themselves by citing the importance of sponsorship in today's sport and pop music worlds. McDonald's said that it had put £14 million into local football sponsorship since 1993 and that its support will make it possible for 10 000 people to become football coaches. The pop industry also criticised the proposals. Julian Henry, the managing director of Henry's House PR company, which represents *Pop Idol*, S Club and MTV, said: 'Record labels have become dependent on brands that want to support new pop talent. With sales of singles dwindling, brand investment is a critical part of the success of a new pop act. Part of the Spice Girls' appeal was that they could reach consumers in supermarkets and garage forecourts as well as on Radio 1 and *Top of the Pops*.' Other companies claim that they are already acting responsibly in their advertising campaigns. A spokesman for Coca-Cola in the UK said: 'We don't target under-12s in our advertising, and marketing for our product for two- to five-year-olds is aimed at parents.'

The Food Standards Agency's 12-member board will discuss the proposals and will canvass 'a broad spectrum of views' before making recommendation for legislative changes but, in the words of Sir John Krebs, chairman of the FSA, 'doing nothing is not an option'.

Source: adapted from Charlotte Edwardes, 'First They Banned Cigarette Advertising. Now They Want to do the Same to Junk Food', *Sunday Telegraph*, 9 November 2003, p. 3.

summary

The classic view about the responsibilities of a firm believes that its main goals and obligations refer to economic behaviour. The firm has to be concerned about performance and growth, including innovations and technology. The modern view, however, states that a firm has to be responsible beyond its economic goals. It has to be responsible for the well-being and interest of its stakeholders: owners, employee, suppliers, customers, managers and local communities. Thus, it is a firm's responsibility to be fair and impartial towards its employees and to help society in eradicating poverty and injustice.

Ethics and social responsibility become particularly important for marketers as they are the ones who have to convey this to the market. Moreover, it is quite often the marketing function that has to take the major responsibility, at least towards the customers, and to ensure the positive performance of the company. Product safety, packaging and labelling has to be undertaken in a responsible way. The marketing message (advertising, etc.) has to be honest and clean, and not manipulative or deceptive. The same is true for pricing – customers should be able to compare prices with competing products. Finally, the company has to participate in the community's social programmes such as education and equality.

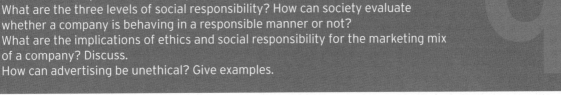

questions

1 Can a company behave legally and still be unethical? Give examples.
2 What is meant by Green marketing. How is it enforced?
3 What are the three levels of social responsibility? How can society evaluate
  whether a company is behaving in a responsible manner or not?
4 What are the implications of ethics and social responsibility for the marketing mix
  of a company? Discuss.
5 How can advertising be unethical? Give examples.

further reading

- J.M. Aurifelle and P.G. Quester, 'Predicting Business Ethical Tolerance in International
  Markets: A Concomitant Clusterwise Regression Analysis', *International Business
  Review*, 2003, 12(2), pp. 253-72.
- J. Fisher, 'Social Responsibility and Ethics: Clarifying the Concepts', *Journal of
  Business Ethics*, 2004, 52, pp. 391-400.
- S. Webley and E. More, 'Does Business Ethics Pay?', see http://www.ibe.org.uk/
  dbepsumm.htm.

references

1 B. Schlegelmich, *Marketing Ethics: An International Perspective* (London: Thomson, 1998).
2 C. Stone, 'Why Shouldn't Corporations Be Socially Responsible?', in W.M. Hoffman and J.M. Moore (eds),
  Business Ethics: Readings and Cases in Corporate Morality (New York: McGraw-Hill, 1990).
3 M. Friedman, 'The Social Responsibility of Business is to Increase its Profits', *New York Times*, 14
  September 1970.
4 H. Mintzberg, 'The Case for Corporate Social Responsibility', *Journal of Business Strategy*, 1983, 4(2),
  pp. 65-74.
5 J.M. Aurifielle and P.G. Quester, 'Predicting Business Ethical Tolerance in International Markets: A
  Concomitant Cluster-wise Regression Analysis', *International Business Review*, 2003, 12(2), pp. 253-72.
6 J.R. Boatright, *Ethics and the Conduct of Business* (New Jersey: Pearson, 2003).
7 S.P. Sethi, 'Dimensions of Corporate Social Performance: An Analytical Framework for Measurement
  and Analysis', *California Management Review*, 17(Spring), pp. 62-72.
8 This section draws on R.E. Freeman, 'A Stakeholder Theory of the Modern Corporation', in L.P. Hartman
  (ed.), *Perspectives in Business Ethics*, 2nd edn (New York: McGraw-Hill, 2002), pp. 177-204.
9 N. Bowie, 'It Seems Right in Theory but Does it Work in Practice?', in L.P. Harman (ed.), *Perspectives in
  Business Ethics*, 2nd edn (New York: McGraw-Hill, 2002), pp. 83-6.
10 J. Blythe and A. Zimmerman, *Business to Business Marketing Management: A Global Perspective*
  (London: Thomson, 2005).
11 M. Josephson, 'Ethics and Business Decision Making', in W. Hoffman, R. Fredrick and M. Schwartz (eds),
  Business Ethics: Readings and Cases in Corporate Morality, 4th edn (Boston: McGraw-Hill, 2001), pp.
  87-116.
12 J.K. Galbraith, *The Affluent Society* (Boston: Houghton Mifflin, 1958).
13 Lynn S. Amine, 'The Need for Moral Champions in Global Marketing', *European Journal of Marketing*,
  vol. 30, no. 5, 1996, pp. 81-94.
14 'EC Wants Public as Environmental Watchdogs', *Business Europe*, 10 January 1992, pp. 1-2.
15 Kirsten Bergstrom, 'The Eco-Label and Exporting to Europe', *Business America*, 29 November 1993,
  p. 21.
16 Stephen Kinzer, 'Germany Upholds Tax on Fast-food Containers', *New York Times*, 22 August 1994, p. C2.

17 G.G. Brenkest, 'Marketing to Inner-city Blacks: Power Master and Moral Responsibility', in Hoffman, W.M., Fredrick, R.E. and Schwartz, M.S. (eds), *Business Ethics: Readings and Cases in Corporate Morality*, 4th edn (Boston: McGraw-Hill, 2001), pp. 394–403.

18 Hoffman *et al.* (ibid.), p. 360.

19 Terpstra, V. and David, K., *The Cultural Environment of International Business* (Cincinnati, OH: South Western Publishing).

20 Hoffman *et al.* (ibid.), pp. 277–82.

chapter 20
Financing and Managing International Marketing Operations

Chapter Outline

When companies decide to market internationally, additional financing is one of the important resources. An often-cited reason for companies not achieving international business objectives is insufficient capital to fund the additional investments necessary for success. This is particularly true for small and medium-sized (SMEs) companies. Marketing and finance are inextricably intertwined with overall corporate planning, goals and objectives; policies and decisions in either one have a profound effect on the other. Without proper financial support, marketing activities cannot achieve their ultimate potential.

As a company moves deeper into the international arena, the interdependence of marketing and financial activities increases and places greater demands on the company. This means (1) an increased need for working capital, (2) assuring timely international payments, (3) enhanced financial risk resulting from fluctuating exchange rates and (4) implementing methods of minimising risks.[1]

This chapter emphasises the financial requirements of international marketing; it discusses the need for increased funds, especially for SMEs, the sources of those funds, the financial risks involved and methods of minimising those risks. The entire treatment is concerned with the strategic marketing implications related to finance.

capital needs for international marketing

Distance, time lags, tariffs, taxes, financial participation requirements, exchange restrictions, fluctuating monetary values and adequate local financial strength are all elements differentiating the problems of financing international marketing activities from those related to domestic marketing. Effective management of the financial functions of marketing can be a strategic factor affecting profits and having great impact on the company's ability to develop marketing channels.

Time lags caused by distance and crossing international borders add cost elements to international marketing that make cash-flow planning especially important. Even in a relatively simple transaction, money may be tied up for months while goods are being shipped from one part of the world to another; customs clearance may add days, weeks or months; payment may be held up while the international payment documents are being transferred from one nation to another; and breakage, commercial disputes or governmental restrictions can add further delay. One study done by a credit management association found that the time required for foreign firms to collect on the average bill from international customers ranged from 54 days for payment from Germany to a high of 337 days from Iran.[2] In countries where shortages of hard currency exist and countertrades are

necessary, capital requirements are even greater since full receipts are not collectable until the countertraded goods are sold. Nearly every international transaction encounters some time lag during which marketing financing must be provided.

For smaller firms, in addition to greater demands for working capital, the international marketer may have to make long-term capital investments. In some instances, markets are closed to a foreign business unless all or some portion of the product is manufactured locally. Thus, international marketing activities frequently require supplemental financing for working capital and capital investment.

working capital requirements

Because of time lags, shipping costs, duties, higher start-up costs, inventory cost, market penetration costs, and increased financial needs for trade and channel credit, international operations typically require higher levels of working capital than domestic activities operating at the same volume levels. Travel costs alone can consume working capital funds; in one instance, a small firm discovered it was spending more on travel in a foreign market than on salaries.

Start-up Costs   Start-up costs for a company entering new international markets frequently require large amounts of working capital. Such costs can come as a surprise to the firm accustomed to operating in a familiar domestic market. A firm may find it must pay for information assumed or acquired without cost in the home country. Also part of start-up costs are legal fees, establishing an office, purchase of licences, and so on. Marketing research can become a major expense, particularly if a company has to research three or four countries before embarking on a business enterprise in any one of them.

Inventory   The marketer's effectiveness in managing inventories has considerable impact on the financial requirements of this function. Adequate servicing of overseas markets frequently requires goods to be inventoried in several locations; one company that uses two factory warehouses for the entire continental Europe needed six foreign distribution points that together handled less merchandise than either European outlet. One of the advantages of a single European market is the use of fewer inventory storage points than were required when there were 25 different countries with rules that hampered speedy delivery.[3] Most other markets are not so integrated.

Slower transportation and longer distances when shipping over water mean inventory turnover can be lengthened considerably over the customary time for domestic operations. Add loading and unloading time, and the time in transit for an overseas shipment from a British manufacturer in Europe to an Asian market, for example Indonesia, can be as much as two months or longer. If your product is entering a congested port, there may be a week's delay just for unloading. The additional time required for delivery increases the capital requirements needed to finance inventories.

market penetration costs

A variety of costs is associated with market penetration. In many cases these costs are higher, relative to sales, in foreign markets than in domestic markets, thereby increasing the capital needs for international marketing.

Promotion and advertising costs, similar in domestic and foreign markets, are generally higher relative to actual sales. Markets are smaller, media usually more expensive and multiple media generally required; these and similar factors increase investment needs.

Manufacturers of durable goods have found they often must provide funds for service facilities before their products are accepted. Japanese car-makers met with little success in Europe until they invested in adequate service facilities and expanded spare parts inventories.

It is never inexpensive to establish a channel of distribution but, again, the complications of international distribution can require extra-large channel investments. Foreign

middlemen are seldom adequately financed and may require extensive long-term credit if they are to carry adequate inventories and offer their customers adequate credit.

Channel credit requirements have surprised many Western firms. Most of the world's middlemen are woefully underfinanced, and if they are to buy goods in economical quantities, **interim credit** must be provided by the producers. The international finance director of a machinery and equipment company says he expects increasing foreign sales volume to require additional working capital to 'support from 50 per cent to 75 per cent of the sales increase'.

Smaller firms' competitive position may be weaker in world markets than in domestic markets because of the number of competitors vying for customers in certain product lines. One UK company that marketed insecticides in Spain through seven local distributors found that within less than three years, six of those distributors had been purchased, or partially purchased, by competitive firms, thus blocking the initial supplier's distribution. The company found similar situations in Latin America, South Africa, Australia and Asia. To retain a competitive position, the company in question was virtually forced to make major investments in buying distributors throughout the world. While many of these ventures are profitable, it requires a huge infusion of funds to maintain market position. In the home market, such investments would probably not have been necessary.

Accounts-receivable financing imposes great strains on international working capital. Middlemen and industrial customers have both learned that they are in a position to pressure manufacturers into continuously longer and longer credit extensions because credit terms are such an important marketing weapon in the battle for competitive position in international markets. Marketing and product advantages are being offset by more advantageous financial terms from competing foreign suppliers. To get goods into the channel of distribution, marketers may have to compensate for the middlemen's lack of capital by providing consignment merchandise, floor-plan financing or long-term credit. Without such financial assistance, most foreign middlemen cannot handle adequate inventories.

A decade or two ago, international marketers had little concern about credit because terms tended to be cash in advance. Many small agricultural marketers or exporters continue to rely on these terms; but, in today's intensely competitive world marketplace, no major marketer can afford a cash-only posture. Middlemen may require both extensive and intensive credit availability to develop the type of distribution systems requisite to international marketing. When Daewoo entered the European market with its cars, it offered two to three years' interest free credit in a number of European countries.

capital investment

Some markets are closed to foreign business unless they produce goods locally. The French Government, for example, gave notice to Ford Motor Company that if it expected to keep its large volume of sales in France, it had to produce there; Ford prudently agreed to build its next European plant in France. Ford, Toyota, Sony or Siemens can easily adhere to these types of demand from local governments. The situation is, however, different for smaller firms. In such cases, the production facility itself is a crucial element to market entry and may be considered part of the marketing system because market requirements alone dictate the expenditure. In addition, such marketing facilities as warehouses, shipping docks, retail stores and sales offices require significant capital investment in physical facilities. In considering financial implications, the cost of the production facility as well as costs of marketing facilities may logically be related to marketing as a cost of market entry.

An important financial issue facing international marketers from smaller firms is the availability and source of capital to finance the additional working capital needed. Besides a company's own resources, there are a variety of public funds available.

sources of government funds for international marketing

Working capital for international marketing operations is usually derived from the assets of the company engaging in international trade or exporting. However, private external sources may be used for financing inventory, accounts receivable, construction of physical facilities and other financing needs. Public sources of funds are likely to play a more important role in financing marketing operations internationally than they do domestically. A number of supranational agencies are engaged in financing international development and marketing activities, plus the foreign marketer may turn to foreign, national, state and local governments for various kinds of financial assistance.

The great majority of sources of public funds for international business are oriented to industrial development activities. Some agencies, however, interpret industrial development broadly and make funds available for a wide range of business activities.

Export Credit Banks   In most Western countries, there are specialised banks for **export credit**. Also, most well-established banks in these countries finance export activities of their clients. Other than these private banks, a number of government or semi-government agencies provide funds for international trade and investments. These agencies operate as loan guarantee programmes. Loans are made through commercial banks and guaranteed by these agencies.[4] Some banks specialise in different regions, such as the European Bank for Reconstruction and Development (EBRD) for Eastern Europe and the Asian Development Bank for Asia.

International Development Agencies (IDAs)   These agencies provide loans and grants to less developed countries for both developmental and foreign policy reasons. **Developmental loans** are extended to support recipient-country development in key economic sectors in agriculture and nutrition, health, training and education, and energy. Foreign policy loans are extended to developing countries and are used to pay for imports needed to run their economies. A significant portion of each loan or grant is used to finance Western exports.[5] Almost all Western countries have their international development agencies that fund or partly finance exports and franchising for all exports that can be related to development sectors such as education, health and infrastructure development.

Eurodollar Market   The eurodollar market is one of the more important sources of debt capital available to the MNC. The term **eurodollar** refers to a deposit liability banked outside the United States, that is, dollars banked in Germany or any country other than the United States. While the eurodollar market refers to dollars, it includes other national currencies banked outside their countries of origin. Because the eurodollar market includes other than US currencies, it is sometimes referred to as the eurocurrency market, even though the predominant currency is the US dollar. These currencies serve as a ready source of cash that holding banks can use as an asset on which a dollar-denominated loan can be made to someone else. Similar markets in Asia and the Caribbean consist of national currencies deposited in banks outside the country of origin.

Debt-equity Swaps   Another source of funds for companies operating in countries with high external debt are **debt-equity swaps**. Banks wanting to lower their debt portfolios, and countries wanting to lower their debt burdens without using scarce foreign exchange, participate in favourable debt-equity swaps with foreign companies. For foreign companies, it is a way to finance business activity in a country at discount rates. Debt-equity swaps have been used to finance joint ventures, to acquire working capital, to buy raw materials and to invest in new facilities.[6]

key terms

export credit
a loan that allows a company to pay for an export contract

developmental loans
loans granted for development projects, e.g. health and education

eurodollar
a deposit liability banked outside the US – that is, dollars banked in any country other than the US

debt-equity swaps
the exchange of a debt instrument in return for equity, which cancels out the debt

487

financial risk and risk management

Several types of financial risk are encountered in international marketing; the major problems include commercial, political and foreign-exchange risk. Some risks are similar to domestic risks although usually intensified, while others are uniquely international. Every business should deal with the fact of risk through a structured **risk-management** programme. Such a programme may call for assuming risks, engaging in some type of risk avoidance and/or initiating **risk-shifting** behaviour. In foreign markets, companies have to compete with local firms that might be heavily subsidised by local governments, thus putting extra financial burden on foreign firms (see Exhibit 20.1).

key terms

risk management
the sophisticated
use of such
techniques as
currency hedging
and interest rate
swaps

risk shifting
risk is not reduced
or eliminated but
rather shifted on
to someone else

Exhibit 20.1 European state subsidies (European state aid spending as a % of GDP, 2002)

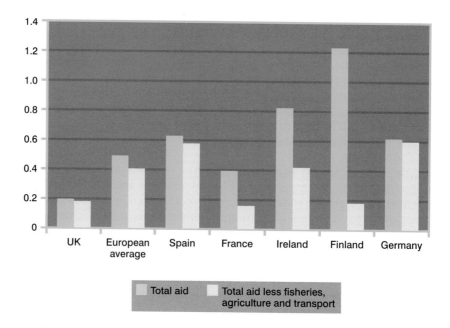

Source: Bob Sherwood, 'Competition Fear Over Subsidies', *Financial Times*, 25 November 2004, p. 3.

commercial risk

Commercial risks are handled essentially as normal credit risks encountered in day-to-day business. They include solvency, default or refusal to pay bills. The major risk is competition, which can only be dealt with through consistently effective management and marketing.

One unique risk encountered by the international marketer involves financial adjustments. Such risk is encountered when a controversy arises about the quality of goods delivered (but not accepted), a dispute over contract terms or any other disagreement over which payment is withheld. For example, a British company shipped several hundred tons of dehydrated potatoes to a distributor in Germany. The distributor tested the shipment and declared it to be below acceptable taste and texture standards (not explicitly established). The alternatives for the exporter of reducing the price, reselling the potatoes or shipping them home again involved considerable cost. Although there is less risk of substantial loss in the adjustment situation, it is possible for the selling company to have large sums of money tied up for relatively long periods of time until the client accepts the controversial goods, if ever. In some cases, goods must be returned or remanufactured, and in other instances, contracts may be modified to alleviate the controversies. All such problems are uninsurable and costly.

GOING INTERNATIONAL 20.1

the debate on export subsidies

The Arrangement on Guidelines for Officially Supported Export Credits, as its name suggests, sets out guidelines to regulate officially supported (i.e. government-backed) export credit guarantees and insurance against the risk of non-repayment. An export credit arises whenever a foreign buyer of exported goods or services is allowed to defer payment. Export-credit insurance and guarantees may take the form of 'supplier' or 'buyer' credits where the exporter's bank or other financial institution lend to the buyer or his bank respectively.

The Arrangement also regulates official financing support where the government provides such loans directly, offers refinancing or supports interest rates. The institutions that undertake these official activities, for or on behalf of governments, are export-credit agencies (ECAs). There are several types of such agency: they can be government owned (as with the Export Credits Guarantee Department (ECGD) in the United Kingdom, which is a government department), or privately owned institutions, such as COFACE in France.

The Arrangement on Guidelines for Officially Supported Export Credits, then commonly known as 'the Consensus', was formerly established in 1978. The Arrangement applies to officially supported export credits with a repayment term of two years or more (most short-term business is now underwritten by the private sector) and sets out, *inter alia*, maximum repayment terms and, where official financing support is involved, minimum interest rates.

The Arrangement details the circumstances in which trade-related tied and partially untied aid may be given in transactions where aid funds are provided on the condition that the goods/services being supported are purchased from the country providing the aid money.

One of the most noteworthy developments of recent years has been the agreement on the 'pricing' of official support reached in June 1997, the so-called 'Knaepen Package'. In essence, these ground-breaking new rules provide for minimum risk-based premium fees that should be adequate to cover the risk of non-repayment by an overseas country/government in markets in which OECD exporters are active.

Another major issue facing the participants is that of project financing, a technique that is used increasingly, particularly for infrastructure projects, where loan repayments are made from the revenue generated by the projects themselves.

■ Are export subsidies justified?

Source: European Business Report, Spring 1Q, 1998, p. 58.

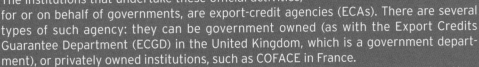

key term

currency inconvertibility deterioration in ability to convert profits, debt service and other remittances from local currency into another currency

political risk

Political risk is related to the problems of war or revolution, **currency inconvertibility**, expropriation or expulsion, and restriction or cancellation of import licences. One of the most frequently encountered political risks arises when a country refuses to allow local currency to be converted to any other currency. This often happens when countries are experiencing economic difficulties and want to conserve scarce supplies of hard currencies, that is, currencies that are easily exchangeable for goods or other currencies. For example, when someone in Russia wants to purchase goods from a company in another country, the seller would probably be reluctant to accept payment in roubles because

roubles have a history of rapid erosion as a result of hyperinflation. The Russian buyer has to convert roubles into a hard currency, the US dollar, euro, British pound or any other currency that is freely accepted for payment by most of the world.[7]

foreign-exchange risk

Until 1973, the international monetary system operated under an agreement (**Bretton Woods Agreement**) that pegged exchange rates for currencies of the industrialised countries to a gold exchange standard. During the period of the Bretton Woods Agreement, most hard currencies were relatively stable and fluctuations were infrequent and small. Thus, a firm's transactions in foreign currencies were fairly secure in terms of exchange rates to other currencies because devaluations of major currencies were infrequent and usually anticipated. Since the abandonment of the Bretton Woods Agreement, currencies are allowed to float freely and exchange rates fluctuate daily. Exhibit 20.2 illustrates the volatility that has occurred in some major currencies between 2000 and 2004. It is not hard to imagine the foreign-exchange risk problems of companies that deal with large quantities of foreign currencies at any given point. Depending on the specific time span, a firm could suffer the loss of substantial sums of money from too much exposure to fluctuating currencies.[8] **Floating exchange rates** have forced all marketers to be especially aware of exchange-rate fluctuation and the extent of their transaction exposure.

key terms

Bretton Woods Agreement
sets fixed exchange rates for major currencies and established the IMF

floating exchange rates
changes in market demand and market supply of a currency cause a change in value

Exhibit 20.2 Trade-weighted exchange rates (Bank of England indices, rebased)

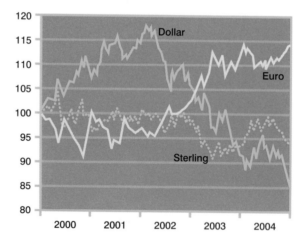

Source: Thomson Datastream and Bank of England, in *Financial Times*, 29 November 2004, p. 3.

A large MNC might encounter several or all of these situations in the course of normal business activity. Most firms try to minimise exchange risks. The most obvious way is to demand payment in the home-country currency, but competitively that is not always possible. When a company demands payment in home-country currency, the exchange risk is shifted to the buyer, who is then similarly exposed. In a fluctuating exchange market such as the one that has existed since the early 1970s, there is a tendency for each party in a transaction to attempt to shift the exchange risk to the other. Thus, demand for payment in the seller's currency may not always be possible. More formal methods of risk avoidance are discussed in the following section on financial risk management.

managing financial risk

When financial risks become too high, companies either stop doing business in high-risk situations or seek ways to minimise potential loss. There are various tools available to manage risks, although none provides perfect protection.

Commercial and political risks are insurable through a variety of government agencies. The principal agencies are: (1) Overseas Private Investment Corporations (OPIC), (2) The Foreign Credit Insurance Association (FCIA), (3) the Export Credit Bank, and (4) the Multilateral Investment Guarantee Agency (MIGA), a World Bank affiliate.[9] Protection against risks resulting from exchange-rate fluctuations is not available from any government agency. It comes only from effective financial-risk management. Some companies avoid risks by refusing to enter transactions not denominated in home-country currency; others accept the consequences of currency oscillations as a condition of doing business.

hedging

Hedging in money is essentially no different from any other kind of hedging in the marketplace. It consists of the forward sale of a currency in danger of devaluation for dollars or euros, or another stable monetary unit.

The same techniques used to buy futures in wheat, soybeans and cattle can be used to reduce risks associated with fluctuations in the values of currencies. The process consists of offsetting risk incurred in the actual sale with buying a futures contract in that currency.

Hedging does not always afford complete protection against price changes. Sometimes factors operate to prevent a hedge from offering complete protection. The primary reason for there being no perfect hedge (i.e. where the spot and future yields would be the same) is that the spread between the spot and futures markets does not always move at the same rate. The two prices may move in the same direction but at different degrees and different speeds. Thus a company that hedges can receive an unexpected profit or incur an unexpected loss. However, in situations where exchange rates are fluctuating, the profits or losses are comparatively smaller than they would have been without a hedge.[10]

foreign-exchange options

In addition to buying foreign-exchange futures to hedge against exchange risk, the international marketer has the alternative of buying **foreign-exchange options**. An option is an agreement between two parties in which one party grants the other the right, but not the obligation, to buy or sell foreign exchange under specific conditions. With a futures contract, there is an obligation to buy or sell foreign exchange. The foreign currency option market functions in much the same manner as options for commodities or stocks. Although using options to hedge can often be more expensive than buying futures contracts, there are circumstances when it would be better to hedge with options. Because hedging with futures contracts or with options is a complicated financial process, the international department of a major bank should be consulted.

marketing and organisation

An international marketing plan should optimise the resources committed to stated company objectives. The organisation plan includes the type of organisational arrangements to be used, and the scope and location of responsibility. Many ambitious multinational plans meet with less than full success because of confused lines of authority, poor communications and lack of cooperation between headquarters and the subsidiary organisation.

In building an organisation, important considerations include the level of policy decisions, length of chain of command, staff support, source of natural and personnel resources, degree of control, centralisation and the degree of involvement of marketing.

A company may be organised by product line, but have geographical subdivisions under the product categories. Both may be supplemented by functional staff support. Exhibit 20.3 shows such a combination. Modifications of the basic arrangements are used by a majority of large companies doing business internationally. Companies are usually structured around one of these three alternatives: global **product divisions** responsible for product sales throughout the world, **geographical divisions** responsible for all products

key terms

**foreign-exchange
options**
the buyer of the
option receives
100% protection
against
unfavourable
movement of
exchange rates

product divisions
when a company is
organised
according to its
different products

**geographical
divisions**
when a company is
organised
according to its
markets

key term

matrix organisation
dual organisational structure (e.g. product as well as markets)

and functions within a particular geographical area or a **matrix organisation** consisting of either of these arrangements with centralised sales and marketing run by centralised functional staff or a combination of area operations and global product management.

Exhibit 20.3 Schematic marketing organisation plan combining product, geographic and functional approaches

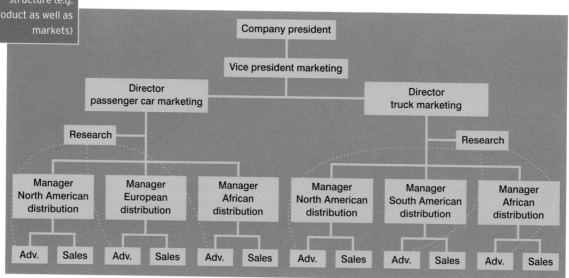

Source: 'An Ever-quicker Trip from R&D to Customer', *Business Week*, Special 21st Century Capitalism Issue, 1994, p. 88.

The extent to which a company can be successful in its international marketing efforts depends on two major factors: first, the nature and suitability of marketing strategy used and, second, the efficient organisation of the firm's international activities. The importance of organisational issues is often not fully recognised or is only partly dealt with. One reason is the underestimation of organising and coordination of different units operating in different markets. These units are of different sizes, type and complexity. At the same time, these units are staffed by people with different backgrounds and abilities. The extent of international marketing success thus forces companies to constantly restructure their organisations. There is no 'right' structure that an international organisation can adopt to be successful. What companies need is to strike the right balance or 'fit' between the companies' objectives, strategies and the local environment or customer needs. The structure that allows this 'fit' and takes care of the ever-changing international marketing environment is the most suitable.[11]

Organisation development is an instrument that is used to achieve marketing objectives and not an end itself. An organisation that looks neat and elegant on a chart is not necessarily the right organisation for a firm in a particular market. A company should thus first establish its goals and marketing strategies, and then explore what type of organisation can help it to achieve those goals and strategies. To achieve the goals of the marketing strategies each function of marketing needs to be properly organised in regard to who will plan and who will perform different tasks, and how these tasks can be performed and coordinated best. As shown by Exhibit 20.4 some of these tasks are more crucial than others. Some of these tasks can be performed outside the company and some activities demand special capabilities, for example, research and advertising. First, an organisation has to realise whether it has its own capabilities to do research or whether it should get it done

Exhibit 20.4 Organising marketing activities

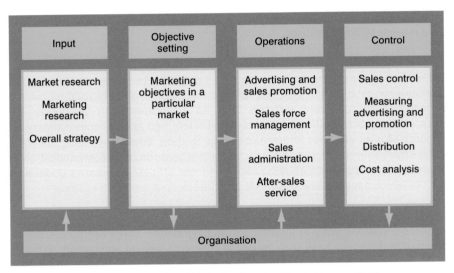

Source: based on Simon Majaro, *International Marketing* (London: Unwin Hyman, 1987).

from outside. Second, the marketing objectives in regard to product, process, distribution, selling and promotion in a particular market would lead to a certain type of organisation. Third, marketing operations such as advertising, sales force management, sales administration, deliveries and after-sales service are to be organised by the firm. Finally, sales control, distribution cost analysis, measurement of advertising effectiveness and other evaluation would give feedback to the organisation for further development and organisational change. A firm has to accommodate these different marketing activities into its structure. The degree of complexity enhances with the number of markets a firm is active in and the number of products it is selling.[12]

issues influencing a structure

The effectiveness and quality of an organisation can be measured only by its ability to achieve its overall goals and marketing strategies. Although there is no best structure available, there are a number of considerations an international marketer should bear in mind while designing an organisation. These issues include centralisation vs decentralisation, communication, position of marketing in an organisation, coordination and the availability of personnel.

centralisation versus decentralisation

Considerations of where decisions will be made, by whom, and by which method constitute a major element of organisation strategy. Management policy must be explicit about which decisions are to be made by the head office and which at local offices. Most companies also limit the amount of money to be spent at local levels. Some multinationals have regional offices and some decision making is done at regional headquarters. Most multinational decisions are made at the head office (centralised) or local offices (decentralised). The chief advantages of **centralisation** are availability of experts at one location, the ability to exercise a high degree of control in planning and implementation, and centralisation of all records and information.

In a number of companies strategic decisions are centralised and operational decisions are decentralised. The choice between centralisation and **decentralisation** is basically a choice between control and delegation; to strike the right balance is often very difficult. The factors that influence this decision are the importance of international activities, the

key terms

centralisation
when most
decisions are
made at the top or
head office

decentralisation
when most
decisions can be
made in
subsidiaries or at
all levels of the
company

size of the firm, the importance of the technology/patents involved, the distance between head office and the local office, and the cultural and management style of a particular company. According to one author, the more a company has an ethnocentric orientation, the more it tends to be centralised.[13]

communication flows

Communication is considered to be one of the most important issues influencing international organisations and their efficient functioning. Coordination beyond national boundaries becomes increasingly difficult due to communication problems such as misinterpretations, ambiguities and costs. An efficient and speedy communication flow is thus essential for an effective international organisation. When discussing the choice of a particular organisational design and structure, consideration of its communication implications is extremely important. Grouping together some offices/subsidiaries under a regional office, all of which have language and cultural closeness, is one such example.

position of marketing

Different organisations have different 'centres of gravity' – some companies are technology oriented and thereby have their technical side, engineering and design, as their centre of gravity. On the other hand, companies that are market oriented tend to have marketing as their centre of gravity. The differences of degree in these two orientations would influence the organisation design and structure. In the second type of organisation the structure might be based on product groups because of different types of customer segment. This can be seen in a company such as Volvo, where the organisation is divided into cars, trucks and aircraft engine divisions. The structure is also dependent on the degree of involvement in international activities. For example, a firm dealing with exports to a couple of markets might have an organic structure based on functions, while a firm that has a number of subsidiaries in several markets, dealing with several products, might have to work with a matrix structure.

coordination

Coordination is perhaps the most important task of an internationally scattered company. Whatever the level of decentralisation and independence of the local offices and subsidiaries, an international firm needs to coordinate and consolidate the activities of its several units. Other than centralised decision making, this is the only way firms can exercise some control over their international activities. From the perspective of the subsidiary, it can easily be considered as permanent pressure from the head office for a constant stream of reports and statements. The dilemma for head office is to apply some sort of standardised tools to measure the performance of the subsidiaries and managers and at the same time allow some freedom or openness to let subsidiaries use their local systems of evaluation and reward. The coordination of purchasing, production and most of the marketing activities can influence the cost structure and efficiency of the company to a great extent. Who is responsible for what and who reports to whom, leads to an overall coordination of a firm's activities.

availability of personnel

For an efficient running of local operations and subsidiaries, firms have to employ locals as well as expatriates. Structures are not just boxes and positions; these boxes have to be manned by efficient personnel. The first issue here is the availability of such personnel in each market. Experienced and skilled marketing personnel are a scarce resource in many foreign markets. Besides availability, whether a firm decides to employ local people or send people from head office depends on the company culture and the extent of control. Whatever course of action is taken, a company has to make the people familiar with the company, its product, its culture and working morale. Some companies thus face enormous

difficulties in recruiting and training local staff in their subsidiaries. Hiring nationals from third countries has recently become quite common, which is a real alternative to local recruitment problems. The problems related to recruitment, training and motivation of personnel are discussed in the next section.

the changing profile of the international manager

The executive recently picked to head Procter & Gamble's US operations is a good example of the effect globalisation is having on businesses and the importance of experience, whether in Japan, Europe or elsewhere. The head of all P&G's US business was born in the Netherlands, received an MBA from Rotterdam's Erasmus University, then rose through P&G's marketing ranks in Holland, the United States and Austria. After proving his mettle in Japan, he moved to Cincinnati to direct P&G's push into East Asia and then to his new position.

Fewer companies today limit their search for senior-level executive talent to their home countries. Coca-Cola's former CEO Guizetta, who began his ascent to the top in his native Cuba, and the former IBM vice-chairman, a Swiss national who rose through the ranks in Europe, are two prominent examples of individuals who rose to the top of firms outside their home countries.

Businesses are placing a greater premium on international experience.[14] In the past, a foreign assignment might have been considered a ticket to nowhere, but such experience has now come to represent the fast track to senior management in a growing number of MNCs. The truly global executive, an individual who takes on several consecutive international assignments and eventually assumes a senior management position at headquarters, is beginning to emerge. For example, of the eight members of the executive committee at Whirlpool, five had international postings within three years of joining the committee. In each case, it was a planned move that had everything to do with their executive development.

The executives of 2010, as one report speculates, will be completely different from the CEOs of today's corporations. They will come from almost anywhere, with an education that will include an undergraduate degree in French literature as well as a joint management/engineering degree. Starting in research, these executives for the twenty-first century will quickly move to marketing and then on to finance. Along the way there will be international assignments taking them to China, India or Brazil, where turning around a failing joint venture will be the first real test of ability that leads to the top. These executives will speak English, Portuguese, Spanish and French, and will be on a first-name basis with commerce ministers in half a dozen countries.

While this description of tomorrow's business leaders is speculative, there is mounting evidence that the route to the top for tomorrow's executives will be dramatically different from today. A Whirlpool Corporation executive was quoted as saying that the CEO of the twenty-first century 'must have a multi-environment, multicountry, multifunctional, and maybe even multicompany, multi-industry experience'.

Some companies, such as Colgate-Palmolive, believe that it is important to have international assignments early in a person's career, and international training is an integral part of its entry-level development programmes. Colgate recruits its future managers from the world's best colleges and business schools. Acceptance is highly competitive and successful applicants have a degree, often in business/management, with proven leadership skills, fluency in at least one language besides English and some experience living abroad.

Trainees begin their careers in a two-year, entry-level, total-immersion programme that consists of stints in various Colgate departments. A typical rotation includes time in the finance, manufacturing and marketing departments, and an in-depth exposure to the company's marketing system. During that phase, trainees are rotated through the firm's ad agency, marketing research and product management departments, and then work for

GOING INTERNATIONAL 20.2

Koreans learn foreign ways: goof off at the mall

The Samsung Group is one of Korea's largest companies and it wants to be more cultur-ally sensitive to foreign ways. To that end, the company has launched an internationali-sation campaign. Cards are taped up in bathrooms each day to teach a phrase of English or Japanese. Overseas-bound managers attend a month-long 'boot camp' where they are awakened at 5.30 am for a jog, meditation and then lessons on table manners, dancing and avoiding sexual harassment. About 400 of its brightest junior employees are sent overseas for a year. Their mission: goof off, just live and observe! They know

international exposure is important, but they feel you also have to develop international taste. To do this you have to do more than visit. You have to goof off at the mall and watch people. The pay-off? One executive of Samsung remarked, after reading a report of 'goofing off' by an employee who spent a year's sabbatical in Russia, 'in 20 years, if this man is representing Samsung in Moscow, he will have friends and he will be able to communicate, and then we will get the pay-off'.

Japanese companies have a similar programme of exposure to foreign markets, which comes early in employees' careers. The day he was hired by Mitsubishi in 1962, a new employee was asked if he wanted to go overseas. Mitsubishi did not need his services abroad immediately but the bosses were sorting out who, over the next 40 years, would spend some time overseas. Japanese executives have long accepted the fact that a stint overseas is often necessary for career advance-ment. Because foreign tours are so critical for promotions, Japanese companies do not have to offer huge compensation packages to lure executives abroad. The new employee who was asked to go abroad back in 1962 is now on his third US tour and has spent a total of 10 years in the United States.

Source: abstracted from 'Sensitivity Kick: Korea's Biggest Firm Teaches Junior Execs Strange Foreign Ways', *Wall Street Journal*, 30 December 1992, p. A1; and 'Why Japan's Execs Travel Better', *Business Week*, November 1993, p. 68.

seven months as a field sales person. At least once during the two years, trainees accom-pany their mentors on business trips to a foreign subsidiary. The company's goal is to develop in their trainees the skills they need to become effective marketing managers, domestically or globally.

On completion of the programme, trainees can expect a foreign posting, either immedi-ately after graduation or soon after an assignment in their home country. The first posi-tions are not in London or Paris, as many might hope, but in emerging markets such as Brazil, Indonesia or maybe South Africa. Because international sales are so important to Colgate (60 per cent of its total revenues are generated abroad), a manager may not return to his home country after the first foreign assignment but instead moves from one overseas post to another, developing into a career internationalist, which could open to a CEO's position. Commenting on the importance of international experience to Colgate's top management, the director of management and organisation said: 'The career track to the top – and I'm talking about the CEO and key executives – requires global experience ... Not everyone in the company has to be a global manager, but certainly anyone who is developing strategy does.'

Companies whose foreign receipts make up a substantial portion of their earnings, and who see themselves as global companies rather than as domestic companies doing

GOING INTERNATIONAL 20.3

**a look into the future: tomorrow's international leaders? an
education for the twenty-first century**

A school supported by the European Community teaches Britons, French, Germans,
Dutch and others to be future Europeans. The European School in a suburb of Brussels
has students from 12 nations who come to be educated for life and work, not as products of motherland or fatherland but as Europeans. The
EC runs nine European Schools in Western Europe,
enrolling 15 000 students from kindergarten to 12th
grade. Graduates emerge superbly educated, usually
trilingual, and very, very European.

The Schools are a linguistic and cultural *mélange*.
There are native speakers of 36 different languages
represented in one school alone. Each year students
take fewer and fewer classes in their native tongue.
Early on, usually in first grade, they begin a second
language, known as the 'working language', which must be English, French or German. A
third language is introduced in the seventh year and a fourth may be started in the
ninth.

By the time students reach their 11th year, they are taking history, geography,
economics, advanced maths, music, art and gym in the working language. When the
students are in groups talking, they are constantly switching languages to 'whatever
works'.

Besides language, students learn history, politics, literature and music from the
perspective of all the European countries – in short, European culture. The curriculum is
designed to teach the French, German, Briton and other nationalities to be future
Europeans.

Source: abstracted from Glynn Mapes, 'Polyglot Students are Weaned Early off Mother Tongue', *Wall
Street Journal*, 6 March 1990, p. A1. Reprinted by permission of the *Wall Street Journal* © 1990 Dow
Jones & Company, Inc. All Rights Reserved Worldwide.

business in foreign markets, are the most active in making the foreign experience an integrated part of a successful corporate career. Their global orientation permeates the entire
organisation from personnel policies to marketing and business strategies. Such is the
case with Gillette, which made a significant recruitment and management-development
decision when it decided to develop managers internally. Gillette's international human
resources department implemented its international-trainee programme, designed to
supply a steady stream of managerial talent from within its own ranks. Trainees are
recruited from all over the world, and when their training is complete they will return to
their home countries to become part of Gillette's global management team.[15]

managing international personnel

Several vital questions arise when attempting to manage in other cultures. How much does
a different culture affect management practices, processes and concepts used in the home
market? Will practices that work well at home be equally effective when customs, values
and lifestyles differ? Transferring management practices to other cultures without
concern for their exportability is no less vulnerable to major error than assuming a product
successful in the home market will be successful in other countries. Management concepts

are influenced by cultural diversity and must be evaluated in terms of local norms. Whether or not any single management practice needs adapting depends on the local culture.[16]

impact of cultural values on management

Because of the unlimited cultural diversity in the values, attitudes and beliefs affecting management practices, only those fundamental premises on which Western management practices are based are presented here for comparison. International managers must analyse normally used management practices to assess their transferability to another culture. The purpose of this section is to heighten the reader's awareness of the need for adaptation of management practices rather than to present a complete discussion of Western culture and management behaviour.

There are many divergent views on the most important ideas on which normative Western business cultural concepts are based. Those that occur most frequently in discussions of cross-cultural evaluations are represented by the following: (1) 'master of destiny' viewpoint; (2) independent enterprise – the instrument for social action; (3) personnel selection on merit; (4) decisions based on objective analysis; (5) wide sharing in decision making; and (6) never-ending quest for improvement.

The *master of destiny* philosophy underlies much of management thought and is a belief held by many in Western culture. Simply stated, people can substantially influence the future; we are in control of our own destinies. This viewpoint also reflects the attitude that although luck may influence an individual's future, on balance, persistence, hard work, a commitment to fulfil expectations and effective use of time give people control of their destinies. In contrast, many cultures have a fatalistic approach to life – individual destiny is determined by a higher order and what happens cannot be controlled. It is very close to uncertainty avoidance in Hofstede's dimension of culture.[17]

Approaches to planning, control, supervision, commitment, motivation, scheduling and deadlines are all influenced by the concept that individuals can control their futures. In cultures with more fatalistic beliefs, these good business practices may be followed but concern for the final outcome is different.

non-Western management styles

The acceptance of the idea that *independent enterprise* is an *instrument for social action* is the fundamental concept of Western corporations. A corporation is recognised as an entity that has rules and continuity of existence, and is a separate and vital social institution. This recognition of the corporation as an entity can result in strong feelings of obligation to serve the company. In fact, the enterprise can take priority over personal preferences and social obligations because it is viewed as an entity that must be protected and developed. This concept ties into the 'master of destiny' concept in that, for a company to work and for individuals to control their destinies, they must feel a strong obligation to fulfil the requirements necessary to the success of the enterprise. Indeed, the company may take precedence over family, friends or other activities, which might detract from what is best for the company.

Consistent with the view that individuals control their own destinies is the belief that *personnel selection is made on merit*. The selection, promotion, motivation or dismissal of personnel by Western managers emphasises the need to select the best-qualified persons for jobs, retaining them as long as their performance meets standards of expectations, and continuing the opportunity for upward mobility as long as those standards are met. Indeed, the belief that anyone can become the corporate president prevails among management personnel within Europe and the United States. Such presumptions lead to the belief that striving and making accomplishments will be rewarded and, conversely, the failure to do so will be penalised. The penalty for poor performance could be dismissal. The reward and penalty scheme is a major basis for motivating Western personnel.[18]

This scientific approach is not necessarily the premise on which foreign executives base decisions. In fact, the infallibility of the judgement of a key executive in many foreign cultures may be more important in the decision process than any other single factor. If one accepts scientific management as a fundamental basis for decision making, then attitudes towards accuracy and promptness in reporting data, availability and openness of data to all levels within the corporation and the willingness to express even unpopular judgements become important characteristics of the business process. Thus, in Western business, great emphasis is placed on the collection and free flow of information to all levels within the organisation and on frankness of expression in the evaluation of business opinions or decisions. In other cultures, placing such high value on factual and rational support for decisions is not as important; the accuracy of data and even the proper reporting of data are not prime prerequisites. Further, existing data frequently are for the eyes of a select few. The frankness of expression and openness in dealing with data characteristic of Western businesses does not fit easily into some cultures.

A number of studies have revealed that more and more companies develop a network of relationships with a number of related companies such as suppliers, distributors, banks and even competitors. In Japan similar networks are called *keiretsu*, in South Korea *chaebol* and in India these are dominated by one family and often called groups such as the Tatas and Birlas.

Japanese *keiretsu*

The **keiretsu**, a unique form of business organisation that links companies together in industrial groups, may be providing Japanese business with a substantial competitive edge over non-*keiretsu* organisations. *Keiretsus* are descended from the **zaibatsus**, huge industrial conglomerates that virtually controlled the Japanese economy before the Second World War. Four of the largest *zaibatsus* – Mitsubishi, Mitsui, Sumitomo and Yasuda – accounted for about a quarter of all Japanese industrial assets.[19] *Zaibatsus* were outlawed after the Second World War and *keiretsus* emerged as a variation. Today there are six major industrial *keiretsu* groups and 11 lesser ones. Together, the sales in these groups are responsible for about 25 per cent of the activities of all Japanese companies, and *keiretsus* account for 78 per cent of the value of all shares on the Tokyo Stock Exchange.[20]

The Mitsubishi Group illustrates the range and complexity of the relationships among its member companies. It is led by Mitsubishi Bank and Mitsubishi Heavy Industries, the country's largest machinery manufacturer, with interests ranging from aircraft to air-conditioning equipment. Altogether, the Mitsubishi Group, with annual sales of €156 billion ($175 billion), involves 160 companies, of which 124 are listed on the Tokyo Stock Exchange. Each is entirely independent, with its own board of directors.

Keiretsus are collections of dozens of major companies spanning several industries and held together by cross-shareholding, old-boy networks, interlocking directorates, long-term business relationships and social and historical links. At the hub of each *keiretsu* is a bank or cash-rich company that provides low-cost, 'patient' (long-term, low-interest) capital. The six top Japanese financial-based *keiretsus* and the number of core industries within each are:

1 Dai-Ichi Kangin – 47 core companies
2 Fuyo – 29 core companies
3 Mitsui Group – 24 core companies
4 Sanwa – 44 core companies
5 Sumitomo – 20 core companies
6 Mitsubishi – 28 core companies

There are three types of *keiretsu*: (1) financial; (2) production; and (3) sales–distribution. The *financial keiretsu* are loose federations of powerful, independent firms clustered

key terms

keiretsu
a host of interfirm relationships and affiliations of varying degrees of formality, in Japan

zaibatsu
a large family-controlled banking and industrial combination, in modern Japan

around a core bank that provides funds to a general trading company and other member firms. They are linked together by cross-holdings of shares, by sales and purchases within the group, and by formal and informal consultations.

The *production*, or *vertical*, *keiretsu* is a web of interlocking, long-term relationships between a big manufacturer and its main suppliers. **Vertical *keiretsus*** are pyramids of companies that serve a single master – a manufacturer that dictates virtually everything; including prices it will pay to hundreds of suppliers who are often prohibited from doing business outside the *keiretsu*. At the pyramid's bottom is a swarm of job shops and family ventures with primitive working conditions and subsistence-level pay and profits.

Production *keiretsus* are typically found in the automotive industry and consist of vertically integrated systems – from the manufacturer to suppliers. Rather than produce the majority of parts in-house as American auto companies do (GM, Chrysler and Ford produce 60 per cent of their parts in-house), *keiretsus* depend on their supplier partners. A large manufacturing firm will have a group of primary subcontractors, which in turn farm out work to thousands of little firms. All subcontractors are integrated into the manufacturer's production process and receive extensive technological, managerial and financial support. Manufacturers and their subcontractors are tied by reciprocal obligation: the subcontractor to high quality and low costs; the manufacturer to providing a steady flow of financial and technical resources. Exhibit 20.5 illustrates the ties that bind Toyota and its suppliers.

The third category, *sales-distribution keiretsus*, consists of vertically integrated manufacturing and distribution companies. The trading company, the centre of a **distribution *keiretsu***, coordinates a complex manufacturing process that involves thousands of small companies that sell through the *keiretsu*'s distribution network.

Exhibit 20.5 Ties that bind: Japanese *keiretsus* and Toyota

Toyota has a typical *keiretsu* family with financial ties to its most important suppliers. Some of those companies, with the percentage of each that Toyota owns, are:	
	%
Lighting – Koito Mfg	19
Rubber – Toyoda Gosel	41.4
Disc brakes – Akebona	13.9
Transmissions, clutches, brakes – Aisin Seiki	22
Clocks – Jeco	34
Electronics – Nippondenso	23.6
Seatbelts, switches – Tokai Rika	28.2
Steel – Aichi Steel Works	21.0
Upholstery material – Kyowa Leather	33.5
Door sashes, mouldings – Shiroki	13.2
Painting – Trinity	30.2
Mufflers – Futaba Industrial	13.2

Source: adapted from 'Japan: All in the Family', *Newsweek*, 10 June 1991, p. 38.

The *keiretsu* controls its own retail system, enabling it to dictate prices, profit margins and exclusive representation through the system. High prices are maintained by establishing customer loyalty and limiting availability of products to *keiretsu*-owned or -controlled retail stores. Retail loyalty is maintained by giving generous rebates, advertising subsidies and a special 'monopoly' rebate to stores that limit shelf space for competing brands.

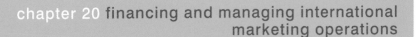
Matsushita, a distribution *keiretsu* of consumer electronics, controls 60 wholesalers that sell to 25 000 *keiretsu* stores. Wholesalers also sell to large consumer electronics stores, department stores and chain stores, all of which are encouraged to limit shelf space of competitive brands in order to receive generous rebates and other benefits; Matsushita pays for loyalty.

Top executives of the group's main bank or trading company characteristically have interlocking directorates and presidents' clubs so that the chief executives of the principal companies can meet. Cross-shareholding is very common among member firms, as is the exchange of cooperative directors.

Strong buyer–supplier relationships exist among group members and at least 30 per cent or as much as 50 per cent of the business of member companies is among group members. Members give preferential treatment to one another as customers and vendors. A *keiretsu* such as Toyota can assemble one of its auto division's cars using parts supplied almost entirely by Toyota-linked suppliers. However, the parent and subsidiary companies both maintain close, cooperative relationships with their major domestic competitors. They buy from and sell to each other, share technology, cooperate on R&D, operate joint ventures, have common banks and shareholders, and coordinate their dealings with foreign competitors.

Korean *chaebols*

The relation structure of *keiretsus* can also be witnessed in other Asian structures. In South Korea, there are industrial conglomerates known as **chaebols**. One structural difference between the *chaebols* and *keiretsu* in Japan is in ownership and control. Member firms in the *keiretsu* are said to own minority equity in each other and are headed by the lead bank or the lead firm in the network. In the case of the *chaebols*, a family and its members own the companies in multi-industries. Furthermore, a circular type of corporate ownership is said to dominate the *chaebol* structure: company A holds shares or equity in company B which holds equity in company C which holds shares in company A.

The Korean entrepreneurial families have been powerful entities since the Second World War, and during the Park regime (1961–73) it is said that the families fostered close relationships with President Park Chung Hee. The presence of *chaebols* has been so overwhelming that the government in the 1980s struggled to contain 'the power of the [*chaebol*] founding families that control much of South Korea's economy'.

A capsule profile of the four largest *chaebols* in South Korea shows the scope of these industry groups. All four can be characterised as conglomerates since ownership is held by the family and control resides therein. Some have their origin in trading activity resembling the *zaibatsu*: however, all are now engaged in many key industries including electronics. A relative newcomer is the Sunkyong Group, founded in 1953. It has grown into a vertically integrated manufacturer of a broad spectrum of products ranging from petroleum to textiles, with annual sales revenue exceeding €18 billion ($20 billion). The backbone of this experiment is said to be the Sunkyong Management System and the Super Excellence movement.

Asian family business structures

Business group formation activities in India are comparable to Japanese *keiretsus* and Korean *chaebols*. In the early part of the twentieth century, the then fledgling entrepreneurial families (such as the Birlas, Mafatlals and Tatas) began to emulate the managing agency system model. In his seminal work, Lokanathan pointed out that the managing agents came to control and manage a large number of similar (industrial) undertakings. Thus, the managing agency system acted as the organisational mechanism that could fill the capital and management needs of the then emerging large-scale industry in India.

Even though the managing agency system was outlawed in 1969, the point to be noted here is that entrepreneurial families such as the Birlas and the Tatas could expand their business activities and stretch their management acumen and competence by means of complicated contractual managing agency agreements.

key term

chaebol
conglomerate of many companies clustered around one parent company

Aditya Birla, in his 52 years of life, had amassed 37 companies into a mammoth enterprise generating €4.5 billion ($5 billion) sales in 16 countries, an empire ranging from textiles to cement, iron and aluminium. When he died suddenly in 1995, the mantle passed to his 29-year-old son.[21]

The Tata Group illustrates how capital allocation to member firms within its network has been based on relational, rather than cost–benefit, considerations. The Tata Group, with its more than €4.5 billion ($5 billion) sales revenue and €230 million ($255 million) operating profits, has a network of autonomous enterprises ranging in business scope from steel and high technology to consumer products and hotels. In its iron and steel sector alone it employs more than 75 000 workers. It is also part of a wide range of international networks and has joint ventures with AT&T, IBM, Mercedes-Benz and Silicon Graphics, as well a number of Singapore-based enterprises.

The Tata Group is continuously rearranging its portfolio of networks. Recently it sold its soap division to Unilever, and has withdrawn from a partnership with PepsiCo. It should be noted, however, that while there are scores of relatively new entrepreneurial firms in India, some of the single-business firms of the 1950s and 1960s have now emerged as cohesive group companies exhibiting somewhat similar organisational characteristics as those of the Tata or Birla Groups. These family businesses are often run by the family members, who are sent abroad for education to Oxford, Cambridge or Harvard. Most Western MNCs have to accept these management styles as they form partnerships with these family firms while entering India. The management style in these companies is quite different from Western management styles. Western companies planning to do business in these countries need to get an insight into these management systems to efficiently control their operations.

summary

Although it is not their formal domain, marketing executives of small and medium-sized enterprises (SMEs) should be acquainted with the requirements, sources, problems and opportunities associated with the financing of international marketing operations. The financial needs of international marketing differ considerably from those of the domestic market. Most specifically, the international marketer must be prepared to invest larger than normal amounts of working capital in inventories, receivables, channel financing and consumer credit. It is possible that market entry may require capital financing of production facilities for purely marketing reasons. International marketers need to be willing to undertake additional financial burdens to operate successfully in foreign countries. Indeed, adequate financing may spell the difference between success and failure in foreign operations. The willingness of marketers to carry adequate inventories in strategic locations and/or to provide consumer or channel credit that they would not be likely to furnish in their home country may be key elements in market development.

Financial risks associated with international marketing are greater than those encountered domestically, but such risk taking is necessary for effective operations. Many companies have been so conservative in their credit and payment terms that they have succeeded in alienating foreign customers. These risks, as well as those of exchange availability or fluctuation and the various political risks, can be accommodated in an effective financial-risk management programme.

The extent to which a company can be successful in its international marketing efforts does not just depend on the nature and suitability of the marketing strategy used. An important factor is the efficient organisation of the firm's international activities. There is no 'right' structure for an international organisation. Companies need to find the right

balance or 'fit' between the company's objectives and strategies, and local environment or customer needs. The structure that allows this 'fit' in an ever-changing international marketing environment is the most suitable.

Important issues to be considered in designing an organisation include the choice of centralisation or decentralisation of decision making, the communication implications of an organisational structure, the position of marketing in an organisation, the coordination of the firm's activities, and the availability of experienced and skilled personnel.

questions

1 Explain why marketers should be concerned with the financial considerations associated with international marketing.
2 Explain how a debt-equity swap works for a company that wants to make an investment in a country.
3 Identify the financial requirements most likely to concern a smaller company when marketing internationally.
4 Discuss the differences between financial requirements for export marketers and for overseas marketing operations.
5 What are the extra problems and risks faced by a smaller international marketer?
6 Review some of the ways financial requirements can be reduced by variations in marketing policies or strategies.
7 What significance do government sources of funds have for marketers?
8 Review the types of financial risk involved in international operations and discuss how each may be reduced.
9 Using exchange data in the *Financial Times* on a date assigned by your instructor, calculate the foreign exchange gain or loss on the following transaction: a British firm borrows 5 million Swiss francs one year before the assigned date, converts those to British pounds and pays 9 per cent interest per annum. How many pounds will be required to repay the loan and interest?
10 Discuss the ways a company can reduce exchange risk.
11 Interview a local company that has a foreign sales operation. Draw an organisation chart for the marketing function and explain why that particular structure was used by that company.
12 The global manager of 2010 will have to meet many new challenges. Draw up a sample resumé for someone (yourself) who could be considered for a top-level executive position in a global firm.
13 What are the characteristics of a *keiretsu* management style?
14 How do *chaebols* differ from *keiretsus*?

further reading

- S. Ghoshal, 'Global Strategy: An Organizing Framework', *Strategic Management Journal*, 1987, 8, pp. 425-40.
- C.S. Katsikeas and R.E. Morgan, 'Differences in Perceptions of Exporting Problems Based on Firm Size and Export Market Experience', *European Journal of Marketing*, 1994, 28(5), pp. 17-35.
- P. Ghauri, C. Lutz and G. Tesfom, 'Using Networks to Solve Export Marketing Problems of Small and Medium Sized Firms from Developing Countries', *European Journal of Marketing*, 2003, 37(5-6), pp. 728-52.

references

1 S. Ghoshal and L. Gratton, 'Integrating the Enterprise', *Sloan Management Review*, 2002, 44(1), pp. 31–8.

2 Michael Selz, 'Small Firms Hit Foreign Obstacles in Billing Overseas', *Wall Street Journal*, 8 December 1992, p. B2.

3 S.T. Cavusgil, S. Yeniyurt and J.D. Towsend, 'The Framework of a Global Company: A Conceptual and Preliminary Validation', *Industrial Marketing Management*, 2004, 33(8), pp. 711–16.

4 'Sources of Export Financing', *Business America*, February 1995, pp. 23–6.

5 Michael Williams, 'How to Secure Funding for Entrepreneurial Projects', *Trade and Culture*, September–October 1994, pp. 52–3.

6 Joseph Ganitsky, 'Investing in Developing Nations Using Debt-equity Swaps', *The International Executive*, May–June 1991, pp. 14–19.

7 Nilly Landau, 'Watch Your Step: How to Put the Best Foot Forward When Managing Your Company's Financial Risks', *International Business*, February 1994, pp. 92–4.

8 'Harsh New Currency World', *International Business*, April 1995, pp. 16–18.

9 'Investment Insurance: Guaranteed Return', *Business China*, 30 May 1994, pp. 2–3.

10 For a complete discussion of financial risk management, see David K. Eiteman and Arthur I. Stonehill, *Multinational Business Finance*, 8th edn (Reading, MA: Addison-Wesley, 1998).

11 Christopher Bartlett, Sumantra Ghoshal and Julian Birkinshaw, *Transnational Management: Text, Cases and Readings in Cross-Border Management*, 4th edn (Boston: McGraw-Hill, 2004).

12 M. Harvey, M.M. Novicevic and T. Kiessling, 'Hypercompetition and the Future of Global Management in the Twenty-first Century', *Thunderbird International Business Review*, 2001, 43(5), pp. 599–616.

13 H.V. Perlmutter, 'The Tortuous Evolution of the Multinational Corporation', *Columbia Journal of World Business*, January–February 1969, p. 12; and Pervez Ghauri, 'New Structures in MNCs Based in Small Countries', *European Management Journal*, vol. 10, no. 3, 1992, pp. 357–64.

14 Lori Ioannou, 'Stateless Executives', *International Business*, February 1995, pp. 48–52.

15 Jennifer J. Laabs, 'How Gillette Grooms Global Talent', *Personnel Journal*, August 1993, pp. 65–75.

16 For a discussion of different management styles, see Maud Tixier, 'Management Styles across Western European Cultures', *The International Executive*, July–August 1994, pp. 377–91.

17 Geert Hofstede, *Culture and Organizations: Software of the Mind* (London: McGraw-Hill, 1991).

18 M.B. Sarkar, S.T. Cavusgil and P.S. Aulakh, 'International Expansion of Telecommunication Carriers: The Influence of Market Structure, Network Characteristics and Entry Imperfections', *Journal of International Business Studies*, 1999, 30(2), pp. 361–82.

19 John Child, 'Management in China', in Peter Buckley and Pervez Ghauri (eds), *Multinationals and Emerging Markets* (London: International Thompson Business Press, 1999).

20 J.R. Sparks and M. Miyake, 'Knowledge Transfer and Human Resource Development Practices: Japanese Firms in Brazil and Mexico', *International Business Review*, 2000, 9(5) pp. 599–612.

21 Pervez Ghauri and Benjamin Prasad, 'A Network Approach to Probing Asia's Interfirm Linkages', in Benjamin Prasad (ed.), *Advances in International Comparative Management* (Greenwich, NY: JAI Press, 1995), pp. 63–77.

section 6
supplementary resources

The Country Notebook: a Guide for Developing a
Marketing Plan

Case Studies

The Country Notebook: a Guide for Developing a Marketing Plan

The Country Notebook Outline

A number of books and articles have described strategic marketing planning at corporate or business unit level.[1] Here we are mainly concerned about a marketing plan for a foreign market or a marketing plan for a particular product in one particular market. The guidelines provided here can be used for different markets; however, depending on the market and the product, the emphasis on different parts of the framework may change.[2]

The first stage in the planning process is a preliminary country analysis. The marketer needs basic information to: (1) evaluate a country market's potential, (2) identify problems that would eliminate a country from further consideration, (3) identify aspects of the country's environment that need further study, (4) evaluate the components of the marketing mix for possible adaptation and (5) develop a strategic marketing plan. One further use of the information collected in the preliminary analysis is as a basis for a country notebook.

Many companies, large and small, have a *country notebook* for each country in which they do business. The country notebook contains information a marketer should be aware of when making decisions involving a specific country market. As new information is collected, the country notebook is continually updated by the country or product manager. Whenever a marketing decision is made involving a country, the country notebook is the first database consulted. New product introductions, changes in advertising programmes, and other marketing programme decisions begin with the country notebook. It also serves as a quick introduction for new personnel assuming responsibility for a country market.[3]

This section presents four separate sets of guidelines for collection and analysis of market data and preparation of a country notebook: (1) guideline for cultural analysis; (2) guideline for economic analysis; (3) guideline for market audit and competitive analysis; (4) guideline for a preliminary marketing plan. These guidelines suggest the kinds of information a marketer can gather to enhance planning.

The points in each of the sets of guidelines are general. They are designed to provide direction to areas to explore for relevant data. In each set, specific points must be adapted to reflect a company's products. The decision as to the appropriateness of specific data and the depth of coverage depends on company objectives, product characteristics, and the country market. Some points in the guidelines are unimportant for some countries and/or some products and should be ignored. Preceding chapters of this book provide specific content suggestions for the topics in each guideline.

Cultural analysis

The data suggested in the cultural analysis include information that helps the marketer make market planning decisions. However, its application extends beyond product/market analysis to an important source of information for someone interested in understanding business customs and other important cultural features of the country.

The information in this analysis must be more than a collection of facts. Whoever is responsible for the preparation of this material should attempt to interpret the meaning of cultural information. That is, how does the information help in understanding the effect on the market? For example, the fact that almost all the populations of Italy and Ireland are Catholic is an interesting statistic but not nearly as useful as understanding the effect of Catholicism on values, beliefs and other aspects of market behaviour. Even though both countries are predominantly Catholic, the influence of their individual and unique interpretation and practice of Catholicism can result in important differences in market behaviour.

Guidelines

I Introduction.
   Include short profiles of the company, the product to be exported, and the country with which you wish to trade.
II Brief discussion of the country's relevant history.
III Geographical setting.
   A Location.
   B Climate.
   C Topography.
IV Social institutions.
   A Family.
      1 The nuclear family.
      2 The extended family.
      3 Female/male roles (are they changing or static?).
   B Education.
      1 The role of education in society.
      2 Literacy rates.
   C Political system.
      1 Political structure.
      2 Stability of government.
      3 Special taxes.
      4 Role of local government.
   D Legal system.
      1 Organisation of the judiciary system.
      2 Code, common, socialist or Islamic-law country?
      3 Participation in patents, trademarks and other conventions.
   E Social organisations.
      1 Group behaviour.
      2 Social classes.
      3 Race, ethnicity and subcultures.
   F Business customs and practices.
V Religion and aesthetics.

A Religion and other belief systems.
 1 Which religions are prominent?
 2 Membership of each religion.
B Aesthetics.
 1 Visual arts (fine arts, plastics, graphics, public colours, etc.).
 2 Importance given to aesthetics.
VI Living conditions.
 A Diet and nutrition.
  1 Typical meals.
 B Housing.
  1 Types of housing available.
  2 Do most people own or rent?
  3 Do most people live in one-family dwellings or with other families?
 C Clothing.
  1 National dress.
  2 Types of clothing worn at work.
 D Recreation, sports, and other leisure activities.
 E Social security.
 F Healthcare.
VII Language.
 A Official language(s).
 B Spoken versus written language(s).
VIII Executive summary.

After completing all of the other sections, prepare a two-page (maximum length) summary of the major points and place it at the front of the report. The purpose of an executive summary is to give the reader a brief glimpse of the critical points of your report. Those aspects of the culture a reader should know in order to do business in the country but would not be expected to know or would find different based on his or her SRC should be included in this summary.

IX Sources of information.
X Appendices.

Economic analysis

The reader may find the data collected for the economic analysis guidelines are more straightforward than for the cultural analysis guidelines. There are two broad categories of information in these guidelines: general economic data that serve as a basis for an evaluation of the economic soundness of a country and information on channels of distribution and media availability. As mentioned earlier, these guidelines focus only on broad categories of data and must be adapted to particular company/product needs.

Guidelines

I Introduction.
II Population.

A Total.
 1 Growth rates.
B Distribution of population.
 1 Age.
 2 Sex.
 3 Geographic areas (urban, suburban and rural density and concentration).
 4 Ethnic groups.
III Economic statistics and activity.
 A Gross national product (GNP or GDP).
  1 Total.
  2 Rate of growth (real GNP or GDP).
 B Personal income per capita.
 C Average family income.
 D Distribution of wealth.
  1 Income classes.
  2 Proportion of the population in each class.
  3 Is the distribution distorted?
 E Minerals and resources.
 F Surface transportation.
  1 Modes.
  2 Availability.
 G Communication systems.
  1 Types.
  2 Availability.
 H Working conditions.
  1 Employer-employee relations.
  2 Employee participation.
  3 Salaries and benefits.
 I Principal industries.
  1 What proportion of the GNP does each industry contribute?
  2 Ratio of private to publicly owned industries.
 J Foreign investment.
  1 Opportunities?
  2 Which industries?
 K International trade statistics.
  1 Major exports.
   a Dollar/euro value.
   b Trends.
  2 Major imports.
   a Dollar/euro value.
   b Trends.
  3 Balance-of-payments situation.
   a Surplus or deficit?
   b Recent trends.
  4 Exchange rates.
   a Single or multiple exchange rates?
   b Current rate of exchange.
 L Trade restrictions.
  1 Embargoes.
  2 Quotas.
  3 Import taxes.

4 Tariffs.

5 Licensing.

6 Customs duties.

M Extent of economic activity not included in cash income activities.

  1 Countertrades.

    a Products generally offered for counter-trading.

    b Types of countertrades requested (i.e. barter, counterpurchase, etc.).

  2 Foreign aid received (relevance for the product in question).

N Labour force.

  1 Size.

  2 Unemployment rates.

O Inflation rates.

IV Developments in science and technology.

A Current technology available (computers, machinery, tools, etc.).

B Technological skills of the labour force and general population.

V Channels of distribution (macroanalysis).

This section reports data on all channel middlemen available within the market. Later, you will select a specific channel as part of your distribution strategy relevant to your product.

A Middlemen.

  1 Retailers.

    a Number of retailers.

    b Typical size of retail outlets.

    c Customary mark-up for various classes of goods.

    d Methods of operation (cash/credit).

    e Scale of operation (large/small).

    f Role of chain stores, department stores and speciality shops.

  2 Wholesale middlemen.

    a Number and size.

    b Customary mark-up for various classes of goods.

    c Method of operation (cash/credit).

  3 Import/export agents.

  4 Warehousing.

  5 Penetration of urban and rural markets.

VI Media.

This section reports data on all media available within the country/market. Later, you will select specific media as part of the promotional mix/strategy relevant for your product.

A Availability of media.

B Costs.

  1 Television.

  2 Radio.

  3 Print.

  4 Other media (cinema, outdoor, etc.).

C Agency assistance.

D Coverage of various media.

E Percentage of population reached by each of the media.

VII Executive summary.

After completing the research for this report, prepare a two-page (maximum) summary of the major economic points and place it at the front of the report.

VIII Sources of information.

IX Appendices.

Market audit and competitive market analysis

Of the guidelines presented, this set is the most product- or brand-specific. Information in the other sets of guidelines is general in nature, focusing on product categories, whereas data in this set are brand-specific and are used to determine competitive market conditions and market potential.

Two different components of the planning process are reflected in these guidelines. Information in Parts I and II, Cultural Analysis and Economic Analysis, serve as the basis for an evaluation of the product/brand in a specific country market. Information in these guidelines provides an estimate of market potential and an evaluation of the strengths and weaknesses of competitive marketing efforts. The data generated in this step are used to determine the extent of adaptation of the company's marketing mix necessary for successful market entry and to develop the final step – the action plan.

The detailed information needed to complete these guidelines is not necessarily available without conducting a thorough marketing research investigation. Thus, another purpose of this part of the country notebook is to identify the correct questions to ask in a formal market study.

Guidelines

I Introduction.

II The product.

A Evaluate the product as an innovation as it is perceived by the intended market.

  1 Relative advantage.

  2 Compatibility.

  3 Complexity.

B Major problems and resistances to product acceptance based on the preceding evaluation. (See Chapter 13 for a discussion of this topic.)

III The market.
  A Describe the market(s) in which the product is to be sold.
    1 Geographical region(s).
    2 Forms of transportation and communication available in that/those region(s).
    3 Consumer buying habits.
      a Product-use patterns.
      b Product feature preferences.
      c Shopping habits.
    4 Distribution of the product.
      a Typical retail outlets.
      b Product sales by other middlemen.
    5 Advertising and promotion.
      a Advertising media usually used to reach your target market(s).
      b Sales promotions customarily used (sampling, coupons, etc.).
    6 Pricing strategy.
      a Customary mark-ups.
      b Types of discount available.
  B Compare and contrast your product and the competition's product(s).
    1 Competitors' product(s).
      a Brand name.
      b Features.
      c Package.
    2 Competitors' prices.
    3 Competitors' promotion and advertising methods.
    4 Competitors' distribution channels.
  C Market size.
    1 Estimate industry sales for the planning year.
    2 Estimate sales for your company for the planning year.
  D Government participation in the marketplace.
    1 Agencies that can help you.
    2 Regulations you must follow.
IV Executive summary.
  Based on your analysis of the market, briefly summarise (two pages maximum) the major problems and opportunities requiring attention in you marketing mix and place the summary at the front of the report.
V Sources of information.
VI Appendices.

Preliminary marketing plan

Information gathered in the previous sets of guidelines serves as the basis for developing a marketing plan for your product/brand in a target market. How the problems and opportunities that surfaced in the preceding steps are overcome and/or exploited to produce maximum sales/profits are presented here. The action plan reflects, in your judgement, the most effective means of marketing your product in a country market. Budgets, expected profits and/or losses, and additional resources necessary to implement the proposed plan are also presented.

Guidelines
I The marketing plan.
  A Marketing objectives.
    1 Target market(s) (specific description of the market segment).
    2 Expected sales 20–.
    3 Profit expectations 20–.
    4 Market penetration and coverage.
  B Product adaptation, or modification – using the product component model as your guide, indicate how your product can be adapted for the market (see Chapter 13).
    1 Core component.
    2 Packaging component.
    3 Support services component.
  C Promotion mix.
    1 Advertising.
      a Objectives.
      b Media mix.
      c Message.
    2 Sales promotions.
      a Objectives.
      b Coupons.
      c Premiums.
    3 Personal selling.
    4 Other promotional methods.
  D Distribution: from origin to destination.
    1 Port selection.
      a Origin port.
      b Destination port.
    2 Mode selection: advantages/disadvantages of each mode.
      a Railroads.
      b Air carriers.
      c Ocean carriers.
      d Motor carriers.
    3 Packing.
      a Marking and labelling regulations.
      b Containerisation.
    4 Documentation required.
    5 Insurance claims.
    6 Freight forwarder.
      If your company does not have a transportation or traffic management department, then consider using a freight forwarder. There are distinct advantages and disadvantages to hiring one.

E   Channels of distribution (micro analysis).
    This section presents details about the specific types of distribution in your marketing plan.
    1   Retailers.
        a   Type and number of retail stores.
        b   Retail mark-ups for products in each type of retail store.
        c   Methods of operation for each type (cash/credit).
        d   Scale of operation for each type (small/large).
    2   Wholesale middlemen.
        a   Type and number of wholesale middlemen.
        b   Mark-up for class of products by each type.
        c   Methods of operation for each type (cash/credit).
        d   Scale of operation (small/large).
    3   Import/export agents.
    4   Warehousing.
        a   Type.
        b   Location.
F   Price determination.
    1   Cost of the shipment of goods.
    2   Transportation costs.
    3   Handling expenses.
    4   Insurance costs.
    5   Customs duties.
    6   Import taxes and value added tax.
    7   Wholesale and retail mark-ups and discounts.
    8   Company's gross margins.
    9   Retail price.
G   Terms of sale.
    1   Ex works, fob, fas, c&f, cif.
H   Methods of payment.
    1   Cash in advance.
    2   Letters of credit.
II Pro forma financial statements and budgets.
A   Marketing budget.
    1   Selling expense.
    2   Advertising/promotion expense.
    3   Distribution expense.
    4   Product cost.
    5   Other costs.
B   Pro forma annual profit and loss statement (first year and fifth year).
III Resource requirements.
A   Finances.
B   Personnel.
C   Production capacity.
IV Executive summary.
    After completing the research for this report, prepare a summary (two pages maximum) of the major points of your successful marketing plan and place it at the front of the report.

V   Sources of information.
VI Appendices.
    The intricacies of international operations and the complexity of the environment within which the international marketer must operate create an extraordinary demand for information. When operating in foreign markets, the need for thorough information as a substitute for uninformed opinion is equally as important as it is in domestic marketing. This information should be systematically collected and analysed before it is presented as a base for decision making.[4]

Summary

Market-oriented firms build strategic market plans around company objectives, markets and the competitive environment. Planning for marketing can be complicated even for one country, but when a company is doing business internationally the problems are multiplied. Company objectives may vary from market to market, from product to product and from time to time; the structure of international markets also changes periodically and from country to country, and the competitive, governmental and economic parameters affecting market planning are in a constant state of flux. These variations require international marketing executives to be specially flexible and creative in their approach to strategic marketing planning.

References

1 See, for example, David Aaker, *Strategic Marketing Management*, 4th edn (New York: Wiley, 1995).

2 For going into a new market see, for example, Franklin Root, *Entry Strategies for International Markets* (Washington, DC: Heath and Company, 1994).

3 Tamer Cavusgil, Pervez Ghauri and Milind Aganwal, *Doing Business in Emerging Markets: Entry and Negotiation Strategies* (Thousand Oaks: Sage, 2002).

4 Pervez Ghauri and Kjell Grønhaug, *Research Methods in Business Studies: A Practical Guide* (Hemel Hempstead: FT-Prentice Hall, 2005).

Case Studies

section 1
case studies

cases

case 1.1 Starbucks: Going Global Fast

The Starbucks coffee shop on Sixth Avenue and Pine Street in downtown Seattle sits serene and orderly, as unremarkable as any other in the chain bought 15 years ago by entrepreneur Howard Schultz. A little less than three years ago, however, the quiet store-front made front pages around the world. During the World Trade Organization talks in November, 1999, protesters flooded Seattle's streets, and among their targets was Starbucks, a symbol, to them, of free-market capitalism run amok, another multinational out to blanket the earth. Amid the crowds of protesters and riot police were black-masked anarchists who trashed the store, leaving its windows smashed and its tasteful green-and-white decor smelling of tear gas instead of espresso. Says an angry Schultz: 'It's hurtful. I think people are ill-informed. It's very difficult to protest against a can of Coke, a bottle of Pepsi, or a can of Folgers. Starbucks is both this ubiquitous brand and a place where you can go and break a window. You can't break a can of Coke.'

The store was quickly repaired, and the protesters have scattered to other cities. Yet cup by cup, Starbucks really is caffeinating the world, its green-and-white emblem beckoning to consumers on three continents. In 1999, Starbucks Corp. had 281 stores abroad. Today, it has about 1200 – and it's still in the early stages of a plan to colonise the globe. If the protesters were wrong in their tactics, they weren't wrong about Starbucks' ambitions. They were just early.

The story of how Schultz & Co. transformed a pedestrian commodity into an upscale consumer accessory has a fairy-tale quality. Starbucks has grown from 17 coffee shops in Seattle 15 years ago to 5689 outlets in 28 countries. Sales have climbed an average of 20 per cent annually since the company went public 10 years ago, to $2.6 billion in 2001, while profits bounded ahead an average of 30 per cent per year, hitting $181.2 million last year. And

This Starbucks store opened in 2000, in the Forbidden City area of Beijing

the momentum continues. In the first three quarters of this fiscal year, sales climbed 24 per cent, year to year, to $2.4 billion, while profits, excluding onetime charges and capital gains, rose 25 per cent, to $159.5 million.

Moreover, the Starbucks name and image connect with millions of consumers around the globe. It was one of the fastest-growing brands in a *Business Week* survey of the top 100 global brands published 5 August. At a time when one corporate star after another has crashed to earth, brought down by revelations of earnings misstatements, executive greed, or worse, Starbucks hasn't faltered. The company confidently predicts up to 25 per cent annual sales and earnings growth this year. On Wall Street, Starbucks is the last great growth story. Its stock, including four splits, has soared more than 2200 per cent over the past decade, surpassing Wal-Mart, General Electric, PepsiCo, Coca-Cola, Microsoft and IBM in total return. Now

at $21, it is hovering near its all-time high of $23 in July, before the overall market drop.

And after a slowdown last fall and winter, when consumers seemed to draw inward after September 11, Starbucks is rocketing ahead once again. Sales in stores open at least 13 months grew by 6 per cent in the 43 weeks through 28 July, and the company predicts monthly same-store sales gains as high as 7 per cent through the end of this fiscal year. That's below the 9 per cent growth rate in 2000, but investors seem encouraged. 'We're going to see a lot more growth,' says Jerome A. Castellini, president of Chicago-based CastleArk Management, which controls about 300 000 Starbucks shares. 'The stock is on a run.'

But how long can that run last?' Already, Schultz's team is hard-pressed to grind out new profits in a home market that is quickly becoming saturated. Amazingly, with 4247 stores scattered across the United States and Canada, there are still eight states in the United States with no Starbucks stores. Frappuccino-free cities include Butte, Mont., and Fargo, ND. But big cities, affluent suburbs and shopping malls are full to the brim. In coffee-crazed Seattle, there is a Starbucks outlet for every 9400 people, and the company considers that the upper limit of coffee-shop saturation. In Manhattan's 24 square miles, Starbucks has 124 cafes, with four more on the way this year. That's one for every 12 000 people – meaning that there could be room for even more stores. Given such concentration, it is likely to take annual same-store sales increases of 10 per cent or more if the company is going to match its historic overall sales growth. That, as they might say at Starbucks, is a tall order to fill.

Indeed, the crowding of so many stores so close together has become a national joke, eliciting quips such as this headline in *The Onion*, a satirical publication: 'A New Starbucks Opens in Restroom of Existing Starbucks.' And even the company admits that while its practice of blanketing an area with stores helps achieve market dominance, it can cut sales at existing outlets. 'We probably self-cannibalise our stores at a rate of 30 per cent a year,' Schultz says. Adds Lehman Brothers, Inc. analyst Mitchell Speiser: 'Starbucks is at a defining point in its growth. It's reaching a level that makes it harder and harder to grow, just due to the law of large numbers.'

To duplicate the staggering returns of its first decade. Starbucks has no choice but to export its concept aggressively. Indeed, some analysts give Starbucks only two years at most before it saturates the US market. The chain now operates 1200 international outlets, from Beijing to Bristol. That leaves plenty of room to grow. Indeed, about 400 of its planned 1200 new stores this year will be built overseas, representing a 35 per cent increase in its foreign base. Starbucks expects to double the number of its stores worldwide, to 10 000 in three years. During the past 12 months, the chain has opened stores in Vienna, Zurich, Madrid, Berlin, and even in far-off Jakarta. Athens comes next. And within the next year, Starbucks plans to move into Mexico and Puerto Rico. But global expansion poses huge risks for Starbucks. For one thing, it makes less money on each overseas store because most of them are operated with local partners. While that makes it easier to start up on foreign turf, it reduces the company's share of the profits to only 20–50 per cent.

Unpredictable market

Moreover, Starbucks must cope with some predictable challenges of becoming a mature company in the United States. After riding the wave of successful baby boomers through the 90s, the company faces an ominously hostile reception from its future consumers, the twenty- or thirty-somethings of Generation X. Not only are the activists among them turned off by the power and image of the well-known brand, but many others say that Starbucks' latte-sipping sophisticates and piped-in Kenny G music are a real turn-off. They don't feel wanted in a place that sells designer coffee at $3 a cup.

Even the thirst of loyalists for high-price coffee can't be taken for granted. Starbucks' growth over the past decade coincided with a remarkable surge in the economy. Consumer spending has continued strong in the downturn, but if that changes, those $3 lattes might be an easy place for people on a budget to cut back. Starbucks executives insist that won't happen, pointing out that even in the weeks following the terrorist attacks, same-store comparisons stayed positive while those of other retailers skidded.

Starbucks also faces slumping morale and employee burnout among its store managers and its once-cheery army of baristas. Stock options for part-timers in the restaurant business was a Starbucks innovation that once commanded awe and respect from its employees. But now, though employees are still paid better than comparable workers elsewhere – about $7 per hour – many regard the job as just another fast-food gig. Dissatisfaction over odd hours and low pay is affecting the quality of the normally sterling service and even the coffee itself, say some customers and employees. Frustrated store managers among the company's roughly 470 California stores sued Starbucks in 2001 for allegedly refusing to pay legally mandated overtime. Starbucks settled the suite for $18 million this past April, shaving $0.03 per share off an otherwise strong second quarter. However, the heart of the complaint – feeling over-worked and underappreciated – doesn't seem to be going away.

To be sure, Starbucks has a lot going for it as it confronts the challenge of maintaining its growth. Nearly free of debt, it fuels expansion with internal cash flow. And Starbucks can maintain a tight grip on its image because

stores are company-owned: there are no franchisees to get sloppy about running things. By relying on mystique and word-of-mouth, whether here or overseas, the company saves a bundle on marketing costs. Starbucks spends just $30 million annually on advertising, or roughly 1 per cent of revenues, usually just for new flavours of coffee drinks in the summer and product launches, such as its new in-store web service. Most consumer companies its size shell out upwards of $300 million per year. Moreover, unlike a McDonald's or a Gap Inc., two other retailers that rapidly grew in the United States, Starbucks has no nationwide competitor.

Starbucks also has a well-seasoned management team. Schultz, 49, stepped down as chief executive in 2000 to become chairman and chief global strategist. Orin Smith, 60, the company's number-cruncher, is now CEO and in charge of day-to-day operations. The head of North American operations is Howard Behar, 57, a retailing expert who returned last September, two years after retiring. The management trio is known as H2O, for Howard, Howard, and Orin

Schultz remains the heart and soul of the operation. Raised in a Brooklyn public housing project, he found his way to Starbucks, a tiny chain of Seattle coffee shops, as a marketing executive in the early 80s. The name came about when the original owners looked to Seattle history for inspiration and chose the moniker of an old mining camp: Starbo. Further refinement led to Starbucks, after the first mate in the novel *Moby Dick*, which they felt evoked the seafaring romance of the early coffee traders (hence the mermaid logo). Schultz got the idea for the modern Starbucks format while visiting a Milan coffee bar. He bought out his bosses in 1987 and began expanding. Today, Schultz has a net worth of about $700 million, including $400 million of company stock.

Starbucks has come light-years from those humble beginnings, but Schultz and his team still think there's room to grow in the United States – even in communities where the chain already has dozens of stores. Clustering stores increases total revenue and market share, Smith argues, even when individual stores poach on each other's sales. The strategy works, he says, because of Starbucks' size. It is large enough to absorb losses at existing stores as new ones open up, and soon overall sales grow beyond what they would have with just one store. Meanwhile, it's cheaper to deliver to and manage stores located close together. And by clustering, Starbucks can quickly dominate a local market.

The company is still capable of designing and opening a store in 16 weeks or less and recouping the initial investment in three years. The stores may be oases of tranquillity, but management's expansion tactics are something else. Take what critics call its 'predatory real estate' strategy – paying more than market-rate rents to keep competitors out of a location. David C. Schomer, owner of Espresso Vivace in Seattle's hip Capitol Hill neighbourhood, says Starbucks approached his landlord and offered to pay nearly double the rate to put a coffee shop in the same building.

The landlord stuck with Schomer, who says: 'It's a little disconcerting to know that someone is willing to pay twice the going rate.' Another time, Starbucks and Tully's Coffee Corp., a Seattle-based coffee chain, were competing for a space in the city. Starbucks got the lease but vacated the premises before the term was up. Still, rather than let Tully's get the space, Starbucks decided to pay the rent on the empty store so its competitor could not move in. Schultz makes no apologies for the hardball tactics, 'The real estate business in America is a very, very tough game,' he says. 'It's not for the faint of heart.'

Still, the company's strategy could backfire. Not only will neighbourhood activists and local businesses increasingly resent the tactics, but customers could also grow annoyed over having fewer choices. Moreover, analysts contend that Starbucks can maintain about 15 per cent square-footage growth in the United States – equivalent to 550 new stores – for only about two more years. After that, it will have to depend on overseas growth to maintain annual 20 per cent revenue growth.

Beyond coffee

Starbucks was hoping to make up much of that growth with more sales of food and other non-coffee items, but has stumbled somewhat. In the late 90s, Schultz thought that offering $8 sandwiches, desserts, and CDs in his stores and selling packaged coffee in supermarkets would significantly boost sales. The speciality business now accounts for about 16 per cent of sales, but growth has been less than expected. A healthy 19 per cent this year, it's still far below the 38 per cent growth rate of fiscal 2000. That suggests that while coffee can command high prices in a slump, food – at least at Starbucks – cannot. One of Behar's most important goals is to improve that record. For instance, the company now has a test programme of serving hot breakfasts in 20 Seattle stores and may move to expand supermarket sales of whole beans.

What's more important for the bottom line, though, is that Starbucks has proven to be highly innovative in the way it sells its main course: coffee. In 800 locations it has installed automatic espresso machines to speed up service. And in November, it began offering prepaid Starbucks cards, priced from $5 to $500, which clerks swipe through a reader to deduct a sale. That, says the company, cuts transaction times in half. Starbucks has sold $70 million-worth of the cards.

In early August, Starbucks launched Starbucks Express, its boldest experiment yet, which blends java, web technology, and faster service. At about 60 stores in

the Denver area, customers can pre-order and prepay for beverages and pastries via phone or on the Starbucks Express website. They just make the call or click the mouse before arriving at the store, and their beverage will be waiting – with their name printed on the cup. The company will decide in January on a national launch.

And Starbucks is bent on even more fundamental store changes. On 21 August, it announced expansion of a high-speed wireless Internet service to about 1200 Starbucks locations in North America and Europe. Partners in the project – which Starbucks calls the world's largest Wi-Fi network – include Mobile International, a wireless subsidiary of Deutsche Telekom, and Hewlett-Packard. Customers sit in a store and check e-mail, surf the web, or download multimedia presentations without looking for connections or tripping over cords. They start with 24 hours of free wireless broadband before choosing from a variety of monthly subscription plans.

Starbucks executives hope such innovations will help surmount their toughest challenge in the home market: attracting the next generation of customers. Younger coffee drinkers already feel uncomfortable in the stores. The company knows that because it once had a group of twentysomethings hypnotised for a market study. When their defences were down, out came the bad news: 'They either can't afford to buy coffee at Starbucks, or the only peers they see are those working behind the counter,' says Mark Barden, who conducted the research for the Hal Riney & Partners ad agency (now part of Publicis Worldwide) in San Francisco. One of the recurring themes the hypnosis brought out was a sense that 'people like me aren't welcome here except to serve the yuppies,' he says. Then there are those who just find the whole Starbucks scene a bit pretentious. Katie Kelleher, 22, a Chicago para-legal, is put off by Starbucks' Italian terminology of grande and venti for coffee sizes. She goes to Dunkin' Donuts, saying: 'Small, medium and large is fine for me.'

Happy staff

As it expands, Starbucks faces another big risk: that of becoming a far less special place for its employees. For a company modelled around enthusiastic service, that could have dire consequences for both image and sales. During its growth spurt of the mid- to late 1990s, Starbucks had the lowest employee turnover rate of any restaurant or fast-food company, thanks largely to its then unheard-of policy of giving health insurance and modest stock options to part-timers making barely more than minimum wage.

Such perks are no longer enough to keep all the workers happy. Starbucks' pay doesn't come close to matching the workload it requires, complain some staff. Says Carrie Shay, a former store manager in West Hollywood, California:

'If I were making a decent living, I'd still be there.' Shay, one of the plaintiffs in the suit against the company, says she earned $32 000 a year to run a store with 10 to 15 part-time employees. She hired employees, managed their schedules, and monitored the store's weekly profit-and-loss statement. But she was also expected to put in significant time behind the counter and had to sign an affidavit pledging to work up to 20 hours of overtime a week without extra pay – a requirement the company has dropped since the settlement. Smith says that Starbucks offers better pay, benefits and training than comparable companies, while it encourages promotion from within.

For sure, employee discontent is far from the image Starbucks wants to project of relaxed workers cheerfully making cappuccinos. But perhaps it is inevitable. The business model calls for lots of low-wage workers. And the more people who are hired as Starbucks expands, the less they are apt to feel connected to the original mission of high service – bantering with customers and treating them like family. Robert J. Thompson, a professor of popular culture at Syracuse University, says of Starbucks: 'It's turning out to be one of the great twenty-first-century American success stories – complete with all the ambiguities.'

Overseas, though, the whole Starbucks package seems new and, to many young people, still very cool. In Vienna, where Starbucks had a gala opening for its first Austrian store last December, Helmut Spudich, a business editor for the paper *Der Standard,* predicted that Starbucks would attract a younger crowd than the established cafés. 'The coffeehouses in Vienna are nice, but they are old. Starbucks is considered hip,' he says.

But if Starbucks can count on its youth appeal to win a welcome in new markets, such enthusiasm cannot be relied upon indefinitely. In Japan, the company beat even its own bullish expectations, growing to 368 stores after opening its first in Tokyo in 1996. Affluent young Japanese women like Anna Kato, a 22-year-old Toyota Motor Corp. worker, loved the place. 'I don't care if it costs more, as long as it tastes sweet,' she says, sitting in the world's busiest Starbucks, in Tokyo's Shibuya district. Yet same-store sales growth has fallen in the past 10 months in Japan, Starbucks' top foreign market, as rivals offer similar fare. Add to that the depressed economy, and Starbucks Japan seems to be losing steam. Although it forecasts a 30 per cent gain in net profit, to $8 million, for the year started in April, on record sales of $516 million, same-store sales are down 14 per cent for the year ended in June. Meanwhile in England, Starbucks' second-biggest overseas market, with 310 stores, imitators are popping up left and right to steal market share.

Entering other big markets may be tougher yet. The French seem to be ready for Starbucks' sweeter taste, says

Philippe Bloch, cofounder of Columbus Cafe, a Starbucks-like chain. But he wonders if the company can profitably cope with France's arcane regulations and generous labour benefits. And in Italy, the epicentre of European coffee culture, the notion that the locals will abandon their own 200 000 coffee bars en masse for Starbucks strikes many as ludicrous. For one, Italian coffee bars prosper by serving food as well as coffee, an area where Starbucks still struggles. Also, Italian coffee is cheaper than US java and, say Italian purists, much better. Americans pay about $1.50 for an espresso. In northern Italy, the price is 67 cents; in the south, just 55 cents. Schultz insists that Starbucks will eventually come to Italy. It'll have a lot to prove when it does. Carlo Petrini, founder of the anti-globalisation movement Slow Food, sniffs that Starbucks' 'substances served in Styrofoam' won't cut it. The cups are paper, of course. But the scepticism is real.

As Starbucks spreads out, Schultz will have to be increasingly sensitive to those cultural challenges. In December, for instance, he flew to Israel to meet with Foreign Secretary Shimon Peres and other Israeli officials to discuss the Middle East crisis. He won't divulge the nature of his discussions. But subsequently, at a Seattle synagogue, Schultz let the Palestinians have it. With Starbucks outlets already in Kuwait, Lebanon, Oman, Qatar and Saudi Arabia, he created a mild uproar among Palestinian supporters. Schultz quickly backpedalled, saying that his words were taken out of context and asserting that he is 'pro-peace' for both sides.

There are plenty more minefields ahead. So far, the Seattle coffee company has compiled an envious record of growth. But the giddy buzz of that initial expansion is wearing off. Now, Starbucks is waking up to the grand challenges faced by any corporation bent on becoming a global powerhouse.

Profit at Starbucks Coffee Japan fell 70 per cent in the first nine months of the year because of growing competition from rival coffee chains. Sales at stores open more than one year fell 16 per cent. The firm expects a loss for the full year.

Questions

As a guide use Exhibit 1.3 and its description in Chapter 1, and do the following.

1 Identify the controllable and uncontrollable elements that Starbucks has encountered in entering global markets.
2 What are the major sources of risk facing the company? Discuss potential solutions.
3 Critique Starbucks' overall corporate strategy.
4 How might Starbucks improve profitability in Japan?

Visit www.starbucks.com for more information.

Source: Stanley Holmes, Drake Bennett, Kate Carlisle and Chester Dawson, 'Planet Starbucks: To Keep Up the Growth it Must Go Global Quickly', *Business Week*, 9 December 2002, pp. 100–10. Reprinted by permission of *Business Week*; and Ken Belson, 'Japan: Starbucks Profit Falls', *New York Times*, 20 February 2003, p. 1.

case 1.2 Nestlé: the Infant Formula Controversy

Nestlé Alimentana of Vevey, Switzerland, one of the world's largest food-processing companies, with world-wide sales of over $8 billion, has been the subject of an international boycott. For over 20 years, beginning with a Pan American Health Organization allegation, Nestlé has been directly or indirectly charged with involvement in the death of Third World infants. The charges revolve around the sale of infant feeding formula, which allegedly is the cause of mass deaths of babies in the Third World.

In 1974 a British journalist published a report which suggested that powdered-formula manufacturers contributed to the death of Third World infants by hard-selling their products to people incapable of using them properly. The 28-page report accused the industry of encouraging mothers to give up breast feeding and use powdered milk formulas. The report was later published by the Third World Working Group, a lobby in support of less-developed countries. The pamphlet was entitled 'Nestlé Kills Babies', and accused Nestlé of unethical and immoral behaviour.

Although there are several companies that market infant baby formula internationally, Nestlé received most of the attention. This incident raises several issues important to all multinational companies. Before addressing these issues, let's look more closely at the charges by the Infant Formula Action Coalition and others, and the defence by Nestlé.

The charges

Most of the charges against infant formulas focus on the issue of whether advertising and marketing of such products have discouraged breast feeding among Third World mothers and have led to misuse of the products, thus contributing to infant malnutrition and death. Here are some of the charges made.

- A Peruvian nurse reported that formula had found its way to Amazon tribes deep in the jungles of northern Peru. There, where the only water comes from a highly contaminated river – which also serves as the local laundry and toilet – formula-fed babies came down with recurring attacks of diarrhoea and vomiting.
- Throughout the Third World, many parents dilute the formula to stretch their supply. Some even believe the bottle itself has nutrient qualities and merely fill it with water. The result is extreme malnutrition.
- One doctor reported that in a rural area, one newborn male weighed 7 pounds. At four months of age, he weighed 5 pounds. His sister, aged 18 months, weighed 12 pounds, what one would expect a four-month-old baby to weight. She later weighed only 8 pounds. The children had never been breast fed, and since birth their diets were basically bottle feeding. For a four-month baby, one can of formula should have lasted just under three days. The mother said that one can last two weeks to feed both children.
- In rural Mexico, the Philippines, Central America and the whole of Africa, there has been a dramatic decrease in the incidence of breast feeding. Critics blame the decline largely on the intensive advertising and promotion of infant formula. Clever radio jingles extol the wonders of the 'white man's powder' that will make baby grow and glow, 'Milk nurses' visit nursing mothers in hospitals and their homes and provide samples of formula. These activities encourage mothers to give up breast feeding and resort to bottle feeding because it is 'the fashionable thing to do or because people are putting it to them that this is the thing to do'.

The defence

The following points are made in defence of the marketing of baby formula in Third World countries.

- First, Nestlé argues that the company has never advocated bottle feeding instead of breast feeding. All its products carry a statement that breast feeding is best. The company states that it 'believes

that breast milk is the best food for infants and encourages breast feeding around the world as it has done for decades'. The company offers as support for this statement one of Nestlé's oldest educational booklets on 'Infant Feeding and Hygiene', which dates from 1913 and encourages breast feeding.

- However, the company does believe that infant formula has a vital role in proper infant nutrition as a supplement, when the infant needs nutritionally adequate and appropriate foods in addition to breast milk, and as a substitute for breast milk when a mother cannot or chooses not to breast feed. One doctor reports, 'Economically deprived and thus dietarily deprived mothers who give their children only breast milk are raising infants whose growth rates begin to slow noticeably at about the age of three months. These mothers then turn to supplemental feedings that are often harmful to children. These include herbal teas and concoctions of rice water or corn water and sweetened, condensed milk. These feedings can also be prepared with contaminated water and are served in unsanitary conditions.'

- Mothers in developing nations often have dietary deficiencies. In the Philippines, a mother in a poor family who is nursing a child produces about a pint of milk daily. Mothers in the United States usually produce about a quart of milk each day. For both the Filipino and US mothers, the milk produced is equally nutritious. The problem is that there is less of it for the Filipino baby. If the Filipino mother doesn't augment the child's diet, malnutrition develops.

- Many poor women in the Third World bottle feed because their work schedules in fields or factories will not permit breast feeding. The infant feeding controversy has largely to do with the gradual introduction of weaning foods during the period between three months and two years. The average well-nourished Western woman, weighing 20 to 30 pounds more than most women in less-developed countries, cannot feed only breast milk beyond five or six months. The claim that Third World women can breast feed exclusively for one or two years and have healthy, well-developed children is outrageous. Thus, all children beyond the ages of five to six months require supplemental feeding.

- Weaning foods can be classified as either native cereal gruels of millet or rice, or commercially manufactured milk formula. Traditional native weaning foods are usually made by mixing maize, rice or millet flours with water and then cooking the mixture. Other weaning foods found in use are crushed crackers, sugar and water, and mashed bananas.

There are two basic dangers to the use of native weaning foods. First, the nutritional quality of the native gruels is low. Second, microbiological contamination of the traditional weaning foods is a certainty in many Third World settings. The millet or the flour is likely to be contaminated, the water used in cooking will most certainly be contaminated, and the cooking containers will be contaminated; therefore, the native gruel, even after it is cooked, is frequently contaminated with colon bacilli, staph, and other dangerous bacteria. Moreover, large batches of gruel are often made and allowed to sit, inviting further contamination.

- Scientists recently compared the microbiological contamination of a local native gruel with ordinary reconstituted milk formula prepared under primitive conditions. They found both were contaminated to similar dangerous levels.

- The real nutritional problem in the Third World is not whether to give infants breast milk or formula, but how to supplement mothers' milk with nutritionally adequate foods when they are needed. Finding adequate locally produced, nutritionally sound supplements to mothers' milk and teaching people how to prepare and use them safely are the issues. Only effective nutrition education along with improved sanitation and good food that people can afford will win the fight against dietary deficiencies in the Third World.

The resolution

In 1974, Nestlé, aware of changing social patterns in the developing world and the increased access to radio and television there, reviewed its marketing practices on a region-by-region basis. As a result, mass media advertising of infant formula began to be phased out immediately in certain markets and, by 1978, was banned worldwide by the company. Nestlé then undertook to carry out more comprehensive health education programmes to ensure that an understanding of the proper use of its products reached mothers, particularly in rural areas.

'Nestlé fully supports the WHO [World Health Organization] Code. Nestlé will continue to promote breast feeding and ensure that its marketing practices do not discourage breast feeding anywhere. Our company intends to maintain a constructive dialogue with governments and health professionals in all the countries it serves with the sole purpose of servicing mothers and the health of babies.' This quote is from *Nestlé Discusses the Recommended WHO Infant Formula Code*.

In 1977, the Interfaith Center on Corporate Responsibility in New York compiled a case against formula feeding in developing nations, and the Third World Institute launched

a boycott against many Nestlé products. Its aim was to halt promotion of infant formulas in the Third World. The Infant Formula Action Coalition (INFACT, successor to the Third World Institute), along with several other world organisations, successfully lobbied the World Health Organization to draft a code to regulate the advertising and marketing of infant formula in the Third World. In 1981, by a vote of 114 to 1 (three countries abstained and the United States was the only dissenting vote), 118 member nations of WHO endorsed a voluntary code. The eight-page code urged a worldwide ban on promotion and advertising of baby formula and called for a halt to distribution of free product samples or gifts to physicians who promoted the use of the formula as a substitute for breast milk.

In May 1981 Nestlé announced it would support the code and waited for individual countries to pass national codes that would then be put into effect. Unfortunately, very few such codes were forthcoming. By the end of 1983, only 25 of the 157 member nations of the WHO had established national codes. Accordingly, Nestlé management determined it would have to apply the code in the absence of national legislation, and in February 1982 it issued instructions to marketing personnel that delineated the company's best understanding of the code and what would have to be done to follow it.

In addition, in May 1982 Nestlé formed the Nestlé Infant Formula Audit Commission (NIFAC), chaired by former Senator Edmund J. Muskie, and asked the commission to review the company's instructions to field personnel to determine if they could be improved to better implement the code. At the same time, Nestlé continued its meetings with WHO and UNICEF (United Nations Children's Fund) to try to obtain the most accurate interpretation of the code. NIFAC recommended several clarifications for the instructions that it believed would better interpret ambiguous areas of the code; in October 1982, Nestlé accepted those recommendations and issued revised instructions to field personnel.

Other issues within the code, such as the question of a warning statement, were still open to debate. Nestlé consulted extensively with WHO before issuing its label warning statement in October 1983, but there was still not universal agreement with it. Acting on WHO recommendations, Nestlé consulted with firms experienced and expert in developing and field testing educational materials, so that it could ensure that those materials met the code.

When the International Nestlé Boycott Committee (INBC) listed its four points of difference with Nestlé, it again became a matter of interpretation of the requirements of the code. Here, meetings held by UNICEF proved invaluable, in that UNICEF agreed to define areas of differing interpretation – in some cases providing definitions contrary to both Nestlé's and INBC's interpretations.

It was the meetings with UNICEF in early 1984 that finally led to a joint statement by Nestlé and INBC on 25 January. At that time, INBC announced its suspension of boycott activities, and Nestlé pledged its continued support of the WHO code.

Nestlé supports WHO code

The company has a strong record of progress and support in implementing the WHO code, including the following.

- Immediate support for the WHO code, May 1981, and testimony to this effect before the US Congress, June 1981.
- Issuance of instructions to all employees, agents and distributors in February 1982 to implement the code in all Third World countries where Nestlé markets infant formula.
- Establishment of an audit commission, in accordance with Article 11.3 of the WHO code, to ensure the company's compliance with the code. The commission, headed by Edmund S. Muskie, was composed of eminent clergy and scientists.
- Willingness to meet with concerned church leaders, international bodies, and organisation leaders seriously concerned with Nestlé's application of the code.
- Issuance of revised instructions to Nestlé personnel, October 1982, as recommended by the Muskie committee to clarify and give further effect to the code.
- Consultation with WHO, UNICEF and NIFAC on how to interpret the code and how best to implement specific provisions, including clarification by WHO/UNICEF of the definition of children who need to be fed breast milk substitutes, to aid in determining the need for supplies in hospitals.

Nestlé policies

In the early 1970s Nestlé began to review its infant formula marketing practices on a region-by-region basis. By 1978 the company had stopped all consumer advertising and direct sampling to mothers. Instructions to the field issued in February 1982 and clarified in the revised instructions of October 1982 to adopt articles of the WHO code as Nestlé policy include the following:

- no advertising to the general public
- no sampling to mothers
- no mothercraft workers

- no use of commission/bonus for sales
- no use of infant pictures on labels
- no point-of-sale advertising
- no financial or material inducements to promote products
- no samples to physicians except in three specific situations – a new product, a new product formulation, or a new graduate physician; limited to one or two cans of product
- limitation of supplies to those requested in writing and fulfilling genuine needs for breast milk substitutes
- a statement of the superiority of breast feeding on all labels/materials
- labels and educational materials clearly stating the hazards involved in incorrect usage of infant formula, developed in consultation with WHO/UNICEF.

Even though Nestlé stopped consumer advertising, it was able to maintain its share of the Third World infant formula market. In 1988 a call to resume the seven-year boycott was made by a group of consumer activist members of the Action for Corporate Accountability. The group claimed that Nestlé was distributing free formula through maternity wards as a promotional tactic that undermined the practice of breast feeding. The group claimed that Nestlé and others, including American Home Products, have continued to dump formula in hospitals and maternity wards and that, as a result, 'babies are dying as the companies are violating the WHO resolution'. As late as 1997 the Interagency Group on Breastfeeding Monitoring (IGBM) claimed Nestlé continues to systematically violate the WHO code. Nestlé's response to these accusations is included on its website (see www.nestle.com for details).

The boycott focus is Taster's Choice Instant Coffee, Coffee-mate Nondairy Coffee Creamer, Anacin aspirin and Advil.

Representatives of Nestlé and American Home Products rejected the accusations and said they were complying with World Health Organization and individual national codes on the subject.

The new twist

A new environmental factor has made the entire case more complex. As of 2001 it was believed that some 3.8 million children around the world had contracted the human immunodeficiency virus (HIV) at their mothers' breasts. In affluent countries mothers can be told to bottle feed their children. However, 90 per cent of the child infections occur in developing countries. There the problems of bottle feeding remain. Further, in even the most infected areas, 70 per cent of the mothers do not carry the virus, and breast feeding is by far the best option. The vast majority of pregnant women in developing countries have no idea whether they are infected or not. One concern is that large numbers of healthy women will switch to the bottle just to be safe. Alternatively, if bottle feeding becomes a badge of HIV infection, mothers may continue breast feeding just to avoid being stigmatised. In Thailand, pregnant women are offered testing, and if found to be HIV positive, are given free milk powder. But in some African countries, where women get pregnant at three times the Thai rate and HIV infection rates are 25 per cent compared with the 2 per cent in Thailand, that solution is much less feasible. Finally, the latest medical evidence indicates that extending breast feeding reduces the risk of breast cancer.

The issues

Many issues are raised by this incident and the ongoing swirl of cultural change. How can a company deal with a worldwide boycott of its products? Why did the United States decide not to support the WHO code? Who is correct, WHO or Nestlé? A more important issue concerns the responsibility of an MNC marketing in developing nations. Setting aside the issues for a moment, consider the notion that, whether intentional or not, Nestlé's marketing activities have had an impact on the behaviour of many people. In other words, Nestlé is a cultural change agent. When it or any other company successfully introduces new ideas into a culture, the culture changes and those changes can be functional or dysfunctional to established patterns of behaviour. The key issue is, what responsibility does the MNC have to the culture when, as a result of its marketing activities, it causes change in that culture? Finally, how might Nestlé now participate in the battle against the spread of HIV and AIDS in developing countries?

Questions

1 What are the responsibilities of companies in this or similar situations?
2 What could Nestlé have done to have avoided the accusations of 'killing Third World babies' and still market its product?
3 After Nestlé's experience, how do you suggest it, or any other company, can protect itself in the future?

4 Assume you are the one who had to make the final decision on whether or not to promote and market Nestlé's baby formula in Third World countries. Read the section titled 'Ethically and socially responsible decisions' in Chapter 5) as a guide to examine the social responsibility and ethical issues regarding the marketing approach and the promotion used. Were the decisions socially responsible? Were they ethical?

5 What advice would you give to Nestlé now in light of the new problem of HIV infection being spread via mothers' milk?

Source: this case is an update of 'Nestlé in LDCs', a case written by J. Alex Murray, University of Windsor, Ontario, Canada, and Gregory M. Gazda and Mary J. Molenaar, University of San Diego. The case originally appeared in the fifth edition of this text.

The case draws from the following: 'International Code of Marketing of Breastmilk Substitutes' (Geneva: World Health Organization, 1981); *INFACT Newsletter*, Minneapolis, February 1979; John A. Sparks, 'The Nestlé Controversy – Anatomy of a Boycott' (Grove City, PA: Public Policy Education Funds); 'WHO Drafts a Marketing Code', *World Business Weekly*, 19 January 1981, p. 8; 'A Boycott over Infant Formula', *Business Week*, 23 April 1979, p. 137; 'The Battle over Bottle-Feeding', *World Press Review*, January 1980, p. 54; 'Nestlé and the Role of Infant Formula in Developing Countries: The Resolution of a Conflict' (Nestlé Company, 1985); 'The Dilemma of Third World Nutrition' (Nestlé SA, 1985), p. 20; Thomas V. Greer, 'The Future of the International Code of Marketing of Breastmilk Substitutes: The Socio-Legal Context', *International Marketing Review*, Spring 1984, pp. 33–41; James C. Baker, 'The International Infant Formula Controversy: A Dilemma in Corporate Social Responsibility', *Journal of Business Ethics*, 1985, no. 4, pp. 181–90; and Shawn Tully, 'Nestlé Shows How to Gobble Markets', *Fortune*, 16 January 1989, p. 75. For a comprehensive and well-balanced review of the infant formula issue, see Thomas V. Greer, 'International Infant Formula Marketing: The Debate Continues', *Advances in International Marketing*, 1990, 4, pp. 207–25. For a discussion of the HIV complication, see 'Back to the Bottle?', *Economist*, 7 February 1998, p. 50; Alix M. Freedman and Steve Stecklow, 'Bottled Up: As UNICEF Battles Baby-formula Makers, African Infants Sicken', *Wall Street Journal*, 5 December 2000; and Rone Tempest, 'Mass Breast-feeding by 1128 is Called a Record', *Los Angeles Times*, 4 August 2002, p. B1.

cases

case 2.1 Daimler–Chrysler Merger: a Cultural Mismatch

It's no surprise that Schrempp is running the show. What is surprising is the way in which he is putting the two organisations together: forcing head-on confrontations, with the survivors left to run the company.

– Time, 24 May 1999, commenting on DaimlerChrysler CEO, Jurgen Schrempp's style of management

Introduction

In May, 1998, Daimler-Benz[1] and Chrysler Corporation,[2] two of the world's leading car manufacturers, agreed to combine their businesses in what they claimed to be a 'merger of equals'. The DaimlerChrysler (DCX) merger took approximately one year to finalise. The process began when Jurgen Schrempp[3] and Robert Eaton[4] met to discuss the possible merger on 18 January 1998. After receiving approval from a number of groups, the merger was completed on 12 November 1998.

The merger resulted in a large automobile company, ranked third[5] in the world in terms of revenues, market capitalisation and earnings, and fifth[6] in the number of units (passenger cars and commercial vehicles combined) sold. DCX generated revenues of $155.3 billion and sold 4 million cars and trucks in 1998. Schrempp and Eaton jointly led the merged entity, as co-chairmen and co-CEOs. DCX sources were confident that the new company was well poised to exploit the growth opportunities offered by the global automotive market in terms of geographical and product segment coverage.

Exhibit 1	Chronology of events in DCX merger
12 January 1998	Schrempp and Eaton meet to discuss the possible merger.
6 May 1998	Merger agreement signed in London.
7 May 1998	Merger agreement announced worldwide.
14 May 1998	Daimler-Benz Supervisory Board agrees to the merger.
23 July 1998	European Commission approves the merger.
31 July 1998	Federal Trade Commission approves the merger.
6 August 1998	DaimlerChrysler announces that its shares will trade as 'global stock' instead of American Depository Receipts.
18 September 1998	97 per cent of Chrysler shareholders and 80 per cent of Daimler-Benz shareholders approve the merger.
12 November 1998	DaimlerChrysler merger completed.

However, analysts felt that to make the merger a success, several important issues needed to be addressed. The most significant of these was organisational culture. German and American styles of management differed sharply. A cultural clash would be a major hurdle

to the realisation of the synergies identified before the merger. To minimise this clash of cultures, Schrempp decided to allow both groups to maintain their existing cultures.

The former Chrysler group was given autonomy to manufacture mass-market cars and trucks, while the Germans continued to build luxury Mercedes. However, analysts felt that this strategy wouldn't last long. When Chrysler performed badly in 2000,[7] its American president, James P. Holden, was replaced with Dieter Zetsche from Germany. Analysts felt that Zetsche would impose Daimler's culture on its American counterpart. A few senior Chrysler executives had already left and more German executives were joining Chrysler at senior positions.

In an interview with the *Financial Times* in early 1999, Schrempp admitted that the DCX deal was never really intended to be a merger of equals and claimed that Daimler-Benz had *acquired* Chrysler. Analysts felt that this statement probably wouldn't help the merger process.

Clash of cultures

DCX's success depended on integrating two starkly different corporate cultures. 'If they can't create a climate of learning from each other,' warned Ulrich Steger, a management professor at IMD, the Lausanne business school, 'they could be heading for an unbelievable catastrophe.' Daimler-Benz was characterised by methodical decision-making while Chrysler encouraged creativity. Chrysler was the very symbol of American adaptability and resilience. Chrysler valued efficiency, empowerment, and fairly egalitarian relations among staff; whereas Daimler-Benz seemed to value respect for authority, bureaucratic precision and centralised decision-making. These cultural differences soon became manifest in the daily activities of the company. For example, Chrysler executives quickly became frustrated with the attention Daimler-Benz executives gave to trivial matters, such as the shape of a pamphlet sent to employees. Daimler-Benz executives were equally perplexed when Eaton showed his emotions with tears in a speech to other executives. Chrysler was one of the leanest and nimblest car companies in the world; while Daimler-Benz had long represented the epitome of German industrial might (its Mercedes cars were arguably the best example of German quality and engineering).

Another key issue at DCX was the differences in pay structures between the two pre-merger entities. Germans disliked huge pay disparities and were unlikely to accept any steep revision of top management salaries. But American CEOs were rewarded handsomely: Eaton earned a total compensation of $10.9 million in 1997. Complications would arise if an American manager posted to Stuttgart[8] ended up reporting to a German manager who was earning half his salary. Chrysler could cut pay only at the risk of losing its talented managers. Schrempp mooted the idea of overcoming the problem through a low basic salary and high performance-based bonus, unlike anything seen in Europe. Base pay would be lower than Germans were used to, but the pay structure would have more variables such as stock options (an American feature).

Germans and Americans also had different working styles. The Germans were used to lengthy reports and extended discussions. On the other hand, the Americans performed little paperwork and liked to keep their meetings short. Americans favoured fast-paced trial-and-error experimentation, whereas Germans drew up painstakingly detailed plans and implemented them precisely. In general, the Germans perceived the Americans as 'chaotic' while the Americans felt that the Germans were stubborn 'militarists'.

Chrysler managers believed in spotting opportunities and going for them. However, post-merger, they were trapped in the German style of planning, constantly being told what to do. Steve Harris, Chrysler's former communications chief (who defected to General Motors) commented, 'The Germans played literally by the book – theirs. You'd go into a meeting and have to turn to Volume 7, Section 42, page 597.' The Germans prided themselves on analytical research that produced a plan, while the Americans reached for the impossible and kept coming up with new ideas to achieve these 'impossible' goals.

Before the merger, Daimler-Benz was known for its top-down management approach. Chrysler, by contrast, seemed to be a humble collection of colourful consensus managers. DCX claimed that the merger process would be complete in 12 months. However, analysts felt that the authoritarian German management methods would prove foreign to the non-hierarchical style at Chrysler, making the integration of the two cultures difficult. From the start, the cultural differences made DCX's post-marriage period of adjustment difficult. No sooner was the merger announced, Schrempp started issuing reams of organisational flow charts to the employees. Every phase was given titles like 'synergy tracking'; and every group had its weekly meeting schedule. DCX also set up a 'post-merger integration' (PMI) structure in which 12 'issue-resolution teams' were assigned to push and cajole their counterparts into combining everything from supplies to research. Every time there was disagreement, the integration process for that group was halted until a solution was found.

Attempts to bridge the chasm

DCX took several initiatives to bring the two cultures closer. Press reports indicated that in Stuttgart, the more formal Germans were experimenting with casual dress.

The Germans were also taking classes on cultural aware-ness. The Americans at DCX were encouraged to make more specific plans, while the Germans were urged to experiment more freely.

Analysts felt that there were many indications that the Americans and the Germans might come closer. The Americans were impressed by their German counterparts' skill with the English language (though they tried to cut down on slang to simplify speech when the Germans were in town). To reciprocate, many Americans were taking lessons in German. When the DCX stock began trading on 17 November 1998, German workers celebrated with American-style cheerleaders, a country & western band called The Hillbillies, doughnuts and corn on the cob. At a Detroit piano bar, the Americans were taken by surprise when they realised that the Germans knew the lyrics of old rock-and-roll songs.

Daimler's hegemony

In 2000, there was a management exodus at Chrysler headquarters in Detroit: two successive Chrysler presi-dents, James Holden and Thomas Stallkamp, both American, were fired. Holden was fired after only seven months in the position. Stallkamp replaced Holden and was forced to resign after only 12 months as CEO. Unreal as it might seem, two highly regarded Chrysler executives were fired from their CEO positions in the space of 19 months. Zatsche, the newly appointed CEO of Chrysler USA, was a Daimler executive and a close confidant of Schrempp. He, in turn, appointed Wolfgang Bernhard, another Daimler executive, as COO. Neither had any real exposure to the US marketplace. This turn of events demoralised Chrysler's workers. According to an employee, most of the workers were disgusted and frustrated because they felt they were being punished. The employees were expecting big layoffs, and were worried that the company would be sold out.

Analysts felt that after the merger Chrysler would no longer exist as an entity. In fact Chrysler was reduced to a mere operating division of DCX. The Daimler-Benz management presence permeated every important function at Chrysler USA. There was no Chrysler pres-ence on the DCX supervisory board or the board of management. By the end of 2000, there were only 128 000 Chrysler employees still working in the US opera-tions, all anxious and demoralised. Ex-Chrysler managers felt that Daimler-Benz was steadily leading Chrysler into a state of chaos.

Schrempp himself said that he never intended the merger be one of equals. He openly acknowledged that if Daimler-Benz's real intentions were publicly known before the merger, there would have been no deal. However, in a press interview, Schrempp largely retracted his statements by saying that if the strategy were to take over Chrysler,

Daimler would never have included them in the name of the new corporate entity. Analysts felt that these contra-dictory statements had severely tarnished Schrempp's image, both in Germany and the US.

Given these chaotic circumstances, Chrysler reported a third-quarter loss of $512 million for the period ending 30 September 2000; and its share value slipped below $40 from a high of $108 in January 1999.

DCX in trouble

Analysts were of the opinion that DCX should eliminate between 20 000 and 40 000 jobs at its North American Chrysler division and permanently close at least one of its 13 plants in the US and Canada because of huge financial losses in 2000. After third-quarter losses of more than half a billion dollars, and projections of even higher losses in the fourth quarter and into 2001, Schrempp told employ-ees that Chrysler had only 13.5 per cent of the US market, but it was staffed as if it had a 20 per cent share.

In early 2001, DCX announced that it would slash 26 000 jobs at its ailing Chrysler division. 'No one wants this to happen. I personally wish it didn't have to happen,' said Zetsche. He called the moves painful but necessary in the face of 'brutal' competition and low US sales. Zetsche said a large part of the job cutting would be through retire-ment programmes, layoffs, attrition and other means. About three-quarters of the job cuts would be made in 2001, he said. In addition, production would be curbed at factories in Canada and four states in the US by slowing assembly lines and trimming the number of shifts.

However, analysts interpreted this move as a failure of the German and American auto-makers to live up to their promise. One of them said, 'Instead of making the billions of dollars in cost savings and synergies at the time of the merger, they're making desperate cuts to get Chrysler back in the black.'

Why the merger failed to realise synergies

Analysts felt that, strategically, the merger made good business sense. But opposing cultures and management styles proved to be a hindrance to the realisation of syner-gies. Daimler-Benz attempted to run Chrysler USA opera-tions in the same way as it would run its German operations. This approach was doomed to failure. In September 2001, *Business Week* wrote, 'The merger has so far fallen disastrously short of the goal. Distrust between Auburn Hills and Stuttgart has made cooperation on even the simplest of matters difficult. Coming to terms with issues like which parts Mercedes-Benz would share with Chrysler was almost impossible. The Germans and the Americans had been out of sync from the start. The two proud management teams resisted working together, were wary of

change and weren't willing to compromise. Daimler-Chrysler have combined nothing beyond some administrative departments, such as finance and public relations.'

Questions

1 Mergers and acquisitions take place to realise the synergies between the two or more companies involved. Why do you think the Daimler-Chrysler merger failed to realise the synergies that were expected from it?

2 Many a cross-cultural merger has failed because proper attention was not given to the difference in cultures between the two companies. What issues should be addressed to make cross-cultural merger a success?

3 Very often companies involved in a merger claim it to be a merger of equals but this is not always the case. 'The Daimler-Chrysler deal was never expected to be a merger of equals.' Comment.

Further reading and bibliography

- 'Post-merger Identity Problems at DaimlerChrysler', *The Hindu Business Line*, 10 November 1999.
- Alex Taylor III, 'Can the Germans Rescue Chrysler?', *Fortune*, 30 April 2001.
- Joann Muller and Christine Tierney, 'Can this man save Chrysler?' *Business Week*, 17 September 2001.
- Joann Muller and Jeff Green, 'Chrysler's Rescue Team', *Business Week*, 15 January 2001.

- Frank Gibney Jr, 'There are Lots of Details', *Time Magazine*, 24 May 1999.
- Stanley Reed, Gail Edmondson and Lowry Miller, 'No More Flying Solo', *Business Week*, 21 December 1998.
- Alex Taylor III, 'The Germans', *Fortune*, 11 January 1999.
- Daimler-Benz, Annual Report 1998.
- www.daimlerchrysler.com.

References

1 Daimler-Benz was formed with the merger of two German automobile manufacturers – Mannheim-based Benz & Co. and the Stuttgart-based Daimler Motor Company (DMC) – in 1926.
2 The US-based Chrysler was a major automobile manufacturer with headquarters at Auburn Hills.
3 CEO of Daimler-Benz.
4 Chairman and CEO of Chrysler Corporation.
5 After General Motors and Ford Motor Company.
6 After General Motors, Ford, Toyota and Volkswagen.
7 Chrysler reported a third-quarter loss of $512 million for the period ending 30 September 2000. Its share value had slipped below $40 from a high of $108. After the merger, Chrysler's market share fell from 16.2 per cent to 13.5 per cent.
8 Headquarters of Daimler-Benz.

This case was written by Sanjib Dutta, ICFAI Center for Management Research (ICMR). It is intended to be used as a basis for class discussion rather than to illustrate either effective or ineffective handling of a management situation. The case was compiled from published sources.

case 2.2 Cultural Norms: Fair & Lovely and Advertising

Fair & Lovely, a branded product of Hindustan Lever, Ltd (HLL), is touted as a cosmetic that lightens skin colour. On its website (www.hll.com) the company calls its product, 'the miracle worker', which is 'proven to deliver one to three shades of change'. While tanning is the rage in Western countries, skin-lightening treatments are popular in Asia.

According to industry sources, the top-selling skin lightening cream in India is Fair & Lovely from Hindustan Lever, followed by CavinKare's Fairever brands. HLL's Fair & Lovely brand was the undisputed monarch of the market with a 90 per cent share until CavinKare Ltd (CKL) launched Fairever. In just two years, the Fairever brand gained an impressive 15 per cent market share. HLL's share of market for the Fair & Lovely line generates about $60 million annually. The product sells for about 23 rupees ($0.29) for a 25-gram tube of cream.

The rapid growth of CavinKare's Fairever (www.cavinkare.com) brand prompted HLL to increase its advertising effort and to launch a series of ads depicting a 'fairer girl gets the boy' theme. One advertisement featured a financially strapped father lamenting his fate, saying, 'If only I had a son', while his dark-skinned daughter looks on, helpless and demoralised because she can't bear the financial responsibility of her family. Fast-forward and Plain Jane has been transformed into a gorgeous light-skinned woman through the use of a 'fairness cream', Fair & Lovely. Now clad in a miniskirt, the woman is a successful flight attendant and can take her father to dine at a five-star hotel. She's happy and so is her father.

In another ad, two attractive young women are sitting in a bedroom; one has a boyfriend and, consequently, is happy. The darker-skinned woman, lacking a boyfriend, is not happy. Her friend's advice? Use a bar of soap to wash away the dark skin that's keeping men from flocking to her.

HLL's series of ads provoked CavinKare Ltd to counter with an ad that takes a dig at HLL's Fair & Lovely ad. CavinKare's ad has a father-daughter duo as the protagonists, with the father shown encouraging the daughter to be an achiever irrespective of her complexion. CavinKare maintained that the objective of its new commercial is not to take a dig at Fair & Lovely but to 'reinforce Fairever's positioning.'

'We have noticed attempts by Fair & Lovely to blur our positioning by changing its communication platform from "wanting to get married" to "achievement", the principal Fairever theme. Since we don't have the spending power to match HLL, a tactical way for us to respond is to reinforce our brand positioning and the commercial will be aired until the company's "objective" is achieved,' a CavinKare official said.

Skin colour is a powerful theme in India as well as much of Asia where a lighter colour represents a higher status. While Americans and Europeans flock to tanning salons, many across Asia seek ways to have 'fair' complexions. Culturally, fair skin is associated with positive values that relate to class and beauty. One Indian lady commented that when she was growing up, her mother forbade her to go outdoors. She was not trying to keep her daughter out of trouble but was trying to keep her skin from getting dark.

Brahmins, the priestly caste at the top of the social hierarchy, are considered fair because they traditionally stayed inside, poring over books. The undercaste at the bottom of the ladder are regarded as the darkest people because they customarily worked in the searing sun. Ancient Hindu scriptures and modern poetry eulogise women endowed with skin made out of white marble.

Skin colour is closely identified with caste and is laden with symbolism. Pursue any of the 'grooms and brides wanted' ads in newspapers or on the web that families use to arrange suitable alliances and you will see that most potential grooms and their families are looking for 'fair' brides; some are progressive enough to invite responses from women belonging to a different caste. These ads, hundreds of which appear in India's daily newspapers, reflect attempts to solicit individuals with the appropriate religion, caste, regional ancestry, professional and educational qualifications, and, frequently, skin colour. Even in the growing numbers of ads that announce 'caste no bar', the adjective 'fair' regularly precedes professional qualifications.

Bollywood (India's Hollywood) glorifies conventions on beauty by always casting a fair-skinned actress in the role of heroine, surrounded by darker extras. Women want to use whiteners because it is 'aspirational', like losing weight.

Even the gods supposedly lament their dark complexion – Krishna sings plaintively, 'Radha kyoon gori, main kyoon kala?' (Why is Radha so fair when I'm dark?) – a skin deficient in melanin (the pigment that determines the skin's brown colour) is an ancient predilection. More than 3500 years ago, Charaka, the famous sage, wrote about herbs that could help make the skin fair.

Indian dermatologists maintain that fairness products cannot truly work as they only reach the upper layers of the skin and so do not affect melanin production. Nevertheless, 'hope springs eternal' and for some Fair & Lovely is a 'miracle worker.' 'The last time I went to my parents' home, I got complements on my fair skin from everyone,' one user gushes. But for others, there is only disappointment. One 26-year-old working woman has

been a regular user for the past eight years but to no avail. 'I should have turned into Snow White by now but my skin is still the same wheatish colour.'

The number of Indians of the opinion that lighter skin is more beautiful may be shrinking. Sumit Isralni, a 22-year-old hair designer in his father's salon, thinks things have changed in the last two years, at least in India's most cosmopolitan cities, Delhi, Mumbai and Bangalore. Women now 'prefer their own complexion, their natural way,' Isralni says; he prefers a more 'Indian beauty' himself. 'I won't judge my wife on how fair her complexion is. 'Sunita Gupta, a beautician in the same salon, is more critical. 'It's just foolishness!' she exclaims. The premise of the ads that women could not become airline attendants if they are dark-skinned was wrong, she said. 'Nowadays people like black beauty.' It is a truism that women, especially in the tropics, desire to be a shade fairer no matter what their skin colour. Although, unlike the approach used in India, advertisements elsewhere usually show how to use the product and how it works.

Advertising

HLL launched its television ad campaign to promote Fair & Lovely in December 2001 and withdrew it in February 2003, amid severe criticism of its portrayal of women. Activists argued that one of the messages the company sends through its 'air hostess' demonstrating the preference for a son who would be able to take on the financial responsibility for his parents – is especially harmful in a country such as India where gender discrimination is rampant. Another offence is perpetuating a culture of discrimination in a society where 'fair' is synonymous with 'beautiful'. AIDWA (All India Democratic Women's Association) lodged a complaint in March and April 2002 with HLL about its offensive ads but Hindustan Lever failed to respond.

The women's association then appealed to the National Human Rights Commission alleging that the ad demeaned women. AIDWA objected to three things: (1) the ads were racist, (2) they were promoting son preference, and (3) they were insulting to working women. 'The way they portrayed the young women who, after using Fair & Lovely, became attractive and therefore lands a job suggested that the main qualification for a woman to get a job is the way she looks.' The Human Rights Commission passed AIDWA's complaints on to the Ministry of Information and Broadcasting, which said the campaign violated the Cable and Television Networks Act of 1995 – provisions in the Act state that no advertisement shall be permitted that 'derides any race, caste, colour, creed and nationality' and that 'Women must not be portrayed in a manner that emphasises passive, submissive qualities and encourages them to play a subordinate secondary role in the family and society.' The

government issued notices of the complaints to HLL. After a year-long campaign led by the AIDWA, Hindustan Lever Limited discontinued two of its television advertisements for Fair & Lovely fairness cold cream in March 2003.

Shortly after pulling its ads off the air, and, coincidentally, on International Women's Day, HLL launched its 'Fair & Lovely Foundation', vowing to 'encourage economic empowerment of women across India' by providing resources in education and business. Millions of women 'who, though immensely talented and capable, need a guiding hand to help them take the leap forward'. Presumably into a fairer future.

HLL sponsored career fairs in over 20 cities across the country, offering counselling in as many as 110 careers. It supported 100 rural scholarships for women students passing their 10th grade, a professional course for aspiring beauticians, and a three-month Home Healthcare Nursing Assistant's course catering to young women between the ages 18 and 30. According to HLL, the Fair & Lovely Academy for Home Care Nursing Assistants offers a unique training opportunity for young women who possess no entry-level skills and, therefore, are not employable in the new economy job market. The Fair & Lovely Foundation plans to serve as a catalyst for the economic empowerment of women across India. The Fair & Lovely Foundation will showcase the achievements of these women not only to honour them, but also to set an example for other women to follow.

A few facts about HLL taken from www.hll.com

Lever Limited is India's largest Packaged Mass Consumption Goods company. We are leaders in Home and Personal Care Products and Food and Beverages including such products as Ponds and Pepsodent.

We seek to 'meet everyday needs to people everywhere – to anticipate the aspirations of our consumers and customers and to respond creatively and competitively with branded products and services which raise the quality of life'. It is this purpose which inspires us to build brands. Over the past 70 years, we have introduced about 100 brands.

Fair & Lovely has been specially designed and proven to deliver one to three shades of change in most people. Also its sunscreen system is specially optimised for Indian skin. Indian skin unlike Caucasian skin tends to 'tan' rather than 'burn' and, hence, requires a different combination of UVA & UVB sunscreens.

The fairness cream is marketed in over 38 countries through HLL Exports and local Unilever companies and is the largest selling skin lightening cream

in the world. The brand today offers a substantive range of products to consumers including Fair & Lovely Fairness Reviving Lotion, Fair & Lovely Fairness Cold Cream and Fair & Lovely Fairness Soap.

Some information on CavinKare taken from www. cavinkare.com
We shall achieve growth by continuously offering unique products and services that would give customers utmost satisfaction and thereby be a role model.'

Goal
In fifteen years (2012) we will be a hundred times our current turnover.

Values and beliefs of CavinKare
Integrity   The company values honesty and truthfulness above everything else in all its interactions. Our thoughts, words and actions shall be the same. We shall try out utmost to fulfill promises and honour commitments.

Fairness   The company shall be fair in all its dealings with people inside and outside. We will follow rules, norms and procedures not only in letter but in spirit as well; we will show common decency in all our dealings with people; we will not exploit undue advantages; we will respect the rights of others.

Excellence   The company values highly all efforts that lead to high standards in everyday work and results. We shall attempt to be the best-in-class in anything we choose to work on. We shall encourage any individual or collective effort in promoting excellence.

Innovation   The company values innovative thinking, innovative approaches and innovative solutions in our regular work life. We will always look for better ways of doing things; we will seek new ideas to solve problems; we will experiment with new concepts, ideas and solutions.

Openness   The company believes that openness to new ideas, thoughts and opinions makes relationships stronger and productive, we shall listen to others; we shall openly discuss among colleagues all that is appropriate; we shall welcome ideas from everywhere.

Trust   The company believes that trust is an important ingredient for effective functioning within the organisation and with the outside world. While we shall protect our legitimate business interests, we

would also approach the people, issues and associations with straightforwardness, optimism and positive outlook.

Stretch   The company believes that people have infinite potential. We have an extraordinary capability to exert and extend the limits of the possible. We shall aim for stretch goals, ambitious targets and ever-receding horizons.

Questions
1   Is it ethical to sell a product that is, at best, only mildly effective? Discuss.
2   Is it ethical to exploit cultural norms and values to promote a product? Discuss.
3   Is the advertising of Fair & Lovely demeaning to women or is it portraying a product not too dissimilar to cosmetics in general?
4   Will HLL's Fair & Lovely Foundation counter charges made by AIDWA? Discuss.
5   In light of AIDWA's charges, how would you suggest Fair & Lovely promote its product? Discuss. Would your response be different if Fairever continues to use 'fairness' as a theme of its promotion? Discuss.
6   Propose a promotion/marketing programme that will counter all the arguments and charges against Fair & Lovely and be an effective programme.
7   Based on CavinKare's statement of values and beliefs, how would you evaluate its advertising/marketing programmes?

Source: Nicole Leistikow, 'Indian Women Criticize "Fair & Lovely" Ideal', *Women's News*, 28 April 2003; Shuchi Sinha, 'Skin Care: Fair & Growing', *India Today*, 4 December 2000, p. 48; Ratna Bhushan, 'CavinKare Changes Tack to Challenge HLL Strategy', *Business Line (The Hindu)*, 10 July 2002; Arundhati Parmar, 'Objections to Indian Ad Not Taken Lightly', *Marketing News*, 9 June 2003, p. 4; 'Fair & Lovely Launches Foundation to Promote Economic Empowerment of Women', *Press Release, Fair & Lovely Foundation* (www.hll.com and search for 'foundation'), 11 March 2003; 'CavinKare Changes Tack to Challenge HLL Strategy,' *Indian Business Insight*, 10 July 2002; Shunu Sen, 'A Fair Way of Advertising', *Business Line (The Hindu)*, 1 August 2002; 'Ad Nauseam', *The Statesman-Asia Africa Intelligence Wire*, 9 March 2002; Rina Chandran, 'All For Self-control,' *Business Line (The Hindu)*, 24 April 2003; Miriam Jordan, 'Creams for a Lighter Skin Capture the Asian Market, Especially in India, as a Cultural Virtue', *International Herald Tribune*, 24 May 1998; Simon Robinson and Peter Hawthorne, 'Colour Blindness Obsessed with Fair Skin. Many African Women Are Using Dangerous Lighteners', *Time*, 30 July 2001; Khozem Merchant and Edward Luce, 'Not So Fair and Lovely,' *Financial Times*, 19 March 2003; and Bhanu Pande and Seema Shukla, 'Big Brother Is Watching', *Economic Times*, 9 May 2003.

case 2.3 The McDonald's 'Beef Fries' Controversy

Hindus and vegetarians all over the world feel shocked and betrayed by McDonald's deception and ultimate greed.

> – Attorney Harish Bharti on filing the lawsuit against McDonald's in May 2001

These are the ways the fries are made in the US, and we don't have any plans to change.

> – Walt Riker, McDonald's spokesperson, in May 2001

A controversy erupts

In May 2001, a class-action lawsuit[1] was filed against the world's largest fast-food chain McDonald's, in Seattle, US. The lawsuit alleged that the company had, for over a decade, duped vegetarian customers into eating French fries[2] that contained beef extracts. The lawsuit followed a spate of media reports detailing how the French fries served at McDonald's were falsely promoted as being '100 per cent vegetarian'.

Although McDonald's initially declined to comment on the issue, the company issued a 'conditional apology', admitting to using beef flavouring in the fries. The furore over the matter seemed to be settling down when, to McDonald's horror, some of its restaurants in India were vandalised. Activists of Hindu fundamentalist groups – the Shiv Sena, the Vishwa Hindu Parishad (VHP) and the Bajrang Dal – staged a demonstration in front of the McDonald's head office in Delhi protesting the alleged use of beef flavouring. They submitted a memorandum to the Prime Minister, demanding the closure of all McDonald's outlets in the country.

Activists also staged protests in front of McDonald's restaurants in south Mumbai and Thane. Mobs ransacked the outlet at Thane, broke the glass panes and smeared the McDonald's mascot Ronald with cow dung. About 30 people were arrested and later let off on bail. Company officials estimated the loss to the outlet at Rs2 million.

Officials at McDonald's India quickly announced that the vegetarian products served in India did not have any non-vegetarian content (refer to Exhibit 1 for details). However, despite this reassurance, the anti-McDonald's wave refused to die down.

Meanwhile, more cases were being filed against McDonald's – this time in California, US, and Canada. It seemed certain that the company would have to shell out millions of dollars to settle the class-action lawsuit representing the 1 million US-based Hindus and 15 million other vegetarians.

Activists protest the use of beef products in the French fries sold at McDonald's in Bombay © AP/WideWorld Photos

Background notes

McDonald's was started as a drive-in restaurant by two brothers, Richard and Maurice McDonald in California, US, in 1937. The business, which was generating $200 000 per annum in the 1940s, got a further boost with the emergence of a revolutionary new concept called 'self-service'. The brothers designed their kitchen for mass production with assembly-line procedures. Prices were kept low. Speed, service and cleanliness became the critical success factors of the business. By the mid-1950s, the restaurant's revenues reached $350 000. As word of its success spread, franchisees started showing interest. However, the franchising system failed because the McDonald brothers observed very transparent business practices. As a consequence, they encouraged imitators who copied their business practices and emerged as competitors. The franchisees also did not maintain the same standards of cleanliness, customer service and product uniformity.

Undeterred by these developments, the company continued with its expansion plans and, by 2001, it had 30 093 restaurants all over the world with sales of $24 billion. By mid-2001, the company had 28 outlets in India, spread across New Delhi, Bombay, Pune, Jaipur and on the Delhi–Agra highway.

The troubled history

McDonald's has had a long history of lawsuits being filed against it. It had frequently been accused of resorting to unfair and unethical business practices – 16 October is even observed as a 'World Anti-McDonald's Day'. In the late 1990s, the company had to settle over 700 incidents of scalding coffee burns. Reportedly, McDonald's kept the

Exhibit 1 What happened in India?

In May 2001, managing directors of McDonald's India – Vikram Bakshi of Delhi's Connaught Plaza Restaurants and Amit Jatia of Mumbai's Hardcastle Restaurants – said at a press conference, 'We are open to any kind of investigation by the authorities, from the state or central governments. We categorically state that the French fries and other vegetarian products that we serve in India do not contain any beef or animal extracts and flavouring of whatsoever kind.'

Bakshi said that the company had developed a special menu for Indian customers taking into consideration Indian culture and religious sentiments. McDonald's officials circulated official statements by McCain Foods India Pvt. Ltd. and Lamb Weston, suppliers of French fries to McDonald's India, stating that the fries were par-fried in pure vegetable oil without any beef tallow or any fat ingredient of animal origin.

People were however sceptical of the company's assurance because it had made similar false promises in the US as well. Their fears were realised when it was revealed that Lamb Weston's supplies had been rejected after they failed to meet standards set by McDonald's. McCain Foods was still in the process of growing the appropriate potatoes and needed another two years to begin supply. The French fries were being sourced from the US.

However, tests conducted on the French fries and the cooking medium by Brihanmumbai Municipal Corporation (BMC) and the Food and Drug Administration (FDA) confirmed the fries contained no animal fat.

Source: ICMR.

coffee at 185° – approximately 20° hotter than the standard temperature at other restaurants – which could cause third degree burns in just 2-7 seconds. An 81-year-old woman suffered third degree burns on her lower body that required skin grafts and hospitalisation for a week. After McDonald's dismissed her request for compensation for medical bills, she filed a lawsuit against the company.

A McDonald's quality assurance manager testified in the case that the company was aware of the risk of serving dangerously hot coffee, but it had no plans to lower the temperature or to post a warning on the coffee cups about the possibility of severe burns. In 1994, the court declared McDonald's guilty of serving 'unreasonably dangerous' hot coffee. The court awarded punitive damages of $2.7 million dollars, which was later lowered to $480 000.

The company also had to settle multi-million-dollar lawsuits in many other cases, the majority of which were spearheaded by two London Greenpeace activists (Steel and Morris). The company was severely criticised for hiring detective agencies to break into the activist group. According to an analyst, 'The company had employed at least seven undercover agents to spy on Greenpeace. During some London Greenpeace meetings, about half the people in attendance were corporate spies. One spy broke into the London Greenpeace office, took photographs and stole documents. Another had a six-month affair with a member of London Greenpeace while informing on his activities.'

Steel and Morris were later found to have libelled McDonald's by a British court. However, the company was also found guilty of endangering the health of its customers and paying workers unreasonably low wages. The case, chronicled completely at www.mcspotlight.org, has become a classic example of a corporate giant's struggle to uphold its image amid allegations of unethical practices.

In the light of the company's chequered history of legal problems, the French fries controversy seemed run-of-the-mill. However, when McDonald's issued a conditional apology, the matter acquired serious undertones. This was because it was one of the very few instances where the company seemed to have publicly acknowledged any kind of wrong-doing.

The beef fries controversy

With an overwhelming majority of the people in the West being non-vegetarian, products often contain hidden animal-based ingredients. Incidents of vegetarians finding non-vegetarian food items in their food abound throughout the world. Whether a person has chosen to be a vegetarian for religious, health, ethical or philosophical reasons, it is not easy to get vegetarian food in public restaurants. According to the manager of a Thai food café in the US, 'We have a lot of customers already. We don't need to have any vegetarian food.' Commenting on this dilemma, a US-based Hindu vegetarian said, 'We can't blame anybody. You have to find out for yourself. If you have any doubts, try to avoid it. Otherwise, you just have to close your eyes and try to eat.'

The French fries controversy began in 2000, when a Hindu Jain software engineer Hitesh Shah, working in the US, happened to read a news article, which mentioned that the French fries at McDonald's contained beef. Shah sent an e-mail to the McDonald's customer service department, asking whether the French fries contained beef or not and, if they did, why this was not mentioned in the ingredient list. Shah soon got a reply from Megan Magee, the company's Home Office Customer Satisfaction Department.

The reply stated, 'Thank you for taking time to contact McDonald's with your questions regarding the ingredients in our French fries. For flavor enhancement, McDonald's French fry suppliers use a minuscule amount of beef flavoring as an ingredient in the raw product. The reason beef is not listed as an ingredient is because McDonald's voluntarily (restaurants are not required to list ingredients) follow the "Code of Federal Regulations"

(required for packaged goods) for labeling its products. As such, like food labels you would read on packaged goods, the ingredients in "natural flavors" are not broken down. Again, we are sorry if this has caused any confusion.'

A popular Indian-American newspaper, *West India*, carried Shah's story. The news created widespread outrage among Hindus and vegetarians in the US. In May 2001, Harish Bharti, a US-based Indian attorney, filed the class-action lawsuit against McDonald's.

McDonald's immediately released a statement saying it never claimed the fries sold in the US were vegetarian. A spokesperson said that though the fries were cooked in pure vegetable oil, the company never explicitly stated that the fries were appropriate for vegetarians and customers were always told that the flavour came partly from beef. He added that it was up to the customer to ask about the flavour and its source. This enraged the vegetarian customers further. Bharti said, 'Not only did they deceive millions of people who may not want to have any beef extraction in their food for religious, ethical and health reasons, now McDonald's is suggesting that these people are at fault, that they are stupid. This adds insult to injury.'

Interestingly enough, McDonald's statement that it never claimed its French fries were vegetarian was proved completely wrong after Bharti found a 1993 letter sent by the company's corporate headquarters to a consumer in response to an enquiry about vegetarian menu items. The letter clearly bundled the fries along with garden salads, wholegrain cereals and English muffins as a completely vegetarian item.

The whole controversy rested on a decision McDonald's had taken in 1990 regarding the way French fries were prepared. Prior to 1990, the company made the fries using tallow.[3] However, to address the increasing customer concern about cholesterol control,[4] McDonald's declared that it would use only pure vegetable oil to make the fries in the future. However, after the decision to change from tallow to pure vegetable oil, the company realised that it could have difficulty in retaining customers who were accustomed to beef-flavoured fries.

According to Eric Scholsser, author of the best-selling book *Fast Food Nation: The Dark Side of the All-American Meal*,[5] 'For decades, McDonald's cooked its French fries in a mixture of about 7 per cent cottonseed oil and 93 per cent beef tallow. The mix gave the fries their unique flavour.' This unique flavour was lost when tallow was replaced by vegetable oil. To address this issue, McDonald's decided to add the 'natural flavour', i.e. the beef extract, which was added to the water while the potatoes were being partially cooked.

The 'beef fries' controversy attained greater dimensions in India

as 85 per cent of the country's population was vegetarian. Non-vegetarian Indians also usually did not consume beef because Hindus consider cows to be holy and sacred. Eating beef is thus a sacrilege. A US-based Hindu plaintiff in one of the lawsuits said, 'I feel sick in the morning every day, like I want to vomit. Now it is always there in my mind that I have done this sin.'

Experts commented that the issue was not of adding beef extract to a supposedly vegetarian food item – it was more to do with the moral and ethical responsibility of a company to be honest about the products and services it offered. According to James Pizzirusso, founder of the Vegetarian Legal Action Network at George Washington University, 'Corporates need to pay attention to consumers who avoid certain food products for religious or health reasons, or because they have allergies. They say they are complying with the law in terms of disclosing their ingredients, but they should go beyond the law.'

Meanwhile in June 2001, another class-action lawsuit was filed in the District Court in Travis County, Austin, Texas, on behalf of all Hindus in Texas, alleging that Hindu moral and religious principles had been violated by their unintentional consumption of French fries that were flavoured with beef. As public outrage intensified, McDonald's released a conditional apology on its website, admitting that the recipe for the fries used a 'a minuscule trace of beef flavoring, not tallow' (refer to Exhibit 2 for McDonald's response to the allegations).

McDonald's said that it issued an apology only to provide more details about its products to customers. A company spokesperson said, 'Customers responded to the news about the lawsuit. In the end, we are responding to those customers. We took a fresh look at how we could help customers get more information about natural flavors.'

Unsatisfied by the apology, Bharti said, 'Apology is good for the soul if it comes from the heart. It is not an unconditional apology. Why do they go around using words like "if there was any confusion" in their apology?' Further, news reports quoting company sources said that the apology did not mean McDonald's was admitting to claims that it misled million of customers by adding beef extract to its fries. Bharti said that the legal battle would continue and that McDonald's would have to issue an unconditional apology and pay a substantial amount of money. By this time, two more lawsuits had been filed in Illinois and New Jersey, taking the total number of cases to five.

The aftermath

The courtroom battle had entered its 11th month when McDonald's announced that it would issue a new apology and pay $10 million to vegetarians and religious groups in a proposed settlement of all the lawsuits in March 2002.

Exhibit 2 McDonald's response to the allegations

It has always been McDonald's practice to share nutrition and ingredient information with our customers, including facts about our French fries. In the US, we consistently communicate this information through in-store posters, wallet-sized cards and various brochures, which offer a wide variety of dietary details.

McDonald's USA is always sensitive to customer concerns. Because it is our policy to communicate to customers, we regret if customers felt that the information we provided was not complete enough to meet their needs. If there was confusion, we apologise.

Meanwhile, here are the details of our French fry production in the US. A small amount of beef flavoring is added during potato processing – at the plant. After the potatoes are washed and steam-peeled, they are cut, blanched, dried, par-fried, and frozen. It is during the par-frying process at the plant that the natural flavoring is used. These fries are then shipped to our US restaurants. Our French fries are cooked in vegetable oil at our restaurants.

McDonald's 1990 switch to vegetable oil in the US as our standard cooking oil was made for nutritional reasons, to offer customers a cholesterol-free menu item. This nutrition announcement received national media coverage, widely broadcasting the facts about our switch and why we made it.

As a local business in 121 countries, our French fry process varies country-by-country to account for cultural or religious dietary considerations. For example, in predominantly Muslim countries – as in Southeast Asia, the Middle East and Africa – McDonald's strictly conforms to halal standards. This means no use of beef or pork flavorings or ingredients in our French fries. In India, where vegetarian concerns are paramount, no beef or pork flavorings are used in our vegetarian menu items.

Our 'McDonald's Nutrition Facts' brochure uses the term 'natural flavor' in the ingredient list for French fries. This description is in full compliance with and permitted by the US Food and Drug Administration (FDA).

Source: www.mcdonalds.com

Around 60 per cent of this payment went to vegetarian organisations and the rest to various groups devoted to Hindus and Sikhs, children's nutrition and assistance, and kosher dietary practices.[6]

The company also decided to pay $4000 each to the 12 plaintiffs in the five lawsuits, and post a new and more detailed apology on the company website and in various other publications. McDonald's also decided to convene an advisory board to advise on vegetarian matters.

In April 2002, McDonald's planned to insert advertisements in newspapers apologising for its mistakes, 'We acknowledge that, upon our switch to vegetable oil in the early 1990s for the purpose of reducing cholesterol, mistakes were made in communicating to the public and customers about the ingredients in our French fries and hash browns. Those mistakes included instances in which French fries and hash browns sold at US restaurants were improperly identified as vegetarian. We regret we did not provide these customers with complete information, and we sincerely apologise for any hardship that these miscommunications have caused among Hindus, vegetarians and others.'

Unhappy with the monetary compensation the company was offering, Bharti said, 'Wish I could do better in terms of money. But our focus was to change the fast-food industry, and this is a big victory for consumers in this country because we have brought this giant to this.'

Though $10 million was definitely a pittance for the $24 billion McDonald's, what remained to be seen was whether the case would set a precedent and make corporates throughout the world more aware and responsible towards their customers or not.

Questions

1   Analyse the various allegations levelled against McDonald's before the French fries controversy. Why do you think the company attracted so much hostility and criticism despite being the number one fast-food chain in the world?

2   Discuss the French fries controversy and critically comment on the company's stand that it had never claimed the fries were vegetarian. Do you think the company handled the controversy effectively? Give reasons to support your answer.

3   Discuss the steps taken by McDonald's to play down the French fries controversy, and critically comment on whether the company will be able to come out of this unscathed.

Exhibit 3 McDonald's: social responsibility statement

The McDonald's brand lives and grows where it counts the most – in the hearts of customers worldwide. We, in turn, hold our customers close to our heart, striving to do the right thing and giving back to the communities where we do business. At McDonald's, social responsibility is a part of our heritage and we are committed to building on it worldwide; some of our efforts to do so are described here.

Ronald McDonald House Charities – McDonald's supports one of the world's premier philanthropic organisations, Ronald McDonald House Charities (RMHC). RMHC provides comfort and care to children and their families by awarding grants to organisations through chapters in 31 countries and supporting more than 200 Ronald McDonald Houses in 19 countries.

Environmental Leadership – We take action around the world to develop innovative solutions to local environmental challenges. Ten years ago, we began a groundbreaking alliance with the Environmental Defense Fund (EDF) to reduce, reuse and recycle. Since then we eliminated 150 000 tons of packaging, purchased more than $3 billion of recycled products and recycled more than one million tons of corrugated cardboard in the US. We continue to set new waste reduction goals and are focusing on reducing energy usage in our restaurants. In Switzerland, we annually avoid 420 000 kilometers of trucking and, in turn, the use of 132 000 liters of diesel fuel by shipping restaurant supplies via rail. In Latin America, we have partnered with Conservation International to create and implement a sustainable agriculture program to protect the rainforests in Costa Rica and Panama. In Australia, we have committed to meet that country's Greenhouse Challenge to reduce greenhouse emissions.

Diversity – We believe a global team of talented, diverse employees, franchisees and suppliers is key to the company's ongoing success. We work to create and maintain an inclusive environment and expand the range of opportunities, thereby enabling all our people to reach their highest potential and generate the most value for McDonald's and the best experience for customers. McDonald's also provides opportunities for women and minorities to become franchisees and suppliers and offers a wide range of support to help them build their businesses. These efforts have paid off: Today, more than 30 per cent of McDonald's franchisees are women and minorities, and in 1999, we purchased about $3 billion worth of goods and services from women and minority suppliers.

Employment – Being a good corporate citizen begins with the way we treat our people. We are focused on developing people at every level, starting in our restaurants. We invest in training and development programs that encourage personal growth and higher levels of performance. These efforts help us attract and retain quality people and motivate superior performance.

Education – As one of the largest employers of youth, education is a key priority. So the company, our franchisees and RMHC proudly provide about $5 million in educational assistance through a variety of scholarship programs. We also honor teachers' dedication and commitment to education with the McDonald's Education Award.

Safety/quality – We are committed to ensuring safety and quality in every country where we do business. Accordingly, we set strict quality specifications for our products and work with suppliers worldwide to see that they are met. This includes ongoing testing in labs and on-site inspection of supplier facilities. Restaurant managers worldwide are extensively trained in safe handling and preparation of our food. Also, we continually review, modify and upgrade the equipment at PlayPlaces and Playlands to provide a safe play environment. Our quality control efforts also encompass animal welfare. Notably, we are working with a leading animal welfare expert in the US to implement an auditing process with our meat suppliers to ensure the safe and humane treatment of animals.

Source: www.mcdonalds.com.

Further reading and bibliography

- David Emery, 'Ratburger – Family Sues McDonald's After Allegedly Finding Rat's Head in Burger', www.urbanlegends.about.com, 4 April 2001.
- Viji Sundaram, 'Where's the Beef? It's in Your French Fries', *India-West*, 9 April 2001.
- 'Lawsuit says McDonald's Uses Beef Fat in French Fries', www.seattleinsider.com, 2 May 2001.
- Pais, J. Arthur, 'Harish Bharti Fears Dirty Tricks', www.rediff.com, 4 May 2001.
- Nanda Harbaksh Singh, 'Hindu Zealots Throw Cow Dung at McDonald's', www.mcspotlight.org, 4 May 2001.
- 'Bharti's Beef With McDonald's', www.rediff.com, 4 May 2001.
- Nirsha Perera, 'Bharti gets Clinching Evidence Against McDonald's', www.rediff.com, 5 May 2001.
- 'Indian Beef Protesters Raid McDonald's', www.europe.cnn.com, 5 May 2001.
- 'McDonald's India Denies Beef Flavouring', www.blonnet.com, 5 May 2001.
- 'No Beef Extract in French Fries, Claims McDonald's', www.rediff.com, 5 May 2001.

- 'Quit India, Sena tells McDonald's', www.hindu.com, 6 May 2001.
- Arthur J. Pais, 'I've Been Violated for Over a Decade!' www.rediff.com, 6 May 2001.
- Venugopal, Arun, 'Even the Pea Soup has Ham!', www.rediff.com, 9 May 2001.
- Laurie Goodstein, 'For Hindus and Vegetarians, Surprise in McDonald's Fries', www.common-dreams.org, May 2001.
- Nirshan Perera, 'Will You Get Any McDonald's Money?' www.rediff.com, 1 June 2001.
- Emma Brockes, 'Life After McLibel', www.mcspotlight.org, 7 June 2000.
- Guha Suman Mozumder, 'Another Class Action Lawsuit Against McDonald's', *India Abroad*, June 2001.
- Deborah Cohen, 'McDonald's Tries to Diffuse Meaty Fries Row', www.mcspotlight.org, 13 August 2001.
- Vivian Chu, 'Big Mac Will Pay $10 million to Patrons if Offended', *Economic Times*, 9 March 2002.
- 'Big Mac Atones for Beef Fries With $10 million', *Business Line*, 9 March 2002.
- Chidananda Rajghatta, 'McDonald's Apologises, to Pay $10 million to Veggies', *Times of India*, 9 March 2002.
- 'McFacts about the McDonald's Coffee Lawsuit', www.lawandhelp.com.
- www.mcspotlight.org.
- www.mcdonalds.com.

References

1 A class-action suit is a suit filed to protect the interests of groups of individuals who are affected or may be affected by a perceived fraud or misconduct of a similar nature. The number of people could be as few as under 10 to millions. Typically, class-action suits in the US drag on for years and very often parties settle out of court within the first year of filing.

2 Thinly sliced, finger-sized pieces of potato, deep fried and served with a sprinkling of salt.

3 Tallow refers to shortening made from beef fat.

4 Cholesterol is a soft, waxy substance found in the lipids (fats) in the bloodstream and in all body cells. It forms cell membranes, hormones and other needed tissues in the body. However, a very high level of cholesterol in the blood causes cardiovascular diseases and leads to heart attacks and strokes. Foods rich in saturated fats cause the cholesterol level to rise thereby increasing the chances of cardiovascular diseases.

5 The book provides a detailed account of the negative aspects associated with the products and operations of fast-food giants such as Burger King and McDonald's.

6 The term 'kosher' is used to describe foods or other animal products that are fit for consumption according to the religious rules of the Jewish community. By ensuring that the food is kosher, the Jews believe that they recognise the value of the life taken, while at the same time integrating religion into their dietary practices.

This case was written by A. Mukund, ICFAI Center for Management Research (ICMR). It is intended to be used as a basis for class discussion rather than to illustrate either effective or ineffective handling of a management situation.

The case was compiled from published sources.

case 2.4 Coke and Pepsi Learn to Compete in India

The beverage battlefield

In 2003 Jagdeep Kapoor, chairman of Samsika Marketing Consultants in Mumbai (formerly Bombay), commented that 'Coke lost a number of years over errors. But at last it seems to be getting its positioning right.' Similarly, Ronald McEachern, Pepsi-Co's Asia chief, asserted 'India is the beverage battlefield for 2003.'

The experience of the world's two giant soft drinks companies in India during the 1990s and the beginning of the new millennium was not a happy one, even though the governments had opened its doors wide to foreign companies. Both companies experienced a range of unexpected problems and difficult situations that led them to recognise that competing in India requires special knowledge, skills and local expertise. In many ways, Coke and Pepsi managers had to learn the hard way that 'what works here' does not always 'work there'. In spring 2003, Alex von Behr, the president of Coca-Cola India admitted ruefully, 'The environment in India is challenging, but we're learning how to crack it.'

The Indian soft drinks industry

In India, over 45 per cent of the soft drinks industry in 1993 consisted of small manufacturers. Their combined business was worth $3.2 million dollars. Leading producers included Parle Agro (hereafter 'Parle'), Pure Drinks, Modern Foods, and McDowells. They offered carbonated cola drinks, orange, and lemon-lime beverages. Coca-Cola Corporation (hereafter 'Coca-Cola') was only a distant memory to most Indians at that time. The company had been present in the Indian market from 1958 until its withdrawal in 1977, following a dispute with the government over its trade secrets. After decades in the market, Coca-Cola chose to leave India rather than cut its equity stake to 40 per cent and hand over its secret formula for the syrup.

Following Coca-Cola's departure, Parle became the market leader and established thriving export franchise businesses in Dubai, Kuwait, Saudi Arabia, and Oman in the Gulf, along with Sri Lanka. It set up production in Nepal and Bangladesh, and served distant markets in Tanzania, Britain, the Netherlands and the United States. Parle invested heavily in image advertising at home, estab-lishing the dominance of its flagship brand, Thums Up.

Thums Up is a brand associated with a 'job well done' and personal success. These are persuasive messages for its target market of young people aged 15 to 24. Parle has been careful in the past not to call Thums Up a cola drink, so it has avoided direct comparison with Coke and Pepsi, the world's brand leaders.

The soft drinks market in India is composed of six product segments: cola, 'cloudy lemon', orange, 'soda' (carbonated water), mango and 'clear lemon', in order of importance. Cloudy lemon and clear lemon together make up the lemon-lime segment. Prior to the arrival of foreign producers in India, the fight for local dominance was between Parle's Thums Up and Pure Drinks' Campa Cola.

In 1988, the industry had experienced a dramatic shake-out following a government warning that BVO, an essential ingredient in locally produced soft drinks, was carcinogenic. Producers either had to resort to using a costly imported substitute, estergum, or they had to finance their own R&D in order to find a substitute ingredient. Many failed and quickly withdrew from the industry.

Competing with the segment of carbonated soft drinks is another beverage segment composed of non-carbonated fruit drinks. These are a growth industry because Indian consumers perceive fruit drinks to be natural, healthy, and tasty. The leading brand has tradition-ally been Parle's Frooti, a mango-flavoured drink, which was also exported to franchisees in the United States, Britain, Portugal, Spain and Mauritius.

Opening up the Indian market in 1991

In June 1991, India experienced an economic crisis of exceptional severity, triggered by the rise in imported oil prices following the first Gulf War (after Iraq's invasion of Kuwait). Foreign exchange reserves fell as non-resident Indians (NRIs) cut back on repatriation of their savings, imports were tightly controlled across all sectors and industrial production fell while inflation was rising. A new government took office in June 1991 led by Prime Minister Narasimha Rao. Inspired by Finance Minister Dr Manmohan Singh, the government introduced measures to stabilise the economy in the short term and launched a

fundamental restructuring programme to ensure medium-term growth. Results were dramatic. By 1994, inflation was halved, exchange reserves were greatly increased, exports were growing and foreign investors were looking at India, a leading Big Emerging Market, with new eyes.

The turnaround could not be overstated; one commentator said, 'India has been in economic depression for so long that everything except the snake-charmers, cows and the Taj Mahal has faded from the memory of the world.' For many years, the outside world had viewed the Indian Government as unfriendly to foreign investors. Outside investment had been allowed only in high-tech sectors and was almost entirely prohibited in consumer goods sectors. The 'principle of indigenous availability' had specified that if an item could be obtained anywhere else within the country, imports of similar items were forbidden. As a result of this policy, India became self-reliant in its defence industry, developing both nuclear and space programmes. In contrast, Indian consumers had little choice of products or brands, and no guarantees of quality or reliability.

Following liberalisation of the Indian economy in 1991 and introduction of the New Industrial Policy intended to dismantle complicated trade rules and regulations, foreign investment increased dramatically. Beneficiary industries included processed foods, software, engineering plastics, electronic equipment, power generation and petroleum generation. A commentator observed, 'In the 1970s and 1980s, it was almost antinational to advocate foreign investment. Today the Prime Minister and Finance Minister are wooing foreign investors.'

Foreign companies that had successfully pioneered entry into the Indian market many decades earlier, despite all the stringent rules, quickly increased their equity stakes under the new rules from 40 per cent to 51 per cent. These long-established companies included global giants such as Unilever, Procter & Gamble, Pfizer, Hoechst, BAT and Philips (of the Netherlands).

Coca-Cola and PepsiCo enter the Indian market

Despite its huge population, India had not been considered by foreign beverage producers to be an important market in the past. In addition to the deterrents imposed by the government through its austere trade policies, rules and regulations, local demand for carbonated drinks in India was very low, compared to countries at a similar stage of economic development. In 1989, the average Indian was buying only three bottles a year. This compared to per capita consumption rates of 11 bottles a year in Bangladesh and 13 in Pakistan, India's two neighbours.

PepsiCo

PepsiCo lodged a joint venture application to enter India in July 1986. It had selected two local partners, Voltas and Punjab Agro. This application was approved under the name 'Pepsi Foods Ltd' by the government of Rajiv Gandhi in September 1988. As expected, very stringent conditions were imposed on the venture. Sales of soft drink concentrate to local bottlers could not exceed 25 per cent of total sales for the new venture. This limit also included processing of fruits and vegetables by Pepsi Foods Ltd. Robert Beeby, CEO of Pepsi-Cola International, said at that time: 'We're willing to go so far with India because we wanted to make sure we get an early entry while the market is developing.'

In May 1990, the government mandated that Pepsi Food's products be promoted under the name 'Lehar Pepsi' ('lehar' meaning 'wave'). Foreign collaboration rules in force at the time prohibited use of foreign brand names on products intended for sale inside India. Other examples of this policy were Maruti Suzuki, Carrier Aircon, L&T Honeywell, Wilkinson's Wiltech, Modi-Champion, and Modi-Xerox.

In keeping with local tastes, Pepsi Foods launched Lehar 7UP in the clear lemon category, along with Lehar Pepsi. Marketing and distribution were focused in the north and west around the major cities of Delhi and Mumbai. An aggressive pricing policy on the one-litre bottles had a severe impact on the local producer, Pure Drinks. The market leader, Parle, pre-empted any further pricing moves by Pepsi Foods by introducing a new 250 ml bottle that sold for the same price as its 200 ml bottle.

Pepsi Foods struggled to fight off local competition from Pure Drinks' Campa Cola, Duke's lemonade and various brands of Parle. Aware of its difficulties, Pepsi Foods approached Parle in December 1991 to offer an alliance. Parle declined the offer, choosing to stand its ground and continuing to fight to preserve its number one position.

The fight for dominance intensified in 1993 with Pepsi Food's launch of two new brands, Slice and Teem, along with the introduction of fountain sales. At this time, market shares in the cola segment were 60 per cent for Parle (down from 70 per cent), 26 per cent for Pepsi Foods, and 10 per cent for Pure Drinks.

Coca-Cola

In May 1990, Coca-Cola attempted to re-enter India by means of a proposed joint venture with a local bottling company owned by the giant Indian conglomerate, Godreg. The government of Rajiv Gandhi turned down this application just as PepsiCo's application was being approved. Undeterred, Coca-Cola made its return to India by joining forces with Britannia Industries India Ltd, a local producer of snack foods. The new venture was called Britco Foods. In 1993 Coca-Cola filed an application to create a 100 per cent-owned soft drinks company, Coca-Cola India.

The arrival of Coca-Cola in the Indian soft drinks industry forced local small producers to consider extreme

survival measures. The small Delhi-based company, Pure Drinks, tried to revamp its bottling alliance with Coca-Cola from earlier years, even offering to withdraw its own leading brand, Campa Cola, as an inducement to Coca-Cola. Campa Cola's brand share at the time was 10 per cent. However, Coca-Cola had its sights set on a different partner, Parle.

Among local producers, it was believed at that time that Coca-Cola would not take market share away from local companies because the beverage market was itself growing consistently from year to year. Yet this belief did not stop individual local producers from trying to align themselves with the market leader. Thus, in July 1993, Parle offered to sell its leading brands including Thums Up, Limca, Citra, Gold Spot and Mazaa. It chose to retain ownership only of Frooti and a soda (carbonated water) called Bisleri.

As a result of Parle's offer, two new ventures were set up to bottle and market both companies' products. The marketing venture would provide advertising, media services, and promotional and sales support. Parle's chief, Ramesh Chauhan, was named chairman and Coca-Cola staffed the managing director's position. Parle held 49 per cent of the marketing venture but took an equal 50 per cent stake in the bottling venture.

Fast forward to the new millennium

Seasonal sales promotions – the 2000 Navrartri campaign

In India the summer season for soft drink consumption lasts 70-75 days from mid-April to June. During this time, over 50 per cent of the year's carbonated beverages are consumed across the country. The second-highest season for consumption lasts only 20-25 days during the cultural festival of Navrartri ('Nav' means nine and 'rarti' means night). This is a traditional Gujarati festival and it goes on for nine nights in the state of Gujarat, in the western part of India. Mumbai also has a significant Gujarati population that is considered part of the target market for this campaign.

As Sunil Kapoor, regional marketing manager for Coca-Cola India stated, 'As part of the "think local – act local" business plan, we have tried to involve the masses in Gujarat with "Thums Up Toofani Ramjhat": with 20 000 free passes issued, one per Thums Up bottle. ['Toofan' means a thunderstorm and 'ramjhat' means 'let's dance,' so together these words convey the idea of a 'fast dance.'] There are a number of [retail] on-site activities too, such as the "buy one – get one free" scheme and lucky draws where one can win a free trip to Goa.' (Goa is an independent Portuguese-speaking state on the west coast of India, that is famed for its beaches and tourist resorts.)

For its part, PepsiCo also participates in annual Navrarti celebrations through massive sponsorships in 'garba' competitions in selected venues in Gujarat. ('Garba' is the name of a dance, which is done by women during the Navratri festival.) In 2000 Deepak Jolly, executive vice-president for PepsiCo India, commented: 'For the first time, Pepsi has tied up with the Gujarati TV channel, Zee Alpha, to telecast "Navrartri Utsav 2000 at Mumbai" on all nine nights. ['Utsav' means festival.] Then there is the mega offer for the people of Ahmedabad, Baroda, Surat, and Rajkot where every refill of a case of Pepsi 300 ml bottles will fetch one kilo of Basmati rice free.' (These are four cities located in the state of Gujarat. Basmati rice is considered to be a premium quality rice. After the initial purchase of a 300 ml bottle, consumers can get refills at reduced rates at select stores.)

During the Navrartri festival, both companies are extremely generous with giveaways in their sales promotions. For example, in 2000 Pepsi Foods offered a free Kit-Kat with every 1.5 litre bottle and a packet of Polos (hard candies like 'Lifesavers') with each 500 ml bottle of Pepsi and Mirinda.

The 2002 summer TV campaign

In 2002 Pepsi Foods took the lead in the clear lime category with 7UP leading its category, followed by Coca-Cola's Sprite brand. On 7 March 2002, it launched a new summer campaign for 7UP. This date was chosen to coincide with the India-Zimbabwe one-day cricket series. The new campaign slogan was 'Keep It Cool' to emphasise the product attribute of refreshment.

A nationwide television advertising campaign was designed with the objectives of growing the category and building brand salience. The national campaign was to be reinforced with regionally adapted TV campaigns, outdoor activities, and retail promotions.

PepsiCo's ad spending for 7UP was not comparable to the level invested in its flagship brand Pepsi-Cola because the clear lime segment in 2002 was minuscule, accounting for just 4.5 per cent of the total carbonated soft drinks market. This was equal to about 250-270 million cases. The cloudy lemon segment is more than twice this size, with 10 per cent market share; carbonated orange drinks account for about 15 per cent.

7UP was being sold in 250 ml, 300 ml and 500 ml bottles, and in 200 ml bottles in southern states. The industry trend was pushing towards 200 ml bottles in order to increase frequency of purchase and volume of consumption. Pepsi Foods rolled out its Mirinda Lemon, Apple and Orange in 200 ml bottles in the Delhi market, following similar market launches in Punjab and Uttar Pradesh in the previous year.

In the past, celebrity actors, Amitabh Bachchan and Govinda, who are famous male stars of the Indian movie

industry, had endorsed Mirinda Lemon. This world-famous industry is referred to as 'Bollywood' (the Hollywood of India, based in Bombay).

Both Coca-Cola and PepsiCo routinely keep close track of the success of their seasonal advertising campaigns in India through use of marketing research agencies. Coca-Cola has used ORG-MARG, while Pepsi Foods has worked with IMRB. ORG-MARG uses its weekly 'Ad Track' to study spontaneous ad recall among 1000 male and female respondents aged 12–49 in 17 cities. IMRB's 'Perception Analyser System' surveys 15 to 30 year olds in four cities. Responses are sought on measures of likeability of the ad and intention to buy.

Pepsi's sponsorship of cricket and football (soccer)

After India won an outstanding victory in the 2002 India-England NatWest one-day cricket series finals, PepsiCo launched a new ad campaign featuring the batting sensation Mohammad Kaif. Although he had been signed up a year earlier, Kaif had not yet figured in Pepsi ads. The spotlight had been on Sachin Tendulkar and Amitabh Bachchan who are famous icons as a cricket player and a movie star, respectively. Sachin Tendulkar is considered to be the best batsman in the history of cricket. He started his international cricket career at the age of 16, and now at age 29 he already figures in the list of top young billionaires in the country. Amitabh Bachchan has the distinction of having being the leading superstar in the Indian movie industry for the last 30 years. Even now, at 60 years of age he commands the highest name rating any star has every received in Bollywood.

PepsiCo's line-up of other cricket celebrities includes Saurav Ganguly, Rahul Dravid, Harbhajan Singh, Zaheer Khan, V.V.S. Laxman and Ajit Agarkar. Saurav Ganguly is presently the captain of the Indian cricket team. All of these players were part of the Indian team for the 2003 Cricket World Cup held in South Africa, where they performed superbly, reaching the finals. They lost to Australia in the finals, but PepsiCo was able to capitalise on the overall team's performance during the month and a half long tournament.

Six months earlier, PepsiCo had taken advantage of World Cup soccer fever in India, featuring football heroes such as Baichung Bhutia in their celebrity and music-related advertising communications. These ads featured football players pitted against sumo wrestlers. In addition, para football tournaments were held in selected cities.

In 2003, similar sports-themed promotions took place, centred around PepsiCo's sponsorship of the World Cup Series in cricket. During the two months of the series, a new product, Pepsi Blue, was marketed nationwide. This was positioned as a 'limited edition', icy-blue cola sold in 300 ml returnable glass bottles and 500 ml plastic bottles. These were priced at 8 rupees (Rs) and Rs15 respectively. In addition, commemorative, nonreturnable 250 ml Pepsi bottles priced at Rs12 were introduced. (1 rupee was equal to 2.08 US cents in 2003.)

To consolidate its investment in the 2003 campaign, PepsiCo also featured a music video with other celebrity endorsers including the Bollywood stars Amitabh Bachchan, Kareena Kapoor, Abishek Bachchan (the son of Amitabh Bachchan) and Fardeen Khan, as well as several cricketers. The new music video aired on SET Max which is a satellite channel owned by Sony. This channel is popular among the 15-25 age group, mainly in the northern and western parts of India.

Coca-Cola's lifestyle advertising

In 2002 and 2003, Coca-Cola India used a strategy of 'building a connect using the relevant local idioms', according to Rajesh Mani, regional marketing manager. The ad strategy, developed by Orchard Advertising in Bangalore, was based on use of 'gaana' music and ballet. ('Gaana' means to sing.)

The first ad execution, called 'Bombay Dreams,' featured A.R. Rahman, who is a famous music director. This approach was very successful among the target audience of young people, increasing sales by about 50 per cent. It also won an Effi Award from the Mumbai Advertising Club. (Note: even though the name of the city has been officially changed from Bombay to Mumbai, local people still continue to use Bombay.)

2003 saw the launch of a second execution of this regional strategy in Chennai (formerly Madras), called 'Chennai Dreams.' This ad featured Vijay, a youth icon who is famous as an actor in the regional movies of south India. The campaign targeted consumers in Tamil Nadu located in the southern part of the country. Thomas Xavier, executive creative director of Orchard Advertising, commented that the success of the ad was due to insight into needs of the target market. 'We were clear that the need of the hour was not for an ad film, but for a Tamil feature film in 60 seconds.'

In 2002 Coca-Cola India worked hard to build up a brand preference for its flagship brand, Coke, among young people in rural target markets. The campaign slogan was 'thanda matlab Coca-Cola' (or 'cool means Coca-Cola' in Hindi). Coca-Cola India calls its rural youth target market 'India B'. The prime objective in this market is to grow the generic soft drinks category and to develop brand preference for Coke. The 'thanda' ('cold') campaign of 2002 successfully propelled Coke into the number three position in rural markets.

The urban youth target market, known as 'India A,' includes 18 to 24 year olds in the major metropolitan

areas. In 2003, the urban youth market was targeted with a campaign developed by McCann-Erickson. The TV ad ran for 60 seconds and featured actor Vivek Oberoi with Aishwarya Rai. Both are famous as Bollywood movie stars. Aishwarya was the winner of the Miss World crown in 1994 and became an instant hit in Indian movies after she decided on a career of acting.

This ad showed Oberoi trying to hook up with Rai by deliberately leaving his mobile phone in the taxi that she hails, and then calling her. The ad message aimed to emphasise confidence and optimism, and a them of 'seize the day', according to Shripad Nadkarni, Vice-President of Marketing for Coca-Cola India. The 2003 campaign used a variety of media including television, print, outdoor, point-of-sale, restaurant and grocery chains, and local promotional events. 'While awareness of soft drinks is higher, there is a need to build a deeper brand connect' in urban centres, according to Sharda Agarwal, director of marketing for Coca-Cola India. 'Vivek Oberoi – who's an up and coming star today, and has a wholesome, energetic image – will help build a stronger bond with the youth, and make them feel that it is a brand that plays a role in their life, just as much as Levi's or Ray-Ban.'

Coca-Cola's specific marketing objectives for 2003 were to grow the per-capita consumption of soft drinks in the rural markets, and to capture a larger share in the urban market from competition and increase the frequency of consumption there, according to Ms Agarwal. It was expected that a new 'affordability plank' in the advertising strategy, along with introduction of a new 5 rupee bottle, would help to achieve all of these goals.

The 'affordability plank'

In 2003, Coca-Cola India dramatically reduced prices of its soft drinks by 15 per cent to 25 per cent nationwide, in order to encourage consumption. This followed an earlier regional action in North India that reduced prices by 10-15 per cent for its carbonated brands, Coke, Thums Up, Limca, Sprite and Fanta. In other regions such as Rajasthan, western and eastern Uttar Pradesh, and Tamil Nadu, prices were slashed to Rs5 for 200 ml glass bottles and Rs8 for 300 ml.

These price reductions were in keeping with Coca-Cola's goal of enhancing affordability of their products, bringing them within arm's reach of consumers and thereby promoting regular consumption. Given the very low per-capita consumption of soft drinks in India, it was expected that price reductions would expand both the consumer base and the market for soft drinks. PepsiCo was forced to match these price reductions, leading PepsiCo's Asia chief to conclude: 'India is the beverage battlefield for 2003.'

Another initiative by Coca-Cola was the introduction of a new size, the 'Mini'. This was expected to increase total volume of sales and

account for the major chunk of Coca-Cola's carbonated soft drink sales, according to Rajesh Mani, regional marketing manager for Coca-Cola India.

The price reduction and new production launch were announced together by means of a new television ad campaign for Fanta and Coke in Tamil. Lower Chennai created the ad concept, with executions by Primary Colors for Fanta and Rajiv Menon Productions for Coke. Both agencies are based in Chennai.

The 30-second Fanta spot featured brand ambassador, actress Simran, well known for her dance sequences in Hindi movies. The ad showed Simran stuck in a traffic jam. Thirsty, she tosses at 5-rupee coin to a roadside stall and signals to the vendor that she wants a Fanta Mini by pointing to her orange dress. (Fanta is an orangeade drink.) She gets her Fanta and sets off a chain reaction on the crowded street, with everyone from school children to a traditional 'nani' mimicking her action. ('Nani' is the Hindi word for grandmother.)

Rajesh Mani commented that the company wanted to make consumers 'sit up and take notice'. This was accomplished 'by using a local star, with local insight, because Tamil Nadu is a big market for Fanta'.

A new product category

In order to encourage growth in demand for bottled beverages in the Indian market, several producers have launched their own brand in a new category, bottled water. This market was valued at 1000 Crore in 2003. (1 Crore = 10 000 000 rupees, US$1 = Rs48, so 1000 Crore = US$ 0.2083 million.)

Coca-Cola's brand, Kinley, was introduced in 2000. Ogilvy & Mather designed a two-ad television campaign. By 2002 Kinley had achieved a 28 per cent market share and was being produced in 15 plants. The biggest of these are located in Mumbai, Delhi, Goa and Bangalore. In 2003 it was planned to double bottling capacity by adding another 10 to 15 production plants. These would be a combination of company-owned plants, franchisee operations and contract packing companies.

The Kinley brand of bottled water sells in various pack sizes: 500 ml, 1 litre, 1.5 litre, 2 litre, 5 litre, 20 litre and 25 litre. The smallest pack was priced at Rs6 for 500 ml, while the 2 litre bottle was Rs17.

The current market leader with 40 per cent market share is the Bisleri brand, owned by Ramesh Chauhan who is the CEO of Parle. Pepsi Foods' brand is Aquafina with about 11 per cent market share. Aquafina is produced in six company-owned or franchised bottling plants in Roha (Maharashtra), Bangalore, Kolkata (formerly Calcutta) and New Delhi. Focusing on metropolitan areas, Pepsi Foods' ad campaign uses both television and outdoor media, and is managed by HTA, Pepsi Foods' agency.

Other competing brands in this segment include Bailley by Parle, Hello by Hello Mineral Waters Pvt. Ltd, Pure Life by Nestlé, and a new brand launched by Indian Railways called Rail Neer.

Coca-Cola's attempts to 'crack' the Indian market

By 2002, Coca-Cola owned 30 bottling plants, 10 franchisees and held a 56 per cent market share of the national soft drink market in India. Yet despite creative and locally responsive marketing efforts and a total investment of some $840 million to build its distribution and manufacturing infrastructure, Coca-Cola had reported losses in India since its return there in 1993. In 2001 the company had written off a loss of $400 million. Total accumulated losses were estimated to be over 2000 Crore (US$0.4166 million).

To make matters worse, in January 2002 the company was ordered by the government to sell to Indian investors 49 per cent of Hindustan Coca-Cola Holding Pvt. Ltd (HCCHPL), the wholly owned holding company for all Coca-Cola operations in India. This move by the government followed action taken by Coca-Cola in 1996 when it had requested and received government permission to increase its investment in the Indian market. Under the new governmental policy passed that same year affecting all new soft drink investments. Coca-Cola had agreed to sell 49 per cent of its equity to Indian partners within two years. This time limit had been extended once already, but a request for a second extension to 2007 was turned down on 3 October 2001. Coca-Cola was hoping that by 2007 it would be in a stronger financial position and would receive a better return on its forced disinvestment.

The government's response to the company's second request was that 'entry conditions cannot be changed'. This response might have been acceptable if investment rules in India were clear and unchanging, but this was not the case during the 1990s when implementation of government rules had been inconsistent. Some companies, like Coca-Cola, were required to reduce their equity in order to allow Indians into the industry. At the same time, other companies – like Philips (of the Netherlands), Carrier (of the United States) and Cadbury-Schweppes (of Britain) – were being allowed to buy back most of their outstanding shares and would likely delist their shares altogether, effectively making their Indian operations wholly owned subsidiaries. This was the status that Coca-Cola was being forced to give up.

Local market analysts commented that there is no apparent logic behind these government policies, other than to allow local investors to become bargain hunters at the expense of Coca-Cola.

Coca-Cola responded by trying to maintain some control over its operations. It applied for government approval from the Foreign Investment Promotion Board (FIPB) to deny voting rights to its new Indian shareholders. Again the government response was that the company had to abide by the legal provisions that were applicable on the date of its original foreign investment in the country. Since all equities back in 1996–1997 had mandatory voting rights, it was considered normal that Indian shareholders in this case should receive voting rights. The Indian Government in May 2002 turned down Coca-Cola's request for a waiver of the disinvestment rule.

Making things even more difficult for Coca-Cola at that time was a change of oversight of the FIPB, from the Ministry of Industry to the Department of Economic Affairs. This change would require Coca-Cola and other foreign companies to build new relationships with bureaucrats, rendering past lobbying efforts useless.

Local business observers faulted Coca-Cola for trying to obtain repeated waivers of the disinvestment rule, pointing to the favourable expectation of an over-subscription for shares in the company's Initial Public Offering. One commentator said 'This is in no way a priority industry, and when it [Coca-Cola] was permitted to do business in India, it was with the condition that it will dilute a 49 per cent stake after five years. Foreign companies keep on saying that in India promises are not fulfilled. Why doesn't this multinational set an example by fulfilling its own commitment in this particular issue?' Another stated unsympathetically, 'They went into this with their eyes open.'

The Indian Government had originally stipulated the 49 per cent disinvestment clause as a condition for its agreement to allow Coca-Cola to buy out local Indian bottlers when the company first entered the market, instead of setting up greenfield bottling plants as Coca-Cola had initially proposed. In contrast to Coca-Cola, PepsiCo had entered India in a different year under a different set of rules. Moreover, it was not held to a disinvestment rule because it had opted to set up several greenfield bottling units.

Coca-Cola India initiated its compliance with the government disinvestment rule in February 2003 by following the private placement route. It agreed to place 49 per cent of equity from its wholly owned subsidiary Hindustan Coca-Cola Holdings Pvt. Ltd (HCCHPL) worth $41 million, in its bottling subsidiary Hindustan Coca-Cola Beverages Pvt. Ltd (HCCBPL). HCCBPL runs the bottling plants originally taken over from local Indian bottlers including Parle. Of the 49 per cent equity placed by HCCHPL, 10 per cent was placed in Hindustan Coca-Cola Beverages (HCCB), in favour of employee and welfare trusts.

The second Gulf War

During spring 2003, as a result of the attack by the United States and Britain on Iraq, a call was launched by the All-India Anti-Imperialist Forum to boycott purchases of American and British goods. The boycott targeted specifically Pepsi, Coca-Cola and McDonald's as a protest against the 'unjust' war. The Forum's president is Justice V.R. Krishna Iyer, a former judge of the Indian Supreme Court. The Forum's general secretary, S.K. Mukherjee, said 'We give a call to all peace-loving people of the world and India to rise up in protest against the imperialist aggression against Iraq ...'. Within two weeks of the announcement of the boycott, sales of Coke and Pepsi in the southern Indian state of Kerala plummeted 50 per cent.

Members of the Forum included more than 250 non-governmental groups. These went on 'shop-to-shop' campaigns to persuade retailers not to stock American products. They visited homes in Kerala presenting the same plea to consumers. Other items on the boycott list included toothpaste, soap, cooking oil and cosmetics. Retailers feared a public backlash if they stocked items on the boycott list. In place of brand name items, retailers were asked to promote local substitutes such as a herbal product in place of toothpaste and mango juice instead of colas. Sunil Gupta, vice-president of Hindustan Coca-Cola Beverages, commented that this action would hurt not only the Kerala region. 'We have one million retail suppliers of our products [in India]. In the event of a boycott, it is the Indian economy that will be hit.'

Learning some hard lessons

In 2002 Coca-Cola's overall sales reached $940 million and company products accounted for more than half the soft drinks market. A three-year cost-cutting programme had brought dramatic results, reducing the company's payroll by 23 per cent. Eight outdated plants, inherited from the Thums Up purchase, were closed. Local purchasing policies brought savings of 57 per cent on import duties. Coca-Cola's well-known but poorly supported Thums Up brand was reinvigorated with an infusion of $3.5 million spent on advertising and distribution. Market share for Thums Up that had slipped from more than 60 per cent of carbonated beverage sales down to a puny 15 per cent was regained. Within a year, Thums Up was back to the number two rank nationwide. Coke still trailed its arch-rival Pepsi, however, with a market share of only 16.5 per cent versus 23.5 per cent.

Compared with per-capita consumption rates in other Big Emerging Markets, India's rate was still very low in 2003 at seven (8 oz) servings per person. This compared with 14 in Pakistan, 89 in China, 278 in South Africa, 471 in Brazil, 1484 in Mexico and 1404 in the domestic US

market. Coca-Cola India's director of finance, N. Sridhar, stated confidently, however, 'We have turned a corner.' In a similar vein, Jagdeep Kapoor, chairman of Samsika Marketing Consultants in Mumbai, concluded 'Coke lost a number of years over errors. But at last it seems to be getting its positioning right.'

Questions

1 The political environment in India has proven to be critical to company performance for both PepsiCo and Coca-Cola India. What specific aspects of the political environment have played key roles? Could these effects have been anticipated prior to market entry? If not, could developments in the political arena have been handled better by each company?

2 Timing of entry into the Indian market brought different results for PepsiCo and Coca-Cola India. What benefits or disadvantages accrued as a result of earlier or later market entry?

3 The Indian market is enormous in terms of population and geography. How have the two companies responded to the sheer scale of operations in India in terms of product policies, promotional activities, pricing policies and distribution arrangements?

4 'Global localisation' (glocalisation) is a policy that both companies have implemented successfully. Give examples for each company from that case.

5 Some analysts consider that Coca-Cola India made mistakes in planning and managing its return to India. Do you agree? What or who do you think was responsible for any mistakes?

6 Which of the two companies do you think has better long-term prospects for success in India?

7 What lessons can each company draw from its Indian experience as it contemplates entry into other Big Emerging Markets?

Dr Lyn S. Amine, PhD, Professor of Marketing and International Business, and Vikas Kumar, International Business and Marketing, ABD Saint Louis University, prepared this case from public sources as a basis for classroom discussion only. It is not intended to illustrate either effective or ineffective handling of administrative problems. Copyright 2003.

Source: Lyn S. Amine and Deepa Raizada (1995), 'Market Entry into the Newly Opened Indian Market: Recent Experience of US Companies in the Soft Drinks Industry', in *Developments in Marketing Science*, XVIII, proceedings of the annual conference of the Academy of Marketing Science, Roger Gomes, ed., AMS: Coral Gables, FL, pp. 287-292. *Business Week, Business Line, Financial Daily, Fortune, India Express.*

section 3
case studies

cases

case 3.1 Swifter, Higher, Stronger, Dearer

Back in 1948, the BBC, Britain's public broadcasting corporation, took a fateful decision. It paid a princely £15 000 (£27 000 in today's money) for the right to telecast the Olympic Games to a domestic audience. It was the first time a television network had paid the International Olympic Committee (IOC, the body that runs the Games) for the privilege.

But not the last: the rights to the Olympics that opened in Atlanta on 19 July 1996 raised $900 million from broadcasters round the world. And the American television rights to the Olympiads up to and including 2008 have been bought by America's NBC network for an amazing $3.6 billion (see Exhibit 1). The Olympics are only one of the sporting properties that have become hugely valuable to broadcasters. Sport takes up a growing share of screen time (as those who are bored by it know all too well). When you consider the popularity of the world's great tournaments, that is hardly surprising. Sportsfests generate audiences beyond the wildest dreams of television companies for anything else. According to Nielsen Media Research, the number of Americans watching the 1996 Superbowl, the main annual football championship, averaged 94 million. The top eight television programmes in America are all sporting events. A staggering 3.5 billion people are likely to watch some part of the 1996 Olympiad – two-thirds of mankind.

The reason television companies love sport is not merely that billions want to tele-gawk at ever more wonderful sporting feats. Sport also has a special quality that makes it unlike almost any other sort of television programme: immediacy. Miss seeing a particular episode of, say, *ER* and you can always catch the repeat, and enjoy it just as much. Miss seeing your team beat the hell out of

Exhibit 1 Chariots for hire – Olympic broadcast rights fees* $bn (world totals)

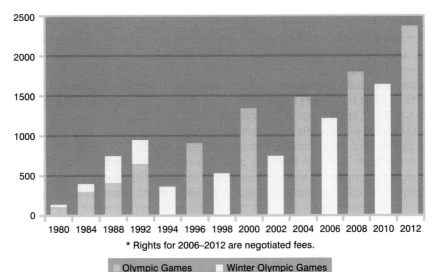

* Rights for 2006–2012 are negotiated fees.

■ Olympic Games   ■ Winter Olympic Games

Source: International Olympic Committee. Used by permission of the International Olympic Committee.

its biggest rival, and the replay will leave you cold. 'A live sporting event loses almost all its value as the final whistle goes,' says Steve Barnett, author of a British book on sport. The desire to watch sport when it is happening, not hours afterwards, is universal: a study of South Korea by Spectrum, a British consultancy, finds that live games get 30 per cent of the audience while recordings get less than 5 per cent.

This combination of popularity and immediacy has created a symbiotic relationship between sport and television in which each is changing the other. As Stephen Wenn, of Canada's Wilfrid Laurier University, puts it, television and the money it brings have had an enormous impact on the Olympic Games, including the timing of events and their location. For instance, an Asian Olympics poses a problem for American networks: viewers learn the results on the morning news.

The money that television has brought into professional basketball has put some of the top players among the world's highest-paid entertainers: a few are getting multi-year contracts worth over $100 million. Rugby has been reorganised to make it more television-friendly; other sports will follow. And, though soccer and American football draw the largest audiences, television has also promoted the popularity of sports which stir more local passions: rugby league in Australia, cricket in India, table tennis in China, snooker in Britain.

What is less often realised is that sport is also changing television. To assuage the hunger for sports, new channels are being launched at a tremendous pace. In America, ESPN, a cable network owned by Capital Cities/ABC, is starting a 24-hour sports news network in the autumn; in Britain, BSkyB, a satellite broadcaster partly owned by Rupert Murdoch, has two sports channels and is about to launch a third. Because people seem more willing to pay to watch sport on television than to pay for any other kind of programming, sport has become an essential part of the business strategy of television empire-builders such as Mr Murdoch. Nobody in the world understands the use of sports as a bait for viewers better than he.

In particular, sport suggests an answer to one of the big problems that will face television companies in the future: how can viewers, comfortable with their old analogue sets, be persuaded to part with the hefty price of a new digital set and a subscription to an untried service? The answer is to create an exclusive chance to watch a desirable event, or to use the hundreds of channels that digital television provides to offer more variety of sports coverage than analogue television can offer. This ploy is not new. 'Radio broadcasts of boxing were once used to promote the sale of radios, and baseball to persuade people to buy television sets,' points out Richard Burton, a sports market-

ing specialist at Lundquist College of Business at Oregon University. In the next few years, the main new outlet for sports programmes will be digital television.

Going for gold

To understand how these multiple effects have come about, go back to those vast sums that television companies are willing to pay. In America, according to Neal Weinstock of Weinstock Media Analysis, total spending on sports rights by television companies is about $2 billion a year. Easily the most valuable rights are for American football. One of the biggest sporting coups in the United States was the purchase by Fox, owned by Mr Murdoch's News Corp, of the rights to four years of National Football League games for $1.6 billion, snatching them from CBS. Rights for baseball, basketball and ice hockey are also substantial.

Americans are rare in following four main sports rather than one. America is also uncommon in having no publicly owned networks. As a result, bidding wars in other countries, though just as fierce as in America, are different in two ways: they are often fought between public broadcasters and new upstarts, many of them pay channels; and they are usually about soccer.

Nothing better illustrates the change taking place in the market for soccer rights than the vast deal struck in early July by Kirch, a German group owned by a secretive Bavarian media mogul. The group spent $2.2 billion for the world's biggest soccer-broadcasting rights: to show the finals of the World Cup in 2002 and 2006 outside America. That is over six times more than the amount paid for the rights to the World Cups of 1990, 1994 and 1998.

Such vast bids gobble up a huge slice of a television company's budget. In America, reckons London Economics, a British consultancy, sport accounts for around 15 per cent of all television-programme spending. For some television companies, the share is much larger. BSkyB spends £100 million ($155 million) a year on sports, about a third of its programming budget.

This seems to pose a threat to public broadcasting, for, in any bidding war outside America, public broadcasting companies are generally the losers. A consortium of mainly public broadcasters bought the rights to the 1990–98 World Cups for a total of $344 million. This time around, the consortium raised its bid to around $1.8 billion, and still lost. Public broadcasters often do not have the money to compete: in Britain, the BBC spends about 4 per cent of its programme budget on sport in a non-Olympic year, about £15 million a year less than BSkyB.

The problem is that the value of sport to viewers ('consumer surplus', as economists would put it) is much larger than the value of most other sorts of programming. Public broadcasters have no way to benefit from the extra value that a big sporting event offers viewers. But with

subscription television and with pay-TV, where viewers are charged for each event, the television company will directly collect the value viewers put on being able to watch.

Because of this, many people (especially in Europe) worry that popular sports will increasingly be available only on subscription television, which could, they fear, erode the popular support upon which public broadcasters depend. In practice, these worries seem excessive. Although far more sport will be shown on subscription television, especially outside America's vast advertising market, the most popular events are likely to remain freely available for many years to come, for two reasons.

First, those who own the rights to sporting events are rarely just profit-maximisers: they also have an interest in keeping the appeal of their sport as broad as possible. They may therefore refuse to sell to the highest bidder. Earlier this year, the IOC turned down a $2 billion bid from Mr Murdoch's News Corp for the European broadcasting rights to the Olympic Games between 2000 and 2008 in favour of a lower bid from a group of public broadcasters. Sometimes, as with the sale of World Cup rights to Kirch, the sellers may stipulate that the games be aired on 'free' television.

Second, the economics of televising sport means that the biggest revenues are not necessarily earned by typing up exclusive rights. Steven Bornstein, the boss of ESPN, argues that exclusive deals to big events are 'not in our long-term commercial interest'. Because showing sport on 'free' television maximises the audience, some advertisers will be willing to pay a huge premium for the big occasion. So will sponsors who want their names to be seen emblazoned on players' shirts or on billboards around the pitch.

It is not only a matter of audience size. Sport is also the most efficient way to reach one of the world's most desirable audiences from an advertiser's point of view: young men with cash to spend. Although the biggest audiences of young men are watching general television, sporting events draw the highest concentrations. So advertisers of products such as beer, cars and sports shoes can pay mainly for the people they most want to attract.

There are other ways in which sport can be indirectly useful to the networks. A slot in a summer game is a wonderful opportunity to promote a coming autumn show. A popular game wipes out the audience share of the competition. And owning the rights to an event allows a network plenty of scope to entertain corporate grandees who may then become advertisers.

For the moment, though, advertising revenue is the main recompense that television companies get for their huge investments in sport. Overall, according to *Broadcasting & Cable*, a trade magazine, sport generated $3.5 billion, or 10 per cent, of total television advertising revenues in America last year. The biggest purchasers of sports rights by far in America are the national networks. NBC alone holds more big sports rights than any other body has held in the history of television. It can, obviously, recoup some of the bill by selling advertising: for a 30-second slot during the Superbowl, NBC asked for $1.2 million.

Such deals, however, usually benefit the networks indirectly rather than directly. The Superbowl is a rarity: it has usually made a profit for the network that airs it. 'Apart from the Superbowl, the World Series [for baseball] and probably the current Olympics, the big sports don't usually make money for the networks,' says Arthur Gruen of Wilkowsky Gruen, a media consultancy. 'But they are a boon for their affiliate stations, which can sell their advertising slots for two or three times as much as other slots.' Although Fox lost money on its NFL purchase, it won the loyalty of affiliate stations (especially important for a new network) and made a splash.

Winning subscriptions

Almost everywhere else, the biggest growth in revenues from showing sports will increasingly come from subscriptions or pay-per-view arrangements. The versatility and huge capacity of digital broadcasting make it possible to give subscribers all sorts of new and lucrative services.

In America, DirectTV and Primestar, two digital satellite broadcasters, have been tempting subscribers with packages of sporting events from distant parts of the country. 'They have been creating season tickets for all the main events, costing $100–150 per season per sport,' says John Mansell, a senior analyst with Paul Kagan, a Californian consultancy. In Germany DF1, a satellite company jointly owned by Kirch and BSkyB and due for launch at the end of July, has the rights to show Formula One motor racing. It plans to allow viewers to choose to follow particular teams, so that Ferrari fanatics can follow their drivers and select different camera angles.

In Italy, Telepiu, which launched digital satellite television in February, plans to offer viewers a package in September which will allow them to buy a season ticket to live matches played by one or more teams in the top Italian soccer leagues. The system's 'electronic turnstile' is so sophisticated that it can shut off reception for subscribers living in the catchment area for a home game, to assuage clubs' worries that they will lose revenue from supporters at the gate. In fact, top Italian clubs usually have to lock out their fanatical subscribers to avoid overcapacity.

Most skilful of all at using sports rights to generate subscription revenue is BSkyB. It signed an exclusive contract with the English Premier League which has been the foundation of its success. Some of those who

know BSkyB well argue that £5 billion of the business's remarkable capital value of £8 billion is attributable to the profitability of its soccer rights.

Winner take all

Just as the purchase of sporting rights enriches television companies, so their sale has transformed the finances of the sports lucky enough to be popular with viewers. On the whole, the biggest beneficiaries have not been the clubs and bodies that run sports, but the players. In the same way as rising revenues from films are promptly dissipated in vast salaries to stars in Hollywood, in sport the money coming in from television soon flows out in heftier payments to players.

In America, the market for sportsmen is well developed and the cost of players tends to rise with the total revenues of the main sporting organisations. Elsewhere, the market is newer and so a bigger slice of the revenues tend to stick to the television companies. 'The big difference between sports and movies is the operating margins,' says Chris Akers, chairman of Caspian, a British media group, and an old hand at rights negotiations. 'Hollywood majors have per-subscriber deals. No sports federation has yet done such a deal.'

Guided by the likes of Mr Akers, they soon will. Telepiu's latest three-year soccer contract gives the television firm enough revenue to cover its basic costs, guarantees the soccer league a minimum sum and then splits the takings down the middle. In Britain, BSkyB is locked in dispute with the Premier League over the terms of the second half of its rights deal: should the league then be able to opt for half the revenue from each subscriber on top of or instead of a fixed hunk of net profits?

The logical next step would be for some clubs or leagues to set up their own pay-television systems, distributing their games directly by satellite or cable. A few people in British soccer are starting to look with interest at America's local sports networks, such as the successful Madison Square Garden cable network, and to wonder whether Europe might move the same way.

If it does, not all teams will benefit equally. In America, football has an elaborate scheme to spread revenues from national television across teams. But in other sports, including baseball, the wealth and size of a team's local market mean large differences in rights from local television. The New York Yankees make almost $50 million a year from local television rights, says Brian Schechter, a Canadian media analyst. At the other end of the scale, the Kansas City Royals, make $4-5 million a year.

Not all players benefit equally, either. Television has brought to sport the 'winner-take-all' phenomenon. It does not cost substantially more to stage a televised championship game than a run-of-the-week untelevised match. But the size of the audience, and therefore the revenue generated, may be hugely different. As a result, players good enough to be in the top games will earn vastly more than those slightly less good, who play to smaller crowds.

A referee's whistle

The lure of money is already altering sport and will change it more. Increasingly, games will be reorganised to turn them into better television. British rugby union officials are squabbling over the spoils from television rights. Rugby league, whose audiences have been dwindling, won a contract worth £87 million over five years from BSkyB this year in exchange for switching its games from winter to summer. Purists were aghast.

Other reorganisations for the benefit of television will surely come. Mr Murdoch wants to build a rugby super-league, allowing the best teams around the world to play each other. A European superleague for soccer is possible. 'At the moment, Manchester United plays AC Milan every 25 years: it's a joke,' complains one enthusiast.

Sports traditionalists resist changing their ways for the likes of Mr Murdoch. So far, the big sporting bodies have generally held out against selling exclusive pay-television rights to their crown jewels, and have sometimes deliberately favoured public broadcasters. Regulators have helped them, intervening in some countries to limit exclusive deals with pay-television groups. Britain has just passed a law to stop subscription channels tying up exclusive rights to some big events, such as the Wimbledon tennis championship. In Australia in March, a court threw out News Corp's attempt to build a rugby superleague as the lynchpin of its pay-television strategy.

But the real monopolists are not the media companies, but the teams. Television companies can play off seven or eight Hollywood studios against each other. But most countries have only one national soccer league, and a public that loves soccer above all other sports. In the long run, the players and clubs hold most of the cards. The television companies are more likely to be their servants than their masters.

Questions

1 The following are the prices paid for the American television broadcasting rights of the summer Olympics since 1980:[1] Moscow – NBC agreed to pay $85 million; 1984 in Los Angeles – ABC paid $225 million; 1988 in Seoul – NBC paid $300 million; 1992 in Barcelona – NBC paid $402 million; 1996 to 2008 – NBC will pay $3.6 billion; 2012 – NBC will pay $1.18 billion. You have been charged with the responsibility of determining the IOC and local Olympic Committees' asking prices for the 2004 television broadcast rights to five different markets: Japan, China, Australia, the European Union and Brazil. Determine a price for each and justify your decisions.

2 Your instructor may assign you to represent either the IOC or any one of the television networks in each of the five countries that have been asked to bid for the broadcast rights for the 2004 Games. Prepare to negotiate prices and other organisational details.

3 The World Football League (WFL), a joint venture between the National Football League (NFL) and Fox Television (owned by Rupert Murdoch's News Corp), has offered you the Edinburgh, Scotland, Claymores franchise. Your Scottish Claymores, should you choose to invest, will be playing against the five WFL teams from London, Barcelona, Amsterdam, Frankfurt and Dusseldorf. What would you be willing to pay for the Claymores? The interested investor will note that a previous incarnation of the WFL with three teams in Europe and seven in the United States folded in its second season in 1992, having lost $50 million.[2]

References

1   See Roy J. Lewicki, Joseph A. Litterer, David M. Saunders and John W. Minton, *Negotiation: Readings, Exercises and Cases*, 2nd edn (Burr Ridge, IL: Irwin, 1993); and John L. Graham and Yoshihiro Sano, *Smart Bargaining: Doing Business with the Japanese*, 2nd edn (New York: HarperCollins, 1989), for details regarding the negotiations.

2   Roger Thurow and A. Craig Copetas, 'NFL Goes Long in its Attempt to Sell World League in Europe', *Wall Street Journal*, 28 March 1997, p. B7.

case 3.2 Motorola in China

With thanks to Motorola

Motorola wants to be a purely Chinese company. We want to be more Chinese than local companies.

– Lai Bingrong, senior vice president, Motorola, Inc.; president, Motorola (China)

The Chinese factor

By 2003, with a cumulative investment of $3.4 billion, Motorola, Inc. topped the list of foreign investors in China. This revealed the importance Motorola attached to the Chinese market. According to Motorola sources, China was a very significant market for the company on account of its size. Mike Zafirovski, president and chief operating officer (COO) of Motorola, said, 'China is a very, very significant partner and the market here is very important for Motorola worldwide as well as a manufacturing base and research centre for the company.'[1]

Motorola's Chinese venture seemed to have been successful. In 1999, Motorola was ranked second, behind Volkswagen[2] in *Fortune*'s[3] list of most favoured foreign enterprises in China. Analysts felt that Motorola's performance in China was incredible, considering the country's difficult social and political environment. It was successful in penetrating the Chinese market and was the leader in the Chinese mobile handset market, with a share of over 20 per cent by the early 2000s.

According to company sources, Motorola was successful in China due to its understanding of the market and the people and because of the strategies it adopted. However, analysts were sceptical about Motorola's success in China in the future on account of increasing competition from both local and foreign players in the mobile handset

market, which was an important product segment for the company. With the growing demand for cell phones and saturating markets for other consumer appliances, many Chinese consumer appliance companies also entered the mobile handset business, thus increasing the competition for multinational companies such as Motorola.

Motorola started feeling the heat by the early 2000s, when it saw its market share declining due to fierce competition in the Chinese mobile handset market. In order to increase its sales and market share, Motorola announced a new strategy in June 2002. Despite this, Motorola continued to lose its market share and analysts were skeptical about its continued dominance in the Chinese market.

Background

The history of US-based Motorola's presence in China dates back to the late 1980s, when Motorola established a representative office in Beijing in 1987. It exported telecommunications gear and semiconductors to China and employed around 600 people to market its products. With increasing competition and production costs, Motorola decided to shift some of its manufacturing activities to China. In 1992, Motorola established Motorola (China) Electronics Ltd and opened a manufacturing facility at Tianjin in north China.

Over the years, Motorola expanded its business in China to various segments, such as personal communication sector (PCS), global telecom solutions sector (GTSS), semiconductor products sector (SPS), commercial, government and industrial solutions sector (CGISS), broadcast communications sector (BCS) and integrated electronics systems sector (IESS).

In 1998, Motorola relocated its north Asia headquarters to Beijing from Hong Kong. By 2000, Motorola was the leader in the mobile handset industry, with around 31 per cent market share. In 2002, revenues from China were reported to be 47 billion yuan ($5.7 billion) - 13 per cent of Motorola's total global revenues - and it employed around 13 000 employees in its 18 R&D facilities and 26 sales offices across China. It was also one of the largest exporters from China - exporting goods worth $3.6 billion.

The recipe for success

Initially Motorola was wary about setting up manufacturing facilities in China and put up a makeshift plant in Tianjin to manufacture paging devices. However, by 2003, Motorola was regarded as the most successful foreign company in China. When asked to comment on the reasons for its success, Lai Bingrong, senior vice president of

Motorola in China said, 'Understand Chinese culture, pay respect to Chinese conditions, do not be self-opinionated, do not always blame others.'[4] Initially Motorola adopted a four-point strategy in China, which was as follows:

1 investment/technology transfer
2 management localisation
3 local sourcing
4 joint ventures/co-operative projects.

Investments and joint ventures

Initially, Motorola set up a plant at a total cost of $120 million in the Tianjin economic and technology development area for manufacturing pagers, simple integrated circuits and cellular phones. In the next phase of its investment of around $400 million, the company built its second plant for manufacturing automotive electronics, advanced microprocessors, walkie-talkie systems and fabricated silicon wafers. In addition to its wholly owned manufacturing plants, between 1995 and 2002, Motorola entered into nine joint ventures with Chinese firms to expand its presence in the market and also increase its production capacity.

Through these joint ventures, Motorola produced pagers, smart cards and mobile handsets that were marketed in China. The joint ventures helped Motorola gain access to the Chinese market without establishing additional manufacturing plants. These joint ventures also resulted in savings for the company.

In line with its four-point strategy, Motorola invested in research and development centres in China. In 1999, Motorola established the Motorola China Research and Development Institute in Beijing. The company announced that its research centre would focus on technological development and innovation. Motorola's R&D institute conducted research in the areas of communication, software, and semiconductors. Motorola also established a production procedure lab, an analytical lab, and software and equipment labs for developing new technologies that would make China a high-technology manufacturing hub. By 2003, Motorola had established 18 research centres in China.

Motorola employed around 650 engineers for its research activities in China. The company also entered into research partnerships with Chinese universities and institutes. Motorola gave scholarships to students and faculties of around eight Chinese universities. It also donated computers, and offered opportunities to college students to work as interns in the company and get acquainted with high technologies.

Over the years, Motorola entered into agreements with two Chinese telephone service providers – China Unicom and China Mobile – for installing telecom networks across the country. It also provided GSM technology to the mobile service vendors Hubei Mobile Communications[5] and Eastern Communications Co. Ltd (popularly known as Eastcom).[6] It was reported that Motorola had won a number of contracts from Chinese mobile service providers to install telecom networks across China.

Management localisation

The company realised that in order to increase its market share, it had to hire more Chinese employees. However, Motorola also realised that the Chinese managers were not familiar with Western management concepts and that the country lacked managerial talent. Though the Chinese were good at basics, they lacked practical application of theories. Thus, Motorola established the Motorola University in 1993 to train young Chinese people to take up global managerial positions. The mission of the university was 'to train and develop world-class staff for Motorola'. The university campus was situated near Beijing airport and had Western-style restaurants, conference rooms, pool tables and tennis courts.

Motorola University had a rigorous training programme known as China Accelerated Management Program (CAMP) for its Chinese employees. CAMP consisted of six weeks classroom learning and 14 months' on-the-job training, which included action learning, project management, coaching and rotation of employees through Motorola's worldwide facilities.

The training was imparted thrice a year and in each cycle the university trained around 15 people. The syllabus for CAMP included sections on market economy, value creation, business process design and benchmarking. In addition to these topics, they were trained in the areas of team building, situational leadership, and presentation style. Candidates had to go through a rigorous selection process to qualify for CAMP. Aspirants who wanted to join the program had to be nominated by their superiors. The employees underwent individual interviews and a test in the English language. After clearing these, they appeared for a 32-part structured interview where they had to answer questions like, 'Do you think you make decisions quickly?', 'If a co-worker wanted to discuss a personal problem with you, what would you do?' etc. Commenting on the selection procedure, one of the university staff said, 'The screening is meant to explore eight skill areas, including cognitive and administrative skills. It also surfaces "soft" characteristics such as motivation, a capacity for empathy, a talent for self-organisation.'[7]

In addition to CAMP, Motorola also provided in-house training to its employees. The engineering recruits were sent to its manufacturing plants in other countries like the US, Singapore and Hong Kong for on-the-job training in designing and other high-tech manufacturing procedures.

It also initiated a career management programme called *'Cadres 2000'*. Under this, Motorola selected around 20 top employees for a leadership training programme and posted them in Motorola manufacturing plants across the world.

Sourcing locally

To the extent possible, Motorola sourced components from the local Chinese players. This reduced its cost and also complied with the government's requirement that MNCs working in China had to source a certain percentage of components from the local firms. Motorola provided training to the local suppliers to improve their standards by extending technological and managerial support. It also helped them to increase their productivity and quality levels, and even assisted them to enter global markets. Motorola also encouraged its foreign suppliers to set up plants in China. According to reports, by 2002, around 45 Motorola suppliers had set up manufacturing bases in China.

In order to inculcate a competitive spirit among its Chinese suppliers, Motorola conducted exhibitions, such as Teaming for Excellence, which allowed its suppliers to showcase their talent and components. By 2002, Motorola had 176 direct suppliers and 700 indirect suppliers, and the usage of local components increased from 58.85 per cent in 2000 to 65 per cent in 2001.

Building an image

Motorola also focused on building its brand among the Chinese. It installed glow signs in busy market areas and placed advertisements in print and television to increase awareness among consumers about the company. It was reported that due to its extensive marketing the Chinese associated Motorola with quality and did not mind paying a premium price for its products. The company also opened up Motorola exclusive showrooms in the upmarket areas such as Shanghai and Beijing, offering the latest mobile handset models.

Motorola also introduced a new retailing concept called *Motorola Towns*. These towns were based on the Nike Town in the US and aimed at providing a unique retailing experience to consumers. In Motorola Towns, mobile handsets were displayed and consumers could walk in and use various technological gadgets without spending any money. According to company sources, the concept was not only about selling the company's products but allowing consumers to learn about the latest technological trends and connect them emotionally with the company. According to company sources, Motorola Towns would provide the company with feedback about its products. Motorola encouraged customers to express honest opinions about the sample products they had used and to suggest any additional features they would like to have.

Along with its marketing activities, Motorola concentrated on building its image as a good corporate citizen in China. Motorola associated itself with 'Project Hope' which was initiated by the China Youth Development Foundation. The project not only aimed at spreading primary education, but also offered financial assistance to school dropouts in rural areas for completing their education. As part of its assistance to Project Hope, Motorola donated huge amounts and established *Motorola Hope Schools*. The company also donated teaching equipment and provided training for the schoolteachers.

According to Motorola sources, from 1994, it provided financial aid to more than 9000 children to complete their school education and constructed around 40 Motorola Hope Schools in about 25 provinces. It also established multi-media labs in the schools and trained more than 500 teachers to enhance the educational standards. To encourage children to read, it set up Hope Libraries in about 30 schools.

To strengthen Project Hope, Motorola undertook a Motorola Hope Tour in which the company's top executives visited underdeveloped areas in the country to learn about the local conditions. Motorola also organised programmes like 'Green China' to protect the environment in the country. Commenting on Motorola's role in the social responsibility area, former Motorola CEO Gary Tooker said, 'We seek a partnership with China for mutual development. Closely linked with this strategy is our promise to be a worthy corporate citizen of China, participating in and contributing to the building of a caring and responsible society.'[8]

Due to its focused strategy in the Chinese market, Motorola was the leader in the mobile handset market with a share of 31 per cent in 2000. However, with increasing competition Motorola started experiencing a decline in its market share and by 2002 this was down to 28 per cent.

Change in recipe

With increasing competition and declining market share, Motorola announced a new five-year *'2+3+3 strategy'* in June 2002. The new strategy was announced by Tim Chen who took over as president of Motorola China in 2002. This strategy was aimed at strengthening the company's position in China as it had become a strategically important market for Motorola. Analysts reported that while Motorola experienced declining sales in the other markets across the world, in China, its sales were on the rise. According to company sources, China's share in Motorola's global revenues was increasing over the years (refer to Exhibit 1).

Exhibit 1 Share of Chinese market in Motorola global markets	
Year	China's share in global revenues (in %)
1999	10
2000	12
2001	13
2002	14
Source: Motorola annual reports.	

Commenting on the new strategy Tim said that it was an extension of Motorola's earlier four-point strategy and added, 'The core of the new strategy is the same as that of the four-point strategy: win-win for Motorola and China. Based on the new strategy, Motorola will continue to be a good corporate citizen in China, to deeply root itself in China and to be integrated into the China society. Our final goal is to become a genuine Chinese company by establishing an unshakable partnership with China. The 2+3+3 strategy will ensure our continuous success in China.'[9]

The new strategy focused on three broad goals for the company in the Chinese market. All the numbers in the new strategy – 2+3+3 – signified specific goals for the company. The new strategy was as follows.

- The number '2' referred to two goals: developing China into a worldwide manufacturing and R&D centre.
- The first '3' referred to three growth areas identified by the company – semiconductors, broadband and digital trunking systems (the mobile-communications systems used by police, taxi drivers, and delivery fleets).
- The second '3' symbolised three goals of Motorola to be achieved by 2006. These were to increase the value of its annual production to $10 billion, and its investments to $10 billion and to purchase $10 billion worth of components from Chinese markets.

However, analysts were divided on whether Motorola would be able to retain its market leadership position in China. While some felt that with its long-standing profile in the Chinese market, Motorola would be able to retain its position, others said that with the increasing local competition, it would be very difficult for it to do so.

Referring to Motorola's new strategy, *Business Week* wrote, 'A critical part of Motorola's strategy is to show Beijing its commitment to the Chinese economy. That's especially important given that local rivals are usually government-owned and have good *guanxi*, or connections, with local officials. Motorola, though, contends that it is as Chinese as any of its rivals, with more than 10 000 employees in the country – roughly the same number as Ningbo Bird.[10] And since Motorola isn't blind to Beijing's desire to boost China's science and technology prowess, it recently announced a $100 million expansion of an R&D center in the capital. Chinese officials appreciate the effort.'[11] Motorola was confident of its success in the Chinese market and to ensure this announced that it would collaborate with its competitors and sell cell phone chips to TCL and Eastcom.

The road ahead

Motorola experienced a slowdown in sales in China with the outbreak of severe acute respiratory syndrome (SARS)[12] in early 2003, which disrupted normal life in China for over a month. It was reported that weekly sales of mobile handsets (which constituted a major share of Motorola's revenues in China) in mainland China were down by 40 per cent in the last week of April, resulting in drop in revenues for cellular companies. Motorola was forced to close down its Beijing office for a week as one of its employees was diagnosed with SARS.

Unlike other multinationals which deferred their investment plans in China, Motorola announced that it would go ahead with its plans to invest further. To show solidarity with the Chinese authorities, Zafirovski visited Beijing in May 2003, defying the travel ban on the country. Addressing reporters, he said, 'We are optimistic about China's economy and our commitment to China is not changed at all. This confidence is based on Motorola's deep rooted investment in China and its close co-operation and partnership with the Chinese government and enterprise.'[13] Motorola also donated $1.4 million worth of communication equipment to fight SARS.

Meanwhile, Motorola announced a decline in its second quarter earnings for the year 2003 due to problems in its Asian operations. While the company blamed SARS for the decline in its earnings, analysts pointed out that increasing competition was the real reason. They said that during the period Motorola experienced a decline in its market share, the local players had increased share to 20 per cent.

For the same period, Motorola's sales declined by around 58 per cent. Commenting on Motorola's position in the Chinese market, Paul Sagawa, analyst, Sanford C. Bernstein, said, 'There are very aggressive Chinese handset manufacturers that are fighting for their lives and fighting for market share, and that's hitting Motorola smack-dab in the forehead. Motorola is dealing with excess inventory, desperate competitors, and cut-throat pricing. That's why it's losing market share.'[14]

A major problem faced by Motorola in China was piling up of inventory. According to company sources, Motorola had an inventory of around 30 million handsets and it would take around six to nine months to dispose them. With increasing inventory, Motorola resorted to heavy discounting and price wars, which only compounded

its woes. It was reported that the average selling price of Motorola handsets declined by 10 per cent in the second quarter of 2003.

In addition to the above problems, Motorola also faced exodus at senior managerial level. In September 2003, Chen resigned to join Microsoft. Analysts were quick to point out that it was a very big loss for the company, as Chen was popular with both Motorola partners and distributors and had also developed a very good rapport with the Chinese officials.

Analysts also pointed out that with the slowing down of demand in the urban areas, mobile companies need to focus more on smaller cities and rural areas. However, for multinationals such as Motorola, which did not have strong distribution networks in the rural areas it would be difficult to make inroads compared to the local players.

Further, the global slump in the semiconductor market after the dotcom burst was also hurting Motorola badly. Motorola invested heavily in the semiconductor chip plant at Tianjin during the dotcom boom. In 2003, Motorola announced that it would sell its chip plant to Shanghai-based Semiconductor Manufacturing International Corp. (SMIC). Analysts were of the opinion that this would streamline Motorola's operations in China and the company would be able to focus more on the mobile handset business. In October 2003, Motorola launched 21 new mobile handset models in China. Analysts were of the opinion that the success of these new models would decide the future of Motorola in China.

Questions

1 According to company sources, Motorola wanted to become more Chinese than the local Chinese companies. Explain the strategies adopted by Motorola to gain popularity with Chinese consumers. How far do you think these strategies helped Motorola become a successful company in China?

2 Though Motorola was successful in China, many analysts feel that with competition in the mobile handset market increasing, it would be difficult for the company to sustain its competitive position. Do you agree with the analysts? What according to you is the future of the mobile handset industry in China and where do you see Motorola in the changing scenario?

Further reading and bibliography

- Pete Engardio, 'Motorola in China: A Great Leap Forward', *Business Week*, 17 May 1993.
- Bernard Avishai, 'In China, It's the "Year of the Manager"', www.fastcompany.com, November 1995.
- Karl Schoenberger, 'Motorola Bets Big on China', *Fortune*, 27 May 1996.
- Bill Menezes, 'Pricing Hurts Motorola', www.wirelessweek.com, 13 July 1998.
- Kuhl, Craig, 'Motorola Takes Chinese Staff Back to School', www.multichannel.com, 10 January 1999.
- Dexter Roberts, 'China's Local Cell-Phone Boys Get Tough', *Business Week*, 20 September 1999.
- Yu Donghui, 'How Did Motorola Succeed in China?', www.ultrachina.com, 2 June 2000.
- 'Motorola Continues Success in China Market With $55 Million GSM Business in Hubei', *Business Wire*, 11 June 2000.
- Mei Fong, 'Motorola Lusts for China', *Forbes*, 13 July 2000.
- He, Zhong, 'Chinese Mobile Phone Market', www.ultrachina.com, 18 August 2000.
- 'Motorola's Investment in China Amounts to 28.5 Billion Yuan', www.pfeng.peopledialy.com, 12 September 2000.
- Donghui Yu, 'Why Motorola Invested Additional RMB16 Billion in China', www.ultrachina.com, 29 September 2000.
- Allen T. Cheng, 'Who Will Win China's Phone Wars?', www.asiaweek.com, 1 December 2000.
- 'Motorola to Invest $10B in China by 2006', www.electronicnews.com, 11 July 2001.
- Steven Fyffe, 'Chasing the Dragon – Motorola fires up its investment in China', www.eb-asia.com, January 2002.
- 'Domestic Mobile Market in Shake-up', www.fpeng.peopledaily.com, 9 May 2002.
- Borton, James, 'Motorola University Scores High Grades in China', www.atimes.com, 4 June 2002.
- 'Chinese Home Appliance Makers Turning to Cell Phones', www.fpeng.peopledaily.com, 5 June 2002.
- 'Motorola China Announces 5-Year Strategy', www.motorola.com, 6 June 2002.
- 'Motorola Marks 10th anniversary of investment in Tianjin', www.motorola.com, 11 September 2002.

- 'China Becomes World's Leading Mobile Phone Market!', www.fiducia-china.com, 2002.
- Bruce Einhorn, Dexter Roberts and Roger O. Crockett, 'Winning in China', *Business Week*, 27 January 2003.
- 'The Local Touch', *The Economist*, 6 March 2003.
- 'SARS Case Shuts Down Motorola Offices in China', www.austing.bizjournals.com, 6 May 2003.
- 'Motorola China not for Turning', www.fpeng.peopledaily.com, 19 May 2003.
- Caroline Daniel, 'Motorola Keeps an Eye on China Numbers', *Financial Times*, 28 July 2003.
- 'News Conference: The New Chairman of Motorola China', www.english.enorth.com.cn, 16 September 2003.
- Bruce Einhorn, 'Motorola's China Challenge', *Business Week*, 23 September 2003.
- 'Motorola to Sell China Fab to SMIC', www.eetimes.com, 23 October 2003.
- Rose, Barbara, 'Motorola to Sell China Chip Plant', www.chicagotribune.com, 24 October 2003.
- 'Motorola Sells $1B Chip Plant in China', www.bizjournals.com, 24 October 2003.
- 'Motorola Slims Semiconductor Unit in China', www.techweb.com, 27 October 2003.
- www.ultrachina.com.
- www.apspg.motorola.com.
- www.motorola.com.
- www.aberdeen.com.

References

1 'Motorola China not for Turning', www.english.peopledialy.com, 19 May 2003.

2 (Germany), Europe's largest manufacturer of automobiles, was the fourth largest automobile producer in the world. Volkswagen manufactured a variety of automobiles including cars, trucks and vans. The company's major car brands included Golf, Passat, Audi, Jetta, Lamborghini, Bentley and Beetle.

3 World's leading business magazine published in the US.

4 'How Motorola Succeeds in China', www.ultrachina.com, 6 June 2000.

5 Hubei Mobile Communications is a subsidiary of China Mobile – China's largest mobile communications operator. It provides mobile voice, data, IP phone, multimedia transmission and many other value-added services in Hubei Province (situated in central China).

6 Eastcom is the largest listed company in the mobile communication industry in China. The company provides integrated solutions in mobile telecommunications network, operation and maintenance of project network, value-added services of communication systems, upstream industry of mobile communications as well as optical industry.

7 Avishai, Bernard, In China, It's the 'Year of the Manager', www.fastcompany.com, November 1995.

8 www.apspg.motorola.com.

9 'Motorola China Announces 5-Year Strategy', www.motorola.com, 6 June 2002.

10 Established in 1992, Ningbo Bird is engaged in development and manufacturing of electronic communication products. Its product range includes system equipments, handheld PCs, mobile phone accessories and pagers, etc.

11 Einhorn, Bruce, Roberts, Dexter and Crockett. Roger O., 'Winning in China', *Business Week*, 27 January 2003.

12 Severe acute respiratory syndrome (SARS) is a viral respiratory illness caused by a coronavirus, called SARS-associated coronavirus (SARS-CoV). It first broke out in Asia in early 2003.

13 'Motorola China Not for Turning', www.english.peopledaily.com, 19 May 2003.

14 'Motorola Blames View on SARS: Street Sees China Price War', www.c114.net, 10 June 2003.

This case was written by K. Subhadra, under the direction of Sanjib Dutta, ICFAI Center for Management Research (ICMR). It is intended to be used as a basis for class discussion rather than to illustrate either effective or ineffective handling of a management situation.
Reprinted with permission. www.icmrindia.org.

The case was compiled from published sources.

case 3.3 Airbus: from Challenger to Leader

In prior years we found customers somewhat cautious about supporting Airbus. This year it has become acceptable and, frankly, even stylish to laud Airbus and to chastise Boeing.

> – Excerpt from Bear Stearns Analyst Report as reported in *Fortune*, August 1999

We are not here to buy market share.

> – Noel Forgeard, chairman, Airbus Industrie, August 1999

Boeing's nightmare

In October 2002, *The Seattle Times*, a local newspaper published in Seattle, US, where Boeing is headquartered, carried a headline story, 'Boeing is slipping to No. 2'. According to the newspaper report, Boeing's sole competitor, Airbus Industrie (Airbus) had bagged an order from easyJet[1] for 120 A-319 jets; easyJet was one of Boeing's most loyal customers (refer to Exhibit 1 for a profile of Boeing).

Analysts felt that after easyJet's shift away from Boeing, other low-cost airlines would follow suit in opting for Airbus. Airbus seemed all set to take market leadership in the low-cost segment from Boeing for the first time. From the mid-1990s onwards, Airbus had steadily increased its market share. By the late 1990s, Boeing and Airbus had an equal share in the market.

Rival Boeing accused Airbus of resorting to heavy price cutting in order to beat off the competition. It also accused Airbus of producing aircraft for which it had not received orders and creating a glut in the market. But Airbus rejected the allegations, saying that it was in the market to make money and not to buy market share. Some analysts were of the opinion that Airbus was able to increase its market share because of the financial support it received from its consortium partners. However, others attributed Airbus's success to its fuel-efficient jets, which were economical to run.

The take-off

The history of Airbus dates back to the late 1960s, when Britain, France and West Germany launched the Airbus Project. Airbus was a desperate attempt by the European governments to end the monopoly of American manufacturers in the aerospace industry. At that time, American manufacturers dominated the global aerospace industry and European aircraft manufacturers were unable to compete with American players.

Exhibit 1 Profile of Boeing

The leading airplane manufacturer in the US, Boeing Airplane Company, was formed in 1916 by William Boeing and George Westervelt. At the time, it was called the Pacific Aero Products Company. The company's name was changed to Boeing in 1917. Boeing began by manufacturing aircrafts for the US military during the First World War. In 1922, Edgar Scott became the company's president and during his tenure the navy awarded Boeing a contract to build a primary trainer (a plane for test flights). In 1927, the Model 40A mail plane, won the US Post Office contract to deliver mail between San Francisco and Chicago. The Boeing Air Transport (BAT) was formed to run the new airmail services. BAT also trained pilots, set up airfields and provided maintenance staff for the new service.

However, Boeing realised that to grow it needed to design and go in for mass production and sell its own aircraft. After the Second World War, the company shifted its focus from the defence industry to commercial jets. In 1952, Boeing launched its first commercial jet, the Boeing 707, a short-range jet. In 1960, William M. Allen became the company's CEO. The same year, Boeing began manufacturing its first jumbo jet – the Boeing 747. During Allen's tenure, Boeing launched one of its most successful jets, the 737. In 1962, Boeing manufactured the Air Force One for the American President's use. In late 1969, Boeing entered the spacecraft manufacturing business by contributing to the Apollo programme.

In the early 1970s, Boeing faced a host of problems due to the recession in the aviation industry. When Airbus Industrie was formed in 1970, Boeing's market share (70 per cent in the early 1970s) began to decline. In the mid-1970s, Boeing launched long-range planes (the 757 and the 767). By the mid-1980s, Boeing expanded its presence in the consumer electronics business through joint ventures, mergers and subcontracting. In March 1984, Boeing took over De Havilland Aircraft of Canada to enter the commuter planes market. In the early 1990s, Boeing completed the manufacture of the 727 and the 737. By October 1994, the company launched the new 737 series, the 737–800.

In the mid-1990s, Boeing's revenues plunged and it had to retrench around 9 300 employees due to the economic slowdown. The company faced a 10-week strike in the fourth quarter of 1995. In late 1996, Boeing and McDonnell Douglas announced plans to merge. In 1997, Boeing had approximately 70 per cent of the world market for passenger aircraft. By the end of 1997, Boeing was severely affected by the Asian economic crisis* that put in doubt over one-third of the $1.1 trillion projected commercial aircraft sales for the next 20 years. The company's internal problems such as excessive bureaucracy, redundant manufacturing processes and an outdated information technology set-up further aggravated the situation. Boeing lost 17 per cent of its market value as a result of the Asian crisis.

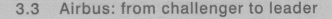

The big three of Europe – Britain, France and West Germany – came together to salvage European pride and industry. Due to differences with the other partners, Britain quit the project in July 1967, and in 1970 the Airbus Project was reorganised and named Airbus Industrie, a Franco-German company under French law.

In 1971, Spain joined the consortium with a 4.2 per cent stake through state-owned Construccciones Aeronautics SA (CASA). Initially, Airbus had its headquarters in Paris; in 1974 the headquarters were shifted to Toulouse (France). Each partner in the consortium was assigned specific production and assembly tasks, and the consortium was responsible for coordinating designing, development, financing and production activities of the partners.

Airbus's first product was the A-300-B – a wide-body twin-jet plane with a capacity of 226 passengers. The next product was the A-300-B2, a 250-seater. By 1975, Airbus was able to garner 10 per cent of market share, and received first-time contracts from Eastern Airlines[2] and Thai Airways.[3] By the end of 1975, Airbus had orders for 55 aircraft. By 1978, Airbus's orders had increased to 133, and it had a 26 per cent market share by value. It also launched the A-310 with a 218-passenger capacity in the two-class configuration. The A-310 had a two-man cockpit with a six-cathode ray tube display, replacing dials – the first of its kind in the aviation industry. In 1979, British Aerospace Systems (BAE Systems) entered the consortium with a 20 per cent stake, and in the same year, Airbus announced that it would launch a single-aisle aircraft with a seating capacity of 130–170; the aircraft was later called the A-320.

In the early 1980s, Airbus experienced difficulties in financing the A-320 project, since all the Airbus partner governments had not approved the programme. While the French Government had approved the project, both British and German partner governments wanted more time to measure the market potential for the plane. Another problem was that the consortium had not yet made money on products already in the market.

By 1985–86, Boeing's market share had decreased to 46 per cent, with Airbus having increased its share to 25 per cent. With Airbus's increasing market share, Boeing began to accuse Airbus of using unfair trade practices by getting heavy subsidies from its European governing partners. The US government too started pressurising the EU to reduce subsidies to Airbus. The then President of the United States, Ronald Reagan, cited Airbus as a classic example of violation of international trade agreements.

In the late 1980s, the US Government filed a complaint against Airbus at the General Agreement on Trade and Tariffs (GATT). It complained of unfair competition against two US airline manufacturers, McDonnell Douglas and Boeing, by Airbus. Airbus, it said, had the financial support of four European governments, which provided cheap loans to the consortium with no repayment conditions. Airbus responded by denying that it received heavy subsidies from the governments concerned. The governments of the four European states also stated that US aircraft manufacturers received indirect government subsidies through the US defense department. After protracted discussions, in 1992 a bilateral deal was signed between the European governments on one side and the US government on the other, that limited the financial help that could be given to Airbus to develop any new model to 33 per cent of its total development costs. The agreement also stipulated that the aid would have to be repaid with interest within 17 years.

Airbus came under strong pressure to corporatise itself. Despite its success in attracting orders and increasing its market share, many were skeptical about its ability to compete with Boeing with its existing structure.

In early 1998, the Airbus partners restarted discussions on revamping the organisational structure of the consortium. In the same year Noel Forgeard[4] was appointed as CEO of Airbus. However, there were serious differences between the consortium partners over the valuation of the assets to be pooled in the new corporate structure. The fact that accounting standards differed from country to country was also a hindrance in the valuation of assets.

In 1999, the stumbling blocks to restructuring were finally cleared, when Aerospatiale was merged with Matra Hautes Technologies, and DASA (Germany) taking over the Spanish partner CASA. Aerospatiale Matra and DASA together formed the European Aeronautic Defense and Space Company (EADS). By 2001, Airbus was incorporated into an integrated company, with EADS and BAE

Exhibit 2 Manufacturing plants of Airbus

Parts manufactured	Location
Cabin interior	Buxtehude, Laupheim (Germany)
Fuselage (forward & aft)	Hamburg, Nordenham, Bremen, Varel (Germany)
Fuselage (cockpit & centre)	Meaulte, Saint Nazaire, Nantes (France)
Wing	Broughton, Filton (England)
Pylon, Nacelle	Toulouse (France)
Empennage – horizontal tail plane	Puerto Real (France), Getafe & Illescas (Spain)
Empennage – vertical tail plane	Stade (Germany)
Final assembly lines	
A320 family	Hamburg (Germany) & Toulouse (France)
A300/A310 & A330/A340	Toulouse (France)
A380	Hamburg (Germany) & Toulouse (France)

Source: www.airbus.com.

Exhibit 3 Turnover of Airbus

Year	Turnover (in billions)
1997	$11.6
1998	$13.3
1999	$16.7
2000	$17.2
2001	€20.5
2002	€24.3

Source: www.airbus.com.

owning stakes of 80 per cent and 20 per cent respectively. In 2002, Airbus employed around 45 000 employees, with manufacturing plants spread all over Europe (see Exhibit 2). In 2002, it reported a turnover of €24.3 billion[5] (see Exhibit 3).

The aerospace industry

The history of the aerospace industry dates back to 1917, when the US government built an aeronautics research center in Langley, Virginia. In the subsequent years, there was close private and public sector collaboration in the industry. The US government's investment in the aero-

space industry was substantial before and during the Second World War. After the Second World War, US manufacturers had distinct technological and financial advantages over their European competitors. Prior to the Second World War, Britain had been the leader in the aerospace industry. However, it failed to retain its leadership position due to the lack of a proper corporate and regulatory climate.

Investment in the aerospace industry involves a high degree of risk. The investment risk can be gauged from Airbus's investment in its A-380 aircraft; the investment required was equivalent to the company's net worth. The cost structure of the aerospace industry is also very high. It is estimated that the cost of development of a new aircraft model, from designing to launching, is around $4 billion. The cost structure in developing a new aircraft can be broken up as follows:

Development	40%
Tooling	20%
Work-in-progress and overhead expenses	40%

Product development of an aircraft begins with a 'paper airplane' – a three-dimensional model, estimating the performance and the operating costs of the aircraft. The manufacturers generally used these models to demonstrate new technology and, most importantly, to assess the response of potential buyers. Generally, before initiating production of new aircraft, companies hold discussions with key airline companies about adaptations and options that need to be incorporated into the prototype. Often, these airlines became launch customers, placing initial orders that guaranteed the minimum volume, while sending signals to potential buyers that the aircraft is worth considering.

In the early 1980s, the American company Lockheed announced that it was stopping production of commercial aircraft to concentrate on the military and space segments. The commercial aircraft market was now divided between the three dominant players – Boeing, McDonnell Douglas and Airbus Industrie. There was further consolidation in the industry when, in the late 1990s, the two American majors Boeing and McDonnell Douglas announced their merger. The merger resulted in a situation of duopoly in the commercial aircraft market with only two players – Boeing and Airbus Industrie (see Exhibit 4 for market share).

In the late 1990s and early 2000s, the worldwide economic recession, compounded by terrorist attacks in the US, resulted in turbulent times for the industry. The September 11th 2001 attacks on the US had a devastating effect on airline companies all over the world, with a decline in the world air passenger traffic. Many airline

 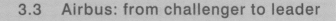

Exhibit 4 Global aerospace industry: market shares (%)		
Year	**Boeing**	**Airbus**
1995	69.7	13
1996	64	32
1997	60	35
1998	50	50
1999	45	55
2000	45	55
2001	47	53
2002	43	57
Source: compiled from various sources.		

companies went broke and filed for bankruptcy. The US government stepped in and announced a bailout package for the US airline industry. The slump in airline services had a very negative impact on aircraft manufacturers, with most airline companies cancelling orders for new aircraft.

Flight to success

In 1970, when Airbus Industrie was set up, the commercial aircraft market was totally dominated by US aircraft manufacturers led by Boeing. Boeing dominated the world market with its 747 jumbo jet family of aircraft. Although Airbus had great difficulty in breaking into the market initially, over the years, it managed to attract more and more customers. Though some attributed Airbus's success to the subsidies it received from European governments, others felt that Airbus succeeded because of its production efficiency and innovative product development.

Innovative product development

In the 1970s, the aerospace industry was in a transition. The regulatory set-up in the American market restricted price wars among existing carriers and the entry of new carriers. However, existing airlines were allowed to fly any number of flights on the route, resulting in an increasing number of flights on the popular routes. Airlines found that the use of Boeing aircraft (Boeing 727s) was expensive for frequent flying. There was a demand for wide-body aircraft with twin engines and twin aisles, and with capacities of 250 passengers.

The first breakthrough for Airbus came in 1978, with Eastern Airlines[6] placing an order for 23 A-300s, and soon Airbus started receiving more orders for the A-300. In the same year, Airbus decided to develop a new model, the A-310, an extension of the A-300, with a budget of $1 billion. Until the late 1980s, Airbus had only two aircraft models on the market – the A-300 and the A-310. Soon it realised

that it needed to increase its product range in order to compete with Boeing in all product categories. During the 1990s, Airbus focused on introducing new aircraft. It launched four product families with nine airplane models during the 1990s; in the same period Boeing launched only two product families, the 717[7] and the 777, and revamped its old models in other product lines. Commenting on the Airbus products, Ned Laird, managing director of Air Cargo Management Group, said, 'Airbus airplanes are newer in design, and in most cases they are cheaper to own than Boeing alternatives.'[8] In 1989, Airbus launched the A-321 with increased seating capacity (185 passengers), and in 1992, the A-319, a 124-seater, was launched. In 1993, Airbus launched the A-319 with a seating capacity of 124 passengers (see Exhibit 5 for the Airbus product range).

Airbus also differentiated itself from Boeing in its aircraft design. For instance, the A-320 was designed with a 7.5 inch wider fuselage than Boeing's 737 (designed during the 1960s), giving the airline extra space to add more seats in a six-across configuration. Richard Aboulafia, director of aviation with the Teal Group, said, 'That inch makes a difference, because North American rear ends aren't getting any smaller.'[9]

The wider choice of aircrafts encouraged airlines to switch to Airbus in order to spread their maintenance costs. Commenting on the economies of using Airbus aircraft, Frederic Brace, vice president, finance, at United Airlines, said, 'Once you get an Airbus in your fleet, you tend to want more of them. They make a good plane that is very economical to operate.'[10]

Over the years Airbus has come out with aircraft in line with the market demand, and incorporating technological innovations, unlike Boeing's aircraft, which were extensions of its 747 technology. Boeing had failed to introduce new technology in its commercial jets after its Super Jumbo 747.

Airbus's A-320, launched in 1984, had new technology, resulting in better operating efficiencies and performance. The A-320 was the first commercial jet with 'fly-by-wire'[11] controls and side sticks, and was designed to meet the requirements of short-distance routes. In 1986, Airbus launched the medium capacity A-330/-340 for long-distance routes. While Airbus was coming out with new models, Boeing was offering its existing 747 and 737 product lines only.

Production efficiency

In 1995, Boeing started offering huge discounts of about 25 per cent on its aircraft in a bid to draw customers back from Airbus. However, though it succeeded in getting more orders than Airbus that year, it was unable to stick to its delivery schedule. Two of its production plants were

Exhibit 5 Product range of Airbus and Boeing		
Category	**Airbus**	**Boeing**
	A-319	757
	A-320	757–200
	A-321	767
	A-318	757–300
		717
Wide-bodied aircraft	A-300–600R	767–200ER
	A-330–200	767-300ER
	A-340–200	767-400ER
	A-330–300	
	A-340–200	
	A-340–300	
	A-340–500	
	A-340–600	
Super jumbo jet	A-380	747–400

Source: www.airbus.com and www.boeing.com.

shut down due to shortage of parts and workforce. As a result of the delays, many clients cancelled their orders with Boeing and returned to Airbus, raising Airbus's market share over that of Boeing.

The main problem for Boeing, as many analysts saw it, was that its production processes dated back to the Second World War period, after which the company had never comprehensively revamped its production processes. It followed traditional aircraft manufacturing methods. In Boeing factories, planes were docked in stalls on either side of the factory floor. Each plane was surrounded by ramps and workers found the parts and installed them, and during the night, partly finished planes were moved into the stall using cranes, for the next stage of assembly.

Compared to Boeing's cumbersome production practices that were decades old, Airbus had very sophisticated production practices. Airbus adopted the line-manufacturing method, which made the process of assembling aircraft easier. Boeing employed 216 workers per aircraft, while Airbus employed only 143 workers. This amounted to a 51 per cent productivity difference between the two companies. Boeing's 119 000 workers manufactured 550 jets, while Airbus manufactured 230 jets with help of 33 000 employees per year.

Airbus also had much fewer HR problems than Boeing. During the mid-1990s, when its orders were up, Boeing hired 38 000 people and trained them. However, due to production problems, it was forced to reduce its workforce and lay off around 26 000 employees in late 1998. By the late 1990s, workforce salaries and overhead expenses in Boeing were around 30 per cent of total overhead costs – very high for any company. In addition, Boeing had difficulties with its employee unions. Boeing unions went on strike over four times between 1998 and 2002, resulting in serious production problems for the company.

The gamble

In order to increase its market share, Airbus decided to enter the super jet category (400 seater). In 1998 it announced that it would be developing a super jumbo jet with a planned initial investment of $10 billion. If it took off, Airbus's A-3XX (later called A-380) would end the monopoly of Boeing's 747 in the over-400 seats category. According to company sources, the A-380 would be a double-decker plane with a seating capacity of 555 passengers (137 more than the Boeing 747). The super jumbo would be priced at $213 million and was expected to fly by 2004 (later, the launch date was postponed to 2006). The main challenge for Airbus was to raise the funds required to manufacture the A-380. Finally, Airbus was able to split the total costs of development of the project as follows: around 40 per cent would be funded by its suppliers, such as Saab (Sweden), 30 per cent would be in the form of government loans bought in by partners, and the remaining 30 per cent would be the consortium's own funds.

Boeing questioned Airbus's wisdom in putting funds into the development of a super jumbo. While both Airbus and Boeing were agreed on the expectation that air traffic would increase 5 per cent annually over the next 20 years, they differed in their expectation regarding the type of aircraft the market would absorb. Airbus felt that airlines would opt to buy larger aircraft to accommodate growing consumer demand, whereas Boeing felt that airlines would be buying smaller aircraft such as the 777, as there would be increased demand for point-to-point services rather than long-haul flights requiring bigger planes. Said Allan Mullay, head of the commercial airplane division at Boeing, 'We think the lineup we have is what airlines want, and there is no economic justification for a bigger airplane.'[12]

Airbus disagreed, saying that with increasing restrictions in airports regarding noise and pollution, airlines would opt for big planes, as they would require fewer take-offs and landings. Said Philippe Jarry, head of Airbus market development, 'Boeing acts as if there are no constraints on airports, runways, or the environment. I'm really surprised that the leading American manufacturer is so concerned about the bottom line that it says, "Flying is more fun in our smaller planes. You should buy more of them".'[13]

The Airbus super jet project received further encouragement when airline companies also showed interest in the aircraft. Companies such as Federal Express were reportedly interested in the super jumbo as freight ship-

ments were predicted to grow fast – in fact, faster than passenger volumes. Commenting on their interest in the A-380, Don Barber, senior vice president of FedEx air operations, said, 'The A-3XX may be an option to increase our capacity per trip.'[14]

Airbus consulted more than 60 airports worldwide to ascertain whether or not its super jumbo jet would take off and land easily. To reduce the weight of the aircraft, a crucial element in take-off and landing, Airbus developed a new material called Glare.[15] During the design of the aircraft, the Airbus staff had to give careful consideration to seating arrangements and arrangements for evacuating 555 people from the aircraft in case of an emergency. Initially, passenger seating was on a single deck or in side-by-side fuselages; however, later on designers hit upon double-deck seating arrangements as it would be easier to get passengers off the plane quickly. Another advantage was that double-deck planes would not require more space on runways. In order to avoid the problem of claustrophobia among passengers, Airbus announced that it would create an ambience of leisure on the plane. The A-380 would have a staircase connecting both decks, and also exercise rooms, and sleeping rooms with bunk beds. It enlisted 1200 frequent fliers from eight cities across the world to assess and provide suggestions for its mock cabins.

In response to fears that operational costs of the super jet would be high, Airbus sources said that the use of new technology meant that the A-380 would be 15 per cent cheaper to operate than the Boeing 747. Airbus also said that the 656-seater A-380 would be reduce operating costs by around 25 per cent. Boeing officials, however, calculated that cost savings through the super jet would amount to half the level claimed by Airbus.

The 747 family

A major concern that arose for Airbus was Boeing's decision to extend its 747 family. In March 2001, Boeing announced that it would be extending the family of 747s with its 747-X planes that would be on par with the Airbus A-380s,[16] and would carry around 522 passengers. It was also reported that Boeing's costs for 747-X would be around a quarter of the A-380's budget. However, by the end of 2001, Boeing abandoned its plans to go for 747-X due to weak market projections for the large super jet. It announced that it would launch a 'Sonic Cruiser' that would travel at 98 per cent the speed of sound. However, this project too failed to arouse any interest among airline companies due the turbulent conditions in the industry.

After the September 11th (2001) attacks, the airline industry was down and out because of the sharp falls in air travel. The worldwide economic slowdown also affected the industry very badly. Both Airbus and Boeing announced declines in their revenues due to recession. However, in October 2002, Airbus had 276 orders, while Boeing had just 186 orders. Analysts felt the lower operational costs of Airbus aircraft might have brought about this situation. However, as far as the A-380 project was concerned, Airbus would need around 100 orders to break even, but it actually had only 50 orders by the end of 2002.

While Airbus was gearing up to consolidate its position through its A-380, Boeing also started refocusing on operational efficiencies in order to regain market leadership. In June 2003, Boeing announced the launch of a new plane – the 7E7, with a seating capacity of 200-250 passengers. Boeing sources said that with the help of new technology and operational processes it would be able to assemble the plane in only three days. With Boeing seemingly set to face up to the challenge from Airbus, it remains to be seen how long Airbus will be able to sustain its leadership position.

Questions

1 When Airbus was set up, it failed to attract customers and did not get any orders over a period of 18 months. Discuss the problems faced by Airbus initially, and analyse the strategies adopted by the company to overcome them.

2 By the early 2000s, Airbus had acquired market leadership in the aerospace industry. Discuss the nature of the competition between Airbus and Boeing. What differentiating strategies did Airbus adopt in order to survive and succeed over the past few decades? How far do you think the advantages are sustainable in the long run? Justify your answers.

3 Analyse the changes in the structure of the aerospace industry over the years and evaluate its effect on competition in the industry.

Further reading and bibliography

- Tim Healy, 'Competition: Battle for Asia', www.asiaweek.com, 29 March 1996.
- 'Can Airbus Partners Unite?', *Business Week*, 22 July 1996.
- Gail Edmondson and Seanna Browder, 'Angst at Airbus', *Business Week*, 23 December 1996.
- Gail Edmondson and Seanna Browder, 'A Wake Up Call for Airbus', *Business Week*, 30 December 30 1996.
- 'Peace in Our Time', *The Economist*, 24 July 1997.

- Janet Guyon, 'The Sole Competitor', *Fortune*, 12 January 1998.
- Ronald Henkoff, 'Boeing's Big Problem', *Fortune*, 12 January 1998.
- Gail Edmondson, 'Up, Up, and Away at Last for Airbus?', *Business Week*, 9 February 1998.
- 'Airbus Highflier Grounded', *Business Week*, 2 February 1998.
- 'Hubris at Airbus, Boeing Rebuilds', *The Economist*, 26 November 1998.
- 'Boeing Admits it "Let Clients Down"', www.news.bbc.co.uk, 8 September 1998.
- 'Fearful Boeing', *The Economist*, 25 February 1999.
- Alex Taylor III, 'Blue Skies for Airbus', *Fortune*, 2 August 1999.
- Gail Edmondson, 'Overhauling Airbus', *Business Week*, 2 August 1999.
- Norbert Burgner, 'The Airbus Story', www.flugrevue.com, February 2000.
- 'Airbus Gets a Boost', *The Economist*, 6 April 2000.
- 'Rivals in the Air', www.news.bbc.co.uk, 23 June 2000.
- 'Airbus Steals Boeing Ground', www.news.bbc.co.uk, 30 November 2000.
- Jerry Useem, 'Boeing vs Boeing', *Fortune*, 2 October 2000.
- 'Airbus Draws First Blood', www.news.bbc.co.uk, 18 June 2001.
- Carol Matlack and Stanley Holmes, 'Trouble Ahead for Airbus?', *Business Week*, 1 October 2001.
- 'Bettering Boeing', *The Economist*, 18 July 2002.
- Stanley Holmes, 'Showdown at 30 000 Feet', *Business Week*, 22 July 2002.
- 'Airbus Just May Win This Dogfight', *Business Week*, 5 August 2002.
- 'Bashing Boeing', *The Economist*, 17 October 2002.
- Carol Matlack and Stanley Holmes, 'Look Out, Boeing', *Business Week*, 28 October 2002.
- 'Boeing vs Airbus', *The Economist*, 17 April 2003.
- 'Boeing Can Assemble 7E7 in 72 Hours', *The Economic Times*, 6 June 6 2003.
- www.flugrevue.com.
- www.airwise.com.
- www.aviationnow.com.
- www.seattletimes.com.
- www.news.bbc.co.uk.
- www.airbus.com.
- www.speednews.com.
- www.boeing.com.

References

1 Europe's second biggest low-cost airliner.
2 Eastern Airlines was one of the largest airlines in the US, which operated on eastern coast routes. It was liquidated in 1991 due to heavy losses.
3 Thai Airways is an airline company operating from Thailand.
4 Former CEO of French missile and satellites maker Matra Hautes Technologies.
5 On 6 June 2003, 1 Euro = $1.18.
6 Eastern Airlines was one of the largest airlines in the US, which operated on eastern coast routes. It was liquidated in 1991 due to heavy losses.
7 Some analysts pointed out that Boeing inherited the 717 aircraft family from McDonnell Douglas, which was acquired by it 1997, so they pointed out that, effectively, Boeing came out with only one new product – the 777 – during the 1990s.
8 'Upstart Airbus Threatens to Leave Giant Boeing in its Jet Stream', *The Seattle Times*, 13 May 2002.
9 'Blue Skies for Airbus', *Fortune*, 2 August 1999.
10 'Blue Skies for Airbus', *Fortune*, 2 August 1999.
11 Fly-by-wire is a means of aircraft control that uses electronic circuits to send inputs from the pilot to the motors that move the various flight controls on the aircraft. There are no direct hydraulic or mechanical linkages between the pilot and the flight controls. Digital fly-by-wire uses an electronic flight control system coupled with a digital computer to replace conventional mechanical flight controls.
12 'Blue Skies for Airbus', *Fortune*, 2 August 1999.
13 'Blue Skies for Airbus', *Fortune*, 2 August 1999.
14 'Blue Skies for Airbus', *Fortune*, 2 August 1999.
15 Glare was made of aluminum alloy and glass-fibre tape, which reduced the weight of the aircraft.
16 A3XX was renamed A380 in early 2001.

This case was written by K. Subhadra, under the direction of Sanjib Dutta, ICFAI Center for Management Research (ICMR). It is intended to be used as a basis for class discussion rather than to illustrate either effective or ineffective handling of a management situation. The case was compiled from published sources.

section 4
case studies

cases

case 4.1 Wal-Mart's German Misadventure

'Don't look now:' low prices all year round!
With thanks to Walmart

I don't think that Wal-Mart did their homework as well as they should have. Germany is Europe's most price-sensitive market. Wal-Mart underestimated the competition, the culture, the legislative environment.

– Steve Gotham, retail analyst,
Verdict Retail Consulting, October 2002[1]

We screwed up in Germany. Our biggest mistake was putting our name up before we had the service and low prices. People were disappointed.

– John Menzer, head of Wal-Mart International
December 2001[2]

German blues

For the world's largest retailing company, Wal-Mart, Inc., the German market was proving difficult to crack. By 2003, even after five years of having entered Germany, Wal-Mart was making losses. Though Wal-Mart did not reveal these figures, analysts estimated losses of around $200-300 million per annum in Germany over the five-year period.

According to analysts, the main reason for Wal-Mart's losses was its failure to understand German culture and the shopping habits of Germans. Though Wal-Mart was famous the world over for its Every Day Low Pricing (EDLP),[3] which turned it into the world's No. 1 retailer, it could not make an impact in Europe's most price-sensitive market – Germany. Wal-Mart also ran into a series of problems with German regulatory authorities for its pricing strategies and faced considerable opposition from German suppliers to its centralised distribution system. It had problems with its German workers too.

However, Wal-Mart was not the only retailer to do badly in Germany in the 1990s. German retailers too faced losses in the period because of the flat economy and rising unemployment. Though Wal-Mart was confident that there would be a turnaround in its fortunes in the German market, by late 2003, this opinion was not shared by most independent analysts.

Wal-Mart's history

In 1962, Sam Walton and his brother opened the first Wal-Mart store in Rogers (Arkansas), US. In the first year of its operations, the store registered sales of over $1 million. Initially, the Waltons concentrated on opening stores in small towns and introduced innovative concepts such as self-service. By 1967, Wal-Mart had 24 stores with sales of $12.6 million.

By 1980, Wal-Mart had 276 stores with annual sales of $1.4 billion. The number of stores increased to 640 with annual sales of $4.5 billion and profits of over $200 million by 1984. In 1988, Walton appointed David Glass as CEO of Wal-Mart. Soon after taking over, Glass started Hypermart USA. It was originally a joint venture with Cullum Companies (a Dallas-based supermarket chain). In the following year Wal-Mart bought out Cullum's stake in the venture.

In 2000, Wal-Mart was ranked 5th in *Fortune* magazine's Global Most Admired All-Stars List. Lee Scott became the CEO of the company in 2000. In 2002, Wal-Mart was ranked No. 1 in the *Fortune* 500 list. It recorded the largest single-day sales in the company's history, in 2002, when on the day after Thanksgiving it reported sales of $1.43 billion. In 2003, Wal-Mart was the world's largest retailer with a total of 4688 stores (3400 stores in the US and 1288 stores in other countries). It reported sales of $244.5 billion for the year 2003 with a net income of $8.03 billion.

Wal-Mart's international operations

In the early 1990s, Wal-Mart announced that it would go global. It wanted to look for international markets for the following reasons.

- Wal-Mart was facing stiff competition from K-mart[4] and Target,[5] which adopted aggressive expansion strategies and started eating into Wal-Mart's market share.
- Wal-Mart also realised that the US population represented only 4 per cent of the world's population and confining itself to the US market would mean missing the opportunity to tap potentially vast markets elsewhere.
- In the early 1990s, globalisation and liberalisation opened up new markets and created opportunities for discount stores such as Wal-Mart across the world.

Wal-Mart expanded its international operations through acquisitions, joint ventures, greenfield operations and wholly owned subsidiaries. In 1991, Wal-Mart entered Mexico through a joint venture with Mexican company Cifra, and opened Sam's Clubs in Mexico. Wal-Mart's globalisation plans got a boost in 1993, when the Wal-Mart International division was created. In the same year it acquired 122 former Woolco stores from Woolworth in Canada. By 2003 Wal-Mart had a presence in nine countries with 1288 stores, which included 942 discount stores, 238 supercentres, 71 Sam's Clubs and 37 neighbourhood stores (see Exhibit 1 for Wal-Mart's international presence).

By 2003, Wal-Mart was the largest retailer in Mexico, Argentina, Canada and Puerto Rico, and one of the top three retailers in the UK. In 2003, Wal-Mart's operating income from international operations was $2.033 billion, 15 per cent higher than in the previous year (see Exhibit 2). However, Wal-Mart was not successful in all the markets it entered. It failed to make an impact in Europe's most price-sensitive market – Germany.

Wal-Mart in Germany

Most American companies entering Europe started with the UK due to the similarities between the US and the UK in culture, language and legal environment. Wal-Mart, however, decided to enter Germany first. Analysts were critical of this decision as the German retailing industry was experiencing slow growth rates and retailers were indulging in price wars which eroded margins badly. Additionally, Germany had high labour costs, high real estate prices and a very inflexible business environment (see Exhibit 3).

But Wal-Mart felt it was right to venture into the German market. Ron Tiarks, president of Wal-Mart's German operations, said, 'Germany, being the third-largest economy in the world, is very important to us and one obviously that we can't ignore.' *Fortune* wrote in 1999, 'Germany offers Wal-Mart a central base from which it can expand to

Exhibit 1   Wal-Mart's international presence in 2003

Country	Mode of entry	Year of entry	JV partner/company acquired	No. of stores
Mexico	Joint venture	1991	Cifra	597
Canada	Acquisition	1994	Woolco Stores	213
Argentina	Greenfield operations	1995	–	11
Brazil	Joint venture	1995	Lojas Americanas	22
China	Greenfield operations	1996	–	26
South Korea	Acquisition	1998	Makro Stores	15
Germany	Acquisition	1997	Wertkauf and Interspar	94
United Kingdom	Acquisition	2000	Asda	258
Puerto Rico	Wholly owned subsidiary	1993	Wal-Mart Puerto Rico, Inc.	52

Source: Compiled from various newspapers and Wal-Mart annual reports.

Exhibit 2   Operating income from international operations

Fiscal year	Operating income ($ billion)
2003	2.033
2002	1.305
2001	0.949

Source: Wal-Mart 2003 Annual Report.

Exhibit 3 A note on the retailing industry in Germany

As the world's third largest economy, Germany has attracted the attention of retailers from around the world such as Marks & Spencers and Toys 'R' Us for several decades. With a GNP of €2 trillion and a population of around 80 million, Germany was rated as one of the biggest retail markets in Europe. In 2002, Germany accounted for 15 per cent of Europe's €2 trillion retail market. The West German retail industry saw tremendous growth rates till the early 1990s. However, after the unification of Germany in 1990, the Germany economy went through a tough phase of restructuring, which had an impact on the retailing industry too. The difference between the levels of economic prosperity in West and East Germany pulled down the average growth rates in the German retail industry. By the late 1990s, the German retail industry was growing slowly.

The German retail market was oligopolistic with a few players dominating the industry. In the early 2000s, the top 10 players accounted for 84 per cent of sales and the top five players in the market garnered around 63 per cent of market share. German consumers reportedly attached more importance to value and price than customer service. According to analysts, the German market was one of the most price-sensitive markets in Europe.

Until the late 1990s, discount stores concentrated only on food and other grocery items; but in the late 1990s, the trend changed and the discount stores moved to non-food items also. For instance, the discount store Aldi emerged as the largest seller of personal computers under its own brand name.

In the early 2000s, with the slowdown in the economy, the German retail industry experienced the lowest profit levels of all the developed countries. The profit margin in grocery retailing was just 1.1 per cent in 2002, and in the food segment it was only 0.5 per cent. Another important feature of the German retailing industry was the domination of

almost anywhere on the Continent. Wal-Mart clearly wants to be a pan-European player, a goal made more feasible by the Euro's promise to ease business across national boundaries.'[6] As Germany was considered a price-sensitive market, analysts felt that Wal-Mart's EDLP philosophy would be successful in the country. German stores usually offered seasonal discount sales and special sales to increase their revenues. With its customer-focused service, it was felt that Wal-Mart would be able gain market share in Germany. However, Wal-Mart faced a number of serious problems in Germany.

Entry strategy gone wrong?

Wal-Mart expanded its presence into Germany through acquisitions. It acquired the 21 hypermarket stores of Wertkauf in 1997. The Wertkauf stores offered both food and general merchandise to the customers. Wal-Mart sources said that Wertkauf stores would provide the necessary footage in the German market. However, as Wertkauf covered only southwestern Germany, it failed to provide the required market penetration to Wal-Mart in Germany. In 1998, Wal-Mart acquired Interspar's 74 hypermarket stores to raise the total number of Wal-Mart stores in Germany to 95.

With the acquisition of Interspar's stores, Wal-Mart became the fourth largest hypermarket retailer in Germany. However, both the Wertkauf and the Interspar

family-owned enterprises. Most of the retailing enterprises were not listed on stock exchanges.

The German retailing industry is highly regulated. Analysts believe that the regulatory environment in Germany hindered the development of retailing in the county. There were many legislations relating to the competition and corporate strategies of retailers. The German Government also pursues protectionist policies to support small and medium-scale German retailers. Some of the legislations which affect the retail industry in Germany significantly are summarised below.

- A retailer can operate for a maximum of 80 hours/week. The store working hours are the shortest in Europe. Retailers are not allowed to work on Sundays and holidays. Because of this regulation Wal-Mart was not able to operate its 24/7 convenience stores in Germany.

- Retailers are not allowed to sell below cost for an extended period of time. However, a merchant can discount goods for a limited period of time.

As regards German consumers, for cultural reasons, they were less friendly and less outgoing compared with American and British consumers. In line with this, in Germany the number of employees per store was low compared to the US and other developed markets.

In order to increase consumer spending, the German government undertook major tax reforms in 2001. This was expected to boost retail sales in the country. However, though government tax reforms boosted consumer spending, it did not benefit the retail industry as expenditure took place in the housing, tourism and communications sectors.

During 2003, too, the German retailing industry was expected to have slow growth because of the macroeconomic conditions. The increasing unemployment affected the food retailing sector in the country.

Source: adapted from various newspaper articles and websites.

stores were not popular with German consumers. A major challenge for Wal-Mart was to change customer perceptions of the stores. Wal-Mart was criticised for acquiring Interspar's stores as they had made heavy losses and had a poor brand image in the public mind.

Wal-Mart also faced a major problem in trying to integrate the operations of the two companies (Wertkauf and Interspar). John Menzer, head of Wal-Mart International, said, 'The challenge of putting the two chains together was more than we thought. We knew Interspar was losing money and we had to turn it around. We had to reconstruct it and lose more money before it could turn around.'[7]

Wal-Mart found out that the store layout and design of Interspar stores did not conform to Wal-Mart's store layout and design worldwide. Interspar stores were of varied sizes and formats and most of the stores were situated in interior areas, where customers opted for general grocery chains. After acquiring the Interspar chain stores, Wal-Mart embarked on a renovation program to bring them up to Wal-Mart standards. Wal-Mart reportedly spent around $150 million to renovate the Interspar stores.

Though acquisitions may not have been the ideal route for Wal-Mart to take in Germany, the company, in fact, had little choice. The German Government was refusing new licenses for food and grocery retailing, so if it wanted to enter the German market, Wal-Mart had to go in for acquisitions.

Problems in the operating environment

Soon after acquiring the stores, Wal-Mart hurried through their renovation and put its brand name on them to make sure its EDLP message went across. But it was unable to cash in on its EDLP selling point, chiefly because of the strong competition from German retailers.

Whenever Wal-Mart lowered its prices on commodities, German retailers such as Aldi, Lidl, Rewe and Edeka also lowered their prices to keep their customers, so Wal-Mart found it difficult to get a foothold. German retailer Edeka put it plainly, saying, 'The prices Wal-Mart offers are not lower than ours.' In response to Wal-Mart's slashing of prices in 2000, German competitor Real – the hypermarket chain – also decreased prices on around 3000 items. One of the German retailers, Rewe, even copied Wal-Mart's slogan – *'Jeden Tag Tiefpreise'*. In 2000, Wal-Mart also introduced its private label, *'Smartprice'*, to Germany. However, the German discount retailers had a strong relationship with consumers, and Wal-Mart's private labels were not considered low-priced by the German public.

The lack of strong vendor relations also affected Wal-Mart's operations in Germany. Wal-Mart's success in its home market was mainly due to its efficient supply chain and vendor relations. Unlike in the US, where the company and its suppliers were accustomed to the centralised distribution, in Germany suppliers were not comfortable with the centralised distribution system that Wal-Mart adopted. As in the US, Wal-Mart in Germany wanted to rely on inputs from suppliers in order to decide on product assortments. However, in Germany, Wal-Mart's relationship with its suppliers was not mature enough to make this possible. Thus, Wal-Mart ended up trying to sell goods which its customers did not want but which suppliers wanted to push.

Wal-Mart also had a number of inventory problems. Initially Wal-Mart had only one stockroom which stocked all merchandise. The company found it difficult to hire employees for its stockroom due to the low wages it was offering. The shortage of workers delayed the movement of goods, leading to excessive stockpiling.

Another operational problem Wal-Mart faced was employee unrest. It was accused of paying low wages and

not providing good working conditions. Wal-Mart did not understand the German work culture. As in its US operations, it discouraged employees from forming unions. After acquiring Interspar and Wertkauf, Wal-Mart prohibited members of the work councils of the erstwhile separate companies from meeting each other. The company also rarely consulted the elected representatives of its employees.

Wal-Mart ran into trouble with German unions when it announced employee lay-offs and store closures in 2002 in order to reduce its personnel costs.[8] In addition, it refused to accept the centralised wage-bargaining process[9] in the German retail industry. Because of this, the trade unions organised a walk-out from Wal-Mart stores which led to bad publicity for the company. Wal-Mart employees also went on a two-day strike in July 2002, demanding the negotiation of wage contracts with the company (see Exhibit 4).

Problems in the external environment

Wal-Mart faced several problems on the legal front as well. It was accused of breaching various German laws. The company was accused of having violated Section (IV) (2) of the 'Act Against Restraints of Competition' (Gesetz gegen Wettbewerbsbeschrankungen or GWB) and Section 335a of the 'Commercial Act' (Handelsgesetzbuch or HGB). Section (IV) (2) of GWB forbids companies 'with superior market power in relation to small and medium-sized competitors' from lowering their prices and engaging in price wars with small companies. Such large companies were allowed to lower prices only after providing justification for the lower prices.

Exhibit 4   Profiles of German retailers

ALDI: The history of Aldi dates back to the 1940s. In 1946, Theo Abrecht and Karl Abrecht inherited convenience stores from their parents. In 1960, Albrecht Discount Stores began to be called 'Aldi', and there were 300 such stores. In 1961, a hard discount format was formulated by Theo and Karl Abrecht. This combined ultra-low prices and high product quality with a very limited product assortment of around 600–700 products with a no-frills shopping experience. In 1962, the company was spilt into two independent operations – Aldi Nord (Aldi North) and Aldi Süd (Aldi South). Aldi's northern operations were headed by Theo Abrecht and its southern operations were headed by Karl Abrecht, who operated independently, coordinating major decisions such as suppliers and pricing. The company continued to be known as the Aldi group. By 2002, the Aldi group had around 3741 stores in Germany and had around 2643 stores internationally. It had a presence in Australia, the United Kingdom, the United States, France, Denmark, Belgium, Luxembourg, Netherlands, Ireland, Spain and Austria.

METRO AG: Metro AG was formed in 1996 after the merger of Metro Cash & Carry (established in 1964), Kaufhof Holding AG (established in 1879) and Asko Deutsche Kaufhaus AG (established in 1880). With the merger, the Metro AG group became world's third biggest supermarket group, with around 2300 sales outlets, and a distribution network in around 26 countries in the world covering not only European countries but also countries such as China, Turkey, Eastern Europe and Morocco. The Metro group divided its business into five segments: Cash & Carry, under the brand names Metro, Makro and Spar (since March 2002); Real (800 hypermarkets) and Extra (supermarkets) in the food sector; Mediamarkt and Saturn, selling electronic goods; Praktiker, selling home improvement products; and Galeria and Kaufhof, general stores offering consumer goods. More than 40 per cent of Metro AG's turnover was generated from its international stores. For 2002, Metro AG reported sales of €51.5 billion, compared to 2001 sales of €49.5 billion.

EDEKA GROUP: The history of the Edeka group dates back to the late 1890s. The Edeka group was the brainchild of Friedrich William Raiffeisen and Hermann Schulze Delizsch. Their idea was to set up a purchase association where goods were made available to buyers at low prices. In October 1907, the Edeka Foundation was formed with 23 purchase associations. In the same year, a central procurement office called Edeka Center AG was established. Over the years, the group was able to maintain low prices because of its strong relations with its suppliers. Edeka procured goods from regional wholesalers. The Edeka group was made up of a number of independent retailers and co-operative societies. Edeka's product range included organic fruits, vegetables, dairy products and cereals. The food products were marketed under the brand name Bio Wertkost. The group's brands also included Rio Grande and Mibell. The group also had a presence in pharmacy retailing, food processing and wine operations, publishing and banking services.

Source: compiled from various newspapers and company websites.

Wal-Mart had lowered the prices of some commodities, namely sugar, milk and margarine, in May 2000. The new prices were reportedly lower than the cost price at which Wal-Mart had bought them. In making this move, Wal-Mart was alleged to have violated Section (IV) (2). In response to Wal-Mart's move, the German retailers Aldi and Lidl also lowered their prices. As the price war continued, the German Federal Cartel Office (FCO) launched an investigation in September 2000. It ordered the retailers to stop selling the commodities below cost price as it would hurt small and medium-size retailers and lead to unfair competition.

In response to the FCO order, Wal-Mart took the case to the Appeals Court in Düsseldorf. The Appeals Court ruled in favor of Wal-Mart, stating that Section (IV) (2) prohibited big players from selling at lower prices,

and Wal-Mart could not be considered as a big player in Germany as it did not have a considerable market share nor market capitalisation. However, the FCO took the case further up to the Supreme Court to argue against the verdict of the Appeals Court. In November 2002, the German Supreme Court gave its verdict, declaring that Wal-Mart's selling goods at prices below cost price would result in unfair competition against small and medium-size retailers, and that Wal-Mart should abandon its pricing strategies.[10]

Wal-Mart was also hauled up for violating the Commercial Act's Section 335a by not publishing financial data such as balance sheet and profit and loss account statements on its operations in Germany. The trade unions alleged that they were not given access to accounts of the company. In order to gain access to financial information, the trade unions filed a suit against Wal-Mart in the state court. In its verdict the court ruled that Wal-Mart should publish the required financial information; it also fined Wal-Mart senior executives for not providing the required financial information. Wal-Mart sources said that since the company was a limited partnership, it was not mandatory for it to publish financial information under German laws. However, according to the trade unions, under the altered German commercial code, even limited partnership firms were required to publish their financial accounts. In November 2002, Wal-Mart filed a suit in the German Supreme Court against the verdict of the state court, asking it to delay the state court's decision until the European Court of Justice came out with its decision on disclosure provisions by foreign companies.[11]

Cultural mismatch

Apart from the operational and regulatory problems, Wal-Mart also faced cultural problems in Germany. It found it difficult to integrate the two companies (Wertkauf and Interspar) that it had acquired. The companies had completely different work cultures; while Interspar had decentralised operations with independent regional units, Wertkauf was highly centralised with the head office making all decisions. Additionally, Wal-Mart found it difficult to integrate the two companies' cultures with its own.

Employee morale in Wal-Mart Germany was also reported to have been badly affected by the changes in internal rules and regulations effected by Wal-Mart. The earlier managements of both Interspar and Wertkauf had given their executives liberal expense accounts. But after Wal-Mart's acquisition of the firms, the executives' expense accounts were reduced. For instance, during business trips, they were required to share rooms – which came as a culture shock to the Germans.

Wal-Mart also faced a language problem in Germany. When Wal-Mart entered Germany, the top management who came from the US did not show any inclination to learn German. Within a few weeks, English became the official language of the company in Germany. This resulted in serious communication problems for the German employees. Making English the official language affected employee morale, with employees starting to feel like outsiders and getting increasingly frustrated. The German public also found it difficult to pronounce Wal-Mart's name correctly. They pronounced it as Vawl-Mart.

In Germany, Wal-Mart's world-famous customer service methods fell flat. For example, Wal-Mart's famous Ten-Foot Rule[12] was not implemented in Germany, as German customers did not like strangers interfering with their shopping. Commenting on this, Tiarks said, 'You can't beat those things into your people. They have to be genuine, or the customer sees right through them.' For the same reason, Wal-Mart also did away with the idea of greeters at German stores. In the US, Wal-Mart used to employ greeters at all its stores to welcome customers as they entered. However, in Germany, the company found that customers did not appreciate this idea at all. Apart from this, the German consumers realised that they were the ones who would be paying more because of 'the guy standing at the door' – which is why they did not appreciate it. Wal-Mart in Germany could not offer loyalty cards[13] as they were banned in Germany.

Future prospects

Even five years after entering the German market, Wal-Mart had not made a significant impact in the German retail industry. Wal-Mart reported losses over all the four years up to 2002 in its German operations (see Exhibit 5). It was reported that between 1999 and 2002 Wal-Mart's sales declined by 5 per cent on average. Increasing costs also pushed up losses for the company. Wal-Mart sources indicated that personnel costs accounted for around 17 per cent of sales; these high costs prompted Wal-Mart to freeze new recruitment. Commenting on the operations in Germany, Wal-Mart CEO Scott said, 'We just walked in and said, "We're

Exhibit 5 Sales and operating profit in Germany		
Year	**Sales ($ million)**	**Operating profit/(loss) ($ million)**
1999	2815	(192)
2000	2468	(181)
2001	2506	(164)
2002	2420	(108)
Source: adapted from www.mventures.com.		

going to lower prices, we're going to add people to the stores, we're going to remodel the stores because inherently that's correct," and it wasn't. We didn't have the infrastructure to support the kind of things we were doing.'[14]

Though Wal-Mart claimed that sales were picking up, analysts felt otherwise, and said that Wal-Mart in Germany had failed on its customer service promise. Independent studies conducted by some newspapers indicated that Wal-Mart was rated seventh out of the 10 major retailers in Germany in terms of overall customer satisfaction (see Exhibit 6).

Exhibit 6 Customer satisfaction ratings of German retailers

Retailer name	Rank
Aldi Group	1
Globus	2
Kaufland	3
Lidl	4
Norma	5
Marktkauf	6
Wal-Mart	7
Metro	8
Penny	9
Real	10

Source: www.hicbusiness.org.

Wal-Mart announced that it would not be looking for further acquisitions in Germany and would concentrate on stabilising its business in the country. Commenting on the company's plans, Dave Ferguson, head of European operations, said, 'What we first have to achieve is that the existing stores are operating optimally.'

To revive its fortunes in Germany, Wal-Mart announced that it would be focusing on bringing down its capital costs. It announced that instead of opening Wal-Mart supercenters, the company would focus on opening smaller stores in Germany. Only time will tell whether Wal-Mart will become a significant player in the German retail market.

Questions

1 Wal-Mart started its global operations in the early 1990s when it opened its first international store in Mexico. Analyse the reasons for Wal-Mart's decision to go global.

2 When Wal-Mart announced that it would be entering the German market, analysts were surprised. Usually, the cultural affinity between the US and the UK led American companies to target the UK first, before launching on to the European continent. Do you think Wal-Mart's decision to enter the German market was correct? Justify your opinion.

3 Even after five years of doing business in Germany, Wal-Mart had failed to make an impact on the German market and had been incurring losses year after year. Analyse the reasons for Wal-Mart's problems in the German market. Do you think the company will be able to improve its performance in Germany?

Further reading and bibliography
- Wendy Zellener, 'Wal-Mart's Newest Accent is German', *Business Week*, 18 December 1997.
- Mike Troy, 'Wal-Mart Germany's New President Faces Culture, Customer Challenges', *Discount Store News*, 9 February 1998.
- John Schmid, 'In Europe, Wal-Mart Pursues a Big Dream', *International Herald Tribune*, 2 October 1998.
- 'Wal-Mart Acquires Interspar Hypermarkets', www.prnewswire.com, 9 December 1998.
- Mike Troy, 'Wal-Mart Germany Beefs Up', *Discount Store News*, 4 January 1999.
- Jeremy Kahn, 'Wal-Mart Goes Shopping in Europe', *Fortune*, 7 June 1999.
- Heidi Dawley, 'Watch out Europe: Here Comes Wal-Mart', *Business Week*, 28 June 1999.
- 'Wal-Mart in Germany is Not Doing Well', www.union-network.org, 7 March 2000.
- 'Wal-Mart Makes Bigger than Expected Losses in Germany', www.union-network.org, 10 March 2000.
- 'The Wal-Mart Effect', *Business Europe*, 17 May 2000.
- 'Wal-Mart's Low Prices too Low for Germany's Retail Regulators', www.enquirer.com, 9 September 2000.
- 'Germany: Stop Bullying Wal-Mart', *Business Week*, 25 September 2000.
- David Marino, 'Wal-Mart Steps up German Invasion', www.fool.com, 26 March 2001.
- 'Wal-Mart Continues to Lose Money in Germany – Responds through Escalating Price War', www.union-network.org, 29 March 2001.

- 'Operations Evolve to Offset Doldrums in Deutschland', *DSN Retailing Today*, 5 June 2001.
- Wendy Zellner, Katharine A. Schmidt, Moon Ihlwan, Heidi Dawley, 'How Well Does Wal-Mart Travel?', *Business Week*, 3 September 2001.
- Daniel Rubin, 'Grumpy German Shoppers Distrust the Wal-Mart Style', www.gaccwa.org, 30 September 2001.
- 'The First "Real" Wal-Mart is a flop?', www.union-network.org, 12 February 2002.
- Isabelle de Pommereau, 'Wal-Mart lesson: Smiling service won't win Germans', www.csmonitor.com, 17 October 2002.
- www.walmartstores.com.
- www.planetretail.net.
- www.forbes.com.
- www.hicbusiness.org.
- www.mventures.com.
- www.wilmercutler.com

References

1 Pommereau, Isabelle de, 'Wal-Mart Lesson: Smiling Service Won't Win Germans, www.csmonitor.com, 17 October 2002.
2 Rubin, Daniel, Grumpy German Shoppers Distrust the Wal-Mart Style', www.gaccwa.org, 30 December 2001.
3 EDLP was a pricing strategy adopted by Wal-Mart to ensure lowest prices among all retail chains on its products.
4 K-mart is a leading US retailer.
5 Target is one of the leading discount retail chains in the US.
6 Jeremy Khan, 'Wal-Mart Goes Shopping in Europe', *Fortune*, 7 June 1999.
7 'Operations Evolve to Offset Doldrums in Deutschland', DSN *Retailing Today*, 5 June 2001.
8 It was reported that Wal-Mart had the highest employee costs among German retailers. The high costs were attributed to heavy recruiting by Wal-Mart anticipating huge business and its misreading of the German retailing environment. For instance, Wal-Mart had to lay off employees who were taken on as greeters as the German public did not take to the idea, and it also had to cut down the number of employees in many stores due to low sales.
9 In a centralised wage bargaining process, the wages across all companies in a particular industry are decided according to the average productivity in the industry.
10 The German Supreme Court felt that Wal-Mart pricing margarine below cost was legal as it was done for only a brief period. However, the court was against Wal-Mart's pricing of sugar and milk below cost prices.
11 Many European firms had filed cases against Germany's alterations to its commercial code which required the firms to publish financial information. The European Court of Justice's decision was still awaited.
12 As per the Ten-Foot Rule of the company, whenever an employee comes within 10 feet of a customer, the employee should look up to the customer, greet him and ask him if he needs any help.
13 Loyalty cards were offered by supermarkets and big retail chains to select loyal customers. The businesses offered special prices for the customers possessing loyalty cards. However, in 2002, many customer groups accused companies of using loyalty cards to track down the purchasing patterns of the customers and started opposing such schemes.
14 Zellner, Wendy, 'How Well Does Wal-Mart Travel?', *Business Week*, 3 September 2001.

This case was written by K. Subhadra, under the direction of Sanjib Dutta, ICFAI Center for Management Research (ICMR). It is intended to be used as a basis for class discussion rather than to illustrate either effective or ineffective handling of a management situation. The case was compiled from published sources.

To order copies, call 0091-40-2343-0462/63/64 or write to ICFAI Center for Management Research, Plot # 49, Nagarjuna Hills, Hyderabad 500 082, India, or e-mail icmr@icfai.org. Website: www.icmrindia.org

case 4.2   Handl Tyrol: Market Selection and Coverage Decisions of a Medium-sized Austrian Enterprise

Company background

Handl Tyrol was established as a family business in the province of Tyrol, Austria, in 1902. The company focuses on the production and marketing of high-quality smoked and air-dried meat and sausage specialties from Tyrol. Handl Tyrol has three business locations: the Pians production facility, Schönwies service center and Christanell GmbH in Naturns/South Tyrol, Italy (a wholly owned subsidiary since 1993); all of which have been certified under the International Food Standard (IFS, Version 04) and the higher level British Retail Consortium Technical Standard (BRC 2002). Both of these certification procedures use the most stringent standards in the European food production industry, with a special focus on the areas of food safety, hygiene and the specific traceability of all goods throughout the entire processing chain. The long-term success of the company has been realised by means of a growth strategy in the form of equity interests and acquisition efforts as well as intensive innovation activities. Austria is Handl Tyrol's home market, and since 1978 the company has worked this entire market through selected food retailers and the restaurant and catering industry, as well as the company's own sales outlets in highly frequented tourist areas and larger cities.

Handl Tyrol's growth objectives

Handl Tyrol's strategic objectives are twofold:

1 to become the home market champion by dominating in those areas where the company excels (quality leadership, relationship to tradition)
2 to become a European champion, that is, Handl Tyrol strives for European market and brand leadership in its market segment.

Handl's internationalisation and expansion strategy

Restricting factors

As Handl Tyrol is a company which produces smoked bacon and ham products backed by a long-standing Alpine tradition, the connection between the product and its origins has to be maintained. This implies that the company has to confine production activities to the area in and around Tyrol when entering new markets. In the case of product adaptations, it is necessary to consider the Tyrolean lifestyle and culture in accordance with the company's slogan ('Der echte Nordtiroler', roughly: 'genuine northern Tyrolean products') and to ensure that the unique taste of Handl Tyrol products remains unchanged. Expansion activities have to be financed by the company's own cash flow in order to ensure the company's continued financial health.

Marketing focus

Handl Tyrol pursues a distinctive niche strategy. The company strives to develop slowly but steadily as a hidden champion and to raise its position to the level of European market leadership. The company primarily concentrates on retail trade advertising and participation in relevant trade fairs (e.g. ANUGA in Cologne – international trade in food and semi-luxury goods – INTERMEAT in Düsseldorf and CIBUS in Parma). Hence, Handl Tyrol follows a push strategy. In 2003 and 2004, the company also increased its image advertising efforts on television and in print media. The consumer group targeted by Handl Tyrol's premium range comprises quality-conscious people who enjoy food and belong to the middle and upper income brackets. In Austria, Handl Tyrol has reached a level of an unassisted brand recall of over 60 per cent. In 2004, the company entered into a sales alliance with the Spanish market leader Esteban Espuna. This alliance has the strategic advantage of providing customers with a competent source of typical air-dried and smoked specialities.

Country selection criteria

Handl's approach regarding the selection and servicing of foreign markets is based on a set of analytic country selection criteria. These have been applied in former expansion strategies, such as when entering Germany,

Spain etc. The selection of countries encompasses a preliminary strategic decision with due attention to the following business criteria: structure and development of the company's international market presence, balance, risk diversification, preliminary decisions as to regional development paths and country portfolios. In addition the company takes into account country-specific economic data such as per capita income, GDP, rate of inflation, per capita consumption of pork, level of internal supply of pork, price level, competition (number of providers, competitors' revenues), presence of Austrian companies in the food industry (experience), import conditions, distribution, risk, meat consumption, geographical location (distance from Austria), business contacts, living and consumption habits, frequency of tourism and retail trade structures.

Market penetration in Germany, Italy and the rest of Europe (except Eastern Europe)

On the basis of its market leadership in Austria since the early 1990s, Handl Tyrol has been working the German and Italian markets more intensively since 2000. The products are listed at approximately 80 per cent of the retail trade chains in Germany. The company operates on the German market through its own distribution network, consisting of three internal employees as well as a dozen retail trade agencies. The competitive situation is becoming increasingly difficult. In addition to meat and sausage producers in general, the producers of the South Tyrolean smoked bacon brand ggA are also penetrating the market and creating fierce price competition. Handl's marketing mix is being expanded as revenues increase, with the main focus being on retail trade-related advertising. Sales activities in Germany are characterised by a major discrepancy between the north and the south due to the south's geographical proximity to the Tyrol, as well as similar consumption habits in those regions.

In Italy, Handl Tyrol's distribution network (consisting of the company's own employees) is continuously expanded as sales activities are steadily increasing. The company's main competitors in Italy are the producers of the South Tyrolean smoked bacon brand ggA as well as salami producers. Sales activities in Italy focus on Handl Tyrol's premium real northern Tyrolean cured sausage and smoked bacon, mainly at the deli counter.

The company works the rest of the European market via its own sales force and various importers, focusing on Luxembourg, Denmark, Belgium, the Netherlands, Finland, France, Switzerland and England.

In general, Handl Tyrol's entire 'Alpine range' is offered in these countries, with the strongest differentiation by Handl Tyrol's genuine northern Tyrolean products.

Market coverage in Eastern Europe
Incremental approach

Since 2002, exports have deliberately been expanded to Eastern European countries due to the high potential of Austrian specialities in these markets. For strategic reasons such as the proximity to the home market, existing relationships with international retail trade groups, consumer preferences and economic attractiveness, Handl Tyrol decided to extend their business into Eastern Europe in a two-step process. In a first step, the Handl Tyrol genuine northern Tyrolean range was exported to the Czech Republic, Hungary, Slovakia, Slovenia and Poland. Other Eastern European countries should be covered in later expansion stages.

With increasing incomes, the residents of the Eastern European countries that are currently served by Handl Tyrol also have higher expectations of food products and are also prepared to pay more for them. In these markets, there are many domestic producers whose quality has not yet reached Western standards. Aside from the other international suppliers of similar meat and sausage products, these producers are Handl Tyrol's most significant competitors. The company is therefore making efforts to establish its name as a high-quality supplier of northern Tyrolean specialties. With this clear positioning and simultaneous differentiation from competing suppliers, the company offers consumers use-specific range solutions. A positive brand transfer can be created, especially by means of self-service goods.

The Eastern European markets are primarily serviced by importers. As revenues grow and contacts are developed further, the company plans to expand its sales network with its own employees.

The retailing landscape in these markets is characterised by vast differences. In Hungary, mainly the large international groups such as Metro, Tengelmann, Tesco, Rewe (Billa/Penny), Spar and Auchan are represented, in addition to several Hungarian retail chains. In Slovakia, Tesco, Metro, Rewe (Billa), Kaufland, Carrefour and Delvita dominate the scene. In Poland, Makro, Auchan, Tesco and Carrefour are represented on the market. The international chains have not yet expanded to Slovenia due to the small size of this market, meaning that domestic suppliers have an especially strong presence there.

Each month, Handl Tyrol exports 2 tons of high-quality meat products to the Czech Republic. Customers mainly include international retail chains such as Spar, Globus and Billa. In Hungary, Handl Tyrol is now listed in three chains – including Auchan – and in numerous smaller companies with various branches. A contract has also been signed with a partner in Slovenia.

The product portfolio in these markets is dominated by Handl Tyrol's genuine northern Tyrolean range. This

positioning and differentiation makes it possible to gain a foothold in the market with an extraordinary range of specialties. The products are adapted in such a way that they are distinguished in the language of each country. If the market requires, Handl Tyrol has the technical flexibility to design products specifically for each country.

Communication activities focus heavily on retail sales in Eastern Europe. In addition to typical flyers, the company also performs public relations work. In the future, the company also plans to increase its participation in specific trade fairs. Sales literature is translated into the language of each country.

Business development and further expansion

With its continuous business development and approximately 400 employees, Handl Tyrol's sales increased 8 per cent to some €78 million by the end of the 2004 business year; 67 per cent of sales can be attributed to the Austrian market. The share of exports was 33 per cent, an increase of 12 per cent over the previous year. Exports were increased by 15 per cent in Germany, 30 per cent in Italy, 30 per cent in the rest of Europe (France, Luxembourg, Belgium, Denmark, Finland), and 100 per cent in Eastern Europe (from 30 to 60 tons).

The management team meets up for a strategic review of its international activities. The management is charged with decisions about the future development of the Eastern European markets.

Question
1   Should the company expand further into the Eastern European markets and which countries should it enter in what sequence?

This case was written by Claudia Klausegger, Wirtschaftsuniversität Wien, Austria, and Rudolf R. Sinkovics, University of Manchester, UK. The authors gratefully acknowledge the excellent support of Sonja Elmaver, marketing manager, Handl Tyrol.

case 4.3 Blair Water Purifiers to India

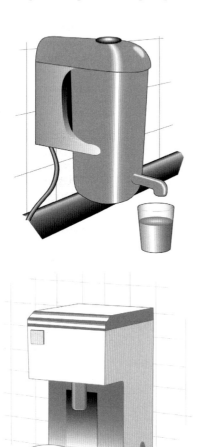

'A pity I couldn't have stayed for Diwali', thought Rahul Chatterjee, 'but anyway it was great to be back home in Calcutta.' The Diwali holiday and its festivities would begin in early November 1996, some two weeks after Chatterjee had returned to the United States. Chatterjee worked as an international market liaison for Blair Company, Inc. This was his eighth year with Blair Company and easily his favourite. 'Your challenge will be in moving us from just dabbling in less developed countries (LDCs) to our thriving in them', his boss had said when Chatterjee was promoted to the job last January. Chatterjee had agreed and was thrilled when asked to visit Bombay and New Delhi in April. His purpose on that trip was to gather background data on the possibility of Blair Company entering the Indian market for home water purification devices. Initial results were encouraging and prompted the second trip.

Chatterjee had used his second trip primarily to study Indian consumers in Calcutta and Bangalore and to gather information on possible competitors. The two cities represented quite different metropolitan areas in terms of location, size, language and infrastructure – yet both suffered from similar problems in terms of water supplied to their residents. These problems could be found in many LDCs and were favourable to home water purification.

Information gathered on both visits would be used to make a recommendation on market entry and on elements of an entry strategy. Executives at Blair Company would compare Chatterjee's recommendations to those from two other Blair Company liaisons who were focusing their efforts on Argentina, Brazil and Indonesia.

The Indian market for home water filtration and purification

Like most aspects of India, the market for home water filtration and purification took a good deal of effort to understand. Yet despite expending this effort, Chatterjee realised that much remained either unknown or in conflict. For example, the market seemed clearly a mature one, with four or five established Indian competitors fighting for market share. Or was it? Another view portrayed the market as a

fragmented one, with no large competitor having a national presence and perhaps 100 small, regional manufacturers, each competing in just one or two of India's 25 states. Indeed, the market could be in its early growth stages, as reflected by the large number of product designs, materials and performances. Perhaps with a next generation product and a world-class marketing effort, Blair Company could consolidate the market and stimulate tremendous growth – much like the situation in the Indian market for cars.

Such uncertainty made it difficult to estimate market potential. However, Chatterjee had collected unit sales estimates for a 10-year period for three similar product categories – vacuum cleaners, sewing machines and colour televisions. In addition, a Delhi-based research firm had provided him with estimates of unit sales for Aquaguard, the largest-selling water purifier in several Indian states. Chatterjee had used the data in two forecasting models available at Blair Company along with three subjective scenarios – realistic, optimistic and pessimistic – to arrive at the estimates and forecasts for water purifiers shown in Exhibit 1. 'If anything,' Chatterjee had explained to his boss, 'my forecasts are conservative because they describe only first-time sales, not any replacement sales over the 10-year forecast horizon'. He also pointed out that his forecasts applied only to industry sales in larger urban areas, which was the present industry focus.

Exhibit 1 Industry sales estimates and forecasts for water purifiers in India, 1990–2005 (000 units)

Year	Unit sales estimates	Unit sales forecast under …		
		realistic scenario	optimistic scenario	pessimistic scenario
1990	60			
1991	90			
1992	150			
1993	200			
1994	220			
1995	240			
1996		250	250	250
1997		320	370	300
1998		430	540	400
1999		570	800	550
2000		800	1200	750
2001		1000	1500	850
2002		1300	1900	900
2003		1500	2100	750
2004		1600	2100	580
2005		1500	1900	420

One thing that seemed certain was that many Indians felt the need for improved water quality. Folklore, newspapers, consumer activists and government officials regularly reinforced this need by describing the poor quality of Indian water. Quality suffered particularly during the monsoons because of highly polluted water entering treatment plants and because of numerous leaks and unauthorised withdrawals from water systems. Such leaks and withdrawals often polluted clean water after it had left the plants. Politicians running for national, state and local government offices also reinforced the need for improved water quality through election campaign promises. Governments at these levels set standards for water quality, took measurements at thousands of locations throughout the nation and advised consumers when water became unsafe.

During periods of poor water quality, many Indian consumers had little choice but to consume the water as they found it. However, better educated, wealthier and more health conscious consumers took steps to safeguard their family's health and often continued these steps year-round. A good estimate of the number of such households, Chatterjee thought, would be around 40 million. These consumers were similar in many respects to consumers in middle- and upper-middle-class households in the United States and the European Union. They valued comfort and product choice. They saw consumption of material goods as a means to a higher quality of life. They liked foreign brands and would pay a higher price for such brands, as long as purchased products outperformed competing Indian products. Chatterjee had identified as his target market these 40 million households plus those in another 4 million households who had similar values and lifestyles, but as yet took little effort to improve water quality in their homes.

Traditional method for home water purification

The traditional method of water purification in the target market relied not on any commercially supplied product but instead on boiling. Each day or several times a day, a cook, maid or family member would boil two to five litres of water for 10 minutes, allow it to cool, and then transfer it to containers for storage (often in a refrigerator). Chatterjee estimated that about 50 per cent of the target market used this procedure. Boiling was seen by consumers as inexpensive, effective in terms of eliminating dangerous bacteria, and entrenched in a traditional sense. Many consumers who used this method considered it more effective than any product on the market. However, boiling affected the palatability of water, leaving the purified product somewhat 'flat' to the taste. Boiling also

was cumbersome, time-consuming and ineffective in removing physical impurities and unpleasant odours. Consequently, about 10 per cent of the target market took a second step by filtering their boiled water through 'candle filters' before storage. Many consumers who took this action did so despite knowing that water could become recontaminated during handling and storage.

Mechanical methods for home water filtration and purification

About 40 per cent of the target market used a mechanical device to improve their water quality. Half of this group used candle filters, primarily because of their low price and ease of use. The typical candle filter comprised two containers, one resting on top of the other. The upper container held one or more porous ceramic cylinders (candles) which strained the water as gravity drew it into the lower container. Containers were made of plastic, porcelain or stainless steel and typically stored between 15 and 20 litres of filtered water. Purchase costs depended on materials and capacities, ranging from Rs350 for a small plastic model to Rs1100 for a large stainless steel model (35 Indian Rupees were equivalent to US$1.00 in 1996). Candle filters were slow, producing 15 litres (one candle) to 45 litres (three candles) of filtered water each 24 hours. To maintain this productivity, candles regularly needed to be removed, cleaned and boiled for 20 minutes. Most manufacturers recommended that consumers replace candles (Rs40 each) either once a year or more frequently, depending on sediment levels.

The other half of this group used 'water purifiers', devices that were considerably more sophisticated than candle filters. Water purifiers typically employed three water processing stages. The first removed sediments, the second objectionable odours and colours and the third harmful bacteria and viruses. Engineers at Blair Company were sceptical that most purifiers claiming the latter benefit actually could deliver on their promise. However, all purifiers did a better job here than candle filters. Candle filters were totally ineffective in eliminating bacteria and viruses (and might even increase this type of contamination), despite advertising claims to the contrary. Water purifiers generally used stainless steel containers and sold at prices ranging from Rs2000 to Rs7000, depending on manufacturers, features and capacities. Common flow rates were one to two litres of purified water per minute. Simple service activities could be performed on water purifiers by consumers as needed. However, more complicated service required units to be taken to a nearby dealer or an in-home visit from a skilled technician.

The remaining 10 per cent of the target market owned neither a filter nor a purifier and seldom boiled their

water. Many consumers in this group were unaware of water problems and thought their water quality acceptable. However, a few consumer in this group refused to pay for products that they believed were mostly ineffective. Overall, Chatterjee believed that only a few consumers in this group could be induced to change their habits and become customers. The most attractive segments consisted of the 90 per cent of households in the target market who boiled, boiled and filtered, only filtered, or purified their water.

All segments in the target market showed a good deal of similarity in terms of what they thought important in the purchase of a water purifier. According to Chatterjee's research, the most important factor was product performance in terms of sediment removal, bacteria and virus removal, capacity (either in the form of storage or flow rate), safety and 'footprint' space. Purchase price also was an important concern among consumers who boiled, boiled and filtered or only filtered their water. The next most important factor was ease of installation and service, with style and appearance rated almost as important. The least important factor was warranty and availability of finance for purchase. Finally, all segments expected a water purifier to be warranted against defective operation for 18 to 24 months and to perform trouble-free for five to 10 years.

Blair Company, Inc.

Blair Company was founded in 1975 by Eugene Blair, after he left his position in research and development at Culligan International Company. Blair Company's first product was a desalinator, used by mobile home parks in Florida to remove salts from brackish well water supplied to residents. The product was a huge success and markets quickly expanded to include nearby municipalities, smaller businesses, hospitals, and bottlers of water for sale to consumers. Geographic markets also expanded, first to other coastal regions near the company's headquarters in Tampa, Florida, and then to desert areas in the southwestern United States. New products were added rapidly as well and, by 1996, the product line included desalinators, particle filters, ozonators, ion exchange resins and purifiers. Industry experts generally regarded the product line as superior in terms of performance and quality, with prices higher than those of many competitors.

Blair Company sales revenues for 1996 would be almost $400 million, with an expected profit close to $50 million. Annual growth in sales revenues averaged 12 per cent for the past five years. Blair Company employed over 4000 people, with 380 having technical backgrounds and responsibilities.

Export sales of desalinators and related products began at Blair Company in 1980. Units were sold first to resorts in

Mexico and Belize and later to water bottlers in Germany. Export sales grew rapidly and Blair Company found it necessary to organise its International Division in 1985. Sales in the International Division also grew rapidly and would reach almost $140 million in 1996. About $70 million would come from countries in Latin and South America, $30 million from Europe (including shipments to Africa), and $40 million from South Asia and Australia. The International Division had sales offices, small assembly areas, and distribution facilities in Frankfurt, Germany; Tokyo, Japan; and Singapore.

The Frankfurt office had been the impetus in 1990 for development and marketing of Blair Company's first product targeted exclusively to consumer households – a home water filter. Sales engineers at the Frankfurt office began receiving consumer and distributor requests for a home water filter soon after the fall of the Berlin wall in 1989. By late 1991, two models had been designed in the United States and introduced in Germany (particularly to the eastern regions), Poland, Hungary, Romania, the Czech Republic and Slovakia.

Blair Company executives watched the success of the two water filters with great interest. The market for clean water in LDCs was huge, profitable, and attractive in a socially responsible sense. However, the quality of water in many LDCs was such that a water filter usually would not be satisfactory. Consequently, in late 1994, executives had directed the development of a water purifier that could be added to the product line. Engineers had given the final design in the project the brand name 'Delight'. For the time being, Chatterjee and the other market analysts had accepted the name, not knowing if it might infringe on any existing brand in India or in the other countries under study.

Delight purifier

The Delight purifier used a combination of technologies to remove four types of contaminants found in potable water – sediments, organic and inorganic chemicals, microbials or cysts, and objectionable tastes and odours. The technologies were effective as long as contaminants in the water were present at 'reasonable' levels. Engineers at Blair Company had interpreted 'reasonable' as levels described in several World Health Organization (WHO) reports on potable water and had combined the technologies to purify water to a level beyond WHO standards. Engineers had repeatedly assured Chatterjee that Delight's design in terms of technologies should not be a concern. Ten units operating in the company's testing laboratory showed no signs of failure or performance deterioration after some 5000 hours of continuous use. 'Still,' Chatterjee thought, 'we will undertake a good bit of field testing in India before entering. The risks of failure are too large to ignore. And, besides, results of our testing would be useful in convincing consumers and retailers to buy.'

Chatterjee and the other market analysts still faced major design issues in configuring technologies into physical products. For example, a 'point of entry' design would place the product immediately after water entry to the home, treating all water before it flowed to all water outlets. In contrast, a 'point of use' design would place the product on a countertop, wall, or at the end of a tap and treat only water arriving at that location. Based on cost estimates, designs of competing products, and his understanding of Indian consumers, Chatterjee would direct engineers to proceed only with 'point of use' designs for the market.

Other technical details were yet to be worked out. For example, Chatterjee had to provide engineers with suggestions for filter flow rates, storage capacities (if any), unit layout, and overall dimensions, plus a number of special features. One such feature was the possibility of a small battery to operate the filter for several hours in case of a power failure (a common occurence in India and many other LDCs). Another might be one or two 'bells or whistles' to tell cooks, maids, and family members that the unit indeed was working properly. Yet another might be an 'additive' feature, permitting users to add fluoride, vitamins, or even flavourings to their water.

Chatterjee knew that the Indian market would eventually require a number of models. However, at the outset of market entry, he probably could get by with just two – one with a larger capacity for houses and bungalows and the other a smaller capacity model for flats. He thought that model styling and specific appearances should reflect a Western, high technology school of design in order to distinguish the Delight purifier from competitors' products. To that end, he had instructed a graphics artist to develop two ideas that he had used to gauge consumer reactions on his last visit. Consumers liked both models but preferred the countertop design to the wall-mount design.

Competitors

Upwards of 100 companies competed in the Indian market for home water filters and purifiers. While information on most of these companies was difficult to obtain, Chatterjee and the Indian research agencies were able to develop descriptions of three major competitors and brief profiles of several others.

Eureka Forbes

The most established competitor in the water purifier market was Eureka Forbes, a joint venture company established in 1982 between Electrolux (Sweden) and Forbes Campbell (India). The company marketed a broad line of

'modern, lifestyle products' including water purifiers, vaccum cleaners and mixers/grinders. The brand name used for its water purifiers was 'Aquaguard', a name so well established that many consumers mistakenly used it to refer to other water purifiers or to the entire product category. Aquaguard, with its 10-year market history, was clearly the market leader and came close to being India's only national brand. However, Eureka Forbes had recently introduced a second brand of water purifier called 'PureSip'. The PureSip model was similar to Aquaguard except for its third stage process, which used a polyiodide resin instead of ultraviolet rays to kill bacteria and viruses. This meant that water from a PureSip purifier could be stored safely for later usage. Also in contrast to Aquaguard, the PureSip model needed no electricity for its operation.

However, the biggest difference between the two products was how they were sold. Aquaguard was sold exclusively by a 2500-person sales force that called directly on households. In contrast, PureSip was sold by independent dealers of smaller home appliances. Unit prices to consumers for Aquaguard and PureSip in 1996 were approximately Rs5500 and Rs2000, respectively. Chatterjee believed that unit sales of PureSip were much smaller than unit sales for Aquaguard but growing at a much faster rate.

An Aquaguard unit typically was mounted on a kitchen wall, with plumbing required to bring water to the purifier's inlet. A two-metre long power cord was connected to a 230-volt AC electrical outlet – the Indian standard. If the power supply were to drop to 190 volts or lower, the unit would stop functioning. Other limits of the product included a smallish amount of activated carbon, which could eliminate only weak organic odours. It could not remove strong odours or inorganic solutes like nitrates and iron compounds. The unit's design did not allow for storage of treated water and its flow rate of one litre per minute seemed slow to some consumers.

Aquaguard's promotion strategy emphasised personal selling. Each salesman was assigned to a specific neighbourhood and was monitored by a group leader who, in turn, was monitored by a supervisor. Each sales man was expected to canvass his neighbourhood, select prospective households (e.g. those with annual incomes exceeding Rs 70 000), demonstrate the product, and make an intensive effort to sell the product. Repeated sales calls helped to educate consumers about their water quality and to reassure them that Aquaguard service was readily available. Television commercials and advertisements in magazines and newspapers supported the personal selling efforts. Chatterjee estimated that Eureka Forbes would spend about Rs120 million on all sales activities in 1996, or roughly 11 per cent of its sales revenues. He estimated that

about Rs100 million of the Rs120 million would be spent in the form of sales commissions. Chatterjee thought the company's total advertising expenditures for the year would be only about Rs1 million.

Eureka Forbes was a formidable competitor. The salesforce was huge, highly motivated and well managed. Moreover, Aquaguard was the first product to enter the water purifier market, and the name had tremendous brand equity. The product itself was probably the weakest strategic component – but it would take much to convince consumers of this. And, while the salesforce offered a huge competitive advantage, it represented an enormous fixed cost and essentially limited sales efforts to large urban areas. More than 80 per cent of India's population lived in rural areas, where water quality was even lower.

Ion Exchange

Ion Exchange was the premier water treatment company in India, specialising in treatments of water, processed liquids, and wastewater in industrial markets. The company began operations in 1964 as a wholly owned subsidiary of British Permutit. Permutit divested its holdings in 1985 and Ion Exchange became a wholly owned Indian company. The company presently served customers in a diverse group of industries, including nuclear and thermal power stations, fertilizers, petrochemical refineries, textiles, automobiles and home water purifiers. Its home water purifiers carried the family brand name, ZERO-B (Zero-Bacteria).

ZERO-B purifiers used a halogenated resin technology as part of a three-stage purification process. The first stage removed suspended impurities via filter pads, the second eliminated bad odours and taste with activated carbon, and the third killed bacteria using trace quantities of polyiodide (iodine). The latter feature was attractive because it helped prevent iodine deficiency diseases and permitted purified water to be stored up to eight hours without fear of recontamination.

The basic purifier product for the home carried the name 'Puristore'. A Puristore unit typically sat on a kitchen counter near the tap, with no electricity or plumbing hookup needed for its operation. The unit stored 20 litres of purified water. It sold to consumers for Rs2000. Each year the user must replace the halogenated resin at a cost of Rs200.

Chatterjee estimated that ZERO-B captured about 7 per cent of the Indian water purifier market. Probably the biggest reason for the small share was a lack of consumer awareness. ZERO-B purifiers had been on the market for less than three years. They were not advertised heavily nor did they enjoy the sales effort intensity of Aquaguard. Distribution, too, was limited. During Chatterjee's visit, he could find only five dealers in Calcutta carrying ZERO-B

products and none in Bangalore. Dealers that he contacted were of the opinion that ZERO-B's marketing efforts soon would intensify – two had heard rumours that a door-to-door salesforce was planned and that consumer advertising was about to begin.

Chatterjee had confirmed the latter point with a visit to a Calcutta advertising agency. A modest number of 10-second TV commercials soon would be aired on Zee TV and DD metro channels. The advertisements would focus on educating consumers with the position, 'It is not a filter'. Instead, ZERO-B is a water purifier and much more effective than a candle filter in preventing health problems. Apart from this advertising effort, the only other form of promotion used was a point-of-sale brochure that dealers could give to prospective customers.

On balance, Chatterjee thought that Ion Exchange could be a major player in the market. The company had over 30 years' experience in the field of water purification and devoted upwards of Rs10 million each year to corporate research and development. 'In fact,' he thought, 'all Ion Exchange really needs to do is to recognise the market's potential and to make it a priority within the company.' However, this might be difficult to do, given the company's prominent emphasis on industrial markets. Chatterjee estimated that ZERO-B products would account for less than 2 per cent of Ion Exchange's 1996 total sales, estimated at Rs1000 million. He thought the total marketing expenditures for ZERO-B would be around Rs3 million.

Singer

The newest competitor to enter the Indian water purifier market was Singer India Ltd. Originally, Singer India was a subsidiary of the Singer Company, located in the United States, but a minority share (49 per cent) was sold to Indian investors in 1982. The change in ownership had led to construction of manufacturing facilities in India for sewing machines in 1983. The facilities were expanded in 1991 to produce a broad line of home appliances. Sales revenues for 1996 for the entire product line – sewing machines, food processors, irons, mixers, toasters, water heaters, ceiling fans, cooking ranges and colour televisions – would be about Rs900 million.

During Chatterjee's time in Calcutta, he had visited a Singer Company showroom on Park Street. Initially he had hoped that Singer might be a suitable partner to manufacture and distribute the Delight purifier. However, much to his surprise, he was told that Singer now had its own brand on the market, 'Aquarius'. The product was not yet available in Calcutta but was being sold in Bombay and Delhi.

A marketing research agency in Delhi was able to gather some information on the Singer purifier. The product contained nine stages (!) and sold to consumers for Rs4000. It removed sediments, heavy metals, bad tastes,

odours and colours. It also killed bacteria and viruses, fungi and nematodes. The purifier required water pressure (8 PSI minimum) to operate but needed no electricity. It came in a single counter top model that could be moved from one room to another. Life of the device at a flow rate of 3.8 litres per minute was listed at 40 000 litres – about four to six years of use in the typical Indian household. The product's life could be extended to 70 000 litres at a somewhat slower flow rate. However, at 70 000 litres, the product must be discarded. The agency reported a heavy advertising blitz accompanying the introduction in Delhi – emphasising TV and newspaper advertising, plus outdoor and transit advertising as support. All 10 Singer showrooms in Delhi offered vivid demonstrations of the product's operation.

Chatterjee had to admit that photos of the Aquarius purifier shown in the Calcutta showroom looked appealing. And a trade article he found had described the product as 'state of the art' in comparison to the 'primitive' products now on the market. Chatterjee and Blair Company engineers tended to agree – the disinfecting resin used in Aquarius had been developed by the United States government's National Aeronautics and Space Administration (NASA) and was proven to be 100 per cent effective against bacteria and viruses. 'If only I could have brought a unit back with me,' he thought. 'We could have some test results and see just how good it is.' The trade article also mentioned that Singer hoped to sell 40 000 units over the next two years.

Chatterjee knew that Singer was a well-known and respected brand name in India. Further, Singer's distribution channels were superior to those of any competitor in the market, including those of Eureka Forbes. Most prominent of Singer's three distribution channels were the 210 company-owned showrooms located in major urban areas around the country. Each sold and serviced the entire line of Singer products. Each was very well kept and staffed by knowledgeable personnel. Singer products also were sold throughout India by over 3000 independent dealers, who received inventory from an estimated 70 Singer-appointed distributors. According to the marketing research agency in Delhi, distributors earned margins of 12 per cent of the retail price for Aquarius while dealers earned margins of 5 per cent. Finally, Singer employed over 400 sales men who sold sewing machines and food processors door-to-door. Like Eureka Forbes, the direct sales force sold products primarily in large urban markets.

Other competitors

Chatterjee was aware of several other water purifiers on the Indian market. The Delta brand from S&S Industries in Madras seemed a carbon copy of Aquaguard, except for a more eye pleasing, counter top design.

According to promotion literature, Delta offered a line of water-related products – purifiers, water softeners, iron removers, desalinators and ozonators. Another competitor was Alfa Water Purifiers, Bombay. The company offered four purifier models at prices from Rs4300 to Rs6500, depending on capacity. Symphony's Spectrum brand sold well around Bombay at Rs4100 each but removed only suspended sediments, not heavy metals or bacteria. The Sam Group in Coimbatore recently had launched its 'Water Doctor' purifier at Rs5200. The device used a third stage ozonator to kill bacteria and viruses and came in two attractive countertop models, 6- and 12-litre storage. Batliboi was mentioned by the Delhi research agency as yet another competitor, although Chatterjee knew nothing else about the brand. Taken all together, unit sales of all purifiers at these companies plus ZERO-B and Singer probably would account for around 60 000 units in 1996. The remaining 190 000 units would be Aquaguards and PureSips.

At least 100 Indian companies made and marketed candle filters. The largest of these probably was Bajaj Electrical Division, whose product line also included water heaters, irons, electric lightbulbs, toasters, mixers and grillers. Bajaj's candle filters were sold by a large number of dealers who carried the entire product line. Candle filters produced by other manufacturers were sold mostly through dealers who specialised in small household appliances and general hardware. Probably no single manufacturer of candle filters had more than 5 per cent of any regional market in the country. No manufacturer attempted to satisfy a national market. Still, the candle filters market deserved serious consideration – perhaps Delight's entry strategy would attempt to 'trade-up' users of candle filters to a better, safer product.

Finally, Chatterjee knew that sales of almost all purifiers in 1996 in India came from large urban areas. No manufacturer targeted rural or smaller urban areas and at best, Chatterjee had calculated, existing manufacturers were reaching only 10 to 15 per cent of the entire Indian population. An explosion in sales would come if the right product could be sold outside metropolitan areas.

Recommendations

Chatterjee decided that an Indian market entry for Blair Company was subject to three 'givens' as he called them. First, he thought that a strategic focus on rural or smaller urban areas would not be wise, at least at the start. The lack of adequate distribution and communication infrastructure in rural India meant that any market entry would begin with larger Indian cities, most likely on the west coast.

Second, market entry would require manufacturing units in India. Because the cost of skilled labour in India was around Rs20 to Rs25 per hour (compared to $20 to $25 per hour in the United States), importing complete units was out of the question. However, importing a few key components would be necessary at the start of operation.

Third, Blair Company should find an Indian partner. Chatterjee's visits had produced a number of promising partners: Polar Industries, Calcutta; Milton Plastics, Bombay; Videocon Appliances, Aurangabad; BPL Sanyo Utilities and Appliances, Bangalore; Onida Savak, Delhi; Hawkins India, Bombay; and Voltas, Bombay. All companies manufactured and marketed a line of high-quality household appliances, possessed one or more strong brand names, and had established dealer networks (minimum of 10 000 dealers). All were involved to greater or lesser degrees with international partners. All were medium-sized firms – not too large that a partnership with Blair Company would be one-sided, not too small that they would lack managerial talent and other resources. Finally, all were profitable (15 to 27 per cent return on assets in 1995) and looking to grow. However, Chatterjee had no idea if any company would find the Delight purifier and Blair Company attractive or if they might be persuaded to sell part or all of their operations as an acquisition.

Field testing and product recommendations

The most immediate decision Chatterjee faced was whether or not he should recommend a field test. The test would cost about $25 000, placing 20 units in Indian homes in three cities and monitoring their performance for three to six months. The decision to test really was more than it seemed – Chatterjee's boss had explained that a decision to test was really a decision to enter. It made no sense to spend this kind of time and money if India were not an attractive opportunity. The testing period would also give Blair Company representatives time to identify a suitable Indian company as a licensee, joint venture partner or acquisition.

Fundamental to market entry was product design. Engineers at Blair Company had taken the position that purification technologies planned for Delight could be 'packaged in almost any fashion as long as we have electricity'. Electricity was needed to operate the product's ozonator as well as to indicate to users that the unit was functioning properly (or improperly, as the case might be). Beyond this requirement, anything was possible.

Chatterjee thought that a modular approach would be best. The basic module would be a countertop unit. The module would outperform anything now on the market in terms of flow rate, palatability, durability and reliability, and would store two litres of purified water. Two additional modules would remove iron, calcium or other metallic contaminants that were peculiar to particular regions. For

example, Calcutta and much of the surrounding area suffered from iron contamination, which no filter or purifier now on the Indian market could remove to a satisfactory level. Water supplies in other areas of the country were known to contain objectionable concentrations of calcium, salt, arsenic, lead or sulphur. Most Indian consumers would need neither of the additional modules, some would need one or the other, but very few would need both.

Market entry and marketing planning recommendations

Assuming that Chatterjee recommended proceeding with the field test, he would need to make a recommendation concerning mode of market entry. In addition, his recommendation should include an outline of a marketing plan.

Licensee considerations

If market entry were in the form of a joint working arrangement with a licensee, Blair Company financial investment would be minimal. Chatterjee thought that Blair Company might risk as little at $30 000 in capital for production facilities and equipment, plus another $5000 for office facilities and equipment. These investments would be completely offset by the licensee's payment to Blair Company for technology transfer and personnel training. Annual fixed costs to Blair Company should not exceed $40 000 at the outset and would decrease to $15 000 as soon as an Indian national could be hired, trained, and left in charge. Duties of this individual would be to work with Blair Company personnel in the United States and with management at the licensee to see that units were produced per Blair Company's specifications. Apart from this activity, Blair Company would have no control over the licensee's operations. Chatterjee expected that the licensee would pay royalties to Blair Company of about Rs280 for each unit sold in the domestic market and Rs450 for each unit that was exported. The average royalty probably would be around Rs300.

Joint venture/acquisition considerations

If entry were in the form of either a joint venture or an acquisition, financial investment and annual fixed costs would be much higher and depend greatly on the scope of operations. Chatterjee had roughed out some estimates for a joint venture entry, based on three levels of scope (see Exhibit 2). His estimates reflected what he thought were reasonable assumptions for all needed investments plus annual fixed expenses for sales activities, general administrative overheads, research and development, insurance and depreciation. His estimates allowed for the Delight purifier to be sold either through dealers or through a direct, door-to-door sales force. Chatterjee thought that estimates of annual fixed expenses for market entry via acquisition

would be identical to those for a joint venture. However, estimates for the investment (purchase) might be considerably higher, the same or lower. It depended on what was purchased.

Exhibit 2 Investments and fixed costs for a joint venture market entry

	Operational scope		
	Two regions	Four regions	National market
1998 market potential (units)	55 000	110 000	430 000
Initial investment (Rs000)	4 000	8 000	30 000
Annual fixed overhead expenses (Rs000)			
Using dealer channels	4 000	7 000	40 000
Using direct sales force	7 200	14 000	88 000

Chatterjee's estimates of Delight's unit contribution margins reflected a number of assumptions – expected economies of scale, experience curve effects, costs of Indian labour and raw materials and competitors' pricing strategies. However, the most important assumption was Delight's pricing strategy. If a skimming strategy was used and the product sold through a dealer channel, the basic module would be priced to dealers at Rs5500 and to consumers at Rs5900. 'This would give us about a Rs650 unit contribution, once we got production flowing smoothly,' he thought. In contrast, if a penetration strategy was used and the product sold through a dealer channel, the basic module would be priced to dealers at Rs4100, to consumers at Rs4400, and yield a unit contribution of Rs300. For simplicity's sake, Chatterjee assumed that the two additional modules would be priced to dealers at Rs800, to consumers at Rs1000 and would yield a unit contribution of Rs100.

To achieve unit contributions of Rs650 or Rs300, the basic modules would employ different designs. The basic module for the skimming strategy would be noticeably superior, with higher performance and quality, a longer warranty period, more features and a more attractive appearance than the basic module for the penetration strategy. Positioning, too, most likely would be different. Chatterjee recognised several positioning possibilities: performance and taste, value for money/low price, safety, health, convenience, attractive styling, avoiding diseases and health related bills, and superior American technology. The only position he considered 'taken' in the market was that occupied by Aquaguard – protect family health and service at your doorstep. While other competitors

had claimed certain positions for their products, none had devoted financial resources of a degree that Delight could not dislodge them. Chatterjee believed that considerable advertising and promotion expenditures would be necessary to communicate Delight's positioning. He would need estimates of these expenditures in his recommendation.

If a direct salesforce was employed instead of dealers, Chatterjee thought that prices charged to consumers would not change from those listed above. However, sales commissions would have to be paid in addition to the fixed costs necessary to maintain and manage the sales force. Under a skimming price strategy, the sales commission would be Rs550 per unit and the unit contribution would be Rs500. Under a penetration price strategy, the sales commission would be Rs400 per unit and the unit contribution would be Rs200. These financial estimates, he would explain in his report, would apply to 1998 or 1999, the expected first year of operation.

'If we go ahead with Delight, we'll have to move quickly,' thought Chatterjee. 'The window of opportunity is open but if Singer's product is as good as they claim, we'll be in for a fight. Still, Aquarius seems vulnerable on the water pressure requirement and on price. We'll need a product category "killer" to win.'

This case was written by Professor James E. Nelson, University of Colorado at Boulder. He thanks students in the class of 1996 (Batch 31), and the Indian Institute of Management, Calcutta, for their invaluable help in collecting all data needed to write this case. He also thanks Professor Roger Kerin, Southern Methodist University, for his helpful comments in writing this case. The case is intended for educational purposes rather than to illustrate either effective or ineffective decision making. Some data as well as the identity of the company are disguised. © 1997 by James E. Nelson. Used with permission.

case 4.4 A Tale of Two Tipples

Over the past 15 years the Australian wine industry has enjoyed unprecedented export success. Starting from virtually zero in the late 1980s, Australian wine exports now account for over 6 per cent of the world trade in wine, placing Australia in fourth position after Italy, France and Spain. Some 1.9 million bottles of wine leave Australia every day supplying 111 markets globally. The spectacular growth in Australian export sales for the period 1992 to 2003 is illustrated in Exhibit 1.

A milestone was reached in 2002 when for the first time export sales surpassed domestic wine sales, a remarkable achievement considering that exports accounted for less than 3 per cent of Australian wine sales in 1984. The United Kingdom remains Australia's largest overseas market for wine, although in value terms the United States of America surpassed the UK for the first time in 2003.

Two wine companies have been instrumental in achieving Australia's export success, Orlando Wyndham, the makers of Jacob's Creek, and Southcorp Wines, the makers of Penfolds Grange. Jacob's Creek has been the country's leading export brand for more than a decade, while UK wine critic Hugh Johnson called Penfolds Grange the 'one true First-Growth of the Southern Hemisphere'. Indeed, Grange has been acclaimed by the world's most influential wine critic Robert Parker Jr as 'a leading candidate for the richest, most concentrated dry red table wine on planet earth' (Caillard, 2004: 223). This case explores the global segmentation and targeting strategies utilised by these two brands, in particular their distinctive and unique advertising and promotional programmes.

Global wine segmentation

One of the key steps in approaching the promotional strategy decision is the identification of market segments. Global market segmentation involves finding homogeneous segments across groups of countries. Five quality/price segments have been identified in the global wine industry: basic, premium, super-premium, ultra-premium and icon (see Exhibit 2).

A key to Australia's export success has been the ability of its wine companies to effectively target selected global segments with competitive brands. Well-known examples include Banrock Station, Lindemans Bin 65, Yellowtail, Jacob's Creek and Penfolds Grange. The communication programmes of the two latter brands have been particularly effective and well integrated.

The Jacob's Creek marketing programme has been targeted towards the mass-market 'premium' global wine segment, with the communication theme ('Jacob's Creek – Australia's Top Drop') designed to resonate across national boundaries. Although advertising and promotion is tailored to meet individual market requirements, the essence of this reasonably priced brand remains unchanged globally.

The marketing effort of Penfolds Grange, on the other hand, is targeted towards the 'icon' global wine segment –

Exhibit 1 Australia's export sales from January 1992 to December 2003.

	Volume (million litres)	Change %	Value A$ million	Change %	Unit value A$/litre	Change %
1992	89	37	259	28	2.91	–6
1993	124	39	343	32	2.76	–5
1994	125	0	376	9	3.02	9
1995	116	–7	406	8	3.51	16
1996	148	28	551	36	3.72	6
1997	172	16	687	25	4.00	8
1998	199	16	884	29	4.44	11
1999	258	29	1192	35	4.63	4
2000	311	21	1484	25	4.78	3
2001	375	21	1757	19	4.70	–2
2002	471	26	2289	28	4.79	2
2003	525	11	2391	6	4.55	–5

Source: Australian Wine Export Council, in *2004 Australian and New Zealand Wine Industry Directory*, Winetitles, p. 17.

Exhibit 2 Quality segments in the global wine industry

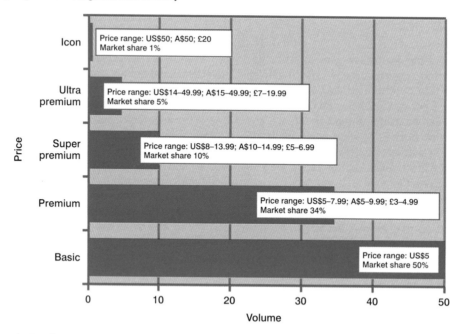

Icon — Price range: US$50; A$50; £20 / Market share 1%

Ultra premium — Price range: US$14–49.99; A$15–49.99; £7–19.99 / Market share 5%

Super premium — Price range: US$8–13.99; A$10–14.99; £5–6.99 / Market share 10%

Premium — Price range: US$5–7.99; A$5–9.99; £3–4.99 / Market share 34%

Basic — Price range: US$5 / Market share 50%

Price (vertical axis) — Volume (horizontal axis, 0 10 20 30 40 50)

a niche segment. Penfolds has created a promotional programme of mutually reinforcing elements that together communicate a sense of romance, luxury and exclusivity. Although the targeted icon segment is relatively small in most countries, the highly priced Grange product (over $A350 per 750 ml bottle) makes the market potentially very profitable.

Jacob's Creek global communications

The Jacob's Creek brand was launched in 1976 when Orlando Wyndham released a claret-style wine named after their historic site in the Barossa Valley of South Australia. Initially marketed in Australia, it took eight years before Orlando ventured overseas with the brand, first to New Zealand and subsequently to the UK. The Jacob's Creek winemaking philosophy is to produce fresh easy drinking wines with consistency of style and lots of fruit at a reasonable price. Jacob's Creek represents 'safe' drinking that won't 'offend' anyone and it is a wine that can be enjoyed immediately without years of cellaring. Several varieties now make up the Jacob's Creek range including Chardonnay, Riesling, Cabernet Sauvignon and Shiraz. It is exported to more than 60 countries with international sales of 7 million cases (63 million litres) in 2003.

Other than the mass-marketing communication elements of broadcast and print advertising, consumer and trade promotions, point-of-purchase displays and website development, Orlando Wyndham has focussed its marketing efforts squarely upon event sponsorship – in particular

sports sponsorship. Associations have been developed in the key sports of rugby (2003 World Cup – Australia), tennis (Wimbledon – UK), golf (British Open, Australian Open) and cycling (Tour Down Under – Australia).

The selected events enjoy international reputations and 'top-drawer' status, perfectly matching Jacob's Creek's theme of 'Australia's Top Drop'. The events attract world-wide television coverage and interest. For example, the Jacob's Creek Open Championship (Australia's premier golf event), linked as it is with the US PGA Tour, ensures a large TV audience in the US and many other parts of the world.

Event sponsorship for a brand such as Jacob's Creek makes sense at a number of levels. It overcomes the potential for increased restrictions on the advertising of alcohol in global markets. More importantly, it offers the opportunity to communicate without words (Quester, 2001: 132). Its message is non-verbal – the association with an event or sport communicates implicit messages that are particularly useful for positioning the brand in a global context. For example, in as far as road cycling is perceived as having a French flavour, Jacob's Creek's sponsorship of the Tour Down Under (a six-day road cycling event in Australia) will help add credibility to the brand by association with France and (by implication) French wine (Quester, 2001: 132).

Penfolds Grange global communications

Penfolds Wines was established 1844 by Dr Christopher Rawson Penfold in Adelaide, South Australia. Now part of

the Southcorp group of companies, Penfold is the home of Australia's most prestigious red wine, Grange. Highly perfumed and concentrated, Penfolds Grange boasts an unbroken line of vintages from 1951. It is a wine of very high quality requiring medium to long term cellaring before drinking. It commands high prices – a single bottle of the 1951 vintage sold recently at auction for $A52 211 (Caillard, 2004: 12). In short, Penfolds Grange is an icon wine.

Integral to the communications programme is the story of the wine's creator, Max Schubert. The early vintages of Grange were severely criticised by some in the industry and some within the company, and in 1957 Penfolds forbade him from making further vintages. Schubert ignored the management directive and continued making Grange in secret. His foresight and persistence were eventually rewarded with Grange claiming its rightful place as one of the great wines of the world. In recognition of his achievements, Max Schubert was named in 1989 as UK *Decanter Magazine*'s 'Man of the Year'.

The awards haven't stopped there. In 1995 the US magazine *Wine Spectator* named Penfolds 1990 Grange as its 'Wine of the Year' (the best red wine in the world) and in 1999 named Penfolds 1955 Grange as one of the top 12 wines of the twentieth century. These accolades not only create a strong international image for Penfolds Grange, but for Australian wine and winemaking in general. Although Grange sells in very small quantities, the brand has been just as important to Australia's export success as has Jacob's Creek.

Unlike the Jacob's Creek promotional strategy, however, Penfolds avoids mass-market communication techniques such as wide-scale advertising. Rather, the company concentrates on ultra-high-quality wine production, while nurturing the romance and exclusivity that surrounds the Grange brand. For example, the company produces a guidebook, *The Rewards of Patience*, that provides a vintage-by-vintage assessment of the drinking and cellaring potential of Grange and other wines. These assessments are made by independent critics, not Penfolds personnel. Now in its fifth edition, the well-produced guidebook also offers the reader information about Penfolds winemaking philosophy, wine investment, and of course the Max Schubert story.

An especially noteworthy element of the promotional programme is the Re-corking Clinics conducted by Penfolds winemaking personnel. Owners of Penfolds red wines which are 15 years and older can take their wine to a clinic where it is assessed and if judged to be in good condition topped up with a more recent vintage of the same wine, re-corked and a clinic label affixed certifying the wine for quality (Caillard, 2004: 274). The service is

entirely free, and dubbed by Penfolds as the 'ultimate in after sales service'. It certainly sends a strong quality message, and is an example of 'buzz' or 'word-of-mouth' marketing. Re-corking Clinics are held every year in Australia. The first clinic outside Australia was held 2001 in London, and since then clinics have been held in New York, Chicago and Auckland.

Questions

1 Both Jacob's Creek and Penfolds Grange are targeted at specific global wine segments. Will this concentrated targeting approach leave the brands vulnerable? If so, what can be done to overcome potential weaknesses?

2 Why has Orlando Wyndham selected sporting events as the sponsorship vehicle for Jacob's Creek rather than, say, music or art events?

3 What are some of the implicit or non-verbal messages that are communicated by Jacob's Creek's association with sports such as rugby, golf and tennis? Do these implicit messages transcend national and cultural boundaries?

4 Will Re-corking Clinics, as conducted for Penfolds Grange, work for Jacob's Creek? Why or why not?

Further reading and bibliography

- A. Caillard (2004) *The Rewards of Patience – A Definitive Guide to Cellaring and Enjoying Penfolds Wines*, 5th edition.
- Jacob's Creek website: http://www.jacob-screek.com.
- Penfolds website: http://www.penfolds.com.
- P. Quester (2001) 'Sponsorship Opportunities and Guidelines', *Australia & New Zealand Wine Industry Journal*, 16(6) pp. 130-7.
- J. Walterfang (2001) *What's in a Name? Wine Country South Australia*, Winestate Publishing, Unley, South Australia, pp. 14-15.
- Winemakers' Federation of Australia & Australian Wine and Brandy Corporation (2000) *The Marketing Decade – Setting the Australian Wine Marketing Agenda 2000 to 2010*.
- Winetitles (2004) *The Australian and New Zealand Wine Industry Directory*, 22nd annual edition, Adelaide, South Australia.

This case was written by Robert van Zanten, Adelaide University, Australia.

case 4.5 Kellogg's Indian Experience

Our only rivals are traditional Indian foods like idlis and vadas.

– Denis Avronsart, managing director,
Kellogg India

A failed launch

In April 1995, Kellogg India Ltd (Kellogg) received unsettling reports of a gradual drop in sales from its distributors in Mumbai. There was a 25 per cent decline in countrywide sales since March 1995, the month Kellogg products had been made available nationally.

Kellogg was the wholly owned Indian subsidiary of the Kellogg Company based in Battle Creek, Michigan. Kellogg Company was the world's leading producer of cereals and convenience foods, including cookies, crackers, cereal bars, frozen waffles, meat alternatives, piecrusts, and ice cream cones. Founded in 1906, Kellogg Company had manufacturing facilities in 19 countries and marketed its products in more than 160 countries. The company's turnover in 1999-2000 was $7 billion. Kellogg Company had set up its 30th manufacturing facility in India, with a total investment of $30 million. The Indian market held great significance for the Kellogg Company because its US sales were stagnating and only regular price increases had helped boost the revenues in the 1990s.

Launched in September 1994, Kellogg's initial offerings in India included cornflakes, wheat flakes and Basmati rice flakes. Despite offering good quality products and being supported by the technical, managerial and financial resources of its parent, Kellogg's products failed in the Indian market. Even a high-profile launch backed by hectic media activity failed to make an impact in the marketplace. Meanwhile, negative media coverage regarding the products increased, as more and more consumers were reportedly rejecting the taste. There were complaints that the products were not available in many cities. According to analysts, out of every 100 packets sold, only two were being bought by regular customers; with the other 98 being first-time buyers. Converting these experimenters into regular buyers had become a major problem for the company.

By September 1995 sales had virtually stagnated. Marketing experts pointed out various mistakes that Kellogg had committed and it was being increasingly felt that the company would find it extremely difficult to sustain itself in the Indian market.

The mistakes

Kellogg realised that it was going to be tough to get the Indian consumers to accept its products. Kellogg banked heavily on the quality of its crispy flakes. But pouring hot milk on the flakes made them soggy. Indians always boiled their milk, unlike in the West, and consumed it warm or lukewarm. They also liked to add sugar to their milk. If one tried having it with cold milk, it was not sweet enough because the sugar did not dissolve easily in cold milk. The rice and wheat versions did not do well. In fact, some consumers even referred to the rice flakes as rice corn flakes.

In early 1996, defending the company's products, managing director Avronsart said, 'True, some people will not like the way it tastes in hot milk. And not all consumers will want to have it with cold milk. But over a period of time, we expect consumer habits to change. Kellogg is a past master at the art, having fought – and won – against croissant-and-coffee in France, biscuits in Italy and noodles in Korea.'

A typical, average middle-class Indian family did not have breakfast on a regular basis like their Western counterparts. Those who did have breakfast, consumed milk, biscuits, bread, butter, jam or local food preparations like idlis, parathas etc. According to analysts, a major reason for Kellogg's failure was the fact that the taste of its products did not suit Indian breakfast habits. Kellogg sources were, however, quick to assert that the company was not trying to change these habits; the idea was only to launch its products on the health platform and make consumers see the benefit of this healthier alternative. Avronsart remarked, 'Kellogg India is not here to change breakfast eating habits. What the company proposes is to offer consumers around the world a healthy, nutritious, convenient and easy-to-prepare alternative to the breakfast eating habit. It was not just a question of providing a better alternative to traditional breakfast eating habits but also developing a taste for grain-based foods in the morning.'

Another mistake Kellogg committed was on the positioning front. The company's advertisements and promotions initially focused only on the health aspects of the product. In doing this, Kellogg had moved away from its successful 'fun-and-taste' positioning adopted in the US. Analysts commented that this positioning had given the brand a 'health product' image, instead of the fun/health plank that the product stood on in other markets. (In the US, for instance, Kellogg offered toys and other branded merchandise for children and had a Kellogg's fan club as well.)

Another reason for the low demand was deemed to be the premium pricing adopted by the company. At an average cost of Rs21 per 100 gm, Kellogg products were clearly priced way above the product of its main competitor, Mohun's Cornflakes (Rs16.50 for 100 gm). Vinay

Mohan, managing director at Mohan Rocky Springwater & Breweries, the makers of Mohan's cornflakes, said, 'Kellogg is able to cater only to the A-Class towns or the more affluent consumers whereas Mohun's caters to the mass market.' Another small-time brand, Champion, was selling at prices almost half that of Kellogg's. This gave the brand a premium image, making it seem unattainable for the average Indian consumer. According to one analyst, 'When Kellogg tried a dollar-to-rupee pricing for its products, the company lost out on getting to the mass consumer.' Even the customers at the higher end of the market failed to perceive any extra benefits in Kellogg's products. A *Business Today* report said that like other MNCs, Kellogg had fallen into a price trap, by assuming that there was a substantial latent niche market in India for premium products.

In most Third World countries pricing is believed to play a dominant role in the demand for any product. But Kellogg did not share this view. Avronsart said, 'Research demonstrates that to be well accepted by consumers even the most nutritious product must taste good. Most consumers view quality as they view taste, but with a very high standard. We approach pricing on a case-to-case basis, always consistent with the total value delivered by each product.' He also said, 'Local brands are selling only on the price platform. We believe that we're demanding the right price for the value we offer. If the consumer wants quality, we believe he can afford the price.' Thus, it was not surprising that the company went ahead with its plans of increasing the price of its products by an average of 28 per cent during 1995–98.

Before the product was made available nationally in March 1995, the demand from Mumbai had been very encouraging. Within a year of its launch in Mumbai, Kellogg had acquired a 53 per cent market share. Following this, the company accelerated its national expansion plans and launched the product in 60 cities in a 15-month period. However, Kellogg was surprised to see the overall demand tapering off considerably. A Mumbai-based Kellogg distributor explained, 'Why should somebody sitting in Delhi be deprived of the product? So there was considerable movement from Mumbai to other parts of the country.' As the product was officially launched countrywide, the company realised that the tremendous response from the Mumbai market was nothing but the 'disguised demand' from other places being routed through Mumbai.

Kellogg had also decided to focus only on the premium and middle-level retail stores. This was because the company believed that it could not maintain uniform quality of service if it offered its products at a larger number of shops. What Kellogg seemed to have overlooked was the fact that this decision put large sections of the Indian population out of its reach.

Setting things right

Disappointed with the poor performance, Kellogg decided to launch two of its highly successful brands – Chocos (September 1996) and Frosties (April 1997) – in India. The company hoped to repeat the global success of these brands in the Indian market. Chocos were wheat scoops coated with chocolate, while Frosties had sugar frosting on individual flakes. The success of these variants took even Kellogg by surprise and sales picked up significantly. (It was even reported that Indian consumers were consuming the products as snacks.) This was followed by the launch of Chocos Breakfast Cereal Biscuits.

The success of Chocos and Frosties also led to Kellogg's decision to focus on totally indianising its flavors in the future. This resulted in the launch of the Mazza series in August 1998, a crunchy, almond-shaped corn breakfast cereal in three local flavours – 'Mango Elaichi', 'Coconut Kesar' and 'Rose'. Developed after a one-year extensive research to study consumer patterns in India, Mazza was positioned as a tasty, nutritional breakfast cereal for families. Kellogg was careful not to repeat its earlier mistakes. It did not position Mazza in the premium segment. The glossy cardboard packaging was replaced by pouches, which helped in bringing down the price substantially.

The decision to reduce prices seemed to be a step in the right direction. However, analysts remained sceptical about the success of the product in the Indian market. They pointed out that Kellogg did not have retail packs of different sizes to cater to the needs of different consumer groups. To counter this criticism, the company introduced packs of suitable sizes to suit Indian consumption patterns and purchasing power. Kellogg introduced the 500 gm family pack, which brought down the price per kg by 20 per cent. Also, Mazza was introduced in 60 gm pouches, priced at Rs9.50.

Kellogg's advertising had not been very impressive in the initial years. Apart from 'Jago jaise bhi, lo Kellogg's hi', the brand had no long-term baseline lines. Later, Kellogg attempted to indianise its campaigns instead of simply copying its international promotions. The rooster that was associated with the Kellogg brand the world over was missing from its advertisements in India. One of its campaigns depicted a cross section of individuals ranging from a yoga instructor to a kathakali dancer attributing their morning energy and fitness to Kellogg. The advertisement suggested that cornflakes could be taken with curds, honey and banana.

In April 1997, Kellogg launched 'The Kellogg Breakfast Week', a community-oriented initiative to generate awareness about the importance of breakfast. The programme focused on prevention of anaemia and conducted a series of nutrition workshop activities for both individuals

and families. The programme was launched in Chennai, Delhi and Mumbai. The company tied up with the Indian Dietetic Association (IDA) to launch a nation-wide public-service initiative to raise awareness about iron deficiency problems. Nutritionists and dieticians from the country participated in a day-long symposium in Calcutta to deliberate on the causes and impact of anaemia caused by iron deficiency. This programme was in line with the company's global marketing strategy, which included nutrition promotion initiatives such as symposiums, educative programmes and sponsorship of research.

Emphasising Kellogg's commitment to nutrition education, Avronsart remarked, 'Product modification, particularly the addition of iron fortification in breakfast cereals, is how Kellogg responds to the nutritional needs of the consumers. In this spirit, Kellogg India is taking a major step to improve the nutritional status of consumers in the country, the specific opportunity being iron fortification for which we have undertaken major initiatives to promote the awareness of the importance of iron in the diet.'

Kellogg also increased its focus on promotions that sought to induce people to try their product and targeted schools across the country for this. By mid-1995, the company had covered 60 schools in the metros. In March 1996, the company offered specially designed 50 gm packs free to shoppers at select retail stores in Delhi. This was followed by a house-to-house sampling exercise offering one-serving sachets to housewives in the city. The company also offered free pencil boxes, water bottles, and lunch boxes with every pack. Plastic dispensers offering the product at discounted rates were also put up in petrol stations, supermarkets, airports etc.

Kellogg identified distribution as another major area to address in order to increase its penetration in the market. In 1995, Kellogg had 30 000 outlets, which was increased to around 40 000 outlets by 1998. Avronsart said, 'We have increased our reach only slightly, but we are now enlarging our coverage.' Considering that it had just one plant in Taloja in Maharashtra, the company was considering plans to set up more manufacturing units.

Kellogg also began working towards a better positioning plank for its products. The company's research showed that the average Indian consumer did not give much importance to the level of iron and vitamin intake, and looked at the quantity, rather than the quality, of the food consumed. Avronsart commented, 'The Kellogg mandate is to develop awareness about nutrition. There is a lot of confusion between nourishment and nutrition. That is something that we have to handle.' Kellogg thus worked towards changing the positioning of Chocos and Frosties – which were not positioned

on the health platform but, instead, were projected as 'fun-filled' brands.

Kellogg then launched the Chocos biscuits, claiming that cereals being a 'narrow category,' the foray into biscuits would create wider awareness for the Kellogg brand. Biscuits being a mass market product requiring an intensive distribution network, Kellogg's decision to venture into this competitive and crowded market with stalwarts like Britannia, Parle and Bakeman, was seen as a bold move not only in India, but also globally. Avronsart said, 'We are ready to develop any food based on grain and nutrition that will satisfy consumer needs.'

The results

In 1995, Kellogg had a 53 per cent share of the Rs150 million breakfast cereal market, which had been growing at 4–5 per cent per annum up until then. By 2000, the market size was Rs600 million, and Kellogg's share had increased to 65 per cent. Analysts claimed that Kellogg's entry was responsible for this growth. The company's improved prospects were clearly attributed to the shift in positioning, increased consumer promotions and an enhanced media budget. The effort to develop products specifically for the Indian market helped Kellogg make significant inroads into the Indian market.

However, Kellogg continued to have the image of a premium brand and its consumption was limited to a few well-off sections of the Indian market. The company had to face the fact that it would be really very difficult to change the eating habits of Indians. In 2000, Kellogg launched many new brands including Crispix Banana, Crispix Chocos, Froot Loops, Cocoa Frosties, Honey Crunch, All Bran and All Raisin. Kellogg also launched 'Krispies Treat,' an instant snack targeted at children. Priced on the lower side at Rs3 and Rs5, the product was positioned to compete against the products in the 'impulse snacks' category. According to some analysts, the introduction of new cereals and the launch of biscuits and snacks could be attributed to the fact that the company had been forced to look at alternate product categories to make up for the below-expectation performance of the breakfast cereal brands.

Kellogg sources, however, revealed that the company was in India with long-term plans and was not focusing on profits in the initial stages. In Mexico the company had to wait for two decades, and in France nine years, before it could significantly influence local palates. With just one rival in the organised sector (Mohan Meakins) and its changed tactics in place, what remained to be seen was how long it would take Kellogg to crack the Indian market.

This case was written by A. Mukund, ICFAI Center for Management Research (ICMR). It is intended to be used as a basis for class discussion rather than to illustrate either effective or ineffective handling of a management situation.

The case was compiled from published sources.

Questions

1 What were the reasons behind the poor performance of Kellogg in the initial stages? Do you agree that a poor entry strategy was responsible for the company's problems? Give reasons to support your answer.

2 Analyse Kellogg's efforts to revamp its marketing mix and comment on the initiatives taken regarding each element of the marketing mix.

3 Do you think the company's decision to launch biscuits and snacks was the right one? Give reasons for your answer.

Further reading and bibliography

- Chhaya, 'A Second Helping', *Business Today*, 7 April 1997.
- 'Kellogg Breakfast Week in Calcutta', *Business Standard*, 17 April 1997.
- Narayan Sanjay and Bhandari Bhupesh, *Business World*, 22 October 1997.
- Chhaya, 'Can Kellogg India Sustain the Crackle?', *Business Today*, 22 October 1998.
- Dubey Chandan, 'Instant Snack – Kellogg India Launches Krispies Treat', *Financial Express*, 17 May 2000.
- Kulkarni Jatar Nita, 'Kellogg's India Dream', *Business Today*, 22 June 2000.
- www.kelloggs.com.

case 4.6 Strategic Alliances in the Global Airline Industry: from Bilateral Agreements to Integrated Networks

Following the process of economic globalisation and regional integration, strategic alliances have become increasingly common in the last twenty years around the world. After the rapid development of corporate linkages in manufacturing industries, the 1990s have witnessed an increase of alliances in service industries. The progressive deregulation of many service sectors has considerably facilitated the development of corporate linkages. Since the early 1990s, airline companies appear to be particularly active in forming alliances. Available studies show that the number of alliances signed by airline companies has continuously increased and that signed agreements have become more complex. This case study analyses the evolution of alliances established by major airline companies.

Strategic alliances: a condition for success?

In the era of economic globalisation, strategic alliances can be regarded as a *sine qua non* condition for success. They represent an important source of competitive advantage and increasingly determine the global performance of firms. Strategic alliances can have different purposes. They can be a means to turn actual and potential competitors into allies and to develop new businesses by associating with providers of complementary goods and services. The objective is to reach critical mass and global presence needed for effective competition. Cooperative agreements also allow to create value through the combination of previously separate resources, positions, skills, and knowledge sources. Firms can also learn quickly about unfamiliar markets.

The competitive environment of airline companies

Following the process of deregulation, the competitive environment of airlines has witnessed considerable changes over the past few decades. Until the 1980s, a majority of airlines were state owned and run for reasons of national prestige. The liberalisation of air transport markets has led to the privatisation of major airline companies such as British Airways. Moreover, national governments gradually reduced their control over route allocation and pricing, thus allowing the creation of private airline companies. Consequently, the environment of airline companies has become increasingly competitive. The

global airline market has historically been dominated by US companies, which can partly be explained by the importance of their domestic market.

The legal environment of airline companies

As in many other sectors, critical size and global market presence have become important factors of competition. However, despite the internationalisation of civil aviation, the airline industry is still characterised by important market entry barriers. National markets are thus dominated by established major carriers that operate at the most busiest and desirable airports. Moreover, government bilateral agreements limit the ability of airlines to directly serve certain markets. In many countries, national legislation restricts foreign ownership of airlines to minority equity investments. In the same way, prohibitive antitrust rules and strong corporate cultures represent important barriers to the formation of mergers and acquisitions. Consequently, airline companies prefer to establish strategic alliances, allowing partner airlines to remain independent and to keep their corporate identity. These hybrid forms of organisation enable airline companies to remain cost efficient and to gain access to new markets without heavy investments.

The formation of bilateral agreements

In the early 1990s, interlining and code-sharing agreements have proliferated as very popular forms of cooperation between airlines. When airlines practice interlining, they establish joint fares and coordinated flight schedules, but each company retains its own identity. Flight segments are clearly labeled as to which carrier is providing the service. Code sharing alliances enable airlines to sell seats on flights provided by other airline companies (e.g. flights from regional airports to an international airport, a so-called 'hub', for onward connection to inter-continental destinations). Airlines can thus expand route networks without adding actual flights. Code sharing involves the issue of one single ticket which may reflect a single carrier through to the final destination, even if the actual passage involves two or more different airlines. Code sharing arrangements can be accompanied by other joint activities such as the coordination of flight schedules, shared airport facilities (check-ins, lounges), joint maintenance, procurement policies, staff training, and connection services (e.g. coordination of baggage checks). Interlining and code-

sharing agreements are contractual alliances that provide marketing advantages without requiring equity investments.

The strategic alliance between KLM and Northwest Airlines

In 1993, KLM and Northwest Airlines signed an extensive cooperation agreement, with the objective to create a unified global airline system. The cooperation has involved a high integration and coordination of flights through extensive code sharing and joint marketing activities, including the creation of a joint frequent flyer program. Cooperation has also been extended to ground handling, sales, catering, information technology, maintenance, and joint purchasing. Covering a wide range of activities, the agreement signed by KLM and Northwest Airlines can be considered as the first integrative strategic alliance formed in the airline industry.

The creation of airline networks

The 1990s have also witnessed the creation of several global alliance networks. In 1994, Austrian Airlines, SAS and Swissair decided to create the 'European Quality Alliance' (Qualiflyer). In 1997, Air Canada, United Airlines, Lufthansa, SAS (which decided to leave the European Quality Alliance) and Thai Airways launched 'Star Alliance'. In 1999, American Airlines, British Airways, Cathay Pacific, Canadian Airlines and Qantas created the 'OneWorld' alliance. In 2000, AeroMexico, Air France, Alitalia, CSA Czech Airlines, Delta Airlines and Korean Air established 'SkyTeam'. Through multilateral cooperation, airline companies attempt to achieve global market coverage and to meet the needs of international customers. Compared to bilateral interlining and code-sharing agreements, global airline networks cover a broad range of activities: code-sharing, coordination of flights, scheduling, advertising, reciprocal frequent flyer programmes, sharing of airport facilities, sharing of computer reservation systems, interchanges of flight-crew personnel and aircraft. They allow to realise added revenues and to improve passenger services and customer satisfaction. Affiliated airlines also use their membership as a marketing and communication tool. Their degree of commitment is generally higher than in bilateral agreements.

The 'Star Alliance' network

An analysis of the strategy followed by the members of global airline networks reveals that most of them had already been linked by bilateral agreements before the creation of the multilateral alliance. Exhibit 1 indicates bilateral links established before the creation of Star Alliance. It appears that the network had emerged from several bilateral agreements.

Exhibit 1 Bilateral alliances formed before the creation of Star Alliance

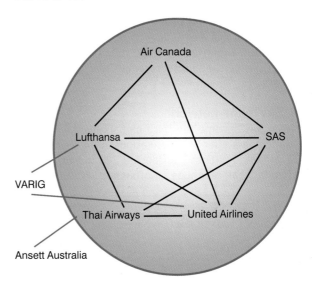

In order to improve their global market presence, member airlines of the Star Alliance network have extended their cooperation to other important carriers: Varig Brazilian Airlines joined in 1997, ANA All Nippon Airways, Ansett Autralia and Air New Zealand in 1999, Austrian Airlines Group (Austrian Airlines, Lauda Air and Tyrolean Airways), Singapore Airlines, British Midland and Mexicana in 2000, Asiana Airlines and Spanair in 2003. The Star Alliance network has become the first airline network worldwide. The 16 affiliated airlines allow a broad geographic coverage. In 2002, the network offered 688 destinations in 124 countries and transported 292 million passengers, reaching total revenues of 67.5 billion US dollars. The Star Alliance network appears to be the most integrated airline network. In order to improve the coordination of activities, the members of the network recently decided to appoint an 'Alliance Management Team' (AMT), which represents the executive body of the partnership. The funding and supervision of this entity are shared by the alliance partners. Its function is to observe contributions and benefits of members, to collect information about member performance and to maintain behaviour norms with the network through neutral coordination. The entity has also become a focal point for communication and exchange between alliance partners.

The 'OneWorld' network

After its creation in 1999, the OneWorld alliance has been extended to Finnair and Iberia in 1999, and to Aer Lingus and LanChile in 2000. After the merger of Air Canada

(member of Star Alliance) and Canadian Airlines (member of OneWorld), Canadian Airlines left OneWorld in order to integrate the 'Star Alliance' network. The OneWorld alliance has become the second largest airline network in the world. Eight member airlines allow to serve 550 destinations in 135 countries. In 2002, they transported 230 million passengers, and total revenues reached 50 billion US dollars.

The 'SkyTeam' network

SkyTeam has become the third global alliance network: its six members offer 512 destinations in 114 countries. In 2002, affiliated airlines transported 228 million passengers, and total revenues approached 40 billion US

dollars. The geographic coverage of SkyTeam is certainly less extensive, but the coordination of activities appears to be easier because of the limited number of members.

The 'European Quality Alliance' network

The European Quality Alliance network ceased to exist, mainly because of management difficulties and because of insufficient geographic coverage. In fact, the multilateral character and the relatively high degree of integration make alliance networks relatively difficult to manage: coordination problems and conflicts concerning contributions and benefits are more likely to arise than in bilateral agreements. Moreover, given the increasing globalisation

Exhibit 2 Major networks established in the global airline industry

Name of network	Affiliated airline companies	Year of foundation	Fleet size	Number of destinations	Number of passengers
Star Alliance	Air Canada Air New Zealand ANA All Nippon Airlines Asiana Airlines Austrian Airlines Group (Austrian Airlines, Lauda Air, Tyrolean Airways) bmi britishmidland Lufthansa Mexicana Airlines SAS Scandinavian Airlines Singapore Airlines Spanair Thai Airways International United Airlines Varig Brazilian Airlines	1997	2058	688 (in 124 countries)	292 million per year (10 700 daily flights)
OneWorld	Aer Lingus American Airlines British Airways Cathay Pacific Finnair Iberia LanChile Quantas	1999	2000	550 (in 135 countries)	230 million per year (8500 daily flights)
SkyTeam	AeroMexico Air France Alitalia CSA Czech Airlines Delta Airlines Korean Air	2000	1224	512 (in 114 countries)	228 million per year (8200 daily flights)

Source: http://www.star-alliance.com; http://www.oneworld.com; http://www.skyteam.com.

of the airline market, it seems necessary to achieve global and not only regional market presence.

Major airline networks

The global airline market is currently dominated by three major airline networks: Star Alliance, OneWorld and SkyTeam (see Exhibit 2). Over the past few years, competition between these three global networks has increased considerably.

The analysis shows that strategic alliances formed in the global airline sector have considerably changed over time: bilateral interlining and code-sharing agreements have gradually evolved into integrated airline networks. Airline companies collaborate within networks while remaining competitors. Moreover, competition between different airline networks has considerably increased. The evolution of the alliance policy of airline companies shows that competition between individual airlines coexists with competition between groups of airlines. Because of the dominant position of the three major airline networks, the membership of one of these networks can be considered as a competitive advantage.

Questions

1 What are the reasons for the formation of strategic alliances and networks in the airline industry?
2 Managing strategic alliances is not an easy task. What are the main advantages and drawbacks associated with the membership of a global airline network?
3 What will be the future evolution of major airline networks?
4 In 2004, Air France and KLM decided to merge. How will this merger affect the SkyTeam network and competition between networks?

Further reading and bibliography

- Association of European Airlines (1998), *Airline Alliances and Competition in Transatlantic Airline Markets*, Final Report.
- U. Mayrhofer (2001), *Les rapprochements d'entreprises, une nouvelle logique stratégique? Une analyse des entreprises françaises et allemandes*, Bern: Peter Lang.
- U. Mayrhofer (2004), *Marketing International*, Paris: Economica.
- OneWorld, published documents.
- SkyTeam, published documents.
- StarAlliance, published documents.
- M. Tayeb (2001), *International Collaborative Partnership*, London: Palgrave.

This case was written by Sylvie Hertrich and Ulrike Mayrhofer, IECS Strasbourg, Graduate School of Management, Robert Schuman University, France.

Sylvie Hertrich and Ulrike Mayrhofer have received the Golden Pen of the Chamber of Commerce and Industry in Paris. This prestigious award distinguishes authors whose case studies are extensively used by European business schools and universities (http://www.ccip.fr/ccmp).

case 4.7 GN Netcom in China[1]

1 This case was written by Klaus Meyer © 2002, 2004.

In autumn 2000, GN Netcom had been a global specialist in development, production and marketing of headsets for professional and consumer markets. It is one of three major divisions of GN Great Nordic A/S that was created as a spin-off in 1987 from one of its sister companies. The other two major divisions in 2000 were GN ReSound, which focused on the manufacture of hearing aids, and NetTest, which produces testing equipment for communication networks.

GN Netcom presented itself as 'among the leading and fastest growing suppliers of hands-free communications solutions, focusing specifically on three market segments: Call centres, Offices, and Mobile and PC audio' (annual report 2000, p. 30). The main products were headsets with microphones and the corresponding amplifiers that were used in offices where staff have a lot of telephone conversations, for example in call centres or in service and sales departments. Using such a headset, office staff had their hands free, for example to search for information via their desktop computer, thus increasing the efficiency of their work. Other headsets were produced for consumer markets, for example for use with mobile phones in cars.

History

GN Great Nordic A/S had a long and prestigious history that dates back to the nineteenth century. The then 'Great Northern Telegraph Company A/S' was established in 1867. Its prime business was the construction and operation of international telegraph networks, including cross-continent and under-ocean connections. A major part of the telegraph network was the line through Russia to the Far East, connecting Europe to Japan. The relatively small Danish company entered China for the first time in 1872 when an overseas cable was landed near Xiamen in Fujian province, initially without the approval of the Chinese authorities.

After the Second World War, the telegraph networks were increasingly taken over by state-owned companies, and GN transformed itself into an industrial conglomerate producing a wide range of products broadly related to communication technology, with most of its business activity in Denmark.[2] Throughout the 1990s, GN Great Nordic, as it was now known, restructured its operations to move from a Danish conglomerate to a telecommunication equipment manufacturing company operating in related global niche markets. For a few years it had operated telephone companies including the mobile phone company Sonofon in Denmark and smaller operations in St Petersburg, Russia.

Throughout this long restructuring period, GN continuously maintained business relationships with both Russia and China.

Sister companies

A major business grew in the 1980s and 90s with GN Danavox producing hearing aids and related products. Following the acquisition of ReSound Corporation and Beltone Electronics in the US in 1999, this business had been renamed to GN ReSound. GN Danavox established a JV in China in 1987, as one of the first Danish companies to establish production facilities in China. The local partner was not prepared to participate to become actively involved in production or sales. Also cultural conflicts arose. When the Chinese partner withdrew, IFU (Danish Fund for Developing Countries) acquired part of the equity in 1989. In 1999, GN ReSound bought out these shares and became sole owner of GN ReSound (China) (Børsen 28.11.2000).

GN ReSound gradually increased the number of employees in China to about 100 in 1998, when they started a major shift of production of older models of hearing aids from Præstø, Denmark, to Xiamen, China - initially without intentions of reducing employment in Denmark (Børsen 10.11.1998). However, in early 2000 about 50 employees were laid off due to relocation of production to China (Børsen 12.1.2000). In the first half of 2000, employment in China increased by about 100 to c.300, and 70 per cent of production had been relocated (annual report 1999, p. 12). GN ReSound has also been active in the Chinese market, with an all-Chinese website (www.gnresound.com.cn).

NetTest (formerly GN Nettest) provided instruments, systems and other services for testing and optimising communications networks. NetTest developed, manufactured and marketed products for optical, data transmission, and telecommunications networks and was a leader for optical network testing. The company's product range spanned advanced handheld instruments to systems that monitor and manage complex networks. Providing hardware for the rapidly growing Internet industry, NetTest capitalised on the vast growth potential of the IT industry. It has been a global niche business with strong market positions worldwide, among other markets in China where it was more active than its sister company in selling to local markets (see Appendix 1). Due to diminishing synergies with other GN companies, NetTest had been prepared for a separation from the parent firm. An IPO had been scheduled for 2001.

GN netcom's global strategy

GN Netcom had its headquarters in Copenhagen; R&D centres were in New Hampshire, California and Denmark, while its own production facilities were based in the UK and the US. Worldwide, GN Netcom had 754 employees in 2000, and achieved a global turnover of DKK1479 million and earnings before tax and interest (EBIT) of DKK272 million (see Appendix 1).

The company had expanded in both Europe and North America through acquisitions of, among other firms, UNEX in New Hampshire in 1996 and ACS in San José, California, in 1998. These companies were largely integrated operationally, though the separate brands were still maintained, as some key technological interfaces were not compatible. The products varied between Europe and North America, as well as between the different North American brands, which reduced scale economies and efficiency of the global supply chain. However, product and brand diversity is retained to continue serving customers that had one type of infrastructure, i.e. amplifiers, installed.[3]

In 2000, GN Netcom acquired two companies in the US: Hello Direct and JABRA. These two new acquisitions were primarily aimed at improving the market position of GN Netcom in North America. Hello Direct was a catalogue-based distributor, serving mainly corporate customers, such as large offices where employees frequently use the phone. JABRA manufactured and sold headsets for consumer markets, especially for use with mobile phones, and as OEM manufacturer to mobile phone companies. These acquisitions, and similar smaller acquisitions in Europe, provided GN Netcom with more control over distribution channels. Following the acquisitions, the operations of these previously independent firms had to be integrated.

Market position in 2000

In the global market GN Netcom was No. 2 behind market leader Plantronics, Inc. GN Netcom had a stronger position in Europe, while Plantronics is stronger in the US and in Asia. There were a number of secondary players in the industry, some of which, like Hello Direct, had been acquired by GN Netcom in recent years. Remaining competitors included 'Andrea', 'Telex', 'Hosiden' and 'Labtec', all of which were rather small compared to the market leaders, with single-digit market shares. After the acquisition of Hello Direct in 2000, GN Netcom was estimated to hold about a quarter of the global market, and Plantronics almost 50 per cent. Hence the global competition in the market had developed towards a duopoly. Four main parameters were considered key for success in the business: cost, quality and product performance, delivery, and service.

GN Netcom had not yet established a strong position in Asia. A regional headquarters had been established in Hong Kong in 1998 to coordinate the business activities in Asia-Pacific. The VP Asia-Pacific, Steen Bøge, was based in Hong Kong. Sales offices for the region were in China, Japan, Australia and Hong Kong. In the year 2000, GN Netcom earned 4 per cent of its revenues in Asia-Pacific, where the largest markets were Australia and Japan. China accounted for less than 1 per cent of global sales. Yet sales had been growing at a rate of 45 per cent over the previous year, far higher growth than in other regions (annual report 2000, p. 33).

GN Netcom's products had been sold to the Chinese market since 1993, initially with an agency agreement and then a joint venture with EAC, a Danish conglomerate with business operations across Southeast Asia. GN later took over the sales network and GN Netcom shared sales offices with NetTest. By 2000, the sales networks had been separated. Marketing and sales in China were coordinated in the country office in Beijing, with additional sales offices in Shanghai and Guangzhou.

The main customers in this region were call centres and, in Hong Kong, Singapore and Australia also the office segment (annual report 2000, p. 33). This includes especially large firms, for example mobile phone operators and the financial sector, including major foreign multinationals investing in China. The products were designed to increase the efficiency of highly qualified, and thus expensive, office staff. Thus, the potential demand is highest where service industries were well developed and where salaries for office staff were high – which explained some of the regional sales pattern. Within China, the most interesting locations were areas with high growth and foreign investment, such as Shanghai. Typically, companies establishing new offices work with a 'solutions provider' or 'system integration' firm that establishes new offices including all the relevant hardware and software. For GN Netcom, these firms are an important channel through which to sell its products.

The marketing is different from that in Europe or North America as decision-making processes over procurement are different in Chinese firms. Many older Chinese firms, moreover, have excess staff, or low staff costs, such that increasing the efficiency of their office staff is not a major concern – and they thus were not (yet) interested in GN Netcom's products.

The Chinese market was fragmented, with considerable regional variations and informal trade barriers within the country. Market information was less available than in mature market economies. Roughly one-third of the market was supplied by imports including GN Netcom and Plantronics, as well as their Korean competitors. The two largest domestic manufacturers provided one-third, and a wide range of small local firms served the remain-

ing third. The domestic firms manufactured mainly products for the lower end of the market, which is below what GN Netcom considered the lower end of its product portfolio. However, its was expected that the membership of China in the WTO, which was anticipated for late 2001, may change the competitive dynamics in the industry.

GN Netcom global operations in 2000

GN Netcom's headsets for the European markets were based on a modular 'click-fit' design, where boom arms with microphones and cord assemblies were manufactured separately. They could be combined in alternative ways, allowing for over 100 product specifications. Production and final assembly was mainly in the UK. GN Netcom (UK) had established relations with a number of subcontractors mainly in the Beijing area, and with GN ReSound in Xiamen. There had been frequent discussions on how to use outsourcing and relocation of production to reduce production costs.

The products for the North American market were based on an integrated design that would not be equally suitable for subassembly. They were not necessarily compatible with the European ones. Moreover, GN Netcom maintained both UNEX and ACS product lines in North America in addition to products under GN Netcom's own brand name. This was to continue serving customers who had the infrastructure for these products installed. Hence, firms who had for example ACS amplifiers installed in their offices were offered new products that matched these amplifiers.

GN Netcom's main production facility in North American was based in Nashua, New Hampshire. However, this operation had over the years outsourced to over a dozen subcontractors in Guangdong province (north of Hong Kong), and four OEM suppliers. The most important of them was DG Ltd[4] based in Dongguan, which had been manufacturing high-volume products, while the facilities in Nashua focused increasingly on smaller volume products. For some products, DG Ltd would produce the entire product, inclusive of packaging, and ship it to Nashua, NH. The business volume with this partner reached US$18 million in 2000 out of about US$60 million spend on procurement in China. GN Netcom accounts for about 10 per cent of sales for DG Ltd, and possibly more in terms of profits.

The competitor[5]

Worldwide, GN Netcom faced one major competitor, Plantronics, Inc., which had been manufacturing lightweight communication headsets since 1962. Highlights in the corporate history were the supply of technology to the first Apollo missions, and the transmission of Neil Armstrong's historic words from the moon in 1969. Plantronics employed 2200 associates worldwide. Turnover had been growing from US$286 million in the financial year ending March 1999 to US$315 million in the next year, and further growth in 2000. It was ranked 43 in the list of 200 best small companies published in *Forbes* magazine in October 2000, with one of the highest returns on equity over the preceding years. An internal GN Netcom report in 1998 concluded that Plantronics' gross margins were 10 to 14 per cent higher, although products were selling at similar prices.

The world headquarters of Plantronics were in Santa Cruz, California. The majority of products were manufactured in a single facility in Tijuana, Mexico. Moreover, they outsourced the manufacture of a limited number of their consumer products to third parties in China and Taiwan. Components for headset products were purchased in Asia, the United States, Mexico and Europe.

Plantronics had for many years been the dominant market leader in the US. Growth had been largely organic without major acquisitions. The main sales segments were call centres (40 per cent) and offices (42 per cent) with the remainder in accessories to mobile phones (13 per cent) and PCs (5 per cent). Plantronics focused mainly on the US market, with about 33.5 per cent of sales in fiscal year 2000 generated abroad. Plantronics did not have an affiliate in China, but its products were available there through imports. Plantronics' view of the global competition was documented in its report to the stock exchange (10-K form, p. 15):

> We believe the principal competitive forces in each market are product features, comfort and fit, product reliability, customer service and support, reputation, distribution, ability to meet delivery schedules, warranty terms, product life, and price. We believe that our brand name recognition, distribution network, extensive and responsive customer service and support programs, large user base and extensive number of product variations, together with our comprehensive experience in designing safe, comfortable and reliable products and dealing with regulatory agencies, are the key factors necessary in maintaining our position as a leading supplier of lightweight communications headsets.

However, the business environment and technology were continuously changing. Mr Ken Kannappan, CEO, summarised the main challenges facing Plantronics as follows:[6]

> We're undergoing a massive level of change from a business that has been focused in the call centre market, purely business to business, with a level of broad consumer awareness that was very low, to a company that is now going into mainstream markets, and needs to build its retail expertise. We need to build up emerging market segments that we

haven't been involved with before, namely mobile and personal computer and grow relationships with the key players in those markets. We're moving up the technology curve very rapidly in terms of wireless and in terms of digital signal processing. All of these changes, in terms of product development and the understanding of markets and needs, in terms of consumer brand awareness and marketing, are major changes for the company.

New developments in 2000

At the corporate level, GN Great Nordic continued its de-diversification and the re-organisation of its businesses:

■ NetTest had been prepared for an IPO scheduled tentatively for 2001, which necessitates GN Netcom to establish its own independent sales network in China
■ GN ReSound relocated more production to Xiamen, China – and in the process closed facilities in Denmark and Austria; this created further need to expand production capacity in China.

At the business level, GN Netcom was rethinking its global strategy. Niels B. Christiansen had been appointed as CEO of GN Netcom as of 1 January 2000, succeeding Christian B. Tillisch. Aged 33 at the time, Christansen had an education in Engineering, and an MBA from INSEAD. He had four years' consultancy experience with McKinsey, and spent two years with Hilti Corp in Liechtenstein with responsibilities for global marketing. He had been with GN Netcom for two years before taking over as CEO (press release 14.9.1999).

The new leadership team brought in new ideas for various aspects of management. They advocated a strategy of continuous improvement across the organisation, focusing of R&D on new developments at the high end of the market, and better global integration of operations across Europe, North America and Asia. As part of this strategic change, a VP Global Operations was appointed for the first time. Tom Kivela, previously head of North American operations, was appointed to this position, and he was based in Nashua, New Hampshire, US. The new management team had to address a number of competitive challenges, as follows.

■ GN Netcom had acquired two companies in North America in 2000, Hello Direct and JABRA. This strengthened its position in the key US markets, and the growing market for headsets for mobile phones. Yet, following the acquisitions, the operations of these previously independent firms had to be integrated.

■ GN Netcom had to address the costs of its operations with production in relatively high wage countries (US and UK), and the geographical dispersion of the production process as many sub-suppliers were based in Asia.
■ GN Netcom was serving its clients from two main distribution centres in New Hampshire, US, and Newcastle, UK, as well as three distribution centres of recently acquired firms in the US. Neither of these distribution centres was geographically well located. In particular distribution in Asia was freight intensive as products were shipped from New Hampshire, even if they were originally manufactured in Asia.

Moving part of the global operations to China appeared to be an avenue to enhance GN Netcom's global position and to address the pertinent challenges. However, this suggestion raised a number of practical questions: Which function should be located in China? Where to locate within China? Which partner to choose, or to go alone? How quickly to move, and if speed was essential, how to ensure fast and smooth implementation? And last but not least, how should the new operations be integrating with the existing operations in Asia and worldwide?

References

2 This period of the history of Great Northern has been analysed by Martin Iversen (2001): *The Diversification of the Great Northern Telegraph Company 1945-1980: From Concessioned Telegraph Company to Modern Industrial Concern*, unpublished manuscript, Center for Virksomhedshistorie, Copenhagen Business School.
3 The products consisted of a headset and an amplifier that would sit on the person's desk. The connecting cable and interfaces (to unplug the headset) had to meet high demands in terms of quality of transmission. Thus special products were developed. Yet, the different firms that were acquired over time (UNEX, ACS, Hello Direct) used different interfaces.
4 A pseudonym to retain anonymity.
5 This section is based on archival sources, including Plantronics' website (www.plantroncs.com, accessed 7.2.2002), an interview with CEO Ken Kannappan in the *Wall Street Corporate Reporter* (www.wscr.com) in 30 April-13 May 2001 on pages 17 & 43-4), and Form 10-K filed by Plantronics with the United States Securities and Exchange Commission for the fiscal year ended 31 March 2001.
6 *The Wall Street Transcript – JP Morgan H&Q Technology Special*, April 2001, pp. 210-12.

Appendix 1 GN Great Nordic: activities by region, 2000

Revenues	Europe			America	Asia	Other
	Denmark	**Other Nordic**	**Other Europe**			
GN Netcom		43.0		53.0	4.0	–
GN ReSound		42.2		49.4	8.1	0.3
NetTest		42.7		45.5	11.8	–
Other[a]	Sonofon	–	GN Comtext, Telegraph Co.	–	–	–
Total, in %	15.1	5.7	30.7	39.2	8.1	1.2
Total, in DKK million	1056	399	2152	2743	568	85
Assets[b]						
Total, in %	7.5	0.6	52.7	38.8	1.0	–
Total, in DKK million	1794	140	12398	9241	236	–

Source: annual report 2000, pp. 24, 32, 40, 46 (for division revenues), p. 64 (for group revenues), p. 75 (for group assets).
Notes: (a) GN Comtext is mainly active in the UK and the Telegraph Company mainly in Eastern Europe. Together they contributed DKK476 million to revenues. Sonofon was sold in 2000 but is still included in the revenue figures for 2000 with DKK972 million, which was mainly earned in Denmark.
(b) The location of assets reflects where the company had undertaken acquisitions in recent years. The assets contain a high proportion of goodwill created through such acquisitions, especially in the case of GN ReSound.

This case has been prepared solely as a basis for classroom discussion; it is not intended to show the effective or ineffective handling of a management situation.

© Klaus Meyer, 2002, 2004.

case 4.8 IKEA: Entering Russia

With thanks to IKEA

In Russia all possible things turn out to be impossible, and all impossible is possible.

Lennart Dahlgren,
IKEA country manager, Russia

When Swedish furniture retailer IKEA's country manager arrived in Russia to set up the first store, the country was in a state of deep shock. It was 17 August 1998, the day the Russian monetary policy finally collapsed. Almost all foreign companies were leaving the country, but IKEA stayed and this may turn out as a very favourable strategic move from a long-term perspective. The decision to stay in Russia in 1998 was, however, taken almost entirely by one man, IKEA's founder Ingvar Kamprad. During one of his visits to Russia, he shared his vision of how IKEA Russia would develop in the coming years: 'IKEA becomes the main supplier of home furniture to the normal Russian families and our sales in Russia will exceed those in our old home country Sweden.' To make this vision come true, he stood in opposition to the whole management group when the decision to enter the country was taken.

The fact that IKEA's owner saw Russia as a long-term investment also enabled the management to apply a long-term view that may become a competitive advantage in the

years to come. As a Russian manager commented: 'We have been on the market here for three and a half years now, and we can note the tendency, and if the tendency grows as quickly as it has done during this time, the market will be unlimited for a company like IKEA, and for most Western companies who are now interested to come here.'

Transferring the IKEA culture and values to Russia

IKEA is a leading home furnishing company with more than 200 stores in 32 countries, selling a range of some 10 000 articles and having more than 84 000 employees within the IKEA group. The company was founded by Ingvar Kamprad in Småland, a province in southern Sweden where people are renowned for working hard, being thrifty and innovative, and achieving big results with small means. Today, the IKEA group is controlled by a private foundation and the company is thus not on the stock market. Ingvar Kamprad's innovative idea was to offer home furnishing products of good function and design at prices much lower than competitors by using simple cost-cutting solutions that did not affect the quality of products. This is a prominent philosophy at IKEA, which is now realizing its ambitious plans in Russia. IKEA has been operating in Russia since 1991 but opened its first store in Khimki, Moscow, only in March 2000. Since that time, three new stores have been opened – one more in Moscow (in December 2001, one in St Petersburg in December 2003, and one in Kazan in March 2004). All Russian operations are controlled as fully owned ventures by the IKEA group.

IKEA is characterised by a strong brand based upon its vision to create a better everyday life for many people. A set of explicit values is linked to the vision and plays a guiding role in the strategy development. The values are the foundation of a culture called internally the 'IKEA Way', which is an expression of IKEA's history, the product range, the distribution system, the management style, the human resource ideas, etc. Brand and cultural values coincide and affect the strategy, organisational processes, product development and customer relationships. Thus the key value of cost-consciousness that lies in the heart of IKEA's flat-package concept dictates the necessity of global sourcing, defines the customer relationship where 'IKEA does a half and customers do a half' and guides the product design, choice of materials and logistics. The value of simplicity is reflected in the fast planning process, behaviours and routines governed by common sense, and straightfor- ward relationships with suppliers and

customers as well as in the product development process. By linking vision and values, IKEA creates a firm platform for entering a new market.

It was the overall company vision that guided the desire to establish business in Russia, and especially the impression that few companies in Russia focused on solving the needs of the many people by offering attractive products at reasonable prices. However, the initial knowledge about the Russian market as IKEA decided to open its first store in Moscow was very scarce. No special marketing research was carried out before setting up the store. A company representative commented: 'If we had done such a research, it should have shown that the consumption level is too low, the individual income level is too low, there are no traditions of retailing, which result in the fact that consumers generally don't go to the chains to shop.'

In each market IKEA enters it must recreate its company culture from scratch. In Moscow that included the replication of the store design and layout in accordance with the latest version of the existing store and an extensive cultural education that was carried out by the team of experienced IKEA people. It involved introducing the newly employed co-workers to IKEA routines and cultural traditions as well as helping them to develop the necessary competences (e.g. teamwork, leadership, skill diversity, etc.) and the IKEA management style. It has its roots in Swedish leadership style and gives responsibility to each co-worker and emphasises 'learning by doing'. In the Russian case, the store played an additional role by becoming the training site for new employees who later got involved in new projects or formed teams for the newly opened stores – a sort of cultural incubator. The extensive in-store training gave some very positive results. According to a store manager, the second store in Moscow could operate well from the first minute it opened because the whole staff was trained in the first store working with corresponding jobs: 'Here they just started and then they went on like this! No downturn, no nothing, no reaction, they just knew what to do!'

The role of IKEA's experienced management staff has also been indispensable in Russia. A main task is to train and prepare the local people who will be ready to lead further the expansion process. As a manager has commented about his management group: 'My main task is really to make this group more Russian and to export people for the upcoming expansion.' The demand for knowledgeable Russian staff is indeed very big with two stores just opened in St Petersburg (12 December 2003) and Kazan (22 March 2004). Development of experienced staff is impossible without extensive training.

As a whole, there is thus a strong emphasis on the vital role of training at IKEA Russia, at an overall manage-ment level as well as the store level. The local staff on the store level with a primarily academic education and a prioritisation of abstract knowledge is faced with the necessity to translate it into concrete sales figures. This includes both cultural training and education in IKEA values and different levels of professional on-the-job training.

Developing and positioning the retail proposition in Russia

Market information was thus not regarded as necessary for selecting the Russian market. According to a manager, IKEA knew that a lot of people live in Moscow so that at least one store should succeed. A survey giving that information was considered as unnecessary. Furthermore it was considered less important to develop specific strategies for the market in advance. Instead entry was based on the view that there is a need to live and learn about the new market before setting the strategies. Within IKEA, setting up a new business was described as very little theory and very much practice. However, once the decision was made to enter the Russian market IKEA specialists were sent to Russia to make investigations, but data about the Russian market was often uncertain and difficult to assess. For example, one initial conclusion was that the IKEA store should be situated near a Metro station since there were hardly any cars in Moscow. Five years later, however, traffic jams was one of Moscow's biggest problems. The country manager argued that instead of information about the market it is better to acquire market knowledge and the best way to get that knowledge is to live and learn in the market.

IKEA introduces more or less the same product range in all new countries – irrespective of what is considered popular by local customers. In Russia IKEA's Scandinavian furniture design is in some contrast to the historically preferred dark wood, massive, lacquered, expensive furniture. In order to support this strategy, IKEA most often identifies the potential needs that are similar across markets: 'We have the IKEA range and we have the market knowledge and the people needs, which are pretty much the same needs in Moscow and in Malmö.' Another IKEA approach was to create needs that could be satisfied within the range, and to inspire customers with numerous new solutions based on the existing range. The theme 'Living with small spaces' was one such solution used in Russia. The storage solutions are among those most popular in Russia since the average apartments are small and often house several families. Cheap and nice looking accessories for the home also became very popular with Russian customers and accounted for a big part of the stores' turnover.

IKEA's basic strategy – neither to adjust the style of the products to the local needs nor follow the competitors'

product development – was central to preserving the IKEA concept and image: 'The range is supposed to be IKEA-unique and typical IKEA.' All range products are divided into four major categories or styles: Scandinavian, Country, Modern and Young Swede, which are clearly distinguished in all business areas across the store. One of the reasons why IKEA was successful with its standard product ranges in Russia was the fact that several of these IKEA ranges emphasise the modern style, which is very different from the traditional Russian style but is attractive and new for the Russian customers since it symbolises change.

An important part of the market approach was to identify the needs that are not fully recognised and to teach customers what IKEA is about. IKEA's retail proposition is based to a large extent on its Swedish roots and history, which is, in turn, very different from Russian traditions. Therefore, learning as much as possible about the local culture and customer needs was considered essential. For example, IKEA practised home visits to customers in order to talk to people, see how they lived and used their homes and to identify potential needs and wants not fully realised by customers themselves. Understanding the local family conditions and furnishing traditions then provided a basis for an effective introduction and marketing of the IKEA concept. As exemplified by a store manager, the main priority in Russia is the normal living costs; then comes the car and TV and afterwards maybe a trip abroad. The idea of changing people's priorities by explaining to them that a beautiful home does not have to cost a fortune, and they can afford both the wardrobe and a trip abroad, is an essential leitmotiv of the marketing campaigns in Russia.

Since IKEA was totally new to many Russian customers, 'to bring people as much as possible in the store in order to learn about IKEA and get a positive attitude' was a main goal from the very beginning. IKEA put a strong emphasis on making the Russian customers feel welcome and important in the store, which was very unusual for Russian stores at the time. The way the range was presented and the opportunity to touch and test everything in the store also made the products much more desirable to the Moscow customers. This was a new and unusual retail approach.

However, a great deal of IKEA's success with the product range can be attributed to their work to influence the customer's decision making. One example of how IKEA has considered the local preferences is in developing the room settings to reflect local conditions in terms of apartment sizes and the local traditions of furnishing. As discussed earlier, it is vital to understand the local customer needs and 'transfer IKEA's range into relevant solutions' for the families where three generations often live together in small apartments of 50–60 square metres. It should also be possible to 'mix and match' the range with the Russian home.

The importance of positioning the IKEA concept in accordance with the desired image from the very beginning was critical. This meant building an image of a low price brand that also guaranteed attractive and modern products of good quality. To achieve this, IKEA has faced many challenges such as high customs fees; necessity to purchase more from the local producers; difficulties in finding and developing suppliers in Russia; still low buying power of Russian customers, etc. For IKEA, it was critical to associate the low price with meaning. For Russian customers low price was very strongly related to unattractive products of poor quality, and one challenge has been to overcome this and explain how it is possible to offer good products at low prices. Therefore, it has also been an ambition to provide the Russian market with the best and most attractive IKEA products.

Marketing communications became an important means to create the right image of IKEA in Russia. The ways to communicate the image were many: the outdoor product ads (prices), image ads in the glossy magazines, TV (though IKEA has used this very restrictively due to high costs), articles in the newspapers (press coverage has become very broad and quite positive towards the IKEA culture and philosophy). Another very important communication means in Russia is the buzz network or word-of-mouth communication that works very effectively. In addition, IKEA had an open and friendly approach towards Russian journalists. This was in sharp contrast to most other large organisations. IKEA was completely open to the journalists and introduced them to the IKEA way and values by organising press trips to Älmhult in Sweden to learn how the range is created. The result was that the press coverage of IKEA in Russia became much more positive.

Government authorities and officials of different ranks were also critical stakeholder groups. Their goodwill and support was crucial for IKEA's expansion in Russia. What played a pivotal role in the present success of IKEA's operations in Russia was the fact that IKEA was the only company that stayed in Russia after the currency devaluation and subsequent economic collapse in August 1998, when almost all foreign companies left the country. That created an immediate effect of trust and willingness to cooperate with IKEA on behalf of the major Russian politicians. IKEA's positive image in Russia plays an increasingly important role in further expansion, since it is crucial for creating new contacts with the local government and finding sites for the new stores in the distant regions.

Internal organisational processes also supported the positioning strategy. Common activities carried out on a regular basis were informal and formal discussions at the store level, where co-workers from one or several

store departments take part. The discussions covered different customer issues and the best ways to present the range to the customers. Market data and experience were also transferred and shared within and between different departments and units at the company. The store managers and department heads meet regularly to share the sales information and the latest decisions regarding the room settings, etc. Data about local customer perceptions and opinions about IKEA's different products and service parameters, collected by the store departments' heads, were also quickly reported to the marketing and sales department at the service office in Moscow. This information in most cases is about product pricing with the goal to lower the price for a specific product. These issues were discussed at the weekly and even daily store meetings since the speed of reaction might be very crucial for the store sales statistics. The topics included outgoing articles, a new range, and different solutions to present it, and discussion took the form of an informal exchange of opinions. The inter-departmental and local–corporate flows of information were prerequisites of the fast decision making at IKEA. For example, the new product development supported the trading organisation and the retailing organisation in Russia with ideas about new products and supplier capabilities.

In early 2004 IKEA thus had four stores operating in Russia, two of them occupying plots on the outskirts of Moscow, one in Khimki to the north of the city, and the other in Tyoplyi Stan to the south, one store in St Petersburg and one in Kazan. The company also opened its Mega Mall shopping complex at the Tyoplyi Stan site. The mall accommodates around 210 000 square metres of retail space and 240 retail outlets. Construction of another Mega Mall is now under way at the Khimki site, which is going to be 10 per cent larger than the Tyoplyi Stan Mall, and will house more than 250 retailers. The Mega Malls were treated as a separate business, which was an addition to IKEA's core concept. Normally, IKEA does not manage or develop shopping centres but this was considered necessary in Russia due to its lack of an existing structure of large branded stores and external as well as central shopping centres of a Western kind. Previously, many Russians shopped for furniture and other products in outdoor markets or at smaller, local stores. From IKEA's perspective, developing a whole mega mall was part of attracting Russian customers to the stores.

The future

As a whole, IKEA has made substantial investments in Russia, and the turnover is increasing rapidly. IKEA was also hoping to see profit in Russia in the near future. It would, however, still be needed to back up further

expansion: 'As soon as we make a profit, I can see at least ten years ahead when we will need all the money that is generated in Russia in Russia. So, the day when we will start to take out profit from Russia and use it in other countries is perhaps 15 years away.'

In the near future IKEA plans to open 13 new stores in Russia, with at least two openings a year. A project team has been made responsible for the expansion – to look for new cities, get permissions, build a store and recruit and educate IKEA co-workers. As a whole, experiences and knowledge in general about the process of opening a new store, as well as specific market knowledge, is important in this expansion phase. One example is the knowledge about potential sites – where to build new stores. The choice of cities is to a large extent based on the local attitude and IKEA's intention is to establish new stores only in cities where the authorities welcome the company. However, as a manager argued, the fact that authorities are hesitant towards the establishment of a new large store in the area can be seen as an opportunity. If it is difficult to enter a new city or region, other retailers will also face difficulties and may give up the attempt. IKEA can, on the other hand, take advantage of its previous experiences regarding this type of challenge and may eventually open a new store in an area with little competition.

The realisation of these vast plans will be to a large extent dependent on the progress in IKEA's local buying and production in Russia. An increased capacity and bigger volumes by the Russian suppliers will allow the company to cut costs and lower prices in Russia as well as to export the Russian-made furniture to its other markets. As a matter of fact, IKEA prices are still very high for many ordinary Russians. For example, even in St Petersburg, the second largest city, the shopping power is 30 to 50 per cent lower than in Moscow, where an average purchase value equals that in Stockholm.

As a whole, almost all IKEA managers have perceived the cultural differences between Sweden and Russia as very substantial. It is clear that the cultural aspect will continue to play a major role when considering that many of the regions and cities that IKEA plans to enter in the future are likely to be even more different from the West when compared to the major cities of Moscow and St Petersburg. As one manager commented, 'Everything we believed would have been a problem when we came to Russia has turned out to be no problem at all. Everything we believed would work nicely was and still is a problem.'

Questions

1 Can you see any alternative entry strategy that IKEA could have applied when entering the Russian market? What would have been the advantages and disadvantages of these alternative strategies?

2 To what extent do you think that IKEA's entry strategy for Russia is based on adaptation and on standardisation? How are those approaches balanced?

3 In what respects do you think that IKEA's market behaviour in Russia has been different due to the fact that Russia is an emerging market?

4 IKEA has a vision of building up a global brand. Can IKEA be regarded as a global brand? How does IKEA's marketing strategy in Russia influence/contribute to the company's brand vision?

5 What do you think the ownership form means for IKEA's entry strategy and its long-term activities in the Russian market?

6 Discuss IKEA's opportunities to achieve long-term success in the Russian market. What are the main challenges that IKEA faces? How can they be managed?

The case study was written by Ulf Elg, Anna Jonsson and Veronika Tarnovskaya of Lund University, Sweden. Reference source: www.IKEA.com.

case 4.9 The 'David Beckham' Brand

David Beckham in his Real Madrid shirt, designed by Adidas

He's a sponsor's dream: a fashion icon, associated with success, a family man. Because of Beckham, football is no longer just about football, but about character and personality.

Michael Sterling, a sports analyst
at Field Fisher Waterhouse, London, 2003[1]

The brand is exceptional and the potential is enormous. No other sportsman or woman has the brand placing or personality of Beckham.

John Williamson, director, Wolff Olins
brand consultancy, 2002[2]

Spanish sojourn

In June 2003, one of the biggest deals ever in world football was signed between Manchester United, a Premier League football club[3] based in Manchester, England (for which David Beckham (Beckham) had been playing since he was a teenager), and Real Madrid, one of the biggest clubs in Spain. The deal, which cost the Spanish club £25 million ($41.31 million),[4] caused one of the biggest sensations ever in the field of soccer. Fans of Beckham as well as the clubs concerned went into a furore over what the outcome of such a transfer would be. Analysts said that the drama and excitement surrounding this transfer was no less than that surrounding a corporate takeover. They were also interested to know what the outcomes of one of the most significant transfers in the world of sport would be. The sensation created was hardly surprising as Beckham was one of the biggest brands in sport, rating only behind all-time legend Michael Jordan (basketball) and Tiger Woods (golf).

Celebrity endorsements were an important part of marketing in the early 2000s. While television and movie stars were usually the first choice, most companies also sought out sports stars to promote their products. Beckham was one of the most sought after celebrity endorsers, not just for his skill at football, but also for his good looks, charisma and the pop star lifestyle he led. He was a great favourite with the media, who faithfully reported whatever he did in his life. He was perceived as the icon of youth and style and many companies seeking to portray such an image sought him out to endorse their products. His appeal was further heightened by the fact that he played for Manchester United, the leading and most commercially successful club in Europe and a great favourite in Asian countries.

Background

David Robert Joseph Beckham was born on 2 May 1975 in Leytonstone, northeast London. He was the only son of David Edward Beckham and Sandra Beckham, who had two daughters. Beckham's father was gas fitter's assistant and his mother worked as a hairdresser. Soccer was a very popular sport in Leytonstone and Beckham's father had at one time nurtured dreams of playing football professionally. He was never able to realise that dream, but he was a good player and regularly played local league matches. His love for football was imbibed by Beckham at a young age. Every summer from the age of 12 the young David Beckham went to Manchester for workouts at Manchester United and in July 1991, at the age of 16, he was signed on as a trainee by the club.

In May 1992, he helped Manchester United win the Youth FA Cup.[5] A few months later, in September 1992, he made his first team debut as a substitute in the Rumbelows Cup. He was signed on in a professional capacity by Manchester United in 1993; however, because of his lack of physical strength and experience he was kept as a reserve for another two years before he made his Premier League

appearance. He played junior level matches for Manchester United during that intervening two years. He also played a few matches for Preston North End, a Lancashire club (to whom he was loaned for a temporary period by Manchester United) where he enthralled everyone with his talent.

In 1999, Beckham got married to Victoria Adams of the Spice Girls and the media once again gave them a lot of coverage, augmenting their popularity The 1999/2000 season was another successful one for Beckham, in spite of constant coverage of his lifestyle, haircut and arguments with Sir Alex Ferguson (manager of Manchester United) by the media. That season Beckham received his fourth Premiership winner's medal, and was voted second best player in Europe and the World. Rivaldo, a Brazilian player who played for Barcelona, won both those awards. Beckham was also runner-up in the BBC 'Sports Personality of the Year', losing out to boxing champion Lennox Lewis.

In the 2000/2001 season, Beckham captained England for the first time in a friendly match against Italy. He continued as captain for a friendly match with Spain and then for the qualifying matches for the World Cup 2002. Meanwhile, he demanded and received a pay rise from Manchester; at £100 000 a week, he became the highest-paid Manchester player. He also gathered fans from all over the world and acquired near pop star status.

He captained England in the World Cup 2002, held in Japan and South Korea. England did not win the Cup, losing to Brazil in the quarter finals, but Beckham made a lot of fans in Japan and other parts of Asia because of his looks and style. Beckham's growing celebrity status became a bone of contention between Sir Alex and Beckham. Sir Alex did not like the pop star lifestyle adopted by Beckham and rifts between them began to be reported in the media. There were also sensationalised rumours that Manchester United was likely to sell Beckham to another club.

Beckham was reportedly hurt at being used like a pawn in a political game. In a counter-move he announced that he would sign a four-year contract with Real Madrid. 'This is an amazing opportunity for me at this stage in my career and a unique and exciting experience for my family. I know that I will always regret it later in life if I had turned down the chance to play at another great club like Real Madrid.'[6] Real Madrid had earlier expressed unwillingness in buying Beckham, but in July 2003, Beckham officially joined as a Real Madrid player. In buying Beckham, Real Madrid also outdid their rivals Barcelona in their attempts to acquire him. In mid-2003, Beckham was made an officer of the Order of the British Empire by Queen Elizabeth II.

Beckham's endorsement deals

Analysts have called Beckham the hottest marketing machine in the world after Michael Jordan. Beckham was one of the most important person-centered brands in the twenty-first century. Analysts felt that he had all the makings of an icon – good looks, talent, image, style and, more importantly, his lifestyle as the husband of a pop star. These factors combined to make him a popular brand in the UK as well as other places. 'He's an interesting phenomenon. There are not many people in sports who can be paralleled, people that literally step out of the sports fame into general fame and will go down in history,' said sports public relations expert Karen Osborne at Cohn and Wolfe, a London-based agency.[7] He was one of the biggest names in sports marketing. *The Observer* estimated Beckham's brand to be worth £200 million ($334.5 million) in 2003.

It was estimated that Beckham's endorsement deals with major companies earned him about £15 million a year. He endorsed products for Adidas, Vodafone, Pepsi, Police sunglasses, and Marks & Spencer among others. Advertisers believed that any product associated with Beckham would 'fly out of stores'. He had reached such heights as an endorser that analysts felt that his endorsement deals almost sidelined the fact that he was soccer player to begin with.

Beckham had a personal endorsement deal with German sports goods maker Adidas (although Manchester United was sponsored by rival Nike). Adidas paid Beckham over £4 million annually. Adidas chose Beckham for the immense charisma he possessed. The company wanted a person who would do for Adidas what Michael Jordan did for Nike. It believed that Beckham had the necessary brand equity to rival Nike and Jordan.

Beckham wore shoes made by Adidas in all his matches. The shoes were made especially for him and were embossed with the names of his first two sons. It was also rumoured that Beckham wore a new pair of shoes for every match. This brought in a lot of publicity for Adidas. In 2003, Adidas was considering offering Beckham a lifelong contract to endorse the company's products even after his retirement from football. The £100 million contract (the biggest contract in sports history) was similar to the one Michael Jordan signed with Nike.

Considering his penchant for hairstyling, it was not surprising that Beckham endorsed Brylcreem hairstyling gel. Brylcreem was associated with the image of a traditional hairstyling gel, normally used by older men. With the threat of increasing competition from companies like Shockwaves and Studioline, Brylcreem was forced to reposition itself. The company wanted to shake off its image of a product used

by older men and increase its appeal to youth. In order to create the new image, Brylcreem chose Beckham as its brand ambassador in 1997.

Soon after the World Cup 2002, Beckham was also signed on by the Castrol Power 1 brand to market auto lubricants in the Asian market. 'Consumer research in Asia has shown that Beckham and Castrol are both strongly associated with attributes such as winning, world class and powerful,' said Kshatriya, who was Castrol's Director of Marketing, Asia-Pacific Business.[8] The company believed that being associated with Beckham would help it increase brand equity in the Asian region as Beckham's popularity in the region had increased after the World Cup.

Vodafone, one of the sponsors of Manchester United, also had a personal endorsement deal with Beckham. Vodafone paid Beckham £2 million per year to endorse the company's phone network. 'David has the rare ability to appeal to such a wide range of people that he is the ideal person to promote our services globally,' said Peter Harris, director of sponsorship and media at Vodafone.[9] The companies thought up various ways to use a celebrity endorser. For instance, in 2002, Beckham granted Vodafone the rights to use his voice in the company's voice mail service. This was the first such deal ever by a celebrity and it kept the media buzzing. Vodafone also used Beckham in their advertisements in Japan where it offered a phone model with a camera, which popularly came to be known as the 'Beckham Phone' (because he endorsed it). It was reported that since Beckham became Vodafone's international face in 2002, global sales increased by one-third.

Beckham also had a £2 million per year deal with Pepsi to promote the cola drink. The company also conducted several contests, wherein participants could win a session with Beckham. Beckham was also part of an 11-member team that featured in Pepsi's advertisements before the World Cup 2002, where the players fought with Sumo wrestlers to win drinks of Pepsi. He was also featured in other television ads with some of his team-mates.

Marks & Spencer also brought out a range of products branded the DB07 range which were quite popular. The range for boys, which comprised T-shirts and other garments, had his initials in lettering style that was similar to what he used on his body tattoos. Beckham was also said to have had a hand in designing the range and none of the products went to the store without his approval.

Beckham also promoted Police Sunglasses; however, he was replaced by George Clooney in early 2003. Beckham initially endorsed the glasses in the UK and Japan, while Clooney was the global face. He also had a £1 million plus royalties deal with RAGE software, a maker of computer games. The company entered into a three-year contract with Beckham to develop various games that featured a character in his likeness. His pictures were also used on the packaging. Beckham was said to have played an important role in contributing to the development of the games' software. After RAGE started using Beckham to endorse its products, the revenues increased by £4.2 million.

Beckham's popularity was not restricted to Europe alone. In fact he was far more popular than any other soccer player in the Far East, especially Japan. Beckham endorsed a number of products in Japan. He and his wife Victoria modelled for a chain of beauty clinics in Tokyo called TBC and for confectioner Meiji Seika Kaisha. He shot a television advertisement for Meiji chocolates and his face also featured on the packing of the company's chocolates. The company revealed that the chocolate sales had doubled in the week after the ads featuring Beckham were first aired. In 2002, the same company had also generated a lot of publicity by building a chocolate statue of Beckham. Fans in Japan, who were rather traditional and family-oriented, seemed to like the fact that he gave a lot of importance to his wife and family. Most of them admired him for that.

Beckham's appeal as a brand

'We use David as a lifestyle icon. He does not appear in our advertising dressed in football kit, he is always appearing in his own casual clothing,' said Michael Caldwell, Director of Corporate Communication at Vodafone.[10] Beckham's appeal as a brand endorser went much beyond his abilities as a football player.

Beckham was a style icon. His rise from a middle-class background to become the richest footballer made him seem approachable and real, and at the same time created an image of exclusivity and luxury. He had a special ability to reach out to the public. Good looking and photogenic, he was the natural choice of advertisers wanting to make an impact on the market. His wife Victoria also played an important role in designing the Beckham brand. The couple were always image conscious and dressed fashionably. They sometimes wore matching clothes and hairstyles, which always kept them in the news. Beckham's ever changing hairstyles also regularly made news columns. In addition to all this, he was a good footballer, known for his signature ability to bend the ball towards the goal.

Beckham also had the clean-cut image of a family man which endeared him to the public, as well as advertisers wanting to portray that image. He did not smoke, drank very little and showed his commitment to his family. This image was especially effective in Asian countries where people gave importance to familial ties. In Japan, Beckham almost acquired the status of a demigod and set instant fashion trends with his changing hairstyles. His fans there

called him Beckhamu-sama (the Honourable Mr Beckham), using an honorific to show admiration and respect. 'A lot of people think that my life is more glamorous than it actually is. I enjoy spending time with my family,' Beckham told a newspaper in China when he was on a promotional tour to the country in 2003.[11] The couple were also media savvy and made an effort to maintain positive public relations.

The couple were looked on as fashion icons and whatever they wore or did immediately became a trend. Even their sons were part of the fashion game and set trends in the market for children's products. Beckham had a unique ability to create news. For instance, when he injured his foot before the World Cup in 2002, there was a complete frenzy among the public. Even the Prime Minister of England, Tony Blair, was said to have remarked in a cabinet meeting that 'Nothing is more important to England's arrangements for the World Cup than the state of David Beckham's foot.'[12] During that time, phone-in shows on radio and television were inundated with talk of orthopedics. The tabloid *Sun* went to the extent of putting a picture of Beckham's injured foot on its front cover, asking people to touch it and make it better.

Real Madrid's gain

The transfer of Beckham from Manchester United to Real Madrid led to a lot of speculation about the effect it would have on the two clubs concerned. Manchester United was the most well known club in Europe. It was estimated that the club had over 53 million fans worldwide. A number of products and services like financial planning, insurance, bed linen, jewellery, wallpaper, mortgages, a magazine and a television channel were offered under the Manchester United brand. The effect the club had was even greater in the Asian region, where it was estimated that the club had over 17 million fans. It also had stores to sell club-related merchandise in some Asian countries.

Real Madrid, which had far better players than Manchester United and was nine times champion of the European club championship (to Manchester United's two times), was a better club, but not as successful as Manchester United commercially. Real Madrid had conducted marketing research in the East Asian countries, which formed a crucial market, to test how it could increase its appeal to them. The club studied the appeal of individual players and found that there were very few people who could compete with Beckham's popularity in the region. It was found that he had the charisma to attract even those people who had no traditional interest in the game. Associating with Beckham would extend the market for the club's merchandise considerably.

Real Madrid was also a competitive club, and had ambitions to overtake all its competitors, both on and off the pitch. Since Florentino Perez, a construction mogul, became

the club's president in 2000, he signed three of the world's best players, Ronaldo (Brazil), Zinedine Zidane (France) and Luis Figo (Portugal), in three successive seasons. Real Madrid had a lot to gain by signing on Beckham. However, their need for him was mostly on the commercial front as the club already had at least four world-class players who were thought to be better than Beckham.

One of the important reasons why the move to Real Madrid was advantageous for Beckham was that the various endorsement and sponsorship deals that he had at an individual level fitted in neatly with the deals of the club. At Manchester United, there were clashes between the club's sponsorship interests and those of Beckham. For instance, Beckham was sponsored by German shoemaker Adidas, whereas the club was sponsored by rival Nike. On the other hand, Real Madrid's strip was made by Adidas, so the interests of the club and Beckham matched. One of Real Madrid's sponsors was Pepsi, which was also the personal sponsor of Beckham, so there was no conflicting move. Vodafone also found the move more beneficial than it would have if Beckham had been sold to AC Milan of Italy as the team was sponsored by Telecom Italia, a rival, whereas Real Madrid worked with Siemens with which Vodafone partnered.

It was also thought to be an effective marketing move on the part of Real Madrid as the club had very low recognition and support in Asian countries where Manchester United was definitely more popular. The likely outcome of the transfer was that most of the fans of Beckham in Asian countries, who were a considerable number, would now support Real Madrid, thus increasing the club's reach. In terms of comparison, analysts estimated that almost 5 million of the 17 million fans of Manchester United in Asia would shift loyalties to Real Madrid. This was because, in Asia, the general trend was to root for an individual player, as against Europe, where people were loyal to clubs. 'Many fans in Asia watch a team because of the individual star players. When those players are transferred quite often they will swap allegiances to a club and they will follow the player,' said Samantha McCollum, consultant at FutureBrand.[13] Therefore, the reason behind Real Madrid's offer was not just Beckham's football skills but his immense marketability.

Michael Sterling, a sports analyst at Field Fisher Waterhouse in London, estimated that Beckham would generate between £6 million and £10 million per year for the club – largely because he would open both the British and Asian markets for them. 'Real Madrid will rival Man U as a brand now. He's a sponsor's dream: a fashion icon, associated with success, a family man. Because of Beckham, football is no longer just about football, but about character and personality,' he said.[14]

Real Madrid offered Beckham a compensation of £4.2 million a year. However, he was expected to turn in 50 per cent of his endorsement amount to the club. He even had fans who did not know a single thing about football. And it was profitable for the club to pay that amount to him, because it was estimated that shirt sales alone would recover the amount in four years according to sports marketing firm Apex.

Analysts felt that it would not harm Manchester United to sell Beckham, who was its star player, because the club was already big enough to survive without having to depend on any one player. A majority of Manchester United's revenues came from ticket sales and media rights which were unlikely to get affected by Beckham's transfer. Merchandising, on which Beckham had considerable power, comprised only 7 per cent of the club's revenues. However, there were rumours that Vodafone, which sponsored the shirts for Manchester United, would probably not want to renew the sponsorship when the contract expired in 2004, as a majority of the Manchester United shirts it sold were replicas of Beckham's shirts, and with Beckham no longer playing for the club, the shirt sales would fall significantly. In England, a club was always bigger than any individual player, and observers felt that Manchester United probably did not like the fact that Beckham began to rival its popularity. Analysts also felt that it was a good move on the part of Manchester United to sell Beckham at the peak of his career, when he fetched the best price.

The sale was not without its critics though. There were a number of people who disliked the club's decision to sell Beckham. The sale of Beckham headed the list of bulletin board topics on a number of websites and discussion forums and was widely discussed in the media. On www.sina.com, one the largest websites in China, fans criticised the sale severely. 'I'll never watch United again,' declared one fan.[15] Some fans were also worried that Beckham would not always find a place on the playing team in a club that was already packed with most of the talented players in the world and resented this.

There have also been people who criticised the amount spent by Real Madrid on purchasing Beckham. 'There are many better ways of spending money that has been earned with great sacrifices other than hiring Mr Beckham,' said Silvio Berlusconi, the Italian premier, who was also president of AC Milan.[16] Another important element which clouded the deal was that the demand for soccer and soccer stars was at an all time low at the time when the transfer deal was in negotiation. Because of the growth of pay channels on cable television the viewership of matches had come down. A number of players were also being laid off by clubs, who were themselves facing

> **Exhibit 1** Breakdown of Beckham's transfer fee
> - £5.25m on completion of Beckham's transfer
> - £12m in installments over next four years
> - £7m based on Real's performances in Champions League (£875 000 every year they qualify, £875 000 every year they reach quarter-finals)
>
> *Source:* news.bbc.co.uk.

bankruptcy, especially in Britain. In this scenario, the amount paid for Beckham seemed unjustified.

The pitfalls of celebrity endorsements

Analysts feel that there is certain risk associated with celebrities endorsing products. There have been times when the image or name of Beckham had been used without his permission in advertisements. For instance, easyJet, the low-cost airline had once used Beckham in its advertisements without his permission. In early 2003, when there were rumours about Beckham being sold by Manchester, the airline ran a newspaper advertisement showing a picture of Beckham with his new hairstyle with the tag line 'Hair Today. Gone Tomorrow'[17] in an indirect reference to his move to Real Madrid. When Beckham and his publicists objected to this, the airline ran another advertisement with Beckham's picture with the tag line 'Not sure where to go this summer? Barcelona? Madrid? Milan? Lowest fares to the hottest cities'.[18]

Beckham's image along with those of fellow players in the England team, such as Michael Owen, had also been used by British American Tobacco (BAT) to promote its Dunhill brand of cigarettes in Malaysia during the 2002 World Cup.

Analysts felt that Beckham also faced the danger of getting overexposed. Overexposure was never a good thing for celebrities as it made them lose their exclusivity and lowered their value. It was also felt that Beckham was more aligned to his endorsement deals and was deviating from his real interest – soccer. In fact this was thought to be the main reason behind Manchester United dropping him from their team. There was also the risk that he gets stuck in a rigid contract and would have to endorse products which he did not innately believe in.

Setting new trends

Analysts were almost united in their agreement that Beckham was one of the biggest marketing phenomena in the early part of the twenty-first century. Not only did he help sell a number of different products that spanned across different product categories, but he also played an important role in setting new trends. For instance, he is credited with being the first sportsperson to display an interest in how he looked and who took an active interest in

grooming and clothes. Traditionally, sports people were associated with a macho image and were not expected to do anything even remotely effeminate. However, Beckham was very open about the fact that he was interested in fashion and grooming, which set an example to New Age men.

There was also talk of creating a global brand with the whole Beckham family, including the children. The couple signed up Simon Fuller, a British music mogul, who had helped the Spice Girls promote themselves earlier. This was thought to be a step in the direction of moving to Hollywood. Fuller was to help them make better contacts in show business and obtain further endorsements. As the children became older, they were also to participate in some commercial projects.

Questions

1 David Beckham was one of the most successful endorsers in the late 1990s and the early twenty-first century. What were the reasons for his success as an endorser? What values did he signify as a brand and what were the advantages that the companies who used him obtained? Answer with special reference to Beckham's popularity in the Far East.

2 Real Madrid paid a huge price to acquire Beckham. However, the club was confident of recovering the amount it paid within a short period by cashing in on his appeal. How did Real Madrid stand to benefit through the acquisition of Beckham? Was the price it paid for him justified?

3 Celebrity endorsements were the biggest market-ing trend in the early twenty-first century. Discuss the phenomenon of celebrity endorsements. What are the implications of using people as brands? What are the advantages and disadvantages experienced by the company as well as the celebrity?

Further reading and bibliography

- Julia Day, 'Beckham Grants Vodafone Voice Rights', *Media Guardian*, 14 August 2002.
- Richard Fletcher, 'Beckham Launches Kit Designs for M&S', *Telegraph*, 15 September 2002.
- 'Castrol Initiates Marketing Plans to Leverage "Power 1"', *Financial Express*, 21 November 2002.
- Michael Elliot, 'Brand it Like Beckham', *Time*, 30 January 2003.
- Denis Campbell, 'Beckham is Most Influential Man in the UK', *Observer*, 2 February 2003.
- Paul Kelso and Giles Tremlett, 'Real Madrid Eye Up Beckham – the £40m brand name', *Guardian*, 26 April 2003.
- 'Beckonomics', *The Economist,* 12 June 2003.
- 'The Beckham Bracket', *The Economist*, 12 June 2003.
- Adam Pasick, 'Battle for Beckham Leaves Soccer Field Behind', *USA Today*, 13 June 2003.
- Mihir Bose, 'Beckham is the Real Thing', *Telegraph*, 18 June 2003.
- Daniel Taylor, 'Beckham Powers the Drive East', *Guardian,* 18 June 2003.
- 'Branded Like Beckham', *The Economist*, 5 July 2003.
- Richard Tomlinson, 'Brand it Like Beckham', *Fortune*, 7 July 2003.
- Geraldine O'Shea, 'Resorting to Celebrity Acts', *Marketing Magazine*, July/August, 2003.
- 'Adidas Offers Beckham 100 Million Pounds', *Mid Day*, 10 August 2003.
- Godfrey Robert, 'Beckham's the Name in Branding Game', straitstimes.asia1.com, 30 November 2002.
- Ginanne Brownell, 'Brand it Like Beckham', *Newsweek International*, 2003, www.msnbc.com.
- 'Beckham Bends it for Castrol', www.blonnet.com, 22 January 2003.
- 'The David Beckham Story', sport.telegraph.co.uk, 30 April 2003.
- 'Beckham is Best-Paid Player', www.rediff.com/sports, 6 May 2003.
- Tom Fordyce, 'Beckham's True Worth', news.bbc.co.uk, 5 June 2003.
- 'Beckham a Marketing "icon", says Real Official', www.rediff.com, 10 June 2003.
- Kristine Kirby Webster, 'Brand it Like Beckham', www.marketingprofs.com, 10 June 2003.
- Tom Fordyce, 'The Inside Track on Beckham's Move', news.bbc.co.uk, 11 June 2003.
- Briony Hale, 'Beckham's Brand Power', news.bbc.co.uk, 11 June 2003.
- Andrew Brown, 'How Big is David Beckham in Asia?', www.cnn.com, 12 June 2003.
- Katie Allen, 'Beckham builds on brand value', Uk.biz.yahoo.com, 13 June 2003.
- Philippa Moreton, 'Beckham's Sponsors and Image Increase his Value to Real', In.sport.yahoo.com, 18 June 2003.
29 Elaine Lies, 'Beckham Gets Pop-star Welcome in Japan', In.sport.yahoo.com, 18 June 2003.

- 'Beckham-mania Hits Japan', www.cnn.com, 18 June 2003.
- Franklin Foer, 'Bye, Bye, Becks', slate.msn.com, 18 June 2003.
- 'Beckham Joins Real Madrid', News.bbc.co.uk, 18 June 2003.
- Adam Sherwin, 'Beckhams' Brand will Include the Children', 24 July 2003. www.timesonline.co.uk.
- 'Flop in the US, famous in Asia', www.straits times.com.
- www.ausport.gov.au.
- www.askmen.com.
- www.celebritystorm.com.

References

1 Ginanne Brownell, 'Brand it Like Beckham', *Newsweek International* 2003, www.msnbc.com.

2 Richard Fletcher, 'Beckham Launches Kit Designs for M&S', *Telegraph*, 15 September 2002.

3 The Premier League was the flagship of the Football Association in England and consisted of 20 of the finest football clubs in the country. The Premiership was launched in 1992, with the objective of improving the standards of football in England.

4 £1 = $1.64 (approximately, in September 2003).

5 Conducted by the Football Association of England, the FA Youth Cup was first started in 1952. Players below the age of 18 can play in the Youth Cup.

6 Mihir Bose, 'Beckham is the Real Thing', *Telegraph*, 18 June 2003.

7 Katie Allen, 'Beckham Builds on Brand Value', uk.biz.yahoo.com.

8 'Beckham Bends it for Castrol', www.blonnet.com, 22 January 2003.

9 Julia Day, 'Beckham Grants Vodafone Voice Rights', *Media Guardian*, 14 August 2002.

10 Katie Allen, 'Beckham Builds on Brand Value', uk.biz.yahoo.com.

11 'Bowled Over By Beckham', *New Straits Times – Management Times*, 27 June 2003.

12 'Mend it Like Beckham', *Time*, 14 May 2002.

13 'Flop in the US, Famous in Asia', www.straitstimes.com.

14 Ginanne Brownell, 'Brand it Like Beckham', *Newsweek International*, 2003, www.msnbc.com.

15 'Flop in the US, Famous in Asia', www.straitstimes.com.

16 'Beckonomics', *The Economist*, 12 June 2003.

17 Julia Day, 'Beckham Asks for easyJet Donation', *Guardian*, 28 May 2003.

18 Julia Day, 'easyJet Risks Further Beckham Wrath', *Guardian*, 16 June 2003.

This case was written by Shirisha Regani, under the direction of Sanjib Dutta, ICFAI Center for Management Research (ICMR). It is intended to be used as a basis for class discussion rather than to illustrate either effective or ineffective handling of a management situation. The case was compiled from published sources.

case 5.1 Iberia Airlines Builds a BATNA

MADRID – One day last April, two model airplanes landed in the offices of Iberia Airlines.

They weren't toys. The Spanish carrier was shopping for new jetliners, and the models were calling cards from Boeing Co. and Airbus, the world's only two producers of big commercial aircraft.

It was the first encounter in what would become a months-long dogfight between the two aviation titans – and Iberia was planning to clean up.

Airbus and Boeing may own the jetliner market, with its projected sales of more than $1 trillion in the next 20 years, but right now they don't control it. The crisis in the air-travel industry makes the two manufacturers desperate to nail down orders. So they have grown increasingly dependent on airlines, engine suppliers and aircraft financiers for convoluted deals.

Once the underdog, Airbus has closed the gap from just four years ago – when Boeing built 620 planes to Airbus's 294 – and this year the European plane maker expects to overtake its US rival. For Boeing, Iberia was a chance to stem the tide. For Airbus, Iberia was crucial turf to defend.

Iberia and a few other airlines are financially healthy enough to be able to order new planes these days, and they are all driving had bargains. Enrique Dupuy de Lome, Iberia's chief financial officer and the man who led its search for widebody jets, meant from the start to run a real horse race. 'Everything has been structured to maintain tension up to the last 15 minutes,' he said.

Throughout the competition, the participants at Iberia, Boeing and Airbus gave the *Wall Street Journal* detailed briefings on the pitches, meetings and deliberations. The result is a rarity for the secretive world of aircraft orders: an inside look at an all-out sales derby with globetrotting executives, huge price tags and tortuous negotiations over everything from seats to maintenance and cabin-noise levels. The rivals' offers were so close that on the final day of haggling, Iberia stood ready with multiple press releases and extracted last-minute concessions in a phone call between the airline's chairman and the winning bidder.

By that point, both suitors felt like they'd been through the wringer. 'With 200 airlines and only two plane makers, you'd think we'd get a little more respect,' said John Leahy, Airbus's top sales man.

Airbus, a division of European Aeronautic Defense & Space Co., reckoned it had a big edge. It had sold Iberia more than 100 planes since 1997. Mr Leahy thought last summer that he might even bag the contract with minimal competition. In June he had clinched a separate deal with Iberia for three new Airbus A340 widebodies.

But Mr Dupuy made Mr Leahy fight for the order – and so enticed Boeing to compete more aggressively. Then, 'just to make things interesting,' Mr Dupuy said, he upped the pressure by going shopping for secondhand airplanes. These are spilling onto the market at cut-rate

prices as the airline industry's problems force carriers to ground older jets with their higher operating costs.

Iberia is one of the industry's few highly profitable carriers, thanks to a thorough restructuring before the national carrier was privatised in early 2001. The world's No. 18 in passenger traffic, with a fleet of 145 planes, it has benefited by flying few routes to North America, where air travel is in tatters, and by dominating the large Latin American market.

The Spanish carrier was looking to replace six Boeing 747-200 jumbo jets more than 20 years old. It wanted as many as 12 new planes to complete a 10-year modernisation programme for Iberia's long-haul fleet. Based on list prices, the 12-plane order was valued at more than $2 billion.

Iberia's Mr Dupuy, 45 years old, a soft-spoken career finance man, first needed to woo Boeing to the table. The US producer had last sold Iberia planes in 1995, and since then the carrier had bought so many Airbus jets that Boeing considered not even competing. But in late July, Mr Dupuy met Toby Bright, Boeing's top salesman for jets. Over dinner in London, according to both men, Mr Dupuy told Mr Bright that Iberia truly wanted two suppliers, not just Airbus.

The Boeing sales chief was sceptical, and he recalled thinking at the time, 'You're running out of ways to show us.' Having worked as Boeing's chief salesman in Europe, Airbus's home turf, he had heard similar lines from customers who eventually bought Airbus planes. So he wondered: 'Are we being brought in as a stalking horse?'

Yet replacing Iberia's old 747s with new 777s would be Boeing's last chance for years to win back Iberia. The argument against Boeing was that an all-Airbus fleet would make Iberia's operations simpler and cheaper. Still, going all-Airbus might weaken Iberia's hand in future deals. Airbus would know that the carrier's cost of switching to Boeing would require big investments in parts and pilot training.

In early November, Airbus and Boeing presented initial bids on their latest planes. The four-engine Airbus A340-600 is the longest plane ever built. Boeing's 777-300ER is the biggest twin-engine plane.

The new A340 can fly a bit farther and has more lifting power than the 777. The new Boeing plane is lighter, holds more seats and burns less fuel. The Boeing plane, with a catalogue price around $215 million, lists for some $25 million more than the A340.

Mr Dupuy, whose conference room is decorated with framed awards for innovative aircraft-financing deals, set his own tough terms on price and performance issues including fuel consumption, reliability and resale value. He won't divulge prices, but people in the aviation market familiar with the deal say he demanded discounts exceeding 40 per cent.

As negotiations began, Mr Dupuy told both companies his rule: Whoever hits its target, wins the order. The race was on.

Mr Bright, who had been appointed Boeing's top airplane sales man in January of 2002, pitched the Boeing 777 as a 'revenue machine'. He insisted that his plane could earn Iberia about $8000 more per flight than the A340-600 because it can hold more seats and is cheaper to operate. A burly 50-year-old West Virginian, Mr Bright joined Boeing out of college as an aerospace designer. He knew the new Airbus would slot easily into Iberia's fleet. But he also felt that Mr Dupuy's target price undervalued his plane.

At Airbus, Mr Leahy also fumed at Iberia's pricing demands. A New York City native and the company's highest-ranking American, he pursues one goal: global domination over Boeing. Last year he spent 220 days on sales trips.

To Iberia, he argued that his plane offered a better investment return because the A340 is less expensive to buy and is similar to Iberia's other Airbus planes. From a hotchpotch of 11 models in 1997, Iberia now flies five types, and replacing the old 747s with A340s would trim that to four – offering savings on parts, maintenance and pilot training.

Even before presenting Airbus's offer, Mr Leahy had flown to Madrid in October to make his case. On 18 November, he once again took a chartered plane for the one-hour flight from Airbus headquarters in Toulouse, France, to Madrid. For two hours that evening, he and his team sat with Mr Dupuy and other Iberia managers around a table in Mr Dupuy's office, debating how many seats can fit on a 777. Those numbers were crucial to the deal because each seat represents millions of dollars in revenue over the life of a plane but also adds weight and cost.

Boeing had told Iberia that its 777 could hold 30 more seats than the 350 Iberia planned to put on the Airbus plane. Mr Leahy argued that the Boeing carries at most five more seats. 'Get guarantees from Boeing' on the seat count, Mr Leahy prodded the Iberia managers.

At Boeing, Mr Bright was eager to soften Iberia's pricing demand. His account manager, Steve Aliment, had already made several visits to pitch the plane, and in late November, Mr Bright sent him once again to protest that Iberia didn't appreciate the 777's revenue potential. Boeing desperately wanted to avoid competing just on price, so Mr Bright pushed operating cost and comfort.

On the Airbus side, Mr Leahy also was feeling pressured because a past sales tactic was coming back to haunt him. In 1995, when Iberia was buying 18 smaller A340s and Mr Dupuy expressed concern about their future value, Mr Leahy helped seal the deal by guaranteeing him a minimum resale price, which kicks in after 2005. If Iberia wants to sell them, Airbus must cover any difference

between the market price of the used planes and the guaranteed floor price.

The guarantee is one of the tools that Mr Leahy has used to boost Airbus's share of world sales to about 50 per cent today from 20 per cent in 1995. Boeing rarely guarantees resale values.

Mr Dupuy had wanted guarantees because they lower his risk of buying, and thus cut his cost of borrowing. What mattered now was that the guarantees also freed him to sell the planes at a good price. Early in the competition, he suggested to both Airbus and Boeing that he might eventually replace all of Iberia's A340s with Boeings – and potentially stick Airbus with most of the tab.

'If we didn't have the guarantees, the position of Airbus would be very strong,' Mr Dupuy said in an interview. Instead, 'we have a powerful bargaining tool on future prices.'

On 4 December, Mr Leahy flew again to Madrid to try to persuade Iberia to close a deal by year's end. Running through a presentation in Mr Dupuy's office, Mr Leahy and five colleagues ticked off fuel and maintenance costs for their plane. They asserted that passengers prefer the plane because it is quieter than the 777 and has no middle seats in business class.

Mr Dupuy then rattled Mr Leahy's cage with a new scenario: Iberia managers would be flying off next week to look at used Boeing 747-400 jumbo jets. Singapore Airlines had stopped flying the planes and was offering to lease them at bargain prices.

Mr Leahy chided Mr Dupuy, saying that was 'like buying a used car,' where a bargain can easily backfire. Mr Dupuy replied that sometimes buying used makes sense because it offers the flexibility of other options. The message: Iberia could dump its Airbus fleet.

Within Iberia, another debate was ending. Mr Dupuy heard from his managers the results of a yearlong analysis of the rival planes. The Airbus was cheaper than the Boeing, and the A340's four engines help it operate better in some high-altitude Latin American airports. But Iberia managers had decided they could fit 24 more seats on the Boeing, boosting revenue. And Iberia engineers calculated that the 777 would cost 8 per cent less to maintain than the A340. Maintenance on big planes costs at least $3 million a year, so the savings would be huge over the life of a fleet.

Unaware of Iberia's analysis, the Boeing team arrived in Mr Dupuy's office on the morning of 11 December with three bound selling documents. One contained Boeing's revised offer, titled 'Imagine the Possibilities ... Iberia's 777 Fleet.' Knowing Mr Dupuy as a numbers guy, the Boeing team peppered him with data showing passengers would choose Iberia because they prefer the 777.

Mr Dupuy told the sales men their price was still too high.

By mid-December, Iberia chairman Xabier de Irala was getting impatient and wanted a decision by the end of the year. On 18 December, Boeing's Mr Bright flew to Madrid. Over a long lunch, Mr Dupuy reiterated his price target.

'If that's your number, let's give this up,' Mr Bright said. Talks continued cordially, but the men left doubtful they could close the gap. That Friday, 20 December, Mr Dupuy told Iberia's board that prices from Airbus and Boeing were still too high and he would push the used-plane option harder.

By the start of the year, Airbus's Mr Leahy, growing frustrated, arranged a Saturday meeting with Mr Dupuy. On 4 January, the Iberia executive interrupted a family skiing holiday in the Pyrenees and drove two hours along winding French roads to meet Mr Leahy for lunch.

Mr Leahy spent four hours trying to convince Mr Dupuy and a colleague that Airbus couldn't offer a better deal. Mr Dupuy argued that Airbus had just given steep discounts to British airline easyJet, so it should do the same for Iberia. Annoyed, Mr Leahy said media reports of a 50 per cent price cut for easyJet was nonsense.

'You get Boeing to give you a 50 per cent discount and I'll send you a bottle of champagne,' he told the Iberia executives.

Mr Bright was frustrated too. In the first week of January, Mr Dupuy proposed visiting Seattle, where Boeing builds passenger planes. Mr Bright's reply: If Iberia was unwilling to budge, there was little reason to come. So, when Mr Dupuy said he would make the 14-hour journey, Mr Bright was encouraged.

On 14 January, Mr Dupuy and two colleagues arrived in Seattle. In the private dining room of Cascadia, a high-end downtown restaurant, they met for dinner with the Boeing salesman and Alan Mulally, the chief executive of Boeing's commercial-plan division. Mr Dupuy was impressed by Mr Mulally's eagerness and was pleased when he urged Mr Bright's team to find a way to close the gap.

The next day, the Boeing salesmen offered a new proposal – including a slightly lower price, improved financing and better terms on spare parts, crew training and maintenance support from General Electric Co., maker of the plane's engines.

When Mr Dupuy left Seattle on 16 January, Mr Bright felt Iberia was relenting a bit on price and that Mr Dupuy wanted to 'find a way to do the deal.' Mr Dupuy was also optimistic about striking a deal with Boeing.

Back in Madrid the next day, he raced off to join Iberia's chairman, Mr Irala, for a meeting with Mr Leahy and Airbus President Noel Forgeard. Mr Irala, a bear of a man who is credited with saving Iberia from bankruptcy eight years ago, told the Airbus executives that Mr Dupuy's price target remained firm. When the Airbus men relented

on a few points, Mr Irala yielded a bit, too, and spelled out Iberia's remaining targets for Airbus. Mr Forgeard said a deal looked possible.

As the meeting broke up, Mr Dupuy was pleased. He felt that Boeing and Airbus were digging deep. And no wonder. The world air-travel market was sinking deeper, and fears of war in Iraq and terrorism had slashed global bookings.

In the next few days, the sales teams from Boeing and Airbus each huddled to refine their offers. Both remained about 10 per cent above Mr Dupuy's price targets. Each called him several times daily, pushing for concessions. Mr Dupuy didn't budge. On 23 January, he told Iberia's board that both companies could do better. The board scheduled a special meeting for the following Thursday, 30 January.

Energised by the Seattle meetings, Mr Bright pushed his team 'to go all out to win this bid,' and they worked around the clock. Mr Bright phoned Mr Dupuy daily from Seattle and occasionally fielded his calls at 3 am, Pacific time. By late January, Boeing had cut its price by more than 10 per cent after haggling over engine price with GE and financing with leasing firms. The 777 was now less than 3 per cent above Mr Dupuy's target – so close that Mr Bright asked for a gesture of compromise from Iberia.

Mr Dupuy was impressed by Boeing's new aggressiveness. But Airbus was also closing the gap so quickly, he said, that he could offer no concessions. To Mr Leahy, he talked up Boeing's willingness to deal. 'I was just talking to Toby ...' Mr Dupuy told Mr Leahy during several conversations, referring to Mr Bright. Airbus improved its offer further.

On Wednesday, the day before the deadline, Boeing and Airbus were running about even. In Seattle, Mr Bright threw some clothes in his briefcase and proposed to Mr Dupuy that he hop on a plane to Madrid. Mr Dupuy said the choice was his, but what really mattered was the price target. That day, Mr Dupuy told Messrs. Bright and Leahy that their bosses should call Mr Irala with any final improvements before the board meeting.

On Thursday morning, Mr Bright offered to trim Boeing's price further if Mr Dupuy could guarantee that Boeing would win the deal. 'I can't control Forgeard,' Mr Dupuy replied, referring to the Airbus president, who was due to talk soon with Mr Irala. Mr Bright made the price cut without the concession.

'You're very close,' Mr Dupuy told him.

Later, Mr Forgeard got on the phone with Iberia's Mr Irala, who said he still needed two concessions on the financial terms and economics of the deal. Airbus had already agreed to most of Mr Dupuy's terms on asset guarantees and, with engine maker Rolls-Royce PLC, agreed to limit Iberia's cost of maintaining the jets. Mr Forgeard asked if relenting would guarantee Airbus the deal. Mr Irala replied yes, pending board approval – and looked over with a grin at Mr Dupuy, who seat nearby with his laptop open. Mr Forgeard acquiesced. Mr Dupuy plugged the new numbers in his spreadsheet. Airbus had hit its target.

That evening, Boeing got a call from Iberia saying the airline would soon announce it had agreed to buy nine A340-600s and taken options to buy three more. Hours later, Boeing posted on its website a statement criticising Iberia's choice as 'the easiest decision.' Mr Bright said later that he simply couldn't hit Mr Dupuy's numbers and 'do good business.'

In the end, Airbus nosed ahead thanks to its planes' lower price and common design with the rest of Iberia's fleet. By offering guarantees on the planes' future value and maintenance costs, plus attractive financing terms, Airbus edged out Boeing's aggressive package. The deal's final financial terms remain secret.

At Airbus, Mr Leahy was relieved, but he faced one last slap. Iberia's news release crowed about Airbus's price guarantees on the planes – a detail Mr Leahy considered confidential. Iberia's Mr Dupuy said he wasn't rubbing it in. But he had, he boasted, won 'extraordinary conditions'.

Questions

1 Critique the negotiation strategies and tactics of all three key executives involved: Dupuy, Leahy and Bright.

2 Critique the overall marketing strategies of the two aircraft makers as demonstrated in this case.

3 What were the key factors that ultimately sent the order in Airbus's direction?

4 Assume that Iberia is again on the market for jet liners. How should Bright handle a new enquiry? Be explicit.

Source: Daniel Michaels, 'Boeing and Airbus in Dogfight to Meet Stringent Terms of Iberia's Executives', *Wall Street Journal Europe*, 10 March 2003, p. A1. Copyright 2003 by Dow Jones & Co., Inc. Reproduced with permission of Dow Jones & Co., Inc. via Copyright Clearance Center.

case 5.2 Halliburton 'Over-billing' Controversy

The Pentagon audit confirms what we've known for months: Halliburton has been gouging taxpayers, and the White House has been letting them get away with it.[1]

– Henry Waxman, Democrat elected from State of California, US

No company is busier in Iraq than Halliburton. And no company in Iraq is as busy battling to clear its name.[2]

– James Cox, journalist, *USA Today*

The allegations

On 20 March 2003, the US-led coalition forces attacked Iraq in pursuance of 'Operation Iraqi Freedom.'[3] The war ended in two months. For all the various requirements of the pre-war and post-war period, the US government declared that it had awarded no-bid contracts[4] to Halliburton Company.[5] Analysts and media reports questioned the US government's decision to award contracts to Halliburton. They said that the company had a tainted past and was infamous for its unethical business practices. The major opposition came from the Democrats (the leading opposition party of the Republican government in the US). They alleged that the contracts had been awarded to Halliburton mainly because of the ties that the Vice President Dick Cheney[6] had with the company.

However, Kellogg Brown & Root (KBR), the engineering and construction subsidiary of Halliburton that was supposed to carry out the military contracts denied these allegations. KBR said that it had bagged the contract because of its excellent track record and expertise. The company commented, 'KBR was selected for this award based on the fact that KBR is the only contractor that could commence implementing the complex contingency plan on extremely short notice.'[7] Dave Lesar, the CEO of Halliburton, said, 'We are proud of our record and of our employees who serve the military. We receive contracts to make omelets and build infrastructure because of our unique skill sets.'[8]

In August 2003, the Department of Defense (DoD) of the US complained that the food that was cooked and served to the US troops in Iraq was done so in extremely unhygienic conditions. A report[9] mentioned that the food was cooked with 'rotting meats and vegetables' and with 'blood all over the floor', and was served in 'dirty pans', 'dirty grills', and 'dirty salad bars'. Moreover, the DoD also charged KBR with over billing of oil that it imported to Iraq.

The DoD said that KBR had overcharged to the tune of $61 million. The auditors with DoD alleged that the company charged $1.09 per gallon more for gasoline. Following this, there were allegations that KBR had overcharged for food as well. The company was put under scrutiny for over-billing.

Meanwhile, KBR denied all the allegations and said that the company was doing a good job under the extremely difficult situation of war. It alleged that it was being targeted for political reasons as the presidential elections were due in November 2004. A few analysts agreed with the company's argument and said that since the charges against the company had not been proved, criticism of the company was not justified. A journalist wrote, 'The difference between a potential overcharge and an actual overcharge is a big one, of course. It's the difference between a suspicion and a proven fact.'[10]

Background note

Founded in 1919, Halliburton was one of the world's largest providers of oil field services. The company was involved in providing oil and gas services to business, industries and government agencies throughout the world. Catering to the energy customers worldwide, Halliburton operated through its two main subsidiaries – KBR and Halliburton Energy Services.

Although a successful company, Halliburton had been dogged by controversy since the late 1980s. In 1995, the company was charged with doing business with Libya in spite of the US ban.[11] It was charged with exporting six pulse neutron generators to Libya between 1987 and 1989. These devices, apart from being oil and gas well survey tools, could be used to detonate nuclear weapons. This fact made the allegation against Halliburton more serious than just violation of trade practices. The controversy continued for a few years and eventually, in 1995, the company pleaded guilty to criminal charges that it had violated the ban. Subsequently, it was asked to pay a fine of $3.81 million.

Halliburton was also criticised for its trade with Azerbaijan and Burma. The US Government had imposed a ban on trade with Azerbaijan as it believed that the country indulged in 'ethnic cleansing'[12] of Armenians. Halliburton had an oil pipeline project in Burma. In 2001, the company had to face the wrath of its shareholders for having a project in Burma as the Burmese army was blamed for killing thousands of pro-democracy protesters to remain in power. The country's military had been widely condemned as

one of the world's most brutal violators of human rights. However, justifying the company's project in Burma, Cheney commented, 'The problem is that the Lord didn't see fit to always put oil and gas resources where there are democratic governments.'[13]

Media reports commented that Halliburton had a strong political network (refer to Exhibit 1 for Halliburton's political connections). Cheney served Halliburton as CEO of the company between 1995 and 2000. Analysts opined that at the time of joining the organisation, Cheney did not have much business experience of running a company. However, his stint as Secretary of Defense (1988-1993)[14] helped him perform his role effectively. During his tenure, Halliburton grew to become the leading oil services company in the US. Cheney brought with him a new direction for the company. During Cheney's tenure, Halliburton got contracts worth $2.3 billion as against only $1.2 billion during the previous five years between 1990 and 1995.

With Cheney's efforts, the number of subsidiaries situated in offshore tax havens grew to 44, whereas it was only nine before his tenure. This meant that the company received an $85 million tax refund in 1999, whereas it had paid $302 million in 1998. Analysts said that these changes were the result of Cheney's personal network with different countries from his time as the Secretary of Defense. By the early 2000s, Halliburton and its subsidiaries employed more than 100 000 people in 120 countries serving almost 7000 customers.

The accounting scandal

Though Halliburton's operations expanded significantly during Cheney's tenure, it did not always result in improved financial performance. One of the major changes that Halliburton witnessed during this period was that the company started receiving contracts of fixed prices rather than on the more usual cost plus[15] basis. The fixed-price contract did not guarantee any profit margin to the company in the event of cost overruns or unforeseen cost increases. All that Halliburton could do was to try to persuade its clients to pay for at least a part of the increased cost. The amount involved in those persuasions was referred to as 'disputed claims'. Prior to 1998, Halliburton did not include disputed claims as revenues and such claims were recognised as revenues only after settling with the clients as it depended entirely on the negotiation ability of the company whether it could get the customers to pay for those extra costs incurred or not. Since the fourth quarter of 1998, the company included a portion of disputed claims as revenues.

Analysts also commented on the timing of the change in accounting practices. They pointed out that Halliburton faced a tough time in 1998 as lower oil prices had affected its

business adversely. The problem was aggravated by the acquisition of Dresser for $5.4 billion. Analysts said that the company reported $175 million of pre-tax operating profits, more than half of which ($89 million) resulted from the change in the accounting policy. They said that since the bottom line of the company was under pressure, without the accounting practice change, the company would have fallen short of its revenue estimates and this would have affected its share price negatively. They alleged that this prompted Halliburton and its auditor Arthur Andersen[16] to change the company's accounting policy.

Analysts also pointed out the accounting technicality involved in the Halliburton case. They referred to paragraph 81 of the American Institute of Certified Public Accountants Statement of Position 81-1 (also known as SOP 81-1), which said that the recognition of amounts of additional contract revenue was appropriate only when it was probable that the claim would result in additional contract revenues and if the amount could be reliably estimated. Paul Brown, chairman of the accounting department at the Stern School of Business at New York University opined, 'In general, companies are not supposed to book sales unless they are certain that they will be paid – and how much they will be paid.'[17] However, Halliburton argued that it had applied the percentage of completion method[18] and had not violated any accounting norms. The company also added that it included disputed claims as revenues only when there was some probability of it receiving the contract money.

Responding to these allegations, Halliburton said that it had not disclosed the change because it was too small to matter. The company said that it had earned $14.5 billion revenues for the financial year 1998, and hence the inclusion of $89 million was not at all significant. The company stood by its accounting practice, whereas SEC continued its investigation for any possible malpractice in the financial reporting.

The contract

In March 2003, the US Government waged a war with Iraq. For all required logistic support, it gave a 'no-bid contract' to Halliburton months before the actual war started (refer to Exhibit 2 for the details of the contracts awarded to Halliburton). The DoD asked the company to get military bases into the Kuwaiti desert ready for possible invasion. About 1800 employees of Halliburton began working in Kuwait and within a few weeks they had erected camps that were capable of supporting 80 000 soldiers. This contract was secretly awarded to Halliburton and was not made public until the war started.

In March 2003, the US Government also awarded another contract to Halliburton to extinguish oil well fires. This contract was to be carried out by Halliburton's

Exhibit 1 Halliburton's political connections

Halliburton Company is known for its political connections. One reason for the company having a strong political network is its expenditure on political parties, especially Republicans. These expenditures became higher after 1995 when Dick Cheney became the CEO. The company had a Political Action Committee (PAC), which contributed donations to the federal candidates. Halliburton also made soft money contributions since 1995. In November 2002, the soft money payment was banned in the US. The cumulative contribution made by the company between 1995 and 2002 is given in Table 1.

Table 1 Halliburton PAC and soft contribution

PAC		Soft	
Democrats	Republicans	Democrats	Republicans
$44 500	$710 002	$0	$432 375

Source: Alternative Annual Report on Halliburton, http://users2.ev1.net/, April 2004.

In addition to the contribution to specific political candidates, Halliburton had spent $2.6 million on lobbying public officials since 1998, employing well-connected lobbyists with extensive histories in the US Defense Department (see Table 2).

Table 2 Halliburton total expenditures on politicians

Election cycle	Lobbying expenditure	PAC & soft contribution	Total
1995–96	–	$218 000	$218 000
1997–98	$540 000	$354 175	$894 175
1999–00	$1 200 000	$376 952	$1 576 952
2001–02	$600 000	$163 250	$763 250
2003	$300 000	$75 500	$375 500

Source: Alternative Annual Report on Halliburton, http://users2.ev1.net/, April 2004.

subsidiary KBR. The company was supposed to extinguish oil well fires, capping oil well blowouts, as well as respond to any oil spills. When this information was made public, the government was criticised vehemently by many analysts and observers. They complained that the contract was given to a company that had a history of doing business with terrorist regimes and was being investigated by the SEC. They also raised their voice against the manner in which the contract had been awarded. As it was a no-bid contract, many analysts alleged that Halliburton was awarded the contract because of Cheney's financial interests in the company.

Responding to these allegations, Cheney said that after his retirement from the company in 2000, he had no financial interests in Halliburton. But a media report[19] mentioned that Cheney was still receiving $1 million every year as a part of his retirement compensation of $20 million. Another report[20] stated that the package of $20 million was approved by the company on 20 July 2000, just five days before he was announced as the vice-presidential candidate. The report also stated that Cheney's compensation for the eight months of 2000 in which he served as the CEO of Halliburton was $4.3 million in deferred compensation and bonuses and $806 332 in salary.

Halliburton claimed that it had got the contract because of its competency as it was the only contractor that could do the work required at extremely short notice. Dave

Lesar, the CEO of Halliburton, commented, 'We get government contracts because of what we know, not who we know.'[21]

By 14 April 2003, the US Government had declared that the major fighting in Iraq was over, following the capture of Tikrit, the birthplace of Saddam Hussein. However, the troops encountered resistance from Iraqi fighters in small towns and cities. A formal declaration regarding the end of war by the US came a fortnight later on 1 May 2003.

After the war, the US forces had the major task of rebuilding Iraq. There was an immediate need for oil as many oil wells had been destroyed in Iraq. The country had no electricity to power its refineries. The Iraqis did not even have the required fuel to make food. The US forces suspected that if oil was not made available in Iraq soon, the problem may lead to a civil war. The US government aptly expanded the scope of the contract earlier given to Halliburton and asked it to start exporting gasoline to Iraq. All the contracts were awarded on a cost plus basis.

The controversy

In August 2003, the DoD charged Halliburton with serving mediocre-quality food to the US army in extremely unhygienic conditions for which it charged $28 per day per soldier. Reportedly the soldiers could have had their food in the best hotels of Iraq for this sum. Moreover, the company was also alleged to have falsely charged $186

617

Exhibit 2 Contracts awarded to Halliburton

Contract awarded by	Job	Value of the contract	Company's fee
US Army Corps of Engineers Task Force Restore Iraqi Oil	Assess and repair Iraq's oil infrastructure, restore production	Anticipated value: $1.9 billion	2 per cent of the total value, performance bonus up to 5%
US Army Corps of Engineers Task Force Restore Iraqi Oil II	Repair oil infrastructure in southern Iraq and restore production	Maximum value: $1.2 billion	0 per cent of the total value, performance bonus up to 3%
US Army material Command's Logistics Civil Augmentation Program (LOGCAP)	Build and maintain base camps, supply food, water, laundry, sanitation, recreation, transport and other services	Maximum value: $4 billion	1 per cent of the total value performance bonus up to 2 per cent
US Army Corps of Engineers Transatlantic Program Center	Design and build facilities for US Central Command (CENTCOM) in area stretching from Horn of Africa to Central Asia	Maximum value: $1.5 billion	Undisclosed

Source: US Army Corps of Engineers, US Army Material Command, Halliburton.

million for meals that were never delivered. According to reports, the company did not keep records of how many soldiers were having their meals at a time. Analysts felt that this was done in order to make the estimate of the food bill impossible to calculate.

Halliburton, however, denied these charges and said that it was possible that there was some overestimation. The company said that in wartime, exact estimation of number of soldiers that would come for lunch/dinner was not possible as soldiers went on leave or troops were shifted to other locations frequently without the knowledge of the company. The company also said that it did not keep records of the number of meals because the commanders did not want the soldiers to 'sign in' for meals due to security reasons. They also did not want the troops to wait in a queue to have food. The company, however, agreed to pay back $27.4 million but underlined that 'this is not any sort of admission of wrongdoing.'[22] Later, the company also suspended $141 million of its food bill. The company said that it would receive the payment from the government only when the controversy over-billing was resolved.

By the end of 2003, the allegations of over-billing against Halliburton increased significantly. Waxman was one of the first people to charge the company with over-billing. According to him, the company charged the US Government $1.59 per gallon (excluding own commission), whereas the average wholesale rate of gasoline in the Middle East countries during the same period was about 71 cents a gallon. This meant that the company was charging almost 90 cents per gallon for transportation. According to Waxman, the reasonable transportation cost was the maximum of 25 cents. He commented, 'When we checked with independent experts to see if this fee was reasonable, they were stunned.'[23] The US DoD audit suggested an even higher amount of over billing. It reported

that Halliburton had overcharged the army by $1.09 per gallon for 57 million gallons of gasoline delivered to the Iraqis, taking the total amount of over billing to about $61 million.

Halliburton claimed that the US army initially wanted all the fuel to come from Kuwait, and it was only because of the recommendation of the company that Turkey was considered as the second option. According to the company, this suggestion saved millions of dollars of the US taxpayers' money as by December 2003, the company was buying two-thirds of its oil requirement from Turkey and only one-third from Kuwait. The company added that the army did not accept the idea of using only Turkey for bringing in fuel as it considered it risky to supply oil to Iraq from such a distant place. It also added that the army wanted the supply of oil from both the north (Turkey) and south (Kuwait) so that even if one route was closed, Iraq's oil supply was not stopped completely. Randy Harl, the president and CEO of KBR, said, 'KBR delivered fuel to Iraq at the best value, the best price and the best terms.'[24]

Halliburton received a major blow in January 2004 when it was reported that two of its employees accepted bribes of $6 million to award the contract to a subcontractor of Kuwait. However, the company took quick action by sacking these employees immediately. The company released a statement: 'We do not tolerate this kind of behavior by anyone at any level in any Halliburton company.'[25]

In another report[26] released in February 2004, two ex-employees of Halliburton were reported to have met Waxman and told him that the company had routinely overcharged the US Government. They alleged that Halliburton had wasted millions of dollars of the US taxpayers. They also gave many examples of wasteful spending by the company, including:

- abandoning of trucks worth $85 000 because of flat tyres and minor problems
- lodging 100 workers at a five-star hotel in Kuwait for a total of $10 000 a day while the US DoD wanted them to stay in tents, like soldiers, at $139 a night
- paying $100 to have a 15-pound bag of laundry cleaned in Kuwait whereas it cost only $28 in Iraq
- paying $1.5 to buy a can of soda, about 24 times higher than the contract price
- purchasing special towels for soldiers at $7.50 a piece when ordinary ones would have cost one-third of the price.

The ex-employees said that Halliburton did not mind paying high prices because the motto of the company was, 'Don't worry about price. It's cost plus.'

On 22 February 2004, the DoD announced that it had opened a criminal investigation against Halliburton for allegations regarding overpricing of fuel delivered in Iraq. The investigation was focused on KBR. On 16 March 2004, the DoD decided to withhold $300 million (about 15 per cent of the total bill) of the food bill until it received the new cost estimates from Halliburton. Responding to this, the company said that if did not receive the payment from the DoD, it would be forced to withhold the payments to its subcontractors.

By June 2004, analysts started saying that Halliburton was so mired in the overbilling controversy that it should no longer be allowed to carry on the work in Iraq. Moreover, its presence in Iraq had reportedly angered Iraqi contractors. A report said, 'Qualified Iraqi businesses are hungry to take over the work that Halliburton has been doing unsatisfactorily, and at a fraction of the cost. The Iraqi people deserve to be the first bidders on contracts to rebuild their country rather than being prohibited from bidding as is currently the case.'[27]

Halliburton, however, claimed that it had performed its work successfully while fighting against all odds. It also said that seven of its employees had been killed in the war. However, the company denied that the allegations levelled against it would have any substantial impact on its domestic and global business. Surprisingly, in spite of the controversy Halliburton's stock price witnessed a steady increase since early 2003.

Further reading and bibliography

- Peter Waldman, 'Pipeline Project in Burma Puts Cheney in the Spotlight', www.burmaformula.org, 27 October 2000.
- Alex Berenson and Lowell Bergman, 'Under Cheney, Halliburton Altered Policy on Accounting', The New York Times, 22 May 2002.
- Press release, 'Halliburton Reports SEC Investigation of Accounting Practice', www.halliburton. com, 28 May 2002.
- 'Halliburton Falls on SEC Probe', http://money.cnn.com, 29 May 2002.
- Jane Bussey, 'Judicial Watch Sues Cheney', Halliburton, http://www.dfw.com, 10 July 2002.
- Press release, 'Halliburton Responds to News of Judicial Watch Lawsuit', www.halliburton.com, 10 July 2002.
- Anne Rittman, 'A Halliburton Primer', Washingtonpost.com, 11 July 2002.
- Dana Milbank, For Cheney, Tarnish From Halliburton http://www.truthout.org, 16 July 2002.
- 'Vice President Denies Wrongdoing in Connection with Halliburton, which is Under SEC Investigation', money.cnn.com, 7 August 2002.
- David Teather, 'Halliburton Staff Sacked "for Taking Bribes"', Guardian, 24 January 2003.
- Press release, 'KBR implements plan for extinguishing oil well fires in Iraq', www.halliburton.com, 24 March 2003.
- Jason Leopold, 'Halliburton and the Dictators: The Bloody History of Cheney's Firm', http://www.ccmep.org, 16 April 2003.
- Sue Pleming, 'Iraq: Halliburton Accused of Overbilling', Reuters, www.corpwatch.org, 15 October 2003.
- 'Halliburton Accused of Iraq Overbilling', http://money.cnn.com, 16 October 2003.
- Douglas Jehl, 'Halliburton Overcharges Government in Iraq', New York Times, 12 December 2003.
- 'Halliburton: $61m Overcharge?', http://www.cbsnews.com/, 12 December 2003.
- 'Halliburton Disputes are a Feature of its Government Contracts', http://www.spacewar.com, 13 December 2003.
- 'Contractor Served Troops Dirty Food in Dirty Kitchens', www.taipeitimes.com, 14 December 2003.
- Paul Krugman, 'Profiteering and Patriotism', New York Times, 17 December 2003.

- 'Halliburton Denies Price Gouging Charges; Oil Services Firm says it Saved Taxpayers Millions', *MSNBC News Services*, 18 December 2003.
- Jim Wolf, 'Democrats Press Rumsfeld for Halliburton Records', *Reuters*, 20 December 2003.
- 'Report: Feds Accuse Halliburton In Iraq Fuel Contract', The Street.Com, 20 December 2003.
- Stephen Glain, 'Waxman hits Halliburton fuel contract', *The Boston Globe*, 16 January 2004.
- 'Halliburton Admits $6 Million Kickbacks', http://news.bbc.co.uk, 23 January 2004.
- 'Halliburton Pays for Possible Overcharge', http://money.cnn.com, 23 January 2004.
- Lesley Stahl, 'Doing Business With The Enemy', *CBS*, 25 January 2004.
- 'More Halliburton Overcharges?', www.cbsnews.com, 2 February 2004.
- Jackie Spinner, 'Halliburton to Return $27.4 million to Government', http://www.washingtonpost.com, 4 February 2004.
- 'Another Halliburton Probe', *Newsweek*, 4 February 2004.
- John Kerry: 'Halliburton Investor', www.latefinal.com, 6 February 2004.
- 'Ex-Halliburton Employees Tell of Overbilling', www.reuters.com, 12 February 2004.
- Andrew Limburg, 'Documenting the Halliburton/ Cheney Crimes and Controversies, Part II', *Independent Media TV*, 14 February 2004.
- John King, 'US Lifts Travel Ban to Libya', www.cnn.com, 27 February 2004.
- 'Piling on Halliburton', *Washington Post*, 3 March 2004.
- James Cox, 'Halliburton CEO says Firm Saves Money for Pentagon', *USA Today*, 19 March 2004.
- Press statement, 'KBR Continues to Work With Government to Resolve Billing Issues', wwww.halliburton.com, 17 May 2004.
- Marian Wilkinson, 'Major Iraq Contract Falls Over', www.theage.com, 20 May 2004.
- '*Time* Reports Cheney Hand in Contract', www.iht.com, 31 May 2004.
- www.halliburton.com.
- www.bigcharts.com.
- www.hoovers.com.
- http://biz.yahoo.com.

References

1 Douglas Jehl, 'Halliburton Overcharges Government in Iraq', *New York Times*, 12 December 2003.

2 James Cox, 'Halliburton CEO says Firm Saves Money for Pentagon', *USA Today*, 19 March 2004.

3 The US Government believed that Osama Bin Laden led terrorist organisation, Al-Qaida, which was responsible for the September 11 2001 terrorist attacks on the World Trade Center in the US may obtain weapons of mass destruction (WMD) from Iraq. As Iraq was ruled by Saddam Hussein, who was openly hostile to the US, the US officials considered it a severe threat to the country's security, and felt the need for pre-emptive war against Iraq to prevent further damage from occurring in the US. In March 2003, the US declared war against Iraq (the second war, the first being in January 1991), called 'Operation Iraqi Freedom,' aimed at freeing Iraq from the ruling Hussein government and gaining control over the WMD. The war ended in May 2003, following the capture of Tikrit, the birthplace of Hussein. Hussein was captured by the US army in December 2003.

4 A no-bid contract is a military or government contract that is made directly with a corporation, bypassing the standard process of bidding. These contracts can be finalised much more quickly than a typical contract. However, they are often viewed with suspicion when the company to which the contract has been issued has any ties with the administration in power at the time.

5 The Houston-based Halliburton Company provides products and services to the petroleum and energy industries to aid in the exploration, development and production of natural resources. Halliburton KBR, the company's engineering and construction division, designs, builds and provides additional services for the energy industry, governments and civil infrastructure.

6 Born on 30 January 1941 in Lincoln, Nebraska (US), Dick Cheney is the vice president of the US. He had been the CEO of Halliburton from 1995 to 2000.

7 Press release, 'KBR Implements Plan for Extinguishing Oil Well Fires in Iraq', www.halliburton.com, 24 March 2003.

8 'Piling on Halliburton', *The Washington Post*, 3 March 2004.

9 'Contractor Served Troops Dirty Food in Dirty Kitchens', www.taipeitimes.com, 14 December 2003.

10 'Anti-Bush Ad Overstates Case Against Halliburton', www.factcheck.org, 8 June 2004.

11 The US ban on commercial trade with Libya was imposed in 1986 when Libya allegedly bombed a German disco theatre killing two US soldiers and a Turkish woman and injuring 229 others. In early 2004, US lifted the ban after Libya acknowledged that it had secret weapons of mass destruction and agreed to dismantle them.

12 An act of either driving out or exterminating the people of the minority race in order to create an ethnically homogeneous state.

13 Peter Waldman, 'Pipeline Project in Burma puts Cheney in the Spotlight', www.burmaformula.org, 27 October 2000.

14 Cheney held the position of Secretary of Defense under George Bush Sr. During his tenure as Secretary of Defense, he was responsible for directing the US invasion of Panama and the first Gulf War. As Secretary of Defense, Cheney also conveniently changed the rules restricting private contractors doing work on the US military bases. He subsequently oversaw the awarding of billions of dollars in Department of Defense contracts to Halliburton, his future employer.

15 Cost-plus contracts are contracts wherein the bill amount is not decided beforehand. The bill amount is equal to whatever the expenses incurred on the contract plus a small profit margin for the contractor. Under this method, the contractor is assured to have a fixed margin even in the case of a sudden or unforeseen increment in the cost.

16 Arthur Andersen LLP was a US-based partnership firm engaged in auditing and consultancy. It came under fire in the Enron scandal in which it was convicted for obstructing justice in relation to the Enron scandal, which left the firm unable to perform audits for publicly traded US companies.

17 Alex Berenson and Lowell Bergman, 'Under Cheney, Halliburton Altered Policy on Accounting', *New York Times*, 22 May 2002.

18 A procedure for computing partial payments on a large contract wherein identifiable portions of the work may be satisfactorily completed, invoiced and paid before the entire project is completed and paid in full.

19 Mairesse Michelle, 'The Spoils of War', www.hermes-press.com.

20 'Halliburton Has Been Very, Very Good to Dick Cheney', www.democrats.org.

21 'Piling on Halliburton', *Washington Post*, 3 March 2004.

22 'Halliburton in Pentagon Payback', *BBC News*, 4 February 2004.

23 Halliburton Accused of Iraq Over-billing', http://money.cnn.com, 16 October 2003.

24 'Halliburton Denies Price Gouging Charges, Oil Services Firm Says it Saved Taxpayers Millions', *MSNBC News Services*, 18 December 2003.

25 David Teather, 'Halliburton Staff Sacked for Taking Bribes', *Guardian*, 24 January 2004.

26 In another report Ex-Halliburton employees tell of over-billing, www.reuters.com, 12 February 2004.

27 Alternative annual report on Halliburton, http:// users2.ev1.net/, April 2004.

This case was written by Avishek Suman, under the direction of Vivek Gupta, ICFAI Center for Management Research (ICMR). It is intended to be used as a basis for class discussion rather than to illustrate either effective or ineffective handling of a management situation. The case was compiled from published sources.

case 5.3 AIDS, Condoms and Carnival

Brazil

Half a million Brazilians are infected with the AIDS virus, and millions more are at high risk of contracting the incurable ailment, a federal study reported. The Health Ministry study is Brazil's first official attempt to seek an estimate of HIV-infected residents. Many had doubted the government's prior number of 94 997. The report by the National Programme for Transmissible Diseases/AIDS said 27 million Brazilians are at high risk to contract AIDS, and another 36 million are considered to be at a medium risk. It said Brazil could have 7.5 million AIDS victims in the next decade.

'If we are going to combat this epidemic, we have to do it now,' said Pedro Chequer, a Health Ministry official. Chequer said the Health Ministry would spend $300 million next year, distributing medicine and 250 million condoms and bringing AIDS awareness campaigns to the urban slums, where the disease is most rampant. Last month, Brazil became one of the few countries to offer a promising AIDS drug free to those who need it. The drug can cost as much as $12 000 a year per patient.

AIDS cases in Brazil have risen so dramatically for married women that the state of São Paulo decided that it must attack a basic cultural practice in Latin America: their husbands don't practise safe sex. Last month, the government of Brazil's megalopolis started promoting the newly released female condom.

Many of the new AIDS cases in Brazil are married women who have children, according to a report released last month at the Pan-American Conference on AIDS in Lima, Peru. Worldwide, women constitute the fastest-growing group of those diagnosed with HIV. And of the 30.6 million people who are diagnosed with the HIV virus, 90 per cent live in poor countries.

One Brazilian mother, Rosana Dolores, knows well why women cannot count on male partners to use condoms. She and her late husband never thought of protecting their future children against AIDS. 'We were married. We wanted to have kids,' says Mrs Dolores, both of whose children were born with HIV. 'These days, I would advise young people to always use condoms. But married couples … who is going to?'

Brazil, with its 155 million people and the largest population in South America, has the second-highest number of reported HIV infections in the Americas, after the United States, according to a report released on 26 November by the United Nations agency UNAIDS.

Public health officials say one reason why AIDS prevention efforts have failed is that many Brazilians just don't like condoms. While use in Brazil has quadrupled in the past six years, it is still the least popular method of birth control – a touchy issue in the predominantly Roman Catholic country. Another reason is that condoms cost about 75 cents each, making them more expensive here than anywhere else in the world, health officials say.

Plus, Latin-style machismo leaves women with little bargaining power. Only 14 per cent of Brazilian heterosexual men used condoms in 1996, according to AIDSCAP, an AIDS-prevention programme funded by the US Agency for International Development. In other studies, many women said they would not ask their partner to use a condom, even if they knew he was sleeping with others.

'Women are afraid of asking their men to have safe sex, afraid of getting beaten, afraid of losing their economic support,' says Guido Carlos Levi, a director at the health department at Emilio Ribas Hospital. 'This is not Mexico, but we're quite a machistic society here.'

The frequency with which Latin men stray from monogamous relationships has compounded the problem. In studies conducted in Cuba by the Pan-American Health Organization, 49 per cent of men and 14 per cent of women in stable relationships admitted that they had had an affair in the past year.

In light of statistics showing AIDS as the number one killer of women of childbearing age in São Paulo state, public health officials here launched a campaign in December promoting the female condom.

The hope is that it will help women – especially poor women – protect themselves and their children. But the female condom seemed unlikely to spark a latex revolution when it hit city stores on 1 January. The price is $2.50 apiece – more than three times the price of most male condoms.

The Family Health Association is asking the government to help subsidise the product and to cut the taxes on condoms that make them out of reach for many poor Brazilians. 'We're looking for a pragmatic solution to prevent the transmission of HIV-AIDS,' group president Maria Eugenia Lemos Fernandes said. 'Studies show there is a high acceptance of this method because it's a product under the control of women.'

While 75 per cent of the women and 63 per cent of the men in a pilot study on the female condom said they approved of the device, many women with AIDS say they would have been no more likely to have used a female condom than a conventional one.

Part of the problem is perception: 80 per cent of women and 85 per cent of men in Brazil believe they are not at risk of contracting HIV, according to a study conducted by the Civil Society for the Well-Being of the Brazilian Family.

Also at risk are married women, 40 per cent of whom undergo sterilisation as an affordable way of getting around the Catholic church's condemnation of birth control, health officials noted.

'It's mostly married women who are the victims. You just never think it could be you,' says a former hospital administrator who was diagnosed with the virus after her husband had several extramarital affairs. He died two years ago.

'I knew everything there was to know about AIDS – I worked in a hospital – but I never suspected he was going out like that. He always denied it,' she says.

While the HIV virus is making inroads in rural areas and among teenagers in Brazil, Fernandes said it doesn't have to reach epidemic proportions as in Uganda or Tanzania. 'There is a very big window of opportunity here.'

Brazil's Health Ministry is adding a new ingredient to the heady mix that makes up the country's annual Carnival – condoms. The ministry will distribute 10 million condoms next month along with free advice on how to prevent the spread of AIDS at places like Rio de Janeiro's sambadrome, where bare-breasted dancing girls attract millions of spectators every year.

'It's considered as a period of increased sexual activity,' a spokeswoman at the ministry's AIDS coordination department said on Monday. 'The euphoria provoked by Carnival and the excessive consumption of alcohol make it a moment when people are more likely to forget about prevention,' she explained. Tourists descend on Brazil for Carnival, which is viewed as a time when inhibitions fall away and anything goes.

India

S. Mani's small barber shop in this southern Indian city looks like any other the world over. It's equipped with all the tools of the trade: scissors, combs, razors – and condoms too.

A blue box full of free prophylactics stands in plain view of his customers as Mr Mani trims hair and dispenses advice on safe sex, a new dimension to his 20-year career. 'I start by talking about the family and children,' Mr Mani explains, snipping a client's moustache. 'Slowly, I get to women, AIDS and condoms.'

Many Indian men are too embarrassed to buy condoms at a drugstore or to talk freely about sex with health counsellors and family members. There's one place where they let down their hair: the barber shop. So, the state of Tamil Nadu is training barbers to be frontline soldiers in the fight against AIDS.

Programmes like the barber scheme are what make Tamil Nadu, a relatively poor Indian state that's home to 60 million people, a possible model for innovative and cost-effective methods to contain AIDS in the developing world.

Six years after it was first detected in India, the AIDS virus is quickly spreading in the world's second most-populous nation. Already, up to 5 million of India's 920 million people are infected with HIV – more than in any other country, according to UNAIDS, the United Nations' AIDS agency.

But faced with more immediate and widespread health woes, such as tuberculosis and malaria, officials in many Indian states are reluctant to make AIDS prevention a priority. And in some states, the acquired immune deficiency syndrome is regarded as a Western disease of decadence; officials deny that prostitution and drug use even exist in their midst.

'Some Indian states are still in total denial or ignorance about the AIDS problem,' says Salim Habayeb, a World Bank physician who oversees an $84 million loan to India for AIDS prevention activities.

Tamil Nadu, the state with the third-highest incidence of HIV infection, has been open about its problem. Before turning to barbers for help, Tamil Nadu was the first state to introduce AIDS education in high school and the first to set up a statewide information hotline. Its comprehensive AIDS-education programme targets the overall population, rather than only high-risk groups.

In the past two years, awareness of AIDS in Tamil Nadu has jumped to 95 per cent of those polled, from 64 per cent, according to Operations Research Group, an independent survey group. 'Just two years ago, it was very difficult to talk about AIDS and the condom,' says P.R. Bindhu Madhavan, director of the Tamil Nadu State AIDS Control Society, the autonomous state agency managing the prevention effort.

The AIDS fighters take maximum advantage of the local culture to get the message across. Tamils are among the most ardent moviegoers in this film-crazed country. In the city of Madras, people line up for morning screenings even during weekdays. Half of the state's 630 theatres are paid to screen an AIDS-awareness short before the main feature. The spots are usually melodramatic musicals laced with warnings.

In the countryside, where cinemas are scarce, a movie mobile does the job. The concept mimics that used by multinationals, such as Colgate-Palmolive Co., for rural advertising. Bright red-and-blue trucks ply the back roads, blaring music from well-known movie soundtracks whose lyrics have been rewritten to address AIDS issues. In villages, hundreds gather for the show, on a screen that pops out of the rear of the truck.

In one six-minute musical, a young husband's infidelity leads to his death from AIDS, the financial ruin of his family and then the death of his wife, also infected. The couple's toddler is left alone in the world. The heart-

rending tale is followed by a brief lecture by an AIDS educator – and the offer of a free pack of condoms and an AIDS brochure.

Tamil Nadu's innovations have met with obstacles. It took several months for state officials to persuade Indian government television, Doordarshan, to broadcast an AIDS commercial featuring the Hindu gods of chastity and death. Even then, Mr Madhavan says, Doordarshan 'wouldn't do it as a social ad, so we have to pay a commercial rate.'

Later, the network refused to air a three-minute spot in which a woman urges her husband, a truck driver, to use a condom when he's on the road. Safe infidelity was deemed 'inappropriate for Indian living rooms,' says Mr Madhavan. A number of commercial satellite channels have been willing to run the ad.

Tamil Nadu has met little resistance recruiting prostitutes for the cause. For almost a year, 37-year-old prostitute Vasanthi has been distributing condoms to colleagues. With state funding, a non-governmental agency has trained her to spread the word about AIDS and other sexually transmitted diseases. As an incentive, the state pays participants like Ms Vasanthi, a mother of three, the equivalent of $14 a month, about what she earns from entertaining a client.

Before Ms Vasanthi joined the plan, she didn't know that the condom could help prevent HIV infection. These days, if any client refuses to wear a condom, 'I kick him out, even if it takes using my shoes,' she says. 'I'm not flexible about this.' More men are also carrying their own condoms, she says.

Thank barbers such as Mr Mani for that. Especially in blue-collar areas of Madras, men 'trim their hair and beard before frequenting a commercial sex worker,' says Mr Madhavan. They can pick up their condom on the way out.

Tamil Nadu launched the barber programme in Madras last March. So far, it has enlisted 5000 barbers, who receive AIDS education at meetings each Tuesday – the barbers' day off. The barbers aren't paid to be AIDS counsellors, but they appear to take pride in their new responsibility.

Over the generations, India's barbers have been respected as traditional healers and trusted advisers. 'If you want to get to the king's ears, you tell his barber,' says Mr Madhavan, the state AIDS director. Reinforcing the image of barbers as healers, the local trade group is called the Tamil Nadu Medical Barber Association.

'I first talked about AIDS with my barber,' says Thiyagrajan, an electrician in his 40s. 'I don't have multiple partners, so I don't need a condom, but I take them for my friends.'

One recent night, a man in his thirties walked into Aruna Hair Arts, greeted Mr Swami, then headed out the door with a fistful of condoms scooped from the plastic

dispenser. 'That's OK,' Mr Swami says approvingly. 'He's a regular customer.'

A local non-governmental organisation helps barbers replenish condom stocks by providing each shop with self-addressed order forms. But the central government hasn't always been able to meet supply, for reasons ranging from bureaucracy to price disputes with manufacturers.

Tamil Nadu has started sourcing condoms from elsewhere. But they're too expensive to give away. So the next stage of the barber scheme, just under way, is to charge two rupees (six cents) for a two-condom 'pleasure pack'. The barbers will get a 25 per cent commission. Thus far, the only perk of participating has been a free wall calendar listing AIDS-prevention tips.

Roughly 30 per cent of barbers approached by Tamil Nadu have refused to participate in the AIDS programme, fearing that they would alienate customers. But those who take part insist that carrying the AIDS message hasn't hurt business. 'We give the message about AIDS, but we still gossip about women,' says barber N.V. Durairaj at Rolex Salon.

London International Group

London International Group (LIG) is recognised worldwide as a leader in the development of latex and thin film barrier technologies. The Group has built its success on the development of its core businesses: the Durex family of branded condoms, Regent Medical gloves and Marigold household and industrial gloves. These are supported by a range of noncore health and beauty products.

With operational facilities in over 40 countries, 12 manufacturing plants, either wholly or jointly owned, and an advanced research and development facility based in Cambridge, England, LIG is well placed to expand into the new emerging markets of the world.

Durex is the world's number one condom brand in terms of quality, safety and brand awareness. The Durex family of condom brands includes Sheik, Ramses, Hatu, London, Kohinoor, Dua Lima, Androtex and Avanti. Sold in over 130 countries worldwide and leader in more than 40 markets, Durex is the only global condom brand.

The development of innovative and creative marketing strategies is key to communicating successfully with our target audiences. Consumer marketing initiatives remain focused on supporting the globalisation of Durex. A series of innovative yet cost-effective projects have been used to communicate the global positioning 'Feeling Is Everything' to the target young adult market, securing loyalty.

The Durex Global Survey, together with a unique multi-million-pound global advertising and sponsorship contract with MTV have successfully emphasised the exciting and modern profile of Durex and presented significant opportunities for local public relations and event sponsorship, especially in emerging markets like Taiwan.

LIG continues to focus on education, using sponsorship of events such as the XI Annual AIDS Conference held last summer in Vancouver and other educational initiatives to convey the safer sex message to governments, opinion formers and educators worldwide.

Japan

London Okamoto Corporation, the joint venture company between London International Group, plc (LIG) and Okamoto Industries Inc. (Okamoto), recently announced the Japanese launch in spring 1998 of Durex Avanti, the world's first polyurethane male condom.

This is the first time an international condom brand will be available in Japan, the world's most valuable condom market, which is estimated to be worth £260 million ($433 million). Durex Avanti has already been successfully launched in the United States and Great Britain, and will be launched in Italy and other selected European countries during the next 12 months.

Durex Avanti condoms are made from Duron, a unique polyurethane material twice as strong as latex, which enables them to be made much thinner than regular latex condoms thereby increasing sensitivity without compromising safety. In addition, Durex Avanti condoms are also able to conduct body heat, creating a more natural feeling, and are the first condoms to be totally odourless, colourless, and suitable for use with oil-based lubricants.

Commenting on the launch, Nick Hodges, chief executive of LIG, said: 'Japan is a very important condom market; with oral contraceptives still not publicly available, per capita usage rates for condoms are among the highest in the world. Our joint venture with Okamoto, Japan's leading condom manufacturer, gives us instant access to this strategically important market.'

The joint venture with Okamoto, which is the market leader in Japan with a 53 per cent share, was established in 1994 with the specific purpose of marketing Durex Avanti. Added Mr Takehiko Okamoto, president of Okamoto, 'We are confident that such an innovative and technically advanced product as Durex Avanti, coupled with our strong market franchise, will find significant consumer appeal in Japan's sophisticated condom market.'

Durex Avanti, which is manufactured at LIG's research and development centre in Cambridge, England, has taken over 10 years to develop, and represents an investment by LIG of approximately £15 million.

Questions

1 Comment on the Brazilian and Indian Governments' strategies for the prevention of AIDS via the marketing of condoms.
2 How is the AIDS problem different in the United States compared to Brazil and India?
3 Would the approaches described in Brazil and India work in the United States? Why or why not?
4 Suggest additional ways that London International Group could promote the prevention of AIDS through the use of condoms worldwide.

Further reading and bibliography

- 'Half a Million Brazilians are Infected with the AIDS Virus', *Associated Press*, 21 December 1996.
- Andrea McDaniels, 'Brazil Turns to Women to Stop Dramatic Rise in AIDS Cases. São Paulo Pushes Female Condom to Protect Married Women from Husbands. But Costs of Devices Are High', *Christian Science Monitor*, 9 January 1998, p. 7.
- 'Brazil to Hand Out 10 Million Condoms during Carnival', *Chicago Tribune*, 19 January 1998, p. 2.
- Miriam Jordan, 'India Enlists Barbers in the War on AIDS', *Wall Street Journal*, 24 September 1994, p. A18.
- www.lig.com (for example).
- www.durex.com.

case 5.4 Key Success Factors of Theme Parks: the Experience of Walt Disney Company

Tourism is a global phenomenon that has experienced significant changes over the past few decades. Following the growing importance of leisure and the increasing demand of consumers for amusement and entertainment, theme parks have known an important development worldwide. The market of theme parks has become increasingly competitive and the performance of many theme parks appears to be insufficient. This case study examines key success factors of the market leader of theme parks, Walt Disney Company.

The leisure society

The late twentieth century and the beginning of the new millennium have witnessed the development of the leisure society. Tourism has become one of the fastest growing sectors of the economies of many developed countries. Its expansion has been supported by the multiplication of tourist attractions. Tourist attractions comprise a wide range of natural and man-made environments appealing to either mass tourism audiences or more specific interests. Following the increase of leisure in developed countries, consumers spend a growing amount of their income on travel and entertainment. They have become increasingly demanding as far as their leisure activities are concerned. The new tourist consumer shows a preference for fully integrated services and requires improved quality at lower prices. Moreover, a large number of individuals search to live different experiences during their leisure time. The demand for attractions that offer amusement and entertainment has considerably increased.

The expansion of theme parks

Theme parks can be defined as amusement parks that are designed around a central theme or a group of themes and where visitors are charged a pay-one-price admission fee. They are man-made tourism attractions that fulfil a wide range of consumer needs. Over the past few decades, theme parks have known a considerable expansion worldwide. Given the highly competitive environment, critical size has become an important issue in the theme park industry. Walt Disney Company appears to be the leading theme park chain, attracting more than 90 million visitors per year.

Walt Disney Company

Theme parks represent an important part of the activities of Walt Disney Company, which is considered as one of the world's leading producers and providers of entertainment and information. The company divides its activities into four main strategic areas: (1) media networks, (2) parks and resorts, (3) studio entertainment, and (4) consumer products. In 2002, the total revenues of the company reached 25.3 billion US dollars. The strategic area of parks and resorts accounted for 6.5 billion US dollars, that is 25.5 per cent of total revenues (see Exhibit 1). In 2002, park and resort activities generated earnings of 1.8 billion US dollars (earnings before interest, income taxes, depreciation and amortisation), which represent 48.4 per cent of total earnings of Walt Disney Company.

Theme parks of Walt Disney Company

Walt Disney Company has established four major theme parks, located in three different continents: (1) Disneyland Resort in California, created in 1955, (2) Walt Disney World Resort in Florida, founded in 1971, (3) Tokyo Disney Resort in Japan, opened in 1983, and (4) Disneyland Resort Paris, launched in 1992 for the European market. They have become some of the major tourist attractions worldwide: Disneyland Resort in California is the first tourist attraction in North America, Tokyo Disney Resort is the first tourist attraction in Asia, and Disneyland Resort Paris is the first tourist attraction in Europe.

Exhibit 1 Distribution of revenues of Walt Disney Company by strategic area (in 2002)

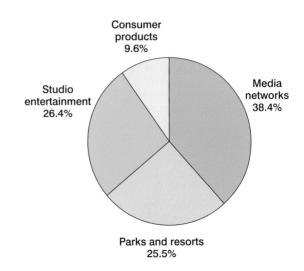

Source: Walt Disney Company (2002), Annual Report.

Success factors of Walt Disney theme parks

The success of Walt Disney theme parks can be explained by eight major factors: (1) originality of concept, (2) geographic location, (3) integrated services, (4) international expansion, (5) innovation, (6) partnerships, (7) yield management, (8) B2B marketing (see Exhibit 2).

Originality of concept

The concept used by Walt Disney Company is unique and original. The theme parks are based on the stories written by Walt Disney, which are highly appreciated by both children and adults. Since 1923, Walt Disney Corporation has created over 1000 different characters, many of whom are known around the world. The first park in California was conceived in order to be used as a film set. Walt Disney theme parks offer an experience that is unique. The use of Walt Disney stories and characters allows the company to differentiate its offer from other theme parks. The concept is focusing on family entertainment, fun, fantasy, and quality services. The value and reputation of the Disney brand has considerably contributed to the profitability of Walt Disney theme parks, allowing the company to apply relatively high entrance fees.

Geographic location

The geographic location of a theme park largely determines the number of visitors. After the creation of Disneyland in California in 1955, Walt Disney Company

Exhibit 2 Key success factors of Walt Disney theme parks

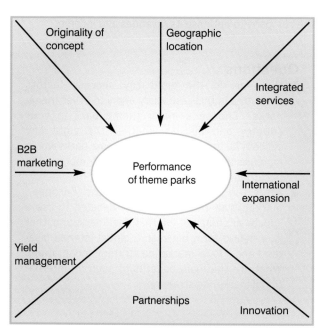

opened a second theme park in Florida in 1971 (Walt Disney World), which has become the most famous resort in the world. Both locations are close to affluent cities that are attractive destinations for tourists. The closeness to large metropolitan areas is thought to guarantee a minimum of visitors per year. Because of the heavy investments required for the creation and the maintenance of theme parks, a high number of regular visitors is a prerequisite for profitability. The geographic location was also an important criterion for the theme parks opened abroad.

Integrated services

Walt Disney theme parks offer a large variety of services such as attractions, parades, hotels, restaurants and boutiques. The environment was created in order to satisfy the whole family, and not only children. Moreover, the company offers attractive packages that include entrance fee, accommodation and transportation. Compared to other theme parks, which mainly rely on local customers, the extensive offer has allowed Walt Disney theme parks to become holiday destinations, attracting people from different regions and countries. Walt Disney theme parks have gradually evolved from parks to resorts where tourists can spend their holiday.

International expansion

The international expansion of the company can be considered as another key success factor. Following the globalisation of markets and competition, critical size increasingly determines the survival and performance of companies. Walt Disney Company thus chose to establish theme parks in major markets of the Triad. After the creation of two theme parks in its domestic market (Disneyland in California in 1955, renamed Disneyland Resort and Walt Disney World in Florida in 1971, renamed Walt Disney World Resort), Walt Disney Company decided to export the concept. In 1983, the first overseas theme park was opened in Japan: Tokyo Disneyland (renamed Tokyo Disney Resort). The theme park is owned and operated by an independent Japanese company (Oriental Land Company Limited). The Japanese site proved to be very profitable from the beginning. In 1999, Tokyo Disneyland attracted the most visitors of any theme park worldwide, admitting 17.5 million people. In 1992, Walt Disney Company expanded into Europe, opening the theme park Eurodisney near Paris. The European experience appeared to be difficult, mainly because the concept was insufficiently adapted to the diversity of European cultures. Following these difficulties, the theme park was adapted to the European context and renamed Disneyland Paris Resort. The theme park near Paris has become the most important theme park on the European continent,

attracting more than 13 million visitors in 2002. The company is planning to establish a fifth theme park in Hong Kong, which is scheduled to open in 2005 or 2006.

Innovation

Walt Disney Company is constantly innovating its offer and renewing attractions in order to increase the number of visitors in its theme parks. After the creation of the theme park Magic Kingdom in Florida in 1971, Walt Disney Company decided to open a second theme park in 1982 (Epcot, based on technology and the representation of different nations), a third park in 1989 (Disney-MGM Studios, focusing on the fields of cinema and television) and a fourth park in 1998 (Animal Kingdom, based on the theme of animals). In the same way, the company opened a second theme park in Paris, Walt Disney Studios, which is focusing on the fields of cinema, animation and television.

Partnerships

Over the past few years, Walt Disney Company has formed several strategic partnerships with other companies. Marketing alliances have been established with major brands. These so-called official partners are associated with an attraction, a boutique or a restaurant in the theme park and Disneyland integrates their name or logo into the place they have sponsored. Partner companies can mention their association with Disneyland in a variety of activities such as advertising, promotions and public relations, and benefit from the status of favoured suppliers. For instance, the new space pavilion opened in 2003 at Epcot (Walt Disney World Resort in Florida) has been sponsored by Compaq. Walt Disney Company has also developed partnerships with service providers such as transportation companies and tour operators, allowing the company to offer attractive overall packages. Finally, the company has strengthened relationships with local communities in order to expand theme parks into full resorts and in order to improve transportation access to its theme parks. In cooperation with the French government, the company has developed an urban project next to its theme park in Paris, called Val d'Europe. Val d'Europe is intended to become an economic centre near Paris, attracting residents, companies and hotels.

Yield management

Walt Disney Corporation successfully applies yield management techniquesin order to face high fixed costs and in order to regulate capacities and flows. Yield management is a method that allows the company to adapt its prices according to the demand. Walt Disney theme parks thus propose relatively high prices during periods when the number of visitors is important. Conversely, attractive offers are elaborated for periods when the demand is weak.

B2B Marketing

Walt Disney Company is particularly active in the profitable business tourism market. It is not only targeting individual customers (business to consumer, B2C marketing), but also organisations and companies (business to business, B2B marketing). All theme parks have conference centres that allow companies to organise meetings, incentives, conferences and events (MICE market). Because of the strategic importance of this market, Disneyland is operating a separate business unit for the MICE market.

Following the globalisation of markets and competition, tourism providers are constantly striving to improve their business performance. The increasing demand for attractions that offer amusement and entertainment has led to an important development of theme parks worldwide. In a highly competitive environment, Walt Disney Company has decided to continuously adapt its offer to the evolution of the tourist market. Since the creation of its first theme park, the originality of the concept used and the geographic location of its parks have guided the strategy conducted by Walt Disney Company. Following the increasing demand of tourist consumers for integrated services and the globalisation of the tourism industry, the company considerably extended its offer and expanded into major foreign markets. In response to the multiplication of theme parks, Walt Disney Company has strengthened product innovation and strategic partnerships. Finally, yield management techniques and B2B Marketing have allowed the company to optimise its revenues and income.

Questions

1 How far do the eight key success factors presented in this case study apply to other theme parks? Choose a major theme park in your country and discuss whether the eight key success factors of Walt Disney theme parks would increase the number of visitors and improve the performance of the theme park.

2 After the difficulties faced in the European market, Walt Disney Company decided to use a 'glocal' approach of international marketing, that is, a hybrid form between a global (standardisation) and a local marketing strategy (adaptation). What are the main benefits of such an international marketing strategy?

Further reading and bibliography

- Costa, J.A. and Bamossy, G.J. (2001), 'Le Park Disney: Creating an "Authentic" American Experience', *Advances in Consumer Research*, 28, pp. 398-402.
- Euro Disney SCA (2002), Annual Report.
- S. Hertrich, and U. Mayrhofer, (2001), *Disneyland Paris: le lancement de Walt Disney Studios*, Paris: Centrale de Cas et de Médias Pédagogiques - Chambre de Commerce et d'Industrie de Paris.
- S. Hertrich, and U. Mayrhofer, (2004), *Disneyland Paris: 2 ans après le lancement de Walt Disney Studios*, Paris: Centrale de Cas et de Médias Pédagogiques - Chambre de Commerce et d'Industrie de Paris.
- U. Mayrhofer (2002), *Marketing,* Paris: Ed. Bréal, Coll. Lexifac.
- U. Mayrhofer (2004), *Marketing international,* Paris: Economica.
- E.P. Spencer (1995), 'Euro Disney - What Happened? What Next?', *Journal of International Marketing*, 3(3), pp. 103-114.
- Walt Disney Company (2002), Annual Report.

This case was written by Sylvie Hertrich and Ulrike Mayrhofer, IECS Strasbourg - Graduate School of Management, Robert Schuman University, France.

Sylvie Hertrich and Ulrike Mayrhofer have received the Golden Pen of the Chamber of Commerce and Industry in Paris. This prestigious award distinguishes authors whose case studies are extensively used by European business schools and universities (http://www.ccip.friccmp).

case 5.5 British American Tobacco: an Insight into Tobacco Marketing

The outlook for the company is better than at any time for 40 years. We have never faced such opportunities before.

— Martin Broughton, CEO, BAT

As evidence against tobacco companies becomes increasingly damning and widespread, tobacco sales in the Western world are diminishing. Mounting lawsuits, better education, and campaigns led by the World Health Organization and government bodies have led to an increased awareness and subsequent decline of smoking in the developed world. This has forced the tobacco industry to seek out markets with greater growth potential. The three main players in the industry are Philip Morris, RJ Reynolds, and British American Tobacco (BAT).

British American Tobacco

BAT is the second largest tobacco group in the world, with a market share of 15.4 per cent and a 2002 turnover of £24.6 billion with profits of £2.6 billion. The company was formed in 1902 when the Imperial Tobacco Company US formed a joint venture in a bid to end an intense trade war. In the last century BAT has acquired many tobacco companies and today has a portfolio of over 300 brands, including Benson & Hedges, Lucky Strike, John Player and Pall Mall. BAT operates 85 factories in 66 countries and employs about 86 000 people worldwide, with the majority of operations being run out of the company's UK headquarters. The company oversees every stage of cigarette production from tobacco harvesting to distribution. 2002 saw the production of some 777 billion cigarettes. The majority of the company's products are sold through retail markets and outlets, including a variety of stores, hotels, restaurants and cafés.

According to the World Federation of Public Health Association (WFPHA), an estimated one-third of the world's population aged 15 and above is now smoking regularly. Tobacco is a known or probable cause of 25 diseases, killing nearly 3.5 million people each year, with a predicted 10 million deaths annually by the year 2025. The proven dangers of cigarette smoking have incited a series of lawsuits in the US, with the UK recently following suit. As a result, governments have been forced to tighten legislation, with advertising and smoking bans becoming more and more widespread in the US. Such regulations are currently being introduced in the EU, with clearer health warnings, advertising and sponsorship bans, and public smoking restrictions now in place. Tobacco consumption has seen a decline in Britain, with 25 per cent of adults now smoking. This subsiding popularity is reflected in the rest of the Western world, a trend set to continue in the future.

Growth in adversity

Despite this, the stock markets have not been adversely affected and the value of tobacco shares continues to rise. Contrary to many Western trends, the global tobacco market continues to prosper with a dramatic increase in cigarette consumption worldwide. This can be largely attributed to demographic and socio-economic change, with natural increase and aging of the population, urbanisation, and increased income being the key factors. Some commentators argue that developing countries don't have the same level of basic information on the harmful effects

Exhibit 1 The world's major tobacco groups		
Company	**Top brands**	**Estimated market share (%)**
Altria (previously known as Philip Morris)	Marlboro, Basic, Virginia Slims, Merit, Parliament, Alpine, Cambridge, Bristol, Bucks, Commander, English Ovals, Saratoga, Superslims	16.4
British American Tobacco	Benson & Hedges, John Player, 555, Hilton, GPC, Kool, Viceroy, Raleigh, Barclay, Belair, Capri, Richland, Pall Mall, Lucky Strike, Dunhill	15.4
Japanese Tobacco Incorporated (RJ Reynolds)	Camel, Doral, Winston, Salem, Vantage, More, Now, Century, Ritz, Monarch, Magna, Sterling	7.2

of smoking, unlike developed countries. As a result, sales in developed countries have fallen due to strong educational programmes and antismoking legislation, whereas in developing countries sales are steadily rising.

Mergers and acquisitions

There is an ongoing trend towards a general industry consolidation, which further strengthens the power of individual tobacco companies and the tobacco industry in general, both commercially and politically. BAT has long been the most international in outlook of all the tobacco multinationals, engaging in strategic acquisitions and increasing production capacity on a global scale. The past number of years has seen BAT invest millions in mergers and takeovers in countries such as Cambodia, Turkey, Hungary and Mexico, adding considerable strength to their international portfolio. In 1999, BAT announced a global merger with Rothmans International, the fourth largest tobacco company in the world. The complementary geographical spread of the companies secured a leading position for the group in Latin America, Africa, Asia and Australasia, and an improved presence in Western Europe. Politically, BAT-Rothmans has greater lobbying power and ability to influence regulators than their combined power as two separate companies.

New markets

International tobacco companies such as BAT have targeted the developing world to replace diminishing sales in Western Europe and North America. Globally, it is estimated that cigarette consumption increased by over 50 per cent from 1975 to 1995 and all of this increase is in developing countries. Analyst projections indicate that this trend will continue for the foreseeable future, providing an extremely lucrative potential market for BAT. Traditionally, Asian and Eastern European countries have had state-owned monopolies on tobacco production and their tobacco industries had been closed to international competitors. The US Cigarette Export Association (of which Brown & Williamson, BAT's US subsidiary was a member) recognised the huge potential of Asian markets and put pressure on the Office of the US Trade Representative (USTR) to act. In 1985, the USTR began to use Section 301 of the 1974 Trade Act to open up foreign markets to US cigarettes, threatening retaliatory sanctions against countries that discriminated against US imports. The fall of the USSR also opened up Eastern Europe, leaving BAT free to enter the market.

BAT and the other major players are intensifying their strategy of overseas production, purchasing previously state-owned factories, setting up joint ventures with existing state enterprises and building new factories. Currently, BAT manufactures more than half of its cigarettes in Asia, Australia and Latin America in an attempt to locate manu-facturing plants closer to the sources of tobacco leaf. BAT spent $25 million to upgrade its 'Liberation Factory' in Cambodia to boost production for the domestic and export markets and purchased a controlling interest in Tekel, the state cigarette monopoly of Turkey, the worlds' ninth largest cigarette market. BAT also made one of the largest foreign investments ever when they purchased Cigarerra La Moderna (CLM), Mexico's largest producer of cigarettes, for $1.7 billion, and have recently opened new plants in Nigeria and South Korea.

Advertising and promotion

BAT's scale allows it to spend millions on aggressive advertising and price competition campaigns. The intensity of its marketing is such that domestic tobacco companies cannot compete, and BAT is succeeding in winning over new and existing smokers. Currently, only 7 per cent of women in non-industrialised countries smoke, making women one of BAT's prime target markets. BAT is making huge investments in advertising campaigns, some of which promote the perceived ideals of the West, such as independence, affluence and sex appeal. This glamourous image, coupled with increasing urbanisation, education, career achievement and spending power have created a new demand among women and young people.

> The younger smoker is of pre-eminent importance: significant in numbers, 'lead in' to prime market, starts brand preference patterning … (Brown & Williamson [BAT], 1974)

Many countries have recognised the connection between cigarette advertising and increased youth smoking rates and have taken steps to restrict or ban cigarette advertising. This has forced BAT to employ indirect forms of advertising such as sponsorship of sports, rock concerts, discos and the arts. It also engages in 'brand stretching', putting its logos on a variety of products and services, including Kent Travel Agency, John Player whiskey, Lucky Strike clothing and Benson & Hedges Quality Blend Coffee. This allows it to skirt advertising restrictions and create a halo effect on its cigarette brands. World Investment Company, a BAT subsidiary that develops consumer products that use its cigarette brand names, carries out testing on such projects.

BAT has gone a step further in Hungary, the sixth biggest cigarette consumer in the world, where it has become an integral part of the communities in which it is based. Its initiatives include an annual donation of £20 000 to BAT House, a shelter for homeless men (this is the equivalent of one morning's profit for BAT Hungary). It also sponsors a town theatre and donates money to a clinic for the treatment of smoking-related diseases. In addition to this, BAT factories are a source of much

needed employment in deprived areas. These factors combined create a positive image and often a grateful attitude in many Hungarian people. This is reflected in the lack of action taken against BAT for advertising outside stores, despite it being against the law.

BAT spends millions of pounds sponsoring sporting events and teams to publicise its brands and create a positive image. BAT Hilton sponsors the Chinese national basketball team and BAT 555 backs the Hong Kong–Beijing car rally. BAT also promotes and sponsors entertainment events that appeal to young people. In Sri Lanka, young, attractive women called 'golden girls' promote Benson & Hedges at lavish discos sponsored by BAT. The girls hand out cigarettes to customers as they dance to the latest pop music, while laser lights emblazon the walls with the Benson & Hedges logo. The company sponsors a similar disco in Beijing three times a week to advertise its 555 brand. Young Chinese women, wearing skimpy clothes bearing the '555' logo meet and greet customers at the door, giving out free cigarettes. While large '555' banners festoon discos, proclaiming 'Be free from worldly cares'. BAT also sponsors pop music magazines and rock concerts and in Sri Lanka, it skirts a radio advertising ban by underwriting a 'Golden Tones Contest' on a radio station with a large teen audience. The company has taken a slightly more direct approach in Kandy, Sri Lanka's largest city, where it hires young women to travel the country in bright red 'Gold Leaf' cars and jeeps, handing out free cigarettes in places that young people frequent, such as college campuses and shopping malls. BAT has also sponsored a scoreboard of a high school and paid for advertising on the front wall of another.

Youth Smoking Prevention Campaign

Despite all of this advertising clearly being aimed at a young market, BAT denies that it is encouraging young people to smoke. In July 2001, BAT launched its 'Youth Smoking Prevention Campaign'. BAT claims that it sees smoking as an adult choice, and that it feels the responsibility to prevent smoking among under-18s. The campaign consists of a 30-second television ad, three one-minute radio scripts, a billboard ad, and a sticker. The stickers and the billboard bear the same image. On one side there is a picture of smoke rings and underneath it is the word 'no'. On the other side is the caption 'We don't smoke', accompanied by a picture of ordinary youths, featuring a boy holding his hat in the air and one of the girls holding up flowers.

The campaign messages are all highly ambiguous. Nowhere is there any mention of the reasons not to smoke, or the harm smoking can do. One of the radio ads informs a young boy that 'smoking at this age is a really bad habit', implying that it is fine when you are older. Each of the messages also enforces smoking as an adult activity, something that makes you more grown up. There is an implication in each of the radio ads that all adult men smoke, again reinforcing the message that smoking is something that youth aspires to. The campaign ads lack the quality and glamour of BAT's brand advertisements and unlike these advertisements there is an absence of role models that are popular among youth, such as sports personalities and pop stars. The use of the word 'no' and the phrase 'everybody should come forward to stop underage smoking' are authoritarian in nature, suggesting a heavy-handed approach to underage smoking. This is exactly the kind of control that youths rebel against, one of the reasons why many young people smoke in the first place.

It appears that BAT's Youth Smoking Prevention Campaign is a public relations scheme devised to stop attempts at legislation and to avoid criticism by appearing to be socially responsible. If BAT were serious about reducing smoking rates among youth, they would not oppose government legislation proposing tax increases and advertising bans – measures that are particularly successful with youth.

The black market

Trade barriers to the tobacco market and increasing taxes and restrictions on tobacco products have incited a dramatic increase in the volume of illegal cigarettes sold through the black market. The figure has tripled since 1989 and approximately 300 billion cigarettes are currently being illegally smuggled each year. This represents one-third of all cigarettes entering into international markets, at a loss of $16 billion per year in government taxes and customs revenue. Smuggling allows BAT to promote its brands and develop brand loyalty in countries that are closed to tobacco imports, and is particularly advantageous in countries that will soon become open to international trade, such as China. The smuggled products are usually available at about one-third of the retail price, encouraging smoking among people who are more sensitive to pricing, such as the youth market. Smuggling also benefits BAT by encouraging governments to reduce trade tariffs and barriers and allow increased cigarette imports, in an effort to curb black market growth and gain revenue. Although BAT and the other major tobacco groups categorically deny any direct involvement in the smuggling of cigarettes, there is substantial evidence to indicate otherwise. A former executive with BAT subsidiary Brown & Williamson was recently convicted of accepting $33 million in kickbacks from a Hong Kong-based smuggling ring. The *Wall Street Journal* reported that BAT executives held 'weekly meetings at which smuggling activities were discussed'. Although BAT denies knowledge of the 'rogue' operation, these smuggling activities have undoubtedly given BAT a foothold in the world's largest cigarette market.

The future

In the future, BAT will continue to expand its operations worldwide. It is continually finding new ways to prise open foreign markets. Pressure from the USTR and trade agreements such as the North American Free Trade Agreement (NAFTA) have helped to open up new markets and strengthen its global position. In fact, Martin Broughton, BAT's CEO, is the chairman of the Chatham House Task Force, a foreign policy group that 'aims to facilitate free trade in China'. China is the largest tobacco market in the world, consuming one-third of all cigarettes, more than the next seven highest consuming countries put together. At present, China wishes to join the WTO, which would open up their cigarette market to companies such as BAT, giving it access and ability to set up factories and joint ventures, thus allowing it to widen its product range.

Conclusion

Smoking rates are still holding steady, despite punitive antismoking legislation, and antismoking education. Some countries, like Ireland, have banned smoking from the workplace, a world first. However, smoking rates in Asian countries like Japan, South Korea, Thailand and Taiwan rose 10 per cent higher than if their tobacco markets had not been opened up to international competition. Since Japan was forced to liberalise its market, foreign cigarette brands have increased their market share from 2 per cent to 22 per cent. Between 1986 and 1996, the smoking rate for Japanese women in their twenties rose from 15.5 per cent to 20.3 per cent. Between 1990 and 1996, the smoking rate among 17-year-old boys rose from 26 per cent to 40 per cent and among girls the figure went from 5 per cent to 15 per cent. The Korean government opened its market to US brands in 1988. Within a year, US companies had 6 per cent share of the market, and smoking rates among teenage boys had risen from 18.4 per cent to 30 per cent

and among teenage girls from 1.6 per cent to 8.7 per cent. The figures in other Asian countries like Taiwan are similar, with US companies securing more than 20 per cent of the market in less than two years, while smoking rates among high school students increased by 50 per cent.

Despite the efforts of governments in the developed world and global health organisations, tobacco companies such as BAT are going from strength to strength. They have the political power to challenge or evade any restrictions that governments of the developing world have tried to place in their way, and the financial resources to reach potential customers on a level at which domestic tobacco companies cannot compete. As smoking levels decline in the West, BAT continues to secure new demographic markets and bring its product to a whole new generation of smokers.

Questions

1 What strategies has BAT employed to secure its position as one of the world's leading tobacco companies?
2 How has BAT continued to promote its brands successfully in the face of increasingly restrictive regulations?
3 Suggest other marketing tactics that could be deployed by tobacco companies in the wake of further marketing communications regulatory restrictions (e.g. advertising bans)?
4 What are the strategic options available to BAT in an increasingly restrictive regulatory climate?

This case was written by Ailbhe Jenkinson, Sinead Kavanagh and Conor Carroll, University of Limerick. Copyright © Jenkinson, Kavanagh and Carroll (2003). The material in the case has been drawn from a variety of published sources.

glossary

accounts-receivable – A comprehensive billing and customer information system that helps you manage your receivables, streamline the collection and control of cash, and separately track individual clients, organisations and funding sources.

act of God – An extraordinary happening of nature not reasonably anticipated by either party to a contract, i.e. earthquakes, floods, etc.

activist groups – See *Green activist*. Refers to these groups, e.g. Greenpeace.

adaptation – Making changes to fit a particular culture/environment/conditions; when we produce special/modified products for different markets.

administered pricing – Relates to attempts to establish prices for an entire market.

advertising campaign – Designing and implementing particular advertising for a particular product/purpose over a fixed period.

advertising media – Different alternatives available to a company for its advertising (e.g. TV, magazine).

after-sales service – Services that are available after the product has been sold (e.g. repairs).

air freight – Sending a product by air.

analogy – Reasoning from parallel cases/examples.

Andean Common Market (ANCOM) – A sub-regional economic integration organisation existing out of Bolivia, Colombia, Ecuador, Peru and Venezuela.

anti-trust laws – Laws to prevent businesses from creating unjust monopolies or competing unfairly in the marketplace.

APEC – Asia Pacific cooperation among 21 member states. APEC promotes free trade and economic cooperation between members.

arbitration – Mediation done by a third party in case of a commercial dispute.

ASEAN – The fourth biggest trade area of the world comprising 10 Southeast Asian countries.

Asian crisis – In 1996/1997, stock exchanges and currency values in a number of Asian countries lost a major part of their value.

back translation – When a questionnaire/slogan/theme is translated into another language, then translated back to the original language by another party. Helps to pinpoint misinterpretation and misunderstandings.

balance of payments – System of accounts that records a nation's international financial transactions.

barriers to exporting – Obstacles/hindrances to export.

barter – Direct exchange of goods between two parties in a transaction.

barter house – International trading company that is able to introduce merchandise to outlets and geographic areas previously untapped.

billboards – Large stands that comprise advertising space, usually found on the sides of roads.

blocked currency – Blockage cuts off all importing or all importing above a certain level. Blockage is accomplished by refusing to allow importers to exchange national currency for the seller's currency.

Boston Consulting Group (BCG) – An international strategy and general management consulting firm, it uses specific models to tackle management problems.

boycott – A coordinated refusal to buy or use products or services of a certain company/country.

brand loyalty – When customers always buy the same brand.

branding – Developing and building a reputation for a brand name.

Bretton Woods Agreement – An agreement made in 1944. It set fixed exchange rates for major currencies and subsequently established the IMF.

bribery – Voluntarily offered payments by someone seeking unlawful advantage.

broker – A catchall term for a variety of middlemen performing low-cost agent services.

business culture – Values and norms followed in business activities.

business services – Services that are sold to other companies (e.g. advertising).

capital account – A record of direct investment portfolio activities, and short-term capital movements to and from countries.

cartel – A cartel exists when various companies producing similar products work together to control markets for the types of goods they produce.

census data – A record of population and its breakdown.

centralisation – When most decisions are made at the top or head office.

centrally planned economic model - A model that is characterised by state monopoly of all means of production, lack of consumer orientation and lack of competition.

chaebol - Korean term for conglomerate of many companies clustered around one parent company, similar to the *keiretsu* in Japan.

client followers - Companies that have followed their clients to other countries (i.e. become international) to service their primary clients while they are abroad.

collaborative relationships - Relationship between companies to cooperate with each other.

collective programming - When groups of people are taught/indoctrinated about certain values.

commercial disputes - Conflicts about commercial agreements (e.g. terms of payment, penalties for delay).

committee decision making - Decision making by group or consensus.

Common Commercial Policy (CCP) - Its aim is to liberalise world trade.

common law - Tradition, past practices and legal precedents set by the courts through interpretations of statutes, legal legislation and past rulings.

Common Market - A free-trade area with a common external tariff, international labour mobility and common economic policies among member states.

compadre - Friendship according to Latin American culture.

comparability and equivalence - Information that is comparable and is understood in the same way.

comparative advertising - Advertising that directly compares you with your competitors.

compensation deals - Involve payment in goods and in cash.

competitive strength - Strength of a product/company as compared to competitors.

conciliation - A non-binding agreement between parties to resolve disputes by asking a third party to mediate the differences.

confiscation - Seizing a company's assets without payment.

congruent innovation - The product concept is accepted by the culture and the innovativeness is typically one of introducing variety and quality or functional features, style or perhaps an exact duplicate of an already existing product - exact in the sense that the market perceives no newness, such as cane sugar versus beet sugar.

consumer goods - Goods that consumers buy to consume.

consumption patterns - How consumers buy a particular product.

containerised shipments - When products are packed into containers for transportation.

content labelling - Mention of the contents/ingredients of a product on the package.

continuous innovation - Alteration of a product is almost always involved rather than the creation of a new product. Generally, the alterations result in better use patterns - perceived improvement in the satisfaction derived from its use.

corporate strategy - Strategy of the company as a whole.

countertrade - When products are exchanged with other products instead of cash/money.

country-of-origin effect (COE) - Any influence that the country of manufacture has on a consumer's positive or negative perception of a product.

country-specific brand - A brand that is sold in only one country.

cultural adiaphora - Relates to areas of behaviour or to customs that cultural aliens may wish to conform to or participate in but that are not required.

cultural change - Change in cultural conditions, e.g. Americanisation.

cultural exclusives - Those customs or behaviour patterns reserved exclusively for the local people and from which the foreigner is excluded.

cultural imperative - Refers to the business customs and expectations that must be met and conformed to if relationships are to be successful.

cultural sensitivity - Being attuned to the nuances of culture so that a new culture can be viewed objectively, evaluated and appreciated.

culture - A set of value and norms followed by a group of people; human-made part of the human environment - the sum total of knowledge, beliefs, art, morals, laws, customs, and any other capabilities and habits acquired by humans as members of society.

currency inconvertibility - The deterioration in the ability to convert profits, debt service and other remittances from local currency into another currency.

current account - A record of all merchandise exports, imports and services plus unilateral transfers of funds.

customer loyalty - When the same customers always buy one company's products.

customer segment - Those consumers who are the potential customers.

customised products - Products that are modified for each customer.

customs union - Creation of a common external tariff that applies for non-members, the establishment of a common trade policy and the elimination of rules.

database - A bank/storage of information on a particular issue.

deal-centred - When a sales person is solely concerned to finish the particular transaction.

dealer - Generally speaking, anyone who has a continuing relationship with a supplier in buying and selling goods is considered a dealer.

debt-equity swaps - The exchange of a debt instrument (such as a bond) by a company, in return for equity, which cancels out the debt.

Decade of the Environment - The 1990s, when environment was considered the most important issue.

decentralisation - When most decisions can be made in subsidiaries or at all levels of the company.

decentralised decision making - When every level of the organisation can make its own decisions.

decentring - A successive iteration process of translation and retranslation of a questionnaire, each time by a different translator.

demand elasticity - When demand for a product changes due to minor changes in the price.

demographic data - Information on the demographics of a country/city/area.

developmental loans - Loans granted for developmental projects, e.g. health and education.

differential exchange rate - The essential mechanism requires the importer to pay varying amounts of domestic currency for foreign exchange with which to purchase products in different categories.

differentiated products - Products that are considered different from other similar products.

differentiation strategy - The marketer is trying to convince the market/customers that his product is different to that of competitors.

direct-mail advertising - Advertising that comes to you through the post, directly addressed to you.

direct marketing - Advertisement sent directly to customers.

discontinuous innovation - This involves the establishment of new consumption patterns and the creation of previously unknown products. It introduces an idea or behaviour pattern where there was none before.

disposable income - That proportion of your income that is not already accounted for, for example, on mortgages, loans, bills, etc.

distribution _keiretsu_ - A network of affiliated wholesalers and retailers that manufacturers of consumer goods use to distribute their products.

distribution network - How the product moves from the producer to the customer.

domestic-made products - Those products sold in the country in which they were made.

domestic market extension concept - Foreign markets are extensions of the domestic market and the domestic marketing mix is offered, as is, to foreign markets.

domestic middlemen - Middlemen (e.g. wholesalers) in the home market of the company.

domestication - When host countries take steps to transfer foreign investments to national control and ownership through a series of government decrees.

dumping - When a product is sold for a lesser price than its actual cost.

dynamically continuous innovation - This may mean the creation of a new product or considerable alteration of an existing one, designed to fulfil new needs arising from changes in lifestyles or new expectations brought about by change. It is generally disruptive and therefore resisted because old patterns of behaviour must change if consumers are to accept and perceive the value of the dynamically continuous innovation.

eco-labelling - A label or logo to show that a company is socially responsible.

e-commerce - Buying and selling through the Internet or comparable systems.

economic change - Change in economic conditions, e.g. recession.

economic nationalism - The preservation of national economic autonomy in that residents identify their interests with the preservation of the sovereignty of the state in which they reside.

economic needs - Things that are required such as minimum food, drink, shelter and clothing.

economic sanctions - When it is forbidden to trade with a country.

economic wants - Arise from desire for satisfaction and, due to their non-essential quality, they are limitless.

efficiency seeking - Firms want to enter countries/markets where they can achieve efficiency in different ways.

electronic commerce - Buying/selling a product via the Internet.

EPRG schema - A schema that classifies firms by their orientation: ethnocentric, polycentric, regiocentric or geocentric. The degree of commitment to internationalisation is what determines a firm's orientation.

establishment chain model - A stepwise internationalisation to foreign markets.

ethnocentric - Intense identification with the known and the familiar of a particular culture and a tendency to devalue the foreign and unknown of other cultures.

ethnocentrism - When we behave in an ethnocentric way; there is an exaggerated tendency to believe our own values/norms/culture are superior to those of others.

eurodollar - A deposit liability banked outside the United States, that is, dollars banked in Germany or any country other than the US.

European Court of Justice - An institution of the European Union.

exchange controls - When rate of exchange (e.g. for money) is controlled or fixed by the authority.

exchange permits - Give permission to exchange money.

exchange restrictions - Obstacles to exchanging money.

exchange variation - Variation in the exchange rate of the two currencies involved.

exhibitions - An exhibition is used to promote product range extensions and to launch activities in new markets.

expatriate - An employee of the company/organisation who is sent to another country to work.

export credit - A loan, that allows a company to pay for an export contract.

export credit guarantee - When a government/organisation commits to give a loan to an exporter.

export management company (EMC) - An important middleman for firms with relatively small international volume or for those unwilling to involve their own personnel in the international function.

export regulations - Rules and regulations for export.

expropriation - Taking away companies from the owners and into state ownership (in this case).

factual knowledge - Something that is usually obvious but that must be learnt.

floating exchange rates - Changes in market demand and market supply of a currency cause a change in value.

focus groups - A group of people who are considered relevant for our product and can provide us with useful information.

focus strategy - When a company decides to focus on a particular market segment or part of the product line.

follower brands - Brands that came later to the market.

foreign brokers - Agents who deal largely in commodities and food products, typically part of small brokerage firms operating in one country or in a few countries.

foreign-country middlemen - Middlemen in foreign markets.

foreign-exchange options - Very similar to an insurance contract, in which, in exchange for a pre-paid premium, the buyer of the option receives 100 per cent protection against unfavourable movement of exchange rates.

foreign-freight forwarder - A company that helps other companies in transportation and export/import matters.

foreign-made products - Those products made in a different country from the one they are being sold in.

foreign-trade zones (FTZs) - Where products are produced mostly for exporting purposes.

frame of reference - *See self-reference criterion.*

free-trade area - Where products can move freely, without tariffs and restrictions.

generic strategy - The core strategy for the company as a whole.

geographical divisions - When a company is organised according to its markets.

geography - The study of the earth's surface, climate, continents, countries, peoples, industries and resources.

global brand - The worldwide use of a name, term, sign, symbol, design or combination thereof intended to identify goods or services of one seller and to differentiate them from those of competitors.

global market concept - The world is the market and, wherever cost- and culturally effective, an overall standardised marketing strategy is developed for entire sets of country markets.

global marketing - Using global market concepts in marketing decisions.

global products - Standardised products.

global sourcing - When you buy components and materials from all over the world.

GM foods - Genetically modified foods.

Green activists - Organisations or individuals who actively want to protect the environment.

green dot programme - A sign (logo) that shows a product adheres to *Green marketing*.

Green marketing - Marketing decisions that take the environment into consideration.

Green movement - Political/consumer movement favouring environment-friendly approaches.

group decision making - When a groups makes a decision together.

guan-xi - Relationship building/friendship according to Chinese culture.

hedging - Insuring against a negative event. Companies use hedging techniques to reduce their exposure to exchange risks.

hedonistic - Carefree and pleasurable.

high-context culture - Cultures that demand implicit communication.

high-priority industries - When some industries are given extra benefits by authorities because they are considered important.

historical data – Information over a period of time.

idiomatic interpretation – Interpretations according to the characteristics of a particular language.

import licence – Permission to import.

import regulations – Rules and regulations for import.

import restrictions – When it is not permitted to import.

income elasticity – When higher or lower income would influence demand for a product.

individualism – When everybody is concerned only with their own well-being.

industrial advertisers – Companies that advertise *industrial products*.

industrial products – Products developed for the industrial market, not the consumer market.

innovation – New product/technology/method.

intellectual property – An immaterial asset that can be bought, sold, licensed, exchanged or gradually given away like any other form of property.

intellectual property rights – Laws governing *intellectual property*.

Inter-American Convention – Provides protection similar to that afforded by the *Paris Convention*.

interim credit – A business loan to fund the acquisition and rehab or remodelling of a structure.

International Monetary Fund (IMF) – Formed to overcome market barriers such as inadequate monetary reserves and unstable currency.

Internet advertising – Advertising on and through websites.

interpretive knowledge – The ability to understand and appreciate fully the nuances of different cultural traits and patterns.

interviews – When we talk to people to get information on specific matters.

ISO 9000 – Quality assurance certification of the production process.

joint venture – When two companies together open/start a third company.

jurisdiction – Overall legal authority.

just-in-time (JIT) – When deliveries are made at a time when the component being delivered is to be used and not before (often in manufacturing).

keiretsu – A host of interfirm relationships and affiliations of varying degrees of formality in Japan.

Kyoto Agreement – Agreement signed by the EU, Russia and a number of other countries, determining the decrease required in pollution over the coming years.

labelling laws – Laws which indicate what should be mentioned on packaging.

leasing – Borrowing/renting.

legal disputes – Conflicts that are resolved through legal means.

letter of credits (LC) – Shifts the buyer's credit risk to the bank issuing the LC.

licensing – To allow another company to produce and sell your product against royalties. A means of establishing a foothold in foreign markets without large capital outlays.

litigation – Taking the other party to court.

local content – Containing locally made parts.

local nationals – Employees of a company that are local to the market.

local responsiveness – When a company adapts its product and strategies according to local needs and requirements.

low-context culture – Cultures that demand explicit communication.

lubrication – A relatively small sum of cash, a gift, or a service given to a low-ranking official in a country where such offerings are not prohibited by law.

Madrid Arrangement – There are some 26 member countries in Europe that have agreed to automatic trademark protection for all members.

managing agent – conducts business within a foreign nation under an exclusive contract arrangement with the parent company.

mañana – Spanish for 'tomorrow'.

mandatory requirements – Requirements that a company must meet.

manufacturer's export agent (MEA) – An individual agent middleman or an agent middleman firm providing a selling service for manufacturers.

manufacturers' representatives – Representative of the producing company in another country.

market barrier – A barrier to trade imposed by the government, against foreign business and imports, in an attempt to promote domestic industry; when market mechanisms work as obstacles to trade.

market-driven economies – Economies/countries that are following the free market economic system.

market planning – A systematic way of producing and selling a product.

market resistance – When customers are reluctant to accept a new product/service.

market seeking – Companies that venture into new countries/become international because they are looking for new markets.

marketing function – Marketing activities (often in a company).

marketing mix – An optimal combination of product, price, place (distribution) and promotion.

marketing research - The systematic gathering, recording and analysis of data to provide information useful in marketing decision making.

Marshall Plan - A plan designed to assist in the rebuilding of Europe after the Second World War.

Marxist-socialist approach - Where a communist or socialist economic system is followed.

matrix organisation - When a dual organisational structure is used (e.g. product as well as markets).

merger - When two companies decide to join together.

methodology - Way of doing research.

middleman - Businessman, other than the producer and customer, involved in the exchange of goods.

misleading advertisement - Advertisement that gives incorrect message/impression of a product/company.

monetary barriers - Putting monetary restrictions on trade, e.g. availability of foreign exchange for imports.

monopsony - The buying-side monopoly.

M-time (monochronic) - Concentrating on one thing at a time. Time is divided up into small units and used in a linear way.

multicultural studies - Studies that are performed in different cultures.

multidomestic market concept - Each country is viewed as being culturally unique and an adapted marketing mix for each country market is developed.

multinational marketing information system (MMIS) - An interacting complex of people, machines and procedures designed to generate an orderly flow of relevant information and to bring all the flows of recorded information into a unified whole for decision making. An MMIS covers multiple countries and operates at each country level.

nationalism - An intense feeling of national pride and unity, an awakening of a nation's people to pride in their country.

newly industrialised countries (NICs) - Developing countries that have grown rapidly in the last few decades and do not fit the traditional pattern of economic development of other LDCs.

ningen kankei - Human relationships.

non-physical features - Characteristics of a product that are not physical but perceptional.

non-profit organisations - Organisations whose purpose is not profit-oriented.

non-tariff barriers - Hurdles or restrictions on trade that are other than tariff rates, e.g. quotas.

ocean freight - Sending a product by ship.

organisational culture - Values and norms of working in an organisation.

outsourcing - When you let other companies take over part of your production process.

own brand - Retailers' own brands (e.g. Tesco tea).

parallel imports - When products are imported into a country without the consent of the brand owner.

parallel translation - When more than two translators are used for a *back translation*, and a comparison of the results is undertaken. (Overcomes problems with back translations.)

Paris Convention - A group of 100 nations that have agreed to recognise the rights of all members in the protection of trademarks, patents and other property rights.

patent - Any product or formula/technology registered with the relevant office that establishes who possesses the right of ownership.

patent rights - Only the owner of these rights is authorised/can use the particular product technology.

pattern advertising - A global advertising strategy with a standardised basic message allowing some degree of modification to meet local situations.

penetration pricing - To charge lower prices to gain some market share in a new market.

personal selling - When a product is sold through personal methods (e.g. sales people).

physical attributes - Physical characteristics of a product.

piggybacking - When a company does not export directly but uses another company's channels to export its products.

pioneering brands - Brands that were first in the market.

planned domestication - When a company plans to successively use local staff or components in a foreign market.

PLC stages - Stages in the *product life cycle*: introduction, growth, maturity and decline.

political climate - Political environment/conditions.

political payoff - An attempt to lessen political risks by paying those in power to intervene on behalf of the multinational company.

political risk assessment - An attempt to forecast political instability to help management identify and evaluate political events and their potential influence on current and future international business decisions.

positioning - Creating an image of your product and its quality in the customers' minds.

premium offers - Special offers or high-priced offers.

price control - When prices are regulated/fixed by an authority.

price differentials - Difference in price of a product.

price escalation - An increase in price.

price fixing - When competing companies agree to set a certain price for their products.

price freezes – When the price of a product cannot be increased.

primary data – Data that has been collected for the systematic research at hand.

privatisation – When a government company is sold to private investors.

proactive market selection – Actively and systematically selecting a market.

problem definition – Explaining the research problem.

product buy-back – When a company promises to buy back some of the products produced in its subsidiaries.

product divisions – When a company is organised according to its different products.

product life cycle (PLC) – Different stages (*PLC stages*) in a product's life; from introduction to decline.

promotional misfires – Mistakes made in the advertising activities of a company.

promotional strategy – Systematic planning to promote a product.

protectionism – When governments do not allow freedom of activity for foreign companies, to protect their own companies.

psychic distance – When a market is considered distant due to psychological barriers.

P-time (polychromic) – Characterised by the simultaneous occurrence of many things and by 'a great involvement with people'.

public-sector enterprises – Government-owned organisations.

qualitative research – Open-ended and in-depth, seeking unstructured responses. Expresses the respondents' thoughts and feelings.

quantitative research – Structured questioning, producing answers that can easily be converted to numerical data. Provides statistical information.

questionnaire design – Formulating exact questions to be asked, often in survey research.

quotas – Limitations on the quantity of certain goods imported during a specific period.

rate of diffusion – How quickly a product spreads out in a specific area.

reactive market selection – When selecting a market at random or without a systematic analysis.

relationship-centred – When the sales person aims to build an ongoing relationship with the customer.

reliability – Whether information/the results of a study are trustworthy.

research design – Overall plan for relating a research problem to practical empirical research.

research hypothesis – A theory that can be proved or rejected via research.

resource seeking – Firms try to enter countries to get access to raw materials or other crucial inputs that can provide cost reduction and lower operation costs.

retailer mark-ups – The profit margin of the retailer.

riba – The unlawful advantage by way of excess of deferment; that is, excessive interest or usury.

risk management – The sophisticated use of such techniques as currency hedging and interest rate swaps.

risk shifting – The level of risk is not reduced or eliminated but rather shifted on to someone else.

sales promotions – Activities to attract consumers and promote products.

sampling – The selection of respondents.

secondary data – Information that somebody else has collected, but we can use it for our purpose.

segmentation – Part of the customer market that is our potential customers/market.

self-reference criterion (SRC) – Considering our own conditions, values and norms.

Shari'ah – Islamic Law.

silent language – Communication without the use of language or words.

skimming – To charge a high price to maximise profit in the early stages of a product's introduction.

social responsibility – When a company is concerned about the implications of its decisions for society in general.

socialist laws – Cluster around the core concept of economic, political and social policies of the state. Socialist countries are, or were, generally those that formerly had laws derived from the Roman or code-law system.

soga shosha – Japanese trading and investment organisations that also perform a unique and important role as risk takers.

special drawing rights (SDRs) – Developed by the IMF to overcome universally floating exchange rates.

stakeholders – Parties that have an interest in the company's activities.

standardisation – Producing the same products for many markets.

state-owned enterprises (SOEs) – Companies owned by the government.

Statistical Yearbook – An annual publication of the United Nations, provides comprehensive social and economic data for more than 250 countries around the world.

strategic alliance – When two companies cooperate for a certain purpose.

strategic planning – A systematised way of relating to the future.

subornation – Involves large sums of money, frequently not properly accounted for, designed to entice an official to commit an illegal act on behalf of the one paying the bribe.

surveys – When we collect information using a list of questions.

sustainable competitive advantage (SCA) – Advantages over other competitors that can be enjoyed over a long period of time in the future.

tactical planning – A systematic way of handling the issues and problems of today.

tariff – A tax imposed by a government on goods entering at its borders.

third-country nationals – Expatriates from the business's own country working for a foreign company in a third country.

time lag – When there is a time gap between two actions.

total quality management (TQM) – A method by which management and employers are involved in the continuous improvement of the production of goods and services.

trade association – Association of companies belonging to the same industry.

trade balance – The relationship between merchandise imports and exports.

trade fair – An exhibition where participants are able to show/sell their products and services to the visitors and general public. Also used to establish and maintain contacts.

trademark – Registered 'mark' or 'logo' for a company or business.

Trade-Related Aspects of Intellectual Property Rights (TRIPs) – The TRIPs agreement establishes substantially higher standards of protection for a full range of intellectual property rights (patents, copyrights, trademarks, trade secrets, industrial designs and semiconductor chip mask works).

Trade-Related Investment Measures (TRIMs) – Established the basic principle that investment restrictions can be major trade barriers and are therefore included, for the first time, under GATT procedures.

trade sanctions – A set of stringent penalties imposed on a country by means of import tariffs or other trade barriers.

trading companies – Such companies accumulate, transport and distribute goods from many countries and companies.

transfer pricing – When a company uses selective prices for internal transactions (e.g. between two subsidiaries).

Triad trade – The process of trade undertaken between the EU, North America and Canada, Japan and China.

unfamiliar environment – Environment with which a company is not familiar, especially when it is a foreign market.

urban growth – Growth of urban areas or cities.

validity – Whether the measures used are reasonable to measure what it is supposed to measure.

value systems – Values that are followed unconsciously.

VER – An agreement between the importing country and the exporting country for a restriction on the volume of exports.

vertical *keiretsu* – A close stockholding relationship between firms at various stages of production or the long-term subcontracting arrangements of a firm with its suppliers of intermediate goods that artificially block the participation of outside firms.

volatility in demand – Changes in demand.

white goods – Often refers to large electrical goods for the kitchen (e.g. refrigerators, freezers).

wholesalers and retailers – So-called middlemen who facilitate the exchange of goods between manufacturer and consumer.

zaibatsu – A large family-controlled banking and industrial combination in modern Japan.

index